THE ROYAL NAVY IN THE COLD WAR YEARS

THE ROYAL NAVY IN THE COLD WAR YEARS 1966–1990

RETREAT AND REVIVAL

EDWARD HAMPSHIRE

Seaforth
PUBLISHING

Copyright © Edward Hampshire 2024

First published in Great Britain in 2024 by
Seaforth Publishing,
A division of Pen & Sword Books Ltd,
George House, Beevor Street, Barnsley S71 1HN

www.seaforthpublishing.com

A CIP catalogue record for this book is available from the British Library

ISBN 978 1 3990 4122 5 (HARDBACK)
ISBN 978 1 3990 4124 9 (EPUB)
ISBN 978 1 3990 4125 6 (KINDLE)

All rights reserved. No part of this publication may be reproduced or transmitted in any form or by any means, electronic or mechanical, including photocopying, recording, or any information storage and retrieval system, without prior permission in writing of both the copyright owner and the above publisher.

The right of Edward Hampshire to be identified as the author of this work has been asserted by him in accordance with the Copyright, Designs and Patents Act 1988.

Pen & Sword Books Limited incorporates the imprints of Atlas, Archaeology, Aviation, Discovery, Family History, Fiction, History, Maritime, Military, Military Classics, Politics, Select, Transport, True Crime, Air World, Frontline Publishing, Leo Cooper, Remember When, Seaforth Publishing, The Praetorian Press, Wharncliffe Local History, Wharncliffe Transport, Wharncliffe True Crime and White Owl

Typeset in 10.75/13.5pt Garamond by Mac Style

Printed and bound in Great Britain by CPI Group (UK) Ltd, Croydon, CR0 4YY

Contents

List of Plates	viii
Introduction	xi
Acknowledgements	xv
List of Abbreviations	xvii

Part I: Retreat, 1966–1975

1	February 1966	1
2	The Battle for the Carrier	35
3	Recovery and Rebuilding	51
4	A New Navy	86
5	Structures, Doctrine and Deployments	106
6	Sea Control	132
7	Cost Control	156
8	The Critical Level	189
9	Retreat to the Four Pillars	230

Part II: Crisis, 1975–1982

10	The Eastlant Navy	254
11	After *Ark Royal*	287
12	False Hope	326
13	The 'Bermudagram'	346
14	The Way Forward	370
15	Pushing Back	400

Part III: Revival, 1982–1990

16	Operation 'Corporate'	436
17	Lessons Learnt	468
18	Maritime Strategy	505
19	Reform and Overstretch	540
20	To the End	583
21	Conclusions	620

Appendices
1. Organisation — 629
2. Budget — 632
3. Personnel — 635
4. The Fleet — 639
5. Warship Procurement — 641

Notes — 645
Bibliography — 700
Index — 712

For my father and for Eric Grove

List of Plates

Between pages 264 and 265

1–12. The Navy's Leadership. *(Crown Copyright)*
13. HMS *Resolution*, the Royal Navy's first nuclear-powered ballistic missile submarine. *(Crown Copyright)*
14. HMS *Warspite*, a first-generation nuclear-powered attack submarine. *(Crown Copyright)*
15. A personnel transfer onto a *Trafalgar* class nuclear-powered attack submarine by helicopter. *(Crown Copyright)*
16. The next generation: HMS *Vanguard*. *(Crown Copyright)*
17. The aircraft carrier HMS *Ark Royal* and HMS *Eagle*, on the first Beira Patrol operations in 1966. *(Crown Copyright)*
18. A Mk 1 Sea King uses its dipping sonar to detect submarines. *(Crown Copyright)*
19. HMS *Hermes* operating as a commando carrier in the 1970s. *(Crown Copyright)*
20. Two landing craft depart HMS *Fearless* to take part in Operation 'Motorman'. *(Crown Copyright)*
21. A Royal Marine artillery unit disembarks in Norway. *(Crown Copyright)*
22. Two Royal Marines take part in an exercise defending North Sea oil rigs. *(Crown Copyright)*
23. HMS *Invincible* alongside at Portsmouth. *(Creative Commons 2.0/Hugh Llewelyn)*
24. A Phantom F4K undertakes test landings on HMS *Eagle* in 1969. *(Crown Copyright)*
25. The first operational Sea Harrier in flight. *(Crown Copyright)*
26. The Sea Harrier FA2 entered service in 1990. *(Crown Copyright)*

27. A Wessex medium helicopter hovers over the stern of the frigate HMS *Rothesay*. *(Crown Copyright)*
28. The *Leander* class frigate HMS *Danae* in 1967. *(Crown Copyright)*
29. The 'County' class destroyer HMS *Norfolk*. *(Crown Copyright)*
30. The *Leander* class frigate HMS *Naiad*. *(Crown Copyright)*
31. HMS *Amazon*, the first Type 21 frigate. *(Crown Copyright)*
32. The Icelandic gunboat *Tyr* approaches the frigate HMS *Bacchante*. *(Crown Copyright)*
33. HMS *Broadsword*. *(Crown Copyright)*
34. HMS *Liverpool* steams alongside an *Iowa* class battleship. *(Public Domain/ US Department of Defense)*
35. HMS *Phoebe*. *(Public Domain/PH2 Tracy Lee Didas, US Navy)*
36. The Type 23 frigate. *(Crown Copyright)*
37. HM Ships *Exeter* and *Jupiter* with the US carrier *Kitty Hawk*. *(Public Domain/PH2 Frank Davison, US Navy)*
38. One of the earliest design concepts for the Type 44 destroyer. *(Crown Copyright)*

Between pages 328 and 329

39. One of the options for the Future Frigate. *(Crown Copyright)*
40. HM Ships taking part in Operation 'Rheostat'. *(Crown Copyright)*
41. HMS *Brecon*. *(Crown Copyright)*
42. RFA *Olna* replenishing a Type 21 frigate at sea. *(Public Domain/Ken Griffith)*
43. RFA *Oakleaf* refuelling ships. *(Crown Copyright)*
44. The Arapaho system. *(Crown Copyright)*
45–56. Inside a Cold War guided missile destroyer. *(All photographs Crown Copyright)*
57. The frigate refit complex at Devonport. *(Crown Copyright)*
58. The other investment was in a nuclear submarine refit complex. *(Crown Copyright)*
59. The headquarters facilities at Northwood. *(Crown Copyright)*
60. The new Trident submarine base at Faslane. *(Crown Copyright)*
61. Junior rates dining facilities on *Ark Royal* in the mid-1970s. *(Crown Copyright)*
62. Almost all administrative processes were manual in warships in the 1970s and into the 1980s. *(Crown Copyright)*
63. The Junior Rates club at HMS *Dolphin* in 1975. *(Crown Copyright)*
64. In the 1970s the improvement of facilities for families became an increasing priority. *(Crown Copyright)*

65. Members of the crew of HMS *Ark Royal* observe a Soviet 'Kresta II' cruiser. *(Crown Copyright)*
66. A Sea Harrier shadows a Soviet Tu-16 'Badger' bomber. *(Crown Copyright)*
67. A Soviet 'Backfire B' strike aircraft. *(Public Domain/US Department of Defense)*
68. A Soviet 'Delta III' submarine. *(Public Domain/National Archives and Records Administration, USA)*
69. A Soviet 'Charlie I' class submarine. *(Public Domain/US Department of Defense)*
70. A Soviet 'Victor III' submarine. *(Crown Copyright)*
71. Soviet *Kirov* class cruiser. *(Public Domain/National Archives and Records Administration, USA)*
72. Confidence-building measures in the age of Glasnost. *(Crown Copyright)*

Introduction

On 15 March 1966 Admiral Sir David Luce, the First Sea Lord – the professional head of the Royal Navy – resigned from his post in protest: he was the first holder of that office in over half a century to do so for reasons of government policy. He, along with the Navy Minister Christopher Mayhew, had left office five days into a general election campaign because of the Cabinet's decision not to procure a new large fleet aircraft carrier and then to phase out aircraft carriers altogether from the Navy by 1975. The cancellation of this enormous new capital ship, combined with the resignation of the First Sea Lord, was a trauma for significant sections of the Royal Navy, consigning the centrepiece around which much of the ocean-going surface fleet would be justified to oblivion. It ushered in a period of introspection and re-evaluation in what was informally known as the 'Senior Service', which had previously assumed not only that its aircraft carriers had a central role to play in the defence of the United Kingdom and its vital national interests, but that the Navy itself was a significant and important part of the British state. The resignation of the First Sea Lord in the first half of the twentieth century over a naval policy decision within government would undoubtedly have been a major cause célèbre and might even have threatened the survival of a government. In 1966 however, the resignation barely created a ripple within the national press which quickly moved on to other matters that seemed more relevant to a country that was changing rapidly, both technologically and socially: the launch of the Gemini 8 space rocket at Cape Kennedy in the United States and Britain's first Asian policeman.[1] Two weeks later, the governing Labour Party easily won the general election and increased its majority from four to ninety-eight, so there was to be no last-minute reprieve of the aircraft carriers due to a change in governing party.

The subject of this book is the 25-year period from David Luce's resignation in 1966 through to the end of the Cold War during 1990 and 1991. This was a period in which the Royal Navy had to struggle with a world that was shifting rapidly and in which it seemed to be playing a less important part. How effectively did the Navy fight its important policy battles, including the unsuccessful battle to order a new aircraft carrier? How well did it adjust to the carrier's cancellation, and to the withdrawal from East of Suez? As the focus of British defence policy shifted during the 1970s increasingly towards countering the USSR on the central European front in a potential land/air campaign, how well did it make the case for a broader and less tightly focussed strategy? How did the Navy approach the 1974–5 and 1981 Defence Reviews? What were the key arguments and positions, and how did these reviews progress and how important were the United Kingdom's allies in shaping the eventual outcomes?

The 1970s to the early 1980s was a period of unprecedented uncertainty for the Royal Navy, which for five years between 1975 and 1980 had a core operational area – the waters around the United Kingdom and the North East Atlantic – that was its smallest since the seventeenth century. However, in an irony that was not lost on many contemporaries, this period also saw one of the Royal Navy's most impressive military victories against the odds, when it ensured the liberation of the Falkland Islands in the South Atlantic, across a 7,000 nautical mile logistical chain and against determined and often effective air attack by aircraft operating at a fraction of this distance from their air bases.

The period covered by this book is therefore an important and revealing one in the naval history of the United Kingdom, and in the afterglow of the Falklands victory the policy climate seemed much more favourable than it had been only a few years before. How did the Navy respond to strategic developments led by the United States, to further centralisation in the management of Defence, and the greater involvement of the private sector in support and logistics? In addition, this book will aim to cover areas that have been somewhat neglected or side-lined into secondary roles: personnel policy, support for the fleet and equipment procurement. How important have these three areas been in the development of wider policy during this period?

This book aims to at least go some way to answering these questions, whilst also providing the reader with a comprehensive history of the Royal Navy and British maritime power during the quarter-century from 1966 to 1991. Other histories have analysed this period, not least the late Eric Grove's seminal *Vanguard to Trident* which covered the period 1945 to 1987.[2] But that book was written nearly 35 years ago, when the outcome of the Cold War was still uncertain, and when the author did not have access to the huge quantity of government records that have since been released. John Roberts' *Safeguarding the Nation* also provides a fascinating compendium of Royal Navy operations and much besides since 1956, but it does not provide an analytical approach to the period in question.[3] There have also been histories from the perspective of different arms of the Navy, including the submarine service in *The Silent Deep* by Peter Hennessy and James Jinks, and that part of the Fleet Air Arm that operated from aircraft carriers in David Hobbs' *The British Carrier Strike Fleet after 1945*.[4] Nick Childs' *Age of Invincible* is another notable account of British naval airpower, but focussing on the eponymous ship and her sisters.[5] Several academic monographs and doctoral theses have been written dealing with a range of subjects that bring in the Navy, including British foreign and defence policy in general, nuclear weapons, the withdrawal from 'East of Suez' and other more specific policy issues at different points over the quarter-century.[6] Other histories have focussed solely on military campaigns, in particular the Falklands conflict of 1982,[7] some have covered warship design history,[8] and a good number of biographies and autobiographies have also been published.[9] However, none has analysed the Royal Navy in depth across the period addressed here, as this book aims to do, making use of the full range of government and private archives that are now available; the aim, therefore, is to fill this gap in the literature.

This book is written broadly chronologically, beginning with the Whitehall battle over aircraft carriers and ending with the collapse of the Soviet Union. It also attempts to cover as wide a range of activity as possible: from 'high policy' and strategy, through to personnel, procurement, support and logistics to operations, so the broadly chronologically-arranged chapters include thematic sections covering aspects of these different subject areas. Some chapters focus more on personnel and organisational change, whilst others focus on warship procurement and operations, and others again on high policy, but both a narrative and analytical thread is maintained as the text progresses and the reader can see how policies and activities develop and shift over time.

The book can be divided into three distinct periods: Part I includes Chapters 1 to 9 and deals with the period 1966 to 1975, when operations still included appreciable numbers of forces in the Mediterranean and 'East of Suez'; Part II consists of Chapters 10 to 15 and covers 1975 to 1982 when the Royal Navy faced its greatest policy challenges in a number of generations; and then Part III which analyses the period from after the Falklands conflict to the end of the Cold War. The first chapter provides a wide overview of the Navy as it stood in February 1966, so as to give the reader an understanding of the breadth and scale of the interlinked organisations that constituted and supported the Royal Navy at the point at which the aircraft carrier was cancelled. The next chapter sets out how and why the projected *Queen Elizabeth* class carriers were cancelled; this was a crucial pivot point in the history of the modern Royal Navy, and many of the policy issues that recur during the period studied here are linked to this particular cancellation, either as direct results or reactions, or indirectly as the Royal Navy adjusted to new roles, capabilities and vulnerabilities. From Chapters 3 onwards, the approach is broadly chronological, although with most chapters focussing on specific areas that were significant at a particular time, such as personnel in Chapter 4, overseas commitments in Chapter 9 and so on. As the book progresses, the reader should see strands of analysis that build towards what is the second pivot point in the period studied here: the 1981 Defence Review under Sir John Nott in Chapters 13 and 14 and its aftermath which is set out in Chapter 15. A range of unresolved policy issues and inconsistencies had mounted for the Navy as its operational radius shrank through the late 1960s and 1970s, and Nott's review exposed many of these to a searching scrutiny for which the Royal Navy was not well prepared. In the last third of the book, both the Nott review and the Falklands cast their shadow over the Royal Navy and British defence policy. The Nott review had been partly reversed in areas, but not coherently and in a planned way, which created its own problems, whilst the positive outcome of the Falklands provided political protection for the Navy but its practical lessons were sometimes complex, painful to digest or difficult to map on to a strategic environment dominated by the Cold War.

Acknowledgements

This book could not have been written without the help of a great number of people. Stephen Prince, Andrew Livsey, Tim Benbow and my father John Hampshire, have read drafts of all the chapters of this book, whilst Kevin Rowlands, Matthew Seligmann, Andrew Harris and Andrew Ward have read selected chapters. I am immensely grateful for all their sage advice, suggestions and corrections as I have been writing and fine tuning the book. Their input has been extremely helpful, and any errors that remain are solely my own.

This book is the result of many hours and days in archives and research libraries over a good number of years. I would like to thank my former colleagues at The National Archives in Kew, as well as the staff of the National Maritime Museum in Greenwich, the National Museum of the Royal Navy in Portsmouth, the Liddell Hart Centre for Military Archives at King's College London, the Churchill Archives Centre at Cambridge (in particular Andrew Riley), the Western Manuscripts section of the Bodleian Library at Oxford, the archives at Southampton University, the Russian Military Studies Centre at Cranfield University, the Marine Technology Special Collection at Newcastle University, the British Aero Collection Trust in Bristol, the British Library, the libraries at the Joint Services Command and Staff College and the Royal Military Academy Sandhurst. Many thanks also go to Robert Avery and David Fields for allowing me access to Robert's archive of the RUKUS talks and for reading sections of Chapter 20 to ensure that I had my facts right.

I would also like to thank my colleagues at the Naval Historical Branch: Stephen Prince, the Head of Branch, for being such an understanding and encouraging manager; Kate Brett, fellow Historian and Deputy Head, for sharing her encyclopaedic knowledge of our archival holdings, operational records and policies on inclusion; Jenny Wraight, the Admiralty Librarian, for sharing her equally extensive knowledge of our library holdings and charts, and helping to find and source those difficult-to-locate books and pamphlets; and historian Andrew Harris for our joint work and discussions on defence policy, defence reviews and matters MOD. I would also like to thank George Gelder, especially for his knowledge of Royal Marines history, and Aedan Butler, Lynne Lewis, Sue Price and Richard Margey, for amongst many other things, putting up with me whilst I was occasionally distracted by the dreaded 'big book'. Alastair Noble of the Air Historical Branch deserves much thanks not only for his help in identifying RAF-related sources but also his encouragement and support, and for discussing and sharing his deep understanding of defence policy in the late Cold War.

Steven Haines, Ann Coats, Duncan Redford and Andy Boyd have also knowingly or unknowingly helped in the research and writing of different parts of the book: many thanks. As this work is to some extent the product of much of my career working along the seam between the two worlds of academia and government, I would also like to thank my managers, supervisors and mentors over the last twenty-odd years, but in particular Stephen Twigge, Andrew Lambert, Joe Maiolo, the late Saki Dockrill, the late Eric Grove and Geoffrey Till. Julian Mannering has been an exceptionally understanding editor during both Covid-19 and as the manuscript became somewhat longer than originally planned. Stephen Chumbley has expertly copy-edited this text. I would like to thank both my parents for their support and encouragement in everything I have done, including this mammoth project. My wife and daughter have been a continuous source of support whilst I have been researching and writing the book, particularly in the last months as the final manuscript took shape and the hours spent in the study increased considerably. It would have all been impossible without their forbearance and understanding; thank you Ellie and Florence.

This book is dedicated to two people: to the late Eric Grove, a mentor, encourager-in-chief and friendly critic during both difficult and good times, he will be sorely missed; and to my father, John Hampshire, whose service in the Navy almost exactly matched the period covered by this book. He encouraged my interest in naval history from an early age, and he has unfailingly read and commented on almost every page of the books, chapters and articles I have had published over my career.

The views and opinions expressed in this book are those of the author and should not be taken to represent those of His Majesty's Government, the Ministry of Defence, HM Armed Forces or any other agency.

Abbreviations

1SL	First Sea Lord
2nd PUS	Second Permanent Under-Secretary
2SL	Second Sea Lord
AAW	Anti-Air Warfare
ABM	Anti-Ballistic Missile treaty
ACAS	Assistant Chief of the Air Staff
ACDS	Assistant Chief of the Defence Staff
ACNS	Assistant Chief of the Naval Staff
ACSA	Assistant Chief Scientific Adviser
ADAWS	Action Data Automation and Weapon Systems (shipborne tactical command system)
AEL	Admiralty Engineering Laboratory
AEW	Admiralty Experiment Works
AEW	Airborne Early Warning
AFCENT	Allied Forces Central Europe (NATO)
AFNORTH	Allied Forces North Europe (NATO)
AMC	Authorised Manpower Ceiling
AML	Admiralty Materials Laboratory
AMTE	Admiralty Marine Technology Establishment
ANZUK	Australia, New Zealand and United Kingdom command
AOR	Auxiliary Oiler Replenishment
APS	Assistant Private Secretary
ARE	Admiralty Research Establishment
ARL	Admiralty Research Laboratory
ASR	Air Staff Requirement
AST	Air Staff Target
ASVW	Anti-Surface Vessel Warfare

ASW	Anti-Submarine Warfare
ASWE	Admiralty Surface Weapons Establishment
ATP	Allied Tactical Publication (NATO)
AUS	Assistant Under-Secretary
AUTEC	Atlantic Undersea Test and Evaluation Centre, Bahamas
AUWE	Admiralty Underwater Weapons Establishment
AWACS	Airborne Warning and Control System
AWO	Advanced Warfare Officer
BAE	British Aerospace
BALTAP	Allied Forces Baltic Approaches (NATO)
BDS	British Defence Staff (Washington)
BOST	Basic Operational Sea Training
BR	Book of Reference
BRITFORLEB	British peacekeeping Force, Lebanon
C3	Command, Control and Communications
CAAIS	Computer Assisted Action Information System (shipborne tactical command system)
CACS	Computer Assisted Command System (shipborne tactical command system)
CAP	Combat Air Patrol
CAS	Chief of the Air Staff
CB	Confidential Book
CBF	Commander British Forces
CBM	Condition-Based Management
Cdo	Commando
CDP	Chief of Defence Procurement
CDS	Chief of the Defence Staff
CENTO	Central Treaty Organisation
CFS	Chief of Fleet Support
CGRM	Commandant General Royal Marines
CGS	Chief of the General Staff
CinC	Commander-in-Chief
CINCCHAN	Commander-in-Chief Channel (NATO)
CINCEASTLANT	Commander-in-Chief Eastern Atlantic (NATO)
CINCFLEET	Commander-in-Chief Fleet
CINCNAVHOME	Commander-in-Chief Naval Home Command
CINCNORTH	Commander-in-Chief Northern Command (NATO)
CINCWESTLANT	Commander-in-Chief Western Atlantic (NATO)
CinC WF	Commander-in-Chief Western Fleet
CL	Light Cruiser
CNGF	Common New Generation Frigate ('Project Horizon')

CNO	Chief of Naval Operations (US)
CNS	Chief of the Naval Staff (i.e. First Sea Lord)
CO	Commanding Officer
CofN	Controller of the Navy
COMASGRU 2	Commander, Anti-Submarine Group 2 (NATO)
COMFEF	Commander, Far East Fleet
COMSIXTHFLT	Commander Six Fleet (US)
CONSTRAIN	Consolidation of Training programme
COS	Chiefs of Staff
COSC	Chiefs of Staff Committee
COSSEC	Chiefs of Staff Committee Secretariat
CPO	Chief Petty Officer
CPRS	Central Policy Review Staff
CSA	Chief Scientific Adviser
CTF	Commander Task Force
CTG	Commander Task Group
CTU	Commander Task Unit
CVA	Aircraft Carrier, Strike
CVS	Aircraft Carrier, Support
DCDS	Deputy Chief of the Defence Staff
DCI	Defence Council Instruction
DCNS	Deputy Chief of the Naval Staff
DD	Destroyer
DDG	Destroyer, Guided-missile armed
DDL	Light Destroyer
DGNMT	Director General Naval Manning and Training
DG Ships	Director General, Ships
DGW	Director General, Weapons
DLG	Destroyer Leader, Guided missile armed
DNOR	Director of Naval Operational Requirements
DNOT	Director of Naval Operations and Trade
DN Plans	Director of Naval Plans
DNW	Director of Naval Warfare
DOAE	Defence Operational Analysis Executive
DS4	Defence Secretariat, Ministry of Defence, Branch 4
DS5	Defence Secretariat, Ministry of Defence, Branch 5
DSO	Distinguished Service Order
DSWP	Defence Studies Working Party
DUS	Deputy Under-Secretary
EASTLANT	Operational Area under CINCEASTLANT's command
EDATS	Extra Deep Armed Team Sweep

EEC	European Economic Community
EEZ	Exclusive Economic Zone
EORSAT	Electronic Ocean Reconnaissance Satellite (Soviet)
FAA	Fleet Air Arm
FAMS	Future Air Defence Missile System
FCO	Foreign and Commonwealth Office
FF	Frigate
FFG	Frigate, Guided-missile armed
FOAC	Flag Officer Aircraft Carriers
FOAS	Fleet Operational Analysis Staff
FOCAS	Flag Officer Carriers and Amphibious Shipping
FOF1	Flag Officer First Flotilla
FOF2	Flag Officer Second Flotilla
FOF3	Flag Officer Third Flotilla
FONAC	Flag Officer Naval Air Command
FOSM	Flag Officer Submarines
FOSNI	Flag Officer Scotland and Northern Ireland
FOST	Flag Officer Sea Training
FOTI	Fleet Operational and Tactical Instructions
FPB	Fast Patrol Boat
FPDA	Five Powers Defence Arrangements
FRC	Fleet Requirements Committee
GDP	Gross Domestic Product
GEC	General Electric Company
GIUK	Greenland-Iceland-United Kingdom gap
GNP	Gross National Product
GRP	Glass Reinforced Plastic
GWS	Guided Weapon System
HMSO	Her/His Majesty's Stationery Office
HQ	Headquarters
ICS	Internal Communication System
IFF	Interrogator: Friend or Foe
JMOPS	Joint Maritime Operating Procedures
JTIDS	Joint Tactical Information Distribution System (US)
LCHMA	Liddell Hart Centre for Military Archives
LCVP	Landing Craft, Vehicle Personnel
LGC	Lieutenant's Greenwich Course
LOLA	Logistics and Loitering Area
LPD	Landing Ship, Dock (Personnel)
LPH	Landing Ship, Helicopter (Personnel)
LSL	Landing Ship, Logistics

LST	Landing Ship, Tank
LTC	Long Term Costings
LTCA	Long Term Costing Assumptions
LTSG	Long Term Study Group
MAD	Magnetic Anomaly Detector
MAFF	Ministry of Agriculture Fisheries and Food
MBT	Main Battle Tank
MC	Military Concept (NATO)
MCM	Mine Counter Measures
MCMV	Mine Counter Measures Vessels
MINIS	Management Information System for Ministers
MIRV	Multiple Independently targetable Re-entry Vehicle
MNF	Multi-National Force (Lebanon)
MOD	Ministry of Defence
MPA	Maritime Patrol Aircraft
NAS	Naval Air Squadron
NASA	National Aeronautics and Space Administration (US)
NATO	North Atlantic Treaty Organisation
NCS	Naval Control of Shipping
NFR90	NATO Frigate Replacement Programme
NGS	Naval Gunfire Support
NHB	Naval Historical Branch
NMM	National Maritime Museum
NMR	Naval Manpower Requirement
NMRN	National Museum of the Royal Navy
NSR	Naval Staff Requirement
NST	Naval Staff Target
OA	Operational Analysis
OBE	Order of the British Empire
OD	Oversea Policy and Defence Committee of Cabinet
OEG	Operational Evaluation Group
OPD	Oversea Policy and Defence Committee of Cabinet
OPDO	Oversea Policy and Defence Committee (Officials Committee)
OPV	Offshore Patrol Vessel
ORC	Operational Requirements Committee
OSIS	Ocean Surveillance Information System
PAS	Port Auxiliary Service
PLO	Palestinian Liberation Organisation
PS	Private Secretary
PUS	Permanent Under-Secretary

PWO	Principal Warfare Officer
QARNNS	Queen Alexandra's Royal Naval Nursing Service
RAF	Royal Air Force
R&D	Research and Development
RAN	Royal Australian Navy
RFA	Royal Fleet Auxiliary
RM	Royal Marines
RMAS	Royal Maritime Auxiliary Service
RN	Royal Navy
RNR	Royal Naval Reserve
RNSTS	Royal Naval Supply and Transport Service
RNV(S)R	Royal Naval Volunteer (Special) Reserve
RNXS	Royal Naval Auxiliary Service
RNZN	Royal New Zealand Navy
ROE	Rules of Engagement
RORSAT	Radar Ocean Reconnaissance Satellite (Soviet)
RUKUS	Russia-United Kingdom-United States Naval Talks
SACEUR	Supreme Allied Commander Europe (NATO)
SACLANT	Supreme Allied Commander Atlantic (NATO)
SACLANTCEN	Anti-Submarine Warfare Research Centre
SAG	Surface Action Group
SALT	Strategic Arms Limitations Talks
SAS	Special Air Service
SAWC	Sea-Air Warfare Committee
SBS	Special Boat Service
SDAF	Scottish Department of Agriculture and Fisheries
SIOP	Single Integrated Operational Plan (for nuclear weapons use)
SLOCs	Sea Lines of Communication
SNFL	Standing Naval Force Atlantic (NATO)
SNOSA	Senior Naval Officer South Africa
SNOWI	Senior Naval Officer West Indies
SofS	Secretary of State
SOKS	Sistyema Obnaruzhyeniya Kil'vatyernogo Slyeda (wake detection system, Soviet)
SOP	Standard Operating Procedures
SOSUS	Sound Surveillance System
SRMH	Single Role Mine Hunter (*Sandown* class)
SSBN	Nuclear powered ballistic missile firing submarine
SSGW	Ship to Ship Guided Weapon system
SSK	Diesel Electric attack submarine

SSN	Nuclear powered attack submarine
STANAVFORLANT	Standing Naval Force Atlantic (NATO)
STRKFLTLANT 1	Atlantic Strike Fleet 1 (NATO)
STRKFLTLANT 2	Atlantic Strike Fleet 2 (NATO)
STUFT	Ships Taken Up From Trade
SURTAS	Surveillance Towed Array System
TACTAS	Tactical Towed Array System
TEZ	Total Exclusion Zone
TF	Task Force
TG	Task Group
TLB	Top Level Budgets
TNA	The National Archives of the United Kingdom
TRALA	Tugs, Repair and Logistics Area
TU	Task Unit
UDI	Unilateral Declaration of Independence
USCG	US Coast Guard
USCGC	US Coast Guard Cutter
US of S	Under-Secretary of State
VCAS	Vice Chief of the Air Staff
VCDS	Vice Chief of the Defence Staff
VCGS	Vice Chief of the General Staff
VCNS	Vice Chief of the Naval Staff
VERTREP	Vertical Replenishment
VSTOL	Vertical or Short Take-Off and Landing
VSEL	Vickers Shipbuilding and Engineering Ltd
VT	Vosper Thornycroft
WESTLANT	Operational area under CINCWESTLANT's command
WOI	Warrant Officer I
WOII	Warrant Officer II
WRNR	Women's Royal Naval Reserve
WRNS	Women's Royal Naval Service

Part I: Retreat, 1966–1975

1

February 1966

As Admiral Luce was preparing to resign as First Sea Lord, what did the Royal Navy look like? Where was it based, how were its assets – material and human – distributed, how did it operate, who were its personnel, how was it supported and how large was the civilian infrastructure that backed it up? In February 1966 the best place to start would be at the huge naval base and dockyard complex at Singapore, the home of the Royal Navy's Far East Fleet and the most powerful force in the Navy. This was a relatively recent phenomenon; as recently as 1955, the Far East station was a relative backwater, consisting of two cruisers and only five destroyers. Most of the Navy was, at this time, operating in home waters or with the Mediterranean Fleet, which in 1955 consisted of two carriers, two cruisers and eleven destroyers, in support of a role focussed on countering the Soviet Union in Europe and the Middle East.[1] In the aftermath of the 1957 Defence Review, the First Sea Lord, Admiral Mountbatten, had deliberately re-oriented the Navy away from direct superpower confrontation in and near Europe, towards fighting global 'brush fire' conflicts as the United Kingdom decolonised but wanted to ensure that friendly governments stayed in place following independence. This 'East of Suez strategy' was focussed on fighting the Cold War, but this was a globalised 'cold' conflict in which Soviet-backed or inspired rebels and revolutionaries would be countered by British forces supporting newly-established governments which usually operated a 'Westminster-style' democratic system, at least initially. These brush fire wars included supporting land and air forces during the Malayan Insurgency of the 1950s and early 1960s, and the Indonesian Confrontation across Borneo and neighbouring seas between 1963 and 1966. The Royal Navy was also heavily used to pre-empt or prevent the overthrow of established governments: not least through the landing of forces to protect Kuwait in the Persian Gulf from a possible invasion by Iraq in 1961, and in 1964 putting down a 'barrack room' revolt in Tanganyika that could have escalated into a military coup.[2]

The Far East Fleet
In February 1966, the British Far East Fleet included the Royal Navy's two largest aircraft carriers: HMS *Ark Royal* and HMS *Eagle*. *Ark Royal*, escorted by two frigates of the 23rd Escort Squadron, was on passage across the Indian Ocean to Mombasa for a period of 'self-maintenance', where her own crew would undertake minor repairs and maintenance alongside at Kenya's main commercial port. Mombasa was a regular stopping-off point for such maintenance periods, a role that would remain throughout the period covered by this book, not least during the 1980s when Royal Navy vessels regularly visited whilst stationed in the Persian Gulf. Embarked on *Ark Royal* was the Second in Command of the Far East Fleet, Vice Admiral Peter Hill-Norton, and his staff, whilst back in Singapore the Commander of the Far East Fleet, Vice Admiral Sir Frank Twiss, was based at the shore establishment and naval base HMS *Terror*.[3] *Ark Royal* had on board Scimitar strike aircraft from 803 Naval Air Squadron ('NAS') of the Fleet Air Arm, Sea Vixen fighters from 890 NAS, as well as a flight of Gannet airborne early warning aircraft and anti-submarine Wessex helicopters from 815 NAS.[4] *Ark Royal* and her escorts were involved in what was becoming known as the Beira Patrol, an attempted blockade of the Mozambiquan port of Beira, through which the rebel white-minority regime of Rhodesia was being supplied. Quite soon, the patrol would reduce to two and later only one frigate supported by maritime patrol aircraft, but at this point the demonstration of Britain's resolve was deemed to require a task group led by an aircraft carrier.[5]

Table 1: British Far East Fleet February 1966[6]

	Active	*Reserve*	*Refit/docking/ maintenance*
Aircraft carriers	1		1
Commando carriers	1		
Guided missile destroyers			1
Frigates/older destroyers	13 (+4 RAN, 1 RNZN)		
Diesel-electric submarines	3		2
Minesweepers/minehunters	12 (+2 RAN, 2 RNZN)	2	4 (+2 RAN)
Depot/maintenance/support ships	2	1	1
Seaward defence boats	2	2	2

At Singapore HMS *Eagle* was in a period of maintenance in the largest dry dock there, the King George VI graving dock. This would finish on 28 February, after which she would sail into the Indian Ocean and relieve *Ark Royal* off Beira. The new and large guided missile destroyer, HMS *Devonshire*, was also in dock maintenance with plans for her to depart with *Eagle* and accompany her to the coast of East Africa. The commando carrier, HMS *Albion*, was off Borneo supporting British Commonwealth forces fighting Indonesian-backed fighters, with many of her troop-carrying Wessex helicopters of 848 Squadron operating ashore from Labuan and Simbang. She would return to Singapore on 28 February and replace *Eagle* in dry dock for a period of maintenance. Two Royal Marine Commandos (each an equivalent to a battalion) were based in the region, 40 Commando in Singapore and 42 Commando in Sarawak, Borneo. The headquarters of the Royal Marines' Brigade was also in Singapore. The large fleet maintenance ship, and converted aircraft carrier, HMS *Triumph*, was making a port visit to Bangkok and was expected to return to Singapore on 25 February. Most of the frigates of the Far East Fleet were involved in Exercise Mill Stream: HM Ships *Dido* and *Berwick* of the 21st Escort Squadron, *Lincoln* of the 24th Escort Squadron, *Euryalus* of the 26th Escort Squadron and *Plymouth* and *Chichester* of the 29th Escort Squadron. Of the other frigates in the Far East Fleet, HMS *Salisbury* was making a port visit to Tawau in Sabah on the island of Borneo, HMS *Ajax* was on post-refit trials, whilst the old frigate *Loch Fada* was at Penang on the west coast of Malaysia. The old destroyers *Barrosa* and *Cambrian* of the 26th and 29th Escort Squadrons were both at Singapore, the former available for tasking, whilst the latter was in self-maintenance.[7]

The major warships of the Far East Fleet therefore included some of the newest ships in the fleet such as the 6,000-ton guided missile destroyer *Devonshire*, and the 2,500-ton *Leander* class frigates *Dido*, *Euryalus* and *Ajax*, as well as the modern 2,000-ton Type 12 anti-submarine frigates *Rhyl*, *Lowestoft*, *Berwick* and *Plymouth*, and the 2,000-ton Type 61 aircraft direction frigates *Salisbury*, *Lincoln* and *Chichester*. The older vessels of Second World War vintage, *Barrosa*, *Loch Fada* and *Cambrian*, had all been substantially modernised over the last decade, with *Barrosa* converted to an aircraft direction destroyer, *Cambrian* fitted with the Sea Cat air defence missile system and modern radar and *Loch Fada* modernised with newer radar and guns in the 1950s. In addition to surface ships, there was one squadron of submarines: the 7th Submarine Squadron consisted of six conventional diesel-electric powered submarines, five of which were 'A' class boats built soon after the Second World War but since modernised and the last was an 'O' class boat, completed only a few years previously. Three – *Ambush*, *Anchorite* and *Oberon* – were taking part in Exercise Mill Stream, whilst HMS *Andrew* was in maintenance, HMS *Amphion* was in refit in Singapore and HMS *Auriga* was on passage out from home waters.[8]

The Far East Fleet did not just consist of these ocean-going warships: there were also three squadrons of mine warfare vessels of the 'Ton' class totalling fifteen ships, one squadron of which operated as patrol vessels stationed at Hong Kong. In addition to *Triumph*, *Manxman* and *Medway* were the Fleet's mine warfare support ship and submarine depot ship respectively, and the Fleet was supported by seven tankers, one fleet support ship, five stores support ships and three armament support ships all operated by the Royal Fleet Auxiliary, registered merchant vessels owned by the British government which ensured that the warships were kept stocked with fuel, stores, victualling and armaments at sea. The Far East Fleet also operated one ocean-going survey ship, whilst within the bounds of Singapore dockyard there were twelve Port Auxiliary Service tugs, with a thirteenth at Hong Kong and a fourteenth larger tug operated by the Royal Fleet Auxiliary for ocean work. These were further supplemented by a water supply boat, an armament supply vessel and a dizzying range of other smaller supporting craft that enabled warships to be supplied within the naval base, operate effectively and train. The Royal Australian and Royal New Zealand Navies also contributed important forces to the Far East Fleet, the former with two destroyers, both of which were taking part in Exercise Millstream, and four mine-warfare vessels, and the latter with a frigate and two mine-warfare vessels.[9]

Threats in Eastern Waters
In February 1966, with the Confrontation fully underway, the Royal Navy's main adversary in the region was the navy and other armed forces of Indonesia. Other regional navies were either friendly, neutral or too far away to be a threat. Occasional Soviet warships would pass through from the west to the naval bases of the Soviet Pacific Fleet, but these were rare occurrences and there was – as yet – no ability to sustain a presence in either the Indian Ocean or the South China Sea and Straits of Malacca.[10] Indonesia had, however, increasingly aligned itself with the Soviet Union during the late 1950s and 1960s, and could be seen as a Soviet proxy in the region: the Navy could therefore argue that the Far East Fleet was fighting the spread of communism just as much as any forces in Europe or the Atlantic.

The Indonesian Navy had been fully re-equipped from the late 1950s onwards with Soviet ships, including the large *Sverdlov* class cruiser *Irian*, seven *Skory* class destroyers, twelve 'Whiskey' class submarines, and eight smaller escorts, six of which were ex-Soviet 'Riga' class vessels. Smaller craft included a mix of vessels, but the most worrying for the Royal Navy must have been fourteen 'Komar' class fast attack craft armed with P15 'Styx' anti-ship cruise missiles. Although the pride of the fleet, the *Irian*, was normally based at the capital Jakarta, most of the fleet was based at Surabaya in the east of the island of Java, some 800 nautical miles from Singapore. A naval intelligence assessment from 1963 acknowledged that this naval force might be 'formidable on paper, but its capabilities are limited due to lack of experience and training as well as by maintenance difficulties,' although it was acknowledged that continued Soviet assistance and support could increase this capability over time.[11]

The Indonesian Navy usually kept its distance from Royal Navy vessels, operating coastal patrols to prevent the insertion of British forces, although in September 1964 the two navies did come close to direct conflict as a British task group led by an aircraft carrier undertook a freedom of navigation exercise through the Straits of Lombok not too far from Surabaya. It had originally been planned to proceed through the Sunda Strait near Jakarta, but the Indonesian Navy declared an exercise zone in the strait and the British decided not to force the issue, aware that both the Australians and Malaysians were concerned about escalation, so the force transited the Lombok strait instead.[12] No confrontation occurred that day, although the passage of the Lombok strait had been undertaken at defence stations and at one point the task group was shadowed by an Indonesian 'Whiskey' class submarine.[13] This incident was a one-off: usually naval forces were used to support operations on land or deter Indonesian raids on some of the smaller islands off Malaysian Borneo. East of Suez, the Royal Navy was not dealing with the sort of 'peer adversary' that it faced in European waters, but with forces which although impressive in some respects were outmatched by British capabilities.

Other Overseas Stations: Middle East, Mediterranean, South Atlantic and West Indies

The Far East Fleet was not the only station east of the Suez Canal. In the Western Indian Ocean and the Persian Gulf, the Flag Officer Middle East, Rear Admiral Peter Howes, was in charge of a smaller force consisting of three Type 81 frigates of the 9th Frigate Squadron, a squadron of 'Ton' class mine warfare vessels and an amphibious force consisting of one veteran Tank Landing Ship, HMS *Striker* and a Tank Landing Craft, HMS *Bastion*, supported by a number of small landing craft. In addition to these vessels were a range of auxiliaries and supporting craft, albeit much fewer in number and role than at Singapore. The Flag Officer Middle East, reporting to a tri-service Commander-in-Chief Middle East, operated from the shore establishment HMS *Sheba* in Aden, now within modern Yemen, with a Senior Naval Officer Persian Gulf in Bahrain at HMS *Jufair*. Of the Type 81 frigates, HMS *Gurkha* was on Persian Gulf Patrol, whilst *Nubian* was at Bahrain undergoing self-maintenance. HMS *Eskimo* was making a port visit to Socotra, a large island east of the Horn of Africa 500 nautical miles from Aden. This was a much smaller force than that of the mighty Far East Fleet, but it was one of the elements of the British presence in the Persian Gulf region, which also included RAF aircraft and a small Army garrison in Bahrain, which fulfilled a series of defensive agreements with the sheikhdoms and small states along the shores of the Gulf, whilst also protecting and supporting the flow of oil, drilled by British companies, which left by tanker from Iranian ports. Unlike at Singapore, there was no great dockyard, so ships needing more than basic self-maintenance would have to either sail east, or west to Gibraltar dockyard at the mouth of the Mediterranean.[14]

The Mediterranean had been for many years the crucible of British naval power, the scene for major naval campaigns and battles from the eighteenth century up to the Second World War, and historically the sea in which the Royal Navy's second most powerful fleet operated after those in home waters. By 1966, however, the British Mediterranean Fleet was a shadow of its former self. Even the title 'Fleet' was an embarrassing misnomer for a force that was smaller and less capable than either the Middle East Station or the small South Atlantic and South America Station and the West Indies Station which will be described below. The Commander-in-Chief Mediterranean, Admiral Sir John Hamilton, who 'double-hatted' as NATO's main maritime commander in that sea and was based in Malta, had responsibility for only one ageing destroyer, HMS *Defender*, and six 'Ton' class mine warfare vessels. Aside from these ships, several even older vessels swung at anchor in reserve, mostly at Gibraltar. The Flag Officer Gibraltar, Rear Admiral Thomas Best, who reported to C-in-C Mediterranean, had responsibility for an important dockyard and naval base, but he had no fully active warships allocated to him, and his dockyard largely operated as an overflow for refit work in United Kingdom yards.[15] In 1966 the Mediterranean primarily served as a transit route for ships deploying to and from 'East of Suez' and was barely active as a Royal Navy functioning operational command. The NATO role at least gave Admiral Hamilton more experience of commanding multiple warships, as during exercises Alliance members would subordinate the command of their warships to the local NATO commander.

The South Atlantic and South America Station, as its name suggests, covered both the huge expanse of the South Atlantic and the Pacific coast of Latin America. For support it made use of South African maintenance and berthing facilities at the naval base of Simonstown in Cape Province. The Commander-in-Chief of the Station, Vice Admiral John Gray, was based at Youngsfield in the suburbs of Cape Town, an uncomfortable position given that South Africa had recently left the Commonwealth and was coming under increasing international criticism for its apartheid system and for sustaining white minority rule in a majority black country.[16] Two Type 41 frigates, *Puma* and *Jaguar*, were supplemented by a Royal Fleet Auxiliary and the Ice Patrol Ship *Protector*, which patrolled the Falkland Islands and other British dependencies in the far South Atlantic. On the 15 February 1966, HMS *Puma* was working her way down the West African coastline, making ports visits to Bathurst in the newly independent Gambia, followed by Monrovia in Liberia.

Meanwhile *Jaguar* was three days sailing away from Stanley in the Falklands, heading for a series of port visits up the Pacific coast of South America before transiting the Panama Canal on 20 March.[17]

The Senior Naval Officer West Indies ('SNOWI'), Commodore H Dannreuther, was based at the British colony of Bermuda, and had command of three warships, the frigates *Rothesay* and *Ursa*, and the destroyer *Dainty*. *Ursa* was at the British colony of the Bahamas, which was home to the Atlantic Undersea Test and Evaluation Centre ('AUTEC'), a US-run underwater trials centre that took advantage of the deep-water basin off Andros Island. *Dainty* was escorting a Royal visit in the Royal Yacht HMY *Britannia* to the West Indies, whilst *Rothesay* was undergoing maintenance in Bermuda.[18] In 1966, much of the English-speaking Caribbean was still under British rule, although Jamaica and Trinidad and Tobago had already gained their independence, and several other islands were in the process of following them.[19] Royal Navy vessels not only 'showed the flag' but, each with a small Royal Marine party, also provided back-up to British governors in the event of riots or other disturbances. They also helped to deter Guatemalan designs on the colony of British Honduras, which the former claimed as its own.

Individually, these four small stations consisted of only a handful of frigates each but taken together they were a significant commitment for the Royal Navy, especially when the roulement of ships in and out of station is taken into account. The Mediterranean Fleet had been the main victim of the gradual increase of the Far East Fleet during the late 1950s and early 1960s, causing tensions when both the French and the Italian Navies easily contributed more ships to NATO exercises in the Mediterranean, and yet were not given command status. The squadron in the Persian Gulf was directly tied to the series of long-standing treaties in the region which ensured British protection for a number of semi-states that retained independent internal self-government, whilst the West Indies Station was strongly linked to the United Kingdom's residual colonial possessions. The South Atlantic Station involved a mix of minor colonial responsibilities such as the Falklands Islands and a more general 'presence' role in the region. Given the priority was the Far East Fleet at the time, it seemed very difficult to envisage the Mediterranean and South Atlantic stations having an independent status for much longer. The future of the South Atlantic Station looked particularly precarious given that it depended on the use of naval facilities in white minority-ruled South Africa.

The Home Fleet
At first glance, the Home Fleet appeared to be by far the most powerful force in the Royal Navy: consisting of three aircraft carriers, three cruisers, three guided missile destroyers and forty-three frigates and destroyers, commanded

by Vice Admiral Sir John Frewen, the Commander-in-Chief Home Fleet, who 'doubled-hatted' in the NATO operational role as Commander-in-Chief Eastern Atlantic and was based at Northwood in Middlesex alongside the headquarters of RAF's Coastal Command. In reality, Frewen's force was much less operationally capable than it would initially seem: of the three carriers, *Hermes* and *Victorious* were in refit, whilst *Centaur* was in preservation pending either scrap or conversion to a commando carrier. Of the three cruisers, *Lion* was in preservation pending a decision on her future and *Blake* was awaiting a decision on plans to convert her to a helicopter cruiser, so only *Tiger* was active, taking part in Exercise Sailor's Pride, an anti-submarine and air defence training exercise between Gibraltar and the Western Approaches.[20] With the three large guided missile destroyers, the story was similar: *London* and *Kent* were in refit, whilst only *Hampshire* was operational, training at Portland, with a visit to Belfast due the following month. Of the forty-three frigates and older destroyers, fourteen were training ships: the Type 12 frigates, *Eastbourne*, *Torquay*, *Scarborough* and *Tenby* formed the 17th Escort Squadron, better known as the Dartmouth Training Squadron, providing officer cadets with their first experience at sea. In February 1966, the first three were preparing for their annual spring cruise, which would include port calls across the Mediterranean, including Malta, Trieste, Corfu, Athens, Izmir and Gibraltar. The frigates *Aurora*, *Dundas*, *Murray*, *Pellew* and *Ulster* comprised the 2nd Frigate Squadron based at Portland, the anti-submarine training squadron whose roles included training sonar operators and torpedo specialists. Two of the ships, *Murray* and *Pellew*, were about to take part in Exercise Sailor's Pride. Five frigates, *Yarmouth*, *Naiad*, *Grafton*, *Hardy* and *Russell*, made up the active ships of the 20th Frigate Squadron, based at Londonderry, and provided the sea-based side of the advanced anti-submarine training school based in that town. A further three frigates, *Penelope*, *Verulam* and *Wakeful*, were trials ships. HMS *Whirlwind*, of Second World War vintage, was about to arrive back to her home port, Portsmouth, to be prepared for decommissioning and disposal as scrap. A further fifteen frigates were in refit or under repair. These were the older destroyers and frigates *Decoy*, *Diana*, *Carysfort*, *Aisne*, *Relentless*, *Zest* and *Undaunted*, as well as the Type 81 frigates *Mohawk* and *Ashanti*, the Type 12s *Falmouth*, *Brighton* and *Whitby*, and also *Arethusa*, *Leopard* and *Llandaff*, which were respectively of the *Leander*, Type 41 and Type 61 classes.[21]

After all these vessels were removed from the inventory, there remained a total of ten frigates and destroyers. Of these, seven were either returning from overseas deployments or working up in preparation for them, and were therefore assigned to the Home Fleet just for these short periods. HMS *Lynx* of the 7th Frigate Squadron was with the Home Fleet for a number of months before going into refit and then returning to the South Atlantic to relieve

Table 2: British Home Fleet February 1966[22]

	Active	Reserve	Refit
Nuclear submarines	1 (sea trials)		
Aircraft carriers			2
Cruisers	1	1	1
Guided missile destroyers	1		2
Frigates/older destroyers	25		16
Diesel-electric submarines (under FOSM)	14		17
Minesweepers/minehunters (under Capt MCM)	6		7
Depot/maintenance/support ships	3		1

her sister ships later in the year. HMS *Zulu* of the 9th Frigate Squadron was working up prior to re-joining the Middle East Station, whilst HMS *Tartar* of the 8th Frigate Squadron was spending a short period with the Home Fleet so her crew could take leave before returning to her previous role on the West Indies Station. The story was similar with *Delight* and *Leander* of the 21st Escort Squadron and *Blackpool* and *Londonderry* of the 29th Escort Squadron: the first two were working up prior to taking the passage to Singapore, whilst the second two had just returned to the United Kingdom to ensure that their crews gained their requisite leave periods at home before setting off for Singapore again in June. This therefore left the three active ships of the 27th Escort Squadron, the *Leander* class frigate HMS *Galatea*, the older destroyer HMS *Agincourt* and the older frigate HMS *Troubridge*, to cover taskings across both home waters and the Mediterranean. As of 15 February 1966, they were all at Gibraltar prior to taking part in Exercise Sailor's Pride.[23]

The Mine Countermeasures Flotilla, based at HMS *Lochinvar* on the Firth of Forth, consisted of the first and third mine countermeasures squadrons with twelve 'Ton' class mine warfare vessels, the diving ship *Reclaim* and the minelayer *Plover*. These were supplemented by twelve minesweepers and two seaward defence boats operated by the Royal Naval Reserve.[24] The Home Fleet was supported by seven tankers and one fleet replenishment ship operated by the Royal Fleet Auxiliary: two of these were supporting the West Indies Station on 15 February and another was taking part in Exercise Sailor's Pride.[25]

This might seem to be a dire situation with only one cruiser, one guided missile destroyer, three other frigates and destroyers and twelve mine warfare vessels to cover all eventualities in home and Mediterranean waters. However, in the event of an emergency, the ships of the Londonderry Squadron would be available for tasking and, if it came to it, would provide the kernel of an anti-submarine escort force. In addition, the four active frigates of the Fishery Protection Squadron, which are described below, could also be re-deployed for anti-submarine duties. It also reflects the nature of naval operations: ships need to be maintained, repaired and refitted and their crews need leave time, meaning that it is never possible to have all ships available at all times. Looked at another way, the deployment of the surface fleet at this time was quite impressive: a significant number of ships were taking part not only in two major exercises on opposite sides of the world, Exercise Sailor's Pride off the Azores and Exercise Mill Stream in the Malacca Straits, but also sustaining a significant aircraft carrier-led force deployed off the east coast of Africa.

In 1954 'Foreign Service' and 'General Service' commissions had been introduced in order to ensure that the long periods away from home that came with overseas deployments were spread as evenly as possible across the fleet, and to ensure that a ship's company was 'block drafted' onto a vessel and could therefore work together for 30 months without the disruption of sailors joining and leaving the ship at different times. Ships on General Service Commissions, which in 1966 included all the aircraft carriers and most of the ships deployed overseas, were assigned a maximum of 12 months overseas and 18 months in home waters in each 30-month commission. Ships on Foreign Service Commissions, which were the two commando carriers and the 24th and 26th Escort Squadrons in February 1966, had 18 months overseas and 12 months in home waters. The three training squadrons in home waters and the Fishery Protection Squadron operated on Home Sea Service terms which assumed either short periods or no periods at all on overseas deployment.[26] When it had been introduced, this scheme had ensured that those serving in the Far East Fleet had not borne the brunt of long periods away from the United Kingdom, but as will be seen in Chapter 4, this system was beginning to come under significant strain.

The Soviet Threat in Home and North Atlantic Waters

The Soviet Northern Fleet, stationed in a number of bases in the White Sea and fjords facing onto the Barents and Norwegian Seas, would be the Royal Navy's main adversary in the event of confrontation or war. Most of the ships of the Royal Navy – not just those in the Home and Mediterranean Fleets – were declared to NATO, but many of these were on two to three weeks' notice, which theoretically gave sufficient time to bring much of the Far East Fleet and ships on other stations home. Whether such an emergency involving the Warsaw Pact would allow for 14 to 21 days to mass forces was another matter. In 1966, this did not appear to be a major issue, for although the Soviet Navy was beginning to build up an impressive fleet of nuclear submarines and ocean-going warships, the removal of Khrushchev as General Secretary of the USSR Communist Party, and the declared policy of peaceful co-existence by his successors Andrei Kosygin and Leonid Brezhnev, had taken away much of the worry of war that had hung over NATO during and immediately after the Cuban Missile Crisis of 1962.[27]

In 1966 the Northern Fleet consisted of three large conventional cruisers of the *Sverdlov* class and six conventional destroyers of the Project 56 'Kotlin' class, plus a number of 'Kildin' and 'Kanin' class destroyers armed with medium-range anti-ship missiles. The fleet was also home to a very large number of submarines including numerous boats of the 'Whiskey', 'Zulu', 'Romeo' and 'Foxtrot' classes. In addition, and most significantly, the Soviet Navy had begun three production lines of nuclear-powered submarines in the late 1950s: the 'Hotel' class ballistic missile submarines, the 'Echo' class cruise missile submarines and the 'November' class attack submarines.[28] Seven 'Hotels', 16 'Echos' and 10 'Novembers' were stationed with the Northern Fleet, a huge force considering that the Royal Navy only had one nuclear-powered submarine in service (albeit with another seven building).[29] These submarines were impressive vessels, and although they were known for being excessively noisy, which was a significant flaw in vessels that are meant to use stealth as a means to conduct successful attacks, they made up for this with both numbers and the long-range 'carrier killing' SS-N-3 'Shaddock' missiles that the 'Echo' class carried. In 1966 it was also thought that these submarines could not reach speeds above 25 knots underwater, but two years later NATO analysts would be disabused of this notion when a 'November' class achieved 30 knots when tracking a US carrier task group.[30] The newest generation of Soviet destroyers (which the Soviets themselves called Large Anti-Submarine Ships) also demonstrated the leaps being made in capability. These 'Kashin' class ships were armed with two twin SA-N-1 'Goa' air defence missile launchers and a helicopter with hangar and were the first major warships to be solely powered by gas turbines; two were based with the Northern Fleet. Finally, the Soviet Navy had a large fleet of smaller vessels including patrol boats, minesweepers and fast attack craft, all of which were well represented in the Northern Fleet. The most powerful fast attack craft were the dozens of 'Komar' and 'Osa' class missile attack craft firing the SS-N-2 'Styx' missile. As has been seen, several had been sold to Indonesia (and to other Soviet-friendly states) with more under construction.[31] A number of both classes were with the Northern Fleet, although the difficult weather conditions in northern waters must have limited their operational range and availability. Air cover for surface units could only come from MiG-15 and MiG-17 land-based naval fighters, which would in practice have tied the surface ships relatively close to naval air bases in the event of general war, though warships would have operated further afield during peacetime and in support of local overseas interventions.[32] The Soviet naval forces of the Northern Fleet were therefore large and impressive but largely focussed on the submarine arm for its wartime offensive capabilities.

In terms of Soviet strategy, the United States Navy assumed that the large Soviet submarine fleet was designed to attack shipping running along western sea lines of communication ('SLOCs') in the event of war: preventing reinforcements reaching Western Europe and perhaps even starving it into submission. Many in the US Navy also believed that the Soviet Navy could also attempt to wrest oceanic sea control from NATO using its long-range cruise missiles to attack carrier battle groups. In reality, Soviet naval strategy was quite different and was in essence strategically defensive. In wartime its focus was to keep nuclear weapon-equipped aircraft carriers, and Polaris submarines, as far away as possible from the Soviet Union and to destroy them, and to protect the Soviet navy's own nuclear submarines in mid-ocean. It did not wish to gain sea control through great sea battles, but to exploit areas of no control where it could, and create an area of sea denial it termed the 'blue belt of defence'.[33] Some naval analysts attempted to shift the US understanding of Soviet naval strategy based on detailed analysis of open and closed Soviet publications, but the protection of SLOCs and a battle for general sea control had a strong grip on the US Navy, all of whose senior leaders had served in the Second World War where the Battle of the Atlantic against German U-boats and great carrier battles in the Pacific against the Japanese loomed large in their understanding of war at sea.[34] In the Royal Navy, the analysis was closer to the Soviet reality: the four key roles of the Soviet Navy were perceived in 1966 to be the destruction of NATO carrier groups, operations against Polaris submarines, strategic nuclear strike and the defence of the coastal zone, including amphibious operations in support of the army.[35] The disruption of SLOCs would only occur after the four primary tasks had been completed. Overall, the Soviet Navy was assessed as being formidable in its home waters but that it would take many years to become a worldwide maritime power and that this was in any case not their objective as their strategy was defensive: 'their requirement is to counter the Western Fleets, rather than compete with them in an area where the West has such considerable initial advantage.'[36] This analysis had broadly remained constant through the 1960s up to this point, although in 1962 in the immediate aftermath of the Cuban Missile Crisis, the British assessment had briefly shifted towards a view that the Soviet aim was 'the acquisition of sea power in global war' having fully 'appreciated the role of sea power in history and therefore its role in their own destiny, which they believe to be world domination.'[37] As tensions reduced the following year, this view disappeared, but it did suggest that assessments could change rapidly as a result of international political developments and move away from an analysis based on publicly-stated Soviet policy and strategy. In any case, the post-Cuba thaw and significant improvement in US-Soviet relations had taken much of the tension out of the confrontation, even to the extent that some feared for the future of NATO, and consequently much of the Royal Navy's active fleet was operational on overseas stations rather than closer to home.[38] In the mid-1960s it was expected to be much more likely that the Royal Navy would end up fighting Soviet-made ships operated by Third-World navies, rather than the Soviet Navy itself.

Other United Kingdom-based Commands
In addition to the Home Fleet, there were 'cross-cutting' functional commands responsible for aircraft, submarines and the Royal Marines that were usually deployed under the command of the relevant Commander-in-Chief or regional Flag Officer either home or abroad. The Fleet Air Arm was under the control of two United Kingdom-based Flag Officers: Flag Officer Aircraft Carriers, Rear Admiral Hugh Janvrin, who, via the relevant Commanders-in-Chief, controlled the four aircraft carriers, and Flag Officer Naval Air Command ('FONAC'), Rear Admiral Donald Gibson, who controlled flying training and the naval air stations. FONAC had responsibility for four major air stations: from Yeovilton in Somerset there flew Sea Vixen fighters for the carriers in 890, 892, 893 and 899 Squadrons, whilst at Lossiemouth in north Scotland the carriers' strike aircraft – the Buccaneers and Scimitars – flew in 800, 801, 803 and 809 Squadrons. In south-west Wales, Gannets in 849 Squadron flew from Brawdy, whilst Culdrose specialised in carrier-borne helicopters, flying the Wessex in 814, 815, 819, 820, 845 and 848 Squadrons. The last two of these squadrons providing troop carrying commando helicopters for HM Ships *Albion* and *Bulwark*, the rest being anti-submarine helicopters armed with torpedoes and equipped with 'dipping sonars' on retractable cables. The vast majority of the aircraft of the Fleet Air Arm flew from either aircraft carriers or commando carriers: at this time only twenty-three smaller ships had their own ships' flights. The four guided missile destroyers had a single Wessex helicopter, whilst the new *Leander* and Type 81 class frigates flew the small Wasp anti-submarine helicopter, which could be armed with torpedoes but was dependent on its parent ship for sonar targeting data. Finally, the two newest survey ships, *Hecla* and *Hecate*, also flew Wasps and the Antarctic patrol ship *Protector* flew two older Whirlwind helicopters. The ships' flights operated from Portland and were all part of 829 Squadron. In total there were seventeen operational squadrons and twelve training or trials squadrons, each commanded by a Lieutenant Commander.[39]

In addition to the Fleet Air Arm, the Royal Air Force's Coastal Command provided land-based maritime patrol aircraft, most of which operated from the United Kingdom, with some aircraft detached for operations in the Far East flying from Singapore, and others earmarked to support the Beira Patrol off east Africa. Coastal Command's operational aircraft consisted of more than thirty Mark 3 Shackletons: these were propeller-driven aircraft derived from the famous Lancaster bomber that had been progressively modernised since the early 1950s when the Mark 1 version had entered service. Although slow and cumbersome, the aircraft was large and had a long-range, and could therefore be used for reconnaissance and to attack lightly defended shipping and submarines. The Mark 3, which had been further updated during the 1960s in three phases, was equipped with long-range radar and could drop bombs, mines and sonobouys, sonars that floated at a pre-set depth whose readings could be analysed back on the aircraft. Despite these updates, the Shackleton was rapidly becoming obsolete, and a new jet-engined maritime patrol aircraft was being developed (which would become the Nimrod). Coastal Command operated seven squadrons, numbers 42, 120, 201, 203, 204, 206 and 210, from RAF Mount Batten, Kinloss and Bally-Kelly air stations and its headquarters were at Northwood in Middlesex, co-located with the Commander-in-Chief Home Fleet, who would take operational control of the aircraft during exercises, times of tension and war under his NATO role as C-in-C Eastern Atlantic.[40]

Submarines were administratively under the control of the Flag Officer Submarines, Rear Admiral Ian McGeoch, based at HMS *Dolphin* in Gosport, across the harbour from Portsmouth Naval Base. Unlike the surface ships, most submarines operated in home and Atlantic waters. A total of twenty submarines were split between the 1st Submarine Squadron at *Dolphin* and the 3rd Submarine Squadron at Faslane in Scotland. A further twelve were in refit at various yards in the United Kingdom. These boats included modernised wartime submarines of the 'T' and 'A' classes, supplemented by the more modern *Porpoise* and 'O' classes. Two of these boats, *Orpheus* and *Porpoise* of the 3rd Submarine Squadron, were about to take part in Exercise Sailor's Pride, whilst others were taking part or in transit to local exercises off Portsmouth, Londonderry and Malta. In addition, the first nuclear-powered submarine, HMS *Dreadnought*, was based at Faslane and undergoing continuing trials three years after her completion.[41] She was a harbinger of things to come in the submarine service, although a lone boat. By the end of the decade she would be supplemented by a further seven boats, four of which were armed with nuclear ballistic missiles. In addition to the submarines operating from Singapore, there were two 'A' class submarines of the 6th Submarine Division operating from Halifax, Nova Scotia, to provide training targets for the anti-submarine orientated Royal Canadian Navy, and a further three boats of the 'T' class at Sydney, Australia undertaking a similar role for the Royal Australian Navy.[42]

The Royal Marines had existed since the seventeenth century as the Royal Navy's own soldiers: used for boarding parties, going ashore against opposition and, originally, for internal ship discipline. The last of these roles had long disappeared, and for many years small Royal Marine parties aboard warships had also manned some of the ship's primary or secondary weapons. Since the end of the Second World War, and the abolition of the Army's own Commando units, the Royal Marines had monopolised raiding, amphibious operations from ship to shore and it was in these roles that their core specialisms now resided. The Commandant General of the Royal Marines, Lieutenant General Norman Tailyour, had recently been made a member of the Naval Staff and was the professional head of his service.[43] As has been seen, the Headquarters of 3 Commando Brigade was in Singapore, where one of the five Commandos, 40 Commando, also had its headquarters. 42 Commando was based in Sarawak, Borneo and 45 Commando in Aden. The remaining two Commandos were based in the United Kingdom with 41 Commando in Bickleigh and 43 Commando in Plymouth, both in Devon. The Marines were also supported by two specialist Royal Artillery Regiments of the British Army, one based in Singapore the other in Plymouth.[44] Operationally, the Royal Marines embarked on the two commando carriers and the few remaining older landing ships and craft dotted around the Fleets. These older vessels were soon to be replaced by two new dock landing ships, HMS *Fearless* and HMS *Intrepid*. The Ministry of Transport also operated a number of old Tank Landing Ships for the routine logistical transfers of military equipment around the globe. They were in the process of being replaced by the *Sir Lancelot* class of logistical landing ships. All these vessels were operated by a shipping contractor, the British-India Steam Navigation Company.[45]

The post of Flag Officer Sea Training ('FOST') had been established in 1958 to provide seven-week intensive training for ships' crews as they joined a newly commissioned ship under the Foreign and General Service regimes. Held by Rear Admiral Philip Frost in February 1966, FOST's remit was to ensure that all ships meet the required standards of efficiency, whilst also providing advice and assistance to crews to improve their performance. The training regime was designed to ensure that crews gained experience of nearly every eventuality from fast craft attack to accidental fires and major power failures. The FOST process had proven to be a considerable success and smaller European navies had already begun to make of use the training. FOST also had subsidiary duties as the senior officer in charge of the naval base at Portland and controlling the large sea exercise areas off Portland.[46]

Finally, there were also local commands covering different sea and coastal areas around the United Kingdom, as well as administering naval bases, dockyards and a range of shore-based facilities, including taking responsibility for much of the training of the sailors home ported at their respective bases. Commander-in-Chief Portsmouth, Admiral Sir Varyl Begg, the Commander-in-Chief Plymouth, Vice Admiral Sir Arthur Talbot, and Flag Officer Scotland and Northern Ireland ('FOSNI'), Vice Admiral Sir George Gregory, were primarily responsible for portions of the still-sizeable reserve fleet, a number of accommodation and depot ships, and a mix of small vessels, including minesweepers, landing craft and seaward defence boats.[47] FOSNI was also responsible for the Fishery Protection Squadron, which consisted of two divisions. The first protected and supported the British deep sea fishing fleets which mostly operated in High North waters and consisted of four Type 14 frigates, HM Ships *Blackwood*, *Exmouth*, *Keppel* and *Palliser*. On 15 February *Palliser* was on her way to Portland, *Keppel* was at Rosyth, whilst *Blackwood* was off Tromso and *Exmouth* was preparing to begin a patrol of the Irish Sea. The second division patrolled the United Kingdom's territorial waters zone, which stretched out to three nautical miles from the shore and consisted of five 'Ton' class mine-warfare vessels converted to patrol vessels, which must have had a challenge patrolling the United Kingdom's huge length of territorial waters to prevent foreign fishing vessels from entering.[48]

The Commanders-in-Chief Portsmouth and Plymouth and FOSNI were also in charge of their local naval bases through the Admiral Superintendents of Portsmouth, Devonport, Chatham and Rosyth dockyards – Chatham's reporting to the C-in-C Portsmouth. Under the Admiral Superintendents were the facilities that made up the wider naval bases. For example, at Portsmouth naval base, Rear Admiral J L Blackham, the Admiral Superintendent, was responsible for the dockyard, which focussed on refitting warships, major repairs and occasionally building warships, the barracks and officers' mess (soon to be renamed HMS *Nelson*) which accommodated servicemen working in Portsmouth, the Royal Clarence Victualling Yard (food and drink) and the armaments depots at Priddy's Hard, Frater and Bedenham across the water from Portsmouth in Gosport.[49] The Captain of the Dockyard, who was also the Queen's Harbourmaster, Captain T L Martin, had responsibility for the berthing, mooring and movements of ships in the naval base, making use of Port Auxiliary Service tugs, lighters, tenders and other craft, whilst a number of different organisations undertook routine maintenance work on ships alongside.[50] These facilities were repeated to varying degrees at Devonport, Chatham and Rosyth, often being somewhat smaller at the latter two bases, as well as at the main two overseas dockyards in Gibraltar and Singapore.

In their respective towns and cities of Portsmouth, Plymouth, Chatham, Rosyth, Gibraltar and Singapore these enormous groupings of establishments and organisations dominated the local economies with a high proportion of the population either directly working for the Ministry of Defence, or being indirectly dependent on it, through local contractors, suppliers, shopkeepers and other service industries. In 1965 the 'Dockyard Vote' with the Defence Estimates came to a total of £178 million and employed 51,554 personnel throughout the United Kingdom, although this total also included the staff at the aircraft repair yards at Fleetlands near Gosport and Belfast.[51] The Royal Navy therefore dominated the economies of these large naval towns, but there were also a huge number of other employees working in less obvious parts of the countries, some of them working many miles inland.

Other Shore Establishments

The most prominent shore establishments outside the naval bases were the training establishments. These included the initial training establishments of HMS *Ganges* in Ipswich, Suffolk and HMS *St Vincent*, Gosport, for boys and young entry sailors, HMS *Raleigh* in Torpoint, Cornwall for other new entry sailors, HMS *Fisgard* also in Torpoint, for apprentices, who would become artificers, the Navy's skilled lower deck workforce, and the Britannia Royal Naval College in Dartmouth, Devon for Officer Cadets ('Special Duties' officers, raised from the lower deck, were trained in Portsmouth, nominally at HMS *Victory*). HMS *Royal Arthur*, in Corsham, Wiltshire, trained petty officers, the Royal Naval College, Greenwich was the Royal Navy's staff college, and the Royal Naval Engineering College at Manadon, Plymouth, educated engineer officers. The WRNS, the Women's Royal Naval Service, were trained at HMS *Dauntless* near Reading. In addition there were a host of training establishments covering almost every specialism for ratings and officers: HMS *Collingwood*, Fareham, Hampshire (for electrical engineering); HMS *Caledonia*, Rosyth (engineering); HMS *Excellent*, Portsmouth (gunnery); HMS *Sultan*, Gosport (marine engineering); HMS *Dryad*, Southwick, Hampshire (navigation); HMS *Mercury*, East Meon, Hampshire (signals); HMS *Daedalus*, Lee-on-Solent, Hampshire (safety and survival, as well as photography); HMS *Vernon*, Portsmouth (torpedo, anti-submarine warfare, diving). A range of training for naval air personnel occurred at the various Royal Naval Air Stations, whilst submarine training occurred at HMS *Dolphin*, the submarine service headquarters, with some additional tactical training at the depot ship HMS *Maidstone*.[52] Many of these establishments clustered around the Portsmouth area, accentuating its economic dependence on the Navy, and also emphasising its position as the 'home' of the service. The Royal Navy also had its own hospitals for treating its personnel, the largest two being at Haslar in Gosport and Stonehouse near Plymouth. There were smaller hospitals in Malta, Gibraltar and Mauritius.[53]

There were not only ammunition depots at the main naval bases, but also several dotted across the United Kingdom, at Beith in Ayrshire, Trecwn near Milford Haven in Pembrokeshire, Broughton Moor in Cumberland, Ditton Priors in Shropshire, Antrim in Northern Ireland, Dean Hill in Hampshire and Wrabness in Essex. These had all been established during the Second World War to make naval armament supplies less vulnerable to the bombing of the major dockyard towns. Similar reasons for dispersal in the event of a war with the Soviet Union were used as justifications for keeping these establishments open. There was also an ammunition depot at Mombasa in Kenya, as well as a torpedo factory at Alexandria in Dunbartonshire and a propellant factory in Caerwent in Monmouthshire.[54] Similarly, there were Royal Navy Stores Depots away from the main naval bases, including Copenacre in Wiltshire which mainly held electronic stores (valued at over £33 million in 1966), Eaglescliffe in County Durham which held machinery spare parts, Perth in Scotland and Llangennech in Carmarthenshire which held air stores, Deptford in London and Woolston near Southampton.[55] These were significant establishments: by 1968 the largest of the Stores Depots, at Copenacre, employed over 1,700 members of staff, although this figure did include some sections of another department which had been transferred from Bath.[56] In addition, there were four oil depots at Lyness in the Orkneys, Invergordon in Ross and Cromarty, at Pembroke Dock and Old Kilpatrick in Dumbartonshire.[57] Only in the previous few months had the separate organisations for armament stores, victualling, naval stores and fuels been combined into a single organisation, the Royal Naval Supply and Transport Service, which employed a total of over 25,000 staff, headed by a civilian Director General.[58] As with the dockyard towns, these depots also had a major economic impact on their hinterlands, particularly as many had been deliberately sited in rural and sparsely populated areas. In 1965 these depots, along with their counterparts located at or near the large naval bases, cost a total of £191.1 million each year to run, and employed 22,184 personnel.[59] In terms of contracts, a few years later in 1968, a total of 28,000 orders were placed that year with a total value of between £160 to £190 million.[60]

The Royal Navy also controlled a large network of research and development establishments, undertaking applied scientific research into the full range of naval technologies. The Admiralty Surface Weapons Establishment at Portsdown in Hampshire and the Admiralty Underwater Weapons Establishment at Portland in Dorset were the largest research establishments and they themselves were relatively recent mergers of smaller establishments that had specialised in gunnery, radar, torpedoes and mines. The Admiralty Engineering Laboratory in West Drayton, Middlesex, undertook a mixture of mechanical and electrical engineering research into areas such as metallurgy, machinery controls, seals, engines, switchgear, telecommunications, cables, electronics and the impact of shock and vibration.[61] The Admiralty Experiment Works at Haslar near Gosport ran a number of model test tanks, whereby scale models were used to analyse seakeeping, cavitation (bubble creation), steering, propeller design and speed and power requirements.[62] The Admiralty Research Laboratory in Teddington, Middlesex, dealt with oceanography, sonar, hydrodynamics, mathematics, computing and psychology.[63] The Admiralty Materials Laboratory in Holton Heath, Dorset, undertook research into plastics, rubbers, metals and chemicals. Other establishments included the Admiralty Compass Laboratory (Slough), Admiralty Oil Laboratory (Brentford, Middlesex), Admiralty Experimental Diving Unit (Portsmouth), Admiralty Fuel Experimental Station (Haslar), Admiralty Hydro-Ballistic Research Establishment (Helensburgh), Admiralty Reactor Test Establishment (Dounreay), The Naval Aircraft Materials Laboratory (Fareham), the Naval Construction Research Establishment (Dunfermline), Naval Ordnance Inspection Laboratory (Caerwent), Royal Naval Physiological Laboratory (Alverstoke), The Services Electronics Research Laboratory (Baldock) and the Services Valve Test Laboratory (Haslemere).[64] Taken together, this was another large group of organisations spread across the country, with a number of them placed some way from the traditional naval sites. In April 1965 they employed 7,721 personnel with another 500 scientists working in central Navy Department roles, costing £27.7 million a year.[65] If the Research and Development work that produced many of the innovations that would be incorporating into the ships, submarines and aircraft of the fleet was at this time largely under the control of government, this was not the case with the defence industry that would be called upon to manufacture these pieces of equipment.

The Royal Navy, the Defence Industry and Other Suppliers
The section of the defence industry most associated with the Navy was the shipbuilding industry. This industry, particularly that part of it which built merchant vessels, was beginning to feel the impact from stiff international competition after an initial post-war boom when almost all competitors, with the exception of the United States, had to deal with severe bomb damage and economic exhaustion. The shipbuilding industry in Britain suffered from both poor management and intransigent trades unions, and by the 1960s was in many cases much less efficient than builders in other countries, particularly those that had built or re-built from scratch their industries since 1945 such as Japan and Norway.[66] As a significant number of shipbuilders built both merchant vessels and warships, this had an impact on the Royal Navy and its warship-building plans. These yards were often suspected of using their lucrative warship orders to help cross-subsidise their shrinking mercantile order books, and the temptations to inflate the costs of naval contracts were considerable.[67] These 'mixed' shipyards were Hawthorn Leslie and Swan Hunter on the Tyne; Harland and Wolff in Belfast; John Brown, Fairfields, Scotts and Stephens on the Clyde; Whites on the Isle of Wight; and Cammell Laird in Birkenhead. All of these shipbuilders were either building or had just completed ships of

the *Leander* and 'County' classes, so were an integral part of delivering the Navy's building programme, even if many were finding it difficult to remain profitable. Fairfield, which was completing a 'County' class destroyer for the Navy, had recently gone into receivership and was in the process of being resurrected with part-government control and a £1 million government loan.[68] An independent enquiry into the future of the industry had been established by the government under Reay Geddes, the Chairman of Dunlop Tyres, which was considering consolidating different yards, introducing new methods and machinery, and other means to make the shipbuilding industry profitable again. As the British share of worldwide merchant ship contracts began to shrink, these mixed yards became increasingly dependent on defence contracts for their survival, thus pushing the Ministry of Defence further into industrial policy, often on behalf of Labour governments many of whose core voters in cities such as Glasgow, Newcastle and Liverpool worked in, or had links to, the shipbuilding industry.[69] There were a number of yards that only built warships and these yards were much more likely to be wholly dependent on the Ministry of Defence for their survival. Within the industry, they had the reputation of being the least efficient yards given this reliance on government orders, although this was somewhat unfair on a yard like Vosper Thornycroft which was able to build a strong order book of overseas naval contracts alongside their British government work.[70] Vickers at Barrow were specialist submarine builders and were the lead yard for the Navy's new nuclear submarines. Vickers in Newcastle built large and medium-sized warships, whilst both Yarrow on the Clyde and Vosper Thornycroft in Southampton were specialist frigate and destroyer builders. Finally, the Royal Dockyards were also still building warships, Devonport and Portsmouth building frigates whilst Chatham built conventional submarines.

In 1961 222,000 were employed in the shipbuilding industry as a whole, but the industry was shrinking rapidly as its yards foundered: in 1958 there had been 297,000 workers in the industry, and by 1977 this number would have shrunk to under 70,000.[71] It is likely therefore that by 1966 employment in shipbuilding was probably close to, or even under, 200,000. Estimating what portion of the industry worked on warships is difficult, but it would have been a clear minority within the industry: only 250 shipyard workers were needed to build a frigate, though at least fifteen yards were used to build these types of ships in the 1960s.[72] In 1965 the Royal Navy was holding open the expectation of some twenty ship orders up to March 1968, including the new strike carrier, three destroyers, seven frigates, four nuclear submarines and other support vessels totalling £200 million in contracts. Between 1968 and 1975 it was planned to order another fifty vessels of up to £500 million in contracts.[73] For warship yards, and the mixed yards whose merchant shipping businesses were suffering, this was a potential lifeline – if of course all these vessels were in fact ordered and built.

There were not only the shipbuilders, and the host of sub-contractors that depended upon them, but also the weapons and other equipment manufacturers. Shorts of Belfast produced the Sea Cat missile system for the Royal Navy, whilst the Hawker Siddeley group not only produced the Sea Slug and Sea Dart missile systems but also made the Sea Vixen fighter and Buccaneer maritime strike aircraft. The British Aircraft Corporation were developing the next generation of missiles for the navy, including what would become Sea Wolf.[74] The electronics companies Marconi, Plessey, Ferranti, Racal and Decca produced radars and other electronic equipment for the Navy, as analogue and later digital technology became increasingly important for the functioning and effectiveness of fighting ships, and companies such as Graseby manufactured sonars and other underwater detection and communication equipment. The huge naval stores infrastructure also had to be supplied with food, clothing, spares and other equipment. For example, the total value of naval stores held in 1966 was over £99 million.[75] The Royal Navy therefore depended on a large web of equipment suppliers, from those that could build nuclear submarines and aircraft carriers, through to the bulk supply of dairy products and other foods to keep sailors fed and healthy around the world.

The Naval Side of the Ministry of Defence
In April 1964 the Admiralty, the government department that had supported and administered the Royal Navy, had been folded into an enlarged and overarching Ministry of Defence. Initially, only relatively small practical changes were made, as the Admiralty renamed itself the Navy Department, and an Admiralty Board was constituted – as a sub-committee of the new Defence Council – in place of the old Board of Admiralty. The Admiralty Board was nominally chaired by the Secretary of State for Defence, Denis Healey, but he did not often attend and his place was taken by the Navy Minister, Christopher Mayhew. Its members included the First Sea Lord, the Second Sea Lord – who had responsibility for personnel matters, the Controller of the Navy – who had responsibility for procurement, the Vice Controller – who had responsibility for support and supply, as well as the Deputy and Vice Chiefs of the Naval Staff ('DCNS' and 'VCNS'), the Chief Scientist (Royal Navy) and the 2nd Permanent Under-Secretary for the Royal Navy. Each member had their own responsibilities: the First Sea Lord was the professional head of the service, and adviser to ministers on naval matters. Unlike during the Second World War, the First Sea Lord no longer retained ultimate operational command of the navy through his Commanders-in-Chief and Flag Officers. By 1958, practical operational command had been vested

in the Commanders-in-Chief themselves, appointed by the Admiralty Board, and operating from shore-based Maritime Headquarters.[76] The First Sea Lord was supported by the Naval Staff via DCNS and VCNS, and also had the Hydrographic Department and Naval Operational Research report directly to him. The Second Sea Lord, Admiral Sir Desmond Dreyer, was responsible for Naval Training, Manpower, Statistics, Officer Appointments, Recruitment and Medical Matters. The Controller of the Navy, Vice Admiral Sir Horace Law, was responsible for the Polaris Executive, Weapons Development, Ordnance Inspection, Weapons Production, the Ship Department – which developed the designs of warships, Marine Engineering, Electrical Engineering, Ship Production and Aircraft development and production. The Vice Controller, Vice Admiral Sir Raymond Hawkins, was responsible for the dockyards and maintenance, shore electrical engineering and the new Royal Naval Supply and Transport Service. The Second Permanent Under-Secretary of State (RN), Sir Michael Cary, a career civil servant with experience at the Admiralty, Air Ministry and Foreign Office (and with the rather unusual hobby of making harpsichords), was the most senior civil servant in the Navy Department and had responsibility for those areas traditionally supervised by civilians in the Admiralty, including the complementing of naval posts, finance, contracts and naval materiel issues in support of the Controller and Vice Controller.[77] The military and civilian personnel who worked in this sprawling empire, which itself was only a sub-set of the wider Ministry of Defence with similar structures for each service, worked from a number of offices split between London and Bath. The Naval Staff and a number of other core departments worked at the Ministry of Defence main building, the former Air Ministry and Transport Ministry building on Whitehall. Other London offices included Empress State Building, a large government high-rise office block in Earl's Court, West London in which parts of the Royal Naval Supply and Transport Service (RNSTS) and the Chief Scientist's office work; and the Old Admiralty Building in which much of the Second Sea Lord's staff still worked. Since the Second World War a significant portion of the Admiralty, and now the Navy Department, had worked in offices located in or near Bath, particularly those in the Controller's area of responsibility.[78] Before the decade was out the Finance and Contracts Departments had been 'centralised' and taken out of Navy Department Control.[79]

The Naval Staff has been described as the Navy's 'brain'. It supported the First Sea Lord in his role as professional head of the service, adviser on naval matters and top level operational commander. It was the Naval Staff that developed the Navy's arguments and compiled evidence to support its case during the Defence Review. Its senior members were part of the many tri-service working parties and committees that studied different elements of the

Review, and it was the Naval Staff that briefed the First Sea Lord in the key discussions and meetings that decided the fate of the aircraft carrier. With the creation of the centralised Ministry of Defence in 1964, the Naval Staff had a dual role: ultimately reporting to the Chief of the Defence Staff within a new and enlarged Defence Staff on tri-service matters, and reporting within the Navy Department structures for single-service matters. In practice, most of its work was single-service focussed. A few areas had been fully centralised, or 'functionalised' in the prevailing jargon, in 1964. The Naval Intelligence Division was incorporated into a new tri-service Defence Intelligence Staff, although within this single structure, the old single-service areas remained largely untouched, at least for now.[80] The Naval Staff itself was split between VCNS and DCNS. The former, Vice Admiral Sir John Bush, focussed on operations and planning, was responsible for the Naval Plans Division, the Naval Administrative Planning Division, the Naval Operations and Trade Division and the Naval Weather Service. DCNS, Vice Admiral Sir Frank Hopkins, focussed more on current and future equipment and capabilities, and was responsible for the Naval Tactical and Weapons Policy Division, the Surface and Amphibious Warfare Division, the Undersurface Warfare Division, the Navigation and Tactical Control Division, the Naval Air Warfare Division and the Naval Staff's statistical adviser. Each of these divisions was headed by a Captain, under whom were a number of Commanders and Lieutenant Commanders who did much of the staff work, including briefings, report writing and recommendations for decision.[81]

Traditionally, the Military Branch of the Admiralty, made up of civil servants, had supported the Naval Staff in its work, but in 1964 it had been incorporated into a new central Defence Secretariat. Initially, the same civil servants still undertook secretarial duties for meetings and advised the naval staff officers on policy matters, it was just that in the new structure, they were now part of the new central Defence Secretariat, working in the DS4 and DS5 divisions and reporting to the Ministry's Permanent Under-Secretary. As a result, their reporting lines were no longer to the Navy's Leadership, but to the Ministry of Defence's. Over time the former close bonds between the former Military Branch and the Naval Staff were gradually sundered as the civil servants' careers depended upon movement and promotion across the wider Ministry, so the previous Admiralty cadre gave way to civil servants who might only work with the Navy for a few years before moving onto other parts of the Ministry. This lack of subordinated civilian support that had a long-term stake in supporting the Royal Navy almost certainly had an impact on the ability of the Naval Staff to undertake its roles effectively.[82] As will be seen in the next chapter, it is notable that the former head of DS4 and former career Admiralty civil servant Pat Nairne proved one of the Navy's most effective – if under-appreciated –

lobbyists on behalf of the naval case during the carrier battle, in his position of the Secretary of State's private secretary. In later years, such civil servants with an understanding and appreciation of the naval perspective became fewer in number and rarely reached the highest positions in the Ministry of Defence. In 1965–6 there were 156 naval officers in the Naval Staff supported by 68 civil servants, but there were a total of 7,998 civil servants in Whitehall and Bath across all the different departments that reported into the Admiralty Board: a substantial number which would gradually reduce as the Ministry of Defence was increasingly centralised over the next 25 years.[83]

Personnel

The Royal Navy's personnel, its officers, ratings, reservists and members of the auxiliary services, were the most important element in the effective operating and fighting of the fleets. How many were there, who were they, and how long were they serving? The table below sets out the total strength of the Naval Service in October 1965, as agreed by Parliament in its annual Vote on military personnel funding. Actual figures were usually somewhat lower.[84]

Table 3: Personnel strength as voted by Parliament

	Officers	*Ratings/ Other ranks*	*Total*
Royal Navy	10,700	75,700	86,400
Royal Marines	700	8,700	9,400
Locally-employed personnel	–	–	2,100
Women's Royal Naval Service	200	3,000	3,200
Queen Alexandra's Royal Naval Nursing Service	200	300	500
Total	11,800	87,700	101,600

As can be seen, the Navy itself dominated the figures, with the Royal Marines providing less than 10 per cent of personnel, and the other supporting services and locally employed personnel making up an even smaller percentage. In comparison to 15 years previously, this was a considerable fall from 141,800 in the naval service in 1950 excluding conscripts, but this should also be seen in the longer-term context of the twentieth century. In 1937 the number of personnel had been almost exactly the same as in 1965, whilst in 1933 it had hit an inter-war low of 88,600, a figure that in itself was similar to the size of the navy as far back as 1860.[85]

The Royal Navy was therefore smaller than it had been in earlier post-war years and trailed the RAF at 122,700 and the Army at 182,400 but was still a relatively substantial size.[86] The biggest problem that it faced in the short-term was increasing, or even sustaining, its current size. In 1965 the Naval Service had been funded for a personnel total of 104,000, but it was 3,000 short of this figure and was suffering from difficulties recruiting and retaining sailors. The other services were having similar problems. One factor was demographics: the number of 15-year-olds in the population available to recruit – 15 was the reference recruitment age given that the school leaving age was then 14 – had shrunk by 15 per cent since 1960 and was expected to shrink further for another decade. On top of this, greater numbers of children were staying on at school until they were 16, so they could gain 'O' level qualifications. More were staying to 18 to gain 'A' levels, whilst more were going to university.[87] A better-educated workforce was not yet fitting well with the 'offer' that the Royal Navy was perceived to be providing to school leavers, a worrying situation given the technological revolution in naval warfare that was then under way. There was another important factor at work: pay. Sailors signed on for nine years from the age of 18, with an option for another five years, and then another eight after that. Back in the late 1950s when naval pay still compared well to that in the wider workforce, nearly two-thirds of sailors 're-engaged' for another eight years, but by 1965 this had reduced to 48 per cent.[88] Many more sailors consequently had to be recruited to fill this shortfall, and even then the new recruits lacked the experience and skills of those that had been unexpectedly lost. All three services were suffering from similar problems. It had been estimated some years before that the armed forces would need around 34,000 recruits a year, but the increased problems in retaining trained manpower now meant that 40,000 to 50,000 would be needed each year – and this from a shrinking workforce.[89]

Ratings
Despite these problems, the Royal Navy and the Royal Marines had still recruited a total of 7,603 ratings or other ranks in 1964–5, plus 1,005 WRNS. Most WRNS only stayed in the service for four years, so the number of recruits needed for that service was even higher by proportion in order to keep numbers up. Of the 7,603 men, 34 per cent were aged 15, 26 per cent were 16, 20 per cent were 17 and 20 per cent were 18 or over. This split was changing rapidly: only two years' previously the 15-year-old cohort had made up 44 per cent of recruits. Excluding artificers only 38 per cent of those who applied to join the Navy were accepted in 1964–5: 29 per cent had been below the minimum educational standard, 13 per cent had been medically unfit, 11 per cent withdrew their applications whilst another 9 per cent were rejected for other reasons including lack of parental consent, being of 'doubtful character', unsatisfactory references or bad work records. Recruitment was managed all

year around, with an unsurprising surge in September as the summer holidays ended, and the smallest numbers in December, July and August.[90]

Those who joined under the age of 16 were trained and educated either at the shore establishments HMS *St Vincent* or HMS *Ganges* before joining their relevant branches. Those who joined at 16 and over went straight to training establishments, whilst Artificers spent a total of four years at technical training establishments as apprentices learning their specific trades followed by one year at sea before qualifying in their chosen field.[91] Once in the Navy, a rating would have joined one of the numerous branches: there were the Artificers, who have already been mentioned and at this time worked to different ranks, pay scales and engagement lengths; the Seaman Branch which included torpedo, gunnery, radar plotting and anti-submarine specialisms; the Communications Branch which included the general, tactical and electronic warfare specialisms; the Engineering Mechanic Branch which manned ships' engine rooms and were informally known as 'stokers'; and the Electrical Branch which maintained and repaired electrical equipment. There was also the Supply and Secretariat Branch which included the cook, steward, writer and stores specialisms; the Sick Berth Branch; the Regulating Branch which was responsible for internal discipline; and finally two air branches, the Naval Air Mechanic Branch and the Naval Airman Branch. The former is self-explanatory and the latter included aircraft handlers, safety, photographic and meteorological specialisms.[92] The balance between the branches was gradually shifting in favour of those requiring technical skills, as the table below shows:

Table 4: Ratings – Split Amongst Branches

	1950	*1965*
Artificer	8.9 per cent	11.7 per cent
Air Artificer	2.9 per cent	4.7 per cent
Engineering Mechanic and Electrical	24.0 per cent	27.6 per cent
Air Mechanic	8.6 per cent	9.6 per cent
Airman	2.3 per cent	2.4 per cent
Total technical branches	46.7 per cent	56.0 per cent
Other branches	53.3 per cent	44.0 per cent

By 1965, those in the various technical branches outnumbered those in the other, non-technical branches: the Navy was becoming ever more technically focussed and this was reflected in its personnel requirements for those with the aptitude to undertake such roles.[93]

The average sailor reached the rank of Leading Rate after five years of service, and Petty Officer after eight and half years' service, just near the point of signing on for another five years. The average Chief Petty Officer gained that rank at 16 years' service, a few years into his second re-engagement and on the track towards leaving with a pension after 22 years, although there were some opportunities to stay on longer on five-year increments.[94] The proportions of ratings at different ranks was a classic pyramid for those who were not artificers (figures for October 1965):

Table 5: Ratings – Split by Rank

	General	Air	Total
Chief Petty Officers	2,997	532	3,529
Petty Officers	7,761	1,309	9,070
Leading Rates	10,439	2,334	12,773
Able Rates	32,604	4,869	37,473
Total	53,801	9,044	62,845

Approximately 60 per cent of ratings were Able Seamen, and for every ten of them there was approximately one Chief Petty Officer, with gradations in-between. None of these figures included the 9,614 Artificers, whose pay and grades made direct comparison difficult with the rest of the Royal Navy: Chief Artificers numbered 1,424, 1st and 2nd class Artificers 5,559, and 3rd class 2,591. This was in no way a pyramid structure, and reflected the different profiles of these specialist and highly trained ratings: once trained, they were much more likely to stay on to pensionable age and many more were in higher grades as promotion depended on the acquisition of technical skills. Higher pay compared to other ratings also played a part in more effective retention.[95]

A small number of ratings were promoted to officers and there were three ways of doing so. The first and most numerous route was as Special Duties Officers. Chief Petty Officers, Petty Officers and equivalent Artificers aged between 25 and 34 were eligible to apply. Once commissioned they would become Sub-Lieutenants but their greater experience would be recognised with a somewhat higher pay rate than General List officers. Their roles were usually that of specialists, usually in technical areas, and in 1964 they already made up 20 per cent of the officer cohort with plans for them to replace more General List officers, leading to a projected percentage rate of 40 per cent. Upper Yardmen were ratings aged up to 25 picked out as particularly talented and appropriate to gain a commission on the General List. Finally, a small number of Supplementary List Seaman and Aircrew Officers were recruited from the lower deck each year. In 1964–5 the numbers commissioned by these routes had been 189 as Supplementary Duties Officers, 24 as Upper Yardmen and 26 as Supplementary List Officers.[96]

Officers

If most ratings, with the exception of the Artificers, were not expected to serve for most of their working lives, with the majority leaving after nine or fourteen years, this was very different for the majority of officers, as can be seen in the table below.[97]

Table 6: Officers – Split by Age

Age	Percentage of total
17–19	5 per cent
20–24	14 per cent
25–29	15 per cent
30–34	18 per cent
35–39	18 per cent
40–44	17 per cent
45–49	10 per cent
50+	3 per cent

These bald figures therefore suggest a flat progression of nearly equal numbers of officers through their career, with each serving around 20 to 25 years and retiring to a comfortable pension. In reality the situation was much more complex, and the officer cadre was in the process of considerable change. There were three types of officer: those on the General List who numbered 5,967 in October 1965 and would expect to serve a 'career length', those on the Supplementary List numbering 1,162 who would serve for only ten years with the option to leave at five (or five, eight and twelve years for Air Supplementary List Officers), and those Special Duties officers who numbered 2,205 and have already been discussed.[98]

Given the age of Special Duties officers it was unlikely that more than a handful would progress beyond Lieutenant or Lieutenant Commander, whilst most Supplementary Duties officers would, it was assumed, have left the service before they reached their early thirties. The General List officers would therefore provide the cohort that would progress to command posts and senior ranks, whilst the others, who made up the majority of officers, would provide a second tier of older specialists from the lower deck and short service officers (a good many of whom would be in flying roles). These three separate strands had been introduced in 1956, so their effect had only progressed halfway through the Navy to those in their late twenties and early thirties. Above this age there would be a much higher proportion of long-career General List officers, who as they retired were more likely to find their roles replaced by Special Duties officers, especially if they had not reached high rank.[99] One significant development that this was bringing about was a social change in the wardroom, as Special Duties officers from modest backgrounds increased in number. Another parallel shift was a change in the officer cadet cohort for the General List. By the mid- to late 1960s intakes to the Britannia Royal Naval College were including much greater numbers of state-educated cadets, largely as a result of the abolition of fees in 1948. This was a seismic change that opened up the Royal Navy's officer class to a wider social grouping for the first time during peace since the Victorian era, although in the 1960s the tenor of the institution was still set by public school expectations and elocution lessons were offered for those whose accents were deemed to be 'regional'.[100]

Officers were split into many fewer specialisations than ratings, numbering four core groups in 1965: seamen, mechanical engineers, electrical engineers and supply officers. Seamen officers made up the largest group with a total 5,233, followed by mechanical engineers at 1,962, electrical engineers with 1,199 and 940 supply officers. These were supplemented by smaller numbers of specialist officers including medical officers, dental officers, instructors, chaplains, shipwrights, wardmasters (medical assistants) and careers service officers, who in total numbered 1,489. Within the largest group were the instructors numbering 650, followed by 419 medical officers with only 43 careers service officers as the smallest specialisation.[101] If the age breakdown of the officer cadre showed a similarly-sized block across all ages until the mid-40s, in terms of rank the structure was, as would be expected, a classic hierarchical pyramid, as shown in the table below.[102]

Table 7: Officers – Split by Rank

Rank	Numbers
Admirals	67
Captains, Commodores, Acting Captains	389
Commanders	1,080
Lieutenant Commanders	2,321
Lieutenants and lower	5,477
Total	9,334

It was therefore clear, when looking at these two tables, that most General and Special Duties List officers could expect to remain with the Navy until able to take a pension, often filling out non-seagoing posts in the later years of their service. Another, more controversial, reform from the 1950s, the Post List, which split seaman commanders deemed suitable for operational command and those best suited for non-command 'staff' roles, will be discussed in Chapter 4. The Royal Navy's officer class was at the mid-point of a 2-year-long reform to replace a group mainly recruited from cadets who served for a whole career, to a mix of those taken from the lower deck, those serving for only a short time, and a smaller elite group who would make a career of the navy and become its leaders in due course.

The Royal Marines

The Marines had to deal with many of the same problems that haunted the Royal Navy in attempting to recruit and retain its ranks. The cohort was shrinking, spending more time in education, and the pay was less competitive in comparison with civilian life. Its percentages for acceptance and rejection for service had some similarities to the Navy, with 36 per cent of candidates accepted, but only 20 per cent were rejected as being below the educational standard compared to 29 per cent for the Navy, and a much higher proportion were rejected for 'other' reasons which included the standard list of malefactors who were of 'doubtful character', lacked parental consent, had unsatisfactory references or had 'bad work records': 18 per cent compared to 9 per cent.[103] In terms of the hierarchy of other ranks in the Marines, this was a pyramid with a much larger base than the Navy, with 6,304 at Lance Corporal and below, 1,165 at Corporal, 735 at Sergeant, 365 at Colour Sergeant and 162 at Regimental Sergeant Major or Quartermaster Sergeant.[104] The Officer cadre was even smaller, with only 28 officers commissioned through direct entry in 1965–6, another 25 for short service, 7 for special duties and a further 16 under special entry for Commando flying service (flying the Marines' Wessex troop transport helicopters). Overall, there were 621 officers at Lieutenant or lower, 200 Captains, 78 Majors, 19 Lieutenant Colonels, 11 Brigadiers and Colonels and 5 Generals.[105] As with the other ranks, this was a much wider pyramid at the base than in the Navy, reflecting the needs of a land-fighting service and therefore probably not too dissimilar to the Army, but it also had the tripartite split of officers of the Royal Navy albeit with fewer risen from the ranks and more recruited on short commissions.

WRNS and QARNNS

The Women's Royal Naval Service had been initially established in November 1917, dissolved at the end of the First World War and then re-established at the start of the Second. They had survived after 1945 primarily because the Navy itself had trouble recruiting sufficient men for all roles, even when conscripts were available. As has been seen, the WRNS numbered 3,200 in 1965 led by 200 officers and served for an initial engagement of four years. Most chose not to extend their engagement, and approximately one-third of WRNS ratings joined and left each year.[106] Official documents stated that they were 'an integral part of the Royal Navy' but they were not subject to the Naval Discipline Act, using their own disciplinary code, and could not go to sea. They served in shore establishments at home and overseas, and in 1965 could work within one of twenty specialisms, five of which were air related (Air Mechanic, Radio Electrical (Air), Radar Plotter, Range Assessor and Meteorological), another six were Supply and Secretariat-related (Writer General, Writer Pay, Writer Shorthand, Stores, Cook and Steward). The remaining specialisms related to communications (Radio and Switchboard Operators) or a range of niche roles from cinema operator through to welfare worker. WRNS ranks were different to, but the equivalent of, Royal Navy ranks. The head of the service was the Commandant, the equivalent of a Commodore, with Superintendent (Captain), Chief Officer (Commander), First through to Third Officer (Lieutenant Commander to Sub-Lieutenant), Chief Wren (Chief Petty Officer), Petty Officer Wren, Leading Wren and Wren (all equivalent to the expected naval ranks). Queen Alexandra's Royal Naval Nursing Service had been established in 1902 and provided nurses for naval hospitals. All full-time QARNNS had officer equivalent status and were qualified nurses, whilst the small number of QARNNS reservists were unqualified ratings.[107]

Royal Fleet Auxiliary
The officers and sailors of the Royal Fleet Auxiliary were employed by the Ministry of Defence, but were traditional merchant seamen as reflected in their training through the Merchant Navy Training Board, Shipping Federation course and various Nautical College courses, and the listing of officers and crew with the Registrar General of Shipping and Seamen. Since 1956, the Royal Navy had increased its emphasis on afloat support rather than supply from naval bases, and this resulted in a shift of focus towards replenishment at sea and supporting warships. The Merchant Navy training was therefore increasingly overlaid with training specific for their unique role, including undertaking replenishment at sea, damage control, using naval communication systems, the quality control of fuel at sea as well as working alongside naval parties, such as those that maintained and crewed the helicopters increasingly used for 'vertical replenishment' or VERTREP.[108] The RFA had its own system of ranks similar to those in standard merchant service, and although it has not been possible to find a breakdown of personnel by rank, in 1965–6 there were a total of 3,311 Royal Fleet Auxiliary personnel afloat and ashore.[109]

Other auxiliary services
In addition to the Royal Fleet Auxiliary, there were a number of other auxiliary services operating in support of the Royal Navy. Personnel figures for the Port Auxiliary Service (PAS) in this period are very limited, but it is known that there were 784 PAS personnel at Portsmouth Naval Base in 1970, 489 at Devonport in 1969, and at Portland, Chatham and Rosyth there were between

239 and 270 in 1969–70. Gibraltar had 166 PAS personnel in 1968.[110] These numbers would have been a little higher in 1966 and would have included similar numbers of personnel in Malta and Singapore, suggesting a total PAS establishment of approximately 3,000. PAS employees were industrial civil servants like dockyard workers and consisted of masters, mates and hands operating harbour tugs, lighters, tenders and other craft involved in making sure the port operations of the major Naval Bases worked smoothly.

Finally, there was perhaps the least well known but possibly one of the most important support services – at least if war had broken out – the Royal Naval Auxiliary Service (the 'RNXS'). It was largely staffed by a mix of male and female volunteers with a core of full-time uniformed civil servants, and would have become a crucial part of the Royal Navy's mobilisation in a crisis. It had begun as a volunteer mine-watching service established in 1952, but in 1962 when the RNXS was formally established, it consisted of around 3,800 personnel operating from 94 units. The RNXS volunteers would provide the core of the Naval Control of Shipping Organisation, which would have managed and organised convoys arriving and leaving British waters, in particular the boarding and berthing of ships at convoy assembly anchorages. For this role, they were equipped with a number of small converted minesweepers and tenders. In addition, there was a secondary role of managing the dispersal of various PAS craft to safer ports and anchorages if there was an imminent threat of nuclear attack on naval bases.[111] The RNXS was also a pioneer of sexual equality at sea, appointing its first female skipper in 1961, Mrs Jo Cook, who later became a Head of Unit. She would be awarded the British Empire Medal in 1968 and retire in 1975.[112]

Reserves

A number of reserve forces provided additional trained and untrained personnel for the Royal Navy in the event of a crisis. The Royal Naval Reserve (RNR) provided trained volunteers to help meet the Navy's personnel requirements in an emergency, most of whom would operate a small fleet of minesweepers. They would undergo fourteen days of training each year and were based at eleven divisions based around different parts of country and would have their expenses paid combined with a regular 'bounty' payment. In 1965 and 1966 there were approximately 4,000 RNR officers and 4,200 RNR ratings, the latter enrolled for five-year periods. The RNR was supplemented by a series of different reserves made up of those that had recently left the Navy. The Royal Fleet Reserve consisted of former ratings, most of whom had left the Navy with a commitment to serve a number of years in the reserves. They totalled approximately 4,800 in 1965–6. The Emergency List and Retired List of Officers had a similar function for those who had been commissioned, and consisted of either former Supplementary List officers or retired General List officers in receipt of retired pay. Former National Servicemen were also subject to be called up again through the Royal Naval Special Reserve. Until only the previous year there had also been the officer-only Royal Naval Volunteer (Supplementary) Reserve, which recruited those who had at any point held temporary naval officer rank or were 20 to 30 year olds with yachting and sailing experience or engineering qualifications; they had often been used to help operate Command Headquarters during NATO exercises.[113] The RNV(S)R, which had shrunk to only 2,000 personnel, had been abolished and their personnel were being integrated into the RNR during 1966. The Royal Marines, WRNS and QARNNS all had their own reserve organisations with requirements similar to the RNR for a number of days of training a year coupled with a bounty. In 1965–6, there were 1,070 Royal Marine reservists, of which 150 were officers, 1,087 WRNS reservists, of which 162 were officers and 60 QARNNS reservists.[114]

* * *

The Royal Navy in 1966 had many similarities to the inter-war Royal Navy: it was a globally-deployed service whose main role was the supporting of British interests around the world, funded at a similar level to the 1930s, and with a not-dissimilar force structure of capital ships supported by escorts and a significant submarine arm. When looked at in a little more detail, however, there were some important differences: the capital ship was now the aircraft carrier not the battleship, the overseas focus had shifted from the Mediterranean to the Far East, and technological revolutions in jet aircraft and radar had transformed the air-naval environment. The Royal Navy was moreover on the cusp of even more substantial changes: guided missiles were, in 1966, only fitted on a small number of ships and in most cases this was the minimal-impact (and somewhat limited capability) Sea Cat air defence system, but this was shifting quickly, as was the adoption of helicopters on most warships. More importantly, the Royal Navy was investing significant sums in building nuclear-powered submarines which could remain underwater for weeks and even months and promised a revolution in undersea warfare, whilst major innovations in sonar technology and electronic warfare were in the very earliest stages of development. Some of these submarines would soon be carrying the United Kingdom's strategic nuclear deterrent, placing them at the very core of British defence policy and strategy. Many of these advances were being achieved with a substantial research and development complex which was partly the product of the Second World War. The Royal Navy and all the public sector organisations that supported it totalled nearly 220,000, with probably a similar number in the defence industry and in towns near naval bases and depots economically dependent on the Navy. Taken together this was a significant portion of the whole nation's workforce.

The Navy of 1966 was also beginning to deal with an unfamiliar problem of attracting personnel to serve when the economy was buoyant: the personal wealth and aspirations for the ordinary working man and women had been transformed since the 1930s, and there were no longer any conscripts to help fill gaps in recruitment and retention. Over the next 25 years the transformation of the Royal Navy in terms of roles, technology and personnel would be even greater than that experienced since 1945, and it would now have to occur without the capital ship – the conventional aircraft carrier – that had been at the centre of naval planning since 1945.

2

The Battle for the Carrier[1]

Admiral Luce and the Navy's Tribes

For Admiral Sir David Luce, the final act of the battle to cancel or approve the new aircraft carrier, as will be seen, would be not only a shattering professional defeat but also a painful personal humiliation that was even more agonising than the bare facts of his resignation suggest. David Luce was a submariner by training, earning the Distinguished Service Order in the early months of the Second World War for his command of submarines in North Sea operations. He was awarded an Order of the British Empire for his involvement in the Dieppe Raid, and earned a Bar to his DSO for his role as Chief Staff Officer for naval forces at the Normandy Landings. He had then commanded cruisers after the war and progressed up the Navy's higher ranks before becoming Commander-in-Chief of the Far East Fleet between 1960 and 1962, and then Commander-in-Chief of all British forces in the Far East between 1962 and 1964.[2] Luce therefore combined a distinguished wartime record that had demonstrated bravery, tactical skill and organisational abilities with a post-war career of high operational command, and was in many respects a natural choice for the position of First Sea Lord. However, he was an introverted and self-contained man, in the manner of many submariners, and was often unwilling to explain himself and his decisions to his subordinates which often gave an impression of aloofness.[3] Just as crucially, as a submariner he was a member of one of two leading 'tribes' within the Royal Navy that were rising in power and influence, and jockeying for position, during the post-war period.

The other rising tribe was that of the aviators of the Fleet Air Arm (FAA), one of whom had been Luce's predecessor as First Sea Lord, Admiral Sir Caspar John. For the Fleet Air Arm the decision on the new aircraft carrier was almost existential in its importance – at this time the FAA was primarily an organisation that operated from aircraft carriers – and former aviators were rising in prominence within the Navy as the aircraft carrier had become the capital ship of the fleet.[4] The submariners were not as powerful a force within the Naval Staff as the aviators at this time, as their rise had only recently begun with the entry into service of nuclear-powered submarines only a few years before. Touted as the new capital ships, these were now a competitor for resources and funding for the aircraft carrier that was the 'incumbent' leading vessel of the fleet and around which much of the larger vessels of the surface fleet were designed to operate as escorts. Luce, early on in his tenure as First Sea Lord, had inadvertently lost the trust of many senior Fleet Air Arm officers through his failure to promote Vice Admiral Sir Richard Smeeton, a former pilot and the Flag Officer Naval Air Command, to full Admiral. From the perspective of Luce and Rear Admiral William O'Brien, the Naval Secretary who administered senior appointments, this was just a matter of the outcome of a confidential vote of existing serving Admirals, but for Smeeton and no doubt many other senior aviators it was a deliberate slight.[5] Luce did not help the situation by not explaining the rationale for his decision, and for the rest of his time as First Sea Lord his relationship with former Fleet Air Arm officers within the Naval Staff and elsewhere in the Navy was prickly and often difficult.

In February 1966, knowing that the new carrier would be cancelled and the existing force soon phased out, Luce himself felt obliged to offer his resignation, but both the Secretary of State, Denis Healey, and the Navy Minister, Christopher Mayhew, tried to dissuade him from this decision.[6] Mayhew's role in the dissuasion process seems to have been more self-serving. Like Luce, he had been at the forefront of the campaign to order the aircraft carrier, and he had already decided to resign himself, and one cannot resist the conclusion that the Navy Minister wanted his resignation, when it came, not to be upstaged by that of his uniformed counterpart. When the Admiralty Board learnt that the First Sea Lord had been persuaded not to resign, its members threatened to collectively resign themselves if he did not. The beleaguered Luce reconsidered yet again and eventually decided to go.[7] After all the agony the event, as with the departure of Christopher Mayhew, received only moderate press attention. Any residual hope that the decision would be reversed by an incoming Conservative government was then removed by the large majority given to the Labour Party as the general election results came through on 1 April. The whole excruciating process did not reflect well on any of those involved: the Admiralty Board had been ruthless, Mayhew self-serving and Luce himself appeared to have little control over even his own personal decisions. It was the culmination of an intense 15-month Whitehall battle over the aircraft carrier and the future of naval aviation, and atmosphere around the Admiralty Board table was angry and disorientated.

The Royal Navy and Carrier Air Power

What was so important about this new aircraft carrier and why were these vessels regarded as the capital ships of the Navy? Since the attack on Pearl Harbor in December 1941, and the sinking of the British battleship *Prince of Wales* and battlecruiser *Repulse* by Japanese torpedo bombers in the South China Sea a few days later, it had been clear that even the most modern, well-armoured and well-defended battleship would have difficulty surviving in high-intensity naval warfare without air cover. The Battles of the Coral Sea and Midway the following year seemed to augur a new kind of naval warfare where the new capital ships were now lightly or unarmoured aircraft carriers able to carry the maximum number of aircraft. These aircraft would either be fighters to counter enemy aircraft, strike aircraft armed with bombs or torpedoes, or alternatively reconnaissance aircraft. After the Second World War ended, the Royal Navy was rebuilt around these new capital ships, with the Navy's battleships rapidly being taken out of service due to their high manning requirements.[8] Only one wartime-completed fleet aircraft carrier, HMS *Victorious*, remained in the Navy by the mid-1960s, heavily modernised with a new flight deck, electronics and radars, her long refit being so expensive and time-consuming that plans to modernise other pre-1945 carriers had been abandoned.[9] A number of other aircraft carriers were completed during the 1950s. These were ships whose construction had been suspended after the war and which were then completed to modified designs. Two 40,000-ton fleet carriers, *Eagle* and *Ark Royal*, had been commissioned in 1952 and 1955 respectively. *Eagle* had undergone a major modernisation between 1959 and 1964 and was now the best equipped and most capable carrier in the fleet, whilst *Ark Royal* had not been modernised to the same degree. Four light fleet carriers of between 23,000 and 28,000 tons, *Bulwark*, *Albion*, *Centaur* and *Hermes*, had been completed between 1953 and 1959. They too had been begun in the war and were completed to modified designs. The first three had become too small for the latest jet aircraft, so *Bulwark* and *Albion* had been converted into 'commando carriers' between 1959 and 1962: carrying helicopters and Royal Marines to undertake 'vertical envelopment' operations (landing troops ashore by helicopter). *Centaur* was withdrawn from the fleet in 1965 and her conversion was also being pondered. *Hermes* had been completed later than the other three and was somewhat larger. She could operate some of the more modern aircraft but it was expected that by the early 1970s, she too would be too small to operate a credible modern force consisting of both the Phantom air defence aircraft and the Buccaneer 2 strike aircraft.[10] The F4 McDonnell Douglas Phantom was a US aircraft modified to fit the British Rolls-Royce Spey engine and the Buccaneer was produced by the British manufacturer Hawker Siddeley.[11] Even accepting that its carrier force was shrinking from seven to four, the Royal Navy therefore needed new aircraft carriers to replace *Victorious*, *Eagle*, *Ark Royal* and *Hermes* before they became too old or too small to operate the most modern naval jet aircraft, in order to provide a capable carrier force out to the early 1990s.

The Naval Staff had been attempting to gain agreement for the construction of a wholly new aircraft carrier since the late 1940s but had been unable to push a favourable decision through government. Aircraft carriers and their air wings were undoubtedly expensive, and while some of the six aircraft carriers begun during the war were still under construction, it was difficult to argue for a new hull. From 1959 and the completion of *Hermes*, the situation became more urgent as the service lives of many of the carriers were expected to be ending soon. Again, gaining approval was especially difficult: the costs would be considerable, and in many parts of the defence establishment, which was at this time split between three ministries supporting each armed service (the Admiralty, War Office and Air Ministry) and a small Ministry of Defence which attempted to co-ordinate the work of the other three, there was opposition to building such large vessels. In the early 1960s the Air Ministry proposed that Vertical or Short Take off and Landing ('VSTOL') aircraft, operated by the RAF, should fly from small carriers, but this was rejected by the Naval Staff as providing a much inferior capability: the planned VSTOL aircraft were subsonic and less capable than the new US Phantom fighter.[12]

The Air Ministry and the Royal Air Force saw the new strike carriers, and in particular a new planned variant of the Buccaneer, as a threat to its own plans for a new generation of bomber. The Buccaneer 2** would have an enhanced ability to undertake attacks against land targets, turning the aircraft from one which was optimised for attacking warships to one which could have an equivalence to the RAF's planned TSR2 long-range bomber.[13] The RAF was about to have the responsibility for operating the United Kingdom's strategic nuclear deterrent taken away from it, and given to Royal Navy ballistic missile submarines, so the planned TSR2 (and the American-built F-111 that replaced it after its cancellation in 1965) seemed like the RAF's last chance to retain a toehold in strategic bombing, a role that had defined that service's early years. Without a long-range bomber, the RAF risked seeming like a service that did no more than support either the Army or the Navy, a position that made its leadership feel especially vulnerable given the attempts by the older services to dismember the RAF in the early inter-war years.[14] For the RAF the battle over a new carrier was as close to being existential as it was for the Fleet Air Arm.

From an ideological perspective this was expressed through the belief within much of the Air Staff and its leadership that all significant air power capabilities should ideally be under its control: the existence of the Fleet Air Arm and the Army Air Corps was not only inefficient by duplicating support structures, it meant that the Navy and Army only had a narrow understanding of what air power could do, seeing it as only as a support capability for warships and land forces, rather than a war-winning capability in its own right. From the perspective of the Navy and Army this was precisely why they wanted their own air capabilities: the RAF was too focussed on a strategic role that justified its existence and over-emphasised the war-winning abilities of air power, rather than practical tactical air power on the battlefield or at sea. The Navy's aviation capabilities were much greater than that of the Army's, so it was inevitably seen as a greater threat to the Air Force. Although the RAF's arguments about the central strategic and war-winning role of air power had varying degrees of support amongst civil servants and ministers, accompanied by some scepticism, the arguments against the duplication of air capabilities across all three services did carry weight with those politicians and officials keen to ensure that the defence budget was kept under greater control.[15]

In the Treasury, senior civil servants had been attempting to reduce the scale of British defence spending since the early 1960s, fearing that the 'warfare state' was diverting money and expertise from modernising and helping to grow the civilian economy, thus reducing Britain's potential economic growth rate.[16] In particular, senior civil servants such as Richard 'Otto' Clarke, the second Permanent Under-Secretary at the Treasury, saw the large military expenditure in bases and capabilities east of the Suez Canal in the Indian Ocean and South East Asia as particularly wasteful. Clarke saw the cancellation of military capabilities that made the 'East of Suez' role viable as a back-door way of ensuring that it was abandoned.[17] Before the return of the Labour Party to government in October 1964, officials had made some tentative steps to consider a future reduction in the British position in the Indo-Pacific region, with senior officials in the Foreign Office recognising that the British presence would have to shrink in the medium to long-term.[18] The arrival of Sir Alec Douglas Home as Conservative prime minister in October 1963 had seen a brief return to a greater focus on a world role, and it was during his short tenure in the post that the Cabinet approved in principle the procurement of a new aircraft carrier, known as CVA01.[19] They were therefore strongly linked with the maintenance of a world role, at least in the eyes of the Treasury. The Navy had seemingly achieved part of what it had been aiming for over many years, but the new ship had not yet been laid down when a general election was called: a new government might easily reverse such a decision.

The Defence Review
Soon after the new Labour government came to power in October 1964, the incoming Prime Minister, Harold Wilson, was persuaded by Burke Trend, the Cabinet Secretary, to launch a defence review to reduce British defence

spending to £2,000 million by 1970. This would mean a reduction of £400 million from the existing planned expenditure of £2,400 million in that year.[20] From the perspective of the Labour government this would enable a greater part of taxpayers' money to be used on building up the welfare state. This had not been a commitment in the Labour Party's manifesto, which had in fact suggested that it would spend more money on non-nuclear defence, but it fitted well with what the Party wanted to achieve in government and partly aligned with the Treasury's more technocratic objectives.[21] The £2,000 million limit was given to the new Secretary of State for Defence, Denis Healey, to fulfil.[22] Healey was the youngest and most junior member of the Cabinet, but he was also able, tough and determined to succeed in bringing defence spending down to the level required.[23]

Healey's task was made much easier by the Chief of the Air Staff's politically astute decision to sacrifice the TSR2, and other aircraft such as a supersonic version of the Harrier short take-off or vertical landing aircraft (the P1154), and a large transport aircraft (the HS681). This ended the British aircraft industry's attempt to remain a major player in the military aircraft industry. Only the Harrier survived the cull, but after this point joint ventures with other countries were the only feasible way to develop major aircraft. The RAF would purchase the F-111 swing-wing bomber instead of the TSR2 and the C-130 Hercules to replace the HS681. If the US–UK foreign exchange rate did not change, and make the new US procurements more expensive (which would only have happened if the Pound Sterling was devalued, in this Bretton Woods era of fixed exchange rates) then this decision would save more than half of the money Healey needed to reach £2,000 million in 1970. The Chief of the Air Staff's decision was ruthless, and bitterly resented in parts of the British aircraft industry, but it was also a masterstroke that took the pressure off the RAF and pleased a staunchly pro-American Defence Secretary. The RAF's leadership was concerned about being forced to accept an expensive British built and designed aircraft such as the TSR2, when the F-111 was, at least on paper, almost as capable but only two-thirds the cost.[24]

Grateful to the RAF for offering up cancellations without being pushed, by March 1965 Denis Healey now needed to find around £200 million by 1970 to reach his target. As was wryly noted by a senior Treasury official, this amount happened to be almost the same as was projected to be spent on constructing the carrier in that year.[25] The Army had little to offer up in terms of major procurement reductions, so the other service aside from the RAF that invested in large, expensive and high-tech procurements, the Royal Navy, was clearly in the Defence Secretary's sights. The Defence Review would last another 11 months, and it would be consumed with dealing with only one issue: whether to cancel or procure the planned aircraft carriers. The Chief of the Defence Staff was Admiral of the Fleet Lord Louis Mountbatten, the Queen's cousin and the Duke of Edinburgh's adoptive father. He was at the end of his unprecedented six-year period in the role, having spent three years before that as First Sea Lord. Mountbatten was loved and loathed in equal measure within the defence establishment: he was charismatic and an effective bureaucratic operator, but his behind-the-scenes methods of operating, and his willingness to be ruthless in the Ministry's office politics, had meant that he had created many enemies over the years. He had also been accused of unfairly supporting and sheltering his own service, with some justice, and with the Royal Navy in the firing line he was perceived to be pushing the aircraft carrier procurement on behalf of his old service.[26] A slick slide show organised by Mountbatten in December 1964 for the new Labour ministerial team to demonstrate the usefulness of carrier air power was sparsely attended, the Secretary of State pointedly staying away.[27] The creation of the newly centralised Ministry of Defence had been driven by Mountbatten, who was keen to place himself at the centre of the new structures: as a result Denis Healey would never truly control this sprawling new department until Mountbatten had been constrained and ideally removed.[28] The Chief of the Defence Staff's association with the new aircraft carrier therefore did not help the case for the latter with the Secretary of State, who was attempting to wrest control of his department from him.[29] Mountbatten was past his prime in any case, reputedly falling asleep in some meetings he was chairing, and making a significant concession in June 1965, alongside Luce, by accepting that the RAF's F-111 bomber was an essential part of the programme.[30] This now meant that the aircraft carrier was seen as an *additional* part of the procurement programme on top of an already-approved F-111, rather than as a competitor with that aircraft. Healey, with Wilson's full support, soon managed to sideline Mountbatten: his posting as Chief of the Defence Staff would not be renewed, and he was sent on a tour of the Commonwealth to investigate immigration policy, not an area in which he had much expertise or in truth, probably much interest.[31] But he went, and the Royal Navy was now without its long-standing protector, and its subsequent performance in the Review would show how much it had depended upon Mountbatten's support even if it did not, at that time, know it.[32]

Mountbatten and Luce's concession on the F-111 was one of many mistakes made in a badly mismanaged campaign by the Navy to retain the carrier. The Naval Staff's positions and decisions seemed poorly thought through and with a singular lack of understanding of the difficult environment that the Navy was in. The Naval Staff laid down two 'red lines' during the bureaucratic battle that hobbled their ability to adjust and modify their position as the policy landscape changed. First, they argued that the maritime role of the carrier –

which included air defence of naval vessels and the maritime strike role against enemy warships – could not be split from the role of the carrier in power-projection on land. They were deemed indivisible and together made up a single capability: the message coming from the Naval Staff seemed to be that if land power projection was not needed, then carriers would not be needed at all.[33] To some extent, the maritime strike and land strike capabilities were strongly linked, not least in the fact that the Buccaneer strike aircraft would undertake both roles. However, it was in land strike that it could be argued there was 'duplication' with the F-111, which had already been accepted by Mountbatten and the Royal Navy. Most of the arguments that then followed over the need for the carriers therefore focussed on the carrier's role in land power-projection operations, and in particular by providing air defence and ground attack capabilities for amphibious landings. This had been a key capability singled out back in 1962 by the Chiefs of Staff Committee for operating 'East of Suez' and as a major justification for carrier air power in the region.[34] If this requirement were removed and reduced only to amphibious operations alongside allies rather than alone, which is exactly what Healey was considering, then the role of the aircraft carrier was now in doubt.[35] This focus also meant that the vital role of an aircraft carrier in defending ships from air attack and attacking enemy warships was pushed into the background.

At the start of the Review, the Air Staff implicitly acknowledged that the strongest part of his argument lay with the duplication of land power-projection, and that attempting to argue that land-based aircraft could defend naval forces or convoys many hundreds of nautical miles away, or attack enemy shipping, would be much more difficult. As a brief prepared by the Air Staff for the Chief of the Air Staff, Air Chief Marshal Elworthy, stated: 'the RAF could make a worthwhile contribution, even in extreme and unlikely situations, to the protection of maritime forces, albeit at some extra expense and considerable effort.'[36] It was in the best interests of the Air Staff that the Navy would continue with its all-or-nothing position. To their immense relief the Navy did, and the role of carrier air power in wholly maritime operations never fully came to the fore. As the Review progressed, and the arguments became so heated that it was beginning to become clear that inter-service relations – particularly between the Royal Navy and Royal Air Force – could be scarred for many years, the new Chief of the Defence Staff, General Richard Hull along with Healey's private secretary, Pat Nairne, a former Admiralty civil servant, devised a proposal for procuring a smaller 'maritime role' carrier. It would fly only Phantom aircraft, primarily for air defence, and have a dual role in maritime strike armed with free-fall bombs and perhaps new anti-ship missiles that were then in development. This would result in a smaller, cheaper carrier of around 30,000 to 35,000 tons, with an admittedly much less effective strike capability, but it would have a much better chance of producing a significant portion of the required savings in 1970.[37] The Admiralty Board and Naval Staff rejected this compromise proposal, sticking to their position that the maritime and power-projection roles were indivisible.[38] In some respects this position is understandable: the Buccaneer was an excellent aircraft that was only just beginning to show its effectiveness; but the Navy's leadership did not seem to see what a precarious position it was in and how willing Healey was to push to obtain his savings, and so passed up probably its best chance of getting a carrier procured.[39]

The second red line, which was only given up in the final weeks of the battle for the carrier, was the Naval Staff's insistence that the existing fleet of destroyers and frigates could not be reduced below eighty.[40] This meant that an offer to sacrifice some of these vessels in order to help reduce the 1970 overhead and therefore squeeze a carrier procurement within the defence budget would not be possible. Given that the nuclear submarine building programme was not likely to be reduced either, this meant that the Navy was effectively stating that it would not contribute any significant programme reductions to the Defence Review at all, leaving the RAF and Army to take all the pain. This looked especially stubborn given that the RAF had already offered up a range of cancellations at the start of the Review, and the Army – which had fewer large procurement projects that it could trim – had offered to reduce its reserves by a quarter.[41] Chronic personnel retention and recruitment problems also made the eighty-escort position untenable in the medium to long-term, and the Navy's plans for the fleet had to be regularly caveated with the proviso that sufficient personnel would be found. Denis Healey himself saw this issue as a major and under-recognised factor in the eventual cancellation of the aircraft carrier: a reduction in the number of ships and therefore the number of crews would have removed this important vulnerability from the Navy's case.[42] With these two red lines, the strong impression was being given that the Navy not only did not accept that the carrier should be cancelled or frigates and destroyers reduced in number, but that it – uniquely of the three armed services – should be spared any meaningful reductions in its budget and capabilities.

The way the Navy's senior officers went about this Whitehall battle was also counterproductive. Admiral Hopkins, the former Swordfish observer who was Deputy Head of the Naval Staff, chaired an early study into the maritime air power role. This study should have provided an opportunity to confirm how difficult it would be for land-based aircraft to undertake air defence and anti-shipping operations, but it was overshadowed by the perception that Hopkins had been overtly partisan in his manner with the RAF representatives. Hopkins also made a serious error in allowing that part of the study that dealt with how land-based aircraft could undertake the maritime role to be written wholly by the Air Force Department, rather than by the study group which had a mixed membership. The Air Force Department's study unsurprisingly argued that the maritime role could be effectively undertaken by the RAF, and this therefore meant that the overall study had ambiguous and unclear conclusions that left the issue entirely open. It was also reported to the Permanent Under-Secretary that a rough estimate (presumably made by the Air Staff) of £550 million could be saved by not building the carriers and using land-based air power instead. The committee led by Hopkins therefore had to conclude to Healey and the Chiefs of Staff that the net conclusion of the study was that 'fixed wing carriers may not be indispensable for purely maritime tasks'.[43] Hopkins' peremptory, dismissive and condescending manner with other study group members resulted in a decision, supported by the Air Staff, that no further studies – and there were many more studies commissioned over the next ten months – were to be chaired by 'interested parties' such as naval or RAF officers, with civil servants or defence scientists usually leading subsequent groups.[44] Once the study was complete the Naval Staff then failed to follow up some of the Air Force Department's claims that had been made in the report, such as an assertion that RAF pilots would be able to fight their aircraft effectively after flying 900 nautical miles, that command and control from ashore at such distances would be possible, and that there would be no issues of air base availability in foreign countries or problems with overflights of neutral countries. The Air Staff were particularly worried about the 900 nautical mile issue and was concerned that the Naval Staff would lobby for operational analysis studies of this subject – they knew that the Air Force Department's claims would probably be shown to be false or at least wildly optimistic.[45] However, the request for such a study never came, the Naval Staff seeming unaware that they had come close to exposing some of the flaws in the Air Staff arguments over maritime air power, and the discussions moved on to ground on which the Air Force was much more comfortable: power-projection.

Whilst Luce was unable to constrain his more aggressive senior officers such as Admiral Hopkins, the Chief of the Air Staff had deliberately avoided situations that would result in his senior staff officers being seen in an aggressive light, particularly at the start of the Review.[46] It helped create an impression of moderation and reasonableness that contrasted with the Navy's approach. The senior officers of the Naval Staff did not manage their staff officers well at a lower level either: it was made clear at the start of the Review to certain middle-ranking staff officers their careers would be over if the carrier was cancelled. This was not a way to induce calm and coherent thinking, and as no such sword of Damocles hung over the staff officers of the RAF's Air Staff, and it is therefore not surprising that as a group they performed better during the Review.[47]

Hopkins' Maritime Air study was followed by a blizzard of short studies on a range of subjects, from different operational scenarios East of Suez through to numerous re-visitings of power-projection and amphibious operations issues.[48] Under pressure from the Prime Minister, Healey was extremely keen to wrap up the Review quickly, so each batch of studies had short deadlines of only a few weeks or a month, not long enough for detailed in-depth analyses that would bring in outside approaches such as operational analysis.[49] From March 1965 it was well known within government that the only battle left in the Review was over carrier air power. Healey was a young and ambitious politician, whose reputation would be significantly damaged if he were seen to have been 'defeated' by the Navy and have allowed the large carrier through: the Naval Staff failed to acknowledge this important factor in driving the Defence Secretary's behaviour, and appeared unable to understand that some form of compromise was going to be necessary.

Cancellation

By October 1965, it was clear that the Navy's leadership would not voluntarily give up on the large aircraft carrier, so the Secretary of State decided to convene a meeting of the Defence Council in which he attempted an ambush on the First Sea Lord. Despite having been told that the Council meeting would be some form of 'showdown' in the carrier debate with the First Sea Lord and Navy Minister on one side and the Chief of the Air Staff and Air Force Minister on the other, the Council actually proceeded on the basis that the Treasury could not wait any longer and that instead a series of studies should be launched on the basis that a hypothetical major cancellation had already been made that would take the budget under £2,000 million. Unsurprisingly that hypothetical cancellation would be the aircraft carrier. Wrong-footed by Healey's sudden change of approach, Luce and Mayhew had difficulty responding to this proposal and at certain points seemed to contradict each other over a suggestion by Solly Zuckerman, the Chief Scientific Adviser, to lease older United States carriers for a number of years to cover the period until land-based aircraft would take over the former carrier role.[50] The meeting was a mess, and it exposed divisions between Luce and Mayhew, as well as alienating Zuckerman who had been a sympathetic voice to the Navy during the Review. Luce fought hard and doggedly through a difficult meeting, but was not bullied into accepting cancellation, even 'hypothetically'. Despite this, there was now no doubt that cancellation was going to be difficult to avoid, even if the atmosphere in parts of the Ministry of Defence was becoming poisonous. In December, Healey made a final effort with a new 'maritime only' carrier proposal, this time with only one carrier procured on the assumption that carriers as a whole would be phased out in 1980.[51] The Admiralty Board remained trenchant, stating that only the large carrier should be built, and if it was not and there was no power-projection capability, then the Navy should not have carriers at all and they should be withdrawn from service as quickly as possible.[52] Maybe the Board thought that they had pushed Healey part of the way towards their position and remaining intransigent would bring further concessions from the young minister. They were mistaken: this had in fact been their last realistic opportunity to keep the aircraft carrier alive, and they had failed to engage with the proposals seriously. Even the Treasury, frustrated at the time being taken to complete the Review, was willing to countenance a maritime role carrier if the Ministry of Defence could make the sums fit into the £2,000 million amount.[53] The Navy was not listening, and was blindly hoping that plugging away at an all-or-nothing approach would finally force Healey to cave in.

Infuriated by the Admiralty Board's inability to compromise, and then their provocative call for all carriers to be withdrawn as soon as possible if the large carrier were not approved, Denis Healey effectively decided to call their bluff and began the process by which the decision not to procure the large carrier and to withdraw the existing carrier force without replacement was made. On 10 January 1966 the carrier decision was taken to the Oversea Policy and Defence ('OPD') Committee of the Cabinet. Two options were first laid out of the 'Official Committee' of that Cabinet Committee, consisting of the Permanent Secretaries of the Ministers who attended OPD. Luce and Elworthy also attended. The first option (Option A) was for the withdrawal of all carriers by the end of 1969, and second (Option B) the construction of one large carrier with *Eagle* and *Hermes* refitted to operate Phantoms so they could operate into the 1980s. The smaller maritime role carrier option was conspicuous by its absence. The first option would be £88 million cheaper and require 6,460 fewer servicemen by 1970, and the Ministry of Defence's line over military capability was that they would be 'more or less equal' in military terms given some additional spending on compensating capabilities including anti-ship guided missiles. The Treasury was unequivocal in its support for the no carriers option. The Cabinet Secretary was, however, relatively sympathetic towards the Navy, and was sceptical of the RAF's claim that it could undertake maritime roles efficiently if the carriers were withdrawn in 1969.[54] He confirmed that ministers would have to make the final decision, whilst Healey, aware that Option A was losing credibility, put forward a middle option (Option C) of running on the carriers until the mid-1970s.[55] The proposals went to the full OPD committee, chaired by the Prime Minister, with Healey presenting the Ministry of Defence's case. Over a marathon seven meetings across nearly four weeks, the OPD committee went through the decisions of the Defence Review as a whole, but most of the discussions and time were taken up with the carrier issue. Over these meetings it became clear that the case in favour of the maritime role for land-based aircraft operating between 200 and 900 nautical miles from their bases was not yet proven, and this was given by Healey as the reason for producing the option of running on the carrier force until 1975. The Buccaneer 2** aircraft was cancelled after Healey gave a steadfast defence of the F-111. Procuring the Buccaneer 2** had been quietly advocated by Pat Nairne, Healey's private secretary, for some months and had been taken up by Burke Trend, the Cabinet Secretary. It had opened up the possibility of inter-operability between the Royal Navy and the RAF, but now it had also gone. Healey's forceful advocacy was pushing the argument in favour of the new 1975 option, but Trend was able to persuade the Prime Minister to allow direct interventions by the First Sea Lord and the Navy Minister to make their cases.[56]

The Navy's leadership was now being given one last chance to put forward a proposal for a new carrier, in front of a Cabinet Committee that had begun to shift towards a compromise position that accepted that the maritime role was best undertaken by aircraft carriers, at least for the next decade. How would it fare? The Naval Staff were permitted to work up a new option, but what they came up with was an incoherent jumble. Unable to give up on the Buccaneer completely, this new option nearly halved the number of Phantoms to be purchased, reduced the Buccaneer purchases to below that of Option C, continued operating the aged Sea Vixen until the early 1970s, withdrew the Gannet airborne early warning aircraft in favour of second-hand US-built aircraft, and reduced the capability of the new Martel anti-ship missile by removing television guidance. Twenty-five Anglo-French Jaguar aircraft would be 'navalised' to operate off carriers from 1973 as would the proposed Anglo-French variable geometry aircraft which would also fly off carriers from the mid-1970s. Up to 1973 this new option would actually mean *less* capability for the fleet, and it would still cost more than Option C overall. No development work on navalising either Jaguar or the Anglo-French variable geometry aircraft had actually be done so far, so this proposal was conjectural in the extreme and its costings could be no more than guesses. Unsurprisingly the costings were therefore challenged during one of the OPD meetings, when they were revised upwards. Given such a difficult proposal to defend Luce could not make any headway with the committee, and Option C remained the favoured approach.[57]

The Navy Minister, Christopher Mayhew, had his own chance a few days earlier to make his case in favour of the carrier. Unfortunately, he was probably the person least likely to help the Navy swing the argument in its favour at that time. His relationship with Denis Healey was not easy but this paled into insignificance compared to the collapse that had occurred in his relationship with the Prime Minister over the previous few months. Leaks had been flowing from the Ministry of Defence during the Defence Review, and Mayhew believed that one of his political enemies, George Wigg, the Paymaster General, had hinted to an ever-suspicious Wilson that Mayhew was the source of those leaks. Healey had been asked to conduct an internal leak enquiry by the Prime Minister, and a painful exchange of private letters began between Mayhew and Wilson. Mayhew, knowing with the progress of the Defence Review and the carrier controversy that his ministerial career was nearing its end, was ill-advisedly blunt in one of his letters and let it be known that he had shown Wilson's last letter to his officials. Wilson replied in a similar vein, but with added sarcasm. Wilson later even hinted darkly that Mayhew might be de-selected at the forthcoming general election: Mayhew had burnt his boats and had no chance of a meaningful ministerial career as long as Harold Wilson was leader of the Labour Party.[58] The Chairman of OPD was obviously not going to be swayed by an appearance by Mayhew, but would he convince any of the other members? Sadly for the Navy, this was not the case. Mayhew's intervention descended at times into an incoherent ramble: it was not clear whether he supported the £2,000 million target or not, he talked rather awkwardly of the 'white powers' in the Far East in language that would have been uncomfortable for the Labour ministers sitting around the committee table, and most significantly he did not make a clear and coherent case for the carrier. Wilson thanked Mayhew for his contribution and the Navy Minister left the room to ponder his resignation.[59] The carrier question went to the full Cabinet a few weeks later, an acknowledgement of the seriousness and importance of the decision, but the decision had effectively already been made. Healey put forward a forceful argument in favour of Option C and the Cabinet agreed to accept his proposal.[60] Mayhew could not even get the dramatic resignation he had wanted. Wilson's hint about de-selection had meant that he did not feel safe enough to resign before the general election was called, and so instead left office at the same time as Luce.

* * *

The cancellation of the large aircraft carrier is a classic study in poor staff work by the Royal Navy: the Navy seemed to have no interest in even thinking through any sort of concessions until it was too late, could not recognise or grasp compromises and 'off-ramps' when it saw them, had no understanding of the political stakes for the Secretary of State and fatally underestimated his resolve. It also had difficulties putting forward coherent proposals at short-notice and failed to follow up when gaps had been exposed in the arguments of its adversaries. Neutral players were unnecessarily alienated and it was deemed sensible to motivate staff officers through fear of the destruction of their careers if they failed. Admiral Luce fought hard in the key committees, but he often had to work against the ineptly unhelpful interventions of Mayhew, the poorly directed aggression of Hopkins, and the weak staff work he was given at key moments. Luce's diffident and introverted manner, and his strained relations with the most determined advocates of the aircraft carrier perhaps helped to create an environment where the Naval Staff's intransigence was more directed at preventing a First Sea Lord they did not entirely trust from giving away concessions unnecessarily, than building a coherent case to convince those outside the Navy. There is no evidence of Luce holding back from fighting hard for the carrier programme from the documents that this author has seen, but there might have been an inner equivocation or just a pessimism below the First Sea Lord's impenetrable surface. At the start of the Defence Review in January 1965, Mayhew had jokingly bet Luce £1 that the aircraft carrier would still be in the defence programme in a year's time, and Luce agreed to take him up on that wager. A year later, the carrier was still there – but only just – and Mayhew was due his £1 from Luce, and a month after that the carrier was gone, with both Luce and Mayhew soon to follow.[61]

What is most telling about the whole debacle is that the Air Staff were never able to fully convince Denis Healey, or the Cabinet Secretary or for that matter the OPD Cabinet Committee, that the RAF would be able to provide effective maritime air defence, airborne early warning and maritime strike for a Royal Navy that expected to be deployed worldwide. At one point, it even seemed possible that the Buccaneer had a chance of replacing the F-111 as the United Kingdom's key tactical land strike capability. However, this was not down to the efforts of the Naval Staff, Admiral Luce or Christopher Mayhew, but due to the lobbying of concerned outsiders: Sir Solly Zuckerman, the Chief Scientific Adviser at the Ministry of Defence and later at the Cabinet Office, General Sir Richard Hull, the Chief of the Defence Staff, and Patrick Nairne, Denis Healey's Private Secretary. And yet no carrier was built and these maritime roles *were* transferred to the RAF due to the inability of the Naval Staff to produce a workable small carrier plan. A cynical assessment of the debacle was made in Dyndal's 2012 study of the battle over the carrier. Dyndal, a Norwegian Air Force Colonel and former Dean of their Air Force Academy, is no air power sceptic, and yet he ultimately concluded that although Healey was not convinced by the RAF's arguments, they served a purpose in providing a justification to cancel the carrier, when the Navy argued its case poorly and proved unwilling to compromise.[62] Although Denis Healey's determination to push through the reductions in the defence budget to £2,000 million whilst also procuring the F-111, was the main reason why the Navy's preferred 60,000-ton carrier was not approved in 1966, the Naval Staff and the Navy's leadership were the prime reason why *no carrier at all* was procured that year and that aircraft carriers were to be phased out of service by 1975.

Eric Grove has described the cancellation of the aircraft carrier as 'perhaps the most traumatic shock to the Royal Navy of the entire postwar period'.[63] Aside from the resignations of the First Sea Lord and the Navy Minister, the Navy now had to adjust to a future where its long-planned capital ship would no longer be built: it would have to rebuild not only its fleet plans, but also its self-image and self-confidence after a painful 18-month Whitehall battle.

3

Recovery and Rebuilding

With the departure of Admiral Luce, the Navy needed new leadership, and it is unsurprising that the Secretary of State, guided by his officials and possibly by Luce himself, settled on Admiral Varyl Begg. He had the great advantage of having been outside Whitehall during the great carrier battle. As was seen in the previous chapter, Begg had recently begun a posting as Commander-in-Chief Portsmouth, having spent two years with the Far East Fleet. He was a surface fleet officer rather than a submariner like Luce, but he had also expressed some scepticism about the large carrier in an earlier period in the Naval Staff.[1] Significant sections of the Navy were still reeling from the cancellation, and Begg faced several overlapping tasks: he had to rebuild the Navy's relationship with the Secretary of State, he had to rebuild a sense of purpose within the Navy itself now that its long-standing capital ship, the carrier, was being removed, and he had to manage the transfer of much of the Fleet Air Arm's aircraft and some of its personnel to the Royal Air Force. Most urgently however, Begg had to address the procurement programme, for the existing runs of 'County' class destroyers and *Leander* class frigates were beginning to become outdated and new designs were urgently needed in order to get new weapons systems to sea. To tackle this issue Admiral Begg appointed a special working party of the Naval Staff to develop fleet options for approval by the Secretary of State.

Future Fleet Working Party
Rear Admiral John Adams, the Assistant Chief of the Naval Staff (Policy), was appointed chair of the new committee. The Future Fleet Working Party, as it was now called, began work on three separate pieces of work: a concept of operations setting out the likely activities of the Navy in the future, a set of ship design options ranging from the largest to the smallest vessels, and

finally recommendations for which ship combinations should be selected. The cancellation of the new aircraft carrier had left the Royal Navy's plans for the future fleet looking incoherent and unbalanced. A class of six large Type 82 destroyers had been planned for the 1970s, alongside a class of small, fast Type 19 frigates. The Type 82, with a specific role providing missile air defence for the carrier, now appeared to lack a purpose, whilst the Type 19 was too small to provide the mix of presence and war-fighting capabilities that appeared to be required for a Navy that would still be operating worldwide as well as in the NATO theatres of the Eastern Atlantic and Mediterranean. With no aircraft carriers, task group command facilities would have to be provided in other vessels, and what capabilities such ships would have also needed to be decided.[2]

Admiral Adams, who had a distinguished war record as a junior officer in the Second World War, had been the first non-submariner to command a submarine squadron and had been the commanding officer of the commando carrier HMS *Albion* during the Indonesian Confrontation, set about his task with enthusiasm and dynamism.[3] However, it very quickly seemed that matters were not proceeding to the liking of the Secretary of State or the civil servants at the centre of the Ministry. The Head of Defence Secretariat Branch 1, which provided policy support to the Secretary of State, stated that the early work of the committee was not 'relevant to our future requirements'; there were concerns that the Working Party was not making any reference to the RAF and its future role in providing air defence, reconnaissance and strike capabilities, nor did the materials produced give an understanding of what types of operation in which the Navy would be likely to be involved.[4] It was recommended that the best way of resolving this problem was for the Secretary of State to discuss the problem directly with Begg.[5]

Adams' team, supported by the Ship Department, were clearly working hard: they drafted a concept of operations, produced over 100 papers and were developing sketch designs for dozens of different warship types, but the Working Party was edging towards recommending 'cruiser/carriers', 17,000-ton ships that looked suspiciously like small aircraft carriers. Central Secretariat civil servants, who had been drafted onto the Working Party as observers, were clearly reporting back to the centre on its progress.[6] Healey then made his concerns felt more directly, stating that any operations East of Suez were likely to be at a lower intensity than the Working Party envisaged, that they were ignoring the contributions that the RAF and Army could make to RN operations, and he doubted that Harrier was an appropriate aircraft for the planned cruiser/carriers, which were in any case probably too large and should be merely cruisers. Healey's concerns that Adams would not produce what he wanted resulted in his commissioning studies chaired from outside the Navy Department on the naval 'ladder of deterrence' and an operational analysis assessing the need for amphibious capabilities.⁷ Both of these studies were clearly designed to constrain the conclusions of the Working Party: the Navy Department was not yet entirely trusted by the Secretary of State. A meeting in July 1966 between the Permanent Under-Secretary and Begg was a final attempt to clarify to the Navy's leadership that the Secretary of State would not countenance a Navy justified by sophisticated high-end operations East of Suez and centred around vessels that looked suspiciously like small aircraft carriers.⁸

Admiral Adams and the First Sea Lord had been sent unusually strong warning signals that the Working Party's early conclusions over warship types were not going to be approved by the Secretary of State. Why then did Adams and Begg persist? Adams clearly believed strongly in the direction he was taking the Working Party, and perhaps he felt that Begg, who had much better relations with Healey than his predecessor, could win over the Secretary of State; but the two meetings with Healey thus far had not provided any hint of a shift in position. If Adams was taking a risk with his future career to push what he felt to be the best solution, it is unclear why Begg had not taken a tighter grip over the Working Party and moved it closer to what he knew Healey wanted. Adams' proposals were put to the Admiralty Board and approved with little opposition and clear support from Begg.⁹ In the end, one can only assume that the proposals were what Adams, the Naval Staff and the Admiralty Board thought were right for the Navy, and that they could push it through, perhaps whilst Healey was distracted by further pushes from the Treasury for defence budget reductions. This was a risky approach to take: Healey was not known for being a pushover, his trust in the Navy could erode further, and the simplest thing the Secretary of State could do if further reductions were on the way would be to park the Working Party report until after a fresh review of the defence budget had taken place.

The Concept of Operations paper, which aimed to provide an operational context from which different warship types would be justified, worked on the continuing assumption that the Navy's core role both East and West of Suez would be peacekeeping and deterrence, and this would be to be achieved through a military presence worldwide, a 'shield force' for NATO and finally, the nuclear deterrent. It chimed with Healey's own view at the time that 'we do not take the view that a deliberate Soviet attack in the West is likely'.¹⁰ The continued improved relations between the West and the Soviet Union were taken for granted, whilst the gradual withdrawal from fixed bases in the Indian Ocean and South East Asia would actually require a greater naval presence to make up for the withdrawn garrisons and closed air stations. Operations, if they occurred, would be small scale and of short duration, and despite a number of forceful nudges from Healey, the RAF and Army were both barely mentioned in the text. Limited war and total war operations would only be undertaken with the support of allies.[11] By July 1966 three options for major ships had been proposed: the first option consisted of six 18,500-ton 'cruiser-carriers' flying Sea King and P1127 aircraft supplemented by the two recently-completed amphibious assault ships; the second was four 10,000-ton command cruisers, three commando carriers and two assault ships; and the third was six 12,000-ton command cruisers and three assault ships. Their running costs in the 1970s would theoretically be £64.5 million, £47 million and £62 million respectively compared to the pre-Defence Review planned fleet of three strike carriers, six escort cruisers, two commando carriers and two assault ships, which would have cost £188 million per year to operate.[12]

The final report which emerged in August 1966 had opted for option one, with the six cruiser-carriers replacing the three *Tiger* class cruisers and two commando carriers. In addition to the two assault ships, four Type 82 destroyers would be built as the best way to get the Sea Dart and Ikara missile systems to sea as quickly as possible, whilst a class of 2,500-ton 'Standard Frigates' based on the Type 19 would also be procured. In the late 1970s, after the Type 82s had entered service, new 'first rate frigates' of 4,500 tons armed with either Sea Dart or Ikara would be ordered. The SSN construction programme would continue until a total of fifteen or sixteen were in service, whilst a class of thirty-two combined hunter-sweeper mine countermeasures vessels would be built. Other vessels included hovercraft for coastal patrol and a large force of twelve fleet tankers and four stores ships.[13] The Working Party had been optimistic in its costings for the major equipment types: quoting £30 million for a cruiser-carrier, £20 million for a Type 82 and £7 million for a Type 19 frigate. The Central Secretariat were especially sceptical about the proposed unit costs, particularly for the cruiser/carrier and the cost of navalising the Harrier, which was put at £10 million.[14]

Given that the defence budget as a whole was reducing to £2,000 million a year (in 1964 prices) by 1970, this was an expensive and ambitious programme, with highly optimistic cost assumptions given the rapid increases in naval systems over the last few years. Assessing the 18,500-ton cruiser-carrier at £30 million a unit when the 6,000-ton Type 82 would only be a third cheaper at £20 million seemed difficult to believe. The charge of over-optimism over costs was soon proven as the Type 82 increased in cost by over 20 per cent in the next seven months.[15] It was not just the optimistic costings that were problematic about the recommendations, but that the two main projected escort classes from the previous programme, the Type 82 and the Type 19, had been retained. From an external perspective, and seen in a sceptical light, this did not look like a radical review from the bottom-up of the future fleet mix to take account of the cancellation of the carriers, but almost a stubborn refusal to make major changes to the Navy's procurement programme whilst also trying to resurrect a ship type, the aircraft carrier, that the Secretary of State and the Defence White Paper had categorically stated was on the way out. This is unfair on the Working Party, which had undertaken numerous in-depth assessments of the requirements for the 1970s onwards and had believed that the lack of full-sized carriers did mean that a large air defence ship (the Type 82) and a large helicopter cruiser were even *more* necessary, but it does acknowledge the need for a better *presentation* of the results to satisfy the intended audience and gain approval. Since the creation of the centralised Ministry of Defence in 1964, the Navy was no longer the 'master of its own house' and needed to convince those who were not naval insiders of the utility of its requirements at the centre of the Ministry of Defence. Over the next few years the Naval Staff would learn from this mistake and become more adept at presenting its requirements more effectively.

It was entirely predictable that the Secretary of State would not be happy with the outcomes presented by Admiral Adams. Both Healey and the Permanent Under-Secretary had made this clear through numerous meetings between March and July 1966, and yet still the Future Fleet Working Party produced a report that would inevitably rile the Secretary of State and fail to be approved. From the perspective of Healey, the inability of Begg to 'rein in' Adams also damaged the new First Sea Lord's standing as he attempted to re-build the Navy's relationship with the Ministry's leadership. Healey ordered that the Report be completely re-written to reflect his requirements for a Concept of Operations that acknowledged greater dependency on other services, particularly the RAF, as well as a proposed fleet mix that was not only cheaper but did not suggest attempts to re-create an aircraft carrier requirement.[16] Begg angrily berated and then dismissed Adams, in effect letting the more junior admiral take the blame for a predictable outcome for which the more senior admiral was equally responsible. The First Sea Lord then took over direct control of a new-look Future Fleet Working Party, which no longer sat within the Naval Staff but was reconstituted as a sub-committee of the Admiralty Board.[17]

Revising the Report

Begg rapidly began the re-writing of the Concept of Operations paper which, as directed, acknowledged the strike, deterrence and air defence capabilities of RAF strike aircraft in support of the fleet, stated that fleet to fleet 'duels' were a thing of the past and that the only operations that naval forces would undertake would be 'operations short of limited war' both East and West of Suez.[18] His recommendations for the future fleet mix were much more cautious and focussed around smaller ships: the 10,000-ton command cruiser had been the smallest of the 'cruiser' options (costing £25 million), whilst the selected 3,500-ton 'Sea Dart frigate' was just about the smallest vessel capable of operating that missile system (£10 million), albeit supplemented with a helicopter and medium gun. Only one Type 82 destroyer would be built, as a test platform for Sea Dart and Ikara, and the modified Type 19 'Standard Frigate' (£7 million) survived as the *Leander* class successor.[19] The new report judiciously did not provide numbers for each of these ship types, and aside from the continuance of the SSN programme did not give recommendations for any other vessel types. This fleet mix was described as providing smaller ships for worldwide peacekeeping and presence roles such as the Sea Dart frigate and the Standard Frigate, which could be supplemented by larger higher-value units as such as the command cruiser and SSNs. The command cruiser was, entirely spuriously, billed as a development of the Type 82 destroyer in order to help demonstrate that this vessel was definitely not a carrier in disguise, whilst the Type 19 was no longer described by this name, and only given the title 'Standard Frigate'. Begg had learnt some important lessons when presenting conceptual warship proposals to Denis Healey.[20]

These were an extremely cautious set of conclusions and recommendations designed to ensure their approval and allow for a rapid transition to detailed design, ordering and construction. They were also a product of an uncertain strategic environment: although the carrier had been cancelled, a considerable presence East of Suez was still envisaged for the foreseeable future, whilst in home waters the lessening of tensions following the fall of Khrushchev suggested that confrontation with the Warsaw Pact was less likely. This resulted in ships such as the Sea Dart frigate and Standard Frigate that were described within the Ministry of Defence, not entirely inaccurately, as primarily 'East of Suez' ships for peacekeeping and presence rather than sustained high-intensity conflict. Doubts were even raised by civil servants about the utility of the command cruiser if it operated purely in a 'West of Suez' environment against Warsaw Pact forces.[21] Despite the First Sea Lord's effort to turn around a new set of recommendations quickly, the Secretary of State was now fully engaged in the beginnings of the new round of defence economies, and so perhaps predictably had little inclination or time to revisit and approve the new report. The Navy Minister attempted to nudge Healey and the new Permanent Under-Secretary through September and October, but to no avail.[22]

Healey finally found time to read the report and attended the Admiralty Board on 9 November. He was still unhappy with the Concept of Operations, arguing that it did not reflect the Foreign Office's position on the future of the British presence in the Indo-Pacific, which had shifted over the last few months and was drifting towards a gradual reduction in engagement with the region. Healey was still not convinced with the Navy's wish to build one Type 82 which he regarded as a relic of the fleet designed around aircraft carriers, took note of the Sea Dart frigate which was now termed the Type 42, and was informed that the lack of design capacity within the Ship Department would probably mean that a commercially-designed 'cheap' frigate would be procured before the Standard Frigate. However, although Healey approved two further *Leander* class frigates and a nuclear-powered attack submarine, he did not approve the new Working Party report, leaving the future of the Navy's new warship programme still in limbo.[23] The lack of much progress on the ladder of deterrence and operational analysis papers added to the worry, as did a lukewarm and equivocal endorsement of the paper, with a further revised and truncated Concept of Operations section, by the Chiefs of Staff Committee in December. With the new defence review well under way, entitled the Defence Expenditure Studies, the Navy increasingly looked like it would be vulnerable to yet more capability cuts especially if a reduction in East of Suez capabilities occurred; the Chiefs of Staff Committee ominously noting that the Report might have to be substantially revised as a result of the outcome of the Studies.[24]

The Navy's agony continued into the first few months of 1967, as Healey repeatedly delayed making decisions and appeared to have little interest in the Working Party report despite numerous revisions to meet his changing criticisms. The Secretary of State reviewed the Concepts of Operations paper in its second revised form, and was still unhappy with it, believing that the section on West of Suez operations in the NATO area did not convince, and that the choice of ships – the command cruiser, the Sea Dart frigate and the Standard Frigate – did not fit with what was needed in the NATO area of operations. However, he did not set out what changes were required in the subsequent meeting with Begg beyond the rather worrying statement for the Navy, which contradicted his earlier conclusion about these ships, that the nature of Britain's maritime commitment to NATO was 'essentially a political, rather than military assessment'.[25] Failed and rather transparent attempts by the Naval Staff to slip in the new ship types into drafts of the 1967 White Paper, despite their lack of approval by Healey, did little to improve the Navy's relationship with the Secretary of State and his senior civil servants, as well as annoying the Treasury who were only partly mollified when they discovered how cheap the proposed vessels were meant to be.[26] The behaviour of the Naval Staff at this time still suggests that Begg did not have a firm grip of this organisation that was meant to provide him with policy advice and support, but instead was now undermining his position with the Secretary of State. In this torpid and dispiriting atmosphere, it seemed likely that the Navy was being lined up for even more reductions as the Defence Expenditure Studies neared their conclusions within the Ministry.

Concluding the Defence Expenditure Studies

The final stages of the Studies came down to three possible options to provide the Treasury with its required cuts: an 'Army option' which reduced the defence budget by £231 million by 1970–1 and resulted in keeping 50,000 troops in Germany combined with a number of Army garrisons East of Suez. In this option, the Navy would be gutted: the cruisers would be cancelled, the amphibious force withdrawn quickly, the Royal Marines disbanded, and the rate of nuclear submarine production halved. It was a difficult option to make practical as the Army's East of Suez garrisons would probably end up in Australia, if they could be persuaded to take the troops, but would have little mobility. The 'Navy option' largely kept the Navy at its current and planned strength whilst reducing the Army to a force that operated just in the United Kingdom and Germany. This saved £198 million by 1970–1. The third option was an 'equal misery approach' which reduced the Army, but not as painfully as in the 'Navy option', whilst withdrawing the existing carrier force in 1970–1 rather than 1975.[27] One interesting intervention from A D Peck, the Deputy Under-Secretary for Budgets and Plans, a former Treasury official who was usually an enthusiast for cost and capability reductions, argued that the Navy should not be singled out for cuts again as it was in February 1966 as it could undermine the 'present and past character' of that service.[28] This note made its way to Healey and appears to have had an effect on the Defence Secretary. Healey took the third option to the Prime Minister, accompanied with an assessment that finding the £200 million or more required by the Treasury would only be possible by a significant pull-out from East of Suez commitments, leaving just a few naval vessels, and RAF aircraft deployed from a series of 'island bases'.[29] With the Indonesian Confrontation having ended in August 1966 and the withdrawal from Aden announced in February of the same year, there were no ongoing operations, so withdrawals at least looked politically and diplomatically possible, and in the coming months the fateful decision was made to withdraw from East of Suez commitments by 1975.[30] Begg had fought hard to keep the Royal Marines and amphibious force, and also pointed out that with cuts of this nature, reduction in civilian Ministry of Defence posts would also be necessary, but the plan to withdraw carriers by 1970–1 stuck, along with another reduction in the destroyer and frigate force. The cruisers and the nuclear submarine programme were untouched.[31] With the Defence Expenditure Studies complete, Healey now felt able to return to the Future Fleet Working Party report, which he approved in a meeting of the Defence Council on 20 March 1967.[32] The command cruiser would now cost £30 million, the Type 42 (now described as a destroyer) £12 million and the Standard Frigate £8 million, whilst the total programme would cost £115 million a year from 1971/72 onwards.[33] The programme was approved, almost as a formality, by the Oversea Policy and Defence Committee of Cabinet in June 1967.[34] After much pain and another defence review, the Navy now finally had its new future fleet.

There was one last act to this exhausting period of almost continuous defence reviews. On 18 November 1967 the pound sterling, which at that time was exchanged at fixed rate to the US dollar, was devalued. Everything bought in dollars across the economy was now 1/7th more expensive: the Treasury needed reductions in spending across the board, and the Ministry of Defence was tasked with finding yet another block of reductions, this time £100 million.[35] The axe fell on two key aspects of Denis Healey's 'Island Strategy': the money to pay for creating an air base on the Indian Ocean island of Aldabra, and the US-made F-111 bomber. The RAF's island strategy, by which strike, air defence and other aircraft would use a series of airfields across the Indian Ocean in order to intervene militarily or support naval vessels, had been predicated on the optimistic assumption that these airfields would be straightforward to build or upgrade. One of the key islands, Aldabra in the western Indian Ocean, which was uninhabited and had no airstrip, would, it was discovered, cost much more than originally envisaged to develop. The United States was initially willing to split the costs in half, but it was then discovered that the island was a haven for rare birds and quickly became a cause célèbre for campaigning ornithologists and naturalists. The US side of the Aldabra deal was now unlikely to get through Congress, and with devaluation the British side was now under threat as the Treasury was looking for quick cost reductions. The building of an airfield at Aldabra was therefore cancelled and the island strategy was no longer viable without such a large part of the Indian Ocean uncovered.[36] The US-built F-111 was similarly vulnerable, and now that it almost cost 1/7th more, not even the recently-agreed smaller order of fifty seemed viable. Healey fought hard in Cabinet to save the aircraft, but to no avail and it was cancelled in January 1968.[37] Along with the F-111 cancellation and the end of the island strategy came a decision to speed up the withdrawal from major commitments East of Suez in December 1971.[38] In only a matter of two years, the British military role in the Indian Ocean and South East Asia had shifted from being at the core of defence strategy and policy to being almost completely given up. The deterrence and peacekeeping fleet that Begg had managed to get approved in March 1967 would now be a force primarily deployed in the North Atlantic and in European waters. This could make operational sense if the post-Khrushchev lessening of tensions continued, but if these went into reverse and Soviet naval capabilities continued to improve, it could make Begg's fleet of cost-effective surface ships look small, under-armed and vulnerable.

The Future of Maritime Air

The cancellation of the strike carrier and the accompanying decision to phase out aircraft carriers by 1975 were, from the perspective of the Fleet

Air Arm, a catastrophe. Former Fleet Air Arm officers had spent the first two post-war decades working their way up the structures of the Royal Navy, gaining influence and the acceptance of carrier air power within a service still dominated by gunnery officers. Admiral Luce's immediate predecessor as First Sea Lord, Admiral Caspar John, had been the first Fleet Air Arm officer to hold that position at the very top of the Navy, and key naval staff and command positions were beginning to include significant numbers of former flyers. In short, the 'flying' tribe of the Navy was in the ascendant before the carrier decision, and the fall and the impact was even greater as a result. It is worth remembering that the flying of helicopters from smaller ships such as frigates was still in its early days and was in any case considered a stopgap until all weather anti-submarine missile systems were available in the 1970s; so lacking any significant shore-based flying capability, the Fleet Air Arm was therefore primarily an aircraft carrier and fast-jet focussed branch.[39]

The most significant immediate impact for Fleet Air Arm fixed-wing aircrew officers was the institution of a programme for voluntary retirement, transfer of a limited number of flyers to the Royal Air Force and finally the transfer out of the armed forces and directly into the burgeoning civil aviation industry, under a scheme arranged with the three main British airlines. The exact number of fixed-wing flyers that would be needed in the future was unclear at that stage: the decision made in 1966 still envisaged running on the carriers until the mid-1970s, which would encompass the full flying careers of younger flyers.[40] On the other hand, the carrier force was definitely going to shrink, probably to only *Eagle* and *Ark Royal* by the early 1970s down from the five strike carriers in service in 1966. In early 1968 it was envisaged that the total personnel numbers of the Fleet Air Arm and those from other branches that worked at air stations would fall from a total of 16,451 to 7,583 ten years later. The number of pilots and observers would fall from 1,112 to 589 during the same period.[41]

Despite the winding-down of the carrier force in the next decade, further orders for carrier jet aircraft were made: thirty Buccaneer S2s were ordered on 12 April 1966, with the final fifteen being ordered a year later, although eight of these were cancelled at the end of 1967. These joined the other thirty-seven Buccaneer S2s in service or being built. Transfers to the Royal Air Force would only begin at the end of 1968, and only five had moved across by the end of the decade.[42] A second tranche of thirty-five Phantoms was also ordered in October 1966 to add to the twenty production orders placed in 1965. However, seven would end up being cancelled with another thirteen being transferred to the Royal Air Force before completion.[43] The Royal Navy still needed a substantial fast jet force for the next decade of expected carrier operations.

Of the five aircraft carriers available in 1966, the future of HMS *Centaur*, the smallest, was quickly decided when plans to convert her to a commando carrier like her sisters *Albion* and *Bulwark* were cancelled; she was therefore decommissioned and became an accommodation ship before being scrapped in 1972. She had been too old and small for a modernisation to take the latest aircraft, so her withdrawal was not unexpected. By contrast, the decision to expand the planned major refit of HMS *Ark Royal* into something much more ambitious than originally planned is on the surface surprising given that the type was being phased out. Initially, it had been planned to refit *Ark Royal* for 22 months, updating her to operate the Sea King helicopter in the place of the Wessex and the Buccaneer 2 in place of the Buccaneer 1. However, this refit had not been approved by the Treasury in 1965, who argued that the expense of a £13.5 million refit to provide only four years of service from 1968 to 1972 was a poor return on the money, and that the future of the carriers was in any case under review. A few weeks after the cancellation of the CVA01, the Naval Staff returned to consideration of *Ark Royal*'s refit to find a much more favourable environment. Although the carriers would be phased out, the Secretary of State had publicly committed not only to the retention of the carriers until 1975, which confirmed the medium-term need for these vessels, but had also stated specifically that the refit of *Ark Royal* would go ahead: the Treasury had now been trumped by a publicly-made commitment.[44] The Naval Staff had also taken the opportunity to expand the requirements of the planned refit before it had been placed before the Secretary of State. The ship would be updated to operate the Phantom in place of the older Sea Vixen, which would mean major changes to the ship's flight deck to increase its angle and provide space for a new 199ft-long catapult and strengthened arrestor wires that the new fast jet needed for effective operations. The opportunity was also taken to improve the ship's electronics fit by installing two new air-search radars of the distinctive Type 965P 'double bedstead' type and an improved communications and electronic warfare suite. The poor state of *Ark Royal*'s cabling and propulsion also meant that more time and money would need to be spent in these areas. The refit would now take 30 months and cost around £26 million, but with the Secretary of State's public commitment to it, the work was quickly approved by the Treasury and £674,000 of long-lead items were immediately ordered.[45] By the end of the year it was becoming apparent that the initial cost estimate had been optimistic and the price was expected to be up to £30 million, and even then this would only be possible if plans to augment the ship's Sea Cat point defence missile systems were shifted from 'fitted with' to 'fitted for'. With a busy refit programme, ensuring that *Ark Royal* would be ready by 1970 now required making the refit nearly the top naval priority in the equipment programme, behind only the introduction of the Polaris submarine-launched nuclear missile system into service.[46]

The refit and later service of another aircraft carrier, HMS *Victorious*, would prove to be more contentious. *Victorious* was an armoured carrier of Second World War vintage that had been almost completely re-built in the 1950s up to the highest standards of the day. Although smaller than *Ark Royal*, she was larger than *Centaur* and was therefore able to operate the Buccaneer strike aircraft alongside the Sea Vixen fighter. She had entered a short refit in the summer of 1967 but a fire on board whilst in dockyard hands resulted in the death of one crewman. The peremptory decision was made to decommission the ship even though the repair work required was not major, and the ship had another four to five years' worth of naval service ahead of her.[47]

Three factors combined to ensure that she was decommissioned early. The first was that as has been seen, the government was planning to withdraw from bases East of Suez four years earlier than originally planned, and this earlier withdrawal therefore warranted a smaller carrier force. Second, the planning of the Navy Department's budget estimates for 1968–9 had been particularly painful: the planned budget was still £10.1 million over the target set by the Ministry of Defence finance department. The immediate paying off of *Victorious* and the parallel cancellation of the last eight Buccaneer aircraft would reduce the total by £4 million and £5.6 million respectively almost filling the gap completely. It is notable that the Navy Department did not make this decision itself but passed it up to the Secretary of State to make – thus allowing for a modicum of distancing from a painful decision.[48] Finally, the Navy was entering one of its now-periodic manning crises, with an acute shortage of engine room ratings driving decisions to withdraw older destroyers from service a few years earlier than planned. *Victorious* had thirty-seven engine room artificers in her complement, the equivalent of seven older destroyers and frigates.[49] Although the withdrawal of *Victorious* had been rejected when the crisis had first emerged in July 1966, by the end of 1967, when the speedier rundown of the carrier fleet was becoming a certainty, the release of her crew to other ships would have helped resolve problems that were threatening to keep warships in port. In the event a fair number of her crew transferred to another carrier, HMS *Hermes*, which was about to deploy to the Indian Ocean.[50] *Victorious* languished, de-commissioned, for a number of years as plans for her to be sold to the Portuguese navy as a military transport for her African colonial campaigns or sold to a German businessman to act as a German-flagged exhibition ship were rejected. The latter option would have been a particularly humiliating end for the ship whose aircraft had help sink the German battleship *Bismarck* in 1941: surprisingly, it was pursued by both the British Embassy in Bonn and the Defence Sales Organisation for some time, despite the objections of the Vice Chief of the Naval Staff and the Second Sea Lord.[51]

In retrospect, the decision to push forward quickly with the *Ark Royal* modernisation, and to increase the capability enhancements despite the rise in cost and time, was the right one. Later political developments in 1967 would result in an earlier out-of-service date for the carrier force, and a more rapid cull of these ships. Originally it had been planned for *Ark Royal*'s sister ship, *Eagle*, to receive the first modernisation to operate Phantoms between 1968 and 1970, but if this plan had remained in place, the decisions of November 1967 would almost certainly resulted in the cancellation of that modernisation meaning that no aircraft carriers would have been able to operate the Phantom with the result that all the surviving aircraft would have transferred direct to the Royal Air Force or been cancelled. The surviving carriers would then have only operated the obsolescent Sea Vixen air defence aircraft, making the case for the retention of carriers after 1971 much more difficult to make. Instead, from 1970, the Royal Navy would possess a modernised aircraft carrier able to operate some of the most effective air defence and strike aircraft in the NATO inventory. *Ark Royal* was a ship with many mechanical weaknesses compared to her better-maintained sister *Eagle*, not least in her machinery and her air-search radar, but if she had not been modernised in that way at that time, then the Navy's strike carrier capability would have not lasted as late as 1978, nearly seven years later than envisaged.

Submarines

If the cancellation of CVA01 had dealt a blow to one of the Royal Navy's rising 'tribes' – the Fleet Air Arm – it also served to help push ahead the position of another 'tribe' who felt that its time had now come. The considerable capabilities of the new nuclear-powered 'hunter-killer' submarines, of which the first, HMS *Dreadnought*, was in service with another three under construction and a further one ordered, were beginning to be fully understood. They were true submarines, able to stay underwater for weeks and even months rather than only hours, and capable of great speeds whilst submerged. The decision, following the cancellation of the Skybolt nuclear-armed missile in 1962, to shift the United Kingdom's strategic nuclear deterrent from the RAF's bomber force to nuclear-powered submarines firing US Polaris missiles, only accentuated the prestige of the submarine in the Royal Navy and the submariners who sailed in them.[52] The decision to place images of HMS *Dreadnought* on the cover of the Future Fleet Working Party report emphasised this shift.[53] One of the few things that both the Navy's leadership and the Secretary of State were agreed upon throughout 1966 and 1967 was that the nuclear submarine programme needed to continue at its current rate: the original Working Party report had recommended the continuance of the programme so that a fleet of fifteen to sixteen such vessels would eventually be in service and this position was maintained by the new Begg-chaired Working Party. As we have seen, Denis Healey, who was happy to kill off the first report and then sit on the second version for many months, was also content for an additional nuclear-powered submarine of the *Valiant* class to be ordered in mid-1966 despite this enforced stasis in the plans for the surface fleet.[54]

When Admiral Begg became First Sea Lord the process of building four Polaris ballistic missile carrying nuclear-powered submarines was already well under way.[55] The first of class, HMS *Resolution*, was launched in September 1966 and commissioned in October 1967 after four months of contractor's and other sea trials. These trials went smoothly and were followed by further trials and test firings of the Polaris missiles off Cape Kennedy in the United States. Each of the boat's two crews ('port' and 'starboard') undertook missile firings, and all were eventually successful, although the starboard crew's firing had to be delayed after the US Navy range escort accidentally collided with *Resolution*'s specially-fitted telemetry mast.[56] Meanwhile, procedures for the launching of the Polaris missiles in the event of a 'supreme national emergency' involved the creation of a closed-circuit television link between Number Ten Downing Street and Western Fleet Headquarters in Northwood, north-west London, which would allow the Prime Minister to give his order to Commander-in-Chief Western Fleet, who in turn would send an authorising signal to the boat on patrol. A parallel NATO authorisation procedure was put in place whereby the Supreme Allied Commander Europe could authorise firing via Northwood, but only with a concurrent authorisation from the Prime Minister. In the event of the Prime Minister being incapacitated, then authority for firing would reside with a First and then a Second Nuclear Deputy, both senior Cabinet ministers. In the absence of any political authority to fire as a result of a pre-emptive nuclear strike, from 1972 all boats carried two sealed envelopes. The first gave instructions and conditions for opening the second envelope, which was a secret message from the Prime Minister providing orders for the boat's crew. The contents of these messages have never been revealed. The actual firing of the missiles required two-person activation at two separate stages: first with the decoding of the authorisation signal, and second with the actual firing. In both stages the two people in question were the boat's Commanding Officer (or Executive Officer) and the Polaris Systems Officer.[57] Consideration was given to deploy, or at least have the capability to deploy, the Polaris boats East of Suez as a means to deter China, retain influence with the US in East Asia and replace existing tactical nuclear stocks in the region, but these plans were abandoned in 1968 and the four *Resolution* class operated their whole careers in Atlantic waters.[58]

The crews of the new Polaris submarines were inheriting the huge responsibility for the successful maintenance of the British strategic nuclear deterrent from the Royal Air Force, placing the Royal Navy's submarine fleet at the centre of British defence strategy for the first time. The nuclear-powered submarines armed only with conventional weaponry were also an important adjunct to the Polaris missile boats. Aside from their role attacking enemy ships and submarines, they also had important tasks in helping to escort Polaris boats out to and back from patrol, checking for any shadowing Soviet submarines, and in detecting and trailing Soviet ballistic missile submarines with the aim of destroying them to prevent the firing of their missiles in the event of general war. Nuclear-powered submarines were now clearly amongst the Royal Navy's capital ships alongside its surviving aircraft carriers, and a strong argument could be made that they were in fact *more* important than the aircraft carriers. The advent of the nuclear submarine fleet was clearly uncomfortable for some of the surface-fleet officers who had traditionally dominated the Naval Staff and the higher echelons of the Navy. The first Commander-in-Chief of the Western Fleet to have responsibility for the operational control of the strategic nuclear deterrent, Admiral Sir John Bush, seemed to have an ambivalent attitude to the *Resolution*'s commissioning. He told her crew that he regarded the boat as 'no different to one of our minesweepers' just before they went on their first nuclear patrol, which could not have been good for their morale.[59] It would take another generation before submariners would rise to the very top of the Navy, but even then the submarine service retained a feeling, not wholly unjustified, that the rest of the Navy did not quite understand the importance and capabilities of the nuclear submarine fleet.[60]

The production of the first ballistic missile nuclear submarines and their conventionally-armed counterparts began to suffer a range of problems and setbacks during the late 1960s, many of which reflected the limitations of British industry and the strains placed on shipbuilders to provide the materials, components, equipment and submarines for the Royal Navy. The launch of HMS *Repulse* in November 1967 at the Vickers Barrow yard resulted in her being grounded in Walney channel for 12 hours, but the greatest problems occurred with the second yard building nuclear submarines, Cammell Laird. The timetable for their two *Resolution* class boats, *Renown* and *Revenge*, began to slip and serious issues of quality control emerged as *Renown* was being built: the misinterpretation of drawings provided from Vickers resulted in some bulkhead gaps being 1in shorter than in the Vickers boats, a difference that raised a series of questions about the possibility of other unplanned differences and their impact on the boat's safety and capability. Noises in the same boat's reactor compartment were detected some months later and it was eventually discovered that eleven pieces of broken metal had ended up in the boat's thermal sleeve. This was either sabotage by disgruntled shipyard workers or the result of gross incompetence, neither of which placed great confidence in Cammell Laird as a nuclear submarine builder. Throughout *Renown*'s service career she would suffer from numerous technical problems, whilst her fellow Cammell Laird boat *Revenge* would be the first to be withdrawn from service in 1992 despite being the youngest in the class.[61]

Another problem affecting both the deterrent and the fleet boats was problems over the quality of steel used in construction. An inspection of *Dreadnought* after her first commission had picked up hairline cracks in her hull. Sonic testing of the affected areas confirmed there was sufficient sound metal to ensure that failure would not occur, but similar tests were carried out on *Valiant* and *Warspite*, whilst a decision was made to rely on US steel for the fourth and fifth nuclear fleet submarines, pending confirmation that British steel was of sufficient quality for later boats.[62] *Dreadnought* suffered further cracking problems during her career, but these were similar to problems found on US Navy boats and there is no evidence that it caused any serious structural issues for the submarines.[63]

In 1967 the Admiralty Board approved the next generation of fleet submarine, which became the *Swiftsure* class. Despite being described as the improved *Valiant* class, it was 'entirely new' in design, having been designed from scratch anew, and the first boat of the new class would be the seventh nuclear-powered fleet submarine to be built. An improved hydrodynamic form, which included a shorter fin, resulted in a greater speed than preceding vessels. The boat also had a deeper diving depth, improved safety characteristics and would be a quieter vessel than her predecessors. Given concerns about the quality of British steel, US HY80 steel would be used for the sixth nuclear submarine (*Courageous*) and *Swiftsure* herself but it was planned that all the later ships in the class would have British steel of an equivalent of HY80. *Swiftsure* would also be different to her later sisters in two other ways. Pump-jet trials were being undertaken on HMS *Churchill*, and if successful, then the second and succeeding members of class would be so fitted. Pump jets were shrouds placed around propellers that reduced 'cavitation' or the making of bubbles and therefore helped reduce the sound made by a submarine, therefore making it more difficult to detect. In addition, *Swiftsure* would be fitted for, though initially not with, the new Tactical Data Handling System which would be fitted to later vessels. Finally, it was agreed that ice operations capability would not be necessary for the new class as both Flag Officer Submarines and the Director of Undersea Warfare in the Naval Staff were both of the mind that this was no longer a priority. Initially it was hoped that *Swiftsure* would cost £27 million but by March 1967 this had increased to a more realistic £29 million with another £2 million set aside as a contingency for any further increases.[64] The order for *Swiftsure* was placed in

November 1967.⁶⁵ It was originally planned that the next boat was be a further and final boat of the *Valiant* class, but this was changed in early 1967 to the newer design.⁶⁶ *Swiftsure* was commissioned on 17 April 1973 and a further five boats were built up to 21 March 1981 and the commissioning of the last of class, HMS *Splendid*.⁶⁷

Cruisers

If the strike carriers had been approved, then it is likely that the cruiser as a warship type would have died out in Royal Navy service by the early 1970s. The old wartime cruisers were expensive to operate and had manpower requirements that were close to that of an aircraft carrier but were also ill-suited to the guided-missile age as they had limited internal volume for modern electronic systems given their heavy belts of armour. Only a handful of cruisers completed during or before the war were still in commission and none were in front-line service. Three *Lion* class cruisers, which had been laid down during the war, but completed between 1959 to 1961 to a much-modified design incorporating new weapons and radars, were still in service but their all-gun armament made them seem ill-suited to the requirements of the 1970s, when longer-ranged guided missiles were expected to be the main anti-ship capability. Designs for new helicopter-carrying escort cruisers had been developed in the early 1960s with the aim of increasing the fixed-wing capacity of the planned strike carriers by taking helicopters off these ships, and by providing additional ships with flagship facilities, but these vessels had been deferred as their procurement would have deflected money and resources from the higher-priority strike carrier design.⁶⁸

Design concepts were then developed from 1964 onwards to convert the *Lion* class into interim helicopter cruisers until the new escort cruisers finally arrived, presumably after the carrier force had been renewed, but given the difficulties that would have been encountered manning the new carriers, it is likely that the *Lion* class would have been retired early and the escort cruisers would never have been revived. The planned class of large Type 82 destroyers would have sufficed as small Task Group flagships, and the carriers themselves would have provided both Task Force command facilities and operated sufficient numbers of helicopters, in addition to their air defence, strike and early warning roles. However, with the cancellation of the new ships and the intended phasing-out of existing carriers by 1975, it now became clear that some form of command ship would be necessary for naval surface task groups. Plans to convert the *Lion* class, which had not been approved before the Defence Review, were dusted off and presented as interim solutions before any new command ships were procured. As has been seen, the nature of what these new command ships would be – cruiser-carriers, commando carriers or command cruisers – had been the most contentious part of the Future Fleet Working Party's report. With vessels that appeared to be small aircraft carriers forcefully rejected by the Secretary of State, and subsequently by the First Sea Lord, the new Working Party re-visited the design concept options that were available and agreed to develop the smallest and cheapest version: a 10,000-ton command cruiser with a flight deck aft and spaces for six to eight helicopters that bore a strong resemblance to the escort cruiser designs of the early 1960s.[69] Admiral Begg was deliberately playing safe with this design and emphasised its cheapness and relatively small size. The command cruiser design continued its development during 1967, the relevant Treasury officials assuring themselves of the need for such a vessel by comparing it to an Army divisional headquarters, a telling indication of the extent of that department's understanding of naval matters.[70] By mid-1968, when Admiral Begg retired as First Sea Lord, the cruiser had been described as a 'tanker with a Type 42 [destroyer] armament', probably with an eye to Treasury concerns about cost rather than as an accurate description the design of such a ship. The 'tanker' aspect presumably related to the ship's hangar space, and the Type 42 armament implied the Sea Dart missile system and a 4.5in medium gun.[71] However, this vessel remained relatively small, at around 12,000 tons and flying only six Sea King anti-submarine helicopters. It would not be until Begg's retirement that the concept of the command cruiser was taken in a new – and more aircraft carrier-like – direction by his successor Admiral Michael Le Fanu.

Guided Missile Destroyers

Since the end of the Second World War, the Admiralty and then the Navy Department had devoted considerable resources to designing and developing guided missiles capable of destroying enemy aircraft. The Sea Slug Mk 1 guided missile was the main outcome of this research and development, and it was fitted to the first four 'County' class guided missile destroyers, which were completed in 1962 and 1963. Sea Slug was a medium-range missile able to intercept aircraft out close to the horizon, it could theoretically deal with 'crossing targets': aircraft flying towards other ships rather than directly at the ships armed with Sea Slug. The demands of the Sea Slug missile had resulted in the 'County' class vessels being impressively large at 6,000 tons, the size of a Second World War cruiser.[72] With the impending withdrawal of aircraft carriers – and their air defence aircraft – from service, such vessels suddenly became much more important for a Navy that expected to be operating outside the range of land-based aircraft at least some of the time.

Unfortunately, the first four 'County' class vessels, the Sea Slug missiles and the GWS 1 missile system that they operated, had two major problems. The first was that the ships did not possess sufficient tactical command and control capabilities to manage the air defence of a task group by themselves. They had always been expected to operate with modern aircraft carriers which would have provided tactical command of the air picture and use their large air-search radars, such as the Type 984 'searchlight' radar fitted to the carriers *Eagle*, *Victorious* and *Hermes*, to help detect and identify targets, which would have been passed by rudimentary data link to the 'County' class ships.[73] How would such ships operate when the last carriers were withdrawn in 1975? The question became even more urgent when the withdrawal of the carriers was accelerated to 1971. Four ships which had been completed as recently as 1962 and 1963 would soon be unusable in their designed role less than a decade after their completion, unless significantly updated. The second problem was that Sea Slug itself, even when directed by carrier command and control, was not an effective missile against the threats it was likely to meet. As the United States had found with its air defence missile programme during the 1950s and 1960s, such medium-range missile systems were highly complex, expensive and difficult to make effective against manoeuvring supersonic targets.[74] The US Navy had the resources to ensure that the teething problems with their missile systems would largely be resolved by the end of the 1960s; the Royal Navy did not. The first fleet exercise to make use of Sea Slug alongside air defence aircraft operating from carriers had shown up the limitations of the system, despite the acknowledgement that it was an improvement on the pre-Sea Slug air defence: the number of missiles carried was 'embarrassingly small', the system had trouble handling more than a few targets and could not deal with low targets, and their vulnerability made it 'most inadvisable to employ these ships in war on detached or general purpose duties'.[75] The Royal Australian Navy, which had seen the problems experienced by Sea Slug at first hand during its long period of testing on the Woomera ranges in South Australia, were so sceptical about the missile system they refused to purchase 'County' class destroyers from Britain, buying US-designed and built major warships for the first time and therefore accelerating that Navy's gradual de-coupling from British warship procurements, and from the Royal Navy in general.[76]

The second quartet of 'County' class destroyers had been designed with a number of changes to improve their air defence capabilities. Sea Slug was updated to a Mark II variant, and the GWS 1 system was replaced by the improved GWS 2 and linked into the Royal Navy's first tactical command system for non-carriers: ADAWS 1. Other improvements included improved air-search radars and modified missile-handling arrangements. Sea Slug Mk II had a range of 32,000 yards compared to 23,000 yards for the Mk I variant. Mk II could also intercept small jet aircraft and large guided missiles flying down to 150ft from the sea's surface, an improvement on the Mk I, which had a minimum intercept height of 500ft and a minimum target size of something comparable to a Canberra bomber. Sea Slug Mk II and GWS 2 therefore provided, on paper at least, a significant improvement in capability over the earlier variant, and in the 1966 the Admiralty Board initially agreed the modernisation of the first four vessels to the standards of the second four.[77] Further economies in defence spending first resulted in the decision to limit the modernisation of the earlier ships to two ships only, and then in 1968 these were also cancelled. The early withdrawal of the carriers in 1971 rather than 1975 had counter-intuitively caused this cancellation: the fleet now needed greater availability of guided missile destroyers in the early 1970s to fill the gap left by the lack of aircraft carriers. As a result, the extra time spent modernising the two 'Counties' could not be spared, and in any case further economies meant that the £15 million saved would also help keep the Navy Department' budget balanced in the coming years.[78] In any case, Sea Slug Mk II had developed a tendency to break up whilst in flight, a problem that was only resolved in 1972.[79] Another factor that might have influenced the decision was the realisation that Sea Slug Mk II had limited capabilities against the growing threat of long-range guided missiles. By the early 1970s it was assessed that the Mk II would only be able to engage one anti-ship missile at a time, and only then if the missile's speed were under Mach 1.5 and it was also flying directly at the Sea Slug launching ship.[80] This was not a capability that would give a task group much protection against the estimated missile threat of the mid to late 1970s, and as the last two ships of the class had only been completed in 1970 their main armament was effectively obsolete only a few years after their entry into service.

With aircraft carriers being withdrawn early, and both Sea Slug Mk I and Mk II being inadequate to deal with the growing Soviet threat to shipping, much rested on the speedy introduction into the fleet of the Sea Slug's successor, Sea Dart. The original plan to build six ships of the existing Type 82 design, to get Sea Dart to sea quickly, had been prevented by the Secretary of State's scepticism over the large Type 82 design. There was only sufficient capacity to design one new escort type, and the Future Fleet Working Party's original plan had been to focus that capacity on the Type 19/Standard Frigate.[81] However, with the Type 82 class cancelled, save one ship which Denis Healey reluctantly agreed to retain over the diplomatic impact on the Netherlands as that state was supplying the ship's large 'Broomstick' air-search radar, the remaining design capacity would now have to be reallocated to develop a new smaller Sea Dart ship.[82] The Standard Frigate would have to wait.

The Future Fleet Working Party had set four Sea Dart ship design concepts in front of the Admiralty Board: the Type 82 and three smaller types. One was the smallest possible vessel able to operate Sea Dart: it had almost no armament aside from a pared-down version of that missile system, which would have severely limited its deployability in general-purpose roles. The next in size was the minimum ship capable of operating Sea Dart (fired from a lightweight single-armed launcher and with only one missile-tracking radar) as well as a medium gun and a small helicopter. This was 3,500 tons and provided a minimal general-purpose capability and little room for future modernisation. The largest was a 4,500-ton destroyer armed with a medium gun, Sea Dart, Sea Cat and a helicopter. This design had the room for future updates and benefitted from the twin-armed launcher fitted to the Type 82 destroyer.[83] Admiral Adams' original working party had recommended this design as a possible follow-up to the Type 82 for construction in the late 1970s, but with the rejection of Adams' proposals, the new-look Working Party under Admiral Begg's chairmanship had to look again. The First Sea Lord was understandably keen to get as many Sea Dart systems to sea as rapidly as possible, given the delay needed for detailed design work. A cheaper Sea Dart ship would help enable this in a cash-constrained environment, and as the minimum ship had no general-purpose capability, the next ship upwards in size, the Sea Dart frigate, was the obvious option.

The Sea Dart frigate quickly evolved into what became known as the Type 42 destroyer: the single-armed Sea Dart launcher was replaced by a new-design twin-armed launcher which was still much lighter than that used on the Type 82, its only major limitation being a magazine and loading system that would allow for a maximum of twenty-two Sea Dart missiles. At the time this was considered to be acceptable as more Type 42s would be procured in place of the Type 82s, and the threat at the time did not seem to warrant larger missile capacities. In addition, the Type 42 was given a second missile-tracking radar aft. Some thought was given to fitting a lightweight anti-submarine mortar on the hangar roof and anti-ship missile canisters amidships, but these were both vetoed as they threatened to escalate the cost of the ship to a point at which the hoped-for additional numbers could not be procured.[84] The decision of the Type 42 also provided credibility for an internal campaign against 'gold-plating' in defence procurement that Begg had begun at the end of 1966, designed to help rebuild the trust of the Secretary of State and the Treasury, whilst also gently pointing out the escalating prices of some of the other services' procurements.[85] The detailed design work on the Type 42 was undertaken at great speed, which enabled the order of the first of class, named HMS *Sheffield*, to be placed as early as 14 November 1968, in such a hurry that the Admiralty Board formally approved the design only after the order had been placed.[86]

Frigates and Older Destroyers

One of the less trumpeted outcomes of the 1966 Defence Review was the phased reduction in the Navy's force of frigates and older destroyers: it was argued that with a smaller and reducing carrier force the number of escorts required should also therefore reduce.[87] Frigates and destroyers were much more than escorts for capital ships or convoys however: they could also operate in their own right as independent ships, in peacetime conducting naval diplomacy and constabulary operations, and in wartime acting as part of task groups to achieve sea control through anti-submarine and other operations. As was seen in Chapter 1, these ships were made up of three types: first were destroyers that had been built during the war and had been modernised in various ways during the 1950s and 1960s. These vessels were ageing rapidly, and almost all were expected to be out of service by the early 1970s. The second group of ships were the first generation of post-war frigates, most of which were the size of wartime destroyers, completed between 1953 and 1962: these would need replacing by the early 1970s. The third group were the second generation of post-war frigates of the Type 81 and *Leander* classes equipped with lightweight Sea Cat 'point defence' anti-aircraft missiles and small Wasp helicopters in addition to the guns and anti-submarine mortars of the second group. None of these ship types had been developed with the sophisticated and bulky guided missile systems that were being developed in the 1960s for planned introduction into the fleet in the 1970s in mind. These new missile systems, which included Sea Dart, Ikara and the Sea Wolf point defence anti-missile missile system, would require new hull shapes and sizes to take the *volume* of their electronic systems and supporting equipment, in place of the *weight* of the older gunnery, mortar and torpedo weapon systems, whilst also ensuring that they remained stable at sea with their radars and other antenna placed as high as possible on masts or other platforms.

The old wartime destroyers needed to be replaced quickly and the reduction down to a force of seventy frigates and older destroyers had not resolved the problem: there were still nine of them in service in 1966, and the oldest and least capable ships of the first post-war generation would also need replacing from 1970 onwards.[88] By 1971 all of the remaining older *Daring*, 'Battle', 'Weapon' and 'Ca' class destroyers and Type 15 frigates would have been withdrawn from operational service. With the decision to assign the Ship Department's drawing offices to work on the Type 42 destroyer, this meant that further work on the proposed Standard Frigate, the planned successor to the *Leander* class, had to be postponed. However, the need for new frigates was still great: the existing *Leander* class was still in production and the Secretary of State had been happy to approve additional vessels, but its design was becoming outdated and would need major changes to adapt to the planned missile systems.

The Controller of the Navy therefore argued for an externally-designed light frigate to fill the gap in frigate production until the Standard Frigate design was ready. With initial funding for design work being shared with the Royal Australian Navy, which had a requirement for a 'light destroyer' ('DDL') optimised for presence, patrol and naval gunfire support, the shipbuilders Vosper Thornycroft and Yarrow were approached for a design.[89] They both had a successful track record in building warships for overseas purchasers, and despite the scepticism of the Ship Department, a design was developed based on Vosper Thornycroft's Mark 18 frigate. This 'commercial frigate' was then christened the Type 21, whilst the Standard Frigate was designated the Type 22. In 1969, the Australians changed their requirements, now prioritising a larger destroyer armed with a US missile system built in domestic yards, so they dropped out of the project.[90] The Type 21 design needed several changes to meet naval standards which increased its upfront cost but probably reduced in-service costs and certainly aided ship survivability, self-maintenance and stability.[91] The first vessel, HMS *Amazon*, was ordered in 1968 and a total of eight were eventually built, entering service between 1974 and 1978. Meanwhile, the Royal Navy had decided to develop the Standard Frigate jointly with the Royal Netherlands Navy: their requirements were similar, the Dutch had operated former British ships during the immediate post-war years and had recently decided to build six frigates to the *Leander* class design, and therefore had a familiarity with operating British-designed vessels.[92]

Amphibious Vessels

One of the most important aspects of Mountbatten's 'East of Suez' strategy devised in 1957–8 was the modernisation of the Navy's amphibious capabilities in order to make interventions in 'brush fire' conflicts achievable when there were no friendly states or British bases nearby. The first priority had been the conversion of the small carriers *Bulwark* and *Albion* into commando carriers, which could carry troops to shore in helicopters. The second stage had been the replacement of the ageing Tank Landing Ships and Tank Landing Craft with vessels that could get troops and heavier equipment to shore after an initial helicopter assault. It was eventually decided to re-visit a capability developed during the Second World War: the dock landing ship. This was a powered floodable dock within which were placed a number of medium landing craft which could be loaded with troops and equipment. This type had been resurrected by the United States Navy a few years before, and the variant the Royal Navy procured had a smaller dock in order to provide greater space for personnel and stores, which became known as the LPD (for Landing Ship, Personnel, Dock).[93] In addition, the amphibious command facilities that had been placed on a converted wartime frigate, HMS *Meon*, would be replaced by much-enhanced facilities on the new LPDs. As a result, these ships replaced three different types of amphibious vessel at once, and as they had substantial command facilities they became major warships in their own right. The Admiralty Board even considered naming one of the vessels *Churchill* in memory of the recently-deceased wartime Prime Minister.[94] In the event that name went to a nuclear-powered submarine, but it is not surprising that *Jane's Fighting Ships* in 1967 described the new LPDs, which were named *Fearless* and *Intrepid*, as Amphibious Cruisers.[95] A number of old Tank Landing Ships were also in use under contract to the Ministry of Transport for ferrying the Army's armour and equipment to and from overseas bases and garrisons. These were replaced by the *Sir Lancelot* class Landing Ship, Logistics, six of which were built between 1964 and 1968. As mentioned in Chapter 1, they were initially operated by a private shipping company, but were handed to the Ministry of Defence and operated by the Royal Fleet Auxiliary from 1970.

Gas Turbine Propulsion

The new generation of major surface ships designed in the years after the 1966 Defence Review all had one element in common regarding their propulsion: they were all solely powered by gas turbine engines rather than traditional steam turbines. Gas turbines did away with the need for manpower-intensive boilers, condensers, pumps and steam turbines and replaced them with a bladed turbine which was turned directly by the hot gases emitted from the combustion of air with fuel. From just after the Second World War, the Royal Navy had experimented with converted aero engines in a handful of fast patrol boats. By the early 1960s the Royal Navy, as well as the West German and Italian navies, were building larger warships powered by a mix of gas turbines and steam turbines, whilst the Soviet Navy had introduced its first all-gas turbined powered class, the 'Kashin' Large Anti-Submarine Ship.[96] The 'County' class destroyers and Type 81 'Tribal' class frigates had propulsion systems of this type: the gas turbines providing a 'sprint' capability for rapid steaming from a standing start before the boilers feeding the steam turbines had produced enough heat to power them. These early big ship gas turbines were bespoke types produced for ships, but when plans were developed to provide sole propulsion from gas turbines, designers reverted to converted aero engines. The small single-screw Type 14 frigate HMS *Exmouth* was converted into a gas-turbine trials ship powered by one large Olympus gas turbine and two smaller Proteus gas turbines, all of which were derived from aero-engines.[97] Beyond the Soviet Navy, she was the world's first major warship to be solely powered by gas turbines and recommissioned in 1968. Early problems with the Olympus intakes causing vibrations that broke the turbine fans seemed serious at the time, but were soon resolved, and her trials proceeded successfully, *Exmouth* being one of the last of her class to remain in service, decommissioning in 1979.[98]

The success of *Exmouth* confirmed that gas turbines could work efficiently and effectively as much for large ships as for fast craft, and the confidence of the Ship Department was such that the Type 21, Type 42, Type 22 and even command cruisers were also powered by gas turbines: Olympus turbines supplemented by Tyne turbines for bursts of speed on the Types 42 and 22, and just Olympus turbines on the command cruiser. The Royal Navy was the western world's leading innovator in this area and was rapidly creating a surface fleet of major ships that would be entirely gas turbine powered. Gas turbines had the advantage of requiring many fewer personnel to maintain them and support their operation and created less underwater noise, decreasing a ship's vulnerability to detection by submarines. However, fuel efficiency could be an issue as a gas turbine operating at low speeds is less fuel-efficient than diesel propulsion.[99] The Royal Navy took some risk by pushing forward wholeheartedly with gas turbines in the late 1960s, but the benefits were well worth it and soon other navies were following the British example.

Hovercraft

In June 1959 the engineer Christopher Cockerell publicly unveiled the first full-scale hovercraft, the *SR.N1*, manufacturing by the flying boat builder Saunders Roe. He had begun development of his invention in 1953 and by 1956 had gained the attention of Lord Mountbatten, the then First Sea Lord, who amongst others began lobbying government for funding to produce a prototype. In 1958 money was received from the National Research Development Corporation and a year later, to great public interest, the *SR.N1* was demonstrated across the United Kingdom and caused considerable publicity when it successfully crossed the English Channel on 25 July 1959.[100] The hovercraft uses a 'cushion of air' ejected into a 'curtain' around the edge of the craft to produce lift and reduce the natural friction that occurs when a boat travels through water. This therefore opened up the possibility of much greater speeds than could be achieved with conventional vessels: *SR.N1* could achieve speeds of 66 knots for a short period, and later craft such as the *SR.N5* and *SR.N6* could achieve 60 knots for between three to seven hours. As hovercraft 'flew' just above the surface of the water, they had 'pilots' trained for both air travel and operating at sea, and were soon powered by small gas turbines, such as the Rolls-Royce Gnome, which usually powered helicopters, providing both the air supply for the cushions and propulsion for aft-facing propellers that generated forward movement.[101]

An Interservice Hovercraft Trials Unit was established at Lee-on-Solent in September 1961 and a series of trials began to be undertaken with hovercraft leased from their manufacturers. The Navy, despite the early backing of Lord Mountbatten, appeared relatively reticent about the new technology and it was therefore the Army that set up the first operational unit, 200 Hovercraft Squadron, as potential transport and patrol craft for the Army's then-extensive roles 'East of Suez'.[102] Once the Navy began to show interest it was quick to ensure that it achieved predominance in the new tri-service trials body: all commanding officers from 1964 onwards were naval officers ranked at Commander, whilst from 1968 onwards the Navy Department gained control of all base support and repair for hovercraft, even when operated by the Army and RAF.[103] Despite their great speed, a major problem remained with the hovercraft: what roles would be suitable for such a craft? Trials were conducted worldwide in the mid-1960s, including in Aden, Libya, Singapore, Thailand, Malaysia, the Low Countries and the Falkland Islands.[104] All were deemed successful at the time, but difficulty in operating in poor weather in the open sea and the emerging realisation that maintenance costs would be high were significant limitations. By the late 1960s it was clear that three possible uses remained for the Royal Navy, given that it had little need for fast attack craft (a role it would have been well suited for): coastal anti-submarine warfare, mine warfare and amphibious landings.[105]

Using hovercraft in the anti-submarine role initially seemed particularly promising: when hovering, the craft would be almost impervious to torpedo attack from a submarine. The problem lay with using sonar. In 1964 the *SR.N3* hovercraft was fitted with a Type 195 dipping sonar of the type used by Wessex anti-submarine helicopters and undertook a series of trials near Nab Tower at the eastern entrance to the Solent estuary. Unfortunately, the dipping sonar could not be used when the craft was hovering, and only way to deploy it was when the craft was stopped, 'immersed' and facing into the wind. This was not an insurmountable problem, although it did leave the hovercraft somewhat vulnerable, but the most important issue was cost and ease of use compared to a helicopter which would be faster and more able to hold stationary when 'dunking' its sonar.[106] It was clear therefore, that though the coastal anti-submarine role was possible, other means were more effective. By the late 1960s mine warfare and the amphibious role remained the most promising areas for hovercraft but it was now becoming clear that they were likely to be niche vessels within the fleet, rather than potential replacements for a range of vessels.

The Beira Patrol

On 11 November 1965 the colony of Southern Rhodesia, landlocked within southern Africa, unilaterally declared its independence ('UDI') from the United Kingdom, renaming itself Rhodesia. Southern Rhodesia, unlike other

British colonies in southern Africa, had had a significant measure of internal autonomy, but based on the effective control of government by the white settler minority. When the Labour government of Harold Wilson set out its conditions for the independence of Southern Rhodesia, which included moves towards black majority rule and the ending of racial discrimination, the colony's government decided to declare its independence from London. A United Nations Security Council Resolution, supported by the United Kingdom, called on all nations to embargo oil and sever their economic ties with the rebel colony. Meanwhile, the Wilson government, which foreswore any military operations to bring Rhodesia to heel, began a series of on-off negotiations with the Rhodesian government to end UDI and move to majority rule. Rhodesia continued to lack any international diplomatic recognition and soon had to fight a black liberation movement supported by Zambia to the north. Despite this situation, Rhodesia was able to survive as its other bordering states were the Republic of South Africa under an 'apartheid' white government, and the Portuguese colony of Mozambique to the east. To the west was Botswana, independent under black majority rule, but constrained by its economic dependence on South Africa and South African companies. Portugal and South Africa were both sympathetic to the regime and were willing to allow trade, including in oil, with Rhodesia. Oil arrived by pipeline from the Mozambiquan port of Beira or over road and rail from South Africa and Mozambique. Even the United Kingdom allowed trade relations although it did ban oil exports. Early hopes that the oil embargo would bring Rhodesia to the negotiating table were unfounded, and by February 1966 pressure was building on the British government to do something to prevent the smuggling of oil. Press reports, encouraged by the Rhodesian government, that oil tankers were successfully bringing oil to Beira, forced the British government to act and at least to be seen to be doing something to prevent such ships from reaching the Mozambiquan port.[107]

Carrier aircraft from HMS *Eagle* had already provided air defence for Zambia in the first few weeks of the UDI crisis following fears that the Rhodesian government might attack its neighbour to the north with its own small air force, and as has been seen in Chapter 1 a patrol was established off Beira to prevent 'pirate' oil tankers entering the port and discharging their cargos into pipelines bound for Rhodesia. The patrol aimed to demonstrate that the United Kingdom took both the oil embargo, and its breaking, seriously. When the carriers departed they were replaced by three RAF Shackleton maritime patrol aircraft flying 12-hour patrols from the French air base in Majunga, Madagascar. In the first five weeks of the Beira patrol, once spotted, the flag countries of any tanker not on a regularly-updated 'innocent list' would have to be contacted and permission requested to board and inspect the vessel.

This cumbersome approach was soon made more straightforward when UN Security Council Resolution 221 gave a stronger legal basis for action to prevent tankers entering Beira after the Greek-flagged ship *Joanna V* refused to submit to inspection and docked unhindered. If a blockading frigate had a reasonable belief that oil was begin carried destined for Rhodesia, force could be used if it was 'reasonable'.[108] Rules of engagement were tightened up in 1967 when warning shots fired by the frigate HMS *Minerva* ahead of the French-flagged *Artois* failed to stop the ship entering Beira. Now, Royal Navy warships could use a 'ladder' of ascending levels of force to stop a ship: first firing across the bows, if this failed an approach to 'point blank' range with a threat of opening fire, firing on the ship's funnel with practice ammunition and finally firing on the bridge and/or engine room of the ship until it stops. After this change and its public dissemination, no more attempts were made to ignore Royal Navy requests for boarding.[109]

The Beira Patrol was nonetheless a frustrating and resource intensive operation for the Royal Navy and Royal Air Force. It was clearly not stopping oil reaching Rhodesia: it was arriving in the former colony by road and rail from South Africa and other ports in Mozambique. Extending the blockade to all of Mozambique and South Africa's ports would require almost the whole of the Royal Navy's frigate, destroyer and carrier force to be on station at once: an impossibility given the need to rotate ships on and off station on a regular basis, and the obvious fact that all of the Navy's other commitments would have to be given up. Opening up the patrol to other navies was also politically difficult, as one of the first volunteers would be the Soviet Navy, which was beginning to establish a presence in the region and was seeking allies amongst those liberation movements fighting white minority rule in southern Africa.[110] The commitment as it stood also tied up a significant portion of the Navy: two warships and three long-range aircraft needed to be on station off Beira in order to detect, interdict and inspect ships. For the Royal Navy, keeping two frigates or destroyers on station required a total of five to six frigates, more than 7 per cent of the whole force. The commitment for the Royal Fleet Auxiliary was even greater proportionately: one tanker and one replenishment ship were needed to supply the patrol at sea, often having to undertake refuelling twice a week, meaning a near constant presence of the tanker at least. Allowing for the rotating of Auxiliaries, a significant part of the RFA fleet was tied up supporting the patrol and doing very little else. It was known by the sailors on the ships, the British government, the Rhodesian government and almost everyone else that the Patrol was ineffective: its only purpose being to demonstrate that the British government was doing *something* to push Rhodesia into accepting majority rule, given that it was unwilling to do anything more substantive.

The Withdrawal from Aden

If the Beira Patrol was a long-lasting and largely thankless operation of limited military utility, the naval operation supporting the withdrawal from the colony of Aden, centred around the port city of the same name, and the western and eastern protectorates of Aden to the north and east of the colony, in November 1967 was in many respects its opposite. The withdrawal proceeded quickly and smoothly with little disturbance, ensuring that British forces were removed ahead of a deadline for independence. However, if the withdrawal itself was a textbook operation, the four years of counterinsurgency that preceded it was not. Since 1963, the British authorities had been fighting a double insurgency in Aden: against two different Egyptian-backed and Soviet-backed rebel groups, both in the city of Aden itself, and in particular in the old Arab quarter of Crater City, and in the parts of the interior where British control had long often been nominal rather than real. In early 1964 the then Conservative government agreed to independence by 1968, and much work was undertaken to attempt unify the colony based on the city of Aden and the protectorates in the interior. The incoming Labour government was hesitant about plans to give power to traditional tribal groups and to push hard against the rebel nationalists who had support from trade union and working-class groups in Aden City, so plans to disengage became muddled and during the spring of 1967 the colonial authorities began to lose control of much of Aden City with open gunfights in the street.[111] A ruthless but effective operation in Crater City by the 1st Battalion Argyll and Sutherland Highlanders managed to quell the violence temporarily in July 1967, and an uneasy peace largely held up to and including the date of withdrawal: the nationalist groups generally thought better of further fighting when the planned withdrawal in November would in any case achieve their immediate objective of forcing the British to leave.[112]

Operation 'Magister', the naval withdrawal from Aden, began on 24 October 1967. The commando carrier HMS *Albion* was already operating off Aden, and in the next few days additional forces arrived, including the assault ship HMS *Fearless* and several Royal Fleet Auxiliaries and Ministry of Transport landing ships of the *Sir Lancelot* and 'LST 3' classes. On the 4 November this force was joined by the carrier HMS *Eagle* and her escorts, detached from the Far East Fleet. The naval Task Force, named TF 318, now came under the command of Rear Admiral Edward Ashmore, Flag Officer and Second in Command of the Far East Fleet. For the duration of the operation, Ashmore reported to the tri-service Commander-in-Chief Middle East, Admiral Michael Le Fanu, who had overall command of the operation. Three days after the arrival of *Eagle*, responsibility for air operations for the colony and the evacuation shifted from the air base RAF Khormaksar to *Eagle* and the Task Force. The military build-up occurred in parallel with diplomatic and other moves to ensure a peaceful withdrawal: discussions with the Egypt-backed National Liberation Front occurred both in Aden (via intermediaries) and were being planned more formally in Geneva, whilst the co-operation of the leaders of the Kamaran and Perim Islands off the Aden coast was achieved with pay-offs negotiated from the minesweeper HMS *Appleton*. The Royal Navy's establishment in Aden, HMS *Sheba*, was fully vacated by 11 November, and the situation on the ground was sufficiently stable that it was agreed to postpone the completion of the evacuation to 30 November, thus allowing a pause between the 16th and 22nd and for the Geneva negotiations to start.[113]

HMS *Eagle*, which largely steamed within a 10-mile circle 25 miles west-south-west of Khormaksar, maintained a combat air patrol in another 10-mile circle 25 miles south of Ras Al Ara to the west of Aden City, which placed aircraft close to the straits of Bab al-Mandab and in a good position to detect and monitor any civilian or military air traffic approaching from Djibouti or down the Red Sea. In addition, either one or two further air defence aircraft were maintained at 'Alert 20' on the deck of *Eagle* to respond to any emergencies. Task Force communications had been a particular problem in earlier operations, such as the landing of troops in Kuwait in 1961 to provide support following Iraqi threats of invasion, so much thought had been given to strengthening these during the planning for the operation in the summer. New teleprinter communications equipment was therefore fitted to the leading ships prior to their arrival off Aden in place of their earlier Morse-based systems, and this allowed over 750 messages per day to be safely handled by the Task Force during the operation. Communications with London were more of a problem and depended upon the availability and sufficient handling capacity of land-based high-frequency radio stations which were often found to be inadequate and in the words of Ashmore, a communications specialist, were 'just not good enough'. The Rear Admiral recommended satellite communications as the best form of communication in any such operations in the future.[114]

The actual evacuation itself proceeded without any incidents. Although some personnel could be evacuated by air, almost all of the military and civilian equipment, and most of the troops, had to be evacuated by sea. This involved the Ministry of Transport landing ships, *Sir Bedivere*, *Sir Galahad*, *Sir Geraint* and the *Empires Fulmar*, *Tern*, *Guillemot*, *Grebe* and *Petrel*, loading stores and equipment in the inner harbour at Aden, whilst supported and protected by smaller landing craft from HMS *Intrepid* (which had relieved her sister HMS *Fearless* on 21 November) armed with light machine guns. Once most of the troops had been evacuated from the port area, machine-gun armed helicopter patrols were maintained as the last stores were loaded. The Army had established a Supporting Co-ordination Centre ashore before the start of the evacuation and this shifted to HMS *Fearless* as the evacuation progressed, although Ashmore pointed out that this had not been part of the original evacuation plan, and grumbled about the staff at the Centre's lack of understanding of naval capabilities or their ignorance of the relatively recent tri-service joint doctrine, Joint Service Publication 4 ('JSP 4' for short), which hindered the co-operation it was meant to be supporting.[115]

The evacuation proved to be so free of incident that the naval forces put on a fleet review towards the end of the process, with the outgoing High Commissioner, Sir Humphrey Trevelyan, and Admiral Le Fanu inspecting the Task Force from HMS *Appleton*. By 1500 hours the 29 November the evacuation was finally finished and had passed off without incident. With Operation 'Magister' complete, Operation 'Monitor' was implemented, which involved the ships of the Task Force remaining on station off Aden to be ready to evacuate any remaining British subjects and 'friendly nationals' should the situation deteriorate in the City of Aden. All remained quiet ashore, and on 4 December the Task Force was shifted from six to thirty hours' notice for operations under Monitor, which allowed the ships to move to an area off RAF Salalah in Oman. On 14 December HMS *Hermes* relieved *Eagle* as the Task Force's aircraft carrier and the notice period lengthened again to 48 hours which allowed the remaining ships in the group to operate further afield and visit Khor Al Quawi at the entrance to the Persian Gulf for Christmas. On 4 January the notice period was extended yet again in the new year, the new British ambassador having arrived safely in Aden and the situation continuing to appear calm.[116] The Task Force was finally stood down on 25 January.[117]

The evacuation of Aden would prove to be the largest Royal Navy operation until the Falklands conflict of 1982. Removing British forces without naval logistics and the warships to protect them would have been impossible – air lift could not (and still cannot) shift large quantities of military equipment – and although the decision to withdraw was not without criticism, the actual evacuation operation itself was conducted without any serious problems or difficulties. Tactically and operationally, it could not be faulted, but geo-strategically it marked the beginning of a shift in the power structures of the Indian Ocean region. Soon after the Task Force was withdrawn the situation deteriorated in Aden as the two former rebel groups began fighting each other for supremacy. The eventual winner was the Soviet-backed Front for the Liberation of Occupied South Yemen, and very quickly Soviet naval vessels would be anchoring near the island of Socotra and using the port of Aden as a logistics hub, providing them with an important base as they extended their presence into the Indian Ocean just as the British were withdrawing.[118]

The Soviet Threat

The warship types approved and developed in 1966 and 1967 reflected the perceived threat environment of that time: continued operations 'East of Suez' with a strong linkages to foreign policy objectives in that region against relatively unsophisticated opponents, coupled with 'deterrence' operations 'West of Suez' against a Soviet Union that was advocating 'détente', a lessening of tensions and negotiations after the turbulent years of the Berlin and Cuban Missile Crises. The continued production of Soviet nuclear submarines and ocean-going warships was expected, but the existing first-generation nuclear submarines of the 'Hotel', 'Echo' and 'November' classes were, as has been seen, noisy and believed to have much slower speeds than their NATO equivalents, and Defence Intelligence assessments in 1966 implied a continuation of the programmes of these less effective vessels. New generations of submarines were expected but none had yet been commissioned or undertaken trials, and it was not unreasonable to assume that in most cases they would be only incremental improvements on their predecessors.[119] At a wider defence level, the Secretary of State and the Ministry of Defence's leading civil servants still emphasised the continuing East of Suez and worldwide role well into the middle of 1967: naval forces would just now be supported by land-based air capabilities, not aircraft carriers. As has been seen above, economic and financial difficulties drove the decision to 'withdraw from East of Suez' not any re-evaluation of the Soviet threat in central Europe or the Eastern Atlantic. However, three factors during 1967 and 1968 would overturn these presumptions of a lessening threat from the Soviet Union and its Navy.

The first factor was the growing worldwide deployment of Soviet military capabilities in support of its allies. This was exemplified by the considerable role played by Soviet naval capabilities in the 1967 Six Day War, when Israel pre-emptively attacked Egypt, Syria and Jordan as those states were amassing troops to invade and potentially destroy Israel in a co-ordinated invasion. Soviet military advisers and the supply of Soviet naval equipment had helped the Egyptian forces in particular launch a credible attack. The loss of the Israeli destroyer *Eilat* (the former HMS *Zealous*, some of whose sister-ships were still in service with the Royal Navy[120]) to a Soviet-made 'Styx' cruise missile launched from fast attack craft, and guided to its target from ashore command and direction facilities, heralded what appeared to be a new age in naval warfare, where small fast craft could destroy much larger warships. This attack made many aware of Soviet naval capabilities for the first time, but these capabilities had been known for some years and the Royal Navy had maintained, and was modernising, a fast boat squadron to train against Soviet fast missile craft. Soviet involvement in the Six Day War also brought attention to the growing worldwide deployment of the USSR's naval forces in support of its foreign policy objectives. In the early 1960s Soviet naval forces barely ventured beyond home waters and the inability of Soviet submarines to escort and protect ships carrying missiles and other equipment to Cuba in 1962 underlined Soviet naval weakness in the open ocean.[121] Since that date however, larger Soviet naval vessels had begun to be deployed further afield, and by 1967 the Soviets had established its 6th Squadron in the eastern Mediterranean with an anchorage at Alexandria, near where the British Mediterranean Fleet had anchored during the Second World War. Although the Six Day War had ended in an embarrassing defeat for Arab forces, the Soviets had been able to show that they were able to credibly support an ally, the *Eilat* attack being one of the few unequivocal successes for Egypt in that short war. Soviet naval forces were also beginning to go further afield, entering the Indian Ocean in 1968 just as British naval forces were running down their numbers in this region, and making a deal with the Somali government to build a base at Berbera, and as has been seen, the new government in Aden to make use of its sheltered anchorages for Soviet replenishment and depot vessels.[122]

The second factor was the appearance of a new generation of Soviet major warships that were not just incremental successors to the vessels that had come before. The 'November' class nuclear-powered attack submarines were succeeded by the 'Victor' class which adopted a Western-style 'teardrop' hull form which improved efficiency and lessened noise-making drag characteristics. They were also equipped with an effective submarine-detecting sonar, enabling them to operate as 'hunter-killers' that could track down and destroy NATO Polaris submarines. The earlier 'Novembers' could only effectively attack surface warships due to the limitations of their sonars. The 'Victor' class would become the most successful Soviet nuclear submarine class, with modified versions entering service until the end of the Cold War. The earlier 'Hotel' class ballistic missile submarines were succeeded by the second-generation 'Yankee' class, which for the first time could launch their missiles from underwater and were again built with a Western-style hull form that reduced noise signature. It would gradually become clear that their ballistic missiles were inferior to US types, but the 'Yankees' were still a great leap forward from the 'Hotel' class with their small battery of inefficient missiles.[123] The final member of the second-generation trio of Soviet submarine types was the 'Charlie' class cruise missile submarine. These succeeded the earlier 'Echo II' class and were much more effective 'carrier-killers': like the 'Yankees' they no longer had to surface to launch their missiles, gaining targeting information, via a floating radio antennae buoy, from maritime patrol aircraft. The 'Charlies', when they appeared, caused considerable concern within the US Navy, who felt that their carrier strike groups were now much more vulnerable. By the mid-1970s it was clear that the 'Charlies' were somewhat slow, which limited their ability to gain a favourable position to launch missiles against a fast-operating carrier group, but in the late 1960s and early 1970s their threat was taken extremely seriously by the US and NATO.[124] Not only submarines, but surface vessels were appearing that were much more effective than their predecessors. The 'Kashin' class destroyers and 'Kresta' class cruisers were much more plausible open-ocean warships than their 'Kotlin' and 'Kynda' class predecessors: the latter had never even being deployed to the Soviet Northern Fleet and spent their careers as second-line warships. By contrast, the 'Krestas' sacrificed half their anti-ship cruise missile battery for increased air defence capabilities, a shipborne helicopter, a better seagoing hull and a greater ability to operate independently. Defence Intelligence described these ships sporting superstructures festooned with aerials, antennae and radar as much more capable than their predecessors, and with a helicopter for missile targeting means that they would 'pose a threat independent of external support' from other warships: in other words they could operate by themselves and still threaten Western naval forces.[125] Such vessels were not only much more of a threat to NATO naval task groups, they were also increasingly being deployed beyond Soviet home waters, 'Charlie' class submarines being particularly evident in the Mediterranean tracking the US 6th Fleet during the 1970s.[126] Major surface warships increasingly began to deploy worldwide and begin to make regular port visits to friendly states such as Cuba, India, Egypt, and after Angola Mozambique.[127] The Soviet Pacific Fleet began to be built up, probably due to the rebuilding of Japanese naval capabilities, the collapse in friendly relations with China and the increasing numbers of US vessels deployed to the region as a result of the Vietnam conflict. This resulted in vessels built in the west transiting east on completion and deployments to the Indian Ocean and Persian Gulf increasingly being undertaken by Soviet Pacific Fleet ships.[128]

Finally, the invasion of Czechoslovakia by Soviet and Warsaw Pact troops on 20 August 1968, after reformist Communists in that country had become a little too reformist for the USSR, shattered any illusions that East-West confrontation would gradually fade away into 'peaceful co-existence'. Although détente was not derailed over the longer term, it was clear that the Soviet Union would continue to have an iron grip over its satellite states and was not afraid to use its armed forces in Europe. Lessening tensions could no longer be taken for granted. From the late 1960s onwards, British defence intelligence analysts seem to have taken the Soviet Navy's publicly stated objectives much less seriously. Annual reviews of the Soviet Navy in regular naval intelligence reports ceased in 1966, so although these reports provided considerable information on Soviet capabilities, opportunities to set out Soviet intent disappeared.[129] Given the dramatic leaps in Soviet naval capability during this period it can only be concluded that Defence Intelligence, perhaps unsurprisingly, just did not believe Soviet statements anymore and focussed on discerning intent from the capabilities, reach and deployment of their warships. In reality, the core roles of destroying NATO nuclear weapon carrying warships and submarines remained at the centre of Soviet naval strategy, except that now the navy had a more credible ballistic missile submarine, the 'Yankee', the protection of these nuclear assets also became a priority. In addition, the dependence on a 'blue belt of defence' to keep NATO vessels at a distance, was losing out to an acceptance of a more general ocean-wide hunt for NATO nuclear weapon-equipped vessels. The nuclear attack role of the new 'Yankees' was also increasingly mentioned, but often in the context of being held back for further deterrence *during* a war, or to help negotiations at the war's end. Attacks on sea lines of communication remained very much a secondary or even tertiary role.[130]

* * *

The new warship types and force structure that Admiral Begg had spent the previous two years creating had been optimised for a less threatening European environment and worldwide operations encompassing traditional 'showing the flag' activities, as well as operations like the Beira Patrol or Aden evacuation that were focussed on maritime diplomacy or operating against less able adversaries. A small air defence destroyer (the Type 42) and commercially-designed cheap frigate (Type 21) were ideally suited for these scenarios. The Czechoslovak crisis showed that although the worldwide role remained, the European and Eastern Atlantic theatres now looked much more threatening and dangerous. The new *Swiftsure* class submarines would be able to cope well in such an environment, but their lack of below-ice operating capabilities did show how countering the Soviet Northern Fleet close to its own bases had still been a secondary requirement in 1967. The later development in the designs of the Type 22 Standard Frigates and command cruisers would reflect the new priorities but these two classes would not enter service for another decade. In the meantime the Royal Navy had now committed to creating a post-CVA01 fleet optimised for a much less threatening environment and it would have to deal with the ramifications of these decisions for much of the rest of the Cold War.

4

A New Navy

Admiral Varyl Begg's tenure as First Sea Lord had been extremely challenging. After the pain of the carrier cancellation he had successfully rebuilt the trust of the Secretary of State in the Navy and had guided his service through another defence review which at times threatened even more heavy reductions. However, he seemed to have only partial control of his recalcitrant Naval Staff at crucial points and had made important procurement decisions based on premises that were partly unravelling as he retired. He was also aware that the Navy's officers and sailors needed to feel a renewed sense of purpose, but both by temperament and by his immersion in the seemingly never-ending run of reviews and expenditure reductions in Whitehall, he was not well placed to lead such a role.[1]

Much of the task of doing this, and of rebuilding the personnel, support and doctrinal structures of a Navy that would now expect to withdraw from its bases East of Suez by 1971 and lose its strike carriers soon afterwards, would fall to his successor, Admiral Sir Michael Le Fanu. With a quick brain and sound intuition, Le Fanu was a natural leader of men who had thrived in operational command roles and had had a notable wartime career that included a Distinguished Service Cross and a Mention in Despatches. His contemporary and friend Admiral Louis Le Bailly described him as a man who sometimes 'played to the gallery' – gaining the affection of his subordinates and the respect of the Secretary of State – in order to puncture the pomposity that could inhabit the higher echelons of the Senior Service. However, in private he seemed to lack an inner self-confidence, was occasionally subject to moods and depression, and was prone to over-working himself when his health was fragile.[2] His hobby of embroidery sealed his reputation as a very unusual Admiral.[3]

Appointed a few months before Le Fanu took over, Admiral Sir Frank Twiss became Second Sea Lord after two years as Commander-in-Chief of the Far

East Fleet. He would prove to be one of the Navy's most radical reformers in post-war personnel policy, instituting changes that would transform important aspects of how the Navy treated its officers and ratings. Sometimes his proposals overreached what the Sea Lords were willing to contemplate, but they did point ahead to changes that would occur in the succeeding decades.[4] Admiral Horace Law remained Controller of the Navy until January 1970, whilst Admiral Francis Turner became Chief of Fleet Support, and in January 1969 Vice Admiral Edward Ashmore became Vice Chief of the Naval Staff. The post of Deputy Chief of the Naval Staff was abolished after a requirement for all the services to trim the membership of their service boards by one person as part of Ministry of Defence headquarters reductions. DCNS was the most junior member, and was in effect, VCNS's deputy. In addition, DCNS had specific responsibilities relating to the Fleet Air Arm, and the scaling-down of that organisation provided a further rationale for its disappearance.[5]

Whilst the period from the end of 1964 to the middle of 1968 had been dominated by the shape of the fleet, its role and purpose, from the autumn of 1968 onwards the Admiralty Board focussed much of its attention on two areas in preparation for the re-orientation of the Fleet towards 'West of Suez'. This chapter looks at the first of these, personnel reforms, whilst the next chapter reviews the second, the organisational structures of the fleet and its administration. During the 1960s not only had the technology and equipment of the Navy changed dramatically, but so had broader society beyond the often inward-looking world of the Senior Service. Admiral Le Fanu would spend a significant portion of his time in post negotiating how much of this new more liberal and affluent society should be reflected in the Navy itself, and how much should be kept at arms-length. The ending of the most archaic aspects of naval life were amongst the most of visible of these reforms.

The Rum Tot, Hammocks and Bell Bottoms
The 'tot' – a shot of strong rum watered down with two parts water – which was issued to all ratings ashore and at sea over the age of 20 (or alternatively they could receive three pennies of 'grog money' in lieu), had been in existence in one form or another since the eighteenth century and formalised in the nineteenth. By the 1960s, for many senior naval officers, it seemed like an antiquated hangover from the age of sail. The tot had been reviewed in 1964, and it had been agreed to abolish the tot ashore, but to hold back from implementing the change as a bargaining chip with the Treasury. In the event, the status quo remained and the issue was re-visited in 1967. By this time, all three of the Navy's remaining Commanders-in-Chief were keen for the tot to be abandoned. Admiral Twiss, the Second Sea Lord and a former Commander-in-Chief of the Far East Fleet, was of the same mind, seeing it as a blight on a

ship's efficiency.[6] They felt that senior ratings in particular were drinking too much alcohol, which was an increasing problem that would have an ever-greater impact in a more technology-focussed Navy. However, it was acknowledged that it was popular with significant parts of the lower deck. It was a social focus for the mess in the middle of the day, and it was perceived as a perk that the Navy received that was not replicated in the other two services. This was an important factor when it was felt by many that they were worse off compared to Army and RAF other ranks. The Admiralty Board failed to make a decision on the issue. They re-confirmed the plan to abolish the tot ashore, but left its actual implementation to a later date. With the tot afloat, no formal decision was made either, but the Board agreed to consider the issue in the future.[7]

When it was reviewed again in late 1969, after leaks to the press about possible abolition, the Board finally agreed to end the tot but its members were clearly nervous about both lower-deck reaction and negative publicity in the media. The money that would otherwise have been spent supplying the tot (£2.7 million over ten years) would be paid into a charitable fund to support naval ratings, and in partial recompense junior ratings would be able to drink some of their beer ration at lunchtime and senior ratings would be allowed, for the first time, to purchase spirits commercially for their messes. This would be accompanied by a detailed plan for the announcement, including a statement in Parliament, a signal to the fleet, a press conference and even a short film to explain the tot and the reasons for its abolition.[8] The Sailors' Fund, as the new charity was named, soon became well established, whilst the press management of the abolition was carefully planned given the sensitivity of the issue. The actual press event for the abolition went ahead successfully, not least because the journalists invited to the conference were all given tots of rum on arrival, but there were mixed headlines in the press and an adjournment debate was called in Parliament on the issue, although as a non-voting debate it had no impact on the decision.[9] 'Splicing the mainbrace' survived as an occasional celebration with rum, but the routine rum tot finally disappeared in 1970, the last being issued on 31 July 1970.

Before the rum tot had been abolished the Navy was also phasing out another long-standing tradition: sleeping in hammocks. In 1968 it was agreed to introduce full bunk sleeping in every ship likely to remain in service for any significant amount of time after 1970. This was seen to be an important factor to help aid personnel retention. It would be phased in over five years up to 1973, and would cost a total £2.05 million.[10] Although hammocks saved space, by allowing sleeping areas to be converted every day into meal spaces and off-duty socialising spaces, they did not fit well with canteen messing which was being introduced across the fleet. Bunks, on the other hand, provided sailors with more familiar bed-spaces and more space that they could personalise and call home. As with the rum tot, hammocks were deeply associated with an older, more tradition-bound Navy, an organisation which was increasingly finding it difficult to recruit and retain the better-educated sailors needed for the new high-technology navy of the 1970s.

Even with the phasing out of hammocks and open messdecks, there were still significant issues with the space allocated to ratings onboard warships. The creation of separate canteens and the spaces for bunks had resulted in a reduction in recreation space. For example, in the standard 24-person junior rates messdeck there was now only a 5ft by 5ft space left over for recreation. If hammocks were seen as a problem for sailor retention, then only allocating 1ft^2 per sailor for recreation space once hammocks were removed would hardly solve the problem. This led to the inevitable issue of finding more space for accommodation overall. Making major changes was difficult in existing warships but in 1969 new standards were introduced which increased the size of recreation areas. These areas had to seat at least two-thirds of those accommodated in each mess, increasing kit stowage space whilst slightly reducing the width of bunks as partial compensation. These improvements did come at a cost: increasing the price of a Type 22 frigate by £200,000. The Admiralty Board considered this a small price to pay for improvements in accommodation for sailors and the recommendations were approved, these standards being applied across the surface fleet for much of the rest of the Cold War.[11]

If there was symbolism in the abolition of the tot and ending of open messdecks and hammock sleeping, there was even more so in the uniform reforms that followed in the early 1970s. Questionnaires were sent to ratings in 1969 asking about their views on uniforms, in particular the traditional Class II 'Square Rig' of bell bottoms, a broad square white collar, a lanyard and black ribbon and a peakless cap with a cap tally with the name of the sailor's ship woven into it. They were not at all popular with ratings and concerns were expressed about such an outdated-looking uniform being a recruitment disincentive, so a Navy Department committee was established and with the advice of the fashion design house Hardy Amies, a series of different new uniform options were designed.[12] They went before the Admiralty Board in 1971 and two variants were selected for trials and evaluation, both of which made the uniform more practical by integrating the collar, simplifying the lanyard and replacing the bell bottoms with fashionable vertically creased flares.[13] A simplified square rig derived from these two variants was eventually agreed in 1974 but only formally adopted in 1977, the Admiralty Board being aware that lower-deck opinion preferred the adoption of the 'fore and aft' rig (a gold-buttoned suit) as worn by petty officers and chief petty officers.[14] Meanwhile, daily working rig was changed dramatically in 1974 by the introduction of the heavy woollen jersey or 'woolly pully', a dark blue variant of the jerseys worn by the Army and RAF. After a tentative start they were enthusiastically adopted as part of day-to-day clothing by both ratings and officers: they were cheaper and more practical than suits and other permitted jumpers and they also had the indirect effect of killing off the lower deck's long-standing 'badge culture': good conduct stripes, distinguishing badges, medal ribbons and 'wings' were not worn on the new woolly pullies, creating a somewhat more egalitarian culture that found favour with younger ratings and by the late 1970s had been broadly accepted across the Navy.[15]

Pay, Recruitment and Retention
In the late 1960s and early 1970s the Navy's leadership not only aimed to modernise or replace what were seen as some of the outdated symbols of naval service, they also attempted to address more concrete concerns of sailors regarding pay and time ashore. Although changes in technology were shifting the personnel requirements towards more highly educated and better technically trained ratings, severe issues with recruitment and retention meant that longer terms of engagement were putting off young men from joining the Navy. Recruitment in 1968–9 had been especially poor and it seemed that without a major change in the current policy, the Navy would be undermanned by 25 per cent within only a few years. The Second Sea Lord proposed introducing a new four-year engagement alongside the existing nine-year engagement, which would – if surveys of potential recruits and the experiences of other services were any guide – increase recruitment by 20 per cent, but with the downside that only a third of this additional 20 per cent would consider re-engaging after the four-year initial period. Twiss also proposed abolishing the nine-year engagement and replacing it with a much more finely calibrated set of terms of service, which would include engaging for either four or eight years (with those under 18 having to opt for eight years, but with the option to shift to four years at the age of 18), a requirement to stay in the service for an additional four years after any promotion, a point at twelve years' service where men could engage for a pension, and an ability to leave with a pension from the age of 37, with no sailors serving over the age of 40 unless they were warrant officers.[16] Most of these more radical proposals were laid out as a possible structure to resolve recruitment and retention issues over the long-term, but the Sea Lords agreed to Twiss's first step of creating a new four-year engagement – on an experimental basis – alongside the nine-year engagement to help solve the immediate problem of recruiting shortfalls, with an acknowledgement that it would simultaneously create its own retention problems.[17]

By 1970 the pressure to reform the engagement period was still there but coming from a somewhat different direction. Recruitment that year had in fact been relatively strong, but given the experience of the new four-year engagement experiment, extending this across all branches was expected only to increase engagement by around 10 per cent, not the 20 per cent hoped for two years previously. This 10 per cent uplift meant that the Navy's trained strength would still shrink, but by not as much as would have been the case without the changes.[18] The main push for further change was instead coming from the report of a committee set up by the Secretary of State for Defence to examine recruitment of under-18s into all three of the armed forces. The committee, chaired by Lord Donaldson, reported in autumn 1970 and recommended a three-year engagement with a right to leave by purchase at the age of 18 for the Army, Navy and RAF. Donaldson and his committee were also keen to ensure that those recruits who had previously signed up for a nine-year engagement at the young age of 15 or 16 now had the means to leave after three years, if they found that military service was not for them. Apprentices would have the option of reducing their service to five years post-training, but would, in addition, be allowed to leave if they wished at 18.[19] The Second Sea Lord, who was now Admiral Andrew Lewis, was clearly concerned that accepting this recommendation would cause severe retention problems, as well as dissatisfaction from other sailors who would see that young new entrants were getting such favourable terms of service, and increase the risk that trainee artificers (i.e. apprentices) could theoretically leave the Navy without having spent any time in trained active service. Instead he recommended that the four-year engagement experiment be extended to all non-artificers of any age, that artificers could leave after either four or five years' service after the completion of their skills training, and that discharge by purchase be gradually moved down to four years' service for all ratings, whichever engagement they were employed under. A certain amount of cross-negotiation with the other two services was necessary to ensure their position had enough commonality to show a united front.[20] After much discussion, but with both Donaldson and ministers keen for the thrust of the recommendations to be implemented, the best that could be achieved was to align Donaldson's recommendations for apprentices closer to those for other servicemen: they could exercise an option to leave in three years' time at the age of 18, but no longer would they be allowed to leave directly at 18.[21]

Another concern of the heads of personnel for all three services was the decision by government to raise the school leaving age to 16. Some of the Navy's best recruiting occurred at the age of 15 and the worst-case scenario was a loss of 800 new recruits a year. The Admiralty Board did not feel able to press for an exemption from the relevant Act, knowing that it would be turned down, but did push for discussions with the Department of Education and Science about ways of lessening the impact of the age increase.[22] Another cross-service change was the creation of what was termed a 'military salary' across Defence. Many of the unpaid benefits and subsidies that were then common in military life, including in the Navy, were removed and replaced by an equivalent uplift in service pay. In addition, pay rates for single-servicemen were equalised with those for married servicemen, who had previously been able to receive marriage allowances to add to their income. Both of these reforms allowed for a more realistic comparison of service with civilian pay. Finally, the government established a permanent pay review body for the Armed Forces in September 1971. Each year their report would recommend pay rises for the military after making comparisons with equivalent civilian pay rates, allowances for inflation and an evaluation of what was term the 'X Factor', and an additional sum to take into account of the 'special difficulties of service life'.[23]

All of these changes, whether initiated by the Navy or across Defence as was becoming more common, were implemented to take greater account of the increases in pay and benefits in the civilian world during the 1960s and 1970s. They improved the pay and conditions of serving personnel and began to inch towards employment structures that were closer to those found in civilian employment, although this did have the effect of making comparisons easier, thus ultimately increasing the chance of a retention crisis if pay did not keep up with civilian life. The working environment of Britain was changing rapidly in the 1960s and the Navy and Defence were being forced to adapt to those changes, even if the choices available had advantages and disadvantages on both sides.

Service Conditions and Ships' Programmes

Another factor that was causing discontent within the Navy, and therefore resulting in retention issues, was the length of time that ships were spending away from their base ports, thus reducing the time that sailors could spend with their families. This was a particular grievance among those sailors with families that the Navy might wish to keep in the service after their first nine-year engagement. The move to a four-year engagement, which would provide an opportunity to leave the Navy earlier, could make the situation even worse. The first steps in dealing with the problem were made in 1968 and 1969 when it was agreed that no deployment from a base port should be any longer than nine months, that no more than 15 months out of any 30-month period should consist of overseas deployments, that all long leave periods (three weeks in the summer and two weeks at Christmas) should be taken at base ports, as would any refits, assisted maintenance periods and major dockings. This major change was only possible on the basis that the Far East Fleet was being abolished in 1971, with all major vessels operating from the United Kingdom.

An outline deployment plan would also be published up to nine months in advance, and the start dates for refits and assisted maintenance periods would also be set many months ahead. In addition, sailors would be able to apply for 'sea service' or 'shore service' alternatives, rather than the pre-existing complex system of different services and commissions.[24]

These reforms helped reduce uncertainty for sailors, and in particular removed the frustration of long-leave and maintenance periods occurring in home ports away from the ship's base port – resulting in long journeys home and sometimes no ability to go home at all if some crew members were required to stay with the ship. But it did increase the difficulty in planning ship's programmes across the fleet. For a number of years this had been under strain as the number of vessels deployed to the Far East Fleet had increased during the 1960s. These pressures were easing somewhat, but the new controls added another layer of restrictions, which led to the next step in the process of reforming service conditions: the abolition of the inflexible Foreign Service and General Service Commissions. As described in Chapter 1, this regime had been introduced in 1954 in order to spread the pain of long foreign-service deployments across the whole fleet, and allow a ship's company to work together for a period of up to 30 months without the disruption of sailors joining and leaving the ship at different times.[25] The process of re-commissioning a ship with a totally new crew, assigning it either to a period of no more than 12 months overseas, with up to 18 months in home waters (the General Service Commission), or 18 months overseas with up to 12 months in home waters (the Foreign Service Commission), was proving too inflexible to work properly, and plans had been considered as early as 1964 to add flexibility to the system.[26] The objective of keeping a crew together over 30 months was increasingly not being met as sailors and officers had to join or leave ships mid-commission in order to take part in training, whilst in other instances sailors were placed in short-term shore billets to wait for a ship's recommissioning, creating turbulence in shore postings. In one extreme example, a particularly bad trough resulted in the new guided missile destroyer HMS *Hampshire* being placed in care and maintenance for nine months due to the lack of specialist ratings. Personnel planners also faced regular peaks and troughs in the drafting load, particularly when large ships such as cruisers and aircraft carriers either recommissioned or decommissioned.[27]

The result was the decision to shift to continuous commissions, with ships' crews being replaced gradually over time through what became known as 'trickle drafting'. Personnel would serve no more than 30 months on a ship and approximately 5 per cent of the ship's crew would be replaced each month.[28] Any reductions in a ship's effectiveness resulting from the arrival of new personnel unfamiliar with the ship would hopefully be offset by improved 'harmony' – a word that began to be used as a description for the terms on which sailors served at sea and at home – and greater flexibility in the planning of ship's programmes. In a comparison with how other navies managed their ships' programmes it was noted that the Royal Navy had been an outlier. None operated anything similar to the complex and rigid General and Foreign Service Commission structures: the US Navy had fewer manpower problems and had many short-engagement personnel, whilst other Western navies were primarily 'home-based navies' with few ships based overseas. Rather pointedly, the Admiralty Board was informed by the Vice Chief of the Naval Staff and the Second Sea Lord that this latter situation would increasingly apply to the Royal Navy as well.[29] The final version of the 'harmony' rules, as set out two months later, stated that the total over overseas deployment of a ship would be no more than 15 months over a 30-month period with no single period over nine months.[30] A series of other secondary rules were also set out, such as that assisted maintenance and docking and refit periods should always occur at the base port, and that outline ship's programmes should be set out nine months in advance.[31] The new system was promulgated in May 1970 and introduced between the end of 1970 and 1974 and was sufficiently successful that it stayed in place until beyond the end of the Cold War.[32]

Officers

The End of the Split List

In 1956, due to a shortage of seagoing commands, the then First Sea Lord, Admiral Mountbatten, introduced the 'Split List' for Royal Navy Commanders and Captains in the Seaman Branch. Some promoted to these ranks would be on the 'Post List' (known informally as the 'wet list') and eligible for seagoing command roles, and others on the 'General List' (the 'dry list') eligible only for shore commands and other postings.[33] Both lists were meant to have a proportion of 'abler' officers, but in reality seagoing commands were essential for most further progression to flag rank, so the Split List became hugely divisive within the seaman officer cadre and was perceived to consign General List seaman officers, however capable, to a second-class existence before they had had a chance to prove themselves in a seagoing command role. In 1965 it was decided to turn the General List into a real second-class marker, by limiting Post List promotions to Commander to those who promoted in their first eight opportunities, with those who promoted later being consigned to the General List.[34] In 1968 further changes were made, allowing a modicum of flexibility, whereby although the previous arrangement for Commanders largely remained in place, the terms Post List and General List were abolished, and those who would have been regarded as General List officers had some opportunities for seagoing appointments if vacancies arose during the first three years of their appointment. The Split List remained in place for Captains.[35]

The Split List had resulted in the creation of perverse incentives for ambitious and capable officers. If they were perceived to be potential 'staff officers' early in their career, by showing an interest in strategy, tactics, military planning and administration, they were at great risk of being regarded as ideal General List officers, thus limiting their chances of gaining command roles and achieving flag rank. Ambitious officers were therefore advised to focus solely on becoming strong warship commanders and avoiding wider reading and intellectual enquiry, a tendency that was increased by the habit of those picked out for the very top being exempted from attending Staff College, so that they could progress through the mix of roles deemed necessary rapidly enough to enable them to promote at the first or second chance. The classic example of an officer consigned to the General List second tier was Rear Admiral J R Hill, perhaps the navy's most intellectually capable senior officer of the era. He played a crucial role in negotiations for the UN Convention on the Law of the Sea and wrote a number of books on naval power, technology and strategy on his retirement.[36] Displaying intellectual leanings early in his career, he was consigned to the General List and never achieved a seagoing command. To some extent he proved the exception to the rule by becoming a rare General List officer appointed to Rear Admiral, but after only two years in this only flag post in charge of the Admiralty Interview Board for aspiring officer cadets, he was told his career was over and retired to write on naval strategy and warfare. Without the chance of seagoing command, Hill was unable to harness his intellectual skills to first-hand experience of operational command and the possibility of reaching the top of the service.[37]

By 1971 the effects of the 1965 and 1968 post-list reforms were becoming clear. Those officers who missed the earlier slots for promotion to Commander were leaving the service early, depriving the Navy of useful personnel unnecessarily. The hope of giving late promotions some sea experience was not being fulfilled and at the same time those staff posts that had been reserved purely for General List officers were now being filled by the new '2nd eleven' General List officers much to chagrin of the flag officers who were calling for the return of the 1956 system. Also, joint and international postings that were theoretically being reserved for General List officers were coming under increasing pressure to shift to Post List officers instead, thus reducing their sea time and lessening their chances of promotion to Post List Captain. In short, the situation was unsustainable, and instead of attempting to fix a broken system for the third time, the Second Sea Lord proposed abolishing promotion by Split List and the institution of selection boards for sea appointments.[38] The reforms were agreed and the Sea Appointments Board, chaired by the Second

Sea Lord, was duly set up, ending an unpopular and damaging system that had persevered for far too long.[39] The impact of forcing your most ambitious and capable officers *away* from intellectual enquiry and from showing planning and administration abilities for more than a decade and a half could only have had a negative impact on the quality of the Navy's leadership in the last two decades of the Cold War.[40]

The Principal Warfare Officer
In the summer of 1968, Vice Admiral Edward Ashmore, the Second-in-Command of the Far East Fleet, began to put forward the argument that the officers on board ships below the posts of Captain and Executive Officer had a too narrow range of understanding of their ship's capabilities beyond their own particular sub-specialisation. As warships became more sophisticated, weapon systems were increasingly linked together by semi-automated tactical command systems, and the time available to react to threats was becoming ever shorter. It was becoming clear that focussing on the ship's Captain, perhaps supported by his Executive Officer, as the sole authority on the all-round fighting of the ship was becoming untenable. At the same time more junior officers were needlessly over-specialised in their own area and did not have a sufficient understanding of the wider 'art of fighting ships at sea'. Ashmore, whose next appointment was as Vice Chief of the Naval Staff, was able to use his new post to establish an Operations Room Working Party on this issue.[41] It reported in June 1971, approving trials of a 'watchkeeping principal warfare officer' or 'PWO' whose task was to take 'command, under the Captain, of the operations room and giving operational instructions for fighting the ship.' The PWO would provide co-ordinated advice on operational matters covering the sub-specialisations such as gunnery, navigation, different missile systems, anti-submarine weapons, radar, sonar and electronic warfare; the PWO would also share the burden of integrated tactical command of the ship with the Captain. Ships of frigate size would no longer have deep sub-specialisation specialists, although these could be in place in ships leading squadrons or in guided missile destroyers and other larger vessels, and junior officers would only be trained to the level needed for their next job and no further. It was acknowledged that a certain amount of risk was being taken in allowing deep and narrow skill-sets to be held by a smaller number of people, but the gains in overall operational capability and breadth of understanding were felt to outweigh any objections.[42] The Admiralty Board agreed and the training regime for seaman officers shifted quickly from a series of specialised 'long courses' in particular sub-specialisations to different levels of training building up to a Principal Warfare Officers course. In order to preserve in-depth knowledge of particular areas, Advanced Warfare Officers ('AWO') courses were also established for

air defence, underwater warfare and communications, designed for those who would serve in ships leading squadrons, major warships or in specialist posts ashore. The PWO/AWO system proved to be a success and was rolled out across the fleet over the next three years, and in a somewhat modified form, remains in existence in today's Royal Navy.[43]

Degree Education and the Staff College

Since 1966 engineer officers had been given in-service degree education and qualifications by the Royal Naval Engineering College at Manadon near Plymouth.[44] By 1969, Admiral Twiss was arguing for the provision of degree-level education for seaman and supply officers as well: with the increasingly technical nature of naval warfare and the growing prestige and importance of degrees for professional status, he felt that the Navy would be left behind by other employers if it did not. A tri-service Royal Defence College had originally been planned to undertake such education, but it had been abandoned as a cost-cutting measure, and it was now left to the single-services to develop appropriate courses.[45] A syllabus for a bespoke Royal Navy degree in 'Modern Studies' was therefore developed with City University, consisting of five elements: systems logic and analysis; statistics and computing; behavioural and organisational studies; technical sciences; and history and political science. The first year of this course would be spent at Dartmouth immediately after midshipmen had completed their first period of sea time, with the succeeding two years in halls of residence at City University; the course would be open to all Seaman and Supply officers who had achieved two A levels before entering the Navy.[46]

This proposal appears to have been largely sustained by the sponsorship and enthusiasm of the Admiral Twiss, as only a few months after his retirement it was made voluntary and eventually limited to a maximum of twenty students a year and changed to a more limited 'Systems and Management' course.[47] The new Second Sea Lord, Vice Admiral Andrew Lewis, argued instead for the continuation of the present system but with a gradually shifting focus towards University Cadet Entry, and in the long run he was correct. By the mid-1990s the majority of officer cadets would have had a university education before joining, but Twiss's proposal is a fascinating alternative possibility, offering an unusually forward-looking 'technocratic' degree to the majority of non-engineer naval officers. Many years later, Admiral Twiss would argue that it was difficult to get the Navy's leadership to think in terms of universities other than Oxford or Cambridge for non-technical officer education, and perhaps it was this academic snobbishness that was behind the scaling down of the Navy's degree-education plans in 1970.[48] It also appears that none of the three services were that enthusiastic about in-service education: the Army investigated but then abandoned a plan to turn Sandhurst into a 'military university' whilst the RAF went in another direction and planned a rapid shift towards graduate entry for most of its officer cadets, although it quickly drew back from this ambition and graduate entry numbers remained lower than planned through the late 1970s.[49]

The Split List system continued to have its pernicious effect many years after its abolition. A major side effect had been the denigration of staff training: as late as 1974 the Second Sea Lord admitted that there was a 'widely held view that the Navy's approach to staff training in the past had not been sufficiently professional or enthusiastic'.[50] There were two main staff courses run by the Navy and delivered at the Greenwich Naval College: the Lieutenant's Greenwich Course (the 'LGC') and the full Staff Course. In 1971 it was finally agreed that all general list officers should attend the Staff Course, and that the previous system whereby often the most talented and promising officers, who were tipped for flag rank and therefore needed to promote and progress through the expected range of jobs as quickly as possible were excused attendance, was ended. Unfortunately, in order to enable full attendance, it was also agreed to halve the length of the Staff Course to six-months – without any consideration of the curriculum elements that would have to be dropped – which did little to inspire confidence that the Navy's leadership understood the importance of staff training any better. By this time Greenwich had survived two external reviews of its courses and approach to education, and had its engineering and general scientific courses and departments moved to Manadon, leaving only the History and International Affairs Department and the Department of Nuclear Science and Technology.[51] Three years later the Admiralty Board agreed that the Navy should aspire to have all full career naval officers attend the LGC, which was then rarely attended by engineers. Although the Board stated that 'all officers should be led to appreciate the importance that the Board now attached to staff training', the Vice Chief of the Naval Staff glumly commented that these aspirations would not be met within the next decade unless officer recruitment and long-term retention were improved significantly.[52] Progress was being made, but only slowly. Despite the efforts of successive Second Sea Lords, the Navy's leadership still laboured under the shadow of long-lasting assumptions that 'staff officer' work was only fit for those who were never destined for the top of the service, and it would take more than the abolition of the Split List for this assumption to fade away.

Ratings

The Operations Branch and User-Maintainers
The introduction of the Principal Warfare Officer changed the way in which the two ratings branches that dominated a ship's operations room dealt with

their officers: they were answering to a common group of professionally qualified officers and increasingly had a common operational purpose. These two branches were the Seaman Branch which dealt with weapons, radar and sonar, and the Communications Branch which dealt with communication systems and electronic warfare. Within the Seaman Branch there had been three roles: seamanship, weapon and sensor operation and ship husbandry. With the introduction of the PWO and the growing dominance of the operations room in ship fighting, the weapon, sensors and communications roles became increasingly inter-linked. The logical step was therefore made to combine the two branches. The change was announced in 1973 and the two branches were merged in 1975, although retaining sub-branches within different relevant specialisms such as electronic warfare and sonar.[53]

A more radical development was the move towards a 'user-maintainer' approach to weapon systems. This had first been suggested by Admiral Twiss as early as 1969 who argued for the seaman and weapons engineer branches to be combined and offered two approaches for ratings: the user-maintainer concept, where those ratings that maintained the equipment could also operate it, or an 'every-rating-a-mechanician' approach where all rating recruits to the branch would have, or be trained to have, skills similar to those trained ratings in the engineering branches who were not artificers.[54] These proposals, which in a clear-eyed fashion were anticipating the shift to an increasingly technologically-focussed navy, were much too radical for the Sea Lords and were not implemented, but it sowed the seeds for later consideration of the user-maintainer concept. A user-maintainer experiment was introduced in a number of limited areas on board the new Type 21 and Type 42 ships as well as the recently-converted 'Ikara *Leander*' frigates. It allowed weapons engineering ratings to undertake some of the operating tasks that had previously been the sole preserve of gunnery and torpedo and anti-submarine ratings. This permitted a small reduction in the number of ratings in ships and was extended across most of the frigate force the following year.[55] Despite the success of this approach in these limited areas, further radical reform was rejected: a merger of the two branches at both officer and rating level did not go ahead. In both their culture and training the two branches were very different; the Sea Lords were cautious about lower-deck opinion and morale, so both remained distinct and separate but increasingly found themselves working alongside one another.[56] The user-maintainer concept and the idea of branch merger would be raised again a number of times over the next two decades without a definitive resolution.

The New Warrant Officer and Appointment by Merit
One of the changes prompted by the moves to regularise pay, ranks and benefits across the three armed forces, was the decision to create a new

Warrant Officer rank above that of Chief Petty Officer, which would parallel that of the Warrant Officer I and II in the Army and Royal Air Force. This development was actually welcomed by senior officers as a means to reward the most capable Chief Petty Officers and provide a non-commissioned rank that could take on a number of managerial roles previously undertaken by officers. The new Warrant Officers would plan, allocate and control work, and have an important role within the divisional system, the aim being to have one warrant officer in each sub-specialisation on a 'medium-sized' ship. The new warrant officers would be chosen by selection boards from the cohort of Chief Petty Officers over the age of 34. The pre-existing rank of Chief Technician, given to those artificers at the very top of their career structures, would be gradually phased out, with either Chief Technicians being selected for warrant officer or retaining their existing pay and benefits and remaining in their current rank but being replaced in time by Warrant Officers. It had originally been planned to create both Warrant Officer I and Warrant Officer II ranks as was standard in the Army, with the WOIs being selected by board and WOIIs only consisting of the remaining Chief Technicians. This was rejected by Flag Officers and Commanders-in-Chief, who felt that the warrant officer rank had to be earnt, and as result only a WOI rank was created. Personnel planners recommended that 623 technical branch WOIs would be needed, alongside 536 non-technical WOIs, the educational minimum for advancement was two O levels (a relatively high bar given the number of sailors recruited into the Navy in the 1950s and 1960s without any O Levels), and it was expected that two thirds of the new WOI cohort would be in position within a year. The new Warrant Officers would be known informally as 'Fleet Chiefs', be addressed as 'Mr' by their superiors and 'Sir' by their subordinates, and although they would mess with the Chief Petty Officers, the long-term aim was to provide them with their own cabins as was standard for commissioned officers.[57]

As the new Warrant Officer rank was being created, and was being populated by men appointed by merit, similar changes were made further down the rating structure. For technical ratings, promotion had been straightforward up to 'technician 1st class', depending only on achieving the relevant technical qualifications, length of service and being recommended by their commanding officer. For non-technical ratings, a 'roster system' was in place that automatically advanced ratings to higher ranks if they reached the top of a roster based on length of time at their current rank, supplemented by the accumulation of 'merit points', many of which rather counter-intuitively focussed on time served not service deserving merit, and a recommendation from the commanding officer. The latter system produced 'a proportion of mediocre CPOs' in the words of Admiral Twiss' report to the Admiralty Board, whilst the former had the tendency to reward technical proficiency over any leadership or management abilities. With the institution of selection boards for the new warrant officer, the opportunity was taken by the Second Sea Lord to propose selection boards for promotion to Chief Petty Officer as well. The board would consider a person's record of service and the number of new merit points he had accumulated. These merit points would no longer be given for time served and would be time-limited, with only those gained in the last five years (three years for promotion to Chief Petty Officer) being considered. For Petty Officers and Leading Rates the roster system would remain, but time-based merit points were abolished. These reforms now ensured that the Director General of Naval Manning had much more flexibility, through the appointment boards, in regulating not only the quality but the quantity and type of WOIs and CPOs created, thus allowing for the numbers chosen to better reflect the current and expected gaps in positions.[58] With the creation of the Operations Branch in 1975, the remaining area where the older approach to promotion remained – the Seaman Branch – was abolished, and all Operations Branch ratings moved to a promotion structure based on the successful completion of courses and the completion of 'Task Books'.[59] One of the most common ways for ratings to time-serve their way up the promotion ladder had now been removed.

Married Quarters, Social Workers and Families
The Royal Navy had generally lagged behind the RAF and Army in the provision of married quarters – subsidised rental housing – for ratings and officers and their families in the earlier post-war years. In 1960–1 the Royal Navy spent as little as a fifth of the money on married quarters as the RAF and Army. By 1968–9 the situation had improved markedly, but the Navy was still spending only two-thirds of amount spent by the RAF, even though its strength was 78 per cent that of the Air Force.[60] As part of the wide range of activities to improve conditions for servicemen and women, the Navy began a programme of married quarters building in the late 1960s and early 1970s combined with a loosening of the criteria for being allocated quarters. The lower age limit was reduced, whilst families now had the option of either moving quarter as the rating or officer moved posting or staying put in a 'port scheme' so that the family did not have to move on such a regular basis. The Navy also acknowledged issues of social problems that were emerging on some of the married quarters estates, and put the reasons down to 'husbands ... [being] away at sea'. Estate wardens and community officers were appointed to some of the larger estates and community centres were built as were play groups for pre-school children. The rate of married quarters building was stepped up dramatically, with a plan to have a total stock of 20,000. In 1971 there were a total of 12,776 with 1,200 having been built in the previous

18 months and nearly 4,000 planned for the next four years. The Navy also continued to lease properties from the private rental sector as a temporary solution, but this was proving increasingly difficult as rental rates were rising in the early 1970s. Most married quarters were terraced or semi-detached houses in what would have been called 'cottage estates' in the civilian sector, but some estates were built as blocks of flats, not least the flagship Rowner estate in Gosport, which consisted of a string of multi-storey slab blocks in built in the fashionable 'Brutalist' style with most flats set out as maisonettes with 'deck access' for residents. Despite this rapid programme of building, the Admiralty Board still had to admit that it could not build as many quarters as it wished to due to financial constraints and that waiting lists for quarters might continue for some years.[61] There were also emerging issues relating to the quality of construction. New officers' quarters built in Portland in 1967 were beset with structural defects on completion.[62]

Sometimes it seemed that the naval leadership's enthusiasm for modernisation and the improvement of conditions for its sailors and their families reached beyond what flag officers and much of the officer hierarchy were willing to accept. In 1968 the Seebohm Report had recommended the professionalisation of social services in local authorities across England and the rest of the United Kingdom. In the following years local authorities began to invest heavily in social services departments, staffed by qualified professionals, along the lines recommended by the Report.[63] In 1973, the Royal Navy appeared to be following this lead: it commissioned Frederic Baron Seebohm, the chair of the committee that had written the eponymous report, to recommend a social worker service for the Royal Navy.[64] The Admiralty Board agreed these recommendations which included the appointment of a Head of Naval Social Services and three regional directors who would each be in charge of eight professional social workers. This service would sit outside the standard hierarchies of naval authority, bypassing the divisional system and individual ship and establishment command structures by reporting directly to the Second Sea Lord. As soon as it was clear what this could mean in practice – an alternative line of authority up to the Admiralty Board and the possibility that the new 'politically engaged' social workers could challenge officers across the traditional hierarchy over sailors' welfare and the treatment of their families – senior flag officers and commanders began to lobby against its full implementation. Simultaneously, the new Head of Naval Social Services lobbied the Second Sea Lord for an increase in her front-line social worker cadre from twenty-four to thirty. The Commander-in-Chief Naval Home Forces, Admiral Lewin, led the lobbying against the new service, recommending the transfer of the new Head of Naval Social Services from the Second Sea Lord to himself, a recruitment pause in the twenty-four social workers, and a restructuring of the new service to ensure greater control by the traditional lines of command. The Head of Naval Social Services refused to work under Lewin and the issue returned to the Admiralty Board in 1976. The Board acknowledged the problems that could come from 'a professionally motivated welfare organisation' that would not be 'fully integrated and responsive to professional Naval advice' and the universal opposition of the Commanders-in-Chief and relevant flag officers, and it therefore agreed to Lewin's recommendations for shrinking, subordinating and de-professionalising the service.[65] The pre-existing system of welfare, which was led by retired middle-ranking officers supported by the WRNS, was retained but these postholders increasingly undertook civilian social work training to improve their skills. Independent professional social workers would not return to the Royal Navy, whilst the first qualified social worker afloat would have to wait for another 35 years, with the appointment of a naval Petty Officer in the role.[66] In retrospect it is not surprising that the Navy's social worker experiment failed, but what is most notable is that it had got so far: the RAF had rejected any social workers out of hand while the Army had decided not to implement a similar report that Seebohm had written for them, whilst outside of the Navy the new and assertive social work profession was beginning to see a popular and political backlash that would continue to build momentum through the late 1970s and the 1980s.[67] The social worker debacle showed a naval leadership attempting to make real improvements for its sailors whilst embracing progressive solutions from civilian life, even if – in this case – they did not fully understand what they were actually approving.

Training Establishments

As the branches were consolidating and the Navy was shrinking in numbers, consideration was given to the rationalisation of training establishments ashore, eighteen of which were operating in 1970.[68] A review of shore training for the surface navy – submarine, air and Royal Marine training were excluded – was undertaken in 1969. Given the awkward title of 'CONSTRAIN' (*Cons*olidation of *Train*ing), it recommended a radical reduction down to five establishments over the next fifteen years (excluding initial officer training at Dartmouth): HMS *Raleigh* at Torpoint for ratings new entry training; HMS *Collingwood* in Fareham for weapons engineering training; HMS *Sultan* in Gosport for marine engineering training; HMS *Dryad* north of Portsmouth for tactical and operations training; and HMS *Excellent*, on Whale Island near Portsmouth, for ship fighting and management training.[69] Two further establishments would remain in existence but be subordinated to one of the 'big five': HMS *Fisgard*, the apprentice training establishment, to *Raleigh* and HMS *Mercury*, the signals establishment, to *Dryad*. Most of the remaining eleven establishments would be shut down and their roles incorporated into those that remained. This dramatic consolidation was much more difficult to achieve in practice as political considerations made the shutting of some establishments impossible. The closure of the engineering school, HMS *Caledonia* at Rosyth, and the shifting of its staff and students to HMS *Sultan* proved impossible given the fact that it was within a government 'development area' and had specific Scottish sensitivities. The school remained open throughout the 1970s and was only combined into *Sultan* in 1985, *Caledonia* itself remaining open in another role. The consolidation of weapons engineering training to *Collingwood* and ship fighting to *Excellent* meant a certain amount of shuffling of training roles between these establishments, but the aim of closing HMS *Vernon* in Portsmouth was not achieved as the Commander-in-Chief Portsmouth was 'loathe to surrender this valuable and attractive area if other uses can be found for it.'[70] *Vernon*'s anti-submarine weapon training role eventually transferred to HMS *Collingwood* in 1979 (with elements moving to *Dryad*), and *Vernon* itself was decommissioned in 1986, but the site remained in naval use until the 1990s with mine-warfare and diving training remaining there for some years.[71] The only significant training establishment closure came with the integration of initial training for Special Duties Officers (those brought up from the lower deck generally due to their specific skills and technical abilities) into that for general and supplementary list officers at the Britannia Royal Naval College, Dartmouth. Integrating their training into that for the more traditional officer entry candidates not only recognised the special role they fulfilled but helped reinforce their equality with other officers. HMS *St George*, the Special Duties Officer training establishment, was therefore closed in 1974 and initial training transferred to Dartmouth.[72] Plans to shift the Nuclear Biological and Chemical Training School (HMS *Phoenix*), the Supply and Secretariat School (HMS *Pembroke*) and the Petty Officer's Leadership School (HMS *Royal Arthur*) to HMS *Excellent* were soon scaled back. Eventually HMS *Pembroke* would be folded into HMS *Raleigh* in the 1980s, whilst HMS *Phoenix* and HMS *Royal Arthur* were not integrated into *Excellent* until the 1990s.[73] As a result, many of the financial savings that had been planned under CONSTRAIN could not be realised: the decision to keep *Caledonia* open through the 1970s limiting the planned reductions that could be made.[74] Much had been nominally consolidated as a result of CONSTRAIN but in most cases establishments had simply remained open and been subordinated to others, whilst few if any civilian or military posts were abolished in the various changes, or any sites sold off. This pattern of organisational rationalisation and nominal consolidation without actually saving any money would be repeated in many of the reforms of the operational structures of the Navy between 1967 and 1971, as will be seen in the next chapter.

* * *

From 1968 to 1971 the personnel reforms instituted by the Navy, and those generally relating to pay driven by the centralised Ministry of Defence structures, were amongst the most far-reaching and radical since the Second World War. Old traditions were swept away, and a range of reforms in pay, engagement, accommodation standards, family support, education and training were aimed not only to prepare and equip the sailor for the Navy in the guided-missile age, but also to provide an environment that would keep them within the service rather than re-join an increasingly affluent and comfortable civilian society. These reforms had some measure of success, but as will be seen in later chapters, recruitment and retention problems would return to haunt the Navy in the later years of 1970s. Also, these were reforms within very much a 'man's world': the WRNS continued its semi-precarious existence, treated by naval personnel planners as a 'regulator' to fill gaps in shore postings when numbers of seamen slumped. Any serious discussion of sending women to sea would have to wait until the mid-1970s as will be seen in Chapters 8 and 20.

5

Structures, Doctrine and Deployments

The other major focus of Michael Le Fanu's time as First Sea Lord was the creation of the operational and organisational structures necessary for the new West of Suez-orientated Navy. Most of the structural changes would last until beyond the end of the Cold War, whilst the operational changes saw the Royal Navy return to home, eastern Atlantic and Mediterranean waters, attending NATO exercises in significant numbers whilst also retaining some form of presence, albeit much reduced, East of Suez. It also began the process of re-learning to operate with the RAF's maritime air capabilities. Naval doctrine continued to develop and the dockyards and other support structures were subjected to significant reforms that reflected the increased complexity of modern warships and the multiplicity of functions within the dockyards themselves.

Reorganising the Fleet: Home Commands and West of Suez
As has been seen in Chapter 1, the operational structures of the Royal Navy were geographically organised in 1966: with those Commanders-in-Chief, Flag Officers and Senior Naval Officers in charge of particular commands having both operational control of ships in their areas and responsibility for their training and readiness. This general structure had been in place since the nineteenth century and would be rapidly swept away in organisational reforms between 1967 and 1969. Despite a range of decisions in the mid-1960s to shut down overseas stations and rationalise home commands, the immediate driver of these reforms was external to the Navy itself. Following the centralisation of defence in 1964, an Independent Study of Defence Organisation was commissioned by the Secretary of State. Its report called for a cross-service standardisation of commands in different regions, with each of the three services having a Commander-in-Chief for the UK, a Commander-

in-Chief in the West, whilst there would continue to be a joint Commander-in-Chief for the Far East. The three Commanders-in-Chief for the West would form part of a Joint Committee, the Commanders-in-Chief Committee (West), to co-ordinate their operations. The report also recommended that the split in responsibilities between each service's UK Commander-in-Chief and Western Commander-in-Chief should be 'functional', with the former being a 'provider' that focussed on the training and administration of forces and the latter a 'user' that solely undertook the operational command of those forces.[1] Given the Royal Navy's long-standing geographical structure, it was the service that had to make the greatest organisational changes to fit in with these recommendations, which were soon approved by the Secretary of State.

Although externally driven, these changes were internally acknowledged by the Navy's leadership to be necessary for other practical reasons: from 1968 the new Polaris submarines, the carriers of the United Kingdom's strategic nuclear deterrent, would be under the operational control of the Commander-in-Chief Home Fleet, whose control would be exercised via the communication systems available at Coastal Command's headquarters in Northwood, in the outer suburbs of north-west London. This cut across the traditional role of Flag Officer Submarines in Gosport as operational commander of the submarine force, and although anomalous in this regard, the importance of the deterrent role and its policy-strategic importance meant that operational command could only be held by a full admiral: Flag Officer Submarines was usually only an appointment for a rear admiral. The abolition of the West Indies, South Atlantic and Mediterranean stations were now in process, being replaced with lesser commitments under the control of the Commander-in-Chief Home Fleet. Also, the Commander-in-Chief Channel NATO command had recently been passed from the Commander-in-Chief Portsmouth to the Commander-in-Chief Home Fleet, which lessened the need for a full admiral Commander-in-Chief role at Portsmouth. Finally, a 'functional' re-organisation of the fleet had been considered and largely rejected in 1961, but some of these reforms had been incrementally introduced, not least the combination of the role of Flag Officer Medway with the Admiral Superintendent of Chatham Dockyard.[2]

All in all, therefore, the Navy had been slowly inching its way towards a major reform of the operational structure for a number of years, but the Independent Study of Defence Organisation had pushed the Admiralty Board into a comprehensive review and an 'all-at-once' change. It was therefore not surprising that interviews with the Commanders-in-Chief and Flag Officers themselves actually produced positive responses to proposals for the 'functional' splitting of the home commands between 'provider' and 'user'.[3] The proposed re-organisation would see the replacement of the three existing domestic Commander-in-Chief roles for the Home Fleet, Portsmouth and Plymouth with two: a Commander-in-Chief Home Fleet with expanded responsibilities and a Commander-in-Chief Naval Home Command. CinC Home Fleet would be in charge of 'sea affairs', with the Flag Officer Second in Command Home Fleet, Flag Officer Submarines, Flag Officer Aircraft Carriers, Commander Amphibious Forces, Captain Mine Counter Measures Vessels, Captain HMS *Vernon* (in his role as Senior Naval Officer in charge of Fast Patrol Boats) and Flag Officer Sea Training under his direct command. Direct operational control of ships West of Suez would be held by CinC Home Fleet, but he could delegate operational control to any of these 'type commanders' when he saw fit. In later iterations CinC Home Fleet was re-named CinC Western Fleet, presumably to avoid confusion with the new CinC Home Command, and the roles of Flag Officer Aircraft Carriers and Commander Amphibious Forces were merged into a single post named Flag Officer Carriers and Amphibious Ships. The post of Flag Officer Naval Air Command, a 'provider' role that took responsibility for naval air training and administration, eventually came under CinC Western Fleet as well. This apparent anomaly reflected the very different requirements for support that aircraft had, and their need to be linked more closely to the operational commands. The Flag Officer Second in Command Home Fleet was also renamed Flag Officer Flotillas, Western Fleet, and was given responsibility for the Western Fleet's destroyers and frigates as well as having command of the Captains in charge of fast patrol boats and mine-warfare vessels (when the Western Fleet was eventually abolished and replaced with a single Fleet structure, Flag Officer Flotillas became Flag Officer of the First Flotilla (known as 'FOF1')). CinC Western Fleet would also take over control of residual overseas commands West of Suez, including Senior Naval Officer West Indies ('SNOWI') and Flag Officer Gibraltar.[4] The largely hollow Mediterranean Fleet and the small South Atlantic and South America Command were dissolved on 5 June and 11 April 1967 respectively. The responsibilities for both sea areas would now fall under CinC Western Fleet.[5]

CinC Naval Home Command (shortened to CINCNAVHOME) would be in charge of 'shore affairs' including the management of ports, logistics, administration and training. The roles of local commanders-in-chief would be merged with the Admirals Superintendent of Portsmouth and Devonport dockyards and shorn of any seagoing responsibilities. Commander-in-Chief Plymouth was therefore merged with the Admiral Superintendent Devonport role to create Flag Officer Plymouth. CINCNAVHOME would double up in the residual role of Commander-in-Chief Portsmouth, but most of these local duties would be undertaken by a new subordinate commander: Flag Officer Spithead. Similar reforms had already taken place some years ago with respect to Chatham and the Nore, with the creation of the role of Flag Officer Medway. Flag Officer Portland had also already been a subordinate command. Flag Officers Plymouth, Rosyth, Portland and Medway would therefore all be subordinated to CINCNAVHOME. Originally, Flag Officer Scotland and Northern Ireland ('FOSNI') was to have been combined with Flag Officer Rosyth on the same basis as the other regional commands, but by 1968 a successful rearguard action by FOSNI had resulted in the post remaining an independent command with local responsibilities in the relevant sea areas, whilst Flag Officer Rosyth remained in charge of just the naval base and dockyard. The survival of FOSNI did ensure that there was a second independent operational sea command, based at Pitreavie, in the event that CINCFLEET and his headquarters were unable to operate.[6]

An important part of these re-organisations included the installation of additional national naval command facilities at the joint Coastal Command/CINCEASTLANT headquarters in Northwood, and the fostering of effective co-ordination and co-operation with the RAF. The two services worked relatively smoothly to create structures whereby land-based aircraft, be they strike, fighter, airborne early warning or maritime patrol, could operate with naval vessels at sea. It was quickly understood that two physically separate military headquarters should be accommodated on the Northwood site. The existing NATO headquarters would remain, whilst a new national headquarters, named the Joint National Operations Planning Centre, would be created to enable command of RN and RAF maritime forces outside the NATO area, but still West of Suez, or to command UK-only exercises and operations. It was agreed that the national headquarters must be controlled jointly by the Royal Navy and the RAF, and in 1969 the decision was made to abolish Coastal Command and replace it with 18 Group within the new RAF Strike Command. Its commanding officer was still a 3* Air Marshal, but no longer had the 'Air Officer Commanding-in-Chief' title that was equivalent to the Royal Navy's Commander-in-Chief role. For national air command matters, the commander of 18 Group reported to the Air Officer Commanding Strike Command at High Wycombe, but with his parallel NATO role as Commander Maritime Air Eastlant, he was subordinate to CINCEASTLANT, the CinC WF's parallel NATO post. The RAF also retained control of the long-term planning aspects of RAF maritime air operations, which would still be undertaken by the Air Staff in Whitehall. This was unsurprising, given that the aircraft were RAF assets and their crews were RAF, but it did mean that CinC WF had less influence over the size, composition and long-term decision-making over the land-based maritime air capabilities compared to the ships and ship-based aircraft of the Royal Navy. The costs of the new national command centre were estimated in 1967 as being at £300,000, and it was planned to centralise all national and NATO operational control there by early 1970 at the latest.[7]

Despite the anger directed at the Royal Air Force by parts of the Royal Navy following the cancellation of the strike carrier in 1966, the joint RN/RAF headquarters at Northwood operated remarkably smoothly from its standing up in 1969 to the end of the Cold War. This was particularly impressive given the complex and mixed chains of command across national and NATO lines. Poor personal relationships and a lack of trust could have made the whole system impossible to work and it is a tribute to the professionalism of the officers of both services who worked in the two 'holes in the ground' under the prosperous suburbs of north-west London. Numerous Royal Navy Commanders-in-Chief who worked there, such as Admirals Lewin, Treacher and Fieldhouse, all paid fulsome tribute to the commanders of 18 Group and clearly had effective working relationships.[8] Matters might not have been as smoothly happy as these tributes suggested: in the early 1970s the Navy's leadership experienced a period of nervousness about its operational headquarters being so far ashore and at an establishment with a history as the RAF's Coastal Command headquarters, and plans were seriously developed for the transfer of CINCFLEET headquarters to HMS *Vernon* at Portsmouth.[9] Eventually, the shift was abandoned when it became clear how many new married quarters would have to be built around Portsmouth (many for RAF officers from 18 Group), the planned available space at *Vernon* was reduced, and when it also became apparent that modernising the headquarters to allow for the direct operational control of ships in the Eastlant area would have been cheaper to implement at Northwood.[10]

The implementation of the new organisational structure was surprisingly swift. Commander-in-Chief Home Fleet gained direct operational control of West Indies forces on 1 May 1967, as well as all operational vessels in home waters (temporarily delegating command and control to subordinate commanders until the new facilities in Northwood were complete). Three weeks earlier he had gained control of the South Atlantic and South America Station, with that station's responsibilities along the East African coast shifting to the Commander-in-Chief of the Far East Fleet.[11] On 5 June 1967, the Mediterranean Command was abolished, the Commander-in-Chief Mediterranean's Flag being hauled down in Malta and his role replaced by a Flag Officer Malta who reported to the Commander-in-Chief Western Fleet. A by-product of these changes was the ending of the Royal Navy's role as the holder of a major NATO naval command, that of Commander-in-Chief, Allied Forces Mediterranean, which had been held by the RN's Commander-in-Chief Mediterranean. The Commander-in-Chief, Allied Forces Mediterranean was replaced by Commander Naval Command South, an Italian Admiral, with the RN's Flag Officer Malta subordinate to him in his NATO role as Commander South East Mediterranean.[12] Although the Royal Navy's permanent presence in the Mediterranean had been shrinking for some time, this complex and sometimes head-spinning re-organisation of both national and NATO roles was a clear acknowledgement that the United Kingdom was giving up the leading role in the defence of the Mediterranean that it had held since the Second World War. The Royal Navy was beginning its rapid retreat from an operational theatre that had been the crucible for some of its hardest-fought battles of the Second World War: the battles of Taranto, Matapan, Crete and Sirte Gulf, and the Malta Convoys.

The re-organisation of the home commands was also relatively quick, with the operational command and control West of Suez under Commander-in-Chief Western Fleet being completed in August 1968, and the more complex changes under Commander-in-Chief Naval Home Command occurring between February 1968 and March 1969.[13] If these huge organisational changes had a major fault it was that even though numerous senior roles had been abolished, it resulted in almost no reduction in either military or civilian personnel, despite the significant shrinkage of in the size of the fleet resulting from the 1966 Defence Review and the 1967 Defence Expenditure Studies. The Admiralty Board repeatedly pressed for 10 per cent manpower savings in the re-organisation, but those delivering the changes seemed unable to produce any more than a handful of reductions. Despite the seismic changes in the structures of naval home command covering large swathes of the Navy's serving personnel, only fifteen officer posts were abolished. If the Rosyth and Plymouth NATO sub-commands were abolished then two dozen further officer posts could be removed, along with a handful of civilian and rating posts, but this was not done: the sub-commands had important operational roles to fulfil and claimed personnel savings were far too small to justify on efficiency grounds.[14]

The need for speedy completion of the changes probably did not help the rationalisation of posts, but the re-organisation, in the United Kingdom at least, did not make any major physical changes – no establishments were shut for example, and most civilian and military post-holders continued do the same job, just with different and slightly lower-ranking Admirals in command. Suggestions that the Flag Officer Sea Training be moved to Plymouth to enable Portland to be run down as a naval base were made but rejected. The Sea Lords might have pushed for reductions in posts, but it was left up to the local Admirals to decide how to pare down their own empires, and perhaps unsurprisingly, they all 'had difficulties in identifying savings'.[15] It was this failure to reduce the Navy's administrative and training 'tail' to reflect the reductions in the 'teeth' imposed in 1966 to 1968 that began the shift in the 1970s towards a growing proportion of the navy's personnel being based ashore rather than at sea. The Navy's total personnel numbers did reduce during the late 1960s but most of this stemmed from reductions in the Fleet Air Arm and the abolition of posts when major overseas bases were shut down and ships withdrawn from service, not from domestic shore reductions. During 1969 and 1970 the Ministry of Defence's headquarters in Whitehall was reduced in personnel numbers by 7,500, although most of these staff were moved to 'outstations' beyond London.[16] No similar-sized reductions were made to the individual service departments beyond some shrinkage in the single-service Staffs: between 1966 and 1970 the total reductions in civilian staff were meagre and mainly concentrated in staff locally employed at overseas bases.[17] When external criticisms of this development were eventually made more than a decade later in the bracing early years of the first Thatcher government, the Navy would be vulnerable to charges of being a naval service that spent much of its time ashore, and this was an accusation that was not completely unfounded, even if it had important benefits with respect to personnel retention and recruitment.

Re-organising the Fleet: East of Suez

Whilst West of Suez the operational structure of the Navy was changing dramatically, East of Suez the changes were, initially at least, much less drastic. The post of Flag Officer Middle East was abolished on 1 September 1967 whilst the tri-service Commander-in-Chief Middle East was reduced to a three-star post would now report to the similarly tri-service four-star Commander-in-Chief Far East. A Senior Naval Officer Persian Gulf post was created for a Captain, who would report into the CinC Middle East. Otherwise the structures remained similar, but the forces slowly shrank in size.[18] At Singapore, the Commander-in-Chief Far East Fleet became a post for a Rear Admiral in May 1971 – Rear Admiral John Troup replacing Vice Admiral Leslie Empson – and downgraded to merely Commander Far East Fleet.[19] The size of that fleet began to shrink from its highpoint of the mid-1960s, but was still a formidable force. In March 1970, the Far East Fleet consisted of the commando carrier *Bulwark*, assault ship *Fearless*, eleven frigates, four submarines, four ships attached from the Australian and New Zealand navies as well as minor war vessels, support ships and auxiliaries.[20] However, the need to rotate ships back to home waters on a regular basis (known as 'roulement') meant that there needed to be a further two vessels in the fleet – working up, working down or in maintenance – for every one on station over 9,000 nautical miles away.

The election of a Conservative government in June 1970 resulted in a change to earlier plans to withdraw completely from the Singapore base. The Far East Fleet would still disappear, but a presence would continue to be maintained with a number of frigates remaining in the region, providing ships for the Beira patrol, Five Power Defence Arrangement commitments and a guardship for Hong Kong.[21] On 1 November 1971 the Far East Fleet was formally abolished,

Rear Admiral Troup hauling down his flag to be replaced by Rear Admiral D C Wells of the Royal Australian Navy, who was placed in charge of a new Australia/New Zealand/United Kingdom ('ANZUK') command of which the Royal Navy was a part.[22] The carrier *Eagle*, which had arrived in the Far East in July 1971, left Singapore for the last time alongside the commando carrier *Albion*, the fleet repair ship *Triumph* and four destroyers and frigates.[23] Rear Admiral Troup's second in command, Rear Admiral David Williams, then became Flag Officer of the 2nd Flotilla ('FOF2'), reporting to the new Commander-in-Chief Fleet in the UK.[24] The 7th and 8th Frigate Squadrons of the Far East Fleet, consisting of five frigates each, were re-allocated to the new single Fleet, and stayed a little longer: the 7th Squadron returning home in January 1972 and the 8th Squadron between February and June that year. They were replaced by five frigates of the 3rd Frigate Squadron under FOF2 between March and May with the large guided missile destroyer HMS *Devonshire* arriving in July. From September the ships of the 3rd Squadron would begin to be relieved by those of the 1st Squadron, another FOF2 unit.[25] Therefore, the demise of the Far East Fleet was not the cliff-edge reduction in capability that it has sometimes been portrayed, but was a removal of capital ships and a halving of escorts, which in practice still committed almost two-fifths of the Navy's force of frigates to supporting the commitment in Singapore due to the demands of roulement. This force posture, which had been created at relatively short-notice as a result of the new government's decision, soon came to be seen as impractical and a poor use of naval units. Unlike with ships operating under the old Foreign Service Commission arrangements, vessels were not away from home waters for 18 months, but were instead away for only nine months under the new harmony rules. As a result, FOF2's ships now spent twice as much time on transit to station in the Far East as they did before 1968. The sailors may have been happier, and retention issues lessened, but the ships were now subject to more wear and tear and operational planners had fewer hulls to allocate for tasks.[26] Another, more subtle, change was a shift in the centre of gravity in the Navy's operational commanders. FOF2, unlike FO Far East, was based in the United Kingdom and not in theatre and inevitably his focus began to shift back to the Eastern Atlantic and local seas, particularly as he had under his command those FOF2 ships still in home waters: working up, working down, engaging in exercises in the eastern Atlantic and Mediterranean whilst transiting to or from the Far East. More broadly the Navy as a whole was shifting its focus from worldwide operations to those in the NATO area: the Eastern Atlantic, the Northern Flank off Norway and Iceland and the Southern Flank in the central and Eastern Mediterranean.

Admiral Lewin, the Vice Chief of the Naval Staff, was given the task of solving this problem: he had to maintain a presence East of Suez whilst also making the best use of the frigate and destroyer force and contributing to NATO exercises and tasks as much as possible. His solution was an elegant one and made a significant contribution to increasing the ability of frigates to do more in home and overseas waters, but it did result in a significant further reduction in the number of ships East of Suez. The roulement of three squadrons in and out of Singapore would cease. Instead, a single cheap 'gunboat' frigate would be permanently based at Singapore with another at Hong Kong in order to provide a visible and permanent presence in the region, whilst each year a 'group deployment' of one FOF2 frigate squadron, led by a flagship (invariably a *Tiger* class cruiser or 'County' class destroyer) would undertake a seven to nine-month tour of waters East of Suez in order to 'show the flag', support defence sales and demonstrate to allies that the Navy's capabilities could be deployed to the region in a time of tension. This would therefore only tie up one of FOF2's squadrons, leaving the others for deployment in home waters, the Mediterranean and other theatres. The expectation was that FOF2 himself would accompany the group deployment for most of its time in the region and in transit.[27] Behind this solution hung the ghost of Admiral Jackie Fisher's concentration of the most capable units of the fleet in home waters 60 years before – in order to face the threat of Imperial Germany – leaving older and less capable units to patrol overseas stations, but applied in a more radical and Europe-centric form to reflect the new NATO strategic focus.

The two 'gunboats' were to be diesel-powered frigates. Diesel fuel was easier to procure and take on board from commercial sources when overseas, and diesel propulsion although noisy underwater gave considerable range for ships to operate without refuelling, thus lessening the call on precious Royal Fleet Auxiliaries. HMS *Chichester*, an ageing Type 61 diesel-powered aircraft direction frigate, was chosen for the Hong Kong role. The governor of the colony was particularly keen on an imposing-looking ship to demonstrate Britain's commitment to a territory surrounded by Communist China, and to support the authorities in the event of public disturbances, of which there had been a number in the 1960s.[28] *Chichester*'s refit effectively reduced the frigate to a gunboat in all but name. Much of her extensive radar suite was removed to be replaced by recreation space for the crew, including a cinema room, and she was crewed with the absolute minimum of personnel, totalling 147 compared to 237 before her refit, with some defence stations posts being left vacant. Her only significant augmentation was the fitting of a relatively modern electronic warfare 'passive intercept' set in order to detect the radar of Chinese warships, which were occasionally prone to test the boundaries of Hong Kong territorial waters.[29] *Chichester* arrived on station in 1973 and provided the presence and capabilities for which the governor had requested. Family of crew members were permitted to live in married quarters in the colony, but for younger crew members a posting on *Chichester* could be more frustrating than for those with families. The ship had to remain at 48 hours readiness to sail, which meant that her complement could not undertake 'expeds' to the hills of the New Territories or other outward-bound activities that were proving increasingly popular in the armed forces (it also circumscribed trips to the burgeoning gambling centre of Macao, a two-hour ferry ride away from the colony!).[30] The ship was somewhat of a paper tiger, unable to operate both her 4.5in gun main armament at the same time as her 40mm guns, as she only had sufficient gunnery ratings to operate one weapon system but not both at the same time. Her light crewing also meant that exercising alongside other Royal Navy vessels could exhaust her crew relatively quickly.[31] This was all 'behind the scenes' however, and the ship proved a success from the perspective of the Hong Kong administration.

The second 'gunboat', to operate from Singapore as part of the command structures created by the Five Powers Defence Arrangements, was an altogether more unusual choice. Yarrow shipbuilders had adapted the basic design used for the Type 61 frigate and its near sister the Type 41, for a Presidential yacht for President Nkrumah of Ghana. The ship was completed in 1968 but was never accepted by the Ghanaian government following the overthrow of Nkrumah in 1966.[32] The ship swung at anchor for a number of years, the British government and Royal Navy unwilling to buy a vessel for which they could not think of a purpose. Lewin's plan for permanently-based utility warships East of Suez suddenly made the ship, which had been well preserved and had almost no wear and tear, a tempting purchase, and Yarrows were only too happy to accept a price and remove the ship from its building yard. The vessel was renamed HMS *Mermaid* and after a longer than expected refit to bring her up to Royal Navy operating standards, she was eventually sent to Singapore, arriving somewhat later than planned in September 1974.[33]

The annual group deployment concept was approved by the Admiralty Board in May 1973, and there was clearly a wish to start the new approach to the East of Suez presence as soon as possible, as the first group deployment departed from home waters only a month afterwards.[34] In fact, it was really just the arrival of two ships of the 5th Frigate Squadron in the Far East to relieve some ships of the 6th Frigate Squadron, but accompanied by a nuclear-powered submarine, HMS *Dreadnought*, and the helicopter cruiser HMS *Tiger* as flagship. Rear Admiral Clayton, Flag Officer of the 2nd Flotilla, led the deployment which was named Task Group 321.1. The Group entered the region via the Cape of Good Hope and it visited a range of ports and took part in a number of exercises with allies across the Indo-Pacific region over seven months.[35] When *Tiger* and *Dreadnought* left Singapore in October

1973 the previous squadron of five frigates left with it although two ships were left behind to act as Hong Kong and Singapore guardships for a few additional months, to be replaced on rotation until their permanent 'gunboat' replacements – *Chichester* and *Mermaid* – arrived on station. Another frigate was detached to undertake the Beira Patrol, which was now no longer a full-time requirement, but partial tasking with ships on patrol less than half of the year.[36]

Almost as soon as Task Group 321.1 returned to home waters, a second group deployment was despatched, with Rear Admiral Clayton yet again in command, which was this time named Task Group 317.1 and consisted of the 'County' class destroyer HMS *Fife* as flagship and five ships of the 7th Frigate Squadron. The Group took the same route as its predecessor, rounding the Cape with a stop off at the island air base of Gan on the way to Singapore, with some ships being detached to the Gulf for port visits. The Task Group returned to the United Kingdom in September 1974.[37] A third Group, Task Group 317.2, left home waters a few months later had a rather more ambitious programme involving visits to Pakistan and Japan, and involvement in the major exercise Midlink 74 in the western Indian Ocean. The cruiser *Blake* was its flagship with Rear Admiral Henry Leach, Flag Officer First Flotilla, in command. The nuclear submarine HMS *Warspite* was also part of the deployment, which otherwise consisted of five frigates of the 3rd Frigate Squadron, and the group returned home in June 1975.[38] A pattern had now been set for these deployments, and a further seven such Task Groups would be created through to 1980. Lewin's concept of group deployments were therefore relatively successful in sustaining a British presence east of the Cape after 1973 when the five frigates came home, but they did mark a significant draw down in capability: the five frigates being replaced in effect by two 'gunboats' and the intermittent presence of a somewhat more capable force for only a few months of the year. Although the Royal Navy had not completely withdrawn from South East Asia and the Indian Ocean, the 1973 reduction did mark another step down in the priorities of a Navy increasingly focussing on the Eastern Atlantic and Mediterranean. However, group deployments also meant that the Navy regularly practised sustained out of area 'cruises' by relatively large numbers of warships, a capability that would be of immeasurable use a decade later, when a task force was despatched to the South Atlantic following the invasion of the Falkland Islands.

Exercises, Standing Forces and British-Dutch Co-operation
Whilst the Navy was re-orientating itself towards the Eastern Atlantic and European northern and southern flanks, significant shifts were also manifesting themselves within NATO's strategy. This could be seen most readily in how

the major annual naval exercises changed as the 1960s gave way to the 1970s. In 1969 Exercise Peacekeeper was the major Atlantic exercise of the year, involving a US-led maritime strike force entering the Western Approaches and English Channel, and undertaking a series of long-range land strikes deep into Germany. This was a further iteration of the 'Rip Tide' series of exercises that had been instituted in the late 1950s, and in 1969 involved carrier strike aircraft flying as close as 50 miles from the border between West and East Germany after a series of scenarios against 'Orange' (i.e. simulated enemy) aircraft, submarines and warships.[39] For an enormous investment in naval capability, including four aircraft carriers (two US, one Canadian, one British), and twenty-one cruisers, destroyers and frigates, the results seemed somewhat underwhelming from the perspective of the observers from SACEUR's sub-commands. The quantity of ordnance the carrier-based strike aircraft could theoretically loose seemed small in comparison to that from SACEUR's land airfields. Despite an upbeat assessment from the NATO Commander Strike Fleet Atlantic (a US Admiral who double hatted as Commander of the US 2nd Fleet), Peacekeeper was in fact the last of its kind, the planning for which had started more than two years previously.[40] From 1970 onwards the annual NATO Eastern Atlantic exercise would generally follow a different concept, which was instead based on an assumption that control of the sea would have to be fought for, and that land strikes by carrier aircraft, if they happened at all, would support the Northern Flank where there were no NATO airbases and standing forces were limited only to the Norwegian and Danish military. The appearance of a new generation of Soviet submarines had influenced a strategic shift by NATO towards defending the sea lines of communications between North America and Western Europe, resulting in a focus on the Greenland-Iceland-United Kingdom (GIUK) gap whereby Soviet submarines could pass into the open Atlantic and NATO forces would have to traverse in order to undertake operations in support of the Northern Flank.[41] Not all Eastern Atlantic exercises after 1969 would follow a GIUK gap focus, some would take an Azores to Western Approaches route, but none would have such a focus on strike operations on the central front again and all would include important elements of convoy work: either of merchant ships or of amphibious forces destined for northern flank landings.

Exercise Northern Wedding 70 the following year exemplified this new approach. The British carrier strike group transited the Irish Sea to meet up with the US carrier strike group and undertake a combined traversing of the GIUK gap.[42] Northern Wedding saw a new and specific focus on convoy management with the use of helicopters from Portland to ferry RNXS and other reserve officers to selected merchant ships in order for them to receive convoy instructions and proceed through a theoretical 'transport corridor' in the English Channel.⁴³ That year's exercise also saw another change: the return of the ships of the Royal Navy. In 1969 the carrier HMS *Eagle* might have been involved in Peacekeeper, but she had been accompanied by only one escort, the rather aged destroyer HMS *Diana*, and a number of submarines to act as 'Orange' units.⁴⁴ In 1970 this had changed significantly: the carrier *Ark Royal* was now accompanied by four frigates and destroyers, the Royal Yacht *Britannia* in its secondary role as a hospital ship, as well as nine mine warfare vessels and the usual submarines acting 'Orange'.⁴⁵ Through the 1970s, attendance at one of the annual eastern Atlantic exercises could become a high point of a ship's commission: a chance to demonstrate their capabilities in front of many ships from many NATO navies and play their part.

Exercise Strong Express in 1972 was the largest of these exercises of the early 1970s and followed a similar pattern to Northern Wedding 70. Considerable efforts were made to interest the media of NATO countries: a glossy press pack including statements from the relevant senior commanders was accompanied by the text of Article 5 of the North Atlantic Treaty Organisation, which committed all members to come to the aid of one that had been attacked, and is at the core of the Alliance's mutual defence. The exercise scenario involved the crossing of the GIUK gap by a combined US-UK carrier strike group escorted by other NATO navies including the Canadians and Dutch, which would then undertake simulated conventional and tactical nuclear strikes in support of the NATO land commander in Norway, CINCNORTH, following an attack by 'Orange' (i.e. enemy) force on that country. The exercise also included amphibious landings at Lofoten and Sorreisa under carrier air cover and ended with 'R-Hour' when protection against nuclear attack was practised. This was the largest exercise since 1968 and included 64,000 personnel, over 300 ships and 700 aircraft. The exercise also practiced the protection of convoys to Norway against Soviet submarine, surface and air attacks, and was linked with land exercises in Norway involving 14,000 troops including US and Royal Marines. Sixty chartered merchant ships were involved in the exercise, simulating convoys to the protected by naval escorts. The British contribution included the carrier HMS *Ark Royal*, the commando carrier *Albion*, the nuclear-powered attack submarines *Conqueror* and *Dreadnought*, the assault ship *Fearless*, cruiser *Blake*, six frigates and destroyers, five conventional submarines, eighteen mine warfare vessels and twelve Royal Fleet Auxiliaries, including five 'Sir' class landing ships. This was second only to the US contribution, which included the USS *John F Kennedy*, a support carrier, two nuclear-powered submarines, two cruisers, fourteen destroyers and destroyer escorts and six conventional submarines as well as numerous amphibious vessels and auxiliaries.⁴⁶ This was a huge demonstration of capability, as well as Alliance solidarity and cohesion, when the Soviet Union was at its most self-confident.

Exercise Swift Move the following year was nominally in the Rip Tide series, but in reality the scenario was similar to Strong Express: a passage through the GIUK gap, strike operations in support of land forces in Norway, with convoy serials and amphibious landings followed by tactical and then strategic nuclear release. The major difference for the Royal Navy was the absence of any British strike carrier and the use of *Hermes* in the support carrier role leading an anti-submarine task group ahead of the US carrier strike force: a precursor to the Royal Navy's standard role in such exercises in the late 1970s and 1980s. *Hermes* had almost every operational Royal Navy anti-submarine Sea King helicopter on board – sixteen in total – in order to have six on task as part of an anti-submarine screen for NATO forces.[47] However, her use in this role meant that she could not contribute to the amphibious elements of the exercise in her other role as a commando carrier. With few operational 'flat tops' available the Royal Navy would have had to make difficult operational decisions with *Hermes* and *Bulwark* in a crisis during the 1970s: what was more important – anti-submarine warfare or amphibious landings? The answer would have depended upon the nature of the crisis but it illustrates how 'double hatting' capabilities can create prioritisation problems in such situations. 1974's Exercise was Northern Merger, with little to differentiate from its immediate predecessors. This time *Ark Royal* was available to form part of the carrier strike force and the landings were in Denmark instead of Norway, but otherwise an outsider would have found it little different to Strong Express and Swift Move.[48] NATO forces in the Eastern Atlantic, including the Royal Navy, were practising a similar northern flank scenario for five years in a row: a clear indication that planning had shifted from carrier strike support for NATO's central front to sea control and strike operations on the northern flank.

The transfer of fixed-wing air operations from aircraft carriers to land-based aircraft resulted in the establishment of a series of exercises to test Joint Maritime Operating Procedures ('JMOPs') between the Royal Navy and the Royal Air Force, where the latter would be providing shore-based air support without aircraft carriers. The first exercise was Lime Jug 70, conducted in the eastern Mediterranean with two destroyers and five frigates supported by eight Buccaneer strike aircraft, eight Phantom and Lightning air defence aircraft, three new MR1 Nimrod and four older Shackleton maritime patrol aircraft flying from either Malta or Cyprus. Acting as the 'Orange' forces were *Ark Royal* in the role of an 'airfield' launching her Buccaneers and Phantoms who were 'playing' Soviet 'Badger' strike aircraft and their long-range missiles, with RAF Vulcans and Canberras acting as Soviet electronic warfare and guidance aircraft.[49] The scenarios were deliberately restrictive and highly planned, primarily as a way to help practice new ways of co-operative working between the Royal Navy and the RAF. The exercise seems to have been a relative success in the context of its constrained and limited objectives.[50] RAF fast jets operating from Cyprus worked under fighter control by the Royal Navy ships well, whilst surface strike operations by Buccaneers guided to their targets by naval ships were moderately successful but did involve inaccuracies on the part of the naval side.[51] Vulnerability to jamming was acknowledged whilst the anti-submarine part of the exercise emphasised the weakness of frigates detecting and attacking submarines in comparison to large anti-submarine helicopters operating from one of the Royal Fleet Auxiliaries. The Nimrod demonstrated its capabilities in comparison to the aged Shackleton, but both aircraft faced challenges detecting submerged submarines: of fifty-eight reported detections only eleven were of submerged submarines actually on the exercise.[52]

The following year Exercise High Wood aimed to be a less constricted exercise and was conducted in November in the Norwegian Sea, an altogether more challenging environment. A similar but larger set of forces were in play: three destroyers and six frigates supported by ten Buccaneers, ten Phantoms and Lightnings and eighteen Nimrods. Orange forces included nuclear and conventional submarines, four frigates and various Vulcans, Canberras, Phantoms and Shackletons acting as Soviet strike, guidance and maritime patrol aircraft.[53] High Wood also marked the first time that 'chaff' decoys, consisting of clouds of reflective metal to deflect guided missiles, were used in a major Royal Navy exercise.[54] The exercise demonstrated that there would be much more work needed to ensure the effectiveness of land-based air assets in support of warships. Command and control arrangements were cumbersome and there was unnecessarily high signals traffic which appears to have overloaded operators. This was one of the factors that resulted in a large number of accidental 'blue-on-blue' interceptions by air defence aircraft, and Buccaneer strike aircraft not receiving up-to-date targeting information and therefore not locating ships to attack. Some of this was also due to reconnaissance aircraft having difficulties finding targets for the Buccaneers to strike.[55] Often, when they did find targets they did not continue shadowing them, as the Vulcan and Canberra crews were not used to the shadowing doctrine that was standard amongst maritime pilots.[56] The aged Shackleton airborne early warning aircraft 'made little contribution to the exercise, detecting one-third of the twenty-seven low altitude aircraft which penetrated the defences of the force they were supporting'.[57] Another factor of significance was aircrew fatigue on RAF aircraft: their crews clearly needed to adjust to the much longer flying times required to get aircraft into the Norwegian Sea from their bases in the United Kingdom.[58]

In anti-submarine warfare, the results were extremely poor: the Nimrods flew twenty-seven sorties in which submarines were potentially contactable, but only two detections were obtained, one radar detection of a conventional submarine 'snorting' (re-charging batteries at periscope depth) and one passive sonobuoy detection, and neither of these was sufficiently localised to allow a simulated attack to be made.[59] The weather was relatively poor with high winds and fog, with high sea states and conditions were generally unfavourable to the use of the Nimrods' passive sonobuoys.[60] HMS *Churchill*, the nuclear submarine simulating a 'Charlie' class cruise missile submarine, 'had things her own way' for two periods during the exercise, able to 'fire' her anti-ship missiles without being detected, deterred or attacked. The poor performance in anti-submarine warfare was also due to a relative lack of Sea King helicopters: RFA *Olwen*, the main platform operating these helicopters in the exercise, had mechanical difficulties and only participated in parts, whilst the poor weather forced those helicopters present to stay in their hangars much of the time.[61] Ship-based anti-submarine warfare was similarly unsuccessful: no independent sonar detections were made, and even when ships were told where submarines were, their mortar and Wasp helicopter attacks were all judged as misses.[62] High Wood 71 was the first joint RAF/Royal Navy exercise in sea areas where operations were most likely to occur, and it showed up the need for much better co-ordination and the relative weakness of anti-submarine capabilities at the time. From now onwards, RAF maritime forces would play significant parts in major NATO exercises, and through the 1970s familiarity would be gained by RAF aircrew in the maritime environment and the particular difficulties in co-ordination, reconnaissance and attack that it posed.

High Wood 71 was to have been followed up by Ocean Span in 1973, a Royal Navy-only exercise using naval Buccaneers and Phantoms operating from ashore either against or supporting the newly converted HMS *Hermes* and a task group, but this was cancelled after the major annual NATO exercise of the year, Swift Move 73, was pushed back into October, only one month before Ocean Span's planned date.[63] Instead, there were repeat exercises in the High Wood series in 1975, 1977 and 1979. High Wood 75 took a naval task group around the British Isles from Portland to the Faeroes via the Irish Sea and then down the North Sea, allowing RAF maritime squadrons from air bases across the United Kingdom from St Mawgan in Cornwall to Leuchars and Kinloss in Scotland opportunities to undertake air support, strike or anti-submarine operations. The main focus of the exercise was the means by which submarines and surface vessels could intercept Soviet 'Charlie' class submarines before they fired their missiles.[64] Exercise High Wood 77 had an emphasis on 'free play', suggesting greater confidence between the RN and RAF, and involved a transit from the Western Approaches, west of Ireland and then up through the Faeroes-Shetland gap to the Norwegian Sea. Australian, New Zealand and US units were also involved in the exercise.[65] The last in the series was High Wood 79, which was an almost entirely free-play exercise with no track chart for 'Blue' forces published and linked into an amphibious exercise and landing near Dundee.[66]

The post-exercise report for High Wood 77 shows how far co-ordination in anti-submarine warfare and other operations had developed since 1971. The exercise was primarily focussed on anti-submarine co-ordination with strike and air defence activities taking a secondary role. All three main anti-submarine capabilities: a nuclear submarine operating with the task group, maritime patrol aircraft and anti-submarine Sea Kings, had successes in detecting and prosecuting attacks on the 'Orange' submarines, both nuclear and conventional. HMS *Dreadnought*, playing a 'Charlie' class submarine, made six approaches to the task group, four of which were detected by the escorting submarine, although that submarine was only able to transmit this information to the commander of the task group in two instances, and numerous times this escorting submarine was detected by 'Orange' submarines thus laying itself open to attack. Nimrods made six detections of *Dreadnought*, whilst Sea Kings – having recently been equipped with sonobouys – made two, even though their parent ship, *Hermes*, was positioned a long distance from the screen, resulting a smaller number of aircraft on station than planned. Conventional submarines made ten approaches on the task group, six being undetected. Effective co-ordination by the US submarine *Billfish*, with Nimrods enabled that submarine to achieve a firing solution on a surface action group using downlinked Nimrod data. These results were patchy but had been achieved in poor sonar conditions – in some portions of the exercise no surface layer was present at all – and were a considerable improvement on High Wood 71. Co-ordination between naval and RAF forces was much better, with a number of the earlier communications issues being resolved or at least mitigated.[67] The issue of large numbers of signals overloading those receiving them had still not disappeared and would in fact be a recurring issue in most later Cold War exercises involving large numbers of ships, aircraft and submarines.

Another reflection of the new focus on sea control in the Atlantic was the establishment of the Standing Naval Force Atlantic ('STANAVFORLANT') in January 1968. This multi-national NATO force of frigates and destroyers aimed to be permanently operational, able to provide an instant presence or convoying force in the event of increased tensions or a descent into war, with ships assigned to the force for a duration of six-months. During that time, each ship in the force would sport the NATO emblem on their funnels and personnel wore a small NATO badge on their formal uniform. For two-thirds of the year the force was deployed within the EASTLANT area, and the remaining time within WESTLANT with ships returning to their home ports for the Christmas leave period.[68] The force provided opportunities for ships of different allied navies to operate together, understand each other's approaches and practice using NATO doctrine. As a demonstration that the British were back in home and European waters, it would be a British frigate, HMS *Brighton*, with a British commander, Captain Geoffrey Mitchell, who would become the first Commodore of the new force. The other three ships were a US destroyer, a Dutch frigate and a Norwegian frigate.[69] Up to the end of the Cold War the Royal Navy would ensure that at least one of its frigates or destroyers was assigned to STANAVFORLANT on a regular basis, a demonstration of its commitment to the Alliance after a prolonged period from the late 1950s to the late 1960s when British warships had often been conspicuous by their absence from NATO exercises. Throughout the early 1970s the strong British involvement in the annual Eastern Atlantic exercises and the new Standing Naval Force Atlantic aimed to demonstrate that the Royal Navy was now focussing on its home and near waters, whilst the Lime Jug and High Wood exercises were increasingly complex attempts to foster Royal Naval and Royal Air Force tactical and operational co-operation. Both of these were significant changes in operational focus: the Eastern Atlantic was no longer a relative naval backwater but at the core of the Royal Navy's shifting missions.

One operational change demonstrated the extent to which the Royal Navy was willing to interweave itself with its European NATO partners and vice versa: from October 1972 at least two Dutch submarines were regularly based in Faslane.[70] During this time they would be part of the Royal Navy's 3rd Submarine Squadron and subordinate themselves to Flag Officer Submarines (acting in his NATO role as Commander Submarines Eastern Atlantic).[71] For the Dutch Navy this enabled a more rapid transit to deep waters and likely patrol areas, as well as providing the means to deepen the British-Dutch naval relationship which was developing in other areas as well. In 1973, the Royal Marines and the Dutch Marines formed a relationship that would prove beneficial to both over the following decades. In the late 1960s, the Dutch Marines had lost most of their remaining amphibious shipping and by the early 1970s their long-term future did not look assured.[72] In a Memorandum of Understanding they therefore agreed to make use of the Royal Navy's amphibious shipping and train, exercise and deploy with the Royal Marines. This not only saved the Dutch Marines in the long-term, but it also demonstrated the Royal Marines' increased focus on NATO activities, provide an opportunity to benefit from sustained cross-fertilisation from another European marine force, and when in future years, the survival of British amphibious shipping and the Royal Marines seemed in doubt, the relationship helped support the case to retain both. The relationship has proved particularly successful and remains in place today.[73]

Tactical Doctrine

By the late 1960s, the Royal Navy had established and developed a comprehensive and generally successful hierarchy of doctrine to support naval officers in their operational and tactical decision-making. Doctrine has been defined as 'considered thought on what works' or more formally as fundamental principles guiding military actions in support of objectives.[74] At the tactical level this is guidance and advice on how to make the complex decisions required of an officer involved fighting a ship. At higher levels it can set out the principles of war and the nature of maritime operations to provide context and frame tactical and operational doctrine.

In 1969, Royal Navy doctrine existed in four inter-linked layers.[75] At the top was the Naval War Manual, the latest version being issued that year and superseding the 1958 edition. In five different parts, split into a total of twenty-two chapters, it set out how defence policy was made and the international alliance system in Part 1; the principles of war and the nature of strategy in Part 2; the Ministry of Defence, Royal Navy Command structures and NATO command structure in Part 3; the main elements of maritime warfare – including the defence of shipping, defence against invasion, limited and 'cold' war, power projection, logistics and support – in Part 4; and the leadership, morale, training and discipline in Part 5.[76] This was an outwardly impressive publication, but after some updates in 1970 it appears to have been neglected and largely forgotten through the 1970s and 1980s.[77] In some respects this is unsurprising, the Naval War Manual partly duplicated what was taught at the LGC which produced its own teaching materials, and it did not contain much that would either directly help an officer preparing for a major exercise, or in much of his day-to-day shipboard operational routine. Subjects were covered at an 'Olympian' level, with NATO dealt with in only a page and a half, ballistic missiles in one short paragraph and the merchant navy in two paragraphs, so beyond providing an introductory overview, other publications or sources of information would be needed. However, as has been seen, not every officer attended the LGC and fewer would retain either the memory or course materials if they had. The withering-away of the Naval War Manual during the 1970s partly reflected the shift in naval operations towards the single NATO role against Warsaw Pact forces, so issues of wider maritime strategy and the broader context appeared to be either self-evident or not especially relevant: NATO's military strategy seemed more significant than any residual 'national' strategy outside the NATO area. This creeping atrophy in strategic awareness and thinking, which began to afflict all three services through the later Cold War years, would only become obvious once the Cold War ended: it would take some seven years to develop a coherent high-level defence strategy in the 1990s without a Soviet threat to face.[78]

The next layer of doctrine focussed on what might be termed the higher tactical level, and here there was a huge store of information for the naval officer preparing for an exercise or for operations. Since 1959 it had been issued in two parts both entitled 'Fighting Instructions'. The first part covered each type of naval warfare in turn: submarine warfare, air defence and so on, in addition to general factors relating to all types of naval warfare. General principles of warfare in each of these areas were set out coupled with overviews of Royal Navy and Soviet capabilities, combined with overviews of key concepts such as anti-submarine screens, Polaris operating cycles and scouting operations.[79] The second part was entitled 'Tactical Problems' and was regularly updated and dealt with over forty different problems, such as helicopter usage, the use of nuclear depth bombs, the conduct of surface action groups and rules of engagement at high levels of tension. Each problem analysed a particular issue and was then followed by recent comments from operational commanders, including ship COs, training establishments and analysis and evaluation units.[80] This approach ensured that at this level, doctrine development was actually a collective activity rather than handed down from on high by office-bound doctrine writers: readers were given real-world commentary and assessments and saw that they might be able to add contributions or propose new 'problems' for assessment and commentary. Captains and Flag Officers were kept engaged in the process by signing off on new problems and any comments on them.[81] The Fighting Instructions remained in heavy use, with regular annual updates to Part II all the way through the Cold War, and ensured that at the tactical level knowledge gained by individual units could be transmitted, commented on and further developed in a way that encouraged mediated debate and discussion. While the War Manual might have been a fading and increasingly forgotten document in the later Cold War, the Fighting Instructions remained in rude health and helped contribute to a Navy that was educating and preparing itself to high state of readiness for fighting a rapidly shifting high-technology war at sea.

The third layer of doctrine consisted of direct instruction on the use of particular system types in the form of 'Fleet Operational and Tactical Instructions' or FOTIs. Examples include 'FOTI 1732: Tactical Employment of Electronic Warfare Equipment' or 'FOTI 1210: Tasking of Helicopters for the ASW or surface strike role'.[82] The presumption was that whilst the Fighting Instructions would be read a few days before an exercise, the FOTIs would be for use within a ship's operations room.[83] It was a number of these important documents that were passed to the Soviets between 1966 and

1971 by Sub Lieutenant David Bingham, a Special Duties officer with debt problems whose wife knocked on the door the Soviet embassy and offered to supply classified material in return for money. The First Sea Lord was deeply concerned by these losses, and it is difficult to tell how much of an impact their loss had: in the short-term this might have been significant, but given the regularity of updating and change it is possible that the impact over the longer term was less severe. Despite this, they are likely to have given the Soviets an important insight into how the Royal Navy approached tactical issues even as the actual detail became outdated.[84]

The final, bottom, layer of doctrine consisted of the many hundreds of manuals to different systems and pieces of equipment, either in the form of Books of Reference ('BRs') at the Restricted level of classification or Confidential Books ('CBs') at Confidential or Secret.[85] These were very much user manuals designed for the individual operator or engineer/mechanic for a piece of equipment, and were necessary just to ensure that the equipment worked and was used competently, safely and effectively on board ship. They would be regularly updated as the equipment itself was updated and developed, and sometimes they would consist of the manufacturer's own user manual, rebound for Royal Navy use.

This Royal Navy-specific doctrine was complemented by, and influenced, joint NATO doctrine, which had originated as joint US/UK/Canada doctrine developed in the immediate aftermath of the Second World War. NATO's cornerstone ATP(1) publication had been initially envisaged as a manual setting out manoeuvring instructions, but grew during development to include other areas of cross-NATO tactical co-operation and co-ordination, and was quickly joined by other NATO naval publications. During the Cold War years, British influence on writing of NATO doctrine was second only to that of the USA.[86] The four layers of Royal Navy doctrine would therefore have been used in different ways by different personnel: operations branch and weapons engineering branch senior ratings and special duties officers would have known their CBs and BRs well and hopefully had some understanding of the FOTIs relevant to their areas. Junior seaman officers would have known their relevant FOTIs and hopefully the relevant sections of the Fighting Instructions and some of the CBs and BRs, whilst PWOs and AWOs should have had a command of most parts of the latest Fighting Instructions, coupled with a good working knowledge of the more heavily used FOTIs. This interlocking and integrated system of tactical doctrine served the Navy well during the rest of the Cold War, and it was partly on this mass of guidance and instructions, supplemented of course by effective training and practice, that rested the Royal Navy's reputation as a highly professional and capable fighting service.

Dockyards, Naval Bases and Fleet Maintenance

Dramatic changes in the Royal Dockyards were agreed during 1968 and 1969: plans were approved for shrinkage, rationalisation and the creation a formal fleet maintenance capability, and all served to not only modernise the dockyards, but turn them into a smaller and less dominant part of what now became known primarily as Naval Bases. From September 1971 the dockyard and its management would now be only one of five different elements within a 'Naval Base' which also consisted of the fleet maintenance base, the barracks, the port area under the Captain of the Port which managed and maintained the berths and waterfront, and the Port Stores and Transport Officer's area which consisted of victualling, fuelling and armaments storage, maintenance and transfer.[87]

Within this new structure, the first and most noticeable change was shrinkage: the Royal Navy was reducing in size, and once the aircraft carriers were withdrawn, the load of refit and repair for surface ships would reduce even if the new refitting tasks for nuclear submarines were included. This was accompanied by a directive from the Chiefs of Staff Committee to reduce the 'support elements' across Defence by 20 per cent. Three options were considered: a gradual rundown through natural wastage, the closure of one home dockyard or a controlled rundown which would include some redundancies. It was thought that a dockyard labour force of between 26,000 and 24,000 would be needed through the 1970s, but it was hoped that the lower figure could be reached by 1973–4 if flexible working was introduced and more use of overtime was made. The dockyard considered to be the most likely candidate for closure was Chatham: shutting Portsmouth or Devonport would reduce the workforce too far, and the closure of Rosyth not enough. However, the closing of Chatham was not recommended: it would require the maintenance of larger workforces than would otherwise be planned at Portsmouth and Devonport, and this might not be possible. Devonport was limited by its small local workforce and would probably not be able to keep its numbers up to the level required, whilst Portsmouth suffered the opposite problem of difficulties in retaining labour attracted to other industrial or port work in the prosperous Hampshire hinterland. Another factor against closing Chatham was that although the cost savings would be greater than the other options over a ten year period (£60 million in 1968 prices), there would in fact be cost increases to pay for shutting the base in the first few years, with savings only accruing after five years. That Chatham had just had millions of pounds spent on it to enable the refitting of nuclear submarines was another reason to keep the yard open. Of the options of rundown by natural wastage and controlled rundown, the latter was proposed as the most effective: skills that needed to be retained would be, and recruitment would not have to be scaled down so far. Redundancies and retraining with new skills might be difficult to negotiate with the trade unions, but this was considered much more preferable to an uncontrolled rundown through natural wastage. If by 1973–4 the workforce was reduced to 24,000, with most of the reductions occurring after 1971–2 when it was expected that the last aircraft carrier refit would have been completed, the savings over ten years would be in the order of £40 to £50 million.[88]

In addition to shrinkage, the refit work of the dockyards was being rationalised with individual yards specialising in different work. Whilst, as mentioned, Chatham had recently been upgraded to refit nuclear-powered submarines alongside conventional submarines, work was ongoing to enable Rosyth to refit the *Resolution* class submarines carrying the strategic nuclear deterrent. Devonport would be allocated frigate refit work, whilst Portsmouth would refit destroyers and Rosyth minor war vessels. The aim was to build up and sustain expertise in particular ships classes at specific yards, as well as increasing efficiency and simplifying the procurement and storage of spares and equipment used in refits. This shift towards specialisation, and away from undertaking refits for home based vessels only, was a long-term success, particularly as it was accompanied by investment in new refit facilities, not least the covered frigate refit hall at Devonport and modernised facilities for destroyer refit at Portsmouth and minor vessel refit at Rosyth. The late 1960s and 1970s also saw a sustained period of investment in the infrastructure of the main home naval bases: barrack accommodation was improved, and administrative offices, repair and maintenance facilities were rebuilt. For example, in Portsmouth new accommodation blocks and dining halls were built in the late 1960s, two large ten-storey office blocks were completed in 1965 and 1972 (since demolished), a huge heavy plate shop in 1975 (now the naval base's Steel Production Hall), two workshop complexes and three lay apart stores between 1975 and 1979, an apprentice training centre was completed in 1980 and host of other stores, workshops and amenity buildings.[89] Similar, and just as substantial, improvements were made to Devonport and Rosyth, not least the huge frigate refit complex at the former, and taken together were the largest investments in dockyard infrastructure since the Second World War.[90]

The maintenance of ships between refits had been relatively straightforward in the pre-war Navy: large ships had the capacity for self-maintenance, with workshops, personnel and stores able to support themselves, whilst smaller vessels and submarines were maintained via depot ships. This situation theoretically continued after the war, with surface ships down to the size of frigate maintaining a wide range of spares, workshops and personnel for self-maintenance, with the remaining depot and repair ships providing support where needed. However, the increased sophistication of warships, and in particular the proliferation of complex and limited production run electronic equipment, meant that ships could no longer hold sufficient spares for every eventuality, whilst fixing and repairing required more highly-skilled crew members than before. The result was two developments through the 1950s and early 1960s: first, an increasing willingness to allow tasks to build up during a commission so that they could be properly fixed in refit which resulted in longer and more expensive refits, and second the ad hoc setting aside of dockyard facilities for between-refit repair and maintenance, manned by a mix of base maintenance parties, craft groups and fleet maintenance units. With the withdrawal from bases East of Suez the last depot ships were facing retirement, leaving the ageing converted aircraft carrier HMS *Triumph* as the fleet's only heavy repair ship. With a fleet that would primarily be home based, the existing incrementally established maintenance services would come under increasing strain and the risk was that the periods of ship non-availability, which had already reached 50 per cent of ship-time, would increase further. The Chief of Fleet Support, the new title given to the Fourth Sea Lord and former Vice Controller in 1967, therefore recommended the establishment of stand-alone fleet maintenance bases in the main naval bases. They would have dedicated facilities, including specially allocated berths, warehouses, cranes and workshops, which would co-locate all of a naval base's maintenance groups under a single Captain, Fleet Maintenance. On the other side, the prime responsibility for between-refit maintenance would be lifted from the ship's company and taken up by the new fleet maintenance base, who could also fly over Fleet Maintenance Units to undertake and support maintenance in overseas stations. This would release each ship from carrying a complete set of spares, and would also help the shift towards 'refit by replacement' whereby broken equipment, such as gas turbines, could be removed from a ship and replaced with a new item quickly, allowing proper repair to be undertaken in slow time ashore, and reducing the amount of time a ship would be unavailable. These reforms were approved in 1969 with plans for implementation the fleet and naval bases by 1974–5.[91]

The last years of the 1960s also saw the end of a dockyard role that had once been their core function for hundreds of years: the construction of warships. In February 1970, HMS *Scylla*, the last dockyard shipbuilding order on the books, was commissioned. Three months before, the Admiralty Board had discussed the future of warship-building at Royal Dockyards and came to the conclusion that no further warships should be ordered at present but left open the possibility of reviewing the position in the future. The reasons were varied and included the need to focus dockyards on their key refitting role whilst also rationalising, consolidating and cutting workforce numbers; the decision to build warships in batches with a single builder which would not be possible with the dockyards given their limited capacity; the belief that dockyard-built ships were more expensive, although differences in treating costs made this difficult to show conclusively; and finally the additional expenditure required to bring dockyards up to date to construct some of the newest ships such as Type 22 frigates. Ordering just a first of class ship from a dockyard was considered, but again was deemed not worthwhile: the Ship Department, the Navy's in-house ship designers, would have to provide detailed designs for the ship and arrange contracts, and it was already overstretched with its main design tasks.[92] As will be seen in Chapter 11, the Navy's leadership would revisit the possibility of dockyard-built warships, but each time it would shy away from committing to do so, not least because the refit programme continued to grow in size and length and provided little if any space for warship building: HMS *Scylla* would therefore be the last dockyard-built warship. Continuing concerns about the efficiency of the dockyards led to proposals, initially made by the junior Navy Minister David Owen in 1968, to create a separate Vote for the dockyards split from the rest of the Ministry Votes to improve transparency and effectively make their accounts public, and then to turn the dockyards into a semi-independent 'trading fund' that would tout for refit business alongside private sector yards. The separate Vote was eventually instituted in 1975, but trading fund never went ahead.[93] The Treasury and Admiralty Board were generally in favour but Ministry of Defence finance officers were not, concerned that the dockyards were natural monopoly suppliers of the most complex and expensive refits and a trading fund would therefore just create much more accounting work for little gain.[94] The status quo therefore remained until even more radical proposals during the 1980s eclipsed the concept of a trading fund.

* * *

The organisational and deployment changes during Le Fanu's period as First Sea Lord were closely linked to the personnel policy changes outlined in the preceding chapter. The shutting down of most of the overseas stations, combined with the consolidation of commands in home waters, was not just driven by the decision to withdraw from East of Suez, but was also influenced by the need to aid retention of personnel which could only be solved by new deployment cycles which meant shorter periods away from home ports for ships. The organisational shifts were achieved with commendable speed, but underneath most of the changes in the titles of flag officers and commanders-in-chief the majority of the personnel, civil and military, would only have seen relatively gradual and perhaps even only cosmetic changes. Operationally, the new focus on home and Mediterranean waters resulted in the Royal Navy returning in considerable numbers to the major NATO exercises and becoming a permanent presence in the multi-national Standing Naval Force Atlantic. As Michael Le Fanu prepared to move up into the post of Chief of the Defence Staff, his successor Peter Hill-Norton was expecting to implement the final stages of the work undertaken by his two predecessors: introducing the new warship types into the fleet, modernising Polaris and tackling the submarine threat from the Soviet Navy.

6

Sea Control

New First Sea Lord and Board

In June 1970, just as the Conservatives returned to government after six years in opposition, Michael Le Fanu was nominated as the next Chief of the Defence Staff, and Admiral Sir Peter Hill-Norton became First Sea Lord in his place. Hill-Norton was a gunnery officer with a wide-ranging wartime record who had commanded his first ship in 1956 and had held two senior tri-service posts prior to 1970: Deputy Chief of the Defence Staff for Personnel and Logistics from 1966 to 1967, and then the tri-service Commander-in-Chief Far East from March 1969. Between these two posts he had spent two years on the Admiralty Board and then a few months as Second Sea Lord, followed by a slightly longer period as Vice Chief of the Naval Staff. This whirlwind of different posts held in short succession did not stop when he became First Sea Lord. Michael Le Fanu's health, which had always been fragile, gave way and it became clear that he would die from leukaemia in the next few months. Le Fanu died in November 1970 and Air Chief Marshal Charles Elworthy remained in post as Chief of the Defence Staff until a successor could be found. Given that the post was then held on a strict rotational basis amongst the three services, it was agreed that the Navy should continue 'its turn' and Hill-Norton was selected as Le Fanu's eventual successor. Hill-Norton's time as Chief of the Defence Staff would be dominated by negotiations and decisions over the updating of the Polaris strategic nuclear deterrent. His unexpected successor as First Sea Lord was Admiral Sir Michael Pollock who had only recently been appointed Controller of the Navy in January 1970.

Pollock's wartime career was amongst the most distinguished of his fellow late Cold War First Sea Lords, having earned three mentions in despatches and a Distinguished Service Cross as a gunnery officer, most notably on the cruiser

HMS *Norfolk* during the Battle of North Cape when the German battlecruiser *Scharnhorst* was sunk. In 1952 he was heavily and successfully involved in organising the funeral of King George VI, providing an early demonstration of his organisational skills.[1] Despite this early promise, in mid-career he seemed to languish somewhat, not receiving a seagoing command at the rank of Commander, despite a number of demanding second-in-command roles, which risked making it impossible for him to proceed to flag rank. However, his second posting as a Captain saw him gain command of the old destroyer HMS *Vigo* and the local Portsmouth flotilla. Pollock clearly made a success of the role, as from this point onwards he held a series of high-profile posts, including command of HMS *Ark Royal* and two years as an Assistant Chief of the Naval Staff during the 1964–6 Defence Review. Although Pollock was a gunnery officer he was given the role of Flag Officer Submarines ('FOSM') from 1967 to 1969, a post that was usually held by submariners. During his time as FOSM, the Royal Navy had successfully taken over the role of carrying the United Kingdom's strategic nuclear deterrent and commissioned five nuclear-powered submarines, and this stood him in good stead for the two dominant themes of his time in post: the Polaris modernisation decisions which are discussed in this chapter, and the planned introduction of a new generation of surface ships, including the Type 82 and Type 42 destroyers and the Type 21 frigate, which is discussed in the next chapter.[2]

The arrival of Pollock in post in March 1971 soon saw turnover in almost all the other senior posts: Vice Admiral Sir Anthony Griffin became Controller in place of Pollock and Admiral Sir Derek Empson became Second Sea Lord in December 1971 in place of Vice Admiral Sir Andrew Lewis. Lewis had only been appointed to that post in March 1970 and now became Commander-in-Chief Naval Home Command in place of Admiral Sir Horace Law. Vice Admiral G F A Trewby was appointed Chief of Fleet Support in July 1971. Vice Admiral Terence Lewin had already been appointed VCNS in January of that year whilst Sir Edward Ashmore became the last Commander-in-Chief Western Fleet in September 1971, his post being reconstituted as Commander-in-Chief Fleet in November.

The United States, NATO and Nuclear Weapons

Modernising Polaris
On 30 June 1969 the Royal Air Force's 'V Force' of nuclear bombers was stood down from readiness: the United Kingdom's strategic nuclear deterrent was now solely in the hands of the Royal Navy's four *Resolution* class Polaris-carrying nuclear-powered submarines. The transition from the V Force to the *Resolution* class had been remarkably quick. HMS *Resolution*, the first of class,

had commissioned on 2 October 1967, and begun its first deterrent patrol on 14 June 1968.[3] Even before these important milestones, the government was already investigating the modernisation or replacement of Polaris.[4]

Evidence that the Soviets were enhancing their anti-ballistic missile defences around Moscow put at risk what had been called the 'Moscow criterion': a minimum threshold for the British strategic nuclear deterrent as a national rather than a NATO capability.[5] To meet the criterion at its most basic level, the nuclear deterrent had to be able to break through Moscow's defences. If the USSR had more interceptor missiles arrayed around its capital than the British had ballistic missile warheads then the criterion was not met: the deterrent value of the British capability would be so weakened by the limited threat that it posed, that it would be unable to perform its purpose and expose the United Kingdom to the risk of nuclear blackmail or a nuclear attack from which it could not respond credibly.[6] The Polaris A3 missile, which the Royal Navy's boats carried, had a range of 2,500 nautical miles, and its weapon 'bus' consisted of three warheads that would spread over the target during re-entry in a regular pattern in order to create the largest possible area of destruction and triple the number of targets for anti-ballistic missiles systems to intercept.[7] This multiple re-entry vehicle (or 'MRV') had significantly improved Polaris' capability when it had been introduced into US service in 1964, but by the mid-1960s the rapid development of Soviet defences meant that the United States embarked on the development of a new system, Poseidon C3, which would have between ten and fourteen re-entry vehicles which could be individually targeted. This Multiple Independently targetable Re-entry Vehicle ('MIRV') system therefore expanded the number of targets a single missile could potentially destroy from one large target with three re-entry vehicles with Polaris A3 to between ten and fourteen targets each with a single re-entry vehicle with the new Poseidon C3.[8] This provided a much larger number of warheads, which would probably be more dispersed than their Polaris predecessors, for Soviet anti-ballistic missile systems to attempt to intercept. Poseidon was therefore the most capable system that the British could potentially operate and it was theoretically available under the existing technology-sharing agreements, but it would tie the United Kingdom just as tightly into the US naval nuclear programme as Polaris had, and be particularly expensive. The British Polaris had its own British-made nuclear weapons within the warhead, and if this had also been done with a British Poseidon, then the challenges of creating much larger numbers of weapons to fit within each MIRV could be beyond British scientific capabilities – at least at an acceptable cost.[9] There were also concerns whether the US would allow the UK to purchase Poseidon: at least one US Secretary of Defence, James Schlesinger, who was in post between July 1973 and November 1975, was known to be against doing so.[10]

Another, less capable but cheaper, option was to keep the Polaris MRV system but replace one of the three re-entry vehicles with a number of 'penetration aids': decoys that would fool Soviet intercepting missiles, combined with 'hardening' the two remaining MRVs to make them more resistant to air-burst defensive nuclear missiles that might be fired by the Soviets into the outer atmosphere. This concept, named Antelope, had been first proposed by the United States in 1967 but had been put aside when the Poseidon option had instead been taken up.[11] If the British were to adopt Antelope, then they would benefit from the work already done on it by the Americans, it would provide a less challenging task for British nuclear scientists creating the weapons and provide a greater margin over the Moscow criterion than Polaris A3. The British version was re-named Super-Antelope to emphasise additional improvements including better hardening for both the warheads and the decoys.[12] A number of hybrid options were also considered at different times by the British, including 'Stag' which married a Poseidon missile to an Antelope front-end and Option M, in which a new US-developed warhead could be married to either the Polaris or Poseidon missile.[13] Yet another option was the purchase of a fifth Polaris submarine, which would allow for two boats to be on patrol and thus increase the number of warheads that could be launched in an emergency. This option was rejected in November 1972: it would disrupt the hunter-killer submarine building programme, the fifth boat would not enter service until 1980 and was argued not to be cost-effective.[14]

A wide range of political and diplomatic considerations complicated this decision that ostensibly looked like a simple trade-off between cost and capability. First, the new Prime Minister, Edward Heath, had stated his ambition whilst in opposition to improve nuclear co-operation with the French and lessen dependence on the United States.[15] It took some time to clarify the extent to which dependence on the US meant that almost any substantive technology sharing with the French would be impossible without US permission, forcing Heath back towards a US-based solution.[16] Second, the rapid growth in the Soviet nuclear arsenal had resulted in a shift in US policy away from ensuring nuclear predominance over the Soviets towards mere 'sufficiency' and something approaching parity, combined with bilateral negotiations to limit any further growth in arsenals. The Strategic Arms Limitations Talks ('SALT') complicated matters for the British: if the Soviets suggested, and the US agreed, to stopping technology transfer to allies, then the British deterrent would become inoperable quickly. This did not come to pass, but it was a latent fear throughout the SALT negotiations.[17] Procuring the MIRV-ed Poseidon could have drawn unwelcome attention to the increasing capability of the British deterrent and might have made it impossible for the United States to hold off Soviet calls for ending technology transfer. In such circumstances, the more discrete Super-Antelope or one of the hybrid options looked like more obvious solutions. Parallel negotiations over the restriction of anti-ballistic missiles defences were also of particular interest: an agreement to limit the capability or size of these defences would mean that the Moscow criterion would not keep on rising and therefore quickly make the new missile system – whether Poseidon, Super-Antelope or something in between – obsolescent. The Anti-Ballistic Missile ('ABM') Treaty of May 1972 restricted both the USSR and the United States to no more than 100 systems to provide defence for each country, and in 1974 a protocol to the Treaty restricted the systems to one site around each capital. Fixing the number of anti-ballistic missile systems (each with only one missile) to 100 gave the British what they wanted and removed the spectre of a one-sided mini-nuclear arms race between the UK and the USSR as the Moscow Criterion kept sliding out of view.[18]

The third complication related to the internal politics of the United States. It was never clear that Congress would approve of the supply of MIRV-ed Poseidon to the British, partly because it might be seen to jeopardise SALT and partly because significant portions of Congress had been pushing for an increase in European NATO members' contributions to common *conventional* defence capabilities and lessen the burden on US forces. At the extremes some Republican congressmen were lobbying for the withdrawal of half of US military personnel from Europe. British-American relations also went through difficult stages during the early 1970s. Heath and Richard Nixon, the President, got on well, but US dismay at what it saw as Britain's near-neutral position over the Arab-Israeli Yom Kippur War in 1973 influenced the National Security Council to argue briefly that only the US should possess nuclear weapons within NATO. In the dying days of Nixon's presidency, his weakness and likely inability to persuade Republican congressmen and senators to support the provision of Poseidon to the UK was another factor pushing the British away from procuring the most capable system available. Despite these problems, US-UK co-operation was sufficiently good to ensure that technology sharing and the use of the Nevada desert for underground nuclear testing of the British-developed new weapons began early and continued throughout the development of the new system.[19]

The Royal Navy had always preferred the Poseidon option, as the most capable system and the one that ensured the tightest co-operation with the United States, throughout much of the prolonged discussions from 1970 to 1973 over which system to procure.[20] However, the Ministry of Defence itself generally recommended either Super-Antelope or the compromise hybrid options, as did influential civil servants such as Sir Burke Trend, the Cabinet Secretary, as well as Lord Carrington, the Defence Secretary. It would be politically less difficult to procure, cheaper and maintained a curtailed amount of British independence. The hybrid options were ruled out in late 1973 due to their projected costs and concerns that even a de-MIRVed Poseidon might be blocked by a Congress increasingly unwilling to listen to the embattled President.[21] Edward Heath had planned to make the announcement of the decision to update Polaris with Super-Antelope (which was itself soon modified and renamed Chevaline after a species of antelope) in the forthcoming 1974 Defence White Paper.[22] However, the coal-miners' strike, which caused a shortage in electricity for business and domestic use, thus resulting in electricity rationing (the 'three-day week') and repeated power cuts, caused the Prime Minister to call a general election which he duly lost. The February 1974 election brought Labour back to power in a minority government, and a further general election in October 1974 produced a small three-seat majority. Opposition to nuclear weapons with the Labour Party meant that Heath's planned announcement could not go ahead – the Statement on the Defence Estimates was cancelled altogether in 1974 – and the returning Prime Minister, Harold Wilson, decided to continue its development under the utmost secrecy so that his left wing would not discover that the nuclear deterrent was being renewed and modernised.[23] The Royal Navy could now expect the missiles its *Resolution* class submarines carried to be updated, not with the US Poseidon that it preferred but with the domestically-developed Chevaline.

Tactical Nuclear Weapons
Tactical nuclear weapons, which are sometimes also called battlefield nuclear weapons, are usually but not always lower-yield and shorter-range nuclear weapons that had been developed in order to make up for deficiencies in conventional weaponry or as a cheaper means of achieving the same military effect. If conventional missiles, gunnery and torpedoes lacked sufficient accuracy, capability or numbers then a low-yield nuclear weapon could – it was surmised by military planners in the Cold War – resolve the issue of accuracy and more than make up for any issues of low capability or numbers through their enormous explosive and destructive power. Both NATO and the Soviet Union procured and deployed tactical nuclear weapons for these reasons. In the context of the Royal Navy, such nuclear weapons would be useful to destroy Soviet surface action groups with a single weapon or could be used underwater as 'nuclear depth bombs' to clear Soviet nuclear submarines that threatened surface forces or convoys. In addition, nuclear bombs carried by carrier aircraft could also be used for nuclear strike operations ashore, either to support land operations or to destroy Soviet naval shore facilities such as naval bases and dockyards.[24] This last capability, which was lessening in importance as NATO strategy shifted towards securing control of the sea from a more powerful Soviet navy, was effectively being phased out in the Royal Navy with

the withdrawal of the carriers, although it remained with the RAF, including Buccaneer strike aircraft originally destined for, or transferred from, the Navy.

The most obvious problem with tactical nuclear weapons was their escalatory potential. The use of such a weapon, especially ashore, might occur for ostensibly sound military-tactical reasons but the result would probably the deaths of tens of thousands, if not more, civilians in addition to the destruction of the military target. This could then prompt a more powerful nuclear response from the other side which could then escalate to a general nuclear exchange and therefore almost certain Armageddon terrifyingly quickly. In the 1950s, NATO's nuclear posture had combined numerous such weapons – which were locally controlled by tactical commanders ashore and at sea – with a 'tripwire' policy of a full and general nuclear response to any incursion into NATO territory. The chances of accidental release and the lack of political control of all such weapons had seriously concerned the Kennedy and Johnson administrations of the early and mid-1960s, so they began lobbying for NATO to adopt a new nuclear strategy which was named 'Flexible Response'. This had been heavily influenced by game theory and the belief that nuclear exchanges could be controlled into a 'ladder of escalation' that allowed the limited use of such weapons as a 'shot across the bows' at different points in a conflict before any general release could occur. The aim was to achieve 'war termination' with either no, or a small number of, nuclear weapons being used.[25] This nuclear strategy was finally approved by NATO in 1967 and became known as Military Concept ('MC') 14/3.[26] Flexible Response required greater centralised control of tactical nuclear weapons and would rely more on conventional military forces as it was expected that the early part of any conflict, operating at the lower level of the ladder of deterrence, would not involve nuclear release.

In the late 1960s, a programme to update the United Kingdom's main airborne tactical nuclear capability was in the process of completion. The WE177 free-fall nuclear bomb, with a variable yield of between 0.5 and 10 kilotons, was replacing the Red Beard bomb that had been carried by RAF aircraft on the Central European front, at Cyprus and Singapore, and Royal Navy carrier aircraft operating worldwide since 1962. With the decision to withdraw from East of Suez and phase out the carrier force, storage for Red Beard in Singapore would not be replaced, and the number of naval-operated WE177s flown from Buccaneer aircraft for anti-submarine and anti-ship use would be reduced from a planned sixty-three to forty-three. However, there was a gain for maritime operations as a whole as these twenty bombs, combined with a further order of sixteen WE177s, would be operated by UK-based RAF Buccaneers under Commander-in-Chief Eastern Atlantic in the maritime role, in addition to more of these weapons for Nimrod maritime patrol aircraft.²⁷ In frustration at development problems with the Mark 24 torpedo, Flag Officer Submarines even proposed adding a nuclear warhead to the old unguided Mark 8 torpedo, as a means to make up for deficiencies in speed and accuracy in both the Mark 8 and the Mark 24.²⁸ This never went beyond the proposal stage, but this did mirror a number of Soviet nuclear-tipped torpedoes, missiles and nuclear depth charges which also sought to compensate for concerns about conventional capability.²⁹

Although both the US and British military had procured tactical nuclear weapons for military purposes, Flexible Response and more general concerns about escalation, resulted in the British treating them primarily as part of the deterrent rather than warfighting capabilities: the use of a tactical nuclear weapon would be a deterrent signal to the enemy that NATO was willing, if necessary, to escalate to the next level in the 'ladder of deterrence' and nothing more.³⁰ One potential exception was the use of tactical nuclear weapons at sea, where the lack of large numbers of civilians made this a theoretically 'safer' and more containable domain for their use, and suggested that escalation would have a better chance of being prevented or controlled. In 1970, the rules of engagement and procedures for using nuclear depth bombs at sea were clearly set out in British naval doctrine. Two types of release were set out: general and selective. General release, which would have been part of a wider strategic use of nuclear weapons was 'exceedingly unlikely' in a limited war.³¹ Even selective release 'will probably require the prior approval of both national and NATO authorities' whilst delegating authority to a seagoing commander was 'most unlikely', although did not exclude the possibility of delegation to a shore-based theatre commander such as the Commander-in-Chief Western Fleet or Commander-in-Chief Fleet.³² For maritime patrol aircraft, selective release would only be possible in certain sea areas (presumably to avoid releasing a weapon in an area known to be patrolled by friendly submarines or by Soviet nuclear deterrent submarines – which would have almost certainly been seen as escalatory), and readers of the doctrine were warned that the time taken to ready the aircraft and receive shore-based approvals would mean that it could be difficult for an at-sea commander to request a timely attack by land-based aircraft.³³ This doctrine reflected British government policy that treated tactical nuclear weapons as deterrents to be sparingly used if at all, and contrasted with wider NATO maritime doctrine in the Standard Operating Procedures of the Supreme Allied Commander Atlantic ('SACLANT'), which probably reflected US doctrine more closely, and stated that 'the final decision whether to use a nuclear weapon ... against a submarine target ... is a function of the on-scene Commander'.³⁴ This created a situation in which national and NATO doctrine was different, and one can only assume that national doctrine would have had primacy over that of NATO in such circumstances.

In a study dated November 1975, eight different types of tactical nuclear use at sea were set out by the Naval Staff, four of which would be 'interpreted [by the Soviets] as a self-defence measure' and therefore hopefully non-escalatory. These were: use against anti-ship cruise missiles, and against aircraft, warships or submarines attacking NATO units at sea. Use against naval units 'involved in the land battle' could be interpreted by the Soviets as either defensive or offensive, whilst use against 'submarine and surface ships at large' would clearly be interpreted as offensive. Use of such weapons against a surface action group shadowing a NATO strike fleet would be interpreted as 'a pre-strategic strike measure' whilst use against Soviet strategic deterrent submarines would be regarded as a pre-emptive nuclear strike. Although the last two were unequivocally escalatory, this assessment hints at a possible shift of British doctrine closer to that of the US and NATO, but it is not known whether British maritime doctrine did indeed shift this way in the late 1970s.[35] In the early 1970s NATO's Nuclear Planning Group assessed the Alliance's tactical nuclear use and delegation policies, and having reviewed maritime scenarios in the Mediterranean and in SACLANT's area, agreed that these should remain as they were, given the much lower likelihood of escalation resulting from their use in most instances compared to land-based scenarios.[36]

Whether Flexible Response and a controlled war game-style ladder of escalation would have actually worked in a tense stand-off is another matter. US concepts of mutually-assured destruction and ladders of escalation had initially appeared alien to the Soviet leadership, but following the tacit acceptance of at least some of the US thinking in this regard with the signing of the SALT I and Anti-Ballistic Missile treaties, and the realisation that with the arrival of US Pershing missiles in Europe the USSR could no longer be regarded as a nuclear free 'sanctuary', the Soviet civilian and military leadership began to accept the possibility of a conventionally-fought war that might only escalate into nuclear conflict if one side was faced with expected defeat. They also moved towards a realisation that nuclear weapons were more of a political tool than a war-winning capability. In the later years of the Cold War, Soviet nuclear planners assumed that the fractious capitalist West would take four to five days to agree to a nuclear strike, and as a result planning for the land campaign worked on the assumption of a rapid advance across Western Europe to take as much territory as possible before a possible Western decision on nuclear release.[37] The evidence with respect to fighting at sea is much sparser but does show that, in the case of tactical nuclear depth charges for Soviet maritime patrol aircraft at least, there was clearly no delegation of release authority to tactical commanders. The weapons themselves could only be armed using secret codes received directly from the Soviet General Staff, and the Soviet naval air arm was never even allowed to conduct full-scale nuclear exercises beyond general mission preparation.[38] It is not known whether permissions for use were delegated anywhere else in the Soviet Navy, but it is a supreme irony that the one domain where the Ministry of Defence and NATO were willing to countenance tactical nuclear use, appears to have been also where Soviet release control was so tightly held.

The US Navy and the Shift to Sea Control

With the Royal Navy shifting its centre of gravity back to operational areas in the Eastern Atlantic and Mediterranean, NATO and the policies and strategy of the alliance's largest and most important member, the United States, became increasingly important. A higher proportion of Royal Navy warships would be operating under the ultimate command of either NATO maritime commanders or the Royal Navy's CINCFLEET, who also held two NATO commands himself (CINCEASTLANT and CINCCHAN), to a degree that had not been the case since the early years of the Alliance. The prime purpose of NATO was to enable the huge military and economic power of the United States to support and help defend Western European states against the Warsaw Pact. As a result, how the US Navy saw its role, interacted with NATO and developed its strategy was suddenly much more important to the Royal Navy. During the late 1960s, the US Navy had focussed operationally on power-projection carrier operations, largely in the war in Vietnam. With respect to the Warsaw Pact threat, it had largely assumed that US and NATO naval preponderance over a Soviet navy that was largely confined to its local waters would mean that in a conflict, control of the seas would be easily obtained to allow power-projection operations against the Soviet flanks.[39] As has been seen, from 1966 and 1967 onwards this assumption no longer reflected the reality of a growing Soviet submarine and surface fleet which regularly operated in the eastern Mediterranean, Pacific and Indian Oceans and was developing anchorages and bases off Egypt, Syria, Somalia and Yemen.[40] The new generation of Soviet nuclear-powered ballistic missile submarines, armed with more effective strategic nuclear missiles, was also adding to a nuclear arsenal that appeared to match that of NATO.

For the new US Chief of Naval Operations (CNO), Admiral Elmo Zumwalt, this meant that the US Navy would have to adjust both its strategy and the type of warships it operated and procured. Zumwalt, a charismatic surface navy officer with considerable Washington experience who had followed a long line of naval aviators as CNO, had to fight multiple battles within the Navy to advance his agenda, which also included significant personnel and disciplinary reforms.[41] With respect to strategy, Zumwalt was partly successful in re-orientating the US Navy towards fighting for 'sea control' primarily against Soviet submarines but also surface action groups (or 'SAGs').[42]

Zumwalt believed that the Soviet Navy was now strong enough to undertake a seaborne campaign to cut off US oil supplies from the Persian Gulf, and would also have a good chance of preventing the effective re-supply of Europe from North America during a period of high tension in Europe.[43] The idea that a conflict at sea could occur as a possible prelude to a land conflict, rather than simultaneously, began to be treated seriously within naval planning circles.[44] This then created a supposed inconsistency between SACEUR and SACLANT war plans: the former presuming a campaign of a few days or possibly a few weeks, the latter assuming a few months. This apparent contradiction confused and disturbed both Lord Carrington, the Defence Secretary between 1970 and 1974, and Sir John Nott who held the same role seven years later.[45] The temptation was to assume that these major NATO commanders were at cross-purposes, but they were in fact describing two different conceptions of conflict with the Warsaw Pact. SACEUR's 'war' would start when the first armed clashes occurred across the inner German border between NATO and Warsaw Pact forces, whilst SACLANT's 'war' began with a period of tense stand-off and confrontation at sea that might last weeks or even a month or more before the armed conflict spread to land forces. The confrontation might take the form of a Soviet attempt to strangle NATO ocean re-supply logistics before they launched a land attack. Another scenario was a prolonged stand-off at sea that might gradually escalate into what Zumwalt's office called a maritime 'guerrilla war' rather than a full conflict, which could then escalate into a full war at sea and then a war on land.[46] The 1962 Cuban Missile Crisis provided an example of this second type of confrontation, and this would be complemented in the 1973 by stand-off between US and Soviet naval forces in the Mediterranean during the Yom Kippur war, which is described in Chapter 9. In the case of Lord Carrington's concerns, the difference in timescales was explained to him by Admiral Hill-Norton, but with Nott the outcome was somewhat different, as will be seen in Chapter 13.[47]

With the shift to fighting for sea control, Zumwalt also planned to re-purpose major units such as the carrier groups for both sea-control and strike operations, whilst building large numbers of cheaper warships, alongside higher value units such as nuclear carriers, nuclear submarines and larger destroyers, to provide the numbers necessary to counter the Soviets at sea as the many wartime generation destroyers were decommissioned. Zumwalt had mixed success in this regard: the *Perry* class utility frigates were procured in numbers but his attempts to build small VSTOL carriers ('Sea Control Ships') failed and his plans for conventionally-powered Aegis air defence ships rather than more expensive nuclear-powered variants only came to fruition after he had left his post.[48] Most importantly for the Royal Navy was that Zumwalt's strategic changes helped to re-focus NATO operations and exercises back towards sea control after more than a decade of relative neglect, although the beginnings of an increased US interest in anti-submarine warfare in the Atlantic, and partnering with the Royal Navy in this area, had pre-dated Zumwalt's tenure as CNO by nearly two years.[49] It could be argued that the intellectual and doctrinal shift required by the Royal Navy was not as significant as that for the US Navy as the Royal Navy had continued to maintain significant anti-submarine expertise, but both faced the fundamental problem that asserting sea control against an enemy equipped with nuclear-powered submarines was extremely difficult. In the early 1970s there were serious problems with both detection and attack that needed to be resolved before there could be confidence that NATO could in fact ensure sea control in a conflict with the Warsaw Pact.

Anti-Submarine Warfare

The underwater environment makes it much more difficult to detect an object in the sea than in the air or on the sea's surface. Radio waves, including those at radar frequency, cannot penetrate water effectively, and visual detection is very occasionally possible at a shallow depth in the clearest of waters – for example in parts of the Mediterranean when the sea is at its calmest – but only when almost directly above the object. As a result, in practical terms detection is only effective through the use of sound waves: either by the transmission of sound outwards and the receiving and processing of reflected sound after it has bounced off a submarine – active sonar – or by the detection of involuntary sounds made by a submarine (its propulsion, generators and other mechanical systems) through sensitive listening devices – passive sonar. However, the nature of the sea adds enormous complications to what might initially seem to be a straightforward process.

The open sea generally consists of three 'layers' distinguished by significant differences in temperature, density and salinity, each of which can have an impact on how sound waves move in the sea, and therefore impinge heavily upon the effectiveness of sonars. The top layer is known as either the surface layer or the isotherm and consists of only 2 per cent of the ocean's water. Here, temperature, salinity and density stay relatively similar throughout this layer as the actions of waves and currents mix and churn this part of the sea. The surface layer usually extends to around 150m below the surface but this can vary significantly depending on local conditions, in some places reaching as deep as a 1,000m or very rarely there might be no surface layer at all. The next layer down is generally known as the thermocline and makes up around 18 per cent of the ocean's water. This layer, which can be around 800–900m in depth, forms a temperature barrier between the surface layer and the deep layer below it: there is little mix from the currents above, and instead the temperature of the water falls increasingly rapidly as the depth increases. With the temperature fall comes an increasingly steep rise in density and salinity. The decrease in temperature then causes significant problems for sound propagation: temperature reductions slow the speed of sound waves whilst also causing a sharp downward refraction which in turn causes a significant drop in the effective range of standard sonars, in some cases reducing their range by over 80 per cent.[50] The third, deep, layer generally begins at around 1,000m depth, but this can vary significantly, and here the temperature has settled at a mere 3 degrees Celsius, a relatively stable salinity and a more gently increasing density. In this zone, as the depth increases so does the speed of sound waves as a result of the slowly increasing density.[51]

When all submarines were diesel-electric, had limiting diving depths and had to surface regularly to re-charge batteries, the thermocline boundary was of little importance. But with deeper-diving long-endurance nuclear-powered submarines, experienced commanders could make sustained use of the thermocline – dipping within it to hide their submarine from detection for long periods of time and rising into the surface layer to confirm detections and prosecute attacks. The nature of the sea also causes additional problems in detection: increased sea states and rain degrades the effectiveness of sonars as background sea noise increases and the motions of the sonar operating vessel creates further noise and distraction.[52] A relatively shallow surface layer can reduce sonar range as sound waves repeatedly bounce off the sea's surface and the thermocline barrier and dissipate. The boundaries between different currents in the surface layer, and in shallow waters near an estuary, can also create vertical 'walls' in the sea that can dissipate or refract sound waves.[53] The cooling and heating of the water in night and day, can also have an effect on sonars operating near the surface of the water, creating short-lived mini-thermoclines that can degrade sonar effectiveness, often causing what is known as an 'afternoon effect' in calm conditions.[54] Marine life can also increase background noise or produce false sonar targets.[55]

Some of the effects of the sea environment can also be positive for detection: the sea bottom can create additional background noise and cause problems, particularly in shallow waters, but there was much research in the 1960s and 1970s into the bouncing of sound waves off the sea bed in order to increase their range to at least 20 nautical miles.[56] The Doppler Effect, the change in frequency as sound sources move, is another factor that could be used, particularly in passive detection.[57] Also, in the deep layer as the density increases with depth, sound speed increases and refraction reduces, so sound waves can then begin to refract upwards to the surface. In the North Atlantic, the distance between the sonar source and its re-emergence into the surface layer and upper thermocline – known as the convergence zone – is approximately 30 nautical miles, creating an 'annulus' or area of detection of around 3 to 5 nautical miles.⁵⁸ Again, research was being undertaken into this approach of increasing detection ranges with ship-based sonar. Finally, at a certain level of the ocean's deep layer, generally between 600m and 1,200m deep, sound can travel for more than a thousand miles trapped within a 'deep sound channel' which tends to repeatedly refract sound back into this channel, thus forcing it to travel horizontally for enormous distances rather than dissipate downwards or upwards.⁵⁹ This phenomenon, discovered in the 1940s, has proved extremely important in the development of fixed seabed arrays. In summary therefore, the underwater oceanic environment is extremely complex, with a host of variables that can decrease the ability to detect nuclear-powered submarines, with only a few mitigating factors and opportunities that were only just beginning to be exploited in the late 1960s and early 1970s. At this time most of the Royal Navy's anti-submarine forces were still more suited to the simpler and more straightforward world before the emergence of the nuclear-powered submarine, which could stay submerged for weeks or months and make the most of the sea's underwater properties to evade detection.

Anti-Submarine Frigates
In the late 1960s the core of the Royal Navy's standing anti-submarine force included the anti-submarine training squadron at Londonderry and the frigates of the Fishery Protection Squadron, but with the arrival of the second generation of Soviet nuclear submarines these frigates, armed with short and medium-range hull sonars and mortars, were hopelessly outmatched. They would have had trouble detecting a submarine at a distance at which the latter would be likely to fire its torpedoes (let alone fire missiles submerged), and then struggle to approach close enough to engage it with mortars that had a maximum range of only 1000 yards. In Exercise Lime Jug, held in November 1970 in the eastern Mediterranean, all but one of eight attacks on conventional submarines with anti-submarine mortars was judged to have been a 'miss', and even the single hit was assessed to have been achieved 'more by luck than judgement'.⁶⁰ With this poor performance against a conventional boat it is unsurprising that mortars were considered of little or no use against nuclear boats. Detections by hull sonars on board ships were similarly poor: during the exercise there were considered to have been twenty opportunities for the seven frigates and destroyers involved to detect submarines, but only five of these resulted in detections and two of these were in unusual circumstances.⁶¹ When the latest 'Charlie' class cruise missile submarine variant could launch its anti-ship missiles from 65 nautical miles distance, this was clearly inadequate.⁶² This was confirmed by the exercise in which seven 'Charlie' class missile launches were simulated, but only one was detected before the boats theoretically launched their missiles.⁶³ Clearly, new technologies were necessary to counter the modern Soviet submarine.

Variable-Depth Sonars and Anti-Submarine Helicopters

In the 1950s and early 1960s a series of new technologies had been developed in order to counter the fastest conventional submarines, and then the first Soviet nuclear submarines. The Canadian variable-depth sonar (VDS) SQS-504, designated the Type 199 in Royal Navy service, was purchased and fitted to ten *Leander* class frigates and two Type 81 frigates in the 1960s.[64] At least one senior flag officer in the late 1950s argued, rather optimistically, that this type of sonar would be as capable or better than similar sonars fitted on nuclear submarines.[65] The Type 199 sonar was lowered from the stern of the carrying ship and could reach a depth to take it below the surface layer and into the upper thermocline. However, the VDS was not wholly successful in Royal Navy service, reputedly because it had difficulties detecting submarines in the complex oceanographic environment of the Eastern Atlantic, and it was subsequently removed from many of the ships that had carried it from the mid-1970s onwards.[66] VDS was not at that stage the leap forward for which anti-submarine specialists had been hoping.

The second new technology was the torpedo-carrying helicopter. From the early 1960s new frigates entering the fleet had been equipped with hangars, flight decks and facilities for operating small Wasp helicopters, but these were severely limited in their capabilities. They carried no sonar and so were completely dependent on targeting information from their parent ships, and could only stay aloft for 30 minutes when carrying two torpedoes.[67] The Wasp went some way towards dealing with the issue of having to close with an enemy submarine at speed, but did not do anything to resolve the detection problem and the limited range and effectiveness of ship-based sonars. Large helicopters with both dipping sonars (somewhat like smaller versions of the VDS) and torpedoes were much more capable aircraft. They had been flown from aircraft carriers since the early 1950s, but three such helicopters would be needed on a carrier to keep one aloft and on station during operations, and carriers tended to operate only six or seven, and two such helicopters would not be enough to operate a full screen. As the aircraft carriers were decommissioning – *Hermes* disappeared into dockyard hands in 1970 for conversion to a commando carrier, and *Eagle* was decommissioned in 1972 – the loss of their helicopters was partly compensated by the conversion of two older cruisers, *Tiger* and *Blake*, to helicopter carriers at great expense. They could operate only four each, and single large helicopter on each of the eight 'County' class destroyers were only a minor supplement. Therefore, in a time of tension in the early 1970s, the Royal Navy could probably muster a task group with one carrier, one helicopter cruiser and two, possibly three 'County' class destroyers, providing a total of ten to fourteen large helicopters – enough to provide a screen of approximately four for that task group, but with none left over for any other naval forces including any convoys.[68] There were just not enough large anti-submarine helicopters and nor were there the ships from which to fly them.

The arrival of the Sea King helicopter, a modified version of the US SH-3D helicopter with Rolls-Royce Gnome engines constructed at Westland Helicopters in Somerset, into service in 1970 gave the Navy a capable machine that went some way to countering the lack of airframes. Vice Admiral Fell, the Flag Officer Carriers and Amphibious Shipping, described them as a 'tremendous step forward in the field of ASW' in comparison to the Wessex Mark 3 that they replaced.[69] The Sea King could undertake flying sorties for up to four hours armed with two torpedoes, more than four times that of the preceding Wessex Mk 3, thus allowing for much greater coverage and time on station.[70] It also had much improved serviceability and availability, although its systems were essentially still that of the Wessex Mk 3: the Type 195 dipping sonar, the Ecko light radar and the Automated Flight Control System which allowed the helicopter to operate at night independently. The sonar had a nominal maximum range of 3.5 nautical miles but in most circumstances it would have been much less than this.[71] The Sea King was an important step forward, but there were still too few of them (and platforms from them to fly from), the avionics would soon need updating and it could be argued that the dipping sonar did not yet provide the range or effectiveness for a good enough screen to protect major surface ships. This was confirmed by an Admiralty Underwater Weapons Establishment analysis of 1966 which argued that anywhere between six and twelve Sea King helicopters would be needed to provide an effective all-round screen for a task group. This was a somewhat pessimistic assessment that assumed the absence of anti-submarine frigates, but given the limitations of such ships and the ineffectiveness of VDS in the eastern Atlantic, a significant number of Sea Kings would be needed, particularly to detect submarines below the surface layer.[72] The capability of the dipping-sonar helicopter in comparison to the traditional anti-submarine frigate with its hull sonar, mortars and light helicopter, was confirmed in Exercise Lime Jug 70, the final assessment stating that 'the advanced helicopter screen was more effective than the closer surface escorts against the long-range torpedo firing submarine attacking the main body [of the task group].'[73] However, this success was relative, and it would not be until the availability of sonobuoys in the late 1970s for anti-submarine helicopter use that the Sea King could begin to become a truly effective nuclear submarine hunter.

Anti-Submarine Missiles
In the mid-1960s the limited Wasp helicopter was considered only an interim anti-submarine capability prior to the development of a quick-reaction anti-

submarine missile system. In March 1965, the Australian Ikara system was selected and modified for Royal Navy use, most significantly by integrating it into a variant of the ADAWS tactical command system. There was much optimism that Ikara would finally provide surface ships with an edge over the nuclear submarine. Ikara could react quicker than the Wasp and could operate in nearly all weathers and more sea states, an important advantage when operating in the North Atlantic and the northern North Sea. The Ikara missile carried a US Mark 44 or 46 torpedo underneath it, and once fired, would drop the torpedo into the sea at a selected position using data from the firing ship. Six systems had been purchased from Australia and it had been planned to fit them in the Type 82 class of destroyers but as has been seen, this class, with the exception of the lead vessel, was cancelled, leaving five unallocated systems.[74] Ikara, as modified for Royal Navy service, had a significant impact on a ship when installed. The launcher was fitted within a large circular drum covered by a retractable awning to protect it from the elements, and the missile needed considerable below-decks space to allow it to be readied for firing. Fitting an ADAWS-capable operations room also had a major impact on the ship below-decks. It had originally been proposed to procure a new warship type, an anti-submarine destroyer dubbed the Type 17, as the main platform for Ikara, but as was seen in Chapter 3, getting a Sea Dart firing ship (the Type 42) and a cheap frigate to sea (the Type 21) was a greater priority and there was limited ship design capacity within the Ship Department, so the conversion of existing warships was considered instead.[75] The *Leander* class – which would total twenty-six ships in service when the last vessel commissioned in 1973 – was the obvious candidate: its armament mix of mortar, medium gun, Wasp helicopter and Sea Cat missile system already looking obsolescent at the start of the 1970s. The concept of an Ikara-fitted *Leander* had been considered and ultimately rejected back in 1963, but the situation was now different and an imperfect solution was all that was possible in the timescales required.[76] Modifying the last few ships under construction was the obvious answer, but the delay to construction times would mean that the number of active frigates in the fleet would dip as older vessels retired whilst the *Leander* production slowed down to shift to the Ikara design. This was deemed to be too great a risk to the fulfilment of current operations and commitments, so instead it was decided to add Ikara when the oldest *Leander*s went through their mid-life refits despite costing twice as much as fitting to new *Leander*s.[77] In the event, these mid-life refits took much longer than anticipated and the ordering of the last *Leander*s was slowed in any case, so any operational benefit must have been marginal, but the decision had been made, and of the oldest ten *Leander*s eight would receive the Ikara system completing their refits between 1972 and 1978 (the agreement for the purchase of a further three Ikara systems had been made by March 1968).

The decision also stored up another problem: as these older ships would be nearing the end of their operational lives after only ten years with Ikara when it would be expected that the system had another ten years of life, a difficult decision would have to made in the early 1980s about either prematurely withdrawing Ikara or building a new class of ships with the system, despite that system having less than a decade's life left in it. For the planners of the late 1960s and early 1970s that was far in the future, but it was also clear that Ikara did not solve the detection problem, in fact it was almost too good for the sonars then available. With a range of 10 nautical miles, it outranged hull-mounted sonars in all but the most favourable of environments. A sophisticated missile system, controlled from a state-of-the-art operations room, would be of little use if its target could not be detected until it was too late. It could be argued that Ikara could be used against submarines detected by dipping-sonar helicopters, but such helicopters were armed with their own torpedoes and would probably be closer to the target. This problem of weapon system 'mismatch' with its sensors – and the general awareness that since the advent of the nuclear submarine, the surface ship had been at a significant disadvantage in anti-submarine warfare – led to investigations into long-range sonars that could 'bounce' or reflect their sound waves off the sea bed, and hydrophones ('passive sonars') trailed from submarines or ships that began from the late 1960s onwards. These further innovations are discussed in later chapters.

Maritime Patrol Aircraft

Another platform for anti-submarine warfare was the land-based maritime patrol aircraft. As has been seen, these were operated by the RAF, and in the late 1960s consisted of the obsolescent Shackleton Mk 3, armed with radar, sonobuoys, magnetic anomaly detectors, torpedoes and depth charges. These capabilities were sufficient to deal with conventional submarines, but the Shackleton's age, limited range and speed, and its limited analysis and processing power, meant that was not effective enough against the Soviet navy's nuclear boats. The successor Nimrod began to enter service in 1970. It was the world's first jet-engine maritime patrol aircraft which gave the aircraft considerable range, and when flown economically on two engines whilst on patrol, it could stay aloft for up to 24 hours.[78] Like the anti-submarine helicopter, to maintain a permanent patrol on station for a sustained period, two or even three further aircraft were needed, whilst to reach far into the mid-Atlantic and up to the Denmark Strait, the most northerly passage of the GIUK gap, the aircraft needed to be air-refuelled. Despite these limitations the Nimrod MR1 had the great advantage of speed and therefore reach. However, in order to save costs and have a Shackleton replacement in service as quickly as possible, the Nimrod was initially fitted partly with equipment inherited from its predecessor.[79]

The most powerful of the Nimrod's capabilities was the Jezebel low-frequency passive sonobuoy that exploited the sound propagation properties of the deep sea layer. A sonobuoy would be dropped from an aircraft; when it hit the water it would unreel a passive or active sonar from its base and an antenna from its top. Sound detections are then relayed back to the aircraft for analysis. The advantage of sonobuoys over dipping sonars was that 'patterns' of multiple such devices could be dropped which allow for the effective and rapid triangulation of the position of a target. Jezebel needed seven minutes from launch before reliable signatures could be detected and in the best conditions a bearing could be found on the noisiest targets (elderly conventional submarines) up to 100 nautical miles away, but with the newest and quietest submarines of the early 1970s, this shrank to a 'few tens of [nautical] miles'.[80] Jezebel had a number of strengths; for example it could operate in two modes (the first for detection and the second for localisation) but it experienced problems detecting submarines operating at low speeds and often had difficulty detecting submarines when surface ships were in the vicinity as they could easily 'drown out' signals from an underwater target.[81] Analogue acoustic processors on the aircraft, which had inherited from the Shackleton, could correlate detections from multiple buoys but in 1970 this could take up to 30 minutes to provide a fix, and the system had difficulties combining signals from different types of buoys.[82] Both the Nimrod MR1 and the Shackleton also carried the large Mk 1C active/passive sonobuoys which were optimised for localising a submarine's position sufficiently well so that a torpedo could be fired. Their maximum active range was 3,000 yards and 8,000 yards in passive mode. A total of fifteen to twenty of these 5ft-high cylindrical tubes were carried on the Shackleton and probably a similar number on the MR1 Nimrod, although the version used by the latter had improved serviceability.[83] By the early 1970s, the Mk 1C was showing its age: the Air Staff had stated that due to its low data rate and limited range it 'severely limits the Nimrod attack capability against targets other than obsolete, noisy, slow-moving submarines'.[84] The Nimrod also carried a magnetic anomaly detector, a system developed during the Second World War that could detect submarines, and other large metal underwater objects, from the air, albeit at a very short-range. The aircraft were also fitted with torpedoes, depth charges and could carry nuclear depth bombs.[85] The Nimrod aircraft itself provided much-increased range and comfort for its crews, but the RAF would have to wait until the arrival of the MR2 in the early 1980s, which would include digital acoustic processors, improved sonobuoys and more effective radars, before it could begin to fulfil its real potential.

Submarines in the Anti-Submarine Role

Probably the most effective anti-submarine capability that the Navy possessed was the nuclear submarine itself. The range of its sonars were much greater than that of surface vessels or sonobuoys, it could easily operate below the isotherm, and it could track and shadow Soviet submarines for days, weeks and even months. Nuclear submarines were ideal vessels for tracking and holding at risk Soviet nuclear submarines that carried strategic ballistic missiles which, until the advent of the R-29 ballistic missile on the Soviet 'Delta I' class in 1973, had to venture out into the mid-Atlantic in order to keep in range of the United States with their R-27 missiles. The type of submarine that carried the R-27, the 'Yankee' class, were also notoriously noisy and therefore relatively straightforward to detect and track.[86] Nuclear submarines were similarly effective at tracking and shadowing hunter-killer or cruise missile boats over long periods of time. However, they were ill-suited to protecting surface vessels such as convoys or major task groups. Concerted attempts were made to attach nuclear submarines to surface task groups – and to this end, nuclear-powered hunter-killer submarines were formally named 'fleet submarines' throughout the 1970s – but communications could be difficult and the risk of the submarine succumbing to an attack by friendly surface forces always seemed high. Most importantly, making use of a nuclear submarine's long-range active bow sonar which could detect some enemy submarines out to over 40 nautical miles also advertised the existence of not only the boat but the task group it was escorting, and skilled submarine commanders could learn to work their way around the escorting submarine and attack the surface group from the flanks or rear.[87] In any case submarine commanders disliked being 'tethered' to surface task groups which severely limited their freedom for manoeuvre and made them more predictable and detectable targets. In addition, nuclear submarines worked best within an underwater network, where SOSUS seabed hydrophones – which are discussed below – or maritime patrol aircraft cued in a target for the nuclear submarine to trail. Without such support the North Atlantic ocean was far too large a space for a few dozen NATO submarines to locate a similar number of Soviet submarines. Nuclear submarines were therefore excellent submarine hunters but they were most effective when operating independently within the 'underwater network': they were not an answer to the surface fleet's anti-submarine problem – beyond the strategic role of detecting and marking Soviet ballistic missile boats – at least unless NATO was willing to cease using high-value surface ships in contested waters completely and concede the surface of the Norwegian Sea, North Sea and Eastern Mediterranean to the Soviets in times of high tension or war. As will be seen, by the late 1970s this was seriously being considered as an option given the increase in the combined threat from both Soviet underwater and air capabilities.

Seabed Hydrophones

By the 1960s the United States had established in the Western Atlantic a network of seabed hydrophones, named the Sound Surveillance System ('SOSUS'), stretching from Iceland to Bermuda. Placed sufficiently deeply below the thermocline in the 'deep sound channel' described above, these hydrophones were specifically adapted to listening for very low frequency sound waves. Low-frequency sound travels much further than higher frequencies, and if analysed in detail the sound of different types of machinery, and even individual pieces of machinery, could be discerned, opening up the possibility of identifying not only a particular class of submarine but also each individual submarine's own unique machinery-sound characteristics.[88] The capture and analysis of low frequency sound waves in the deep sound channel could enable extremely long-range detection of submarines, although with the drawback that only a bearing could be provided – not the exact range. Triangulation with multiple hydrophones could isolate a position down to an area of between 750 and 3,000 square nautical miles: this was still a very large area, but it would at least provide a search area for an aircraft, ship or submarine and it could also show where there were no submarines.[89] The US network in 1967 consisted of thirteen base stations each of which controlled a low-frequency array of between forty and forty-eight hydrophones, with a potential detection range of a few hundred nautical miles or more, depending on sea conditions. Each base station was connected by secure land communication to an evaluation centre at Norfolk, Virginia, co-located with the US Naval Commander in the Western Atlantic at which a shipping plot of the whole Western Atlantic was kept and updated, information co-ordinated with other information sources.[90] Coverage of the Western Atlantic was good, but the hydrophones could not reach into the Eastern Atlantic due to the mid-Atlantic ridge, which created a barrier to the ocean beyond. It was plausible to lay cables across the mid-Atlantic ridge back to the US but the cost would be much more than making use of new base stations in Europe.[91] Not only did the US Navy wish to extend SOSUS into the Eastern Atlantic it was also planning to upgrade the system in the next few years with longer and deeper hydrophone cables with greater carrying capacity.[92]

The building of a base station in the United Kingdom made economic sense for the United States: it would be a cheaper alternative to dozens or more cross-Atlantic cables. From the British perspective involvement in, and direct access to, SOSUS would provide much more direct information on Soviet submarine positions. It could also provide opportunities for the integration with the communication systems of new Nimrod maritime patrol aircraft, and it could all be done at a fraction of the cost of 'going it alone' with a UK-developed system. The total cost of the UK SOSUS base station and its cables, arrays and hydrophones was $67 million with $200,000 annual running costs excluding pay for the estimate of 264 personnel, although the split of costs between the UK and USA had not yet been decided at that stage.[93] Formal discussions and negotiations began in 1968, surveying the sites for the cables and arrays began in 1971 and RAF Brawdy in Pembrokeshire was chosen as the base station site.[94] The United States also requested 'joint sector manning' – a mix of British and US personnel – at Brawdy, along the lines of Canadian involvement in the base station on their territory.[95] The SOSUS system also began to be integrated into a much larger and more capable operational information and intelligence-gathering system called the Ocean Surveillance Information System, which integrated SOSUS information with submarine, ship and maritime patrol aircraft sensor information as well as satellite information.[96] Military communication satellites would then enable the connection of all these together to create a distributed information analysis system below and above the surface of the seas and oceans worldwide. This was particularly important as the Soviet Navy began to operate regularly in the mid-Atlantic, Caribbean, Pacific and Indian Ocean in the 1970s. The Royal Navy, with its base station at Brawdy, was therefore benefiting from being part of this new worldwide system, by the 1970s a US Fleet Ocean Surveillance Information Centre was established in the US Embassy in Grosvenor Square in London.[97] The creation in 1974–5 of the Royal Navy's submarine command and control organisation at Northwood, known as CTF 311, was enabled by the channelling of the information coming from SOSUS, and presumably other elements of OSIS, to create a combined picture of the underwater operating environment which could be more easily co-ordinated with the United States.[98]

With the increased focus on the Soviet naval threat and on securing sea control in the Eastern Atlantic, anti-submarine warfare inevitably became the major focus of the Royal Navy's energies as most of its forces shifted away from operations East of Suez. Despite this, the battle against the submarine continued to appear loaded in favour of the nuclear submarine and against the surface ship throughout the late 1960s and 1970s.

Oceanographic Research and Hydrography
With the arrival of the nuclear-powered submarine it quickly became clear how little was known about the deep sea, including its thermal layers which had a significant impact on sonar effectiveness and range, seawater salinity, the effects of underwater currents and the nature of the seabed. When submarines stayed under the surface for weeks and months, understanding these factors became especially important as they would become not only the geography they navigated but also the medium through which they sailed. In addition, they played a crucial role in preventing detection or helping the detection

of other submarines.⁹⁹ Between 1964 and 1967 a series of reforms had been put in place that increased the importance of oceanography in the Navy, its associated research establishments and the wider scientific community in the United Kingdom. The Royal Naval Weather Service and the Hydrographer's Department were merged in 1965, with the former head of the first becoming a director within the second, responsible for both meteorology and oceanography.[100] This was a reflection of the close links between the scientific study of the weather and of the oceans, and also signalled a significant change for the Royal Navy's hydrographers as the marine surveying of the coastline and seabed, was now accompanied – increasingly on a level footing – with the study of the sea itself. The new directorate produced 'underwater handbooks' and 'oceanographic atlases' setting out the oceanography of a particular sea area including temperature, density, currents and the nature of the seabed, whilst also building up a forecasting capability so that changes in these factors, which would have an impact on sonar performance, could begin to be predicted. It also undertook a range of work to support the development and testing of sonars and helped support the Polaris programme.[101]

All of this new and expanded work was supervised by an Admiralty Board Sub-Committee on Oceanography, specifically tasked with expanding oceanographic research and increasing the number of staff involved in this work.[102] Once the new arrangements had bedded in, an internal educational effort was launched across the Navy and expertise built up at the Admiralty Research Laboratory and other research establishments. Civil research into oceanography was also reformed as part of the government's creation of research councils for funding and directing university research, with representatives of the Hydrographer's Department on the relevant committee of the new Natural Environment Research Council, thus allowing for the more effective promotion of civil research into areas of interest to the Royal Navy.[103] This expansion of oceanographic research and co-ordination was not undertaken in a vacuum: the SACLANT ASW Research Centre at La Spezia in Italy had been established in the late 1950s, and undertook its own research with its own vessels and a multi-national team of scientists, whilst co-ordinating its work with national naval bodies. The United States' effort in oceanography was the best funded and most capable internationally, focussed on Wood's Hole Oceanographic Institution in Massachusetts, guided and partly funded by the US government's Interagency Committee on Oceanography.[104]

The Royal Navy's fleet of survey ships was also renewed during this period of growing interest in oceanography, the hydrographers receiving three modern vessels of the *Hecla* class equipped with helicopters and the latest surveying and oceanographic sonars and instruments. These were supplemented a few years later by four new coastal survey vessels of the *Bulldog* class, and then in

1974 by a modified *Hecla* class vessel, HMS *Herald*. The Admiralty Cable Layers *St Margaret's* and *Bullfinch* were increasingly used for sonar trials and supporting oceanographic research, whilst commercial cable layers were also sometimes chartered for such work.[105]

* * *

The early 1970s was a period of significant shifts in Cold War naval strategy – where the assumption of NATO sea control in the open oceans could no longer be taken for granted, and of important decisions in the modernisation of the nuclear deterrent. The huge challenges of anti-submarine warfare in the age of the nuclear submarine were also beginning to be tackled, but it was also clear that these boats still held a significant advantage over surface vessels. Innovations in detection and attack were promising but not yet delivering the transformative new capabilities that would diminish the vulnerability of surface ships to underwater attack. For the Royal Navy, much would depend upon the new warship types and weapon systems that would be entering service in the early 1970s. Would they be capable enough, and would there be enough of them, to enable the Navy to complete its tasks in peace, tension and war?

7

Cost Control

Although matters of nuclear policy had taken up a significant portion of the First Sea Lord's time in the early 1970s, more immediate issues regarding the control of naval expenditure took up much of the rest. During the late 1960s, warship construction had largely consisted of a drumbeat of modified versions of proven designs such as the *Leander* class frigates, 'County' class destroyers and follow-on nuclear-powered submarines. In the early 1970s, not only were a range of new designs under construction, such as the Type 21 frigate, Type 82 and Type 42 destroyers and *Swiftsure* class submarines, but a further tranche of new designs needed to be approved and construction begun: the new cruiser, the Type 22 frigate and the next generation of mine-warfare vessels. When the inevitable difficulties of shepherding these new and complex designs through the design and construction process were combined with major changes in defence policy without providing sufficient funding, ailing shipyards, poor industrial relations, cost underestimates and finally an oil crisis and high inflation, it is not surprising that it soon became clear that a defence review would be inevitable. The period of Pollock's leadership has been described as an 'Indian Summer' for the Royal Navy, but with respect to warship procurement and the Navy's budget this was definitely not the case: it was a slow and painful slide into unaffordability which little, it seemed, could to be done to prevent.[1]

The Navy and the Defence Budget

Within the Ministry of Defence there were two periods of budget-setting and negotiation each year. Just after the start of the new financial year in April, each part of the Ministry drew up their planned Long Term Costings for the next decade starting with the next financial year. This was a process focussed on the short, medium and long-term and was supported by a series of Long

Term Costings Assumptions based upon the expected procurement and personnel requirements.[2] What was termed 'production and development' took up approximately two-thirds of the Navy Department's budget, the rest primarily being on personnel and pay, for which there was much less flexibility to make major changes. Once the Long Term Costings had been settled, about four or five months before the end of the financial year, negotiations would begin on the planned budget, known as the 'Estimates' for the next financial year. The figure agreed in the Long Term Costings would provide a starting point but policy changes, new cost calculations and inflation would all have had their impact, whilst the Treasury might have since decided to rein in or reduce spending. The 'sketch' or preliminary Estimates would also be subjected to the insertion of 'shadow cuts' to help ensure that spending stayed within the budget during the year by instituting reductions based on an estimate of the likely increases in costs, and of 'wedges' which instituted small 1 per cent or 2 per cent reductions in many areas to encourage efficiency and swallow possible unexpected underspends. The Navy Department would then submit sketch Estimates to the centre with much 'scrutiny' and further assessment undertaken until a final figure was agreed. Once the Estimates for each part of the Ministry had been agreed, then the full Defence Estimates would be published and put before Parliament for votes to authorise the necessary funds for the coming year. Sometimes supplementary Estimates would be voted on by Parliament as a result of particular policy or operational developments. The most significant change in this period to this approach to budget setting and approval was the institution of new integrated 'Votes' in the published Defence Estimates for 1970–1, which combined the spending categories of the three services making it difficult to split out, for outsiders, how much each service would be spending. The new vote structure also formalised the move of some areas which had been recently centralised, such as contracts, victualling and finance away from the Navy Department and into the centre.[3] In addition, in 1971 the creation of Defence-wide Procurement Executive which incorporated the Navy Department's Ship and Weapons Departments, resulted in the Controller of the Navy now 'double-hatting' as a member of the Admiralty Board and as the most senior naval representative on the Procurement Executive's own board. This had the effect of nominally transferring the procurement and research and development budget out of the Navy Department from 1972–3 onwards, although in practice the Navy Department, as the 'customer' for the Procurement Executive's naval programmes, retained a significant portion of the responsibility for ensuring that the overall procurement programme was not overloaded.[4]

The last 18 months of Harold Wilson's Labour government of 1966–70 saw relatively small reductions in planned future spending coupled with efficiencies across Defence, with a cut of just over 1 per cent in the Navy's projected budget for 1970–1 being agreed in May 1969, but here the early stages of the future spiral in costs were beginning to become evident. There were cost rises in the development of the new Sea Wolf missile system – the successor to Sea Cat – and in the new Mark 31 lightweight anti-submarine torpedo which had been significant enough to force a reduction in research and development staff to compensate, spending on fissile materials for nuclear reactors had to be deferred, whilst the Mark 24 heavyweight torpedo project was stretched out and subjected an additional shadow cut, all to ensure that the development budget stayed within its agreed amounts. Revised unit costs of the Cruiser, Type 22 frigate and new mine countermeasures vessel saw all of these types increase in cost considerably, another warning signal for future years.[5] The Sketch Estimates negotiations for 1970–1 at the end of 1969 were largely uncontentious, with the Navy having to find only £2.5 million in reductions to meet its set budget target of £571 million at November 1969 prices. The full Ministry of Defence Estimates for 1970–1 stood at £2,206 million at 1969–70 prices.[6] These small reductions and adjustments were all eminently manageable and little different to the annual negotiations over the Estimates and costings that had occurred since the creation of the combined Ministry in 1964. From the following year, however, significant problems in cost-control began to emerge.

In the April 1970 Long Term Costings discussions, it was becoming apparent that a large bulge in procurement spending would be necessary in the mid-1970s. Would a significant increase in the Navy Department's budget be permitted by the Ministry during this period? A few on the Admiralty Board were sanguine: there had been a similar bulge in the mid-1960s when the nuclear deterrent and attack submarine programmes had begun. However, in that instance there had been cross-Defence agreement on the crucial importance and primacy of Polaris and the nuclear submarine programme; this time there was no such unquestioning agreement on affording a top priority to the frigates, destroyers and cruisers planned for the new surface fleet. Other, more cautious members pointed out that there would have to be sufficient design capacity in the Ship Department and shipbuilding capacity in the industry as well as buy-in from the centre for an uplift in naval spending: such a bump seemed 'questionable' to them. The more realistic scenario would be a 'smoothing' of the bump and the pushing of much of the programme back into the later 1970s.[7]

In June 1970, the Labour government was unexpectedly defeated in a general election, and a new Conservative administration entered office with Edward Heath as the Prime Minister, and Lord Peter Carrington as the new Defence Secretary. Lord Carrington was a former First Lord of the Admiralty (Navy Minister in charge of the Admiralty prior to the creation of the centralised Ministry of Defence) and was sympathetic to the Royal Navy and an advocate of a strong navy.[8] The new government issued a Supplementary Statement on Defence Policy in October 1970 announcing a range of new measures in defence. The Royal Navy would now continue to operate HMS *Ark Royal* as a fixed-wing aircraft carrier until the late 1970s, with the transition to relying on RAF air cover and support being more gradual. *Ark Royal* had been slated to be converted into a commando carrier after *Hermes* had emerged from her refit to convert her for the same purpose. With *Ark Royal* now continuing as a fixed-wing carrier for up to six years longer than originally planned, one of the two first-generation commando carriers, either *Albion* or *Bulwark*, would have to continue in service until at least 1976, the earliest date that a new-build replacement was envisaged to enter service. This also meant that three 'flat tops', with their significant personnel requirements, would remain in service rather than two. This was partly compensated for by the cancellation of the conversion of *Lion* to a helicopter cruiser like her sisters *Blake* and *Tiger*, but these changes – including the running-on of naval fixed-wing aviation for a number of additional years – meant additional costs which were not fully met by the rather meagre and delayed defence-budget increases announced in the Supplementary Statement. An announcement was also made confirming the purchase of the Exocet anti-ship guided missile system for the fleet, and the Statement also mentioned the aim of operating VSTOL aircraft from the planned cruisers if this could be made practicable.[9] Further changes to the Navy's capabilities were made but not publicly announced: plans to build a replacement commando carrier were postponed, the older *Albion* retained as the second commando carrier and *Bulwark* scrapped in 1974 (the decision on *Albion* and *Bulwark* was later swapped around, with *Albion* being scrapped early), the assault ships *Fearless* and *Intrepid* would have periods of reduced readiness, the first 'County' class destroyer, HMS *Hampshire*, would be retired in 1975, seven years earlier than would have been expected, and the fleet repair ship *Triumph* would be placed in reserve in 1973.[10] The Army was having some of the cuts that had been announced in 1968 and 1969 halted, the Territorial Army was being expanded, whilst the RAF had secured the government support for the British-French Jaguar ground attack aircraft and what would become the Tornado multi-role aircraft partnered with Germany and Italy. The Statement also confirmed that British forces would retain a worldwide role with contributions to the Five Powers Defence Arrangements with Malaysia and Singapore continuing and a presence in the Mediterranean being retained. Despite these major changes the Ministry of Defence would only receive an extra £35 million in 1972–3 and £69 million in 1973–4, with no additional funding in the forthcoming 1971–2 financial year.[11] Despite the strategic benefits from a continued commitment to a global role, from a planning perspective the Navy now had to deal with the worst of both worlds: retaining commitments which it had assumed would largely disappear, accompanied by no fundamental change to the equipment decisions of 1966 to 1968, and little new money to fulfil those commitments.

This public announcement was accompanied a few months later by a less-heralded decision from the Secretary of State to bring forward the ordering and construction dates of follow-on Type 21 frigates and Type 42 destroyers as part of the new government's 'dash for growth'.[12] This provided some welcome certainty for those shipbuilders in need of work to survive and many jobs in areas of the country desperately needing them, but it was now unexpectedly front-loading the shipbuilding programme, pushing the 'bump' in procurement spending further forward in time, and making it more difficult to continue the regular annual 'drumbeat' of orders for frigates and destroyers that had been in place since 1950. In the event, the bringing forward of these orders did have this exact effect: another Type 42 destroyer would not be ordered until 1976 and the next frigate order – for the first Type 22 – would not take place for another three years. Meanwhile, 'substantial' delays were manifesting themselves in weapons production, not least with Sea Dart and the delivery of Sea Slug Mark 2 missiles.[13] The decision was also made to cancel the domestically-developed Mark 31 lightweight anti-submarine torpedo and replace it with the US Mark 46. The existing Mark 44 torpedo was proving inadequate in service and needed to be supplemented quickly by a more effective weapon. The Mark 31 would take too long to enter service and would only provide a marginal improvement on the Mark 44.[14] The US Mark 46 could be bought immediately and enter service quicker, whilst British research development could focus on a long-term successor, later named Stingray, which would enter service in a decade's time and provide a major change in capability. The Mark 46 was an improvement on the Mark 44, but it would prove to be unable deal with the newest fast Soviet submarines of the 'Alfa' and 'Papa' classes, so the development of Stingray was urgent.[15] The Mark 46 decision had considerable operational benefits and would save money over the five years, but it did mean another significant up-front cost of £24 million for the purchase during 1972 to 1975.[16]

The cost of new construction of warships had risen yet again, with an additional £130 million over ten years being added to the programme. Each new cruiser would now cost £52 million instead of £43 million, follow-on Type 42s would now cost between £16.4 and £18.4 million each instead of £14.5 million and the first Type 22 would now be almost as expensive, having increased in price by £4 million in a single year from £12.4 million. Some of this was inflation but over half of the additional costs were due to higher steel and labour costs, and the crystallisation of real costs following tendering processes from contractors and sub-contractors.[17] These changes all served to make further painful cuts necessary to fit the Navy's planned spending within the levels planned for the next decade. The Type 42 and Type 22 programmes were 're-phased', in other words pushed back with more of the spending occurring later in the ten-year Long Term Costings period or dropping off the charts altogether by shifting beyond the ten-year point. The purchase of additional Sea King helicopters was deferred, the number of Exocet missiles to be purchased was reduced, the last order of Sea Slug Mark 2 missiles was cancelled, some RFA tankers were deferred or cancelled, whilst funding was taken out of Research and Development (again) as well as from fleet support and marine services. Even then, the Navy Department's Long Term Costings would be £16 million over target in 1972–3, £55 million the following year and £59 million the year after that.[18] The new Vice Chief of the Naval Staff, Vice Admiral Lewin, argued that there was very little that could be done, the Navy Department had 'reached the end of the road on cancellations and deferments' if its NATO and international commitments were to be kept, and that 'our future credibility compared with the Russians was put at risk'.[19] Although Lewin was striking an alarmist tone, there was little that could be done beyond setting out different options for reducing the Navy's sketch estimates so that they fitted within the available budget.

Seven months later, when the sketch Estimates for 1972–3 came to be discussed, the funding situation had not necessarily been resolved by the new government's decision to front load warship orders as part of the 'dash for growth' which had resulted in the fifth and sixth Type 42s being ordered earlier than planned as well as four more Type 21 frigates. Other warship orders had to be deferred, including the first cruiser which would now be ordered in 1973, whilst a series of less visible reductions were made, including reducing war stocks, savings in the planned Northwood command and control centre, and reductions in practice targets and training systems.[20] Even then, the Estimates would still be £6 million over the budget for the year, and a series of additional minor reductions or deferments would be necessary to halve this amount. There were looming storm clouds on the horizon however, as the Controller warned that there was 'an unprecedented pattern of early bill presentation by contractors': this would mean paying out money earlier than planned and suggested that business for these contractors was not good, as they had the spare resources to fulfil their contracts early.[21] The following year saw further deferments and cancellations in the procurement programme in order to keep within the ten-year budget levels: the planned seventh and ninth Type 42 destroyers were cancelled and the envisaged building rate of mine warfare vessels in the mid-1970s was reduced significantly and the refit for HMS *Albion* was cancelled, saving £25 million and resulting in her early decommissioning. A series of overspends in new procurements were amongst the main causes for these decisions. Yet again, the trimmed budget could not meet the required targets, with overspends rising from £9 million in 1972–3 to £39 million in 1975–6, so further options for cuts had to be put to ministers: cancelling the eighth Type 42 and a further purchase of Wasp helicopters whilst deferring the Northwood upgrade once more as well as planned orders for new fleet tankers, fleet maintenance ships, diving vessel and inshore survey vessels for a number of years.[22] Nearly all these options were taken up. A similarly dispiriting cycle was in evidence for the following year as cost increases in the Type 42 and Type 21 programmes forced the pushing back of further orders, the continued reduction in stores, spares and war stocks and delays to modernising the Royal Fleet Auxiliary.[23] To add to the woes, a dockyard strike in late 1972 had lost 80,000 man-weeks of labour, costing the Navy Department over £8 million.[24]

The Navy Department was not alone in suffering major problems in its equipment and support programmes, the Army and Air Force Department were faced with similar overruns in this period although by 1972 there were concerns on the Admiralty Board that the Royal Navy's share of the budget was falling behind the other two services.[25] In any case, it was becoming inescapably clear that the perpetual deferments – pushing planned purchases and equipment production into the later half of the Long Term Costings – were building up pressure for a new defence review in order to make longer term planning sustainable. When this was combined with Treasury attempts to reduce the defence budget by £130 million for the 1974–5 financial year as part of Anthony Barber's attempt to rein in public spending after the 'Barber boom' began to run out of control, it became clear that something more than the usual round of 'salami slicing' cuts would be necessary.[26] In the event, only £56 million could be found by the Ministry, but a few months later fears of a run on the Pound resulted in Barber proposing yet another round of government spending cuts.[27] As will be seen in the next chapter, a Defence Studies Working Party had already been established in 1972 and it gradually turned into the guiding body for a new defence review which would eventually commence under a new Labour government in March 1974. Before moving onto the conduct of the Review, the rest of this chapter will review the state of the shipbuilding industry and then assess the different major procurements then in progress or planned.

The Shipbuilding Industry
The British shipbuilding industry was tasked with building the ships and submarines that had been ordered, and by the end of the 1960s it was in a parlous state. The commission under Lord Geddes, that had been tasked with analysing the state of the industry and recommending reforms, had produced a report in 1966 that had recommended the consolidation of the fragmented

industry by combining yards that were geographically close to one another. The objective was that the better yards could spread their expertise and knowledge to other yards in the same group, and lift up the poor performers. Geddes' ambitious plans were not fully realised: the main warship yards – Vickers at Barrow, Yarrow and Vosper Thornycroft – were successful at retaining their independence, much to the relief of the Ministry of Defence, whilst the other yards were consolidated into five main groups: the lower Clyde, the upper Clyde, east Scotland, the Tyne and Tees estuaries and two groups on the Wear.[28] Most significantly, the industry's poor performance at attracting orders turned out to be even weaker than Geddes' worst-case scenario. Major British shipowners such as Holts, P&O and BP had stopped ordering ships from domestic shipbuilders in the 1960s, because they were usually delivered over-price and late, and there was no sign that the post-Geddes industry was attracting them back.[29]

The mixed yards such as Swan Hunter and Cammell Laird that built both warships and merchant ships were increasingly reliant on government orders as commercial contracts failed to materialise. Both of these yards made huge losses in 1969 and 1970 of over £9 million and £8 million respectively. The warship yards were not necessarily in good shape either as naval orders were either too few or were for designs that were not fully developed resulting in many expensive changes, as will be seen with the Type 21 and Type 42. Yarrow had made a total loss of £5 million in 1969 and 1970, and while Vosper Thornycroft was not in such a parlous state, it too had made a loss in 1968 and its profits had been relatively anaemic in 1969. Only Vickers, with its guaranteed production line of nuclear submarine orders was making consistent profits between 1966 and 1971.[30] This poor position resulted in subsidies being poured into the industry by the new Shipbuilding Industry Board that had been created as a result of Geddes' recommendations. A high proportion of these subsidies were no more than life support, being swallowed up offsetting losses rather than used to invest in new plant or facilities.[31] The Ministry of Defence became involved as well, providing a £4.5 million loan to Yarrow shipbuilders in 1971, thus helping to support a key warship builder that appeared at risk of sliding into long-term unprofitability.[32] A 1972 report on the industry by Booz, Allen and Hamilton, a management consultancy, laid bare the problems of the industry: long-term planning was so poor as to be non-existent in many yards, purchasing and stock management was deficient, as was marketing, labour management and trade union relations. Most companies were reluctant to innovate or purchase new technology, and many were increasingly dependent on government largesse for survival.[33] It was on the shoulders of this crisis-stricken industry that the Navy's shipbuilding programme would depend, the only bright spot being that two of the most stable and successful British yards were Vickers and Vosper Thornycroft, both of them being warship builders.

Submarines

One advantage that the nuclear-powered submarine building programme had over the other naval procurement strands was that it was accepted across the Ministry of Defence, and to some extent at the Treasury as well, that these boats were a key defence priority and that a rolling programme of regular orders was needed in order to build up their numbers. Up to January 1968 it had been planned to order one nuclear submarine a year, but following a review of the submarine construction programme this was slowed down, the eventual rate being settled at one order every 18 months in 1970.[34] The change was not just a cost-saving measure pushed by the Treasury and taken at the very end of the long run of defence economies between 1964 and 1968, but it was also an acknowledgement that only one yard could be reliably trusted to build nuclear-powered submarines: Vickers at Barrow. Cammell Laird, the second nuclear submarine yard, had not proved as efficient as Vickers and, as has been seen in Chapter 3, their *Resolution* class boats had suffered numerous problems, as did their last boat, *Conqueror*, whose gearbox had broken during trials as a result of sabotage by a shipyard worker.[35]

The order of *Swiftsure*, the first of the new 'Improved *Valiant*' or 'SSN0X class', had been easily agreed with the Treasury in late 1966 following robust support from the then Secretary of State, Denis Healey, the boat being described to the Treasury as merely an incremental improvement on the *Valiant* class.[36] In reality, although there were some incremental changes on the preceding class, the *Swiftsure* class introduced a significant number of important innovations. Most importantly, the hull shape was changed from the US-style 'teardrop' to a tubular shape which although it was shorter overall allowed for a larger pressure hull. The machinery spaces were redesigned, reduced in size and placed on 'rafts' that reduced the extent of noise travel, thus making the boats quieter and less vulnerable to detection by passive sonar. The reactor was the same pressurised water reactor of earlier classes but with a new, more powerful and longer-lasting core. The weapon spaces were also redesigned. The overall objective was to create a more efficient, effective and above all quieter submarine.[37] During the 1970s and 1980s the Royal Navy's nuclear submarines were amongst the quietest built during the Cold War, although this was to some extent at the expense of speed.[38]

At this time it was envisaged that there would be five boats of the *Swiftsure* class, and that the next boat, SSN12, would be the first in a new class code-named SSN0Y. This class, also of five boats, would incorporate only 'evolutionary improvements' on its predecessor and would itself be succeeded by a new class in the early to mid-1980s, the SSN0Z, which would include a new reactor and new weapon systems. Early SSN0Y design studies envisaged a boat with an identical hull form and displacement to the *Swiftsure* class and only incremental changes to weapons and sensors, whilst SSN0Z would be somewhat larger at 6,500 tonnes.[39] The SSN0Y design would develop over time and eventually become the *Trafalgar* class, the first boat of which entered service in 1983 after six rather than five *Swiftsures* had been built. After the decision to order one nuclear boat only every 18 months in 1970, the Navy's Long Term Costings Assumptions began to include a new class of ten small conventional diesel-electric submarines to undertake the training and other roles of the current conventional boats in the fleet.[40] In many respects they were also to provide additional numbers within the submarine force, now that completions of nuclear boats would be spaced out more widely. Always a lower priority than the nuclear boats, the new conventional boat design remained in development throughout the 1970s the first of class ordering date continually being pushed back, eventually emerging as the *Upholder* class, the first of which was ordered in 1983.[41]

The Cruiser

Major changes in the new cruiser's design occurred during 1969 and the first months of 1970, following the arrival of Michael Le Fanu as First Sea Lord: the proposed number of helicopters gradually increased from six to twelve, and the option to operate a small number of Harriers on a one-for-one replacement basis for Sea Kings was proposed. Twelve helicopters were justified as a way to ensure a fully-effective anti-submarine screen for a task group, whilst the cost of enabling Harriers to be flown (expanding aircraft lifts, adding weapons storage) was argued to be only £1 million.[42] The Treasury were willing to accept the increase to twelve helicopters, which it was argued by the Navy made an island deck arrangement necessary, and reluctantly accepted the relatively small additional cost of allowing the possibility of Harrier operations, but were still extremely sceptical about anything that might result in the return of fixed wing flying on naval warships. They regarded the 'old' Fleet Air Arm as having been an extremely expensive duplication of the RAF's capabilities and did not want a return to this situation. Treasury officials initially hoped that the Royal Air Force would defeat the Navy's attempts to procure Harriers, but when they saw that the RAF was not opposed, they pushed for the aircraft to be RAF rather than Royal Navy operated.[43] Denis Healey in his dealings with the Treasury fully supported the expansion of the Cruiser to a twelve-helicopter vessel and was willing to countenance Harriers if studies and assessments were to find their operation from ships to be practical.[44] The 1970 general election and arrival of a new Conservative government delayed the ordering of the first cruiser as the concept had to be put to a new group of ministers, but in essence Healey's approval was not challenged and, as has been seen, the first ship was eventually ordered in 1973. Twelve helicopters never featured in any of the concepts for the Cruiser that this author has found, and it is highly likely that this was used as a way to enable space for what was initially three Harriers in place of three nominal Sea Kings. By 1972 the three Harriers had increased to five.[45] The Royal Navy had indeed ensured the resurrection of the aircraft carrier by the 'back door': Treasury officials clearly had suspicions that this was happening but by conceding early on the twelve-helicopter requirement and the fitting of the ship *for* Harriers, if not with, they allowed momentum to build in support of fixed-wing aircraft and then the development of a navalised version of the RAF's ground attack Harrier.

In addition to the increase in aircraft during her design development, the Cruiser had lost a 4.5in Mk 8 gun which had been in the design in March 1968 but disappeared a year later.[46] As late as November 1972 it would have been fitted for, but not with, Exocet anti-ship missiles and have the older Type 965 air-search radar, but by the time the ship was launched the Exocets had been removed and the Type 965 replaced by the more capable Type 1022 radar.[47] The first ship of the class was named *Invincible*, after a former battlecruiser, rather than an established aircraft carrier name, as a deliberate attempt to disassociate the ship from carriers. The ship was built at Vickers, the yard that not only built all the Royal Navy's nuclear submarines but was also leading the Type 42 programme. The other yards deemed capable of being lead yards on warship building, Yarrow and Vosper Thornycroft, did not have slips large enough to build ships larger than destroyers.

HMS *Bristol* and Sea Dart

The Type 82 destroyer had survived in the programme primarily to sustain British-Dutch naval co-operation at a sensitive time. The Dutch were partners in the Standard Frigate project and were keen for their Type 988 'Broomstick' air-search radar to be purchased by the Royal Navy. The radar would have been fitted to the cancelled CVA01 and the Type 82s, so the sole remaining Type 82 provided the only opportunity for this Dutch piece of equipment to be fitted in a Royal Navy ship.[48] In the event the Broomstick radar was not fitted, replaced by the venerable Type 965. The sole ship of the class, named HMS *Bristol*, was advertised as a test-bed for the new weapon systems that would be fitted to her and was commissioned in March 1973.

The ship spent the first seven years of her service in effect operating as a test and trials ship, including acceptance trials for Sea Dart and its GWS 30 system, Ikara and its GWS 41 system, the new Mark 8 4.5in gun and its automated firing system, as well as a host of other much smaller trials being undertaken by research establishments. She also had to deal with a serious fire in her steam propulsion unit, resulting in her dependence on her gas turbines for another two years and thus an operating radius limited to northern Europe.[49] *Bristol* had been equipped with a range of labour-saving devices aimed at reducing the size of the crew – she had eighty fewer sailors than the similarly-sized 'County' class destroyers – but not only did some of these fail to work as intended, the reduction in junior rates caused problems with ship husbandry on such a large vessel. The captain called for a reduction in the number of senior rates, who appeared to be under-employed, and an increase in juniors during her next commission.[50]

Because of the delays to *Bristol*'s construction, she was not the first ship to be commissioned fitted with Ikara: the entry of Ikara into service is set out below with HMS *Leander*, the first ship to operate the system. *Bristol* was, however, the first Sea Dart warship in the fleet and her trials were extensive, with a good number of years needed to iron out problems with new air defence missile and the wider GWS 30 system. The formal acceptance of the system had to be delayed by two years in July 1970; there were issues with the missile's flight reliability, ignition systems and missile producibility.[51] Even as late as 1976 only just over half of her Sea Dart firings in the previous six-months had been successful. There were also problems with the Type 909 guidance radars for the missile system, and trials continued on these radars until as late as 1976.[52] Issues with her 4.5in gun's automatic firing system and other elements of the weapon lingered even longer, with the Mk 8 gun, despite being fitted to more than a dozen warships still not being formally accepted into service when the Falklands conflict started.[53]

From July 1976 to February 1978 *Bristol* was refitted as a fully-operational warship, but still the trials continued: she was fitted with the first 'Abbeyhill' passive intercept electronic warfare system and the new NATO Link 11 tactical communication system, which resulted in a long series of ultimately successful trials during 1979 and 1980.[54] *Bristol* in the early 1970s seemed like a white elephant and was associated in the Navy with being not much more than a trials platform, but her large magazine and her economy in crewing compared to the Ikara-fitted *Leander* and the Type 42 which had in effect replaced her cancelled sisters, did give the sole Type 82 some important operational advantages, not least when the air threat grew and recruitment and retention crises returned in the late 1970s.

HMS *Sheffield* and HMS *Amazon*

As was seen in Chapter 3, the Type 42 destroyer and Type 21 frigate were to be the new immediate focus for surface-ship construction following the demise of the CVA01 aircraft carrier and the decision to procure only one

Type 82 destroyer. Admiral Begg had ensured that the two new ship types were ordered as quickly as possible: the Type 42 would – it was hoped – bring the largest possible number of Sea Dart air defence missile systems to the fleet as quickly as possible, crucial now that carrier air cover would not be available in a few years' time, whilst the commercially-designed Type 21 would enable a continued production line of frigates to replace the already obsolescent *Leander* class and fill the gap before the internally-designed Type 22 was ready. The contract for the first Type 42, HMS *Sheffield*, was signed on 14 November 1968, only 20 months after the Defence Council had agreed on the outline concept for the ship. The contract for HMS *Amazon*, the first Type 21, was signed only four months later on 26 March 1969. At this point it was planned that the more complex *Sheffield* would be accepted for service by 14 February 1973 and the cheaper, simpler *Amazon* by 20 April 1972.[55] In 1969, the forward programme envisaged two Type 42s being ordered each year until 1974 followed by one a year until 1979, for a total class of sixteen. The number of Type 21s, which in 1968 was still being envisaged as a joint venture with the Royal Australian Navy, would only be three for the Royal Navy and the same number, at least initially, for the Australians. The three British Type 21s would enter service in in 1972 and 1973 with a planned unit cost of £7.3 million each.[56] After the RAN dropped out, having modified their requirements, the number of vessels planned for the Royal Navy increased to four with the additional ship entering service in 1974.[57] As the design for the successor Type 22 frigate was repeatedly pushed back, the number of Type 21s in the forward programme was increased first to six in January 1970,[58] and finally to eight in January 1971. When the new Conservative government was formed in June 1970 only *Sheffield* and the first four Type 21s had been ordered. The new government's 'dash for growth' resulted orders for five more Type 42s and the last four Type 21s all being placed between May and November 1971, six of the nine contracts being signed on the same day: 11 November.[59] The two classes would also be constructed under the new batch system, whereby the lead yard would produce a detailed design, which would then be used to construct succeeding ships, reducing minor differences between vessels of the same class and making the supply and maintenance of equipment much easier. The ships would also be procured under competitive tendering. Both batch building and competitive tendering had been successful in helping to bring down costs and speed up delivery for the last four *Leander* class frigates, so there was no reason to believe that this would not be the case with the new classes.

Unfortunately, this would be far from the case. In a two-part post-mortem on the construction of the first Batch of six Type 42s and the eight Type 21s, written in 1975 and 1976, it was confirmed that construction costs of the fourteen ships had increased between 25 per cent and 71 per cent and their delivery had been delayed by between 15 and 27 months.[60] *Sheffield* herself suffered a real terms cost increase (taking account of inflation), of 52.1 per cent from her original estimate when the contract was placed, whilst *Amazon* was an astonishing 70.7 per cent more expensive.[61] They were delivered 51 months and 37 months late respectively.[62] The excesses for the follow-on ships were generally less extreme in cost terms but just as bad, if not worse, with respect to delivery dates. What had gone so horribly wrong?

There were five reasons for these cost overruns and late delivery. First, the two designs were too immature when the first-of-class orders were placed, and problems were encountered in developing the detailed specifications. Begg's decision to order early made sense within the political environment of the Ministry of Defence, but not from a design perspective. With the Type 42, electrical specifications and gas turbine requirements had not been set when the ships were ordered, and as these matured and inevitably grew in complexity, size and cost they had considerable knock-on effects to the design.[63] Many pieces of equipment were of new types and so the cost estimates made by Ministry and shipyard accountants were more likely to be inaccurate.[64] Vickers was the lead yard and was responsible for producing the detailed design drawings for the class, but they were also lead yard for the nuclear submarine programme and the Cruiser, and were clearly overwhelmed undertaking all three roles, as well as building one additional Type 42 for Argentina and supporting the construction of a second at an Argentine yard. The Ship Department was not impressed by some of the early detailed drawings that Vickers produced, and these had to be re-done and more resource allocated to the work.[65] With the Type 21 the situation was somewhat different: the Ship Department had taken on trust Vosper's statements that the design was well-developed but had discovered that this had not been so.[66] The Ship Department also demanded a series of changes to the Type 21 to ensure it met the standards required for Royal Navy warships, many of which Vospers thought were unnecessary. Both of these factors served to cause delays and increase costs. Vospers were finding the work a strain and had to embark on a shake-up of its management team for the Type 21.[67] The Ship Department was not without fault: communication with sub-contractors was not good, and the supervision of them was not tight enough, resulting in more unexpected delays and cost overruns.[68] All in all, a total of 574 design changes to *Sheffield* were made after the order and 534 to *Amazon*, a huge number that reflected just how underdeveloped both these designs had been in 1968.[69]

Second, there was a 'buyer's market' for shipbuilding in the late 1960s and the yards had underbid to get the contracts, which were on a fixed-price basis. Then, with the multiple changes that were required, these yards soon found themselves building the ships at a growing loss. Vospers, which had also landed a large order for seven Brazilian frigates in 1970 and had limited slips for construction, took the Ministry of Defence to court over the Ship Department's required design changes and the knock-on delays to its Brazilian order.[70] Vickers played an equally tough game, even threatening to halt work on HMS *Sheffield* in the months before the Queen was due to launch the ship, in order to force the Ministry to provide more funds.[71] When building their second ship, HMS *Cardiff*, Vickers was clearly becoming overwhelmed by the weight of work across various classes, with this vessel suffering from slow progress and low prioritisation within the yard. When the Ship Department hinted at moving *Cardiff* for completion at another yard, Vickers countered by proposing a new, more expensive, cost-plus contract for the ship. *Cardiff* was soon under tow to Swan Hunters for completion.[72] Relations between the yards and the Ministry of Defence could clearly be difficult and tense, which could not have helped with the resolution of problems and smooth running of the two procurements.

Third, the Ministry of Defence had been slack in writing its contracts with Vospers, Vickers and other shipbuilders: for example they included no penalty clauses for late delivery of machinery by sub-contractors.[73] As it became clear that they would be making a loss on building the Type 42s and Type 21s, the shipyards tried to make use of as many loopholes in the contracts as possible to cancel out the losses and make the construction of the ships financially worthwhile. 'Exceptional Dislocation and Delay' clauses had been badly written and these were repeatedly made use of to push for additional funds. The lead yards also took advantage of what had initially seemed like a minor and innocuous cost-plus element to their contract, which allowed for additional funding to pay for the creation and maintenance of 'identicality records' for each piece of equipment fitted to ships. The Ship Department suspected that these were heavily inflated in order to gain further additional funds.[74]

Fourth, the new government's 'dash for growth', and its decision to order large numbers of vessels all at once, destroyed any of the benefits that might have accrued from the new batch system. Instead of a regular drumbeat of annual orders to a limited number of selected and trusted yards, the government spread the orders of Type 42s as widely as possible across the different shipbuilding centres of the United Kingdom. Not all of these yards were well equipped to build these ships, the lead yards now had to produce more versions of more drawings of the detailed design, and instead of working with perhaps only one other yard, they now unexpectedly had to deal with many more. Overworked and facing losses on their own ships, the lead yards inevitably neglected some of their lead-yard responsibilities. As a result, some of the 'identicality' requirements for ships of the same batch had to be loosened, and a return to the old system of local detailed design partly returned through the back door.[75]

Fifth, the two procurements had to deal with bad luck to be building warships when high inflation struck the economy (which was unsurprisingly stoked by the government's deficit-fuelled 'dash for growth'), followed by the oil crisis of 1973. Labour shortages, particularly of skilled electricians, were also a major problem. At Yarrow, the follow-on builder for the Type 21s, there were particular issues with inadequate numbers assigned to building ships. There were similar problems at Vickers.[76] Strikes, many of which were over pay rises to keep up with runaway inflation, also disrupted building work. These types of problems were also in evidence for other major government building contracts in this period: the warship building industry was not unique in this regard.[77] Also, a serious fire on HMS *Sheffield* a few months before her launch by the Queen, was another piece of bad luck which resulted in huge efforts to ensure that the launch date was not changed, much of which added additional costs to the build.[78]

In the 1976 post-mortem, it was speculated that if the price estimates for the two classes had been closer to the eventual reality, then 'the ships might have been ruled out of court' and never procured as being too expensive for the capability they provided.[79] Whether this would have resulted in the paring back of further capabilities in the two designs or an acceptance that the number of destroyers and frigates would have to shrink in size even further, is impossible to know. However, the net effect of ordering these two designs too early was that many fewer ships were built than had been planned, and as will be seen as this chapter progresses, lower priority procurements were repeatedly delayed and some were eventually cancelled.

HMS *Sheffield* was finally accepted for service in February 1975 and underwent a period of trials: as first of class and for her variant of the GWS 30 Sea Dart missile system and the ADAWS 4 tactical command system. The second ship, HMS *Birmingham*, followed in early 1976, with two more commissioning in 1978 and the last two of the first batch of six ships in 1979. Once HMS *Amazon* was accepted into service in 1974, the production of the remaining ships of her class was much less delayed: all had been completed and were in service by the end of 1978. The Type 21s were popular in service – they were relatively roomy, elegant ships with a small crew – but although they had space to fit the Exocet missile system, they were not large enough to operate the large and bulky Sea Wolf air defence missile system that was being fitted to the Type 22 so suffered from being relatively new ships armed with the previous generation of self-defence capability.[80] However, they had been procured as a stopgap class and were well-adapted to act a presence vessels in peacetime and second-rate light escorts in war. In the first few years there were teething problems with their new CAAIS tactical command system, but these were soon resolved.[81] For the Type 42s, their operational problem was more serious. They were sophisticated vessels that managed to cram much into a relatively small hull (with almost no margin for future additions of equipment) and had been designed to deal with the Soviet air threat as it had existed in the late 1960s and first few years of the 1970s. But, as will be seen in the next chapter they entered service just as the ageing Soviet Tu-16 'Badger' bomber was being replaced by the supersonic long-range Tu-22M 'Backfire' bomber armed with Kh-22 missiles.[82] The Type 42's small magazine of only twenty-two missiles was deemed inadequate to deal with the new threat and Sea Dart/GWS30 itself would be hard pressed to intercept the faster and longer range missiles. In operational analysis conducted in 1977 it was estimated that a task group consisting of three Type 42s, three *Leander* class frigates and six 'high value units', facing an attack from thirty-six Kh-22 missiles launched from eighteen 'Backfires', would receive between two and three hits on the Type 42s and between two and three hits on the other nine units. The number of hits would be even higher if Soviet radar-jamming aircraft were present.[83] This was not effective air defence: all the Type 42s could be wiped out in a single attack and their defensive screens repeatedly breached. As soon as the Type 42 had entered service it was moving rapidly towards obsolescence as an air defence ship able to cope with the type of cruise missile attacks expected from Soviet naval aviation.

HMS *Leander* and Ikara
As was described in Chapter 3, with the cancellation of all but one of the Type 82 class, the Royal Navy had to find platforms for the five remaining Ikara anti-submarine missile systems it had agreed to purchase. The decision was made by March 1968 to undertake extensive mid-life refits of the eight earliest *Leander* class frigates in order to operate the system (three more Ikara systems had been purchased by March 1968), and the first ship to enter refit was the oldest ship in the class, *Leander* herself, although the initial plans had placed her sister ship *Dido* as the lead vessel.[84] Her 4.5in gun forward of the bridge was replaced by large protective superstructure within which was placed the missile launcher, which would be enabled to fire by the retraction of moveable roof structure. The ship's large air-search radar on the mainmast was removed and the vessel's operations room was completely rebuilt in order to operate Ikara and the sophisticated ADAWS 5 tactical command system that was required to coordinate Ikara targeting and guidance. She was equipped with the new Type 184M medium-range scanning sonar that would provide detection data for ADAWS to turn into firing solutions for Ikara, whilst the Link 10 tactical communication system would allow for the transfer of

information from other ships' sensors to supplement or take the place of Type 184M detections.[85] These changes transformed what had been a relatively simple general-purpose ship into a state-of-the-art specialised anti-submarine frigate with a strong co-operative capability with other ships, a much more capable 1970s successor to the Type 14 frigates that had dominated the anti-submarine and fishery protection roles a decade before. The Ikara *Leander*s were much prized in the mid-1970s for their sophisticated operations rooms – tactical command systems of the capability of ADAWS had only so far been fitted to the last four 'County' class destroyers, HMS *Bristol* and the Type 42s, and it would not be until 1979 that the Type 42s were operational in the fleet in any significant numbers.[86]

Ikara proved to be a capable system on its initial trials: *Leander*'s commanding officer, Captain B K Shattock, declared in May 1974 that 'we are all enthusiasts on board for the excellent system that GWS 41/ADAWS 5 has turned out to be',[87] and in comparison to using the Wasp helicopter as a torpedo-delivery system it was a significant step-change: Ikara's time of reaction from detection to reaching target was 90 seconds compared to at least six minutes for the helicopter, it could be operated in almost all weathers unlike Wasp and it would be available nearly 24 hours a day – except for 10 minutes of maintenance time per day – a considerable improvement on Wasp. However, Ikara had some significant problems, as was mentioned in the previous chapter: it was severely hampered by the limited range of the Type 184M sonar, which was only somewhat better than the maximum range in good conditions of its predecessor, the Type 184, which was 5,500 yards.[88] When Soviet 'Charlie' class submarines could launch their missiles from underwater many tens of miles away, the main Soviet anti-ship torpedo, the wake-homing 53–65M, had a maximum range of 22km at 40 knots speed or 12km at 70 knots,[89] and Soviet submarine commanders had been observed firing their torpedoes in exercises at between 12,000 and 5,000 yards away, this was clearly inadequate.[90] In 1975 the Joint Maritime Operational and Tactical School admitted that in exercises over the previous few years, most of which would have included Ikara ships, those submarines playing the part of 'Charlie' class boats had not been detected before they fired their missiles in *any* instances.[91] The new Ikara *Leander*s were fitted with the NATO standard Link X tactical communications system, which allowed for target and other data to be transferred from one ship to another, thus opening up the possibility of using another ship's data to launch a missile, but this capability would be limited until Link X (or its successor Link 11) was available across the fleet, which was not expected until the end of the 1970s and the early 1980s. Finally, the Mark 44 and Mark 46 torpedoes that the Ikara missile carried, and then dropped close to the target, had major shortcomings. The Mark 44 was too slow and operational analysis had estimated that it only had a 16 per cent chance of success against a submarine travelling at 18 knots and no chance at all against a submarine travelling at 25 knots or more. It also did not work well in shallow waters.[92] The Mark 46 was a faster and more capable torpedo, but it had its own limitations: its warhead lethality was poor and it did not work well in shallow waters, whilst it was still not fast enough to deal with the newest and fastest Soviet submarines of the 'Alfa' and 'Papa' classes.[93]

After a number of years of trials and exercises, tactical doctrine was developed to make best use of Ikara, and it was recommended that two Ikara ships would be necessary for each task group, one operating in front and the other behind the task group centre, with the freedom to manoeuvre quickly so that they could bring their Ikara missile launcher to bear at short-notice.[94] Ikara, as it entered service during the 1970s, was therefore an extremely problematic weapon system: despite its sophistication it depended on inadequate sonars for detection and made use of poorly performing torpedoes, and it would not be until the 1980s before either new sonars or new torpedoes would be available to make up for these deficiencies.

HMS *Cleopatra* and Exocet

Up to 1970 it was expected that the next eight oldest *Leander* class frigates after the Ikara conversions would only receive minimal refits, whilst the final ten *Leander*s in mid-life refits would have their old 4.5in mountings replaced by the new Mark 8 fitted to the Type 21s and Type 42s and their Wasp helicopters replaced by what would become the Lynx helicopter.[95] However, once the Exocet anti-ship guided missile had been purchased in 1971, these plans changed. With the gradual withdrawal of the strike carrier force through the 1970s, the procurement of anti-ship guided missiles became a priority for the Navy. Initially, long-range cruise missiles, rather like those fired by Soviet cruisers and cruise missile submarines, were considered, but these depended upon long-range land-based targeting aircraft to provide mid-course guidance for the missiles, and there was little chance that the money would be found to develop either the long-range missile or the targeting aircraft to support it. Instead, medium-range cruise missiles were considered, whose maximum range was limited to the horizon line or just beyond it. Two missile systems were in contention, the French Exocet system and ship-launched version of the British air-launched Martel missile. 'Ship Martel', although it had similar capabilities to the French system, was 18 months behind Exocet in its development and the Navy's need was urgent, so negotiations to purchase Exocet began in September 1970.[96] Initially a total of 37 quadruple sets of launchers and 300 missiles were to be purchased at a cost of £66 million in 1971 prices.[97] Housed in containers on a ship's deck, usually in groups of four,

Exocet was a 'fire and forget' missile which used its own nose-cone radar to detect and home onto the target whilst flying at a low 'sea-skimming' altitude, which made detection by radar difficult until the last minute. Whilst not able to reach the great distances of Soviet long-range missiles, its range was similar to that of the Soviet 'Styx' missile fitted to destroyers and fast attack craft.[98] Threat of Exocet attack would also serve the purpose of holding marking ships at distance in times of tension: a form of tactical deterrence, and they were also regarded as a longer range more capable replacement for, or supplement to, a ship's general purpose medium gun.

The Navy was keen to get as many of these missiles to sea as quickly as possible, but a number of ship types initially slated to be fitted with Exocet, such as Type 81 frigates, *Tiger* class cruisers, *Fearless* class assault ships, the commando carriers and the new Type 42 destroyers, had to be dropped due to the required refit being too expensive or complicated.[99] The new Type 21 and Type 22 frigates would have Exocet, whilst the first vessels to receive the missile system would be the four newest 'County' class destroyers. This left those *Leander* class ships not equipped with Ikara as the obvious choice for the system. Initial plans to fit Exocet at the extreme stern of the *Leander*s were rejected as this would have required the ship's helicopter to be in flight or in the hangar for the firing to take place: a constraint considered sufficiently serious to shift the Exocet to the forecastle and sacrifice the 4.5in mounting.[100] Other more modern equipment would also be fitted, as well as additional Sea Cat missile systems, an enlarged hangar for the new Lynx helicopter and a fit of modern electronics as well as the CAAIS tactical command system. The first *Leander* class ship to emerge from refit with this new weaponry was HMS *Cleopatra* in November 1975. She was followed by another six ships between 1977 and 1981.[101] The 'County' class destroyer HMS *Norfolk* was the first ship fitted with Exocet, in place of her 'B' mounting just below her bridge, and trials with the system in the Mediterranean in 1974 were successful.[102] The placing of Exocet missiles in cannisters above decks created concerns about the risk of small-arms fire or blast fragments igniting a missile that was not safely stored in a protected and controlled magazine below the waterline – invoking the ghost of earlier naval concerns about the ammunition explosions that sank battlecruisers at Jutland in 1916 and the engagement with the German battleship *Bismarck* in 1941 – but this was partly resolved by the fitting of armoured protection plates to the side of the launchers from 1975 onwards.[103]

A few years later, attention turned to the refit plans of the last ten *Leander* class frigates. With many more Exocets to fit, these too would have the missile system in place of their forward mounting, but the decision was also made to replace Sea Cat with Sea Wolf, a much more effective short-range air defence missile system, but one which, as will be seen below, was growing increasingly bulky and complex.[104] The costs of the Exocet refits were also increasing significantly, and through the 1970s there were clearly concerns that modernising such ships was a false economy when a new-build vessel for only a little more money would have double the life – around 20 years compared to only 10 to 12 for modernising an existing ship. The first evidence of this concern was the short-lived 'SSGW frigate' concept, which is described below, and was a means of getting large numbers of Exocets to sea in new vessels. In the later 1970s the Director General, Ships, the Navy's most senior constructor (naval architect) also had concerns about the cost effectiveness of modernising the *Leander*s so expensively, and suggested building new frigates instead, but the Naval Staff persisted with the *Leander* modernisation programme.[105] These increasingly complex refits were becoming one of the main reasons to justify the continuing existence of four domestic dockyards, whilst at the same time the *Leander* class were popular, seaworthy ships and there was perhaps an understandable reluctance to lose these relatively new ships because of their obsolescent equipment fit.

The Type 22 Frigate
A lack of design capacity in the Ship Department had meant that the eventual successor to the *Leander* class was delayed and as a stopgap the Type 21 frigate was procured instead. The *Leander* successor had its origins in the pre-1966 Defence Review Type 19 frigate. After the design work on the Type 42 had been completed, attention then returned to the Standard Frigate, which was now being considered in co-operation with the Dutch Navy, who had recently built their own *Leander* class frigates and had purchased other British warships in the postwar years. In 1968, the Standard Frigate had a proposed armament that largely updated that of the *Leander*s, and had some similarities to the Type 21: one medium gun, the new light helicopter (later named the Lynx), and one launcher for the PX430 Confessor, the successor to Sea Cat which would later be renamed Sea Wolf.[106] Confessor began as a British-French-Dutch co-operative project and it initially aimed to make use of existing Sea Cat launchers to fire a missile that could intercept supersonic anti-ship missiles.[107] This was a considerable leap from the subsonic aircraft that Sea Cat could theoretically deal with, and as a result the system grew in bulk rather rapidly and therefore required its own much larger and stronger launcher. It did continue the Sea Cat 'point defence' philosophy of intercepting its target at close range, rather than medium-range point-defence missiles such as the US Sea Sparrow or area defence systems such as Sea Dart and the US Tartar. This meant that Sea Wolf missiles remained relatively small, thus allowing for manual loading into launchers and the ability to carry many more such missiles in a deep magazine (up to fifty-four on a Type 22 in total, compared to eight and no re-loads in a Sea Sparrow launcher[108]), but its short-range did

mean that there would probably only be one chance to intercept a missile in the last seconds of its flight. At one point, Sea Sparrow with British radars was considered as an alternative option that might keep the Dutch involved in the Type 22, but the US missile's bulky nature meant that reloads could not be carried. Sea Sparrow also had a longer warm-up time than Sea Wolf which impacted its ability to intercept targets quickly.[109] This concept was soon rejected. The French had backed out of Sea Wolf in 1966 and Dutch followed soon afterwards, the latter accepting Sea Sparrow and the former developing their own medium-range missile, Crotale.[110]

Co-operation with the Dutch on the Standard Frigate also faltered as their requirements soon diverged from that of the Royal Navy. The Dutch wanted to retain a medium gun and adopt Sea Sparrow while the British shifted to ship-to-ship guided missiles instead and stuck with Sea Wolf. A compromise was patched up in 1968 whereby both navies would develop their own variants of the Type 22 with differing armament and sensor fits but keeping the same hull.[111] As it was clear that the partnership was unravelling, the Dutch made one last attempt to keep it alive. They were willing to accept a single common design, including Sea Wolf and no medium gun, as long as Sea Wolf made use of Dutch electronic technology in a jointly-designed 'Gamma' system instead of the UK-only Marconi GWS 25. This was extremely tempting, in that such a ship, using Sea Wolf, had a good chance of becoming a NATO Standard Frigate, but Marconi was unwilling to concede Dutch involvement and the Ministry of Defence in turn was unwilling to push the issue with one of its major contractors.[112]

The Dutch finally accepted that they would have to design their own frigate – the 'Standaard Frigate' – which eventually entered service between 1978 and 1983 as the *Kortenaer* class. Shorn of Dutch partnership, the Type 22 began to grow in size and sophistication. The most important driver of this increase was the Sea Wolf/GWS 25 missile system, which continued to grow in size and bulk, with launchers, guidance radars and below decks processors requiring more space and creating more topweight on the ship design. The decision in 1970 to fit two Sea Wolf/GWS 25 systems, which would provide all-round air defence and some redundancy in the event of battle damage or breakdown, was probably the most important driver of space and weight increase: each time the missile system grew, twice that growth now needed to be accommodated on the ship.[113] The decision in late 1972 or early 1973 to add provision for a second Lynx helicopter demonstrated how large the ship had become: it could accommodate two such helicopters side by side in the ship's hangar, but it also enabled a significant increase in helicopter availability.[114] As a result of these, and other changes, the Type 22 grew from 2,900 tonnes in 1969 to 4,030 tons in 1975 when the first ship of the class had her keel laid.[115]

This increase in cost and the consequent realisation that fewer ships of the class would be built than initially planned, combined with the increasing focus on anti-submarine warfare, prompted a gradual perception in the Naval Staff that the Type 22 was too expensive, not capable enough and the wrong ship for the Eastern Atlantic task. In 1972, just before the order for the first of class was placed, the Type 22 was offered up for possible cancellation as a means of controlling the budget.[116] This was hardly a vote of confidence in the design. Two years before a new ship concept had appeared in the Long Term Costing Assumptions: the large 'ASW Ship'. By 1973 it had grown to 12,000 tons and would be capable of operating six Sea King dipping sonar helicopters and fitted with a 'bottom bounce' sonar. At first glance this appeared to be a resurrection of Varyl Begg's original command cruiser concept before it had been enlarged under Le Fanu to take Harriers.[117] In fact, it was a realisation that the most effective anti-submarine weapon system available to the surface fleet was the large dipping-sonar and sonobuoy-fitted helicopter operating in some numbers to form screens around a surface task group, and that there were just not enough of helicopter platforms in the fleet.

The Type 22's contribution to the core anti-submarine role by contrast was relatively meagre: until 1973 it was planned to be fitted with the same Type 184M sonar that so limited the capability of the Ikara system. From this date the next-generation Type 2016 was planned to be fitted instead. It was a much more capable system than the Type 184M, with a double beam: one for detection within the surface layer and a second angled at 7 degrees to penetrate the thermocline with a 'bottom bounce' capability. Its typical effective range of 9km was a significant improvement but still too short to detect missile-firing submarines or torpedo firings at long-range. It was more effective in shallow water than the Type 184M.[118] Two Lynx helicopters would be much better anti-submarine systems than the single Wasp helicopter on board the current generation of ships, but the Lynx remained a torpedo-delivery system without its own dipping sonar or sonobouys and was therefore still largely dependent on the Type 22's own sonar with all its limitations for detection. The Type 22 was therefore more of a large and extremely capable general-purpose platform suited to a global patrol role or limited-war situations, but even then this was partly undermined by the absence of a medium gun, and by 1973 the NATO anti-submarine role was becoming increasingly dominant in Royal Naval deployments and doctrine. In this context, the large ASW Ship seemed doctrinally much more relevant.

Another late competitor to the Type 22 was the 2,500-tonne 'SSGW frigate', which would have been armed with eight Exocet, a medium gun and Lynx but no self-defence missile system. In 1972 it was proposed presumably as a means to get Exocet to sea quicker and provide a cheaper supplement to the Type 22: the Type 22's programme would be reduced by a quarter and the cancelled vessels replaced by more than double the number of SSGW frigates which would cost £16.5 million per unit in Autumn 1971 prices compared to the Type 22 at £12.4 million.[119] An expensive vessel with heavy medium-range offensive weaponry but no means of self-defence could not have been particularly attractive and the idea was soon discarded, but it was clear that the Type 22 after its growth in size during design development was seen as too small for effective anti-submarine warfare, but too large and expensive for the patrol and anti-shipping tasks.

In the event, the Type 22 was not cancelled and the first two vessels, *Broadsword* and *Battleaxe*, were ordered in February 1974 and September 1975, whilst the ASW Ship, which looked rather like a competitor to the Cruiser, was dropped from the long-range programme during the 1974–5 Defence Review. Adopting the ASW Ship would also have meant accepting that the number of frigates would drop considerably over the long-term as they were replaced by smaller numbers of these large vessels: a decision with consequences both for Royal Navy deployments in the wide range of single ship-taskings, and for the number of vessels attributed to NATO. There also appears to have been considerable momentum behind the Type 22: any alternatives would not have been available to order for some years, and the Naval Staff would have been unlikely to countenance yet more stopgap Type 21s. The forces pushing to retain the existing pyramid force structure of the ocean-going surface fleet were much stronger than those, however tactically sound, arguing for more radical change.

Minor War Vessels

The Naval Staff's policy on patrol craft in the late 1960s and early 1970s was marked by much uncertainty and changes in plan. Ageing converted 'Ton' class minesweepers needed replacing in both Hong Kong and for fishery protection patrols of UK territorial waters, whilst the use of ocean patrol vessels in place of frigates to support the deep-sea fishing industry was also being considered as a possibility. The Future Fleet Working Party had proposed the building of three fast target craft to train the Fleet in countering Soviet fast attack craft, followed by a class of up to ten fast patrol craft, probably armed with anti-ship missiles, to cover the UK patrol role. This plan still held in 1968. The three target craft became the *Scimitar* class, a linear development of the preceding 'Brave' class of the 1950s, powered by gas turbines but too small to mount guided missiles. However, by 1968 doubts appear to have been mounting about the appropriateness of short-ranged fast missile craft in the patrol role, and an alternative programme was mooted with only three new missile craft and nine slower but longer range patrol craft.[120] An abbreviated concept of operations in the Royal Navy's Fighting Instructions of 1969 saw uses for fast craft in the Baltic and Norwegian Seas, but envisaged their most likely use in limited war operations.[121] They were seen as coastal craft that could protect friendly coastal shipping and attack enemy shipping, and their operation from rapidly-established temporary bases as well as operations in the High North and Baltic had been practised since the early 1950s,[122] but their short endurance, the decline in coastal shipping, the low likelihood of Soviet surface ships operating in British waters during wartime and their limited anti-submarine weaponry had made them a capability with only a secondary or tertiary role, and therefore vulnerable to removal from the programme.

By 1969 the fast craft had disappeared entirely and were replaced by six ocean patrol craft, four inshore patrol craft and five Hong Kong patrol vessels, all to be delivered by 1975.[123] By 1971 there had been yet another change. Fast craft had returned, but this time they were to be either US-built *Tucumcari* class hydrofoils or a British-designed or built variant, combined with patrol craft built to the RAF's *Seal* class design. Both types were externally designed, hinting at a possible overloading of Ship Department design staff with other higher priority work.[124] The following year, and with the naval budget under pressure, yet another somersault had been performed with the hydrofoils largely disappearing and the number of *Seal* class boats being reduced, with later vessels being of a different and new class.[125] Having made four major changes in nearly as many years, the Navy needed to procure at least some craft urgently, so four *Seal* class vessels were finally ordered in 1972 to replace the converted 'Ton' class in the inshore fishery protection role. Joined by one of the RAF's discarded vessels of the same class, they were not a success, their ability to stand difficult seas was severely limited.[126] With impending changes in international maritime boundaries, and the birth of the offshore oil industry in the North Sea, seakeeping in the open seas would soon be at a premium, and the five RN *Seal* class were quickly moved to secondary duties. They were not much to show for the lost, ambitious and multiple plans of the preceding years, the only ghost of what might have been, was Vosper Thornycroft's speculative 45-knot, steel-hulled, fast patrol boat *Tenacity*. She started construction just as the Naval Staff was shifting away from the fast patrol boat type; unable to find a buyer, she was purchased by the Royal Navy in February 1973 and undertook fishery protection duties moderately successfully until being placed on the disposal list in 1980.[127]

Where the policy on patrol craft was uncertain and suffered from numerous changes, that for mine countermeasures vessels was much clearer. The Soviet Navy continued to pose a significant mine threat to NATO: it was estimated that the USSR had a stock of over 400,000 mines with another 50,000 supplied to other Warsaw Pact navies; unlike NATO navies most Soviet warships had minelaying capabilities, including their submarines.[128] Glass Reinforced Plastic (or 'GRP') hulls opened up the possibility of moving away from wooden hulls to a stronger and more robust hull-form, and after joint development between Vosper Thornycroft and the Procurement Executive, a satisfactory form of GRP was now ready to trial on a full-sized hull.[129] A GRP hull shape was created, based on the 'Ton' class minesweeper, and machinery and equipment from a scrapped vessel, HMS *Derriton*, was transferred to the new ship, which was named HMS *Wilton*.[130] For some time there had been fears that GRP-hulled vessels could not stand up to heavy seas. The building of HMS *Wilton* was therefore a calculated risk to prove a concept. The risk taken paid off: not only could *Wilton* perform well in trials in up to sea state ten and was despatched to the Mediterranean to take part in mine-clearance operations in the Suez Canal, but the process of developing and designing *Wilton* created a world-leading centre of expertise at Vosper Thornycroft in the process of building GRP vessels.[131]

The next step was to design and build a new class of GRP vessels to replace the existing fleet of 'Ton' class minesweepers and minehunters. Whilst traditional sweeping was sufficient to deal with tethered mines and influence sweeps could deal with standard acoustic and influence mines, mines on the seabed and other sophisticated mines needed to be hunted using specialist mine hunting sonars such as the Type 193M and un-crewed tethered mini-submersibles such as the French PAP104X to inspect the suspect mine and then lay a charge to destroy it. The PAP104X would be controlled from the ship's operations room, which would have the CAAIS tactical command system, which had hitherto been fitted to frigates.[132] The dual sweeping and hunting role required not only two separate groups of equipment but propulsion that could manage sustained steady speed sweeps combined with the ability to stop, manoeuvre and 'hover' at low speeds during hunting operations. Two Deltic diesels, a pulse generator and three power generators were placed on rafts to reduce vibrations and noise, driving two low noise large screws and a bow thruster.[133] This required a complex vessel, and combined with a GRP hull, this would not come cheap: *Wilton* had cost nearly four times the price per ton of a wooden 'Ton' class, although she was a prototype and this cost would be halved during the development of the new GRP mine warfare vessel.[134] Despite this, the price of the first of the new class was estimated to be £4 million in 1971.[135] In 1968 a twenty-ship class was envisaged, with a first ordered in 1973, followed by three a year until 1978 and a final two in 1979.[136] As was the fate of many other 'second priority' classes during the early 1970s, the order dates for the class slipped back repeatedly, until finally in 1975, the first of class HMS *Brecon*, was ordered. Vospers created a full-scale mock-up of the first ship in order to reduce the numbers of errors in construction, which would have been much more difficult to make right in GRP than with steel.[137] Eventually thirteen ships would be built of the 'Hunt' class albeit at a much slower rate than originally envisaged, entering service between 1980 and 1988. The size of vessels grew during design development: from 540 tons as a concept in 1968 to 650 tonnes in 1972 and 685 in 1975.[138] The 'Hunt' class was a successful design, with most of the class still in service today, with the Royal Navy or other navies, more than 30 years after their construction. They were however, expensive, and in the later years of the 1970s design work began on a cheaper 'single role' minehunter without sweep capabilities.

The Unbuilt Ships

As the most important parts of the shipbuilding programme – the nuclear submarines and the new cruisers, destroyers and frigates – began to escalate in price and their rates of ordering continued to slow, the procurement of a host of second-tier ship types was repeatedly put back with the fate for all being their eventual cancellation. The Large ASW ship and the fast patrol boat/hydrofoil have already been discussed, but there were also a significant number of larger vessels that were to spend the 1970s in planning purgatory before being culled either in the 1974–5 Defence Review or soon afterwards. The most significant such design was that for two new commando carriers.[139]

The 1970 decision to retain *Ark Royal* in service and to retain a somewhat greater capability East of Suez, in fact resulted in the de-prioritisation of the amphibious ships that only a few years earlier had been considered the backbone of the British East of Suez capability. Plans to order the first of two new commando carriers in 1972 were dropped, whilst the readiness of the existing amphibious assault ships, *Fearless* and *Intrepid*, were reduced with one entering reserve and the ships alternating between reserve and active service thereafter. A requirement for one commando carrier remained in the programme, to be ordered in 1979 and enter service in 1983 when *Hermes* would eventually retire from service.[140] As had occurred with the patrol craft requirement, the long-term programme for new amphibious vessels went through a period of dizzying and sometimes perplexing changes from 1972 to 1976 – a sure sign that any orders would be placed at all was becoming increasingly unlikely. First, the order of one vessel was replaced by three competing assumptions of one vessel, two or none at all.[141] Then, in 1973 a large 'CVS' or anti-submarine helicopter carrier appeared in the long-term programme as a means to increase the number of helicopters in the fleet. This, and the commando carrier type, disappeared the next year and was replaced by two ships described as 'LPH/CVS's – dual-role ASW and commando carriers, not unlike the role that *Hermes* herself would increasingly fill from 1976 onwards. These would be utility versions of the new cruisers and would be ordered once the three cruisers had been completed.[142] By 1974 four new *Sir Lancelot* class Logistic Landing Ships were briefly in the programme, probably as a measure to support the shipbuilding industry, but the following year these had disappeared and so would the commando carriers following the decision in the 1974–5 Defence Review not to replace the amphibious warfare capability.[143] The precarious position of the Royal Marines – without any specialised shipping to bring it ashore – was confirmed by this Defence Review, but an important part of this precariousness had its origins in 1971 when *Ark Royal* was spared and the planned 1972 commando carrier cancelled.

An even larger ship came tantalisingly close to being procured in 1968: a huge 22,000 ton Fleet Depot Ship would have entered service in 1972, replacing the 29-year-old HMS *Forth* as a combined nuclear submarine and general fleet depot ship.[144] Such a large vessel resulted in various shipyards grouping together to bid for the contract during 1967 and a design assistance contract was let at about the same time.[145] However the requirement, which was partly tied to the need to base nuclear-powered submarines – including potentially the Polaris boats – outside home waters, had disappeared by June 1968 and the ship was cancelled, further reducing naval orders for the increasingly desperate shipbuilding industry.[146] Plans for two Fleet Maintenance Ships, each with accommodation and facilities for a full Fleet Maintenance Unit, to replace the converted aircraft carrier HMS *Triumph*, eventually went the same way. A 10,000-tonne design had soon grown to over 13,000 tonnes and by 1970 had inherited an additional role as a diesel-electric submarine depot ship.[147] In 1972 they were still in the long-term programme with plans to order in 1976 and 1979, but by June 1973 this had slipped to 1978 and 1979 and the following year both had been cancelled under the auspices of the Defence Review.[148] A Mine Countermeasures Forward Support Ship to replace the wartime cruiser-minelayer HMS *Manxman* stayed in the programme the longest. Initially a requirement for two 6,000-ton vessels able to support ten mine countermeasures vessels each, by 1970 the ships had shrunk to 4,000 tonnes and by 1972 only a single vessel was required.[149] The following year the vessel shrank again to only 1,400 tonnes and would probably have been an updated version of HMS *Abdiel*, a ship of the same size and a similar role which had entered service in 1967.[150] The new ship, whose order date was repeatedly pushed back, had finally disappeared from the long-term programme by 1978.

Through the 1970s the Royal Navy gradually accepted the transfer to the shore of the roles that depot, maintenance and support ships had previously undertaken: a much more realistic proposition when all vessels were to be based in the United Kingdom. Maintenance and support on the quayside also allowed the gradual shifting of some roles from uniformed servicemen to Ministry of Defence industrial staff, which saved money as they were cheaper to employ, but perhaps reduced flexibility and 'responsiveness'.[151] On her return to the United Kingdom from Singapore in 1972, the aged HMS *Forth* was renamed HMS *Defiance* and based at Devonport dockyard where she became the depot ship for the newly formed Second Submarine Squadron whilst also acting as the base for Devonport's Fleet Maintenance Unit, which specialised in maintaining the Fleet's *Leander* class frigates worldwide.[152] The combination of submarine and surface ship maintenance in one hull was a product of an increasing focus on bringing these two support functions closer together, and was in some respects acknowledged the ghost of the cancelled combined submarine and surface vessel depot ship. In 1978 the former *Forth* was scrapped and her role replaced by shore facilities which were also named HMS *Defiance* in 1981.[153] The mine countermeasures support role also moved away from being based in ships. In 1980 the first Mine Countermeasures Support Unit was formed, its role to being to travel by air to mine warfare vessels operating beyond home waters to undertake support and basic maintenance functions.[154] Although routine maintenance and support could be undertaken ashore or with 'flying in' teams in most circumstances, the ability to provide major maintenance and repair facilities to vessels on operations could never have been done by flying in teams and as a result HMS *Triumph* was retained in reserve until 1981 for possible activation in such circumstances. She was never used in such a role but a year after her scrapping, the oil rig support ship MV *Stena Seaspread* was taken up from trade to undertake what would have been *Triumph*'s role for the Falklands campaign.[155] *Stena Seaspread*'s sister ship, *Stena Inspector*, was later purchased and became RFA *Diligence* in 1983, remaining in service in the fleet maintenance role until 2015.

Auxiliaries

The Royal Fleet Auxiliary had benefited from a burst of sustained investment from the late 1950s to the end of the 1960s, as it shifted from a freighting fleet to a service that specialised in replenishing warships at sea. During the 1960s four new classes had entered service: two 'Improved Tide' class and three *Olynthus* class tankers with helicopter landing decks and hangars for vertical replenishment ('VERTREP'), three 'Ness' class stores support ships which had flight decks but not hangars, and two *Resource* class fleet replenishment ships. The *Resource* class specialised in ammunition and explosives but also carried food, whilst two of the 'Ness' class carried general stores. The last 'Ness' class, *Lyness*, was an aviation stores ship.[156] The 1970s saw some enhancement to this modern fleet, first with six, later reduced to five, 'Rover' class small fleet tankers, which were versatile ships that could carry over 340 tons of general stores in addition to her fuel, and then with two, originally three, *Fort Austin* class fleet replenishment ships to replace older 1950s-vintage vessels. The *Fort Austin* class were a modified version of the 'Ness' class which carried a mix of ammunition and naval stores and benefitted from a hangar capable of operating up to four helicopters. Two ships were ordered relatively quickly in 1971, which demonstrated their perceived importance for supporting the fleet and eventually entered service in 1978.[157] The Navy also purchased or chartered a number of larger support and mobile reserve tankers of the 'Leaf' and 'Dale' classes, undertaking the vital but mundane task of transporting oil for the fleet from the Gulf, round the Cape and back to the United Kingdom. They would often transfer oil to the small fleet tankers supporting the Beira Patrol in the western Indian Ocean on their way to the Cape.[158] A class of new fleet tankers was mooted during the 1970s, initially as a class of eight vessels entering service between 1978 and 1985, which was then reduced to five by the late 1970s.[159] As their ordering was repeatedly pushed back it became clear that the older 'Tide' and *Olynthus* classes would have to soldier on through the 1980s and perhaps the early 1990s. These ships were eventually superseded by a new class of combined tanker/replenishment ships which later became the *Fort Victoria* class. Given the delays these new tankers suffered during the 1970s, the Royal Fleet Auxiliary was fortunate that much of its fleet had been renewed in the 1960s, but it did create the potential problem of block obsolescence of much of the RFA's fleet in the late 1980s and early 1990s unless sufficient numbers of *Fort Victoria* class vessels were built.

* * *

During the 1970s the Royal Navy had to tackle the problems of bringing vessels into service that encompassed major new technologies in sensors, weapons and propulsion combined with improved living standards. In its rush to get these new technologies procured it placed orders for two new classes of warship – the Type 42 and Type 21 – before either design was sufficiently mature, resulting in the 'development' and 'manufacture' phases running almost concurrently, a spiralling in costs and slowing in production, all whilst high inflation, labour and material shortages and industrial action exacerbated an already difficult situation in the shipbuilding industry. Two other important follow-on designs, the Cruiser and the Type 22 frigate, grew in size, capability and cost whilst under protracted design development. The increase in the Cruiser's size reflected a long-term plan to convert the ship into a small aircraft carrier, which at least was a part of a planned – albeit not entirely overt – process within the Naval Staff, but the Type 22's increase resulted from an incremental capability and cost spiral over five years. This increase was particularly egregious as it was fast becoming clear that in all but the worst weather conditions large anti-submarine helicopters were much more capable anti-submarine platforms than frigates, even those equipped with two light helicopters and a modern sonar such as the Type 22. Conservatism in favour of the familiar frigate and the basic fact that it was already in the programme saved the class, even though different replacement or supplementary options were considered throughout the 1970s.

These difficulties with the four leading surface-ship types resulted in their own programmes being repeatedly pushed back and reduced in scale, whilst lower priority ship orders of minor war vessels, amphibious ships and support ships mostly suffered the eventual fate of extreme delay or cancellation after years of push-backs. By comparison, the nuclear submarine programme benefitted from regular orders, design changes that could be explained as incremental, and above all a clear commitment to a production line of such vessels by those at the top of Defence and the government.

Another significant problem was structural: the Long Term Costings system within Defence which had been established on the creation of a single combined Ministry in 1964 was fundamentally flawed. There was nothing inherently wrong with a ten-year forward plan for spending by each service, but it worked within a context that made it impossible for it to work as intended. Through the 1970s, the size of planned ten-year programmes began to inflate, even though there was mounting evidence that even the earliest, more conservative plans, had been painfully over-optimistic. The 1968 Long Term Costing Assumptions had envisaged thirty-three frigates and destroyers being ordered between 1968 and 1978, with thirty-five entering service in the same period.[160] In reality this was a significant overestimate: a total of only twenty-five were actually ordered and twenty-five entered service during this time.[161] By 1973 many of the problems highlighted in this chapter had already manifested themselves, but the Long Term Costing Assumptions issued that year optimistically envisaged a total of thirty-seven destroyer and frigate orders between 1973 and 1983, and a total of thirty-four completions.[162] Reality would again be quite different: there would be twenty orders and twenty-four completions.[163] Although the difference between the planned and actual order and completion rates for the cruisers and nuclear submarines was proportionately much better,[164] reflecting their high priority position within the programme, the rates for patrol, mine warfare and support vessels was much worse than for destroyers and frigates.[165]

Why did the Naval Staff continue to make these significant overestimates when they knew that their previous experience, the lack of any significant real-term increase in the defence budget and decreasing shipbuilding capacity all meant that their being fulfilled was highly unlikely? The perennial problems of modern defence procurement which are still with us today, are part of the explanation: an optimism bias on the part of contractors and the Royal Navy who are both keen for procurements to go ahead, combined with the curse of 'defence inflation'.[166] The rate of defence inflation has generally been historically higher than standard inflation within the wider economy as defence is 'overweight' in personnel costs and high-technology be-spoke equipment – which are more likely to increase in cost at a faster rate than other goods within the 'basket' that is used to calculate economy-wide inflation which are more likely to be commodified and reduce in relative price over time.

There was also a more insidious and specific problem that affected the Navy more than the other services. Throughout much of the period covered by this book, the government held publicly to a total number of destroyers and frigates in the fleet: sixty-eight in the early 1970s, sixty from 1975 and then fifty from the mid-1980s. At the same time, the cost and size of minimum-capable ships increased disproportionately, the escalation in size and unit cost of frigates from the *Leander* class to the Type 22 shows this clearly; a 40 per cent increase in tonnage and a more than tripling in unit cost.[167] If ship numbers in such circumstances were inevitably going to reduce when the defence budget was not increasing or only increasingly marginally, then for the Long Term Costing Assumptions to reflect reality, then they should factor in a natural and gradual reduction in ship numbers over time. However, this would come up against the reality of contemporary defence politics: if the number of ships was going to reduce, then what commitments would be dropped in the future, and what would be the political or diplomatic impact? The Treasury would then argue that if the commitment is to be dropped at some point in the future, why not now? What will be politically and economically different in five or ten years' time that is not relevant today? To concede a reduction in the future would be tantamount to conceding a reduction in the present, and the Navy's leaders saw no benefit in 'an unforced error' without gaining anything in return. No other services had so much of their equipment so tightly tied to 'commitments' such as guardships, patrols and attendance at major exercises as the Navy did. The Army in Germany was tied to a minimum number of personnel which did have some similar effects, but this was protected by the Brussels Treaty, whilst the total escort figure was only a national figure, that could be changed by a Defence Secretary, usually following a defence review. The Royal Navy and, to a similar but somewhat lesser extent, the other services had a strong incentive to inflate their long-term planning assumptions beyond what was realistic in order to keep to present-day equipment number commitments, even though they might make little sense within the context of five or ten years' time. Such a situation created an increasingly overweight procurement programme across the whole of Defence, and would soon begin to build pressure for a full defence review which could cut the Gordian knot by re-assessing commitments, capabilities and operational concepts, and then force cancellations or reductions on the three services.

The situation in which the Admiralty Board found itself at the time seemed unfamiliar and disturbing, but the problems they faced were essentially those that have been encountered by successive defence decision-makers through to the present day: high technology bespoke capabilities consisting of a combination of complex systems and sub-systems, that were not fully defined at the point of decision which resulted in unexpected cost escalation. This then created a 'bow wave' effect on the rest of the procurement programme and pushed lower priority projects into the future, further building up costs over time and creating inescapable pressures for a comprehensive review of the need for these procurements to push them back towards affordability.

8

The Critical Level

If Admiral Pollock was an unexpected First Sea Lord whose time in charge was dominated by the question of modernising nuclear weapons and building a new generation of warships, Admiral Sir Edward Ashmore's period as the professional head of the Navy was dominated by the 1974 to 1975 Defence Review and its aftermath. Ashmore took over from Admiral Pollock on 1 March 1974, the day the results for the 28 February general election were confirmed. Harold Wilson formed a minority government on 4 March and the Defence Review began in earnest only a few days later. Ashmore, who had earned a DSC for his role in the Malta convoys of the Second World War, was a signals specialist with Russian-language training, a pair of specialisations that meant he had a relatively unusual route to the top of the Navy, which included a period as Chief Signals Officers to the NATO AFNORTH command in Oslo and Assistant Chief of the Defence Staff (Signals) back in Whitehall. He also held more traditional postings for senior officers heading for the top, including a period as Director of Naval Plans, as Second in Command of the Far East Fleet, and then Vice Chief of the Naval Staff, before becoming Commander-in-Chief of the Western Fleet just as it transformed into Commander-in-Chief Fleet.[1] His NATO experience, combined with being a signaller and Russian linguist, gave him a very particular 'Cold Warrior' profile; and as such he appeared well-suited to navigating the transition towards a Navy primarily focussed on the Eastern Atlantic and High North. This chapter will deal with this Defence Review and the decisions that followed in its wake, including a series of reviews of 'supporting elements' such as the Royal Marines, reserves, the WRNS and the Hydrographic Service. It also covers two 'conflicts' that were ongoing during this period: that in Northern Ireland and also the second Cod War. The chapter that follows this will focus on those 'out of area' commitments that were given up or reduced following the Review.

The Defence Studies Working Party 1973–1974

As was described in previous chapter, the costs of major naval procurements were increasing at a worrying rate in the early 1970s. The Royal Navy was not alone however; similar issues were in evidence in all three services.[2] At the same time, the pressures on the rest of the public sector were also becoming more acute. Spending was increasing, not only because of the government's state-subsidised 'dash for growth', but also because of the growth in domestic public services, in particular new benefits to support the disabled and infirm, payments to the unemployed who had now increased to an unprecedented one million by the start of 1972, increases in National Health Service spending, the costs of increasing the school leaving age to 16, and a major school rebuilding programme.[3] In this context, the Treasury was not only hoping to ensure that defence spending was kept under control, but that it was decreased as a percentage of Gross National Product ('GNP') over the next decade in order to pay for these domestic public spending increases, and those that were likely to follow in the coming years. The Treasury also looked to the contributions of other western European states to defence and argued that the United Kingdom was spending a much higher proportion of its GNP than other European NATO members – at just under 6 per cent compared to 4.2 per cent for the NATO average: 'Britain has for years set an example to our Allies. In our present position of relative economic weakness we cannot afford to continue to lead.'[4] Defence was being told that it could no longer argue it was a special case and be treated any differently to other government departments. The Ministry of Defence's assumption that defence spending would increase in proportion to increases in GNP, which were expected to be around 3.5 per cent over the coming years, could not be taken for granted.[5] This was a radical push by a Treasury that was attempting to juggle the implications of the 'dash for growth' with the pain of the oil crisis, both of which were stoking inflation in an overheating economy. Within this context Defence was a ripe target for reductions. This was a view also held by a number of senior Conservative ministers including Sir Keith Joseph, the Secretary of State for Health and Social Services, who was deeply sceptical about the current level of defence spending in comparison to the needs of his own department.[6]

The Defence Secretary, Lord Carrington, agreed that the longer-term trends in defence spending were concerning and that the Long Term Costings needed to be reformed. He therefore agreed to study the different options available for long-term defence spending. The Permanent Under-Secretary did not want to repeat the public rancour of the previous run of defence reviews under Denis Healey.[7] It was therefore agreed to begin internal inter-departmental studies led by a steering group with Treasury, Ministry of Defence and Central Policy Review Staff (the 'CPRF', the Cabinet Office's internal think tank) members, but with the co-ordinating work set by a Defence Studies Working Party. The Working Party's remit included assessing the resources required for the military's different roles within the context of the differing demands on the totality of government resources. The Working Party was jointly chaired by two senior civil servants, one from the Treasury and the other from the Ministry, and it first met on 16 January 1973. Over most of the rest of that year, as the Yom Kippur war between Israel and Arab states and the oil crisis that followed accentuated the economic difficulties that the United Kingdom faced, the Working Party assessed a range of studies into defence spending and the roles of defence. Its purpose was not to decide on which option to settle on – that would have meant a full defence review which would have to be announced publicly – but to set out the available options, which would be decided upon by ministers the following year.[8]

Just as the Working Party was starting its analysis, the Ministry of Defence's own Long Term Studies Group had completed its analysis of long-term trends in defence, and came up with the dispiriting conclusion that even if defence spending increases matched expected GNP growth, both the size and quality of personnel and equipment could not be maintained to ensure that it did not fall behind the expected growth of Warsaw Pact forces.[9] A Treasury-commissioned report had also fed into these studies, and came up with the equally dispiriting conclusion that over the next decade the GNP of the five Western European NATO states (West Germany, France, Belgium, Netherlands and Italy) would grow by 99 per cent whilst that of the UK would grow by 55 per cent. Even then, if defence spending increased at the same rate as GNP, British defence spending would still be higher as a percentage of GNP than for any of these five economies by the end of the decade.[10] The Treasury was using this comparative approach with other European states in order to press what it really wished to achieve: the setting out of different force structures based on a series of budget options, each one of which would be less than the current £3.5 billion a year, which equated to approximately 5.4 per cent of GNP. The most extreme suggested option was a reduction to 2.8 per cent of GNP by 1980–1: a halving of spending in only five years that would have had a huge diplomatic impact within NATO and Western Europe, and probably a significant impact on the defence industry at home.[11] At this stage however, the Foreign and Commonwealth Office were absent from these studies.

With the arrival of General Sir Michael Carver as Chief of the Defence Staff in place of Admiral Hill-Norton, the Chiefs of Staff Committee decided to gain a firmer grip over the studies being fed into the Defence Studies Working Party and a new steering committee under the Chiefs of Staff was created through which all submissions would have to pass.[12] Eventually, the Working Party's Interim report was formally submitted to the Prime Minister,

Chancellor of the Exchequer and Defence Secretary at the end of November 1973.[13] The inter-service sniping that Carver wished to eradicate was clearly still in evidence at this stage: the Chief of the Air Staff wanted to add a qualifier to the role of protecting merchant shipping, stating that this protection would only occur after 'taking account of defence priorities and resources', a strong hint that the Air Staff was hoping that Defence would back away from or shrink this role, thus reducing the need for surface escorts and therefore reducing the requirement for RAF air defence assets to defend those escorts. It would also shift the focus of anti-submarine warfare towards the barrier patrols and 'attack at source' operations that the RAF preferred. The First Sea Lord objected and Pat Nairne, the leading civil servant on the Working Party, had to broker a compromise form of wording which eventually read 'when necessary and to the greatest extent practicable'.[14] The Assistant Secretary at Chiefs of Staff Secretariat summed up this petty squabbling pithily with a single word: 'pathetic'.[15] It was clear that at this stage at least, Carver had some distance to go before the single-service Chiefs were able to provide a unified line.

What the Interim Report did not do was set out the rationales for the different capabilities that defence possessed. It was assumed that the Working Party's activities in 1974 would consist of completing this second stage, which would then provide the justified and costed options to enable Ministers to decide. In the event, the Prime Minister called a general election earlier than planned, which was then lost by the Conservatives, the Labour Party entering government on 4 March as a minority administration. The Chiefs of Staff believed that a new defence review would be inevitable given both the state of the economy and the general election manifesto of the incoming Labour party which argued that the United Kingdom's defence budget should be reduced to a level closer to that of its major European allies.[16] The Chiefs were correct in their assumption.

The Defence Review 1974–1975

Beginning the Review
The Cabinet Secretary recommended a defence review to the returning Labour Prime Minister, Harold Wilson: the United Kingdom's defence commitments would no longer be met credibly by its capabilities from 1975 onwards. The new Defence Review's structure piggy-backed on that set up for the Defence Studies of 1973: the DSWP stayed in place and was now tasked with managing most of the legwork of the Review, with a remit expanded to look at short-term spending, as well as the medium and longer-term perspective it had taken in the 1973 work. A new steering group was created, this time managed by the Cabinet Secretary himself, to assess and review the findings of

the DSWP.[17] The Treasury, having already created an expectation of options based on possible percentages of GNP during the previous year, was able to push through a similar approach at the start of the Review. They proposed the setting out of four options as: a reduction to 4.5 per cent of GNP by 1978–9, a reduction to 4.5 per cent of GNP by 1983–4, a reduction to 4 per cent of GNP by 1978–9 and finally, a reduction to 4 per cent of GNP by 1983–4.[18] These four options were then accepted by the relevant ministerial Cabinet Committee, the Defence and Oversea Policy Committee, which also agreed to the submission of the Steering Committee's final recommendations in July and an agreement to consult internationally with NATO allies *before* these ministerial submissions.[19] The third of the four options was considered so radical that it had even exceeded the presumptions of the Labour Party's manifesto, but it remained in the options list, with the Treasury keen to use it as a minimum baseline to force the Ministry to reveal what defence capabilities would look like at this level, and then obliging the Ministry to argue for anything higher than this.[20] Permitting international consultations before ministers made their decisions was an important point that would add external pressures against any radical reductions in defence spending. The Defence and Oversea Policy Committee had also requested that the submission to them also include a listing of commitment groupings in their order of importance for British defence: NATO commitments in general, commitments to the Mediterranean and NATO's AFSOUTH Region, commitments in the Far East, commitments to CENTO and the Middle East, commitments to the Caribbean and South Atlantic, and finally the importance of reinforcement and assault forces, 'including the function of responding to the unforeseen'.[21]

The Critical Level

So far, the Treasury had been successfully driving the Review: imposing a way of reaching decisions based on particular budgetary levels that the Ministry would then have to fit its capabilities within. In some respects, this repeated the formulae of the 1964–6 and 1966–7 reviews when a single budgetary number was selected for the Ministry to reduce down towards. However, this time around the Treasury was being more ambitious. By setting out a range of budgetary options, and aiming to have the costings of different capabilities set out almost as a shopping list to be added or taken away from the total, the Treasury was not letting the Ministry decide how it would trim capabilities itself; it wanted to be directly involved along with other government departments represented on the steering group in such decisions from the very first step.[22] The Treasury's aggressive budgetary-based approach was the very opposite of how the Chiefs of Staff and the Defence Secretariat wanted the Review to be run. Within the Ministry there was a fear that the Treasury's financially-led approach would mean capability cuts without any parallel reductions in military tasks. From their perspective, government should instead set what tasks it wanted the military to undertake and then the military would come back with the costs of providing the capabilities to ensure that the tasks could be carried out. If this was more expensive than expected, then either that cost would have to be accepted, or ministers should decide which tasks, which were often part of declared 'commitments', should be dropped.[23] The Treasury disliked this approach as it placed the Ministry of Defence and the Services in the position of deciding whether tasks could be carried out or not, and limited the challenge that could be made to these decisions. To a department permanently sceptical of the Ministry of Defence's efficiency, this defeated much of the point of attempting to control defence spending.

In May Carver therefore adopted a bold approach: he added a fifth option based on a completely different presumption that became known as the 'critical level', a minimum at which existing core commitments to NATO could be met without undermining NATO strategy. Carver was starting with commitments and then working back from them, rather than starting with a budget figure.[24] From this point onwards, the analysis that the Ministry of Defence produced for the DSWP focussed primarily on what was required to maintain this critical level for NATO commitments. The assessments for the other four options were dealt with entirely differently. The 4 per cent level by 1978–9 was ignored altogether as being diplomatically and practicably impossible to achieve, the 4.5 per cent by 1978–9 and 4 per cent by 1983–4 were grouped together as the 'baseline' – an absolute minimum possible over the next decade for which the Ministry would only produce rather broad 'strategic essays' rather than detailed force levels, whilst the 4.5 per cent by 1983–4 level began to merge with the 'critical level'.[25] With the Defence Secretary's fulsome backing, this approach moved the Review away from the Treasury's preferred territory of budgetary levels towards ground on which the Chiefs of Staff felt much more comfortable: setting the size and shape of Defence on a series of minimum commitments, with the capabilities required to meet these commitments partly set by the Chiefs themselves. Roy Mason, the Defence Secretary, accepted this approach because he fundamentally disagreed with a large reduction in defence spending, which he felt was being driven by the Labour Party's increasingly militant left wing.[26] He had also been insistent from the start that 'MOD should take and keep the initiative within Whitehall' over the Review, and acquiescing to the Treasury's formulation of the options would have done the opposite of this.[27] Also, preliminary NATO consultations on the possible review outcomes had started early in May 1974 and as soon as allies began to hear about the possible worst-case scenarios, murmurs of disapproval could be heard from the Alliance partners.

The Supreme Allied Commander Europe, US General Andrew Goodpaster, bluntly stated that the result of the Review was a 'shattering blow to the flanks of the Alliance'.[28] There was also concern that it would set off a cascade of defence-spending reductions across the Alliance, further weakening it when Soviet capabilities seemed to be inexorably rising.

Carver's re-framing of the Treasury's options and the addition of his own, had created a new three option arrangement: the 'critical level' which would be a little above the 4.5 per cent of GNP level (which had been the Treasury's most generous option), and then the 'baseline' level which was clearly painted as the one that would cause a crisis within NATO. Carver's critical level gained additional support from the CPRS, who agreed that going below this level would result in a 'significant all-round reduction in our contribution to NATO' and would also open the possibility that a hard choice might have to be made between the maritime eastern Atlantic commitment or the land commitment on the Central European front.[29] Having to make such a choice would have smashed Carver's unified line amongst the services and meant a return to the vicious rivalries of the 1964 to 1968 period, and no one within Defence was willing to contemplate that.

The critical level, which was associated with fulfilling NATO commitments, became the reference point from which the others were assessed. Carver had skilfully re-engineered the options debate and forced the Treasury onto the defensive. He also ensured that the three services did not publicly fall out with one another, in order to ensure that the painful internecine fighting of 1964–7 did not happen again.[30] The Treasury had over-reached itself, partly through its ignorance of the diplomatic impact of major reductions within NATO, and it would be unable to impose another budgetary level target in a defence review until the end of the Cold War. As will be seen, the next defence review – in 1981 – was entirely focussed on reducing projected future spending to fit with already-planned budgets, not to reduce down to an externally agreed target.

The Navy

The Navy's contribution to the Ministry of Defence's submission to the DSWP started with an assessment of the Soviet threat. The large numbers of new nuclear submarines and major surface units entering the Soviet Navy was set out, and given as evidence that pointed to the Soviet 'attainment of a position of superiority in important sea areas by 1980 or soon after which would permit the adoption of a high risk policy of power politics worldwide'.[31] The section that followed on NATO maritime strategy set out a position in which the 'very grave' consequences of aggression in Europe as 'one reason why the Russians have turned their attention to the sea. NATO is much more heavily dependent on the sea and seabed resources than the Warsaw Pact. This gives Russia the option to damage NATO economically and politically by maritime pressure or action at any level; this option will be the more attractive, the weaker NATO's maritime strength becomes.' If a NATO with a weakened maritime capability decided to respond to Soviet maritime pressure by action on land, this 'would be much more likely to lead to escalation' and that this 'would probably be unacceptable to those NATO nations most directly affected'. As a result, 'maritime weakness would therefore deprive NATO of a range of possible responses to what is now seen as the most likely form of Soviet aggression; as well as of effective means to support operations on the European mainland in times of tension or war'.[32]

With the recent experience of the Soviet-US naval stand-off at the end of the 1973 Arab-Israeli war – which is described later in the next chapter – the concept of an East-West confrontation at sea short of a shooting war was not just theoretical but seen as a distinct possibility. In addition, the maritime domain, given that it was one in which populations did not live, was more likely to become environment of testing, confrontation, coercion and escalation, in which ships and submarines intermingled, shadowed and marked each other, in a way in which land forces facing each other across a 'hard' land border could not. Although not explicitly stated, this fitted into a broader strategic concept of a long period of maritime tension and perhaps even fighting at sea, weeks or maybe months before any land warfare started, acting almost as a preliminary whilst the US attempted to reinforce Europe. The document also stressed the symbolic value of maritime forces, particularly in supporting states on NATO's weak flanks, as a commitment to reinforce in times of tension.[33] Very little of this strategic assessment ended up in the documents passed to the steering group and ministers, which talked more generally about deterrence and NATO's Flexible Response approach, and when it did become more specific, focussed on the fact that any static barrier defence could be outflanked and that defence in depth was of the utmost importance.[34] Both of these aspects were much more relevant to the land environment in central Europe than to the Eastern Atlantic or other NATO maritime areas.

With respect to equipment, work soon began on two fleet options which were somewhat below critical level and closer to the base line. Fleet 1 would mean the reduction in the number of destroyers and frigates to fifty-eight, with a build rate of approximately two a year. Nineteen frigates and one destroyer (the 'County' class destroyer HMS *Hampshire*) would be paid off by the end of 1977, with another ten by March 1982. Only another two more Type 42s would be ordered, with the rest being cancelled, and the second Type 22 in the programme would also be cancelled. The Cruiser programme would be slowed down with the second and third ships being constructed at 2½-year intervals. One assault ship would be paid off as would the commando carrier

Bulwark. A plan to convert *Intrepid* into a basic commando carrier would also be cancelled. The number of conventional submarines would be reduced as older boats of the *Porpoise* class were paid off, and the total number of new conventional boats would also be halved. The Hong Kong patrol vessels would be cancelled without replacement, whilst the existing mine countermeasures fleet would be reduced in size, as would the new programme of GRP vessels. Five tankers, three stores ships and seven LSLs would be withdrawn without replacement, whilst the Antarctic patrol ship *Endurance* would be withdrawn without replacement and the planned diving ship cancelled.[35] This was quite a significant, and rapid, reduction, with most of the disposals occurring in 1976 and 1977. It also included a number of 'bleeding stump' proposals would clearly come up against strong opposition: the Foreign Office would not support the removal of all the Hong Kong patrol craft and the Antarctic Patrol Ship, whilst the Army relied on the LSLs to transport its armour to and from the British Army of the Rhine. Fleet 2 was an even more radical reduction to forty-eight destroyers and frigates, a slower SSN programme, the immediate withdrawal of *Ark Royal* and heavy reductions across the fleet. Outside of Fleets 1 and 2, the cancellation of the planned large ASW ships and the two combined LPH/CVS would also be costed, as would the cancellation of two planned hydrofoils and the early paying off of the older cruisers *Tiger* and *Blake*.[36] Over April, the Naval Staff refined these proposals and added an even more extreme option: Fleet 3, which included cancelling the Type 22, withdrawing all large surface ships except *Hermes* (with *Tiger* and *Blake* surviving until 1979–81), reducing the total submarine fleet to only twelve plus the four SSBNs, and the early disposal of all older frigates as well as the Batch 2 and 3 *Leander* class ships between 1976 and 1986, to bring the total frigate and destroyer force down to thirty-three by the late 1970s.[37]

Setting Out the Options
In the final DSWP report to the Steering Committee, these naval options had been adjusted and finessed further, with a critical level option that was somewhat more generous than the original Fleet 1. Fleets 2 and 3 had disappeared from view, but might have re-emerged if Carver's critical level gambit had failed. As presented to the Steering Committee, there were a total of seven options for Defence from A to G, although within these were the three core options of the critical level (Option C), the 'first level' (4.5 per cent of GNP by 1983/84 – Option D) and the baseline level (Option E). Option A was the Ministry's answer to the issue of prioritising different geographical areas in order of importance: it argued for either a total withdrawal (Option 1A) from all non-NATO commitments, saving £147 million a year by 1978–9, or a partial withdrawal (Option 1B), which would save £73 million by 1978–9

and £84 million by 1983–4. Option 1A would clearly be politically impossible as it involved removal of all military forces from Hong Kong, Cyprus, Belize and the Falklands by 1978–9, whilst Option 1B would involve nearly halving spending in Hong Kong and Cyprus, whilst withdrawing almost entirely from Malta and Mauritius/Indian Ocean.[38] By placing this option first, the driving presumption was set that any commitments beyond NATO should be shed if at all possible. There was no discussion of the benefits of keeping these capabilities, and the first two sentences set the tenor of the whole section: 'The United Kingdom commitment to NATO Alliance is the linchpin of our defence policy. Every possible saving in purely non-NATO expenditure and its back-up must therefore be rigorously sought.'[39] No mention was made of the fact that the United Kingdom still had significant interests worldwide, most of which were now trade-related. From now on, the safety of this trade would implicitly be dependent upon the United States' international defence presence, to which the British would contribute little after 1976. This was a dangerous position to be in. Only five years later, following the Iranian revolution and the outbreak of war between Iran and Iraq which would put international oil supplies sailing from the Gulf in jeopardy, the American government was no longer willing to protect British shipping for no recompense, and requested the return of a British naval presence to the Gulf and western Indian Ocean.[40] The British government responded with a naval commitment that exists to this day, having belatedly re-discovered that there was more to British national security than the defence of Central Europe.

Option B tackled the question of reinforcement forces. The original terms of reference had framed this with respect to reinforcement and assault forces, and 'responding to the unforeseen'. The 'unforeseen' and assault forces were largely absent from this option, which only discussed the reinforcement of the southern and northern NATO flanks. Option B2 involved the abandonment of all reinforcement capabilities, including disbanding the Royal Marines and scrapping the amphibious capability and the RAF's strategic air transport force, saving £100 million in 1978–9 and as much as £180 million in 1983–4. Option B1 recommended a two-thirds reduction in the size of the reinforcement capability, which would consist of a force of Army brigade group size, one Royal Marine Commando group, one battalion and supporting elements contributing to NATO's Air Mobile Force, one squadron of RAF Harriers available for short-notice deployment, fifty-six strategic transport aircraft, and a reduced amphibious force consisting of *Hermes* (having only a secondary amphibious role to her anti-submarine carrier role), two assault ships – one of which would be in reserve and the other would also be used as a sea training ship – which would not be replaced, and six LSLs to transport Army equipment. With Option B1, the role in support of the southern flank would be given up as it was much less important militarily than the US role in the Eastern Mediterranean, whilst the British role in northern flank reinforcement was proportionately more significant. The total savings of Option B1 were £40 million in 1978–9 and £125 million in 1983–4.[41] The Option B section was clearly written in a such a way to push the reader towards Option B1, which despite heavy reductions in reinforcement capabilities, did retain some, although primarily for northern flank reinforcement in a NATO context. Framing this issue based on *NATO* reinforcement, had some logic given the previous section's assertion that the NATO commitment was the linchpin of British defence, but despite this, the issue of responding to the unforeseen had disappeared entirely. It is in this omission that there can be seen the beginning of the descent towards a strategic myopia. In effect, only the expected threats would be prepared for and deterred, whilst minimal provision would be given to the unexpected. However, as was discovered with the Argentine invasion of the Falklands in 1982, and in many military emergencies since, it is in the nature of deterrence (whether nuclear or conventional) that when it is sufficiently effective, the 'expected threat' does not crystalise, therefore making the unexpected and the unforeseen *more* likely to occur. This has been termed the Quinlan paradox by the historian Peter Hennessy, after the senior Ministry of Defence civil servant who first enunciated this seemingly counter-intuitive concept some years after the Falklands conflict.[42]

Having used these first two 'options' to frame the analysis, without much discussion of the advantages and disadvantages of capabilities beyond NATO and the utility of preparing for the 'unforeseen', the paper then proceeded to the three core options: C, D and E, covering the critical level, first level and base line respectively. Under Option C, the critical level was defined as 'the minimum level of military forces which the United Kingdom could contribute to NATO and at the same time preserve the confidence of the Allies in the continuing credibility of NATO strategy'.[43] Discovering this minimum was not so straightforward, as it could not be stated with any confidence the withdrawal of which particular piece of equipment would cause such a crisis of confidence within NATO. The paper noted that 'the assessment of the composition of forces at the Critical Level therefore calls for a delicate exercise of professional judgement about each of the force components against the basic criterion … [set out] above'.[44] In short, only the military could assess where the critical level lay. This statement therefore made clear that the Chiefs of Staff were pushing both the Treasury, and to some extent the Ministry's own civil servants, away from making any assessments on force levels. The Navy's critical level in 1978–9 was confidently stated to be two amphibious ships (one assault ship and one commando carrier), three cruisers/support carriers, sixty-five destroyers and frigates, eleven nuclear submarines (excluding SSBNs), fourteen conventional submarines, twenty-five mine warfare vessels, twenty-two RFAs and ten survey ships. Total military personnel would number 71,000 and civilian personnel within the Navy Department, 72,000. The reserve forces would be reduced by half.[45] This was a halving of amphibious ships, a reduction in destroyers and frigates by 13 per cent, conventional submarines by 26 per cent, mine warfare vessels by 17 per cent and RFAs by 31 per cent. The other services offered up similarly proportioned reductions: the Army would reduce its military personnel by 18 per cent and its new-equipment budget by 30 per cent, whilst the RAF would reduce its tanker force by 40 per cent, its strategic transport fleet by more than half, its support helicopter force by 25 per cent, its tankers by one squadron and its maritime patrol aircraft by 25 per cent.[46] These were painful reductions for all three services, but it is notable that each managed to protect what they regarded as much of their core capabilities: the Navy protected its cruisers and the SSN programme, the RAF's air defence, strike, attack and reconnaissance fast jets were left largely untouched, whilst nearly all of the Army's personnel reductions came from the abolition of all overseas garrisons (excluding the British Army of the Rhine) by 1979–80, and a reduction of BAOR itself by 8,000.[47] If Option A1 – partial abandonment of overseas commitments, Option B2 – partial abandonment of the reinforcement capability, and Option C – the critical level, were taken together, then a total of £480 million a year would be saved in 1978–9 and £750 million in 1983–4.[48]

At the next level, Option D, which was the reduction to 4.5 per cent of GNP by 1983–4 involved additional cuts to the Navy's forces, and was similar to the 'Fleet 1' option created back in March. It included withdrawing from service all remaining amphibious vessels, 70 per cent of the Royal Marines, five more destroyer and frigates, one submarine, three mine warfare ships and three RFAs (as well as the cancelling of orders for fifteen new vessels). The Royal Navy and Royal Marine Reserves would be abolished in their entirety. The result of this would be that reinforcing NATO's northern flank in a period of tension or war would have to be abandoned, anti-submarine forces in the Eastern Atlantic would be reduced by 25 per cent, and amongst other things, a reduction in the ability to undertake off-shore tasks. The reductions required for the baseline level were even more drastic and involved a 40 per cent reduction in the ships allocated to NATO, and halving of the submarine fleet.[49] The Ministry's report deliberately kept the baseline reductions vague and focussed on the implications for NATO, whilst even the First Level reductions did not have the detail of the critical level section. The report was clearly pushing its reader in the Steering Group towards the critical level.

Option F set out ways in which spending could be re-allocated below the critical level. Its first approach was to propose some major capability reductions for each service and the savings that would accrue from them to reallocate elsewhere. For the Navy there were three possible reductions: one was placing half of the anti-submarine forces in reserve, which would save £50–60 million a year, another was the cancellation of the Cruiser and the Sea Harrier, which would save £30 million over eight years and £10 million over six–seven years respectively. Finally, there was the option of a navy mostly made up of submarines, or a navy with no submarines at all; neither of these were costed.[50] These three proposals resulted in some lengthy papers in the Annex to the report, setting out why none of these were advisable: ships in reserve would take two and a half months to reactivate, which would be too long to be useful in a crisis; the Cruisers provided essential anti-submarine helicopters and command facilities for task groups, whilst for a relatively small price (£25 million) the Sea Harrier provided important reconnaissance and interception against Soviet 'Bear D' intelligence/data link aircraft; an all-submarine fleet would be much smaller given the expense of SSNs whilst these vessels were ill-suited for low intensity operations such as boarding and small landings, could not protect surface shipping, and much less effective in presence roles. A Navy without submarines would be without its most effective sea denial weapon and its most effective offensive capabilities against other submarines and ships.[51] The last part of the Option F section raised some interesting possibilities. It suggested that if Ministers wished to remain at the critical level in two out of the three core areas of UK home defence, land-air defence of Central Europe and sea-air Eastern Atlantic operations, but reduce to the baseline level the third core area, then this might be possible. The paper argued that these types of possible shifts had 'nothing to recommend them', as the defence of the United Kingdom interlinked all three roles, and that reductions below the critical level in any of the three would result in a loss of confidence in NATO strategy.[52] Despite this conclusion, the concept of focussing on two roles at the expense of the third in many ways presaged the approach taken in the 1981 Defence Review six years later, with sea-air Eastern Atlantic role being the target for reductions. The final option, G, reviewed nuclear forces separately, giving the option of either not modernising the Polaris submarines and giving up a strategic deterrent in the 1990s as they went out of service, or scrapping the force. If the latter were done, a total saving of £1,000 million would be made over the next ten years. Aside from cancelling an update to the Navy's tactical nuclear weapons, saving £21 million over ten years, the report strongly recommended keeping the nuclear deterrent forces as they were.[53] What was largely absent was any analysis of potentially duplicated capabilities, which had been a key element in the 1966 Defence Review and would equally important in the 1981 six years into the future. This defence review had, in effect, created three separate 'critical levels': one for each service, decided by that service.

The Report as a whole was therefore recommending the critical level (Option C), combined with a withdrawal from as many overseas commitments as practical and the abolition of most but not all reinforcement forces (Options A and B), combined with the retention of the nuclear capability (set out in Option G). From now on, British defence would be defined by what would later be known as the Four Pillars: the defence of the UK base, the land-air commitment to central Europe, the sea-air commitment to the Eastern Atlantic and strategic nuclear forces.[54] This created a number of vulnerabilities, for the Navy at least, as it slewed away aspects of defence for which much of the ocean-going surface fleet were best fitted for: overseas presence and power projection away from fixed bases. For a Navy that was rapidly reorientating itself to Eastern Atlantic operations against the Soviet navy and in particular its submarine force, this change logically fitted with the modernisation and reform of strategy, equipment, personnel and support that had been ongoing over the previous six years. However, if such views were present within the naval leadership and the Naval Staff, there is little evidence of pushback by the Navy from what was in fact a weak position. Throughout the Review, the Navy had been seen as the service that was the most likely to suffer reductions.[55] When the CPRS had suggested a more radical approach: either reducing forces in Germany dramatically or cutting the Navy equally hard, the Treasury characterised this approach as one asking 'do we still need a Navy?'[56] Carver's critical level had therefore protected the Navy from what could have been much heavier reductions.

The Navy, with the possible exception of its submarine service, was having difficulty getting across its utility within government. Today this would be termed 'sea-blindness' and it was partly the result of the shift towards a European focus in foreign, defence and economic policy from the late 1960s onwards. Poor British economic performance would be improved by building trade links with fast-growing Western Europe, where the cost of trade could be much cheaper with these nearby states than with those states thousands of miles away, as was the case with much of the British Commonwealth. The reduction in defence commitments outside the Euro-Atlantic region was also logical and understandable: maintaining large naval, air and army bases with substantial capabilities many thousands of miles away from home was increasingly expensive and seemingly less relevant as the United Kingdom re-orientated itself politically. The Navy was the service most clearly associated with these worldwide links, and to some extent with an Empire that had now largely disappeared. In this context a defence 'continental commitment' fitted with this economic and political shift whilst the Navy's long-standing worldwide role increasingly looked outdated and even perhaps obsolete.[57] Whilst it could be argued that this did not matter to the Navy if the majority of its forces had an important role in the Eastern Atlantic, the land-focussed culture that the shift created made it much more difficult to convince politicians and decision-makers about the Navy's concept of how war with the USSR was most likely to develop, and to counter increasing scepticism over the survivability of surface ships in high-intensity war. These were complex arguments to make, and the Navy's leadership would have to go 'against the grain' of Defence and government thinking in these areas for the rest of the Cold War.

The DSWP's report, and its proposals for Options A, B, C and G, were supported in their entirety by the Steering Committee, which then passed these recommendations up to Ministers at the Defence and Oversea Policy Committee of Cabinet.[58] The DSWP discussed how the outcomes would be presented to the Committee: a slide presentation and script was prepared, and a number of crucial points were agreed as important to communities to ministers. The first was the design of most of the United Kingdom's defence capabilities around the Four Pillars, which were 'of equal importance ... but not of equal magnitude' with regard to the required resources.[59] With respect to the Royal Navy, the presentation to ministers emphasised the recent sharp reduction in the size of the US 2nd Fleet, which had responsibility for the Atlantic and US East Coast, and the importance of having sufficient vessels to deter the Soviet Navy at short-notice. The critical level was formally stated to be the current force level, less a reduction in surface vessels to reflect giving up a permanent presence in the Mediterranean, a shrinkage in the conventional submarine force and a reduction of the Royal Fleet Auxiliary by a third. A reduction of the Royal Navy's Eastern Atlantic contribution by half had been contemplated, stated the script, but 'the implications to NATO would be extremely serious. No other European nation could fill the gap.'[60] Even if they could, it would take a long time to build this up and there was no indication that the US Navy was willing to fill the gap either. Placing a large portion of the surface navy in reserve would not be feasible either as they 'would be of little or no deterrent value, and could not be deployed effectively in time of tension'.[61] A removal of all open-ocean naval forces would mean that the strategic nuclear deterrent would be seriously undermined and 'would in fact amount to the almost total abolition of the Royal Navy. If we, as Europe's major maritime nation, with all our sea interests, took such a step, what would deter the Russian Navy in the Eastern Atlantic?'[62] In preparing for the presentation, the DSWP noted that 'in considering maritime operations in the Eastern Atlantic ... Ministers would more readily understand references to specific examples of the pressures that might be exerted in a period of international tension, e.g. interferences with oil installations, harassment of shipping and the disruption of essential supplies, than generalisations about the Soviet threat'.[63] It was notable that much more explaining of the role of the Navy was deemed necessary for ministers than for the other services.

When the report came to the Defence and Oversea Policy Committee, the Cabinet Committee chaired by the Prime Minister which not only included the Defence and Foreign Secretaries but also the Chancellor of the Exchequer, it was the Navy's Eastern Atlantic role that came under direct attack from the Chancellor. Denis Healey, unlike the CPRS, believed that a choice over the Central European front and the Eastern Atlantic had to be made there and then. He knew that if he could force a discussion onto the subject of the choice between the two, then the 'critical level' would have been pushed to one side and the defence budget might be pushed below the 4.5 per cent-by-1983–4 level. Healey was forthright in his attack on the Navy's proposed post-Review force structure: 'to continue to make a major contribution both to the Allied forces in the Central Region and to the Eastern Atlantic and Channel would be inconsistent with our economic situation.' Healey was not persuaded that the ships of the Royal Navy at the critical level would 'be capable of carrying out the tasks assigned to them' and that 'a change in strategy is perhaps inevitable'.[64] The Chancellor had clearly judged the Navy to be the weak link in the Ministry's argument and had therefore focussed his attack in that direction. Unfortunately for him, this meeting was not one that was going to make major decisions.

The Defence Secretary gave a strong defence of the critical level as a whole and the Navy's role within that, whilst the Prime Minister was no doubt distracted by the impending general election. The government was in a minority and wanted to take the chance of another election in order to gain seats, a majority and therefore a much better chance that it could pass major legislation and last a full Parliament. At the end of the meeting, Harold Wilson stated that any decision on the Defence Review would have to wait the outcome of the election. He then spent much of the rest of that day planning his next television broadcast to the country, and the following day Parliament was formally dissolved and the election campaign began.[65] When the Committee met again in October, after the general election had given the Labour Party a small majority, Healey had already shot his bolt and it was clear that the critical level would hold, and so therefore would the Navy's maritime role in the Eastern Atlantic. The Prime Minister began the meeting by focussing on the withdrawal from the Mediterranean and other non-NATO commitments. The Defence Secretary was supported by the Foreign Secretary, and the Prime Minister settled the matter by aligning with these ministers.[66] In any case, a new economic crisis was looming and re-opening the outcome of the Defence Review at this late stage would have distracted both the Prime Minister and the Treasury from focussing on this crucial issue. Only a few days later, Healey would be presenting a budget to Parliament – his third that year – in a desperate attempt to calm the markets.[67] In comparison, defence was a secondary matter.

The Review Outcomes

Compared to the long-running defence reviews of 1964 to 1967, the 1974–5 review was completed in a commendably short time: a recognition of the success of Carver's 'critical level' approach and perhaps also a reflection of the unwillingness of the Treasury to push harder for further reductions given their pre-occupation with the worsening economic situation and the strong statements by allies, not least the US, against additional reductions. An initial statement was made in Parliament by Roy Mason in December 1974 and was followed by the 1975 Statement on the Defence Estimates, which included a significant portion of its length on the outcome of the Review.[68] The Statement focussed on three factors that had resulted in the Review's decision to reduce defence spending to 4.5 per cent of GNP by 1983–4: the previous Conservative government's decision to maintain more capabilities worldwide than had been planned by its Labour predecessor, the relatively poor performance of the British economy in comparison to its European peers, and finally the fact that British defence spending would be at 5.8 per cent of GNP in 1974 when the figure for France was 3.8 per cent and West Germany 4.1 per cent.[69] It was stated that following consultations with NATO allies it had been agreed to reduce planned spending over the next decade by £4.7 billion in total. There would be small real terms increases in 1975–6 and in 1976–7, but after that annual expenditure would remain steady over the following years at £3.8 billion until 1983–4. Previous plans had assumed spending rising to £4.45 billion by 1979 and then staying at this level 1984.[70] In short, the Review had not actually *reduced* expenditure but it had ensured that spending would no longer increase in line with expected GNP increases until 1979, and therefore flat-line in the 1980s at a lower level than had previously been envisaged. Within this new lower budget, it was envisaged that equipment costs would form a higher percentage of total defence spending by 1979–80 with 40 per cent of the budget rather than 35 per cent and personnel costs would fall from 47 per cent to 43 per cent.[71] The Royal Navy had managed to ensure that the planned personnel reductions only resulted in a 6 per cent decrease in its total strength by 1979 (a reduction of 5,400, 4,000 lower than had previously been planned[72]), in comparison to a 8 per cent reduction for the Army, which would be accompanied by a restructuring of all its headquarters and units, and a painful 18 per cent reduction for the Royal Air Force. Compulsory redundancies would occur for all three services but the Navy was lightly hit, with less than 1,000 such redundancies expected out of a total strength of 74,000 in April 1974.[73]

The headline equipment reductions announced in the Review included a reduction in the number of commando carriers from two, *Hermes* and *Bulwark*, to only one, *Hermes*, which would be commando carrier in a secondary role, with her ASW support carrier role now pre-eminent. The number of commando helicopter squadrons would be reduced from two to one, and a planned replacement for the existing Wessex 5 helicopter would be cancelled. The number of Royal Marine Commandos would reduce from four to three, with 41 Commando based in Malta being disbanded between 1977 and 1979. Of the two assault ships, one would alternate in care and maintenance or refit whilst the other was in service.[74] The total number of destroyers and frigates would reduce by one-seventh, with mine warfare vessels reducing by the same amount. This involved the withdrawal of the oldest post-war frigates of the Type 41, 61 and earlier Type 12 classes, as well as – more controversially – the 13-year-old guided missile destroyer HMS *Hampshire*. This was justified by her poor material condition due to a lack of a major refit during her service life, and the obsolescence of her Mark 1 Sea Slug missile system.[75] Conventional submarines would reduce by one-quarter, whilst *Ark Royal* would continue in service until the late 1970s. The exact reduction in the Royal Fleet Auxiliary fleet was kept vague but five RFAs would be removed from the forward programme (one maintenance ship, three tankers and one afloat support ship), whilst the forward programme for destroyers and frigates would be reduced by nine ships, including two Type 42 destroyers that had been planned to be ordered in the coming year.[76] Behind the scenes, the Large ASW ship was also cancelled but the Cruiser, nuclear submarine, Type 42 and Type 22 programmes continued, even if fewer ships would be procured over the next ten years than had been envisaged. No replacement commando carrier would be built, whilst the two support carriers, as utility follow-ons from the Cruisers, were also removed from the programme.[77] Mason, with the support of the First Sea Lord, had also attempted to shift the costs of running the Royal Yacht onto other government departments, most notably the Foreign and Commonwealth Office and the Department of Trade, but the Prime Minister did not support this and neither did the Permanent Under-Secretary at the Ministry.[78] The idea was killed by the steadfast support for the status quo by Carver, who argued with some justification that both the RAF and Army paid for their elements of their support to the Royal Family (the Royal Flight and ceremonial duties), and so the Navy should therefore continue to do the same.[79]

Operationally, as has been seen, the impact was more significant, as many of the remaining worldwide commitments were removed or reduced. The Singapore force – which included the newly-arrived *Mermaid* – would be removed, along with the flight of Nimrod maritime patrol aircraft sent out there only a few years previously.[80] Involvement in exercises in the Indian

Ocean and South East Asia regions would be significantly curtailed, whilst the Royal Navy's communications station in Mauritius would be closed, as would be the RAF's staging post on the island Gan in the Maldives. Naval and RAF maritime forces would withdraw from Malta by 1979 (which would have occurred even if the southern flank commitment had been retained[81]) and the Royal Navy's commitment to the Caribbean would be reduced. The post of Senior Naval Officer West Indies ('SNOWI') would be abolished and the two frigates based in the region reduced to one.[82] This single frigate would be detached from Eastern Atlantic duties for a number of months and would now be described as the Belize guardship, despite retaining a wider Caribbean role. In the Mediterranean, the Defence Review had proposed the total withdrawal of British forces from Cyprus, but this had been strongly opposed by the United States and as a result it had been ultimately decided to retain the Sovereign Base Areas for the time being.[83] Therefore, aside from retaining the Cyprus base, the commitment to defending NATO's southern flank was removed, saving a total of £240 million over the next ten years.[84] NATO's Defence Planning Committee had criticised the withdrawal of British support to the southern flank, arguing that it would affect NATO military cohesion and effectiveness in the Mediterranean, but this did not alter the British decision.[85] The Review had been expected since the first general election of 1974, and much to the relief of Britain's NATO allies, the forces for the Central European front had not been significantly reduced. The United States was however insistent that the post-Review force was the absolute minimum of capability that would tolerate; the US Secretary of State, James Schlesinger, even threatening to restrict UK access to 'five-eyes' intelligence information and restrict nuclear co-operation if any further reductions were made.[86]

In one important area the Navy was clearly protected from reductions: the government had committed publicly to maintaining all four domestic dockyards, so they were protected from closure even though there were concerns that they might not be fully employed in the post-Review environment.[87] From a political perspective this was understandable given the government's small majority and its dependence on unionised workforces, such as the dockyard workers, for its core vote, but this left the dockyards at risk of serious potential over-capacity, particularly if the increasingly expensive frigate half-life refit programme were to be scaled back or ended. This was an issue that would return five years later during the next defence review.

* * *

In many respects, the 1974–5 Defence Review was a success for the three armed services. Under Carver's forceful leadership they had ensured that the

Treasury's maximalist approach to cuts had been defeated, and those cuts that were made were those that each service were willing to contemplate, as each had individually set its own 'critical level'. However, this did lead to each service retreating into its own preferred areas and letting capabilities that it regarded as peripheral or secondary wither, thus acting against a 'whole-of-defence' approach that would assess capabilities across service boundaries. The most obvious aspect of this was the decision to reduce the RAF's tanker fleet down to a level that made the use of Buccaneers in the long-range land strike role from UK bases into the Central European theatre plausible, but left very few aircraft available to support long-range maritime patrol, air defence and strike operations across the Greenland-Iceland-UK gap at the same time. The tacit assumption that one or the other would be needed in a time of crisis, but not both, was highly optimistic and could be seen as confirming the RAF leadership's prime focus on the Central European theatre. On the Navy's part, the Naval Staff was – as will be seen in the next section – lobbying for the procurement of the Harrier for the new cruiser, and requesting additional RAF maritime air defence or strike aircraft would have undermined that objective, so both services retreated to where they were comfortable thus allowing a reduction in the overall Eastern Atlantic air capability (notwithstanding the real benefits that maritime Harriers would provide if procured).

The Defence Review also saw the final withdrawal from as many overseas commitments outside of the Eastern Atlantic-Central European area as was deemed to be politically possible, another indirect result of the focus on the 'critical level', as interpreted by Carver. The Navy suffered more from this approach than the other two services, but this was not entirely apparent at the time, and the general perception across the three services that the old worldwide role was outdated and too tightly linked to the now disappeared empire, should not be underestimated. The Navy's worldwide capabilities had in fact been relatively minimal in terms of their logistical 'footprint' ashore by this time: for example, the majority of the personnel in Malta when the British presence was run down after 1975, were RAF ground crew supporting the two to four Nimrod aircraft based out there,[88] whilst the reduced facilities at Singapore had been shared with Australia and New Zealand, who provided a significant proportion of the personnel.[89] The post-1971 naval worldwide presence had been focussed primarily on presence rather than capability, and was therefore as much a defence-diplomatic as a warfighting tool, and it is not accidental that when it was decided to rebuild this presence from 2017 onwards, a similar cost-effective approach was taken of using patrol and presence vessels spread across a number of locations supported by very small and lightly staffed support facilities ashore. Finally, Carver and the Chiefs of Staff had been almost *too* successful in fighting for the critical level, and as will be seen in Chapter 10, much of the period from 1976 to 1978 was spent attempting to prevent, and then reluctantly accepting, further reductions in the defence budget as the United Kingdom was forced to turn to the International Monetary Fund for financial support, and then to accept its stringent public spending requirements in order to receive its funding. The next five years would be particularly difficult for the Ministry of Defence, as reductions were layered upon reductions and the 'critical level' was quickly breached and then just as quickly forgotten.

Approving the Sea Harrier
One outstanding naval procurement had remained in limbo during the Defence Review process: that of the navalised Harrier VSTOL aircraft for the Cruiser. Flying navalised Harriers from the Cruiser had been discussed as far back as 1968 and had been announced as a possibility by the incoming Conservative government in 1970. A Naval Staff Requirement had been raised in 1972 and a project definition study had been undertaken between August 1972 and April 1973. The Operational Requirements Committee, a central Ministry committee, approved full development subject to the agreement of the Chiefs of Staff. This was forthcoming in November 1973, the Chiefs describing the Sea Harrier as a 'valuable additional capability', but by this time a final decision was postponed as what became the Defence Review began to take shape. From this time until February 1975, the project was kept alive through the approval of packets of funding to pay for ongoing development at Hawker Siddeley, the designer and manufacturer. During the Defence Review the Sea Harrier had not been considered as being within the critical level, so would therefore have been in line for cancellation, but it survived uncancelled, largely due to the Navy Department declaring it to be one of its highest priorities.[90] With the Review nearing completion, a decision on the Sea Harrier was necessary soon, ideally before the Statement on the Defence Estimates was published in March 1975.

It was clear however, that within the Ministry of Defence approval of the aircraft was fiercely contested. The Minister of State, Bill Rodgers, and in particular his Private Secretary, were strongly against the procurement. The aircraft might be a 'valuable additional capability' but it had not been unequivocally placed within the 'critical level' during the Review. Rodgers and his private office also believed that Admiral Ashmore and the Navy Department had taken advantage of the strong line Carver had taken over external unanimity by the Chiefs of Staff during the Review so that the destructive bickering of the 1964 to 1968 reviews was not repeated. Ashmore, from Rodger's perspective, was therefore threatening to break the unanimity pact unless the other Chiefs accepted and supported the Navy's line that the maritime Harrier was an essential. Rodgers and his private office also believed that all the Chiefs aside from Ashmore were against the approval, or at least neutral.[91] The situation was, however, more complex than this. Ashmore had argued that the importance of the maritime Harrier was such that he was willing to accept lower levels of expenditure in other parts of the Navy's budget in order to accommodate the aircraft procurement.[92] The Permanent Under-Secretary, Sir Michael Cary, also tentatively supported procuring the maritime Harrier, with the strong possibility of overseas sales – in particular to Iran – being an important factor in the procurement: if the maritime Harrier were not purchased for the Royal Navy, then it would be unlikely that overseas purchasers would retain their interest.[93] If it was not good enough for Britain's own Navy, why should the Shah of Iran purchase such an aircraft? Mason's own Private Secretary seemed to accept that the maritime Harrier was a de facto part of the critical level, given the First Sea Lord's staunch defence of the aircraft and willingness to sacrifice other capabilities to procure it.[94] Mason himself does not appear to have objected to the Harrier in principle, but he was clearly irritated that it had emerged as an issue so late in the Defence Review process, writing in the margins of a memo written by his Private Secretary: 'I am not mucking up all my work on the Defence Review by throwing this spanner in the works'.[95] Mason pushed discussions on the maritime Harrier back into 1975, and wanted the case for the aircraft re-submitted.[96]

So why was the maritime Harrier so important for the Navy? The projected role of the Sea Harrier was to provide a 'quick reaction capability' to complement the RAF's maritime air defence aircraft. As stated in the Navy's case for the aircraft, 'experience has shown repeatedly that gaps in the Fleet's essential air cover can occur as a direct result, for example, of the time taken to transit to the force, limited time on task, the need to return to base to rearm, the demand on tanker aircraft support and communications and weather difficulties.'[97] Specifically, the primary role of the Harrier was to intercept Soviet reconnaissance and targeting 'Bear D' aircraft. Soviet long-range missiles fired from submarines, ships and some aircraft required mid-course guidance and correction from just such an aircraft.[98] The 'Bear D' needed to fly between 60 and 80 nautical miles from a NATO task group for between 10 and 15 minutes in order to relay the ship positions back to the launching ships, submarines or aircraft, which would then signal to the missiles the updated course data. In the final stages of flight the missiles would use their own radar trackers to guide themselves onto the target. Destroying the 'Bear D' relay aircraft would then break this relatively fragile chain in the missile targeting process. The aim would be to have one Harrier on deck ready to take off and intercept a 'Bear D' within the 10-minute envelope of time before targeting data was sent back to the launching units. With respect to air defence against Soviet cruise missile attack, this was the only role that the Harrier could fulfil effectively: its range and relatively slow speed would make interception of either the aircraft before they launched their missiles, or the missiles themselves, extremely difficult particularly with the small numbers of aircraft envisaged. Other secondary roles for the Harrier included reconnaissance, a quick reaction capability against enemy warships (if an air-launched anti-ship missile were procured), and even quick reaction sonobuoy barrier laying to complement the RAF's Nimrods.[99] The total cost of the procurement would £102.3 million to provide a total of twenty-five aircraft, and there had already been considerable interest from Iran, India and other states in buying these aircraft for their navies.[100] Most obviously, but left unsaid in any of the Navy Department's papers arguing in favour of the aircraft, the maritime Harrier would also reintroduce fixed-wing aircraft to the fleet, and therefore to some extent it was going back on the decisions of a previous Labour government in 1966 to remove fixed-wing aircraft from carriers.

Given the niche role of the Sea Harrier, and the strong opposition it engendered in parts of the Ministry, it is interesting that a note composed anonymously (perhaps within sections of the Central Staffs or by the Air Staff) was passed by Rodgers to Mason critical of the maritime Harrier. It was gingerly described as a document 'that has come my way' and was clearly intended to persuade ministers to cancel the maritime Harrier, but what was most interesting about it was that it provided such a weak set of arguments against the aircraft. The note questioned how the aircraft was so essential if it was only a 'valuable additional capability' and a 'non-critical level investment', but this assessment was only relevant if the essential nature of the role of the Sea Harrier could be questioned, and as was noted, opinion was split over whether the maritime Harrier was within the critical level or not. The paper held the maritime Harrier to a higher standard than other procurements, by asking whether the 'Bear D' might be improved in future years to be able to operate at greater ranges from its targets, and suggested rather weakly that more studies be undertaken into the aircraft's role. A more substantive question was how a single aircraft could deal with two rather than one 'Bear D' aircraft, but the Navy did at least have a partial answer in that if a force of five Harriers were on a Cruiser, one aircraft would be on patrol in the air 97 per cent of the time with an aircraft ready to launch 91 per cent of the time, providing a good chance that two Harriers would be available within 10 minutes.[101] The truth was that the RAF's maritime air defence capability was not sufficient to provide air cover for naval task groups operating in the Eastern Atlantic, and there were no convincing answers to the Navy's concerns about transit time, time on patrol, the need to re-arm and the need for tanker support, beyond significantly increasing the number of RAF air defence aircraft allocated to

SACLANT, which neither the Air Force Department or the Navy Department wanted. The joint RN-RAF exercises described in Chapter 5 were in the process of improving co-operation and co-ordination, but with respect to air defence at least, the numbers of allocated aircraft were inadequate. The Harrier could not be a full solution, but it was at least an attempt to fill the gap, which now loomed larger following the reduction in the RAF's tanker fleet during the Defence Review from three to two squadrons.[102] The remaining tanker aircraft would now be even more hard-pressed to support both the maritime role in the Eastern Atlantic and the SACEUR-tasked Buccaneers in the land strike role in Germany.

Mason was convinced of the case for the maritime Harrier, but there had been considerable public and governmental interest in the aircraft, so it was felt that securing the approval of the Defence and Oversea Policy Committee was necessary. Mason had a difficult tightrope to walk in convincing the committee of the need for the aircraft whilst also not giving the impression that the 1966 decision to transfer maritime air defence to the RAF was being reversed. The Secretary of State argued that the maritime Harrier was a 'valuable additional capability for the fleet' and that the £102 million cost could be more than compensated by a possible £200 million deal with Iran for an *Invincible* class cruiser and maritime Harriers, but accepted that it was not integral to the operational concept of the cruiser, which was primarily anti-submarine warfare. If the operational concept of the Cruiser were to be changed to accept maritime Harriers in the air defence (or for that matter strike) role, then Mason would then be clearly going back on the 1966 decision. Many of those who had taken that decision nine years ago would be around the committee table, not least Harold Wilson, the chair and Prime Minister, and Denis Healey, the Chancellor, who had been Defence Secretary at the time. Therefore, the maritime Harrier had to be presented as merely a 'valuable additional capability' that was not formally necessary for the Cruiser to undertake its allotted role, whilst simultaneously being considered within the Critical Level and the Navy regarding it as essential.[103] For many of those around the committee table, these presentational gymnastics were not understood but the export opportunities were, and despite the vociferous opposition of the Chancellor, the maritime Harrier was approved. The young special advisor to the Prime Minister, Bernard Donoughue, who was attending the committee as an observer, was so disgusted by what he saw as a decision to spend an unneeded £102 million when government finances were close to collapse, that he walked out of the committee just after the decision was made.[104]

The eventual decision in favour of procuring the maritime Harrier, although it returned organic fixed-wing air power to the fleet, could also be seen as a demonstrating one of the failings of the Defence Review. By focussing on the 'critical level' and allowing it to become a level defined by each individual service, within the wider parameters of the Central European front, the Eastern Atlantic and home defence, it allowed the RAF indirectly to reduce its maritime capability by halving its tanker fleet, which highlighted the fact that the Air Staff regarded its maritime role as of distinctly secondary importance compared to its roles over central Europe and the United Kingdom. In the absence of a return to full fixed-wing naval aviation with catapult-launched aircraft, which was close to impossible from 1966 until the 1990s, to provide effective maritime air capabilities to support the Navy in the Eastern Atlantic, both maritime Harriers *and* many more RAF-operated land-based maritime aircraft in the patrol, strike, air defence and airborne early warning roles would be necessary. This would become evident as a sustained five-year programme of detailed operational analysis was embarked upon, the results of which would be difficult reading for both the Navy and the RAF.

The Sea-Air Warfare Committee and Operational Analysis of Maritime Operations

In the aftermath of the Defence Review, the Air Staff had persuaded the Chiefs of Staff to re-invigorate the structures for ensuring air-naval and air-land co-operation in the creation of 'concepts of operations': the vital documents that linked NATO strategy with tactical doctrine and provided a template for the types of equipment that would be required for the armed forces in the future. The Sea-Air Warfare Committee ('SAWC') had existed for many years, as a means for the Royal Navy and RAF to co-operate in their maritime roles. The new arrangements, which were agreed in autumn of 1976, created a new Land-Air Warfare Committee and made both committees sub-committees of the Chiefs of Staff. The committees would be chaired by 2* appointments which would alternate between the two relevant services. The Air Staff hoped that this would provide a means for it to become more tightly involved in the planning of land and sea operational requirements. In addition to creating concepts of operations, the committees would also produce two reports a year setting out the work underway, and provide terms of reference for the Deputy Chief of the Defence Staff (Operational Requirements).[105]

Most significantly, SAWC now became the co-ordinating body for a large number of operational analysis studies relating to maritime operations coming under the umbrella of a 'balance of investment study'. Three areas provided a particular focus: anti-submarine warfare, maritime air defence and anti-ship operations. Subsidiary areas of analysis included the balance between hull sonars and towed-array sonars, and between ASW frigates and air defence destroyers. This would then inform studies into appropriate force mixes to

Eastern Atlantic operations. These studies included analysis of the RAF's maritime capabilities as complements and alternatives to warships and organic Fleet Air Arm air capabilities.[106] One of the first studies to be produced, and which in fact had been commissioned before the SAWC was reformed, was an analysis of maritime air defence: in the form of directly defending a convoy near the Azores, defending an ASW naval force to the west of Scotland and south of Iceland, and also the use of air defence 'barriers' or Combat Air Patrol zones which would aim to intercept Soviet 'Backfire' bombers before they reached naval forces. The study looked at both Type 42 destroyers in the convoy defence role, and RAF aircraft Phantoms and Tornados (armed with either British Skyflash or US Phoenix air defence missiles. Harriers flying from the new cruisers were not included in the study.[107] The results provided unsettling reading for both the Navy and the RAF. Type 42 destroyers would struggle to protect naval forces against sophisticated co-ordinated attacks by large 'Backfire' forces; barriers of Phantoms or Tornados in addition to combat air patrols above either the convoy or the ASW naval force, would be necessary to defend the naval forces.[108] Fitting electronic countermeasures to all naval vessels was strongly recommended, as was a more effective airborne early warning capability.[109] Disrupting or destroying guidance and communication aircraft was considered to be an important capability that needed more investigation: a pointer to the rationale for purchasing the Sea Harrier.[110] Just to defend the convoy effectively, a total of between six and eight Type 42s would be necessary, a substantial number given that only six had been ordered as of June 1976.[111] Presumably a similar number would have been needed to defend the ASW naval force as well.

It was clear that naval forces would be highly vulnerable to air attack, and the Navy would be heavily dependent on RAF maritime air defence forces. This was where the conclusions were equally difficult for the RAF: the new Tornado was assessed to be little better than the existing Phantom for maritime air defence (although it required many fewer tankers to maintain effective combat air patrols),[112] whilst a huge number of aircraft would be needed to provide air defence. A combat air patrol operating as a barrier force between Iceland and Scotland making use of a total of thirty aircraft supported by ten tanker aircraft would only be able to provide a maximum of between four and six aircraft on patrol at any one time, depending on how far the patrol was placed from Lossiemouth, the RAF's operating base.[113] Combat air patrols for the ASW naval force and the convoy would be able to destroy approximately only one 'Backfire' bomber for every two aircraft on patrol, a number that suggested a significant number of Phantoms or Tornados would be needed.[114] Providing a combat air patrol of six aircraft for the ASW naval force would also require another thirty Tornados supported by ten tankers. A combat air patrol over the convoy near the Azores would need even more aircraft: forty-five Tornados and thirty tankers to provide a patrol of 3.75 aircraft 750 nautical miles away.[115] These numbers, when totalled up, were far beyond those air defence aircraft allocated to SACLANT and therefore available for maritime operations: only thirty Tornados for all maritime operations whilst the relatively small number of tankers the RAF possessed were also required for a range of other roles including air defence of the United Kingdom and support for RAF Germany's operations on the Central European front.

It was clear that many more Type 42 destroyers would be needed as well as perhaps as much as a tripling of the Tornados or Phantoms and their supporting tankers: until these were provided naval forces operating in the Eastern Atlantic would be highly vulnerable to air attack by 'Backfires' making use of flight refuelling to give them ranges into the mid-Atlantic. The report recommended that in terms of economy it would make sense for Type 42s to provide the main defence for convoys between the Azores and the Western Approaches whilst the RAF's maritime aircraft focussed on barrier patrols and patrols defending ASW naval forces further north.[116] In retrospect, the report did overstate likely 'Backfire' capabilities: it assumed that they would be armed with the AS-6 anti-ship missile, when in fact the aircraft was only ever armed with the older AS-4. NATO analysts believed that the newer AS-6 would inevitably be fitted, assuming at the time that it was a more capable missile, but this was never done as the AS-6 was in fact a smaller, slower and shorter range version of AS-4 designed for the older Tu-16 'Badger' bomber.[117] Despite this, the report made for grim reading and strengthened the hands of those arguing in favour of the maritime Harrier, but they also included cost-benefit analyses that implied that the barrier patrols would be more effective than patrols over naval forces or convoys, particularly when operating closer to the UK. In these barrier patrols the RAF's maritime aircraft would be cheaper to use than Type 42s, although effective electronic countermeasures reduced this cost-benefit balance significantly.[118]

This report was then followed by a range of memoranda and working papers that investigated aspects of maritime air defence in more detail, whilst others investigated anti-submarine warfare and anti-ship operations. These numerous studies would continue over the next six years to build up a picture within the Ministry of Defence that stressed the vulnerability of naval surface forces in the Eastern Atlantic. The operational analysis over-stressed these vulnerabilities – defence against the 'Backfire' armed with AS-4 or 'Badger' with AS-5 or AS-6 would not be as difficult as against the presumed 'Backfire' with AS-5 or AS-6 – but there was a significant vulnerability nonetheless, especially when the small size of the Type 42's missile magazine was taken into account as well as the limited number of available maritime air defence aircraft. In addition to this, and many other air defence studies that followed, a similar number of anti-submarine warfare studies were also produced, as well as studies on a wide range of operations including anti-ship warfare.

The Royal Marines

The Defence Review had hit the Royal Marines the hardest of the different parts of the Royal Navy. The contrast with the previous defence reviews was particularly painful: the outcome of the Defence Reviews of 1964 to 1968 had been a qualified success for the Royal Marines and the amphibious shipping from which they were landed ashore. The carrier force might be disappearing, but commando carriers and assault ships would now be the largest surface vessels in the fleet. The latter vessels were new, whilst one of the former had been replaced by converting the conventional carrier *Hermes*. In addition, a new-build commando carrier was placed in the forward construction programme in 1968. However, as the Navy's attention moved to the Eastern Atlantic and home waters, the future of the amphibious force became less certain. As was seen in Chapter 7, the planned new commando carrier was cancelled in 1971 in order to provide the funds and personnel to operate *Ark Royal*, which the new Conservative government had decided to keep in service until the end of the 1970s. With the end of the Far East Fleet, the Royal Marines increasingly focussed on NATO's vulnerable flanks: in the south, the Eastern Mediterranean and the Aegean islands were of particular importance. These were areas in which the Soviet Navy was operating in increasing numbers and where confrontations or clashes amongst these islands could conceivably occur during a period of high tension. In the north, planning revolved around the reinforcement of Norway (which did not have permanent NATO garrisons) in the event of similar tensions with the USSR. As a result, 45 Commando was moved from Stonehouse in Plymouth to Arbroath in Angus, Scotland and began to specialise in Arctic warfare.[119]

The two leading histories of the Royal Marines emphasise the importance of the northern flank role for the Royal Marines in this period, but up until 1975 it was in fact the Mediterranean, southern, flank role that was pre-eminent, with the northern flank only gaining prominence after 1975.[120] The commando carriers and assault ships were involved in a series of major exercises in, and deployments to, the Mediterranean between 1970 and 1976, with the first of these occurring even before the abolition of the Far East Fleet. Annual exercises in the Deep Furrow/Deep Express series involved landings at Saros Bay on the north side of the Gallipoli Peninsula, under a scenario of a Warsaw Pact attempt to seize the Bosphorus by a land invasion from Bulgaria. 41 Commando, based in Malta, would invariably take part, usually alongside one other UK-based Commando.[121] The other major annual exercise was in the Dawn Patrol series and involved a cross-Mediterranean set of scenarios, including an amphibious landing, usually with a Royal Marine force involved. The exercises are described in Chapter 9. In parallel, at least one major amphibious vessel was involved in the major NATO Eastern Atlantic exercise, which usually involved an amphibious element in Norway and a link to AFNORTH's annual Norwegian land exercise. In the early 1970s *Fearless* was a regular attendee, taking part in Exercises Strong Express 72 and Northern Merger 74, with *Hermes* taking part in Swift Move 73, albeit in her role as an anti-submarine carrier, not a commando carrier. These exercises have already been described in Chapter 5.

Despite this busy schedule of exercises and operations, the future of the amphibious capability, and by extension the Royal Marines, seemed increasingly insecure. The doubts felt by Rear Admiral Fell, the outgoing Flag Officer Carriers and Amphibious Ships in 1970, about the utility of the amphibious capability on the NATO flanks expressed some of these concerns. 'The doctrine of the deterrent value of a "presence" of amphibious ships on or over the horizon is only realistic in the right place. I do not think the Northern Flank of NATO comes into this category. The full strength of the Striking Fleet would be required to support any operations in North Norway. There is greater defence in depth on the Southern Flank as the situation is marginally better in this area, but even so the enclosed waters of the Aegean Sea are not all that attractive.'[122] Fell was a former Fleet Air Arm officer, who probably felt much more comfortable with the aircraft carrier side of his command, but the decision to cancel the new commando carrier in 1971 demonstrated that he was not a lone voice amongst the service's senior officers: the Navy's leadership was now willing to de-prioritise the renewal of amphibious capabilities whilst it focussed on nuclear submarine, cruiser, destroyer and frigate procurement. Organisationally, a number of changes were made within the Royal Marines in early 1970s. Not only was the basing of the brigade HQ and the commandos brought back to the United Kingdom (with the exception of 41 Commando in Malta), but the Commando Logistics Regiment was created in 1971. This provided an umbrella unit for the various Army logistics sub-units that supported the Commandos, and in 1974 this regiment became a unit under direct Royal Marines operational control.[123]

The Defence Review, which had forced the individual services to focus on what they regarded as their core areas, brutally exposed the peripheral position of the Royal Marines, at least from the perspective of significant parts of the Navy's leadership. Resurrected plans for replacement commando carriers were scrapped, *Bulwark* would be withdrawn from service in 1976, whilst *Hermes*' main role would now be anti-submarine operations and not amphibious warfare. The two assault ships would now alternate in service, with one vessel being in extended readiness or refit, and would now combine their amphibious role with that of being Dartmouth training ship, with officer cadets embarked for portions of the year and undertaking training cruises to support their training. The 1975 Statement on the Defence Estimates baldly stated that alternative means for the transport of Royal Marine commandos to Norway were being investigated, whilst the Marines' southern flank role disappeared as the Navy largely withdrew from that sea.[124] In short order, the force of four major amphibious vessels had been halved, but the surviving vessels (the commando carrier *Hermes* and the single active assault ship) also now had supplementary roles that would reduce their time available for amphibious exercises and training. The number of Royal Marines was reduced to approximately 7,000 in the Review whilst 41 Commando in Malta would be abolished as that base was wound down between 1977 and 1979.[125] The ongoing commitment to Northern Ireland, which is described below, where the Royal Marines provided additional battalion-equivalent units that could be deployed to the Province, played an important part in preventing any further reductions in the Royal Marines' strength and helped keep 41 Commando alive, albeit at a reduced size, through to 1979.[126]

The Reserves

Not only had the future of the Royal Marines been under scrutiny in the Defence Review, the Royal Naval Reserve had also been undergoing a review of its future role, commissioned by the Admiralty Board, and led by Rear Admiral C G Mitchell.[127] The Mitchell report was completed in December 1974, but it was quickly overtaken by the Review outcomes which recommended a substantial reduction in the size of the RNR. The final proposals for the newly reduced RNR were placed before the Admiralty Board in July 1975. Some of the changes were welcome: they would no longer report to the Second Sea Lord, but to an operational Commander-in-Chief, CINCNAVHOME, and the size of the reservist's bounty would be increased to match that of the Territorial Army (which would involve an additional £300,000 each year.[128] In addition, in 1976 the WRNR was to be fully integrated into the RNR).[129] However, the number of mine warfare vessels that they operated reduced from eleven to six, with the eleven RNR divisions 'sharing' these six ships between them. A total of eighteen mine warfare ship crews would be provided by the RNR: twelve for the six ships and a further six to provide back crews for the regular navy in time of war.[130] The personnel of the RNR was also reduced, but much less drastically. It would fall from 7,000 in 1975 to 6,400 in 1978.[131] The RNR would lose its 2* Admiral as their superior RN officer, replaced by a Captain (although somewhat confusingly the two most senior RNR officers, both ranked as a Commodore, remained[132]) and was to be more tightly integrated into the Navy's operational structures, reporting to CINCNAVHOME rather than the Second Sea Lord. Mine warfare as a key role was retained, but one area of continued RNR predominance, supported in a time of crisis by selected emergency list officers, was the Naval Control of Shipping Branch, which would manage the process of organising and operation of the convoy system in times of tension or war with the Soviet Union. This was increasingly important as naval strategy emphasised the role of reinforcing Europe via convoy against possible Soviet aggression, with the RNR dominating the NCS Branch and becoming heavily involved in NATO-wide training and exercises in this area.[133] The reforms were painful, but they left the RNR in a position to defend its relevance and importance more effectively over the next 15 years.

The Women's Royal Naval Service

Another supporting service found its future being questioned whilst the Defence Review was underway. In 1973 the Director of the Women's Royal Naval Service ('WRNS'), Mary Talbot, persuaded the Second Sea Lord to commission a review into the future of the WRNS. The Pritchard Report, named after its civil servant chairman, recommended that WRNS should be subject to the Naval Discipline Act, bringing them in line with their male counterparts, and a wider range of roles should be made available to them.[134] The consideration of sea service for WRNS had been in the draft remit for Pritchard's investigation, but this had been removed before the final version had been agreed, quite possibly by Talbot herself, who was conscious of how controversial sea service was within the senior ranks of the WRNS.[135] When the Sea Lords reviewed the Pritchard Report in February 1975, aware of recruitment and retention problems beginning to return, they ordered a serious consideration of WRNS sea service in non-combatant vessels.[136]

The question of sending women to sea had first arisen in 1970 as recruitment and retention problems had raised the possibility that an all-male seagoing force might not be sufficient to crew the fleet.[137] The decision in 1972 by the United States Navy to allow women to sea in non-combatant ships had prompted a further review in the Royal Navy.[138] Also, as women were beginning to be apprenticed within the dockyards and were finding other roles within a range of organisations supporting the Navy, it seemed only appropriate to review the long-standing bar on sea service.[139] Within the WRNS the question was a particularly important one that split senior WRNS officers. With the increased civilianisation of many roles in defence, some areas that had been the preserve of WRNS, such as writers, were being given to junior civil servants, whilst a major area of traditional WRNS specialisation, radio operators, was rapidly decreasing in numbers. Turnover of WRNS was also extremely high, with the average rating WRNS only serving for three years and seemed likely to reduce further.[140] Even more frustratingly for the WRNS leadership, many in the Royal Navy's Manning Directorate only regarded the WRNS as a 'manning regulator', to backfill certain shore-based roles when male recruiting and retention was suffering, and then to remove them from these roles when the situation improved. For WRNS officers and ratings who stayed for a career, this created an unstable environment where more rewarding and interesting work might be offered, then taken away on a repeated basis. Some in the Manning Directorate were seriously thinking about the abolition of the WRNS as their roles and purpose shrank. Conversely, WRNS going to sea could result in more interesting and rewarding careers, and perhaps save the WRNS from dissolution.[141]

The Manpower Planning Directorate was tasked with considering the practicalities of sea services for the WRNS, and began to assess the different types of ship that might be appropriate for WRNS. Offshore Patrol Vessels were rapidly discounted as their living conditions were perceived – without any evidence given – to be 'too rugged for women'. Trials ships such as *Matapan* and *Torquay* were removed from consideration as they were believed to be too old for the conversion of messes and washing facilities to be worthwhile. The Ice Patrol Ship *Endurance* was also left out as 'her pattern of employment made her unsuitable for women'.[142] Again, no further detail was given as to why this might be so. By 1977, consideration of the issue was still ongoing, but only the large survey ships of the *Hecla* class and the planned Seabed Operations Vessel were still seen as realistic possibilities. Plans had been drawn up for the conversion of living and washing spaces to be modified on the *Hecla* class, but the conversion never went ahead.[143] The Hydrographer of the Navy intervened to halt the experiment on his ships. His overriding concern was for the survival of his branch, whose existence was being reviewed – as will be seen in the next section – and for which there were also considerable retention problems as Hydrographic Branch officers and men would be more likely to be away for longer periods than the rest of the Navy. With the introduction of WRNS on board these ships, the Hydrographer was concerned that opposition from the wives of sailors and officers would precipitate a retention crisis and jeopardise the viability of the Hydrographic Service.[144]

This left only the planned Seabed Operations Vessel as a potential vessel: she would be operating primarily in the Eastern Atlantic within the continental shelf and therefore not subject to prolonged periods away from home.[145] By this time, the momentum had drained from the proposal. A paper had been planned to be put to the Admiralty Board in 1976 but this was delayed a year as work slowed to a snail's pace. Retention problems had temporarily slackened, most of the personnel of the Admiralty Board had changed since

1975 and within the Manpower Planning Directorate itself there had been increased scepticism. With only eight WRNS planned to go to sea on the Seabed Operations Vessel it was now dismissed as no more than a gimmick. Ironically, it was the WRNS Chief Officer in the Directorate, whose views represented the more traditionalist wing of the women's service, who gave the final coup de grace. She stated that 'until society accepts women in the combatant role (never – I hope) I do not believe that sea service as a part of a ship's c[ompany] is ... suitable.' It was 'pointless' token gesture.[146] The Director of Naval Manpower Planning halted work on mixed crewing on the vessel, and the issue disappeared for another decade: waiting until perspectives had changed and a graver recruitment and retention crisis loomed.[147]

The Hydrographic Service

The Hydrographic Service was being pulled in two different directions as the Defence Review had progressed during 1974: the impending reduction of the Royal Navy's commitments outside the Euro-Atlantic region suggested that fewer ocean-going survey ships would be needed and that the Hydrographic Service might shrink significantly. On the other hand, there were growing civil requirements for surveying work, both to support the emerging oil and gas industry in the North Sea and to survey ports and estuaries as merchant ships became ever larger, with deeper draughts, thus requiring new surveys of channels prior to dredging.[148] The rise of the importance of oceanography to support the nuclear submarine fleet and anti-submarine warfare meant that the Service's survival as a military organisation was never in doubt, but in 1974 it seemed poised between either shrinkage to this core military role or expansion to support the range of other, civilian, roles that were appearing.

In November 1974 the Admiralty Board discussed the future of the Hydrographic Service, with VCNS arguing that the balance of civil and defence hydrographic work was shifting. He proposed reducing the number of ocean survey ships by two and inshore ships by one by March 1976, so that the 'critical level' could be met. These discarded ships would then be available to the civil departments for civilian survey work, subject to the costs being borne by those departments. Defence survey work would continue at its current level in home waters, work near Hong Kong might be funded by that colony's government, whilst work in the Caribbean and Mediterranean would be undertaken on an information exchange basis with the US. All work East of Suez would be civil rather than defence in nature. This proposal was approved by the Admiralty Board.[149]

Despite this decision appearing to favour the shrinkage of the Hydrographic Service to its military core, five months later an Inter-Departmental Study Group reviewing the same issue, whose establishment had been announced in Parliament in July 1974 and whose Chair was the Under-Secretary of State for Defence, released its own report.[150] It came to the opposite conclusion, arguing that the ships of Hydrographic Service should be increased by the addition of four more coastal survey vessels and four more inshore survey vessels. These new vessels, and the work that they would undertake, should be funded by civil authorities 'under the customer-contractor principle', what today would be called a 'Trading Fund' within government. Shipping operators and the offshore oil industry were deemed unlikely to wish to pay sufficient funds, whilst revenues from the sales of charts would not make up the shortfall either.[151] As a result, the burden would have to fall on those government departments with an interest in the civil maritime sector, such as the Department of the Environment, the Department of Energy and the Department of Overseas Development.[152] The annual cost of maintaining in service the vessels that the Admiralty Board had agreed to dispose of (and which the Study Group were told had been cut as part of the Defence Review) was calculated to be approximately £2.5 million. If some or all of this money was not found, then the Ministry of Defence stated that Royal Navy survey ships would be unable to contribute at all to oil and gas industry survey work until 1979.[153]

It was now clear what the purpose of the November 1974 Admiralty Board decision had been: to force the Study Group to come up with a practical solution, and funding proposals, to the increased civil need for survey work. Given that it was chaired by the junior minister responsible for the Navy, it is unlikely that the Study Group would have demurred. By proposing the withdrawal of certain vessels and then wrapping them into the Defence Review outcomes, the Admiralty Board was making clear to other government departments that either a separate civil hydrographic service would have to be set up with the Navy's discarded vessels, or they would have to contribute funding to the Hydrographic Service within the Royal Navy. Two separate government-run hydrographic services made little sense, so the final answer, however difficult for the civil departments to stomach, would have to be transfers from their budgets to support survey work being carried out by the Ministry of Defence. The oil and gas survey work was apparently particularly urgent, but both the Treasury and Ministry of Defence refusing to allow the modification of the survey ship HMS *Hecla* for this type of work until the Department of Energy proved willing to pay for its costs.[154]

The inevitable result was an agreement announced in 1977 that the Department of Energy and the Department of Overseas Development would contribute to Hydrographic Service work, beyond its NATO military requirements.[155] Just as inevitably, despite the recommendations for additional vessels in the Study Group report, the surveying fleet was not in the event expanded and remained at its pre-1974 size of four ocean survey ships, four coastal survey ships and five inshore survey vessels. Then, just when it seemed that the Hydrographic Service would be undertaking a mix of paid-for and defence work, the situation changed yet again. A year later increased Ministry of Defence requirements for oceanographic services as a result of 'new types of sonar systems' (probably towed-array sonar) and the need to better understand the sound propagation properties of water in different sea areas, meant that the civil work had to be de-prioritised and the long-term future of the hydrographic fleet as a military organisation was once again secure. At the same time, some of the requirements of the other government departments had fallen away: after the initial excitement at the beginnings of the offshore oil and gas industry the Department of Energy concluded that little additional surveying capability was actually needed, although the need for inshore port surveys had remained.[156] After these lurches back and forth in policy, and no doubt a worrying period for the Navy's hydrographers, the situation essentially returned to its pre-1974 position, but with the added advantage from the perspective of the Ministry of Defence of a new agreement with other government departments that they would have to pay for any work they might want done in the future.

Northern Ireland
As was seen, the conflict in Northern Ireland played an important part in preserving the numbers, and securing the survival, of the Royal Marines during the 1970s. The six counties of Northern Ireland had remained within the United Kingdom after the rest of the island of Ireland gained its independence in 1922. The province had a majority of Protestants and a minority of Roman Catholics, with representatives of the former invariably running things from the devolved assembly in Stormont, at the outer edge of Belfast. Continued discrimination against Catholics resulted in civil rights marches in 1968 and 1969, which in turn caused riots between the two communities as Protestants felt threatened and Catholics fought back. The Provisional Irish Republican Army, which had the support of sections of the Catholic community and was willing to use violence to push for a united Ireland, began to used armed force, as did a number of Protestant paramilitary groups. With civil order breaking down, the British military was sent to the province with the aim of restoring peace. 41 Commando, based in Malta, was part of the country's 'spearhead force' of the Strategic Reserve and was therefore one of the first units to deploy, arriving in Belfast in September 1969. It stayed only six weeks, but the following year 45 Commando arrived and stayed for a tour of four months. From this point onwards the four Commandos would be regularly deployed to Northern Ireland, operating as part of the rotation of British Army battalions in and out of the Province.[157]

There were essentially two types of deployments for the units. The first was urban, which involved patrolling streets and the crewing of observation posts in major cities such as Belfast or Londonderry. Patrols would deliberately keep moving to avoid become static targets for IRA shooters and operate in groups of four (known as 'bricks'), taking care to ensure that at least one soldier out of four would be out of sight, thus making a gunman unsure whether he was himself a target. Improvised Explosive Devices ('IEDs') would often be placed in the doorways of abandoned houses or other likely spots for soldiers to take cover, so these areas began to be avoided by soldiers. In such deployments, riot duty might be a possibility as would be dealing with thrown bottles or bricks by the local Catholic population. The second type of deployment was rural, primarily in the Crossmaglen border region of Armagh. Here, the situation was the closest it came to a low-level guerrilla conflict. Patrols would also be undertaken here and observation posts manned, but the rolling rural countryside made ambushes relatively easy, and IRA fighters might be armed with surprisingly heavy weapons. The high-hedged lanes of the area, which often crossed and re-crossed the border without any demarcation, were extremely dangerous for those deployed there, and quite soon patrols would deploy and return by helicopter. IEDs were also an issue, but this time attached to farm gates and styles rather than doorways.[158]

By the spring of 1972, there were still a number of 'no-go' areas in Catholic areas of Belfast and Londonderry, so a decision was made to surge additional forces into these urban areas in order to wrest back control and return these areas to the control of the civil authorities. Operation 'Motorman', as the operation was code-named, would bring in a large number of additional troops and allow the removal of barricades. 40 Commando was already in Northern Ireland, but 42 and 45 Commandos arrived as part of the surge force. During the night of 31 July 1972, four landing craft from HMS *Fearless* landed four specialist clearance vehicles to undertake the barricade-clearing in Londonderry in Operation 'Glasscutter'.[159] HMS *Intrepid*, *Fearless*' sister ship, performed the same function at Belfast. The IRA had been informed of the operation by the British government beforehand, so instead of a fight to the death on the streets of the two cities, the Provisionals melted away before the clearance vehicles went in, and control was regained of the streets without significant loss of life. Despite this, 1972 was the bloodiest year of the troubles the Royal Marines themselves losing three personnel killed and a further seventeen injured.[160]

The Royal Navy was given two new tasks as part of the battle to stop the smuggling of weapons and explosives into the province from the Republic of Ireland. In May 1972, the British Army started patrols of Carlingford Lough – which formed the border between County Down and the Republic – using small dory boats, but by the end of the year this had been regularised as a Royal Navy patrol under the code name Operation 'Interknit'.[161] Two fleet tenders, each with a number of light fast craft including a rigid raider and an outboard-powered inflatable, would alternate on patrol with the remit to stop and inspect any suspicious craft on the British side of the Lough.[162] The two vessels were modified fleet tenders whose names, *Loyal Factor* and *Loyal Governor*, were changed to *Vigilant* and *Alert* due to the Protestant paramilitary connotations of the word 'loyal'.[163] Another patrol, Operation 'Grenada', also aimed to interdict arms and explosives but in the Irish Sea and along the Northern Irish Coast. Mine warfare vessels and later *Seal* class patrol vessels were used in this role.[164] Both Operation 'Interknit' and Operation 'Grenada' continued until the end of the Northern Ireland troubles in the 1990s.

The Second Cod War

Whilst the Royal Navy was in the process of retreating from commitments around the world, much closer to home a dispute over fishing rights with Iceland, which would soon draw in the Navy, had been brewing for many years. Between 1958 and 1961 the Icelandic government had attempted to enforce a 12-mile territorial waters limit around Iceland as a means to preserve the fishing stock for its own fishing industry, which made up an important part of the island's economy. At that time, Iceland's territorial waters were accepted to cover the area out to four miles and British distant seas fishing vessels had made a good living from fishing the coastal waters around Iceland, just beyond the four-mile limit. Against a background of claims by many states for larger territorial waters at the first International Law of the Sea Conference, in 1958 the Icelandic government claimed a 12-mile limit and started to impound mainly British trawlers that fished within this limit and happened to come into Icelandic harbours. Next, Icelandic coastguard vessels began harassing trawlers, preventing them from fishing and attempting to board the boats. This had resulted in the involvement of the Royal Navy in protecting British trawlers, using frigates from the Fishery Protection Squadron to block the Icelandic vessels from disturbing the fishing boats. This initial dispute was eventually resolved in March 1961 when the British government conceded the 12-mile limit around Iceland. Fears that Iceland, which was sited in a geo-strategically crucial position across the entrance to the open Atlantic from the Norwegian and Northern Seas and also had been a recalcitrant and difficult member of NATO, would leave or threaten to leave the Alliance combined with the understanding that there were still good fishing grounds beyond the 12-mile limit, led to the British concessions.[165]

For another decade, aside from a few isolated incidents, relations over fishing rights were relatively calm, but an Icelandic general election in 1971 brought a socialist-communist coalition to power, who demanded a shift to a 50-mile limit. This would encompass almost all of the good fishing grounds around Iceland, and if successfully defended, would destroy the livelihoods of a good number of British fishing communities. It was likely that the next sitting of the International Law of the Sea Conference, due in 1973, would shift in the direction of Icelandic demands but as international law stood twelve miles was still the agreed limit. Negotiations between August 1971 and July 1972 resulted in an impasse and both sides prepared for more confrontations at sea.[166]

On 1 September 1972 the Icelandic government declared their 50-mile limit. Initially, the seventy trawlers and their two support ships provided by the Ministry of Agriculture, Fisheries and Food, continued fishing within the 50-mile limit, temporarily hauling in their nets when an Icelandic gunboat approached. However, five days later, the Icelandic gunboats began to cut the nets of British trawlers when they saw that they did not stop fishing. The British government was still negotiating with Iceland, so was initially reluctant to escalate the situation by bringing in warships. As a result, the British trawlers had to face the Icelandic vessels with only the MAFF support ships to aid them. The cutting of nets was used sparingly by the Icelandic gunboats initially, as a means to demonstrate to British negotiators what Iceland could do, and thus bring a settlement in Iceland's favour quickly. Cutting the nets required close manoeuvring in difficult seas, and inevitably the first (minor) collision occurred on 17 October. The firing of blank rounds at trawlers by another Icelandic gunboat the next day created a sense of mounting escalation, and a second Royal Navy frigate joined a first, already stationed just outside the 50-mile limit. Meanwhile negotiations continued. In the new year the cuttings re-commenced, and with few means to prevent the Icelanders use their cutting tool, new vessels were added to the fishing fleet, MAFF-chartered 'defence tugs'. Their role was to interpose themselves between the Icelandic gunboats and the fishing vessels, and in this role they were moderately effective, but required good co-ordination and co-operation with the fishing vessels, which was not always possible or forthcoming. With net-cutting proving more difficult, the Icelandic gunboats were now more prone to firing rounds to force fishing boats to move off. By April, British fishing vessels had begun disrupting the work of Icelandic fishing vessels, such was their frustration with the actions of the gunboats. Talks in April failed to come to any conclusion and the confrontations between British trawlers, their defence tugs and Icelandic gunboats continued. By 15 May, British skippers began to argue that fishing within the 50-mile limit was becoming impossible, and looked to the two frigates just beyond the limit to intervene. They vehemently disagreed with the decision by their trade body, the British Trawler Federation, not to ask for Royal Navy help, and argued that they might be forced to leave the waters around Iceland for good. Two warships, HMSs *Cleopatra* and *Plymouth*, supported by RFAs, gained agreement from Ministers, via the Flag Officer Scotland and Northern Ireland (FOSNI'), to enter the 50-mile limit on 19 May, and they then proceeded to an area east of Dalatangi on the far eastern tip of Iceland. The naval operation to support British trawlers around Iceland – code-named Operation 'Dewey' – had begun.[167]

The rules of engagement chosen for Operation 'Dewey' permitted warships to screen trawlers from the gunboats and interpose themselves between them. They could use helicopters to 'buzz' the Icelandic ships, place armed parties on trawlers and undertake counter-boarding of trawlers that had been arrested. Gunfire could only be used in self-defence, except for special circumstances when an 'Option Delta' was requested from FOSNI, to allow a carefully graduated minimum use of gunfire preceded by clear warnings. A third frigate joined the small force on 20 May: initially HMS *Lincoln* and then HMS *Jupiter* from the 22nd. Quite quickly it became apparent that the confrontation would be more aggressive and fraught than between 1958 and 1961: a riot occurred outside the British embassy in Reykjavik on 24 May, British military aircraft were no longer permitted to land in Iceland, and early attempts by Icelandic gunboats to arrest the trawler *Everton* resulted in repeated shots being fired into the trawler's bows, causing serious flooding. The flooding was repaired with help from defence tugs and a repair party from HMS *Jupiter*, and the damaged trawler doggedly returned fishing within the 50-mile limit the next day. Attempts by the Navy to ensure that the trawlers fished in designated areas proved almost impossible to enforce as the trawler skippers were always keen to find new and undisturbed waters to fish, thus making the task of the frigates and defence tugs that much more difficult.[168]

The force of three frigates, each vessel being relieved by a replacement after a couple of weeks from a pool of seven or eight under the control of FOSNI, were increasingly drawn into situations where collisions either occurred or came close to occurring. The gunboat *Aegir* collided with the frigate *Scylla* on 7 June, with the same vessel causing a near miss with HMS *Jaguar* on the 10th. The *Odinn* was heavily damaged in a collision with the defence tug *Lloydsman* on 21 June, and on 17 July the *Aegir* again collided with a frigate, this time *Lincoln*. On the same day *Arethusa* was rammed by *Odinn* causing minor damage but failing in its objective in cutting nets. On the 2 August the defence tug *Lloydsman* collided with the gunboat *Albert* whilst defending trawlers. Eight days later *Odinn* collided with *Andromeda*. With the exception of the *Odinn-Lloydsman* collision, most of these were minor glancing contacts with no injuries and usually only superficial damage. The Icelandic vessels were sometimes successful in cutting nets but with the British frigates and the defence tugs protecting the trawlers they had to adopt a range of tactics, including stop-start sudden manoeuvres, hugging the coast and mixing with Icelandic fishing vessels in order to reach the trawlers. To support surveillance of the Icelandic gunboats RAF Nimrods, supported by Britannias to conserve the former's flying hours, conducted regular patrols over the Icelandic fishing grounds. Relations between the Royal Navy and the trawler skippers could be difficult at times, the latter frustrated by the restrictive rules of engagement of the warships. However, in at least one incident a trawler, the *Lord St Vincent*, was suspected of fishing within the 12-mile limit causing a pursuit over two days by the gunboat *Aegir* with the frigates *Sirius* and *Andromeda* attempting to interpose themselves.[169]

After a short lull over much of August, the confrontations resumed: on 29 August the *Aegir* collided with HMS *Apollo* with minor damage to both ships. On 10 September *Thor* collided with *Jaguar*, again with minor damage to both. Within Iceland, the politics of the dispute was pushing the government into more aggressive gestures, such as threatening the breaking of diplomatic relations, combined with a guarded willingness to find at least a temporary solution behind the scenes. Diplomatic moves began to be made to resume discussions: a visit by Joseph Luns, the NATO Secretary General, was followed by approaches from the British Ambassador about a resolution. On 26 September, the Prime Minister, Edward Heath, made a proposal to withdraw warships and defence tugs in return for Icelandic ships ceasing their interference and agreement on a limit to the total catch by British trawlers. Whilst placating his communist coalition partners by renewing threats to break off diplomatic relations, the Icelandic Prime Minister also eventually agreed to talks with the British government. The result was a two-year interim agreement during which British warships and defence tugs would not enter the 50-mile limit, harassment would cease and the British catch per annum would not exceed 130,000 tons. The communists objected to the agreement but Iceland's Prime Minister managed to push the agreement through the country's parliament, the Althing, with support from opposition parties.[170]

The Second Cod War was over, but with a new International Law of the Sea Conference beginning in December, and an agreement lasting only two years, it seemed likely that the confrontation would resume in 1975. The Cod 'War' with Iceland was a delicate balancing act, which attempted both to support British fishing crews undertaking legal activities at sea, and ensure that British activities were not so provocative that a NATO-sceptical Iceland decided to leave the Alliance, potentially jeopardising control over Greenland-Iceland-UK Gap during a crisis. The conflict had also diverted a total of seven to eight frigates, more than 10 per cent of the total, away from other duties to provide the numbers in rotation to keep three ships on station in support of the trawlers. This meant that many fewer ships could take part in NATO exercises and overseas visits than had been planned, although the recent withdrawal of the five frigates from Singapore and their replacement with periodic group deployments, as seen in Chapter 5, had made the deployment decisions less painful than they might have been.

* * *

The 1975 Defence Review marked an important turning point for British defence policy as for the first time military resources were unequivocally focussed on deterring the Soviet Union on the Central European front and in the Eastern Atlantic. As was seen in Chapter 5, it had been the Navy itself that had effectively nullified the Conservative government's decision to base five frigates and destroyers in Singapore, by replacing that admittedly impractical commitment with only one vessel supplemented by annual group deployments. Even if the wider defence and political environment had not been enough to pull the Navy's leadership in this direction, the limitations on roulement as a result of new crewing patterns imposed by retention issues in the late 1960s, meant that sustaining a large naval force in Singapore was impossible over the long-term, but a sustained presence in the Mediterranean would have been plausible and useful to NATO. The requirements of the second Cod War and the Northern Ireland crisis also forced the Navy to focus more of its forces in home or near waters, even if they were not directly involved in NATO activities. The shift to the Four Pillars of the Defence Review also set the groundwork for the major crisis for the Navy that would occur at the next defence review: the return of an overcommitted procurement programme, the issue of surface ship vulnerability, the over-capacity of the dockyards, and the need to find the most effective mix of anti-submarine capabilities.

9

Retreat to the Four Pillars

One of the Defence Review's most significant decisions was the withdrawal from as many overseas commitments beyond Central Europe and the Eastern Atlantic as soon as possible. Despite the supposed 'withdrawal' from East of Suez in 1971, in reality there had remained a significant network of overseas commitments in the Mediterranean, Indian Ocean, Hong Kong, Pacific and Caribbean. This chapter will therefore review the maritime side of these commitments from the late 1960s onwards: their character and the forces used and, where this did occur, their winding down and closure after 1975.

The Mediterranean
As was seen at the start of this book, the Mediterranean had declined by 1966 into a neglected transit zone for a Royal Navy that had focussed its capabilities and its deployments on Singapore and the Indian Ocean. This began to change in 1968 as several factors coalesced into returning the Royal Navy's interest to a sea that had been of strategic importance to British maritime power for over 250 years. First was the entry of the Soviet Navy into the Mediterranean. During the 1950s and the early 1960s the Soviet Navy had largely confined itself to the seas bordering their territory: the Barents Sea in the north, the Baltic Sea, the Black Sea and the coastal area of the Pacific bordering the Soviet Far East. The Cuban Missile Crisis had shown that Soviet naval forces needed to have a worldwide capability if they were to support potential allies globally. It was not however until 1967 that the Soviet Navy began to gain the capabilities to operate in the far seas, with new surface ship and submarine classes better suited to global deployment. This new generation of Soviet nuclear-powered submarines of the 'Victor' and 'Charlie' classes were a considerable advance on the previous generation: they could engage other submarines, and had Western-

style 'teardrop' shaped hulls that helped with speed, whilst the 'Charlie' class were armed with SS-N-7 Amethyst anti-ship missiles that could be launched from under the water. This encouraged the Soviets to start deploying 'Charlie' class submarines from the Northern Fleet into the Mediterranean, which proved to be an ideal theatre for these submarines. The first practice firing of an Amethyst missile in the Mediterranean – from the Soviet submarine *K-313* in May 1972 – brought home these capabilities to NATO naval analysts. Cat-and-mouse trailing of the US 6th Fleet, which was based in the Mediterranean, then became a regular occurrence over the rest of the decade.[1] The Soviets also deployed naval vessels to support its allies in the aftermath of the 1967 Six Day War between US-backed Israel and the Arab states of Egypt, Syria and Jordan. This resulted in a long-term deployment of Soviet vessels into the Mediterranean, using the Egyptian anchorage off Alexandria for the 5th Squadron (or Eskadra) of the Black Sea Fleet.[2] Up to 1967 the total number of Soviet 'warship-days' spent in the Mediterranean had never been higher than 5,600; from 1968 it would reach 11,700 and it would stay between 15,000 and 20,000 throughout the 1970s.[3] With the Mediterranean becoming a scene of NATO-Soviet confrontation, a Royal Navy presence, even if it were a much smaller force than the powerful US 6th Fleet, would still be welcomed.

The second reason, and immediate trigger, for an increased naval focus on the Mediterranean was a crisis in a landlocked Central European state under Soviet control. The 1968 'Prague Spring' in Czechoslovakia resulted in an invasion by Warsaw Pact troops and a brutal suppression of the reformist government and its supporters. In straitened circumstances, Harold Wilson's government wanted to be seen to react to the crisis and help strengthen NATO resolve, but did not have the funds after two painful defence reviews to commit additional land forces and all the basing, support, social and foreign exchange costs that would come with posting more battalions to Germany. The redeployment of warships, however, was a much cheaper proposition: the ships would just be deployed to a different sea area and the additional expense might be no more than some additional replenishment costs. Denis Healey, the defence secretary, announced the deployment of a destroyer and two frigates to the Mediterranean, the regular presence of a major amphibious vessel, and a decision to keep Shackleton maritime patrol aircraft at Malta past 1969 (they would be replaced by Nimrods from 1970 onwards).[4] Although the naval deployment only had a moderate diplomatic impact – West Germany would have much preferred additional battalions – it did confirm that the British had regained their interest in the middle sea.[5] By 1970, the Labour government had committed to six destroyers and frigates and one submarine operating in the Mediterranean, the largest Royal Navy force since 1964.[6]

This relatively substantial force had been slimmed down after Edward Heath's Conservative government decided in 1971 to retain five ships at

Singapore rather than withdraw entirely. The Mediterranean commitment was therefore reduced to one guided missile destroyer and two frigates, but the sea retained its significance for naval deployments from home waters. As was seen in the previous chapter, despite being declared to SACLANT, amphibious forces spent a significant part of their time in the Mediterranean and invariably took part in NATO's major exercises. The Deep Furrow series (renamed Deep Express when combined with concurrent land exercises in Turkey) focussed on the eastern Mediterranean and possible Soviet attempts at a break out from the Black Sea involving a land attack on the Dardanelles.[7] The Dawn Patrol series usually involved operations focussed on the central Mediterranean, including escorting amphibious forces or convoys, and serials covering anti-submarine and anti-ship warfare. Amphibious landings were also included, either in Italy or along the western Greek coast.[8] These were major exercises involving most of the US 6th Fleet and substantial numbers of Italian, Greek and Turkish warships. In 1974 Dawn Patrol shifted its focus west and for the first time included a significant portion of the exercise in the Atlantic before undertaking a Gibraltar transit, and phases in the western Mediterranean, culminating in a transit of the Straits of Messina and a landing at Kyparissia on the western Peloponnese.[9] This change reflected a strategic shift in the Mediterranean as the Suez Canal was being prepared for re-opening (see later in this section). The sea would now become not only a transit route for US reinforcements to the southern flank of NATO, but also a crucial world trade route again, not least for oil tankers from the Gulf across the Atlantic to the Americas.

The crucial importance of ensuring a good flow of Middle East oil worldwide was made clear during the 1973 oil crisis when Arab states restricted supply following the Yom Kippur War. This made Gibraltar a doubly important gateway strategically. Unfortunately, this was only slowly recognised by the Ministry of Defence. The conclusions of a 1971 study by the Defence Planning Staff had been that Gibraltar and its straits were of no strategic importance to the United Kingdom, although they were to NATO.[10] Despite the impending opening of the Canal, there were no changes to this assessment throughout the 1974–5 Defence Review, and as a result the Mediterranean continued to be a theatre where support to the southern flank of the Alliance was being given but where few British national interests were at stake. This ambiguous position therefore left the British commitment to the Mediterranean – which aside from facilities in Cyprus was mainly a maritime commitment – in a fragile position and one, as has been seen in the previous chapter, that was vulnerable to withdrawal in a review theoretically based on distilling down to the essential minima of British defence. The neglecting of the strategic importance of trade routes and maritime choke points was another sign of a strategic myopia that was developing in a Ministry of Defence and government focussed on the Central European front against the Soviets above all else.

The Yom Kippur War Naval Confrontation

In 1973 Egyptian and Syrian armed forces launched a bold surprise attack against Israel in an attempt to reverse their losses in the earlier 1967 Arab-Israeli war and also, if their plan had succeeded, destroy or drastically diminish the state of Israel. After initial advances into Israeli-held territory, the defenders began to fight back successfully and were able to surround and partially defeat the Arab forces. Both sides had called upon their superpower allies to support them. The United States, whilst most Western European states including the United Kingdom stood back, supplied arms to Israel, whilst Egypt and Syria, which had already benefitted from considerable Soviet support before and during the war, requested additional supplies and stores. Although little known at the time and today, a prolonged naval confrontation between US ships of the 6th Fleet and Soviet ships of the 5th Eskadra off the coasts of Israel and Egypt has been described as 'the most severe maritime crisis of the Cold War', and which might have escalated into general conflict and whose nearest comparable situation was the much better known 1962 Cuban Missile Crisis.[11] Chief of Naval Operations, Admiral Elmo Zumwalt, with only a modicum of hyperbole, stated that 'I doubt that major units of the US Navy were ever in a tenser situation since World War Two ended'.[12]

In October 1973, the Soviet 5th Eskadra consisted of over fifty warships including eleven submarines and two cruisers and a mix of destroyers and smaller ships, which although they were largely supplied by Soviet vessels from the Black Sea, had the benefit of the use of anchorages off Alexandria in Egypt and Tartus in Syria. Soviet warships were initially involved in evacuating civilians from Egypt as hostilities began. It was not until the US airlift of military supplies to Israel began on 13 October, which itself was a response to the beginning of Soviet military resupply to Egypt on 9 October, that tensions between the two forces heightened.[13] Once Soviet maritime resupply using merchant ships sailing from the Black Sea had started, major naval units of the 5th Eskadra, instead of the usual unarmed intelligence-collection ships, began to shadow and mark the US carrier groups in the eastern Mediterranean as a warning against an attempt to interfere in Moscow's logistical movements to Egypt. Soviet ships would train their missile launchers on US ships, including the carriers, 'illuminating' the ships with their targeting radars, whilst both US and Soviet aircraft would undertake low-level overflights and illuminate targets. Once US resupply to Israel by aircraft began and was followed up two days later by an Israeli counter-attack in the Sinai peninsula, tensions heightened significantly. Threatened by air attack from Israeli aircraft near the Syrian port of Latakia, two Soviet minor warships fired back at the aircraft. As the Egyptians faced defeat by the Israelis the Soviet leader, Leonid Brezhnev, threatened a unilateral intervention in the conflict if the US did not agree to a joint peacekeeping force to enforce a UN-ordered ceasefire. Soviet warships were sent to Port Said in Egypt, troops in the region were placed on alert, and more ships armed with anti-ship missiles began marking the US carrier groups in an attempt to prevent a feared US pre-emptive strike to stop a Soviet intervention operation. The US government moved to the DefCon 3 alert level and on 25 October attempted to defuse a situation that seemed on the very edge of a fighting war at sea, by pushing the Israelis to accept the UN ceasefire proposal and by halting the military resupply effort. Tensions did not immediately subside: the 5th Eskadra began anti-carrier exercises on 26 October, using US warships as 'targets', whilst yet more Soviet warships entered the region and began shadowing and marking the US vessels, bringing the total number of Soviet vessels to over ninety against the US Navy's sixty.[14] In his diary, the Chief of Staff to the Commander 5th Eskadra, Captain 1st Class Yevgenii Simenov, wrote on 30 October that 'Our forces have very powerful cruise missiles and they are directed at only five objects – three aircraft carriers and two helicopter carriers. All others are secondary. Everybody's waiting only for a signal. The pressure has risen to the breaking point.'[15] If hostilities had appeared imminent, US carrier aircraft would have aimed pre-emptively to destroy every missile-firing Soviet warship at sea, whilst Soviet forces would have aimed to fire their missiles directly at the US carriers as quickly as possible – a reflection of the Soviet 'battle of the first salvo' doctrine, even if it would have probably meant ultimate destruction for the Soviet surface vessels. Once the US government had a confirmation that a landing by Soviet troops – as a unilateral intervention – was not going to happen, they ordered their naval forces in the region to move westward and away from Egypt and Israel. A few days later, Soviet forces then began to reduce the number of its ships shadowing US forces and began to rest their crews. At last, the stand-off began to dissipate as warship numbers dropped and aggressive marking by missile-armed warships gave way to shadowing by the familiar and unarmed intelligence-gathering ships the Soviets usually deployed.[16]

The confrontation lasted approximately three weeks, during which warships and submarines manoeuvred, shadowed and marked each other in increasingly tense circumstances, in ways that would have been impossible to imagine across the hard boundary of the 'Inner German Border' between Warsaw Pact and NATO land forces. Few shots were fired, but the Soviets used their inferior forces – although their numbers were greater, the 5th Eskadra primarily consisted of smaller warships, few of which were able to defend themselves against concerted air attack given their lack of air cover – to achieve their military-political ends by pressuring the US to stop the re-supply of its ally and force it into a ceasefire. Much greater risks were taken by these opposing naval forces, as the sea was a domain in which few civilians were present and was what would today be called a 'global commons': a zone of free movement without international borders. Soviet and US forces inter-mixed, shifted their positions and lay close to one another day after day, jostling for advantage and attempting to achieve their political objectives through conventional deterrence and coercion. As with the 1962 Cuban Missile Crisis, which included a similarly tense maritime stand-off, this provided an example of where a prolonged maritime confrontation could become the crucible of superpower rivalry in a much more likely and plausible way than across the static borders of Europe. Inferior forces could achieve their objectives, despite their nominal weakness, through the astute use of threat and manoeuvre before any weapons had been fired. It provided a potential model for a maritime focus on forces for such circumstances, with the aim of achieving political objectives without necessarily resorting to general armed conflict. However, as will be seen in the succeeding chapters, a more static land-orientated approach to superpower confrontation increasingly focussed on surprise attacks across land came to dominate Ministry of Defence thinking.

Re-opening the Suez Canal: Operations 'Rheostat I' and 'II'
By the end of the 1973 Yom Kippur War large numbers of naval mines had been laid by Egypt around the entrances to the Suez Canal, adding to those laid in the earlier war of 1967. As Egypt began to drift away from Soviet support and towards the West, plans were made for the disarming and removal of these mines and for operations to make the Suez Canal passable for the first time since its closure in 1967. Egypt's own minesweeping capabilities were sufficient to clear defensive minefields near the entrances to Port Said, but they did not have the expertise to deal with more sophisticated mines. The British government offered the services of the Royal Navy to Egypt, and by 11 March 1974 a force consisting of HMS *Abdiel*, the mine warfare support ship, and the mine hunters HMS *Maxton*, *Bossington* and *Wilton*, arrived in Egyptian waters. The force started by clearing mines in Port Said harbour, and then proceeded methodically to clear the canal of mines with support from US mine countermeasures helicopters that undertook 'precursor' sweeps in front of the minehunters. HMS *Maxton* became the first ship to traverse the Canal in six years when she passed through into the Gulf of Suez on 14 July 1974. In addition to US precursor sweeps, a French mine warfare force focussed their efforts on the shallow waters on the canal edges supported by British and Egyptian clearance diving teams. A Soviet mine countermeasures force also undertook clearance work, in their case focussing on the southern entrance to the Canal in the Gulf of Suez. A year later, Operation 'Rheostat II' involved *Abdiel* again, this time with *Sheraton* and *Hubberston*, undertaking a second clearance operation through the Canal, to make sure no mines had been

disturbed and become dangerous following Egyptian dredging operations. No mines were located, but a range of other metal objects dumped in the Canal over many years were recovered. The Canal was finally opened to international traffic on 5 June 1975.[17] It was a supreme irony that the Canal, open for the first time in six years and under the control of a pro-Western state for the first time since 1956, was deemed to be no longer vital to British defence despite the crucial role it would quickly take up as a transit point and choke point for oil supplies arriving from the Middle East.

Cyprus and Lebanon
Cyprus had been a British colony up to 1960, but after gaining independence following an insurgency against British rule the new state was not necessarily stable: relations between the ethnic Greek majority and the ethnic Turkish minority deteriorated when the former attempted to change the constitution to reduce the representation of the latter. Violence had broken out between the two groups in 1964, each side tacitly backed by Greece and Turkey, with the new constitution enacted and the ethnic Turkish population increasingly concentrated in the north and east of the island. Cyprus had remained tense over the next decade, with strong Greek influence on the government, the US and Britain attempting to prevent both open war between Greece and Turkey over the issue and Cyprus falling under Soviet influence, whilst Britain maintained two Sovereign Base Areas in the south and south-east of island, which included an air station and other facilities.[18]

In July 1974 a new Greek military Junta attempted to depose Cyprus' President, Archbishop Makarios, and replace him with Nicos Sampson, a journalist and Greek nationalist fighter. The resulting upheaval from this coup precipitated a Turkish decision to invade Cyprus to protect the Turkish minority, who appeared likely to suffer more under the rule of the new Cypriot leader. Neither Britain nor the United States wished to intervene to force the Turks to retreat. However, there were over 35,000 British tourists on Cyprus at the time of the Turkish invasion, Cyprus having become a popular package holiday destination in the 1960s.[19] Most, with the support of British troops flown in from the United Kingdom, were able to make their way to one of the British Sovereign Base Areas and were evacuated by the Royal Air Force, but around 1,500 became trapped in or near the northern port of Kyrenia, one of the first towns taken by the Turkish invaders. A task group headed by HMS *Hermes*, to be joined by the destroyer *Devonshire* and the frigates *Andromeda* and *Rhyl*, was despatched to pick up these stranded British subjects. *Hermes* had just returned to the Mediterranean after a visit to the United States, Canada and Bermuda and was steaming towards Malta. On 16 July the ship was ordered to Malta at speed and then remain there ready to deploy, but this was overtaken by new orders on the 17th to proceed directly to Cyprus, accompanied by the three escorts, which had been brought together from various taskings across the region.[20] Nine hundred were picked up by *Hermes*' Wessex helicopters from the six-mile long beach near the town, whist the remaining 600 were taken from the port itself by the ships' boats of the group. The operation was completed in a single 24-hour period on 23 July, and the British tourists picked up in this way were later dropped off in the British Sovereign Base Areas to fly home to the United Kingdom.[21] The evacuation had been conducted efficiently and effectively in a situation that was both dangerous and tense during an invasion by a foreign state and inter-communal violence. The Turkish advance was halted after around a third of Cyprus had been occupied, and the main island divided along a no-man's-land that became known as the 'Green Line'. Greece and Turkey, both ostensible NATO allies, had come close to war and neither US nor British diplomacy had been successful in helping to resolve the confrontation, which settled over time into the stasis that exists today. The humiliation of the invasion and ineffective Greek response ruined the credibility of the military rulers and Greece soon began its return to democratic rule, but Greece also withdrew from the military structures of NATO for a number of years, whilst Turkey's trust in the US as an arbiter over Cyprus was severely compromised.[22] The eastern Mediterranean, from which most British forces were soon to be withdrawn as a result of the Defence Review, was turning into a major crucible of instability on NATO's flanks. This was further confirmed by the outbreak of civil war in Lebanon a few months later.

Lebanon, on the eastern shore of the Mediterranean, was another small state that was tipping into ungovernability in the early 1970s. The state was a delicately-balanced mix of Shia, Sunni and Druze Muslims, and Maronite and Orthodox Christians. It had become a major tourist and business destination for the wealthy of the Middle East in the post-war years, with the British government setting up its Arabic language school in the capital, Beirut. The arrival of Palestinian refugees ejected from Jordan in 1970 combined with the increased attention of its larger and more powerful neighbour Syria, had resulted in growing tensions and a breakdown in trust between the dominant Maronite and Sunni elites. The presence of Palestinian Liberation Organisation ('PLO') leaders also resulted in Israeli interventions in Lebanon, which was then followed by cross-border raids by the PLO. Violence broke out in Beirut in spring 1975 between different communities and by the autumn the capital city had become divided into militia fiefdoms with the national army, which was soon to disintegrate, unwilling or unable to dislodge them.[23] On 9 October, the commando carrier HMS *Bulwark*, having just completed its involvement in the NATO amphibious exercise Deep Express 75 off the

Turkish coast, was ordered to hold her position just west of Malta pending a possible decision to assist the evacuation of British nationals from Lebanon. In the event, the British subjects that left were evacuated either by air or road.[24]

The situation worsened in June 1976 when Syrian forces invaded the country, concerned that an alliance of PLO, Druze and Leftist forces might crush the Maronites and jeopardise Syrian leverage in Lebanon.[25] Two frigates, HMS *Mermaid* and HMS *Exmouth*, which had just completed their annual training exercise off Gibraltar, accompanied by RFA *Stromness* and RFA *Grey Rover*, were sent eastwards to prepare to evacuate the remaining British subjects from Beirut. Plans were being laid for land convoys to escort up to 1,500 British subjects to Damascus, the capital of Syria, and the first convoy successfully reached Syria on 19 June. The four ships stood by to provide a back-up means of evacuation if the road routes were blocked. As the situation in Beirut worsened, taking the ships or their boats alongside in the Beirut harbour was deemed too hazardous, and plans were made for the ships' boats to land on beaches further out from the city centre. The road convoys were delayed by fighting for two tense days as the ships readied themselves for a possible beach evacuation, but on 22 June the second convoy made it to the Syrian border and the ships were later stood down.[26] The Cyprus and Lebanon evacuations demonstrated the continuing importance of naval forces for evacuating British nationals, particularly if other means had been compromised by fighting. Although the resources committed by using warships were much greater than for air or land evacuation, sometimes they were the only way to get the most isolated or endangered British subjects out of the country.

Malta and Gibraltar
The Defence Review had decided on a general withdrawal from most bases in the Mediterranean, and the most significant base to go was at Malta. In 1972 an agreement had been made with the Maltese government for a further seven-year lease of facilities on the island for a total of just over £50 million a year, paid in increments twice yearly.[27] From 1976 British forces in Malta began to be gradually run down, and rather than exit from the agreement early, it was decided to end the British presence just before the agreement ran out on 31 March 1979. 41 Commando, which was being disbanded as a result of the Review, would vacate its base on the island on 31 March 1977, leaving behind a party of 200 Marines as a local protection force during the run down. In 1978 the RAF's Nimrod maritime patrol aircraft and Canberra reconnaissance aircraft would be withdrawn and RAF Luqa run down, eventually being transformed into Malta's civil airport. From March 1977 the 2,500 British military personnel and their 5,000 dependents would gradually leave the island, with the service schools closing in July 1978 and medical centres in

September.²⁸ The final withdrawal of the British presence began on 9 March 1979 when the destroyer HMS *London* arrived and the Flag Officer Malta, Rear Admiral O Cecil, transferred his flag to the warship. On 1 April 1979, HMS *London* departed the Grand Harbour with crowds lining its bastions.²⁹ The Royal Navy's 173-year presence in Malta had finally ended.

Gibraltar dockyard and naval base, at the entrance to the Mediterranean, remained but even here its strategic significance, as was seen in the previous chapter, appears to have been misunderstood within the Ministry of Defence. The 1974 report of the Defence Review Steering Group, recommending outcomes for the Defence Review, had stated baldly that it was 'no longer of any great military importance to us, although it has some value for NATO.'³⁰ The Gibraltar naval base was not abandoned as it was a significant employer on the territory and the dockyard also provided a useful overflow facility for the home dockyards, which were struggling to cope with the growing and increasingly complex frigate refit programme.³¹

South East Asia and the Indian and Pacific Ocean Regions

Singapore and Hong Kong
As was seen in Chapter 5, with the dissolution of the Far East Fleet and the Conservative government's decision to retain a naval presence in Singapore, the Royal Navy continued to send a force of approximately five frigates, often led by a destroyer, to Singapore to maintain the British presence and fulfil British commitments to the 1968 Five Powers Defence Arrangements ('FPDA'), under which the United Kingdom, Australia and New Zealand agreed to support and develop the defence capabilities of Malaysia and Singapore. This included maintaining a British-Australian-New Zealand command structure at Singapore led by a two-star appointment rotating amongst the three countries. The naval senior officer was a Commodore, initially British but then also rotating, and two of the five Royal Navy ships were assigned to FPDA duties, which usually involved taking part in regular exercises with the Malaysian Navy and the Singapore Maritime Command.³² With the decision to withdraw the five frigates and primarily replace them with periodic group deployments, there was a clear need to maintain at least one vessel at Singapore to ensure that FPDA commitments could be maintained. As was described in Chapter 5, the vessel chosen was a diesel-powered frigate built for, but never delivered to, Ghana.³³ She was purchased, renamed *Mermaid* and after much delay arrived at Singapore Naval Base in September 1974. She was permanently assigned to the FPDA Commodore and spent much of her time as Singapore Naval Base guardship alternating with port visits and deployments within the region. She visited Subic Bay, Manila, Hong Kong and Japan, and in April 1975 was one

of two Royal Navy frigates, the other being HMS *Achilles*, which supported the US Navy's ship-borne evacuations from South Vietnam.[34] The Naval Base at Singapore was now a shadow of its former self but was still managed by a Royal Navy Captain, and included a stores organisation, a helicopter support unit and two Fleet Maintenance Units, which was a not-insubstantial commitment, although many key posts were held by Australian and New Zealand officers. Assisted Maintenance Periods and Docking and Essential Defect periods were amongst the maintenance tasks undertaken, with the focus being support for frigate deployments.[35] Following the outcome of the Defence Review, this infrastructure began to be dismantled, with much of the support capability either returning home or being handed over to other FPDA members. Negotiations started for the retention of an oil depot and two berths for future use, whilst over 1,300 married quarters were handed over to the Singaporean government, as was over £500,000-worth of moveable assets.[36] *Mermaid* sailed for the United Kingdom on 24 September 1975, and after 18 months of service in home and northern waters, she was sold to the Malaysian Navy in April 1977. She was to be the last British warship permanently based at Singapore for more than 40 years. Royal Navy ships would continue to visit, and a few years later most of the old dockyard was redeveloped to become a major container port with the two berths in one corner of the port being retained for Royal Navy (and US, Australian and New Zealand naval) use.[37]

The colony of Hong Kong, which during the 1970s had begun to take off economically, providing a stark contrast to Britain's own economic problems, had long had a small force of patrol vessels supplemented by a frigate acting as guardship. The patrol vessels were primarily used to patrol Hong Kong's territorial waters and sea boundaries with China, whilst the guardship provided a permanent demonstration of the British military presence, which the governor had particularly valued during disturbances and riots in the late 1960s.[38] As was seen in Chapter 5, the new permanent guardship was the old frigate HMS *Chichester*, which had had her crew and some of her capabilities reduced, in all but name becoming a short-range gunboat. *Chichester* did not operate under the standard two- to three-year refit cycle, instead being maintained locally or in Singapore with one two-week long Assisted Maintenance Period every 65 weeks and one four-week Docking and Essential Defects period in the same timeframe.[39] Initially, a refit or replacement by another modified frigate had been planned after five years but by 1974 it was being envisaged that her refit might take place in Hong Kong itself with the support of a Fleet Maintenance Unit flown in from the UK.[40]

The Defence Review had cancelled a planned order for replacements for the existing Hong Kong patrol boats, which were currently ageing former minesweepers. Although this seemed like a dangerous willingness not to protect Hong Kong's territorial waters it was in fact the opening salvo in an attempt by the British government to make Hong Kong's government pay a higher proportion of the cost for the defence of the colony. Faced with paying up to 75 per cent of the costs of the British military commitment as a whole compared to the previous portion of 30 per cent, the governor initially agreed to reduce the patrol craft to three in order to keep *Chichester*, but with the costs of maintaining the frigate becoming more apparent and the Ministry of Defence threatening to withdraw all five craft, the governor eventually agreed to relinquish *Chichester*.[41] However, the governor did agree to pay for 75 per cent of the cost of five new patrol vessels. Each would be armed with a 76mm gun and with a maximum speed of 25 knots, thus giving them an armament that would at least give Chinese destroyers pause for thought now that *Chichester's* medium gun would no longer be available. After some delay in ordering, the five new craft entered service between 1984 and 1985.[42] *Chichester* herself left Hong Kong in March 1976 only three years into what had been expected to be as long as a 10-year deployment to the colony. She was decommissioned on return to the United Kingdom and scrapped in 1982. The Navy prepared plans to re-instate the guardship in the late 1970s but the Foreign and Commonwealth Office never submitted a formal request to the Ministry of Defence for its return.[43] In addition, the balance of personnel in the Hong Kong squadron was shifted, with half of the crew of each patrol craft now being locally recruited and employed, although usually in more junior roles or acting as interpreters.[44] Another effect of the Defence Review was the senior naval officer in the colony was downgraded from a Commodore to a Captain.[45]

Indian Ocean
By 1975 the British presence in the Indian Ocean consisted of a small naval relay station on the colony of the Seychelles (which would become independent in 1976) a much more substantive communications relay station operated by the Royal Navy on Mauritius (which had become independent in 1968),[46] a transit airfield operated by the RAF on Gan in the Maldives (independent in 1965) and the British Indian Ocean Territory, a group of islands including Diego Garcia which had been separated from Mauritius and the Seychelles in 1965. Their inhabitants had been removed and Diego Garcia became a major staging base for the United States military, with British forces having access to some of the US facilities.[47] Royal Navy ships would also make use of basic facilities in Mombasa in Kenya or Bombay (modern Mumbai) in India for self-maintenance and occasional docking and essential defect periods.

Up to 1975 the flow of Royal Navy warships around the Cape of Good Hope and through the Indian Ocean to and from Singapore – as has been seen, the Suez Canal had been shut since the 1967 Arab-Israeli War – had meant that the Indian Ocean states had received regular port visits. The roles undertaken by passing frigates resembled those undertaken in the Caribbean, but the great distances involved meant that visits were inevitably much fewer than on the West Indies station. Disaster-relief operations were undertaken in Mauritius in 1972 and 1975 following cyclones.[48] Ships' helicopters were used to spot the growing of illegal narcotics on Mauritius in 1972 and 1974.[49] Royal Navy warships were also used to 'stand by' beyond the horizon line during disturbances on both Mauritius and the Seychelles. In January 1968, just before Mauritian independence, HMS *Euryalus* landed marines and armed sailors ashore following riots, the significance of her presence being indicated by the ship's commanding officer attending the Governor's security council.[50] After quiet had returned, local school children were given guided tours of the frigate. HMS *Arethusa* stood by off the Seychelles in April 1972 whilst HMS *Leopard* did the same in April 1974.[51]

The survey ship HMS *Hydra* spent a total of six years operating in the Indian Ocean, Persian Gulf and Pacific undertaking hydrographic surveys. Her crew was replaced on a rotating 'trickle drafting' six-month basis, and her maintenance was undertaken with the support of Fleet Maintenance Units flown in from the United Kingdom.[52] In the Indian Ocean her work generally involved repeated surveys around the Seychelles. The RFA tanker *Ennerdale* foundered off the Seychelles on 1 June 1970 and the Royal Navy was heavily involved in the clean-up operation.[53] In the major states bordering the Indian Ocean region, the Royal Navy's influence was diminishing as the number of its warships present in the area declined. The Cape of Good Hope became a crucial way station to reach the Indian Ocean after 1967 and runs ashore in South Africa became part of the routine of an East of Suez deployment. However, the increasing controversy of white minority-ruled South Africa's apartheid policies, meant that not only was it difficult to envisage full naval co-operation with South Africa lasting much longer, but runs ashore were severely circumscribed for those Royal Navy sailors from ethnic minority backgrounds. As will be seen in Chapter 20, the Navy's liaison officer in Cape Town in 1972 was unwilling to jeopardise relations with South Africa's government by accepting that black and Asian sailors would not be able to join their white comrades on runs ashore in racially-segregated areas.[54]

In India, whose Navy had been equipped in the 1950s and 1960s almost entirely with British-built or British-designed ships, and where links between the two navies had been close, there was a rapid pivot away from these imperial-era ties to an increasingly close relationship with the Soviet Union. The first step was made in 1965 when the British government had refused to extend credit to the Indian government to help pay for its programme of

Leander class frigates and a planned submarine programme. India then turned to the USSR to support the building of a range of warship types.[55] The next step in the distancing of the British-India relationship was the decision to halt arms supplies to India when India and Pakistan went to war in September 1965. The USSR continued supplying its new ally and then brokered a peace between the two states in January 1966.[56] China, which had grown hostile to the USSR following the death of Stalin in 1953, clashed with India over its Himalayan border areas in 1967. Despite Harold Wilson's attempt to provide support to India through the British 'nuclear umbrella', which led to his strangely Victorian and diplomatically maladroit assertion that the borders of Britain reached up to the Himalayas, India needed a credible counter to China and built on its initial contacts with the Soviet Union.[57] India remained vehemently 'non-aligned' in the global Cold War between East and West, but from the late 1970s British designed *Leander* class frigates began to be fitted with Soviet naval weaponry and Soviet-built destroyers of the 'Kashin' class were purchased.[58] Port visits by Royal Navy vessels continued, but the Indian Navy became increasingly reluctant to engage in joint exercises for fear of revealing the capabilities of the Soviet weaponry on their ships.[59] India's great rival, Pakistan, was no doubt happy that India's shift to the USSR had given the western powers more reason to ally with it, but British influence here was also in decline. In discussions with senior Pakistani naval officers, the Flag Officer in charge of the 1976 Group Deployment, Rear Admiral A S Morton, was told that US influence on the Pakistani Navy was inevitably growing: the Royal Navy was less in evidence in exercises and port visits just as the number of US vessels in the region was increasing, whilst second-hand US warships were cheaper to buy and in plentiful supply.[60]

The Beira Patrol, which continued to be a considerable commitment for the Royal Navy given the need to transit via the Cape to reach the patrol area, was now being undertaken on a less onerous basis. In March 1971 the government allowed the patrol to be undertaken by one warship rather than two, and two years later the patrol was made non-continuous, the rather tenuous rationale being that Rhodesia was finding it more difficult to refine any crude oil it received from Beira. This was a relief for Royal Navy operational tasking managers, but a decision that even more clearly laid bare the meagre practical utility of the patrol, given the rebel Rhodesian regime's ability to bypass Beira by receiving imports from either South Africa or other Mozambiquan ports. The end of the conservative authoritarian regime in Portugal in 1974 resulted in a rapid collapse in that country's colonial empire, including Mozambique. Beira was therefore no longer available to Rhodesia for imports and the Beira patrol therefore lost its reason to exist. The last ship on the patrol, HMS *Salisbury*, left her station on 25 June 1975, the day that Mozambique became independent.[61]

The outcome of the Defence Review resulted in the withdrawal from the different aspects of this residual British presence in the Indian Ocean: the RAF station at Gan was closed, the Beira patrol had already ended and the communications centre in Mauritius was shut down in 1976 resulting in the loss of many hundreds of local jobs.[62] The political sensitivities of the closure of such a substantial local employer were such that the Mauritian Prime Minister, who had been lobbying for better payments for sacked local staff, was invited to lunch with the Prime Minister and Defence Secretary to discuss the issue when he visited the United Kingdom.[63] Diego Garcia remained but was primarily a US base with the United Kingdom acting largely as the 'landowner'. There would now be almost no permanent British military presence in this huge region for the first time in more than 300 years. With a growing presence of both US naval vessels detached from the Pacific, and Soviet naval vessels beginning to sustain a significant presence in an ocean in which the leading local powers, such as India, still lacked the ability to sustain forces in the deep ocean. The Indian Ocean world was changing rapidly, and the United Kingdom was no longer part of it.

Australia and New Zealand
Strategically, Australia faces in three directions: to the Indian Ocean in the west, South East Asia to the north and the South Pacific to the east. With a relatively small naval force, the Royal Australian Navy had remained partially dependent on the Royal Navy's Far East Fleet to defend and provide a presence in these regions, and many of its vessels were integrated into the Far East Fleet's structures. As a result it made operational sense for its equipment, training and support systems to be still heavily influenced by the Royal Navy in the late 1960s. The British decision to withdraw from Singapore by 1971 had been strongly fought by the Australian government, which was now faced with rebuilding its military alliance structures for the 1970s in the expectation of a much-diminished British presence.[64] Some steps away from the British link had already been made: Australia had committed its military to fighting in Vietnam whereas the United Kingdom had not, whilst the RAN had decided to purchase US-built *Charles F Adams* class guided missile destroyers in 1962 instead of the equivalent British 'County' class.[65] This had created a 'dual navy' in which the new US-built destroyers – which usually deployed with the US Navy off Vietnam – were dependent on US logistics and spares, and the rest of the Navy on British equipment support.[66] Despite this, the British link remained, and the next generation of Australian destroyer, dubbed the DDL or light destroyer, was planned to be of British

design. Initially the DDL would have been a light patrol frigate designed by the British warship builder Vosper Thornycroft. This eventually became the British Type 21 frigate, as was described in Chapter 3, but in 1968 the RAN changed its requirements to a much more capable vessel armed with the US Tartar air defence missile system. In partnership with the Yarrow-Admiralty Research Department, a British consultancy, the new DDL design was developed for construction in Australian yards. Although armed with US Tartar, the ship had a strong family resemblance to British warships being designed at the time such as the Type 42 and Type 22.[67] In many respects it is surprising how long this British-Australian warship survived: a new Labor government elected in 1973 cancelled the DDL and agreed to purchase the simpler but less capable US Navy FFG-7 design instead, pointing the way to the obvious conclusion that the US Navy would be the RAN's most important operational partner in the future.[68] British economic and industrial travails through the 1970s did not help perception of the United Kingdom during this period: news of strikes and power cuts in the 'mother country' not only seemed to re-affirm the migration choices of those who had decided to settle in Australia – a country much of whose population was made up of first- or second-generation British emigrants in 1970 – but also appeared to point to the declining need to retain such a strong British link. The 1975 Group Deployment, which included numerous Australian port visits, was deemed to have helped counter this perception by Rear Admiral Fieldhouse, but this could only have had a relatively short-lived impact and no matter where some sympathies might lie, Australia's strategic future could only lie with the United States: an allied state committed to the region with sufficient military resources to support the defence of Australia.[69]

New Zealand had a much smaller navy than that of Australia, so its potential contribution to US task groups would likely be limited to only one or two ships at most. Although in terms of strategic orientation New Zealand broadly followed the Australian lead away from a British focus towards the USA, it remained equipped with British equipment for longer: buying four British-built frigates which entered service between 1960 and 1971, but by 1979 it was expecting future warship procurement to align with Australian and US capabilities and logistics rather than British.[70] The New Zealand government, when under Labor leadership, took a strong line against nuclear testing, sending two of those new British-built frigates to Mururoa Atoll in the south Pacific to protests against French nuclear tests in 1973.[71] Some years later, in 1985, the New Zealand government's refusal to allow British or US warships carrying nuclear weapons to make port visits in New Zealand caused political controversy, but underneath relations between the RNZN and Royal Navy remained solid, if gradually distancing, through the 1970s and 1980s.[72]

The Pacific Islands and Brunei

To the north-east of Australia lay yet more British island colonies stretching out across the South Pacific. To the east of Papua New Guinea, a colony administered by Australia until independence in 1975, lay the Solomon Islands which gained independence from Britain in 1978. Further to the south east was the New Hebrides, a British-French condominium which would become independent as Vanuatu in 1980. Beyond lay Fiji which gained its independence from the United Kingdom in 1970, and further to the south-east was the protectorate of Tonga and to the north-east the Gilbert and Ellice Islands which would gain independence as two separate states, Tuvalu and Kiribati, in 1978 and 1979 respectively. Even deeper into the Pacific were the tiny Pitcairn islands which is still a British overseas territory today. As the leading historian of the end of Britain's Pacific Empire, W David McIntyre, states, none of these had strategic value to Britain, but had been acquired primarily at the urging of Australia and New Zealand in the late nineteenth century.[73]

These territories were even more widely dispersed than the British Indian Ocean colonies and as they were not on any transit routes used by the Royal Navy, were visited infrequently during the late 1960s and 1970s. In 1969 and 1975 HMS *Jaguar* and HMS *Hydra* respectively provided humanitarian relief supplies to Fiji; in the first instance during a drought and in the second following a hurricane.[74] *Hydra* was also present in the waters around Fiji, the New Hebrides and the Solomons in 1972 and 1974 undertaking hydrographic surveys.[75] The New Hebrides received more regular visits than most, with at least five frigate visits between 1970 and 1976.[76] In 1977 naval ordnance experts undertook Operations 'Hemicarp' and 'Hemicarp II' to dispose of unexploded wartime ordnance on the Gilbert and Ellice Islands prior to independence.[77] Between June and August 1980 a company of Royal Marines in partnership with French troops took part in Operation 'Titan' on the New Hebrides: undertaking patrols on the islands to ensure a peaceful transition to independence. They were flown over by VC10 aircraft, as the islands were so remote from Royal Navy patrol areas that no British warship was present at independence, in contrast to the standard approach in either the Caribbean or the Indian Ocean.[78] In most instances these newly independent states moved into Australia's sphere of influence, a logical step given that it was the closest major state, with Royal Navy ship visits, which had been infrequent enough, quickly receding into memory.

Brunei, which consists of two coastal sections of land on the island of Borneo surrounded by the Malaysian state of Sarawak, was a British protectorate ruled by a Sultan as an absolute monarch. It gained its independence in 1984 but despite being much closer to Singapore than many of the Pacific colonies it received relatively few visits by Royal Navy ships during the 1970s, most notably by the frigate HMS *Hermione* in September 1973.[79] From 1971 units of the British Army's Gurkha Brigade were deployed to the protectorate and provided the core of its defence capability, becoming unusual as a dependent territory with a garrison, thus lessening the importance of a periodic naval presence.

The Caribbean

Prior to 1976 there had been two frigates on the West Indies station, under the command of the Senior Naval Officer West Indies, whose headquarters was at HMS *Malabar* in Bermuda (which was ironically many hundreds of miles from the West Indies themselves). Its commitments included the defence both dependent territories and Associated States (self-governing territories, most of which were moving towards full independence), assistance with any evacuations of British subjects, demonstrating the United Kingdom's ability to maintain security in the region, exercising with local military forces and finally disaster relief and other 'military aid to the civil power' duties.[80] Both of the frigates had a Royal Marine party embarked, often to provide training for local forces or to act in support of local police in the event of riots or other disorders. Bermuda itself was situated in the western Atlantic, 800 nautical miles from the east coast of the United States. The colony of the Bahamas consisted of hundreds of islands that spread from the seas east of Florida, running parallel to the island of Cuba, and ending to the north of Haiti. At the end of the Bahamas archipelago were the Turks and Caicos Islands, a separate and much smaller colony. Arcing south-west from the tip of Puerto Rico were the Leeward Islands, the British colonies amongst these being the British Virgin Islands, St Kitts-Nevis-Anguilla, Antigua and Barbuda, Montserrat and Dominica. Then crossing south until reaching the coast of Venezuela were the Windward Islands, whose British colonies were St Lucia, Barbados, St Vincent, Grenada, and Trinidad and Tobago. In the Caribbean sea and to the south of Cuba was Jamaica, with the much smaller Cayman Islands to the west. On the Caribbean coast of Central America, between Mexico and Guatemala, was the colony of British Honduras, whilst British Guiana lay on the continent of South America, east of Venezuela and south-east of Trinidad and Tobago. The Colonial Office had attempted to push most of the island colonies into a single Federation of the West Indies in 1958 as a prelude to full independence, but the larger and wealthier colonies of Jamaica and Trinidad and Tobago perceived themselves to be subsidising the other smaller colonies, and by 1962 they had left and become independent in their own right within the British Commonwealth.[81] Barbados and British Guiana both became independent in 1966, and the presumption was that those colonies with a viable economy would become independent over the next 10 to 20 years.[82]

Most had internal self-government, with the British government providing a Governor and dealing with foreign and defence affairs, and the British military only supporting law and order if governors and governments requested such support.

The two Royal Navy frigates were the most visible manifestation of the British presence in the region, there being no Army garrisons and a minimal RAF presence beyond the special case of Belize (which is discussed below). Most of the remaining colonies were small and had limited resources of their own. For example, many lacked their own airports, airstrips or helicopters to provide access to remote areas or small islands, and often made use of the frigates' helicopters to evacuate casualties to hospitals, help with infrastructural improvements or provide other 'military aid to the civil power' support. For example, after fears in December 1971 of an impending volcanic eruption on Mount Soufriere on St Vincent, HMS *Berwick* sent over 23 tons of provisions to the island, whilst HMS *Phoebe* stood by to evacuate the population. The situation was particularly sensitive as St Vincent's elected government did not want to be seen to be dependent on British support.[83] In the event, no eruption took place but two years later the helicopters of the assault ship HMS *Intrepid*, on a training cruise, lifted 11 tons of materials up to the top of the volcano in order to build a seismological observatory.[84] Two years after that, her sister-ship HMS *Fearless* lifted technical equipment up to the new observatory in order to improve its capabilities.[85]

One major commitment for the West Indies Squadron was the Bahamas patrol, which began in 1963 and continued until independence a decade later. Following the overthrow of the Batista regime in Cuba by Fidel Castro, Cuban exiles began to use the many small southern-most islands of the Bahamas, to hide and traffic weapons or even kidnap Cuban fishermen. The initial purpose of the patrol was to catch and remove such dissidents, usually landing Royal Marine detachments to sweep islands.[86] For example, in January 1971 HMS *Sirius* landed marines from 41 Commando on Williams Island in Exercise Fettle to search for Cuban exiles, whilst the previous year the survey ship HMS *Fox* had searched for a suspected arms cache on the Anguilla Cays 70 miles north of the Cuban coast.[87] Given the increasing presence of Soviet naval vessels in the water around Cuba, the patrol no doubt enabled the tracking of such vessels through the Caribbean.[88] The Bahamas was also the site of the Atlantic Undersea Test and Evaluation Centre ('AUTEC') operated by the United States Navy but with the Royal Navy given equal access to the facilities, although after independence the British had to pay a fee for access.[89] The nearby Andros trench provided a controlled deep sea testing facility that was regularly used to test anti-submarine weapons, sonars and submarines. The ships of the Bahamas patrol were sometimes involved in supporting

AUTEC trials. More prosaically, the Bahamas patrol also became involved in supporting the Bahamas police in destroying or removing illegal lobster pots across the islands.[90] Following independence in July 1973, which was attended by the frigate HMS *Minerva* (amongst whose crew was the Prince of Wales who was therefore in a position to lead the ceremonial side of the handover) the patrol commitment ended.[91]

As the colonies gained internal self-governance and full franchise elections became a regular occurrence, so the risks of disturbances or riots grew, or at least the *fears* of governors and governments that riots could occur grew. St Vincent was particularly turbulent during the late 1960s, with frigates 'standing by' just over the horizon line a number of times when disturbances were feared. In one instance HMS *Rhyl*'s marine party paraded through the capital's streets as a means of forestalling possible riots.[92] Even if not called upon to land marines, their proximity gave governors and governments increased confidence that situations would not run out of control. On Antigua, HMS *Bacchante* was moored in sight of the capital, St Johns, during elections on the island in February 1971.[93] A year later, HMS *Gurkha* stood by beyond the horizon as the political situation remained fragile.[94] During the celebrations for St Lucian independence in February 1979, HMS *Scylla* was present as part of the ceremonials, but also had her Wasp helicopter at 30 minutes' notice to fly in case the British Foreign Office Minister, Ted Rowlands, and other dignitaries came into danger and had to be extracted at short-notice.[95]

The island of Anguilla, which was administered from St Kitts and Nevis (which was due to become self-governing as a prelude to independence), broke out into disturbances in March 1969 as a result of fears of domination by the larger islands. This resulted in Operation 'Sheepskin', involving HM Ships *Minerva*, *Rhyl* and *Rothesay* landing their Marine detachments, augmented by soldiers flown out from the United Kingdom, to help restore order and then to find a resolution that would command the support of the majority of Anguillans.[96] Fear of further tensions resulted in HMS *Minerva* being placed at 24 hours sailing distance from the island when a formal review of the island's future was published in May 1975.[97] Anguilla's future was finally resolved when it became a dependent territory of the United Kingdom in 1980.[98]

The 1974–5 Defence Review dissolved the post of Senior Naval Officer West Indies. Instead of two permanently stationed frigates in Bermuda reporting to an independent senior naval officer, in a miniature version of the dissolved Fleets and Stations that used to cover much of the globe up to the mid-1960s, only one frigate would now normally be present in the Caribbean. Acting as a guardship, this vessel would be detached from the NATO Eastlant Area for a number of months at a time.[99] The naval signals relay station on the Bahamas, that had provided the main communications link between SNOWI and his miniature fleet, was also shut down.[100] HMS *Malabar* remained as a stores base with its commanding officer being the Senior Naval Officer, Bermuda, but the guardship would now usually only visit Bermuda at the start and the end of the deployment.[101] The loss of the second frigate did reduce some flexibility in the region, but since the independence of the Bahamas and the abolition of the Bahamas patrol, it could be argued that the need for a second ship was no longer so pressing. The economic impact on Bermuda of the scaling down of the British presence was limited, as United States military bases remained on the island, whilst tourism and offshore financial services were beginning to provide substantial revenues for the territory.

Belize
The colony of British Honduras, on the mainland of Central America and bounded by Mexico to the north and Guatemala to the west and south, had long been claimed by the latter country. However, the population of British Honduras did not wish to be integrated into Guatemala, and the British government began to prepare the colony for independence. It attained internal self-government in 1964 and the colony was renamed Belize in 1973 in expectation of its independence. The Guatemalan government, which was a US-backed military-led regime, had been fighting a bloody insurgency in its rural areas since 1966.[102] It also continued its claims to the territory and combined occasional threats of attack or invasion with, usually fruitless, appeals to the United Nations. The Guatemalan threat was taken seriously and throughout the 1970s remained Britain's greatest colonial concern in the Caribbean. The British placed a small garrison in Belize and the concept of operations for the defence of the colony involved that small force defending the main airport long enough to enable air reinforcements – of brigade size – to arrive from across the Atlantic under Operation 'Optic'.[103] The two ships under Senior Naval Officer West Indies were regarded as an important reinforcement during periods of high tension, and additional naval forces would be used under Operation Optic to support the airlifted land forces.

In January 1972, when it became clear to the Guatemalan government that British Honduras was moving towards independence, the British government received a number of warnings from the British ambassadors to nearby Nicaragua and Costa Rica that the Guatemalans were planning to attack British Honduras after statements by both the Governor and Prime Minister of the colony that independence was only a matter of time.[104] This was combined with an intemperate discussion between the British consul in Guatemala and the Guatemalan President, Colonel Carlos Arana Osorio, the latter stating that he would 'not accept lying down, the independence of Belize if this came about without Guatemalan concurrence, no matter what the sacrifice'.[105]

What appeared to be a Guatemalan troop build-up, or alternatively a 'counter-insurgency exercise', began to be seen near the border and this proved to be sufficient evidence to begin to reinforce British Honduras. Rather than begin Operation 'Optic' itself, it was decided to describe the reinforcement as merely a rehearsal for it, under the title Exercise Cadnam. In addition to airlifting two companies into British Honduras, the frigate HMS *Phoebe* was despatched, as was the aircraft carrier HMS *Ark Royal* which was fortuitously already in the mid-Atlantic. The aim was to get close enough to the colony to launch four Buccaneer strike aircraft to undertake an overflight of Belize City, the largest settlement, as a show of resolve.[106] This was accompanied by public and private diplomatic moves to make clear to the Colonel that Britain would defend British Honduras.[107] The combined military and diplomatic messaging served its purpose, and a second stage of reinforcement – the despatch of RAF Harriers and Tigercat air defence missiles – was not needed.[108] As the crisis subsided, moves began to restart talks with the Guatemalan government and lower tensions further.

By 1975 negotiations with the Guatemalan government, who had now shifted towards arguing for cession of a remote southern province, Toledo, had stalled. Within the United Nations General Assembly a resolution was being discussed that would argue in favour of Belizean independence as soon as possible.[109] The Guatemalans, supported by most of Latin America, were lobbying for the resolution's rejection and by autumn 1975 evidence was mounting that military action might be possible. Intelligence reports had stated that 450 troops had been moved close to the border with that province, and a US diplomat in Guatemala had warned the British Governor.[110] The Guatemalan government was also in the international arms market for rapid purchases of small arms and ten aircraft suitable for parachute operations.[111] The Guatemalan President also made it clear to US diplomats that his country would not tolerate the humiliation of an adverse vote at the United Nations. Finally, on 10 October, the whole Guatemalan Army's armoured personnel carrier force (admittedly just ten vehicles) was sent from the capital to the border with Toledo province.[112]

The high risk of a Guatemalan attack resulted in a range of actions from the British government. The two frigates on station in the Caribbean, *Nubian* and *Minerva*, were positioned within two days' steaming from Belize, although they were shifted somewhat further away in the days leading up to the UN vote, so as not to provoke the Guatemalans.[113] Meanwhile, additional troops, three helicopters and enhanced mobile air defence equipment were placed on short-notice standby in the United Kingdom, and then flown out via Canada and the Bahamas under the auspices of Exercise Snow Scene in the days before the UN vote.[114] In the event, the General Assembly vote was overwhelmingly in favour of Belizean independence but the Guatemalans did not act.[115] It is difficult to know whether the naval and flown reinforcements truly had a deterrent effect, but a major earthquake in February 1976 focussed Guatemalan attention back to domestic issues and their military forces were withdrawn from the border. This would be the last naval operation co-ordinated by the Senior Naval Officer West Indies. At the end of March 1976 he and his staff were withdrawn from the HMS *Malabar* naval base in Bermuda and from this point onwards, the Royal Navy's presence in the region would consist of only one guardship.[116]

A further Belize invasion scare occurred in July 1977, as once again negotiations had stalled and the Guatemalan government returned to bellicose language, short-notice arms purchases and the stationing of additional troops along the border.[117] The Guatemalan Army could now deploy a battalion of parachute troops and a force of marine commandos along the coast: it was feared that a surprise parachute assault might outmanoeuvre the small garrison and seize the capital and airport before reinforcements could arrive. July 7th, just after the latest round of talks finished, was perceived to be the date of maximum danger.[118] Deploying the helicopter carrier *Hermes* and her escorts closer towards the Caribbean (she was currently in the Eastern Atlantic) was considered but rejected as potentially too provocative whilst the garrison was unreinforced, so the Guardship, HMS *Achilles*, was sent to Belize and would undertake a port visit on the 7th.[119] The stores ship RFA *Regent* was also deployed there, bringing additional ammunition and supplies for the garrison. As occurred two years' previously, additional troops and air defence equipment were flown in, this time supplemented by six RAF Harriers.[120] The Guatemalans, who had reportedly armed and readied some of their military aircraft for action and had cancelled all military leave, did not act in the face of this new reinforcement, and over the next few months scaled de-escalation by both sides gradually reduced tensions once more.[121]

* * *

The Defence Review had ended or reduced many of the Royal Navy's commitments beyond the Eastern Atlantic, which were now increasingly termed 'out of area' as if to emphasise their peripheral nature. Many of these commitments were gradually diminishing in any case and only demanded a relatively small force, such as the patrol vessels in Hong Kong and the, now, single guardship in the Caribbean, but the giving up of the Mediterranean commitment just as it was *increasing* in strategic importance both to NATO and to the United Kingdom was a short-sighted decision that confirmed an increasing shift towards a tight, almost tunnel vision-like, defence focus on

NATO's Central European front. Other long-running problems, such as Belize, did not seem to have an end in sight, with each crisis resulting in an increase in capabilities required to deter the Guatemalans. Although the British withdrawal between 1975 and 1979 diminished the British military's worldwide presence, some commitments continued into the 1980s: the Caribbean including Belize, the Falkland Islands in the South Atlantic and a number of hydrographic surveys. Royal Navy vessels also continued to undertake periodic deployments to the Mediterranean, but without the permanent presence that had existed up to 1979.

Part II: Crisis, 1975–1982

10

The Eastlant Navy

The Defence Review had significantly reduced the Royal Navy's core operational area: for the first time in 300 years, British sea power would primarily operate in the waters near the United Kingdom, stretching out into the Eastern Atlantic, with single guardships only as far as Gibraltar and the West Indies. This, by necessity, focussed the Royal Navy on countering Soviet naval capabilities: as has been seen, this shift had been occurring since 1967, but now the transition was almost complete. The Royal Navy's adversary would be a large, seemingly powerful and technologically sophisticated naval force, mainly focussed on its submarine arm. Not only was the Navy operating almost solely in a high-threat environment, but it would find that its role and purpose would come under greater scrutiny and challenge than at any time since the seventeenth century. If at sea the Navy appeared vulnerable to the Soviet Northern Fleet, in the corridors of Whitehall it was similarly vulnerable as policy-makers increasingly focussed on the Central European front in Germany and air-based solutions in the Eastern Atlantic that were ostensibly cheaper. Without realising until almost too late, the Royal Navy – or at least its ocean-going surface fleet – would find itself in its most precarious position since the start of the Cold War.

A New Concept of Operations
In the closing stages of the Defence Review, once many of the major decisions had been taken, the Naval Staff's Fleet Requirements Committee set out a new 'Concept of Operations' for the period 1985 to 1999 as a means to provide a policy framework for establishing the 'size and shape' of the Fleet in the post-Defence Review world. Once the 'size and shape' had been established, then planning could begin to procure the next generation of warships, train the manpower to operate them and establish the maintenance, stores and

equipment requirements to support them.[1] This was the first such exercise to be undertaken since 1968, and over the previous seven years there had been considerable changes in the threat picture: the Soviet Navy had demonstrated its ocean-going capabilities, whilst new classes of impressive nuclear submarines and surface ships had entered service and were increasingly to be found sailing in the Mediterranean, Indian Ocean and Eastern Atlantic. Setbacks for the United States in Vietnam and the first oil crisis of 1973 had seemed to put the Western Powers on the defensive, whilst the Soviet Union had not only basked in the defeat of its superpower adversary in a Communist counter-insurgency in South East Asia, but was also lending military aid to friendly states in Africa and the Middle East.[2]

The Concept of Operations paper had a more limited geographical focus: providing a strategic overview of the deterrence of Soviet armed forces within the Eastern Atlantic region only. It was estimated that the Soviet Navy would operate 180 nuclear-powered submarines by 1985, 80 of which would be able to fire cruise missiles and another 55 ballistic missiles. It would also field over 1,000 land-based maritime aircraft and 100 major surface units. This powerful force might conceivably be used to undertake an aggressive anti-shipping campaign in the Atlantic, but it was considered more likely that naval forces could be used in a time of tension to intimidate and blockade Western European states: 'they will have the potential to weaken NATO, economically and politically, by maritime pressure or action at any level of their own choosing. They may seek to undermine NATO's confidence and will to resist by threatening, in a time of tension, to cut off Europe from America by sea.'[3] The Soviets did have the disadvantage of difficult access into the open ocean, with the Northern Fleet having to pass through the 'chokepoint' of the Greenland-Iceland-United Kingdom Gap ('GIUK Gap') and the Baltic Fleet in a similar position with the Danish Skagerrak. This would provide one of the main means by which Soviet intimidation or military action could be prevented or mitigated.[4]

In times of tension, sea control of the North Atlantic was necessary for a range of reasons: to allow for the passage to patrol areas of the ballistic missile carrying strategic deterrent submarines, to enable the reinforcement of NATO forces in Europe from the United States and to deploy the NATO strike fleet as a deterrent force supported by European naval forces. Aside from the strike fleet, European NATO forces, led by the Royal Navy, would provide most of the naval forces in the Eastern Atlantic, English Channel and North Sea, whose main aim would be to 'contain the Soviet submarine threat and blunt Soviet aggression.'[5] Meanwhile, US naval forces would focus on the Western Atlantic, Southern Atlantic and possibly even the western Indian Ocean if Soviet vessels were operating there. The case was made for retaining the Royal

Navy's anomalous four-star NATO Channel command ('CINCCHAN' a post which was held by Commander-in-Chief Fleet by this time), which bypassed both US five-star commanders and thus gave the British a direct military voice reporting to the Atlantic Council, noting that British maritime forces must be sufficient to justify retaining this role.[6]

The difficulty of the Eastern Atlantic operational environment by the mid-1980s was acknowledged. If a shooting war began, the Concept of Operations argued that it would be difficult for any NATO forces to survive in the Norwegian Sea, or for that matter anywhere north-east of the GIUK Gap. Norway would remain a weak point on NATO's northern flank. Its refusal to allow the stationing of NATO troops or nuclear weapons meant that it could be easily overwhelmed by Soviet forces, but at the same time the vulnerability of naval forces in the Norwegian Sea meant that reinforcement with amphibious forces would be difficult, and only really possible during times of tension before conflict had begun.[7] This analysis very much reflected the tenor of the times, and was perhaps too pessimistic: if the environment was difficult for NATO forces it would have been difficult for the Soviets as well: Norwegian terrain could have made any land advance slow and painful, and classic Soviet amphibious flanking assaults would have been hard to pull off along a rugged and hostile coastline with NATO submarines operating. However, the Norwegian Sea would still have been an extremely challenging environment for the Royal Navy to operate in, and significant losses might have to be accepted if the decision were made to commit forces to it.

Having undertaken an analysis of the types of operations that would needed at different levels of tension – ranging from surveillance and intelligence gathering and 'presence forces' in the UK's Exclusive Economic Zone, through to the forces necessary for both low and high intensity naval operations, including war – the paper then assigned levels of importance to different tasks that would be required in order to undertake these operations.[8] The three most important tasks were anti-submarine warfare, the defence against guided missiles and the protection of the strategic deterrent. Three secondary tasks were also set out: naval presence, the reinforcement of the northern flank and the protection of maritime routes in the Channel command. These six core tasks were focussed on the 'higher level' end of the operational spectrum, but it was acknowledged that other tasks at the lower levels were also necessary.[9]

The Concept of Operations was in many ways an unsurprising document that re-affirmed the existing direction of travel for the Royal Navy. There was no radical departure from earlier approaches, beyond the final removal of most of the tasks associated with operations beyond the Eastern Atlantic and home waters. It set out roles for the Royal Navy that emphasised the importance of Royal Navy-assigned commands in NATO, of the NATO strike fleet, of the primacy of the Royal Navy in the Eastern Atlantic region and the need to undertake tasks that reached at the 'higher levels', and would therefore require a fleet mix consisting of at least some sophisticated vessels able to undertake complex anti-submarine warfare and air defence tasks and also to protect the strategic nuclear deterrent. The next document, the 'Size and Shape' paper, was much more radical: following through from the strategic-operational framework of the 'Concept of Operations' it set out the fleet mix required for the mid-1980s to the end of the 1990s.

It was this document that clarified what a dangerous place the Eastern Atlantic would be for the surface ships of the Royal Navy, at least until US Navy forces arrived. The coming into service of the long-range 'Backfire' bomber had changed the military calculus dramatically during 1974–5, even creating problems in the second stage of Strategic Arms Limitation Talks (SALT II), as United States lobbied hard to have the new bomber classified as a strategic weapon.[10] In fact, the 'Backfire', after a protracted development process, was a tactical system, but it was an impressive one at that. Its operational reliability problems were not necessarily known by NATO at this stage, and some aspects of its capability were being overestimated by US Department of Defence analysts.[11] Despite this, it was a much more formidable aircraft than the preceding 'Badger': faster, theoretically capable of launching three long-range cruise missiles and with a somewhat larger radius of operations.[12] Regimental attacks by 'Backfires', launching between twenty and sixty cruise missiles at a time, threatened to overwhelm the air defences of the two planned British naval task forces, which would no longer benefit from a strike carrier's fighter cover. Operational analysis studies, as part of the Sea-Air Warfare Committee's studies concluded that a total of thirty-seven (modernised) Sea Dart air defence missile systems would be needed in order to provide sufficient air defence coverage to ensure that three-quarters of the ships in the two task forces would survive one such attack, and that around half would still be operational after a second attack. These missile systems would be needed in addition to forty-five ship-based VSTOL Harriers *and* forty land-based air defence aircraft. Given that one regimental attack was expected each day of hostilities, this meant that a huge investment in air defence systems would be needed just to ensure that task forces could remain effective for no more than two days of high intensity conflict.[13]

The situation with anti-submarine warfare was particularly stark, but in other ways. The anti-submarine role was split into three main tasks: (1) direct support – provided by the two task forces and primarily as escorts for reinforcement convoys from North America, (2) attrition of Soviet submarines as they patrolled or passed into the open ocean (this included 'barrier operations' along the GIUK gap), and (3) coastal anti-submarine warfare and protection of the nuclear deterrent submarines as they left or returned to their home bases. In the direct support role, the best means of detection was deemed to be the SOSUS seabed underwater detection system supplemented by towed-array sonars, a new form of passive sonar system towed behind a warship and capable of extremely long-range detection. Ship-borne hull sonars were considered to be of much less significance but had a minor role in self-defence when the submarine was attacking with torpedoes rather than submarine-launched missiles. As has been seen, the best means of prosecuting attacks was with large anti-submarine helicopters or the land-based long-range maritime patrol aircraft operated by the Royal Air Force. Nuclear submarines were considered to be moderately effective, but unlike aircraft were vulnerable to counter-attack by Soviet submarines. Communication and coordination with surface units was also difficult, and 'blue-on-blue' losses would be a risk.[14]

Anti-submarine ships in the task forces would need to be fitted with towed-arrays as well as self-defence or reactive anti-submarine capabilities such as short-range anti-submarine torpedoes, large anti-submarine helicopters and bow sonars. In the attrition role, surface ships were almost entirely absent save small and lightly armed towed-array frigates whose role was to pass their detection information onto maritime patrol aircraft for prosecuting attacks. Beyond the GIUK gap, the environment was considered too dangerous for these vessels to operate, so only nuclear submarines fitted with towed-arrays would be deployed. In the coastal and deterrent support role, both conventional and nuclear submarines would be needed along with land-based maritime patrol aircraft and large helicopters.[15]

In the anti-ship role, where the marking and counter-marking of Soviet surface ships was expected as tension mounted towards war, 36-knot escorts were recommended as 'fast marking ships', nuclear submarines would be needed to mark Soviet submarines, whilst VSTOL Harriers armed with anti-ship missiles would prosecute attacks supplemented by land-based anti-ship strike aircraft.[16]

Most of the surface fleet would be employed in the two task groups, each of which would be headed by an *Invincible* class cruiser. The task groups would consist of armed air defence destroyers and almost as large and well-armed towed-array frigates. Royal Fleet Auxiliaries would assume an additional role as supplementary platforms for large anti-submarine helicopters to free up the cruisers to operate Harriers in air defence or probe operations.[17] This concentration of the surface fleet in the convoy escort role, with a secondary anti-ship capability, would eventually turn into a serious risk for the Navy, for if the Soviet navy did not attack the convoys in the open ocean, how many of these larger surface ships would be needed? This problem did not crystallise for another five years, but what was immediately clear was that a large and expensive fleet would be necessary to survive a brutally dangerous threat environment for only a few days if general war broke out, even if the

Soviets restricted themselves to conventional weaponry. In a nuclear conflict the situation would be even worse.

A Larger or Smaller Surface Fleet?

From this assessment, which was backed by comprehensive operational analysis commissioned by the Naval Staff, came a force requirement for the following equipment: three *Invincible* class cruisers, twenty-nine towed-array frigates (surprisingly, despite the paper's scepticism about the utility of large anti-submarine ships, seventeen of these would be better-armed Task Force frigates, and twelve would be smaller attrition frigates with towed-array and a point defence missile system only), thirty-four improved Sea Dart systems (either thirty-four ships with single systems, or seventeen large 'double-ended' vessels), eleven fast 'marking' ships, ten helicopter support RFAs, twenty-four nuclear-powered attack submarines and six conventional submarines. The aircraft required would be forty-five improved Harriers, forty land-based air defence aircraft, nineteen land-based anti-ship aircraft (some of which might be long-range bombers – a British 'Backfire') forty-five land-based maritime patrol aircraft, all supported by sixteen tankers, fifty-nine large anti-submarine helicopters and a small number of light helicopters. These would be supplemented by fifty-six mine-countermeasures vessels (including ten hovercraft mine warfare vessels), two seabed operations vessels to inspect and disable Soviet static seabed arrays, and ten minelayers taken up from trade.[18]

This was a hugely expensive Navy, and way beyond anything that could be expected from the defence budget in the 1980s and 1990s; but this force, modified somewhat to include the survival of some form of amphibious capability, additional light helicopters with anti-ship missiles and offshore patrol vessels, was termed the 'baseline force' to act as a comparison with existing plans. These plans were themselves optimistic. In 1990 it was expected that British maritime forces would consist of four nuclear deterrent submarines, sixteen nuclear-powered attack submarines, five conventional submarines, three cruisers, two assault ships (both of which would be about to leave service), twenty-five air defence destroyers (one Type 82 and twenty-four Type 42s, the last ten of these being of a modified batch), eight Type 21s, seven Type 22s and twenty-four ageing *Leander* class frigates, twenty mine countermeasures vessels, twenty patrol vessels, one diving vessel, thirteen survey ships, sixteen RFAs, fifteen Sea Harriers, forty-one Sea King large helicopters, fifty-four Lynx light helicopters, thirty-six anti-ship Tornado aircraft, thirty air defence maritime Tornados, twenty-seven Nimrod maritime patrol aircraft, eight AWACs aircraft and twenty-four tankers.[19]

Even if the 'baseline' numbers for ships, submarines and aircraft were a long distance from what was planned, let alone practical, the Size and Shape of the

Fleet paper had set out some important changes in the equipment balance. Passive sonars (SOSUS and towed-array) would be much more important than hull-mounted active sonars, and the cruisers would mainly become Harrier ships with large anti-submarine helicopters largely operating off RFAs. The role of land-based air defence aircraft would diminish somewhat, but the balance in resources would shift towards nuclear submarines and long-range maritime patrol aircraft and away from anti-submarine frigates, whose main role would now be as towed-array platforms. Mine warfare would increase in importance, including offensive minelaying by submarines near Soviet northern fleet bases and defensive minelaying undertaken in coastal waters by car ferries taken up from trade. The starkest conclusion was the high proportion of surface-ship assets that would be required for air defence. Existing plans had already been shifted somewhat in favour of additional Type 42 destroyers whilst curtailing the Type 22 programme, but the baseline numbers were in a different league altogether.[20]

Attempting to marry this proposed baseline to the resources available given the recent Defence Review, inevitably created the greatest problems for the Fleet Requirements Committee. A table appended to the paper provided the projected costs (in September 1973 prices) of each of the capabilities, based on the annual running cost of a particular warship, plus one-eighth of its procurement cost. This latter figure was an attempt to take account of procurement costs within annual running costs, and therefore provide a rudimentary annual 'full economic cost' for a capability. Therefore, a nuclear submarine, which in 1973 cost £66 million to procure and £7 million a year to run, was deemed to cost for a year's operation, for the purposes of the exercise, £8.25 million + £7 million = £15 million. Some results were eye-watering: if twenty-four nuclear submarines were needed instead of sixteen, then the additional eight boats would cost £120 million a year under this formula. By far the most worrying cost was that of air defence. Only six Type 42 destroyers had been ordered as of 1975, with the first having just been commissioned. They cost £32 million to build and £6 million a year to operate, providing an annual notional cost of £10 million. Operating thirty-four such ships would cost £340 million a year. If larger destroyers were procured, each with two Sea Dart systems, this would mean fewer hulls, but they were likely to be formidably expensive vessels, approaching that of a nuclear submarine, suggesting a cost somewhere around £280–£320 million a year for a dozen Type 42s and eleven larger 'double-ended' ships. The cost of forty-five additional shipborne Harriers and organic airborne early warning, essential to reducing the number of aircraft so that the air defence ships had fewer missiles to engage, was placed at £112 million a year, whilst the three command cruisers would cost £47 million a year each. This meant that £253 million would need to be added to the cost of air defence ships, producing a total annual cost of over half a billion pounds, only to enable two task groups to survive for a handful of days.[21] This is placed in context when it is realised that the total Navy Department budget for 1973 was £740 million.[22] Procuring the numbers of vessels recommended by the paper was well beyond the resources that could reasonably be envisaged for the Navy, and this task became even more difficult during 1976 and 1977 as the United Kingdom's economic crisis forced further curtailments of government spending and incremental reductions in the defence budget.

Why did the Naval Staff allow itself to become tied to policy documents that, in the event, turned into a ticking time bomb for the future of the surface fleet? In many respects, the Navy was facing a problem similar to that of the Army on the Central European front: actually fielding a force that would credibly contain or defeat a Soviet attack would be prohibitively expensive for a democracy with a range of other domestic spending priorities, so making do with what could be afforded would have to be enough.[23] Making the wider 'enough to deter' case was both difficult, and in practice was never coherently made. The Army benefitted from a defensive backstop in the revised Brussels Treaty that tied the British to basing no fewer than 55,000 troops in Germany.[24] The Navy possessed no such protective agreement. However, the absence of any mention of 'out of area operations' beyond the Eastern Atlantic is not surprising, despite the likelihood that some residual commitments in the West Indies and Hong Kong would remain by the mid-1980s. In mid-1975 the issue was no longer a high priority: the Defence Review was complete and a coherent and comprehensive defence of the Navy's force mix would not be immediately needed. However, these two documents had, amongst other changes, defined the new direction of travel for British anti-submarine warfare: towards passive detection using SOSUS or towed-array sonar, and destruction by nuclear submarines, large anti-submarine helicopters or long-range maritime patrol aircraft.

Soon after the Navy's Concept of Operations and force structure paper had been written, the Chiefs of Staff asked for a strategic concept for maritime operations to be prepared in order to feed into future force structure discussions.[25] The Chiefs were clearly not entirely happy with the Concept of Operations, and given the RAF's growing role in maritime operations, a paper that incorporated their perspective was therefore proposed. Instead of being a purely Royal Navy document, this new strategic concept was prepared at the centre of the Ministry by the Assistant Chief of the Defence Staff (Policy) and therefore incorporated both Navy and RAF analysis and was put together by staff officers on the central rather than single-service staffs. The Strategic Concept took nearly 18 months to write and incorporated some of the higher-level elements of the RN's Concept of Operations paper. The six NATO maritime objectives were set out and these were extrapolated into peacetime, periods-of-tension and wartime tasks, the last of these being directly derived from the six NATO objectives and consisting of (1) the destruction of Soviet SSBNs, (2) the protection of NATO territory from attack from the sea, (3) the protection of the NATO striking fleet, (4) the protection of reinforcement and resupply, (5) the protection of NATO merchant ships and finally (6) amphibious operations. The Strategic Concept then acknowledged that two of the United Kingdom's capabilities in support of fulfilling these tasks were being given up, the UK's carrier strike and amphibious capabilities, and that the threats from Soviet nuclear submarines and its land-based naval air arm were increasing.[26]

NATO's maritime objectives would be best met by exercising sea control, and because of the limits in resources available, the best way to achieve sea control would be the attrition of Soviet naval forces either through 'attack at source' operations, barrier patrols at choke points or through the defence of task groups or reinforcement convoys.[27] When it came to higher level discussions of force mix, the report argued in favour of conventional submarines for shallow water anti-submarine warfare to supplement nuclear-powered submarines, and it also stated that 'future technological developments, particularly in Soviet missile and surveillance capabilities, are not likely to favour surface ships and the future trend points to an increased emphasis on submarines and aircraft for offensive operations'.[28] Land-based aircraft would be of increasing importance, and tanker aircraft would be essential if the most were to be made of land-based air assets.

The report was clearly the result of much painful argument, discussion and compromise within the Central Staffs and between the Navy and Air Force Departments, and as such it was a very different document from the RN's own single-service Concept of Operations. The focus of the force mix discussion was much more based upon warfighting requirements than on operations in peacetime and times of tension, and the RN's naval presence task had largely disappeared. As a result, the crucial importance of having the right type of forces for operations in a period of tension – which could have a crucial role in preventing any war from occurring – was partly lost.[29] Both documents acknowledged the high-threat from submarines and aircraft, but the new Strategic Concept made explicit what was hinted at in the earlier paper: that surface ships would have difficulty surviving in wartime in such a high-threat environment. The increased reliance on air power was acknowledged but the role of organic maritime air power – anti-submarine helicopters and Harriers – was generally minimised, and the problem of ensuring that land based airpower was in the right place at the right time to support surface ships was largely ignored.[30] Another blind spot was its assertion that there was no technological breakthrough on the horizon that could change current maritime strategy – entirely ignoring the extremely positive results coming from the trials of the first surface-ship towed-array sonar on HMS *Lowestoft*, which are discussed in more detail below and in Chapter 18, and which would have a profound impact on surface ship anti-submarine warfare from the mid-1980s onwards.[31] Where the Navy's Size and Shape paper had recommended a very large fleet well beyond any realistically available budget, the joint Strategic Concept paper had instead shifted towards a sub-surface and land-based air answer to maritime operations whilst acknowledging the importance of the surface fleet but stating that this importance would reduce over time.

The Strategic Concept would inform later Ministry analyses and was the first major central study that stated clearly the vulnerability of the surface fleet and that the answer was not necessarily a larger surface fleet: its influence would, in the coming years, be significant. Logically, as the new Strategic Concept had undermined the premises of the 1975 Concept of Operations, a new version of that latter document should have been written, but it is perhaps indicative of how the Strategic Concept was received by the Naval Staff that this was not immediately undertaken. As it was, the Royal Navy would enter the 1980s without a generally accepted concept of operations from which to justify the size and shape of the fleet. Although the need for such a document was recognised within the Naval Staff by May 1979, it took another eleven months for a very rough draft to appear.[32] The Naval Staff was clearly split over which direction the document should go. Captain R T Newman, a former submariner working in the Central Staffs in the Operational Requirements area, boldly stated that only a short war should be planned for, that the importance of the NATO strike fleet and of reinforcement convoys had reduced over the years, that the RN capability should focus on supporting the nuclear deterrent, protecting the amphibious force prior to general war breaking out and providing an anti-submarine capability across the Eastlant area. The most effective anti-submarine assets were nuclear submarines, maritime patrol aircraft and towed-array equipped ships. Most surface ships should be numerous but small towed-array vessels depending on their own soft and hard self-defence capabilities against air attack, and that it was rash to assume that surface ships could operate safely anywhere east of the GIUK gap. A much smaller number of more capable balanced surface forces would be needed to protect the amphibious force and for 'out of area' operations. The 'balanced fleet' was dead and should therefore be replaced by a largely Eastlant orientated force.[33]

Another submariner, Hugo White, who was Assistant Director of Naval Plans, came to a different view, arguing that the balanced fleet concept should be maintained because 'NATO may not last, we may not fight the war we are planning to avoid but another instead, and anyway the US might shift its strategy without warning'.³⁴ He did concede that the 'ship shop' (part of the Naval Staff that set and monitored Staff Requirements for new construction) was split over the future shape of the fleet, and the contributions that followed from other senior staff officers consisted of a wide range of opinions between the poles that Newman and White had set. Over the next five months the draft was comprehensively re-written and discussed but no final version had been fully approved by October 1980, the last version concluding with sections that appeared to support Newman's vision of a specialised fleet but also focussed on the need for a range of different capabilities (implied to be on a mix of different types of platforms) to avoid a serious impact from the unexpected obsolescence of one or other capability. This, in effect, led back to a version of White's call for a balanced fleet, so this draft document still contained considerable ambiguities that would have had some outside of the Naval Staff scratching their heads.³⁵ Eventually a truncated version entitled 'the roles of UK maritime forces' was produced for the Naval Staff's Fleet Requirements Committee. It did not include sections that could point to a future size and shape of the fleet and went no further than this internal Naval Staff committee, so as a result had no purchase within the wider Ministry of Defence.³⁶ As a result, the 1978 Strategic Concept was the only significant high-level document that addressed the question of the type of navy the United Kingdom needed as the Naval Staff began preparing for the new defence review at the start of 1981.

US–UK Concept of Maritime Operations and the Long War–Short War Controversy

In parallel with the Joint Staffs Strategic Concept, the Naval Staffs of the US Navy and the Royal Navy were developing a joint concept of naval operations, at the request of the US Naval Staff. The document only provided minimal help to the Naval Staff as a counter to the Strategic Concept: as a concept of operations it followed the US model and was therefore a higher-level document that only had a weak and abbreviated section that dealt with possible force structures; its focus was much more on co-ordinating command and control and with the possibility of expanding the document to become a NATO-wide concept at some point in the future.³⁷ When it was produced it was described merely as a 'staff level working paper' so that the Air Staff could not accuse the Naval Staff of producing an 'official' document on maritime operations without their involvement.³⁸ However, the document did set out the USN and Royal Navy's perception of Soviet maritime strategy, their own strategy, objectives and maritime tasks, and it was particularly valuable in setting out two possible scenarios based on either a short-warning war, or a slow ratcheting up of tensions as a result of a political crisis.

The Navy's Leadership 1: (a) Admiral of the Fleet Lord Louis Mountbatten, Chief of the Defence Staff 1959–65. *(Creative Commons 3.0/Allan Warren)*; (b) Admiral Sir David Luce, First Sea Lord 1963–6. *(Wellington City Council Archives)*; (c) Admiral Sir Varyl Begg, First Sea Lord 1966–8. *(Crown Copyright)*; (d) Admiral Sir Michael Le Fanu, First Sea Lord 1968–70. *(Crown Copyright)*

The Navy's Leadership 2: (e) Admiral Sir Peter Hill-Norton, First Sea Lord 1970–1. *(Crown Copyright)*; (f) Admiral Sir Michael Pollock, First Sea Lord 1971–4. *(Crown Copyright)*; (g) Admiral Sir Edward Ashmore, First Sea Lord 1974–7. *(Crown Copyright)*; (h) Admiral Sir Terence Lewin, First Sea Lord 1977–9. *(Crown Copyright)*

The Navy's Leadership 3: (i) Admiral Sir Henry Leach, First Sea Lord 1979–82. *(Crown Copyright)*; (j) Admiral Sir John Fieldhouse, First Sea Lord 1982–5. *(Crown Copyright)*; (k) Admiral Sir William Staveley, First Sea Lord 1985–9. *(Crown Copyright)*; (l) Admiral Sir Julian Oswald, First Sea Lord 1989–93. *(Crown Copyright)*

HMS *Resolution*, the Royal Navy's first nuclear-powered ballistic missile submarine. The missile launch hatches can just be discerned aft of the boat's sail. *(Crown Copyright)*

HMS *Warspite*, a first-generation nuclear-powered attack submarine, returning from what was then the longest patrol undertaken by a Royal Navy boat, which had included service in the Falklands campaign. *(Crown Copyright)*

Above: A personnel transfer onto a *Trafalgar* class nuclear-powered attack submarine by helicopter. The boat has clearly been on patrol for some time as some anechoic tiles, which reduce her sonar signature, have been lost from the upper hull. *(Crown Copyright)*

Right: The next generation: HMS *Vanguard*, the first of the new boats carrying the Trident ballistic missile, is rolled out from the construction hall at Barrow in 1992. *(Crown Copyright)*

The aircraft carrier HMS *Ark Royal* (foreground) relieves her sister, HMS *Eagle*, on the first Beira Patrol operations in 1966. *(Crown Copyright)*

A Mk 1 Sea King uses its dipping sonar to detect submarines. The carrier HMS *Ark Royal* is in the background. Dipping sonars provided an important means of detecting submarines away from the hull noise of a ship. By the end of the 1970s, Sea King helicopters were also carrying sonobuoys, another, more flexible, form of detection. *(Crown Copyright)*

HMS *Hermes* operating as a commando carrier in the 1970s with vehicles, stores and helicopters on her flight deck. *(Crown Copyright)*

Two landing craft depart HMS *Fearless* to take part in Operation 'Motorman', the clearing of areas of Londonderry under Provisional IRA control in 1972. Under the striped awnings are hidden British Army AVRE 'bulldozers' for breaking through barricades on the streets of Londonderry. *(Crown Copyright)*

A Royal Marine artillery unit disembarks in Norway as part of a NATO exercise in the late 1970s. *(Crown Copyright)*

Two Royal Marines take part in an exercise defending North Sea oil rigs. The defence of these installations became a new role for the Marines in the late 1970s. By 1980 the Comacchio Company was formed to undertake these types of roles in addition to protecting naval units and establishments. *(Crown Copyright)*

A newly-completed HMS *Invincible* alongside at Portsmouth during the 1980 'Navy Days', when the base and ships alongside would be opened to members of the public. *(Creative Commons 2.0/Hugh Llewelyn)*

A Phantom F4K undertakes test landings on HMS *Eagle* in 1969. The Phantom would never fly operationally from this carrier as she was withdrawn from service in 1972 without being modernised to take this aircraft. *(Crown Copyright)*

The first operational Sea Harrier in flight. Although this aircraft was subsonic and at this time lacked many of the capabilities of larger traditional carrier aircraft, she did mark the Navy's return to organic fixed-wing flying and proved essential to British success in the Falklands conflict of 1982. *(Crown Copyright)*

The Sea Harrier FA2 entered service in 1990. She was a considerable improvement over the first variant, the FRS1. The more bulbous nose houses the capable Blue Vixen radar and this photograph shows to good effect the four long-range AMRAAM air-to-air missiles. *(Crown Copyright)*

A Wessex medium helicopter hovers over the stern of the frigate HMS *Rothesay*, presumably preparing to undertake personnel or equipment transfer, whilst the ship's own Wasp light helicopter also hovers to starboard. The Wessex and Wasp were the mainstay of the Navy's shipborne helicopter fleet during the 1970s. *(Crown Copyright)*

The *Leander* class frigate HMS *Danae*, newly commissioned in 1967. Twenty-six ships of this class were built for the Royal Navy, but by the end of their production run they were obsolescent in their unmodernised form and were unable to effectively counter either nuclear-powered submarines or supersonic aircraft. *(Crown Copyright)*

The 'County' class destroyer HMS *Norfolk* was the first ship in the fleet to be fitted with Exocet anti-ship missiles. She is seen here firing a missile in 1974. Although the Exocet lacked the range of Soviet anti-ship missiles it would have allowed for the effective 'holding at risk' of Soviet warships during periods of high tension. *(Crown Copyright)*

This photograph of the *Leander* class frigate HMS *Naiad* clearly shows the Ikara missile launcher forward of the bridge structure and protected from the elements by an open circular deckhouse. *(Crown Copyright)*

HMS *Amazon*, the first Type 21 frigate, is shown newly completed. The Type 21s were a commercially-designed class which aimed to fill the gap between the older *Leander* class and the more sophisticated Type 22 frigate. *(Crown Copyright)*

The Icelandic gunboat *Tyr* approaches the frigate HMS *Bacchante* during the third Cod War. A number of Royal Navy frigates were damaged in encounters with such vessels whilst protecting British fishing vessels around Iceland. *(Crown Copyright)*

HMS *Broadsword*, the first Type 22 frigate, was almost the size of a pre-war light cruiser. Although her design was set too early to incorporate either the towed array or medium dipping-sonar helicopter, later Batches were enlarged and modified to incorporate these and other capabilities. *(Crown Copyright)*

HMS *Liverpool*, of the second batch of Type 42 destroyers, steams alongside a US *Iowa* class battleship during the NATO Exercise Northern Wedding 86. She shows some post-Falklands conflict modifications including additional light weaponry on new deck sponsons, although the Phalanx close-in weapon system has not yet been installed. *(Public Domain/US Department of Defense)*

HMS *Phoebe* was one of five *Leander* class frigates fitted with the new, highly effective, towed-array sonar during the early 1980s. The array's 'drum' can be seen aft at the stern of the frigate as she enters Hampton Roads in the United States in 1990. *(Public Domain/PH2 Tracy Lee Didas, US Navy)*

The Type 23 frigate was the outcome of a search for a cheaper frigate that was also equipped with the towed-array sonar. The second in the class, HMS *Argyll*, is shown at sea soon after completion. *(Crown Copyright)*

HM Ships *Exeter* and *Jupiter* accompany the US carrier *Kitty Hawk* in the Western Indian Ocean in September 1985. The two Royal Navy ships were deployed on the Armilla Patrol at this time. *(Public Domain/PH2 Frank Davison, US Navy)*

This 1980 illustration of one of the earliest design concepts for the Type 44 destroyer shows its early derivation from the 'stretched' Type 22 hull. Unsurprisingly, further design work resulted in a much larger ship to accommodate the Sea Dart, Sea Wolf and Ikara missiles systems. The Type 44, which would have been a particularly expensive ship for the capability it provided, was cancelled in 1981. *(Crown Copyright)*

The prime role of the Soviet Navy was to defend the USSR and other Warsaw Pact members from nuclear strikes from NATO SSBNs whilst providing a maritime nuclear strike capability to attack NATO. The second role was to prevent any NATO conventional attacks from the sea and support Soviet ground forces when required.[39] The risk to NATO sea lines of communication ('SLOCs') was less clear: earlier drafts suggested that a campaign against NATO SLOCs throughout the open oceans was likely, but the naval side of Defence Intelligence vehemently disagreed, arguing that if they were to attack convoys it would be in the Eastlant and Channel areas closer to bases and where the chances of success would be higher.[40] The paper also showed that NATO was confident that the Soviet Navy was unable to detect NATO SSBNs and would not be able to do so for another decade.[41] NATO's strategy was based first on deterrence and then on fighting to defend or restore Alliance territory, with forces that were available to deploy promptly and flexibly. This had an impact on naval forces, whose deployment in peacetime would be very different to war, unlike land and land-based air forces, most of which would already be at or near their 'starting positions' if conflict were to break out. NATO's maritime objectives were first to prevent Soviet forces denying or inhibiting NATO use of the ocean areas 'essential for the prosecution of the war', and second to support ground forces by helping to defend to vulnerable northern and southern flanks, launching diversionary attacks and providing air and amphibious support to forces operating inland. From this were derived the naval tasks: sea control for the direct protection of shipping, sea denial in the form of barrier operations or attacks at source, and thirdly the support of land operations. The prioritisation of these would depend upon the nature of the confrontation and conflict.[42]

The US-UK document had initially followed with three possible scenarios for a confrontation or conflict with the USSR: a 'short-warning' contingency, 'escalating situations' over a 7 to 14-day timeline, and then a longer 'operations in a period of tension' lasting over 30 days.[43] When the document finally appeared these had been reduced to two: a 'short-warning' and a 'long-warning' scenario. In the former, the primary role of naval forces would be to avoid any pre-emptive attacks and then to counter-attack Soviet naval forces. It was assumed that it would take three days for Soviet naval forces to reach areas of conflict, but seven days for the NATO Strike Fleet – which would be the main capability for attacking Soviet naval forces – to arrive from the US Eastern Seaboard. During this one-week gap, European NATO forces would have to undertake sea control and denial operations by themselves (and with inadequate air cover) until the Strike Fleet arrived. In the long-warning scenario, which was not a long *war* scenario, it was assumed that tensions would gradually build up over time resulting from a 'political crisis or limited conflict outside of Europe' and would involve a prolonged stand-off between

NATO and Warsaw Pact naval forces. In this scenario, which clearly had its antecedents in the Cuban Missile Crisis and the Yom Kippur War stand-off, was focussed on the 'need to attain a maritime posture which will deter the Pact from initiating hostilities' although such a posture might be quite different from that needed to fight a conflict if hostilities broke out.[44]

The joint concept of operations is valuable not only in demonstrating how close the USN and Royal Navy were working to formulate a joint understanding of how they would seek to deter and fight a conflict at sea with the Warsaw Pact, but it is also a clear and effective explanation of what was becoming bowdlerised as the 'short war' and 'long war' concepts.[45] They were not contradictory, as has been implied in certain accounts.[46] The document made it clear that the latter was describing a prolonged *confrontation* and not necessarily a war and was anchored in the experiences of real-world maritime crises that had nearly turned into conflicts over the previous two decades.[47]

There appears to have been another motive for the US Navy's sudden wish to develop a joint doctrine with the Royal Navy in late 1977. The new Carter administration had been keen to distance itself from its predecessors' involvement in the Vietnam War, and therefore returned the focus of US defence policy towards countering the Soviets in Europe: combining a renewed push for increased European defence spending with more pre-positioning of military equipment on the continent.[48] In these circumstances the false conflict between the 'long' and 'short' war scenarios began to take on a crucial importance for the US Navy: if the idea of a 'bolt from the blue' no-warning short war (as short as two days in some analyses) took hold as the driving factor behind US strategy, then the whole concept of reinforcement convoys across the Atlantic fell away, thus resulting in a significant shrinkage in the US Navy.[49] Incidentally, the conceptual justification for significant portions of the Royal Navy would disappear as well. The joint US-UK doctrine therefore seems to be part of an attempt to re-educate the new President and his Secretary of Defense, Harold Brown, whilst demonstrating that the US Navy's conception of a potential war fitted with that of the NATO ally most able to share the burden of Atlantic maritime warfare. It is not clear how influential the joint document was, but by 1979 the idea of a much longer lead time into war had been accepted even to the extent that the US Navy's new 'swing strategy', which had been approved by Harold Brown, involved transiting much of its overstretched naval capability from the Pacific into the Atlantic in a time of high tension, thus assuming a two to three-week period before US naval forces would arrive in the Eastern Atlantic in significant numbers.[50] This in itself would create problems for the Royal Navy, as air cover from the US carrier strike group might not arrive until a number of weeks after a confrontation in the Atlantic had begun, thus forcing it to depend on the subsonic Harrier and the relatively small number of RAF air defence aircraft flying from land bases.

The long war-short war arguments were filtering over the Atlantic and increasingly informed Ministry of Defence perceptions from the mid-1970s onwards: the no-warning 'bolt from the blue' scenario being assumed to be the lodestar which defence planning must follow. This made some sense if one only looked at a possible crisis from the perspective of the Central European front, ignoring increasing tensions elsewhere in the world. On the Central front a sustained period of high tension in a 'long-warning' scenario would mean merely increasing the readiness of forces and reinforcing with troops and equipment from the United Kingdom – the 'fight' would not begin until Soviet forces crossed the inner German border. The Royal Air Force accepted the short war orthodoxy in 1976 in the aftermath of the Defence Review, and it directly affected their approach to maritime tasks: 'we do not make provision to support a concept of an escalating war at sea over a period of 90 days or so without conflict on land, nor accept that seaborne transatlantic reinforcements could be attacked without any reaction elsewhere by NATO, particularly by the United States.' Also, 'maritime operations ... are secondary to operations in the Central Region, where the conflict could be decided within some 6 to 7 days and where nuclear escalation might take place within 4 or 5 days'.[51] Even if one agreed with the bold assessment that a maritime-only war was an impossibility, this conclusion increasingly resulted in a focus solely on the no-notice/short-notice short war, and ignored the possibility that there might be a long period of high tension requiring the flying of high-intensity maritime patrol or maritime strike sorties for many days or weeks, before any warfighting began in which aircraft availability would reduce as maintenance was increasingly required and aircrew suffered from fatigue. Scenarios instead focussed on maritime operations starting from a standing start and becoming a warfighting situation immediately and lasting for only five to seven days. Given that the Navy's planning generally assumed the possibility of a long-war/long-warning conflict, the ability for the two services to co-operate was severely circumscribed if they did not agree on the type of war that would be fought.

The long war-short war debate also elided into a completely different set of disagreements in the late 1970s and early 1980s between the US Navy and the CIA over Soviet strategy in time of war. Since Admiral Zumwalt had been CNO, and before, the US Navy's presumption had been that a major Soviet naval objective would have been NATO convoy interdiction – in effect a third Battle of the Atlantic. CIA analysis of open source and other intelligence had pointed instead towards a more defensive Soviet naval strategy of their forces retreating to protect their SSBN 'bastions' in the Atlantic and Pacific Arctic, the leaving the oceans largely free of Soviet submarines intent on disrupting re-supply convoys.[52] Again, this argument between two arms of US government could potentially have made significant parts of the Royal Navy appear irrelevant. However, as with the long war-short war controversy it ignored the likelihood of a sustained period of tension and confrontation before a shooting war, and as in 1973 during the Yom Kippur stand-off, Soviet naval forces would probably have been perfectly willing to operate far from local waters in order to threaten US naval forces and achieve their political objectives. In addition, one would have thought that an intelligent Soviet naval commander might have deliberately sent some boats into the Atlantic to interdict shipping as a way of keeping NATO forces distracted and away from the bastions. Even if this attempt at strategic deflection (and showing NATO naval leaders what they would have expected to see) failed, it would have been a foolhardy SACLANT who would not have at least provided some convoy escorts to reinforcement forces in the Eastern Atlantic and the Mediterranean. Looking at all of these factors through the prism of the Central European front was helping to create a strategic myopia that focussed on the low probability-high impact risk of a 'bolt from the blue' land thrust into West Germany, whilst increasingly ignoring the higher-probability and potentially equally high impact risk of a prolonged military-political confrontation in a period of mounting tension, as had been seen during the Cuban Missile Crisis and the Yom Kippur War.

Budgetary Strains

In the three years that followed the Concept and Size and Shape papers, and whilst the US-UK document was being written, the funding of defence came under increasing strain, making it more difficult to begin to fulfil the vision of these documents. As the United Kingdom stumbled its way towards a bail-out by the International Monetary Fund in the winter of 1976, further reductions were made in the defence budget. In March 1976 cuts of £177 million in 1977–8, £193 million in 1978–9 and £164 million in 1979–80 were made in the overall departmental budget, immediately throwing some of the assumptions of the 1975 Review up in the air.[53] Re-negotiating the contribution of the Hong Kong government to its own defence helped in a minor way to absorb these reductions, but each of the services had to contribute additional economies. The Navy launched a 'fine tooth-comb study' to find multiple small-scale reductions.[54] It also focussed some of its reductions on support facilities: Antrim and Bandeath armament depots, the Lyness and Pembroke Dock oil depots, and Royal Naval Aircraft Yard at Wroughton would all close. There would also be reductions in fuel and stock purchases and the shore and support services infrastructure.[55] This was accompanied by the absorption of the Port Auxiliary Service into the Royal Maritime Auxiliary Service, and an amalgamation of various Admiralty research establishments and the closure of a number of their sites.[56] In February 1977 further reductions were announced, taking the 1978–9 cuts in Defence up to £230 million.[57] The Ministry had pushed hard against Treasury requirements for yet more major cuts so soon after a defence review, raising the possibility that either the Central Europe front 'pillar' or the Eastern Atlantic 'pillar' might have to be given up to provide the highest of the cuts the Treasury was proposing.[58] The Chiefs of Staff, accompanied by the Defence Secretary, even exercised their right to a meeting with the Prime Minister for the first time since 1968, but to little avail. Despite the Chiefs' concerns about the growing Soviet threat and the potential impact on NATO solidarity, the cuts went through.[59] Staff cuts were made across a range of naval support services, whilst the RN Supply and Transport Service rationalised.[60] These reductions were painful for the Royal Navy, as they undoubtedly were for the other services. In addition to the rationalisation of support and auxiliary services and the reductions in stocks, the equipment programme was reduced in its size from 1976 to 1978: a series of planned orders did not go ahead, including a fifth Type 22 frigate which had been planned to be ordered in 1978.[61] As will be seen later in the chapter, this was the first of a new batch of ships that would link into the United States' OSIS intelligence gathering system and was an important symbol of US-UK intelligence co-operation. Two years of well below-inflation pay rises in all three services was also instituted in 1976 and 1977.[62] By 1978 the government, having partly passed through the economic crisis, agreed to an increase in the defence budget of 3 per cent a year, but the preceding years' cuts had been painful, disruptive and morale sapping and did not make up for the damage done.[63] How would the Royal Navy begin to introduce the new ship types demanded by the Size and Shape paper in such a financially constrained environment?

Anti-Submarine Warfare

Between 1975 and 1981 the underwater capabilities of the Soviet Northern Fleet continued to grow: a total of ten 'Victor II' and 'III' nuclear-powered attack boats entered service in addition to six 'Alfa' class boats of the same type, five 'Charlie' class cruise missile submarines and seventeen 'Delta II' and 'III' classes ballistic missile submarines.[64] These boats were linear developments of previous Soviet submarine types and were generally noisier than NATO submarines, but with the 'Victor IIIs' and the most recent 'Deltas' in particular, quieting technologies had improved and detection by submarines with traditional hull-mounted sonars had become more difficult.[65] By contrast, the 'Alfas' were extremely fast, if noisy, boats that could outrun any NATO nuclear submarine, if not necessarily all the torpedoes they might fire. In 1980 the first of another radical new submarine class entered service, the 'Oscar' class cruise missile submarine. Displacing an enormous 22,500 tonnes submerged, the 'Oscar' class were armed with a battery of twenty-four long-range anti-ship cruise missiles, the equivalent of more than a regiment of 'Backfire' strike aircraft (each armed with a single missile). Although not yet in service, NATO intelligence analysts would no doubt have been aware of other new submarine classes under construction, indicating the shift from the 'second generation' of Soviet boats to a new and more sophisticated third generation. In 1978, it was estimated that the Soviet Navy would have a total of 212 nuclear-powered submarines in service by 1985, with more than half of these in service with the Northern Fleet.[66] The Royal Navy would therefore be at the forefront of countering this growing and increasingly capable fleet.

For the Royal Navy, the rapid rise to prominence of the towed-array sonar had eclipsed what had been the great hope in anti-submarine warfare in the late 1960s: the hull-fitted 'bottom bounce' sonar. However, the trials of an experimental version of such a sonar, the Type 2016, on HMS *Matapan*, had proved the effectiveness of such a sonar, but not to the extent that at one point had been hoped. As oceanographic research developed during the 1970s, a significant part of which was promoted and undertaken directly by NATO at SACLANTCEN based in Las Spezia in Italy, it became clear that both the seabed itself was much more variable than had been originally envisaged, meaning that sound emissions might 'bounce' in many different ways or not at all, and that the sound propagation abilities of the ocean itself were much more complex than had originally been assumed. The *Matapan* trials had not provided a dramatic breakthrough: effective and sustained detection below the top thermal layer of the ocean (the isotherm) was not possible with the sonar, and although ranges were increased out to a maximum of 30 nautical miles in the Eastern Atlantic, this was intermittent, dependent on oceanic conditions and on the position of the narrow zone of detection when it had 'bounced' and returned to the isotherm.[67] The first sonars with some bottom bounce capability, the Type 2016, were fitted to the first four Type 22 frigates, five modernised *Leander* class frigates and the last three Type 42 destroyers, but the system was classed as fully operational only in 1983.[68] The other great anti-submarine hope of 1967–8, the Ikara missile system, was also conspicuous by its absence in the 1975 papers. This was another system, as was seen in Chapter 7, that had not lived up to early hopes. The cancellation of 'stretched Ikara' in early 1977, which would have carried the next generation of lightweight torpedoes and therefore dealt with one of Ikara's weaknesses, seemed to confirm – at least at this stage – that this particular system was not going to be a significant part of the Navy's anti-submarine arsenal through into the 1980s and 1990s.[69]

If the fortunes of bottom bounce sonar and Ikara had waned since 1967, the future appeared to lie with SOSUS and towed-array for detection, and large anti-submarine helicopters and maritime patrol aircraft for the prosecution of attacks on submarines. The SOSUS network of hydrophones had the advantage of sitting underneath the isotherm, making the detection of submarines also below this layer at longer ranges much more assured. However, SOSUS coverage was not complete at the time, it could result in impractically large sea areas to search, and the arrays were clearly vulnerable to tampering or destruction in a period of high tension. This last problem resulted in the requirement for the Seabed Operations Vessel, which is described in the next chapter, whilst the first two problems would be partly covered by using towed-array-equipped ships as supplements to SOSUS, or in those areas where SOSUS devices could not be placed or maintained, such as in the deep ocean.

Towed arrays had been initially developed for submarines as an improvement on the strings of hydrophones that had been placed along the sides of their hulls. Hydrophones are 'passive' listening devices that pick up any sounds in the water. They have the advantage of not emitting any noise of their own (as 'active' sonars would), and if they are sensitive enough can detect sounds from greater distances than active sonars that depend on an emitted sound pulse being returned to the emitting ship. In addition, if the line of hydrophones is long enough then sound waves of very long wavelength, which are most likely to have travelled considerable distances, can be detected. Placing a line of hydrophones along the hull of a submarine was obviously limited to the length of the submarine, so by the 1960s US submarines had started to deploy hydrophones on long flexible lines that be towed from the stern of a submarine. They could either be clipped on when the boat departed for its patrol or stored in reels attached to the submarine. The Royal Navy introduced its first submarine towed-arrays in the mid-1970s, and these were of the 'clip-on' variety: the first submarine towed-array was a purchase of the Type 2024 sonar which depended upon a US processor which entered service in 1977, whilst the second was a domestically developed system, the Type 2026, with improved capabilities.[70]

Moving from submarine to surface-ship towed-arrays was the logical next step and development work started on a British surface-ship array in 1971–2. Such a towed-array attached to a surface vessel held out the promise of enabling surface ships to reliably detect submarines over long distances and without giving away the location of the detecting ship. The 1975 Size and Shape paper had emphasised the importance of surveillance (providing a wider picture of a whole area), and an early decision was made in the development of the new array to create a system that combined this surveillance role with a more straight forward tactical capability. More effective surveillance would be gained through greater bandwidth and range, so the array was made much longer than previous versions. Digital technology allowed for the complex processing of raw data to be quicker and more effective.[71] The first test version of the new array went to sea in the frigate HMS *Lowestoft* in 1978. A large drum was fitted on the ship's stern and the array could be reeled in and out as required. The trials were a particular success: the additional length not only provided greater range, but the increased number of hydrophones meant that the effectiveness of detection remained high even if some of these fragile listening devices broke, as was often the case during long deployments of the ship's 'tail'.[72]

The capability leap over previous detection devices was considerable and marked a ground-breaking change in the 'balance of detection power' between NATO surface vessels and Soviet submarines. The Royal Navy's Operational Evaluation Group assessment of the *Lowestoft* trials started with the statement 'the Sonar 2031 will open up a completely new capability which should allow above-water ASW forces to gain the initiative over the Soviet nuclear submarine for the first time ever'.[73] Over the next four years, the experimental device was developed into two operational towed-arrays for surface ships. The first was an interim towed-array to get the sonar to sea as quickly as possible. A range of vessels were considered for adaption, with *Lowestoft*'s *Rothesay* class sisters being considered first but rejected as too old, whilst the new Type 21 frigates were rejected due to the lack of space. Eventually, *Leander* class frigates that had already been modernised with Exocet cruise missiles were selected.[74] *Cleopatra* was the first ship to be fitted with the towed array, sacrificing her helicopter hangar to the sonar's processing and analysis 'box'. She was followed by *Sirius*, *Argonaut* and *Phoebe*, their processing 'boxes' being placed forward below their Exocets, thus leaving their helicopter capabilities intact.[75] A modified version of the sonar, with thinner and more robust 'tail', a smaller drum and more sophisticated processing power, would be fitted to the second batch of Type 22 frigates, which as will be seen below, had already been selected for fitting with the US Outboard surveillance system.[76]

The 1975 Size and Shape paper had also emphasised the importance of the Nimrod maritime patrol aircraft for anti-submarine warfare, seeing it as the prime means of prosecuting attacks on submarines in the areas within its 1,000 nautical mile range from RAF bases in Scotland (Kinloss) and Cornwall (St Mawgan). The Nimrod had suddenly emerged as such a potent anti-submarine asset because the Air Staff of the RAF had finally agreed to the updating of the aircraft's sensors. When the Nimrod MR1 entered service in 1970 it had done so fitted with much of the already ageing detection equipment that had been installed in its predecessor, the Shackleton. These sensors had been optimised for detecting diesel submarines, leaving the Nimrod MR1, like the Shackleton, with a limited capability to detect and track nuclear submarines which could remain underwater for weeks or months. The Nimrod MR1 had been seen as an interim step towards a more sophisticated aircraft, and by the mid-1970s development work had begun on updated the aircraft's sensors to include much greater processing power, the ability to drop the more sophisticated multiple hydrophone Barra sonobuoy, the CAMBs sonobuoy, and a miniaturised version of the veteran Jezebel passive sonobuoy. This was accompanied by a new semi-automated passive radar intercept system. The first modified Nimrod, the MR2, flew its first test flight in 1977 and the rest of the fleet was modified to the new standard between 1979 and 1984. At long last, the RAF's maritime aircraft had capabilities that matched its range and speed and could now play a significant part in the battle to track, contain and, as necessary, destroy Soviet nuclear-powered submarines.[77] The Nimrod's large battery of sonobuoys and its ability to cover long distances provided it with two significant advantages over anti-submarine warships, but its obvious impossibility of fitting a towed-array and the limitations of its range and persistence meant that it could not completely supplant the combination of surface ships and anti-submarine helicopters.

In parallel with the updating of the Nimrod maritime patrol aircraft, the Sea King anti-submarine helicopter which operated from aircraft carriers and the two *Tiger* class cruisers was updated during the 1970s and 1980s. The Sea King HAS Mark 2, which entered service between 1976 and 1980, introduced improved Rolls-Royce Gnome 1400-1 engines and a six-bladed tail rotor. The helicopter retained the Marconi Type 195 active dipping sonar but was now able to drop sonobuoys. Almost all the HAS Mark 1s were updated to this standard and twenty-three new Mark 2s were built by Westland Helicopters.[78] The technological developments that were helping to increase the capabilities of the Nimrod also helped to create a leap forward in anti-submarine capability for the next variant of the ASW Sea King, the HAS Mark 5 which first entered service in 1980. Thirty new-build HAS Mark 5s were completed by Westlands between 1980 and 1986, whilst fifty-five HAS Mark 2s and one Mark 1 were converted to the new type. The new MEL Sea Searcher radar combined with Decca navigation equipment and the Orange Crop passive detection system improved surface search capabilities, whilst the miniaturisation of sonobouys now allowed the Sea King to drop and monitor more of these powerful passive detectors whilst still retaining the capability to deploy an active dipping sonar. Acoustic signals from the sonar equipment were processed and displayed by the GEC LAPADS equipment which also enabled the Sea King to monitor sonobouys dropped by Nimrod aircraft.[79] The increased capabilities of both the Nimrod aircraft and the Sea King, as predicted by the 1975 Size and Shape paper, firmly placed aircraft in the forefront of the detection, identification and destruction of Soviet submarines and gave the Royal Navy increasingly effective capabilities against the second generation of Soviet attack, cruise missile and ballistic missile submarines.

Surveillance and Shadowing

Throughout the 1970s, and as Soviet overseas deployments grew in frequency, Royal Navy warships were increasingly being used to shadow ships transiting the North Sea, the English Channel and waters north of Scotland. Shadowing by surface ships, which was directed by CINCEASTLANT in Northwood, occurred under Operation 'Larder' and had three specific roles: to track and counter the USSR's expanding maritime activity, to collect intelligence and higher-value intelligence than otherwise, and to enable RN ships to react more quickly to hostile moves.[80] This mix of intelligence gathering and conventional deterrence would usually be allocated to a frigate and destroyer, but if these were unavailable offshore patrol vessels or Royal Fleet Auxiliaries might be deployed. The largest and longest-sustained shadowing operation was Operation 'Algy', which involved seven Royal Navy vessels shadowing ships of the Soviet Northern Fleet as they emerged from the Barents Sea to take part in the huge Okean 75 exercise in April 1975.[81] Spanning three oceans and involving 220 ships and submarines, plus numerous land-based aircraft, Okean 75 included deployment, reconnaissance and strike phases, culminating the demonstration of a ballistic missile launch from a submerged submarine in the Barents Sea, observed by the Chief of the Soviet Navy, Admiral Gorshkov, and General Grechko, the Soviet Defence Minister.[82]

The most eventful element of Operation 'Algy' was the shadowing of a Soviet naval squadron led by the frigate HMS *Danae* commanded by Captain Brian Young. Including the frigate *Nubian* and the auxiliary *Gold Rover*, Young's small group – supported by the ships' helicopters and US and RAF maritime patrol aircraft – worked hard to keep contact with the Soviet force consisting of two modern 'Kresta II' class cruisers, a new 'Krivak' class frigate and an older 'Kanin' class destroyer, as they manoeuvred through the growlers and melting icebergs of the Norwegian Sea. The Soviet squadron repeatedly attempted to evade the British ships, splitting up into single units and then reassembling later, and attempting to mask which vessel was the flagship through the use of false flags and signals. The British were able to keep sight of their adversaries long enough to ensure that they saw the Soviet vessels undertake a number of exercise routines including tracking and attacking their own submarines, and mock firing of missiles. Although many Soviet naval vessels were handled in a workmanlike way, betraying their lack of open ocean experience, the squadron that Young's force tracked demonstrated considerable ship-handling skills, even some panache, in their manoeuvres coupled with willingness to use feint and bluff to shake off their shadowers.[83] The Soviet Navy was beginning to show a confidence and self-assurance in surface operations that it had previously only shown under the water.

The growing significance of shadowing and marking Soviet warships had been reflected in the 1975 Size and Shape paper: effective shadowing would not only mean that if tensions rose any Soviet vessels at sea could be marked and constrained quickly, but also that Soviet operating routines could be analysed over the long-term thus building up a better and more detailed picture of NATO's adversary. One recommendation of the paper that quickly died was the proposed 36-knot 'marking ship': fast frigates had been investigated in the 1960s (the Type 19 frigate) but had been abandoned due to their high noise and the short life of key machinery components. Such single role vessels would also be expensive investments in a role that could be effectively undertaken with slower escorts equipped with shipborne helicopters.

The emphasis on surveillance was reflected in the decision to develop a dual role surveillance and tactical towed-array, as has been described above, but also helped lead to the British purchase of six 'Outboard' surveillance systems from the United States. Outboard, which was fitted to some US *Spruance* class destroyers, was the ship-based element of the US Navy's Ocean Surveillance Information System ('OSIS'). OSIS was a 'system of systems' that combined information from maritime patrol aircraft, surveillance satellites and shore-based radio intercepts, at a number of co-ordination and analysis stations, one of which was in the United Kingdom at the US embassy in Grosvenor Square.[84] Adding Outboard to OSIS provided the US Navy and NATO with a mobile radio intercept system. It could intercept voice, telegraphic and data signals, analyse these signals and then undertake direction-finding in order to isolate the position of the sources of these signals, be they ships, aircraft or submarines on the surface. The frequency range of the intercept equipment covered as much of the spectrum as possible, including very-low-frequency signals which had a greater chance of travelling over long distances as they were reflected downwards from the earth's ionosphere. In practical terms this meant the installation of miles of additional cabling on board a warship to link up two dozen rectangular sensors placed around the ship's hull, and the need for large amounts of space for computer processors and analyst stations within the ship, coupled with direction-finding antennae.[85]

The agreement for the purchase of six Outboard systems and their integration into OSIS was signed with the United States in 1976, and thoughts began to turn to how best to take the systems to sea.[86] Both the Type 21 and Type 42 ships were too cramped to take the equipment, so adapting the Type 22 frigate was investigated. Two options were considered: the first, which would be the quickest, involved the modification of the third and fourth hulls of the class.

It would be too late to change the hull size of these vessels, but if the Exocet missiles were removed and crew habitability standards reduced significantly then Outboard could be fitted. This was considered to be too much of a sacrifice, so the second option was chosen. This involved lengthening the Type 22 hull by ten metres amidships and fitting the Outboard equipment in the space created. The Type 22 would therefore shift to a modified second 'batch' for the fifth to tenth ships.[87] In the event, the government did not agree to any further orders of Type 22 frigates until 1979, so the Outboard frigate remained in limbo for another three years.

Whilst on the surface of the oceans the Royal Navy was undertaking increasingly ambitious shadowing operations and procuring sophisticated intelligence-gathering warships, underneath the surface was where the most impressive feats of long-distance shadowing and trailing were taking place. With a nuclear submarine force that was largely operating in the North Atlantic and growing in numbers and experience, Royal Navy nuclear-powered 'hunter-killer' submarines were able to undertake a series of lengthy trails of Soviet submarines and gain much useful intelligence in the process. In March 1975 a Soviet 'Echo II' class submarine, a first-generation cruise missile boat, was trailed by HMS *Courageous*, commanded by Captain Richard Sharpe, for over 320 miles with the target itself seemingly unaware of the tail. Surpassing even this feat was the trailing of a Soviet 'Delta' class second-generation ballistic missile submarine by HMS *Sovereign*, Commander Richard Farnfield, between 6 October and 1 December 1978. Despite a few breaks of contact for a couple of days at the start and end of the trail, *Sovereign* collected considerable amounts of information on Soviet ballistic missile patrolling routines, noted that the boat was undertaking a contour survey of parts of the seabed perhaps for future use by other boats and ventured as far as the Cape Verde Islands off west Africa. Other notable trailing operations were conducted other 'S' class boats in 1980 and 1981: *Spartan* trailed a number of Soviet second-generation boats in July 1980, successfully shaking off a trail by an 'Alfa' class boat, a particularly notable performance given that class's maximum speed of 40 knots. *Superb* trailed a total of twelve Soviet submarines during a May 1981 patrol, and towards the end of the same year witnessed, undetected, a new Soviet 'Oscar' class cruise missile submarine undertake its missile-launching trials. In other instances trailing operations could be much less successful: for example, *Sceptre* suffered considerable damage from a collision with a 'Delta' class submarine in late 1980 during a trailing operation.[88] The Royal Navy's nuclear-powered 'hunter-killer' submarines and their crews were proving themselves in some of the most testing and risky circumstances of the Cold War, but the other half of the nuclear submarine fleet – the ballistic missile armed 'bombers' of the *Resolution* class – needed improvements to their main weapon systems in order to maintain the credibility of the nuclear deterrent.

Chevaline

In September 1975 senior ministers within the Labour government agreed to continue with plans for a domestically-developed modernisation of Polaris, code-named Chevaline, which would ensure that the British deterrent would continue to meet the 'Moscow criterion' for effective deterrence into the 1980s.[89] This decision had been made by a few senior Cabinet ministers, including the Prime Minister, Foreign Secretary, Defence Secretary and Chancellor of the Exchequer, despite a manifesto commitment not to develop a successor to Polaris and an increasing preference for unilateral disarmament amongst some MPs and many activists. Development was therefore kept highly secret, with some Cabinet ministers on the left deliberately being kept in the dark. As was described in Chapter 6, Chevaline involved the replacement of the existing Polaris warhead with two smaller warheads plus a third capsule known as a 'penetration aid carrier' which would hold a number of decoys that would create a 'cloud' effect that would confuse the Soviet anti-ballistic missile defences around Moscow.

The work required to produce the new warhead, the penetration aid carrier, the decoys and the 'bus' to carry all of those atop the missile all had to be developed in the United Kingdom, stretched the technical, resource and personnel capabilities of the Atomic Weapons Research Establishment ('AWRE') to the limit. Escalating spending requirements combined with poor cost controls resulted in the Royal Navy being given responsibility for the overall project management of Chevaline. Having the system's ultimate 'customer', who was also one step removed from the research work at AWRE, helped slow the rate of escalation in costs and ensured that the cost increases that did occur were properly tracked. However, those costs continued to rise as British government scientists and engineers attempted to develop and make operational technology of a complexity and difficulty that had not been attempted since the 1950s.[90]

The Chevaline programme did continue to remain a tightly-kept secret throughout the period in which Labour was in power (1974–9), but the escalating costs combined with the United Kingdom's precarious economic and financial position resulted in continued reviews of the programme, each time considering whether cancellation would not be a better option.[91] The Chancellor, Denis Healey, who had ironically started the earliest research on Chevaline's predecessors in 1970 when he was Defence Secretary, had doubts that the Moscow criterion was still relevant. The Foreign Secretary, David Owen, would have preferred to purchase the much cheaper but much less capable nuclear-tipped Tomahawk cruise missiles from the United States instead, and only reconciled himself to Chevaline because of the 'psychological shock' to the public if the deterrent were seen to have been downgraded.[92] Even the Prime Minister, Jim Callaghan, expressed his doubts as the costs rose. However, the small group of ministers soon reconciled themselves to continuing the programme, first because of their belief in its necessity, and second because at each cost increase they were assured that the system was almost developed and that cancellation at such a late stage would have wasted the many hundreds of millions of pounds already spent.[93] It is also possible that cancellation at this late stage would been more likely to reveal the existence of a programme the government had denied many times.

Chevaline continued in development and by 1978 was ready for its first tests. Tests on the rocket and the different elements of the new 'nose' were undertaken at Woomera in Australia and Cape Canaveral in the United States, whilst the testing of the nuclear warheads themselves were undertaken in Nevada in co-operation with the US Lawrence Livermore National Laboratory.[94] These latter tests were publicly acknowledged but were described as doing no more than to 'maintain the effectiveness of our nuclear weapons'. The tests during 1978 and 1979 generally proved successful. However, further cost increases were now being accompanied by delays, which would mean that the in-service date slipped back to 1982. This meant that there would be a three year 'capability gap' between the in-service date of the new Moscow ABM system in 1979 to the deployment of the new system on the Polaris submarines.[95] Between 1975 and 1981 the cost of Chevaline had increased from £738 million to £1 billion (at 1981 prices), an appreciable amount but given the complexities of the work involved it is perhaps surprising that the increased were not any higher.[96]

Major Exercises

The annual NATO Eastern Atlantic exercise had become the most important part of the operational calendar for the Royal Navy, now that its presence in the Mediterranean had reduced significantly. As with their predecessors in the early 1970s, they generally occurred during either September and October, and included the transit of a US carrier strike group across the Atlantic, a series of anti-submarine, anti-air and anti-ship exercise routines, a forced passage through the GIUK gap, followed by the escorting of an amphibious force and a landing linked to annual AFNorth Exercises, usually in Norway. Generally a British aircraft carrier would take part in the exercises: from 1975 to 1978 it was *Ark Royal*, acting as the flagship of NATO's STRKFLTLANT 2, STRKFLTLANT 1 being the US carrier battle group. Following the withdrawal of *Ark Royal* from service, *Hermes* would lead the Royal Navy's contribution, generally in an anti-submarine carrier role. Significant numbers of destroyers, frigates and submarines would also take part in different capacities, either as 'Blue' forces (NATO) or 'Orange' forces (Warsaw Pact). Soviet air and naval forces increasingly took an 'observing' role, often attempting to disrupt the exercises with their own overflights and naval manoeuvres. Each exercise would generally end with operations simulating a nuclear attack, in order to practice dispersed operating and locking down against the fallout. One aspect of these exercises that was particularly in evidence during the mid to late 1970s was a caution regarding operating too close to the High North and Soviet waters, fearing the charge of provocation from the Soviet Union during an era of détente and prolonged negotiations over nuclear and conventional force reductions. Exercise Ocean Safari 75 did include considerable operations within the Norwegian Sea, but the amphibious landing was only a 'paper exercise' that occurred in theory rather than in practice.[97] Exercise Teamwork 76 did include an amphibious landing, but at Esbjerg in southern Norway, some distance away from any likely Soviet attack.[98] Ocean Safari 77 avoided the High North altogether with the exercise focussing on resupply convoys from the Azores through to the Western Approaches.[99] Northern Wedding 78 conducted its main amphibious landing on the Shetlands with a 'paper' landing theoretically occurring on Norway.[100] Ocean Safari 79 lacked amphibious operations altogether.[101] As détente began to disintegrate in 1980 this changed somewhat, with Teamwork 80 including a landing at Trondelag in northern Norway.[102] However, this general trend away from amphibious landings and an unwillingness to undertake too many elements of the exercises east of the Greenland-Iceland-UK gap, not only emphasised the increasingly fragile position the Royal Marines found themselves in, but could also be interpreted as reflecting a lack of self-assurance within a western alliance that was on the defensive after the withdrawal from Vietnam, the oil crisis and the Watergate scandal.

The High Wood Exercises conducted in 1975, 1977 and 1979 were similarly cautious about operating too far to the north-east. These United Kingdom-run joint RAF/RN exercises, as has been described in Chapter 5, used a series of scenarios usually based on the Western Approaches, Irish Sea or north of Scotland. High Wood 77 included a 'dash east' to save a 'paper' commando carrier in the Norwegian Sea, whilst High Wood 79 – the last such exercise – was integrated into Exercise Whiskey Venture, an amphibious exercise off Jutland in Denmark.[103]

The Third Cod War
The cold waters around Iceland continued to make their demands upon the ships of the Royal Navy: not just in Cold War surveillance, tracking or

exercises but in the protection of the last remnants of Britain's once extensive distant waters fishing fleet. As has been described in Chapter 8, the Second Cod War had ended with a two-year agreement on 13 November 1973 that restricted – within a 50-mile limit around Iceland – the fishing vessels' total catches, the grounds where they could fish and the types of boats used. Given that negotiations over the International Law of the Sea were heading in the direction of a 200-mile Exclusive Economic Zone ('EEZ'), the agreement provided a breathing space but it was likely that there would be a resumption of Icelandic actions against British trawlers once the two-year period had ended. At the March to May 1975 negotiations in Geneva over the Law of the Sea, the 200-mile EEZ limit had been agreed in principle by almost all states, including the United Kingdom, but although the full Law of the Sea treaty had not yet been agreed, the Icelandic government took the opportunity to announce that it would enforce a 200 mile limit even if a formal agreement had not yet been made internationally. The British government, although accepting this limit in general, was hoping for a long period of transition to the new distance.[104]

When the two-year agreement ended on 13 November 1975, further clashes with the Icelandic coastguard were inevitable. The British and Icelandic government began talks over a new agreement, but the atmosphere in Iceland was febrile and only two days later two British trawlers had their lines cut by coastguard vessels. The fishermen demanded naval protection, and after unarmed British government support ships and civilian defence vessels had proved unable to protect the fishing vessels, the Royal Navy was again deployed. Operation 'Dewey' resumed on 25 November and a force of two frigates and one tanker would be permanently kept on station, with a third on standby at Rosyth naval base. The naval vessels were supported by RAF Nimrods and Hastings providing long-range surveillance capabilities under the code name Operation 'Heliotrope'.[105]

The confrontation between the Royal Navy, government defence vessels and British fishing vessels on one side and Icelandic coastguard vessels on the other, occurred in two periods: from late November 1975 to 20 January 1976, when talks between the two governments resumed, and then from 6 February, when those talks collapsed, to 30 May 1976. The Royal Navy deployed frigates of all classes except the most recent Type 21 vessels, supported at different times by RFAs *Tidepool*, *Olwen*, *Tidereach* and *Blue Rover*, RMAS ocean-going tugs and seven civilian defence vessels chartered by the British government. Compared to the previous Cod War, the Icelandic coastguard vessels were much more aggressive and willing repeatedly to risk collision with Royal Navy warships, the most serious damage occurring during the second period of confrontation.[106]

HMS *Yarmouth*'s bows were heavily damaged in a collision with the Icelandic coastguard vessel *Baldur* on 28 February when attempting to prevent the vessel reaching British trawlers. On 27 March the *Diomede*, in confrontation with *Baldur*, suffered a 12ft gash in her port amidships as that vessel attempted to ram the frigate thirty times, four of which were successful. This particular incident resulted in a change of approach by Flag Officer Scotland and Northern Ireland, the operational commander, who ordered – with the agreement of Ministers – that frigates should avoid damage and, if necessary, tell British fishing vessels to disperse when Icelandic coastguard vessels approached. This new policy caused consternation amongst the fishermen and at the start of May the previous policy of holding off Icelandic vessels resumed. The frigate *Mermaid* was damaged by the *Baldur* during the night of 6 May causing a 5ft gash above in the side amidships, and in the heavy weather began to take in water in the engine room through the hole. In the same incident, which brought in several frigates and Icelandic vessels, *Falmouth* was rammed by *Tyr* (which was also damaged), and the *Gurkha* also received damage in a night of multiple rammings by Icelandic vessels in rough seas. The captains of the Icelandic vessels were received as heroes by the Icelandic public, whilst the Navy was committing increasing numbers of ships in support of a dispute that would inevitably result at some point in the acceptance of a 200-mile limit and the effective end of the British distant sea fishing fleet in northern waters. However, the night action of the 6 May did make the Icelanders realise that the British were determined and had resumed their earlier more aggressive holding off policy. This was enough to bring the Icelandic government back to negotiation, albeit from a position of relative strength. During the third Cold War there were twenty-seven ramming incidents involving frigates and five involving civilian defence vessels from a total of fifty-six collisions. In addition, there had been thirty-five line-cuttings of fishing vessels and three attempts to arrest British fishermen.[107]

On 1 June 1976, in an agreement negotiated in Oslo, both sides agreed that over the next six-months British fishermen could catch 30,000 tons of fish within the 200-mile limit with a daily average of twenty-four trawlers. After that point, new negotiations would be necessary. The British distant-waters fishing industry accepted the inevitable, knowing that for some time that the 200-mile limit would eventually exclude them from Icelandic coastal and offshore waters. In June 1976 the British government also accepted a consolidated 200-mile limit for the EEC as a whole, which meant that vessels from other EEC member states would be able to fish within UK waters to within 12 miles. The British distant waters fishing industry largely died, and UK waters now had to be shared with the fishing vessels of the French, Spanish and other EEC member states. The Third Cod War cost the Royal Navy £1 million in repairs to ships with some countervailing savings in overseas deployments for frigates cancelled. The RAF Nimrod fleet was heavily affected operationally, having to suspend anti-submarine training during Operation 'Heliotrope'.[108]

The Offshore Tapestry

The mid-1970s saw a significant increase in the offshore protection tasks of the British government. The protection of British fishing vessels (and the prevention of foreign vessels fishing illegally) had been a significant if secondary role for the Royal Navy, acting on behalf of the relevant government ministry, the Ministry for Agriculture, Fisheries and Food ('MAFF'). In the 1960s and early 1970s the Fishery Protection Squadron, which had protected the British distant-waters fishing fleet, was largely made up of old Type 14 frigates, which had largely reached the end of their operational lives, while the newer frigates in naval service were larger and more sophisticated and would have been too expensive to use in the role.[109] In addition, a number of converted 'Ton' class minesweepers acted as coastal fishery protection vessels, protecting the twelve nautical mile territorial waters limit from overseas fishing vessels.

Not only were replacements for the Type 14s needed, but the offshore protection task had become more complicated and wide reaching. As has been seen, the UN Law of the Sea conference had proposed national EEZs of 200 nautical miles, and EEC members agreed to set up EEZs of this distance (or at equidistance when neighbouring states were within 400nm of each other) on 1 January 1977. This created a sea area around the United Kingdom and its European dependencies totalling 270,000 square miles that had to patrolled and protected. In addition, the discovery of oil and gas in the North Sea meant that by 1978 a total of 130 structures within British EEZ waters now had to be defended against possible terrorist attack in peacetime or military attack in wartime or periods of high tension.[110] This issue had been raised by NATO's 'Eurogroup' (which consisted of the representatives of NATO's European members) in May 1975, and this had raised the profile of oil and gas protection operations. Norway preferred to keep such protection duties as a civil affair – particularly whilst it was negotiating over maritime boundaries with the USSR in the Barents Sea – but the United Kingdom was keen to combine the role with the newly expanded fishery protection task.[111] The British approach to the problem of defending these structures was not to provide for the individual defence of every oil or gas rig, which would have been far too expensive and would not have been warranted by the risks, but to 'provide a reasonable measure of deterrent patrolling' with utility warships – such as the Type 14s or their successors – and maritime patrol aircraft, coupled with a capability for immediate response in an emergency made up of existing naval and RAF forces.[112] A secondary impact of the rise of the offshore oil industry on the Royal Navy was pressure on its cohort of experienced divers, who could now command much higher pay in the oil and gas industry supporting the installation and repair of rigs at sea, and were leaving in significant numbers.[113]

The most cost-effective short-term replacements for the Type 14s were assessed to be lightly armed offshore patrol vessels ('OPV's) based on trawler hulls and derived from the Jura class vessels operated by the Scottish Department of Agriculture and Fisheries ('SDAF').[114] This decision therefore saw the return to a 'trawler' solution that had first been proposed in the early 1970s, but had been abandoned for the 'convenience' of adapting the RAF *Seal* class instead (see Chapter 7). Five vessels were rapidly ordered in July 1975, with the first vessel, HMS *Jersey*, starting operational patrols in November 1976. The standard competitive tendering process was by-passed in order to allow for orders to be placed at Hall Russell shipbuilders quickly.[115] The first two vessels cost £3.3 million to build, and £1 million a year to run at 1976 prices.[116] They displaced 1,250 tons at full load, and with a complement of only 34 they were much more economical to run than their Type 14 predecessors which had a crew of 135, as well as being more suited to the changeable and often rough North Sea. Two further vessels were ordered in 1977, identical but fitted with stabilisers, and all were in service by the end of 1979.[117] In the gap between the order of the first vessels and their entering service, *Jura* was borrowed for fishery patrol alongside the old ocean-going tug RMAS *Reward*, which was re-commissioned as a Royal Navy warship for the role.[118]

Four vessels based on the RAF's *Seal* class (known as the *Kingfisher* class) had already been constructed, but they had been considered inadequate for the OPV role and even had worse sea-keeping than the converted 'Ton' class minesweepers that they were replacing in the less-demanding coastal role. A second batch of five were cancelled. The *Kingfisher* class were quickly relegated to BRNC Dartmouth and RNR duties.[119] The old 'Tons' therefore needed replacing, and after some consideration of hovercraft and hydrofoils for the coastal patrol task, it was decided to procure more offshore patrol vessels, therefore producing what was called an 'all tier 1' patrol force in which all units could undertake both coastal and offshore patrol duties.[120] The design that emerged, the OPV 2, was a fully navalised and improved patrol vessel, the most notable enhancement being the addition of a helicopter landing deck large enough for a Sea King and the potential for a range of modifications that could shift their role into that of corvettes or light frigates.[121] The requirement was for eight OPV 2s, as a hull-for-hull replacement of the 'Ton' class coastal patrol vessels, but they were expensive ships, costing £10 million each at 1980 prices, approximately the cost of just under four *Jersey* class.[122] Two vessels were ordered in 1980 named *Leeds Castle* and *Dumbarton Castle*.

The OPVs were only half of the new offshore protection capability, the other half being provided by the four RAF Nimrod maritime patrol aircraft that had operated in the Mediterranean until the withdrawal from Malta.[123] With their speed, range and radar they provided long-range surveillance to track fishing vessels, and if necessary, take photographs of and shadow overseas trawlers that had entered the UK EEZ. The Nimrods would then vector the on-station OPV onto the relevant trawler for inspection and possible boarding. In addition, the Scottish Department of Agriculture and Fisheries operated three of its own offshore vessels that could undertake fisheries duties though not oil rig protection as they were unarmed. The seas around the United Kingdom were split into four areas: one centred on the Shetlands, another around Rockall, the west coast of Scotland and the Irish Sea, a third covering the Channel and around the Scillies, and the last the North Sea. Each sea area would have one OPV active, whilst a Nimrod would patrol each area on an annual average of once a week, although in practice there would be two to three patrols a week during the periods of most intense fishing and fewer during quieter periods.[124] The annual cost of operating the Nimrods was estimated to be £3.5 million in 1975 prices. The Nimrod flying hours totalled 180 a month up to 1980, reducing to 140 thereafter on the request of MAFF and SDAF.[125]

The threat to offshore terminals in wartime was a NATO task which would involve all alliance members operating in the North Sea, but the counter-terrorism role was one that was strictly national. The publicity value of a successful terrorist attack on North Sea oil rigs would have been considerable, and at least two threats to undertake such attacks was made, whilst a bomb was planted by the Provisional IRA at the BP oil terminal on the Shetlands just before a Royal visit.[126] The Special Boat Service trained a team to undertake counter-terrorist operations on oil rigs (which was replaced by the new Royal Marines Comacchio Company in 1980), and regular exercises began to simulate bomb attacks or hostage situations. The first of these was Exercise Purple Oyster on 11 June 1975, which involved a pre-emptive response to a terrorist threat, consisting of Special Forces surveillance and insertion, helicopter transfers of military personnel and underwater rig inspection.[127] In practice, most oil rig protection duties involved keeping vessels, including fishing vessels, 500m away from the rigs as set out in the Continental Shelf Act 1964.[128] Offshore Tapestry forces also had a significant role to play in supporting the emergency services if there were disasters at sea, with a Nimrod providing a crucial role co-ordinating the emergency response to the Piper Alpha oil rig fire of 6 July 1988.[129]

Almost all of these activities were classed as providing Military Aid to the Civil Authorities, under which the forces deployed were doing so on behalf of the MAFF, SDAF, the Department of Energy and the Welsh Office, who were presented with bills from the Ministry of Defence on a regular basis. These departments had also paid for much of the construction costs of the *Jersey* class and the new OPV 2s, and could have been forgiven for thinking that with the OPV 2s at least, the Royal Navy was attempting to leverage a wider naval capability out of vessels paid for by others.[130] The Offshore Tapestry might not have been the most high-profile of the Royal Navy's roles, but it provided a direct peacetime link between significant sections of the British economy and the military's role in protecting and supporting them.

The Naval Leadership
At the start of 1976 Admiral Anthony Griffin, the Controller of the Navy, left to become the Chairman of the soon to be nationalised British Shipbuilders Corporation. He was replaced by Vice Admiral Richard Clayton, who would expend much time and energy attempting to bring the two main departments of the Controller's empire, the Weapons Department and the Ship Department, closer together and better able to co-operate.[131] Terence Lewin's time as Commander-in-Chief Fleet was cut short by Admiral Ashmore. It seems that in 1975 he was already considered the front runner as Ashmore's replacement, and Ashmore did not want to create a precedent whereby those who held the post of CinC Fleet would automatically presume to become First Sea Lord. Ashmore had been promoted through this route and he clearly feared that a second promotion from this post would help to close down other ways towards being the professional head of the Navy. As a result, Lewin was moved to be Commander-in-Chief Naval Home Command (CINCNAVHOME) – the only available post that would not be considered a demotion – in November 1975, Admiral Derek Empson then retiring. Admiral Treacher replaced Lewin as CinC Fleet and stayed in this post until 1977.[132]

The unexpected death of Marshal of the Air Force Sir Andrew Humphrey at the age of 56 just after taking up the post of Chief of the Defence Staff ('CDS'), created a new problem in the periodic shuffling of the most senior military posts in Defence. The Secretary of State, Fred Mulley, decided that Admiral Ashmore, who had been acting CDS during Humphrey's short illness, would be promoted to CDS in Humphrey's place and act in this role for a few months before Air Chief Marshal Sir Neil Cameron could then take over to serve a full two years. After this point, as it would be the Navy's natural 'turn' in the rotation of the three services holding the position, Lewin would then be positioned to become CDS. If Ashmore had served a full term as CDS, the Navy's 'turn' would have been lost early and Lewin would have retired before the 'turn' came around again. Ashmore by his own admission had been keen to serve a full term as CDS, but Mulley, advised by a number of retired CDSs, wanted to ensure that the RAF had their 'turn'. In addition, Lord Mountbatten, one of the retired CDSs, in particular wanted to ensure that Lewin had the chance to reach the very top. As result of such complicated manoeuvrings, Ashmore spent six-months as Chief of the Defence Staff, followed by Sir Neil Cameron, with Admiral Lewin as Cameron's expected successor.[133]

* * *

The concepts of operations and fleet size and shape papers of 1975 had set out a comprehensive and radical roadmap for creating the Navy of the late 1980s and 1990s. Recent developments in anti-submarine warfare, increased experience and expertise in surface and underwater shadowing and trailing, and a range of operational challenges were testing a Navy coming to terms with, and adapting to, an operational focus on the North Atlantic. The largest question-mark remained over the lack of a generally accepted concept of operations and size and shape paper, following the completion of the 1978 Strategic Concept. The Navy lacked a justification for much of its fleet and not did seem to be in a hurry to rectify this worrying omission.

11

After *Ark Royal*

The Retirement of HMS *Ark Royal*

On 4 December 1978 at 7.15am, HMS *Ark Royal*, the Royal Navy's last remaining conventional aircraft carrier, arrived at the breakwater protecting Plymouth Sound, embarked thirty-two journalists and then proceeded to berth numbers six and seven at Devonport naval base, coming alongside at 9.00am. Over 3,000 family members were waiting on the jetty to welcome home the ship's crew, and as customs officers had arrived aboard the carrier on her passage home and pre-checked the whole crew's customs declarations, crewmembers were able to meet their loved ones directly as they disembarked in front of the news cameras. With numerous journalists present, the ship's main engines were then rung off at 9.25am. *Ark Royal*'s final hours in active service therefore made newspaper and television news headlines across the United Kingdom, ensuring that the British public were fully aware of an end of an era for the modern Royal Navy.[1]

Ark Royal had in fact missed many of the major conflicts and incidents of the previous 20 years and suffered from engine problems for much of her career. However, the success of the 1976 'Sailor' BBC television series, during which the carrier visited the United States as part of the bicentenary of the US Declaration of Independence and the public encountered members of the crew of the ship in a 'fly on the wall' documentary, had given the ageing ship a high public profile.[2] The documentary, which won a number of awards and received impressive viewing figures, was repeated in 1978 during *Ark Royal*'s last six-months in service and the press continued their interest in the vessel and her crew, naming her the 'love ship' following offers of marriage by crewmen to local women during a two-week visit to Fort Lauderdale in Florida. This documentary, along with the Silver Jubilee Fleet Review at Spithead on 28 June 1977, were the highest-profile elements of a four-year public relations campaign led by Captain Keith Leppard, a former Fleet Air Arm pilot on his last posting before retirement.³ Leppard had helped push the Navy out of its aloof and distant relationship with the media, and into directly approaching a wide range of television, radio and newspaper organisations and programmes, from local papers through to the 'Blue Peter' children's television programme. The *Broadsheet* magazine for retired naval officers was established, recognising the important role that former officers could play as 'influencers' in their communities and social networks, whilst the dry and probably little-read *Naval News Bulletin* that had been issued to messdecks for some 20 years was abolished, with the role of informing the lower deck increasingly relying on the lively 'tabloid' *Navy News* newspaper. With the departure of Leppard, this golden age of Naval public relations quickly fell away, not least as the Ministry of Defence decided to abolish the single-service public relations departments and centralise this activity in Whitehall.⁴ However, the Navy's public relations work in the 1970s did create a lingering public profile that would help the Navy when it needed it most, during the painful 1981 Defence Review and the Falklands conflict the following year.

In 1979, after *Ark Royal* had been decommissioned, the Admiralty Board even allowed discussions to proceed over the possibility of retaining the ship as a floating museum when they knew that it would be prohibitively expensive: somewhat cynically (or cannily depending on one's perspective) the publicity generated by such discussions was deemed to be important in themselves for the profile of the Navy.⁵ The 'HMS *Ark Royal* Preservation Society' even offered £1 million to buy the ship but was turned down by the Ministry of Defence.⁶ In the event, and as expected by the Admiralty Board, the former *Ark Royal* was finally sold for scrap in July 1980 and was broken up at Cairn Ryan in Scotland from August onwards.⁷ The *Ark Royal* name did not disappear however. As the old *Ark Royal* was on passage back to the United Kingdom, she received a signal on 1 December, confirming that an announcement had been made to name the third *Invincible* class cruiser *Ark Royal*.⁸ Perfectly timed, the decision ensured that a name with considerable public recognition would live on in naval service, and perhaps even provide a modicum of protection from sale or early retirement for this third and last ship of her class. The 'Sailor' documentary, and the publicity for the Navy that followed in the succeeding years, had taught the service's leadership a lesson in the importance of public relations.

Back in the autumn of 1978, the old *Ark Royal* had taken part in the NATO Atlantic Exercise Northern Wedding in September and a further exercise with the US Sixth Fleet in the Mediterranean in October. These were her last operational duties and following her final port visit, to Palma in Spain, she returned home to Devonport Dockyard. Before approaching Devonport, her aircraft began disembarking on 27 November, her ten Phantoms and twelve Buccaneers flying to RAF St Athan for transfer to the RAF.[9] A total of eleven Phantoms were transferred, being struck off the Royal Navy's books on 11 December 1978, and seventeen Buccaneers which were struck off on 8 December.[10] The additional aircraft had been based ashore providing training and trials support for the shipborne aircraft. A week later, the two squadrons that had operated these aircraft, 892 and 809, were disbanded.[11] The Buccaneers were initially to have allocated to a dedicated maritime strike squadron but were in event distributed amongst the four existing Buccaneer squadrons in the UK and Germany.[12] The Phantoms were integrated in the RAF's Phantom force, which was split between Germany and the United Kingdom, a number of the aircraft being allocated to the fighters declared to SACLANT for maritime air defence.

If many of the Buccaneers and Phantoms were continuing their operational careers with the RAF, there was no such consolation for the airborne early warning ('AEW') Gannets that *Ark Royal* had operated. They were older aircraft, the most recent having been ordered in 1961 and the majority having been ordered as early as 1954. By 1978 only a handful were still flying, with many in storage or being cannibalised for spares. In the event, two were handed to the RAF as static trainers and two more were handed to the Royal Aircraft Establishment at Farnborough in December 1978, but the remaining aircraft were scrapped, dismantled or used as static plane guards at the entrance to RN and RAF air stations.[13]

With the disappearance of *Ark Royal* and the Gannet, airborne early warning for the fleet now depended entirely on the ageing and much modified land-based Shackleton AEW aircraft, which were fitted with re-purposed former Gannet radars. A replacement was needed, and despite attempts by the US to persuade the UK to buy the AWACS aircraft primarily for early warning over the Central European plain, a British solution was agreed in March 1977 whereby the Nimrod airframe would be re-purposed for the AEW role with a new air-search radar that could undertake both maritime and land early warning duties.[14] In the event, the AEW Nimrod development would become one of British defence's most costly and unsuccessful procurements: the delivery date stretched further into the future, costs spiralled and it became clear that the Nimrod airframe was too small to contain all the necessary equipment to make the aircraft effective. It would finally be cancelled in December 1986, with the venerable Shackleton continuing in service until 1991.[15]

The Navy was acutely aware that there were only limited Shackletons (and envisaged a future in which there would be limited AEW Nimrods) and had continued to investigate quietly the installation of airborne early warning radars to Sea King helicopters to fill any gaps in RAF coverage. Studies by Westland Helicopters in 1972 had set out a number of possible options; the first involved using refurbished Gannet radars in 'radomes' (*rad*ar-d*omes*) placed underneath the Sea King's body. As the radar was too large to fit in this space when the helicopter was not airborne, one option involved placing the radome on a long tether at take-off, then reeling in the tether after the aircraft was in the air. A second option involved attaching the radome to the helicopter just before take-off, from a well created in a carrier's flight deck, with the Sea King dropping the radome into a net on the side of the flight deck just before landing. A third, much less complex and less cumbersome option involved using a slatted Elliott-Marconi radar aerial that was thin enough to be folded under the helicopter's body but which could not be protected by a radome and whose detection capabilities would not be as good as those for the former Gannet radars. Westland set out the costs of mocking-up helicopters for these different mechanisms, but no funding from the Navy was forthcoming.[16] The issue was investigated twice more in the 1970s: in 1974 the incoming Vice Chief of the Naval Staff, Vice Admiral Lygo, requested an investigation into options, and the issue was revisited in 1978 when the last Gannets were retired. Each time the answer was in the negative, and the reasons were varied. Back in 1968, the RN had attempted to push for a cheap maritime AEW capability using a helicopter, when faced with the Air Force Department's proposal for an expensive jet-engined aircraft for both land and maritime AEW, but the requirement was not high enough on the Navy Department's priority list, so the helicopter languished and development on the fast jet continued, but as a low priority.[17] When the issue was revisited in the mid-1970s, the First Sea Lord, Admiral Ashmore, expressed the fear that a time-consuming battle with the RAF to procure organic AEW would distract from the higher priority of procuring the Harrier and a Sea King replacement.[18] In 1978, the Director of Naval Air Warfare, Captain Linley Middleton, despite ostensibly supporting the procurement of helicopter AEW, provided the Vice Chief of the Naval Staff with a detailed list of operational reasons why such a procurement had considerable disadvantages. These included the slow speed of Sea Kings – only 75 knots – when operating at the 10,000ft optimum height for the radar which would limit their range and reach; the maximum range of radar coverage would be 120 to 140 nautical miles, some miles less than the expected cruise missile release range for Soviet strike aircraft; the capability issues of the Elliott-Marconi radar; and finally the apparently considerable weight issues associated with fitting the MR2 Nimrod's new radar instead.[19] For the Naval Staff, the potential pain and difficulty involved in attempting to push through a Sea King AEW outweighed what were considered to be the limited capabilities provided. As a result, outside of the range of the venerable Shackletons, the Navy lacked any form of airborne early warning of enemy attack, a capability gap that would cause considerable problems for the Falklands Task Force in

1982 (which would include Middleton who by then was captain of the Task Force flagship HMS *Hermes*), which in turn would eventually prompt the rapid and long-delayed conversion of Sea Kings to AEW aircraft.

Operational Deployments

Surface Capital Ships
By 1977 it was becoming clear to the Fleet's operational planners that there would be a significant shortage of surface capital ships between 1978 and 1980: the two-year gap after *Ark Royal* was retired and the new cruiser *Invincible* would enter service. In 1974 it had been planned to operate with two 'flat-tops' up to 1981 with an increase to three after that date: *Invincible* would be ready for service as the old *Ark Royal* retired and when *Illustrious* entered service in 1981 the force would then increase to three, with the last ship of the class replacing *Hermes*. However, it now looked like *Invincible* would not complete until December 1980 and would only be fully operational in September 1982. In addition, *Hermes* would enter refit in the last six-months of 1979 meaning that there would be no active 'flat top' in the fleet for 18 months. This would mean a significant capability gap in terms of both fast jets and anti-submarine forces declarable to NATO. Little could be done about the gap between Phantom and Buccaneer withdrawal and Harriers entering service on ships, but the gap in anti-submarine helicopter coverage could be resolved by running on HMS *Bulwark*, which was due to retire in 1978, as an anti-submarine helicopter carrier until 1980. Running on *Ark Royal*, equipped only with anti-submarine Sea Kings, was considered but rejected as it would require a refit and the dockyard capacity was not available.[20] Between 1978 and 1982 the Royal Navy would therefore be in a period of vulnerability with respect to its surface capital ships: *Bulwark* was old and obsolescent, whilst *Hermes* was more capable but also ageing. If the in-service dates of *Invincible* or *Illustrious* drifted further, or *Bulwark* suffered a major breakdown, then the risk that no carriers would be operational became greater.

Group Deployments
Group deployments were now a settled feature of the Royal Navy's annual operational schedule, although increasingly looking vulnerable as the Navy became more focussed on the Eastern Atlantic. They were led by either a 'County' class destroyer or one of the surviving cruisers, *Tiger* or *Blake*, whilst *Ark Royal*, *Hermes* and *Bulwark* remained in the Atlantic and Mediterranean to fulfil the Navy's major NATO obligations. In 1975, the Flag Officer of the 2nd Flotilla, Rear Admiral John Fieldhouse, led that year's group deployment from the destroyer HMS *Glamorgan*. It was the most ambitious so far, and involved a

circumnavigation of the globe, including a Mediterranean passage, crossing the Indian Ocean and visits to Singapore and at least five separate Australian port cities. Fieldhouse noted the beneficial effect of the visiting force – even though it was largely made up of ageing frigates – in countering the relentlessly negative image of the United Kingdom that was seen on the media of Australia and New Zealand. The force then made a Pacific crossing, participating in US-led exercises and undertaking smaller exercises with New Zealand and Canadian frigates. After dispersing to a range of west coast US ports, the group then passed through the Panama Canal, and then visited a number of Caribbean states, *Glamorgan* herself arriving at Venezuela where opportunities for defence sales resulting from that country's new oil wealth were clearly an important driver of the visit. After nine months at sea, the force crossed the Atlantic and returned to their home ports of Devonport and Portsmouth on 14 April 1976.[21]

Amidst further incremental cuts in the naval budget, the next group deployment, led by Rear Admiral Morton in *Glamorgan*'s sister *Antrim*, was a much more modest affair reaching only the western Indian Ocean to be present at the independence of the Seychelles and to take part in the US-Pakistan-Iran Midlink Exercise.[22] The 1977 Group Deployment was split into two parts, with the first solely in the western hemisphere including a number of port visits in South America and West Africa that had a strong focus on defence sales, not least the potential sale of Type 21 frigates to Argentina (which was in the event were vetoed by the Foreign Secretary, David Owen, in 1978).[23] The continuing success of the Navy's public relations strategy was demonstrated by the embarking of a TV film crew from the BBC documentary 'Panorama' investigating developments in anti-submarine warfare.[24] The second part of the 1977 deployment included the now standard route of the Mediterranean, Suez, Gulf, Indian Ocean and Singapore, Australia and Hong Kong. The ships participated in a number of exercises with allies, including the Midlink 77 Exercise with the US, Iran and Pakistan, Compass 77 with the US Navy and Sindex 77 with the Royal Australian Navy.[25] The 1978 deployment had a western focus, including the Caribbean, a Panama Canal transit and port visits to the US, Mexican and Canadian western seaboard. The 1979 deployment returned to East of Suez with a route similar to that of the second part of the 1977 deployment.[26]

In 1980 an attempt was made to develop a more ambitious and politically-engaged programme for that year's deployment, with Rear Admiral D C Jenkin as the flag officer. Partly because of this ambition, it had a much more troubled gestation and its implementation seemed to suggest that the days of the worldwide group deployments might be numbered. To take advantage of détente with both the Soviet Union and China, port visits to both Vladivostok and Shanghai were initially planned. Unfortunately, the Soviet invasion of Afghanistan removed

Vladivostok from the itinerary as part of the United Kingdom's formal protest. The deployment suffered for most of its duration from poor liaison with the Foreign and Commonwealth Office, local British diplomats and defence attaches. Jenkin complained that the 'FCO at present do not see group deployments as having any real part to play in the furtherance of their diplomatic strategy'.[27] Jenkin had to formulate his own aims and objectives without FCO interest or involvement. Many defence attaches had done little or no preparation for port visits, and co-ordination with the Defence Sales Organisation was even worse. This resulted in the group preparing demonstrations and displays of the Corvus 'chaff' decoy launchers at both Manila and Tokyo, but they received little interest from the defence attaches and no British sales reps or potential customers turned up to view what the Navy had prepared. Similar attempts to show equipment in Shanghai resulted in a 'muddle' although Jenkin, with some forced optimism, insisted that they 'must have helped arms sales in China.'[28] The port visit to Bombay was not a success either, reflecting the shift in the Indian Navy towards its long-term relationship with the Soviet Navy as links with the Royal Navy continued to decline. Jenkin noted that 'friendliness [was] lacking and everything we did seemed to irritate' and that 'our visit did more harm than good.'[29] Only with the institution of Operation 'Armilla' in the Gulf which is described below, did a 'sense of purpose' return to the group. Otherwise, Admiral Jenkin glumly noted, both the mess-decks of the ships and the sparsely attended press conferences during port visits heard the repeated question: 'what is this deployment for?'[30] Jenkin, in his final post before retirement, might have been excessively pessimistic in his report of proceedings, but the travails of the 1980 group deployment did indicate that, as the long-standing links to navies in the Indo-Pacific region began to fall away, these expensive and tiring deployments were becoming increasingly difficult to justify. For a Navy which was training in the Eastern Atlantic to a high pitch of readiness, numerous exercises with much less sophisticated and well-trained navies in the Indo-Pacific seemed to provide little practical operational benefit, especially when the FCO seemed so little interested in providing the necessary support. There was no 1981 deployment, probably cancelled to save both money and fleet fuel consumption during a period stringency.[31] It seemed likely that Jenkin's group deployment would be the last, and the Royal Navy's future presence in the Indo-Pacific would consist of no more than Operation Armilla in the Gulf, the small naval force at Hong Kong and the occasional single or two ship deployment.

Hong Kong

1979 and 1980 saw two new commitments for the Royal Navy. The first, in Hong Kong, was essentially an augmentation of an existing commitment but provided a use for a handful of fast craft that were nearing the ends of their operational lives. The second, was the result of the start of a conflict in the Persian Gulf between Iran and Iraq, and the need to protect British trade in this economically and politically crucial region. In mid-1979 Hong Kong was undergoing a migrant crisis: laws within the territory were making it increasingly feasible for those mainland Chinese who had the money to pay people smugglers to transport them in speedboats onto Hong Kong island and escape arrest. The existing Royal Naval presence, five 'Ton' class minesweepers converted into patrol vessels, were too slow to catch such fast boats, whilst the Hong Kong police did not yet have fast enough craft themselves or sufficient helicopters. As a result, the Navy offered a fast patrol craft, HMS *Scimitar*, and two rather elderly hovercraft, to aid the civil authorities. *Scimitar* was manned with crews on a six-monthly rotation from the United Kingdom, but quite soon the people smugglers responded with 50-knot craft that the Royal Navy vessel could not always reliably catch. Difficulties with the crew rotation system, combined with a decision by the territory's Executive Council to invest in additional helicopters for the police resulted in *Scimitar*'s withdrawal in December 1980.[32] The two hovercraft, *P236* and *P237*, were more successful: they were able to operate in the shallows around Hong Kong's many small islands and inlets and catch migrants who had been set down on otherwise hard-to-reach beaches and shorelines. However, their age and the high levels of maintenance required meant that by January 1982 *P237* was beyond economical repair, and *P236* was withdrawn from service a few months later. They were scrapped locally without replacement: changes to Hong Kong's migration laws had slowed the flow of migrants from the mainland, and the new problem was 'boat people' from Vietnam, which hovercraft were much less suited to interdict. Police helicopters and light craft, supported by the five 'Ton' class, took their place.[33]

The Gulf and Establishing the Armilla Patrol

On 22 September 1980, Iraqi forces invaded Iran: it was an opportunistic attack on a new and fragile revolutionary regime, and had been undertaken with the aim to regain Iraq's control of the Shatt Al 'Arab and therefore its sea access to the Persian Gulf, as well as bolster Saddam Hussein's credibility in the Arab world.[34] Despite some initial gains in the first days of fighting, the Iranians proved tenacious in the defence of their homeland and the war would eventually last for eight years and end in a bloody stalemate. However, the first few weeks of fighting saw Iranian raids on Iraqi offshore oil installations and the blocking of the Shatt Al 'Arab. On 22 November 1980 the Iranian regime declared a blockade on Iraq and ordered that all ships that passed within 12 nautical miles of the Iranian coast and its islands to the west of the Straits of Hormuz would be liable to attack.[35]

The United States began to prepare a naval force to protect US-flagged and operated vessels, and President Carter asked Margaret Thatcher for the British to provide a naval presence in the Gulf to protect its own vessels.[36] Given the leading role that British companies played in the oil industry, and the nature of the request from Britain's closest ally, this was an offer that was almost impossible for the government to refuse, despite concerns from civil servants at the Ministry of Defence that this could become an open-ended and long-running commitment.[37] The destroyer HMS *Coventry*, then taking part in the 1980 Group Deployment, was detached with RFA *Olwen* and arrived on 7 October. A week later, she was joined by the frigate HMS *Alacrity* which had also been detached from the same deployment. From this point onwards, a rotating deployment of two warships, usually one frigate and one destroyer, would be maintained until the end of the Iran-Iraq War. In 1980 the role of this small unit was to maintain a British presence in the region and provide assistance to British merchant ships in the Persian Gulf and Gulf of Oman. The patrol would focus on the eastern side of the Straits of Hormuz and remain 12 nautical miles away from the Iranian coast. The rules of engagement were highly restricted, with firing in self-defence only permitted once efforts had been made to provide a warning to the firing vessel or aircraft. Fire-control radars could not be locked onto Iranian or Iraqi targets and no forms of illumination (searchlights or star shells) could be used. These rules were more restrictive than the US rules of engagement but less so than those of France and proved adequate in the first years of the patrol.[38] Operation 'Armilla', as the deployment was named from November 1980, demonstrated the role that naval power could play in support of British diplomacy and trade in situations outside war, but had little impact on defence policy-making. In the last months of 1980 the operation seemed no more than a small deployment of warships, of an unknown but probably short-lived duration, with a severely constrained remit and rules of engagement. In these early days of Operation 'Armilla' the patrol was quiet and uneventful with no contact with Iranian forces aside from occasional overflights by Iranian maritime patrol aircraft. Captain Peter Coward, *Coventry*'s commanding officer, noted that much effort was made to make his ship's weapon systems permanently ready at 30 minutes notice as required and that 'recreational banyans' – in effect ships' picnics ashore – in Oman were an important part of adding interest to what must have been a monotonous and tiring deployment. The ship was almost constantly shadowed by a Soviet 'Krivak' class frigate when on patrol, a reflection of the now significant presence of Soviet naval vessels in the Indian Ocean.[39]

Reforming the Structure of the Fleet
The squadron structure for Royal Navy frigates and destroyers was also modified during 1980 and 1981. From the mid-1960s, frigate squadrons had

consisted of an eclectic mix of ships, thus ensuring that when they deployed together they would make a balanced force. This was most in evidence on the Group Deployments after 1973, which aimed to have a single squadron at its core. By 1979 it was becoming clear that administratively this arrangement was proving difficult to justify as each squadron was having to manage an increasingly wide array of spares and other equipment, and squadron Captains were having to understand and manage a diverse range of ships. Significantly, ships were now generally being deployed on an ad hoc basis, with vessels from different squadrons being brought together – both for the most recent group deployments and for new tasks such as for Operation 'Armilla' – rather than as whole squadrons. Therefore, the old mixed-squadron system was replaced by one in which a squadron now contained only ships of one class: for example, all Type 21 frigates were placed together in the 4th Frigate Squadron.[40] The reform acknowledged that, as the Royal Navy shrank and its deployments became smaller, squadrons were now primarily administrative rather than operational formations. However, there were still benefits to retaining squadron-leading ships, commanded by full Captains, as they provided a cadre of seagoing senior commanding officers who had the experience and rank to take command of ad hoc formations at short-notice. This would prove increasingly important as the large but ageing *Tiger* class cruisers and 'County' class destroyers, which were invariably commanded by Captains, were withdrawn from service as they had previously been natural choices for task-group leadership.

With the withdrawal from service of HMS *Ark Royal* and the disbanding of NATO Strike Fleet 2, of which she had been the centrepiece, another but more minor structural change was made to the Fleet. The Flag Officer Carriers and Amphibious Ships ('FOCAS') was renamed Flag Officer Third Flotilla ('FOF3') in January 1979. The new FOF3 essentially retained the role of his predecessor but without any responsibility for a carrier strike group. As the new *Invincible* class cruisers entered service they came under his operational command, as did the remaining amphibious forces, and a number of other vessels within the surface fleet that did not easily fit within the squadron structures of FOF1 and FOF2. This revised structure would remain in place to the end of the Cold War and ensured that the Navy retained three operational 2 star commanders available for task force command.[41]

Air Defence of the Fleet

Aircraft
With the withdrawal of *Ark Royal,* the main capability for the long-range air defence aircraft of the fleet rested with those RAF Phantom and Lightning air defence aircraft allocated to Supreme Commander Atlantic, which in practice

would mean their operational control in exercises and warfare by the Royal Navy four-star admiral acting as CINCEASTLANT. During the 1980s it was expected that these Phantoms and Lightnings would be replaced by the new Tornado F2 fighter variant. The Phantom and Tornado were formidable aircraft, but there were a number of limitations to their effectiveness. The first and most important was force size: only thirty Tornados were to be allocated to SACLANT (and therefore under CINCEASTLANT's control), which as was seen in Chapter 8 given the distance from their bases to the likely theatres of operations, would mean that there only be enough to provide combat air patrols for Royal Navy surface forces operating along the GIUK gap on 'barrier patrols', *or* one naval task group operating in the Eastern Atlantic. The force could not do both activities. In addition, tactical control would be exercised from CINCEASTLANT's command in Northwood and not from the task group commander in theatre which could prove difficult to manage in a rapidly evolving tactical situation, which given the distances involved, the ability for additional back-up air defence aircraft to be called upon at short-notice was minimal.[42] Finally, the RAF's air defence force was jointly responsible for air defence of the United Kingdom and that of the Royal Navy's surface fleet, with both SACLANT and SACEUR having a call on these aircraft. The Air Force Board was frank that it had not tested how to prioritise SACLANT with SACEUR/national air defence taskings in a simulated crisis, but did not seem willing to test this, beyond a more general assessment that UK defence and the Central European front were a higher priority than its maritime role.[43]

The 1975 Size and Shape paper had therefore argued in favour of purchasing additional Sea Harriers to fill this gap but faced with a constrained budgetary environment throughout the second half of the 1970s, the Navy Department was only able to procure another ten to make a total of thirty-four.[44] In mid-1979 and with the advent of a new government, the Naval Staff pushed again. It argued that with thirty-four Sea Harriers it could only provide air groups of five aircraft each, for two of the three *Invincible* class cruisers. The argument in favour of thirteen additional aircraft was couched in terms of reconnaissance and dealing with shadowing or targeting aircraft rather than facing supersonic Soviet bomber forces in imitation of the original justification for the initial Sea Harrier order. The Minister of State for Defence Procurement, Lord Trenchard, was unconvinced of the arguments in favour of an additional purchase, arguing instead for additional pilots rather than aircraft and questioning why thirty-four aircraft could only support such a small number of aircraft embarked on ships. As before, the Admiralty Board placed such importance on this new additional Harrier purchase that it was classed as the Navy's second-highest priority for funding after nuclear submarines in 1979. Despite this, the Minister continued to block their purchase and he was also sceptical of the Navy's request for early research work into a Harrier replacement, preferring that they take part in the RAF's Harrier replacement programme. In mid-1980 the Naval Staff would attempt again to secure procurement, but with economies being forced on defence spending again, this stood little chance.[45] The inability to procure additional Harriers opened up the question of the need for a third *Invincible* class cruiser. Why was it required if only two Harrier air groups could be formed for this class of three ships?

Electronic Warfare
One element of fleet air defence that had received greater investment as the end of the fleet carrier capability approached was 'electronic warfare'. During April and May 1979 the first trials in the English Channel were undertaken of what at first glance seems an obscure and relatively unimportant system which was categorised under the innocuous-sounding title of 'electronic support measures': the UAA-1 passive intercept. UAA-1, which had been codenamed Abbeyhill during development, was in fact one of the most important technological developments for the Royal Navy in the late 1970s and 1980s. UAA-1 was a 'passive' detection system that could detect radar waves at a much greater distance than any conventional radar. Normal radar depends upon sending radar waves out and then receiving those that reflect off an object: the waves therefore have to travel twice the distance from the radar emitter to the object. Passive intercepts receive radar waves that have only travelled one way, so the amount of signal dissipation is half that for active radar. It is the equivalent of the distance one can see at night when using a torch in a field, compared to the distance away one can see someone else using a torch in that field.[46] In addition, use could also be made of the scatter of radar waves reflecting off the ionosphere in the upper atmosphere to further increase the range of such intercepts.[47] Standard passive intercepts could detect radar waves up to four times further than radar could detect objects, whilst effective use of ionosphere scatter could increase this range even further. This detection can serve two purposes: first, the early warning of an enemy, through detecting its radar on ships, aircraft or missiles and providing a bearing (within a set margin of error); and second, the building up of a picture of radar activity, including the classification of different radar wave emitters including frequency and pulse width, thus building up a library to allow for rapid identification in an early warning situation. Given the potential for long-range detection, intercept systems like UAA-1 could provide early forewarning of a possible threat. NATO navies rarely used such passive intercepts to guide weapons, but they did enable analysis and assessment of incoming threats to provide more time for an effective response.[48] Passive intercept kits had been fitted to naval vessels for some time, but the existing UA8/9 'Porker' set was an early

1960s-vintage analogue system that required the operator to manually match up the detected waves with a 'library' of stored radar signatures; this could be time-consuming when every second counted in a potential engagement. UAA-1 on the other hand was a digital system that undertook the measurement of waves and part of the subsequent matching automatically. Developed by Mullard Research Laboratories, a British electronics company, the system was world-leading when introduced, with US and other competitors taking some years to bring their own versions into service.[49]

UAA-1 provided a revolutionary increase in capability. Not only did it enable detection in a wider range of the spectrum but it also had a direction-finding capability much more accurate than its predecessor. UAA-1 was trial fitted to three destroyers and frigates between 1979 and 1980, with the destroyer HMS *Bristol* undertaking the first sets of trials. During trials in the Channel, *Bristol*'s UAA-1 set detected a US F-111 bomber over 100 miles away, far beyond the line of sight and radar range and she could detect radar signals with UAA-1 more than ten minutes before her long-range radar set (the Type 965 AKE-II). This was a considerable improvement on the old UA8/9 system. The new system seemed almost to be too sensitive, sometimes suffering from much 'background clutter' particularly in the I band area most often used by commercial maritime traffic.[50] However, the trials were still a considerable success, and Abbeyhill would prove its worth during the Falklands conflict three years later.

Improving Sea Dart and the Type 42 Destroyer

The new passive intercept technology provided a new means of detecting enemy targets from a much greater distance than hitherto, but those targets still needed to be destroyed or neutralised: jammers and decoys – the other elements of the electronic warfare arsenal – could only provide a part of the answer. With no additional Harriers nor any likely additions to the land-based air defence force, much therefore depended upon guided missile defence against the Soviet cruise missile threat. With the decision to end any further improvements to the obsolescent and under-performing Sea Slug missile system in 1973, the medium-range missile defence of the fleet now depended solely on the Sea Dart system.[51] Sea Dart was a much more capable system than Sea Slug and could deal with crossing targets and supersonic missiles, but the latest generation of Soviet air-launched cruise missiles were faster and were likely to be launched in much greater numbers, risking overwhelming the Type 42, with its small magazine, limited lines of engagement and known problems dealing with sea-skimming missiles. The 1975 Size and Shape paper had envisaged the procurement of either very large numbers of additional Sea Dart ships or smaller numbers of 'double-ended' Sea Dart ships armed with two such systems. In the absence of any additional Sea Harrier orders, the next generation of air defence destroyer would play an even greater role in fleet air defence.

A series of Naval Staff Targets were therefore issued in 1976–7 to improve every aspect of the Sea Dart and its launching system: an improved 'Sea Dart Mark II' missile, a new guided missile system (GWS 31), a new tactical command system (CACS), and a new air-search radar, the Type 1030. The Fleet Requirements Committee sought to bring these new systems into service during the 1980s and 1990s in three ways: in mid-life refits to the existing Type 42 destroyers, in new batches of the Type 42, and then finally in a new destroyer design, the Type 43. As development work began on the new systems and missile, it quickly became clear that none would be ready for the planned mid-life refit start date for the first of class, HMS *Sheffield*, which was due to start in 1983. Instead, her electronic warfare capabilities would be augmented. Plans to fit the Sea Wolf point defence missile system in place of her forward 4.5in gun were also dropped on cost and technical grounds.[52] Even these more modest improvements were opposed by those assessing operational requirements across defence: by August 1980 the Assistant Chief Scientific Adviser (Studies) was arguing against any form of modernisation for what he saw as a an expensive class with limited capabilities.[53] It therefore seemed possible that the first six Type 42s would not be modernised at all.

From the seventh Type 42 destroyer onwards, some incremental changes had been made for the second batch of ships, including an updating of the ADAWS tactical command system and the fitting of the Type 1022 air-search radar as an interim replacement radar until the Type 1030 was ready (in the event it never appeared), but it was increasingly clear that the basic Type 42 was just too small for any major additions of capability.[54] In 1976, a 'simple redesign' of the Type 42 was proposed for the eleventh ship onwards to improve seakeeping and provide capacity for updates in the future. The ship's length would be increased by 42ft and the beam by 2ft, with ship-launched torpedoes, decoys and sonar updated, with the operations room re-arranged. Additional costs were calculated to be minimal, only £2 million more than a Batch 2 Type 42 in 1976 prices.[55] It is likely that any more radical (and expensive) improvements would not have been approved in the financially constrained environment of the late 1970s. A fourth batch for the fifteenth to eighteenth vessels was proposed at one point, utilising the lengthened hull to increase air defence capabilities. One option involved fitting the Sea Wolf point defence missile system.[56] Another would have replaced the 4.5in gun with a second twin-arm Sea Dart launcher, doubling the number of missiles carried.[57] In the event it was decided to bring forward the construction of the more capable successor class, the Type 43: the seventeenth to eighteenth vessels were cancelled and it was not deemed worthwhile designing a fourth batch just for two ships, and the fifteenth and sixteenth vessels transferred to the third batch equipment fit.

The Type 43 Destroyer

Early sketch designs of the new Type 43 destroyer proposed a large 6,000-ton double-ended Sea Dart ship, also armed with Sea Wolf and Exocet missile systems, and a possible helicopter landing pad for either a light or medium helicopter in the centre of the ship. The Fleet Requirements Committee provisionally agreed to these characteristics during discussions between 1977 and early 1979.[58] However, the earlier focus on improved air defence capabilities was changed following an Admiralty Board decision in early 1979 to re-focus the shipbuilding programme towards anti-submarine capabilities as intelligence pointed to the Soviet construction of new and more capable nuclear submarine classes such as the 'Mike', 'Sierra' and 'Akula' designs. It was also becoming clear that the feared 'Backfire' bomber could also launch nuclear-tipped anti-ship cruise missiles. To counter this, NATO task groups would be more likely to operate in dispersed formations to lessen the effect of such nuclear attacks. In addition, the need for the new towed-array frigates to operate on the edges of a task groups operating area to provide them with manoeuvring room for their arrays, meant that the air defence umbrella provided by both the existing Sea Dart and Sea Dart Mark II would be too small to protect such a widely spaced force.[59] Finally, despite the cancellation of the original version of the 'stretched Ikara' anti-submarine missile system in 1977, there had been strong lobbying within the Naval Staff to resurrect the system and equally strong lobbying to have this new version of Ikara on the Type 43, with the new Ikara variant being inaccurately described as interchangeable with an anti-submarine helicopter despite their very different requirements, in terms of ship space, electronic equipment and operations room requirements.[60] The Deputy Director of Naval Construction at the time, David Brown, has stated that a version of the ship with the sophisticated US Aegis air defence system was informally considered at one point during the design process.[61] The Type 43 would have had a much more effective air defence capability with Aegis and its associated Standard missiles than GWS 30 and double-ended Sea Dart, and this would have provided the most plausible answer to the 'Backfire' threat. However, it would have been as expensive, if not more so, than the planned Type 43 programme – it is difficult to imagine any more than four or five being built – and would have almost certainly required a wholesale change towards the US-built Standard missile system and its associated sensors and tactical command and control. Given that these powerful ships would have become the centrepiece of the Royal Navy's air defence capability it would have left British-designed Sea Dart looking irrelevant, and raised the possibility of the whole class of Type 42s either being rapidly converted into US Standard missile firing ships or withdrawn from service early. British Aerospace, as well as various British sensor and electronics contractors such as Marconi and Ferranti, would have lost out significantly. The shift was probably too radical to consider at the time and was not taken any further, but it poses an interesting counter-factual and would have left the Royal Navy's surface fleet much less vulnerable to both 'Backfire' bombers and critics within the Ministry.

When the Fleet Requirements Committee met in May 1979 to approve the Type 43 design, it was given a range of equipment options, and instead of the heavily-armed air defence option that it had indicated as its preference in previous meetings, its members chose a 'general purpose' variant armed with only one GWS 31 Sea Dart launcher (with a magazine of thirty-two missiles) and a resurrected stretched Ikara anti-submarine missile system instead of a helicopter. The ship would also have multiple Sea Wolf point defence missile systems. Delays with the new CACS command system would mean that the first Batch of the Type 43s would be fitted with the legacy ADAWS system. As further design work was undertaken, the size of the ship increased to around 8,000 tons, and a towed-array sonar was also fitted for good measure.[62] The resulting ship was deeply unsatisfactory, costing as much as a nuclear-powered fleet submarine, and tactically unsound: the Sea Dart system implied a ship at the centre of a task group operating at a steady fleet speed to best facilitate the air defence of high-value units, whilst a towed-array implied a ship operating at the edge of a task group, shifting from slow running to reduce cavitation whilst its towed-array was in use, to fast 'catch-ups' in order to keep in contact with its task group. Tactical doctrine with regard to Ikara, as it had been developed since the mid-1970s, had emphasised placing Ikara-armed ships to the rear or front of a task group and giving them the freedom to manoeuvre at speed in order to improve launch angles for the Ikara missile system at short-notice.[63] The Type 43 variant chosen by the Fleet Requirements Committee would therefore have been split three ways in its tactical deployment and would have either made use of none of its three core capabilities well, or focussed on one to the detriment of the other two. In addition, without a helicopter, the ship would be unable to prosecute any of its own towed-array contacts. A towed-array could detect and perhaps classify a target, but except at short-ranges it was unlikely to provide sufficient information on its exact position to allow torpedoes to be fired: the dipping sonar, sonobuoys or magnetic anomaly detector of a helicopter was ideally suited to do this. In addition, Ikara (even in its planned 'Super-Ikara' form armed with Stingray torpedoes) was too short-range a system to reach towed-array contacts that could be 50 to 100 nautical miles away – Ikara's range was only ten nautical miles. The cancellation of Sea Dart Mark II in April 1980 not only left a question-mark over the GWS 31 system as well, it also begged the question of the capability being gained with the Type 43 for such a large expenditure. Even with the most optimistic financial estimates it was difficult to imagine the Navy being able to afford not only a nuclear submarine production line into the 1980s but also both a frigate and a large destroyer production line as well.

The Type 44 Destroyer
Only a few months after the 'general purpose' Type 43 variant had been chosen, the Vice Chief of the Naval Staff was already having doubts about the ineffective giant that he had approved, pondering that the £2.3 billion expected cost of procuring a class could be better spent on maritime air defence Tornados for the RAF, or that the existing Type 42 programme should continue instead.[64] The most senior civil servant in the Navy Department had wider concerns about the cost of the ship distorting the rest of the shipbuilding programme.[65] It was therefore not surprising that the Type 43 was cancelled as part of a round of procurement reductions in 1980, but not before the design had been radically re-cast again. This time, the ship was much reduced in size to around 4,500 tons, but with much the same capabilities crammed onto the modified hull of a Batch 2 Type 22 frigate. The rationale for this radical change was the lack of design staff in the Ship Department, and therefore the need to adopt a variant of an existing warship type so that as much of the detailed design work as possible could be passed to the lead shipbuilder.[66] The vessel was now even more implausible as a viable warship, but because this shift was not generally known outside the Navy Department and the Procurement Executive's Sea Systems Controllerate, following the 'cancellation' of the Type 43 it could be presented as a new, cheaper, ship: the all-new Type 44. This fooled no one: a senior defence scientist was so dismayed by the progress of the Type 43/Type 44 designs that he was adamant that 'the Navy Department must not be allowed to build it'.[67] A senior naval staff officer working in the central Staffs warned that the Type 44 concept did not make sense to those in the centre, and wondered aloud whether air defence destroyers were now affordable or even necessary, given the need to disperse task groups widely to avoid nuclear weapons.[68] The Assistant Chief Scientific Adviser (P) raised a more fundamental point: 'the UK element of the European maritime force lacks the ability to defend itself (or other units) adequately' which therefore placed the whole policy of operating any surface naval forces within range of Soviet strike aircraft in question.[69] The baleful progress of the Type 43 and Type 44 design development had now become so damaging that the concept of air defence destroyers was now being questioned across important portions

of the Ministry. Predictably, the Type 44 too would quickly grow in size and cost, and also be cancelled within months.

If the Naval Staff was incapable of approving a warship that was tactically sensible, let alone affordable, during the closing months of the 1970s, it did not suggest that it would be well-placed to deal with the sort of searching questioning of underlying assumptions and concepts that would be expected during a defence review. The Naval Staff itself was in flux during these years: a four-year period during which former Fleet Air Arm officers had held the crucial post of Vice Chief of the Naval Staff came to an end in 1977, when a surface fleet officer, Vice Admiral Morton, took over the role.[70] Submariners were rising in prominence across the Navy and they generally had a very different perspective on the role of the surface fleet from either former flyers or surface fleet officers. No coherent single perspective on the future and role of the surface fleet was evident, and short-sighted lobbying on behalf of single systems such as stretched Ikara, helped to up-end the viability of the only plausible ship design (albeit painfully expensive: probably no more than four to six could ever have been afforded) that would have provided organic air defence in the absence of a significant naval air arm.

Anti-Submarine and General-Purpose Ships

The Type 22 Frigate

May 1979 saw the commissioning of HMS *Broadsword*, the first Type 22 frigate. At 4,500 tonnes she was as large as a Type 42 destroyer and was the first major warship built for the Royal Navy, aside from aircraft carriers and amphibious vessels, not to have a medium-gun armament. As was seen in Chapter 7, the design gestation of *Broadsword* had been long and painful and it could be argued that despite her considerable sophistication compared to previous frigates, she was rushing towards obsolescence. Her design had been frozen just before it became clear that large anti-submarine helicopters such as the Sea King would be much more effective at detecting and destroying submarines than smaller Lynx, and two to three years before it also became apparent that towed-array sonars would be the most important submarine detection sensor in the 1980s. *Broadsword* was large, but she neither had a hangar large enough for a Sea King, nor was she fitted with towed-array. Despite this, a double hangar for two Lynx helicopters did provide a dramatic increase in capability over the aged Wasp helicopter that had been operated in older frigates. The Lynx, an Anglo-French design, had much greater range, speed, payload and manoeuvrability than her predecessor and as such really began to fulfil the real potential of ship-based maritime helicopters. Where the Wasp had no anti-submarine detection capability and depended upon the sonar of her parent ship and could only fly for a few minutes when armed with an anti-submarine torpedo, the Lynx was not restricted in this way and in time would operate devices that had been limited to maritime patrol aircraft, such as magnetic anomaly detectors, although the option to operate sonobuoys was never taken up. Whilst the Lynx was not as an effective submarine hunter as the Sea King, it was, however, a fast, manoeuvrable and extremely capable predator of fast attack craft, being armed by the new Sea Skua light anti-ship missile system, which would prove its worth in the Falklands conflict of 1982 and the Gulf War of 1990–1.[71] *Broadsword* was also armed with the Sea Wolf point defence missile system, the successor to Sea Cat and a much more sophisticated weapon optimised for the short-range interception of anti-ship cruise missiles. Four ships were built to the original design. *Broadsword* was therefore a highly-capable warship and a substantial step up from the *Leander*s and Type 21s that had preceded, but she had serious limitations as an anti-submarine platform that needed to be rectified. The fifth ship onwards would therefore be fitted with a towed-array, the new Type 2050 bow sonar, as well as the Outboard surveillance system discussed in the preceding chapter. This resulted in the Batch 2 design, which stretched the hull amidships abaft the bridge to fit the computer processing and analysis elements of Outboard. The new, thinner cabled, Type 2031Z towed-array needed less deck space than the versions fitted to *Lowestoft* and the *Leander*s, so could be deployed from underneath the helicopter flight deck. However, orders were not forthcoming for the first ships of this new batch until a few days before 1979 General Election.[72]

Future Frigates and 'Garage Ships'

If the plans for new air defence ships were collapsing in on themselves, the parallel planning for the next generation of anti-submarine ships to succeed the Type 22s was proceeding little better. The 1975 Concept of Operations had opened up the possibility of a small number of large and capable anti-submarine fleet escorts and it was in this direction that conceptual work initially focussed. By April 1978 the Long Term Costing Assumptions put together by the Navy Department envisaged a third batch of four Type 22s, reverting to the Batch 1 hull-size but armed with an updated version of the Sea Wolf missile system. This would then be followed by a Type 23 class of very large anti-submarine frigates whose equipment and armament were still to be determined but would share a hull with the large Type 43 destroyer.[73] The following year initial plans had changed again, with a Type 22 class extending to twenty-two ships, the later vessels using the lengthened Batch 2 hull and fitted with the new Link 16 communications system, updated Sea Wolf, a successor missile to Exocet and a greater capacity for dual helicopter operations.

This class would then be succeeded by a Type 23 with similar capabilities to these later Type 22s but operating the Sea King replacement helicopter instead of two Lynx aircraft.[74] These assumptions for later Type 22s and larger Type 23s in both 1978 and 1979 were unfeasibly optimistic with regard to what could actually be afforded in the timescales envisaged. Given the considerable cost of such ships whilst the hugely expensive *Swiftsure* and *Trafalgar* nuclear submarine and Type 43 programmes would also be proceeding, it has to be wondered how realistic the cost estimates for such vessels were, or whether the Naval Staff deliberately padded out these Assumptions in the hope that at least parts of the programme would survive the inevitable return to budgetary reality. By May 1980 all mention of additional batches of the Type 22 or any Type 23 design had disappeared from the Long Term Costing Assumptions, as all three services were subjected to cost control measures and economies and the Naval Staff was forced to confront what could realistically be afforded.[75]

In parallel with the Type 22 programme and the projected Type 23, considerable thought and conceptual work went into vessels that were much more in the spirit of the 1975 Concept: large 'garage ships' designed to operate large anti-submarine helicopters, and possibly even Harriers, to increase the number of organic aircraft available to a RN task group. The request for work on this concept had originally come in 1977 from Vice Admiral Lygo, the outgoing Vice Chief of the Naval Staff. It took some time to understand exactly how such a ship would operate. After rejecting a ship working alongside an *Invincible* class cruiser as an additional aircraft platform (which would have tied up a large and expensive ship in an operationally limited role), and a vessel to lead its own anti-submarine task group (which would duplicate the role of the *Invincible* class itself) the role of convoy escort was selected. Recent Maritime Tactical School studies had made clear that at least four or five convoy escort/support groups would be needed in a situation of conflict or high tension, but that many major ships, including the three *Invincible*s, would be tied up leading anti-submarine task groups, supporting the NATO Strike Fleet or escorting amphibious forces to Norway. A number of utility aircraft carriers could instead act as the core of a convoy escort group, consisting of one such ship, a number of basic towed-array frigates (a frigate concept that was beginning to evolve into the new, 'small', Type 23) and one Type 22 Batch 2 Outboard frigate as a communications and sensors platform.[76]

Four options were put to the Fleet Requirements Committee in May 1979. All were single-screw, 22-knot diesel-powered ships, displaced 21,000 to 25,500 tonnes, all could undertake refuelling of other ships with 10,000 tonnes of fuel oil (partly negating the need for an accompanying RFA), and ranged from a ship capable of operating nine Sea King helicopters from a large three spot flight deck aft, to the most expensive option, a vessel with a through deck, two aircraft lifts and hangar space for nine Sea Kings and six Harriers. Costs, at 1978 prices, were between £50 million to £150 million excluding VAT, first of class costs, stores and aircraft purchases. By comparison, a Type 22 Batch 2 frigate cost between £75–80 million and an *Invincible* class £170–180 million. Costs were kept down through the propulsion choice and keeping aircraft direction and communications capabilities to RFA standards (at least for three of the four options). The effect of relatively noisy diesels was partly mitigated by the single screw and the fitting of the 'masker' noise-reduction system. Increasing the speed to 26 knots would add £20 million to the cost: more expensive gas turbines would then be necessary as fast diesels that would provide the necessary speed could not operate effectively below 12 knots. Including the Sea Wolf point defence system would add another £12.5 million, whilst increasing aircraft direction capabilities to *Invincible* class standards would add a further £15–20 million. The committee decided not to include a Harrier capability, although it was acknowledged that the wide spacing of naval forces due to the risk of tactical nuclear attack meant that Sea Harriers were preferable to Sea Dart for area air defence, because for much of the time Trans-Atlantic convoys would be outside Soviet bomber range. The focus therefore lay with anti-submarine capability, where a large anti-submarine helicopter such as the Sea King, because of its range and its ability to counter-attack quickly after an attack, was acknowledged as one of the most effective ways of destroying submarines. Four such helicopters were necessary to provide one on station at all times over a five-day period, so the committee agreed that the minimum number of helicopters should be twelve. They accepted the second of the four options, the cheapest of the through-deck ships and agreed to the fitting of Sea Wolf. There was some discussion of squeezing four such ships into the building programme between the fifteenth Type 42 and first Type 43, whilst cancelling the eleventh to fourteenth Type 22s. In the event, no decision was made on the 'garage ship's' place in the programme but design work was ordered with a view to raising a Naval Staff Target and reporting on the development of studies in a year's time.[77]

A year later however, and the environment for building helicopter carriers was completely different: as will be seen in the next chapter, the defence budget was under severe pressure, and when the garage ship was compared to the planned new class of 'one-stop' replenishment-oilers which would operate with both task groups and convoy escorts, and could accommodate four large helicopters, it looked like an expensive luxury. The garage ship was not formally cancelled, but it was placed as a lower priority in the programme than the one stop ships.[78] Through 1980 and 1981 the one-stop ship, which eventually became the *Fort Victoria* class, gained some of the attributes of the garage ship, not least a role as the centre of a small anti-submarine force and self-defence missiles in the form of Sea Wolf, but the vessel never approached the garage ship's helicopter capacity of twelve. The garage ship was in some ways a lost opportunity, but the Naval Staff never seems to have fully grasped that this type of ship was a replacement for the large anti-submarine frigate, rather than an augmentation to the existing escort force. With a frigate programme potentially clogged with six large Outboard-equipped intelligence gatherers whose cancellation would have caused diplomatic problems with the United States, in retrospect it is unsurprising that the garage ship could not be fitted into an already overheating shipbuilding programme.

Saving the Shipbuilding Industry: the Type 24 Frigate
If the appearance in service of the first Type 22 heralded the arrival of the largest frigate ever produced for the Royal Navy, the slow collapse of the British shipbuilding industry threatened to put at risk the Navy's plans for warship construction into the 1980s. From the perspective of the Naval Staff, this threat came not from the risk of no ships being built at all, but instead from the construction of warships that the yards desperately needed to construct, but that the Royal Navy did not want.

It was clear within government by the middle of 1978 that the British shipbuilding industry, which employed nearly 90,000 workers, was in rapid and terminal decline. Nearly all the industry had been nationalised in 1977, the aim being to save it, partly through 'rationalisation' and partly by enabling best practice from the better yards to feed into those in the most difficulty. In the event, the same year saw a 'perfect storm' as new and efficient yards in South Korea and Japan began building ships just as a glut of unused shipping was available on the market in the aftermath of the Oil Crisis.[79] A scarcity of orders for merchant shipping meant that desperate yards underbid for contracts, often with subsidies from government, and could not make a profit on the work, forcing them back to government for more subsidies, thus creating an expensive death spiral for shipbuilding.[80] The publicly-owned company running the industry, British Shipbuilders Corporation Ltd, proposed plans for a radical and rapid rationalisation of the industry, reducing building capacity by one-third, closing a number of the least efficient yards and making over 12,000 shipyard workers redundant in less than two years. Even then, the management of British Shipbuilders stated that £456 million would be needed to support this transition, and thereafter an annual subsidy of between £100 million and £150 million a year would be needed for at least the next half decade.[81]

For a minority Labour government, backed by trade-union support and sustained in power largely by the votes of the unionised working classes, such radical surgery accompanied by continued heavy subsidies was impossible to countenance, especially with a general election likely in the next 12 months. Gerald Kaufman, the Minister of State at the Department of Industry, was made chairman of a Cabinet committee specifically established to find ways of keeping shipbuilding afloat, at least until the next election. His committee began by commissioning a survey of the situation. Its findings were stark and it was summarised by Kaufman and the Cabinet Secretary for the Prime Minister: 'the report makes for gloomy reading. The world shipping market has slumped, and it's getting worse ... Even without this, the prospects for the United Kingdom industry would be grim. Management has been poor, and productivity dreadful ... To make matters worse, we have tended to be best at building simple types of merchant ships which makes us especially vulnerable to competition from new entrants into the business.'[82] Kaufman's committee set to work trying to help secure orders for British shipyards, with varying levels of success, from the Polish, Tunisian and Pakistani governments.[83] The next, and most desperate, step was to provide British government orders for the yards. A number of the endangered yards were 'mixed builders', able to construct warships as well as merchant vessels: these included Cammell Laird and Swan Hunter. Eric Varley, Kaufman's boss and the Secretary of State for Industry, then began lobbying the Ministry of Defence to build additional ships in its programme for 1978 and 1979, including additional Logistic Landing Ships and survey ships. Both the Navy Department and the Ministry of Defence resisted these requests, not least because such vessels were not priorities, other more important parts of the Ministry's budget would go unfunded if they were built, and the manpower to operate them would not be available when they completed, resulting in other perfectly good ships having to be decommissioned.[84]

Another idea was even more radical, and although it was opposed by most of the Navy Department, it found an advocate in Admiral Clayton, the Controller of the Navy until early 1979 and the Admiralty Board member responsible for warship and weapons procurement. It was suggested that the Department of Industry fund the construction of four, possibly eight, frigates designed specifically for export sale to the navies of other countries. If the sales did not materialise, then the British government would buy the ships and incorporate them into the Royal Navy. It was believed that giving such vessels the imprimatur of Royal Navy operation would help overseas sales. This export frigate was designated the Type 24, despite no Staff Target or Staff Requirement having been set. The Yarrow and Vosper Thornycroft divisions of British Shipbuilders worked with the Ship Department to develop a design for building by the 'mixed yards' such as Cammell Laird. Warships optimised for export were not the type of vessels that the Royal Navy needed, their relatively cheap propulsion would be too noisy for anti-submarine work, many fittings, processes and applications ranging from paint to watertight subdivision and magazine safety would not meet Royal Navy standards, and the weapon and sensor fit might be economical and ostensibly impressive but not optimal for operations in the North Atlantic.[85] The Navy Department stalled when it received the jointly-developed sketch designs, and it is telling that the Type 24 never even went to the Fleet Requirements Committee: there was no requirement in the Fleet for such vessels.[86] The Secretary of State for Industry pushed harder, and in January 1979 he managed to persuade the Ministry of Defence to agree to order the 'long-lead' items for the first four Type 24 ships, with the Department of Industry paying. Eric Varley conceded that such items *might* have to be diverted to existing ship types if no orders came and the Type 24 design was not sufficiently developed to place orders, but he was confident that orders would in fact materialise from forthcoming defence sales visits to Canada, Australia and New Zealand in April.[87] In the event, and perhaps unsurprisingly, the visits were unsuccessful, and the Navy Department and Ministry of Defence continued to stall over the further development of the Type 24 design, making it impossible to place full orders for such ships.[88] With the general election a few days away, it is likely that the long-lead items – if they were ordered at all – were diverted to existing types, almost certainly the 13th and 14th Type 42 destroyers and the 5th and 6th Type 22 frigates, all of which were ordered on 25 April 1979, days before the general election.[89] These orders served to provide work for unionised shipyard workers, some of the Labour Party's core voters, just before the election.

The new Conservative government had much less interest in saving the shipbuilding industry, so the Navy Department, with Admiral Clayton having recently moved to a new role, stopped co-operation with the naval architects of British Shipbuilders and began developing a rival design, the Type 25, to demonstrate what could be procured for Royal Navy service at a similar price to the Type 24, which was expected to cost £56 million in early 1979 prices. The Type 25 was envisaged as a two-thirds of the Type 22 and would be optimised for North Atlantic anti-submarine operations and fitted with towed-array sonar. The Type 24 lingered on for a few more months, its design re-developed into the 'Type 24B' capable of operating towed-array, but now with expensive but quiet propulsion that would make the design difficult to sell overseas. By 1980 it was confirmed that the Royal Navy would not be building any Type 24 frigates, and although the design was unveiled at arms fairs that year by British Shipbuilders it attracted little interest and quickly disappeared from the company's sales brochures. The purpose of the Type 25 having been achieved, this design also slid away from view rapidly, although some of the design work undertaken did feed into studies for the newest version of the Type 22 successor, the new 'small' Type 23, as it began development at the end of 1980.[90] The Type 24 was a politically-driven act of desperation aimed at rebuilding a lost export market in British warships. It was skilfully if cynically undermined by the Navy Department, which managed to achieve orders for four ships it *did* want and might not otherwise have obtained. Meanwhile, the British shipbuilding industry continued on its descent towards general collapse.

Missiles and Torpedoes

The Tigerfish Torpedo
Providing the submarine service with an effective heavy homing torpedo for anti-ship warfare or the Soviet Union's largest submarines was proving especially difficult. As the growing force of nuclear-powered attack submarines was now the most capable arm of the Navy, this was becoming by the late 1970s a particular embarrassment.[91] After 15 years in development the Ondine Mk 24 Mod 0 heavy torpedo provisionally entered service in 1974. It only had an anti-submarine capability, but the modified Mod 1 variant approved for development in the same year could, in theory, be used against surface ships, attack stopped and silent targets, and operate at the greater depth of 1,450ft.

Unfortunately Ondine, later renamed Tigerfish, became a case study in project-management failure by the Admiralty Underwater Weapons Establishment. Subject to three internal reviews during the development of the torpedo, the last review, the Kiely Report, set out the main reasons for the prolonged development period and continued reliability problems. The most important reason was that AUWE had not grasped how complex the development of the torpedo would be. There had been precious little consolidated project management of the torpedo programme, with each section of AUWE operating in its own silo and communicating little with other areas. This often meant that individual parts and sub-systems might work well, but insufficient attention had been given to integrating these into the whole torpedo. The defence industry was used only as contractors for elements of the programme, there was no 'prime contractor' with responsibility for the whole development: that role was undertaken by default and inadequately by AUWE itself. As technical failures continued to manifest themselves with the torpedo, the individual departments within AUWE became increasingly defensive and compartmentalised – inclined to perfect their element of the programme, blame problems on elsewhere and hide issues from senior management. The decision to proceed with the Mod 1 variant after the Mod 0 variant had only just entered service meant that few lessons were learnt from trials with the Mod 0. The provisional approval of Mod 0 in 1974 in effect placed in service a torpedo that the Kiely report defined as no more than a 'working research vehicle'. Unfortunately, the approval of Mod 1 meant that too little attention was given to rectifying the problems with Mod 0 which had been put aboard the fleet's submarines as a nominally operational weapon system. The Mod 0 teams, seeing this variant as only a stopgap, began to be content to settle for a weapon that was at least somewhat better than the preceding and obsolete Mark 23 torpedo, whilst the Mod 1 teams considered their role merely a 'simple updating' of Mod 0 without an appreciation of the fundamental technical problems facing the earlier version. The development of Mod 1 was not helped by a 1977 revision of the staff requirement which added the fire-control equipment to the programme. In practice this meant that by 1982, after eight years of theoretically being 'in service', Tigerfish had extremely low-levels of user confidence and a failure rate 'as a tactical weapon system in excess of 70 per cent' rising to 80 per cent if all technical failures were included. Fire control problems were still being encountered and the torpedo discharge often failed with the weapon leaving the torpedo tube at the incorrect speed or the wrong attitude. 'Random failure amongst the hundreds of electronic, electro-mechanical and mechanical units in the torpedo' was still a regular event, and the guidance wire repeatedly entangled itself in the outboard torpedo dispenser. These failings also meant that it was proving very difficult to train operators: successful firings were rare, so as a result operator errors remained unusually high resulting in further failed tactical launches.[92]

The many problems of Tigerfish were eventually solved during the 1980s as proper project management was introduced and defence industry involvement increased, but the weapon still suffered from its relatively limited capabilities having been derived from an original 1959 operational requirement.[93] It had a maximum speed of 35 knots which was adequate for surface targets but meant that it would have had trouble catching up with Soviet attack submarines of the second and third generations. The need to develop a successor was apparent by 1980, and although both the Royal Navy and the Ministry of Defence's Operational Requirements Committee preferred to purchase the US Mk 48 torpedo, in late 1981 the Secretary of State approved the development by GEC/Marconi of a new torpedo later named Spearfish; the additional costs of this weapon over that of the Mk 48 being negotiated downwards in the first five years of development to meet Treasury five-year spending limits.[94] It entered service in 1992 and is still operational, much updated, with the Royal Navy today.

Anti-Ship Missiles
The threat from Soviet surface ships appeared to be growing in the late 1970s. The main long-range capability against such vessels was provided by the RAF's Buccaneer strike aircraft flying from bases in the United Kingdom, or from the strike aircraft of the US carriers in the NATO Atlantic Strike Fleet. The

main new Soviet warship types that appeared during much of the 1970s had not been armed with anti-ship missiles: the 'Kresta II' and 'Kara' class cruisers, and the 'Krivak' class frigates. However, this soon began to change. The large *Kiev* class ships, which entered service in 1975, were as much cruisers as they were aircraft carriers. Their unreliable Yak-38 'Forger' aircraft did not pose too much a threat to warships as their anti-ship missiles (the AS-7 'Kerry') only had a range of 10km, but the ships' battery of eight SS-N-12 'Sandbox' long-range anti-ship missiles did.[95] In the first years of the 1980s they would be joined by the *Slava* class cruisers and the huge *Kirov* class battlecruisers, the former armed with sixteen SS-N-12s and the latter with twenty new SS-N-19 'Shipwreck' long-range anti-ship missiles. The smaller *Sovremennyy* class destroyers would be armed with shorter-range SS-N-22 'Sunburn' anti-ship missiles.

Exocet, as described in Chapter 7, was entering the fleet in numbers, but two further and separate anti-ship missiles were in development or being procured. The first was US Sub-Harpoon, an anti-ship missile launched from a submerged submarine's torpedo tubes. This had been procured to provide the submarine force with a rapid response weapon against surface ships and helped fill an important gap in submarine capability given the ongoing issues with Tigerfish. The other contender was Sub-Martel, produced for Hawker Siddeley and a development of the aircraft-launched Martel anti-ship missile system. The submarine service preferred the US weapon system, which would be cheaper, available sooner and had less development risk. A contract to purchase Sub-Harpoon was therefore signed, entering service with the Royal Navy in 1982, five years after its introduction in the United States Navy.[96]

Sub-Harpoon was a logical choice from the stand-alone perspective of the submarine service but resulted in a situation where there were three separate anti-ship missiles systems in the Navy and RAF's inventory: Exocet aboard ships, Martel on the Buccaneer and Sub-Harpoon on submarines. The Anglo-French Martel was itself becoming obsolete, its television and data-link guidance version placing the Buccaneer aircraft in harm's way after missile launch and preventing a sea-skimming profile, whilst its radar-homing version had to be pre-selected to a specific frequency before launch and was only viable if the target's active radars were kept on. Hawker Siddeley, later merged into the nationalised British Aerospace in 1977, therefore began development work on what later became the Sea Eagle, a modified version of Martel with a radar homer and a sea-skimming profile, producing a missile somewhat like Exocet. The RAF, in setting out an Air Staff Target (AST 1226) for the Martel successor, soon agreed to the development of this missile.[97]

The Ministry of Defence therefore seemed to be little closer to any sense of commonality in anti-ship missiles as three would continue in service into the 1980s and beyond. An answer appeared to come from attempts within

NATO to produce a common anti-ship missile that could be launched from the surface of the sea, the air and from underwater. The Second Generation Anti-Ship Missile began a feasibility study within NATO under a British chair, with the aim of producing a weapon that might be procured across the Alliance with a production run of over 1,000 missiles, a range of 60 to 110 nautical miles and a sea-skimming approach with improved capabilities against electronic countermeasures. The United Kingdom, France and Germany were main backers and contributors at this stage. The rationale for British involvement was the fear of being left out: if the missile went ahead without UK involvement, it would have no influence over its development. In addition, the projected missile was the first collaborative project from NATO's Naval Armaments Group in what was hoped might be the first of many such joint ventures. Soon re-named the Anti-Ship Euro-Missile, development would be increasingly pushed further in the future with an in-service date shifting from 1985 to the early 1990s before the end of the 1970s.[98] In the event, the manufacturers of Harpoon and Exocet both continued development of improved versions of their established missiles – the Royal Navy hedging its bets by obtaining observer status on the development work for the latter – and the NATO anti-ship missile never saw the light of day, the British backing out in 1980 and its development being halted at the end of the Cold War.[99] All three services also kept a watching brief on the US development of the Tomahawk long-range cruise missile, in its non-nuclear anti-ship and land-attack elements, the Royal Navy professing some interest but arguing that without some form of over-the-horizon targeting system it would be little better than other missile systems in the anti-ship role, and even somewhat slower, despite its very long-range. Renewed interest in 1981 and a tri-service 'Staff Target' for a possible equivalent in British service did not result in orders, which were not eventually forthcoming until the mid-1990s after the 1990–1 Gulf War had shown the effectiveness of the missile in the land attack role.[100]

The Stingray Torpedo
Whilst the Tigerfish torpedo was designed to be fired by submarines, a new lightweight anti-submarine torpedo was desperately needed to replace the less-than-effective Mark 44 and Mark 46 torpedoes. Fired from aircraft and ships it was the main means by which submarines could be attacked effectively: however good sonars were, if the torpedo lacked the necessary capabilities, then Soviet nuclear submarines could only be threatened by NATO submarines, leaving surfaces forces largely defenceless. Development work had begun in the mid-1970s, and the progress had been good, but costs had rocketed, calling into question the future of the torpedo. The new Conservative government had to deal with the future of the weapon, and the issue was put

in front of a Cabinet committee specially convened for the purpose only a few days into the new administration. The MISC 2 committee, chaired by the Prime Minister, was being asked whether this torpedo project, which was supporting the employment of over 3,100 people at the defence company Marconi, should be cancelled. A Naval Staff Requirement had been issued in 1968, and a design contract was awarded in 1977 with the aim of producing a fast torpedo that could operate from a relatively shallow depth to extreme depths against new fast Soviet submarines. The Mark 44 and Mark 46 had a minimum operating depth of 60m and 90m respectively, whilst the Stingray could reportedly operate at a depth between 45m and 750m, the latter being believed to be the maximum of the fast Soviet 'Alfa' class hunter-killer submarines. However effective Stingray might potentially be, the development costs had spiralled in the two years since the design contract had been given to Marconi. Since 1977 planned development costs had increased by 45 per cent and production costs by 27 per cent, producing a total cost of £787.8 million in September 1978 prices. Despite options to cancel Stingray and adopt newer US torpedoes instead, Margaret Thatcher agreed to the continuation of the project, accepting the 'professional advice of the Chiefs of Staff' even if it meant significantly increased costs. In this early stage of her premiership, the Prime Minister was willing to defer to the Ministry of Defence in such matters much to the frustration of the Treasury and the Chancellor of the Exchequer.[101] Stingray would eventually enter service in 1983 and prove to be very capable weapon; modernised variants are still in service with the Royal Navy and other navies today.

Mine Countermeasures and Seabed Operations

The 'Hunt' Class
In spring 1979 a new era began in Royal Navy mine warfare. Just as the last traditional cruiser, HMS *Blake*, and the last strike carrier, HMS *Ark Royal*, decommissioned and were laid up awaiting scrap, the first ship of the new 'Hunt' class dual role minesweepers/minehunters, *Brecon*, began builder's trials.[102] As was described in Chapter 7, the investment in the new shipbuilding techniques required for building glass reinforced plastic vessels by her builders, Vosper Thornycroft, had been considerable, and they were determined to make sure that the first of class was a success. The builder's trials were indeed successful, and the ship was handed over to the Royal Navy on 6 December 1979, commissioning on 21 March the following year. Trials with the Royal Navy demonstrated the effectiveness of the new ship type. *Brecon* was highly manoeuvrable and responsive at both low and high speeds and was well able to steam in higher sea states than her 'Ton' class predecessors. Her

sweeping and hunting capabilities also married well on a single hull. However, she was a lively sea boat forward, with the messdecks in the bows becoming almost uninhabitable in heavy weather. Hammocks had to be used for sleeping and many ratings migrated aft to the ship's storerooms when the Sea State rose above six or seven. *Brecon's* generators also caused trouble, with all three seizing up and having to be replaced during her trials.[103] These initial teething problems were safely resolved and the Royal Navy was soon receiving a steady flow of GRP ships from Vosper Thornycroft, and later Yarrow shipbuilders.

The Single Role Minehunter and 'River' Class Minesweepers
The 'Hunts' were capable but expensive ships and by 1977 it was clear that the necessary numbers would not be built if all new build mine countermeasures vessels were of this class. A 1975 assessment had argued that over fifty mine countermeasures vessels would be needed to undertake all the tasks required of the mine warfare fleet.[104] Half of the vessels were needed for operations off the west and east coasts of Scotland, with the other half for the Channel. The Channel vessels would be less likely to be called upon to undertake sweeps, so conceptual work began on 'Single Role Minehunters' without the winches and sweeping gears of the Hunts, with a projected saving of 25 per cent per hull.[105] After some delays in placing orders, these vessels would begin to enter service from 1989 as the *Sandown* class, named after seaside towns.

In the 1970s a hitherto unknown type of Soviet mining threat was identified by NATO: the 'rising mine' which was code-named 'Cluster Bay' in the West. Details of this type of mine were only made publicly-available by the Russians in the mid-1990s when they started offering such mines on the international arms market. The PMR-2 'Influence Anchored Rocket Mine' targeted submarines and was laid by submarines. The mine would be launched from a submarine torpedo tube, float at a pre-assigned depth, and be attached to the seabed with a mooring cable and anchor that would spool out from the mine after it left the torpedo tube. The mine's own detection system would wait to detect a submarine passing above. Once detected, the equivalent of a small torpedo would be launched from the mine and speed to the target, exploding with either a contact or proximity fuse. The mine could operate at between 200m and 400m depth. The RM-2 mine had similar characteristics to the PMR-2 but was a primarily an anti-ship mine and could be laid by ships. Different variants could be laid by aircraft or had an extra-deep laying depth of up to 900m.[106]

NATO states had nothing like these weapons until the late 1970s, and they added a new and even more worrying aspect to the already impressive Soviet mining capability. Rising mines could be laid anywhere on the continental shelf and were well suited to offensive minelaying operations to interdict

NATO reinforcement convoys or defend nuclear 'bastions' against NATO submarines. In the early 1970s, the Royal Navy's programme to renew its mine countermeasures capability had increasingly focussed on sophisticated but expensive vessels built from GRP. Despite the sophistication of the rising mines, countering them was a relatively unsophisticated operation involving a deep sweep with paired vessels to break the mine's mooring cable and then disable or destroy it on the surface. However, the existing 'Ton' class minesweepers did not have powerful enough winches to manage such deep sweeps safely, whilst the new 'Hunt' class multi-role mine countermeasures vessels would, in times of tension, be fully engaged with hunting and sweeping in the coastal waters of the North-Western Approaches, and were in any case needlessly sophisticated for the sweeping task.[107]

Instead, the use of converted deep sea trawlers – which would have sufficiently powerful winches and the ocean-going capability – was considered. Exercise Northern Wedding 78 had tested the concept of chartered deep-sea trawlers crewed by the Royal Naval Reserve ('RNR') in this role and was considered a success.[108] The RNR's existing ships were six ageing 'Ton' class vessels (each with three RNR crews) and once these were withdrawn from service, they would have no ships. Crewing deep sweep trawlers were a good replacement that made use RNR crews' pre-existing mine warfare skills. A total of thirty-two were estimated to be needed in periods of tension or warfare, and it was thought that twenty of these could be taken up from trade in the event of an emergency. This left a requirement for an additional twelve vessels. If these vessels were fully naval vessels then they could ensure the maintenance of skills, provide ships for the RNR and act as the nuclei for emergency mine warfare squadrons largely raised from vessels taken up from trade. In order to provide a rapid introduction of this new capability, two *Suffolk* class ocean-going stern trawlers were chartered and manned by RNR crews until the first of these twelve vessels entered service. Buying or long-term chartering of trawlers, aside from the two *Suffolk* class, was ruled out as the bulk purchase of such large numbers of trawlers would denude the British deep-sea trawling industry of vessels. In addition, second-hand trawlers would already have been heavy ocean-going service and might only have a few years' life left in them. Instead, the recommended solution was 'new build' ships built at various commercial yards. These would be simple ships, based on a trawler design but with improved communications and deep sweep gear, plus some increased accommodation space and a modicum of improved ship safety through the splitting of ship into two watertight compartments. At July 1978 prices all twelve vessels could be procured for £24.5 million.[109]

The first step of commissioning the two *Suffolk* class trawlers was quickly taken. HMS *St Davids* and HMS *Venturer* were accepted for service on 25 November 1978, the former as the sea tender to the South Wales Division RNR, the latter to the Severn Division RNR.[110] The vessels were quickly utilised in their new deep sweep role during the Exercise Centex in the summer of 1979.[111] The next stage, the ordering of new build trawler/minesweepers, was a much longer time coming. The order for the first four vessels, of the River class, was not placed until October 1982 with the other eight following in 1983.[112] In February 1985 the 10th Mine Counter Measures Squadron was finally established made up of the first three ships in the class.[113] All twelve vessels were in service by the end of 1986, the first of class being HMS *Waveney*.

HMS Challenger: the Seabed Operations Vessel

Throughout the 1970s, the Royal Navy's forward programme had included a new diving ship to replace the ageing diving support vessel, HMS *Reclaim*. A temporary replacement had been procured in the form of the commercial vessel, *Seaforth Clansman*, but a permanent solution was needed.[114] The opportunity was taken not only replace *Reclaim*'s capabilities but also build a much more capable vessel with the ability to inspect and repair SOSUS arrays and investigate other seabed artefacts. A secondary role as a vessel able to conduct rescues from stricken submarines was also included.[115]

A design contract was placed with Scotts Shipbuilding Company at Greenock on the Clyde in 1977, but an order was not made until late May 1979. The ship, to be named HMS *Challenger*, would have a number of capabilities far in advance of the moonpool-equipped *Seaforth Clansman*. She would be able to operate in depths down to 300m in Sea State 5, with 50-knot winds and 3-knot currents. She would be able not only to operate a manned submersible from a moonpool but an unmanned submersible towed from the stern. She would also have a helicopter deck capable of landing a large Sea King helicopter. Concerns about mounting expense had resulted in a review of the procurement, which delayed the project, paradoxically increasing costs even further (to a total of £62.5 million by September 1978), but the final assessment was that, despite her expense and the fact that Scotts' design fell short of requirements in a few minor ways, the vessel was necessary and a commercially sourced alternative would not be able to undertake the roles required of a seabed operations vessel.[116] Also, Scotts' initially seemed like a good choice for the procurement, they had recently fulfilled orders for sophisticated vessels with complex station-keeping propulsion, just as would be needed for *Challenger*.[117] The Admiralty Board approved the vessel in its first meeting under the new government and construction began soon afterwards.[118]

Unfortunately, *Challenger* would never become fully operational, serving in a form of partially-capable limbo between 1984 and 1990. Scotts was a mixed yard in dire financial trouble with poor industrial relations, which had also encountered numerous technical difficulties in completing the specialist commercial vessels that had appeared to make the yard such a good choice when the order had been placed in 1979.[119] The defects in her construction were so great and numerous they could never be resolved despite many years of remedial repair work. For example, her saturation diving system, even after having its pipework fully replaced, was only cleared for use at the relatively shallow depth of 50m as late as April 1989.[120] Eighteen months later, as the Cold War was ending, she was decommissioned and placed on the sales list.[121] During this time *Seaforth Clansman* continued to undertake the diving ship role perfectly satisfactorily. *Challenger* suffered from being built at a shipyard which was unhappy, inefficient and incapable of building such a sophisticated vessel, but also from over-exquisite requirements, when *Seaforth Clansman* could perform 90 per cent per cent of her role at a fraction of the cost.

The Twilight of Fast Craft

Hovercraft
Great things had been expected of hovercraft during the 1960s and much of the 1970s, but by the end of the latter decade, the possible roles for these innovative craft began to shrink in number. They were too vulnerable in heavy weather to operate in the deep ocean or some coastal waters and they were expensive to maintain and operate. As was seen in the previous chapter, two ageing craft had a second lease of life operating around the islets and beaches of Hong Kong intercepting migrants, but roles in home waters were few and far between. Liaison with the United States Navy regarding hovercraft and other innovative vessels was close and regular, the USN being dependent on the RN's smaller craft to provide training for their hovercraft crews, but the direction in which development was proceeding across the Atlantic was not one that looked promising. The United States Navy and Marine Corps, having dropped development in most other areas, were increasingly focussing on the use of hovercraft in amphibious warfare, specifically to take troops to shore from dock landing ships at much greater speed than traditional landing craft.[122]

Back in the United Kingdom, where the 1975 Defence Review had resulted in the decision to withdraw, at the end of their service lives, the two remaining dock landing ships without replacement, this did not seem like a profitable direction to take the Hovercraft Trials Unit. Instead hovercraft were assessed for use as mine countermeasures vessels to help make up the total number of hulls required for the modernised mine warfare force. The craft were deemed to be almost invulnerable to mine explosions and had low influence signatures which meant that mines were less likely to be detonated by their presence. They also had sufficient space to take most types of sweeping gear. However, mine-hunting sonar – such as the Type 193T – could not be operated, and it was mine hunting that was most in demand rather than sweeping. The sweeping of rising mines, which would most likely be laid in oceanic waters, could be more effectively undertaken by a wide range of other vessels, and much more cheaply. The only other potential use of hovercraft in mine warfare was as a 'precursor' sweeper, to sweep ahead of other mine countermeasures vessels.[123] In 1976 a fifth hovercraft was added to the Trials Unit's strength when VT2, built by Vosper Thornycroft, was chartered for trials. *VT2* (which was given the pennant *P234*) was the RN's largest and fastest such craft at 100 tons and a maximum speed, in good conditions, of 60 knots. After undertaking trials with the West German Navy at Kiel in March 1979, *VT2* was purchased by the Royal Navy and entered refit to be modified as a mine countermeasures 'precursor'. She emerged in August 1981 fully equipped for this role but her service life was short. She participated in Exercise Roast Beef with other mine countermeasures vessels in January 1982, but it was announced less than two months later that the whole Hovercraft Trials Unit would be disbanded and all five hovercraft were to be put up for sale.[124] Money had been wasted on the VT2 refit, but most of the craft were ageing, needed replacing and in a time of acute financial pressures, the Trials Unit and its craft were an easy target for end of year savings. Thus the use of the hovercraft in the Cold War Royal Navy ended quietly, in stark contrast to the fanfare with which the craft had been met only two decades previously.

Hydrofoils
As the Royal Navy's interest in hovercraft fell away, there was a brief flurry of enthusiasm in hydrofoils. Hydrofoil craft used 'hydrofoil lifting surfaces' to lift a vessel out of the water, reducing its hull drag and increasing its speed significantly. The United States Navy had shown an interest in the type during the mid-1970s, reluctantly procuring a class of six *Pegasus* class craft. Further orders were however cancelled, and the remaining craft were assigned to duties in the Caribbean. As was seen in Chapter 7, for a short period in the early 1970s, the Royal Navy's forward programme for patrol craft had included hydrofoils, but they were removed after US interest dimmed. Advocates for the hydrofoil remained in the Ship Department, the Deputy Director of Naval Construction, David K Brown, being a particular enthusiast.[125] With £6 million left from an underspend in the 1978 naval construction budget, a single craft was ordered from Boeing Marine Services, despite the lack of any

operational requirement from the Naval Staff. The craft, named HMS *Speedy*, could reach 43 knots on foils but was limited to only 8.5 knots on her hull. She displaced only 117 tons, was powered by two gas turbines and two diesels, had an operational range of 570 nautical miles, and was transported across the Atlantic on the deck of a merchant ship in November 1979. She then spent a number of months being fitted out for naval service at Vosper Thornycroft and was commissioned in June 1980.[126]

Unfortunately, HMS *Speedy* proved to be a disappointment. Although fast on foils, she was not a comfortable craft to be onboard at speed, but her greatest failing was her inability to operate effectively in weather conditions above Force Five. Trials in the Baltic with the West German Navy were somewhat curtailed by weather conditions and the Bundesmarine were polite but careful not to comment on her abilities, their own navy having backed out of the USN's *Pegasus* programme in 1977. Operating with the Fishery Protection Squadron in 1981 demonstrated her limitations: at Force Five and Six *Speedy* had to return to harbour whilst her accompanying fishery protection vessels could remain on station and had no problems with these conditions. When the weather reached this state, defined as 'fresh breeze' and 'strong breeze', *Speedy* could not successfully get onto her foils; this left her wallowing at a maximum of 8.5 knots on her diesels, a situation that made her little use for fishery protection duties. As with the Hovercraft Trials Unit, the need for economies at the end of the 1981–2 financial year resulted in a decision to withdraw the craft from service after less than two years in commission and with her trials programme only partly complete. Boeing Marine Services lobbied hard to prevent this occurring, and they eventually agreed to lease back the former HMS *Speedy* to use for drumming up sales in the North Sea oil industry (this could not have been particularly successful given the notoriously choppy sea conditions in the North Sea). The Navy saved £500,000 a year by the decision to decommission the Navy's one and only hydrofoil.[127] The Royal Navy's remaining fast craft, the three target craft of the *Scimitar* class and HMS *Tenacity*, were also culled during this period. In a Navy under increasing financial pressure, these vessels – which were ageing and would soon need major refits for further service – appeared to be at best 'desirable' vessels rather than essential, and with their decommissioning the Royal Navy was without any fast light craft for the first time since the start of the Second World War.

The Dockyards

The dilemmas facing the Navy's leadership over the Royal Dockyards remained and, if anything, intensified during the second half of the 1970s. Reductions in the dockyard workforce that had been planned in 1975 were partly rescinded following the additional repair and refit requirements created by the Third

Cod War, a number of major fires which put back existing refit plans and problems recruiting and retaining existing dockyard workers.[128] The refitting programme now included increasing numbers of major modernisations of *Leander* class frigates, partly as a response to the lack of sufficient orders of new vessels and the wish to prevent relatively new hulls from becoming obsolete. As each new modernised *Leander* variant emerged, increasing work was required as weapon systems, sensors and other equipment were replaced, and major structural changes were made to accommodate them. In 1978–9 such major refits of this type were expected to take up over one-third of the total refit capacity of the yards; this burden was placed over the top of the general run of routine refits for ships across the fleet.[129] These problems were exacerbated by the repeated overrunning of refits, which not only further delayed succeeding work but also had an increasing impact on the operational availability of warships. The radical solution of turning the dockyards into semi-independent trading funds, which had been mooted back in 1970, was finally rejected in 1977 as it would not change the problematic monopoly-supplier/monopoly-customer situation of the dockyard-Ministry of Defence relationship, and would have required an 'arms-length' approach to the dockyards which the Chief of Fleet Support was unwilling to countenance.[130] Also left unmentioned was the political environment of the time, where the concept of a profit-and-loss-orientated trading fund would have resulted in protests from both unions and increasingly radicalised backbenchers for a government that was now in a minority and needed the support of all its MPs (alongside a few from other parties) to push legislation through Parliament.

With no transformation of the dockyard system in sight, more prosaic and short-term solutions were the only ones available: requests in 1976 and 1977 for either a delay in four *Leander* modernisations or an increase in the dockyard workforce of 600, were coupled with the deferment (and eventual abandonment) of plans to build a Type 42 destroyer at Devonport Dockyard in the mid-1980s. This had been programmed as a way to provide some competition for the newly-nationalised monopoly shipbuilder, British Shipbuilders, and to provide some additional capacity if the number of warship building yards fell under the new nationalised structures.[131] The uplift in activity also provided hope that the ever-vulnerable Chatham would remain viable as a dockyard, after concerns during the previous year that by the 1980s there would be insufficient refit work to justify four home dockyards. Chatham remained the most at-risk yard of the four: Devonport was regarded as the navy's strongest yard due to its size, ease of recruitment locally, its modern facilities and its developing nuclear submarine and frigate refit capabilities. Rosyth had SSBN refit facilities and any closure would have had an undesirable political impact as Scotland's only dockyard. However, the growth of the North Sea oil industry in the late 1970s meant that concerns about insufficient skilled workers in the local area willing to work in dockyards continued to threaten the yard's long-term viability and the forthcoming SSBN refit programme.[132] Finally, Portsmouth Dockyard was at the centre of a number of shore establishments with the dockyard and naval base at the hub. Shutting the yard would then raise question marks about the long-term future of the base and the numerous 'stone frigates' clustered in Hampshire. In short, Chatham's survival was still in the balance, the Admiralty Board reviewing its viability annually, with any future reduction in refit activity leaving it exposed to the Navy agreeing to – in the brutal words of the Chief of Fleet Support – 'get out of Kent' as a cost-saving measure.[133]

The smaller Gibraltar dockyard was in a similar position to Chatham: its survival based on regular reviews and a flow of standard refits that would otherwise have been allocated to the overworked home dockyards. The costs of recruiting and training 500 dockyard workers in the home yards to replace the workforce lost at Gibraltar, if it were closed, would considerably reduce the financial benefits of closure, which were estimated at £3 million in 1977 prices. As with Rosyth, political sensitivities had to be weighed with any closure, when the relations between the United Kingdom and Spain were in flux after the recent death of General Franco.[134] Gibraltar dockyard had a stay of execution but its long-term survival remained in doubt. One former naval base *was* sacrificed following the 1975 Defence Review: Scapa Flow. Although not used in this role since the Second World War, the Royal Navy's residual rights to re-use Scapa if needed were revoked in 1976, severing a final link with the famous base of the Grand Fleet in the First World War and Home Fleet in the Second.[135]

As Jim Callaghan's Labour government reached its final months, a dockyard workers' strike in all four home yards that began in May 1978 further disrupted the refit programme that year: an average of 12.5 per cent of annual capacity was lost in the yards, with the programme slipping by between two and four weeks at Devonport, Chatham and Rosyth. At Portsmouth the disruption was even worse with a loss of 29 per cent capacity, a delay of 15 weeks on that dockyard's refits, and a continuing work-to-rule even after the strike had come to an end. The operational impact was significant: a range of submarines had to be withdrawn from major exercises such as Northern Wedding 78, and that year's Open Gate and Dawn Patrol exercises. One assault ship would have to be withdrawn from Cold Winter 79 and a frigate from Display Determination 79. In addition, the gap between the withdrawal of *Ark Royal* and the return to service of *Bulwark* widened, and Commander-in-Chief Fleet was unable at times to maintain the required number of vessels in home waters as Fleet Contingency Ships.[136]

The strikes spurred attempts by the Chief of Fleet Support to produce a Royal Dockyards White Paper, which would have included a commitment to pay private-sector wage rates, expanding a 'payment by results' wage scheme agreed at Chatham to all yards, in return for an agreement to keep all four home dockyards in operation. The White Paper concept was rejected by the Minister of State, John Gilbert, but work continued on producing a general 'policy statement' incorporating elements of the rejected draft White Paper.[137] Attempts to deal with the backlog in the refit programme included the possibility of taking out some work to contract with the shipbuilding industry, and the cancellation of major refits for the first three Type 42 destroyers.[138] The latter proposal was rejected, but by early 1979 refits by external contractors for the frigate *Torquay* and the submarine *Oracle* were underway with plans for sister ships of both these types, and the two assault ships, to follow into the early 1980s.[139] If the dockyards could not improve efficiency and timeliness in refits, the Navy was now willing to go to outside yards to undertake the required work, even if it required diverting funds from elsewhere to do so.

The dockyards as they stood in 1979 only seemed viable in their current form if the current heavy load of refit work continued, in particular, the complex and expensive mid-life refits of frigates and destroyers. If these were to end or be significantly reduced, a situation of severe under-capacity would rapidly turn into one of considerable over-capacity, and the futures of both Chatham and Gibraltar dockyards – which had been in the balance for more than a decade – would soon return to the agendas of Admiralty Board meetings.

* * *

In December 1978 what had been decided 12 years' previously had finally came to pass. The conventional aircraft carrier, with its air defence, strike and airborne early warning aircraft, had eventually left naval service without any replacement. Other ways to provide these capabilities needed to be in place, and in some respects they were: RAF aircraft under the operational control of the Commander-in-Chief Fleet (with his NATO CINCEASTLANT 'hat' on) undertook these roles out to their maximum ranges from bases in the United Kingdom, and a production line of Type 42 air defence destroyers had been established and was turning out ships with some regularity. However, a more searching analysis of the Navy's position makes it clear that in many key areas there were looming capability gaps, opportunities not taken and confusion about the shape and role of the fleet, particularly the surface fleet.

The conceptual work for a new air defence destroyer had resulted in an expensive compromise of dubious tactical utility when technological and doctrinal developments placed question marks over the utility of this type of ship altogether. Attempts to harness the capabilities of large anti-submarine helicopters in 'garage ships' had been watered down, whilst plans for organic airborne early warning helicopters had been repeatedly shelved. No additional Harriers had been procured either, one of the cornerstones of the 1975 Size and Shape paper. Nuclear-powered 'hunter-killer' submarines could be argued to be the new capital ships of the fleet, but they still lacked an effective torpedo to deal with surface ships and the largest enemy submarines. The new GRP mine warfare fleet was beginning to take shape and prove successful if expensive, whilst an alternative naval future of hovercraft, hydrofoils and fast attack craft began to slide out of view. The dockyards were currently overworked with expensive and far-reaching refits of ageing ships, but if these were reduced or cancelled this feast would turn to famine, and quickly starve the weaker dockyards out of existence. The Royal Navy was in a fragile position and had failed to grasp a number of nettles since 1975, but most worryingly of all, it did not seem to be aware of the extent to which it was vulnerable and lacked a coherent understanding of what it needed to do, to be effective in the contemporary Cold War environment.

12

False Hope

The arrival of a Conservative government in May 1979 seemed to hold open the promise of a new start for Defence: pay had fallen behind inflation for a number of years whilst the previous government had seemed reluctant even to acknowledge in public a Soviet threat that was so important to most in the military. Many within the Ministry had high expectations of a new government that, in opposition, had heavily criticised the previous administration's defence policies and promised increases in both resources and pay.[1] Its first actions set a vigorous new tone. Five days into the new government, the new Secretary of State for Defence, Sir Francis Pym, managed to wring a commitment from the Prime Minister that British defence spending would increase by 3 per cent in real terms each year until 1986, as had been proposed for NATO by the US President in 1978. Diplomatically, this would put Pym and the British delegation in an advantageous position at the forthcoming NATO conference in Brussels, when most other European NATO members were trying to reduce their defence commitments. It also drew praise from the US Secretary of State, who called the new government a 'shot in the arm' for NATO.[2] Financially, the Treasury was deeply unhappy and would spend much of the rest of the year arguing with the Ministry of Defence over how the 3 per cent increase should be interpreted and implemented, trying to claw back as much of the money as it could.[3] In Margaret Thatcher, it seemed that Defence now had a Prime Minister who was willing to provide support and back that support up with increased spending.

The Royal Navy had two specific reasons, aside from the general increase in defence spending, to feel especially positive about the new government. The first related to the new government's plans for service pay which promised to bail the Navy out of an impending recruitment and retention crisis, whilst the second was linked to the new Defence Secretary's plans to alter the focus of the United Kingdom's military effort.

Personnel

In the second half of the 1970s the Navy's leadership had continued to spend much time grappling with the challenges of adjusting its personnel and policies towards the higher-technology and more complex navy that was taking shape. One problem resulted from the increasing responsibilities put on operations room Leading Rates, moderately junior sailors who were being trained to master electronic consoles and systems despite relatively low pay. Attempts to increase pay were prevented by Ministry of Defence requirements to keep wage rates the same across the three services, and as a result increasing numbers of these important personnel left the Navy for a better-paid life in the civilian world.[4] Another challenge was the need for more naval engineer officer posts ashore to supervise and support the large refit programme in the dockyards. The snag was that the most useful engineers for these posts were those with recent seagoing experience, but posting more engineers ashore meant less sea-time across the fleet and therefore fewer engineers with recent sea experience, a seemingly circular problem the Second Sea Lord's departments found difficult to resolve.[5] The Navy also embarked on an ambitious study to work out the requirements for senior officers in the 1990s and then work backwards to adjust promotion requirements and numbers at each rank in the present day. Much analysis was done on this subject, which eventually recommended a 10 per cent reduction in the need for Captains and Commanders by the 1990s, but its practical worth was undermined by the Admiralty Board setting an overly-optimistic projected size for the fleet in the 1990s which in turn resulted in an overestimate of the future total of personnel afloat and the support requirements ashore.[6] However, by far the most serious immediate personnel problem in the late 1970s was pay across the whole Navy.

The Labour governments of 1974–9 had been willing to spend money on defence, particularly on procurement and in support, but one area where spending was reduced and was especially painful for servicemen and women, was a pay freeze that was instituted after 1975 for two years. Between 1975 and 1977 inflation averaged 16.2 per cent per annum but service pay was not lifted at all. An ordinary seaman with six years' experience in 1977 would have suffered the equivalent of a 26 per cent pay cut in only two years.[7] A significant pay rise was approved in 1978 but this still left the ordinary seaman with pay 5 per cent lower in real terms than in 1975.[8] These real wage reductions had a major impact on retention figures as sailors, particularly those with transferable skills such as artificers, left to join those industries that were awarding pay rises that matched inflation.

In response to this problem, which was having an impact on all three services, the new Conservative government gave a significant pay rise to military personnel in its first month in office. Pay was increased by 30 per cent; for the ordinary seaman with six years' service this meant a rise from £6.92 in April 1978 per day to £8.98 in 1979.[9] Inflation over the same period had been 13.4 per cent but this still meant a significant increase that ensured that nearly all the pay lost to below-inflation pay rises during the 1970s had been more than cancelled out.[10] The Ministry's budgeted cash limits were increased by £269 million to pay for the pay rises, whilst another £100 million was thrown in the direction of defence procurement to cover projected cost increases there. The pay rise would be instrumental in ending the naval manning crisis that had been developing since late 1977, but its impact would not be felt for a number of months. In the meantime, drastic measures were needed and the Admiralty Board reluctantly agreed to the placing a number of warships in the Standby Squadron, in effect a form of partially active reserve. These vessels included the last cruiser in service, HMS *Blake* (with a crew of nearly 900), and five 'Tribal' class frigates. This would free up dozens of vital junior warfare officers and marine and weapon engineering ratings to help crew new ships entering service. However, the Vice Chief of the Naval Staff admitted that it was 'essentially a damage control exercise to buy time'.[11] The Board was unwilling to take this drastic step, and it was told that this was the first significant withdrawal of ships from service due to personnel shortages since the late 1940s (which ignored the withdrawal from service of HMS *Hampshire* in the mid-1960s described in Chapter 4), but they could see no other alternative. The government's pay rises were welcomed but it was also acknowledged that other factors that affected retention would also have to be dealt with in due course: a greater predictability of service, less time separated from families and greater job satisfaction.[12]

These factors would be a recurring feature of the personnel retention strains from which the Navy would suffer during the 1980s, and this assessment that it was more than just pay that affected morale and retention was confirmed from a surprising quarter. A poll of servicemen undertaken by Conservative Central Office of all places had come to the same conclusions in late 1979. It was a rather strange affair, in that it had been undertaken without formal Ministry of Defence approval, with the polling work hurriedly stopped and the results suppressed after the Permanent Under-Secretary learnt of its existence.[13] However, a rapid start was made to deal with one particularly damaging problem: a crisis in the number of junior officers able to undertake watchkeeping duties aboard ship. Stemming the voluntary outflow of young officers would be a longer-term proposition requiring a mix of incentives and improved job satisfaction, so a new three-and-a-half year commission was introduced with the aim of bringing in additional seaman officers for a short period of time, but long enough to become qualified for watchkeeping duties rapidly. The reform was introduced in 1980 and succeeded in defusing what

This painting shows one of the options for the Future Frigate, the short-lived successor to the cancelled NATO NFR90 programme. The Future Frigate was abandoned in the early 1990s when the United Kingdom joined the Common New Generation Frigate programme in partnership with France and Italy. *(Crown Copyright)*

The minelayer HMS *Abdiel* and three 'Ton' class minehunters moored at the Egyptian port of Ismailia whilst taking part in Operation 'Rheostat', the clearance of the Suez Canal in 1975. *(Crown Copyright)*

HMS *Brecon* was the first ship of the 'Hunt' class mine countermeasures vessels. With technology and processes pioneered by the British shipbuilding industry and the Royal Navy, her hull was made from glass reinforced plastic, which was non-magnetic, light and hard wearing, and a considerable improvement on her wooden-hulled predecessors. *(Crown Copyright)*

A stern view of RFA *Olna* replenishing a Type 21 frigate at sea as they head south to the Falklands in May 1982. This photograph shows the RFA's hangar and helicopter, the latter having become an increasingly important part of replenishment at sea from the 1960s. *(Public Domain/Ken Griffith)*

RFA *Oakleaf* refuels both the assault ship HMS *Intrepid* and a Fred Olsen Line car ferry during Exercise Teamwork 88. The ferry had been taken up from trade for the exercise to act as an amphibious transport; this was increasingly common in 1980s NATO exercises. Such vessels taken up from trade had proved their utility in the 1982 Falklands campaign. *(Crown Copyright)*

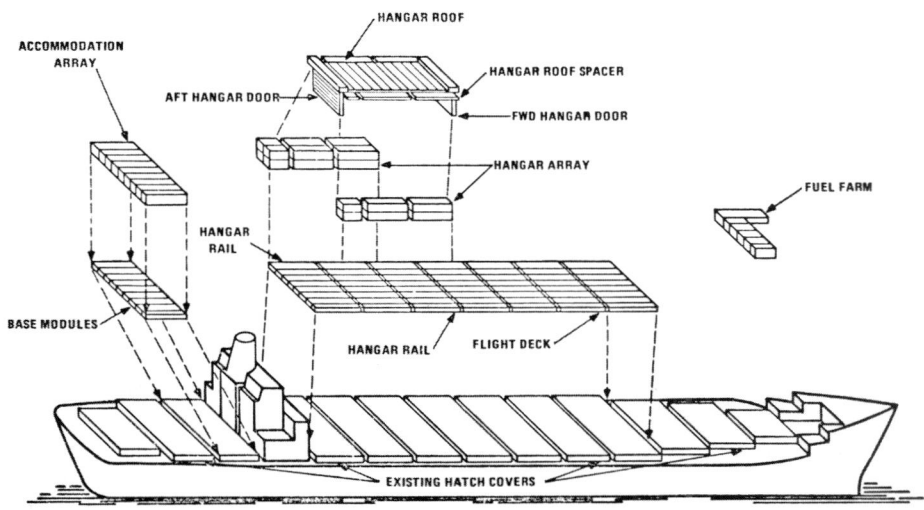

The Arapaho system, developed in the United States, was a way to convert container ships into auxiliary warships in an emergency. The system was tested on RFA *Reliant* when she acted as a helicopter support ship in the Falklands in the mid-1980s. *(Crown Copyright)*

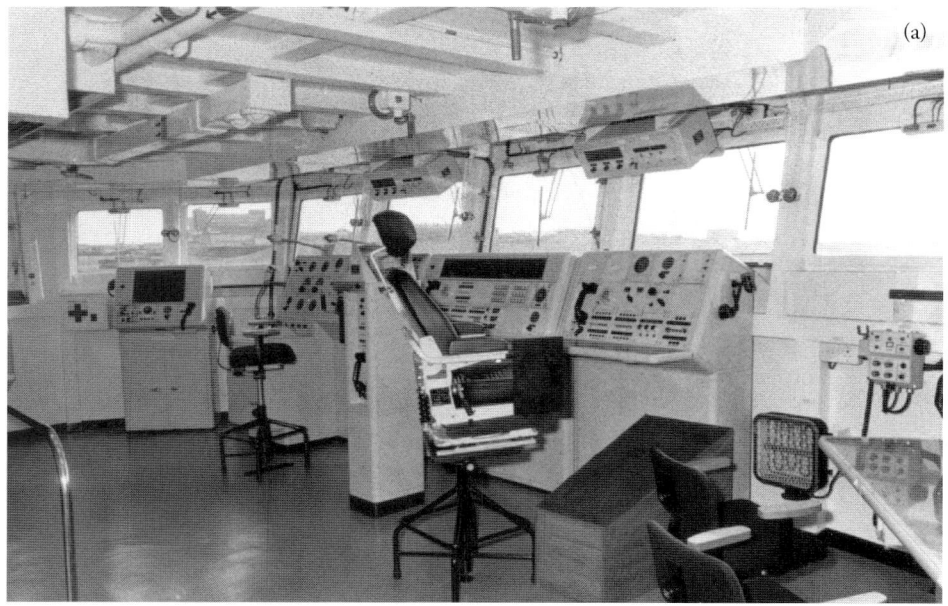

Inside a Cold War guided missile destroyer: the newly completed HMS *Glasgow* in 1979.
(All photographs Crown Copyright)

(a) The ship's bridge; (b) the ship's operations room. During the Cold War, ships would increasingly be fought from the operations room deep within the ship rather than from the bridge.

(c) the machinery control room; (d) the control room for the ship's forward missile tracker radar. From the 1970s, warships were increasingly vessels that required skills in operating and maintaining electronic equipment.

(e)

(e) the captain's cabin; (f) the Petty Officers' bar and mess.

(f)

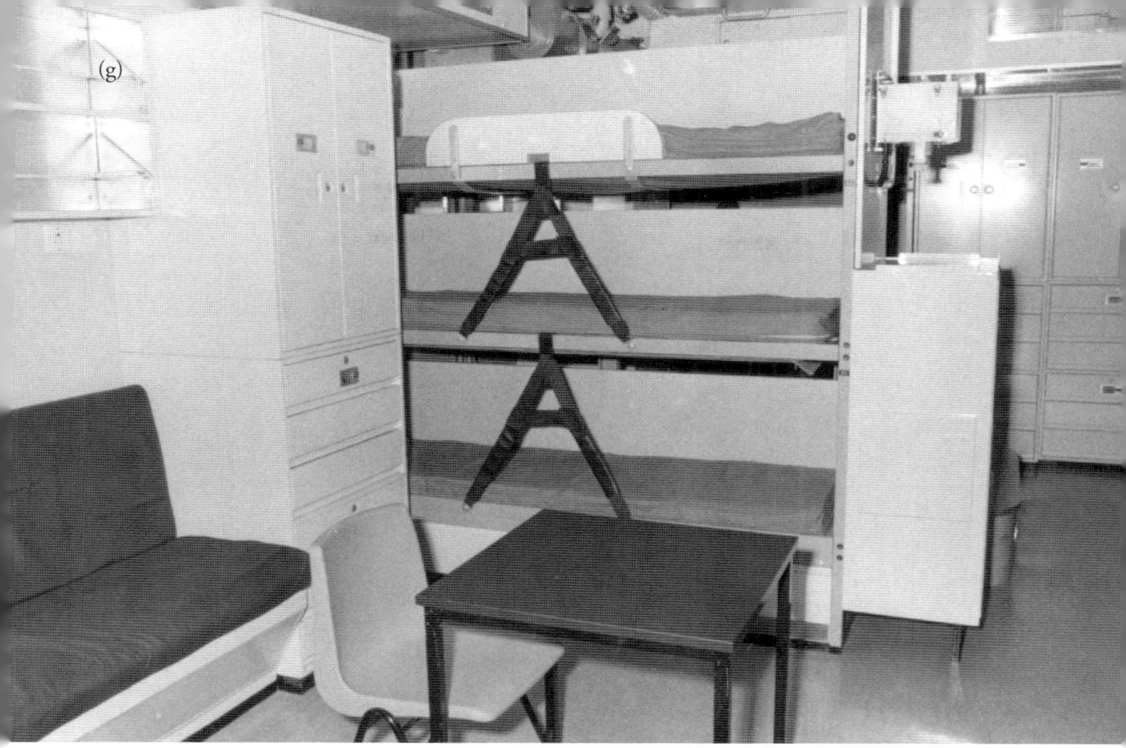

(g) a junior rates' mess; (h) junior rates dining room. Improved accommodation standards were approved in the late 1960s and implemented in ships such as *Glasgow*: such standards were considered to be an important part of retaining personnel in the Royal Navy when employment opportunities in the wider economy might tempt sailors to leave the service.

(i) the ship's galley; (j) the ship's workshop. Warships were expected to improvise the repair much of their simpler equipment internally: lathe-equipped workshops were therefore standard on most vessels of frigate size or larger.

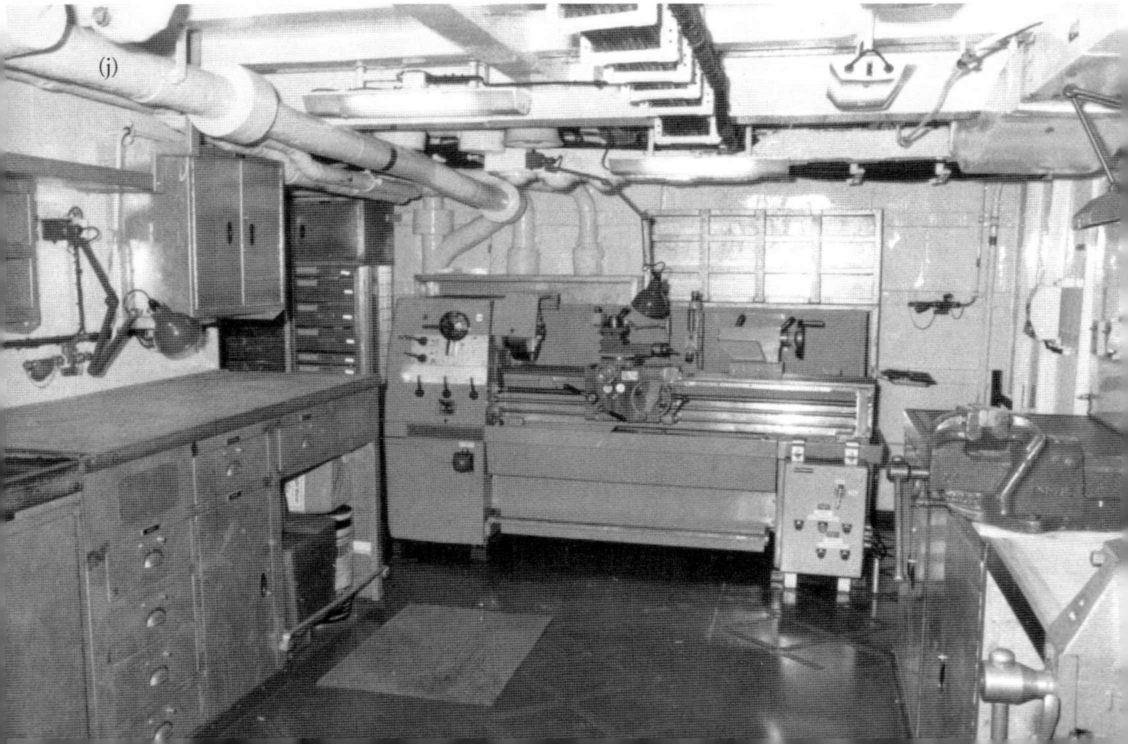

(k) the Sea Dart missile magazine with two test rounds present; (l) the ship's helicopter hangar looking aft towards the hangar door.

The frigate refit complex at Devonport, one of two major investments in the dockyard during the 1970s. *(Crown Copyright)*

The other investment was in a nuclear submarine refit complex, shown here with the submarine HMS *Superb* entering the dock for refitting. *(Crown Copyright)*

A further major project was the upgrade of the headquarters facilities at Northwood, in the north-west suburbs of London. This photograph shows the entrance to the NATO side of the HQ complex for the Commander-in-Chief Eastern Atlantic, the main NATO role for the Royal Navy's Commander-in-Chief Fleet. *(Crown Copyright)*

During the 1980s, the most important infrastructure project was that for the new Trident submarines at Faslane. This image shows an artist's illustration of the new complex once completed. *(Crown Copyright)*

Junior rates dining facilities on an aircraft carrier: *Ark Royal* in the mid-1970s. Huge quantities of food and drink would be consumed by the crew of a major warship such as this. The logistical challenge to supply such victualling was considerable. *(Crown Copyright)*

Almost all administrative processes were manual in warships in the 1970s and into the 1980s. Dollars are being issued to sailors on HMS *Ark Royal* prior to a run ashore in the United States. *(Crown Copyright)*

Money was also spent improving shore facilities for sailors. This is the Junior Rates club at HMS *Dolphin* in 1975, the submarine base in Gosport. *(Crown Copyright)*

In the 1970s the improvement of facilities for families became an increasing priority. The Rowner estate in Gosport was one of the most ambitious projects, eschewing the usual cottage estates and terraces for brutalist slab blocks. The estate was passed to the local authority as being surplus to requirements less than 20 years after being completed. *(Crown Copyright)*

The Soviet Adversary.

Members of the crew of HMS *Ark Royal* observe a Soviet 'Kresta II' class cruiser in the Mediterranean. *(Crown Copyright)*

A Sea Harrier shadows a Soviet Tu-16 'Badger' bomber. 'Badgers' were used in both the missile-launching strike role and for reconnaissance and missile targeting. This is one of the latter aircraft, a 'Badger D'. *(Crown Copyright)*

A Soviet 'Backfire B' strike aircraft. The appearance of these long-range bombers armed with anti-ship missiles in the mid-1970s significantly increased the Soviet threat to NATO surface naval forces. *(Public Domain/US Department of Defense)*

This 'Delta III' nuclear-powered ballistic missile submarine was part of the Soviet Northern Fleet's strategic nuclear deterrent force. Under the 1980s Maritime Strategy, NATO attack submarines would have tracked and, if necessary, destroyed such boats in northern waters during the early stages of a conflict. *(Public Domain/National Archives and Records Administration, USA)*

'Charlie I' class cruise missile submarines worried NATO navies when they first appeared at the end of the 1960s. Unlike earlier Soviet boats, they could fire their missiles from underwater thus helping to protect them from detection. Their relatively slow speed did limit their ability to keep up with carrier strike groups, but they remained a threat that could not be ignored. *(Public Domain/US Department of Defense)*

Left: A Soviet 'Victor III' submarine: these boats were the most numerous and active nuclear-powered attack submarines in the Soviet Northern Fleet of the 1980s. *(Crown Copyright)*

Right: The Soviet *Kirov* class cruisers were huge warships that combined large numbers of long-range anti-ship missiles with a significant area air defence capability and extensive command facilities. By the end of the Cold War, two such vessels were part of the Northern Fleet: the *Kirov* and the *Kalinin*. This is the *Kirov* in 1989 with a 'Krivak' class frigate in the background. *(Public Domain/National Archives and Records Administration, USA)*

Confidence-building measures in the age of Glasnost: Marshal Yazov, the Soviet Defence Minister, visits Portsmouth in 1990. On the far right in naval uniform is Admiral Chernavin, the Commander-in-Chief of the Soviet Navy. They are hosted by Vice Admiral Alan Grose. *(Crown Copyright)*

had threatened to be a crisis in junior officer retention although at cost of providing much expensive training for only three years of service.[14]

The increase in pay for servicemen was also accompanied by a government-wide 20 per cent reduction in the numbers of civil servants. This had the aim of eliminating waste and inefficiency in government – in effect making those who remained work harder – but the Navy Department of the Ministry of Defence already had problems with low-levels of civil service recruitment and high 'wastage' as employees left to work in other departments or industries with better pay. A short-term government ban on civil service recruitment was also accentuating these problems. The Chief of Fleet Support was particularly concerned as many dockyard workers were leaving government employment: a 'further enforced reduction in numbers could make it impossible to provide adequate backing for the Fleet. The situation was potentially very grave.'[15] The Admiralty Board was trying to build the case for an expansion of the Navy, and the reductions in those who supported the fleet, coupled with poor recruitment of new blood, appeared to be undermining this aim.

The Navy and Defence Policy-Making
The second reason for Naval optimism was the attitude of the new Defence Secretary, Sir Francis Pym. A leading light of the 'wet' or moderate faction in the Conservative Party, he was a keen advocate of a greater worldwide role for British armed forces and much less of a focus on the NATO Central European front. These views had held much attraction to many in the Conservative Party, and reductions in the British Army of the Rhine had been mooted whilst in opposition as one of the ways to reduce defence spending once in government.[16] These views had also manifested themselves in the first months of the Heath government although little had eventually come of them.[17] This time however, Pym was seemingly determined to push through a radical re-orientation of British defence strategy; and the Royal Navy could end up being the main beneficiary of any such shift. Pym had the strong support of the Foreign Secretary, Lord Carrington. Assessments were made of the impact of reducing the British Forces Germany, which included the British Army of the Rhine and RAF Germany, below the notional 54,000 level which had been set by the amended Brussels Treaty of 1954.[18]

Pym was advised by the new Chief of the Defence Staff, Admiral Lewin, who had been promoted from First Sea Lord in July 1979. It is not clear how much the advice Lewin gave shaped Pym's views, but a naval Chief of the Defence Staff certainly provided the Navy some advantage in that its perspective and world-view would be more likely to reach the Secretary of State in a direct and unvarnished form. In any case, by January 1980 both Lewin and Pym essentially shared the same position – and were happy to communicate this formally to the Foreign Office – that if any reductions were needed from any of the Four Pillars it should be the Central European front in Germany and not the Navy.[19] Unsurprisingly, it was the view of many of the most senior naval officers that a confrontation on the Central European front was much less likely than one on the high seas. Vice Admiral William Staveley, the new Vice Chief of the Naval Staff, argued that the Soviets would be more able to achieve their aims through a 'phoney land war' in Europe but a real and prolonged sea war in the Atlantic.[20] On the other hand, Lewin had to be seen to be demonstrably above the fray of inter-service rivalry. He was required only to provide advice on the basis of his role as the head of the collective body of the Chiefs of Staff. If the Chiefs of Staff agreed, he could relay that collective position. Only if one of the Chiefs disagreed and no collective position could be forged, could the Chief of the Defence Staff provide his own view.[21] This severely limited his ability to propose anything that the Chiefs had not already discussed. Lewin took this obligation seriously, and he would end his posting as Chief of the Defence Staff as a determined advocate of greater centralisation of power away from the individual services and towards the centre.[22]

With the elevation of Lewin to Chief of the Defence Staff, Admiral Henry Leach was appointed the new First Sea Lord. Leach had worked underneath Lewin on two separate occasions and had proved himself an excellent 'Whitehall warrior' on behalf of the Royal Navy: a master of administrative detail and logical thinking who had also developed a strong understanding of the labyrinthine financial structures of the Ministry of Defence. He had been instrumental in the decision to select Chevaline in the mid-1970s and was regarded by Lewin as 'sound' on matters of the nuclear deterrent and therefore just the right person to have in post when the decisions over the Polaris replacement were being made.[23] Henry Leach, the last First Sea Lord to see action in the Second World War, who had been present at the Battle of North Cape and whose father's ship HMS *Prince of Wales* had been lost to Japanese torpedo bombers for want of air cover, had also shown a tendency to be bracingly direct and determined in his defence of the Royal Navy through the corridors of Whitehall.[24] Leach's skills would be crucial over the three turbulent years that followed. With Leach moving from Commander-in-Chief Fleet, Vice Admiral Eberle took his place, whilst Eberle's previous post as Chief of Fleet Support was taken by Vice Admiral William Pillar. Admiral Clayton, the Controller of the Navy who had pushed so hard for the Type 24, was moved to become Commander-in-Chief of the Naval Home Command, replacing Admiral David Williams who was pushed out of contention for further senior postings and appointed to the pre-retirement role of Governor of Gibraltar. The new Controller of the Navy was Vice Admiral John Fieldhouse, whose previous post had been Flag Officer Submarines.[25]

Defence Budget Battles

Through the rest of 1979 Sir Francis Pym fought hard to bring extra money into Defence, but this proved increasingly difficult as MOD projects, particularly those relating to equipment, seemed to be increasing in cost exponentially. Two battles with the Treasury occupied Pym's time in the second half of 1979.[26] The first was the impact of the Treasury's rise in VAT on the Ministry of Defence. As a major purchaser the Ministry would now have to spend an extra £200 million per year to pay its tax bill to the Treasury. The issue went to the Prime Minister and she supported Pym against the Treasury, stating that 'Defence is different from other [government] departments.'[27] The Ministry was duly compensated by the Treasury. The second issue was more complex, and more bruising for the Defence Secretary: how would the 3 per cent rise in defence spending be calculated. It would not be a surprise that the Treasury preferred the lowest option (based on 'cost' value) and the Ministry of Defence the highest (based on the 'volume' value, the Ministry's own idiosyncratic formula for calculating defence spending). Eventually, a compromise was brokered. The Treasury's preference for 'cost' won out, but a top-up – ostensibly to pay for the early stages of procuring the Polaris successor – would be provided from the Treasury's reserve to bring the figure in 1980–1 up to the volume level. It did mean that a new lower baseline would be in place from which to calculate future annual 3 per cent increases.[28] This newer baseline would immediately cause problems in the new year, as will be seen, as discussions turned towards the Ministry's budget over the next half-decade.

More significantly, the protracted arguments about defence spending made it clear that there was a fundamental problem with the Ministry of Defence keeping within its budget year by year. Reductions to commitments might have to be contemplated. Pym was tasked with undertaking a review of the 'Four Pillars' to see if all four could be sustained over the long-term, having failed in his battle to re-orientate policy away from the Central European front.[29] Sir Francis Pym's attempt to shift the focus of defence spending away from British forces in Germany had rapidly collapsed as his plans met the realities of NATO diplomacy, despite initial support from both the Prime Minister and the Foreign Secretary.[30] In early February 1980 the West German government was informed of the possibility of British troop reductions in Germany. The German reaction was vehement: they regarded the notional 54,000 minimum of British forces in the Federal Republic as sacrosanct and a demonstration of British resolve against the Warsaw Pact.[31] Within a few months, the West German press had discovered the rumours and their reaction was excoriating, with headlines stating that the United Kingdom had deceived and betrayed Germany, NATO and the United States.[32] The damage was so significant that any talk of any major reductions quickly fell away, as did the Royal Navy's dreams that the United Kingdom's 'continental commitment' would be sacrificed to focus on a sea-air strategy. With reductions almost impossible in Central Europe, cuts in the deterrent and home defence impossible, the Eastern Atlantic looked again like the most unstable of the Four Pillars.

Pym's Four Pillars review meant an analysis of the Navy's main commitment aside from the nuclear deterrent, the Eastern Atlantic, but a subtler threat to the Navy's position was emerging. Pym's intransigence had not only vexed the Treasury, but was beginning to irritate the Prime Minister. Over the Christmas break, the Prime Minister was given a series of briefs about the Ministry of Defence from a number of different sources prior to a planned visit. It was quite clear that a concerted campaign of lobbying, perhaps encouraged by the Chancellor of the Exchequer, was being made to provide Margaret Thatcher with a 'better' understanding of the problems within the Ministry of Defence. In the New Year she was going to make her first visit to the Ministry, but the three briefings put before her all focussed on the issue of waste and inefficiency at the Ministry of Defence. These subjects were close to the heart of the new Prime Minister, but up until now she had behaved as if such activities occurred in other departments of state, not in the department that supported the country's armed forces. It was also significant that two of the three focussed on the Royal Navy in their attacks on Ministry waste. It could not have been accidental, given the Defence Secretary's clear preference for a Navy-focussed strategy.

The first brief came from the businessman Sir Derek Rayner. He was Managing Director of the clothes shopping chain Marks and Spencer but had spent a number of frustrating years in the early 1970s as the head of the Ministry of Defence's Procurement Executive, in charge of ordering and delivering military equipment. He was also being used by the Thatcher government as a roving identifier of waste across government, starting what he modestly entitled the 'Rayner Project' with interviews with Permanent Secretaries. Rayner, in his note, pointed out that a minister, silently pointing at Pym, would 'need brutal determination to refuse to allow oneself to be taken over; the smooth, glamorous atmosphere of the Services can quickly envelope the Minister and he may soon find himself taken over heart and soul.' A minister might believe that 'defence is different' but that in fact it was a government department like any other. The attitude of the military was that 'if you wanted more, you should have more money' and that there was 'too little self-examination'. The military were prone to wanting the very best instead of the good, generally argued for over-insurance against breakdown and failure, and often requested too many expensive modifications to designs under development.[33]

Rayner's note was followed by another from the Civil Service Department, the small department based near the Cabinet Office that co-ordinated civil service personnel matters across government. This note stated that inter-service rivalry and a lack of centralisation meant that the efficient allocation of resources amongst the services was extremely difficult. Lobbying by the individual services was endemic, and the briefing only gave one example: that of the First Sea Lord's unequivocal public support, when visiting Portsmouth, for keeping open the dockyard there. Such public lobbying would not be tolerated in any other government department. The briefing note also touched on procurement practices, asking why aircraft design was undertaken by the defence industry, but that ship design was undertaken 'in-house' by the Ship Department of the Navy Department. It also wondered aloud, perhaps in a nod to the failure of the Type 24, why so many new Royal Navy ship designs had poor export potential.[34] Rather pointedly, there were no criticisms of single-service lobbying or the procurement policy of the other two armed services.

Finally, the Prime Minister received a note from an unusual external source: the editor of *Jane's Fighting Ships*. Captain John Moore was a former submariner and had been a high-profile editor of the famous directory of warships for a number of years. He was also a near neighbour and close friend of Sir Ian Gow, the Prime Minister's Personal Private Secretary, a Member of Parliament who acted as Thatcher's eyes and ears within the House of Commons. Moore took the opportunity to write a long letter to Gow, for passing on to Thatcher, that was in effect a polemic against waste in the naval side of the Ministry of Defence. He argued that the Navy Department's bureaucracy was too large and top heavy: there were three Assistant Chiefs of the Naval Staff where there had only been one in 1962 and there were now twelve stages for a procurement to go through before it could be approved, when there had only been two 20 years earlier. Admiralty research establishments were too numerous, overstaffed and had failed to produce any effective torpedoes over the last 20 years. The Navy was focussing too much on large and unduly complex surface ships, when converted merchant ships could be used and warship design could be undertaken by shipyards, instead of by the 'hardware barons of [the Ship Department in] Bath'. Rather contentiously, he argued that the Type 22 frigate was an anti-submarine frigate that did not have any anti-submarine weaponry (ignoring the two torpedo-armed helicopters the ship could operate), that the new 'Hunt' class mine countermeasures vessels would be too few and too expensive, that merchant ships should be used for amphibious landings and that warship building was too little focussed on obtaining exports to bring down costs.[35]

Moore's letter was scathing in tone, and whilst it contained sensible points, it unfairly painted the Royal Navy as ludicrously bloated, conservative and ineffective. There were clear inefficiencies, but for example, the additional layers of approval for warships had been introduced as a result of the centralisation of defence decision-making in the mid-1960s, something which the Navy could do little about and was the same for all three services. There was certainly an argument to be had – and which did occur some 18 months later – about over-complexity and the large size of warships, but Moore provided little hard evidence that 'cheaper' would be 'better'. There was also an underlying subtext to much of his argument: large surface warships competed for funds with the large nuclear-powered submarines that Moore, an ex-submariner, was keen to have procured in greater numbers. Moore's polemic might not have mattered much if the letter had not been read by the Prime Minister, but it was. In fact, she was so impressed with it that she sent it, along with Rayner's note, to a no doubt nonplussed Chancellor of the Exchequer, Sir Geoffrey Howe, for information.[36] At least the Chancellor would have now felt that the Prime Minister was coming around to his way of thinking. Moore's impact would have been less if other similar letters had been sent and read setting out the individual inefficiencies of the Army and the Royal Air Force, but there is no evidence that any were received by the Prime Minister. In fact, Moore sent two more letters on a similar vein, both of which were read by Margaret Thatcher and passed on to Geoffrey Howe during 1980.[37]

These briefings were also covered by a short memo by one of the Prime Minister's private secretaries, Clive Whitmore. By way of summary it reinforced the issue of a lack of central direction and a 'logical' way to divide up resources amongst the services. The Ministry of Defence seemed incapable of coming to clear decisions on important strategic alternatives such as 'should we be investing greater effort in our armoured capability in central Europe and less on anti-submarine warfare or vice-versa? The MoD is stuck in an historical groove and does not know – and perhaps does not want – to get out of it.' Whitmore finished by stating that 'the problems are very close to the surface in the Ministry of Defence, and you should have little difficulty in exposing them'.[38] Unfortunately for Francis Pym, the Prime Ministerial visit to the Ministry did not go well either, with a senior civil servant noting that in a meeting with the Chiefs of Staff, the hapless servicemen had 'failed to score a single run and were beaten by 10 wickets' by a combative Mrs Thatcher.[39]

The Prime Minister's attitude towards the Defence Secretary – who in any case came from a different wing of the party and was a potential leadership rival – had begun to harden during 1980. By accident, or perhaps by design, Margaret Thatcher's Christmas briefings coupled with her visit to the Ministry had started to sow doubts in her otherwise steadfast support for the Ministry of Defence's view of the world, its continued requests for additional funds, and more subtly the role and efficiency of the service that Pym seemed to favour most: the Royal Navy.

Introducing Chevaline

On 24 January 1980, the Defence Secretary finally made public the Chevaline programme to upgrade and improve the Polaris submarine-launched ballistic missile system, which was described in the previous chapter. Sir Francis Pym revealed the Chevaline code name and explained that it would mean the addition of 'advanced penetration aids' and the 'ability to manoeuvre the payload in space' to each ballistic missile.[40] The submarines from which these missiles would be launched, the four *Resolution* class, were the Navy's hidden capital ships – maintaining the United Kingdom's strategic nuclear deterrent through the continuous stationing of at least one boat in the Atlantic Ocean ready to fire its terrifying payload on orders from the very top of government. Chevaline, which as was seen in Chapter 6, had been adopted in place of the purchase of the second-generation US Poseidon ballistic missile system, and was now planned to cost over £1,000 million in 1980 prices, up from a planned £175 million in 1972. This increase was not as great as it first seemed, as high inflation between these two dates meant that £1,000 million would actually have been £240 million in 1972 prices; a large increase, but not a cripplingly huge one.[41] The nature and timing of Pym's announcement had been condemned as an attempt to embarrass the Labour Party, which was deeply split over its nuclear policy. The announcement would inevitably reveal that the preceding Labour government had secretly begun development of Chevaline despite a manifesto promise in 1974 not to approve any new nuclear weapon systems. Recent research has shown that a genuine wish to have a more open debate on nuclear policy was as much, if not more, of a driver of the decision to reveal Chevaline than any short-term political advantage.[42]

The technical challenges to get Chevaline working were considerable. In the months before the announcement, the Chevaline missile had been undergoing a series of trial launches at Cape Canaveral in the United States. In April 1979, the 'P3' trial had highlighted problems with the second stage separation and with the system that guided the weapon in space. The 'P4' trial was more successful, but the 'P5' trial on 1 September had to be aborted 90 seconds into flight due to a motor failure. 'P6' on 8 November was a success and by this time, earlier problems with separation and space guidance had been at least temporarily resolved. Two further trials after Pym's announcement, 'PT1' and 'PT2' in March and April 1980, had similarly mixed results. The first was delayed from March until April and failed to deploy all its elements correctly, but 'PT2' was more successful and it deployed as intended. From November 1980 the first flight trials from a submarine, HMS *Renown*, also off Cape Canaveral, resulted in only one successful trial out of three attempted. Again, problems with the second stage separation were encountered. These issues resulted in creeping delays in the final operational introduction of Chevaline.

Another series of flight trials occurred in July 1981, followed by four final flight trials in January and February 1982. These last four were wholly successful and the Chevaline system was finally deployed on its first patrol from August 1982. Industrial disputes at the Coulport nuclear weapons depot did mean that the boat had to undertake its first patrol with only six Chevaline (formally designated Polaris A-3TK) missiles on board with ten older standard Polaris (Polaris A-3T) missiles filling up the remainder of *Renown*'s vertical missile launch tubes. *Revenge* had been Chevaline-upgraded by June 1983, whilst *Resolution* and *Repulse* followed in 1985 and 1987 respectively.[43] Over 15 years since it had been assessed that the British strategic nuclear deterrent was being compromised by anti-ballistic missile defences over Moscow, the Royal Navy finally had a fully operating class of Chevaline-modified submarines.

The Next Generation: Trident

Chevaline had been a means to maintain the deterrent value of the Polaris system on the 'R' boats into the early 1990s, but both the submarines – which would be over 20 years old by the end of the 1980s – and the missiles would need to be replaced. The previous Labour government, although secretly willing to approve and pay for Chevaline, was extremely reluctant to commit to a completely new missile and new submarines. A document known as the Duff-Mason report, after its authors, had put forward a number of options, but Jim Callaghan's government had not made any final decisions.[44] With the arrival of the Conservative government into power, civil servants briefed the Prime Minister on the state of both the Chevaline programme and the current situation regarding the next generation of strategic deterrent. She was given a copy of the original Duff-Mason report and over the next seven months members of the MISC 7 Cabinet Committee, chaired by Margaret Thatcher, assessed whether the nuclear deterrent should be renewed and what form it should take. The Duff-Mason report was re-written and having quickly agreed that Polaris-Chevaline must be replaced, but not without some opposition, the Committee then analysed the relevant options with additional input from the Defence Planning Staff.[45]

The Committee was given nine possible options. Two were cruise missiles and they were dismissed early in the process; the first would have been air-launched and the second launched from nuclear-powered submarines. The air-launched version was considered to be too vulnerable to Soviet air defences and the second would be too expensive as eleven special cruise-missile carrying submarines would be needed to launch the necessary 400 missiles, which if the existing hunter-killer submarine programme were maintained, would be beyond the capabilities of the shipbuilding industry. Finally, both options were compromised by the fact that existing information-sharing agreements with the United States only covered ballistic, not cruise, missiles and US technology would be necessary for the development of the cruise missiles. Another option considered placing Chevaline on new submarines, but Chevaline had a limited range and would over time become more vulnerable to Soviet defences. An upgrade to Chevaline was option number four, but this, as with the third option, would tie the United Kingdom to old Polaris technologies and equipment that were becoming obsolete and were no longer being produced. The fifth option would be to buy Poseidon from the United States. This had the advantage of equipping the Royal Navy with a MIRV ('Multiple Independently targeted Re-entry Vehicle') system for the first time, but Poseidon too was becoming obsolete, and there would be maintenance and service-life issues with accepting 'second-hand' missiles from the United States. The sixth option was to eschew US partnership altogether by collaborating with the French and buying their M4 missile, but disentangling the UK from the Polaris Sales Agreement and the Mutual Defence Agreement would have been complex and diplomatically difficult, whilst the M4 was not a MIRV system which limited its effectiveness. As a result, this option was set aside only as a possibility if UK-US relations deteriorated dramatically, which seemed unlikely.[46]

This then left three Trident options for the Committee to consider: Trident C4 with a British warhead, Trident C4 with a British warhead and a British-designed Chevaline-like re-entry system, and Trident D5 with a British warhead. Trident C4 was the current generation of Trident system, whilst D5 was the much more capable next generation but was not planned to come into service until the late 1990s, too late for the United Kingdom's requirements. This ruled out the D5 option, whilst after the experience of Chevaline, a further development of that system when a much more effective US MIRV system was available, seemed both unnecessary and expensive.[47] The modified Duff-Mason report therefore recommended Trident C4 with a British warhead and a US-designed MIRV. The MISC 7 committee discussed the options on 17 December 1979, and eventually agreed to the Trident C4 recommendation. It was calculated that the earliest date that orders could be placed for the new boats would be 1983 and that Trident would not enter service until 1990 at the earliest. Discussion over whether four or five boats should be procured was deferred to a later date.[48] Agreement in principle from the United States to purchase Trident C4 was forthcoming some days later, although the formal decision and announcement was delayed due to President Carter's fears that any such announcement might derail the SALT II talks with the Soviet Union.[49] In the event, the Soviet invasion of Afghanistan made the ratification of SALT II extremely unlikely and any fears of diplomatic repercussions dissipated. The US agreement to support the British purchase was announced in July 1980.[50]

The British government had agreed in principle to renew its submarine-launched strategic nuclear deterrent and had therefore guaranteed that the Royal Navy would be the operator of the most powerful weapons in the British military arsenal until the end of the century and probably beyond. The decision also meant a large outlay in expenditure taken from the defence budget throughout the 1980s. It did not seem likely that the defence budget would be increased significantly to cover these costs, so the Trident decision also opened up the likelihood of future battles over defence spending as the remaining funds shrank.

The Pym 'Mini-Review'

The increasingly poisonous battle between the Defence Secretary and the Chancellor of the Exchequer was renewed at the start of 1980, as discussions began to focus on future defence spending for the year 1980–1 forward through to 1983–4. Sir Geoffrey Howe opened the debate by suggesting the lowest possible basis from which to calculate the 1980–1 and 1981–2 3 per cent increases.[51] This basis worked from the Ministry of Defence's expected underspend in 1979–80 and did not include the one-off sum agreed to support initial spending on Trident feasibility studies. Pym was described as being in a 'volcanic state of mind' by officials, and the two ministers were barely able to face each other in the same room.[52] The situation was in fact worse than the headline figures suggested: the Armed Forces Pay Review Body was likely to recommend a higher pay rise for servicemen and women than expected, and Pym was ready to wave through a similarly high pay rise for 'industrial civil servants' – those government employees at the Royal Dockyards and Royal Ordnance Factories. Margaret Thatcher was particularly unhappy with this prospect.[53] In addition, procurement costs were continuing to increase above the rate of general inflation. These expected, but so far hidden, increases would mean that in practical terms, the Ministry of Defence would be facing a real-terms cut of around 2.5 and 3 per cent.[54]

It was becoming increasingly clear that a range of cuts in defence capability would be necessary in order to keep within agreed budget levels. The Ministry of Defence's own long-term costings for the next decade illustrated an underlying problem that had existed for many years: these costings were based on budget assumptions that were grossly inflated. The issues set out in Chapter 7 had not been resolved but had continued and worsened through the 1970s: over-optimistic costings for equipment were combined with heroic assumptions for the recruitment and retention of personnel to create the 'fantasy orders of battle' described in Chapter 11 that would have been impossible to realise without huge increases in both general defence spending and service pay. In February 1980 they were an enormous £1.2 billion higher than the amounts that had been set out by the Treasury's Public Expenditure Survey figures which had been agreed across government.[55] It was therefore inevitable that the services would be disappointed when their own plans proved too expensive. The lack of reality in MOD long-term planning did not just extend to finance – the services paid almost no attention to the wider impact of their planned equipment and operational changes. If the services' plans had been realised, 11.5 per cent of the whole of the United Kingdom's workforce would have either been in the services, MOD civil servants or working for defence contractors (the two biggest of which were nationalised: British Aerospace and British Shipbuilders) by the late 1980s. By the mid-1990s this figure would have been over 14 per cent.[56] Without realising what it was actually doing, the MOD would, if it had got what it wanted, have created an enormous state-controlled military-industrial complex that would have swallowed up a significant proportion of the economy's productive capacity and workforce. Such a 'warfare state' might have been politically acceptable in the 1950s, but there was no way economically or politically that this was possible in the 1980s, especially with a government ideologically committed to a reduction in state involvement in the economy.[57] The Navy was no more or less guilty of this line of thinking than the other services, but it would become clear that not only was it vulnerable because it had so many expensive procurement items in the programme, but also because strategically, its Eastern Atlantic role seemed the most vulnerable of the 'Four Pillars' of defence.

The detail of the Navy's long-term programme for construction had been ambitious to the point of surrealism as the Conservatives entered government. In April 1979 it had planned to have ten *Trafalgar* class nuclear-powered fleet submarines completed between 1983 and 1991, with eight follow-on SSN-0Z class all ordered by 1991 and entering service in the 1990s. A class of ten patrol submarines would enter service between 1986 and 1996. When it came to the programme for destroyers and frigates, any sense of realism that might have remained fell away fast. The 15th and 16th Type 42 destroyers would be in service in 1986 and 1987, whilst twelve large Type 43s would be completed between 1990 and 1996, all having been ordered between 1983 and 1990. The Type 22 class would consist of twenty-two ships completed between 1980 and 1992, with the original, large Type 23 class consisting of eight ships completed between 1992 and 1996. The programme for mine warfare vessels assumed a highly optimistic thirty 'Hunt' class and twelve 'River' class entering service between 1980 and 1994.[58]

Between 1980 and 1996, the programme therefore assumed twenty-eight submarines, three aircraft carriers, twenty-two destroyers (twelve of them – Type 43s – as expensive as nuclear submarines), thirty frigates (eight of which would be the same size as the Type 43) and forty-two mine warfare vessels would be built, in addition to a full programme of minor war vessels, support ships and Royal Fleet Auxiliaries. Especially when combined with the need to replace the four Polaris boats, this would have been well beyond the capacity of the shipbuilding industry, assumed heroic levels of budget increases for the Navy, and utterly unrealistic expectations of recruitment and retention given the Navy's experience of the last two decades. Although the other services' long-term programmes were not necessarily dissimilar, the Royal Navy's looked especially unrealistic, particularly with its obviously overweight programme of large and expensive destroyers and frigates.

As it became clear to the Prime Minister that the defence programme was looking unsustainable, Sir Robert Armstrong, the Cabinet Secretary, took a sideswipe at Royal Dockyard employees in a briefing paper for the Prime Minister just before Christmas 1979: they 'have a reputation for low productivity and over-manning' and he was sceptical about any improvement in this situation. Armstrong had also questioned the wider affordability of all four of the defence 'pillars' that had been set during the 1975 Defence Review. Unlike Pym, who had been hoping to reduce or even remove the Central Europe pillar, it is perhaps telling that the Cabinet Secretary singled out the Eastern Atlantic pillar: 'this maritime contribution costs us a great deal. Is this cost justified? If so, do we do enough in NATO to publicise this fact?'[59] Pym was heavily associated with a maritime/air approach to strategy, and a move away from large fixed forces on the Continent, so these criticisms were not only targeted at the Navy, but also, indirectly, at the Secretary of State. It was becoming clear that there were drawbacks in having a Defence Secretary that actively supported the Navy's view of the world: that minister had to be seen to deliver and to have the confidence of the Prime Minister, otherwise the Navy could suffer along with its patron. Equally, Armstrong was raising pertinent questions: the dockyard workforce did not have a reputation for efficiency, and its union representatives could be bloody-minded in their approach to negotiations over working conditions and pay. The Navy did contribute a very significant proportion of NATO's naval force capabilities in the Atlantic, yet this sometimes appeared to be a politically invisible commitment when mooted reductions of much less militarily significant forces in Germany caused howls of concern from NATO allies.[60]

In the event, a compromise between Pym and Howe was agreed towards the end of January 1980 that broadly sat at the halfway point between their two positions. The defence budget for 1980–1 was agreed to be £8,000 million, compared to Pym's opening position of £8,062 million and Howe's of £7,956 million, whilst the Treasury agreed to increase cash limits to cover the cost of increasing service pay above 14 per cent.[61] However, an important point had been reached: Margaret Thatcher, for the first time and perhaps influenced by the briefs given to her over the Christmas break, had also kept her distance and unlike in previous battles had not weighed in to support her Defence Secretary. A subtle shift had occurred, and it would presage a greater shift by the Prime Minister away from involvement in defence matters and her earlier almost unquestioning support for the Ministry.

The practical impact of this compromise on the Royal Navy was considerable. The Navy's budget target for 1980–1 was reduced by 6 per cent, and it would have been higher if unforeseen costs for Chevaline rocket motors had not been borne by the Ministry's central budget contingency.[62] Producing its planned revised and reduced expenditure for the next ten years, the Navy Department had taken the decision to defer a range of equipment orders, and made a number of major procurement decisions: the planned order of 'long lead' items for six 'Castle' class Offshore Patrol Vessels was cancelled, major modernisations of two 'County' class destroyers (*Antrim* and *Norfolk*) and the last five Batch 3 *Leander* class frigates were cancelled, as was the conversion of the old destroyer *Kent* into a minelayer and the stores ship RFA *Tarbatness* into an amphibious transport. The last refit of the helicopter carrier *Bulwark* was also cancelled ending her active service earlier than planned. Two of the most significant decisions were the cancellation of Sea Dart Mark II air defence missile (saving £137 million over ten years) and the reduction in the size of the planned Type 43 guided missile destroyer from a 'double-ended' air defence vessel with two twin-armed missile launchers, into a smaller single-launcher ship using the Type 22 Batch 2 hull saving £140 million. As was seen in the previous chapter these two changes called into question the air defence of the fleet in the 1990s: the new shrunken Type 43 would be barely any more effective than the existing Type 42 class as an air defence vessel, but at a much greater price. This therefore placed more onus on the Harrier for fleet air defence (the ten additional Harriers ordered in May 1978 provided a partial support to their increasingly important role), and made the Type 43 vulnerable to cancellation, given that it would share many of the inadequacies of the existing Type 42 in dealing with massed Soviet cruise-missile air attacks in the eastern Atlantic. Finally, and probably most importantly for a Navy increasingly relying on its submarine arm, the decision to stretch out the 'hunter-killer' nuclear submarine programme and defer forthcoming orders saved £200 million but was a serious concession that pushed further into the future the Navy's long-term plan for eighteen such submarines in the fleet.[63]

In effect, these cuts had been the first, and most painful, phase in what was known later as the Pym 'mini-review.' The Navy had saved a total of £560 million and had been hit the hardest of the three services, but the Army had been forced to accept the cancellation of the planned MBT 80 tank and a surveillance drone as well as reductions in orders for Blowpipe and Rapier missiles, whilst a range of RAF fast jet orders were deferred and older aircraft kept flying for additional years.[64] It was expected that further cuts would be forthcoming and the Navy Department had been ordered to prepare outline plans for removing a further £840 million from its budget.[65] As had been expected, a significant proportion of these potential cuts did have to be made a few months later as it became clear that the Ministry's spending had been galloping ahead of budget, overspending by £700 million in only three months. This time the cuts were also guided by Pym's report on the future of the 'Four Pillars' which had finally been completed. The Secretary of State had been unable to come to a clear decision. The nuclear deterrent and home defence were non-negotiable, whilst with the Eastern Atlantic and the Central European front 'no black and white choice would be sensible.' Although Pym wanted to cut the latter, diplomatic considerations prevented him from doing so. The Brussels Treaty had been interpreted for many years as requiring a minimum of 54,000 servicemen in Germany, which placed a limit on the reductions that could be made to the Army and to the Royal Air Force in Germany.[66] As a result, there was no other choice but to reduce the Navy and reduce the British contribution to NATO's Eastern Atlantic role.[67]

This then presaged the second phase of the Pym mini-review. For the Navy, the impact was severe but did at least bring its long-term programme somewhat closer to a sense of realism. The nuclear submarine programme was revised, taking better account of the capacity of the shipbuilding industry. The SSN0Z class would start construction three years later, and two more *Trafalgar* class boats would be constructed, four of that class being built at a second nuclear submarine-building yard; an optimistic assumption given the problems Cammell Laird had as the nuclear 'second yard' in the 1960s.[68] Orders for the fifteenth and sixteenth Type 42s were cancelled – they had only been re-inserted into the programme in early 1979 when the redesign of the Type 43 had meant the pushing pack of the first order of that class by 18 months. Much more serious was the decision to push back the order of the Type 43, now redesignated the Type 44, by a number of years more. This made an already vulnerable procurement even more prone to cancellation as a five-year gap was now being placed between the last order of a Type 42 and the first of the Type 44. There were similar changes in the frigate programme, as the fifteenth to twenty-second Type 22 frigates were removed from the programme, and orders for the Type 23 – now a cheap light anti-submarine frigate rather than the large vessel previously envisaged – were pushed back a number of years.[69] The new mine warfare building programme was also more realistic, with thirty 'Hunts' replaced by seventeen of that class, followed by six or more cheaper Single Role Minehunters.[70] In addition, orders for Sea Skua and RAF Sea Eagle anti-ship missiles were halved, the stocks of sonobuoys reduced by

10 per cent, and two support tankers were cancelled. The orders for the twelve 'River' class deep-sea minesweepers were deferred, as was the replacement for Wessex commando helicopter.[71] Overall, this new programme was much more realistic, but it still did not entirely convince: developing a second nuclear yard would be a major, and expensive, undertaking and probably one that would have been beyond the ailing shipbuilding industry. The Type 44 was an undeveloped design based on highly optimistic assumptions that was only relatively minor improvement on the Type 42; there was a high chance that it would end up being as expensive as the Type 43. At the time these reductions appeared heavy and particularly harsh on the Navy, but this was only the start of what was to come over the next year.

The 1980 Statement on the Defence Estimates

Whilst significant chunks were being taken out of the Navy's long-term programme, work was proceeding on the Statement on the Defence Estimates: an annual document that set out current British defence policy. This year saw a transformation in the document: Pym wanted to emphasise clearly the nature and extent of the Soviet threat, de-emphasise detente and clearly set out the British contribution to NATO and how that contribution fitted into NATO strategy.[72] Also, for the first time the Statement was issued in two parts; the second part being a volume of largely previously unavailable defence statistics. The document had an unusual emphasis on seapower and Britain's naval capabilities. It devoted a significant portion of its text to the Eastern Atlantic and Channel role of the Navy within NATO, making clear the importance of Atlantic reinforcement in a period of increased tension and the recent increases in capability of the Soviet Navy. Under the home defence category it also focussed on the role of mine countermeasures forces against Soviet submarine mining.[73] At the Cabinet Committee meeting chaired by the Prime Minister where the draft of the Statement was discussed, Pym was clear that despite the cuts to the Navy, he still believed that it would be in the best long-term interests of the United Kingdom to withdraw almost completely from Germany to concentrate on the Eastern Atlantic and the Channel. He argued that British forces only provided 10 per cent of NATO capability in Germany, but provided 80 per cent of NATO capability in the Eastern Atlantic, and that the Royal Navy possessed 'expertise of a high order'.[74] The Statement on the Defence Estimates was approved by the Committee, but Pym's comments were not explicitly endorsed by other members. The Statement was however a political success, drawing praise from the centre-right press for its detail and candidness, when previous statements had veered towards the anodyne in order to avoid offending the then-Labour government's left wing.[75] The focus on maritime capabilities and the Eastern Atlantic role in the 1980

Statement remains as a publicly-available hint of Pym's ultimately unfulfilled strategic ambitions.

* * *

By the summer of 1980 Pym's credibility was quickly disappearing. His warnings that two British shipyards – Scotts and Cammell Laird – would go under if government orders were not forthcoming did not elicit any note of support from the Prime Minister.[76] Even more damagingly, as an act of desperation the Ministry of Defence imposed a moratorium on contracts with the private sector across the board. Apart from proving almost unworkable and resulting in ships returning to harbour, aircraft being grounded and exercises cancelled, it very quickly began to cause huge problems for suppliers who were already reeling from the recession.[77] The moratorium had to be rescinded and Pym's position was further undermined. In December 1980 the Prime Minister and Chancellor of the Exchequer decided that a new approach was needed, and on 5 January 1981 Sir Francis Pym was demoted to Leader of the House of Commons and Sir John Nott became the new Defence Secretary.

Sir Francis Pym had wanted to effect a dramatic re-orientation in British defence strategy in favour of a maritime, to a lesser extent, air role and away from land forces in Western Germany. The Royal Navy, in this scenario, would have returned to the greater prominence in defence it had held in the early 1960s. However, the Ministry of Defence was assailed by a severe recession and high inflation, coupled with lax spending controls and unrealistic long-term planning assumptions. Pym's failure to control the inevitable budget overspends rapidly undermined his credibility with the Prime Minister, whilst the diplomatic implications of any reduction in troop numbers in Germany made it impossible to undertake the great re-orientation he had envisaged. As Pym was dragged down by this crisis in defence, so to some extent was the Royal Navy with which he had so closely associated himself. In addition, those lingering doubts about the Royal Navy and its role that had built up since the mid-1970s had not faded away: were convoy escorts needed if a war would end before reinforcements arrived across the Atlantic? Could the Royal Navy's surface ships survive the carnage of regimental attacks of Soviet cruise missile-carrying 'Backfire' bombers if its air defences were so meagre? Might not the funds for this significant defence commitment, which seemed to produce so little recognition within NATO compared to land and air forces, be more usefully spent elsewhere?

Only a year earlier, the position for the Royal Navy had seemed more positive than it had been for years: it had a sympathetic Defence Secretary who had accepted the Navy's strategic preferences and wanted to push more of the defence budget in its direction, and a similarly sympathetic Prime Minister who supported the Ministry against the Treasury. By January 1981 this was no more than a memory: as a new Defence Secretary was appointed and the Prime Minister became increasingly frustrated, the Ministry of Defence entered a spending crisis and the Royal Navy began a two-year period of multiple crises of its own.

13

The 'Bermudagram'

Launching the Defence Review

John Nott was appointed the new Defence Secretary on 5 January 1981. Only a few days before, the Prime Minister and Chancellor of the Exchequer had both agreed that a defence review was necessary, and that Francis Pym was not the man to undertake it: he had been unable to control what seemed to be runaway defence spending and had, as a result, eventually lost the confidence of Mrs Thatcher.[1] Nott was an intelligent, peppery and sometimes irascible politician who had been willing to make difficult decisions at his previous post, the Department of Trade, and was, like the Prime Minister, considered 'one of us' on the party's economic policy right wing.[2] With the demeanour of an accountant and an earlier career as a merchant banker, it was evident that Nott had been brought in to get the Ministry back under control. In his first few weeks in office it became clear just how serious the short-term situation was, and as early as 20 January he was both announcing minor cuts in capability and requesting additional funds from the Treasury. In March, as the government's financial year neared its end, Nott would still be scrabbling for short-term economies just like his predecessor.[3] Nott entered a government department that seemed to be enmired in a permanent rolling funding crisis.

In his first letter to Nott as Defence Secretary, the Chief of the Defence Staff, Admiral Lewin, made clear the extremely difficult situation in which Defence found itself. He argued that despite significant increases in Soviet defence capability over the last decade, British defence spending had not been increased materially for over 30 years, that operational activity had been cut by over 30 per cent in many areas to bring in additional short-term savings, and that the Treasury was imposing further controls on the budget. Lewin concluded that therefore there was no alternative but a review of defence commitments.[4] By commitments Lewin in practice meant the balance of investment in each of the

'Four Pillars' of defence policy in the NATO area. The nuclear pillar was not negotiable, whilst the defence of the United Kingdom (which in practice meant air defence, civil defence and the defence of territorial waters) was also seen to be similarly non-negotiable. As under Pym, this therefore left a choice between the Central Front in Europe and the Eastern Atlantic.[5] This time, the Navy would not have a sympathetic Secretary of State to provide a modicum of protection.

In his first few days Nott seemed to have been bullish about making savings across all of defence in order to ensure that the Ministry kept within its long-term budget. Six years later, Sir Frank Cooper, the Permanent Under Secretary, recounted to the journalist Hugo Young how this had shifted towards a focus on the Royal Navy's capabilities.[6] Young stated that, according to Cooper, Nott

> took a very weird line over the Defence Review, from which, says C[ooper], 'we' had to rescue him. [Nott] stirred everything up, giving the impression that absolutely everything was under review, but had no idea how to get out of it. The department, as per tradition, helped him towards an anti-navy solution. Why is the department anti-navy? Basically because nobody has ever been able to agree with the role it sees for itself: stretching worldwide, ready to step in all over etc. etc.[7]

Frank Cooper might well have been building a bigger role for himself in retrospect by claiming that civil servants had helped to bring Nott 'towards an anti-Navy solution', although as will be seen he was clearly the driving force behind the key document of the review – known as the 'Bermudagram'. What is clear is that a decision that reduced the size and role of the surface fleet did accord broadly with the majority view, as much as it can be divined, at the Ministry by the early 1980s.[8] Also, as will be seen, the most important report that fed into the decisions that Nott made – written by General Johnston – was essentially a survey of Ministry informed opinion largely based on interviews with senior civil servants, defence scientists and officers from all three services. Cooper's assertion that the Ministry was 'anti-Navy' is also revealing. By anti-navy he made it clear himself that he was referring to the maintenance of a worldwide role and the ability to deal with unexpected crises, something associated most with the general line of the majority of the Naval Staff, although not necessarily all RN staff officers, with many submariners and some others being a significant dissenting element. To some extent, therefore, the phrase itself is unfair and too generalising. Also, it would be difficult to argue that the Ministry was 'traditionally' anti-Navy in 1976 when Cooper became Permanent Under-Secretary ('PUS'): his predecessor, Sir Michael Cary, who had died unexpectedly from a heart attack in post, had previously worked for both the Admiralty and the Air Ministry and had not objected to the Navy's procurement of the Sea Harrier in 1975, despite strong opposition in some parts of the Ministry. In addition, the other leading candidate for Cary's post had been Patrick Nairne, another former Admiralty civil servant who, it will be recalled from Chapter 2, had attempted to negotiate a small-carrier compromise during the battle for CVA01 in 1965–6 (Nairne, Cooper's great rival in the Ministry, transferred to run the Department for Health and Social Security after Cooper got the post[9]). Certainly, the Europe and land-air focus of the Ministry increased significantly after Cooper became PUS, and not just due to Cooper himself, an ex-Air Ministry official who took an increasingly robust line on the need to focus on this theatre and reduce overseas commitments, but as a result of the shifts within defence policy following the 1974–5 Defence Review, and the withdrawal from most of the remaining commitments East of Suez. As was seen in the previous chapter, the outcome of the Pym mini-review, in which the most actively pro-Navy Secretary of State for Defence for a decade had been forced into greater reductions of the Royal Navy than the other services, shows the extent to which the Navy was the service most vulnerable to reductions.

Cooper's statement does indicate that by 1981, for the Royal Navy to argue in favour of its traditional roles it had to go 'against the grain' of what had become the Ministry consensus over the last six years. As a long-serving PUS he also promoted and supported the careers of the next two generations of the most capable senior civil servants in the Ministry including those of Michael Quinlan and Richard Mottram, both future PUSs at the MOD, and David Omand, a future head of GCHQ.[10] This issue would therefore not necessarily disappear with the retirement of Cooper at the end of 1982, although the end of the Cold War would later change the situation. Civil servants such as Quinlan and Mottram became somewhat more favourable towards the Navy's surface fleet, seeing it as having increased importance in a world without superpower confrontation and a lack of a single specific threat to the United Kingdom.[11]

The situation in 1981 was even more difficult for the Royal Navy because, as was seen in Chapter 10, it had not been able to produce a concept of operations that had been accepted across the Ministry. The most recent document dating from 1978 was a painful compromise written in the Central Staffs that had acknowledged that the surface fleet needed to shrink in the future, although it did make the case for a class of diesel-electric submarines, something which had been in the Navy's Long Term Costings for many years but had never moved beyond early conceptual studies. Lacking a concept of operations that it was comfortable with, the Naval Staff therefore had no document from which to argue for a size and shape for the fleet, and therefore a balance of investment between the different types of maritime capability. In addition, some of its major planned procurements, including the troubled

Type 44 destroyer and indecision over the best anti-submarine platform, did not give confidence that the Naval Staff itself had a coherent understanding of what sort of fleet it wanted. In addition, the 1978 document was almost certainly well-read within senior circles of the Ministry, and had helped to build a consensus around a shrinking surface fleet in the 1980s and 1990s.

It was worse than this though; in Chapter 10 it was recounted that in 1976 the RAF had also adopted a strategy towards a future war with the Warsaw Pact that matched that of the Army: that any future conflict would be a short war lasting no more than five days, that the primary theatre of war would be the Central European front and that the Eastern Atlantic was secondary. It was also heavily implied that such a five day war would start with very short-warning and could just as likely be a little- or no-warning 'bolt from the blue'. As was also seen in the same chapter, this position also began to be accepted within some parts of the Navy, particularly in the submariner community. This very narrow perspective on the likely nature of a future war, which excluded a huge range of different possible transition to war scenarios, was therefore not only now the standard position for civil servants but also for the other two armed services, even though it resulted in a range of inconsistencies, including the fact that the Army was dependent the transfer of one whole division (made up of Territorial Army units) from the United Kingdom during a period of tension in order to support the British Army of the Rhine.[12] The Navy was now very much alone in arguing for anything other than this short-war/short-warning scenario.

Finally, the early decision by Nott to transfer the budget for procuring Trident into that for the Navy Department, which was confirmed in mid-March when Nott released his initial conclusions from the review but had been under consideration since he had become Defence Secretary, turned a difficult situation into one that was potentially disastrous for the Navy.[13] With Trident in the Navy's procurement budget, significant parts of the existing programme would have to be removed. If the submarine programme was protected, and there was every sign that this would be the case, then the surface fleet would be the main casualty. Nott's rationale in March for the transfer of Trident into the budget was that it demonstrated that the Department was treating the cost of Trident 'as part of the cost of our contribution rather something special or additional to service programmes'.[14] Space now had to be found for Trident within the ten-year Long Term Costings that were already highly inflated and increasingly unrealistic. The decision was wholly negative for the Navy and reflected Nott's acceptance of a review that would focus most on the Senior Service rather than being an 'equal pain exercise', but it should not have been entirely unexpected, especially after Nott had reportedly tried and failed to achieve a special subvention from the Treasury to help cover Trident costs.[15]

The Greenwich Conference

John Nott, within a week of becoming Defence Secretary, requested an informal discussion on future defence policy with his most senior officials and the Chiefs of Staff. A location was quickly set for Greenwich, at the Chief of the Defence Staff's residence, the meeting occurring on 16 January.[16] In addition to the Chiefs, the Permanent Under-Secretary, the Chief Scientific Adviser and the Chief of Defence Procurement were to attend. The day consisted of a series of informal discussions and working lunches with no advisers or staff officers present, only these eight most senior people in the Ministry. Discussions began with ten-minute introductions by each of the service chiefs.[17] In an incident that has since become notorious, during Admiral Leach's discussion of the role of the Navy, Nott abruptly interrupted the First Sea Lord and asked 'why do we want surface ships?' Interrupted, Leach remained silent and did not answer, and Lewin eventually intervened by stating that the First Sea Lord would need much more than five minutes to do justice to that question. This aggressive questioning, to which no other Chief was subjected, made it clear that at a fundamental level, the new Secretary of State had already made his mind up about how the Defence Review would proceed.[18]

This early exchange is interesting, as it shows that despite the fact that Leach was one of the ablest senior officers of his generation, he could not articulate a rejoinder to Nott's question. At one level, Nott was showing how little he knew about warships and how, unlike most major capabilities in other services, they have multiple roles in peace, periods of tension and war. However, at another it also demonstrates how ill-equipped Leach was to deal with basic questions relating to the purpose of the Royal Navy. Having spent his whole working life within the Navy, he found it difficult to understand how such a question could be even asked, but such questions were increasingly being asked by those outside the Naval Staff in the Ministry of Defence and in other parts of government. An inability to respond with an effective answer, however reductive, gave an impression of not knowing why the Navy was the size and shape it was. There was one positive aspect to this episode. Nott's aggressive questioning at least gave the Navy an early warning that the Defence Review could be one in which it would be the main target for possible reductions.

Initial Responses

Nott had hoped that the Greenwich Conference would result in some suggestions for possible reductions, but these were not forthcoming from the Chiefs, who were all well aware that voluntarily offering up early reductions had not done the services any good in previous defence reviews.[19] As a result, Nott commissioned Lewin to produce proposals for efficiency savings and reductions. Lewin was heavily restricted in what he could suggest by his role as representative of the three service Chiefs: he could not formally give his own advice, but that collectively of the three Chiefs of Staff. When Lewin's paper appeared in late February it was evident that it had been produced as a compromise acceptable to all three services as well as the Central Staffs. The paper started by setting out an approximate balance of resources within the Ministry: 41 per cent was spent on Central Europe, mostly on British Forces Germany, 23 per cent on the 'UK Base', 23 per cent on the Eastern Atlantic and Channel, 4 per cent on the strategic nuclear deterrent, 4 per cent on out of area operations and 5 per cent on pensions.[20] Lewin was blunt on the nature of the threat from the USSR, which was 'massive and increasing'. The alliance with the US was essential, as was ensuring that oil continued to flow from the Persian Gulf.[21]

Lewin stated that the current level of defence spending was inadequate to fulfil the UK's military commitments, but that if the economic situation required reductions in capabilities or tasks, then the key decision was whether a review would focus on cost effectiveness of military capabilities or on political and diplomatic factors. If cost-effectiveness was the key driver then the maritime contribution should be favoured and the continental commitment reduced: the United Kingdom provided 70 per cent of NATO's ready sea and air forces in the Eastern Atlantic and Channel for 23 per cent of the defence budget, whilst British Forces Germany contributed approximately 10 per cent NATO's land forces in the region for over 40 per cent of the defence budget.[22] If political factors were paramount then maritime forces should be reduced and British Forces Germany sustained, thus lessening the diplomatic difficulties with West Germany and the rest of the Alliance. Lewin then suggested some innovative ideas for shifting British forces in the Central Area without withdrawing them: including pulling them back from the inner German border to form a strategic reserve force (which would have shorter logistics chains and be more easily reinforced from the United Kingdom), or moving them to Denmark and Schleswig-Holstein in northern Germany, shortening logistics lines even further and perhaps providing an increased role for the Royal Marines on the Danish islands in the Baltic. The former plan had been proposed by the Army itself, and would have enabled a more militarily sensible positioning of British forces so that they could respond to a Soviet attack more flexibly, but both were politically extremely difficult to achieve. They would look like the United Kingdom was trying to edge out of its NATO land commitments: either into a secondary area of likely Soviet attack (Denmark) or into a position where it would be allowing other Alliance members to take the first and most painful hit from any attacking Warsaw Pact units. Other NATO members would have to fill the gap at the inner German border, and it was unclear whether any would be willing to do so. Withdrawing either land or air forces from Germany was a theoretical possibility, but aside from the acute political difficulties, these units would have to be accommodated in new barracks and air bases at home, requiring significant up-front costs.[23]

With respect to the maritime and northern flank commitments, Lewin mentioned the possibility of suggesting offsets to other NATO members for the British preponderance in the Eastern Atlantic. Offsets are, in effect, a form of subsidy where the procurement of foreign equipment (sometimes at favourable prices) is undertaken instead of a direct financial transfer. This proposal seems to have been unlikely to have borne fruit. Another alternative would be increasing the amount of pre-positioned equipment in Europe to lessen the need to send equipment by sea. Lewin also suggested a range of other economies: reducing research and development spending down to the ratios of Germany or France, and combining a number of single-service organisations into 'purple' tri-service bodies such as staff colleges, medical services, band services, education, catering and recruiting.[24]

Lewin had effectively set out the available options for the review, and his analysis of the choice between a focus on military effectiveness and politico-diplomatic considerations, put its finger the real nature of the British continental commitment: British Forces Germany existed to deter the Soviets and assure NATO allies, rather than as a real warfighting body. To undertake the latter would require a major increase in defence spending to levels that would have been impossible to defend domestically.[25] The very fact that the best equipped and most capable NATO land/air forces, the US 7th Army and the 17th Expeditionary Air Force, were largely based in southern Germany owed more to the zones of occupation in the late 1940s than to any sensible positioning to counter the most likely Soviet thrust towards the Channel ports. In essence therefore, the British Army and RAF in Germany were more important as political statements than as fighting units, and the political pain of undertaking the most militarily cost-effective option for British defence would probably be too difficult to bear. Aside from the Army's General Staff proposing a shift of the British Army of the Rhine towards a strategic reserve posture, the other significant move made by the three services in the first few weeks after the Greenwich conference, was the RAF's canny production of a paper that emphasised that the forces available for the air defence of the United Kingdom were inadequate and had suffered from a long period of neglect by previous governments.[26] This helped to deflect any attention from economies in the RAF's forces in the UK, and also had the indirect, albeit minor, benefit for the Navy of partly protecting those aircraft that would also provide air cover for the fleet.

The Naval Staff decided to put the case for a maritime-led strategy directly to Nott towards the end of January. The paper they submitted essentially recapitulated the arguments that had convinced Pym back in late 1979. It was argued that a 'long war' or long-warning conflict would be more likely: the nuclear threshold had been set high by the United States and as a result any conflict was likely to be longer rather than shorter, and might not involve any fighting on the Central European front, at least initially. It was also argued that the United Kingdom's proportionate contribution to NATO forces in the eastern Atlantic was much more valuable to Alliance defence and cost effective than the British contribution to the land-based defence of the Central European front.[27] It seemed illogical to concentrate budgets in areas where the impact was least. British forces in Germany did little more than show the UK commitment to its continental Alliance partners, whilst the forces in the Eastern Atlantic 'ensure the US remains linked to Europe and also … protect[s] our national interest'.[28] In addition, given Soviet support for various Third World governments and liberation movements, and the increasing presence of Soviet naval vessels and Soviet military advisers in continents such as Africa, any rise in tension and possible confrontation was more likely to occur beyond the European continent.[29] These arguments had no effect on Nott, who was quickly turning towards a focus on the Central European front and the defence of the United Kingdom over the maritime role in the Eastern Atlantic. In the meantime, the Naval Staff undertook a hard, and realistic, look at its own forward programme for the first time in years.

Reviewing the Future Navy
A small group within the Naval Staff began to analyse different long-term options for the Royal Navy's force mix, based on a more realistic picture of the likely naval portion of the defence budget in both 10 and 20 years' time. The work was led by Captain 'Sandy' Woodward, the Director of Naval Plans, just before he left for the job of Flag Officer First Flotilla and a promotion to Rear Admiral. By looking ahead to 2000, assuming that the defence budget would not increase by any more than its long-term trend line, and that the Royal Navy's portion of the budget would remain the same, the reality of the situation was made clear and the unrealistic fantasies perpetuated by the Long Term Costing assumptions were laid bare. From the available naval budget, assessed to be £3.4 billion a year to 2000 at September 1980 prices (with £2.6 billion available for procurement and ship support), four possible fleet plans were produced.[30] They are summarised in the table below.

Every option included maintaining three *Invincible* class aircraft carriers and four ballistic missile nuclear submarines ('SSBNs'). The Option A fleet prioritised the need to maintain a balanced fleet with steady proportions of money spent on building and supporting both submarines and surface ships. In line with the 1975 Defence Review decision, the amphibious

Table 8: Naval Staff internal size and shape review

	Option A: 'balanced fleet'	**Option B: 'forward operations fleet'**	**Option C: '65 escort fleet'**	**Option D: 'frigate-less fleet'**
Submarines	4 SSBN, 15 SSN, 10 SSK	4 SSBN, 17 SSN (26 by 2020), 10 SSK	4 SSBN, c. 10 SSN (reducing to 0 by 2020)	4 SSBN, 15 SSN, 10 SSK
Aircraft carriers	3 CVS	3 CVS	3 CVS	3 CVS + 3 'helicopter support ships'
Destroyers and frigates	37, down to 'steady state' of 35 soon after	30, down to 'steady state' of 14 by mid-2000s	Under 65	30 down to 'steady state' of 21 soon after
Amphibious vessels	none	2 LPD replacements, 4 LSL replacements	none	none
Mine warfare vessels	Under 50 (c. 12 'Hunt', 12 SRMH, + Hovercraft) + 2 County class DLG as minelayers	c. 12 'Hunt', smaller number of SRMH + 1 DLG minelayer	c. 12 'Hunt', c. 20 SRMH + 1 DLG minelayer	c. 12 'Hunt', c. 15 SRMH
RFAs	6 AORs + residual others	5 AORs	10 AOR + residual others	6 AORs
Personnel	50,000	?	?	?

capability would be phased out by the 1990s. This option demonstrated the impossibility of keeping to the existing policy of sixty to sixty-five destroyers and frigates out to the 2000s, combined with plans to sustain a fifty-strong mine-countermeasures fleet and an aspiration towards an eighteen-strong nuclear-powered attack submarine ('SSN') fleet. Option B created what was described as a NATO northern flank 'forward operations' navy, with maximum investment in nuclear and conventional submarines combined with retaining the amphibious force to support US littoral operations in the region. In this navy the ability to protect convoys would be largely given up as would be the building of air defence destroyers, leaving a small residual fleet of medium-sized frigates, somewhat like the defunct Type 25, by the mid-2000s. With such a small surface force, the three carriers could not be protected or supported by the Royal Navy's own escorts, whilst the amphibious force would only be able to operate under US escort. Option C went in the other direction and aimed to focus all resources on attempting to retain an escort force of sixty-five, with a mix of capable and cheaper ships, to 2000. This would only be possible by phasing out SSNs and SSKs altogether, thus threatening the viability of the SSBN force. In operational terms, SSBNs were best 'deloused' by SSNs when entering and leaving home waters, whilst from a procurement perspective, a production line of other nuclear submarines was also needed to ensure that vital shipyard skills in building such vessels were retained in the gaps between procuring SSBNs. Option D had some characteristics of Option C, but based on the assumption that convoy protection was best undertaken by either helicopters or maritime patrol aircraft, meaning that anti-submarine frigates would be phased out by 2009. Most escorts would be air defence destroyers, and there would be three utility helicopter carriers, dubbed Helicopter Support Ships, carrying anti-submarine helicopters in service with another two under construction by 2000.[31]

Woodward's study was an internal Naval Staff exercise which aimed to inject a sense of necessary realism in the Navy's position over the Defence Review, making it clear what was achievable and what was not: retaining the 60 to 65-strong destroyer and frigate policy would be folly, whilst sustaining a balanced fleet as expensive and larger vessels replaced older and smaller ones would inevitably require a reduction in numbers in almost all ship types. It also seemed to suggest, perhaps somewhat unfairly, that it would be difficult to carve out money from the budget to replace the amphibious capability whilst also attempting to sustain a capable submarine and escort force. These options therefore laid out the implications of the likely budget realities over the next two decades. If the Navy's share of the budget decreased or the defence budget slid below its current trajectory, then the position would be even worse. With the decision to place the costs of Trident within the Navy Department's budget this worst-case situation came to pass, and each of these four fleet options began to look unduly optimistic in their assumptions, even if in other respects they were helping to shift the Naval Staff towards more realistic understanding of the Navy's predicament. It is notable that this study was kept to a very small distribution of staff officers for fear of the impact on naval morale.[32]

The Force Mix Study

Whilst these initial papers were being presented and discussed, all were aware that the most important document for shaping the outcome of the review would the 'Force Mix' paper being written by Lieutenant General Johnston, the incoming Deputy Chief of the Defence Staff (Operational Requirements) ('DCDS(OR)'). It had been commissioned in the dying weeks of Francis Pym's period as Defence Secretary, and Nott had allowed it to continue. Johnston's Force Mix Study was undertaken in the four and half short weeks between his appointment on 20 January and his presentation of the study to the Chiefs on 23 February.[33] Johnston had consulted senior figures within the three services and with senior defence scientists, in particular Sir Ronald Mason, the Chief

Scientific Adviser. Defence Operational Analysis Establishment ('DOAE') reports were also mentioned as an important source for his analysis.[34] One of the major themes that ran through his report was the view that because of significant increases in Soviet capabilities in nearly all domains, the most effective means of defeating Soviet forces was to 'attack at source': for cruise missiles this meant destroying aircraft before they launched their missiles or destroying the airfields from which the aircraft would fly, for submarines this meant destroying Soviet boats as they passed through the Greenland-Iceland-UK Gap before they came close to any NATO shipping. Weapon systems and platforms that focussed on these longer-range tasks would be favoured over 'close support' capabilities. Also, Johnston argued that all three services focussed too much on 'platforms' – ships, aircraft and tanks – rather than weapon systems, resulting in expensive platforms such as nuclear submarines, the Lynx battlefield helicopter and the SP70 self-propelled gun, that fired underperforming weapons (in these cases the Mk 24 torpedo, the TOW missile and an identical shell to that fired by the SP70's predecessor).[35] The section of Johnston's report that dealt with the Central Region and countering Soviet land and air forces was in many ways prescient. He argued that deep strikes against Soviet airfields by RAF bombers were now too risky given advances in Warsaw Pact air defences and that therefore the future would therefore lie in air or submarine-launched cruise missiles to undertake such tasks. He also argued for further investment in the Phoenix air surveillance drone as relatively cheap and flexible means of providing a tactical picture of the battlefield for land forces.[36]

When it came to his recommendations for the Eastern Atlantic pillar, his conclusions seemed blunt and radical – and aligned the Secretary of State's position as it was developing – but were in some respects no more than repeating back to the Navy Department assessments to which it had accepted and agreed over the last six years, most of it derived from the reams of DOAE analysis undertaken for the Navy during the late 1970s. The 1975 Naval Concept of Operations Paper had, as has been seen in Chapter 10, argued that in anti-submarine warfare the day of the 'traditional' anti-submarine frigate using a light helicopter and hull sonar to detect and prosecute targets was over. Medium helicopters and land-based maritime patrol aircraft were much more effective at prosecuting attacks on submarines, whilst the towed-array sonar, complemented by sonobouys and dipping sonars, were much more effective for detection than hull-mounted sonars. Johnston fully accepted this analysis, and as a result, smaller, cheaper towed-array frigates would be needed but not any more of the large Type 22 frigates, and aircraft would provide most of the anti-submarine capability. The cheap ships would be 'forward operating bases' for anti-submarine helicopters, whose 'motherships' would be larger vessels such as the new *Invincible* class aircraft carriers. This assessment partly aligned with the Navy Department's own view, as it had begun in the closing weeks of 1980 to focus on a new cheaper Type 23 towed-array frigate, with a replenishment oiler acting as a platform for anti-submarine helicopters. Some incoherence was brought into this analysis by Johnston's assessment that the new medium anti-submarine helicopter was only a 'close support' platform (despite a tactical radius of over 70–80 nautical miles, which was relatively well matched to the detection range of the towed-array) and should therefore be 'cut back', even though rather confusingly he supported its operational concept.[37]

As was seen in Chapter 11, the Naval Staff's Fleet Requirements Committee had accepted in 1979 that air defence of ships by shipborne medium-range guided missiles was going to be much less viable in the 1980s and 1990s, given the wide dispersal of forces necessary for towed-array operations and in an environment where tactical nuclear weapons might be used. Johnston took this to its logical conclusion by stating that therefore medium-range air defence missiles like Sea Dart did not have the range to defend a naval task group in the 1980s and 1990s. Favouring an approach that intercepted the 'archer rather than the arrow', he therefore argued for investing in a more effective air-to-air missile for the Sea Harrier and that the Sea Harrier should be eventually be replaced by a more versatile supersonic VSTOL aircraft. This assessment therefore also harked back to the 1975 paper, which had envisaged *Invincible* class carriers as primarily Harrier platforms for air defence. More investment in organic air defence aircraft would therefore be accompanied by the phasing out of the air defence destroyer.[38]

Johnston saw RAF land-based maritime strike aircraft – the Buccaneer and in due course the Tornado coupled with the Sea Eagle missile – as the most effective weapon for countering Soviet surface forces, arguing for the retention of the Buccaneer for as long as possible in the role, and believing that ship-launched anti-ship missiles like Exocet only had a marginal role as a counter-marking capability in the transition to war period. He concluded that medium guns should be fitted to new warships, recognising their general-purpose role in different situations. He favoured retaining the *Invincible* class, believing that the Sea Harrier had a significant role to play, and that a small carrier had an importance in out of area operations beyond the range of land-based aircraft. Johnston argued that the North and Norwegian Seas were so vulnerable to Soviet air attack that amphibious operations would have little chance of success, and that the Royal Marines should instead be inserted in the High North by air and that as much equipment as possible should be pre-positioned in Norway. This analysis did no more than reiterate the conclusions of the 1975 Defence Review and could not have been unexpected.[39]

Nine years later Nott would describe Johnston as 'the best brains on the Central Military Staff' at the time, citing his conclusion that all three services should focus on weapons rather than platforms, as one of his most important, and a considerable influence on his thoughts over the Review.[40] Read in black and white, most of the conclusions – which included disinvesting in the Types 42, 44 and 22 and investing more in maritime patrol aircraft, land-based air and Sea Harriers – seemed brutal to many in the Navy Department, but was no more than what the Naval Staff had itself concluded over the previous decade but had not acted upon. The results should not have therefore come as a surprise, but despite paying lip service to the limitations of the anti-submarine frigate and of medium-ranged ship-launched air defence missiles, the Naval Staff had continued to attempt to procure large anti-submarine frigates and air defence destroyers. It had not challenged the operational analysis assessments when they had been produced, and neither had they followed through with the types of ships – aside from the Type 23 – that would have had a place in this environment, such as procuring a smaller number of anti-submarine helicopter-carrying 'garage ships' to replace those parts of the frigate force without towed-array, or even considering the procurement of the much more effective, but expensive, US Aegis air defence system for a small number of large destroyers in place of modernising Sea Dart and continuing a production line of Type 42s and Type 44s.

A number of criticisms of Johnston's paper could be made: in the central theatre the Army was relatively gently treated and his assumption that the Central Front would always be the decisive theatre in any conflict with the Soviet Union, was made without supporting evidence and almost as an obvious given. His partial dismissal of the large anti-submarine helicopter seemed to misunderstand its role, underplaying its importance in prosecuting attacks based on detections from towed-array frigates, and its increasing use of miniaturised sonobuoys to supplement dipping sonars. As will be seen in Chapter 15, this misapprehension would be corrected following the commissioning of operational analysis comparing land-based aircraft and shipborne helicopters in the anti-submarine role; but this would be after the Command Paper had been published. He also over-estimated the practical operational reach of land-based maritime patrol aircraft. In most respects Johnston's paper broadly reflected the views of the majority of Ministry civil servants, defence scientists and the Central Staffs. The assessments of DOAE could be legitimately criticised, especially their sometimes dismissive attitude towards the 'human factor', where issues of military judgement, training, fatigue and morale could have a significant impact on military performance.[41] However, Johnston also noted that his assessments had not been met with virulent opposition from those with whom he had talked: although there was 'no complete consensus ...' he did '... find a marked general agreement with the views expressed in this paper'.[42] Johnston had also made a point of the need for ministerial direction on a 'fifth pillar' for out of area operations. This was not an irrelevance for the Ministry of Defence, given the recent commitment to sending warships to the Gulf as part of Operation 'Armilla'.[43] The acceptance of a fifth pillar would have clearly acknowledged the Royal Navy's importance for such activities beyond Central Europe and the Eastern Atlantic.

Nott certainly received the Johnston paper favourably and had a discussion with the General regarding the document a few days after he had read it. His assistant private secretary, David Omand, had also fulsomely recommended the report to Nott in his cover sheet, providing a clear framing to the Secretary of State that the report was authoritative and aligned with senior Ministry opinion;

> Lt Gen Johnston has 'broken ranks' to clear personal military judgements. These judgements command a wide measure of support – in particular they accord with the views of the Chief Scientific Adviser. I think you will find there is little you would want to disagree with on political grounds. By retaining all four pillars but shifting how the Eastern Atlantic pillar would be fought, the paper gives you a way into detailed equipment readjustments without the problems of starting with controversial a priori judgements about maritime versus continental strategy.[44]

A note of dissension, despite Omand's claim, was soon made respecting the strategic underpinning of the report. Johnston's assumption that a land attack across Central Europe was the most likely military action to be taken by the Soviet Union was quickly challenged by the senior policy civil servant in the Naval Staff (M G Power, the Assistant Under-Secretary (Naval Staff)). He argued that Johnston's paper hinged on the argument that 'the concentration of ground and air forces opposite the Central Region of Europe is such that this region will be the decisive area for any Warsaw Pact/NATO confrontation'. Power stated that

> there is a ring of confidence in that statement which many people might distrust. Intelligence assessments seem to be as fallible as economic assessments. According to the Foreign Secretary only one of the 54 occasions since World War II in which British troops have been used was foreseen... Many professional military officers in MOD and laymen seem to think that the Central Region although important is not the most likely area of confrontation but could be a most likely area of stalemate: and that there are numerous other opportunities in the world

where the USSR could exploit their military and political strength with greater advantage and less risk to themselves.⁴⁵

This prompted an immediate response from his equivalent on the General Staff supporting Johnston's supposition: a conflict might not start in the Central Region but that region would be 'the arena in which the W[arsaw] P[act] would seek to settle matters, whether by actual conquest of heartland territory or simply by inflicting a comprehensive military defeat on NATO's forces. Can there be any serious doubt about that? Where else would they, could they, do either of these things? If they do not see it that way (which is what matters), why do they maintain a greater relative superiority of conventional forces there than anywhere else?'⁴⁶ Although both these documents sit within files created by Nott's private office, it is not clear whether he ever saw them – they certainly lack his telltale acerbic comments made in blue felt tip pen, or the usual short comments by his assistant private secretary framing the note for his minister. Even if they were seen, Nott's positive reception of the Johnston report helped to close down further substantive discussion on Soviet intensions and strategy. The Johnston report also helped to get around Lewin's framing of the review as a choice between the most cost-effective use of British military capabilities and what was most politically acceptable to allies. It also short-circuited discussion of where the decisive theatre would be, and whether a conflict was likely to be long-warning or short-warning, a long war or a short war – and the balance of investment that should go into each possibility – and instead took as read Johnston's assessment of the Central European front as the only decisive theatre. It therefore avoided any discussion of what Soviet intentions were: an aggressive territorial land conquest in Central Europe with a very high chance of nuclear conflict (with extremely high casualties and much risk even if it stayed conventional) or the protection of Soviet interests and the Soviet state combined with undermining Western capitalism by encouraging splits in Western alliances, supporting rebels and revolutionaries and taking advantage of such situations to support socialist or communist allies?

The Johnston study has been presented, by both scholars and Nott himself, as the analytical foundations on which Nott based his judgements in what became known as the 'Bermudagram'.⁴⁷ However, whatever the merits or otherwise of General Johnston's analysis, Nott had already made up his mind. Johnston arrived in the Ministry of Defence on 20 January, and could only have been half way through his analysis when, Nott, in a confidential meeting with the Prime Minister and the Foreign Secretary on 10 February, set out the likely direction of his Review:

The main area of savings would therefore have to be the Royal Navy [as major reductions to BAOR were politically unfeasible and with the RAF 'there was no scope for savings']. The Navy needed more submarines and more minesweepers but its present surface capability was excessive and extremely expensive. The procurement of through-deck cruisers [i.e. *Invincible* class cruisers] had, to take one example, been grossly extravagant (Mr Healey, who had been responsible, now admitted as much). The Navy's programme of refits was similarly extravagant. It should be slowed down. The numbers of destroyers and frigates should be steadily cut back.[48]

Nott then stated that the new carriers could be offered to the US as an out of area capability, and that the West Germans, who were keen to have a greater naval role in NATO, 'would fill the resulting gap in the North Atlantic.' Lord Carrington, the Foreign Secretary, who had actually been responsible for the order of *Invincible* during his time as Defence Secretary in the last Conservative government, rather than Denis Healey, argued that reducing the Navy was 'on objective grounds the wrong decision' but that diplomatically and politically a 'review of NATO' that aimed to revise Brussels Treaty force levels would be impossible to 'get off the ground'.[49] The Prime Minister agreed. Here, in a nutshell, were the basic outcomes that would be set out in the 'Bermudagram' a little more than a month later (excepting the highly unlikely possibility that the West German Navy would reorient itself to become a largely Eastern Atlantic force). Before any substantive analysis had been completed, Nott had already decided on the outcome of the Review. For at least the next three months Nott would either ignore or strongly disagree with anything that did not fit the template he had presented to Thatcher and Carrington.

Maritime Operations: Presenting to the Secretary of State
Having been dissatisfied with a presentation by Defence Intelligence on Soviet maritime capabilities, which he felt had been too negative and had not included any assessment of how British forces would counter them, Nott commissioned two briefings on Royal Navy and RAF maritime capabilities in the first days of March.[50] The first presentation covered maritime warfare in the Eastlant region, for which the Navy Department and Air Force Department would each produce a paper. Parallel briefings were also commissioned covering the Central Front and the defence of the UK Home Base for discussion after the maritime briefings.[51] For the maritime briefings, the two Departments had only three days to prepare their case. Rear Admiral Derek Reffell, the Assistant Chief of the Naval Staff (Policy), gave the Navy's presentation. Reffell made some astute points about the enormous size of the Eastlant sea area, the difficulty of detecting – let alone attacking – enemy forces, particularly underwater,

and the important role of naval forces for conventional deterrence and during times of tension. Reffell then listed seven tasks for the Royal Navy in time of war: maintenance of the nuclear deterrent, containment of Soviet forces as close to their bases as possible (primarily using nuclear-powered submarines on forward operations in the Norwegian and Barents Seas), the defence of reinforcement shipping (such reinforcements acting as a form of deterrence in a high-tension environment), anti-submarine support to the NATO strike fleet, defence of merchant shipping, deployment and defence of amphibious forces, and the protection of offshore resources such as oil rigs.[52]

The first section of Reffell's talk covered anti-submarine warfare where he emphasised the crucial importance of SOSUS and towed-array for detection in forward operations, barrier operations as well as area operations. He emphasised the time-consuming nature of confirming targets with SOSUS and its vulnerability to disablement by Soviet forces: 'we must be prepared to operate without SOSUS information' during wartime, and that a significant number of Soviet submarines would make it into the North Atlantic before war began, thus making the barrier concept an unsafe one to rely upon.[53] The second section dealt with air defence and here he focussed on the importance of a layered defence including Harriers, Sea Dart, Sea Wolf and 'soft kill' electronic warfare technologies. Surface warfare, covered in the last section, depended upon nuclear-powered attacked submarines and land-based aircraft, with the anti-ship missiles on frigates and destroyers largely being of relevance to deal with shadowing warships at the point at which a high-tension confrontation turned into a shooting war.[54] Reffell's talk had many strengths and it was most effective in its anti-submarine section, clearly pointing out the problems of relying solely on SOSUS, maritime patrol aircraft and barrier patrols. However, he was defending a position based on multiple types of platform and multiple layers of defence, which could appear to a non-specialist to be diffuse and over-complex when, as will be seen with the RAF's talks, seemingly simple and clear single platform type solutions appeared to be a viable alternative. Also, as one might expect, Reffell did paper over the real weaknesses of the Navy as it stood in 1981: the majority of the frigate force was of marginal effectiveness in the anti-submarine role, the Harrier had significant limitations as an air defence capability against long-range strike aircraft (especially if mid-course correction for Soviet anti-ship missiles shifted from using targeting aircraft – which the Harrier was designed to attack – towards orbital satellites[55]), whilst the main submarine anti-ship torpedo, Tigerfish, continued to have major problems in reliability and accuracy, partly undermining the role of SSNs in surface warfare.

The presentation by Air Vice Marshal P B Hine, the Assistant Chief of the Air Staff (Policy), followed that of Reffell.[56] It was shorter and punchier, partly benefitting from the exposition of the maritime environment that the

Navy's presenter had been required to undertake to set the scene. At the start of the presentation Hine acknowledged Reffell's characterisation of maritime operations in the Eastern Atlantic as being joint operations between the Royal Navy and the RAF, but after this point his discussion mentioned only RAF capabilities. To some extent this could be justified by the content of Reffell's preceding presentation, but it did give an impression that the RAF could undertake maritime operations alone without the joint approach nodded to at the start. For example, Hine's presentation made much of the SOSUS fixed passive detectors in supporting Nimrod operations, but did not mention towed-arrays at all – either on surface ships or submarines. Hine noted the geographical advantage that NATO had in the run of islands – Greenland, Iceland, Faeroes and the United Kingdom – that cut across any Soviet naval attempt to reach the open ocean, but also made the point that many of the RAF's maritime assets could be re-deployed to land operations 'if the situation so demands', whilst not commenting on the difficulties that would be faced with tasking if RAF assets were required in both the land and maritime domains at once, and the issues of ensuring sufficient training to operate effectively in both environments.[57]

Hine's presentation focussed on the improved capabilities of the Nimrod MR2. It ignored the problems of dependence on SOSUS and submarines passing through barriers before hostilities mentioned by Reffell, and focussed instead on the size of the search area (up to 6,000 nautical square miles) or size of the barrier (250 nautical miles long) that could be patrolled by a single Nimrod MR2.[58] With the aid of transparencies overlaid on charts of the Eastern Atlantic, Hine repeated a visual device that had worked well in the 1964–6 Defence Review: the use of concentric circles to denote the tactical radii of RAF aircraft and thus implying that their effectiveness would be equal and sufficient in all parts of the circles. This gave a highly simplified impression and ignored the extremely difficult sonar conditions in the GIUK gap, the area where the main barrier patrols would be established, and it also obscured the obvious point that detecting submarines on the edge of the Nimrod's tactical radius would be much more difficult given the short amount of time that the aircraft could remain on station compared to areas closer to its operating bases. He did however admit that current sonobuoys would have problems detecting the new third generation of Soviet nuclear submarines that were then under construction. Hine, like his naval counterpart, then dealt with air defence and then anti-surface ship warfare next. Transparencies with concentric circles were again used to denote the range of the thirty-two Phantom fighters co-assigned to SACLANT, again implying full coverage, and ignoring issues of timely response, the problem of tasking prioritisation alongside their national air defence/SACEUR roles, and the inadequacy of the aged Shackleton in the airborne early warning role (although it was planned that an AEW variant of the Nimrod would undertake this role from the mid-1980s).[59] Another unmentioned problem was the strain both maritime air defence and maritime strike operations would put on the RAF's limited air-to-air refuelling tanker force, which would now be even more overstretched as a result of the Tornado having an operational range 20 per cent less than planned.[60] The tasking prioritisation of tankers would therefore severely affect the availability of these crucial aircraft for maritime operations under SACLANT.

Both papers showed gaps in both naval and land-based air capabilities, despite the planned arrival of new technologies and capabilities in the 1980s, not least the improved Nimrod and the surface-ship towed-array sonar. RAF maritime capabilities were significant and increasing, and were an important element of the UK's contribution to SACLANT's operational area, but these capabilities were less effective at greater range, could not reach out into the mid-Atlantic, were largely dependent on SOSUS and there were potential tasking clashes with tanker aircraft and air defence aircraft that could have severely limited the number of available aircraft in a situation of high tension. However, the Royal Navy needed land-based air to augment its air defence, provide long-range anti-ship strike capabilities, supplement its anti-submarine capabilities and provide a crucial element within the Cold War underwater submarine detection system in the Atlantic. Whether either of the presentations made any contribution to the decisions that were then taken is unclear, although one thing is certain: Nott did not notice (or chose not to notice) the complexities of anti-submarine warfare in the Eastern Atlantic, and especially the GIUK gap area, that had been pointed out by Reffell.

The 'Bermudagram'
The initial conclusions of the review were set out in what later became known as the 'Bermudagram', following the document's issuance on 16 March 1981 just after the Defence Secretary had returned from Bermuda.[61] In fact, the document had been drafted in London by Cooper, Cooper's private secretary Richard Mottram, and Omand, whilst Nott was in Bermuda. The Secretary of State had not commissioned it and was unaware of its drafting, but he gave it his full support on reading it on his return.[62] Although it evidently set out his intent respecting the Defence Review, it was a demonstration that his civil servants were driving much of the process, both in terms of its pace and to a significant extent its content. The 'Bermudagram' was accompanied by a mock 'supplementary statement on defence' drafted by the same officials setting out the radical outcomes that should come from implementing their draft 'Bermudagram'.[63] As has been seen, the Navy had expected to be hit

harder than the other services, but the results were in fact much worse than even their most pessimistic scenarios.

The 'Bermudagram' itself was a ten-page document that set out Nott's 'political guidance' to the Chiefs of Staff so that a costed defence programme could then be formulated. The document started by emphasising the 'national economic dilemma' the United Kingdom found itself and the 'creeping impact of successive cuts' resulting in Defence's capital stock becoming 'out of step with the changing nature of the threat' and unbalanced with 'too many resources tied up for tasks which no longer have a matching priority (and related inconsistencies in assumptions about warning times and duration of hostilities between different theatres of operations)'.[64] The existing 1981 Long Term Costings needed to be re-written – these plans focussed too much on units rather than weapons or firepower, and too little had been invested in less-expensive second or third line reserves or capabilities. Trident was the first priority but every effort had to be made to keep its costs within its long-term budget. The Central European commitment remained essentially undisturbed but Army numbers would be reduced to the absolute minimum necessary to comply with the Brussels Treaty, whilst Nott wanted analysis of a re-balance of the British Army of the Rhine in favour of anti-tank helicopters and anti-tank weapons, and costings made on the purchase of additional GR3 Harriers.[65]

The shift in the Eastern Atlantic was significant: the first priority was the deployment and protection of the strategic nuclear deterrent including access to their bases, followed by the protection of the continental reinforcement ports. The next priority was the 'disruption of Soviet maritime activity with the aim of containing it north of the Greenland-Iceland-UK gap' in conjunction with the United States Navy.[66] However, this would be undertaken at the expense of the direct protection of convoys. The rationale for this was that US reinforcement forces would arrive from the Gulf of Mexico, across the South Atlantic and via the Azores, presumably meaning that US reinforcements would be escorted without any contribution from the British. The reference to US forces arriving from the Gulf of Mexico was describing the previous Carter administration's 'swing' strategy of bringing carrier strike groups through the Panama Canal from the Pacific in the event of a crisis in the Euro-Atlantic region. It was a brave decision to only counter Soviet submarines at the GIUK gap and that any transatlantic shipping would have no escorts at all (at least none from the Royal Navy, anyway), whilst the Army division, consisting of Territorial Army units, which would be transported across the Channel if tensions were building, would have no escorts either. Nott was also assuming that no Soviet submarines had already broken out into the Atlantic undetected before hostilities had started, another risky assumption. Outside of the Euro-Atlantic region, Nott asked for an 'imaginative and positive' look at the naval role worldwide, including the possible use of the new support carriers 'in a wider role alongside the United States Navy'.[67]

The submarine and torpedo programmes would largely continue as before: the SSN building programme should proceed was fast as possible without jeopardising timescales on Trident procurement, whilst the planned new conventional boats should proceed, as should the Stingray lightweight torpedo and investigations into UK or US options for a new heavyweight torpedo. 'There should be a sharp change of direction in our surface ship plans' based on the assumption that there would be no escorts for any convoys (reinforcement or mercantile): no more Type 42s would be built and the Type 44 would be cancelled, whilst any investments in Sea Dart would be limited to a 'minimum level which enables us to get some value from our existing investment in Type 42s'.[68] The Type 22 programme would stop as soon as possible and be replaced by the 'very much smaller' Type 23 frigate. Nott also wanted to investigate an even smaller vessel – a corvette – as a minimum towed-array ship. Nott wanted, if possible, to increase the number of Nimrods by bringing some of the airframes in storage back into service (presumably by updating them to MR2 standards), the stated rationale for this was that 'in the briefing CDS and I had last week at Norfolk, Virginia, I was impressed by the contribution of Nimrod and Orion aircraft in the anti-submarine role.'[69] The Sea King replacement would be cancelled as would any additional Sea Harrier purchases. Sea Eagle for the Tornado would be procured whilst the balance of investment in the Tornado procurement would be shifted to increase the number of F2 air defence variants at the expense of GR1 strike aircraft. The Royal Marines would be retained with three Commandos but there would be no specialist amphibious shipping. This meant the withdrawal from service of not only the *Fearless* class assault ships but also the *Sir Lancelot* class logistic landing ships which undertook much of the routine movement of Army equipment across the Channel and worldwide. Nott wanted the reserves of all services to be increased, and greater consideration of the use of civilian assets including taking ships up from trade, fitting weapons to civilian vehicles and adapting airliners for in-flight refuelling.[70]

In terms of what was described as 'overheads' in the 'Bermudagram', Nott called for 10 per cent reductions in officer numbers by 1991 to be focussed as much as possible in headquarters and staff jobs. Civilian MOD employees should reduce to 200,000 by 1 April 1984. Nott called for the streamlining and merger where possible of medical services across the three services. Finally, Nott confirmed that the Trident procurement would be placed within the budget of the Navy Department and that of the Procurement Executive, rather than 'as something special or additional to the service programme.' Nott gave the Ministry just over a month to provide costings for a programme following the decisions made in the 'Bermudagram' document.[71] A one page Annex then set out what percentage of the defence budget should be allocated to each service and to the Procurement Executive. The Navy's percentage had been 27 per cent up to 1980–1 and would be 28 per cent by 1985–6 (including Trident) and 27 per cent by 1990–1 (also including Trident).[72] Three days later Frank Cooper sent out a much more detailed set of targets to the service departments setting out exact amounts, down to the nearest million pounds, for each year over the next decade. In total, the new figures required savings of £12.4 billion over the next ten years with £7.6 billion coming from the Navy Department.[73]

The 'Bermudagram' is a remarkable document: the major decisions of the Defence Review, as was then envisaged, had been made only two months after Nott had entered the department and the review had begun. In fact, Nott had only seen the Johnston report less than two weeks previously, and aside from the briefings he had received a few days later, there had been very little other analysis put in front of the Defence Secretary. This was astonishingly quick (the 1974–5 Defence Review had lasted six-months between the start of the review and its preliminary conclusions), and despite some perceptive analysis in parts of the document, it showed. From the perspective of the Navy, the results were dramatic. Despite Nott emphasising the importance of the US Navy's presentation of maritime patrol aircraft capabilities on his visit to the United States, in reality his decision to build up the Nimrod fleet and effectively phase out the medium anti-submarine helicopter by not procuring a replacement for the Sea King was as much based on assessments in Johnston's report and advice from Sir Ronald Mason the Chief Scientific Adviser, who was an advocate for maritime patrol aircraft as replacements for frigates and anti-submarine helicopters that flew from them. Operational analysis had convinced Mason that MPAs could entirely take over the role of frigates and anti-submarine helicopters, based on their quicker reaction and greater range.[74] But this analysis had been commissioned for other, much more tactical, purposes and relied upon SOSUS for cuing in the Nimrods to attack submarines. Without SOSUS, MPAs would have considerable problems finding submarines across wide areas of sea or long barriers. One obvious issue was therefore the very real possibility that the Soviets would try to disable or destroy as many SOSUS arrays as they could before hostilities began.[75] With respect to the US Navy's preference for barrier operations over convoys, this could be argued to have more to do with the internal politics of the US Navy: following the retirement of Admiral Zumwalt, the USN had rapidly moved away from his concepts of sea control and convoy defence – which would have involved larger numbers of smaller and cheaper 'sea control' carriers focussed on operating anti-submarine helicopters – towards a more strike-carrier-focussed and offensive strategy echoing the US Navy's approach to the naval war in the Pacific, and strike operations in Korea and Vietnam.[76] Making use of maritime patrol aircraft and conducting barrier operations or attacks at source, meant that the US Navy's carriers could focus less on anti-submarine operations and more on these maritime or land strike roles. This lack of attention towards anti-submarine warfare had been noted by Royal Navy officers operating with the US Navy in the Atlantic since the first joint NATO exercises of the 1950s.[77] Inadvertently, the US Navy had provided support to Nott's plans to reduce the Royal Navy's surface fleet dramatically. As will be seen in Chapter 15, when operational analysis was finally conducted comparing the effectiveness of maritime patrol aircraft and helicopters, it was shown that the latter were a much more cost-effective solution in a number of circumstances, in particular the defence of warships or convoys.

Nott acknowledged the importance of the towed-array sonar, but the rushed nature of the document showed that he and Cooper only had a basic understanding of the types of vessels that could operate the array. The Type 23, at this stage in its development, was very close to the minimum vessel for any sort of towed-array operations. As will be seen in the next chapter, it lacked its own helicopter and the fitting of the Sea Wolf system or any ship-to-ship guided missiles were still regarded as options rather than necessities. The idea of a towed-array corvette as an even more basic vessel, lacked any sense of realism and probably resulted from confusion following briefings on the progress of the Type 23 design. The phasing out of the area defence missile capability without any further analysis, reflected both a willingness to take the risk of focussing ship defence on short-range point defence missiles or soft kill capabilities such as jammers and decoys, and the parlous state of the Type 44 programme. Nott's snap decision prevented any further discussion of other options, including adopting US systems and approaches to air defence (something that had been accepted by both France and Italy in the 1960s as indigenous area air defence missile systems had proven too expensive and complex to develop unilaterally), again showed a regard more for rapid decisions that became faits accomplis rather than evidence-based consideration of alternatives.

Although Nott mentioned the *Invincible* class ships for use in global deployments, he had also effectively sealed their fate by deciding not to replace the Sea King or buy additional Sea Harriers. Their core role had always been anti-submarine operations and without dedicated anti-submarine helicopters, or many Sea Harriers, they would have increasingly seemed liked white elephants. In May 1981 Nott confirmed to the Prime Minister that the Sea Harrier would not be modernised at all, and as result would be obsolescent by the late 1980s.[78] Even if the carriers remained operational into the 1990s, their aircraft would soon have been taken out of service, and from this point onwards, premature sale to foreign navies would have been their most optimistic fate. The withdrawal from service of amphibious vessels were similarly painful but were a confirmation of the 1974–5 Defence Review's decisions. The withdrawal of the *Sir Lancelot* class was another demonstration of the rush in which the main decisions of the review had been made. How would the British Army's vehicles and equipment be transported to and from the continent, or to training grounds in Canada or residual commitments such as Belize?

* * *

The 'Bermudagram' was therefore a rushed document that mixed some elements of sound analysis: the primacy of supporting and protecting the nuclear deterrent, the need to focus on port defence, the future importance of surface towed-array sonars, the assessment that the Navy's current area defence policy was a mess, and the need to consider using civilian assets more intelligently. However, this was combined with hasty and dangerous assumptions based on little evidence, most obviously regarding anti-submarine warfare. That Nott assumed, the day after the 'Bermudagram' had been distributed, that both Leach and Lewin would resign as a result of these conclusions, reflected an over-optimistic perspective on how the review would then develop, and is a further indication of haste and the lack of thought involved: difficulties such as an aggressive and intransigent First Sea Lord were being wished away rather than being dealt with realistically.[79] As will be seen, this haste would soon result in the unravelling of significant parts of the review over the next year, which in turn would help undermine Nott's position within government even before the Falklands conflict began.

14

The Way Forward

The 'Bermudagram' of 16 March 1981 had, from the perspective of the Secretary of State at least, set the overall policy and focus of the Review. The task from this point onwards was for the three services to build new Long Term Costings around the assumptions of that document. Given the inconsistencies within the document, and the determined and repeated attempts by the Navy Department to modify the decisions of the 'Bermudagram', this would not be a straightforward process.

The New Long Term Costings
Over the next month, the different departments in the Ministry focussed on providing costings that accorded with Nott's prioritisations and guidance. When the extent of the reductions required of the Navy had sunk in, Keith Speed, the Under-Secretary of State for the Royal Navy, who was a strong supporter of the Senior Service, sent a letter to Nott setting out the reductions to its programme over the last few years, including cancellations, cutbacks and programme re-phasings. These new and draconian reductions on top of the cuts imposed by the Pym 'mini-review' of late 1980 did not 'in my view match the realities of an island nation almost wholly dependent on the sea', and that the expenditure on British forces in Germany was far out of proportion to the military capability that it provided.[1] The letter had little impact on Nott who, in his view, had already made up his mind and the finality of the 'Bermudagram' – requiring an immediate shift to producing a new ten-year costed programme – made it extremely difficult for Speed, the First Sea Lord or the Naval Staff to have their arguments listened to. Such arguments, including that one very rarely ends up fighting the war one expects in the place you expect it, and that either a long-warning or a long-war (or both) were more likely, did not make any difference.[2]

All the departments had considerable difficulties working out the revised programme, as the two parts of the 'Bermudagram' did not cohere. The first part was the textual element signed by Nott specifying what type of capabilities would be prioritised, and the second part was the numerical element set out in year-by-year detail by Cooper in his note three days after the 'Bermudagram'. The Navy Department referred to the textual element as 'Phase 1' and the numerical element as 'Phase 2'. The problems dealing with the potential discrepancies between the two were heightened for the Navy Department given the savings it needed to find and the requirement to fit in the Trident programme. In the pre-Defence Review Long Term Costings a total of £37.8 billion would have been theoretically spent over a decade by the Navy Department. By enacting the measures specifically set out in the text of the 'Bermudagram' (Phase 1) a total of £796 million would be saved, whilst Phase 2 provided the greatest hit with a total of £6.8 billion taken out of the programme, producing a £31 billion total budget over the decade. Another £817 million would need to be found just for 1982–3. Neither the Army nor Air Force departments had been able to meet their Phase 2 target levels but given that their task was much less challenging, their excesses were £133 million and £215 million respectively.[3]

What did this mean for the Navy's programme? The Navy Department dealt with Phase 1 and Phase 2 separately, partly to demonstrate how painful Phase 1 would be by itself, let alone following the Phase 2 strictures. This meant the cancellation of any substantive Type 42 modernisations, stretching out the nuclear submarine programme to the slowest possible, restricting the Type 22 programme to ten ships, and ordering no replacements for the assault ships and the *Sir Lancelot* class logistic landing ships. As requested, the mine warfare programme was largely retained, and despite its impracticability a stream of minimum corvettes was added to the programme alongside the already minimal Type 23 frigate. Four hundred and fifty officers would be made redundant, whilst the reductions in the shipbuilding programme would result in a further 1,500 redundancies in shipyards over those expected. The Navy Department was adamant about keeping a Sea King replacement in the programme, but by reducing the avionics fit of the EH101 they no longer deemed it to be an 'advanced' but a utility helicopter. The implementation of Phase 2 would however be drastic compared to Phase 1: eight frigates and six destroyers would be disposed of immediately, three more would be laid up. Work would be ceased on the last three Type 42s, two Batch 2 Type 22s and HMS *Ark Royal* and all six ships would be scrapped. All Type 42s and Type 21s would be disposed of (it was not clear whether this was immediately or over the ten-year period) and the planned conventional submarines would be cancelled, as would Nott's suggested corvettes. The Royal Yacht *Britannia* would be decommissioned, and three new mine warfare vessels would be cancelled as would four of the twelve planned EDATS trawlers. The hydrographic fleet would be reduced in size, development work on Sea Wolf and Exocet successors would end, the Skynet satellite system would be cancelled, and one Royal Marine Commando would be disbanded, as would the Band Service. Two dockyards would close: Gibraltar and either Chatham or Portsmouth, one armament depot would close as would one stores depot and two fuel storage facilities. The ocean-going fleet would halve in size as would the number of personnel required to go to sea. Redundancies of over 2,000 ratings would be required. Aware that the Navy Department had not offered up enough savings to reach the Phase 2 targets, the following additional reductions were offered: cancelling the Type 23 and the next class of SSNs, disbanding the Royal Marines, cancelling Stingray, Sub-Harpoon, the Sea King replacement and reducing war stocks.[4] This would leave the Navy with its largely pre-existing planned force of nuclear submarines and mine warfare vessels, two *Invincible* class carriers, one destroyer and sixteen frigates by 1991.

These were huge reductions and presented the Centre with a forest of 'bleeding stumps', a Ministry of Defence phrase denoting painful (sometimes deliberately and self-consciously painful) cuts with a high profile impact. The civil servant tasked with co-ordinating the responses from the departments, presumably ignorant of anti-submarine warfare, wondered why the Sea King replacement was spared when surface ships were cut by two-thirds.[5] Omand, in a note to Nott, believed that the Navy Department could be deliberately holding back on support, personnel and overhead reductions in order to maximise the impact of the front-line cuts.[6] The decommissioning of *Britannia* and the breaking up of so many partly built ships on the slip must have seemed especially over the top. Cooper was more direct than Omand: the responses were 'fairly predictable. They are designed to take ground offered or demonstrate the total impossibility of the situation. They are also designed – to put it crudely – to test your intentions and resolve ... The Navy had taken a simple stance – by behaving only too literally in the early part of the period it has severely cut the Navy in the latter part.'[7] Cooper suggested, with a logic that contradicted the 'Bermudagram', that the SSN force should be cut and the Type 23 programme speeded up so the ship could enter service earlier, but he also recognised that the Navy had a particular problem in the first few years of the costings. As it was in the middle of a large, capital-intensive re-equipment programme including *Trafalgar* class submarines, *Invincible* class carriers, Type 42 destroyers, Type 22 frigates and new mine warfare vessels, heavy reductions in the early years could only be undertaken by cancelling vessels already under construction. Cooper suggested transfers from the Army and RAF budgets in these first few years to lessen the pain as it transitioned to a much smaller force (and reduce the embarrassingly large number of ships being broken up on slips).⁸ The Permanent Under-Secretary was clearly trying to steel the Secretary of State to maintain his radical course: in addition to his statement respecting the test of his resolve he also emphasised the support that Nott's plans apparently had across the Ministry, as Omand had done a few weeks previously: 'it is interesting that privately everyone (including the Services) believes that it would be possible to present a coherent story broadly on the basis of your first "Bermudagram"!'⁹ Although a strong case could be made that the 'Bermudagram' went along the grain of the majority opinion of the Ministry of Defence (certainly since the Air Force Board confirmed in 1976 its position that the Eastlant theatre was clearly secondary to the Central Front) stating that 'everyone' supported it cannot be true, not least within the majority of the Naval Staff, and in those presumably extensive parts of the Ministry where civil servants were neutral on the issue.

Whilst the initial results of the costings exercise were coming in, Nott and his private office began to draft his response. The earliest drafts included even more radical thinking in terms of the future of the Navy. He favoured scrapping *Ark Royal* straight after her launch, or preferably selling one of the other two. Any remaining carriers would have a residual 'out of area' role as commando ships or flying the remaining Harrier force which would be operated by the RAF. A later draft even suggested getting rid of all the carriers straight away, but given how new they were this would have been particularly embarrassing. The Royal Marines would be detached from the Navy and placed within a special operations command with the Parachute Regiment and SAS, answering operationally to the Chiefs of Staff but placed under the Army for budgeting and support purposes. He stated that the surface fleet would only be a 'presence capability in and out of the NATO area, and … it would not be required to undertake operations against Soviet maritime forces save in close association with US forces, upon whom we rely for high quality force protection'. All operations against Soviet maritime forces would be undertaken by submarines or the RAF. As the draft developed the sections on the transfer of the Sea Harriers and Royal Marines from the Navy were removed, but the emphasis on the surface fleet as a presence force outside the Eastern Atlantic remained.¹⁰ This ignored the clearly demonstrated utility of the surface-ship towed-array, which was proving to be almost as good at detecting Soviet submarines as towed-arrays on SSNs but on vessels that were much cheaper to build and operate than SSNs. The Type 23 had the added advantage that its procurement did not suffer from the SSN's problems of limited shipbuilding capacity. It also placed the new frigate in a strange position. The design had begun development as a specialist light towed-array frigate, so if its role was now to be a worldwide presence vessel *as well*, then it was very likely it could expand – with capabilities ideal for this role such as its own helicopter, medium gun and anti-ship missiles – into a vessel not too dissimilar to the Type 22 that Nott had regarded as too large and expensive. The towed-array corvette was proving to be a dead end as well: any realistic reduction in size or capabilities on the basic Type 23 as it stood in June 1981 meant that the processing of signals would have to be placed ashore, which then increased costs in other directions as shore communications and processing centres would have to be built.[11] The push for radical absolutism – no surface ships to be involved in any anti-Soviet maritime role – was stretching the intellectual coherence of the review beyond breaking point.

Someone pushing Nott further down the route of radical absolutism was the Chief Scientific Adviser. Sir Ronald Mason sent Nott a commentary on the results from the first stage of the costings exercise. Assessing the 'changing face of warfare', Mason stated that 'it seems that the point has been reached at which we must withdraw the surface warship from the prospect of this type of conflict, replacing its function as far as possible by a combination of submarines, maritime aircraft, anti-ship missiles and fighters. This should make possible the fulfilment of the remaining roles, in peacetime and lesser conflicts, by smaller ships with less complex equipment, which could largely be supported by present start of the art technology.'[12] Mason also thought that the days of crewed aircraft were numbered and that all remaining unguided weapons should be replaced by their guided equivalents. 'The clear trend, already well established, for weapons to become both more lethal and more costly, places increasing emphasis on ensuring that they are directed with maximum economy at targets which are correctly identified and precisely located. Surveillance, command and control and target acquisition thus become increasingly important, and reference has already been made to the influence of such systems on naval warfare.'[13]

Mason's analysis had much that was prescient, and it was describing with some accuracy the defence-technological environment that was then being created and would, in parts, dominate the 1990s onwards. However, his absolutism and his dislike of nuance and complexity pushed his conclusions beyond what was justified by the evidence. Forty years after his note was written, crewed aircraft are still considered relevant, and probably will be so for some decades, whilst his assessment that surface ships were not needed, automatically assumed that the cost of defending a surface strike force would always outweigh its operational benefits in all likely circumstances. Neither did Mason consider that relying solely on area or barrier patrols in a sea region of considerable oceanographic complexity was either brave or foolhardy. Maritime patrol aircraft depended on SOSUS to isolate potential targets, and SOSUS could well be partly or wholly disabled prior to a conflict. The United Kingdom would never have the shipbuilding capacity or money to build enough nuclear submarines to provide sufficient towed-array sonars to narrow the gap between the initial detection of and then the final targeting of submarines, particularly if SOSUS had been fully or partly taken out of operation.

Operational analysis ('OA') had probably played a significant part in the development of Mason's position. Since 1976, a blizzard of OA had been produced on behalf of the Sea-Air Warfare Committee ('SAWC'), the joint RN-RAF body that had gained an increased role in ASW planning after the 1974–5 Defence Review. A large number of working papers, memoranda and reports were produced by the Defence Operational Analysis Establishment based on a number of projects commissioned by SAWC. For half a decade, various studies had analysed the ability of air, surface and sub-surface platforms and systems to detect and destroy Soviet submarines; the effectiveness of Soviet cruise-missile attacks on naval forces; and the ability of Soviet submarines to break through anti-submarine defences. Gradually, these studies began to build a picture of surface ship vulnerability and began to build an apparent case for barrier patrols and area operations as a more effective means of ASW than direct defence through convoy. For example, one major study which compared the effectiveness of different ASW capabilities expected to be in service in 1995, produced tentative conclusions that area operations were more effective (for which maritime patrol aircraft would be the main ASW force) than convoys and direct defence (for which surface ships were generally used).[14] However, the devil was in the detail of the assumptions of these studies. The interim report was based on oceanographic conditions during the winter for the GIUK gap,[15] when the surface layer would generally be 800ft deep, making the task of detecting submarines potentially much easier, especially for sonobuoys.[16] Conditions in the spring changed dramatically however, with the surface layer varying between 50 and 400ft depending on the location and the underwater 'weather'.[17] Such complexities made operational analysis at the time extremely difficult to reach conclusions, given that they added a whole range of additional variables that were beyond the resources of the DOAE to process. Other factors such as the rate and level of degradation in SOSUS effectiveness before and after the start of a conflict also had significant impacts on the results, whilst at the same time OA did not provide any variable for the 'human element', including morale, training and exhaustion. These subtleties would have had much less impact than the bald results of these studies, which appeared to burnish the case for maritime patrol aircraft in anti-submarine detection and attack. It was these headlines that no doubt had a significant impact on Mason's assessment of Eastern Atlantic ASW.

Nott was, however, entirely taken with Mason's paper, writing in blue felt tip pen on the front: 'this is a fascinating note. One of the best I have seen. I don't know whether it is right but I suspect that it is as right as it is possible to be.' To the probable horror of his civil servants Nott then suggested that Mason should be put in charge of writing important sections of the planned White Paper. 'It should form the scientific framework which leads into the operations, R&D and equipment conclusions. It could stand much as it is written here. I propose that the CSA should take overall charge at least of this section of the paper and possibly with DUS(P) the White Paper itself.'[18] Nott's lack of certainty as to whether Mason was correct, combined with his certitude that he was, provides an interesting insight into Nott's frame of mind in April and May 1981.

This was confirmed by his response to the note written by the Directors of Defence Policy in the Defence Planning Staff under the direction of Lewin, commenting on the initial outcomes of the costings process. Nott's blue felt tip pen was also wielded on this note: stating 'rubbish' in the margins three times, and scrawling 'Who are they? Utterly NEGATIVE' referring to his unawareness of the existence of the three Directors of Defence Policy within the Central Staffs. This paper was clearly influenced by some of Lewin's long-standing concerns, as it argued that the Brussels Treaty needed to be renegotiated in order to deal with overstretch of British forces in Germany. The paper also pointed out that the marrying of the Phase 1 textual guidance with the ambitious Phase 2 target figures was proving difficult, with the heavy reductions of the latter often making it impossible to follow the former. Despite the heavy use of the felt tip pen at the start of the note, Nott did not make any annotations or marks against the section of the report that cast doubt on relying solely on barrier patrols to stop Soviet submarines: 'regardless of warning time, an effective percentage of Soviet offensive naval capability is and can be expected to be deployed in advance of heightened tension and without direct support [i.e. convoys or sea lane patrols] it is unlikely that any but the fastest merchant ships would agree to sail in the face of the Soviet submarine threat.'[19] Perhaps because the document had the hallmarks of a paper produced under Lewin's guidance, there was no follow-up by Nott to these important points of doubt: no request for analysis or briefings. Nott had chosen his course, had accepted the barrier patrol philosophy despite its problems, and would persist with his radical absolutism.

Resubmitting the Plans

Dissatisfied with the results so far, Nott asked the three services to revisit their planning and push harder to meet the Phase 2 financial requirements. Finance officers from the Centre worked closely with the Navy Department to try to ensure that their costings were better balanced, and the revised result was produced on 1st May. The Navy's ten year costings were still over Cooper's annual targets, especially in the late 1980s, but a total of £7.3 billion over ten years would still be saved over the pre-Nott LTC costings.[20] The results with respect to the future fleet were still dramatic.

Table 9: Revised fleet size 1 May 1981[21]

	1981	1986	1991	1996
SSBN	2 (+2)	3 (+1)	2 (+2)	3 (+2)
SSN	8 (+4)	13 (+3)	13 (+4)	13 (+3)
SSK	12 (+4)	12 (+3)	6 (+2)	5 (+1)
CVS	1 (+1)	1 (+1)	2	1 (+1)
LPD	1 (+1)	0	0	0
DD	10 (+3)	10 (+4)	11 (+3)	7 (+3)
FF	33 (+13)	18 (+6)	16 (+6)	15 (+6)
MCMV	26 (+7)	30 (+8)	30 (+6)	28 (+7)
Survey	6 (+5)	4 (+1)	3 (+2)	4 (+1)
RFA	13 (+2)	9 (+1)	6 (+1)	6 (+1)

Note: lists operational vessels with vessels in refit or reserve in parentheses

The results were a drastic reduction in the size of the ocean-going surface fleet over the next five years, with further tapering downwards as more ships were withdrawn from service without replacement in the late 1980s and early 1990s. To fit within Cooper's numbers, *Ark Royal* would be launched and then broken up, the seventh through to twelfth Type 22 frigates would be cancelled, the last two Type 42s would not be ordered (although were very unlikely to have been ordered in any case), the Type 23 programme would be thinned out by cancelling three orders and the Type 44 destroyer would be cancelled as would a planned frigate support ship, saving almost £1.5 billion over ten years.[22] *Hermes* and *Bristol* would be withdrawn from service in 1983 and 1985 respectively, whilst the two assault ships would be decommissioned in 1982 and 1984 and three 'County' class destroyers in 1981 and 1982. The *Sir Lancelot* class logistic landing ships would be scrapped without replacement by April 1984. By 1985 all of the *Rothesay* class frigates, Batch 1 and Batch 3 *Leanders* would be out of service, whilst those Batch 2 *Leanders* without towed-array would be placed in reserve. This would save £366 million over a decade. In 1986 this would leave a destroyer and frigate force consisting of the fourteen Type 42 destroyers (with no modernisations), eight Type 21 frigates, six Type 22, and eight *Leanders*, four of which would be equipped with towed-array, and result in a near 40 per cent reduction in escorts declared to NATO. *Britannia* and the ice patrol ship *Endurance* would be withdrawn from service (saving only £5.5 million over ten years), the hydrographic fleet would be halved as it would cease undertaking any civil work, saving £21 million. The defensive mining capability would also disappear, saving £162 million. The submarine fleet would also suffer, but less dramatically: the seventh and last *Trafalgar* class submarine would be cancelled, the build rate of the new conventional submarines would be reduced, and Polaris rocket motors would not be updated, saving £445 million in total. The closure of Gibraltar dockyard in 1982, Chatham dockyard in 1984 and the downgrading of Portsmouth to a forward operating base with docking facilities would save £1.2 billion. The reduction in personnel necessary to fulfil the new programme would save another £1.1 billion and other support reductions, including the closure of stores and oil fuel depots would save further £1.2 billion. The balance would come from other support cost reductions including drastic reductions in the size of the Royal Fleet Auxiliary, reduced aircraft orders, reduced works programmes and miscellanea.[23]

Despite the scepticism of Omand and Cooper, there had not in fact been that many areas where the additional support reductions could be made. However, aside from the breaking up of *Ark Royal* after launch, all the scrapping of ships under construction had been removed from the programme and the total number of destroyers and frigates in a decade's time would be somewhat higher. The earlier plans to scrap all Type 42s and Type 21 early had been replaced by the rapid decommissioning of older frigates sooner and the disappearance of the unrealistic corvette design. Major mid-life refits would be abandoned, and a higher proportion of personnel would go to sea, whilst shore postings for both officers and ratings would reduce. In terms of the overall surface fleet, there was a moderate increase in capability compared to the previous iteration and a removal of the most politically embarrassing elements. The *Ark Royal* problem – the ship was due to be launched by the Queen Mother in only a month's time – might be solved more easily than originally envisaged. It was realised that the Australian Navy was interested in a replacement for its sole aircraft carrier, HMAS *Melbourne*. If this was so, then the first or second ship of the *Invincible* class might be sold and the embarrassing sight of the monarch's mother launching a ship, that would then immediately be broken up, could be avoided.[24] Nott had asked the Navy Department to provide costings for withdrawing all three carriers from service straight away. They had calculated that a total of £789 million would be saved, including reduced support, personnel and aircraft costs, through to 1990–1. Nott had also asked for the cost of cancelling the Sea King replacement altogether, even as an aircraft with reduced avionics. The result was a saving of £371 million over the next decade. Given that the revised costings had focussed on reducing the political embarrassment of the Navy's reductions, it was unlikely that these two options would have been acting upon given their defence industrial and political impact, but they provide an interesting insight into the areas that Nott was still targeting in late-April 1981.[25]

Following a meeting with the Admiralty Board a week after the revised costings had been produced, Nott's position began to soften somewhat. He had been surprised at the drastic impact of attempting to adhere to Cooper's figures,[26] and he was perhaps beginning to think about the presentation of these reductions to allies and to the British public. He was also running out of time to finalise the new costings, so that he could both inform allies and meet his planned date of July for the White Paper. It is also notable that this was the first time he had been presented with arguments in favour of the Navy's position without Cooper, Mason or his private office by his side.[27] The Admiralty Board were also able to present a coherent set of arguments to Nott about the dangers of the approach he was taking to the Defence Review. Their most effective arguments were those that questioned the strategic and military underpinnings of the review, rather than the employment and industrial implications, which were of much less interest to this Conservative government than its Labour predecessor. The Admiralty Board had to accept the Central Front was to be prioritised, as the Oversea Policy and Defence Committee of Cabinet had agreed to this, but they argued that the Committee had to be given a realistic picture of what the alternatives should be, and thus a costing should be prepared that reversed the cuts on the Army and Navy, with the former bearing 63 per cent of the reductions. Nott agreed to this request. It was next explained that an effective continental strategy would still depend on maintaining a maritime link with North America. As was stated to Nott by the Board:

> The Cuban missile crisis had taught the Russians the importance of sea power in securing resupply routes; under Gorshkov this lesson had been well learned. Maritime power was a highly effective means of projecting political and military influence both inside and outside the NATO area; and of sustaining our national influence in the Alliance. The US Department of Defence had indicated in its 1981 statements that the USN was unable to meet all its obligations satisfactorily; it was a one and a half ocean navy with a three ocean commitment. Against this background the US looked to us as the premier European navy to be the mainstay in the Eastern Atlantic.[28]

Reducing the Royal Navy's contribution would above all, in the view of the Board, damage the UK's position with the United States and might lead to a reduction in US technological and intelligence sharing. Given the sensitive position of negotiations with the US over Trident, this could be a very significant matter. The Board also argued that:

> It was important that the GIUK gap barrier should not be considered as a 'Maginot Line.' Intelligence indicated that 50 per cent of Soviet

submarines and 80 per cent of SSNs would be south of the gap by D-2 [two days before hostilities break out]. It was unrealistic to imagine that it could be sealed off. Defence in depth was needed by highly mobile ASW forces. The medium organic helicopter [i.e. the Sea King Replacement] was the linchpin of this concept.[29]

It was also suggested that military taskings in places such as the Caribbean and Mediterranean, where warships could respond quickly, cheaply and discretely to crises, would be much more difficult to respond to with such a shrunken force of surface vessels. Although not necessarily conceding these military points, Nott did agree to consider a proposal by the Deputy Under-Secretary (Navy), the Navy Department's most senior civil servant, to draw up costings that would only add 5 per cent onto the 1 May figures but which would reinstate the seventh *Trafalgar* class, cancel the scrapping of *Ark Royal*, add in two more Type 22s, reinstate the four Type 23s and return the conventional boat programme to earlier levels. In addition, the Single Role Minehunter programme would return to its earlier level and the EDATS trawlers placed back in the programme. This would add a total of £1.4 billion back into the programme.[30] Aside from the reinstatement of *Ark Royal*, this accorded with Nott's original phase 1 proposals from the 'Bermudagram': focussing on submarine, Type 23 and mine warfare forces. It was, therefore, a well-judged choice that fitted with the Defence Secretary's own preferences, and by adding two Outboard-equipped Type 22s back into the programme it might lessen the chance of diplomatic difficulties with the United States over the earlier sale of this highly classified information gathering equipment. Sensibly, the Type 44 programme had been given up for dead and resurrection attempts focussed on the third carrier.

Whilst the Admiralty Board was beginning its fight against the most serious of Nott's reductions, Lewin was still pushing at the strategic underpinnings of Nott's review. He was still arguing for a renegotiation of the Brussels Treaty, using arguments that had been similar to the Naval Staff's at the start of the Review. 'Although it is on the Central Front that we face the greatest concentration of Soviet strength there is a general consensus among the military authorities of the Alliance, that this is the least likely area for the Soviets to attempt a military trial of strength with the West. It would involve an immediate confrontation between the Super Powers and the highest risk of nuclear escalation.' Lewin went on to state: 'The greatest risk to Western interests is Soviet adventurism outside the NATO area' and noted that the United States had been adjusting for this fact by distributing its naval forces away from the Atlantic.[31] Given that accepting these arguments would have meant restarting the Review from scratch when the White Paper was due to be published in only two months' time, it is unsurprising that they were not accepted by Nott, who was already pressing ahead with the presentation of the Review outcomes.

Leach sent a forthright letter to the Defence Secretary requesting a meeting with the Prime Minister. The First Sea Lord stated that 'I consider your proposals for the Navy of the future to be irresponsible and damaging to the short and long-term interests of our country. My advice has been disregarded. I must ask for the opportunity of expressing my views personally to the Prime Minister before ministers meet with her to discuss your proposals.'[32] Nott passed Leach's request and letter to Number 10 but the Prime Minister's private office prevaricated, stating that the time could not be found in the Prime Minister's busy schedule. A meeting with all of the Chiefs of Staff had also been proposed, so Leach's meeting might happen after this larger discussion. Either way, these meetings would happen after the key Oversea Policy and Defence committee had already met, discussed and approved Nott's defence review proposals.[33] As a result, Nott did allow Leach to write a short memorandum to the Prime Minister summarising his concerns, which he asked to be forwarded to the other members of the Cabinet committee. After setting out the cuts to which the Navy would be subjected, the First Sea Lord finished by stating:

> The proposal has been devised ad hoc in two months. It has been neither validated nor studied in depth. No alternative options have been considered. It has all been done in a rush. Such unbalanced devastation of our overall Defence capability is unprecedented; it must cause serious doubts concerning United States reactions in the context of your own conventional assurances and successful negotiation of the Trident project so important to our country.
>
> We are on the brink of a historic decision. War seldom takes the expected form and a strong maritime capability provides flexibility for the unforeseen. If you erode it to the extent envisaged I believe you will undesirably foreclose your future options and prejudice our National Security.[34]

However prescient these words seem in hindsight, they would have little impact with the Prime Minister. Nor did his eventual meeting with the Prime Minister, which finally occurred on 8 June, with Nott present. Leach made his case, arguing for a large reduction in the British Army of the Rhine and accepting that this would cost considerable sums to provide the necessary accommodation back in the United Kingdom. Nott countered his points, and without commenting further the Prime Minister thanked both for their time and showed Leach to the door.³⁵ By the middle of May it seemed clear that the outcomes of the review would largely stand. Keith Speed, the Under-Secretary of State for the Navy, and as has been seen, a strong supporter of the Navy's case in the Review, took the first step towards his resignation by making a speech to his constituents on 15 May arguing passionately against the planned reductions in naval capability.³⁶ John Nott wrote over the note covering the speech transcript: 'Testament of the Heart!'³⁷ Speed refused to resign from the government despite this obvious breach with government policy.³⁸ Interestingly, Nott had initially wanted to keep Speed on, the Secretary of State's second instance of equivocation over the Review outcomes (the first had been his willingness to consider the Admiralty Board's 5 per cent proposals), but Margaret Thatcher correctly perceived that to do this would help undermine the whole review process, and perhaps encourage other acts of ministerial insubordination in a government that was deeply unpopular in the country. Speed was sacked in a meeting with the Prime Minister on 18 May. Naval staff officers lined the corridors in his honour as he left the building.³⁹

Briefing the Prime Minister

On 14 May, Nott sent the Prime Minister three notes. One was a short note on the *Ark Royal* problem and the presentational difficulties of scrapping a ship just after it had been launched by the Queen Mother. The second was the Secretary of State's formal setting-out of the conclusions of the Review and the third, which covered both of the others, provided an introduction and basic summary of the formal conclusions. The cover note focussed on the need for speed in the Review and skilfully played to Thatcher's wish to push against consensus and compromise within government: 'otherwise the initiative for reaching necessary decisions will be wrested from me by those who counsel delay, excessive consultation with the Allies, new option exercises etc. etc. – and all the other Whitehall devices for avoiding harsh and unpleasant changes.'⁴⁰ Nott confirmed that the defence programme needed radical change, and that long-term ten-year reform was needed to avoid the short-term cuts that had reduced operational activity in the last months of 1980. Arguing that there was little scope for cuts in the RAF and that a major withdrawal of the Army from Germany would be politically impossible, he argued that 'I have become increasingly sceptical (as has much scientific and other strategic opinion inside and outside Government, despite the outrage to Naval tradition) of the viability of the surface fleet in the Atlantic, in face of the increasingly long-range submarine and air launched missile forces of the Russians, for the fleet's prime role, that of anti-submarine warfare.' Instead, ASW should be entrusted to submarines and maritime patrol aircraft, 'and switch from expensive frigates to cheaper ships with towed-array (listening devices for ASW).'⁴¹ Nott did admit that he needed more time to assess the usefulness of the anti-submarine helicopter. This shift would result in a reduction in shipbuilding, withdrawing a number of older ships from service early, closing two dockyards and other depots and establishments. The surface fleet's primary role would shift to 'deterrence by presence' inside and outside the NATO area with the new *Invincible* class used for this purpose, primarily outside the Eastern Atlantic. Nott re-emphasised that he was not reducing the defence budget but was ensuring that the planned programmes could fit within it.⁴²

The full paper under this cover note set out the impact on the Navy in much more detail: Nott had not formally accepted the 5 per cent adjustment suggested by the Admiralty Board, so the figures in the document matched those of 1 May, as did the conclusions. Only two *Invincible* class would enter service, the Type 42 would not be replaced or modernised in any major way, the two assault ships would be withdrawn in 1982 and 1984, and twenty-two destroyers and frigates would be withdrawn from service in the next few years in order to reduce their numbers to thirty-eight by 1986 and thirty-one in 1991 (and presumably below thirty-one by 1996). The only part of the 5 per cent adjustment that Nott had accepted so far was the ordering of two further Outboard Type 22s. Personnel numbers would fall from 68,000 to 50,000 by 1986 and 48,500 by 1991.⁴³ The augmentations to the RAF given the increased reliance on their maritime patrol aircraft for anti-submarine warfare were meagre. Only three more Nimrods would be updated to MR2 standards and there were no plans to fit them with air-to-air refuelling facilities which would have had a significant effect in improving their range and time on station. Sea Eagle would be procured for maritime surface strike, but SACLANT would not be receiving early Tornado squadrons for the maritime role, so the Buccaneers would continue in service for a number of years more, and as a result they would presumably be modernised to operate the Sea Eagle in place of Martel.⁴⁴

Some of Nott's analysis was correct: Sea Dart and Sea Harriers would probably have been insufficient to provide effective air defence against mass Soviet cruise missile attacks, and the majority of the frigate force was deeply inadequate in the anti-submarine role, but his solutions looked poorly thought through and unconvincing. It is notable that Nott did not mention the barrier concept in the notes to the Prime Minister. It seems that he was beginning to realise the difficulties in arguing for its efficacy, given the rather obvious problem of submarines passing through the barrier before hostilities started, and the less obvious problem of sonar propagation problems in the main barrier area, the GIUK gap. This therefore meant that at least some close defence of shipping against submarines would now be necessary, although this was not specifically mentioned in the note, with either Nimrods replacing helicopters in this role or shipborne anti-submarine helicopters being retained. The shift to relying on maritime patrol aircraft had been undertaken on the assumption that they could replace the anti-submarine helicopter, but this had not yet been demonstrated, nor had any consideration been taken of the impact of total or partial loss of SOSUS on Nimrod effectiveness. With only three additional aircraft and no air-to-air refuelling, the Nimrod force would in any case be much less effective that it could or should be. The reduction in the number of carriers from three to two was also predicated on the assumption that anti-submarine helicopters would not be needed, but the final decision on the fate of these aircraft had been delayed, so logically the same should have been the case with the three carriers, given their core role as ASW helicopter platforms.[45] In fact, there was a good argument for more such carriers: three would probably not be enough, although in a cheaper utility form such as the 'garage ship' of the late 1970s or in conversions of ships taken up from trade, and probably in place of a significant portion of the frigate force.

Although Nott stated that the surface fleet would not be able to operate safely in the Atlantic, he was willing to countenance developing the Type 23 and continuing the surface towed-array programme. This suggested that such vessels could in fact operate in the Atlantic.[46] Perhaps the assessment of the 1975 concept had been adopted: that only submarines would be safe to operate east of the GIUK gap but surface ships would be viable west of it? However, this was not articulated in any of the Review documents, so this inconsistency could not be resolved. Neither did he explicitly state that these towed-array frigates would only be used in peacetime, which would raise the difficult question of their role and purpose in times of high tension, and the extreme risks being taken if such ships departed from the North Atlantic leaving formerly trailed submarines free to attack shipping. Nott's answer to the inadequacy of the Type 42s in dealing with mass cruise missile attacks was to abolish the air defence destroyer altogether. Other options could have been investigated, including procuring a small number of ships with the US Aegis phased-array radar and tactical command system, which would be much more able to deal with multiple cruise missile targets. Combined with a vertical launch system for missiles, would have provided both the ability to track large numbers of targets and launch sufficient missiles to intercept them. In any case, the Type 42s would be well suited to air defence outside the NATO area where it could deal with less concentrated and intense air threats, and Nott had at least nominally committed himself to retaining a naval capability in the 'out of area' role.[47]

Given the speed with which Nott wanted to proceed, an issue which concerned the Cabinet Secretary, Robert Armstrong,[48] the key members of the Oversea Policy and Defence Committee of Cabinet initially met informally to consider Nott's note on the Defence Review. Nott made his case for the review outcomes in front of the Prime Minister, the Chancellor of the Exchequer, the Foreign Secretary and the Secretary of State for Industry on 18 May. Alongside his proposals for the size and shape of the three services, Nott also argued for a continuation of 3 per cent annual increases in the defence budget until 1987/88 along with a further £600 million up to 1984–5. Nott stated that 'he had almost no room for manoeuvre over the next three years and he could not bring the defence programme under control and give it fresh direction without the resources he was asking for'.[49] Despite all of the changes Nott was instituting across defence, and especially on the Navy, he was still forced to ask for additional funds like his predecessor Francis Pym. He would be saving money in the long-term, but would still need additional funds in the short-term.[50] It was an undeniable indication of the enormously overheated ten-year programme that had existed before the review, and that despite all the planned capability reductions, it would *still* be over budget even if 3 per cent annual increases were granted for six years. The Chancellor, focussing on the overall numbers and Nott's request for additional funds, argued against special pleading by Defence as other departments and nationalised industries were asking the same. He did not want to acquiesce and then face imposing cuts on defence in only a few years' time as the MoD's budget overheated yet again. He rejected Nott's request for £600 million and 3 per cent until 1987–8, and argued that Cabinet would need to discuss this.[51]

Nott's detailed proposals to reduce the Navy had been known within the Foreign and Commonwealth Office for some weeks.[52] The Foreign Secretary, who had strongly supported Pym and Lewin's attempt to reduce spending on British Forces Germany and focus on naval forces a year earlier, and who would state in his autobiography seven years later that 'we British should concentrate upon the maritime area' in the defence of Europe, caved in again and accepted Nott's arguments.[53] Lord Carrington stated that 'difficult decisions' would be necessary, that the Navy's programme needed to be run down more than that of the Army and that any significant reductions on the Central Front would be 'politically disastrous.'[54] Nott's defence review proposals, in terms of equipment and personnel reductions at least, had been broadly supported by the ministers present, even if the Chancellor was adamant that the Secretary of State should not get any additional funds. Even the Navy's traditional ally, the Foreign and Commonwealth Office, would not provide any defence against the significant reductions that the Royal Navy would face. The Oversea Policy and Defence committee would formally meet at the start of June to consider Nott's proposals in full.

Finalising the Review Outcomes

Following the informal ministerial meeting it must have seemed that there was little that the Navy's leadership could do: there would be minimal opposition to the capability reductions, and if the Chancellor had his way there might even be further reductions in equipment as the £600 million supplement was not provided. However, only three days afterwards on 21 May, Nott seemed willing to consider the resurrection of some of the Navy's 5 per cent proposals from earlier in the month. He asked officials to provide costings for completing *Ark Royal* (but only having two carriers in service), building a seventh *Trafalgar* class, speeding up the Type 23 and SSK programmes, running down Chatham and Gibraltar more slowly, keeping HMS *Endurance* and the Royal Yacht in service, reinstating the Navy's offensive mining capability and most significantly of all a less-steep rundown to a force of fourteen destroyers and twenty-two frigates by 1991.[55] These changes were costed, and if all were implemented a total of £1.9 billion would be added to the ten-year programme. The most expensive element was the slower frigate rundown, which would cost an extra £765 million over ten years. Some of these add backs were relatively cheap: the extra SSN would cost £158 million and speeding up the Type 23 and conventional submarine programmes would cost £77 million and £154 million respectively. Completing *Ark Royal* but sticking with a two carrier force would cost £70 million.[56]

Soon, these purely naval add-backs would be accompanied by a handful of additions for the other services, including procuring Sea Eagle for the RAF and the Wavell communications system for the Army. These were then prioritised, with completing *Ark Royal*, retaining the Royal Yacht, Wavell and Sea Eagle as top priorities classed as 'necessary', and the slower frigate rundown, accelerated Type 23 and SSK programmes, seventh *Trafalgar* class boat and defensive mining a second tier defined as 'highly desirable.' Meanwhile, retaining HMS *Endurance* – the Ice Patrol Ship and a visible marker of the United Kingdom's commitment to the Falklands Islands and its other territories in the South Atlantic – languished in a fourth category entitled 'Contingent Items', and even though it would only cost £8 million up to 1985–6 to retain in service, a line in pen had been placed through it (either by Nott himself or by one of his private secretaries) which suggested that it was no longer considered for this category either.[57] However, the original 1 May future fleet (in Table 9) remained in place as one potential variant to put to the Oversea Policy and Defence Committee, with the newer version – including the addbacks – as another variant. Embarrassingly, even though the Queen Mother had launched HMS *Ark Royal* on 2 June, the ship was still formally slated to be broken up before completion.[58]

The papers for the Oversea Policy and Defence Committee ('OD') were sent in draft form to the Prime Minister and other OD attendees in early June and included the two versions as alternatives. Both a 'fast adjustment' option and a 'slow adjustment' option used the same 1 May fleet numbers. The only difference was that the slow adjustment option resulted in somewhat greater spending in the first five years of the ten-year spending period, and was based on 3 per cent annual increases until 1987–8 on a 'volume' basis (which is broadly an inflation adjusted calculation), whilst the fast adjustment would result in 3 per cent increases until 1985–6 only. Although both options appeared to result in an identically shrunk fleet by 1985–6, the 'slow adjustment' option would presumably mean a more gradual shift to the 1985–6 figure. Nott's calculations were based on what was called in Treasury jargon a 'relative price effect' of 2 per cent, in other words that overall 'defence inflation' would be 2 per cent higher than inflation in the economy as a whole. Nott favoured the second option as the one that would be politically possible and achievable given public and backbench opinion over such reductions in the Navy.[59] Given the large number of redundancies from the reductions in the Navy, it is not surprising that Nott would want to spread the reductions out over a somewhat longer period. 4,600 would lose their jobs in Chatham with another 745 in London and the home Counties, 6,800 in the Portsmouth area, 1,050 in the West Country and the same number in South Wales with 1,260 losing their jobs in Gibraltar. This was not just through dockyard closures but also as a result of the closure or reduction in size of depots, stores and training establishments. A total of 6,500 Royal Navy service personnel would be made redundant, 1,500 of them officers.[60] One mysterious absence from the submission was the add-backs that had been painfully negotiated and compiled over May. Despite their absence, many of them were added into the new Long Term Costings over the course of the second half of 1981 (after OD and Cabinet had approved the figures).

The Treasury submitted a more austere counter proposal with a defence budget increasing by 3 per cent on a cash basis (i.e. not inflation adjusted) and only until 1983–4, with a relative price effect of 5 per cent.[61] The Prime Minister was advised by Robert Wade-Gery, the Deputy Cabinet Secretary, that although neither of Nott's options were reducing the defence budget, and would in fact increase it steadily for another six years, they did 'offer the first real prospect for years of bringing defence plans into line with resources. "Overstretch" has been the bane of our military posture since the war. It will be worth breaking some eggs to get away from it at last – as after the initial shock both the Services and our Allies should come to appreciate. The choice of the surface fleet to bear the main brunt of cuts is of course controversial. But any alternative choice would probably be even more so.'[62] The Foreign and

Commonwealth Office only opposed the proposals on the basis of their impact on Gibraltar, Belize, the Falklands and Cyprus but was willing to discuss these issues bilaterally and did not oppose the main thrust of Nott's document. Another possible issue would be the decision to reduce the hydrographic fleet by half and abandon domestic surveying. Wade-Gery pointed out that the government had supported retaining this capability the last time it was discussed before the Pym mini-review, and that the Secretary of State for Trade might oppose this element of the paper.[63] He duly did so a few days after the OD meeting, emphasising the risks to safety of navigation in the Straits of Dover and southern North Sea if hydrography for civil purposes ended.[64]

The OD meeting itself on 8 June went Nott's way. The Chancellor's austere option gained very little support from the members of the Committee, who probably baulked at the large number of redundancies required to fulfil the 'fast adjustment' during a period of 2.5 million unemployment, preferred the 'slow adjustment' option which spread some of the pain over an extra year or two, even if it mean an identical force structure and size across the services by 1985–6. Given the controversial nature of the decisions being made, it was agreed that the proposals should be put in front of the full Cabinet. However, storm clouds were beginning to gather for Nott. Short-term spending within the Ministry of Defence was still running far above budget and the Defence Secretary was forced to consider withholding or 'constraining' cash payments to contractors towards the end of the financial year. For the Prime Minister this began to chip away at Nott's credibility to deliver his proposals and hinted that discussion of ending 'overstretch' in Defence was premature.[65]

Aware that the Chancellor would make another attempt to push his more austere version of the Review at Cabinet, and that some ministers not involved in defence and foreign affairs might feel that the Ministry was being treated more leniently than other departments, Nott proposed a compromise on the day before the Cabinet meeting. He would accept 3 per cent increases until 1985–6 on a volume basis – his fast adjustment option – but at the same time he warned that this would be more difficult to sell to backbenchers and the public.[66] Nott's paper to Cabinet was in essence identical to that put to OD, but incorporated Howe's proposals in one of the appendices, and acknowledged that short-term cash was an issue within the Ministry of Defence and that therefore 'there must be a fair review of this year's cash limits [for the MOD]', a reference to the system by which the Treasury controlled short-term spending by allowing inflation adjusted uplifts at levels agreed by the Chief Secretary to the Treasury.[67]

When Cabinet met on 18 June, its members had already battled their way through a weighty discussion on economic strategy the day before, with the economy in the depths of recession, and the country suffering the highest unemployment seen since before the Second World War. The Defence Review was the last item on the agenda, and the 'broad thrust' of Nott's proposals were approved with the caveat that government could not commit itself to defence programme figures beyond 1985–6: in effect agreeing to the fast implementation option which Nott was now proposing as his preferred option. In addition, the final settling of the defence budget could not be made until the government-wide Public Expenditure Survey had been completed. A clearly exhausted Cabinet agreed to cover individual issues, such as the future of civil hydrography, bilaterally outside of Cabinet or at OD.[68] The Cabinet minutes do not show much dissension from those around the table, but contemporary newspaper reports did state concerns were expressed about both the speed of the review and the lack of consultation with allies so far, with Lord Carrington, Francis Pym and Jim Prior making these points, but only Pym stating that the Navy had been cut too far in the Review.[69] Whether these points were made or not, or whether they were a part of the media briefing campaign by the Prime Minister's opponents, they did not alter the Cabinet decision. Howe's alternative proposal had not been approved, and as at OD it had received minimal support, but he would have plenty of opportunities to quibble with the detail of the proposed numbers, not least because the Public Expenditure Survey negotiations would require the conversion of the MOD's inflation adjusted totals into real cash figures.

Informing, and Negotiating with, the United States

Following the Cabinet meeting, Nott submitted a draft copy of the planned White Paper dated 18 June. In most respects it was the same as the document that would be published by the Stationery Office one week later; with one significant exception. When discussing the size of the fleet, the draft document stated 'the destroyer/frigate force, currently numbering fifty-nine, will contract over the next five years to about forty.'[70] The 'to about forty' phrase was in square parentheses suggesting that it might be liable to change – the actual number agreed by both OD and Cabinet was thirty-eight by 1985–6, of which ten would be in reserve or refit at any one time. Why was the particular issue of destroyer and frigate numbers still up in the air after Nott's review had been approved by the highest body in British government? The only substantive events that occurred between the Cabinet Meeting on 17 June and the announcement of the Review outcomes on 25 June when this figure had changed to fifty, were Nott's visits to the United States to inform the US Secretary of Defense and to NATO headquarters to speak with the Secretary General. The NATO Secretary General would be unlikely to have the leverage to force a major change in policy; the key event was the meeting with Caspar Weinberger, the new Secretary of Defense.

On the day before the Cabinet Meeting, Nott received a note from Frank Cooper, setting out how the situation had changed in the US Department of Defense since their last visit in March. Back in March the senior officials in the department were still those of the outgoing Carter administration, and the US strategy of the late 1970s which – as was seen in Chapter 10 – focussed on short-war scenarios, as much prepositioning of equipment in Europe as possible, and only committing substantial US naval forces to the Atlantic by 'swinging' them from the Pacific in a period of high tension, was still in place. The new Republican administration had a very different set of priorities. Cooper's contact in the Pentagon was Bob Murray, the Under-Secretary of the Navy appointed by Carter who would stay until towards the end of the transition to the new Republican administration, resigning in September 1981. Cooper reported that Murray had 'confirmed that the Navy is, at the moment, by far the most popular Service in Washington.' Also, 'the Navy lobby in Washington is very strong and probably more effective than that of any of the other Services – with the possible exception of the US Marines. He said that arguments about precision-guided weapons and surface ships being vulnerable had been all the rage in Washington about two years ago, but they were now out of favour.'[71] Cooper stated that the Pentagon was very well informed about Nott's plans in the Defence Review, hinting that senior naval officers might have leaked these, although Keith Speed's resignation the previous month had created headlines in the United States and made it obvious that the Royal Navy was the main target of the Review.[72] Murray had stated that Weinberger would ask about what improvements were being made to the Royal Navy and also that any contribution by the Royal Navy in southwest Asia – the Gulf and western Indian Ocean – would be very welcome.[73] Nott was clearly now worried about the US using its leverage with the Trident programme to push for a reversal of elements of the review, and stated as much in a note to the Prime Minister just before the Cabinet meeting: his proposed compromise with Howe was 'the absolute limit that the Party will stand and I still have to persuade the Americans this weekend that our Naval reductions should not be vigorously opposed (possibly by a direct message from [President] Reagan to yourself) or Trident called into question'.[74]

It was clear that some of Weinberger's emphasis would be on destroyer and frigate numbers, the reduction of which would have the most impact across NATO, and the gaps left in the Alliance's force requirements would most probably have to be filled by the United States Navy. As the new administration was trying to increase the size of the US Navy and improve its capability, merely backfilling Royal Navy reductions would not play well domestically and defeat much of the object of increasing the USN's ships to 600.[75] It seems that as early as 12 June the issue of escort numbers could be well be crucial in the forthcoming meeting with Weinberger. On that day, David Omand had suggested that higher frigate numbers in the mid to late 1980s could be a concession to the US that would be feasible. The First Sea Lord suggested using commercial yards for refitting the additional frigates as a way to deal with the problem of the reduced Royal Dockyard capacity for a larger fleet.[76] By the 17th Omand was able to give Nott a series of options for further add-backs into the destroyer and frigate force, based on proposals helpfully put forward by the Head of DS4, the Central Secretariat section which worked alongside the Naval Staff and dealt with naval issues.[77] These are summarised in the Table below.

Table 10: Number of destroyers and frigates declared to NATO (both active and in Standby Squadron)[78]

	Destroyers + Frigates = total	1981–2	1985–6	1990–1
1	'Core fleet'[79] (i.e. baseline agreed before 10 June, and similar to 1 May fleet)	13+46=59	15+24=39	16+23=39
2	Add-backs approved in principle (accelerate Type 23 programme, provide basic 'docking and essential defects' periods to extend life of 19 *Leander/Rothesay* class frigates for 1–2 years)	13+46=59	15+31=46	14+30=44
3	In addition to 2, place three non-towed-array Batch 2 *Leanders* in Standby Squadron rather than deep reserve	13+46=59	15+34=49	14+33=47
4	In addition to 2 and 3, place unmodernised Batch 3 *Leanders* in Standby Squadron rather than dispose of	13+46=59	15+38=53	14+38=52

There are some anomalies with Omand's proposal. He assumes that the add backs in row two had been accepted 'in principle' but these escort numbers were not those approved by OD and Cabinet, which were essentially those of the 1 May fleet structure (close to those in row one). Perhaps OD and Cabinet's agreeing to the 'general thrust' of the Defence Review proposals gave Nott the freedom to make such changes to the planned programme, but this would put additional costs into the ten-year plan that could not have been included in the numbers submitted to OD and Cabinet. The spectre of 'overstretch' was returning, if it had ever been banished in the first place, and the size of the fleet was edging back upwards.

Omand suggested that option three be accepted, with option four a possibility, if Nott came under pressure in his meeting with Weinberger. Taken together, these were considerable concessions that would result in a fleet that did not look as decimated as it would have been under the original plan.

However, a higher proportion of the escort fleet would now be in reserve in the Standby Squadron. The additional cost of both options 3 and 4 was considered to be only an extra £7.3 million to £9.6 million per year between 1983–4 and 1990–1, although this does seem somewhat optimistic given the personnel needed to crew these additional vessels, even if they were all in the Standby Squadron and their refits were undertaken commercially.[80] As these attempts to increase the frigate force were being undertaken, the DUS(Navy) attempted to push for running *Endurance* on as the Ice Patrol Ship until at least 1990 but this was ultimately unsuccessful, although *Britannia* was reprieved.[81]

Nott's visit to Washington, accompanied by Quinlan and Omand, occurred over the weekend of 20 and 21 June. It was not much more than a short hop across the Atlantic and involved only a dinner with Caspar Weinberger on Saturday evening and a formal meeting for an hour the next morning, followed almost immediately by departure for the airport. The group was not to meet anyone else in the administration or the military.[82] The evening meeting was civil and polite, with Nott setting out the rationale for his decisions and his decision to keep within the Brussels Treaty limits in Germany and reducing the size of the Navy. Weinberger noted that the press reports of Royal Navy reductions, with the almost certain likelihood that the gaps would have to be filled by the US Navy, 'would give rise to domestic difficulties for the US administration.'[83] Nott equivocated when asked about total planned escort numbers, with 'numbers varying over the next few years' and a dip in the late 1980s, but that 'the numbers he had were only illustrative at this stage, and many details remained to be worked out.'[84] The Secretary of State then offered Omand's option 3 concession (and perhaps also option 4) of adding more vessels 'to the Standby Squadron, and declared to NATO, rather than disposal for sale or scrap.'[85] Probably aware that drawing this out from Nott at the informal dinner rather than the main meeting had been a significant concession, Weinberger then offered to help by suggesting that the United States could allow the United Kingdom access to some of their facilities for the storage and processing of Trident warheads.[86] Although never stated directly, by offering help on Trident straight after Nott's escort concession, Weinberger was making a point – ever so gently – about the ultimately transactional nature of the sale of Trident.

The next morning, at the formal meeting, Weinberger returned to the subject of escort numbers. This time he made it clear that if there was a fall in numbers by the mid-1980s 'by the order of 13 to 15 then he foresaw difficulties with Congress' whilst reductions in the range of seven to nine 'would not be a cause for alarm'. As the existing force was fifty-nine strong, a fifty-escort fleet would therefore be the minimum with which the US would be happy. Weinberger then asked whether the new Type 23 would be compatible with the US Aegis naval air defence system. This was a significant question to ask and was almost certainly not expected by the Secretary of State.[87] The Aegis system was in the early stages of entry into service, and by using phased arrays instead of standard rotating radar antennae and much sophisticated digital technology, it promised to provide an answer to the Soviet mass cruise missile threat when married to the latest variant of the US Standard air defence missile. In effect, the Secretary of Defense, aware that the Royal Navy's air defence destroyers would over time be withdrawn without replacement, was offering either to sell the Aegis system itself or at the minimum offer the software and hardware to allow British warships to 'operate and contribute within the Aegis air defence control environment' given that Royal Navy vessels operating in the Eastern Atlantic would probably be doing so under US Navy air defence cover.[88] This was an extremely important offer, that could have dealt with many of the concerns about Type 42 and Sea Dart effectiveness by either replacing it entirely with the US system or harnessing it to Aegis capabilities. It was not taken up by Nott and was an incredible missed opportunity to put naval area air defence on a firmer footing (albeit at the expense of the British guided missile industry and at the risk of tying in dependence on US systems into the future).

Weinberger also suggested that the US Navy might purchase one of the three *Invincible* class, if it were compatible with US systems, given delays in their own carrier programme. Nott again demurred, this time because a purchase by the Royal Australian Navy of one of the ships was a distinct possibility.[89] Weinberger also wanted further discussions about destroyer and frigate numbers, and follow-up meetings between officials were agreed. The Secretary of Defense wanted greater clarity over the short-term readiness of the Royal Navy escorts declared to NATO: in effect, how many would be active and how many would be in the Standby Squadron and therefore taking longer before they could deploy.[90] The meeting with the NATO Secretary General occurred a few days later without controversy, although Nott did reconfirm the newly minted fifty figure to the Secretary General.[91] On 25 June the Secretary of State stood in front of Parliament and presented the outcome of his Review to its Members. After he sat down, the new Defence White Paper, entitled 'The Way Forward' was officially released, confirming the outcomes of the Review, and hastily redrafted to include the increased size of the fleet that had been conceded by Nott in his dinner with Weinberger only five days previously.

* * *

The 1981 Defence Review has been deeply controversial and even infamous in political and naval circles. The Falklands crisis only ten months later appeared to many to negate its findings and reverse its decisions, whilst its very controversy put off the government from conducting another review for nearly a decade.[92] Initial academic analysis of the Review, undertaken before official documents were released but based on extensive interviews with participants, sought to provide a more balanced view of a process that had been popularly seen as an embarrassing failure.[93] David Boren argued that it was a successful attempt to wrest control of defence policy planning from the Chiefs of Staff, who were constrained by single-service loyalties and the structures of the Ministry of Defence into producing compromise that resulted in 'equal pain' outcomes, to civil servants able to provide more radical and effective answers that accorded better with strategic, political and economic priorities.[94] Boren is certainly correct that the 1981 Defence Review, led by the Secretary of State supported by Cooper, Mason and to a lesser extent Quinlan, saw a dramatic shift from the CDS-led process of the 1974–5 Review, which had clearly gravitated towards a compromise approach led by the Chiefs of Staff under the effective leadership of Carver. The speed of the 1981 Review, the emphasis on a rapidly-produced policy direction document (the 'Bermudagram'), the small amount of time devoted very late in the process to consulting with allies, all point to a wish to ensure that a radical approach was preserved and that there was as little time as possible devoted to inter-service or service-to-Secretary of State argument and negotiation. This enabled a focus on most of the reductions in present and future capabilities to a single-service, the Royal Navy. The decision to place Trident within the Navy's budget did have the intended effect of helping to ensure that an 'equal pain' review would be impossible in such circumstances.[95]

Boren's assessment of the strategic rationale for focussing the Review on the Navy is however, somewhat simplistic, stating that it reflected a contraction of the UK's global interests, and a focus on NATO whilst reducing resources devoted to 'out of area' operations.[96] This analysis has an element of truth to it, but only addresses one aspect of the Review. Nott *did* retain naval forces for out of area operations, although his choice of using the specialist ASW carriers of the *Invincible* class in this role does look like an attempt to find something to do for a brand-new capability which was now apparently irrelevant in its key role. The surviving frigate force would also be used in such operations, but the parallel push to reduce commitments in Belize (which continued during and after the Falklands conflict, as will be seen in Chapter 16) and capabilities to support the Falklands commitment did suggest a longer-term plan to reduce these as much as possible. At the start of the Review process, latching onto the 'barrier strategy' enabled Nott to keep all four defence pillars in place, rather than sacrifice the Eastern Atlantic pillar outright, by stating that submarines and land-based maritime air would be the main means by which the military tasks of this pillar would be undertaken. However, the obvious and fundamental flaws in this approach – most clearly the high probability that Soviet submarines would have traversed through such a barrier before hostilities started – meant that this had been dropped by the time discussions had broadened beyond the Ministry of Defence. The approach then taken was that surface ships would not be used in the Eastern Atlantic at all, with anti-submarine warfare undertaken by submarines and land-based air only. Despite this, the Type 23 design – a specialist anti-submarine towed-array frigate – was continued and became an important part of the delivery of the Review outcomes. The assertion that land-based maritime aircraft would be able to replace surface ships in anti-submarine warfare also ignored the likelihood of the degradation in effectiveness of the SOSUS system, which was essential in helping maritime patrol narrow down potential target positions. Whether such patrol aircraft could defend surface ships effectively or prosecute detections by surface-ship towed-array contacts had not been demonstrated either. This was one of the reasons why the EH101 (Sea King replacement) helicopter was not categorically cancelled in June 1981 and would later be reprieved. However, Boren did acknowledge that basing so much of the Review's analysis on the results from operational analysis projects had been a mistake. The extrapolation of more general results from very specific scenarios with a range of assumptions which, if changed, could significantly change outcomes, resulted in faulty deductions from analysis that had been commissioned for other reasons.[97]

By contrast, as has been seen, this author has argued that Nott's position on the Eastern Atlantic was incoherent, contradictory and untested. However, it might be argued that this did not matter. Underlying Nott's decisions was the assumption that the Eastern Atlantic theatre was much less important than the Central Front in Europe, and therefore it could be postulated that greater risks could be taken and therefore military coherence mattered less. As Nott himself stated at an academic conference 25 years later, 'it was either a sea or a land decision'.[98] With the RAF's leadership declaring the Eastern Atlantic a secondary theatre in 1976, and this position being undoubtedly supported by the Army, the centre of gravity of the Ministry of Defence was gradually shifting away from a balance across the Four Pillars. The negative outcome for the Navy of the 1980 Pym mini-review also reinforced this perception combined with the political and diplomatic difficulties of attempting to reduce German land/air commitments below the Brussels Treaty levels. The widespread assumption that a short-warning/short-war threat was the most likely (which privileged the Central Front as the prime site for defence investment), despite historical evidence to the contrary in the examples of the Cuban Missile Crisis and the Yom Kippur stand-off, also fed into this increasing perception that the Eastern Atlantic and out of area theatres were less important for Defence. The Ministry of Defence was settling into a strategic myopia where the unexpected would not happen, and therefore capabilities that had the flexibility to respond to the unforeseen were not needed. The future would be stable, expected and politically, diplomatically and strategically static. The next 12 months, and for that matter the next decade, would prove how wrong these assumptions would be.

Andrew Dorman was the second scholar who based his research on interviews with participants, and his analysis of the progress of the Review broadly stands up in the generality, even if some of his details are incorrect. He highlights Nott's relatively lukewarm commitment to the barrier 'strategy', arguing correctly that to have conceded its fundamental flaws would have put the whole Review process in jeopardy. He also correctly saw that the original much lower numbers for escorts were lifted up to fifty as a result of lobbying, although he attributed this to NATO rather than US influence, and the shift actually occurred much closer to the White Paper publication date than he had assumed.[99]

Dorman also highlighted the often-forgotten fact that Nott's review was not a budget-cutting defence review, despite the Secretary of State's reputation as and demeanour of a 'bean-counter'.[100] The long-term programme was so overloaded that despite all his reductions in future procurement and current capability, he was still asking for additional money to help fund the remainder of the Defence budget. As has been seen in this chapter, this assessment is correct: Nott was forced like his predecessor Francis Pym to repeatedly deal with short-term overspending whilst attempting to place the long-term programme on a sustainable track. Boren has noted that the Navy's overloaded procurement programme made it especially vulnerable, and this was correct.[101] The Navy's forward programme, even trimmed as it was during 1980, was nowhere near being a plausible document, and unlike the RAF and its Tornado procurement, it was not protected by the diplomatic issues of attempting to cut back on a multi-national project. Even worse than a forward procurement programme that had many scratching their heads, was the lack of a concept of operations that the Navy Department was happy with, and Boren also alights on this deficit as another reason for the Navy's predicament.[102] A document written by the Naval Staff was in draft form, and had been for some time, whilst the only recognised document within the Ministry was the 1978 Concept drawn up by the Central Staffs and has been seen in Chapter 10, was deeply unsatisfactory from the perspective of the Navy.

Given this extremely difficult position to defend, how well did the Navy's leadership and Staff deal with the environment they found themselves in? Boren argues that the Navy's 'unhelpful' approach to the Review hindered its ability to fight its corner.[103] Nott himself also argued that the Navy's position lacked imagination and offering new solutions.[104] This is somewhat uncharitable, as the offer of reductions or concessions early in a review was generally seen as not providing any benefits or shielding from further cuts later on. However, Boren's criticism does at least have some weight as the Review progressed and it became obvious that the Navy would be the main target. Given the potentially momentous changes to the structure of the surface fleet, the approach of the First Sea Lord was to focus on strategic issues of the possibility of a long-warning and/or long war, and to argue more generally for a balanced fleet able to deal with the unexpected. At one level this was an attempt to deal with attacks on the Navy's programme by working from first principles but given that this gained little 'traction' with Nott, there was no attempt to make a change in tactics. More radical fleet structures – including focussing on garage ships and smaller towed-array frigates for anti-submarine warfare at the expense of the traditional anti-submarine frigate – had been considered a few years before, but these were not pursued as possible alternatives, nor was the Aegis option for air defence offered as a possibility. Despite this, the Navy Department did fight hard to keep the EH101 alive, rightly convinced by the efficacy of helicopters in anti-submarine warfare, and also pushed for the Type 23, which Nott and Johnston were also keen to have procured. The Navy did at least push for the capabilities that were the most effective and important for the anti-submarine mission, even if there was not much imagination on show. However, where the Navy was most effective was in partially reversing the initial conclusions of the Review. Leach was made of much tougher material than Luce 15 years previously. He did not countenance resigning, although Keith Speed's resignation did publicly highlight the potential cuts to the Navy nationally and internationally. Leach, playing dirty by the standards of the day, could well have discussed the issue with his US counterparts as Cooper suspected, but given that Nott was unwilling to listen to the Naval Staff's arguments and, as was seen in the previous chapter, had effectively made up his mind in early February, this is perhaps not surprising. If arguments made internally are gaining no traction, then using external players with influence to make the case can provide much greater leverage, and it certainly did in this case. The additional ships returned to the Navy's future force structure were admittedly old and would be in reserve, but the fifty figure was now a clear publicly-made commitment, and further discussions between the US Department of Defense and the Ministry seemed to hold open the possibility that some of these additional ships could be made active.[105] One of the great ironies of the Review process was that if this had been undertaken six-months earlier, with the Carter administration still in place, which was focussing its energies on pre-positioning equipment in Europe, emphasising the 'short-warning/short war' approach, and de-emphasising the role of the US Navy in a conflict with the USSR, then the Secretary of State would not have been subject to lobbying from across the Atlantic to reverse some of his naval reductions. Timing matters, and the Royal Navy was in this respect exceedingly lucky: it should be very thankful for the intervention of Caspar Weinberger and the US Department of Defense.

Overall, the Navy had been in an extremely difficult position from the very start of the Review. Significant reductions in the future programme were necessary in order make it fit within the budget, whilst existing force levels were also unsustainable. Neither the Foreign Secretary nor the Prime Minister were willing to take the political and diplomatic pain of attempting to renegotiate the terms of the Brussels Treaty and reduce British forces in Germany substantially. This therefore meant that, assuming that the nuclear deterrent would remain and that the defence of the UK Base remained a priority, the Eastern Atlantic pillar looked by far the most vulnerable and the Navy was the prime candidate for reductions. That the Royal Navy came into the Review with an extremely weak hand – an overheated and incoherent procurement programme, no accepted concept of operations, a large body of operational analysis evidence showing the Navy in a negative light – made it especially vulnerable. However, John Nott attempted to undertake his Review too fast, and came to unjustifiably radical decisions on maritime capabilities based on the flimsiest of evidence. It was almost inevitable that any Review process in these circumstances would have produced an outcome where the Navy was hit the hardest, but the extent and pain of the 'Bermudagram' was the result of the Secretary of State's wish for a quick, seemingly simple and clear-cut outcome, which his leading civil service advisers duly provided. This was Nott's great mistake. A lack of plausible military arguments for what were essentially politically- and diplomatically-driven decisions, albeit ones that went along the grain of the Ministry, made the Secretary of State vulnerable to external lobbying and the slow dismantling of many of the elements of his Review. This began in May 1981 and manifested itself most clearly in the successful US push for more escorts to be added back into the programme. It would continue after the White Paper had been completed. In his eagerness to push hard against the Navy, he neglected the possibility of economies in a number of other areas. As early as February 1981 he had declared to the Prime Minister that there was 'no scope for savings' in the RAF.[106] Nott perhaps presumed that he would only have the political capital within the Ministry to fight one service, instead of two or all three, but this meant that when the rolling back began and was accompanied by calls for further economies in Defence, the other two services, particularly the RAF, were hit relatively hard, the Navy being considered to have already suffered enough. As a result and as will be seen in the next chapter, by March 1982, a greater balance in the pain across the services had been achieved, with the Navy's strengths in dealing with the unexpected, both inside and outside the NATO area being better recognised, if only by default. Nott was therefore forced into a series of credibility-sapping reversals, which when combined with his repeated requests for more short-term funding, resulted in the eventual destruction of his political career as the Chancellor and then the Prime Minister began to doubt his ability to deal with what appeared to be the chronic problems within the Ministry.

15

Pushing Back

Following the publication of the White Paper on 25 June 1981, the long-term future for the surface fleet seemed very different from that envisaged only a few months before. The immediate outcomes of the Review were serious but not catastrophic. It was in the long-term programme, stretching out into the 1990s and 2000s, that Nott's decisions would have their real effect. In September 1981 this was spelt out in clear terms within the Navy Department. In the late 1990s, the surface fleet would consist of two carriers, ten Type 42 destroyers and ten Type 22 frigates with the balance made up of Type 23s, supported by an indeterminate number of combined tanker/replenishment ship auxiliaries (the 'AOR'). However, in the early 2000s, all but the Type 23s would be withdrawn from service without replacement resulting in a frigate-only force. In 'the early years of the 21st century ... the AOR and the Type 23 (with any derivatives of greater or lesser capability) will, on present plans, be the only surface ships, apart from MCMVs, remaining in the fleet.'[1] Although there was theoretically all to play for in the future and such replacements might be funded by a future government, much stronger arguments would have to be made to place them in a programme that would initially be designed without the need to provide space for them. The previous chapter has shown how, in the last busy days before the White Paper was published, some of Nott's reductions on the surface fleet were reversed largely through pressure (or the fear of pressure) from the United States. This chapter will set out how the Navy adapted to change in many of those areas affected by the outcome of the review. It starts with the continuing shift in destroyer and frigate numbers and readiness in the months after the publishing of the White Paper.

Destroyer and Frigate Numbers

Although the White Paper had stated that the number of destroyers and frigates would remain at about fifty until 1985–6, by the end of June, the assumption within the Ministry was now that the total number of destroyers and frigates would remain at fifty 'in the early 1990s', yet another addition to capability that had not been set out in the information given to the OD committee, Cabinet and the Treasury.[2] At this stage it was expected that all Type 42s and Type 21s would remain in service past 1992, there would be a class of eight Type 22s and that the first Type 23 would enter service in 1988, followed by others thereafter. All the Ikara *Leander* and *Rothesay* class frigates would be disposed of by the mid-1980s, with eight of the former entering the Standby Squadron for a time, and the remaining *Leander*s in the late 1980s onwards, but with some of these vessels also moving to the Standby Squadron in the mid-1980s.[3]

Ships in the Standby Squadron, which was based at Chatham dockyard, would be at 30 days' notice for operational service, although the readiness period could be reduced, albeit at greater expense. The Squadron had been established in 1979 as a way to keep destroyer and frigate numbers nominally at the then-agreed level of sixty-five, even when there had been insufficient crews to do this and keep the ships in active service. Each ship in the Standby Squadron would be subject to routine maintenance and upkeep, occasional periods of docking to inspect and clean the hull, and low-level trials of any repaired or replaced equipment. The ships in the Standby Squadron would have a crewing level of around one eighth that of active ships, effectively a form of 'nucleus crew' system. In early 1981 it had been estimated that ten ships in the Squadron could be supported and maintained with a total of 12 officers, 117 senior rates and 227 junior rates. 60 per cent of the cost of maintaining the Squadron was for these personnel.[4] The Standby Squadron in June 1981 consisted of ten vessels: one elderly Type 41 class frigate, one equally aged Type 61 class frigate, five 'Tribal' class frigates, two *Rothesay* class frigates, and the newer *Leander* class frigate HMS *Juno*, which was in a temporary purgatory prior to a limited refit as a navigation training ship. Aside from *Juno*, they were all nearing the end of their Royal Navy careers.[5] Based on the plans as at the end of June 1981 it could be expected that after these vessels were disposed of, their place would be immediately taken by the remaining *Rothesay*s and the Ikara *Leander*s, followed by newer *Leander*s after this. The Standby Squadron would be in full use, with probably eight to ten ships, throughout the 1980s. However, this did not happen. By January 1982, the Standby Squadron had been emptied and effectively disbanded.[6] In addition, the total destroyer and frigate force remained above fifty. Even more curiously, a number of ships that had been placed on the disposal list in September 1981, such as the Ikara *Leander* ships, *Naiad* and *Dido* and the 'County' class ships *London*, *Glamorgan* and *Norfolk*, were not placed in the Standby Squadron, which one would have assumed would have been the obvious place for them.[7] The answer seems to lie in additional, and seemingly effective, pressure by the US government on the Ministry of Defence.

The US government had two major concerns about the impact of the Defence Review: one was the loss of one of the new *Invincible* class ships, which – as will be seen below – the US Navy rated very highly, and the other was the number of active and available destroyers and frigates in the fleet.[8] Nott had hoped to clear up this problem in discussions with Caspar Weinberger on his visit to the United Kingdom in August, where the Secretary of State had taken pains to explain the level of readiness of ships in the Standby Squadron.[9] However, as explained in the previous chapter, back in June Nott had also agreed to joint meetings between US and British officials and service personnel to discuss the implications of the Defence Review. As these meetings were dominated by naval issues, either relating to Trident or to US concerns about the carriers, destroyers and frigates, the meetings were left to the Navy Department within the Ministry of Defence. By late August, it was becoming clear that this lack of attention had been a mistake. The US Navy was passing to the Ministry of Defence large quantities of its own analysis on force mixes 'which do not appear to have been examined by the UK', whilst the Navy Department had agreed to investigate increasing the readiness of ships in the Standby Squadron, which would of course cost more and require additional personnel. The Navy Department also agreed to 'examine the possibilities of better cooperation [with the United States] over amphibious lift in the context of the Northern Flank'.[10] This might have been referring to the Royal Marines making use of US amphibious vessels but it could also have been an early expression of US lobbying in favour of retaining the two assault ships; the language in the minute is somewhat opaque. There was also much discussion of Trident issues, but it was clear that the US representatives were tightly tying concessions in these naval areas to the Trident programme. Dov Zakheim, a US Department of Defense official, stated that he

> was sensitive to the need not to be seen to be dictating to a foreign government how to spend its cash; nevertheless he made it clear that the US Government would have difficulty in making special concessions [over Trident] to the UK unless there was some hope or assurance that the areas of US concern could draw some benefit. He added that Congress (which had to approve any special concessions to Britain) and the American media were continuing to be very critical of the weakening of the RN surface fleet and he for his part looked to the UK for some help in reassuring them that the British were doing all they could to maximise their naval effort. Evidence of the UK effort to keep to the 50 ship formula, increase the readiness of surface ships in the Standby Squadron and to maintain a significant defence presence in the Indian Ocean would be a great help.[11]

As will be seen later in this chapter, the US administration would later link the retention of the two assault ships to a continued British presence in the western Indian Ocean. Nott was extremely unhappy with what appeared to be effective lobbying by the US to increase the size of the (nearly) active fleet: 'There can be no enhancement in our surface capability – it may have to be reduced further.'[12] He was more happy about US proposals to buy surplus British RFAs: the later 'Tide' class tankers and the 'Ness' class replenishment ships were being considered for sale, and the latter would eventually be sold to the United States, serving in the US Military Sealift Command for another quarter of a century.[13] David Omand recommended that a close eye was kept on the Navy Department to make sure that they did not 'exaggerate their ability to deliver on force levels'.[14] Nott was concerned about the attitude of the Navy's leadership: 'It is clear that at the top of the RN they have not yet accepted the main thrust of the White Paper.' Leach was still lobbying hard for *Invincible* to remain in the fleet, arguing that she could be, if necessary, placed in the Standby Squadron.[15] Cooper was also suspicious of the US/UK working party, arguing that 'there is increasing evidence to suggest that American officials see them as a convenient method of obtaining a close insight into the UK defence programme and a means of influencing the future shape of that programme in ways which do not necessarily accord with our own priorities. There is an obvious temptation to some of our own people to encourage American officials to support parts of the British programme which appear to be under threat.'[16] Cooper recommended that combining discussions over Trident with more general discussions on maritime issues had been a mistake, and that the two should be split apart into two separate meetings.[17]

The signs from the United States about unhappiness with the Review outcomes were becoming clearer, despite Weinberger's determination to remain emollient with Nott each time he met him face to face. This was also linked to a change in US perceptions about a future war with the Soviet Union. It was now perceived that nuclear strikes by both sides would be unthinkable and as a result any fighting would be likely to be conventional. It was in the interests of NATO to prolong any such conventional conflict so that reinforcements could reach Europe from North America, so in a complete contrast to the preceding Carter administration, the long-war scenario was now considered to be the most likely, and the convoying of troops and equipment across the Atlantic now played a crucial part in planning for any future war. Barrier operations were not considered to be sufficiently effective, whilst direct protection of convoys with SSNs and surface ships with towed-array was shifting towards the centre of US maritime strategy.[18] It soon became clear that the US administration had a very particular role in mind for the Royal Navy in this new strategy: as the Alliance's anti-submarine specialists the British would provide two anti-submarine hunting groups. One would protect US carrier battle groups as they advanced into the Norwegian Sea, and the other would operate in the Western Approaches and down the Azores to protect reinforcement convoys from North America. When asked what British naval vessels they most valued, John Lehman, the new Secretary of the Navy and Admiral Train, SACLANT, argued that anti-submarine frigates with helicopters, the new *Invincible* class and the Nimrod were the most prized. By contrast the Royal Navy's SSN fleet was regarded as the least important as Lehman and Train believed that the US Navy already had sufficient numbers of such boats.[19] In other words, its platform priorities were almost the opposite of those that had emerged from the Defence Review process. Nott's review had looked tailored to fit Carter administration assumptions. It now looked utterly out of step with the new Reagan administration which in so many other ways was running on the same intellectual lines as Margaret Thatcher's government. The Secretary of State was now not only financially exposed as ever more naval items were added back into the defence budget, but ideologically and politically vulnerable.

The US Department of Defense was still making clear linkages between Trident concessions and in October 1981 even went as far as suggesting, at the US/UK liaison meetings over Trident and the Defence Review, that these concessions be matched in value by augmentations in maritime capability. As these concessions might be up to $600 million in value, translated into sterling they were very close to the estimated additions to the Navy Department's budget, and in many respects were counteracting part of the impact of transferring Trident to the Navy's budget in the first place.[20] A form of undeclared offset for Trident was therefore being suggested by the United States government. At the same meeting that this was put forward by US officials, the US shifted from wanting ships in the Standby Squadron but with a shorter period of readiness, to adding more active units into the surface fleet instead. The British delegation, which was led by civil servants and starred officers who were both from or attached to the Naval Staff, agreed to provide the US with 'detailed costs of adding ships to [the] active fleet by ship/year.'[21]

Nott and Cooper's concerns resulted in the ending of the meetings between Zakheim and the Naval Staff, but although the British side suggested successor discussions on naval force levels led by a senior civil servant from the centre, Richard Hastie-Smith, the US Department of Defense lost interest and no further meetings on this subject occurred.[22] The US side had in some measure achieved what they had set out to do: increase the number of destroyers and frigates in the Royal Navy available to NATO compared to the position in June 1981. By January 1982 the Standby Squadron had emptied, and the number of destroyers and frigates in the fleet still totalled fifty-two. Five ships were in refit with the other forty-seven active.[23] In October 1981 it had been envisaged that the Standby Squadron would remain empty until 1984 when eight *Leander* class frigates would be placed in it.[24] However, plans were developed in January 1982 for a further two or three vessels being kept on the active list in future years instead of in the Standby Squadron for an extra £22 million a year, in place of earlier plans to lift the readiness level of all the Standby Squadron ships up a notch. These plans were communicated to the US in February with the acquiescence of Hastie-Smith.[25] The First Sea Lord, in his message to the Navy on 23 March 1982, stated that the destroyer and frigate force level would be 'fifty of which up to eight will be in the Standby Squadron'.[26] The important words here being '*up to*' as at that time none were in the Squadron at all and no ships would be until 1984. Rather than a rapid shift of ships into the Standby Squadron after the Review outcomes, what was now being envisaged was a standby squadron of around five ships between 1984 and 1990.[27]

Trident D5 and Assault Ships

When negotiating the size of the British destroyer and frigate force upwards in the summer and early autumn of 1981, US officials had clearly attempted to link the procurement of Trident with additional British naval capabilities. Their leverage was greater than would otherwise have been the case, because one of the Reagan administration's first defence decisions had thrown into doubt the United Kingdom's purchase of the Trident C4 system. The new administration released additional funds to support the earlier adoption into service of the next generation Trident D5 ballistic missile system, the successor to the C4. The D5 was now planned to enter service in the late 1980s and the C4 would be withdrawn in the mid-1990s, much earlier than had been planned. This now left the British government in a quandary. If it proceeded with the C4, the submarines would only have entered service when they would have been withdrawn by the US Navy. This would result in increasing costs and difficulties in maintaining the C4 boats as the US support infrastructure would be otherwise being dismantled. Alternatively, the D5 could be procured instead of the C4: this would ensure that obsolescence would held off for longer, and the Royal Navy would receive a much more capable weapon. The D5 would have a range of 6,000 miles compared to the 4,500 miles of the C4, meaning that a missile could be launched close to the coast of the United Kingdom and reach anywhere in the Soviet Union. Each missile could carry up to fourteen MIRVs, which would meet the all-important Moscow Criterion with only eight missiles and have a much better chance of destroying the Soviet command and control system in Moscow.[28] The procurement of a Polaris replacement was now wide open again. By ensuring that the Zakheim/ Naval Staff committee – which had combined Trident questions with a range of other maritime subjects – no longer met, Nott and Cooper were clearing the ground for formal negotiations and decisions over whether to accept D5 or continue with C4.

The MISC 7 Cabinet Committee met in November 1981 with the recommendation that the D5 system be procured. Each submarine would have sixteen tubes, but only ten would normally house ballistic missiles when on patrol. The submarine would have the new PWR 2 Pressurised Water Reactor and a missile compartment based on the US *Ohio* class submarines.[29] Other options included twelve D5 vertical tubes or continuing with the C4 procurement. Refitting the *Resolution* class to take C4 had been quickly ruled out on the grounds of cost and the age of the hulls. When the committee came to discuss the options, some ministers raised concerns on the grounds of cost, and to the surprise of officials, the committee could not come to a decision and decided to revisit the issue in the new year. It is not known who objected within the committee, but externally both Francis Pym, now Leader of the House of Commons, and Lord Carrington, the Foreign Secretary, raised similar cost-based concerns. The C4 was a system that was nearing the end of its development, many of its costs were known or could be predicted with a margin of error. In contrast, the D5 had only just started development and its eventual cost was unknown: the potential for escalation outside of the control of the British government was great.[30] The committee met again in January, with the same options laid out, but with the possibility of procuring C4 on a boat large enough to be modified up to D5 standard at a later date. In the event, the committee agreed to D5 but only on the proviso that the final decision would be made by Cabinet, that negotiations should start with the US government before the Cabinet decision and that the issue of procuring three instead of four boats be revisited yet again.[31]

British negotiators therefore returned to the United States in February 1982 to discuss the purchase of the D5 system. The Reagan administration again took a transactional approach to these talks, leveraging as much as possible in terms of conventional defence commitments from the British in return for a 'cut price' deal on the D5. The British for their part were optimistic: it was well known that the Reagan administration was very happy to see the United Kingdom remain a nuclear power, and it was thought possible that a deal 'more advantageous' than the Polaris Sales Agreement might be negotiated. The US side, when talks started, was happy to allow British companies to compete for D5 sub-contracts, and to waive or reduce some potential surcharges and overheads. However, a revised Research and Development levy proved more difficult. This had been partly waived in the C4 negotiations in return for a commitment by the British to pay for the local air defence of US airbases in the UK (with Rapier missile systems) and an agreement that 5 per cent of the R&D costs would be paid. However, the additional costs of the D5 meant that, according to the US negotiators, a total of $222 million in pro-rata R&D costs still needed to be paid. This was well above the 5 per cent level agreed in 1980 and was unacceptably large for the British. The US negotiators then revealed their real intent: the $222 million could be waived and the 5 per cent levy reinstated, if the British agreed to a number of conventional defence commitments. The first two the Americans raised were the retention of HMS *Invincible* in Royal Navy service and for the British to delay their military withdrawal from Belize and remain there after independence. The US was afraid that a British retreat from Belize in 1981 could tilt the balance in Central America against their allies and in favour of Cuba and leftist regimes and make greater US intervention in the region more likely.[32] In order to appease the US over Belize, it was also agreed that the British would investigate the creation of an enhanced training programme for Belize forces following their withdrawal and that the British West Indies Guardship would remain and provide naval back up in Belize if required for a number of years after independence.[33]

Nott refused to back down over *Invincible*, arguing that the ship had already been promised to the Australians, but what happened next has been disputed. Margaret Thatcher, in her autobiography published in 1993, stated that because of the pressure linked to Trident from the United States, Nott offered to retain the two assault ships instead.[34] Keeping these vessels, which were well suited to reinforcing the Norwegian military on the northern flank, fitted neatly with the US Navy's new more aggressive forward strategy in the High North, so the concession had a logic to it. However, later accounts based on Leach's own account and interviews have stated that Nott had been persuaded to keep the ships following a demonstration of their capabilities in Portsmouth.[35] This second interpretation is ostensibly backed up by the official record, with Nott annotating a document from the First Sea Lord setting out the costs of retaining the two ships, stating 'We just have to have some "pluses" – I am worried about the ending of the capability, and did not understand the remarkable versatility of these ships when I was persuaded to include in the "Bermudagram" the ending of our amphibious capability.'[36] Nott argued that for everything short of war, they were valuable vessels. However, in 1984, when Nott had left politics and had decided in a series of tape-recorded discussions with the historian David Kynaston to discuss his time as Defence Secretary, he only stated that the amphibious assault ships were offered to the US as a sop given that he did not want to renege on his offer of *Invincible* to the Australians. As set out in the transcriptions of these interviews, Nott had told the US negotiators that 'the Australians have got it [*Invincible*] but I said we could actually put into the negotiations *Fearless* and *Intrepid* [the two amphibious assault ships]'. Initially the US delegates were not keen, but during their second set of discussions they accepted the offer.[37] An academic interview with former US official Richard Perle in 1991 supports this statement. Perle noted that the two ships had been retained as a result of an 'explicit verbal agreement' that included 'some frigates' as well.[38] This is a very different version to that given in both Leach's autobiography and Lewin's biography, where it was stated that Nott was extremely pleased with a presentation by the Royal Marines of *Fearless*'s capabilities when the Secretary of State was invited to visit the ship.[39] Making use of Prime Minister's Office papers, Kristin Stoddart has argued that the assault ship concession was 'largely cosmetic', as the decision to retain these vessels had already been made, and this was the justification given by Nott to Thatcher when the negotiations were finalised in February 1982.[40] Given that Nott began investigating the possibility of keeping the assault ships in December 1981 this could be, on the surface, a plausible answer. However, the Secretary of State suddenly deciding to change his mind, solely based on a demonstration – however impressive – by the Royal Marines, is difficult for this author to take seriously.

First, agreeing to keep these two vessels was going to be expensive. It was initially estimated to cost £120 million over ten years, only a little less than the expected cost of developing the new heavyweight torpedo (£150 million).[41] Nott was under considerable pressure from the Treasury to remain within the costings he had put to OD and Cabinet in June, and yet here was the Secretary of State adding in another significant expense, on top of more active destroyers and frigates, and (as will be seen later in the chapter) additional hydrographic vessels, logistical landing ships and new heavyweight torpedoes. In October Nott had been talking tough about not acceding to US wishes over active destroyer and frigate numbers (the enhancement of which was going to cost in the low tens of millions of pounds), why was he suddenly caving in over something five times the price just to have 'some pluses'? That Nott stated that he did know about the capabilities of the assault ships when he agreed to the 'Bermudagram', suggests either a worrying disengagement from major decisions (and that he truly was being driven along by Cooper and Omand with little understanding of what he was doing), or instead a certain disingenuousness over a decision made for different reasons.

Second, Nott had clearly set out in a government White Paper that the assault ships would go. Going back on this announcement to Parliament, in both verbal and written forms, was a considerable embarrassment and a severe dent to the Secretary of State's credibility. It also seems extremely unlikely that, in this context, Nott would have allowed himself to go to a presentation of the assault ships' capabilities unless he had either already made his decision to keep the ships, or was at least considering to do so. Which politician with any political nous whatsoever would permit themselves to be shown how well something works if he or she had already decided to get rid of it in front of Parliament, the press and his or her backbench colleagues? There must have been considerable pressure on Nott to take such an excruciating U-turn.

Third, Nott had known since at least June 1981 that the US administration was sorely disappointed about the sale of *Invincible*, so investigating the possibility of providing an alternative that would placate the Department of Defense would have been entirely natural. An initial request to look at the costs of retaining the assault ships was made in December 1981, only weeks after it had been confirmed that negotiations would have to be reopened across the Atlantic for purchasing D5 instead of C4. As in June 1981 when Omand furnished Nott with back-pocket concessions over destroyers and frigates for his discussions with Weinberger, it would only have been prudent to do something similar over talks regarding D5.

This conclusion can only be circumstantial as the official record is opaque, although the taped recorded conversation with Kynaston in 1984 in Nott's own private papers gives a strong indication: it does not make any mention of a 'demonstration of capabilities' as a reason to keep the ships.[42] Nott declaring to the Prime Minister that the decision over the two ships was 'largely cosmetic' was another piece of disingenuous behaviour by a Secretary of State whose credibility was shrinking each time he asked Cabinet for additional funds for Defence. What is certain is that the United States took a coolly transactional approach to the Trident negotiations, and gained considerable concessions from John Nott between June 1981 and February 1982: the destroyer and frigate force was increased from forty to fifty, and the size of the Standby Squadron was shrunk over time and the number of active vessels within this fifty increased. It is almost certain that the assault-ship concession was wrung out from Nott in the same way. That the formal announcement to Weinberger of the two ships' retention was, at the express request of the Department of Defense, couched in terminology and terms that would be understood by Republican Congressmen and Senators, demonstrates the importance of this concession in placating domestic Congressional opinion.[43] In return, the Royal Navy's operation of the United Kingdom's strategic nuclear deterrent had been guaranteed for another generation, in new submarines operating the most up to date version of the Trident ballistic missile. The United States wanted the UK to have the Trident nuclear deterrent, but it also wanted it to have a significant surface fleet as well.

Ocean Venture, Operation 'Activate' and HMS *Invincible*

As John Nott was presenting the outcome of the Defence Review in Parliament on 25 June, the opening stages of a huge multi-theatre exercise were taking place in the Caribbean and South Atlantic. Exercise Ocean Venture, which wrapped together a series of different NATO and non-NATO exercises across numerous different theatres, would not only showcase a new and more aggressive approach to undertaking exercises but also pointed ahead to how the US Navy, with the strong support of the new Republican administration, would operate in times of high tension and war. The Royal Navy would build for itself an important role within this new approach, which in turn would help lever further concessions from Nott, and to an extent, provide long-term justification for a number of Navy roles through the rest of the 1980s.

In December 1979, in the aftermath of the Soviet invasion of Afghanistan and collapse of détente, Lewin, attending a meeting of the Military Committee of NATO, had proposed a 'wide ranging maritime exercise to demonstrate NATO will' in the Atlantic.[44] SACLANT agreed with this proposal and planning work began on an exercise, tentatively dubbed LARGEX 81, to take place in the Atlantic during the autumn of 1981. The next month SACLANT decided to make this exercise even more ambitious by rolling it up with a number of NATO exercises across the Mediterranean, Baltic and Eastern Atlantic (such as Ocean Safari 81 which was already at the planning stage and would cover the Western Approaches and Azores) with a series of non-NATO exercises in the South Atlantic and Caribbean. This new combined exercise was given the name Ocean Venture.[45] The US Navy specifically wanted to use Ocean Venture to re-orientate its force structures and planning to counter the Soviet naval threat in the North Atlantic: by giving the US 6th Fleet, which usually operated in the Mediterranean, more experience in supporting the US 2nd Fleet in the North Atlantic, and by demonstrating that the NATO strike fleet in the Atlantic was now willing to advance deep into the Norwegian Sea and threaten the Soviet Union itself through its northern flank.[46] The advance of the main carrier strike force deep into the Norwegian Sea was in support of Exercise Magic Sword North an AFNORTH land/air exercise, and involved a series of ruses using false signals to suggest that the strike force would be heading south-east, when in fact it was proceeding north-east closer to the Soviet High North under total radio and emissions silence.[47]

This was the first NATO exercise to include a significant portion of its operations in the north Norwegian Sea since Exercise Strong Express in 1972 and seems to have been the first to use such ambitious deception techniques. The US Navy, now under the enthusiastic oversight of the new Secretary of the Navy, John Lehman, was not just using these exercises for training purposes but as a direct way to demonstrate its capabilities to the Soviet Union, and include an element of surprise to wrong-foot the Soviet Northern Fleet. Admiral John Fieldhouse, the new Commander-in-Chief Fleet, and Vice Admiral John Cox, the Flag Officer 3rd Flotilla, were heavily involved in the planning of the exercises, and given Fieldhouse's keenness for the use of ruse and deception on exercises inherited from his days as a submarine commander, the planning for Magic Sword North accorded well with his preferences and approach to operations.[48] The different elements of Ocean Venture are summarised in the table below:

Table 11: Phase of Exercise Ocean Venture and linkage with Ocean Safari[49]

Phase	Dates	Scenario	Participating States
Phase 1	15/6–25/9/81	SLOC protection and anti-insurgency operations in South Atlantic and Southern Caribbean	US, Brazil, Argentina, Columbia
Phase 2	3–20/8/81	Caribbean operations	US, UK (Belize guardship), France, Netherlands
Phase 3	1/8–7/9/81	US east coast operations	US, Standing Naval Force Atlantic
Phase 4a	20/8–1/9/81	Transit of *Eisenhower* carrier battle group from US to GIUK gap	US, UK (*Invincible*, *Bristol*, 2 SSN, 5 SSK, 6 DD/FF, RFAs, maritime air), Canada, West Germany, Netherlands, Portugal, Standing Naval Force Atlantic
Phase 4b	23/8–1/9/81	Transit of *Forrestal* carrier battle group from Mediterranean to GIUK gap	
Phase 5: Magic Sword North	2–4/9/81	Both carrier battle groups in Norwegian Sea supporting AFNORTH	US, UK (*Bristol*, RFAs), Canada, Norway, Standing Naval Force Atlantic
Phase 6: Magic Sword South	7–8/9/81	Carrier air support to Commander BALTAP and AFCENT from North Sea	US, Denmark, West Germany, Netherlands, Norway
Ocean Safari 81	8–18/9/81	SLOC protection operations: Western Approaches, Bay of Biscay and Portugal	US, UK (*Invincible*, *Bristol*, 8 DD/FF, 2 SSN, 2 SSK, RFAs, MCMV, maritime air)
Phase 7	1–19/9/81	Large escorted amphibious force transits from US to Mediterranean	US, France, Spain
Phase 8	29/9–13/10/81	Projection of US/NATO forces into Baltic to conduct freedom of navigation operations	US, West Germany, Netherlands, Denmark

Ocean Venture was a huge meta-exercise, which effectively incorporated *two* major Eastern Atlantic exercises one immediately after another: Ocean

Venture Phases 4 to 6 which harked back to the more aggressive northern flank exercises of the late 1960s, and Ocean Safari 81, which was the latest in a number of Western Approaches to Azores exercises. On to these were grafted South Atlantic, Caribbean, Baltic and Mediterranean elements, that meant that almost the whole Atlantic was included, alongside its tributary seas in northern and southern Europe. Undertaken at a scale close to the Soviet Okean 70 and Okean 75 exercises, this was a clear demonstration to the USSR of the power and reach of NATO and its allies. In Ocean Venture Phase 4, Royal Navy vessels were involved in two ways. *Bristol* and *Invincible* accompanied the US carrier striking fleet from the east coast of the United States. Vice Admiral Fox in his NATO role as Commander Anti-Submarine Group Two used *Bristol* as his flagship, the large destroyer finally finding an operational role as a command ship; her communications facilities and considerable space making her a natural choice.[50] HMS *Invincible*, having recently completed Part IV trials, was on show as a specialist anti-submarine carrier, equipped with the new Mark 5 anti-submarine Sea King helicopter fitted with the new Sea Searcher radar, LAPAD processing equipment and miniaturised sonobuoys that until this point could only have been used by much larger maritime patrol aircraft.[51]

Also included in the exercise were the new Type 42 destroyer *Coventry*, the old 'County' class destroyer *London* (in her last major exercise before decommissioning) and the frigates *Broadsword*, *Arrow*, *Arethusa*, *Apollo* and *Plymouth*.[52] *Broadsword*, another new ship which had recently completed her trials (some of her sensors and weapon systems were not yet cleared as operational) and the Ikara *Leander Arethusa* were placed together on barrier patrol duties in the GIUK gap, joining Admiral Fox's anti-submarine group later on in the exercise. This part of Ocean Venture focussed on tracking both nuclear submarines and conventional submarines. Although the United States had stopped building conventional boats in the 1960s, the Soviets had continued to build a small number of 'Tango' class conventional boats in the 1970s, and these were succeeded by the capable 'Kilo' class from 1980.[53] Anti-submarine conditions were poor in GIUK gap: the surface layer was shallow and weak, with the thermocline sometimes reaching the surface. The new Mark 5 Sea Kings did have success in detecting and keeping track of the Soviet 'Papa' class cruise missile submarine, *K-162*.[54] This one-of-a-kind boat was built from a strong but light titanium alloy, was extremely fast (albeit noisy), armed with sub-surface launched anti-ship missiles and had been tracking the carrier battle group.[55] By contrast, the frigates on the GIUK patrol line had difficulty locating the 'Orange' submarines sent against them in the exercise; *Arethusa* in particular, had trouble making any effective use of her variable-depth sonar.[56] *London*, *Coventry*, *Apollo* and *Plymouth* played the role of the main 'Orange' surface action group ('SAG') opposing the NATO task forces. Acting as a force of Soviet destroyers led by a cruiser, they managed to detect and mark both the *Eisenhower* carrier battle group coming from the Western Atlantic, and the *Forrestal* carrier battle group arriving from the south. They were counter-marked by HMS *Arrow* which was part of the Standing Naval Force Atlantic. By the end of Phase 4B of the exercise, the 'Orange' SAG had picked up a real Soviet warship of its own, as a Krivak class frigate tagged behind them before the SAG dispersed and departed for home.[57]

Following the GIUK transit, the combined US carrier battle group headed north to undertake Phases 5 and 6 of Ocean Venture. *Bristol*, *Invincible* and their RFAs accompanied the US and other NATO ships, but the rest of the Royal Navy forces departed for home. This part of the exercise involved the most daring and innovative elements of Ocean Venture: the transit north into the Norwegian Sea and up to North Cape with the main force operating under emission silence, whilst decoy ships would be used to suggest that the force was moving southward. This proved to be a considerable success, with the Soviets only noticing at the last moment that over eighty NATO warships and auxiliaries were within striking range of the USSR. A mixed flight of aircraft from the two supercarriers surprised a group of Soviet 'Bear' bombers undertaking refuelling just outside the 12-mile limit of the USSR's territorial waters.[58] This exercise was demonstrating in no uncertain terms that the days of holding NATO exercises way back from Soviet waters were over.

Two months prior to the High North phases of Ocean Venture, a much smaller operation by a British destroyer had involved four weeks of deployments within the Barents Sea, almost as a pathfinder for Ocean Venture, named Operation 'Activate'.[59] HMS *Glasgow*, accompanied by RFA *Olwen*, observed Soviet naval vessels on exercise and on trials. *Glasgow* was newly fitted with the UAA-1 passive intercept system and the operation no doubt provided many opportunities to build up a 'library' of Soviet emissions. Soviet naval vessels undertook close marking of *Glasgow* at certain times, and on 27 May the cruiser *Admiral Isakov* even gave *Glasgow* a glancing blow in the bows as a rather robust form of 'warning'. This would be the first in a number of Barents Sea information-gathering operations that would be undertaken at regular intervals by Royal Navy ships until the end of the Cold War. By the mid-1980s Outboard-equipped Type 22 frigates would prove the ideal vessels for such operations.[60]

A number of the ships involved in Ocean Venture Phases 4, 5 and 6, then proceeded to take part in Ocean Safari. This included *Invincible*, *Bristol* and *Broadsword*, as well as seven fresh Royal Navy frigates and destroyers, two nuclear submarines and two conventional boats alongside RFAs, a considerable mine countermeasures force and land-based maritime aircraft.

This was a more conventional exercise focussing on the protection of shipping either through close escort or through the 'defended lane' concept whereby sea areas would be protected rather than convoyed shipping. At the south of the exercise area a French carrier battle group would support operations against 'Orange' forces but under national rather than NATO control.[61] Royal Navy forces were not involved in the Baltic phase of Ocean Venture so with the completion of Ocean Safari, the British involvement in this huge, combined set of exercises was complete.

From the perspective of the United States, the most impressive British element of the whole set of exercises had been HMS *Invincible*.[62] If the US was to have a credible force for penetrating into the High North so close to the bases of the Soviet Northern Fleet and its many submarines, it had to have an effective anti-submarine capability, and since the withdrawal of the last *Essex* class anti-submarine support carriers in the 1970s, the US Navy lacked such vessels. As was explained by John Lehman to the British junior defence minister Peter Blaker on his visit to the United States in October 1981, the new British carriers were planned to be the centrepiece of the two anti-submarine groups. If one of the three new carriers were sold, then having two operational anti-submarine groups would be impossible, given time required for refit and maintenance for one or other of the remaining carriers.[63] However, there was something particularly important about *Invincible* and her sisters that had been ignored during the Defence Review and was little appreciated by outsiders during their operational lives. A hint is given in her captain's comments after Ocean Venture that during the exercise no submarine had been successful in launching an attack on 'this high value unit which does not behave like one'.[64] This mysterious statement is clarified in the report of the captain of her sister ship, *Illustrious*, a few years later. During exercises in 1983, 'Orange' submarines had considerable difficulty locating the new carriers. Even some of the US Navy's most advanced acoustic arrays had been unable to detect the ship at 17 miles range when she was steaming at 18 knots.[65] Through excellent hull design, which meant that there was very little cavitation (bubbles created from the hull or propellers of a ship which would otherwise increase the ease with which it can be detected), combined with extremely effective noise reduction on the ship, including the placing of machinery and other noisy equipment on rubberised pallets, the *Invincible* class came close to disappearing from the screens of submarines' sonars. Given Ocean Venture's emphasis on feints, decoys and emissions silence, it is not surprising how valuable such a ship seemed to the United States Navy. As has been little appreciated by those outside naval circles, effective anti-submarine warfare by surface ships requires considerable investment in such 'under the bonnet' capabilities that are invisible to casual observers.

Type 23 Frigates, Replenishment Ships and Helicopters

The original Type 23 had been conceived as a large anti-submarine frigate of around 6,000 to 8,000 tons, but as was seen in Chapter 11, by late 1979 this rather optimistic concept had been rejected. Given plans for production runs of large and expensive Type 44s and SSNs through the late 1980s and 1990s, only a tiny number of these mammoth Type 23s would have been constructed and the total escort fleet numbers would have plummeted to well below forty by the mid-1990s. As a result, a new Type 23 design began to be developed as a means to get as many towed-array sonars to sea as possible. In July 1980, a ship 50 per cent the price of a Type 22 was initially envisaged, and was described three months later, in its lowest capability form, as a 'passive [sonar] OPV'.[66] It was now becoming clear from the trials on *Lowestoft* that the towed-array passive sonar would prove revolutionary in effective anti-submarine warfare by surface ships in the 1980s and 1990s. The earliest versions of this new Type 23 design therefore included the Type 2038 towed-array (the planned successor to the Type 2031 on *Lowestoft* and the *Leander* class towed-array modernisations), helicopter support facilities but no hangar, a light gun (with a 76mm OTO Melara medium gun as an alternative), a basic active sonar and a suite of electronic warfare and communications capabilities. Even at this early stage, diesel-electric propulsion with gas turbines for boost was considered the quietest and most effective propulsion option. This baseline ship was expected to cost approximately £60 million in September 1980 prices, almost half the cost of the Batch 2 Type 22 frigate (excluding her Outboard systems). Adding one Sea Wolf six-cell launcher would increase total costs by around 20 per cent, adding a helicopter hangar another £2 million and adding anti-ship missiles a further £4 million.[67]

Given that the effective prosecution of a towed-array contact required either a large helicopter or a maritime patrol aircraft to provide final localisation and then attack with torpedoes, such a vessel would have been insufficient as an anti-submarine platform acting alone. A small helicopter such as the Lynx, lacking either sonobuoys or dipping sonars, would not be able to undertake that role. Within the range of Nimrod air bases, these aircraft could conceivably act in this role, but Nimrod numbers were finite and could be quickly overstretched in intensive anti-submarine operations across the Eastern Atlantic area. Outside of Nimrod range, the new Type 23 would be dependent on the helicopters of the new carriers, which were few in number – and after the Defence Review, even fewer – or helicopters operated by other vessels such as Royal Fleet Auxiliaries. As a result, the Type 23 concept became increasingly attached to a sophisticated replenishment ship which would have a hangar capable of operating up to four Sea King helicopters or their replacement. This replenishment ship would combine the roles of tanker and stores and ammunition vessel in one (known as an 'AOR': Auxiliary Oiler/Replenishment).[68] By adding the ability to operate and support a large number of anti-submarine helicopters, it was also the successor of the 'garage ship' considered in 1979 and 1980 and described in Chapter 11.[69] Doctrinally, a significant proportion of the AOR force, which in early 1981 was planned to number anything up to ten ships by the late 1990s,[70] would therefore become the core of an anti-submarine force, working with a number of Type 23s (operating at some distance from the AOR to enable the most effective operation of the towed-array). The Type 23, thus conceived, would be a utility escort optimised for anti-submarine detection and for supporting the prosecution of attacks, with limited capabilities in other areas. The Naval Staff's Fleet Requirements Committee had approved further development of the concept in March 1981, giving a ceiling of approximately a £72 million cost per hull, an increase above £60 million which would certainly allow for a number of additions to the design. The addition of some form of point defence was strongly recommended for Eastern Atlantic operations.[71]

In the last weeks of the Defence Review, the design gradually began to be augmented. John Nott ordered that the Type 23 be re-designed 'with an eye to sales overseas' and similar phrasing was used in the White Paper.[72] Given Nott's strong focus on Eastern Atlantic roles for the Royal Navy's ships, this proved extremely difficult to reconcile, and the gap between commercial requirements and those for a specialist anti-submarine ship proved just as difficult to bridge as it did with the defunct Type 24 described in Chapter 11.[73] Following a meeting with the Chairman of Vosper Thornycroft in July 1981 John Nott finally realised how divergent the requirements were and agreed that the Type 23 design effort should focus on the former, in effect leaving the shipbuilding industry to their own devices regarding export-friendly ship designs.[74] Vosper Thornycroft was probably well able to cope with this decision, having its own very successful export business, but most other warship builders were now going to be depending solely on orders for Royal Navy vessels in order to survive. Given the numbers of likely orders following the Review, and the number of ailing shipyards, this could not have been a positive prospect for British Shipbuilders, the overall parent company of most shipbuilders. As the Type 23 began to grow in size and capability, thoughts of an even simpler 'corvette' or support ship equipped with a surveillance towed-array, dubbed a 'towed-array tug', were – as was seen in the last chapter – entertained by Nott, but they never got far. The towed-array corvette would have been so small and simple that processing would have had to occur ashore, which would have resulted in additional costs for building processing stations and created additional problems of sustaining communications.[75] This was a particular concern when at least one un-named minister was apparently advocating the

Navy being restricted to shallow-water operations with corvettes only, and the RAF somehow adopting towed-array sonars by towing them from Nimrods to obviate the need for ocean-going ships at all![76] International co-operation with the Dutch was also considered. It was proposed that there would be a maximum commonality in requirements and components between the Type 23 and the planned Dutch 'M' class frigate. These discussions faltered over the Dutch preferences for lean crewing and the new Royal Navy focus on placing as much training as possible at sea, which would increase the number of personnel on the ships.[77]

Two other major changes in late 1981 served to expand the capabilities of the Type 23 further. Fitting Sea Wolf had always been one of the options for the design, despite the significant increase in costs. By November 1981 a lightweight version of Sea Wolf with four missiles per launcher and the lightweight VM40 tracker radar was considered the front runner.[78] Following plans by the US Navy to install 'vertical launch' missile silos in their warships in order to increase the number that could fire in short timescales, the Ship Department began to investigate the requirements for doing so with Sea Wolf, possibly for retrofitting during the ship's service.[79] From the perspective of the Royal Navy, an additional benefit was the removal of the need for crew members to load missiles manually into the launcher, exposing them to possible fallout from tactical nuclear weapons and slowing down the ability of the ship to deal with heavy attacks or attacks coming in closely packed waves. Aside from modifications to the missile itself with a booster to enable initial launch in a vertical position, the replacement of a trainable launcher, with its requirements for arcs of fire and manual re-loading, allowed missiles to be fired in a 360-degree direction without the need to manoeuvre either the launcher or the ship, and fire more missiles more rapidly. Interestingly, the ghost of the Battle of Jutland and of the loss of HMS *Hood* in 1941, when capital ships were lost due to major explosions of ammunition, still appeared to haunt the Navy's ship designers. There were qualms by constructors about giving up the relative protection of a below-waterline magazine by adopting an above-decks structure containing significant quantities of high explosive.[80] But a Rubicon had already been crossed with the fitting of Exocet missiles in above-decks cannisters in the early 1970s, and with the provision of armour to prevent splinter damage (and the use of fire-suppressing foam around each missile tube[81]) the change was accepted.

In addition, the decision not to provide a hangar was formally changed in November 1981.[82] This decision was backed up by earlier statistical computer analysis by an outside consultancy, which argued that when hunting submarines providing hangars on Type 23s for helicopters would be more efficient than merely using them as 'lily pads' requiring those helicopters to return to the AOR for re-storing and maintenance: helicopters would be able to reach contacts made with towed-array much quicker from a Type 23 on the edge of a convoy, than from the AOR at its centre.[83] That the work to justify this change had been done by an outside private sector consultancy no doubt helped counter any scepticism from ministers. However, this did add another source of vulnerability to the Type 23 as the Sea King replacement, the EH101, was still at the early stages of development: if the project, which was a UK-Italy joint venture, had failed before the first Type 23 was ordered, then the whole programme would be in danger. Similarly, the relevant central committee which would authorise the development of both the frigate and the helicopter, the Operational Requirements Committee, had made it clear that the helicopter would not be approved without the frigate. Both were therefore put in front of the committee together for approval.[84]

The procurement of the new helicopter had therefore become symbiotic with the frigate. Earlier analysis by the Chief Scientific Adviser had indicated that active dipping sonars in helicopters might not be needed for the localisation of already-detected submarines as Barra buoys and magnetic anomaly detectors would be sufficient.[85] The Johnston Report had argued that maritime patrol aircraft ('MPAs') could undertake anti-submarine roles in place of the medium anti-submarine helicopter, which might not be needed at all; this position had been supported by the Air Staff but opposed by the Naval Staff. Just as the White Paper was being published Johnston was given the task of producing a report on the 'future of anti-submarine warfare'.[86] The results of his analysis clearly changed his position on the shipborne helicopter, and by September 1981 he was stating that such helicopters were essential for the Type 23 to turn a contact into a kill.[87] The key point that shifted the argument was the availability of the MPA to 'firm up' contacts and prosecute attacks quickly enough after detection by towed-array.[88] There would just be insufficient Nimrods able to reach towed-array frigates quickly enough, and procuring sufficient numbers would have been prohibitively expensive. Additional external evidence was gradually amassed that MPAs were not sufficient to deal with the submarine threat by themselves. The US Sea War 85 study made it clear that without SOSUS, land-based aircraft would have considerable difficulties locating submarines. If SOSUS arrays feeding into Brawdy were destroyed on 'D Day' (the first day of full hostilities) then anti-submarine defence would have to be primarily undertaken by 'inner convoy defences' which would mean ship-based anti-submarine capabilities including helicopters.[89] An earlier Center for Naval Analyses study called SeaMix I had concluded that if Soviet submarines pre-deployed into the Atlantic before hostilities started, then the focus of anti-submarine warfare would be on the close protection of task groups and convoys rather than area operations, whilst surface ships and shipborne helicopter would account for the majority of the kills on the newest (and quietest) third-generation Soviet submarines.[90] Other factors also increased the utility of the frigate and helicopter combination: the Soviets were beginning to reinvest in new conventional submarines many of which would be operating in shallower waters around the United Kingdom. In these conditions sonobuoys were of less use but dipping sonars and active hull sonars had significant utility, thus strengthening the case for the EH 101 and the Type 23.[91]

By increments the Type 23 had been turned from a utility single-role convoy escort which would only be operationally effective working with other vessels, to a medium-sized frigate which was not too far from a Batch 1 Type 22 but with the addition of towed-array and a large helicopter. The Ministry's central committees finally approved the design as it then stood in May 1982, whilst the Falklands conflict was being fought.[92] The Navy had benefitted from the fact that the Type 23 had been an important part of the outcomes of the Defence Review, so there was a political imperative to get the ship approved and ordered quickly: this was not a ship that would remain in long-term conceptual or development limbo like the Type 43 or Type 44.[93] However, 'underneath the bonnet' the new frigate design still retained elements of its origins as a cheap utility vessel: most significantly its self-repair facilities (workshops and spares) were less comprehensive than on earlier frigates.[94] Despite this, by incremental changes the Naval Staff and the Ship Department had developed the Type 23 into a capable general-purpose ship able to operate in convoy and task group anti-submarine roles, as well as alone in global defence diplomacy and 'small war' operations. However, such flexibility did not come cheaply; whether such surreptitious 'spiral development' would mean that this now more expensive ship could be built in enough numbers to maintain the escort fleet at fifty through the 1980s and 1990s was another matter. Equally, the AOR with its combined tanker/replenishment capabilities, facilities for numerous anti-submarine helicopters, Sea Wolf air defence system and large operations room for commanding anti-submarine operations, was an extremely effective – and expensive – ship that, as will be seen in Chapter 19, accelerated the shift of Royal Fleet Auxiliaries closer towards being warships by another name. Would there be the funds to build the six needed to work with the projected twenty-four Type 23s that would be necessary to sustain the escort force at fifty in the mid-1990s?

Submarines and Torpedoes

The submarine service had emerged from the Review with much less damage to its future capabilities than most of the other arms of the Royal Navy. The long-term aim to produce a fleet of seventeen nuclear-powered attack submarines was an important confirmation of the importance of these vessels, both for Cold War operations such as the tracking of Soviet submarines, but also their Hot War capabilities as the Navy's main anti-ship and offensive anti-submarine capability. The submarine service was not left untouched however. Although the fourth *Trafalgar* class submarine was ordered the day after the Defence Review was published, there was no commitment to a seventh *Trafalgar* class submarine. Compared to the rest of the Navy however, these were minor setbacks, the nuclear building submarine programme, including expected ordering and acceptance dates had not been changed: seven *Trafalgar* class would be in service by 1990 with the first Trident submarine in service by 1991–2.[95] If Nott's numerous add-backs into the Navy's programme, which mainly benefitted the surface fleet, had not occurred then the Royal Navy would have been a primarily submarine and mine-warfare focussed force by the 2000s.

One significant capability reduction did occur after the Review which caused considerable concern within the Ministry about the reaction from NATO and the United States. This was the early withdrawal from service of the first British nuclear-powered submarine, HMS *Dreadnought*. Before the announcement of the closure of Chatham dockyard in the White Paper, it had been decided to refit *Dreadnought* at the nuclear submarine refit facility in that dockyard, and she had been towed there for this purpose. She had already been inactive since the summer of 1980, and an inspection of her material state had confirmed that any refit would take so long that it could not be completed at Chatham before the yard shut at the end of March 1984. This left the Ministry in an embarrassing situation. If part of the refit was undertaken at Chatham, and then was completed at another dockyard, probably Rosyth, then 'it would be taken as clear evidence that we had misjudged and mishandled the [Chatham] dockyard rundown'.[96] There was also the risk that a disgruntled Chatham workforce, which was in any case being run down in the lead up to closure, might result in the refit taking even longer, perhaps even leaving her in 'an immovable state' and in the worst case scenario risking nuclear safety. The other alternative was to tow *Dreadnought* to either Rosyth or Devonport to undertake the whole refit at one or other of these yards, but fitting her into an already cramped refit programme risked threatening the refit cycles of the *Resolution* class boats of the nuclear deterrent force. As further economies were forced on the Ministry of Defence in the last two months of 1981, the Admiralty Board therefore proposed *Dreadnought* for decommissioning rather than refitting. This therefore forced an embarrassing choice on the Secretary of State: undertake a split refit and make the Ministry look incompetent, force *Dreadnought* into the refit programme elsewhere thus jeopardising the refit streams of the all-important nuclear deterrent boats, or withdraw the boat from service and face the embarrassment of informing allies that this had been done. Peter Blaker recommended the third option, focussing on the practicalities: a three-year refit for *Dreadnought* would only extend her life for a further three years, as she was planned to leave the fleet in 1988; she was a unique boat with obsolescent and noisy machinery whose role in her last years of service would probably be restricted to training for surface ships and in the anti-ship role; and the refit would be extremely expensive, costing £70 million.[97] Nott accepted these arguments, and it was agreed that she should be withdrawn from service.[98] The difficulties came over announcing this decision. Over the next two months Nott and Blaker equivocated over who would inform Admiral Harry Train and also when it should be done, such was the perceived sensitivity of announcing further capability reductions following the Review. Admiral Lewin eventually agreed that he should be the one to inform Train, as were such a decision to come from a minister it would 'create a high profile situation' with a NATO commander who was still angry about the Review outcomes. Lewin duly sent his signal on 5 February 1982, and the withdrawal from service of HMS *Dreadnought* was announced publicly a few days later.[99] Despite these worries, there seems to have been little serious protest from SACLANT, and thus ended the career of the Royal Navy's first nuclear submarine: as a moderately embarrassing side effect of the decision to close Chatham dockyard.

The response from NATO leaders was less painful than envisaged, but by this time concerns about the new conventional submarine programme began to occupy ministers' minds. Geoffrey Pattie, the Parliamentary Under-Secretary for Defence Procurement, started to worry about the progress in the development of this class. He argued that the boat was too large, that its propulsion system was inadequate, and its tactical command system was not as effective as it could be. Pattie seems to have been worried by a draft Peter Hennessy article on the subject and above all by concerns that the new submarine design seemed unlikely to win the competition to build replacement submarines for the Australian Navy. Pattie's proposed answer was to cancel the submarine and build German designs under licence (Vickers had built German submarines under licence for Israel in the early 1970s).[100] He was also deeply sceptical of the competence of the Royal Corps of Naval Constructors and appeared to be pushing for a privatised design process.[101] In reality, the problem revolved around the significant differences between designing a submarine for the Royal Navy's very specific requirements: boats that would supplement nuclear submarines, be effective training platforms for surface vessels, and also be able to undertake operations in the High North. This meant that the new boats would need more space than was usual devoted to weapons control, sensor fit, fuel and stores.[102] These Cold War requirements did not fit well with submarines for export to other navies who often had very different needs, and this was not unusual for many late-Cold War designs for the Royal Navy.

Ministerial concerns were resolved by a well-attended presentation on the new class of submarines to which Pattie and Nott were invited, as were General Johnston, the Chief Scientific Adviser and the First Sea Lord as well as assorted admirals and civil servants. Pattie's concerns appear to have been partly ameliorated and Nott emphasised that a major rethink now would jeopardise the conventional submarine programme, whilst any leaks of concerns about the design might wreck any chance of exports and damage the submarine's lead yard (Vickers Shipbuilding) commercially.[103] Pattie's worries had focussed very much on the submarine's exportability, but what he missed was that despite a relatively traditional propulsion system, the new design managed a submerged maximum speed of 20 knots compared to 16 knots for the preceding *Oberon* class, an increased diving depth and only two thirds of the crew of the *Oberon*s (forty-six compared to seventy-one), in addition to an unusually comprehensive weapon and sensor fit.[104] The heavy involvement of the lead yard, Vickers, in the detailed design of the class was an unusual element of this procurement, which reflected a shift away from reliance on the design expertise of the Navy's Ship Department.[105]

One of the greatest weaknesses of the Royal Navy's submarine fleet had been its underperforming anti-ship armament. The Tigerfish torpedo (formerly Ondine), which was described in Chapter 11, had never performed satisfactorily, and as a result, the submarine service still relied on Second World War-vintage Mark 8 torpedoes for anti-ship work, and lacked a reliable heavyweight torpedo for destroying or disabling large Soviet submarines. The costs of procuring a domestically-produced replacement for Tigerfish were yet another item omitted from the figures that Nott had presented to OD and the Cabinet in June 1981, so the Secretary of State had to return to OD in September 1981 with proposals for a new heavyweight torpedo. The June figures had included the costs of purchasing the US Mark 48 heavyweight torpedo, which had the advantage of already being in service, was in the process of being further updated, and was the weapon preferred within the Ministry of Defence, including the Navy. It was not a perfect weapon: it did not perform well in shallow waters and under ice, but it was available and proven.[106] Nott, mainly for defence industrial reasons and for fear of backbench protests for not buying British, instead argued to buy a heavyweight torpedo developed by the British company Marconi Defence Systems. There would be more control over the development of future variants, and it would have a longer service life as the Mark 48 was already a decade old and might be replaced by a newer type within the next decade. Some of the technology used in the new torpedo was also being used in the Stingray lightweight torpedo which was under development. If the heavyweight were cancelled, then the costs of Stingray were likely to increase by £20 million. Netting out this additional expense, it was estimated that the new torpedo would be £100 million to £150 million more expensive than purchasing the Mark 48, which would cost £1.61 billion to purchase.[107] Nott argued that the benefits outweighed the costs, even if the British option would result in a spike in spending in the mid-1980s that had not been factored into existing costs. The Prime Minister supported Nott: concerns about criticism in Parliament and presumably backbench rebellions pushed ministers down the road of the domestic option. The fact that Marconi had offered a fixed price deal on development and production costs was also attractive.[108] A final decision would theoretically be made later, but in practice it had already been made. The new torpedo would eventually enter service during the last few years of the Cold War, and prove to be an effective and long-serving weapon. Despite this, Nott had now succeeded in adding another £100 million or more to the defence budget, chargeable to the Navy Department's procurement allocation.

Hydrographic Vessels and the Logistic Landing Ships

The Naval Staff had also left two 'poison pills' hidden within the fleet structure that had been created on 1 May 1981, and which Nott and his office had erroneously thought could be safely ignored or easily dealt with; another sign of the problems caused by the haste in which the Review was undertaken. Nott had assumed that the Department of Trade could be easily pushed aside when it protested the withdrawal of all the inshore and coastal survey vessels from service. However, the role of domestic surveying was, rather obviously, essential in ensuring that commercial vessels – from ferries to supertankers – could safely enter British ports. Survey work often needed to be undertaken regularly as sandbanks could move and shift over time or after major storms. A few days after the release of the White Paper, Nott had to concede in principle the retention of the inshore and coastal vessels of the Hydrographic squadron, and another series of costs were added into the defence budget over and above the figures approved by Cabinet.[109]

The other issue was that of the Logistic Landing Ships ('LSLs') of the *Sir Lancelot* class. These had originally been commercially operated but transferred to RFA operation in 1970. The LSLs transported the British Army's equipment from Britain to the continent or to Northern Ireland, along with occasional longer distance transport to British garrisons in places such as Cyprus, Belize and Brunei, as well as to training grounds in Canada and Kenya. Nott and the civil servants at the centre had rashly assumed that such transportation could be undertaken more cheaply by commercial Ro-Ro vessels. The 1 May Fleet had assumed that all six ships, which would need replacing within the next ten years, would be rapidly withdrawn from service without replacement, but it is unclear whether the Navy or the Army were being expected to foot the bill for the planned commercial freighting of equipment. As the White Paper was published their future was still unclear, but by 29 June joint studies were underway by the Army and Navy to see how much the LSLs would cost to run on in comparison with commercial freighting.[110] When these studies were completed in early September it was discovered that the LSLs were actually cheaper to run than the commercial freighting option which would have cost £27 million more a year.[111] This was because the LSLs were run to full capacity, were exempt from regulations regarding the carriage of dangerous materials (such as explosives), and were crewed by cheaper Hong Kong Chinese crews who were exempted from National Union of Seamen terms of service. Both the Army and Navy therefore agreed that the most cost effective option was to run on the existing ships, but predictably each argued that the other service should pay the £12.5 million costs per year of operating the ships.[112] Nott and Omand preferred a fifty-fifty split between the two services, but Nott deferred to Cooper, and as a result the £12.5 million annual cost was transferred to the Navy to add to their increasing load of capability commitments.[113] At least this was one naval capability retention that had actually saved Nott some money, as the costs of the numerous other naval add backs began to mount.

The Future of the Royal Marines
During the early months of the Defence Review, as was seen in the previous chapter, the Secretary of State had mulled the integration of the Royal Marines into a larger intervention force including the Parachute Regiment. This had been put to one side given the costs of such a merger, but the Review had reduced the Marines' ability to conduct amphibious operations following the decision to withdraw the two assault ships from service and HMS *Hermes*, which still retained a secondary commando carrier role. In February 1982 the Commandant General of the Royal Marines ('CGRM') put a paper to the Admiralty Board's Sub Committee on the future of the Marines. The Review had assumed that the Marines' personnel numbers would fall by 1,350 between 1980 and 1985, but that by 1991 the Royal Marines would make up over 12 per cent of the Navy's total personnel, a proportionate increase on both 1980 and 1985.[114] CGRM set out the tasks assigned to the Marines. The first was amphibious operations in support of NATO, which consisted of Op Plan 113, the reinforcement of Atlantic island commands such as the Faeroes, Madeira or Azores; Op Plans 108 and 109, the reinforcement of Norway, Denmark or Schleswig-Holstein in northern Germany; and Op Plan 203 which included a full scale amphibious assault alongside the US Marine

Corps of Soviet-held NATO territory. The other Royal Marine roles included: nuclear and oil rig protection, transition to war duties including defence of key points and contributing to regional military commands; out of area operations and commitments including the Falklands and Hong Kong; national tasking for the Special Boat Service; tasks in support of the Navy, including providing detachments for selected ships' companies; tasks in support of the Army including one Commando undertaking one four and a half month tour of Northern Ireland every thirteen months; 'Spearhead' force commitments for short-notice operations; and ancillary roles such as the Royal Marine Band Service and staff posts in the Ministry and NATO.[115]

CGRM then worked through a number of options in order to bring both costs and headcount down to the levels agreed in the Defence Review. These included allocating one Commando to the training role and basing them at either Lympstone (the Commando Training Centre) or Poole (the amphibious and technical training base); allowing the three remaining Commandos (40, 42 and 45) to become 'underborne' and operate with numbers lower than the formal establishment of 688 but with the risk of a loss of capability; or reductions elsewhere within the Royal Marines. Summing up, CGRM stating that the existing structures worked well and that if reductions were needed they should be in the Band Service, in reducing or abolishing the provision of detachments for ships' companies or, in extremis, allowing underborne Commandos. Each Commando operating at fifty personnel below their establishment would save £1.5 million.[116] The paper had been prepared before the decision had been made to retain *Fearless* and *Intrepid*, so the situation looked less pessimistic than it had initially seemed, and in relative terms the Royal Marines, in personnel and budget terms, were not being reduced, proportionally, as steeply as the Navy. However, coming not so soon after the disbanding of 41 Commando in 1979, horizons for the Royal Marines seemed to be shrinking over the coming years. The abolition of detachments on naval ships, which was one of the major economies that was eventually implemented, saw the end of a centuries old operational link between the Marines and the Navy, and a role that had been at the core of Royal Marine tasks until the rise of Commando operations in the 1940s and 1950s.[117]

The Dockyards

In the early months of 1980, the then Defence Secretary, Francis Pym, had commissioned a study into the Royal Dockyards. The study was chaired by Keith Speed, the Under-Secretary of State for the Navy, and it reported in May 1980. Its findings and recommendations were not a radical departure: the long-standing plan to turn the dockyards into a trading fund was reconfirmed, it was recommended that more basic refit work should be placed with commercial shipyards, and that increased pay flexibility should be allowed in order to counteract specific employment issues in the different yards.[118] Despite the Admiralty Board having considered closing Chatham dockyard a number of times during the late 1960s and 1970s, and the Chiefs of Staff studying the implications of closing Gibraltar dockyard in 1977, Speed's report recommended keeping all existing dockyards open.[119] As it had reported before the Nott review had started, the heavy major refit programme for frigates and destroyers was still in place, meaning that the planned refit load would be substantial over the next decade. The table below sets out the ten-year refit plans for the dockyards as assessed in the summer of 1980:

Table 12: Dockyard refit plans for 1981–2 to 1990–1 as at August 1980[120]

	Major refits	*Ordinary refits*
Devonport	10 SSN, 6 conventional submarines, 16 destroyers and frigates	31 destroyers and frigates
Portsmouth	7 major ships, 4 destroyers, 6 conventional submarines	15 destroyers and frigates 1 *Challenger*, 3 *Britannia*
Chatham	11 SSN, 5 frigates	16 frigates
Rosyth	5 SSBN, 1 SSN, 3 conventional submarines, 5 frigates	7 destroyers and frigates
As yet unallocated	7 destroyers and frigates, 4 conventional submarines	2 LPDs
Gibraltar	-	Single stream of frigates + MCMVs
Total (excluding Gibraltar)	22 SSN, 5 SSBN, 19 conventional submarines, 7 major ships, 37 destroyers and frigates	2 LPDs, 69 destroyers and frigates, 1 *Challenger*, 3 *Britannia*

The outcome of the Defence Review threw nearly all of these calculations out. Major refits for destroyers, carriers and the Type 22 frigates would not occur, whilst the rapid shrinkage of the frigate and destroyer force would result in a much lower refit load. The dockyards were now faced with a rapid shift from feast to famine: with the load reducing by nearly half there was no way that the existing dockyards could be justified. Chatham and Gibraltar – candidates for closure for many years – were almost inevitable casualties, but the end of major refits for carriers and destroyers, and the phasing out of these ship types by the 2000s meant that Portsmouth's refit capacity as a yard specialising in these types of warships could not be justified either. Portsmouth would remain an operating base for warships but would no longer undertake refits beyond docking and essential defect periods. It was estimated that closure of Chatham and Gibraltar, and ending Portsmouth as a dockyard, would result in a total of 4,600, 1,100 and 4,200 redundancies respectively by the mid-1980s.[121]

Chatham had always been the most vulnerable of the Navy's dockyards, and as has been seen in previous chapters, the Sea Lords had considered whether closure was possible as far back as the late 1960s. Despite this vulnerability, after the 1974–5 Defence Review, a new and wide-ranging development plan had been written for Chatham, which envisaged a long-running programme of new building works and refurbishment of existing facilities through into the late 1990s. The plan, which was largely completed in September 1975 envisaged a total spend of £47 million over the next decade or more.[122] Chatham would see a peak of spending around 1981, including major upgrades to the nuclear submarine refit complex, brand new office blocks, new factory buildings, a finishing trades complex and a new apprentice training centre, amongst a range of other improvements and new building work.[123] In the event, it appears that not much of the programme was completed due to spending constraints through the late 1970s and early 1980s. This relative lack of investment, in comparison to spending for example on the frigate refit complex in Devonport, indicated where the priorities lay for the Navy's leadership, who had known for many years that Chatham was the major domestic yard most vulnerable to closure. It was furthest away from the likeliest operational areas of the Western Approaches and the GIUK gap and was smaller than either Devonport or Portsmouth. Even its modern nuclear submarine refit facility could not save it.

Whilst the closure of Chatham had significant, but for the government bearable, domestic political implications, the rundown of the much smaller dockyard in Gibraltar would have a significant diplomatic impact. The naval dockyard was an important employer in the overseas territory, which was claimed by neighbouring Spain, and which any major hint of weakening British support might affect Gibraltarians' confidence in their long-term future. Gibraltar's refitting capacity was relatively minor. During the 1970s, when the domestic British dockyards were struggling to fulfil the increasingly ambitious major refit programme for frigates, Gibraltar took on secondary work such as the refitting of mine countermeasures vessels, and minor refits of older frigates. The specific diplomatic and political issues involved with Gibraltar resulted in a willingness to provide a little more notice before the rundown of refit work, the opening of consultations with unions and local politicians, and the free transfer of some land from the dockyard back to the Gibraltarian government. A reduced naval base would remain at Gibraltar, which had a strategic role for NATO in guarding the entrance to the Mediterranean (and a similar, but unacknowledged, importance for British maritime trade), whilst the three dry docks would be available for commercial work with some government contracts being placed the way of the new commercial owners to ease them into what was hoped would be a profitable business. There would also be encouragement and support to develop new industries, including tourism, financial services and high-tech manufacture.[124]

Whilst Chatham and Gibraltar were shutting down entirely, the situation in Portsmouth was more complex. It would remain a major naval base and home port for a proportion of the fleet, but it would now lack full refitting facilities, which would be focussed at Devonport and Rosyth only. By September 1981, the Controller of the Navy had worked up a case for the future of Portsmouth after it had relinquished its dockyard status and therefore ended its ability to refit warships. Portsmouth would remain the home port for the *Invincible* class, the Type 42 destroyers, eleven minehunters and thirteen diesel-electric submarines as well as the new home for the Standby Squadron, and it would retain its ability to conduct routine maintenance and undertake 'docking and essential defects' work. It was proposed that Portsmouth be re-tasked as a 'setting to work base/weapon support group'. This meant that the naval base would become the specialist base for the latter part of trials for weapon systems on new or newly-refitted ships, including some repair and modification facilities for such systems. In effect, the last and often most technically demanding element of post-refit trials would be moved from where the ship had been refitted to Portsmouth as a single specialist centre, where such work would be combined with similar such work for new ships. This also ensured that some elements of refit capability could be retained at the naval base.[125] There were some reservations by the Controller about how this would be made to work effectively, but both he and the Chief of Fleet Support agreed to the proposals in late March and early April 1982.[126]

As the Falklands conflict progressed it became clear that the repair and refit load would be too much for the remaining dockyards. The Prime Minister considered postponing the announcement of compulsory redundancy notices in the dockyards in order to ensure that the post-Falklands rush of work could be undertaken quickly. John Nott fought this, fearful that his plans for the full rundown of Chatham, Gibraltar and Portsmouth would be put in jeopardy. He argued against too long a postponement, finally agreeing to a one-month delay at Portsmouth.[127]

Sensing an opportunity to push back further on the outcomes of the Review, the Naval Staff began preparing arguments for increasing refit capacity across the dockyards. The shift upwards in refits required, since the decision to increase the number of frigates a few weeks before the Command Paper was published, had implied for a number of months that newly reduced refit capacity would prove inadequate. Since then, Nott had reprieved the two assault ships and the LSLs, and had definitively decided to keep *Britannia* after weighing up its future in the later months of 1981. In planning the forward refit and maintenance programme it was beginning to become clear, whether the Falklands added to this load or not, that capacity was too small. What the Falklands did was create an environment where such decisions were now able to be easily revisited within the government: the short-term refit programme was 'in disarray' as ships had been sent south and much capacity had been used to modify merchant ships taken up from trade.[128]

With the end of the Falklands conflict and the saving of Portsmouth as a refit base seeming increasingly possible, the plans for repurposing Portsmouth as a specialist weapons support base soon became ensnared in a territorial conflict between the Controller of the Navy and Vice Chief of the Naval Staff, as to whether the former or Commander-in-Chief Fleet's organisation would have control over the workforce.[129] Plans to shut the dockyard were therefore put back to early 1985, as staff work began on the forward refit programme and Long Term Costings, and all decision-making was frozen.[130] By November 1982 the weapons support base proposal had disappeared and the Chief of Fleet Support, having assessed that the 'refit overload' would be as high as 13 per cent over the long-term, proposed that refit work be retained at Portsmouth, but under a different approach, with refits only taking place for Portsmouth-based warships under the workforce concept developed for Portsmouth as a Naval Base. It was hoped that this would mean that the old trade demarcation rules of the dockyards, which had limited the types of work different workers could undertake, would no longer be applicable and thus increase the flexibility of the workforce. These proposals would cost £22 million a year and mean the retention of 1,500 dockyard workers and were accepted by the Admiralty Board.[131]

Table 13: Dockyard Refit Plans for 1984–5 to 1993–4 as at September 1983[132]

	Major/Restorative refits	*Ordinary refits*
Devonport	13 SSN, 9 conventional submarines, 7 carriers/assault ships, 12 frigates	19 destroyers and frigates
Portsmouth	5 destroyers	9 frigates
Rosyth	6 SSBN, 5 SSN, 5 conventional submarines, 7 destroyers and frigates	14 frigates, 1 LPD, 2 *Challenger*
Total	18 SSN, 6 SSBN, 14 conventional submarines, 7 carriers/assault ships, 24 destroyers and frigates	1 LPD, 42 destroyers and frigates, 2 *Challenger*

The revised refit plans by 1983 saw Portsmouth therefore re-emerge as a centre for both major and ordinary refits, albeit on a lesser scale than before the review. The refit load for carriers, assault ships and submarines was similar, but both the major and ordinary refits of destroyers and frigates had reduced, and by a greater proportion than would otherwise be expected. Major refits of these vessels had been replaced by what were termed 'restorative refits' for destroyers and frigates, and their operational lives would theoretically be shorter. Initially it had been planned that ordinary refits would be completely replaced by docking and essential defects periods, but as can be seen by 1983 the ordinary refit had returned, presumably as these were required for the gradual updating of sensors, weapons and other equipment.[133] The original presumption that almost no equipment improvements, beyond the most basic, would be made throughout a ship's career had proved in the event to be unrealistic.

Personnel, Training and Ship Availability Reforms
One of the least noticed, least understood but most radical aspects of the changes to the Royal Navy as a result of the 1981 Defence Review was the planned transformation of ship manning, training and ship operational availability. John Nott had quickly latched onto the low 'ship-to-shore' ratio of the Navy: by 1981 more of its personnel were in shore-based than in sea-going billets. To some extent this was the result of the recent retirement of large, manpower-intensive warships such as the carrier *Ark Royal*, the cruisers *Tiger* and *Blake* and the first batch of 'County' class destroyers, and their replacement by less manpower-intensive vessels without a concomitant overall reduction in personnel. In other respects however, a more radical look at how the Navy used its personnel was overdue: shore-based training courses ran for long periods and some shore-billets seemingly underused their sailors. Increasing the amount of time spent at sea as a partial recompense for the shrinking of the fleet was also an important priority for Nott: a policy that would have required an increased number of warship orders to sustain over the long-term. Significant and relatively rapid reductions in personnel were forced upon the Navy in order to 'encourage' these reforms. The Navy's headcount would reduce from 72,300 in 1981–2 to 62,300 by 1986–7 and then down to 53,800 by 1991–2. This would theoretically produce a net saving £700 million over the decade ahead.[134]

The Navy Department created a 'Way Ahead Committee' to investigate and recommend the means by which these reductions could be implemented. The Committee recommended that the only way to increase the ship-to-shore ratio significantly and manage the reductions would be to turn much of the surface fleet into floating training establishments. This was particularly difficult as the old but large and roomy warships that would have easily been able to accommodate sailors under training were being rapidly retired. The committee recommended that Part II and Part III training for Operations Branch Ratings would move to sea, as would the Petty Officer Mechanics' Course. A range of other training courses would be shortened including the

Officer of the Watch, Assistant Warfare Officer and Lieutenant's Greenwich courses. Six shore training establishments, *Excellent, Vernon, Fisgard, Phoenix, Pembroke* and *Caledonia*, would all close. In order to accommodate all the sailors under training on board ship, a new system of 'batch drafting' was devised whereby every 18 months 50 per cent of a ship's able and ordinary seamen would be changed over, so that a new cohort could arrive to be trained. The possibility of installing training simulators of varying sizes and sophistication on board ships was seriously considered, whilst the remaining Royal Marine detachments on board ships would be removed in order to both provide more accommodation for ratings under training, and as has been seen, save money for the Marines.[135]

There were serious concerns that these reforms would accelerate the number of sailors leaving the Navy, so it was ordered that every ship would have a minimum of 40 per cent figure for the time spent at its own base port, therefore placing a cap on how high the ship-to-shore ratio could rise and implying a Navy much more tied to its UK naval bases. These reforms would have theoretically reduced the overall total 'ship-days' available to the Commander-in-Chief Fleet for operations by 20 per cent from 1981 levels. Given that the active fleet of frigates and destroyers was initially planned to reduce by nearly a third, this was a significant increase in proportional availability, but it would have been achieved at a cost. It is unclear how operationally effective the Navy's ships would be if a considerable portion of their time was spent training ratings. Long-term deployments might not have been sustainable in such circumstances, suggesting an end to the worldwide group deployments that had dominated operational planning in the 1970s, and which Nott had then revived and announced in the 1981 White Paper.[136] The Admiralty Board was particularly worried about a vicious cycle being created whereby longer periods of time at sea, combined with only limited Docking and Essential Defect periods in place of full refits, would over time reduce the service life of warships. The problem might have been even more acute with the newest frigates built to the new expectations of only a 15 to 18-year operational life. The Committee acknowledged that risks were being taken with the proposed reforms, but they were the only way to meet Nott's demands for fewer ships, shorter ship lives, fewer refits, much reduced personnel numbers and increased periods of time at sea. The Committee also argued that additional funds would be required in the first three to four years to implement these changes, thus adding yet another stream of spending over and above the original June 1981 figures.[137]

The reforms were never implemented in full, but they did jolt the Navy into thinking more actively about how best to ensure that its sailors were most usefully and efficiently employed. The push for more efficient crewing and shorter ship-lives would also have an impact on the design of the new Type 23 frigate, which eventually emerged at the end of the decade as a relatively lean-crewed vessel.[138] Another less positive impact was the creation of what was later termed the 'Nott hole' by the Navy's personnel planners: in order to meet Nott's exacting personnel reductions, a dramatic reduction in recruitment combined with a tranche of redundancies was forced on the Navy in 1981–2. This created a much smaller cohort of recruits than usual, which in later years would have a negative impact on the numbers of personnel with certain lengths of service, and therefore the numbers available to fill available petty officer, chief petty officer and warrant officer roles. The 'Nott hole' would not finally disappear – utterly unlamented – from the personnel planners' charts until the 2010s.

Negotiating for Money Again

In the autumn of 1981, Nott was forced back into new negotiations with the Treasury over the defence budget. The levels agreed in June 1981 had been made on a 'volume', or inflation-adjusted, basis but as the Treasury was shifting such calculations onto a cash basis (supplemented by their own 'cash limit' adjustments which were usually set at just below the inflation rate), Nott's figures had to be converted from volume to cash.[139] Nott had argued for a 'fair' adjustment but when the Treasury had undertaken this conversion and added in the cash limits, the defence budget was now £400 million lower than had been assumed on a volume basis. The Treasury offered an adjustment of between £250 million to £300 million, but this still left another £100 million for the Defence Secretary to find at short-notice from the following year's budget.[140] A much larger amount of money would be needed over the ten-year period. The Treasury were not happy with Nott's requests for additional funds, arguing that Defence could not be a special case compared to other departments, and pointing out that considerable additional short-term spending had already been agreed in June.[141] Nott duly submitted a list of the cancellations and reductions necessary for Defence to meet the Treasury's requirements. These consisted of a good number of 'bleeding stump' reductions (for example, the Navy Department submitted the cancellation and breaking up on the slip of the twelfth and thirteenth Type 42 destroyers) combined with a steadfast refusal to come close to any major reductions from the Air Force Department, the department which had benefitted the most from the White Paper and therefore stood to lose the most.[142]

Predictably, and probably with some accuracy, the Treasury argued that these were not realistic and that less headline-worthy reductions could actually be made in areas such as administration and staff costs.[143] Much of the disagreement focussed on the next three to four years of defence spending, where by 1984–5 the difference between Defence's figures of those proposed by the Treasury reached as high as £895 million in just that year.[144] An in-depth analysis of how the Ministry calculated its cost estimates set out the fault lines between the two departments: the Treasury believed that the Ministry allowed contractors too great a profit margin on what they provided for Defence, whilst the Ministry argued that it was not possible to push prices down because most defence equipment was not amenable to productivity savings due to its bespoke nature and short production runs. Overseas purchasing could also increase in price significantly if exchange rates moved in a disadvantageous direction.[145] The matter was partly resolved just prior to a Cabinet meeting on public expenditure, when an additional £300 million would be made available for the current financial year, and £375 million for the next, with agreement pending for the next two years after that.[146] This would require considerable programme reductions to fit within even these quite large additional sums. Although Nott argued that much of the Ministry's overspends had come from defence prices rising quicker than inflation and contractors making faster progress than expected and therefore needing to be paid early; but hidden within his figures there must have been some impact from his decisions to include a significant number of add-backs into the programme, especially within the Navy Department.[147] Theoretically, in most cases these add-backs were meant to fit within existing budgets, but often the relevant service department might take an optimistic interpretation of either the cost of the add-back or their ability to make savings in other areas, and when this optimism proved unfounded, the costs would rise quickly and therefore be added within the capacious category of 'defence prices rising higher than general inflation'. In reality, a significant portion of the overspending was therefore due to Nott bending to political pressure from various directions to return capabilities back into the budget.

The reductions necessary for the Secretary of State to meet the targets agreed in Cabinet, fell most heavily on the RAF. A total of £697 million savings were made for the 1982–3 financial year, with £302 million of these coming from the Air Force Department, £187 million from the Navy Department, £154 million from the Army Department and £54 million from outside the service departments. The RAF was forced to reduce the annual Tornado production rate from fifty-two to forty-four, the lowest it could go without incurring significant contractual and diplomatic problems, defer improvements to air defence ground radars and other allied equipment, reduce and defer deliveries of radars and electronic warfare capabilities for the new Tornados, make various reductions in simulator spending, airfield survival works, as well as a range of other deferrals and reductions. The Royal Navy deferred the eighth Type 22 by eight months, put the Type 23 programme back again, deferred the third and fourth 'Castle' class offshore patrol vessels (they would, in the event, never be built), put back spending on satellite communications equipment as well as both the torpedo projects, dispose of the hydrofoil HMS *Speedy* and the trials ship HMS *Londonderry*, re-phase the mine countermeasures vessel programme, cancel the DATUM 'data highway' project to allow rapid software changes to weapon systems, and disband the Hovercraft Trials Unit. As has already been seen, the cancellation of the refit of HMS *Dreadnought* and her withdrawal from service were also added into the figures, although this had been driven as much by other factors. The Army made a series of small reductions across a wide range of areas including ammunition, stores, communications equipment, chemical/biological/radiological/nuclear capabilities, works, clothing, combat engineering equipment, out of area stockpiles, whilst cancelling the Blowpipe missile for Gazelle light helicopters.[148] A significant proportion of these reductions were actually storing up problems for future years: deferring spending, or rephasing projects so that they lasted longer, inevitably resulted in a greater total spending, just stretched out over a longer period of time. Nott was administering a series of quick fixes to get Defence through the next few years: any ambitious talk of dealing with Ministry of Defence overspending over the long-term had long since disappeared.

* * *

This additional tranche of capability reductions shredded what remained of Nott's credibility with Conservative backbenchers and with the Prime Minister, who was now beginning to distance herself from the battered and damaged Secretary of State.[149] John Nott would already be considering retirement from politics and a return to the more placid world of merchant banking well before the Falklands conflict tested him even further.[150] The Secretary of State was now reaping what he had sown by conducting the Defence Review too quickly. On top of the problems that high inflation and a struggling industrial sector had caused for the defence budget, Nott had in his haste made a large number of assumptions that had proved to be incorrect. He had assumed that the United States would not use its leverage with Trident to enforce concessions and that its approach to defence would not change as Carter was replaced by Reagan; he had left out key procurements such as the new heavyweight torpedo from original costings; he had assumed that internal protests over reductions in hydrographic vessels and logistic landing ships that impacted other areas could be waved away; and he had completed the Review without coming to a conclusion about the relative efficacy of anti-submarine helicopters and maritime patrol aircraft, which would have a significant cost and capability impact on amongst other areas, the development of the Type 23 frigate. During a period of high inflation, recession, increasing unemployment and a deeply unpopular government, these errors were cruelly punished, and they helped contribute to the ending of Nott's political career.

Part III: Revival, 1982–1990

16

Operation 'Corporate'

At 2300 hours local time on 1 April 1982, Argentine commandos landed by boat at Lake Point on the island of East Falkland, part of the British Overseas Territory of the Falkland Islands in the South Atlantic. They split into two groups and advanced inland. One headed towards the Governor's residence, Government House, in Stanley, the capital, whilst the second group headed to Moody Brook, the barracks for the territory's small Royal Marine garrison. They were followed the next morning by a full naval invasion force spearheaded by Argentine Marines and although the small garrison fought valiantly, by the end of the day the Falkland Islands were in Argentine hands. On 3 April another dependent territory, South Georgia, 840 nautical miles to the south-east of the Falklands, was also taken. Again, an impressive defence by the small Royal Marine party demonstrated the British non-acceptance of these illegal invasions but was unable to prevent the takeover.[1] The British government had been humiliated as sovereign territory over 7,000 nautical miles away from the United Kingdom had been seized in a day without any means to provide reinforcement or support. In one of the defining moments of Margaret Thatcher's period as Prime Minister – and also one of the defining moments for the Royal Navy since the Second World War – the British government decided not to let the invasion stand and a naval and amphibious task force was readied to retake the islands if negotiations failed. By late April 1982 the Task Force had entered the waters around the Falklands, and by 14 June after a hard-fought naval and land campaign the islands had been retaken and all Argentine troops had surrendered.

This chapter will provide an overview of the conflict. The naval side of the campaign itself has been covered well in a number of publications, so this account will focus on providing enough detail and background to provide the context for the chapter that follows on the lessons-learnt from the campaign.[2]

In addition, this chapter will also cover the Royal Navy in the South Atlantic after the conflict ended, a significant commitment that has often been overlooked by authors.[3]

The Invasion

Both the Falkland Islands, with a population consisting of approximately 2,000 descendants of British settlers from the nineteenth century, and uninhabited South Georgia, had long been claimed by Argentina, whose government argued that the islands had been illegally settled by the British when the territory had legitimately been part of the Spanish empire. Argentina saw itself as the inheritor to the Spanish claim, and the issue had developed distinctly nationalist overtones from the 1960s and came to be seen as 'unfinished business' from Argentina's own struggle for independence from colonial powers in the 1810s and 1820s. Argentina's ruling military junta was, in 1982, increasingly desperate for a unifying and patriotic victory to rally round a country suffering from high inflation and an extremely brutal 'dirty war' against perceived enemies of the state. A quick and successful invasion of the Falklands would provide this visible and heroic nationalistic success, so planning began in the first months of 1982 for an invasion of the islands. The recent announcement by the British Government of the withdrawal from service of HMS *Endurance*, the South Atlantic patrol vessel, confirmed in the minds of the Argentine political and military leadership the lack of British will to retain the islands. For over 15 years on-and-off negotiations between Britain and Argentina over the future of the islands had not resulted in any breakthrough with the Falkland Islanders themselves refusing to accept any transfer of sovereignty to Argentina. By 1981, the British government's attitude towards the islanders had increasingly moved towards frustration over their intransigence, with Nicholas Ridley, the minister in charge of negotiations, telling the islanders on a visit to the Falklands that they would have to 'accept reality' at some point. Yet more messages were therefore being sent to the Argentine junta that the British were not prioritising the defence of the islands.[4]

The crisis began in March 1982 with the occupation of a whaling station in South Georgia by Argentine scrap metal workers. They had been taken there by an Argentinian naval ship, and after the workers raised the Argentine flag, the Argentine Navy had taken the opportunity to land a section of marines. *Endurance* was then sent to investigate the situation. These actions, combined with protests against the Junta in Buenos Aires, pushed their leadership into launching the invasion earlier than had been planned. If they did not do so soon, then more British naval vessels would appear at South Georgia and their presence would make any invasion of the Falklands a much riskier venture.[5]

Initially, with the Chief of the Defence Staff Admiral Lewin in New Zealand on an official visit, the leadership of the Ministry of Defence seemed unable to make a decision and were inclined to believe that nothing could be done, until famously the First Sea Lord, Admiral Leach, persuaded the Prime Minister that a military response was possible – and should be done – and that a naval task force could be readied to send south.[6] Thus galvanised, Mrs Thatcher ordered that a task force be readied to sail south, initially under the assumption that it would add pressure on the Argentines in the negotiations that had been initiated by the United States to resolve the crisis. In fact Admiral Fieldhouse, the Commander-in-Chief Fleet, had anticipated a decision to send a task force and had been in contact with the Flag Officer of the First Flotilla, Rear Admiral John 'Sandy' Woodward, since 29 March – the day on which it was becoming clear that some form of Argentine military action in the South Atlantic was possible even if it was not known what that action would be – and had begun to make preliminary plans to prepare ships to sail south.[7]

First Phase: Assembling and Sustaining the Task Force

Preparing and Sending the Task Force
In preparing a task force to head south, naval planners would have looked in home waters and around the globe to see which ships were available and which would be most appropriate for operations in the South Atlantic. Preliminary planning had begun three days before the invasion, and it was clear immediately that the initial mainstay of any Task Force would come from the ships participating in the annual Springtrain exercise in the approaches to the Mediterranean. Springtrain was a large national exercise involving four destroyers and thirteen frigates. The ships participating included two 'County' class destroyers, *Antrim* (Woodward's flagship) and *Glamorgan*, the Type 42 destroyers *Coventry* and *Glasgow*, with *Sheffield* just about to join following a period on the Persian Gulf patrol; the Type 22 frigates *Broadsword*, *Battleaxe* and *Brilliant*; the Type 21 frigates *Arrow* and *Active*; the *Leander* class frigates *Aurora*, *Dido*, *Euryalus* and *Ariadne*; and the older Type 12 frigates *Lowestoft*, *Plymouth*, *Rhyl* and *Yarmouth*. The RFAs on the exercise were *Fort Austin*, *Tidespring* and *Grey Rover*, with *Blue Rover* returning from the Gulf with *Sheffield*.[8] *Fort Austin* had already been detached on the 26th to support *Endurance*. It was decided not to send any Ikara *Leander*s south; the Argentine submarine threat was considered to be minor and these ships had little in the way of capabilities against anything other than submarines. As a result, *Aurora*, *Dido* and *Euryalus* were sent home after transferring stores and spare victuals to those ships heading south. The unmodernised gun *Leander*, *Ariadne*, was also sent back home, as was (for the time being), *Active*.

The modern Type 42s and Type 22s were natural candidates for the Task Force, but *Battleaxe* was due a Docking and Essential Defects period, so she was not sent to the South Atlantic either.[9] Her sisters *Broadsword* and *Brilliant* were, as were all three Type 42 destroyers, HMS *Arrow* and two of the Type 12s, *Plymouth* and *Yarmouth*. They would be accompanied by *Tidespring* and *Appleleaf* (which was at Gibraltar but not taking part in Exercise Springtrain). The two 'Rover' class RFAs returned to the United Kingdom with those ships not chosen for the force. *Brambleleaf* was returning from the Far East and Gulf, and was attached to Woodward's growing fleet.[10]

Back in the United Kingdom, the carriers *Hermes* and *Invincible* were both at Portsmouth, having taken part in a number of exercises in local and northern waters between January and March; the latter being in an assisted maintenance period and the former's crew mostly taking a period of leave. On 1 April both ships were given orders to be ready to sail in 48 hours. The maintenance period was therefore completed at great speed and the crews of both ships were recalled from around the country.[11] The amphibious element of the Task Force was largely in home waters. *Fearless* had just completed her involvement in the annual NATO northern flank amphibious exercise, Exercise Alloy Express, whilst *Intrepid* was in the process of being de-stored and placed in un-crewed reserve. Four of the six *Sir Lancelot* class logistics landing ships ('LSLs') were alongside in the United Kingdom, two at Marchwood Military Port in Southampton Water, and two at Devonport. RFA *Sir Tristram* was in Belize and RFA *Sir Bedivere* was in Vancouver. All six would be involved in the conflict, but *Sir Bedivere* would arrive in theatre last, following a Panama Canal transit. RFA *Stromness*, a stores ship that had been slated for conversion to an amphibious support ship before the Pym mini-review of 1980, was re-activated from reserve to perform the amphibious role that had been cancelled more than 18 months before.[12] The other ships in United Kingdom waters chosen to join the Task Force were the Type 21 frigates *Alacrity* and *Antelope* (the former was on operational sea training off Portland, and the latter was on exercise), and the stores ship RFA *Resource*.[13]

The Royal Navy's available nuclear-powered submarines had been amongst the first vessels to head south. Press reports on 26 March that HMS *Superb* had left Gibraltar assumed that the submarine was heading to the Falklands. However, this was not the case – *Superb* was heading north for operations tracking Soviet submarines – and the British government was happy to allow such speculation. On the 29th, *Superb*'s sister, *Spartan*, was ordered south and she departed Gibraltar on 1 April. Another sister boat, *Splendid*, was taken off trailing a Soviet submarine and ordered to Faslane to take on stores for the South Atlantic; she sailed on the 2nd. The third nuclear submarine, *Conqueror*, was ordered to prepare on the 1st and sailed from Faslane on the 4th taking a number of SBS personnel with her. The fourth boat was *Valiant*, which was turned around during an Atlantic crossing for re-storing back at Faslane. She too was soon heading south.[14] *Spartan* arrived in the area of operations on 12 April, *Splendid* on the 14th, whilst *Conqueror* arrived off South Georgia on 18 April.[15] In late May, *Splendid* would begin the journey back home and be relieved by *Conqueror*'s sister *Courageous*; whilst the conventional boat *Onyx* would arrive in the South Atlantic at the same time.[16]

It would have been impossible to sustain and support the warships without the decision to make use of 'Ships Taken Up From Trade' ('STUFT') by the Department of Trade on behalf of the Ministry of Defence. These vessels would not be confiscated without compensation: the Government would have to pay the owners, who in most cases would also supply their crews to operate the ships whilst under Government direction. For example, a stern trawler taken up for minesweeping duties cost £3,000 a day and an ocean-going tug £10,000 a day.[17]

Over the course of the conflict, two passenger liners, the *Queen Elizabeth II* and the *Canberra*, were taken up from trade as troop transports; six roll-on roll-off ferries as vehicle transports; four roll-on roll-off container ships as aircraft transports; five cargo ships as stores ships; twelve tankers as support oilers; two ships as repair vessels; three salvage tugs; two ships as despatch vessels; as well as a liner as a hospital ship, a passenger/cargo ship as a minesweeper support ship, one mooring vessel and three vessels as base storage ships, two for oil and one for water. In addition, five stern trawlers were taken up from trade as minesweepers but crewed with Royal Navy personnel.[18] Many of these vessels had to undergo rapid modifications in order to make them useful as STUFT vessels. The most dramatic changes occurred on the four ro-ro container ships, which were transformed by the addition of basic flight decks and hangars partly made from containers, as aircraft transports. Many ships had helicopter pads added, and most were repainted to remove their commercial markings.[19]

Sustaining the Task Force
Of crucial importance would be the island of Ascension, almost halfway between the United Kingdom and the Falkland Islands. It was another overseas territory, but one that was not inhabited save by employees of the British Broadcasting Corporation, Cable and Wireless, PanAm Airways, NASA and the US Air Force, who all operated on the island on a leasehold basis. The island had a runway capable of taking large aircraft, but nothing for ships apart from an exposed anchorage and a single stone jetty suitable for small craft only. As British military personnel began to arrive to turn Ascension into a major logistics hub for operations, the island was gradually transformed. Ascension provided an anchorage for Royal Navy vessels on the way south to the Falklands, an air base for RAF reconnaissance aircraft and a means to shorten the air bridge to the South Atlantic as air drops of light but crucial stores and equipment

became increasingly important. It also provided somewhere to re-sort the many stores that had been packed into ships at great haste, and re-pack them so that they could be either more easily transferred across the Task Force or landed ashore in an organised state once a bridgehead had been established.[20] Once the Task Force had entered the area around the Falklands, an intermediate transfer area was established to the north-east beyond the area of operations. This area of sea was initially dubbed the Logistics and Loitering Area (or 'LOLA') and then renamed the Tugs, Repair and Logistics Area ('TRALA'): it provided a relatively safe place for ships to be refuelled at sea or to transfer stores, and as the campaign progressed, for repairs to be undertaken.[21]

The supply of fuel for ships and aircraft was another important task. The need for large quantities of aircraft fuel at Ascension, which could not have been easily bought on the open market, had resulted in a request to the United States. This had been granted and US oil tankers would regularly visit the island and discharge aviation fuel over duration of the conflict.[22] For the supply of fuel oil for ships, the Task Force had initially relied on stocks held at Freetown in Sierra Leone, at a plant owned half by that country's government and half by combination of oil majors. After the initial days of the campaign, oil was then purchased and refined from a range of regional ports with storage facilities and refineries. These included Dakar in Senegal, Lagos in Nigeria, Abidjan in Ivory Coast, Madeira, St Vincent in Cape Verde, the Azores and even Rio de Janeiro. In the early stages of planning, making use of facilities in Simonstown in South Africa (including for ship repairs) had been considered, but the obvious political objections of being seen to make use of apartheid South Africa's military bases caused this to be quickly ruled out.[23] Oil would be obtained by one of the twelve STUFT support tankers, which would then transfer their oil to RFAs closer to the Task Force in the LOLA/TRALA or at Ascension.[24] Ammunition and stores transfer usually occurred at Ascension or South Georgia (once the latter had been retaken), but in the last few days of the campaign, the STUFT ammunition support ship *Lycaon* transferred her ammunition to RFA *Stromness* in the TRALA in order to shorten the final leg of the supply lines down to the troops advancing on Stanley.[25]

After the despatch of the initial ships of the Task Force, planning immediately began to provide additional ships to send south. The first ships might need reinforcing, and then in time replacing, having spent a number of months in the South Atlantic. It was also possible that battle damage replacements would also be needed. On 13 May, the frigates *Argonaut* and *Ardent* arrived, escorting some of the amphibious force. On the 18th, the frigates *Ambuscade* and *Antelope* also joined, followed a day later by the Type 42 destroyer *Exeter*. There then followed the 'Bristol group' of ships led by the Type 82 destroyer HMS *Bristol*, whose group included the destroyer *Cardiff* and the frigates *Minerva*, *Penelope*, *Andromeda*, *Active* and *Avenger*.[26] The naval planners in Northwood were envisaging a series of ship reinforcements thereafter, working on the assumption that either the conflict might still be going on, or that although a victory had been won there would still be a need to retain a significant force in the South Atlantic to deter any further Argentine actions. In mid-July, a 'Southampton group' of six destroyers and frigates was planned to arrive, followed by a 'Newcastle group' in mid-September.[27] More cycles of ships would then follow, including repaired and patched-up vessels that would have returned from the South Atlantic a few months before. The construction of ships nearing completion was speeded up, as were ships in refit. The decommissioned commando carrier *Bulwark* was even investigated for re-activation as a utility helicopter carrier. Although it was believed that she could be reactivated by August given sufficient funds and resources, the greatest obstacle would have been spares, which had largely been disposed of since her decommissioning, as she had been the last of her class in service.[28]

The command structure chosen for the Task Force gave ultimate command to CINCFLEET, Admiral Sir John Fieldhouse, in Northwood. Under him was Vice Admiral Peter Herbert, Flag Officer Submarines, in charge of the submarines in the South Atlantic (TG 324.3); Rear Admiral 'Sandy' Woodward as commander of the Carrier Battle Group (TG 317.8); Commodore Michael Clapp as commander of the Amphibious Group (TG 317.0); Brigadier Julian Thompson as commander of the Landing Group (TG 317.1); with Captain Brian Young detached from the Carrier Battle Group to command the advance force chosen to retake South Georgia (TG 317.9). This structure was set by 7 April, although an earlier version originally had Woodward in charge of all the other Task Groups except the submarines under Herbert. The new structure gave Fieldhouse a shorter line of command into the different elements of the Task Force. Once Major General Moore arrived in theatre as Commander Land Forces (the new TG 317.1) at the end of May, Thompson reverted to command of just 3 Commando Brigade (TU 317.1.1) with Brigadier Tony Wilson becoming commander of 5 Infantry Brigade (TU 317.1.2).[29]

Capability Assessments

Whilst the Task Force was sailing south, a series of analyses were undertaken comparing the capabilities of Argentine and British forces. The ability of Argentine aircraft to refuel in flight had largely been dismissed, which therefore resulted in an underestimation of the air threat. It was thought that the Argentine Navy's greatest weakness was the poor night fighting capabilities of their carrier's Skyhawk aircraft. Defence against Argentine ship-based Exocets was more of a worry, and there were some doubts about the ability of Sea Dart or Sea Wolf to intercept these anti-ship missiles. It was thought that 'chaff' metal decoys could be the 'deciding factor'. Unsurprisingly for a navy that specialised in anti-submarine warfare, much attention was paid to the Argentine submarine threat. Their two German-built Type 209 submarines might be a threat to British nuclear submarines if they managed to get close enough.[30]

A more disturbing paper was submitted to the Naval Staff by the Admiralty Surface Weapons Establishment, which had undertaken a statistical analysis of the effectiveness of naval weapon systems back in 1980. By combining statistics for weapon availability with their likelihood of hitting targets they came up with some worrying results, especially regarding Sea Dart. The missile system had been plagued by availability issues since its introduction: sometimes its Type 909 tracker radars did not work, other times the missiles malfunctioned and at other times again the tactical command system or target indication radar failed to work properly. When this was combined with Sea Dart's only middling ability to intercept sea-skimming anti-ship missiles, they had calculated that Sea Dart only had 16.3 per cent overall efficiency (i.e. its chance of hitting a target missile). The statistics were somewhat better with British ship-launched Exocet and some variants of Sea Cat, and there were as yet no full sets of testing data for Sea Wolf, but the analysts at the Establishment were still especially pessimistic about air defence. They concluded that 'in view of the inadequacy to deal with even low-level threats where extensive manual co-ordination and intervention are required, even under peacetime conditions, the question arises as to whether there is any point in carrying any missiles at all, or at most a bare minimum'.[31] This analysis had been compiled two years' earlier but had not been distributed outside a small number of staff at the Establishment (its impact on Defence Review discussions in 1981 if it had been distributed would not have helped the Navy at all). Perhaps understandably, it was decided not to distribute this potentially explosive document beyond the small number of staff officers who had already seen it. The Task Force was sailing towards a much more significant air threat than it thought: Argentine land-based aircraft would have much greater range than assumed. At the same time, unknown to nearly all those heading south, the Ministry's specialists in naval above-surface warfare had serious doubts about the efficacy of their air defences.

Second Phase: the Maritime Battle

The Liberation of South Georgia: Operation 'Paraquet'[32]
The British government decided early on that the retaking of South Georgia should occur before the Falklands. Although South Georgia was over 800 nautical miles from the Falklands, and very cold, once captured it could act as a support base and rendezvous for Task Force vessels; it was certainly much closer

than Ascension which was 3,400 nautical miles from the Islands. Its capture had a political purpose in providing a possible bargaining chip if nothing else could be achieved; it also had the advantage of providing activity whilst waiting for the main Task Force to enter the South Atlantic.[33] A small Task Group was therefore detached from the Task Force to push ahead and undertake the operation. It was led by Captain Brian Young in HMS *Antrim*, and included the frigates *Brilliant* and *Plymouth*, the Ice Patrol Ship *Endurance* and the Royal Fleet Auxiliary tanker *Tidespring*, which had two valuable Wessex helicopters to supplement the single such machine on *Antrim*, and was also the troop transport for the operation with 200 Royal Marines on board. The attempt to land special forces on the Fortuna Glacier on South Georgia was aborted due to the appalling weather. The mission to bring back the SAS party went horribly wrong when one of the three Wessexes sent to pick up the personnel crashed on take-off from the glacier. Luckily, no one was severely injured, and the crew and passengers were transferred to the other helicopters. Then a second Wessex crashed whilst flying at low-level over the glacier in poor visibility. The last remaining Wessex was overloaded with personnel so had to return to the Task Group, unload its human cargo and return to the glacier to pick up the personnel from the two helicopters and their erstwhile passengers. This was successfully done despite the snowstorm around them and the overloaded last Wessex returned to *Antrim*. No one died, but the extraction had almost turned into a disaster, and the assault force had lost two-thirds of its medium helicopters.[34]

The Argentine submarine *Sante Fe* had been operating around South Georgia. She was spotted on the surface by the Group's Wessex helicopter near the entrance to Stromness Bay after a signal from the submarine had been detected by HMS *Plymouth* and helicopters from *Antrim* and *Brilliant* had been launched to find the target. The Wessex that arrived first was armed with relatively old-fashioned aerial depth charges and these were dropped on and around the submarine at a low depth setting, which damaged the submarine's fuel tanks making it impossible for her to dive. Her commander therefore decided to make for the pier at Grytviken on the surface. Very soon, the Wessex was supplemented by the Wasp helicopters from *Plymouth* and *Endurance*, as well as the better-armed Lynx from *Brilliant*. The *Sante Fe* eventually reached the pier but by now she was on fire and listing having been repeatedly strafed by the small force of helicopters and hit with one AS12 air-launched anti-ship missile.[35] The actual assault on South Georgia had been planned to take place some days later, and *Tidespring* with her troops aboard had been held back 200 miles from the island. However, Captain Young thought that the shock and effectiveness of the attack on the *Sante Fe* provided him with a window of opportunity during the confusion to launch a coup de main on Grytviken and overwhelm the small garrison before it had the chance to strengthen its defence. A hastily gathered force of SAS and marines who were on *Antrim*, *Brilliant*, *Plymouth* and *Endurance* was therefore put together and an assault rapidly mounted that made use of the surviving Wessex, along with the Wasp and Lynx helicopters. The first wave of only twenty-four troops were landed in one mini-helicopter assault whilst naval gunfire support from *Antrim* and *Plymouth* forced the defenders to stay undercover. The assault force ran through a minefield to reach the Argentine garrison which, demoralised and overwhelmed, promptly surrendered. The second small Argentine force, at the settlement of Leith, also surrendered on hearing of the action at Grytviken.[36] The British had managed to retake South Georgia more quickly and with greater economy of force than expected due to the commanders' ability to use their initiative and take advantage of a favourable situation at short-notice. They had also managed to destroy one-third of the Argentine Navy's active submarine force. Despite its near-disastrous beginning, if the rest of the campaign was conducted with the aggression and elan that had been shown in the final parts of the South Georgia operation, then it must have seemed that victory was now possible.

From the Creation of the Total Exclusion Zone to the Sinking of the Belgrano
To both geographically limit any potential conflict and add clarity as to where civil shipping and aviation might be in danger from attack, the British government declared a Maritime Exclusion Zone, a 200-mile circle drawn from the centre of the Falkland Islands, from midnight on 12/13 April. All Argentine military vessels or aircraft within the zone would be treated as hostile, civilian Argentine vessels and aircraft would be regarded as there to supply Argentine forces, whilst vessels and aircraft of other countries should expect to have Royal Navy ships or aircraft taking all appropriate measures to ensure that they did not supply Argentine forces.[37] When it came to the point where the Task Force was about to enter the Zone, it was decided to strengthen its applicability. From 30 April, in the Zone – which was renamed a Total Exclusion Zone ('TEZ') – any civilian vessel or aircraft would be treated in the same way as an Argentine military vessel or aircraft. Any such vessel or aircraft would 'therefore be regarded as hostile and liable to be attacked by British forces.' In addition, Stanley airfield was regarded as having closed, and as a result any aircraft, civil or military, on the ground there would be regarded as operating in support of the occupation and thus liable to be attacked. Finally, as a way to make clear that Argentine warships and aircraft were at risk outside the TEZ, it was stated publicly that any of their ships or aircraft that approached Royal Navy vessels outside the Zone would be treated as threats and would be 'dealt with accordingly'.[38]

The nuclear submarines had been in the region for some time, with HMS *Splendid* given permission to attack the Argentine carrier *25 de Mayo* if she operated within the submarine's patrol area north of 35 degrees latitude and west of 48 degrees longitude, a large target zone that extended far beyond the TEZ. However, inaccurate intelligence directed *Splendid* south and away from the Argentine carrier group, which was north north-west of the Falklands.[39] The two carrier groups at one point appeared poised to fight the first carrier-on-carrier engagement since the Second World War. Argentine reconnaissance aircraft made sporadic contact with the British Task Force, but these were either fleeting or occurred too late in the day as the Argentine carrier's US-built Skyhawk A4Q strike aircraft lacked a night-fighting capability. During the night an Argentine Tracker was intercepted by a Sea Harrier on reconnaissance patrol and led the British aircraft to the Argentine carrier force. One of the Argentine Navy's Type 42 destroyers locked its Sea Dart tracking radars onto the aircraft which promptly retreated out of range. However, the British Harrier force did not have anti-ship missiles (procuring Sea Eagle for the Harriers having been abandoned in the Defence Review), and attacking with freefall bombs would have probably resulted in unacceptable numbers of losses, so no air attack was ordered.[40] The Royal Navy's main anti-ship capability therefore remained the nuclear submarine. The Task Force expected an Argentine air attack from the carrier force for the next few days, but none came as locating the British ships remained a problem for the Argentines.

On the same day that the Task Force entered the TEZ, an attack by RAF Vulcan bombers was made on the airfield at Stanley, which was followed up by attacks by Harriers armed with free fall bombs, and shore bombardment by *Glamorgan*, *Alacrity* and *Arrow*. The Vulcan raid, which was undertaken from a high altitude to avoid Argentine air defences, managed one hit on the runway, whilst the Harrier raids did manage to damage ground infrastructure.[41] The runway was not out of action for long, and a number of other attacks on the airfield over the conflict would be made, but none would succeed in hitting the runway again. Stanley airfield was of limited use to the Argentines: it lacked sufficient hard standings and infrastructure, and suffered from considerable cross winds which made it an unlikely operating base for Argentine fast jets, but it could be used for landing supplies and for emergency landings.[42] Although of limited direct success and controversial in the 40 years since the conflict, the Vulcan attack, which had been fully supported by all the Chiefs of Staff including the First Sea Lord, did demonstrate that a long-range bombing capability could be used by the British. It was a useful reminder to the Argentines that other targets – perhaps on the Argentine mainland – could be attacked if necessary, therefore guarding against any Argentine attempt at conflict escalation by attacking British forces, assets or citizens beyond the

TEZ. The shore bombardment by the three British warships resulted in attacks from Argentine Daggers (Israeli variants of the French Mirage but with limited avionics) causing some near misses and strafing of the three British warships. A second wave of these aircraft was intercepted by Sea Harriers on combat air patrol ('CAP') and one Dagger was destroyed.[43]

Whilst these attacks were underway, two Task Force frigates, *Brilliant* and *Yarmouth*, had been sent out from the Task Force to investigate a submarine contact. That submarine was *San Luis*, which attempted to attack the frigates but whose torpedo launch system malfunctioned at the critical moment. The frigates and their helicopters then spent a frustrating few hours hunting the *San Luis*. They came closer than they thought to destroying the submarine: one helicopter fired a torpedo that just missed the enemy boat, but after sitting on the bottom for many hours in an area littered with old wrecks, the Argentine submarine escaped.[44] Two waves of Argentine Canberras (medium bombers of 1950s British vintage) also attempted to find and attack the two frigates. The first did not press home their attack, whilst the second was set upon by the Sea Harrier CAP, with one aircraft being destroyed.[45]

The first day of fighting between the British Task Force and Argentine forces had included long-range and short-range bombing, shore bombardment, air on air engagements, air to sea engagements, as well as a potential carrier-on-carrier battle and an attempted submarine attack. It was also important in setting the tenor for the rest of the conflict: Argentine air losses were sufficient to persuade their air command to limit the use of their aircraft and hold them back for the decisive battles, whilst the Sea Harrier had gained an instant reputation as an effective interceptor (but a much less effective bomber).

Meanwhile, the British submarine force had been deployed north and south of the islands to track and potentially intercept three Argentine naval task groups that were attempting a form of 'pincer movement' against the Task Force. To the south was a group led by the former US cruiser *General Belgrano*, to the north was the *25 de Mayo* group and the third group consisting of corvettes was operating to the north of the *25 de Mayo*. *Splendid* had still not regained contact with the *25 de Mayo* group, but *Conqueror* had been trailing the *Belgrano* group for more than 24 hours. The Argentine Navy clearly lacked experience in dealing with submarines, especially nuclear boats: no ships in the group had been using their sonar, and they had not made any use of the Burdwood Bank, an underwater rise which if she had passed or loitered over would have made it extremely difficult for *Conqueror* to continue trailing the cruiser and her escorts. The surface group had been zigzagging: a long-established tactic to confuse submarines as to ships' directions thus making positioning for torpedo release difficult. However, this was well within the ability of the British submarine to counter. Woodward had received intelligence that the Argentine Navy was planning to attack the Task Force on 2 May, so Argentine military intent was now clear. Woodward, knowingly going beyond his authority, ordered *Conqueror* to attack the cruiser. This was immediately countermanded by Northwood, but Woodward's action had highlighted to Fieldhouse, as it was intended to do, that the *General Belgrano* was a clear threat and that an attack on the Argentine fleet would be necessary to deter them from attacking the Task Force.[46] *Conqueror's* commanding officer, Commander Christopher Wreford-Brown, requested permission to fire, and after some deliberation at both the military and governmental levels, this was granted. Not trusting the effectiveness of his Tigerfish torpedoes, Wreford-Brown decided to use modified Mark 8 unguided torpedoes of Second World War vintage. Two from the salvo of three hit the cruiser, one aft causing explosions in the ship's canteen and disabling her generators, the other forward below the ship's 'A' turret. The third hit the bows of an escorting destroyer but did not explode. The *Belgrano* was not at defence watches, her watertight doors had not been shut, and as a result flooding was extensive. The crew abandoned ship and the old cruiser finally sank 45 minutes after being hit. 323 Argentine service personnel died.[47]

Conqueror's attack had demonstrated the power and capability of the nuclear-powered attack submarine: it could track surface ships underwater for long periods of time and use its speed where necessary to keep contact. With an enemy unversed in dealing with such vessels, it was able to approach close enough undetected to launch relatively short-range and elderly torpedoes to devastating effect. The submarine operations to track the Argentine fleet had also shown not only the strengths of the nuclear submarine, but also highlighted some issues: the waters of the South Atlantic were much less familiar to the boats and their crews than the North Atlantic, so knowledge of oceanographic conditions and the use of physical features of the sea was less than in the north. The lack of SOSUS and maritime patrol aircraft also meant that the SSNs were operating outside the familiar 'North Atlantic detection system' that increased their ability to detect and track targets. As will be seen in the next chapter, some boats were not fitted with towed-array, or did not possess sufficient processing capacity for the arrays they did possess, which also hindered detection. Taking these issues into consideration it is even more impressive that the SSNs were able to track the Argentine surface groups as well as they did – the latter's inexperience of nuclear submarine warfare undoubtedly helped the British submariners. The sinking of the *Belgrano* had a crucial strategic deterrent effect: the Argentine Navy would not risk its main surface fleet units in the open seas for the rest of the campaign. Any attacks on the Task Force would now have to be undertaken by land-based aircraft or the two remaining operational submarines.

From the Sheffield Attack to the Launch of Operation 'Sutton'

On 4 May, Argentine maritime patrol aircraft detected the Task Force to the south-east of the Falklands. Two French-built naval Super Etendard strike aircraft, each armed with an Exocet anti-ship cruise missile, were tasked with finding the Task Force based on the patrol aircraft's detection information, and hopefully damage or even sink the aircraft carriers that were at the centre of the British effort to retake the Falklands – in doctrinal jargon, the centre of gravity of the British forces. Over the previous few days the Task Force had been subjected to a number of false alarms, many of which had resulted from passive intercepts by the new UAA-1 electronic warfare system that was fitted to the three Type 42 destroyers, all of which were placed closer to the air threat, and acting as radar pickets in the absence of airborne early warning aircraft. The extreme sensitivity of the UAA-1 system, and a lack of familiarity in its best use, were partly responsible. When yet another alarm was sounded, by HMS *Glasgow* on the picket line, it was dismissed by the air warfare controller in HMS *Invincible*. This time however, it was a genuine attack, the low-flying Etendards 'popping up' briefly to confirm their detection of the Task Force before launching their missile and the aircraft's radars being detected by the UAA-1. There was low cloud cover hindering any chance of visual detection. The operations room in *Glasgow* was still convinced that it was an attack, and when they detected a missile launch they warned other ships and prepared to launch chaff decoys.[48]

Sheffield, the most southerly of the picket ships, was in the process of communicating with its SCOT satellite system which masked the passive detection abilities of its own UAA-1. The ship's anti-air warfare officer was absent from the operations room at the time, and no alert was sounded. One of the two Exocets was now flying towards *Sheffield*, which was not readying herself for action. A few seconds before the missile hit there was a visual sighting, but the stunned bridge team – although they informed the operations room – did not have time to sound a general alert.[49] The missile hit amidships causing major fires in compartments at the centre of the *Sheffield*, with flames spreading partly due to the placing of fuel tanks well above the waterline. The destroyer's fire main had lost pressure, her communication systems failed and although power generation remained in parts of the ship, she was unable to move, fight or combat the fires raging below decks as effectively as she should. The frigates *Yarmouth* and *Arrow* were despatched by *Hermes* to support *Sheffield*, but it was soon decided that the fires could not be put out and the ship was abandoned. After the fires had burnt out she was placed under tow for transfer to Ascension, but holed just above the waterline, she sank in choppy waters on 10 May.[50] Twenty of *Sheffield*'s crew died in the attack. The loss of the *Sheffield* demonstrated that Argentine force were capable of striking a significant blow to the British Task Force, and for the British political leadership and public it was a jolt that confirmed that the conflict would be no walkover and many would die on both sides. There had clearly been failures of readiness in the Task Force, but this was soon dispelled by the attack on *Sheffield*. Her loss was partly the result of a lack of airborne early warning capabilities, the result of policy decisions described in Chapter 11, thus making it necessary to risk an important unit too close to the threat direction. However, the tactical positioning of the Task Force, with all other vessels placed forward of the crucial aircraft carriers, did mean that missiles such as the Exocet would have considerable difficulty reaching high-value units through layers of destroyers, frigates and auxiliaries.

The same day also saw the loss of a Sea Harrier during an attack on Stanley airfield. Given the meagre results from these attacks, and the risk of losing more precious Harriers, the aircraft were now restricted to air defence and interception duties. Two days later two more Sea Harriers were lost in thick fog, probably due to collision.[51] The poor weather prevented Argentine air attacks, but they also enabled Argentine Hercules flights to land at Stanley airfield on 6, 7 and 8 May.[52] The Sea Harrier CAP was unable to intercept the aircraft. The air blockade of the Falklands was therefore distinctly permeable, but when combined with an effective sea blockade, and the Argentine decision to increase the number of troops on the islands without proper logistical support, it was sufficient to ensure that Argentine troops did not receive enough stores to keep them both well supplied and fed during the conflict. Poor distribution of food stores to the troops dug in in the countryside around Stanley made a difficult situation worse.[53]

It was becoming clear to the British that the Argentines were deliberately conserving their aircraft for the crucial battle over the inevitable landings. On 9 May, one of the few times in this period that aircraft were sent out to attack British warships, two Skyhawks collided and were destroyed. It was not known until after the war that this was as a result of an accident, as only two aircraft were in the flight (two others had turned back earlier due to problems refuelling in the air). It is possible that they were manoeuvring to avoid a Sea Dart launch from HMS *Coventry*, which was operating north of the Falklands alongside HMS *Broadsword*, but the crash site of one of the aircraft was beyond Sea Dart range, which might suggest just an unfortunate accident in poor weather.[54] The two warships were acting as a 'missile trap' with the role of enticing Argentine aircraft out to attack them, but using their medium-range Sea Dart and short-range Sea Wolf in a '42/22 combo' to defend themselves and destroy attacking aircraft. Given the lack of short-range 'point defence' on board the Type 42s this was one of the few ways that these vital air defence ships could be defended if attacked directly.

On 12 May, three waves of Skyhawks attacked *Glasgow* and *Brilliant* whilst they were on duty north of the Falklands in the 42/22 combo role. In the first wave of four aircraft, despite faults with *Glasgow*'s Sea Dart, two were destroyed by *Brilliant*'s Sea Wolf missiles and a third whilst attempting to evade either missiles or aircraft debris. The second wave had more success: *Glasgow*'s Sea Dart was still not working, whilst weaving manoeuvres by the approaching Skyhawks confused *Brilliant*'s missile system computer which was designed to deal with straight running anti-ship missiles. The system was not shifted to the manual mode, allowing for operator visual targeting, until it was too late. One 1,000lb bomb passed into *Glasgow*'s engine room 3ft above the waterline, damaging one of her gas turbines and causing fuel leaks. The hole low in the ship's side also resulted in flooding which was contained. *Brilliant* was lucky that a bomb bounced over her and safely into the sea. One of the Skyhawks, the one which had successfully hit *Glasgow*, was lost to friendly fire as it passed too close to Argentine air defences on its return home. *Glasgow* had been seriously damaged and was only capable of operating at reduced speed.[55] On 15 May, after being patched up by *Stena Seaspread*, the Task Force's STUFT repair ship, she spent nine more days on the picket line operating with reduced propulsion, only returning to the United Kingdom for full repairs on 24 May when her last operational Olympus gas turbine looked at risk of seizing up.[56]

In the period prior to the landings at San Carlos on 21 May, there were a number of minor engagements around the Falkland Islands. The fishing trawler *Narwhal*, with an Argentine officer embarked, had been tracking the Task Force and communicating its movements back to the mainland. On 7 May the trawler was attacked by Sea Harriers. She was heavily damaged and later sank. One crew member was killed but the rest survived.[57] The ammunition transport *Isla de los Estados* was destroyed by gunfire from HMS *Alacrity* on the night of 11 May as the frigate undertook a night-time run through Falkland Sound between the two major islands of West and East Falkland.[58] The ship exploded and only two crew members survived. On the 16th two further transports were attacked, this time by Sea Harriers. *Rio Carcarana* was damaged and abandoned by her crew off Port King in Falkland Sound, whilst *Bahia Buen Suceso* was damaged and immobilised in Fox Bay on West Falkland.[59] On 14 May SAS special forces were landed by helicopter on West Falkland at the Pebble Island airstrip. Eleven Argentine aircraft were destroyed or disabled, including six Pucara ground attack aircraft, four Turbo Mentor light aircraft and one Skyvan light transport.[60] The unit was then extracted by helicopter without any casualties.

The Argentine Navy also attempted another torpedo attack by submarine during these operations, with *Alacrity* being targeted by the *San Luis* after she had completed her night-time run through Falkland Sound. *San Luis*' torpedo was probably decoyed by the 'Foxer' towed decoy of HMS *Arrow*, the frigate detached to meet *Alacrity* as she exited the Sound. At the time it had been assumed that the Foxer had been damaged by snagging on submerged rocks near the coast, and it was not until after the conflict that it was confirmed that a torpedo attack had occurred. Both frigates had been entirely oblivious of the Argentine submarine.[61]

On 18 May, the amphibious force, consisting of *Fearless*, *Intrepid*, a number of the logistics landing ships and various STUFT vessels, began to enter the Total Exclusion Zone, and preparations began to ready the amphibious assault force for landings. This involved much cross transfer of troops and equipment amongst vessels. During these cross-decking operations, one Sea King was lost due to a bird strike, resulting in the deaths of twenty-two personnel, many of whom were members of the SAS.[62] Also arriving were the RAF's GR3 Harriers. Originally planned to supplement the Sea Harriers in the air defence role, they would primarily be used in their designed role as ground attack aircraft. On the 18th and 19th the frigates *Antelope* and *Ambuscade* and the Sea Dart destroyer *Exeter* joined the Task Force.[63] The 'Bristol' group would arrive on 23 May, just after the landings, and would include two more Type 21s, three *Leander*s and *Bristol* herself, a ship equipped with important satellite communication systems and which could act if necessary as a flagship should *Hermes* be disabled or sunk.

Before the amphibious force had even entered the Total Exclusion Zone, discussions were under way, both on *Fearless*, the amphibious command ship, and in Northwood, the Task Force command headquarters, about potential landing sites. West Falkland was ruled out quickly: it was closer to Argentina and therefore at greater risk of air attack and it would require another amphibious assault from West to East Falkland. Lafonia, the peninsula in the south-west of East Falkland, was also disliked as it would have given the Argentine defenders a choke point at Darwin and Goose Green. A site close to Stanley was also ruled out early because strong Argentine resistance could not be counted out. The site had to be far enough away to allow the establishment of a safe bridgehead. This left very few options for landings, and when the expertise of Major Ewen Southby-Tailyour – a Royal Marine who had spent much of an earlier posting to the Falklands sailing around the islands – was taken into account, San Carlos was left as the only viable option. By 12 May it was agreed by the Chief of the Defence Staff that the objective should be to retake the Falkland Islands as quickly as possible: a landing that resulted in stasis would leave the Argentines in a better position to negotiate a foothold in the islands. With San Carlos Bay set as the landing site, the detailed planning of the amphibious operation began.[64]

Third Phase: Operation 'Sutton' – the Landings at San Carlos

21 May

In preparation for the landings at San Carlos, special forces had been inserted in the area by helicopter on the night of 18/19 May to observe the planned landing area. In addition, a series of diversionary attacks named Operation 'Tornado' were made at or near Choiseul Sound south of Stanley, with the destroyer *Glamorgan* undertaking shore bombardment, and special forces units landing and firing tracer rounds to simulate a major landing.[65]

The amphibious force for the landings and its transports detached themselves from the Task Force in the late evening of 20 May. They consisted of three waves: the first wave included *Fearless* and the STUFT ferry *Norland*, with 40 Commando, 2 Para and the Brigade headquarters on board, the second wave consisted of *Intrepid* and RFA *Stromness* with 45 Commando and 3 Para on board. The third wave consisted of five logistic landing ships and the STUFT *Europic Ferry* and included logistics, engineers, artillery and land mobile Rapier air defence missile systems. The reserve consisted of 42 Commando on the STUFT liner *Canberra*. They were escorted by a group led by *Antrim* made up of both Type 22 frigates, *Broadsword* and *Brilliant*, the Type 21 *Ardent*, the *Leander* class frigate *Argonaut* and two Type 12 frigates, *Plymouth* and *Yarmouth*.[66]

At 4.40am on the 21st, a larger group of special forces was landed in order to neutralise the small Argentine force at Fanning Head, which commanded the entrance to San Carlos Water. After a fierce firefight, the Argentines retreated to the interior having lost a third of their force: they had been taken completely by surprise. Later in the day, the retreating Argentines did manage to shoot down two British Gazelle helicopters. Both landed in the water and the crew members of the two aircraft were shot at as they swam from the damaged machines. Only one person survived the ordeal.[67] The main landing force was delayed by a few hours due to faulty navigation on HMS *Fearless*.[68] 40 Commando and 2 Para, on landing craft from both *Fearless* and *Intrepid*, landed at San Carlos settlement near the south of San Carlos Water, with 40 Commando securing the settlement and 2 Para advancing to the top of the Sussex Mountains that divided San Carlos from the Argentine garrison at Goose Green. The second wave had two objectives: 3 Para was to secure the small settlement of Port San Carlos in the east of San Carlos Water, whilst 45 Commando was to land at Ajax Bay on the western shore of the Water. The small number of defending troops at Port San Carlos retreated when they saw 3 Para landing, whilst Ajax Bay was also taken unopposed. The third wave of logistics forces landed without any difficulties, and in some cases overtaking elements of the second wave.[69]

The landings were a clear tactical success: opposition around San Carlos had been weak; the Argentine command at Stanley was unaware of what had occurred, having focussed their attention on Choiseul Sound, whilst the garrison at Goose Green was also in the dark, distracted by more diversionary attacks by special forces, supplemented by shore bombardment from HMS *Ardent* which had started after 7.00am. Attempts to send up reconnaissance aircraft to ascertain what was happening, also failed, at least initially. Two Pucaras flew from Goose Green and attempted to attack *Ardent*, but one was shot down by a Stinger fired by special forces and neither had spotted the landing force further up Falkland Sound. A second pair of Pucaras was intercepted by the Sea Harrier CAP and one was destroyed by cannon fire. Neither saw the main landing force. A GR3 Harrier attack on the Argentine helicopter base at Mount Kent destroyed the helicopters there, limiting the ability of the enemy to send in air-mobile troops to attack the growing British bridgehead. One GR3 was lost either to an Argentine Blowpipe missile or to ground fire. It was only when an Aermacchi MB339 sent up from Stanley flew over San Carlos Water from the north that the Argentine command knew for certain that the landings had occurred, and this was at 10.45am, over five hours after the initial landings.[70]

The continued presence of *Ardent* in Falkland Sound during daylight had been enough in itself for orders to be sent out for air attacks against the frigate, even before the main landing had been confirmed. The first attacks were undertaken by six Argentine Daggers. Three aircraft found and attacked *Broadsword* and *Argonaut*, one being shot down by the former's Sea Wolf, but none scored any hits on the two frigates. The other three aircraft were more successful, with one of their bombs hitting *Antrim*, passing through the ship's Sea Slug magazine and coming to rest without exploding. Repairs and bomb defusing meant that *Brilliant* had to take over *Antrim*'s role as forward air controller, despite not being crewed for this role. Five more Daggers followed soon after the first six. Both *Antrim* and *Broadsword* were strafed by cannon fire, the former suffering minor fires and injuries to sailors.[71] The next air attacks occurred two hours later. When two Argentine Air Force Skyhawk A4Bs entered Falkland Sound, one attacked the abandoned *Rio Carcarana* in error and the other attacked *Ardent*. Although its bombs missed the frigate, the aircraft managed to clip the frigate's surveillance radar and knock it 30 degrees out of alignment.[72] Four more Skyhawks followed the first two, but were unfortunate to encounter the Sea Harrier CAP. Two Skyhawks were destroyed by the Harriers' Sidewinders, and the other two jettisoned their bombs and escaped.[73]

The next group of attacks was amongst the most effective of the day. Four Daggers were intercepted by the Sea Harriers, with one being destroyed by a

Sidewinder. The other three pilots thought that their colleague had crashed into the hills, so proceeded to their targets, just as another three Daggers entered Falkland Sound. Both *Broadsword* and *Brilliant* were strafed by cannon fire. The former now had fifteen crew injured and the tracker radar for her aft Sea Wolf damaged. *Brilliant* suffered more damage, with cannon fire damaging cables feeding some of the systems in her operations room.[74] Most of her weapon systems became inoperable, but she was still able to act as forward air controller. Five A4Bs Skyhawks attacked *Argonaut*, which was hit by two bombs. One hit the frigate's propulsion, causing fires and immobilising her, whilst the other entered the forward magazine which caused two Sea Cat missiles to explode, killing two crewmen. Further fires were started as was some flooding. Unable to move, *Argonaut* remained in San Carlos Water for another nine days as her machinery was repaired and bombs defused.[75] A further three Daggers were unlucky to run into the Sea Harrier CAP. All three were destroyed.[76]

Exposed to the south in Falkland Sound, *Ardent* had been the most vulnerable target, and was attacked by six naval Skyhawk A4Qs. The first group of three managed to hit the frigate in the stern with three bombs, but two were intercepted by Sea Harriers after the attack and were destroyed, whilst the third was damaged and although able to make it back home was destroyed in a crash landing (the pilot survived by ejecting). The three bombs destroyed much of the frigate's aft section, including her helicopter and Sea Cat missile system. Flooding combined with fire, resulted in a power failure that disabled the ship's main gun. *Ardent* retreated to the partial cover of Grantham Sound, just as the second group of three naval A4Qs arrived in Falkland Sound. The ship was hit by a further three or four bombs, causing yet more fires and flooding, and killing or injuring many of the damage control team. Fears that the flooding might worsen, resulting in the ship plunging by the stern, caused the ship's commanding officer to order abandon ship. *Ardent* sank the next morning, the first British naval loss in the Battle of San Carlos.[77]

Whilst these air-naval battles were being fought, the amphibious force and its supporting logistics ships were able to unload a significant portion of its stores and equipment. Argentine aircraft had attacked escorts rather than the landing force: if any of the latter had been hit whilst still laden with stores or ammunition, the results could have been serious. In the event, the destroyers and frigates had done what they were meant to do: protect their charges by absorbing most of the attacks and causing attrition on enemy aircraft. One frigate had been lost, and three other ships had been damaged but the forces were ashore. Losses of Argentine aircraft had been heavy. The percentage of aircraft lost within a flight that had encountered the Sea Harrier Combat Air Patrol was extremely high on 21 May: all three aircraft from one flight of

Daggers had been lost in one engagement, as had half of the naval A4Qs that had attacked *Ardent*, and half of a flight of Air Force Skyhawks had also suffered the same fate. For Argentine pilots, a 50/50 (or higher) chance of destruction if engaged by the Combat Air Patrol could not have done anything for morale and a willingness to press home attacks.

22 to 24 May
On 22 May low-lying cloud in Argentina, despite clear skies in the Falklands, had meant that no air attacks were launched and the landing force continued unloading stores and other equipment. An Argentine Boeing 707, drafted in for reconnaissance duties, was targeted by the Sea Darts of HMS *Coventry*, but the blast doors from the hoists to the launcher failed to open due to salt water encrustation on a sensor. Similar shadowing of the 'Bristol' group by a different 707, resulted in a successful launch by HMS *Cardiff*, but the missile failed to destroy the aircraft, exploding nearby.[78] Special forces were also inserted onto East Falkland by the frigates *Brilliant* and *Plymouth* in the evening, whilst the Argentine patrol boat *Rio Iguazu* was attacked and run aground by Sea Harriers and the transport *Monsunnen* was attacked and also run aground by HMS *Yarmouth*.[79]

The 23rd saw a return to Argentine air attacks. The Type 21 frigate HMS *Antelope*, recently arrived in theatre, escorted *Europic Ferry*, *Stromness* and *Norland* back into San Carlos Water for their second unloading of stores, having received them from other supply ships on the 22nd. Sea Harriers intercepted four Argentine transport helicopters carrying military equipment from West Falkland to Goose Green, destroying one and causing two others to land and be abandoned. Lynx helicopters from *Antelope* and *Argonaut* attacked the hulk of the already heavily-battered and abandoned *Rio Carcarana*, proving the effectiveness of the new Sea Skua missile (at least against static targets). The air attacks resumed at around midday. Four Air Force A4s targeted *Antelope*, two bombs hitting the ship but failing to explode and one of the A4s crashing into the sea after clipping the mainmast of the frigate after already having been damaged. Of the three surviving aircraft, two were heavily damaged by gunfire and Rapiers.[80] Four Navy A4Qs then attacked, but by dropping their bombs from a greater height, their chances of hitting ships was going to be low, and they had no success.[81] A Dagger raid that had failed to find ships to attack was intercepted by the CAP, two of its three aircraft jettisoned their bombs and escaped but the third was destroyed by a Sidewinder.[82] Efforts to disarm one of the two bombs on board *Antelope* failed and it exploded, killing the bomb disposal team and eventually sinking the ship, only 24 hours after she had first entered Falklands waters.[83]

Three days after British forces had landed, Argentine air attacks finally began to focus on attacking logistics and amphibious vessels. Showing more co-ordinated and sophisticated tactics, flights approached from multiple directions, including from the south-east over land via Choiseul Sound. Five Skyhawks approached over land and were able to bomb *Sir Lancelot* and *Sir Galahad*, although the bombs did not explode, and *Sir Bedivere* was glanced by another bomb which damaged some of her aerials.[84] They were followed by a flight of Daggers which strafed *Fearless* and *Sir Galahad* and bombed *Sir Lancelot* (again, the bomb did not explode).[85] A second flight of Daggers was intercepted by the CAP, destroying all three aircraft.[86] Three further flights, all made up of Skyhawks, were also unsuccessful. The first aborted as the CAP approached, the second aborted because of the strength of anti-aircraft fire, and the third dropped bombs but missed with one of the aircraft being destroyed, probably by a Blowpipe missile. One of these aircraft, heavily damaged by anti-aircraft fire, was lost on the return flight to Argentina.[87] The British were lucky that the damage to the amphibious vessels had not been more serious; the two logistic landing ships being patched up and soon operational again. If the Argentines had shown this ability to co-ordinate attacks on the 21st or perhaps the 23rd, when the logistics ships were still full, then the impact could have been much greater. The Argentines were adapting to the tactical environment, but doing so too slowly to make enough of a difference to the campaign.

25 May
The next day, which was Argentina's national day, the Navy braced itself for a series of concerted attacks on its shipping. Early engagements that day brought a number of successes for the Task Force: one aircraft of a flight of two A4Bs was engaged and destroyed by *Coventry*'s Sea Dart.[88] A flight of four A4Cs arrived at San Carlos Water but one aircraft was destroyed by either a Rapier or *Yarmouth*'s Sea Cat, and another by *Coventry*'s Sea Dart.[89] None of the aircraft had succeeded in dropping its bombs. It was now clear to the Argentines that *Coventry*, supported by *Broadsword* as its Sea Wolf-armed 'goalkeeper', which was operating to the north of the islands, was a significant threat to their air operations that day, so a flight of A4Bs was sent to attack the two ships. Aware that *Coventry*'s radars had difficulty dealing with shore 'clutter', the aircraft approached over West Falkland and then Pebble Island, this giving the British warships only a short time to defend themselves. The attackers split into pairs, the first two aircraft approaching too low for Sea Dart to acquire the targets. They dropped their bombs, all of which missed, except one which ricocheted onto *Broadsword*'s flight deck, damaged the ship's helicopter and then bounced into the sea. The CAP had been held back because of fears that they would risk a friendly-fire incident with *Coventry*'s Sea Dart. The second attack was much more successful: again, Sea Dart could not

acquire a target and neither this time could Sea Wolf as whilst manoeuvring *Coventry* had blocked *Broadsword*'s line of sight. Three bombs hit *Coventry*, two of which knocked holes in the ship's bottom, causing her to flood rapidly and lose stability. The bombs also started fires amidships. The crew abandoned ship as she began to heel, and it sank 15 minutes later. Nineteen crew died. Another Type 42 destroyer had been taken out of action.[90]

Soon after this attack two Argentine Super Etendards approached the Task Force from the north, each one carrying an Exocet missile. This time, when both aircraft 'popped up' to confirm the location of the Task Force, they were detected by the destroyer *Exeter* and the frigate *Ambuscade*. The pilots launched their missiles flying low at 26 nautical miles, before *Exeter*'s Sea Dart was able to acquire a target, and turned for home. *Ambuscade* fired 'chaff' decoys which lured both missiles away from the two warships. Once they had flown through the chaff cloud they were then presented with a new large target, the *Atlantic Conveyor*, a container ship taken up from trade as an aircraft transport and stores vessel. Lacking any form of defence, including chaff decoys, the *Atlantic Conveyor* had no way of protecting herself. One of the Exocets (and probably the other as well) flew into the container ship and exploded, causing major fires that rapidly spread across the ship as it lacked the sub-divisions and firefighting capabilities of a warship. Once it became clear that the ammunition on board the ship was in danger of being consumed by the fires, the ship was abandoned. Twelve of the personnel on board, including the ship's master, died. The burnt-out hulk eventually sank a few days later.[91]

The Super Etendard pilots had undoubtably been trying to sink one of the carriers, but instead they had destroyed a ship that was the most important British naval loss of the campaign. *Atlantic Conveyor* was carrying three Chinook heavy lift helicopters and six Wessex medium helicopters, as well as the equipment for a shore-based Harrier and helicopter airfield, and various essential stores and equipment for the land campaign. The land force would no longer be able to fly most of its equipment and personnel across East Falkland to the Argentine garrisons guarding the approaches to Stanley, but would have to proceed on foot across moors and bogs before facing the Argentine forces' main defences. However, the Argentines only had one of their five air-launched Exocet missiles left, and they had still failed to damage either of the British capital ships.

Fourth Phase: supporting the Land Campaign

From San Carlos to Teal Inlet
After the 25th, the quantity of Argentine air attacks reduced. Air attacks on land forces on the 27th hit an arms dump at Ajax Bay, whilst unexploded

bombs caused the field hospital there to be temporarily evacuated. San Carlos settlement was attacked, killing five and injuring twenty more. One Skyhawk A4B was destroyed by anti-aircraft fire in this last raid.[92] On 28 May *Argonaut* was finally able to leave San Carlos Water, her propulsion repaired and unexploded bombs made safe and removed. *Sir Lancelot's* unexploded bomb was also made safe the same day. On the 29th the tanker *British Wye*, which was ferrying oil to the Task Force, was attacked by an Argentine Hercules carrying 500lb bombs 400 miles north of South Georgia and 1,000 miles from the nearest Argentine air bases. The Hercules' range had been increased by the addition of internal fuel tanks in the transport aircraft's cargo bay, which also allowed bombs to be placed on external racks normally reserved for fuel tanks. The bombs either missed or bounced off the tanker's hull, but the ship had been defenceless against the only aircraft that could be sent such long-ranges in an attempt to interdict British supply lines. A second attack was attempted two days later on the Royal Fleet Auxiliary *Fort Grange*, but was aborted when it was seen that the vessel was painted grey and presumed to be a warship.[93] Argentina possessed a limited number of Hercules aircraft, which were also being used both to fly supply runs to the Falklands and refuel aircraft, so few aircraft could be spared for such attacks. In response British supply vessels were routed further east. As the Argentine Hercules could theoretically reach South Georgia at their maximum range, the damaged HMS *Antrim* was allocated as South Georgia guardship.[94]

Much later in the campaign, on 8 June, a further attack would be made on a tanker. Unfortunately for the Argentines and the ship's crew, the MV *Hercules* was totally unconnected to the Task Force or to the United Kingdom in any way. It was also outside both the TEZ and the Argentine equivalent which extended 200nm out from its coast. The Liberian-registered tanker was hit by one bomb which did not explode. The vessel sailed to Rio de Janeiro where it was anchored and its Italian crew removed. The ship was eventually scuttled by its US owners, after removal of the unexploded bomb was considered to be too hazardous.[95]

On 30 May, in a rare instance of the Argentine Air Force and Naval Air Arm co-operating, a last Super Etendard Exocet attack was made, accompanied by Skyhawk A4Cs which were meant to follow up the Exocet launch with a bombing attack. This time the attackers approached from the south using two air-to-air refuelling aircraft to reach south of the Task Force. The aircraft were detected by *Exeter*. The nearest ship was the frigate *Avenger*. The sole Exocet-carrying aircraft launched its missile at a target between the two ships – certainly not one of the carriers which were many miles to the north-east – which might have been a chaff cloud put up by *Avenger*. The Exocet either crashed into the sea or was destroyed by *Exeter*'s Sea Dart (the crew of *Avenger* were certain that it had been destroyed by one of the ship's 4.5in shells), and the four A4Cs then flew behind, aiming to undertake a follow-up bombing attack. Although the surviving pilots swore that they had found the carrier *Invincible*, it was in fact *Avenger*. One of the A4Cs was destroyed by a Sea Dart and a second either by small arms fire from *Avenger* or debris from the first A4C. Bombs were dropped but they missed the frigate. The last Argentine air-launched Exocet had been expended, and the chances of damaging or destroying one of the carriers was now vanishingly small.[96]

Towards the end of May the second group of land forces arrived in the TEZ, having sailed south in the liner *Queen Elizabeth*. They trans-shipped to *Norland*, *Fearless* and *Canberra* at South Georgia and were landed with their equipment at San Carlos between 31 May and 2 June. These forces made up 5th Infantry Brigade and included 1st Bn Gurkhas, 1st Bn Welsh Guards, 2nd Bn Scots Guards, and artillery, Army Air Corps and RAF Regiment units. Also arriving in the South Atlantic was Major General Jeremy Moore and his staff, who took operational control of the land campaign from the 30th and command the break-out from the bridgehead.[97] Before Moore's arrival, the attack on the Argentine Goose Green garrison had been made on 28 May, whilst special forces were placed at Teal Inlet on the north coast of East Falkland, which had been selected as a halfway point for the transit across the island.[98] The first groups of infantry had also set off for Teal Inlet, with 3 Para arriving on 29 May with 45 Cdo following a day later.[99] The RAF GR3 Harriers began to be used more frequently in ground attack roles once the bridgehead had been established, supporting the attack on Goose Green, and the SAS at Mount Kent. Two GR3s were lost in these operations but their pilots were rescued.[100] Sea Harriers undertook two bombing raids on Stanley airfield but with little to show for their efforts. A number of repeat Vulcan raids were also undertaken, but again having no success in hitting the runway even though they had used valuable air-to-air refuelling capabilities and runway time at Ascension.[101] Shore bombardment by Task Force ships became a regular duty, with major bombardment of Argentine positions near Stanley and other areas on the night of 27/28 May and on 30 May. Between 1 and 6 June a number of night-time shore bombardments were undertaken in the area near Teal Inlet, Stanley, Pebble Island, Fox Bay, Port Howard, Port Fitzroy and Mount Harriet.[102]

Raids on ground targets by Argentine Canberra bombers in the first days of June achieved little success but an air-transport Hercules, undertaking an ill-advised reconnaissance mission to the north of Falkland Sound, was destroyed by Sea Harriers on 1 June, and on the same day a Sea Harrier was downed by Argentine air defences around Stanley.[103] Five days later, a makeshift refuelling base for helicopters and Harriers was set up near San Carlos, giving both additional range to British aircraft and a safe place for emergency landings. June 6th saw a tragic 'blue-on-blue' incident when HMS *Cardiff* shot down an Army Gazelle helicopter with Sea Dart.[104]

From Fitzroy to the Surrender
By 6 June, British land forces were beginning to position themselves for the assault on the hills leading to Stanley in the east of East Falkland. To supplement the advance by 3 Cdo Brigade from Teal Inlet it was planned that 5th Infantry Brigade would join 2 Para at Fitzroy to add a southern thrust to the British advance. Unable to proceed to Fitzroy over land due to the amount of equipment they had to take with them, the Welsh and Scots Guards could only be taken there by ship, in the absence of sufficient helicopter or vehicle transport.[105] *Fearless* was sent to Fitzroy with the Welsh Guards on board, but a lack of landing craft on arrival meant that only two companies could be sent ashore before daylight. The remaining two companies were sent to Fitzroy on RFA *Sir Galahad* instead, and on the evening of the 7th *Sir Galahad* arrived at Fitzroy. However, the Welsh Guards on board, not aware of the danger of being in such a vessel in daylight and lacking sufficient landing craft to offload rapidly, had wanted to be unloaded at Bluff Cove 16 miles away where the rest of the Welsh Guards were stationed. Communications concerning *Sir Galahad*'s movements were poor, and those at Fitzroy had not been expecting her and her two companies of soldiers. Only a single landing craft was available to do this. Disembarkation from Fitzroy to Bluff Cove by landing craft took far too long: the field ambulance unit on board was offloaded first, and a broken ramp on the landing craft slowed proceedings down further. It was now daylight and the logistic landing ship was dangerously exposed, as was her sister ship *Sir Tristram* which was nearby offloading stores.[106]

Argentine observers on the hills nearby warned their air command about the presence of the two landing ships in daylight, and as a result air attacks were planned on the two ships at Fitzroy. The Argentines were particularly fortunate that day: *Hermes* was stationed further to the east than usual to allow her to clean her boilers in relative safety. It was assumed that *Invincible*'s aircraft, in concert with the new vertical take-off strip at San Carlos, would be able to sustain a CAP over the area. However, the strip was put out of action by a damaged GR3 Harrier that could not be moved, and as a result the CAP was deficient just as an Argentine air attack was approaching. In addition, for the first time since the landings a British frigate had been risked in daylight outside the air defences of San Carlos: HMS *Plymouth* had been detached to undertake shore bombardment of Mount Rosalie on West Falkland. Eight Skyhawks and six Daggers were sent to attack the two landing ships. Three of the former and one of the latter had to return home due to technical difficulties, an increasing problem with Argentine aircraft. The remaining Daggers approached first, and finding *Plymouth*, they attacked her successfully hitting her with four bombs. Incredibly, none caused serious damage. One passed through the ship's funnel, two more landed near the ship's anti-submarine mortar aft but failed to explode, and the last also hit aft, bouncing off a depth charge stowed on the flight deck before falling into the sea. The depth charge exploded and caused fires which took some time to put out. *Plymouth* steamed at speed to the protection of air defences in San Carlos Water.[107]

Meanwhile, the Skyhawks had found Fitzroy and attacked *Sir Galahad* and *Sir Tristram*. The former was hit by two or three bombs and the latter by two.[108] In *Sir Galahad*, ammunition waiting to be unloaded exploded as fires broke out below decks. The two companies of Welsh Guards awaiting to disembark were caught in this inferno below decks and thirty-nine were killed, as were another four Army personnel and seven RFA crew. The ship was eventually abandoned after it became impossible to fight the raging fires. *Sir Tristram* also suffered from fires, particularly in her aft section. Fears that the ammunition on board would explode resulted in the decision to abandon her, but in the event the fires burnt themselves out and the heavily damaged ship was eventually transported back to the United Kingdom and repaired. Two further flights of Skyhawks were sent over Fitzroy and Bluff Cove in the afternoon, the first caused no damage, but the second flight found the utility landing craft *F4* and sank it killing six men on board. This time the CAP was able to get to the aircraft, destroying three with the fourth returning home heavily damaged.[109] The tragedy at Fitzroy should have been avoided, but a botched transfer of troops by sea, poor communications, an unwillingness to disembark from a vulnerable ship during daylight by troops unused to amphibious operations, and a certain amount of complacency after a number of days' lull in air attacks, all contributed to the disaster. Finally, the question of whether battalions of the Welsh (and Scots) Guards were the right units to send to the South Atlantic, given their lower level of training, should also be included any balance sheet of responsibility for the human and material losses.[110]

After the attack at Fitzroy, it was clear that the tempo of Argentine air attacks was slowing. The air attacks that did occur were largely focussed on the logistics area at San Carlos or on land forces. Aircraft serviceability was increasingly becoming a problem. One Canberra aircraft was destroyed by a Sea Dart fired by HMS *Cardiff* on 12 June, two days before the end of hostilities and the last Argentine aircraft destroyed in conflict.[111] All other attacks, by Daggers, Canberras and Skyhawks, failed either to reach their targets, successfully release their bombs, or hit any militarily significant targets, with the exception of one attack by A4B Skyhawks on British positions on Mount Kent. The bombs landed at 3 Commando Brigade's HQ just as an

'O Group' meeting was finishing. Three helicopters were damaged but the peaty soil prevented much additional damage. If some of the bombs had landed closer to the site of the briefing, much of the land force's leadership could have killed or injured.[112]

As land forces neared Stanley and began the land assault across the hills and ridges leading to the capital, naval gunfire support duties became the main front-line operational activity for the Task Force. The older frigate *Yarmouth* and the newer Type 21s *Active*, *Ambuscade*, *Arrow* and *Avenger*, undertook a number of bombardments between the 8th and the 13th, as did the large destroyer *Glamorgan*. One of these bombardments resulted in the death of three Falklands civilians as a result of a stray shell landing in a house in a residential area of Stanley.[113] From 28 May, when *Avenger* had been near-missed by an Exocet launched from land whilst undertaking naval gunfire support operations, an 'Exocet box' had been established to the south of Stanley: covering any area within Exocet range of the concrete coastal roads in the south-east of East Falkland. All ships of the Task Force were instructed to keep clear of the 'box' at all times. These missiles had been taken off Argentine warships and placed on trailers which allowed them to be towed to different sites where concrete roads existed – luckily for the British there were few of these, as most of the road surfaces on the Falklands were dirt or gravel. After conducting shore bombardment duties on the night of the 11th, *Glamorgan* had clipped the edge of the Exocet box, and the Argentines duly fired a missile at the 'County' class destroyer. *Glamorgan* turned towards the threat in order to present the smallest possible radar picture, and the heel resulting from her rapid turn resulted in the missile hitting the ship obliquely above the mass of the hull, skidding off the ship's deck and exploding in the hangar. The resulting fires were serious, and at one point the ship's stability was threatened by large amount of firefighting water trapped high on upper decks, but it could have been much worse for the ship if the missile had hit one deck lower and exploded in the destroyer's large Sea Slug missile assembly area. Thirteen crew members died in the attack, most of whom were in the hangar at the time. The ship, aside from the loss of her helicopter and one Sea Cat launcher, was still operational and removed itself at speed back to the protection of the Task Force.[114]

Two days later, HMS *Penelope* was subject to a mysterious missile attack whilst she was escorting the STUFT *Nordic Ferry* near Fitzroy. It has never been clearly ascertained what the missile was: it did not have its own internal radar as none was detected by the frigate, so could not have been an Exocet. The missile splashed into the water, possibly downed by *Penelope*'s air defences. The missile might have been fired from a Canberra (a number of which were flying over East Falkland at the time) or possibly a hand-held missile launched on land.[115] Aside from GR3 Harrier ground attack missions and further naval gunfire support by gun-armed frigates in support of land forces, these were the last significant operations involving maritime forces in the conflict. The final land assault on Stanley involved a series of hard-fought battles across the ridges to the west of the capital, led by the Royal Marines and the Paras. On 14 June, Argentine forces surrendered as British land forces overwhelmed the last Argentine defences in the hills above Stanley.

Fifth Phase: after the Surrender

Although General Menendez, the Argentine commander on the Falklands, surrendered his forces on 14 June, he could not guarantee that the threat to the Falklands was over, as he did not have command of, or responsibility for, mainland Argentine forces including the Air Force and Navy. This meant that a threat to British forces remained – a last-gasp revenge attack was not out of the question – so a significant contingent of the Task Force had to remain in place. Meanwhile, the surrender of other sections of the Argentine garrison had to be organised. HMS *Intrepid*, with 40 Commando on board, and HMS *Cardiff* were sent to Port Howard to organise the surrender of the Argentine garrison there, whilst HMS *Avenger* was sent to organise the surrender of the Argentines at Fox Bay. The *Canberra* and *Norland*, along with *Intrepid*, were allocated to lead the repatriation of Argentine prisoners of war, and the Argentine government belatedly agreed to this on 18 June. At the same time, efforts were made to provide aid and relief and restore normal conditions for the islanders. The clearance of sea mines began on 21 June by the stern-trawler minesweepers, whilst the building of a Harrier strip was begun near Stanley runway. Once complete, it was assumed that one carrier, the *Hermes*, could then depart for home. Amongst the ships to return home first were those that had sailed from Gibraltar with Admiral Woodward in early April: *Glamorgan*, *Plymouth* and *Arrow*. The first two were still showing their battle damage, and the last had been suffering from hull cracks from the unforgiving seas of the South Atlantic. It was planned that the ships of the 'Bristol' group would remain until July, when they would be relieved by the ships of the 'Southampton' group. *Invincible* would remain until late August, when she would be relieved by her sister ship HMS *Illustrious*, which had been hurried through the final months of her construction and trials to allow her to head south.[116]

The uninhabited islands of Southern Thule, located 450 miles to the southeast of South Georgia, had been occupied by the Argentines since 1976. The garrison was thought to be over 100 strong, three-quarters of whom were military personnel. It was also believed that resistance was unlikely. HMS *Yarmouth* and RFA *Olmeda* left South Georgia on 17 June with two troops of 42 Cdo on board, and supported by *Endurance* and the tug *Salvageman*, they arrived on 20 June to undertake Operation 'Keyhole'. The force had planned to radio the garrison to surrender, but in the driving snow and poor weather, they could not be reached. *Endurance* approached within half a mile of the main settlement, and a white flag was seen, and the few Argentines left in the garrison surrendered without any resistance, having earlier thrown their weapons and equipment into the sea.[117]

Longer term assessments for naval forces in the Falklands began to be made. The 'Southampton' group would be succeeded by another force of six destroyers and frigates, which would be replaced by another such group two months later, and so on. The average length of deployment was five months.[118] As later groups succeeded earlier ships, there was time to include various modifications taking account of lessons from the Falklands. These included the fitting of additional 20mm and 30mm guns (which were initially swapped between ships returning and those heading south), improvements to Sea Dart and UAA-1 modifications, the installation of a 'walkaboard' version of the Lamberton digital secure speech system, the replacing of wooden and aluminium ladders with steel equivalents and the fitting of larger escape hatches.[119] This significant force, as well as a bolstered garrison and a military-capable airfield, would not come cheap. By September Nott was expressing scepticism about the need for a force of six destroyers and frigates, but it remained at or near this level until at least the first months of 1984.[120] Negotiations with the Treasury allowed additional sums to be added to the defence budget to cover the defence of the Falklands for three years. £400 million was added to the budget in 1983–4, £300 million the following year and £200 million the year after. From this point onwards, it was assumed that the Falklands garrison and its ships would be supported within the normal Ministry of Defence budget without any Treasury additions.[121]

With the final departure of the last aircraft carrier after Stanley airfield had been re-opened in November 1982 and the first RAF Phantoms had flown down to the South Atlantic,[122] there still remained the issue of providing anti-submarine helicopters to help defend the ships operating near the Falklands from submarine attack. Flying from Stanley airfield would not give such helicopters the range to protect the warships operating offshore, whilst flying Sea Kings from Royal Fleet Auxiliaries would only provide a partial answer, as the planned force involved the presence of helicopter-capable RFAs only part of the time. The only full-time RFA would be one of the small 'Rover' class tankers which had flight decks but no hangars for helicopters. As a result, innovative solutions were sought to provide a cost-effective anti-submarine helicopter capability.

Since the late 1970s, both the Royal Navy and US Navy had been fitfully investigating the use of merchant vessels as helicopter platforms to help with convoy defence. By 1978 some US Department of Defense money had been released to undertake a demonstrator programme, and regular liaison was established with the US over progress on trials. When the two assault ships had been formerly reprieved from disposal in early March 1982, discussions began concerning the use of such vessels to support amphibious operations as well.[123] The ARAPAHO system, which had been developed in the US, involved fitting a number of pre-fitted containers and other units to create landing pads, hangars, maintenance facilities and additional accommodation. It had been considered for those ships taken up from trade as aircraft transports in the conflict, but instead a more ad hoc process was used on the initial assumption that it would be quicker and cheaper. It was later discovered that this approach had been in fact much slower to use and required more dockyard intervention to both install and remove.[124] As a result, after the conflict had ended, an ARAPAHO-equipped container ship was considered as a means to provide up to five anti-submarine Sea King helicopters to support ships in the Falklands patrol role, especially when RFAs with helicopter hangars were not available.[125] The first sea trials of the ARAPAHO system were undertaken in September 1982.[126] It was decided to lease the system for 18 months rather than purchase it outright, and the lease was signed on April 1983 at a cost of $32,000 per month (the lease was later extended by another 18 months).[127] The container ship MV *Astronomer* was leased as the ARAPAHO platform, and crewed by RFA personnel with a naval party to support flying operations and self-defence. The ship, named RFA *Reliant*, was converted at Cammell Laird shipbuilders and arrived in the South Atlantic in February 1984.[128] Another RFA vessel permanently operating in the South Atlantic was RFA *Diligence*, the former *Stena Inspector*, in the repair and maintenance role previously undertaken by *Stena Seaspread*.[129]

In assessing the needs for local patrol vessels in the Falklands over the next ten years, a number of options were considered. The vessels were required urgently, as the alternative would be using an additional frigate for a task much more suited to cheaper and smaller vessels. The requirements for seakeeping were challenging: the ship would have to be able to conduct operations in the coastal waters of the Falklands all year round, cope with rapid changes in sea state (from force 2 to force 8 in less than four hours) and the ability to operate in at least sea state 6 in waters close to rocks, shoals and beaches. Possible solutions included re-purposing mine warfare vessels, using offshore patrol vessels, 'Bird' class patrol vessels, RMAS vessels, the new Hong Kong patrol craft (which were being constructed at the time), or ships taken up from trade. After much discussion, it was decided to charter three oil rig support ships as an interim solution and then build two further 'Castle' class offshore patrol vessels for the long-term patrol task. There had been concerns about using the existing two 'Castle' class ships as they had been 75 per cent funded by the Ministry of Agriculture, Fisheries and Food ('MAFF') and that ministry would understandably would not wish that these vessels be deployed away from domestic fishery protection.[130] Three oil rig support ships were therefore purchased from Seaforth in March 1983, and they were commissioned as HM Ships *Protector*, *Guardian* and *Sentinel*, serving until the autumn of 1986 when they were replaced by the two original 'Castle' class offshore patrol vessels operating in rotation; the earlier objections of MAFF having been overcome.[131]

Over the 1980s, the size of the main Falklands force of destroyers and frigates gradually began to shrink as Argentina was perceived to be less of a threat, and land-based capabilities were built up on the islands. By June 1984, the number of destroyers and frigates on station was reduced from four to three, then down to two by January 1986. *Reliant* left the Falklands in April 1986, followed a few months later by the three patrol vessels. The first 'Castle' class arrived in November 1986, the same month that the number of destroyers and frigates reduced to only one, whilst RFA *Diligence* was replaced by *Stena Seaspread* on charter in January 1987. This was still a significant commitment: keeping one frigate on station required others to replace the vessel on roulement, whilst the two 'Castle' class vessels stayed for much more sustained periods with one replacing the other every two years, although their crews were relieved on a much more regular basis.[132] Each frigate would normally be accompanied by one 'Rover' class small tanker, with another tanker and a stores ship making occasional visits.[133]

* * *

The British success in the Falklands conflict would have been impossible without the Royal Navy and its supporting vessels. Despite the focus on Cold War operations in the Eastern Atlantic, the Navy still possessed a significant expeditionary capability, and could create yet more through taking ships up from trade. It was clear that there were important deficiencies in some capabilities such as ship-based air defence, but the performance of these systems had not been as bad as had been feared by ASWE. In the end, the Navy simply possessed more than enough warships to replace losses, local air superiority was sufficient to deter the pressing home of Argentine air attacks, at least after the initial engagements, and the Argentines themselves made some significant operational and tactical errors. British training and morale was also an important factor in ensuring final success. With the conflict over, the Royal Navy now made use the successful outcome to help push for both war replacements and general enhancements to capability that had been shown to be lacking in the South Atlantic.

17

Lessons Learnt

This chapter will focus on the maritime 'lessons-learnt' from the Falklands and their impact on British naval and defence policy in the years that followed. Both during and after the fighting, a significant lessons-learnt process was undertaken within the Ministry of Defence, involving the Central Staffs, and defence scientists as well as each of the three service departments. Some of these lessons were made public, whilst others remained classified but fed into a range of changes across the Ministry and the Royal Navy over the next decade, with their influence still being felt up to and beyond the end of the Cold War. The Falklands conflict was one of the very few times that the British military's equipment, training and support structures were tested during the Cold War, and the only major instance in which this happened during the age of the nuclear submarine, guided missile and electronic warfare. Learning from the conflict would therefore provide valuable information on how a war against the Soviet Union and its allies could be fought and how different equipment could perform. After setting out the way the lessons-learnt process was organised, the chapter will then assess these lessons across a range of subject areas, from command and control and maritime air defence through to logistics and personnel.

The Lessons Learnt Process
Whilst the conflict was still in progress, the very earliest lessons-learnt studies were initiated. Within the Task Force, close analysis of the actions leading up to the loss of HMS *Sheffield* occurred in the days after the attack and their results, although incomplete, helped speed up work already underway respecting electronic countermeasures for Exocet attacks. On 13 May, the Vice Chief of the Naval Staff ordered all parts of the Navy Department and other Navy directorates to start recording any lessons being learnt as the conflict progressed with the aim

of collating them after the fighting had stopped.[1] On the day of the surrender of Argentine forces, the Secretary of State initiated the first post-conflict lessons-learnt exercise by sending a scientific evaluation team to the Falklands to speak to those involved in the conflict. He also set in train a wider range of lessons-learnt analysis, stating that 'it is vital that we use the unique opportunity provided by the Falklands Islands crisis to learn as much as we can about equipment and tactics'.[2] The team consisted of five scientists from different research and development establishments, led by a senior analyst from the Defence Operational Analysis Establishment.[3] Very quickly an RAF representative was added and an RN representative was included at the last minute. The team returned to the United Kingdom on 13 July and produced a summary report a few days later.[4] Its findings were less useful than hoped as many key Task Force members had already returned home, but its analysis of the air campaign at least was relatively thorough.[5] Some of the analysis was 'automatically' generated without having to be commissioned from above: in the Royal Navy, following the completion of any operation or major activity, it was standard practice for the senior naval officer involved to send a 'FORMEX 100', a lessons-learnt document to inform future activities of a similar nature. Admiral Woodward's FORMEX 100 for the Falklands was over an inch thick, made up of twenty-five sections, and was completed only two weeks after the conflict ended.[6] Although its findings were provisional, it then fed into the 'CTF 317 report' compiled by Fieldhouse's staff through the summer and early autumn of 1982, incorporating lessons-learnt from his other Falklands commands, including Flag Officer Submarines and the amphibious force and Royal Marines.[7]

Even at this stage therefore, the lessons-learnt process was rapidly assuming its long-term shape. Studies were commissioned at two levels: at the higher level by the Secretary of State, Chief of the Defence Staff and the Central Staffs; and then at the lower level within the individual service departments. The latter naturally fed into the former, which in turn would provide definitive analyses for possible onward dissemination and feed into the defence planning processes, but the lower-level studies also served their own purposes within the service Departments. In the Navy Department, lessons-learnt analysis was important for improving areas wholly within its responsibility such as personnel policy, training and logistics. It was also in the Navy Department's interests to keep a track of these lessons identified and lobby to ensure that improvements were actually implemented.

Ten days after the Secretary of State's commissioning of the scientists' trip down to the South Atlantic, Admiral Lewin and Frank Cooper, the Permanent Under-Secretary, initiated six studies to be written by the Central Staffs with single-service input. They were to cover operations and logistics, equipment, intelligence, procurement, public relations and finally a study on possible official and staff histories.[8] The Admiralty Board created a Way Ahead Executive Sub-Committee, its standard response to requests for the implementation of complex requirements from above, to manage the submission of materials upwards to the Central Staffs and to commission its own analyses.[9] By August, in addition to work supporting the Central Staffs, a total of eleven naval-specific study areas had been commissioned, ranging from command, control and communications to logistics and naval gunfire support.[10] Through 1982 and 1983 the weight of studies required within the Navy Department resulted in the Operational Evaluation Group ('OEG'), the small team of naval officers in CINCFLEET's staff which took on much of the analytical work for the lessons-learnt process within the Navy, being expanded by the addition of scientists on loan from the Research and Development organisations. The OEG was renamed the Fleet Operational Analysis Staff to reflect its increased size and capabilities.[11]

Aside from the internal Central Staffs studies and the large number of single-service analyses, a number of external reports were commissioned. The most important of these was 'The Falklands: the Lessons' command paper, which was published in December 1982, and drove much of the lessons-learnt work in the first months after the conflict. In addition, friendly powers, not least from the United States and France, wanted information on the performance of equipment and capabilities, as did NATO in Brussels.[12] Analysts from the United States undertook research to produce their own report on lessons-learnt from the Falklands, with an additional separate study of special forces.[13] The main US study was criticised within the Naval Staff for being focussed – perhaps not unsurprisingly – on emphasising aspects that helped the USN fight its battles in the Pentagon. The US report criticised the RN's small carriers, subsonic Harriers and small warships as being less capable and more vulnerable to attack than larger US warships and supersonic carrier aircraft. There was some truth to this, but these conclusions were clearly aimed at forestalling any attempts within the Department of Defense to use the Falklands to push the USN back towards the smaller and cheaper sea control ships and utility escorts that had been developed in the 1970s, and from which the current US naval leadership was attempting to distance itself.[14] The French were particularly interested in the air campaign, to be expected given the involvement of their Super Etendard and Mirage aircraft and Exocet missiles, and received detailed breakdowns of Argentine air losses by different missiles and aircraft.[15] The defence industry was especially keen to find out about how their particular pieces of equipment and systems fared, and the Ministry of Defence organised a series of bespoke notes and classified briefings to each supplier on the performance of its own equipment.[16] Over the longer term, each service department commissioned an internal classified *staff* history written by their own historical branches, whilst work began to commission an external *official* history of the conflict for public and academic use.

Command, Control and Communications

Fieldhouse was clear that command, control and communications ('C3') during the campaign had been 'by any standard ... a success'.[17] The use of 'exclusion zones' around the Falklands by the government, as a way to keep the conflict both limited in geographical scope and ensure clarity and simplicity in terms of engaging enemy forces and keeping neutral shipping out, was considered a particular success. The use of 'rules of engagement' ('ROE') agreed by ministers – a relatively new innovation that had not been used by the Royal Navy in armed conflict before – was deemed a success in broad terms by facilitating 'political control especially in the early stages when it was crucial', but the actual day-to-day management of minor changes to ROE was a significant load for staff officers and created considerable confusion with a profusion of caveats, exceptions and suffixes being regularly added by Whitehall and Northwood.[18] A wider range of pre-existing ROE options in the Fleet Operational and Tactical Instructions, and more self-control in ROE changes was recommended for the future.

Some of the Navy's communication systems had worked well in the conflict: the NATO standard Link 10 played a crucial role in air defence operations, in particular preventing potential 'blue-on-blue' incidents. The SCOT satellite communication system fitted to the newer ships in the Task Force had been 'a major area of success' with two important caveats. First, a way was needed to ensure that its use did not mask passive intercept radar detection devices from receiving I band signals, a problem that had been known about since 1980 but little promulgated within the fleet. This problem had contributed to the loss of the *Sheffield*.[19] Second, a more effective means was needed to prevent the overcrowding of satellite broadcast circuits. Rigorous vetting of non-operational traffic combined with higher transmission speeds and faster teleprinters would be required in the future. Concerns were also expressed about British dependence upon US communications satellites: if co-operation had been withdrawn long-distance communication would have been extremely difficult. This issue would become an important factor in the renewal of the British Skynet communications satellite system. The greatest communications shortcoming was in the lack of a secure speech tactical radio system, something which the Argentines exploited to the full by listening into intra-Task Force tactical communications. The secure analogue Parkhill system had poor speech quality and synchronisation delays so was difficult to use, whilst the newer digital Lamberton system was only fitted to a handful of ships and therefore little utilised. Some US systems were borrowed for the conflict but overall, the systems in regular use were inadequate and easily read by the enemy. Internal communication systems within ships had particular problems and were often the first systems to stop functioning after the shock of a hit to a ship. Lack of communications between important posts on a damaged warship such as the operations room, ship control room and sickbay had been an issue, most notably on HMS *Ardent*, whilst the new and sophisticated ICS3 internal system on *Invincible* was so trouble-prone that in the event of *Hermes* being sunk or damaged, it had been argued that *Invincible* would have been unable to act as a replacement flagship. Similar problems were found with ICS3 on *Illustrious* and just before she headed south to act as the Task Force flagship after hostilities had ended, her ICS3 was shut down and replaced by old-style teleprinters with operators placed across the ship. *Invincible* also suffered from multiple and repeated computer failures, not least once during an Exocet attack.[20] Despite these significant shortcomings, the systems that needed to work to ensure that the Task Force could function tactically, were just about sufficient for operations in the South Atlantic so in that regard must be seen as a success, albeit qualified. The problems with ICS3 would eventually be ironed out, whilst a utility version of Lamberton was quickly issued to ships heading south after the end of the conflict. By late 1983 forty-seven ships in the fleet were fitted with either the utility or full versions of Lamberton.[21]

A lack of experience in 'joint' operating amongst the three services was also noted in the lessons-learnt reports. A focus over the preceding decade on predictable and oft-repeated Central European or Eastern Atlantic scenarios where much of the 'joint' co-ordination was done through NATO structures, had meant that 'jointery' at the tactical and operational level had atrophied. One tragic outcome of this lack of experience in working across domains was the loss of a British Army Gazelle light helicopter shot down by a Sea Dart missile by HMS *Cardiff*. Differences between Royal Navy procedures, which assumed that all helicopters would use their Interrogator Friend or Foe ('IFF') transmitters at all times, and Army procedure that assumed that IFF was only necessary near land-based Rapier air defence missile systems, had not been reconciled by the overworked staffs on board HMS *Fearless*.[22] The impact of this accidental loss was magnified by the late acknowledgement that this incident had occurred. Despite strong circumstantial evidence that the Sea Dart had hit the Gazelle, early evidence given to the House of Commons Defence Committee had implied that this was not the case. Internally within the Ministry 'it was considered that no useful purpose would be served by publicising this conclusion, and that, for the sake of the next of kin, the element of doubt should be allowed to linger.'[23] It was not until 1986 that it was publicly admitted that the Gazelle had been downed by Sea Dart.[24]

Ship to shore communication between the Task Force at sea and the land command on East Falkland had also been poor, another reflection of the ossification of joint operations experience and the equipment to make it work. In addition to improving such communication capabilities, it was recommended that more automation was needed, both in providing a computer-aided command centre for flag officers afloat and for automated message handling systems (an early description of what was beginning to emerge at IBM and Hewlett Packard as 'email') to prevent the overwhelming of the flag officer's staff and communications ratings.[25] One system that came in for considerable praise were the HP 9845 'calculators' linked to some Link 14 communication terminals. These were in fact much more than calculators – they were one of the earliest pioneering desktop computers which were being used to support 'autoplot' capabilities in some of the ships' operations rooms.[26]

Back in Northwood and Whitehall the boundaries of joint or single-service command areas had not always been clear. With the creation of the final Task Force structure, operational command became the direct responsibility of the Chief of the Defence Staff, with Fieldhouse reporting directly to Lewin. This had many advantages in shortening the command chain between the commander and political decision-makers. However, in this situation the role of the Naval Operations Staff and its linkages into CDS's staffs were unclear, whilst the Assistant Chief of the Defence Staff (Operations) primarily made use of the Defence Operations Staff. If the tempo had increased or the joint aspects of the operation had become more complex then this central staff function could have been overwhelmed. At the same time, the Naval Operations Staff had appeared under-employed and not properly integrated into either the Central Staffs or Fieldhouse's CINCFLEET organisation in Northwood.[27] These problems hinted at the need for a greater centralisation of operational staffs into tri-service structures, in order to make better use of the available staff officers to prevent duplication or some officers being over- or others under-employed. This recommendation was not acted upon in an environment where NATO structures provided much of the necessary 'jointery' within Defence, but it anticipated the creation of the Permanent Joint Headquarters in the 1990s when non-NATO operations had become more common.

Most of the lessons-learnt analysis focussed on systems and processes rather than the human side of command in the campaign. Given that the campaign had been successful, and that those in command of it – Fieldhouse and Woodward – had written or initiated much of the analytical work within the Royal Navy, this is perhaps to be expected. That stated, the command arrangements had been sufficiently successful not to have jeopardised the outcome of the campaign. The structure, despite its centralisation on Fieldhouse in Northwood rather than making use of an in-theatre Task Force commander, worked well enough, whilst the rapport both Lewin and Fieldhouse both had with the Prime Minister ensured that the military-political link remained strong even during the worst days of the conflict.[28] Some criticism has been made of the decision by Fieldhouse to make Woodward the commander of the carrier group of the Task Force, pointing out that FOF3, Rear Admiral Derek Reffell, as the flag officer in charge of carriers and amphibious vessels, was a more appropriate flag officer to command the carrier group.[29] However, although Reffell had considerable experience in amphibious warfare, he had only been in post since March.[30] Woodward had been an excellent submarine commander, but his knowledge and understanding of amphibious operations was limited and this had shown in his sometimes strained relations with the Royal Marine and amphibious commanders Brigadier Thompson and Commodore Clapp.[31] Fieldhouse had involved Woodward in his earliest initial planning even before the invasion had occurred and he was already at sea commanding ships during the annual Springtrain exercise in the Mediterranean, both of which provided him with 'man on the spot' credentials. Other more subtle elements might also have been at play: both Fieldhouse and Woodward were submariners and although they did not know each other well, they were both of the same 'tribe' and Fieldhouse certainly knew of Woodward's abilities.[32] In 1979 he had wanted to have Woodward as his Chief of Staff when he became CINCFLEET. Woodward, who had already been offered the 'plum' job of Director of Naval Plans, turned him down, much to Fieldhouse's annoyance.[33] Woodward, despite his prickly manner, was a determined and ruthless commander and his experience in operating at close quarters against Soviet submarines was the closest one came to real combat command experience in a Navy where almost all Second World War and Korea War veterans had either retired or were no longer in sea postings.[34] Such experience, and a willingness to drive his subordinates hard, could well have been an important factor in the decision to appoint Woodward despite his shortcomings.

Another way to look at the dilemma posed by the command structure created by Fieldhouse is to see it in terms of the balance between 'mission command' – the willingness of a high-level commander to trust their subordinates and give them considerable autonomy to achieve agreed objectives – and 'grip' – a commander's tight control of operations to ensure that they obtain the results they require. With respect to the decision to appoint Woodward rather than Reffell, the fact that operations would be occurring 7,000 nautical miles from the United Kingdom, meant that a considerable amount of mission command would be inevitable, and mission command can only work effectively if the high-level commander knows and trusts his subordinates. This was more the case with Woodward and was much less so with Reffell. With the different flag officers available to him, Fieldhouse took the choice most likely to ensure that the relationship would be strongest between the overall commander and the most senior officer in theatre, rather than between the senior officer in theatre and the amphibious commanders. Given Woodward's sometimes abrupt behaviour, combined with his limited knowledge of air and amphibious warfare, the divided command structure meant that any tensions could at least be partly countered and potentially dissipated by the centralisation of structures on CINCFLEET rather than on Woodward. Fieldhouse's decision in favour of Woodward is to some extent vindicated by the, wholly misplaced, frustration felt in Northwood by the time needed by Thompson to begin the advance across East Falkland.[35] Such frustrations could have easily multiplied with a carrier group commander, much less well known to Fieldhouse, who would have inevitably (and probably correctly at the tactical and operational levels) supported his amphibious colleagues in issues of dispute when communicating with Northwood.

If the conflict had ended in disaster and defeat it is likely that the centralisation of command on Fieldhouse and the decision to appoint Woodward would have come under considerable scrutiny, and perfectly legitimate criticisms could have been made. However, as it was, the conflict ended in victory and the structures had worked sufficiently well despite their idiosyncratic nature, tailored as they were towards the balance of personalities, capabilities and trust relationships amongst the senior commanders.

The Navy's individual unit commanders – the commanders and captains of the carriers, submarines, destroyers, frigates and assault ships – were an experienced and capable cadre, many of whom were commanding their second, third or even fourth major warship. The preponderance of captains commanding ships in the conflict is notable: aside from the carriers, assault ships and large 'County' class destroyers which were all commanded by captains as a matter of course, a significant number of the other frigates and destroyers were as well. As a result, of the thirty-three major warships and nuclear submarines sent to the South Atlantic nineteen were commanded by captains.[36] Not only were a number of ship squadron leaders with a captain in command, most of the Type 42 and Type 22 ships – new, large and capable vessels – were also commanded by captains. The captains of the two 'County' class destroyers were notably experienced in surface-ship command. Captain Brian Young of *Antrim* was seen earlier in this book leading a small group of frigates and an auxiliary, expertly tracking a Soviet Surface Action Group through the growlers of the High North during Exercise Okean 75 (see Chapter 10). Captain Michael Barrow had commanded three frigates before *Glamorgan*. Captain L E Middleton had also commanded three frigates before becoming captain of *Hermes* whilst Captain E S J Larken of *Fearless* had commanded two submarines and a destroyer. Admiral Woodward had particularly valued the depth of experience of these long-serving officers. Of the other captains with ship commands in the Falklands, most had had at least two previous commands of either submarines or ships the size of frigates or larger.[37] This was a formidably experienced cohort of unit commanders and it is therefore not surprising that they were effective not only as ship commanders during the stress of battle, many fighting their vessels capably after serious damage, but also being able to sustain morale and capability after almost three months continuously at sea. Their cumulative experience was deemed by Admiral Staveley, VCNS during the conflict, to have played an important part in the success of the campaign.[38] However, an entirely rosy picture should not be painted: relationships and command styles were not always perfect. Middleton had a particularly authoritarian approach which had a negative impact on the GR3 Harrier and Sea Harrier pilots during the conflict.[39] Issues that could affect warships in peacetime as well as war, such as petty thieving by crew, were not entirely absent during the conflict either.[40]

Intelligence

The greatest defence intelligence failures occurred before the Argentine invasion: there had been a lack of forewarning and this had been coupled with a lack of pre-collected information on Argentine capabilities. Following the conflict, the Defence Intelligence Staff expanded their 'indications and warnings' system of reporting beyond the Warsaw Pact, to include five potential threats to British sovereign territory: the threat to the Falklands from Argentina, the threat to Hong Kong from China, the threat to Gibraltar from Spain, the threat to Diego Garcia from Mauritius and threats to the Sovereign Base areas on Cyprus from developments in the internal situation in both parts of Cyprus. In addition, the threat to Belize from Guatemala was also assessed given the ongoing British commitment to the defence of that newly independent state. The recent total focus on the Soviet threat, as if no British national interests existed beyond Central Europe and the Eastern Atlantic, was now being rolled back in favour of a more balanced approach to defence intelligence priorities, although rightly, the threat from the USSR remained the primary focus. Other recommendations from the lessons-learnt exercise relating to intelligence included the closer siting of intelligence analysis to operational commands and the interesting conclusion that special forces should not be used for strategic or operational level intelligence collection, which presumably would have strayed onto the territory of the Secret Intelligence Service.[41] However, it was acknowledged that the SAS and SBS had proved of crucial importance in collecting *tactical* intelligence on Argentine dispositions and capabilities before the San Carlos landings. Despite its earlier unpreparedness, after the invasion the Defence Intelligence Staff had been praised for providing a wealth of information at short-notice on Argentine material capabilities.[42] It was recommended that an Intelligence Branch be set up within the Navy to support flag officers' staffs and provide analysis and briefs to units (the Navy had allowed its intelligence branch specialisations to wither away in the 1960s and 1970s). Finally, special communications channels dedicated to intelligence dissemination only, to ensure that such information was not crowded out by other signals, was also recommended.[43]

Air Defence and Electronic Warfare

The Sea Harrier
In the post-conflict analyses the Sea Harrier was generally praised as an effective aircraft that had performed far above expectations, but this was tempered by realism and an awareness of the aircraft's limitations. It was acknowledged that no air superiority had been achieved during the conflict, but that despite this both the amphibious operational area and the high value units had been successfully defended.[44] Sidewinder AIM9L had achieved twenty-three kills from twenty-seven firings, a highly impressive ratio (more recent research has reduced this to twenty out of twenty-six, still a strong total[45]). CINCFLEET described the aircraft as a 'great success' but it was also acknowledged that the Sea Harrier was not fast enough to intercept reconnaissance aircraft, nor had it been able to intercept Super Etendards or their Exocet missiles. A major limitation was the on-aircraft Blue Fox radar which had limited range, no look-down capability and poor low-level performance. The radar was made to work adequately but procuring a successor with a pulse doppler and a good look-down capability was considered a high priority.[46] The Sea Harrier's strong performance in the conflict ensured that it would, in the event, be updated and remain in service into the 1990s. F/A 2 modifications, including the Blue Vixen pulse doppler look-down radar and the AMRAAM air-to-air missiles, were approved in 1984 with the first aircraft entering service in 1993.[47]

Shipborne Air Defence Missiles
Sea Dart had provided the most concerns prior to the conflict, but ASWE's worries that the missile and the GWS 30 system as a whole were almost worse than useless were not borne out by the campaign. ASWE's own post-conflict analysis had accepted that it had made a useful contribution to operations, whilst earlier analysis from July 1982 described its performance when taking account of its known limitations as 'reasonably successful'.[48] It had also forced Argentine aircraft to fly low, thus accentuating fusing problems with their bombs and increasing the risks taken when attacking ships.[49] However, Sea Dart and GWS 30 were still seen as flawed in a number of areas including problems with low-flying targets and limited magazine space, and the conflict had shown up some additional issues. The operations rooms in Type 42 destroyers had difficulties in achieving a clear and accurate air threat picture out to 30 nautical

miles. Poor data presentation on some of the system displays of the ADAWS tactical command system made it difficult to assimilate information rapidly and risked overloading key personnel, whilst fears of problems with the Type 909 missile guidance radars caused operators to over-compensate for these radars' perceived shortcomings, which meant that gaining a timely acquisition of targets was often made more difficult. Ironically, the Type 909 radars performed well with few problems during engagements. When unexpected issues occurred, such as launcher systems failing to operate effectively, operators lacked sufficient knowledge to switch to manual backups or override procedures: 'operator knowledge of how to get the best out of the system in a crisis situation must be improved.'[50] The dramatic losses of *Sheffield* and *Coventry*, combined with sufficient successes for Sea Dart, meant that improvements to the missile and its system to address its shortcomings were now seen as important post-conflict improvements. The modernisation of the earliest Type 42s to the standards of later ships was therefore soon approved, and later modifications to Sea Dart and GWS 30 also went ahead.

The Sea Wolf point defence system was perceived to have been successfully employed in the Falklands. It had made dramatic intercepts during engagements on 12 May. However, the system also had its share of problems. Dealing with weaving and manoeuvring aircraft had initially proved difficult for a system designed to deal with straight-flying anti-ship missiles, but these had been overcome by testing back the United Kingdom and then signalling to the Task Force instructions for typing amended code into the missile system computers whilst the conflict was occurring. If the CAAIS tactical command system was not operational, then Sea Wolf had proved difficult to control. Allowing an interface with the Link 10 tactical communications system was recommended, as was the investigation of increased range for the Sea Wolf missile. The Sea Cat missile system had scored very few kills in the conflict, and suffered from long-known problems of lack of proximity fusing and low speed. Older manual variants of the system had proved more effective than the newer versions on Type 21 frigates or modernised *Leander*s which relied to a greater or lesser degree on automation, which did not work in a heavy radar-clutter inshore environment, thus resulting in a reliance on manual aiming and guidance.[51]

Air Defence Gunnery
Before the Falklands conflict, light guns had been seen as minor weapons designed to provide a proportionate capability against low-threat targets, their air defence role having been largely discounted. The confined inshore waters of San Carlos and Falkland Sound, combined with the use by the Argentines of freefall bombs had resulted in a reconsideration of this decision.

Light weapons played a minor role in deterring or disrupting the approach of attacking aircraft, even if few had been successful in destroying them. As was seen in the previous chapter additional light weapons were fitted to ships heading to the South Atlantic, but this was generally seen as a specific response to a focused and unusual threat. It was assessed that a balance was needed between the impact on crew numbers on fitting additional such guns and their actual effectiveness.[52] It is therefore perhaps not surprising that by the 1990s such mountings had returned to pre-Falklands levels of only two per frigate or destroyer. Even before the loss of *Sheffield* to an anti-ship missile, an Urgent Operational Requirement had been raised for the purchase of two US Vulcan Phalanx Close-in Weapon Systems that used a radar-directed rapid fire rotary multi-barrelled mounting to destroy approaching missiles. The weapon was assessed at the time to have a 70 per cent chance of hitting a missile within 75m and 95 per cent within 25m. Debris from a missile hit at such a close range could still cause considerable damage, but this would probably be much less than a direct missile hit.[53] After the conflict, further Phalanxes would be procured for the *Invincible* class carriers and the Type 42 destroyers, whilst the last four Type 22 frigates would receive the more capable but heavier Dutch Goalkeeper system; these mountings augmenting existing air defence systems.[54]

Airborne Early Warning
The airborne early warning capability, as was seen in Chapter 11, had been sacrificed following the withdrawal of *Ark Royal* in 1978 and not replaced. Fitting Sea King helicopters with long-range search radars had been considered but had been rejected. With the RAF's aged Shackleton aircraft lacking the range and robustness to operate in the South Atlantic, the Task Force lacked any airborne early air threat detection capability, meaning that Super Etendards carrying Exocet missiles were able to approach the Force without being engaged before they released their missiles. As a partial compensation, the Force's limited number of air defence ships were used as 'fleet pickets' closer to the air threat, a doctrinal approach that had not been seen since the late 1950s, and which resulted in the loss of *Sheffield* in such an exposed position. Whilst the conflict was in progress, the Sea King solution was revisited as an 'Urgent Operational Requirement' and Searchwater radars – otherwise fitted to the new Nimrod MR2 maritime patrol aircraft – were fitted to the helicopter and within a couple of months a workable solution was developed and tested. This capability was not available in time for the conflict, but the first AEW Sea Kings went south with *Illustrious* in August 1982.[55] Helicopter-based AEW still had shortcomings compared with fixed-wing equivalents: their limited operational altitude meant that the range of their radars was not as great, and therefore less likely to detect Soviet bombers before they launched their

missiles, but it did mean that this capability was now available to Royal Navy forces operating beyond the range of the RAF's airborne early warning aircraft, and as an important addition over and above the Shackleton capability that was dependent on ageing airframes and obsolescent radars, and would not be replaced until the late 1980s.[56]

Electronic Warfare
Another form of long-range detection was the electronic intercept: the passive radar detection capability described in Chapter 11. The new UAA-1 system had only been fitted to a number of ships, and even before the conflict a number of updates and improvements had been planned. Satellite communication protection filters, so that the use of the SCOT satellite system did not mask UAA-1, were rapidly ordered and sets were to be fitted to all ships carrying the system. In addition, the lack of a jamming capability had been keenly felt: 'chaff' decoys had been relatively successful but on occasion had merely deflected a missile onto another ship. Jammers would serve to disrupt guidance radars and provide another means to undertake a 'soft kill' of an attacking missile. Plans were advanced for further improvements to UAA-1, including improved direction-finding, a greater coverage of the frequency spectrum down to 0.5 GHz and up to 40 GHz, new displays and greater automation of signal sorting. This improved system would enter service as UAA-2 in the late 1980s. New jammers would enter service from 1983 onwards (designated Type 670 and Type 675).[57]

Other Air Operations
RAF Nimrod MR2s had undertaken patrol tasks from Ascension but their inability to be refuelled in the air had limited their range and restricted them to areas beyond the TEZ. The lack of satellite communications on MR2s was another shortcoming (some MR1s did have this capability). Early reports on the Searchwater radar had stated that 'too much may have been expected of this equipment', in particular it had problems with target identification; later reports had replaced this with the more bland statement that 'overall, Searchwater gave good performance'.[58] Other capability improvements were also needed in electronic support measures and missile decoys, as well as high frequency communications. After the Falklands the MR2 was re-equipped to enable air-to-air refuelling, and fitted with satellite communications and air-launched Harpoon anti-ship missiles, the last of which gave the aircraft the ability to engage targets on the surface as well as underwater. The fitting of Stingray anti-submarine torpedoes and AIM 9L Sidewinders for self-defence was also accelerated.[59] These were all significant improvements to the Nimrod that would make it a much more formidable aircraft in the Eastern Atlantic.

Some of these improvements might have occurred in due course, but the Falklands had created an environment where such enhancements could be paid for much earlier.

The twenty-three Victor tankers had done sterling work refuelling Vulcans and other aircraft heading south or returning to the United Kingdom. However, it had been universally recognised that there had been too few of these precious aircraft. Fourteen-hour sorties were not uncommon and many crew had only been able to gain sufficient deep sleep afterwards and recover quickly for more flying by taking 'Farnborough sleeping pills'. The utilisation rate of the aircraft had reached 2.7 times higher than usual.[60] By 1984 the RAF's tanker fleet had been augmented by six TriStars and the conversion of a number of VC10s into tankers.[61] The fitting of AAR capability to the Vulcans had been undertaken successfully at short-notice, but it was acknowledged that a runway denial weapon was necessary as the standard freefall bombs used in the Vulcan raids had not been as effective as hoped.[62]

The GR3 Harriers had originally been deployed south to augment the Sea Harriers in air defence, but as these latter aircraft had not suffered losses at the rates that had been feared, the GR3s were primarily used in their designed ground attack role. Their cluster bombs and 1,000lb bombs, as well as their 30mm cannon, had all worked well, but their communication systems had not always performed satisfactorily. Laser-guided bombs did not arrive in theatre until after the conflict had ended, but there remained concerns that their employment might not have been as effective as hoped as they depended on ground laser target markers which were too heavy, difficult to deploy and often unreliable. A rearward attack-recording camera was also requested so that the effects of bombing could be recorded.[63] There were clearly tensions between the air planners on *Hermes* and the GR3 pilots, who felt that they were being marginalised and not used in the most effective way. Reconnaissance missions seem to have been particularly neglected. Given that there was only one air tasking officer, and that *Hermes*' staff officers had not focussed on fixed-wing strike missions before, this possible neglect is perhaps not surprising, but *Hermes*' captain's authoritarian approach – and perhaps a certain amount of interservice rivalry – might well have made this worse.[64]

Submarine Operations and Anti-Submarine Warfare

The most stunning success in the naval campaign was the sinking of the Argentine cruiser *General Belgrano* and the subsequent decision by the Argentine navy to keep the rest of its surface fleet in port or confined to territorial waters: a classic example of successful operational-level deterrence in warfare. The destruction of the cruiser confirmed the considerable capabilities of the nuclear submarine, most specifically its ability to operate underwater for months without the need to surface and appeared to justify the Admiralty's decision to push to first procure these boats – with much US support – in the 1950s. However, underneath this undoubted and operationally decisive success, there were some significant areas of concern. The most obvious, and much discussed soon after the conflict, was Commander Wreford-Brown's decision to rely on Second World War vintage Mark 8 torpedoes against the cruiser instead of the modern Tigerfish. There were good tactical reasons to do so as Mark 8s would be more capable of piercing the armour of the equally aged *Belgrano*, but Tigerfish's reputation for unreliability was also a factor.[65] As was seen in Chapter 11, given that torpedo's travails during its protracted development through the 1970s, it is understandable that he made this decision. In fact, his caution with the Tigerfish seems to have been justified by the torpedo's failure when two were fired by the conventional submarine *Onyx* to sink the stricken landing ship *Sir Galahad* after its fires had burnt out. Tigerfish could not operate in waters less than 100 fathoms (180m) deep and still had problems with reliability and mis-launches.[66] However, it is also worth noting that Mk 8s required the attacking submarine to approach closer than 2,000 yards in order to have confidence that they would hit, which would be 'suicidal against competent ASW oppositions.'[67] It was therefore crucial that the problems with Tigerfish were ironed out as soon as possible.

There were also other, less publicised, concerns. The main bow sonar of the nuclear submarines, the Type 2001, was considered to be insufficiently effective in its passive mode: *Spartan* had lost an opportunity to attack a submerged Argentine submarine due to the poor performance of the passive Type 2001 (she did not have towed-array either, so was at a considerable disadvantage to the other British boats that did).[68] Those submarines fitted with towed-arrays had been much more effective at detecting and tracking Argentine units, but the clip-on arrays of the Type 2024 were at risk of snagging when the depth went under 100 fathoms and some of the submarines did not have broadband analysers for their towed-arrays, which meant that only a small number of frequencies could be analysed at any one time. So, in addition to recommending both a significant improvement to and a replacement for the ineffective Tigerfish, the lessons-learnt analyses argued for a 'reelable' towed-array to be fitted to all nuclear-powered submarines, combined with wide band analysers and improvements to the Type 2001 bow sonar. The detection capabilities of conventional boats, following *Onyx*'s patchy record of detecting Argentine boats, also needed to be improved.[69]

The threat from Argentine submarines was one which the Task Force had been almost perpetually aware of and concerned about, but for which there was little evidence at the time of attacks from one of the Argentine Navy's four submarines.[70] Information began to emerge in Spanish and some English-language sources from 1983, revealing a handful of attempted attacks and problems of equipment failure and target location by Argentine naval forces.[71] During the conflict the British had fired 33 torpedoes, 47 depth charges and 127 mortar projectiles mostly chasing spurious submarine contacts, from a total of 235 reported anti-submarine incidents.[72] The standard shipborne sonar, the Type 184M, had failed utterly to detect submarines even when other information sources suggested that they were in the locality. The earlier versions of the lessons-learnt reports were blunt in their analysis: 'the abysmal performance of this set is of the greatest concern ... recommend sonar 184 be replaced by an improved sonar.'[73] No more Type 184M sets were fitted on British warships after 1982: the last three Type 42 destroyers were equipped with the more capable Type 2016 sonar instead. The Type 184M was given a minor upgrade to Type 184P in the mid-1980s, but this flawed sonar remained in service with older ships in the Royal Navy until the end of the 1980s.[74]

The Type 195 dipping sonar fitted to Sea King helicopters was somewhat better but was not especially reliable, being prone to failures after only 30 hours of use. These problems helped to spur the development of a replacement: the Type 2069 dipping sonar. It entered service on the next anti-submarine version of the Sea King, the HAS Mk 6 in the late 1980s.[75] Overall, the current situation regarding the performance of the surface ships in anti-submarine operations was described as 'lamentable'.[76] As a partial counter to the poor performance of these systems, magnetic anomaly detectors ('MAD') – which were standard on maritime patrol aircraft – were recommended for Lynx helicopters. Trials had already taken place and plans existed for just such an augmentation to the Lynx. MAD was an effective means of confirming whether a sonar contact was in fact a submarine and would therefore have saved the unnecessary firing of many anti-submarine torpedoes, depth charges and mortars. They had been standard equipment on maritime patrol aircraft for years.[77]

For a surface fleet that had spent the last decade specialising in anti-submarine warfare this was deeply embarrassing and frustrating. In the later versions of the reports that went outside the Navy Department, the emphasis was on the surface ships' poor performance specifically against the quieter diesel-electric submarines of the Argentine Navy, implying that they would be more effective against nuclear boats, but the reality was that the existing capabilities would not have been much better against these latter vessels. The Type 184M, as was seen in Chapter 7, was extremely poor at detecting any submarines below the isotherm, and above it had a limited and extremely variable range. It was also prone to mutual interference, a major problem when almost every frigate and destroyer in the fleet was equipped with this set. The reliability issues of the Type 182 and 195 would not go away when faced with nuclear submarines either, at least until replacements were in service. The only bright spots had been the excellent performance of submarine towed-arrays – which suggested that their surface equivalents would be just as good – and the reliability of the new Type 2016 sonar on the two Type 22 frigates *Broadsword* and *Brilliant*. Unfortunately, as these two ships had been used almost continuously as 'goalkeepers' with their Sea Wolf systems protecting Type 42 destroyers or carriers, they had had little opportunity to make sonar detections with their new set, but at least their sets were producing operational defects at a rate much lower than the previous generation of systems.[78]

Naval Gunfire Support and Anti-Ship Operations

Although the conflict did not see the surface fleet against surface fleet engagement that some had been expecting, and within the Argentine Navy many had been hoping for, there were a number of minor ship engagements throughout the conflict aside from the *Belgrano* attack. The Argentine ammunition transport *Isla de los Estados* had been destroyed with gunfire. The Argentine corvette *Guerrico* had been damaged with a Carl Gustav anti-tank weapon during the South Georgia invasion. Two further Argentine vessels were attacked by Sea Harriers: the trawler and intelligence-gatherer *Narwhal* which sank and the transport *Bahia Buen Suceso* which was immobilised.[79] Most significant for the lessons-learnt analysts, were the successful attacks by Lynx helicopters using the new Sea Skua missile. Sea Skua had not yet formally been accepted into service, but seven had been fired against three targets damaging one patrol vessel, the *Alferez Sobral*, and (it was thought at the time) damaging another, as well as heavily damaging the transport *Rio Carcarana*.[80] These actions seemed to demonstrate the effectiveness of Sea Skua, which would be confirmed in further post-conflict trials and more spectacularly in the 1990–1 Gulf War when Sea Skua-armed Lynxes managed to destroy numerous Iraqi fast attack craft at the Battle of Bubiyan and other engagements.[81]

Naval gunfire support ('NGS') had been an important part of the Navy's role in the conflict after the successful establishment of the beach-head at San Carlos, with nearly 8,000 rounds of high explosive and starshell being fired. Early naval assessments of the effectiveness of NGS had been particularly positive, stating that it had 'played a critical part in interdicting enemy ground forces'[82] with 'an unequalled performance, exceeding peace time practice standards' with NGS making a 'significant contribution to the collapse of Arg[entine] morale'.[83] Later analyses were somewhat more circumspect, acknowledging its importance in affecting Argentine Army morale, but also accepting that when spotting was undertaken from the air or the predicted fire technique was used, especially in the first days, the shells would often fall wide of their mark. Once land spotters from 148 Commando Forward Observation Battery were in place, the quality of the fire improved significantly and individual targets on the front-line were destroyed with much greater accuracy.[84]

The most effective NGS gun was the old Mk 6 4.5in, which had originally entered service just after the Second World War. The Mk 8 gun, fitted to more modern Type 42 and 21 ships, was much less effective, with a mean failure rate of 1 in every 50 firings and relatively short barrel life.[85] The Mk 8 had in fact never been formally accepted into service since its first firings on board HMS *Bristol* in 1973. Over 250 modifications had been produced since then, but most ships had not been given the full run of these modifications, and formal acceptance had never been achieved.[86] It is a mark of the low priority medium guns had been given in the Navy that a weapon fitted to nearly all the most modern frigates and destroyers in the fleet was still not up to its designed standard a decade after its introduction. The number of shells expended had been much more than had been expected with a single night's firing using up the equivalent of up to three years' quantity of ammunition that would be used in peacetime firing exercises.[87] Starshell had not been as effective as hoped and spotters had to use night vision goggles to do their jobs, whilst the high explosive shells used were designed for anti-ship work and much less effective in the peaty earth of the Falklands.[88]

Amphibious Warfare

The 'lessons-learnt' documents relating to the transfer of troops ashore all looked towards their relevance in the NATO northern flank environment. It was stated that the problems faced by amphibious forces were 'not dissimilar to those posed in the NATO setting of Norway'.[89] Although there were in fact a number of major differences in terrain – Norway had steep fjords and sea cliffs, the Falklands sloping moorland and short beaches – whilst the geographical distances from the United Kingdom were hugely different, this comparison between the two was not surprising given the political fragility of the Navy's amphibious forces following the aftermath of the Defence Review. As was seen in the previous chapter, the two *Fearless* class assault ships ('LPDs') were to be retained until the late 1980s, but although it seemed likely that the LSLs would remain in service no formal decision had yet been made, and in any case there were no long-term plans for replacements of either type.[90] It was stated that the 'wisdom of reprieving the LPDs is clear': only the assault ships could have provided the command, communications, helicopter facilities and troop and vehicle carrying facilities to ensure success.[91] The LSLs had proved to be valuable secondary amphibious ships but they had serious shortcoming reflecting their designed role as mere military transports: they lacked military communication systems, had limited helicopter facilities and were severely strained when holding troops in 'overload' conditions. It was recommended that the LSLs be upgraded to the standards of the Royal Australian Navy's landing ship *Tobruk*, an enlarged and militarised version of the LSLs.[92] A formal request was therefore put in for a reversal of Defence Review plans to withdraw the LSLs from service.[93] Repeated emphasis was put on the importance of building and retaining expertise in amphibious landings through continued and repeated training and involvement in major exercises, whilst the rest of the armed forces should have greater awareness of amphibious warfare and capabilities.[94]

One significant omission was that there were no direct calls for commando carriers. The lack of a dedicated platform for commando helicopters had been a major concern of Commodore Clapp and Brigadier Thompson during the conflict and they were deeply concerned about their inability to make use of *Hermes* in this role despite believing initially that they would be able to.[95] As a result, any attempt at 'vertical envelopment' landings using helicopters to land a first wave of troops would not have been possible. It seems that the Naval Staff did not want to push for a capability they were extremely unlikely to get, but in truth the helicopter facilities of the two assault ships were distinctly limited: their lack of hangars meaning that other vessels such as RFAs had been necessary. The commando carrier concept would not die away entirely and justifications for its restitution were made by the Royal Marines and RN amphibious specialists through the 1980s, the capability finally emerging in the procurement of the new commando carrier, HMS *Ocean*, after the end of the Cold War.[96] Another issue had been the adequate supply of commando helicopters, with HAS Mk 2 anti-submarine Sea Kings often being drafted into the role of logistics and troop transport during the conflict.[97] The Royal Navy therefore requested the purchase of more Mk 4 Commando Sea Kings to replace the ageing and less capable Wessexes.

Logistics

Logistics had been one of the unequivocal success stories of the conflict. The Task Force, amphibious force and troops had been sustained more than 7,000 nautical miles from the United Kingdom over a period of approximately three months and could have been supported for quite a few months longer if it had been necessary. In the midst of the conflict the Ministry of Defence was confident of its ability to sustain the land campaign for a total of 60 days in addition to supporting a brigade-sized garrison for another year. Carrier-based operations could have been sustained until the end of September 1982.[98] In the event, this did not prove necessary, but shows the depth of logistical capability, stores and spares available to the Task Force.

The storing of the ships of the Task Force in preparation for war had been undertaken effectively and speedily: the Royal Naval Supply and Transport Service 'achieved wonders' enabling ships to achieve greater than expected endurance through, amongst other things, the stowage of stores outside designated areas on board ship.[99] Early and clear political decisions allowed this work to be undertaken without being subordinated to the committee-driven and bureaucratic procedures set out in the Ministry of Defence warbook. If the warbook had been used, it was argued that 'it is unlikely that clearance to work overtime and shiftwork and to make and load explosive stores would have been given in time to meet the swift reaction of the support areas'.[100] If the warbook were to be used in the future, very swift approvals from the key committees would be necessary in a transition to war scenario.[101] Another warning was made about the risk of relying on overseas suppliers in emergencies: 'who for political as well as logistic reasons may be unwilling to help at a particular time.'[102]

The importance of Ascension in properly organising stores was crucial – some stores had been loaded largely unsorted in great haste – and the island base provided space and time to re-arrange and re-pack these materials.[103] Although not mentioned in the lessons-learnt literature, at least at the higher levels or on the Naval side, the RAF's effective airdrop service from Ascension to the Task Force proved especially useful for small high value supplies and the regular supply of letters from families back in the United Kingdom.[104] Although the overall logistics effort worked impressively well, there were areas of supply shortage, including shortages of decoy rockets (as well as ships' magazines being too small), insufficient high explosive 4.5in ammunition, the need for additional Sidewinder AIM9L missiles from the United States, and by the end of the conflict a shortage of Sea Cat missiles. There had also been some close calls: the failure of *Conqueror*'s communications wires almost resulted in the need for her to end her patrol and be repaired by *Stena Seaspread*.[105]

Ships taken up from trade ('STUFT') was another area that was hailed as a great success. The process for taking ships up from trade could take as little as two weeks, with most being undertaken in Royal Dockyards and ten others under contract. These contract STUFT ships were converted with paperwork that was 'virtually non-existent and contractual (and financial) propriety was ignored for most of the ten [contract] STUFTs'.[106] The process was remarkably effective and relied on the knowledge of the British-flagged merchant marine within the Naval Staff's Directorate of Naval Operations and Trade ('DNOT'). DNOT would obtain details of likely ships from government brokers, the Director General Ships would review their suitability and make the decision of which ships to take up, which would be formalised through an Order in Council. The Chief Engineer's Department would then decide what levels of 'militarisation' would be needed and whether the conversion would be done by government or private dockyard. The work itself would be overseen by the Ship Department.[107] This approach had not been adopted on the fly but had been part of plans for taking ships up from trade that had been developed during the Cold War as an element of transition to war procedures but speeded up significantly to match the time requirements of the Falklands crisis. The waiving of the usual requirements for setting staff requirements, gaining financial approval and tendering for contracts were essential in ensuring that this work could be done at such speed.[108] The Ministry of Defence was also extremely lucky that there was a world slump in maritime trade in 1982; if this had not been the case, then there might not have been enough ships available to take up from trade.[109] Another problem for the future was the rapidly shrinking number of British-flagged merchant ships as shipowners and operators increasingly fled to 'flags of convenience' to escape from the standards and costs set out by the registries of the major trading nations. It was not altogether clear whether there would be sufficient British-flagged vessels available by the end of the 1980s for another such emergency, whether it be the threat of conflict with the Warsaw Pact or another unexpected crisis well beyond British waters.

The Falklands campaign had demonstrated that the Royal Navy had retained a significant long-distance maritime logistics capability despite the reductions in force levels: these were an inheritance from earlier East of Suez commitments, and had been partly sustained through the worldwide group deployments of the 1970s, the Beira Patrol and latterly the Armilla Patrol in the Gulf, and also by the continuing need for the logistics requirements to keep warships at sea for long periods during a time of tension in the Eastern Atlantic. The success of STUFT also resulted in Vice Admiral Staveley, the Vice Chief of the Naval Staff, developing the concept of a 'core fleet' made up of warships which would be supported in wartime by a 'STUFT' fleet of aircraft transports supplementing aircraft carriers, ro-ro ships supporting amphibious vessels, a range of vessels augmenting the Royal Fleet Auxiliaries, and ocean-going trawlers bolstering the numbers of mine warfare vessels.[110] This concept had echoes of emergency expansion of the Royal Navy in the Second World War, where trawlers were taken up from trade and then adapted into utility convoy escorts, ocean liners became armed merchant cruisers and oil and bulk carriers were converted into utility aircraft carriers. In the later Cold War, such conversions and adaptations could not be allowed to take months or even years, but needed to be ready in weeks, and the Falklands STUFT process appeared to be a plausible answer to the perennial problem of both having ships of high-enough quality to hold their own against the enemy's major capabilities, and the need for large numbers of vessels for sea control operations against submarines or raiders. However, it rested on fragile foundations as it depended on the fast-shrinking British flagged merchant fleet. Nevertheless, clear recommendations were made for STUFT to be repeatedly practiced as part of NATO's exercises in the Eastern Atlantic and High North, and as a result STUFT ships became a regular element of at least the amphibious phases of NATO exercises in the mid and late 1980s.[111]

Training, Personnel and Battle Stress

The headlines relating to training and morale during the conflict were effusive: CINCFLEET's final report for example stated that naval personnel had made 'magnificent achievements' and some had undertaken 'acts of great personal courage', whilst 'morale [had been] universally reported as high in all HM Ships throughout the fighting'.[112] Once into the detail of analysis some nuanced points emerged. Overall, 'the present training system achieved its aim in preparing men for their assigned roles'.[113] However, some weapons training had not been effective enough: personnel were good at fighting with their weapons systems in the standard 'automated' modes, but had considerable trouble when these systems had to switch to manual or override modes due to the cluttered radar environments of San Carlos Water. One of the most significant lessons was the importance of on-the-spot expertise, especially weapons and marine engineering technical expertise. The practical 'craft skills' of experienced artificers and engineers had been crucial in a number of instances: 'many ships produced technical innovation and improvisation to the extent that tasks normally only undertaken in DED [Docking and Essential Defects periods] were successfully tackled at sea.'[114] The Navy's existing focus on building up and sustaining cadres of highly skilled ratings and officers in seagoing billets had been proven to be the correct approach for the conflict in the South Atlantic, where there were had been no naval bases nearby and afloat maintenance facilities were limited to the STUFT ship, *Stena Seaspread*.

With respect to personnel numbers, and having sufficient quantities of the right kind of personnel, the Royal Navy had been fortunate in many respects: 4,850 additional personnel out of a total of 68,400 in the naval service had been required to supplement existing crews, including HMS *Intrepid* which was in reserve awaiting refit and 200 short of her normal complement, allocate personnel for Ascension and to naval parties for STUFT vessels, as well as undertake additional staff or administrative roles at CINCFLEET such as casualty reporting and information processing and analysis.[115] The war complements of the headquarters staff at Northwood had been inadequate, and also had to be supplemented. These additional roles were generally met from the shore establishments, especially the training schools where the recent defence review had reduced the throughput of trainees, but their directing staff had not yet been slimmed to fit these new smaller cohorts. Many were therefore able to be sent southwards or to Northwood without impacting seriously on the standard training programmes. If the conflict had occurred a year later, this would not have been possible and training disruption would have been serious, especially as there had been political delays in calling up reserves to backfill posts emptied to cover 'Corporate'-related roles.[116]

At the individual ship level, it was clear that although ships were theoretically crewed with numbers deemed necessary for a swift transition to war, in practice this had not been the case. Those vessels that had joined the Task Force from the Springtrain exercise had been forced to 'poach' selected specialist crew members from those ships not heading south, in order to deal with gaps due to illness or imperfect 'trickle drafting' processes, whereby crew members left and arrived in small numbers throughout a ship's commission. Within the operations room it was found that two Principal Warfare Officers were inadequate for operating under prolonged defence watches. Sustained periods at defence watches interspersed by up to 12 hours at action stations caused 'serious problems of fatigue which can degrade a ship's performance'.[117] Other areas of strain were in available numbers of helicopter controllers and fighter controllers. It was recommended that a minimum of two were required of the former in helicopter-carrying ships, and two of the latter in air defence destroyers. Helicopter maintainers and flight-deck crews also needed to be supplemented in war in order to cope with the rapid turnarounds of modern aircraft such as the Lynx. Overall, it was argued that 'trickle drafting' was the enemy of combat effectiveness, as crews – especially operations room crews – had to re-learn how to work together with each significant arrival of new crew members and created problems of sustaining morale and combating combat stress.[118] 'Few ships admitted to being over-manned and none which was battle-damaged.' Ships deliberately placed junior engineering ratings in machinery spaces whilst at defence and action stations; it helped to disperse crew around a ship and therefore lessen casualties if hit, expediting battle damage control actions and it allowed manual operation of normally automated systems if needed. The clear consensus was that, with the experience of the Falklands, machinery rooms should be crewed, at least in battle conditions.[119]

With the civilian crews of STUFT ships, both morale and working relationships with naval parties had been good in the vast majority of instances, although it had been found that alcohol consumption had been high: unsurprising given that the civilians had neither been trained for, nor had expected to be involved in, high intensity conflict.[120] The morale of the Hong Kong Chinese crews of the LSLs had been particularly low especially after their ships had first been subjected to air attack, but again this was not surprising given that they had initially been promised that they would not be involved in any opposed landings or direct operations. With the speedy post-conflict decision not to withdraw the LSLs from service, it was also agreed to replace their Chinese lower deck crews with United Kingdom British crews over the next half decade.[121]

The ability to cope with the 'Face of Battle', the fear, confusion and horror of air attacks, battle damage and dealing with casualties, was given considerable attention in the Navy's lessons-learnt processes. Almost no one in the Task Force, with the sad exception of Ian North, the civilian master of the *Atlantic Conveyor*, who had survived the torpedoing of two ships in the Battle of the Atlantic before succumbing to the South Atlantic after his ship was hit, had any direct experience of warfare at sea.[122] 'Few had any concept of the effects of action damage. Evidence of this includes complaints of tiredness and discomfort, inclination to take cover prematurely, elementary drill errors, all of which were apparent in the early days but which diminished as war experience grew. Men were ill-prepared for the inevitable stress of action and for the effects of physical and mental shock.'[123] Preparing crews for the mental shock of battle damage was therefore important. Analysis of officer and rating behaviours in damaged warships had shown 'a thread of similarity in reports'. In warships that had been damaged, especially those that had suffered severe structural shock, 'nearly every officer and man onboard seems to have displayed shock symptoms, whether injured or not. There are many instances of impaired judgement, perhaps as a result. Ships which were damaged, but not severely shaken by explosions, coped better.'[124] It was recommended that further research would be needed to overcome this problem, and that undamaged ships nearby 'must be prepared to give moral support and advice, as well as providing extra equipment'.[125]

Two years later, the Navy Department, after much research based on interviews and assessments of crew members across the Task Force, produced a report entitled 'Preparation for the stress of battle'. It noted that nothing very new had been revealed by the campaign but that 'some sharp reminders have been delivered'.[126] It was noted that at a particular level of 'stimulation' in combat a person's efficiency drops and leads to impaired judgements. This level could vary from person to person, but it was recommended that maintaining peak efficiency through training was the first and most important step and that only then should the ability to maintain that efficiency whilst under stress be tested. There were four types of battle stress: (1) acute battle shock, which either virtually paralyses the person or causes them to run away or to concentrate solely on minutiae at the expense of everything else; (2) battle anticipation; (3) combat exhaustion, which was common after three to four weeks of intense combat activity and required up to two weeks for recovery, but over long periods of repeated exposure to activity results in a deterioration in effectiveness from a lackadaisical or foolhardy approach to the dangers of combat; and (4) delayed reaction stress, which could manifest itself days, months or even years after exposure and result in depression, anxiety, addiction or violence. There were deemed to be four causes of stress: (1) the unexpected, (2) the unknown, (3) the sights and noise of battle, and (4) mental and physical exhaustion. In a rather robust but practical response to this issue, it was stated that stress could be combated through fitness, realistic training and leadership.[127]

The importance of the commanding officer was especially emphasised in the report. As was seen earlier in this chapter, the Task Force was blessed with a highly experienced group of COs. 'In war the attention of the ship's company will become focussed on the Captain in a way unlikely to be experienced in peacetime, and in the conditions of uncertainty and fear induced by the stress of war the responsibility of ship command is immense.'[128] In these instances, the highly experienced CO was a crucial benefit: 'experience in command, even though not in war, is a great asset if the test comes. The deduction must be that command experience should not be overdiluted, and that success in one command should be a pre-requisite for the next.'[129] Given the burdens under which commanding officers operated, it was important that they were able to delegate to their executive officer, that they paced themselves and that they communicated their intentions to their officers before action occurred. COs of damaged or sunk ships recalled a loss of a sense of time during battle, so pre-battle discussions and briefings with officers and senior non-commissioned officers were crucial in ensuring that the chain of command could work effectively if the ship were damaged, and not just because of the fragility of internal communication systems mentioned above. The Royal Navy was effectively re-learning lessons of combat experience learnt from the Second World War and other wars before it. Although little was entirely new, the conflict had brought these half-remembered and sometimes forgotten lessons back into the open and had helped to create a more systematic approach to understanding and countering battle stress. A range of recommendations came out of the 'Stress of Battle' paper, including mandatory battle stress training for all crew members down to leading rate, improved battle damage training, more training for medical staff in spotting battle stress, the ending of trickle drafting and additional training for COs and Executive Officers in presenting operational information to ships' companies.[130] Combat training was overhauled over the following years, and with a large number of Falklands veterans with considerable experience available, the Navy's training establishments ensured that these lessons were kept at the forefront of their curricula.

Damage Control and Ship Survivability

The destructive effect of bombs and missiles on a modern, lightly-scantled and unarmoured warship had been considerable: the 'vulnerability of warships to action damage was vividly demonstrated'.[131] Early reports emphasised the need to understand better the impact on ship stability of bomb and missile damage, and recommended that the existing data needed to be reviewed and re-evaluated.[132] By August 1982 the lessons-learnt reports that went outwards from the Navy Department were somewhat more sanguine, stating that 'the resistance of warships to action damage was largely as predicted'.[133] A certain amount of defensiveness within the Ship Department becomes evident, with emphasis placed on the inadequacy of aluminium as construction material. Aluminium had never been accepted as safe by the Ship Department and had only been present in quantity in the commercially-designed Type 21 frigates. The popular perception was that aluminium had caused superstructures and decks to melt in high temperatures.[134] In fact the problems with it were more prosaic but just as serious: aluminium internal doors were more likely to bend and buckle after structural shock, aluminium was more likely to shatter under shock than steel, aluminium was difficult to weld at sea and was therefore less easy to repair, and finally tests at Porton Down had confirmed that high explosive rounds hitting aluminium resulted in a 'much enhanced fireball at double the pressure … compared with steel.'[135] Aluminium, with its clear disadvantages, was therefore given a good amount of attention in the lessons-learnt reports which perhaps lessened the focus on other areas of concern.

For example, Lord Trenchard, the Minister of State for Procurement, was particularly exercised by the Navy Department's report on the attack on HMS *Sheffield*: it did not give sufficient attention to the importance of the positioning of diesel fuel storage tanks on the ship. These were high above the waterline and some were breached with the missile hit which resulted in a much more rapid spreading of the fire. He regarded it as 'a prime factor responsible for the total loss of *Sheffield*' and was angry that the report focussed on the impact of combustible furnishings, which only became important later on in the progress of the fire on the ship.[136] Trenchard felt that there were recommendations for replacing combustible materials in furnishings and lagging, but none that future warship designs should place flammable oils storage in safer positions below the waterline. He made it clear that he thought, perhaps with some justice, that the Navy Department was avoiding highlighting what he saw as fundamental design flaws in the Type 42 in order to focus on a secondary and easily solvable problem with fabrics.[137] Later reports acknowledged the significance of above waterline oil storage and the need to return it to lower in the ship.[138] Concerns about furnishings did not disappear however, so the wholesale replacement of mattresses with non-flammable replacements was quickly undertaken in the months after conflict.[139]

There were a number of other issues with materials and equipment that needed to be dealt with in both current warships and future warship types:

glass mirrors, Formica interior panelling and wooden spurnwaters all resulted in splinters which caused serious injuries to ships' crews. This resulted in the replacement of wood with steel in new ships under construction wherever possible. Some escape hatches were too small to use whilst wearing breathing apparatus which made both escape and fire-fighting difficult; there were also too few access points to different parts of the ship to aid firefighting. Leith Cardle doors, which were easier to close with one hand action, had been easily distorted by explosive shock, making them extremely difficult to open or close. Tragically one person had died 'with his leg trapped in the bottom of this type of door, which had distorted to allow the upper dogs to engage, thus preventing rescue'.[140] It was recommended that such doors be redesigned to allow for the manual operation of individual clips in an emergency, and this was done in the new Type 23 frigates. Acrid smoke had easily penetrated bulkheads and was one of the main reasons why damage control and rescue operations had been hampered after serious damage, and it was recommended in new-build warships to create multiple fire-control zones, each of which was 'gas tight' and with its own fire pump and water main for firefighting. Again, this was carried out in the new class of frigates. Splinter damage had been a cause of electronic and power failure, and it was strongly recommended that major cables not be routed along the outer edges of a ship's hull as had been the case with the Type 22. In addition, it was recommended that light armour (possibly Kevlar) be considered to protect against splinter damage in vital areas such as operations rooms, ship control centres and magazines, and those magazines should also be made floodable as per earlier Second World War practice. Centralised hydraulic fluid piping systems were not recommended, as the fluid was often flammable and the piping prone to break on shock. Hydraulics should not be used at all or, if completely necessary, individual fluid systems should be 'stand-alone' and not connected to a ring-main.[141]

At the level of individual clothing and equipment for crew and specifically damage control teams, recommendations included that crew clothing should not be synthetic (which was much more flammable than wool or cotton), that emergency communications and lighting which were simple and robust – such as battery-powered analogue phones and head-strapped miner's lamps – were those most likely to survive the shock of impact, that ships should be provided with more waterproof suits for work in flooded compartments. Anti-flash gear had proved especially successful in reducing burns, whilst the Navy's 'woolly pully' woollen pull-over had provided a significant amount of fire protection compared to other clothing.[142] Another less publicised success was the maintenance of electrical capacity in *Sheffield* right up to her end: both the forecastle and stern of the destroyer had working electrics days after the Exocet hit.[143] In this instance at least electrical supply, if not necessarily all electrical devices, had been made robust and battle damage resistant. As with dealing with battle stress, the Navy was re-learning many lessons from the Second World War, combined with some new lessons: electrical equipment – at least of late 1970s and early 1980s vintage – was fragile and prone to going off-line with the shock of bomb or missile impact, even if the impact was at the other end of the ship. Simple, robust replacements – and much use of additional human beings – had proven to be the best replacement and supplement to these systems. As many of these recommendations as possible were implemented in the current fleet during refits and maintenance during the mid-1980s, whilst the design of the new Type 23 frigate was recast to incorporate major survivability changes, not least the increase of segregated fire-control zones from three to five, and additional measures to ensure that smoke could not move from one zone to another.[144]

Mine Warfare
The first mine warfare vessels south had been ships taken up from trade, specifically ocean-going stern trawlers rapidly fitted with sweep rigs, the first 'Hunt' class vessels not being ready for operations and in theatre until after the Argentine surrender.[145] The successful deployment of the trawlers appeared to confirm the Royal Navy's decision to rely on STUFT trawlers to supplement more sophisticated and expensive mine hunters. The trawlers did have their limitations: the Argentine mines had all been basic moored contact mines, but if they had been acoustic or magnetic then these vessels would have been much less able to destroy or render them safe. The conflict also highlighted the deterioration of the Navy's de-gaussing capabilities: only half the ships of the Task Force were in-date for their de-gaussing and the facilities for doing so in Portland were inadequate for servicing the fleet.[146] Of twenty-one mines declared by the Argentines, sixteen had been swept or were otherwise accounted for, whilst two detached sinkers had been found implying that at least two further mines had either been swept unnoticed, had already exploded or had broken loose at some point.[147] The mine clearance operation had therefore been relatively successful, and was even more impressive considering that the bulk of the Navy's mine warfare capability – the 'Ton' class mine hunters and sweepers – had not been used as they had been incapable of operating in the heavy seas of the South Atlantic.

Engineering
The conflict was judged to have justified the move to gas turbine propulsion operating in self-contained units. The comparison between the impact of a bomb hit in the machinery spaces of *Argonaut*, an old steam turbine frigate, and *Glasgow*, a gas turbine destroyer, was telling. *Argonaut* had no

propulsion at all for several hours whilst rapid repairs were made in San Carlos Water under the threat of air attack. By contrast, although *Glasgow*'s after engine room was partly flooded the ship could propel herself out of harm's way using her undamaged Olympus gas turbine.[148] The replacement of one of *Invincible*'s gas turbines whilst the ship was heading south was another reflection of the flexibility of this propulsion system. Since commissioning July 1980 *Invincible* had steamed 120,000 nautical miles, nearly all of these during the South Atlantic campaign.[149] One disadvantage of gas turbines was a greater reliance on diesel generators for electrical power generation. The diesel generators in the Type 42s had required frequent maintenance and repair.[150] In addition, individual gas turbines had had relatively low availability, at between 89 per cent and 93 per cent although this was offset by unit propulsion which meant that other turbines could continue in operation. Some key parts of the turbines had worryingly low reliable lives before needing to be replaced. There were also warnings about shifting from the current regimes of routine maintenance to the cheaper 'condition-based-maintenance' approach. The 'maintenance fat' of the current routine regime meant that more replacement parts were kept aboard ship, and during the sustained period at sea in the South Atlantic, these spare parts had proved invaluable and had lessened the logistics load on RFA stores ships.[151] Overall therefore, the adoption of gas turbines had resulted in numerous advantages in flexibility and survivability, but no innovation is without its problems, and multiple recommendations were made to improve the reliability and operational life of the turbines and many of their key components, as well as the diesel generators that were now being much more heavily worked.

The provision of *Stena Seaspread* and *Stena Inspector* as forward support ships had proved a success. The former ship had undertaken major repairs in the open sea, including the placing of new steel plate over damaged sections, re-wiring a damaged Sea Wolf system without access to detailed wiring drawings, recovering 20mm guns from sunken ships and rebuilding the gas turbine downtakes of HMS *Glasgow* after her bomb damage on 12 May. Other impressive achievements were the replacement of one of *Avenger*'s propeller blades underwater, and the replacement of one of *Invincible*'s Olympus gas turbines on the journey south. After the conflict had ended, *Stena Inspector* had replaced the Type 992 radar aerial and pedestal of the destroyer HMS *Birmingham*.[152] This success, and the obvious need for continued forward support for the ships remaining in the South Atlantic after the conflict had ended, resulted in *Stena Inspector* being commissioned as RFA *Diligence* and remaining on the Falklands station until December 1986 when she was relieved by her sister ship *Stena Seaspread* under charter.[153]

Procurement Processes

The conflict had seen the rapid speeding-up of existing procurements including getting the new carrier *Illustrious* and the frigate *Brazen* ready for service, the ordering of additional numbers of weapons or other equipment that were already in production, and the procuring of new 'Urgent Operational Requirements' as the conflict progressed. As was seen with ships taken up from trade, normal procedures were rapidly set to one side. With *Illustrious* and *Brazen*, the rush to push these ships into service had meant that both were ready as part of the relief Task Force, and if the conflict had lasted another two months, they would have been directly involved in hostilities. There were sacrifices made in order to achieve this: their standard of finish had been lower and it was therefore expected that they would be more expensive to preserve and maintain over their service lives. A few pieces of equipment were defective as the two ships were hurried into service: for example *Illustrious*' port-side replenishment at sea masts did not work satisfactorily. The new carrier had 11,000 defects on acceptance and the new frigate a total of 1,600. In normal circumstances there would only be approximately 200 on a new ship the size of *Brazen*. Many of these defects were minor and easily corrected, but the shaving of three months of their final stages of construction was not without its longer-term impact. It was also noted that the relevant shipbuilders had been working well below their capacity before the conflict started, so had the human and material resources at hand to step up production when the call came from the Ministry.[154] It could not be assumed that such a capacity gap would exist in the future.

When it came to the speeding-up of existing production runs and procuring new items at short-notice, initially it was thought that the benefits of setting aside the usual bureaucracy of procurement – which had dramatically speeded up purchase and delivery – could be carried over into future peacetime procurement practice. The normal procedures were described as 'circuitous, often tortuous and always depressingly lengthy', whilst during Operation 'Corporate' when 'financial restrictions and lengthy tendering for contracts were largely set aside ... there was ... a very fast and efficient interchange between all decision-making authorities in the MOD (and between [the] P[rocurement] E[xecutive] and industry)'.[155] There was inevitable push-back from within the Ministry: most of the rapid procurements were undertaken on a 'price to be agreed' basis with no oversight regarding value for money. Over the long run, despite the benefits in terms of speed, the costs to the taxpayer of such an approach would be considerable, whilst the meeting of capability requirements was not as strongly assessed as normal. When seen from the perspective of the classic 'project management trinity' of cost, speed and capability it was clear that cost controls had been entirely removed and capability requirements lessened in order to focus almost wholly on speed of delivery. This was justifiable during a short-term crisis but difficult to continue when peacetime conditions returned. Even so, a review of the acceptance trials process was agreed with the aim of some streamlining based on experience from the conflict.[156]

It had also been notable that the ability of industry to speed up production on existing manufacturing lines had been limited: the number of Sea Dart missiles produced monthly was increased from nine to twelve over a four-month period, whilst Sea Cat production was doubled to twenty a month over a three-month timeframe. However, these were only short-term expedients which would create a future backlog of work: constraints in skilled personnel and long-lead components limited the increases that could be made and would inevitably mean a period of low production some months in the future as such components ran out and skilled workers became exhausted. The most successful procurements were of new requirements where the purchases had been 'off the shelf' with manufacturers already having numbers in storage, such as Vulcan Phalanx guns, Super RBOC chaff launchers and BMARC light guns.[157]

Media Relations

The Navy Department acknowledged after the conflict that its relations with the press had not been good. The Royal Navy had initially not wanted any journalists aboard the Task Force and had only relented after pressure from the Cabinet Office. Even then, those journalists who were allowed aboard were subject to varying restrictions enforced by Ministry of Defence press liaison officers who managed to both frustrate the journalists whilst also lacking any rapport with, or respect from, the senior naval officers of the Task Force. Film images from the war only arrived in the United Kingdom two weeks after they had been produced, which allowed Argentine-produced images to dominate television pictures back in Britain and the rest of the world.[158] Admiral Lewin and the Ministry of Defence were also willing to use briefings to the media as a way to spread misinformation and deceive the Argentines; most famously with Sir Frank Cooper's briefing to journalists a day before the San Carlos landings that a 'D-Day style' operation was not going to happen.[159] In retrospect, the extent to which the media could be controlled, and its reporting monitored, edited and held back was partly a result of the huge geographical distances between the conflict and the United Kingdom and the limitations of communications technology at the time. It was the last significant conflict involving a major Western power in which such control over words and images could be exercised. After an internal inquiry, CINCFLEET's final report acknowledged – rather tersely as if through gritted teeth – that 'greater awareness of the press and their requirements is needed in the Royal Navy' and that a more active involvement of press liaison teams in any future conflicts would be needed.[160] A comprehensive internal study was produced within the Ministry of Defence, whilst external academic studies were commissioned well into the mid-1980s, indicating that the Ministry had decided that it needed to ensure its relations with journalists were better the next time it was involved in a major conflict.[161]

* * *

The lessons-learnt process was a mammoth undertaking, involving the work of numerous specialists, staff officers and those involved in the fighting over the months and years after the Argentine invasion. As a process it was thorough but definitely not flawless, but the analysis undertaken primarily within the Navy Department, for internal use within the Department, and analysis undertaken by subject-matter specialists was generally more accurate. However, even here there could have been a tendency to run along the tramlines of earlier experience. For example, the assessment that the Exocet that hit *Sheffield* had never exploded, could well have been influenced by the problems encountered by that missile when it was under trial by the Royal Navy in the 1970s. More recent analysis has shown that the Exocet warhead probably did explode.[162] Lord Trenchard's pushing for the Ship Department to acknowledge the role of above-waterline oil tanks in the rapid progress of the fire on *Sheffield*, highlights a situation where a department might have been attempting to protect its reputation in its analysis. The higher-level analyses, often undertaken by staff officers collating or editing earlier specialist reports, particularly where evidence could play a role in influencing procurements or force structure and size, were more likely to show marks of building a case for or against particular decisions. Given the Navy's searing experience in the Defence Review only a year earlier, it is perhaps unsurprising that whilst the Falklands conflict was still underway, the Navy's leadership was planning to use it to lever more reversals from the Review: cancelling the sale of *Invincible*, increasing the size of the escort force and maintaining the facilities at Portsmouth Dockyard.[163] By 11 May, detailed lists of capability updates for different ships were being sketched out prior to lobbying for their implementation. Even at this early stage these included updating the Batch 1 Type 42s up to Batch 2 standards with improved radar and other systems.[164]

The Size and Shape of the Fleet
The recommendations reviewed in the preceding sections of this chapter reflected important lessons from the conflict, but these were largely focussed on technology, process and personnel matters. What were the major, strategic and

high policy-level lessons that were learnt from the conflict, and what impact did they have on overall defence policy? The main document driving the early stages of the lessons-learnt process had been the promised White Paper, which became 'The Falklands Campaign: The Lessons' and was released in December 1982.[165] It essentially summarised the internal lessons-learnt process – or at least those parts that the Ministry wanted to make public – and set out decisions over equipment that had come from those lessons or which replaced losses in the conflict. The Lessons White Paper confirmed that HMS *Invincible* would not be sold, that the lost ships would be replaced – with the two Type 42 destroyers and two Type 21 frigates replaced by four Type 22 frigates and *Sir Galahad* replaced by a new vessel of an updated design. *Sir Tristram* would be repaired. All lost aircraft, including Harriers and naval helicopters, would be replaced with seven additional Harriers (later increased to nine[166]) and six Sea Kings also purchased, that the total size of the frigate and destroyer force would remain at fifty-five until at least 1984, with the ships that had been slated for the Standby Squadron placed in active service. The point defence capabilities of the carriers, assault ships and modern destroyers would be enhanced, airborne early warning helicopters for the fleet would be created using Searchwater radars, whilst weapons stockpiles would be significantly augmented.[167] These were important changes: not only would three carriers be maintained but they would have more than enough Harrier aircraft to justify substantial air groups in the two active carriers, with more for 'surging' in a crisis. The active number of frigates and destroyers would now reduce at a much slower rate. Although the planned figure of fifty such ships remained in public statements, this figure would now be arrived at 'later in the decade' rather than in 1982 as had been planned before the conflict. The Standby Squadron, which had had no ships assigned to it since the end of 1981 was formally removed from planning assumptions, with no ships expected to be in reserve through the 1980s.[168]

Behind the scenes, the changes were also significant: the long-term future of air defence destroyers which looked bleak before the conflict, had now been assured with the Ministry of Defence committing to being part of the NATO Frigate Replacement programme for the 1990s ('NFR90'), which included an area air defence variant that the Royal Navy planned to procure as a replacement for the Type 42.[169] The four remaining Batch 1 Type 42s would be modernised to Batch 2 standard, which would have not occurred otherwise, thus effectively reinstituting something not far from the extensive (and expensive) mid-life refit that Nott had sought to abolish in the 1981 Defence Review. The Sea Dart missile system would receive improvements to its capability, which had definitely not been envisaged before the conflict, and Type 42 destroyers would receive the US Phalanx Close-in Weapon System to defend against guided missiles.[170] Redundancy programmes and personnel reduction planning were halted whilst the reduction of Portsmouth naval base to a forward operating base would be postponed and later reversed, ensuring that a destroyer refit capability remained.[171]

Politically it is difficult to see how most of these improvements to the Navy's capability could have been refused: the public and Conservative Party backbench outcry would have been huge if the sale of *Invincible* had gone ahead, if the lost ships had not been replaced, if glaring deficiencies in airborne early warning and ship self-defence had not been remedied, and if successful capabilities were not recognised and further units of those types not purchased. In addition, the Falkland Islands had to be defended from a residual Argentine threat: leaving the islands in what would have been perceived to be a defenceless state would also have been politically impossible. The retention of fifty-five frigates and destroyers until 1984 was largely driven by the need to provide additional warships to the defend the islands until the diplomatic situation cooled.

Strategically these augmentations were justified by a report written by the Chief of the Defence Staff with his Principal Staff Officer, who was now Hugo White, the former Captain of HMS *Avenger* during the Falklands, and endorsed by the Chiefs of Staff, that clearly stated that 'a balanced core fleet is required, sufficient in numbers and in mixture of platforms and weapons in ASW, AAW, ASVW and MCM operations together with afloat support'.[172] The need for such a balanced fleet, which the Defence Review had partly attempted to dismantle, was based on the need to deal with the unexpected: the Falklands might be unique in its remoteness but 'not in its unexpectedness, because history tells us that we are often not able to predict with any assurance the next likely area of conflict'.[173] This was a direct swipe at the Defence Review's attempt to pull nearly all of Defence's capabilities towards preparing for only a very limited number of scenarios, mostly involving an attack by Soviet troops across the inner German border. The Chief of the Defence Staff did not argue that the threat from the Warsaw Pact should be downgraded: 'a substantial shift in defence policy is not justified' but that the 'middle and long-term programme should be nudged towards greater strategic mobility and flexibility to meet the unexpected'. Lewin also argued that the conflict's 'singularity should not obscure its relevance to operations elsewhere'.[174] The harshness of its environment, the rapid expenditure of stocks and problems of air defence in coastal waters, could all be applied to NATO's northern flank and, in part, to the central region.

Lessons Learnt?

Despite the changes towards an acknowledgement of the importance of the unexpected and the need for a spectrum of capabilities, some at the top of the civilian leadership of the Ministry of Defence still seemed to have a tin ear regarding the political impact of the Falklands conflict on defence policy. Only two months after the surrender of Argentine forces on the islands Sir Frank Cooper put forward an argument that British forces should withdraw from Belize as quickly as possible. The former colony in Central America had been granted its independence in 1981 but the problem of the continued Guatemalan claim on the state had not been fully resolved. It had been planned that British forces would withdraw in the middle months of 1982 but this was repeatedly postponed as the Falklands crisis turned into a full conflict. From Cooper's perspective, the end of that crisis now meant that it was now the perfect time to remove – as quickly as possible – another 'out of area' commitment that could turn into a conflict unexpectedly.[175] The belief that the unexpected could be removed from defence policy just by the ending of 'commitments' that the Ministry did not want, betrayed the clean, logical and tidy thought processes of those who wanted the Ministry to work within only the realms of the predicted.

The careers of both Nott and Cooper were in their final months, but their inability to understand that being seen to withdraw from protecting a small, poorly defended state in Latin America from a far-right military regime only a few months after the end of the Falklands conflict would be politically impossible, does demonstrate the extent to which thinking beyond the Soviet threat did not come naturally within the Ministry by the early 1980s. Both Nott and Cooper, as well as Sir Ronald Mason, who had been the driving forces behind the Defence Review, seem to have had difficulties coming to terms with reversal of much of that review following the conflict. Two years after his retirement, when speaking to an historian in a tape-recorded interview about his time in government, Nott expressed his frustration that an unexpected military campaign had appeared to discredit the Defence Review that he had conducted only a year before. The Falklands had been 'an event of pure strategic tragedy. An event which was of a nature that, hard as one tries, one cannot think of any other example in the whole of history which was so capable of distorting the right strategic choice for the defence of Great Britain.'[176]

Cooper, whose long tenure as the Ministry's Permanent Under-Secretary did much to help set the culture of British Defence was, in his retirement, dismissive of the 'world role' of much of the surface fleet, as was shown in the quotation at the start of Chapter 13. Cooper, in post-retirement interviews, also saw politicians as being 'too involved in the nitty-gritty' of policymaking and who should instead behave more like a chairman of the board.[177] To some extent this is the over-compensation of a civil servant from a department where until 1964 the officials had been largely subordinate to military-dominated boards, but it perhaps hints at his perception of the relationship between himself and Nott. If so, it is deeply concerning that Cooper's political antennae were so poor. The political impact of a withdrawal from Belize was so significant that removing British troops was continually delayed throughout the 1980s, and only occurred in 1993 under a new Prime Minister and after Guatemala had tacitly accepted Belize's independence.[178]

Whilst Nott and Cooper held their counsel on the review and the Falklands aftermath until their retirement, Sir Ronald Mason was more forthright whilst still in post. He strongly disliked the Chiefs of Staffs' arguments in favour of more flexibility in capabilities, instead arguing for greater 'hitting power' at longer range. He did not want any further investment in area air defence capabilities – implying that the Type 42s should indeed be withdrawn from service without replacement – whilst any additional funds for maritime air defence should only go on point defence and electronic warfare. He disliked both the concept of 'layered air defence' and of 'flexibility' in capabilities, arguing instead that the focus should remain on the Soviet threat and countering it with long-range weaponry. In a maritime context, this would make the air defence of merchant vessels extremely difficult, unless each one was expensively armed or fitted with electronic warfare capabilities. He also argued that the campaign had shown that Royal Fleet Auxiliaries were not needed and could be replaced by ships taken up from trade.[179] On this point, the Chief Scientific Adviser's arguments departed from the evidence base: STUFT storeships had rarely transferred stores directly to warships, whilst the modifications required to turn STUFT storeships into vessels that could do so would have been so extensive and time-consuming as to defeat the object of doing so. STUFT oilers were more feasible for direct transfer to warships, but only slowly and after considerable training of their crews by experienced RFA officers.[180] For this reason, their transfers were generally only to RFAs during the conflict.

With this example Mason was beginning to sound somewhat unmoored from the evidence-based scientific advice he was meant to be giving, and on occasion his communications in places read like less-than-veiled attacks on the benefits the Navy was accruing from the post-conflict equipment decisions. However, he did acknowledge the significance of the unexpected in the conflict and the problems of basing equipment requirements on a handful of over-tightly circumscribed scenarios, made astute remarks about the need for higher standards of robustness in equipment and emphasised the importance of high levels of training and morale.[181] Despite this, his focus on single predictable threats and long-range weaponry was swimming against the current tide at the Ministry in the last months of 1982. The Naval Staff described one of his notes as 'a scurrilous piece of paper' with 'a string of unsubstantiated general statements'.[182] This was somewhat unfair, but Mason did not help his argument by loose assessments about STUFT support ships that could be easily disproven, which only served to call into question the other points he was making. Such carelessness might reflect his frustrations at the shifts in policy so close to his retirement, but this was certainly unusual behaviour for a Chief Scientific Adviser.

* * *

Mason's statements did not make much difference to the decisions made in the December 1982 White Paper, but they did illustrate that much of what the Naval Staff wanted and the change of approach they were pressing for, went against the grain of a Ministry that was focussed on deterring a Soviet threat defined as a land attack across the inner German border. Out of area operations could not disappear entirely, it was politically and strategically impossible for them to do so, but the focus of the Ministry of Defence largely remained on the Soviet threat on the Central Front.[183] The lessons-learnt process had been undertaken with considerable thoroughness and in some great detail in the months, and years, after the conflict had ended. At nearly every level, these lessons fed into the Navy: from training, damage control and managing morale, through to major equipment procurements and enhancements. Some of these reversed decisions made in 1980 and 1981, and might be seen as an extension of the pre-Falklands process to claw back Nott Review outcomes, but many others required new training or capabilities that had not been envisaged before the conflict had begun. Together, both US Department of Defense interventions in 1981–2 and the Falklands conflict of April–June 1982, served to place the Royal Navy in a much better place than could ever have been envisaged in May 1981 when the first force structures had been developed from the decisions of John Nott's 'Bermudagram'.

18

Maritime Strategy

Although the Falklands conflict had been important in ensuring that major capabilities were retained in both the short and the long-term, the shift in the United States' maritime strategy during the early 1980s had as great an impact in justifying and validating the role of the Royal Navy in the Ministry of Defence through the rest of the decade. The new US strategy, which was gradually devised and revised during the first five years of President Reagan's two administrations, gave the British a clear purpose in providing the anti-submarine defence of the US carrier strike fleet as it advanced into the Norwegian Sea, protection to reinforcement shipping arriving from across the Atlantic, and undertaking offensive operations underwater in the High North. This chapter will start by setting out the nature and extent of the Soviet maritime threat in the early 1980s, then describe in more detail the US Maritime Strategy and the British role within it, the key Eastern Atlantic NATO exercises of the 1980s, the operational introduction of surface towed-array sonar into the fleet and its impact on submarine detection, and then finish with Royal Navy planning for the steps in the transition to war from high tension through to impending nuclear exchange.

First, however, the Navy saw a transition in its leadership as Admiral Leach retired in the last weeks of 1982 to be replaced by Admiral Sir John Fieldhouse, the Commander-in-Chief Fleet. Even without Fieldhouse's experience as the overall operational commander of the Task Force during the Falklands Conflict, he would probably have been the natural choice as First Sea Lord. His three predecessors, Admirals Leach, Lewin and Ashmore, had all been Commander-in-Chief Fleet, so much so that it had now become the standard route through to be the professional head of the service. Fieldhouse was also a submariner, and given the growing prominence of the submarine service within the Navy it was perhaps an overdue recognition of this leading position. The last submariner First Sea Lord had been Admiral Luce, who had retired more than 16 years earlier. The promotion of Fieldhouse, as was usual, also saw a staggered changeover in many of the other leading posts within the Navy. The former Vice Chief of the Naval Staff, and Leach's right-hand man during the Defence Review, had been Vice Admiral Sir William Staveley. He was a former Flag Officer Carriers and Amphibious Ships, and had come from a long line of naval officers, his grandfather being Admiral Doveton Sturdee, victor of the 1914 Battle of the Falklands.[1] Staveley was promoted to Commander-in-Chief Fleet in October 1982, and his successor in the VCNS role was Vice Admiral Peter Stanford, a seasoned Whitehall operator with an intellectual bent rare amongst senior naval officers, who had been Secretary of the Chiefs of Staffs Committee between 1975 and 1979.[2] Admiral Sir Desmond Cassidi had been Second Sea Lord since 1979 and in December 1982 he became Commander-in-Chief Naval Home Command, a post he would hold for the next three years before retirement. Cassidi was a former Fleet Air Arm pilot, commanding officer of HMS *Ark Royal* and Flag Officer, Naval Air Command.[3] His successor as Second Sea Lord was Admiral Sir Simon Cassels, a former commanding officer of the old cruiser *Tiger* and Flag Officer, Plymouth.[4] Meanwhile, Admiral Sir Lyndsey Bryson remained as Controller of the Navy, a post he had held since 1981 in succession to Admiral Fieldhouse, and Vice Admiral Sir James Kennon remained Chief of Fleet Support. Both Bryson and Kennon were quite different from the others that had been promoted into the Navy's most senior positions. Bryson was a naval engineer educated at the Royal Technical College in Glasgow, who had previously held posts as Director General Weapons (Naval) and Chief Naval Engineer Officer. Incredibly, he was the first engineer to hold the post of Controller, despite its responsibility for procurement and engineering.[5] Kennon was also the first supply officer to become Chief of Fleet Support, he was a qualified interpreter in French and Italian and had been Mountbatten's Military Assistant when he had been Chief of the Defence Staff.[6] The Admiralty Board was at last beginning to open up to officers outside the seamen branch, with specialists in engineering and logistics finally being given the most senior posts in the areas in the Navy. It would be these senior officers who would steer the Navy through its adjustment towards supporting the US Maritime Strategy, whilst also attempting to sustain a credible deterrent force against a Soviet Navy that seemed to be growing in size, capability and reach.

The Development of Soviet Naval Capabilities

In the 1970s and early 1980s it seemed that the Soviet Navy's capabilities were undergoing such a significant step-change that this was heralding an important strategic shift: it seemed to some analysts, and was stated in US official publications, that the Soviets now planned to contest sea control from NATO in the open oceans rather than merely attack sea lines of communications or defend their nuclear deterrent forces.[7] Given the multiplicity of new and impressively formidable classes of ship entering service during this period, it is not surprising that some came to this conclusion. In fact, the new types of vessel entering service were more a reflection of increasing size due to the complexity and volume of the most modern weapons, sensors and systems. Also, as will be seen, there *was* a major technological and strategic shift taking place. However, it was not focussed on an attempt at sea control, but instead on new third-generation submarines which would be the quietest ever built by the Soviets, and what would be described in the West as a 'bastion' strategy to protect Soviet SSBNs operating in the High North and carrying newer longer-range ballistic missiles. What was not possible to see in the early 1980s, was that these large and new vessels could not be built in the numbers needed to replace their predecessors, and that the Soviet naval-industrial base was beginning to atrophy and stutter when coming up against the limits of a non-capitalist command economy.

Submarines
In June 1981, the first Soviet 'Typhoon' class ballistic missile submarine (known as Project 941 in the Soviet Navy) went to sea to undertake initial trials. The *TK-208* was the largest submarine ever built. She was armed with twenty solid-propellant R-39 ballistic missiles (known by NATO as SS-N-20), but such was the space required for these missiles, the designers had built two internal pressure hulls side by side along the length of the boat. The missiles in their launch tubes were placed between these two pressure hulls, whilst between and above the two pressure hulls and behind the missile tubes was a third smaller pressure hull containing the boat's command and control facilities. Above the boat's control room was the sail. A fourth pressure hull was placed forward and linked the main pressure hulls, and included the boat's torpedo tubes. All four hulls were then wrapped in an outer protective hull. This unique design had partly been driven by the need for the boat to have a sufficiently shallow draught to enter its home ports on the Kola Peninsula. It also resulted in a huge and extremely wide submarine displacing 23,000 tons on the surface, more than three times that of the Royal Navy's *Resolution* class ballistic missile submarines. A further five such boats were completed before the end of the Cold War, their enormous size driven by the need to house their twenty R-39 ballistic missiles, the largest such missiles ever built. Alongside the new 'Typhoon' class, the Soviets also maintained a parallel programme of 'Delta IV' class boats (Project 667BDRM), a linear development of the preceding classes, and armed with sixteen smaller liquid fuel R-29RM ballistic

missiles (NATO: SS-N-23). Although less radical than the 'Typhoons' these were capable boats, and seven were completed before the end of the Cold War. All boats of both the 'Typhoon' and 'Delta IV' classes were based with the Northern Fleet.[8]

During the 1980s it became clear that the US nuclear 'triad' of bombers, land-based ballistic missiles and submarine-launched ballistic missiles was shifting its balance so that the last of these was beginning to gain dominance in numbers of warheads. The submarines' ability to hide from attack in the deep ocean lessened the chances of a pre-emptive strike on NATO nuclear forces by an enemy being successful, at least in comparison to static missile silos on land or bombers in the air. In the 1980s, it seemed that the Soviet submarine nuclear force might achieve a similar degree of importance, but the Soviet General Staff had concerns about command links with the submarines and about the extremely high cost of the 'Typhoons'. As a result, the 'Typhoon' class were curtailed in number and Soviet Naval offers of converting cruise missile submarines into ballistic missile boats were turned down. Instead, a significant portion of the Soviet protection against vulnerability from a pre-emptive attack would come from road- or rail-mobile land-based launchers for the Topol ballistic missile which entered service in 1989.[9]

Soviet cruise missile submarines, those that launched anti-ship missiles with the aim of destroying NATO carrier battle groups, also saw a dramatic shift in their construction programmes. The 'Charlie I' and 'Charlie II' class programmes, which had been run throughout the 1970s, came to an end. They had proven too slow to keep up with fast US carrier groups and had been dependent on a military satellite system that was not reliable enough for targeting.[10] Since the late 1960s the Soviets had been developing a longer range cruise missile to replace the P-6 missile that had been fitted to 'Echo II' class boats in the 1960s. This new missile, the P-700 Granit (known by NATO as the SS-N-19 'Shipwreck'), would have the advantage of being launched underwater and have a greater range than the P-6. The 'Oscar' class cruise missile submarines (known as Project 949 in the USSR) were therefore designed around this new 'carrier-killer' missile. Launch tubes were placed either side of the boat's sail, creating another wide submarine type, this time able to launch twenty-four P-700s. As with the 'Typhoons', these were extremely resource-intensive to build, with two 'Oscars' being the resource cost equivalent of an aircraft carrier, and therefore were criticised as a poor use of funds. The first boat was commissioned in December 1980 and a total of eight were completed before the end of the Cold War, five of which were with the Northern Fleet.[11] These were serious threats to NATO naval forces, and would have been one of the Royal Navy's main adversaries when attempting to defend the US carrier strike fleet in northern waters if war had broken out.

There was also a multiplicity of new classes of Soviet hunter-killer nuclear-powered submarines entering service in the 1980s. The first to appear was the one-off 'Mike' class (Project 685), a large experimental hunter-killer submarine with extremely deep diving characteristics. Her maximum diving depth was 1,000m, around three to four times that of most combat submarines and similar to that of deep ocean mini-subs. The boat's hull was made of titanium alloy and included a significant number of experimental systems. Within the Soviet Navy it had been hoped to build more of such boats, but presumably the expense and her unclear role meant that only a single boat was approved, the *K-278*. US intelligence organisations speculated on the purpose of the design, fearing that being armed with new torpedo-launched cruise missiles, she could be a land attack submarine, but in reality she was an experimental design with much automation and a small crew of only sixty-nine, albeit with a full fighting capability as a hunter-killer.[12] In 1989, the *K-278* (renamed the *Komsomolets* in 1988) would tragically sink in the Norwegian Sea due to an accidental fire, with forty-two of her crew lost.[13]

After the first appearance of *K-278* in 1984, a second class of titanium alloy submarines appeared the same year, the 'Sierra' class (Project 945) hunter-killer. This was a smaller submarine, designed and built in Gork'iy on the River Volga. Her small size, which was made possible by a small crew and titanium alloy construction, was a necessity given the restrictions on size required for passage on the Volga and the canals that linked it to the Black, Baltic and White seas. The boat was extremely manoeuvrable and was also faster than Western equivalents.[14] The design had been chosen in 1973 to be the centrepiece of 'Project Argus', an ambitious integrated system for anti-submarine defence, over designs produced by the more experienced Malakhit bureau in Severodvinsk in the north, perhaps because of blunders over the Malakhit-designed 'Alfa' class described in Chapter 10.[15] As with all the other new designs described thus far, the boat's greatest drawback was its huge demand for resources – the process of making submarines with titanium alloy required an argon-rich atmosphere for welding – which made it slow and resource-intensive to produce thus making one-for-one replacement of 1960s vintage boats extremely difficult, if not impossible.[16] Only three boats were completed by the end of the Cold War, all of which served with the Northern Fleet. This problem was resolved by the continued production of the most advanced variant of the preceding 'Victor' class hunter-killers throughout the 1980s, and by the building of a larger and less-resource intensive steel variant of the 'Sierra', the 'Akula' class (Project 971), designed by the Malakhit bureau. This had initially been developed for Far East production, as the submarine yard in this region did not have the facilities to build boats with titanium alloy. The first boat, *K-284*, was therefore constructed at Komsomol'sk-na-Amure in the Soviet Far East, entering service with the Pacific Fleet in 1984.[17] However, it was only in 1985, after it became clear that the 'Sierra' programme was in trouble and the 'Akula' design had been proven, that series production began on the rest of the class. Seven were completed by the end of the Cold War, but only two of these were assigned to the Northern Fleet.[18]

As a result, very few third-generation hunter-killers were actually in service with the Northern Fleet during the last years of the Cold War, and so the mainstay of the Soviet nuclear submarine force in the Eastern Atlantic and Norwegian Sea remained the previous generation submarines of the 'Victor' class, particularly the last and most advanced variant, the 'Victor III'. Despite this, there was an awareness in NATO that the 'Sierras' and 'Akulas' were just 'over the horizon' and that in the 1990s, when series production of the latter started to bear fruit, the anti-submarine challenge would then increase significantly. In the event, NATO navies were 'saved by the bell' as a result of the end of the Cold War, just when the 'Akulas' were entering sustained series production.[19] The 'Akulas', 'Sierras' and to some extent the 'Victor IIIs' had initially been a surprise to US analysts, who had assumed that the Soviet submarine quieting would remain far behind that of NATO. British intelligence analysts had been warning since the late 1970s that this situation would not continue, but it was not until the first 'Sierra' and first 'Akula' appeared that the United States realised that the NATO acoustic advantage would be eroded once these boats entered series production.[20] It is thought that this Soviet advance came about as a result of the Walker spy ring in the United States, where information gained through espionage warned the Soviet Navy about the ease at which they could be tracked by NATO sonars.[21] As a result, the Soviets not only invested considerable time and effort in making their submarines less detectable, they also investigated non-acoustic methods of detecting submarines. These ranged from heat signature detection and electro-optics (using lasers to detect a large moving object under the water), through to 'internal wave' detection from space or from the air. In the late 1970s Western scientists realised that the water displaced by a submarine as it travelled through the water created a large 'v' shaped 'wave' or rise in the sea's surface above and behind the boat. Amongst the systems for non-acoustic detection developed by the Soviets was SOKS ('Sistyema Obnaruzhyeniya Kil'vatyernogo Slyeda' or wake detection system), which aimed to detect a different types of wake, this time those created underwater by submarines. SOKS was fitted to a significant number of 'Victor III' and 'Akula' class submarines. It is not clear how successful the Soviets were in perfecting these modes of detection, but their gradual discovery by NATO intelligence agencies during the 1970s and 1980s further increased concerns about the shrinking capability gap between Western and Soviet submarines.[22]

Soviet construction of conventionally-powered boats also continued through the 1980s, as it had done during the 1970s, but instead of only one boat a year being constructed, the new 'Kilo' class soon began series production at three shipyards with two to three being laid down annually. A total of twenty had been completed by the end of the Cold War.[23] As was seen in Chapter 15, NATO exercises in the early 1980s, starting with Ocean Venture in 1981, began to emphasise anti-submarine operations against conventional boats. This required different capabilities in ASW platforms as conventional boats were quieter than their nuclear counterparts which made underwater detection more difficult. However, they also spent more of their operational time on the surface, thus re-emphasising the importance of radar on maritime patrol aircraft.

Surface Ships
If the Soviet submarine programme was worrying Western analysts for the high quality of the boats produced, if not their numbers, then something similar was occurring with the construction of the largest Soviet surface ships. The *Kiev* class hybrid-aircraft carriers continued to enter service through the 1980s, with a third ship of the class appearing in 1982 and a fourth in 1987. Two of the class were based with the Northern Fleet, including the fourth ship, *Baku*, which included improved weapons and radars, some of which presaged a much more ambitious vessel. This was the *Riga*, which was much larger, with a standard displacement of 43,000 tons, and had a full flight deck including arrestor wire recovery of aircraft and ramped take off: a hybrid type of operation that sat between the catapult and arrestor wire carriers of the US Navy and short take off and vertical landing approach of the British *Invincible* class. The *Riga* would fly the much more capable Su-33 'Flanker-D' fighter, able to conduct effective air defence operations, unlike the Yak-38 'Forger' on the preceding *Kiev* class. The substantial anti-ship missile battery remained, but partly hidden under removable flight deck plates. With such a ship, it seemed that the Soviet Navy was truly now able to contest sea control from US carrier battle groups in the open ocean. However, construction of such a large and complex vessel was protracted, and after two changes of name she eventually commissioned in December 1990 as the *Admiral Kuznetsov*, just as the Cold War was ending. A sister-ship, the *Varyag*, started construction in 1985 but was eventually sold to China in 2001, and completed in the Dalian shipyard in 2012 as the *Laioning*.[24] Even more concerning for NATO analysts in the dying days of the Cold War, was the beginning of construction of a new and yet larger design of carrier. The *Ul'yanovsk* would have had a displacement of 62,580 tons and combined both the *Riga*'s take-off ramp with two aircraft catapults. With nuclear propulsion, deck-edge lifts and a small 'island' superstructure sat on a wide overhanging flight deck, the *Ul'yanovsk*

would have looked like, and had most of the capabilities of, a large US aircraft carrier. The ship was laid down in November 1938 but construction was halted on the collapse of the Soviet Union and the hull, which was 20 per cent complete, was broken up in 1992.[25]

If the Soviet carrier programme was largely a matter of what might have been, the Soviet cruiser programme in the 1980s definitely bore fruit, but just like the Soviet third-generation nuclear submarine programmes, it produced a relatively small numbers of ships. In December 1980 the first *Kirov* class cruiser (Project 1144) was commissioned into the Northern Fleet. With a displacement of 24,000 tons and carrying twenty P-700 Granit long-range cruise missiles, ninety-six S-300 (NATO: SA-N-6 'Grumble') area air defence missiles and a full range of secondary armament, the *Kirov* was dubbed a 'battlecruiser' by Western commentators.[26] In fact, the design had originated as an 8,000-ton nuclear-powered ship with an all-round capability in anti-submarine warfare, anti-ship warfare and air defence. After repeated and unsuccessful attempts to provide such a capability on this sized hull, it was finally accepted the design had to grow in order to fit the range of weapon systems required.[27] The addition of the bulky P-700 anti-ship missile, twenty of which were countersunk in launch tubes into the hull forward of the bridge structure at a 45-degree angle, inevitably resulted in a significant growth in projected displacement. The design had then grown even further in size to accommodate full command facilities and communication systems to link with satellites and shore-based command and control centres. The S-300 air defence system was also a major leap forward from its predecessors: it was a true area air defence system able to deal with multiple crossing targets, and as such could provide much of the area defence for the cruiser's supporting surface action group. A 96-missile magazine was deemed to be necessary to undertake this role. The resulting ship, at 24,000 tons, was therefore nearly triple the displacement of its predecessors. Two further vessels to a slightly modified design were completed before the end of the Cold War, with two out of the class of three being stationed with the Northern Fleet. A fourth ship, the *Pyetr Vyelikiy*, was completed after the end of the Cold War for Russia and a fifth ship was cancelled in 1990.[28] Again, these were capable but extremely resource-intensive vessels to build, so although construction was relatively quick at between five and six years, they denied resources for the building of greater numbers of other less capable vessels.

In parallel with the *Kirov* class, the *Slava* class cruisers (Project 1164) were also constructed. They were less than half the size of the *Kirov*s; they had an anti-ship armament consisting of sixteen of an earlier generation of anti-ship missile, the P-500 Basal't (NATO: SS-N-12 'Sandbox'), and a still substantial magazine of sixty-four S-300 area air defence missiles. It had originally been planned to build ten in the class, but only three were completed by the end of the Cold War, just one of which, the *Marshal Ustinov*, was part of the Northern Fleet.[29] Although lacking the size and command facilities of the *Kirov*, the *Slava* class at least provided additional hulls with an effective area air defence capability.

Two new classes of ships of destroyer size also began to enter service in the early 1980s. The *Sovremennyy* class (Project 956) were general-purpose ships armed with medium-range cruise missiles, two twin medium guns and air defence missile systems. They had been derived from an Army request for ships with gun armament to support amphibious operations and had grown into ocean-going warships during the design process. Their Achilles' heel was their problem-prone steam propulsion system, which had been imposed on the design after it became clear that enough gas turbines could not be built to support all the shipbuilding programmes, and to protect the survival of Leningrad steam turbine plant.[30] Thirteen had been completed by the end of the Cold War, seven of which served with the Northern Fleet.[31] The second class were the 'large anti-submarine ships' of the *Udaloy* class (Project 1155). An enlargement of the earlier 'Krivak' class frigates to provide a true ocean-going anti-submarine escort, the *Udaloy*s were more successful. A total of eleven had been completed by the end of the Cold War, six of which served with the Northern Fleet.[32] A modified version of the *Udaloy* class (Project 11551), armed with anti-ship rather than anti-submarine missiles, as a replacement for the troubled *Sovremennyy* programme, was also developed. However, only one vessel was ever completed, nearly a decade after the end of the Cold War.[33] The increased complexity and size of Soviet major surface vessels in the 1980s meant that relatively few of these vessels were in fact completed before the end of the Cold War, with only a total of eighteen ships from the *Kiev* to *Udaloy* classes completed between 1980 and the end of the Cold War serving with the Northern Fleet. The Northern Fleet was therefore primarily a submarine force, and becoming more so, as in the late 1980s large numbers of the oldest missile destroyers began to be decommissioned without direct replacement.[34]

Minor surface vessels continued to be built in considerable numbers by the Soviet Navy, with a particular focus on short-range fast craft armed with anti-ship missiles. The shift to offensive operations in the High North meant that such craft now had to be added into NATO assessments of the Soviet naval threat. Missile corvettes of the 'Nanuchka' class (Project 1234) and later derivatives continued to be built into the 1980s, with eight serving with the Northern Fleet.[35] The harsh weather conditions of the northern seas made these craft much less of threat than in the Baltic or Black Seas, but nonetheless they could not be entirely discounted, particularly in littoral operations and in the fjords of north Norway.

Maritime Strike Aircraft

The Soviet Tu-22M long-range strike aircraft (known as the 'Backfire' by NATO) continued to concern NATO's planners into the 1980s. The original run of Tu-22M2s continued until 1983 with a total of 211 being built for naval service. A modified version then appeared, the Tu-22M3, with improved turbofan engines which increased the aircraft's range significantly; the new variant having a combat radius of nearly 1,500 miles when adopting a high-low-high mission profile. Production of the new type began in 1978, and it achieved initial acceptance in 1981 but full operating capability was not achieved until as late as 1989. A total of 268 were built.[36] A total of approximately 200 aircraft of both 'Backfire' variants served with the Navy, with production continuing until 1993.[37] The 'Backfire' was distributed to all the main Soviet fleets, with Tu-22M2s arriving in the Northern Fleet's 5th Maritime Air Division in the late 1970s, consisting of one regiment of around twenty aircraft based in the Murmansk region and another in the Archangel'sk region. Aircraft from different fleets regularly practiced rapid re-deployment to other commands, so the Northern Fleet 'Backfires' could have been augmented by those from the Baltic or the Black Sea in the event of a crisis.[38] As NATO forces were potentially reaching closer to the USSR itself by pushing up into the Norwegian Sea and perhaps into the Barents, they risked encountering much more heavily armed 'Backfires'. The aircraft could carry one Kh-22 anti-ship missile (NATO: AS-4 'Kitchen') out to 1,200 miles, two out to 870 miles but three out to over 550 miles.[39] In addition, at these shorter ranges 'Backfires' were more likely to be escorted by fighters, such as the Soviet Air Force's Su-15s or MiG-23s.[40] If NATO forces wished to operate in the Norwegian Sea, they would have to contend with a formidable air threat of bombers armed with two or three long-range anti-ship missiles, and escorted by capable air defence aircraft.

The US Maritime Strategy and the Royal Navy

The Maritime Strategy developed by the United States Navy between 1978 and 1986 was a response to a loss of strategic coherence during the 1970s. After the departure of Admiral Zumwalt, whose own strategic innovations had been deeply divisive within the US Navy, there had been perceived to be a sense of drift and a feeling that USN did not understand what its role would be in war. Its carrier battle groups were constrained by their nuclear role, in which the Single Integrated Operational Plan for nuclear war ('SIOP') set specific strike objectives which tied the carriers in tension or war to particular sea areas. Meanwhile, in the US Navy Department, strategies, such as they were, seemed to come and go with some regularity and appeared driven by the need to provide justifications for new procurements of types of ships that the

Navy wanted, rather than the other way round. The Carter administration's downplaying of a role in the rest of the world following the withdrawal from Vietnam, and its focus on the Central European front within the context of a short war, made the US Navy look even more vulnerable to reductions if it could not provide an intellectually coherent strategy.[41]

There were three key drivers that influenced the iterative development of the US Maritime Strategy from the late 1970s onwards. The first was the military-strategic, and this was personified in the late 1970s and early 1980s by Admiral Hayward, the then Chief of Naval Operations. The second might be termed political-strategic, and involved the new Republican administration of President Reagan from 1981 onwards, with the Secretary of the Navy John Lehman as the most visible driving force. The third was a revolution in intelligence assessment of the Soviet Navy pioneered by the Center for Naval Analyses and the CIA and only gradually accepted by the US in the early 1980s. Each of these elements influenced the development of the maritime strategy to different degrees in different ways at different times. As the Royal Navy was, to some extent, a significant beneficiary of this new US strategy, briefly assessing each of these different drivers will help to understand how the Navy benefitted. It will also help to explain how different emphases within the strategy over time, sometimes complicating and even confusing the transatlantic naval relationship.

Admiral Hayward, whilst serving as Commander-in-Chief of the Pacific Fleet between 1976 and 1978, had despaired of both the restrictions of SIOP and the lack of strategic direction from Washington. He therefore began to develop a strategy for the Pacific Fleet based on a number of presumptions that had either been discounted or dismissed in recent years. The first was that sustained conventional conflict was just as likely, if not more so, to occur than a nuclear conflict. Over 30 years of nuclear confrontation had not produced a nuclear exchange, suggesting that the nuclear threshold was in fact high and might not come into play at all during an armed conflict between NATO, its allies and the Warsaw Pact.[42] The second was that an aggressive forward strategy that used his carriers' conventional strike assets against Soviet Far Eastern targets including naval forces and their bases would force the Soviets to concentrate their assets in defending their base areas rather than attacking sea lines of communication. Hayward also saw this concept, which was named Sea Strike, just as much as a deterrent posture during a period of tension, as a real warfighting plan.[43] Sea Strike was sufficiently influential that it helped to inform the US Navy Department SeaPlan 2000, a study that looked at the roles of general-purpose naval forces and marked the first significant example of new strategic thinking from first principles for some years.[44] A year later Hayward had been promoted to Chief of Naval Operations, and he began to move beyond Sea Strike and SeaPlan 2000 into developing a global maritime strategy. From Hayward's perspective he did not want to first decide on platforms or weapons (or their numbers), but ensure that the strategy itself was sound before putting together cases for equipment.[45] However, working within the Carter administration, with its continued focus on a short war, prepositioning and the Central European front, meant that it was extremely difficult for this nascent strategy to gain support. At least by 1979, Carter's Secretary of Defence, Harold Brown, had toned down his approach to defence policy and was beginning to accept arguments for strike capabilities and pull back on naval reductions, even if he still hewed to the short war strategic approach.[46]

The arrival of the Reagan administration changed this situation further. The new President appointed John Lehman as Secretary of the Navy and Casper Weinberger became the Secretary of Defense. Whilst out of power, the Republicans had developed an opposition policy based on support for the Navy and a commitment to return to a '600 ship navy', a commitment that had been made by Donald Rumsfeld, the Secretary of Defense under Gerald Ford, and to which the new administration wanted to hold.[47] Lehman became the driving force behind plans for the revitalisation of the US Navy, which he saw as the United States' most flexible and easily deployable offensive capability and a clear, visible, symbol of American power. This fitted more broadly into Reagan's wish to roll back what he saw as the timidity and defeatism of the Carter years, rediscover US self-confidence in international affairs and be unequivocal about its opposition to Communism and the Soviet Union.[48] Lehman was not an easy person to work with, and made a number of enemies, but he was also an Anglophile, having spent three years at the University of Cambridge, and did much to ensure that the US Navy kept a significant focus on the North Atlantic, when by tradition and history it was much more inclined to prefer operating in maritime-air led regions like the Pacific and Mediterranean.[49] The Hayward-Lehman maritime strategy, as it was developed in 1981 and early 1982, remained focussed on a more aggressive and forward-pushing use of carrier strike groups: off Kamchatka in the western Pacific and in the Norwegian Sea in the North Atlantic.[50] As was seen with Exercise Ocean Venture in 1981, placing carriers into the north Norwegian Sea and even the Barents Sea, was used as a means of not only exercising such operations, but as a form of deterrence and signalling. In wartime or in a period of high tension it would also force the Soviets onto the back foot and to keep forces in local waters to defend the homeland rather than attack sea lines of communication. The US Navy now had additional confidence that its surface forces would survive in such areas close to the USSR following the introduction into service of the Aegis air defence system on board the first *Ticonderoga* class cruisers.[51]

The third driver was intelligence. Through the 1970s and into the early 1980s, the accepted position on Soviet maritime strategic intent was that their Navy would, as a leading priority, attempt to cut the sea lines of communication between North America and the European members of NATO. It was assumed that a 'third Battle of the Atlantic' would be fought into order to keep these sea lines open and ensure that Europe was both resupplied and that reinforcements from the USA could bolster NATO forces on the other side of the Atlantic. A number of internal and external analysts, after reviewing Soviet open-source literature, had argued that the Soviet stance, despite its ocean-going nature in peacetime and tactical and operational aggressiveness, was in fact strategically defensive. On the outbreak of war, Soviet naval forces would coalesce around the defence of home bases and the underwater strategic nuclear deterrent. From the mid-1970s with the arrival into service of the R-29 ballistic missiles, Soviet SSBNs now had sufficient range to be able to launch their missiles from the Arctic Circle near their northern bases, so SSBN protection could now occur in home waters and would not be needed out in the open oceans. This allowed for the creation of defensive areas near home waters and in the Arctic that came to be called bastions by Western analysts.[52] This assessment was not believed by most US naval leaders until it came to be corroborated by human intelligence sources in 1981 and 1982. Hayward's first exposure to this assessment did not go well for the intelligence officers, but gradually he and Lehman began to accept the situation, and adapt the nascent Maritime Strategy to take account of these new insights.[53] As a result, the role of 'strategic anti-submarine warfare' or strategic ASW in forward operations began to be emphasised. In most instances this meant the use of NATO SSNs in High North and Arctic waters to detect and track Soviet SSBNs, with the aim of either destroying such boats one by one and depleting the Soviet second strike capability or trailing so many of them that Soviet leaders would not have confidence that their second strike capability would survive in a general nuclear exchange.[54]

The Maritime Strategy therefore developed over time, with carrier strike groups initially being at the centre of planning but with a partial shift towards strategic ASW by SSNs from 1982 onwards. The creation and honing of strategies is by necessity an iterative process, and the focus of the strategy shifted during the mid-1980s. Carrier strike groups never disappeared from plans, although sometimes US Navy Department wargames placed them west of the Greenland-Iceland-UK gap as a means of bringing forward additional capability during the 'war termination' phase of a conflict.[55] At other times the carrier strike groups returned to centre stage as concerns mounted, as a result of wargaming, that strategic ASW did not have the intended effect on the Soviets, presumably making nuclear exchange more, rather than less likely.[56] The strategy was much discussed within the US Navy in the early 1980s, and different variants were developed and presented to internal and, within limits, external audiences. A special supplement to the United States Naval Institute's *Proceedings* magazine in 1986 set out the strategy for general external consumption across the whole US Navy and the interested general public. Its 48 pages included articles by Lehman and Admiral Watkins, Hayward's successor as the Chief of Naval Operations, General Kelley, the head of the US Marine Corps, and a bibliography on contemporary US naval strategy. By 1985 and 1986 the strategy was being discussed, analysed, supported and critiqued in Congress, academia and parts of the media in the United States.[57] Despite this interest and controversy, what did the strategy mean in practical terms for the Royal Navy on the other side of the 'Atlantic bridge'?

From the perspective of the Royal Navy, as a partial outsider to these developments, but an important partner and beneficiary, the development of the Maritime Strategy provided significant advantages in terms of providing key capabilities to support the Strategy, but also some disorientation and frustration as the focus of the strategy shifted and changed over time. Under the initial carrier strike focus of Hayward, the Royal Navy's anti-submarine capabilities were deemed essential to protect the Atlantic carrier strike group as it pushed north towards the Barents Sea. At this time, as was seen in Chapter 15, the US Department of Defense official Dov Zakheim had even suggested that British SSNs were not a high priority for the US Navy, but that its surface or air ASW forces were the most needed assets. As the changes in the intelligence picture were accepted by the US, the British SSN fleet became a more important supplement to US submarines, with the added advantage of being based much closer to the presumed operational areas in the High North.

The 1980s were another period of impressive submarine trailing operations by Royal Navy boats, with a seemingly greater focus on the Norwegian and Barents Seas, indicating the influence of the Maritime Strategy. A patrol by HMS *Conqueror* in the Norwegian Sea managed to trail, and undertake simulated firings on, no fewer than four Soviet ballistic missile submarines. HMS *Superb* was only the second NATO submarine to detect and gain intelligence on a Soviet 'Typhoon' class submarine, whilst her sister, HMS *Splendid* undertook a long-term trail of a 'Typhoon' that resulted in the loss of her towed-array, after it became wrapped around the Soviet submarine's hull and was lost. This created unwelcome publicity when it was leaked to the media. HMS *Trafalgar* trailed a Soviet 'Victor III' attack boat across the Atlantic in April 1987, whilst in February 1988 HMS *Torbay* trailed four Soviet submarines in the Norwegian and Barents Seas.[58]

Senior British naval officers, as was seen in Chapter 15, had been intimately involved in the planning of the High North elements of Ocean Venture, contributing HM Ships *Invincible* and *Bristol* to operations, as well as an intelligence-gathering operation with HMS *Glasgow* in the months beforehand. As a result they were well aware of the early development of the new forward strategy in the High North. However, between 1981 and 1983, the extent to which the new strategy had filtered through the whole US Navy appeared to be patchy when viewed from the British side of the Atlantic. The regular biannual Royal Navy-US Navy liaison meetings give a flavour of this sense of regular shifts within the United States, and the impression that very different positions would be given depending on who was being leading discussions in the US side. In October 1981 the liaison meeting was extremely productive from the British perspective: the lead on the US side was Rear Admiral T J Cassidy, a naval aviator, and his team included an officer with anti-submarine and towed-array experience. Fruitful discussions were had on towed-array operations, anti-submarine warfare and the sort of air defence the US Navy could provide Royal Navy ships operating in the Strike Fleet's ASW support group.[59] The next meeting, in March 1982 was a complete contrast. This time the US lead was Vice Admiral Bob Foley, who dominated proceedings, appeared to show little interest in High North operations, saw the North Atlantic as a secondary theatre and emphasised the importance of the Indian Ocean, Mediterranean and above all, the Gulf, where he thought that World War III was most likely to start (despite the fact that internal USN studies supporting the development of the Maritime Strategy were showing that the Gulf was the *least* important theatre). He had little interest in discussing anti-submarine operations and was most appreciative of the Royal Navy's presence in the Gulf and Caribbean.[60] The September 1982 meeting focussed on the Falklands conflict, and when the next biannual meeting occurred, the picture had changed again. Rear Admiral S H Packer USN led these talks, and the focus returned to the High North, but more from the perspective of strategic anti-submarine operations by submarines against the Soviet 'bastions'. The Royal Navy's attack submarine capability was emphasised, but tactical anti-submarine operations for the fleet were dismissed as merely a variant of air defence operations, as it was assumed by the US attendees that Soviet submarine commanders would only attack with anti-ship missiles rather than torpedoes.[61] The British delegations had long experience of working with the United States Navy and were aware that it was a large organisation with many competing perspectives. It was generally found that those liaison visits that occurred in the United States were the most productive, as after the formal talks, the Royal Navy officers could then undertake bilateral discussions in the Pentagon with the 'right people' and gain a clearer understanding of developments.[62]

Despite these apparent oscillations, the impact of the new Maritime Strategy could be felt both in NATO and in the planning undertaken by the Royal Navy in the 1980s. The NATO Maritime Tasks as set out in the Alliance's Concept of Maritime Operations, provided some space to enable the Maritime Strategy to fit within its remit. In wartime, the second role for NATO maritime forces, after defending NATO territory from Soviet attack, was to support the land battle directly by carrier-borne air support or amphibious landings, a description that fitted well with the carrier-led aspect of the Maritime Strategy in the High North. Protection of reinforcement and resupply shipping remained, as priorities three and four.[63] Later changes in the mid-1980s saw a renaming and reorientation of some of the main NATO task groups and forces in the Eastern Atlantic to reflect the new strategy. A series of new forces were created: the Carrier Striking Force made up of the main US carrier groups, the ASW Striking Force – which was the new name for the old Anti-Submarine Group Two under Royal Navy command – and an Amphibious Strike Force paired with a Marine Strike Force, made up of US, RN and Netherlands amphibious shipping and marines respectively.[64] The emphasis on 'strike' in all four of these new forces reflected the offensive and forward nature of these forces, and the (nominal) parity between the four emphasised the higher profile of the British contribution to the total Strike Fleet.

The impact of the Maritime Strategy on British doctrinal thinking can be seen in the development of an Operational Concept for Maritime Anti-Air Warfare in late 1982 and 1983, led by Captain Richard Sharpe and involving a carefully crafted compromise with the RAF, it nonetheless incorporated the new forward approach. Working within the three key principles of containment, defence in depth and keeping the initiative, the concept envisaged a major Royal Navy contribution to three campaigns: in the Norwegian Sea, the Eastern Atlantic area and the shallow waters around the United Kingdom, including the Channel, North Sea and Western Approaches. At that point in the US Navy's development of the Maritime Strategy, it was unclear when the US carrier striking group would enter the Eastern Atlantic and northern waters, as it seemed that it would be given a series of other tasks to undertake first. As a result, European naval forces, led by the Royal Navy, would have to contend these sea areas until the arrival of the Americans. They would aim to control the GIUK Gap, protect reinforcement shipping and undertake forward operations so that the Norwegian Sea was 'not allowed to be dominated by the Soviets before the carriers arrive'.[65] How achievable this would have been without the air cover provided by the US carriers is unclear, although the forward operations could have included nuclear submarines either in the strategic or tactical anti-submarine role. If the Norwegian Sea campaign failed, then the ability to control the situation in the Eastern Atlantic would have been fatally undermined. In the shallow water zones the greatest threats would be from mines and conventional submarines.[66]

With respect to the specifics of countering the Soviet air threat, the concept focussed on the importance of defence in depth. Challenging the claims that had been made by the Chief Scientific Adviser during and after the Defence Review, the concept clearly stated that multiple layers of defence not only accorded with NATO maritime doctrine but also insured 'against technological breakthroughs by the enemy that could defeat a single layer concept'.[67] However, the lack of US carrier air cover was a particular concern and it was admitted that UK naval surface forces will not normally be expected to conduct operations in the open sea north of the United Kingdom unless USN or land-based fighters were available to counter the 'Backfire' bomber.[68] It was also thought that the land-based air defence capability would be inadequate until the new Nimrod AEW aircraft was in service (at the time planned for 1985) and the RAF's tanker fleet expanded and modernised, to provide the RAF's air defence aircraft sufficient range to cover enough of the North East Atlantic.[69] Without US carriers in the Eastern Atlantic, the European surface ships would have found it extremely difficult to operate effectively in the Norwegian Sea or east of the GIUK gap.[70] The old problems of maritime air defence had not disappeared and would continue to vex the Royal Navy's planners through the 1980s, but the Maritime Strategy at least made it much more likely that US strike carriers would enter the North East Atlantic and undertake operations, even if belatedly, thus providing some protection against those within the Ministry who doubted the ability of the Royal Navy's surface ships to survive against Soviet 'Backfires'.

Towards the end of 1984, in one of the last documents produced by VCNS before his post was dis-established, an assessment of the Naval Programme was produced at the request of the Minister for the Armed Forces. Its aim was to frame discussions on that year's Long Term Costings. At the start it included a concise exposition, in admirably lucid and plain language, of the Royal Navy's maritime strategy and its operational concepts. The first line of the maritime strategy section stated categorically that British national security was best preserved by maintaining full United Kingdom support for NATO. The Royal Navy would deter Soviet aggression, either in Europe or around the world, and help sustain Alliance cohesion and will through its presence and assurance operations. The most important aspect of Britain's maritime posture was the maintenance of the Atlantic bridge with North America. The United Kingdom's continuing dependence on the sea was not going to change and neither would any threats that focussed on that dependence. However, the exact nature of these threats would be uncertain: planning based on a small number of scenarios would be folly and would reduce the flexibility to respond in crises. Balanced capabilities that ensured that sea denial, sea control and power projection operations could be undertaken would provide that flexibility.[71]

This was a forthright exposition of the framework of Britain's maritime strategy at the very highest level, and most importantly it emphasised the importance of not being tied into tightly drawn scenarios that favoured an easy but dangerous focus on just deterring and preparing for the expected. The document then linked through to NATO's Concept of Maritime Operations from 1980 and the revised Conduct of Maritime Operations Paper, and stressed the importance of the geography to contain the USSR and its allies, the need for defence in depth and finally, the importance of maintaining the initiative.[72] It then stated that the United Kingdom would have a major role in three NATO maritime campaigns in the event of Soviet aggression: in the Norwegian Sea, in the Atlantic and in the shallow seas around the United Kingdom. It set out four categories of tasks and activities for British maritime forces: strategic nuclear deterrence, direct defence of the United Kingdom, maritime operations under NATO command and maritime operations under national command. These were expanded upon in an Annex, and in the sections on operations under NATO command, a list set out possible tasks in order of importance. At the top was taking part in NATO Maritime Contingency Force plans, followed by the provision of an anti-submarine task group to support the NATO Strike Fleet, then submarine forward operations, followed by anti-submarine area operations, the protection of reinforcement shipping, amphibious operations, acting against hostile bases and finally mine warfare.[73] This list had the key elements of the US Maritime Strategy integrated firmly within it, with the Norwegian Sea and forward operations by submarines taking precedence behind the standard nod towards NATO contingency planning. The Navy had undeniably embraced the core tenets of the Maritime Strategy and integrated them into how it understood and approached its role in tension and war.

The Maritime Strategy had therefore provided a much clearer role for the Royal Navy during the 1980s. Even if a short-warning/short war scenario were to occur, then the advance into the Norwegian Sea would threaten an attack on the Soviet northern flank, and importantly, on the Soviet Union itself – in the variant of the strategy that emphasised carrier strikes on northern cities and naval bases – or on its nuclear deterrent submarines in the more submarine-focussed version. No longer would the Navy be forced to defend its ocean-going surface fleet purely on the basis of transatlantic convoying operations which depended in a long-warning/long war scenario which the majority of the Ministry of Defence was unwilling to accept as a likely possibility.

The Operational Introduction of Surface Towed Arrays

As was discussed in Chapter 10, towed-array sonars were first fitted to British submarines in the 1970s. The Type 2024 ensured that towed-array went to sea in SSNs quickly, but it was only a stopgap solution: its links to the submarine's tactical command system and the tactical displays were both rudimentary.[74] The successor Type 2026, developed with the Dutch, included a range of improvements such as more sensitive hydrophones, a stronger cable, a more effective linkage to tactical command systems and higher sensitivity processors for both narrow and broad band low frequencies. The contract was awarded in 1977–8 and it entered service in 1987. Like the Type 2024 it was a clip-on array, but experiments were also undertaken with a reeled array. The successor Type 2046 towed-array would not enter service until the mid-1990s.[75] These systems had soon proved themselves as capable detectors of both submarines and surface vessels. The nuclear-powered boat HMS *Sovereign* tracked a Soviet 'Charlie' class cruise missile submarine for 707 miles in 1977 with a Type 2024 and HMS *Swiftsure* tracked a Soviet diesel-electric submarine for 18 hours in 1978 with the same sonar.[76]

Trials of the first surface towed-array on the old frigate HMS *Lowestoft* had demonstrated that these new detection systems would be transformative for anti-submarine warfare by surface ships. No longer would sonar detection by warships be fleeting and often uncertain. As with the submarine towed-arrays it was shown that it was now possible to trail Soviet submarines for many hours and days. Contemporary published guides to naval weapons credited the Type 2031I (the first operational version) with a tail over 1,600m long and a detection range of approximately 100km, the equivalent to approximately two convergence zones in the Norwegian Sea.[77] Following the first six-months of trials on *Lowestoft*, in which she spent a number of periods working with HMS *Dreadnought* as her 'target' submarine, the assessment of the Navy's Operational Evaluation Group had been emphatic:

> It seems clear that the Sonar 2031 will open up a completely new capability which should allow above-water ASW forces to gain the initiative over the Soviet nuclear submarine for the first time ever. Although HMS *Dreadnought* is noisier than the more modern Soviet SSNs, this capability was to some extent demonstrated in the trial by HMS *Lowestoft*'s ability to hold contact with the target SSN, at ranges between 4 and 91 miles, for 70% of the 77 hours serial time.[78]

Lowestoft then spent three years on further trials of towed-arrays: comparing thick and thin cable arrays for surface towed-arrays and trialling the new Type 2026 submarine array.[79] In 1983 she was fitted with a pre-production Type 2031I sonar and was heavily involved in the major Eastern Atlantic exercises of that year: United Effort 83 and Ocean Safari 83. During these exercises *Lowestoft* was able to hold nuclear submarine contacts for considerable periods of time *and* simultaneously. The report of *Lowestoft*'s Squadron Captain of these trials made clear the impact the new sonar had on the senior US naval commander: 'Even allowing for American verbal extravagance a recent signal from COMSIXTHFLT [Commander US Sixth Fleet] made some highly significant statements in praise of *Lowestoft*, speaking of a "capability heretofore unknown to [the] Sixth Fleet".' This exercise and others 'achieved remarkable results and attracted considerable interest in the USA and consequently opened many doors for the UK'.[80]

By this time *Lowestoft* was showing her age with structural hull cracks appearing as the frigate undertook a range of exercises through 1983 and 1984, working with maritime patrol aircraft and other surface ships in order to hone towed-array tactics.[81] A refit to keep her in service through to 1988 was considered but rejected and she was decommissioned in March 1985.[82] As was seen in Chapter 10 it had originally been planned to convert *Lowestoft*'s Type 12 frigate sisters into towed-array ships, but their age told against them and four *Leander* class frigates, *Phoebe, Sirius, Cleopatra* and *Minerva*, were chosen instead.[83] *Phoebe* was the first to emerge from refit in 1982, but she was fitted for, but not with, the Type 2031I system as there had been delays in the production of the Sonar Display Room by Marconi.[84] In the event, both *Sirius* and *Cleopatra* completed their refits in late 1983 and were fully worked-up by February 1984, with *Argonaut* following soon afterwards having been placed in the programme instead of *Minerva* due to her being put into refit earlier than planned, as a result of repair to damage sustained in the Falklands campaign. *Phoebe* was the last to re-enter service with the new sonar in 1984. When *Lowestoft* was decommissioned in 1985 her pre-production sonar was transferred to the Ikara *Leander*, HMS *Arethusa*, in a refit that completed at the end of 1986.[85] As was seen in Chapter 10, approval had been given to fit modified towed-array sonars to Type 22 frigates. This modification partly consisted of improved processing equipment developed by Dr T E Curtis of the Admiralty Underwater Weapons Establishment. The extra funds for these modified sets were approved for three Batch 2 Type 22s in March 1982,[86] with further sets subsequently being agreed for the remaining Type 22s and the first Type 23s.

After the latest *Lowestoft* trials in autumn 1983, a full test of the British towed-array was programmed into NATO's main series of North Atlantic exercises in the spring of 1984. A family of exercises was centred on the main 'Teamwork 84' Exercise in the north east Atlantic. The scenario involved the escorting of an amphibious force and transports through the Greenland-Iceland-United Kingdom ('GIUK') gap against 'Soviet' bombers, surface ships and patrol lines of conventional submarines. Prior to Teamwork 84, the NATO Exercise United Effort 84 involved the escorting of the amphibious force from the east coast of the United States to the entrances of the GIUK gap on a route via the Azores. This would be a purely anti-submarine exercise, with four 'Soviet' SSNs as the opposition, and would be a perfect opportunity to test the new towed-array capabilities alongside US towed-arrays and other anti-submarine sensors.[87] The final part of the Exercise 'family' involved the landing of troops and equipment from the amphibious force near Tromso, Norway, whilst under air and surface attack from 'Soviet' forces, followed by cold weather land exercises for the Royal Marines in Norway entitled Avalanche Express 84 and a land-air exercise run by AFNorth entitled Busy Eagle.[88]

United Effort would therefore provide the best opportunity for the new towed-array to demonstrate its capabilities, during a series of different scenarios over a number of weeks. The British contribution to this exercise included the carrier HMS *Illustrious* as flagship for the Flag Officer of the 3rd Flotilla, Rear Admiral Fitch, who was COMASGRU 2 (Commander Anti-Submarine Group 2) commanding the main anti-submarine hunting group operating forward of the amphibious force and its close escorts. Under Fitch's control were six destroyers and frigates equipped with towed-array, two of which were British: HMS *Cleopatra* and HMS *Sirius*.[89] During much of United Effort and Teamwork, the weather had been poor: high seas, grey skies and occasional rain; the commanding officer of *Cleopatra* laconically but confidently stating that this 'provided an adequate foundation for towed-array frigates'.[90]

Expectations were high for the Type 2031 sonar following the successes of the previous year. The US Navy exercise commander, Admiral Metcalf, conforming to the stereotype of the blunt American military commander, threatened 'to "have" a portion of my Squadron Operations Officer's anatomy if the results were not as briefed', recounted the commanding officer of HMS *Cleopatra*.[91] Luckily for the SOO the results were good, and in fact even better than had been expected by the Americans. The commanding officer of HMS *Sirius* described the results as a 'spectacular passive sonar success', also commenting that 'Much new ground was broken, and that 2031 displayed an ability to detect and track nuclear submarines at ranges well in excess of those experienced heretofore.'[92] *Cleopatra*'s commanding officer also noted that this capability was much greater than the US towed-arrays then in service: the SQR-15 and SQR-18a.[93]

Why was Type 2031 so effective? It was clear to *Cleopatra*'s commanding officer that the decision to procure a joint tactical and surveillance towed-array sonar (TACTAS and SURTAS in the abbreviated jargon), was the key to the success: the longer array allowed for a much wider frequency range for detection, whilst the increased processing capacity required must have helped isolate weaker signals.[94] Some of the success came from the effectiveness of this processing capability on board the ship, where Dr Curtis' development work dramatically increased the quality and strength of contacts. Trials in the autumn of 1981, when *Lowestoft* was fitted with improved processing equipment, were described by the ship's commanding officer as 'legendary' and that after these specific trials morale on board had 'soared and my team felt that at long last the frigate had once again the chance to jump back into the forefront of submarine detection.'[95] Such success created its own problems. First was the prosecution of attacks on these very long-range sonar contacts. Aside from *Cleopatra*, all the ships had their own Lynx helicopter, but capable as the Lynx was, it lacked its own submarine-detection systems and was dependent on the ship's active sonar for target localisation. Given the relatively poor performance and short-range of the shipboard sonar this meant that the Lynx could do little to act against long or medium-range towed-array contacts. Maritime patrol aircraft could provide valuable support localising targets, when they were available and within range, but a more responsive answer was provided by ensuring that the towed-array patrol ship was paired with a helicopter-equipped Royal Fleet Auxiliary whenever possible.[96] During Teamwork 84 much of the task of localising and intercepting the target had fallen to the Sea King helicopters on board HMS *Illustrious*. This task was made more complex by the unprecedented numbers of aircraft on board the small carrier – more so even than had been on her sister-ship *Invincible* during the Falklands War. This was due to the initial non-appearance of the US strike carrier USS *Independence*, retained in the Mediterranean in support of operations off Lebanon. As a result, a short-notice decision was made to place five more Sea Harriers and three more Sea Kings on board *Illustrious* as a partial compensation for the lack of the full air cover, anti-submarine and strike capabilities the US aircraft carrier provided. The British ship had a total of twenty-two aircraft on board, twelve of which were Sea Kings.[97]

The Sea Kings had the advantage of passive and active dipping sonars to make their own detections, as well as magnetic anomaly detectors to confirm that the targets were in fact submarines rather than marine wildlife. However, the long-ranges put particular strain on the Sea Kings and placed greater emphasis than usual on their role in anti-submarine warfare, as surface ASW units were invariably many miles distant when a towed-array contact was investigated. This also shone some light on inadequacies in the capabilities of the dipping sonars. The performance of 814 Squadron, the carrier's Mark 5 Sea Kings, was considered only adequate in the exercise.[98] Detection ranges had now increased dramatically thanks to the new towed-array, so the localisation and prosecution side of the equation (generally undertaken by aircraft) now looked exposed and needed to catch up. Sonobuoys were gradually being fitted to Sea Kings as they were upgraded from Mark 2 to Mark 5 versions, whilst trials had been completed for fitting and operating the Jezebel passive sonobuoy in Sea

Kings.⁹⁹ Further improvements to the Sea King were integrated into the Mark 6 Sea King which is discussed in the next chapter.

The advent of the towed-array sonar also resulted in some major 'workplace' cultural changes on board ship, that made its day-to-day operation whilst on towed-array duties very different from that of other surface vessels. For *Cleopatra* and *Sirius* to conduct their towed-array operations effectively, the two ships had to operate on 'silent running' procedures similar to that for submarines on patrol. The ships' propulsion was set on low revolutions to reduce noise, and any other ship activity that resulted in noise had to be curtailed, controlled or muffled. The use of radar and radio was also severely limited, to prevent detection from 'enemy' passive intercept capabilities. To some extent, this resulted in the 'submarine-isation' of the surface ships involved, a cultural shift that seemed difficult to adjust to, at least initially. When this was combined with *Cleopatra* and *Sirius*' role as showcases for the new technology, which resulted in a relentless programme of exercises and demonstrations, it was becoming clear that morale on board the frigates was deteriorating. The commanding officer of *Sirius* was blunt in his assessment:

> HMS *Sirius* is spending 216 days actually at sea this year [1984], and 264 away from her base port. Over 90% of the time at sea, in fact 194 days, has been, or will be, spent in defence watches in nine NATO exercises, usually with the array streamed and silent on all active emitters. This leaves a large proportion of the Ship's Company with nothing to do. The result is that the Op[eration]s Dept become disillusioned with permanent 84 hour weeks, often with no contacts to plot; the W[eapons] E[ngineering] Dept cannot maintain much equipment, they cannot transmit on any sensors or radio; and the M[arine] E[ngineering] Dept find life at 56 rpm day after day tedious in the extreme.¹⁰⁰

This problem was particularly acute for these first towed-array frigates, and no doubt reduced somewhat as the novelty of the Type 2031's capabilities wore off and it was integrated into the standard routines of patrols and exercises, but the cultural shift towards surface 'silent running' was clearly a significant one that required much thought by commanding officers in order to sustain morale during towed-array patrols.

By the end of 1985 the *Leander* towed-array squadron was fully stood up, operating at five hulls until 1989 when *Arethusa* was withdrawn from service, with the remaining four ships being withdrawn in quick order between 1990 and 1992. By this time, all six Batch 2 Type 22 frigates were in service and had been followed by four Batch 3 frigates of the same class, also fitted with towed-array sonars. These ten ships operated Dr Curtis' modified version of the Type

2031 towed-array. They used improved computer hardware which reduced the weight of the processors by 60 per cent and their power requirements by 80 per cent. They could also operate effectively at a higher tow speed than those arrays fitted to the *Leander*s.[101]

Operationally, the attempt to undertake continuous patrols worked well from 1984 to 1986, but began to fall apart in 1987 as the towed-array patrol work had been largely left to the old *Leander*s. These ships were run extremely hard and their availability diminished after a few years. The new Type 22 towed-array ships were some of the most capable ships in the fleet, so were generally busy on exercises, being deployed on Operation 'Armilla', or making use of their Outboard systems. As a result, only the second towed-array Type 22, HMS *Beaver*, undertook any patrols in the 1980s. This left the patrol work to *Cleopatra*, *Sirius*, *Phoebe* and *Argonaut*, with *Arethusa* added in late 1986 but withdrawn from service only two and half years' later. Each patrol period generally lasted for a month and during 1985 and 1986 attempts were made to undertake near continuous patrols all year round, with the exception of the Christmas period and the early Autumn when the main NATO Eastern Atlantic exercises ran. By mid-1985 some problems were beginning to come to light: the 'silent running' approach not only had an impact on morale, it also meant that the effectiveness of the ship's weapons crews had dropped off considerably, and therefore needed much additional time off-patrol to build back up to an acceptable standard.[102] By 1986 the ships were beginning to show other signs of their heavy operating routines. HMS *Cleopatra* had to end her March 1986 patrol early after weapons engineering defects were followed by a 'major tow cable failure'.[103] The same year, shortages of available frigates meant that *Argonaut* had to combine her patrol task with being the Fleet Contingency Ship, which would be theoretically ready to respond to short-notice requirements such as shadowing Soviet warships near UK waters.[104] The experiment was not repeated. In June 1987, *Argonaut* was called out on two 'reactive patrols', Operations 'Impresario' and 'Mimulus', to track submarines at short-notice as there was no ship on standard patrol. The ship's commanding officer argued that this was not as effective a way of deploying towed-array ships, in comparison to having one ship already at sea.[105] Assisted Maintenance Periods and Docking and Essential Defects periods for the ships increased in length, as did routine refits which stretched to more than 18 months in some instances. The old ships were exhausted, and by 1988 this was finally accepted and the number of patrols reduced to four or five each year, with HMS *Beaver* now supplementing the *Leander*s with one patrol annually.[106] Continuous towed-array patrols would have to wait until the Type 23s were in service in some numbers.

The introduction of the towed-array into the surface fleet was in many ways revolutionary: surface ships so equipped now had submarine detection capabilities that leapt way ahead of any sonar that had previously been used by surface ships or maritime patrol aircraft. Finally, impressing the United States Navy was not just a matter of national pride and gaining satisfaction that the British contribution was being recognised by the leading state in NATO, it also helped to open up other doors to co-operation. As VCNS had mentioned to the Minister of State for Defence in 1978, when discussing submarine innovations: the United Kingdom has to 'recognise that the US [has] tended to be more forthcoming if we had something to offer in exchange, or possibly, had demonstrated an earnest intent by generating our own research effort in a particular field'.[107] Surface towed-array was one important example of where the Royal Navy now had 'something to offer': not only was it a major step forward in the technological battle between surface ships and submarines, but it provided a new lever for fruitful US-UK naval co-operation when the forward strategy into the Norwegian Sea emphasised the importance of protection against submarine attack.

Major NATO Exercises

The 1980s saw a gradual transformation in many aspects of NATO Eastern Atlantic exercises.[108] As was seen in Chapter 15, Exercise Ocean Venture, which partly subsumed Ocean Safari 81, included a deep thrust into northern waters for the first time since the early 1970s, which had been directly prompted by the collapse of détente in 1979. This trend continued through the decade, as exercise scenarios were adapted and changed over time. The Royal Navy's involvement in Exercise Northern Wedding 82 in September 1982 was limited by the fact that much of the fleet was either in refit and repair after the Falklands conflict, operating down south as part of the task group retained there at the end of fighting, or being preparing to head south on roulement in the next few months. As a result, the Royal Navy was only able to offer the towed-array sonar trials ship HMS *Lowestoft* and four Ikara *Leander* frigates, HM Ships *Leander, Dido, Arethusa* and *Euryalus*. In addition the assault ship HMS *Fearless* was provided, recently repaired after Operation 'Corporate', and not otherwise needed as part of the fleet's roulement plans to the South Atlantic.[109]

Up until 1988, NATO exercises remained in the routine of undertaking Ocean Safari – which focussed on transatlantic reinforcement shipping protection, usually in the Western Approaches or towards the Straits of Gibraltar – every other year, with either Teamwork or Northern Wedding exercises in the years in between. These latter exercises had a much greater focus on traversing the GIUK Gap and then proceeding into the Norwegian

Sea and undertaking amphibious landings in Norway. Ocean Safari, Teamwork and Northern Wedding all generally occurred in September (the exceptions being Ocean Safari 83 in June and Teamwork 84 in March), but when it was an Ocean Safari year, then the annual Cold Winter amphibious exercise gained increased importance as the only major NATO exercise of this type. For example, for Cold Winter 85 the Royal Navy contributed a carrier, four destroyers and frigates and one submarine in addition to the usual amphibious shipping. Cold Winter 87 was similar with four destroyers and frigates and a number of mine warfare vessels taking part.[110] 1989 saw some changes to the exercise schedule, belatedly reflecting the strategic shift towards a greater High North focus: the Ocean Safari and Northern Wedding exercise series disappeared; instead Teamwork would occur biennially, with the new North Star exercise occurring in the years in-between. This new series did not have an amphibious element of itself, but was linked with the amphibious Cold Winter in 1989. That year was especially busy for NATO navies, as not only did the first North Star take place, alongside an associated Cold Winter, in March, but it was followed up by Sharp Spear 89 which focussed on shallow water operations around the United Kingdom. 1990 returned to the less busy format of a spring Cold Winter and an autumn Teamwork.[111]

The British contribution to these core exercises remained relatively steady through the 1980s after the partial hiatus of 1982. One aircraft carrier would generally take part, as would an amphibious assault ship if the exercise included a landing. The number of destroyers and frigates would generally oscillate between seven and four, and from 1984 at least two of these would generally be towed-array ships. There were some exceptions: only two frigates were present at North Star 89, but that year's associated Cold Winter included another two frigates which brought the total back up to a relatively respectable four. The Ocean Safari exercises would generally include two SSNs, whilst the Teamwork and North Wedding series, with a greater littoral element, usually included one SSN and one SSK. The exception was Teamwork 84, which saw a particular emphasis on the countering of conventional boats, presumably in response to increased Soviet production of such vessels.[112] Mine warfare vessels were involved in nearly all the exercises, either for clearing coastal mines prior to an amphibious assault or undertaking the deep-sea sweeping of rising mines.[113] Despite the lessening of Cold War tensions, 1989 and 1990 saw a crescendo of British naval involvement. As has been seen, 1989 saw three major Eastern Atlantic exercises that year, each with a Royal Navy carrier involved. In September 1990, Teamwork 90 had the largest Royal Navy presence in a NATO exercise since the 1970s with both *Ark Royal* and *Invincible* present, alongside nine destroyers and frigates (four of which were towed-array ships), the assault ship *Intrepid* and twelve mine warfare vessels as well as one nuclear and one conventional submarine.[114] This huge showing was partly the result of the absence of US naval forces as a result of the crisis in Kuwait following the Iraqi invasion, and the beginnings of the marshalling of US and allied forces to liberate the state. The British naval contribution to the crisis response was limited to destroyers, frigates and mine warfare vessels, thus permitting the presence of two carriers at Teamwork 90.[115]

The Royal Navy's involvement in these exercises was significant – it was almost always the second largest contributor to them – but it was the US element that was always the most important. A minimum of two US carrier battle groups were generally present (the exceptions being Teamwork 84 and Teamwork 90 recounted above), and their aircraft were inevitably at the core of the both the strike and air defence capabilities in the exercises. The Royal Navy's Sea Harriers had a secondary role in intercepting shadowing and targeting aircraft, but in practice were often used to shadow and ward off real Soviet aircraft which were present either to collect intelligence or attempt to disrupt the exercise. When the Ocean Safari series focussed on southern approaches to Europe, there was sometimes significant French involvement (operating under national command due to France sitting outside NATO command structures). For example, in Ocean Safari 83 the French carrier *Foch*, with escorting ships, played a major part in the exercises.[116] The United States also contributed large numbers of destroyers and frigates, as well as the exercise command ship, which was invariably the USS *Mount Whitney*, with the commander of the US 2nd Fleet/NATO Strike Fleet and his staff on board. Their amphibious contribution also put all the other navies in the shade, although the British effort was not insignificant, not least when it included ships taken up from trade, which was increasingly common in the 1980s, reflecting both Falklands experience and pre-Falklands trends in supplementing warships in emergencies.[117] Dutch, Belgian, German and Norwegian naval forces were also significant participants in these exercises, often operating under CINCFLEET's operational command from Northwood with his NATO 'hat' on as CINCEASTLANT. The Standing Naval Force Atlantic ('SNFL'), the multinational NATO standing squadron, was also involved in these exercises most years, with at least one British frigate or destroyer taking part under SNFL command.[118]

The increased focus on the High North did not just manifest itself in a greater willingness to conduct operations in or near the Arctic and amphibious landings in north Norway, it was also reflected in the development of innovative tactics in order to blunt the threat from Soviet land-based strike aircraft. Placing the US carrier strike group within wide fjords in north Norway like Vestfjord had first been considered in 1978 following US Navy wargames and was first attempted by British amphibious vessels during Exercise Alloy

Express in March 1982. The experience of the Falklands had also encouraged this approach, as the presence of ships in San Carlos Bay had forced Argentine aircraft into a 'funnel' in order to approach targets. By placing major warships in a fjord, long-range anti-ship cruise missiles would be much more difficult to use, forcing Soviet 'Backfires' into either dropping freefall bombs from a high altitude, thus exposing them to attack from large numbers of US air defence aircraft, or approaching from the open ocean direction of the south-west thus creating a zone into which air defence could be concentrated. In Cold Winter 85 HMS *Invincible* was placed in Lyngenfjord in north Norway, with 42 Cdo embarked, and acting as a commando carrier but also operating Sea Harriers and some anti-submarine aircraft.[119] In Northern Wedding 86, the carrier *Nimitz*, battleship *Iowa* and British light carrier *Ark Royal* all entered Vestfjord with escorts and undertook exercise serials from the protection of the fjord. This was repeated in Ocean Safari 87 and Teamwork 88.[120] The use of fjords for ship defence showed how innovative approaches making use of geography, could be used to gain tactical advantage, although the fjord approach did carry risks. The carriers might prove more vulnerable to conventional submarine attack in a constrained environment where passive sonars such as towed-array would be much less effective, there might be vulnerabilities to surface raids by fast attack craft, whilst airborne early warning above the mountain line was essential given that the range of ship radars would be dramatically curtailed by the geography of the fjord. However, these problems could be dealt with by effective defences at the entrance to a fjord, including the use of active sonars and helicopters armed with light anti-ship missiles, thus creating a complex interaction of threats, countermeasures and possible counter-threats in the High North littoral zone.

Another innovation in the late 1980s was the inclusion of more 'freeplay' into exercises: in other words allowing mock engagements with the minimum of restrictions and artificialities that reduce realism. Major NATO exercises had always contained a tension between their role as opportunities to train and practice operating together, and attempts to add realism to proceedings so as to better prepare for war. During the 1970s and early 1980s the former generally won out in most exercises. Just sparing time to practice operating together and using NATO, rather than routine national, chains of command was considered important enough. From the 1980s however, there was a push towards realism again: now that the outlines of the US maritime strategy had fully entered the thought and operational process of NATO and its members, freeplay would allow for the honing of tactical skills and encourage innovation and free thinking. Ocean Safari 87 was the first major NATO exercise for some years to include elements of freeplay.[121] Teamwork 88 took this a step further and for an important segment of the exercise, the warships on exercise split into two groups across the mid-Atlantic and 'fought' each other in a series of engagements designed to allow as much freeplay as possible during a four-day period prior to the crossing of the GIUK Gap. However, this was occurring outside of the main expected operational areas in the Norwegian Sea and it bore little resemblance to any sort of threat likely to come from Soviet forces.[122]

During much of the 1970s, the major Eastern Atlantic exercises had been given very little publicity, but this changed significantly during the 1980s as John Lehman's conception of exercises as peacetime deterrent (and reassurance) operations resulted in much more public relations activity. This publicity probably reached its height during Northern Wedding 86, which from the British perspective was directly linked into celebrations in New York on the 100th anniversary of the Statue of Liberty. HMS *Ark Royal* arrived on the US East Coast in time for the anniversary, where President Reagan inspected an international fleet review. Two of her Sea Harriers led the flypast and then hovered in front of the statue to 'bow' in front of it which was 'much praised and publicised in the American media' according to the carrier's commanding officer.[123] The press conference by Vice Admiral Julian Oswald, Flag Officer of the 3rd Flotilla, was attended by all three major US networks, the new CNN rolling news channel and the major British news networks. Oswald then hosted a dinner with the US Secretary of Defence, Caspar Weinberger. Following visits to Fort Lauderdale that recalled her predecessor's visit a decade before, and some trials at AUTEC, *Ark Royal* transited the Atlantic with the US carrier strike group. Northern Wedding itself was reported in much of the British national media following a press briefing by CINCFLEET, whilst a press conference was held on the carrier USS *Nimitz* whilst she was still in Vestfjord.[124] Such levels of coverage were indeed unusual but were the result of a confluence of the Statue of Liberty anniversary, the first major operational voyage of the new *Ark Royal* which (probably deliberately) associated itself with the famous 1976 deployment which had been subject of a still well-remembered documentary, and also a more optimistic, perhaps even 'gung-ho' perception of US and Western military power in the months after the US bombing of Libya after that state had sponsored terrorist attacks on US citizens during 1985.

Planning for War

Although the US Maritime Strategy had been developed largely on the basis of any conflict remaining non-nuclear for a considerable period of time, every major NATO exercise still ended with rehearsals for nuclear exchange and withstanding nuclear fallout, whilst the early 1980s were also a period of increased superpower tension. Not only did Ronald Reagan heighten the rhetoric of anti-communism in a series of speeches, but with Yuri Andropov as Soviet General Secretary from 1982 and 1984, the USSR had a leader who was especially concerned, if not paranoid, about the risk of a pre-emptive NATO attack.[125] In this context, it is therefore an appropriate place to assess the process by which the Royal Navy would shift from peacetime, to preparing for armed conflict, and then from conventional to nuclear war with the Soviet Union.

The transition from peace to war with the Warsaw Pact had been meticulously planned since the early days of the Cold War. A 'War Book' was created by the Ministry of Defence; it was regularly updated and would set out step by step how the United Kingdom and its armed forces would prepare for such a war, whether it be conventional or nuclear, or would transition from one to the other.[126] No full United Kingdom War Book has been declassified for the period studied for this book, but a document has been released at the National Archives that sets out amendments to the Royal Navy's own subsidiary War Book. These amendments are therefore just some of the pieces of a jigsaw puzzle, the whole picture of which is still obscured.

These proposed amendments were drafted in 1978, and had been requested as a result of the outcome of Exercise Hilex 8, a NATO headquarters-only high level training exercise, in which it had become clear that the War Books needed to be updated.[127] This Naval War Book largely consisted of a series of orders, presumably sent out to naval establishments and warships, at different stages of increased tension and warfare with the Soviet Union and its allies. Only a portion of these orders were amended, but they give an understanding of the different stages of increased preparedness as the world began to descend into global war. Each order had a three-digit serial number, with those that would be activated first at the earliest stages given serial numbers beginning with one, ascending up to serial numbers beginning with four. Those in the 100 series were clearly precautionary and preparatory in nature. Serial 102 required the reporting of any complement deficiencies in Royal Navy ships. Serial 120 ordered preparations for the implementation of 'Plan Loft', which involved the rapid reinforcement of the British Army of the Rhine from the UK. The Royal Navy would have an important role in managing the required cross-channel transportation for this reinforcement. As part of this serial, staff lists for those destined for duty at District Transport Movement Operation Centres and Reinforcement Port Naval Parties were to be reviewed and brought up to date. Serial 129 included the preparation of war buoyage in British ports, whilst serial 123 ordered the review of oceanographic war plans, the implementation of the control of dissemination of oceanographic information from military sources, and the review of plans for implementing the control of ice information.[128]

Series 200 saw the next step: the actual implementation of those actions that had been prepared for. Serial 207 sounded especially ominous. The following would be sent out across the Royal Navy:

> The government has a firm indication that Warsaw Pact forces are being placed into a war footing and therefore acts of aggression against NATO territory or NATO forces may take place in the near future. If attack develops and contact with command is lost, ships are to act in accordance with their war orders, transferring to NATO or national commanders as detailed therein. Shore establishments should, where necessary, make contact with and take instructions from: (a) peacetime authorities if still existing; or (b) wartime authorities if set up; or (c) government organisation in the regions, if authorities in (a) and (b) cannot be contacted.[129]

One must assume that very similar orders would have been sent out to Army and Royal Air Force establishments and units at the same time. The British military would now be moving to a full war footing. Other orders in the 200 series included serial 211 which informed active service personnel that they may be redeployed without notice. Serial 246 implemented Plan Loft, whilst serial 247 (which would presumably be promulgated alongside 246) stated that CINCFLEET was taking operational control of all ships taking personnel and stores to Europe for reinforcing British Forces in Germany. Fifteen ports would be involved in this process and would include shipment to ports in the Netherlands, Germany and Denmark. Serials 245 and 248 essentially confirmed the Navy's operational control over these fifteen ports: the first allowed local Flag Officers to charter whichever local vessels and craft they needed to implement war plans, whilst the second implemented measures 'for naval control and seaward defence of shipping and port installations involved in sealift reinforcement' and other military movement plans.[130]

The next stage, series 300, saw preparations for imminent conflict. Serial 306 ordered the immediate 'distribution of naval control of shipping publications and crypto material to merchant ships joining the naval control of shipping organisation'. Serials 322 and 323 ordered the implementation of both meteorological and oceanographic war plans. Meteorological and oceanographic information from all sources would now be controlled, whilst preparations would be made for the imminent control of all ice information from any source. In effect, the censoring of information that could be of help to the enemy at sea was being put in place. This must therefore have had an impact on civilian research institutes and universities as much as on Ministry of Defence sources of such information, which would have included the

Hydrographic Office.[131] The only suggested amendment in series 400 made it clear the stage that had been reached by this point. It stated:

> A NATO general alert has been declared. Assigned forces are to act as instructed by their NATO commanders and forces under national operational command as directed by CINCFLEET or CINCNAVHOME as appropriate.[132]

With a NATO general alert called the expectation was that a general war with the Soviet Union and its allies was imminent. It is not known what the other orders in the 400 series would have been, but it should probably be assumed that a Third World War would be on the cusp of breaking out. The amendments summarised here are showing only some aspects of the Navy's War Book – those that needed updating since the last revision – so there is likely to have been much more on different aspects of transition-to-war planning, but what is there does give an indication of both the levels of preparation and implementation of the transition to war, and the delegated powers that would have been given to local Flag Officers and the Royal Navy's two Commanders-in-Chief to organise ports for war operations.

Another glimpse of how the Royal Navy would have prepared for war is given in a 1976 document entitled 'The Logistic Support of Naval War Operations'. Despite having been written in the year that the balance of Ministry of Defence informed opinion shifted towards a 'short war/short-warning' scenario, this document was predicated on a scenario that would involve three months of increasing tension, three weeks of 'intermittent action' at sea, followed by one week of 'intensive action'. In other words, it assumed a long-warning/long war approach but with the long war shifting from a lower intensity to higher in its final stages. It also dealt with the problems and role of the logistics supply organisation after a nuclear strike: 'the main requirement will be to provide such support as is needed for the survival of the nation, maintenance of law and order, and control of sea areas using resources available at the time.'[133] It was also recommended, wherever possible before a nuclear strike, to load requisitioned merchant ships with stores that would have value for the Navy 'post-strike'. The possibility of civil disturbances in London during the period of high tension was also contemplated, so plans were laid for the control of naval logistics to be transferred from London to MOD offices in Bath if this transpired, and the MOD's offices in London proved impossible from which to work. After a nuclear strike it was expected that regional government would be in force, and that 'naval personnel not required by Area Flag Officers for continuing Naval operations will be placed under the control of the appropriate

Regional Military Commander. Other naval resources will be controlled by the Regional Commissioner, and Area Flag Officers will liaise with him through the Naval Regional Member.'[134]

The plan set out in this document aimed to mesh both with NATO and national operational plans and requirements, with some naval bases such as the Clyde, Plymouth and Gibraltar being specifically set aside to support certain NATO contingency plans. Ships undergoing refit would have their work sped up – as occurred during the Falklands conflict – although the repairs of action damage and OPDEFs ('Operational Defects') would be prioritised over docking and essential defect rectification and refits. The Royal Navy hospitals at Plymouth and Haslar in Hampshire would prepare for dealing with casualties by discharging as many patients as possible, whilst emergency hospital beds would be made available in unused barracks accommodation wherever possible. Maximising the availability of support craft during such a crisis would be undertaken by using overtime working as much as possible as well as short-notice recruiting, refits of such vessels would be deferred for as long as possible and additional wear and tear would be accepted by reducing craft down time to a minimum. Taking ships up from trade would be undertaken by charter (with crews) prior to activation of the relevant authorisations for requisitioning in the War Book. After requisitioning had been allowed, the ships would be taken over without their crews. Naval bases would be split into 'main' bases at Portsmouth, Devonport, Chatham and Rosyth and 'advance' bases on the Clyde, Gibraltar, Portland and Bermuda.[135] Other 'minor' ports would operate from second-tier commercial harbours and have a major role in the Naval Control of Shipping organisation for the supply of the United Kingdom, on the assumption that many major ports such as Felixstowe and Liverpool would either have been targeted in a nuclear strike or would be at high risk of such a strike. In the event of a nuclear attack, the supply of food and other key supplies to the remnants of the population would depend upon the functioning of secondary ports such as Grimsby, Falmouth, Sheerness and Milford Haven, with the Royal Naval Auxiliary Service ('RNXS') playing a key role in the management of the convoy systems bringing these supplies into ports. The RNXS would also manage the evacuation of harbour craft and as much commercial shipping as possible to safer places if a nuclear attack was imminent.[136]

The Royal Navy at this time was a service at high levels of readiness to begin operations at short-notice, a stance that reflected its core Cold War role, but which had also stood it in good stead during the Falklands crisis. Another snippet of information is a January 1978 assessment of the number of frigates that would be available in the event of an emergency. From a force of fifty-six, thirty-four ships were either operational or in a Docking and Essential Defects period, five were on trials or on BOST (Basic Operational Sea Training), three were in the Standby Squadron, six were in major refit and a further eight were in normal refits. This would mean that in 48 hours, 61 per cent of the frigate force would be available for operations with an additional 12 per cent available at least to go to sea even if they weren't fully operational, whilst within 15 days 63 per cent would be available for operations with another 14 per cent able to go to sea.[137] The total number of destroyers and frigates reduced first to fifty-five and then to fifty during the 1980s, and strains on personnel and crewing did increase during the late 1980s, but it is likely that these proportional availability levels did not dramatically reduce from the 1978 figures. This was a Navy prepared to mobilise a significant proportion of its capability at short-notice: either to counter Soviet actions as international tensions increased between East or West in the long-warning/long war scenario, or to respond to a rapidly escalating crisis if the short-warning/short war scenario was taking place.

These three pieces of evidence only give a partial picture of the total planning for the Navy's transition to war in the last two decades of the Cold War, but are an indication of how conflict would have been prepared for and the actions that would have been taken. They also show aspects of how the Navy would have fitted into a post-strike United Kingdom, with millions dead, many more suffering from radiation sickness, and the country under emergency regional government with significant powers granted to the military and the remaining forces of law and order. Both the Naval War Book and the Logistics Plan, given the many steps required to fulfil them, implicitly (and in the case of the latter explicitly) assumed that a long-warning war would be the most likely occurrence. If not, then it is difficult to see how a short-warning transition to war would not have overwhelmed the War Book processes, with their multiple stages of preparation and implementation.

* * *

The changed strategic environment for the Navy as a result of the development of the US Maritime Strategy provided another factor on top of the successful outcome of the Falklands conflict, which helped to protect the Navy and give a clear driver and justification for much of the surface fleet. It now had a clear and valued role in providing anti-submarine protection to the NATO carrier strike fleet. The demonstration of the superior capabilities of the British surface towed-array therefore came at just the right time, marking a once-in-a-generation shift in the long-running technological and tactical battle between the submarine and surface ship. No longer were nuclear submarines just fleeting and uncertain contacts on ship's sonar screens, they could now be tracked and trailed for days and sometimes weeks in the same way that NATO nuclear submarines had been able to do with Soviet boats for more than a decade. Yet if the strategic environment seemed more positive for the Navy, its place in Ministry of Defence structures, its budget and its key procurements were much less certain.

19

Reform and Overstretch

The Royal Navy now had a more defensible and coherent strategic backing for its forces during the 1980s, but would it be able to provide the capabilities to ensure that the strategy could be carried out, and that British obligations to NATO and to its other maritime commitments could be maintained? The budgetary position of the Navy initially looked adequate until 1985, but this position had only been sustained through the government's commitment to 3 per cent real-terms increases in defence spending each year. Once this was withdrawn, the situation became much more constrained, and a series of important procurements were delayed during the late 1980s, gradually creating an environment where some government commitments – not least the fifty escorts and eighteen nuclear attack submarine levels – could no longer be met into the 1990s. This chapter covers the reform of the Ministry of Defence during the first half of the 1980s, the development of the budgetary situation during this decade, and then the progress of individual procurement areas one by one.

Admiral Fieldhouse was First Sea Lord during the 3 per cent years, and when he moved on to become the Chief of the Defence Staff in 1985, he was succeeded by Admiral Staveley. He in turn was succeeded as CINCFLEET by Admiral Nicholas Hunt, a former Director of Naval Plans who had previously commanded frigates and an assault ship.[1] Admiral Bryson had been succeeded by Admiral Derek Reffell in 1984 as Controller of the Navy. Reffell had been Flag Officer of the Third Flotilla during the Falklands conflict and before that the Assistant Chief of the Naval Staff (Policy). In the role of Chief of Fleet Support, one supply officer was replaced by another as Vice Admiral Anthony Tippet succeeded James Kennon. Tippet had trained as a naval lawyer and had worked in both intelligence and logistics posts.[2] His two successors were not supply officers however, as the post reverted to seaman officers as a matter of course: Tippet was succeeded by Benjamin Bathurst and Jock Slater, both future First Sea Lords. The Second Sea Lord remained Admiral Cassels until 1986 when he was succeeded by Admiral Richard Fitch, a navigator and former naval assistant to Admiral Ashmore as First Sea Lord. Fitch had previously been Flag Officer of the Third Flotilla, Director of Naval Warfare in the Naval Staff and commanding officer of HMS *Hermes*.[3] In the post of CINCNAVHOME, Admiral Cassidi was succeeded by Admiral Peter Stanford, the last VCNS before that post's abolition in 1985. The Admiralty Board therefore looked more 'traditional' towards the end of the 1980s than it had at the start: the brief appearance of submariners, engineers and supply officers around the table being replaced by the usual predominance of surface fleet seaman officers.

Defence Reform

Strengthening the Chief of the Defence Staff

After a period of relative stasis in the structures of the Ministry during the 1970s, three major reforms were undertaken during the following decade. The first, which occurred in early 1982, was the increase in powers of the Chief of the Defence Staff ('CDS'). This had been driven by Admiral Lewin, who had been frustrated at his inability to provide useful advice to the Secretary of State given the constraints he worked under as CDS. At that time, as the Chair of the Chiefs of Staff Committee, he was bound by the collective responsibility of that committee as the joint advisers to the Secretary of State. This therefore made it extremely difficult for him to give candid advice when he had to hold to a joint line agreed by the Chiefs. If there were disagreements, then this joint position might be little more than a lowest common denominator, which would be of little use to ministers. CDS could set out each of the Chiefs' separate positions and then follow this up with his own position on the matter, but this was not an effective way to give clear advice on significant issues. This problem had been especially acute during the 1981 Defence Review when Lewin felt unable either to support Nott and Cooper in their decision-making nor effectively relay his own personal views about the progress of the Review. The Central Staffs were not under his control either, being directed by him only as Chair of the Chiefs of Staff Committee; this meant that CDS was relatively unsupported within the Committee and the Central Staffs would be at risk of ineffectiveness if the Chiefs could not agree on what work the Central Staffs should undertake.[4]

Lewin proposed reforms based on five principles: first, that CDS would now become solely responsible for military advice to the Secretary of State. Second, CDS would now seek the opinions and views of the single-service Chiefs but would no longer be bound by a collective responsibility in the

Committee. Third, the single-service Chiefs would remain the professional heads of their services and retain responsibility for advice to the Secretary of State relating to their own single-service. They would also retain the right to access to the Secretary of State, and in extremis, to the Prime Minister. Fourth, the Central Staffs would now be responsible to CDS in his own right, rather than in his capacity as Chair of the Chiefs of Staff. In practical terms this meant that CDS could now call on the Central Staffs to undertake studies based on terms of reference or criteria set by himself rather than jointly agreed by the Chiefs. Finally, CDS would become chair of the appointments committee for the most senior posts in all three services. This would allow him to ensure that those senior officers who had advanced tri-service positions when serving in the Central Staffs were not punished by their own services for doing so by having their chances of advancement removed.[5] In terms of the organisation of the Central Staffs, the number of direct reports to CDS was reduced from six to three, with the Assistant Chiefs of the Defence Staff now reporting to the Deputy Chief of the Defence Staff, and being given new responsibilities covering programmes, commitments and command and control.[6]

The implementation of these reforms essentially meant that the way in which the 1981 Defence Review had unfolded would not be possible in the future. The Permanent Under-Secretary, the Chief Scientific Adviser and the Chief of Defence Procurement, the other three key advisers to the Secretary of State, had been relatively unconstrained in their ability to give advice, whereas Lewin as CDS had been unable to contribute at the level that he wanted given splits among the Chiefs. This meant that a single authoritative military voice in the Review had been largely absent. The reforms of the mid-1980s described below also downgraded the role of the Chief Scientific Adviser, who no longer had direct access to the Secretary of State. Sir Ronald Mason's advancing of operational analysis taken out of its context, and his shift from being a source of impartial scientific advice to being a determined policy advocate (backed up by a shaky evidence base), had appeared to play a role in this demotion.[7] This further changed the dynamic within the Ministry of Defence, and indirectly strengthened the hand of CDS further. In this respect therefore, the 1981 Defence Review had been the consequence of a very particular confluence of circumstances respecting the key advisers to the Secretary of State which would be unlikely to be repeated following these changes.

MINIS

After the retirement of Sir John Nott in January 1983, Michael Heseltine had been made Secretary of State for Defence. Ambitious, a possible Conservative leadership contender from the left of the party, and with a background in business having run his own successful publishing company, Heseltine embarked on two major structural reforms within the Ministry of Defence. The first was Management Information System for Ministers and Top Management, generally known as MINIS, a system which would provide regular and understandable management information to minister and senior officials.[8] Such systems, sometimes termed a management 'dashboard' to describe the information as it was presented to a company's senior managers, had been commonplace in large businesses since at least the 1960s, and ensured that managers had reliable and regular key performance indicators from which to manage their businesses. From Heseltine's perspective, MINIS was therefore an obvious and essential means to improve defence decision-making.[9] The improvement of government management information had interested Heseltine in previous appointments, and it appealed to Heseltine's business-like approach.[10] It also gave him a project that would not only prove his effectiveness but might be transferrable to other departments across government.[11]

Within a few weeks of arriving at the Ministry, Heseltine had set out to Parliament what he intended to do, and very quickly sent out a series of tabular questionnaires to all the two-star (Rear Admiral, Assistant Under-Secretary or equivalent) areas across the Ministry. This was such a huge undertaking that it was decided to exclude the Procurement Executive from the process, whilst front-line units were also excluded, an acknowledgement that factors other than management efficiency governed their effectiveness.[12] After this first tranche of information had come in and been analysed, Heseltine then requested a second tranche which asked for more detail on the subordinate areas below each two star: their structure, activities, staff numbers, staff costs and budget responsibilities. In addition, pointing the way ahead to personnel management systems that would spread across Whitehall in the 1990s, he asked for 'achievements' in the previous financial year and 'objectives' for the next.[13] Having digested all this material across the Ministry, making use of a new 'MINIS Unit' created out of the Management Audit function, Heseltine set out his initial conclusions to CDS and the Permanent Under-Secretary ('PUS') for further downward transmission. He thanked the two star areas for the information they had provided, but commented that 'so much of the work done by the Staffs covered by MINIS seems to be governed by the federal nature of the MOD'.[14] The Secretary of State made it clear that he wanted clear objectives to be set across all parts of the Ministry, and that authority over decision-making must match the responsibility given to each senior manager. Earlier reforms aimed at delegating the ability to spend money further down the management chain would be speeded up in order to support some of the changes that Heseltine wanted. For the first time in the Ministry of Defence's history, a Secretary of State was driving administrative reform himself, all previous reforms and major changes having been initiated either by CDS, PUS or after external reports by committees or commissions.[15]

MOD Centralisation

The initial outcomes from the implementation of MINIS suggested further reforms within Defence. As had been hinted by the Secretary of State in his communication to CDS and PUS, it was argued that too many resources were spent on co-ordinating and supervising work being done outside the Ministry, and that authority over spending and resources should be devolved down to managers, giving them more responsibility over their own areas. At the same time, the split between the Centre and the three service Departments had meant that lines of accountability and responsibility were blurred and it was therefore less efficient than previously believed. Overheads should be cut, delegation encouraged and resources used more efficiently.[16]

Perhaps inevitably, the result was a series of proposals that focussed much more on the centralisation of powers than on their delegation. Those parts of the Naval, General and Air Staffs that focussed on planning and resource priorities (including the procurement of equipment) would be centralised into a new Defence Policy and Operational Staff at the Centre. In practice this would mean a significant reduction in the size of the Naval, General and Air Staffs. The post of Vice Chief of the Naval Staff held by a Vice Admiral was disestablished, a new Assistant Chief of the Naval Staff ('ACNS') being created to take its place. The Director of Naval Plans and the Director of Naval Operational Requirements, along with their directorates, were added to the central Defence Staff. They still had a strong link back to the Navy Department, as both post holders (renamed Director, Plans and Programmes (Sea) and Director, Operational Requirements (Sea)) were still formally responsible for representing the views of the First Sea Lord to the Centre. ACNS took over the remaining sections of the Naval Staff, which now included senior captains in the roles of Director of Naval Warfare, Director of Staff Duties and the civilian Secretariat. The Director of Naval Operations and Trade remained within the Naval Staff but worked to the Assistant Chief of the Defence Staff (Commitments) in the Centre. Public relations, logistics management, systems analysis and security also fell under the purview of ACNS.[17] The heads of the individual services would now primarily just have responsibility for the 'management of their individual Services ... [and] for their total fighting efficiency and morale'.[18]

CDS would now take responsibility for all military operations, not just those that were joint in character, thus placing CINCFLEET operationally under CDS on national operational matters, although CDS could delegate control of minor operations to the single-service operational commanders if he so chose. To some extent this was formalising what had occurred in practice during the Falklands campaign, when the First Sea Lord and his Staff had largely been cut out of the command loop between Fieldhouse and Lewin. Each service board would set up an Executive Committee to streamline the work under their responsibility and reduce the overlap in responsibilities between the new expanded Centre and the remaining areas within their departments. For the Navy, this new Executive Committee became the Navy Board, which for all practical purposes replaced the business of both the Admiralty Board and the Admiralty Board Sub-Committee (the latter having been established in 1976 to deal with second-tier Board business). The new Navy Board did not have any ministerial representation, so the Admiralty Board remained as an occasional forum to brief ministers on the Navy Department's work. The secretariat for the new Navy Board was initially provided by the Centre, rather than by the Navy Department's own residual civilian Secretariat, a further indication that the Centre was keen to reach down into the remaining responsibilities of the single-services.[19] One significant change to the Navy Department was that the Fleet Air Arm lost its Directorate in the Naval Staff. The Director of Naval Air Warfare was disestablished, with the post's role being split between the Director of Naval Warfare in the Naval Staff and the two new 'Sea' posts in the Defence Staff. This caused some concerns within the Navy's flying community but for some others it was a timely integration of flying matters into the wider mix of Naval Staff business.[20]

The way the new Board undertook its business changed as well. Whereas the old Admiralty Board and its Sub-Committee had dealt with matters as and when they occurred, punctuated by the annually occurring Sketch Estimates, Long Term Costings and Long Term Dockyard Loading discussions, now the new Navy Board primarily focussed on annually recurring items, led by an 'Audit of the Royal Navy' and annual reports on procurement, 'manpower', and the Fleet's 'combat effectiveness'. After a few years, this approach did begin to break down somewhat and revert to its previous format, before coalescing again in 1990 into 'Command Reports' to the Board covering the Fleet, CINCNAVHOME, the Royal Marines, Flag Officer Naval Air Command, and the presentation of the Navy's Annual Management Plan.[21] Discussions on the annual Sketch Estimates and the ten-year Long Term Costings remained, but their nature had changed fundamentally. Prior to the reforms the Navy Department's DUS(N) and VCNS would present on the planned budget for the next year and next decade, to gain approval prior to negotiations with the Centre for their final acceptance. Now, the 2nd PUS and one of the Deputy Chiefs of the Defence Staff from the Centre would attend the Navy Board and discuss *their* proposed Navy Department programme for procurement, personnel and other areas.[22] The realities of this power shift were somewhat more nuanced than they first seemed: the programme that was being presented to the Sea Lords by the Centre as something close to a fait accompli, would have been largely created based on the advice and support of the Director, Plans and Programmes (Sea) and the Director, Operational Requirements (Sea), both of whom would have been in regular contact with the Naval Staff and were working under their obligation to represent the First Sea Lord's views in the proposals that emerged. In addition, the elements relating to personnel and fleet support would still have been put together by the Navy Department.[23]

The changes in the Centre were considerable and resulted in the largest shift in the organisation of the Central Staffs and Secretariat since 1964. The Secretary of State now had only two principal advisers, CDS and PUS, the Chief Scientific Adviser and the Chief of Defence Procurement (the Head of the Procurement Executive) now being placed under PUS in the structures. The staff officers and civil servants taken out of the single-service Staffs were not placed in a single Defence Staff organisation, but were split between an enlarged Defence Staff under a new four star post, the Vice Chief of the Defence Staff ('VCDS'), who reported to CDS, and a new Office of Management and Budget under the 2nd Permanent Under-Secretary ('2nd PUS'). VCDS had three military and one civilian DCDSs reporting into him: covering commitments and operations, operational requirements, long-term policy and nuclear issues, and personnel and long-term programmes. Meanwhile, 2nd PUS had four civilian Deputy Under-Secretaries reporting to him, one covering resources and programmes, one finance, one administration and the last civilian management issues.[24] This strange new structure, having theoretically dealt with the old single-service-Centre split, created a new split between two huge organisations in the Centre: one military-led and the other civilian-led. Heseltine appears to have envisaged the 2nd PUS in charge of the Office of Management and Budget as an equivalent of a private sector Finance Director, with VCDS in charge of the Defence Staff as presumably an Operations Director, but the complexities of defence decision-making meant that this new structure, whilst removing a number of duplications, had created a number of its own, not least between 2nd PUS's resources and programmes area and three of VCDS's direct reports. The Secretary of State clearly wished to ensure that some 'creative tension' existed within the system, but it remained to be seen how effectively this would work and whether the resulting tensions that might ensue outweighed any 'creativity' that had been theoretically unleashed by the reorganisation.[25]

The reforms were pushed through at some speed, with a considerable effort made to ensure that the new structure was in place and operational by 2 January 1985. This not only involved structural changes but many moves of office within a Ministry of Defence main building that was not yet made up of large open-plan spaces, but still consisted of many small offices opening off lines of long corridors. One naval staff officer recalled the situation in the last months of 1984:

The reorganisation entailed much moving of accommodation during a dreary and unusually cold start to the year, the passages of Main Building becoming cluttered with unwanted furniture. Much of the interior of the building was happy but redecoration of offices could only be achieved if major works had taken place, which, with skill, could be simulated. ACNS took the initiative by putting forward suggestions for making the building more user friendly. Pictures for offices were signally absent and the main custodian made it quite clear that although there was an abundant supply, her task was to keep then in store unseen. Fortunately a more helpful attitude prevailed in Old Admiralty Building and a couple of offices obtained some long neglected prints.[26]

Assessments of the success of the reforms after that had some time to bed in, provided a mixed picture. Sir Robin Ibbs, the government's adviser on efficiency, stated that the new structure had done little to help the management of costs and that there had been too little delegation of responsibility down to managers. The outgoing VCDS argued in favour of delegating the operational control of more minor military operations back to the single-services, suggesting an overload in the DCDS Commitments area. The 2nd PUS now had a huge range of responsibilities, so had less time to provide policy or financial advice to ministers, whilst in the Navy at least there were concerns that the distance from those making decisions in the Defence Staff and Office of Management and Budget to those actually responsible for fighting efficiency in the single-service Departments, was at risk of becoming too great. Despite this, some aspects of the recent reforms were deemed to have worked well, not least the clarity of CDS's role as a ministerial adviser and ultimate operational commander.[27] As might be expected, more reform would soon be on the horizon. The New Management Strategy was developed in 1988 and 1989 and implemented across defence in April 1991. It aimed to follow through on some of the objectives of MINIS and the 1985 reforms by shifting to a number of 'Top Level Budgets' ('TLBs') across defence, with senior officials or officers responsible for these TLBs with lower-level budgets underneath; an annual departmental plan would be produced setting out aims, methods of achieving them, and the resources available; and an annual cycle of objective setting and performance review was introduced across the Ministry and throughout management chains.[28] The New Management Strategy was clearly a development of the original Heseltine reforms: attempting to follow through on early financial delegation proposals whilst embedding objective setting, performance management and private sector management approaches across the Ministry.

Heseltine's reforms in 1985 had resulted in structures that looked much more centralised than before, but underneath the tri-service splits remained in much of the Ministry. The centralisation of planning and operational requirements had retained single-service sections that had to look back to their respective departments for expert advice. However much some in the Centre might have wanted to take decision-making away from the single-services, the Ministry could not do without the expertise and experience of those who would eventually have to use the equipment and ultimately deliver the MOD's objectives.

Rationalising Research and Development

Other, much less far-reaching but still significant, reforms also took place within naval research and development between 1982 and 1984. During the period of this book, the many naval research and development establishments had been gradually merged until only three major establishments remained: the Admiralty Underwater Weapons Establishment ('AUWE') at Portland, the Admiralty Surface Weapons Establishment ('ASWE') at Portsdown, and the Admiralty Marine Technology Establishment ('AMTE') operating at a number of sites. The AMTE itself was a recent creation, having been brought about by the merger of five smaller establishments in 1977. These were the Admiralty Research Laboratory at Teddington, the Naval Construction Research Establishment at Dunfermline, the Admiralty Experiment Works at Haslar, the Admiralty Materials Laboratory at Holton Heath and the Central Dockyard Laboratory at Portsmouth. In 1979, the Admiralty Marine Engineering Establishment was also merged into AMTE.[29] This merger had not resulted in the closure of the sites of these establishments – moving their test tanks and laboratories would have cost much more money than was available for such radical shifts in personnel and equipment – but their incorporation into a single dispersed organisation, it was hoped, would be able to save money through the merger of some support functions and the rationalisation of work programmes. In 1982 it was decided to place the three establishments under a single director, and by 1984 the inevitable occurred and ASWE, AUWE and AMTE were merged to create a single Admiralty Research Establishment ('ARE'). As with the creation of AMTE, most of the existing sites remained open but were placed within a single organisation, operating out of nine sites across the United Kingdom.[30] ARE, as had its predecessors since 1971, reported into the Procurement Executive, but was linked into the Navy Department through the Sea Systems Controllerate in the Procurement Executive, whose head, the Controller of the Navy, sat on the Admiralty Board and Navy Board. As with the newly-reformed structures within the Ministry's Main Building, the Navy Department's linkages to other parts of the Ministry that dealt with naval matters were partial and sometimes opaque, but appeared to work well enough to ensure that the Royal Navy was still the predominant influence over its own budget and equipment development decisions.[31]

The Defence Budget and the Royal Navy

In the years immediately following the 1981 Defence Review, the Navy's budgetary position appeared to lurch from famine to apparent feast and back to famine again in only a few years. When reviewing the Navy's position in February and March 1982, the Admiralty Board was made aware of the extremely difficult situation that would be faced by 1985 and 1986. Although the Defence Secretary had been able to secure some additional funds to support the various add backs to the defence programme – including retaining the assault ships, keeping the destroyer and frigate force at fifty and a slower rundown in personnel than originally planned – most of these changes had to be funded from the Navy's budget. As a result, in the weeks before the Falklands crisis, it seemed that by 1986 at the latest, the Standby Squadron would have to be resurrected, the total number of destroyers and frigates reduced to around forty, and the painful reductions in fuel usage that had occurred in 1980 would have to be repeated at various points in the late 1980s. The budget bid to cover the 1982 estimates had to be close to the target set by the Ministry's finance section, and the next few years were also relatively close to their targets, but it was five years into the future that the money the Navy would need to fulfil its programmes ballooned in value far beyond their targets. It seemed that the concessions achieved by heavy US lobbying in 1981 and early 1982 had done no more than achieve a stay for execution on the Navy.[32]

Twelve months later the situation had been apparently transformed. Some of this was due to post-Falklands funding which had secured replacements for lost ships and equipment, and for a few years at least, partly covered the new commitment to naval forces in the South Atlantic. But the decisions to shift from C4 to D5 Trident, which required a delay in spending on the deterrent replacement, and to refurbish missiles in the United States rather than the United Kingdom, had meant that considerable sums had been freed up over the whole ten-year programme. This had only been realised some months after these changes had been negotiated, as new financial information on Trident costs was received from the United States which calculated a much cheaper missile programme than originally envisaged. John Nott's decision to place the Trident procurement in the Navy's budget now had the unexpected advantage that when savings were accrued, the Navy was the sole beneficiary. Between 1987 and 1990, the Navy now had more than an additional £200 million per year free to spend on additional items, the years before and after this there were still significant additions of between £39 million and £153 million each year.[33]

The changes to the Navy's programme were dramatic: the new Long Term Costings for the next decade included a series of new items, such as two further 'Hunt' class mine countermeasures vessels, plans for a sixteen-ship class for the succeeding Single Role Mine Hunter with two ships ordered each year and orders for two further 'Castle' class offshore patrol vessels to undertake Falkland Islands patrols. There was a series of orders for Harrier, Sea King and Lynx aircraft in order to cover expected 'attrition losses' over the lives of those aircraft already in service, as well as additional commando Sea Kings in order to maintain the ability to take two companies of Marines ashore simultaneously when the venerable Wessex V was withdrawn in the late 1980s. In addition, there would be no need to place ships in the Standby Squadron from 1985 onwards and two of the remaining Type 12 frigates would remain in service until 1988 to ensure that the destroyer and frigate fleet remained at fifty ships. Finally, after an initial order for the first Type 23 frigate in 1984, it was expected that three Type 23s would follow each year thereafter. Development work would also begin on a Sea Harrier replacement for the late 1990s, and for a new short-range air defence missile system that would not only be able to defend the ship it was on, but other ships in close company, such as unarmed merchant vessels or military transports.[34]

Unfortunately, although the Navy's most senior civil servant stated that they must be careful to ensure that these additional items would not lead 'once again to over-heating' in the programme, it was all too good to be true.[35] First, the Trident re-phasing and re-costing had saved significant sums, but some costs had just been shifted further back beyond the ten-year timeframe that the Long Term Costings operated within. These particular costs had not gone away, they would just have to be shouldered by the next generation of the Navy's leadership, long after those around the Admiralty Board table had retired. Second, it was rather complacently stated that the US had a good record at keeping the costs of their missile projects under control, implying that the Trident missile procurement would be less likely to suffer from any subsequent uplifts. It was acknowledged that foreign exchange movements might cause problems, as the Trident purchase was being paid in dollars, but no indication of any mitigation in terms of a cash buffer or hedging was mentioned.[36] In the event, as will be seen below, the Navy was extremely lucky, as the exchange rate shifted strongly in favour of the pound in the late 1980s.

Finally, and most significantly for the short-term, the Naval Staff had not taken into account one of the standard tactics of the Treasury when budget increases had been guaranteed, and which had been used repeatedly against Francis Pym and John Nott. The 3 per cent annual increase in the defence budget had been guaranteed until 1985–6, and not unsurprisingly, the Ministry of Defence had calculated the impact of these rises based on a 3 per cent rise on top of another 3 per cent rise and so on, taking into account expected inflation. The Ministry also reached back to John Nott's 'The Way Forward' command paper from 1981 which stated that the 3 per cent rise would result in a total 21 per cent rise by 1985–6, and was hewing to this formulation to support continued increases.[37] The Treasury, in its negotiations with the Ministry for the 1983–4 Estimates instead insisted that that year's 3 per cent rise should be calculated from the amount actually spent in the previous year, rather than the budgeted sum. In 1982–3 the Ministry had underspent by £400 million, so as a result, the 3 per cent rise was calculated from a lower figure than had earlier been assumed.[38] A significant portion of this underspend would have been the result of what were euphemistically called 'realism adjustments': underspends resulting from the late delivery of contracted goods or equipment. What was most damaging about the Treasury's approach was that these late goods had not disappeared, they would just be spent in future years' budgets instead. By re-basing to the underspend, the Treasury was therefore guaranteeing that the Ministry would not only have to find space in its budget for the new late deliveries, but it would have to do so with a smaller than planned amount of money. This in turn would be likely to result in the rephasing of existing projects thus creating more late deliveries, and if these occurred at relatively short-notice or there were problems shifting to the new delivery dates, then more underspends would accrue. As these issues mounted up over a number of years, the reality was that the 3 per cent increase would be gradually taken up more with delayed items than with real capability improvements. A cynic might be forgiven for thinking that the Treasury had been using the rebasing of budget increases in order to undermine the purpose of the budget increase in the first place, although the Treasury might respond that if the Ministry was better able to deliver on time, it would not suffer these problems. An outside observer might equally wonder why the Ministry of Defence did not take account of this likely Treasury approach, given that it had been used only a few years before.

Another significant factor that marked battles between the Treasury and the Ministry of Defence was the issue of 'defence inflation', which was generally higher than general inflation. Defence inflation was calculated by analysing what the Ministry purchased and assessing how much it increased in price year on year. Given that the Ministry was a heavy consumer of expensive and bespoke equipment, whose prices were likely to increase above the general inflation rate, and a low consumer of commodified goods whose prices were likely increase below the general inflation rate or fall, this is perhaps not surprising. However, this meant that all things being equal, its costs would rise above general inflation every year. The Treasury saw 'defence inflation' as nothing more than a sign of Defence incompetence and profligacy, whilst for the Ministry it was an inevitable fact of defence spending. In late 1982 defence inflation was running at 2.8 per cent on top of general inflation, and was therefore swallowing up nearly all of the annual 3 per cent increase.[39] It is unlikely that defence inflation would have run much lower than this in succeeding years, so when this was combined with the Treasury's standard approach of rebasing to the underspend each year causing the build-up of realism adjustments, it is possible to see how the three services would look at constrained budgets that were failing to deliver promised programmes, whilst those outside the Ministry would have just seen ever rising spending.

Whatever the merits or demerits of Treasury re-basing and the impact of defence inflation, the result was that £116 million had been removed from the Navy's budget in 1984–5. A significant sum remained in later years, enough to ensure that the destroyer and frigate force remained at fifty active ships and that the personnel rundown was slowed, but the additional offshore patrol vessels could not be procured and a two-ship per-year programme for the Single Role Minehunter could not be sustained. Capability improvements to the Type 42 destroyers had to be delayed and not all of the aircraft orders could be placed, including the additional commando-carrying Sea Kings to ensure a two company lift.[40]

In the years that followed, the situation became increasingly tighter as resources were pushed into retaining the fifty-escort force, which generally meant keeping older ships with larger crews in service for longer, whilst investments were neglected, not least in ordering new ships that would have lower crewing requirements and need much less spending on them for upkeep. After the 3 per cent real rises ended after 1985–6 this issue became particularly acute as the budget usually did no more than rise with inflation.[41] Given the pressures of defence inflation this would have felt, to those inside the Ministry including the Navy Department, like real terms cuts each year. The only consolation for the Navy was that its predicament in the earlier years was not as bad as the other two services, as it still benefitted from the Trident budget reduction from the first months of 1983.[42] Each year, the Navy Department was asked to place a number of potential projects in a category known as the 'regulator' from which a small number would be chosen to place in each year's Long Term Costings. Year after year, a number of projects were placed in the regulator, including replacement assault ships, Sea Wolf for Type 42 destroyers, and additional stores, spares and weapons, but which were never chosen for investment, often because the amounts were so large – over £600 million for replacement assault ships – that they could not be fitted into the spare space within the Ministry's budget.

The 1985 Long Term Costings resulted in some painful delays to projects, including deferring the orders of the second, third and fourth Type 23 frigates, deferring the third and fourth Trident boats by nine and eighteen months respectively, deferring the Spearfish programme, delaying the SSK programme by six-months, a reduction in fleet activity levels by 5 per cent in 1986–7 and 1987–8 and the early withdrawal from service of the minelayer HMS *Abdiel* without replacement. The deferments and delays were particularly concerning: not only would older vessels have to continue in service for longer (costing more to maintain), but the stretching of production lines further into the future would increase the total value of the procurement overall, even if it saved money in the short-term. The delays to the Trident boats were especially concerning as they also meant that the new SSN class that would start construction after the Trident boats had completed would also be put back by 18 months.[43] Overall, a total of £1.03 billion had been removed from the ten year Naval budget as part of the Long Term Costings exercise so that it could fit within both targets and more stringent budget levels resulting from the end of the 3 per cent annual increase.[44] This also had the effect of squeezing out some procurements that had been considered important only twelve months before, such as the Enhanced Offshore Patrol Vessel (or OPV 3, which is described below), now that the programme's core of nuclear submarines and frigates were being delayed. Replacements for the Ice Patrol Ship *Endurance*, the Royal Yacht and amphibious shipping also appeared to slip even further away from obtaining funding.[45]

By 1986, the year in which the 3 per cent increases formally ended, the frustrations within the newly reduced Naval Staff were mounting. Yet another year of delays to Type 42 improvements, the continued inability to procure enough aircraft to cover losses through attrition, in addition to a range of improvements to ships that had been recommended as part of the post-Falklands lesson learnt process, caused one senior staff officer to lament that 'it will be some nine years from the end of the [Falklands] campaign before the bulk of the action [to implement lessons-learnt from the conflict] is complete, an intolerably lengthy period in which to rectify important lessons arising from our only modern experience of war'.[46] The next year the position had not improved: plans to add lightweight Sea Wolf air defence missile systems to the aircraft carriers and the Batch 3 Type 42 destroyers had been delayed, development of the Spearfish heavyweight torpedo had also been put back alongside reductions in weapons stocks and fuel reserves. The fitting of the Vulcan Phalanx close-in weapon system on HMS *Bristol* was cancelled, making it difficult to deploy the ship on front-line duties any longer.[47] By July of the same year she had been relegated to training duties as the Dartmouth Training Ship for officer cadets.[48]

At the same time the order rate for new ships had been nowhere near that envisaged in the Assumptions that accompanied the planning for the Long Term Costings. With the first Type 23 ordered in 1984, it had been assumed that three more ships would be ordered the following year, with three more the year after, until a class of at least eighteen and potentially twenty-four (if they replaced the Type 21 frigates as well) had been ordered. In reality, the order rate was half that required to keep the destroyer and frigate force at fifty. Three more ships were ordered in 1986, then there was another hiatus before a further three were ordered in 1988. Three more were approved the following year, but with the end of the Cold War a larger gap was permitted, until another three were ordered in 1992.[49] As early as 1986 it was becoming clear that it would be impossible to keep to the fifty figure for much longer. Of the eighteen remaining *Leander* class frigates, all but six would be more than 20 years old by 1990, and four of the newest ships in the class had been unmodernised since completion and were therefore obsolete, being no more than heavily crewed gunboats. By 1994 only ten Type 23 frigates would have been completed, but by then almost all the *Leander* class would be out of service. Many had been heavily used during the 1980s, not least the towed-array-equipped ships, and all were steam-propulsion ships in a Navy that was shifting rapidly to gas turbines. A force of forty destroyers and frigates was probably the most realistic option after the early 1990s. The submarine building programme did keep to its planned rates in the 1980s, ensuring that by 1991 there would be eighteen attack boats and four ballistic missile boats in service. Given the overriding priority of the Trident boats, and the commitment to squeeze three *Trafalgar* class boats into the programme before the Trident boats began construction, there was much less room for delays or cancellations, so at least the submarine arm – still the Navy's leading offensive capability – was being re-equipped. However, problems were being built up for the 1990s: the five oldest attack boats would be more than 20 years old by the end of 1991. In comparison the procurement of the *Upholder* class conventional boats suffered, with the first boat ordered in November 1983 but not entering service until seven years later and only three more being ordered by the end of the Cold War.[50]

After the inevitable round of short-term and long-term savings for the 1988–9 Estimates and 1988 Long Term Costings, for the first time in many years, the First Sea Lord could not state with confidence that the Navy could carry out all of its commitments over the coming year.[51] 1989 was somewhat better, with some additional funding following a relatively favourable Public Expenditure Survey settlement for the Ministry of Defence, but painful adjustments had to be made as it proved difficult to fit programmed equipment projects into the funding available. The third, fourth and fifth *Fort Victoria* class Royal Fleet Auxiliaries were delayed, as was the order date of the first replacement assault ship.[52] The situation was similarly difficult at the start of 1990: orders for single-role mine hunters were deferred, as were those for follow-up *Fort Victoria* class ships (again), whilst the orders of the remaining SSKs were also delayed with the last boat being cancelled, resulting in a class of only nine rather than ten boats. Type 23 deferrals did nothing to deal with the problems keeping the destroyer and frigate levels up, which had declined to forty-seven by April 1990.[53] The replacement assault ship, having come painfully close to being approved in 1988, was now cancelled, so staff discussions had to start afresh to justify the capability, despite agreement as early as 1983 that such vessels were needed.[54] Through the last years of the Cold War it was becoming clear that unless major reductions were made in either commitments or procurement projects, or both, then it would be impossible to put together credible ten-year budget plans for the Long Term Costings. A new defence review at some point in the late 1980s or early 1990s would therefore be inevitable, Cold War or no Cold War, in order to rebalance the budget and the programmes.[55]

Procurement

Submarines

The most important procurement programme across the whole of Defence from the mid-1980s onwards was the building of the new *Vanguard* class ballistic missile nuclear submarine, and the construction of the missiles and warheads to go with them. The decision to refurbish the Trident missiles in the United States had saved an estimated £500 million from the costs of the procurement.[56] When this was combined with extremely favourable foreign exchange movements between 1985 and 1990 (with the rate shifting from just above £1 to $1 in March 1985 to just below £1 to $2 in November 1990),[57] the whole Trident missile and *Vanguard* class submarine procurement became a highly unusual event in British modern defence history: a major project that was delivered within its original budget, even if the date of delivery for the four boats was somewhat later than originally planned. By the end of the Cold War, three boats had been ordered with the order for the fourth boat placed in July 1992.[58] The four submarines entered service between August 1993 and November 1999. The last boat, *Vengeance*, would be launched in September 1998, finally freeing up the submarine building slip at Barrow for the next generation of attack boats.[59] By this time all of the *Valiant* class and all but two of the *Swiftsure* class would be more than 20 years old, if they survived in service that long.

In 1983, HMS *Trafalgar*, the first boat in the new class of SSNs succeeding the *Swiftsure*s, entered service. In many respects the *Trafalgar* class was a linear development of its predecessor with a similar maximum underwater speed of 29 knots and the same number of torpedo tubes. However, there were significant improvements: a new active/passive bow sonar, the Type 2020, that replaced the now aged Type 2001. The Type 2026 towed-array sonar replaced the Type 2024, in addition to the next generation of flank-array sonars and intercept sonars. Later boats in the class had a new reactor core which was quieter than its predecessor. This new technology resulted in a somewhat heavier boat, but exceptionally effective design work meant that the *Trafalgar* class had the same length and diameter as the *Swiftsure* class. It was in quieting that the new classes impressed the most: hull form and shape, surface coatings, internal machinery all served to reduce the noise created by the submarine; this quietness could be maintained even at high speed. From the second boat onwards, they were fitted with a 'Pre-Swirl Pump Jet' or propulsor which not only reduced cavitation (and therefore noise) but also made the replacement of propellor blades more straightforward.[60]

Reflecting the increasing importance of High North operations during the 1980s, all the *Trafalgar* class were fitted with retractable hydroplanes and strengthened fins to enable ice operations. Anthony Wells, a former Royal Navy officer who, unusually, served as an intelligence analyst for both the Royal Navy and the US Navy, regards the pump jet as a technological breakthrough of similar importance to the angled flight deck on aircraft carriers, helping to create 'an extraordinarily capable submarine' that he regards as influencing the shift of the US Navy away from ever larger nuclear attack submarines such as the USS *Seawolf* towards the smaller but still capable boats of the *Virginia* class in the 1990s.[61] During the 1981 Defence Review it had been expected that there would be six boats in the class, but the decision to delay the Trident boats created the space for a seventh boat to be ordered and therefore bringing the whole fleet of nuclear-powered attack boats up to eighteen. The Ministry played a hard game with Vickers over contract negotiations for this last boat, suspending talks until the shipbuilder offered a £25 million discount on their original price.[62] All seven boats were commissioned between 1983 and 1991, and should be seen as the apogee of the Royal Navy's Cold War nuclear submarine programme, building on the experience gained from the *Valiant*, *Resolution* and *Swiftsure* classes.

For the submarine service, and for the Royal Navy, the *Vanguard* and *Trafalgar* classes were undoubtedly the highest priorities in construction. As the naval procurement budget came under increasing pressure during the 1980s, it was the *Upholder* class diesel-electric submarine of the three that suffered the most. In 1982 it was thought that the class might have to be curtailed at only four boats, but the rephasing of the new Trident boats freed up substantial amounts of funding in the short and medium-term, ensuring the full programme of ten boats returned to the programme for the rest of the 1980s.[63] Despite this, only the first of the class, HMS *Upholder*, had been ordered by 1983. Construction at Vickers proceeded slowly, unsurprising given the work being done concurrently on the *Trafalgar* and *Vanguard* classes. The next three boats were ordered as late as January 1986, being built at Cammell Laird, which four months later had become a subsidiary of Vickers. Delays in the later stages of construction meant that *Upholder* was commissioned in

1990, with her three sisters following between 1991 and 1993. As the Cold War ended, only four boats had been ordered and the remainder of the class was subsequently cancelled.[64]

Aircraft Carriers and Fixed-Wing Aircraft
The third and last *Invincible* class carrier, HMS *Ark Royal*, entered service in 1985. She included some incremental improvements on her sister ships. She had a ski-jump increased to an angle of 12 degrees, and was fitted with three rather than two Phalanx close-in weapon systems.[65] Once *Ark Royal* had entered service, under the policy of having only two carriers active, HMS *Invincible* soon went into refit. She would re-enter service in 1988 and HMS *Illustrious* then followed into preservation and then refit.[66]

The Falklands had revitalised the Sea Harrier. Prior to the conflict, the chances of further updates and improvements had been negligible, but its strong performance had assured its future. In 1980, one Sea Harrier had been modified as a testbed for the Sea Eagle air-to-sea anti-ship missile, but the possible fitting of the missile had been rejected during the 1981 Defence Review.[67] The test aircraft had been lost during the fighting, but the inability of the Task Force to strike Argentine naval units with anything other than unguided bombs, resulted in the decision to reconsider the Sea Eagle. The surviving Sea Harriers were supplemented by an order of nine aircraft to replace losses in the conflict, whilst in the year immediately afterwards all the front-line aircraft were made Sea Eagle capable. The surface fleet now had a modern stand-off anti-ship weapon which, with the Sea Harrier as launch aircraft, had a range that went beyond the horizon, something that had been lacking since the demise of the last fixed-wing carrier in 1978. Development then began on an updating the Sea Harrier. Approval was given for the development of the modified FRS 2 variant as a 'mid-life update', which was later renamed F/A 2.[68] The first test aircraft of this type flew in 1988, and in March 1990, an order was placed for eighteen new F/A 2s, whilst thirty-two FRS 1s were converted to F/A 2 standards. The conversions were completed from 1993 onwards, whilst the new-builds entered naval service between 1995 and 1999.[69] The F/A 2 would be armed with the AMRAAM air-to-air missile in addition to the Sidewinder, the Blue Vixen radar which overcame many of the deficiencies of the earlier Blue Fox outlined in the Falklands lessons-learnt process, and an improved Pegasus jet engine.[70]

The F/A 2 was a much-improved aircraft, but it still suffered from some of the limitations of the original FRS 1. The Blue Vixen radar and the longer range AMRAAM made it more likely that Soviet aircraft would be detected earlier and intercepted at greater range – ideally before they launched their anti-ship missiles – but the F/A 2's limited range and speed gave it little margin for error and favoured head-on engagements. The original role of the Harrier in attacking shadowing and guidance aircraft for missile-armed strike aircraft diminished in importance as it became clear that 'Backfires' were gaining their targeting information from Soviet EORSAT and RORSAT satellites rather than aircraft.[71] The anti-guidance aircraft role was still relevant as there were earlier generations of maritime strike aircraft still in the Soviet inventory in the 1980s, but it was likely that these would be withdrawn during the following decade. The F/A 2 would still be an extremely valuable aircraft but there would still be some reliance on either US carrier battle group air cover or on the RAF's air defence capabilities.

In order to enable more effective tactical co-ordination with the US Navy's aircraft and warships, the Royal Navy began to develop a version of the US Joint Tactical Information Distribution System ('JTIDS'), costing a total of £250 million and enabling the use of the NATO standard Link 16 communication network, the next generation system succeeding the Link 11. JTIDS would allow communication and the transfer of data amongst ground stations, warships, strike and air defence aircraft, as well as airborne early warning and electronic warfare aircraft. The RAF had embarked on its own plans to integrate with the US Air Force's version of JTIDS in order to enhance UK air defence. Its version would cost £500 million, but initially the naval systems would not have been able to communicate with the air force systems and vice versa, an incredible demonstration of the inability of either service in either country to operate jointly. A dual-mode system would need to be developed and it was not entirely clear that either the Navy or RAF would prioritise the money to do this. Ironically, the cross-service interoperability issue was only resolved when the US Navy and US Air Force agreed to integrate their systems as the former adopted the latter's version. JTIDS was delayed during the late 1980s and was expected to be introduced into service in the early 1990s.[72]

If US carrier air cover were not available, then the RAF's national air defence capabilities should have been able to fill the gap and supplement the Sea Harrier. Unfortunately, there were significant limitations to these capabilities from the perspective of the Royal Navy, despite the replacement of the Lightning and Phantom with the more capable Tornado ADV during the mid-1980s. The Tornado ADV was much criticised as a large and cumbersome aircraft that would be much less manoeuvrable than fighters and multi-role aircraft such as the F-15 or F/A-18, but from the perspective of maritime operations, its long-range air defence role – using long-range air-to-air missiles to destroy bombers before they launched their stand-off missiles – was just what was needed to deal with the 'Backfire'.[73] It was a role analogous to that of the US Navy's F-14 Tomcat carrier aircraft. However, there were considerable problems with this capability, notwithstanding the usual naval concerns about the lack of short-notice readiness and availability when other non-maritime air defence tasks might be prioritised. The Tornados needed long-range radar in order to guide them towards their targets. The RAF's national air defence Linesman system, which had gone live in 1973, had largely been designed before the responsibility for maritime air defence had been given to the RAF.[74] The system provided radar coverage over nearly all of the United Kingdom's Air Defence Area (of which the Danish Faeroes were a part), which went as far as approximately 65 degrees latitude north, but did not reach Iceland to the north-west. However, coverage at this range only included aircraft or missiles travelling at 30,000ft or above, due to the curvature of the earth and the distance from radar stations in the Shetlands, Faeroes and Outer Hebrides.[75]

The gaps in coverage under 30,000ft and beyond the UK Air Defence Area should have been covered by the RAF Airborne Early Warning aircraft force. The replacement for very aged Shackleton aircraft in this role was to have been the Nimrod AEW Mark 3, but even though the aircraft had been delivered, there were problems with the avionics. The Ministry of Defence placed the onus on the contractor, GEC, to deliver the capabilities agreed and further funding was blocked in 1985. After over £850 million had been spent on the project, the new Secretary of State, George Younger, decided to cancel it. It was thought that the Nimrod Mk 3 would never achieve its operational requirements, even if considerable additional investments were made. The US AWACS E3 Sentry (an aircraft less optimised for maritime AEW than the Nimrod Mk 3) would be purchased in its place, but would not enter service until the early 1990s, so in the meantime the Shackleton would have to continue in its role.[76] The Shackleton had a limited range, decreasing reliability and availability, and was operating obsolescent search radars that had been taken from decommissioned Royal Navy Gannets in the late 1960s and early 1970s. The coverage that they could provide was therefore thoroughly inadequate, and the inadequacy of the Shackleton was emphasised by the tragic loss of one aircraft and its crew in 1990.[77] As a result of this deficient air defence capability, it is likely that Royal Navy forces would probably have had to remain south and west of the Faeroes during a period of conflict and perhaps high tension prior to the introduction of the F/A 2, until the US carrier strike fleet had arrived and could provide air cover.

In the RAF's other maritime roles, the story was less dispiriting. Although the allocation of Tornados to the maritime strike role had been deprioritised, the aircraft not becoming available until the 1990s, the Buccaneer remained in service and was updated to operate the Sea Eagle anti-ship missile. The Buccaneer also had the advantage of a greater operational range with a similar payload than the Tornado, so its retention in service had at least a short- and medium-term benefit.[78] The RAF's Nimrod MR2 maritime patrol aircraft also entered full service during the early and mid-1980s. It was a significant improvement over the MR1 and, when they were within range and were available, provided valuable support to submarines and towed-array frigates in their tracking of Soviet submarines into the Atlantic. One of the results of the Falklands campaign was the decision to increase the number of air-to-air refuelling aircraft, a crucial capability for all of the RAF's maritime capabilities, which increased range and time on station for patrol, strike, warning and air defence aircraft. The slippage in the project to replace the aged Victor tankers with converted TriStars and VC10s during the 1980s was such that the whole force would not enter service until the late 1990s. As with elements of the Navy's programme during the 1980s, the RAF had decided to de-prioritise the tankers in order to focus on those areas deemed to be at the core of the procurement programme, such as the Tornado. In addition, problems had been encountered with the TriStar conversion which further slowed the project.[79] The RAF's maritime contribution during the 1980s was therefore a mix of increased capabilities and effectiveness with respect to the Nimrod MR2 and improvements to the Buccaneer, but significant and important shortfalls in air defence and airborne early warning that had a material impact on the ability of the Royal Navy to operate in the Eastern Atlantic. It therefore made the Navy more dependent on US carrier airpower for the defence of surface ships against Soviet air attack, although the situation would have improved following the introduction of the F/A 2 Harrier in the early 1990s.

Helicopters and RFA Argus
During the 1980s both of the Navy's front-line helicopter types, the Lynx and the Sea King, received significant upgrades in capability. The Lynx HAS 3 entered service with ships' flights from November 1982 onwards.[80] It included an improved engine, gearbox and rotors and standardised the fitting of the Sea Skua anti-ship missile and the Orange Crop passive intercept. Towards the end of the 1980s, incremental improvements included a digital centralised tactical system and the Lamberton secure radio system.[81] The Sea King HAS 6 entered service in 1988 and incorporated a range of improvements that made the aircraft a much more effective anti-submarine platform. This included the new Type 2069 dipping sonar, and a digital avionics processor that was able to combine sonobuoy, dipping sonar and radar data into an integrated tactical picture. Lamberton was also installed. By the end of 1991 three of the five front-line ASW Sea King squadrons had been updated to HAS 6 standards, with the other two in the process of moving over. Five new airframes were built as HAS 6s, with the rest being converted from HAS 5 aircraft.[82]

Meanwhile, the Sea King successor, the EH101 (later named Merlin), was suffering from prolonged difficulties at the development stage. It had been approved by the Operational Requirements Committee in the Centre in May 1982 as conflict raged in the South Atlantic. In 1983 the planned order had been reduced from seventy-four to fifty to reduce the costs of the project down from £2.2 billion to £1.5 billion (in 1985 prices), and the development contract was placed with Westland Helicopters in March 1984. Due to differences in requirements and standards between the two joint partners in the project, Britain's Westland and Italy's Agusta, no clear specifications had been developed until as late as 1988. No prime contractor had been given full responsibility for integrating all the elements of the EH101 into a single system, and the EHI holding company nominally developing the project was not initially strong enough to fulfil this function: its chair and vice chair changed every year and alternated from Westland to Agusta and back again, whilst the small staff of the company were only seconded for relatively short periods from their parent groups. The financial fragility of Westlands added a further level of uncertainty to the project. In April 1987 it was announced that an additional twenty-five Merlins would be procured, but these would be of a utility variant for the RAF, rather than additional airframes for the Navy. Given that theoretically a total of twenty-four might be needed for Type 23 ships' flights, plus at least another three or more squadrons for carrier antisubmarine work, it was unlikely that the fifty aircraft would be sufficient for the Royal Navy's requirements, *if* the fleet remained the same size.[83]

Whilst the Navy's existing helicopter fleet was receiving updates, and a future medium helicopter was at least in development, a significant questionmark was faced with the future of naval helicopter training. The existing helicopter training ship, RFA *Engadine*, was nearing the end of her operational life. She provided vital experience in operating aircraft at sea for helicopter pilots, without such training clogging up the decks of aircraft carriers. From 1982 onwards, the conversion of a merchant ship, along the lines of RFA *Reliant*, to undertake this training role was mooted, with *Contender Bezant*, a STUFT roll-on roll-off cargo ship used in the Falklands, being a prime contender for conversion. Approval was gained in 1984, and the ship was converted at Harland and Wolff shipyard, completing in 1988. During this conversion the vessel was transformed, with additional superstructure added abaft the existing bridge structure, and a large flight deck extending from this forward superstructure right aft and taking up three quarters of the ship's length. A small island structure was created, an aircraft lift added, and the ship given limited replenishment at sea capabilities. The Royal Navy had gained a significant capability, much in excess of either *Engadine* or *Reliant*, that could be used in a range of roles, including as a hospital ship or even a support helicopter carrier. Such a flexible, capable but expensive ship (costing £18 million to buy and £45 million to convert[84]) was very much a product of the 3 per cent increase years and attempts to undertake a similar conversion to procure a utility aviation support ship that could be used in amphibious helicopter operations proved fruitless in the constrained environment of 1985 onwards.[85]

The Amphibious Capability
Although the Royal Marines largely retained their size, structure and role during the 1980s, the Royal Navy's amphibious capability would be the Cinderella of naval procurement in this decade: never achieving much renewal despite its essential role in the re-taking of the Falklands in 1982, and always overlooked in favour of submarine, aircraft and frigate procurement. The rebuilding of the heavily damaged *Sir Tristram* began in 1984, a 120-ton hull plug was inserted amidships in order to increase her load capacity, aluminium was removed where possible, a new bridge structure constructed, and her flight deck amidships being made large enough for Chinook helicopters to use. The work completed in 1986, whilst a new-build replacement for *Sir Galahad* of the same name began construction that year. She was of a modified version of the original 'Knights of the Round Table' class: longer and larger than her predecessor, with a 'bow visor' door and an aircraft lift on her amidships flight deck to allow helicopters to be stowed below on her vehicle deck. Whilst the two ships were in the hands of shipbuilders, two roll-on roll-off ships were chartered commercially and renamed *Sir Lamarock* and *Sir Caradoc*.[86] Once *Sir Tristram* and *Sir Galahad* had entered service there was, however, very little in the way of major capability enhancement for the amphibious force during the rest of the 1980s.

Investigations into replacements for the bulk of the existing amphibious force started in 1983, once it was clear that not only would the two assault ships and the LSLs remain service, but that the amphibious capability would be required over the long-term.[87] A visit to the United States to investigate their plans for amphibious shipping, showed that a revolution in amphibious warfare was in progress. The United States Navy and Marine Corps had developed an operational concept that assumed that its amphibious vessels would remain 'over the horizon' from the landing zone, rather than the two to four miles that had been the previous standard distance. This meant that vertical envelopment with helicopters became more important, and that the transport of second wave troops, equipment and stores would have been undertaken from a much greater distance and much more quickly than hitherto been assumed. The US answer was the use of hovercraft in the landing role to provide the speed needed to move from just over the horizon to the shore. There were drawbacks: each amphibious hovercraft was expensive, noisy and large, taking up much space in an assault ship's dock. For the United States this was a feasible option to pursue, given the large and growing size of their defence budget, but it made any viable replacement capability for the Royal Navy potentially a much more expensive operation. The building, under license, of an American design for an assault ship was considered as an option, although the cost would have been £300 million per unit, not too different from the cost of designing and developing ships domestically.[88]

Following the US visit, a series of options for replacing the assault ships and LSLs were set out. The NATO requirement for the UK's amphibious contribution was for the availability and use of 6,400 troops, 1,860 vehicles and equipment, 24 medium commando helicopters and 18 light helicopters, 4,500 tons of war maintenance reserves and 4,700 tons of stores. Five options were set out, all of which enabled the use of a total of twelve LCU utility landing craft. The first was a like-for-like replacement of the existing force, costing £650 million. The second was a similar new fleet but built to minimum commercial standards costing £430 million, whilst the third was a comprehensive life-extension programme for the existing ships. This was the cheapest option at £390 million, but would mean that money would have to spent on replacements between a decade and two decades later, whilst new ships would have lasted for longer. Two other possibilities were considered: two amphibious command ships (which could have a secondary role in the frigate force) would support four utility amphibious vessels with LCUs in small docks or on deck, in a possibility which split the command and control role of the existing assault ships from their amphibious capability. This would have cost £570 million. Another option was to build six 'standard ships' on commercial lines, with command and control capabilities, probably in removable containers, available for two of the ships. This would have also cost £570 million.[89]

By June 1984 a 'Way Ahead' Committee recommended its first preference for a like-for-like replacement of the old for new vessels but was willing to consider containerised command and control; their second choice would be for six 'standard ships'. An interim option involving the use of the one carrier, a new Aviation Support Ship and various ships taken up from trade was also considered feasible, but only as a stopgap. However, the rapid running down of the United Kingdom's merchant shipping fleet did call into question how much longer such ships would be available to supplement warships.[90] The report was developed in parallel with a study by the Centre on 'specialist reinforcement forces', which included both the Army's 5th Airborne Brigade and the Royal Marines, in late 1984, as well as the development of an amphibious concept of operations.[91]

There had been some expectation of orders for replacement amphibious shipping in 1984 or 1985, given that the oldest LSL, *Sir Lancelot,* was due to retire in 1988, but this was not forthcoming. There were reassurances that the amphibious capability was still a priority, but the situation did not improve when it was confirmed that the 3 per cent increases in defence spending would not continue past 1985–6, and budget expectations became much less optimistic. The sale of HMS *Hermes* brought some welcome funds to the Navy, but it removed the last warship capable of undertaking amphibious helicopter assault, albeit one in deep reserve that would have required many months to reactivate.[92] For a number of years, the amphibious replacement programme, which was costed at approximately £600 million, sat in the Long Term Costings as a high priority programme, but it was unfunded, and generally placed as a 'category II' requirement behind the first priority submarine and frigate programmes.

The possibility of procuring Aviation Support Ships had been announced in Parliament in December 1986, but although tenders were invited from yards in 1989, no orders were placed.[93] It had been hoped to procure the first of two Aviation Support Ships at £105 million each, but this was a wildly optimistic costing. Only two yards responded to the tenders and neither was willing to build the ships at such a price.[94] £140 million was considered the minimum to build the vessel as it was conceived in the late 1980s.[95] Feasibility studies were requested for replacing the two assault ships in 1987, but no contracts for further work were forthcoming.[96] From the end of 1986 it had finally seemed that the replacement programme would get underway, but by January 1990 these hopes had been dashed.[97] The assault ship project was redefined again, this time separating out the cost of the command system from the ship itself.[98] Everything was therefore thrown back in the air again. As the delays built up, the least favoured option of a life extension to the existing amphibious shipping became the most likely possibility to prevent a gap in capability. There was a high chance that such a programme would not be value for money as it was only marginally cheaper than the least expensive new build option and it provided capability for a much shorter period of time. However, it was still cheaper over the ten-year Long Term Costings period, however poor a use of taxpayers' money. An initial investigation into the life extension of *Sir Lancelot* had also been commissioned in 1987.[99] In the event, that ship was sold commercially, but life extension for the LSLs remained the default policy and one was eventually carried out on RFA *Sir Bedivere* between 1994 and 1998. As could have been predicted, it proved so expensive to undertake on a ship that was already 30 years old, it was finally agreed that constructing new builds would be better value for money, and these were eventually procured in the 2000s, 20 years after the first studies had been commissioned.[100] Rather more happily, the changed strategic environment after the end of the Cold War made amphibious shipping a higher priority and one aviation support ship, HMS *Ocean*, and two assault ships, *Albion* and *Bulwark*, were completed in 1998, 2003 and 2004 respectively.[101]

Air Defence Ships

The Falklands conflict had shown the utility of area air defence ships, and the performance of Sea Dart – imperfect but capable in some circumstances – had been sufficient to ensure that a refit programme was quickly approved for the four surviving ships of the first batch to bring them up to the standard of the second batch with their more effective air-search radar. The class was also, over time, fitted with Vulcan Phalanx close-in weapon systems as a last-ditch defence and an acknowledgement of the limitations of Sea Dart. Plans were developed for the addition of two lightweight Sea Wolf launchers amidships on Batch 3 ships, where Phalanx systems had previously been placed, which necessitated removing one Phalanx and placing the other forward between the medium gun and the Sea Dart launcher. These improvements were repeatedly delayed – in a constrained budget they had never been a top priority – until finally approval was given in 1988. HMS *Edinburgh* was refitted 'for but not with' the new lightweight Sea Wolf systems, having the Phalanx system moved forward, and gunwales added to her forecastle to reduce spray onto the Phalanx. By the time the refit had completed, the Sea Wolf enhancement project had been cancelled as part of the 1990–1 'Options for Change' Defence Review, so no other vessels were modified in this way. The Type 42s would receive enhancements to their sensors, systems and to Sea Dart in the post-Cold War period, but they would never receive Sea Wolf.[102]

The NATO Frigate Replacement Programme for the 1990s, generally known as NFR90, was an attempt to create a cross-NATO approach to surface-escort construction. Eight NATO states signed up to the project, with the United Kingdom announcing its involvement in 1985. From the perspective of the Royal Navy, the NFR90 would replace the Type 42 destroyers, and most importantly confirm the continuation of air defence ships within the Navy, even if they would probably be classed frigates rather than destroyers. NFR90 aimed to support the development of a more integrated NATO defence industry and the harmonisation of operational requirements; at about the same time development began on a European Fighter Aircraft for the 1990s, which would eventually develop into the Eurofighter 'Typhoon'.[103] Given the divergences amongst the different partners, in retrospect it is not surprising that the NFR90 project fell apart in 1990. The project was theoretically controlled by a multi-national project management office made of seventy staff representing each of the eight partners, but it was never able to reconcile different requirements. As a result, one of the key documents it was meant to produce, the project definition, was too vague to provide a template from which the defence industry could work. Another weakness was that the development of the ship's air defence system (the Future Air Defence Missile System, 'FAMS') was undertaken in an entirely different structure with no common authority between the two, which meant co-ordinating the impact of changes from one to the other was hugely problematic. In addition, an unrealistic cost target was set, in a quasi-currency that was difficult to understand (the ECU), and when combined with equivocation from partner states as to whether they would actually sign up to the frigate, estimated costs rose and little settled understanding of the cost-capability trade-offs were developed.[104] Such was the Navy's disillusionment with the project, that it began in 1987 quietly to investigate the possibility of building an additional batch of Type 23 frigates, optimised for area air defence, in place of the NFR90.[105]

Underneath the NFR90 project management office was a defence industry consortium which was tasked with developing the design. Based in Hamburg, the consortium had eight shareholders, six of which were themselves consortia of each country's major shipbuilding and naval weapons manufacturers. This resulted in an extremely diffuse structure with sixty-seven ultimate shareholders, in which almost all companies involved only had a very small stake in the project, thus making them even less likely to commit resources and time to developing the design.[106] The British backed out first, in October 1989, creating, in the words of the Royal Navy Rear Admiral with responsibility for supervising the British side of the project, a 'sense of betrayal' amongst the other partners. The British would probably have procured the largest number of ships and their absence reduced NFR90's financial viability. This withdrawal had been partly pushed on the Ministry of Defence by the Treasury, which had been especially worried about the lack of co-ordination between the NFR90 and FAMS project and design teams, the risk that the first ships might go to sea without a FAMS capability, and the additional costs that would entail from such a decision (for example, running on older ships and future retrofitting of FAMS in the first ships). There were also concerns about the structural strength of the design's hull and the ship's tactical command system. The French and Italians followed soon afterwards. The coup de grace was delivered by the West Germans, who backed out of the project in November 1989 following the fall of the Berlin Wall.[107]

With the four largest states having backed out, it was clear that there was no future for the project and within months the NFR90 consortium had dissolved. Feasibility studies then began for different options for ships to replace the Type 42s. The new ship was dubbed the 'Future Frigate' and options included vessels based on either Type 22 or Type 23 hulls, a single hull design that could accommodate either an air defence variant or an anti-submarine variant, as well as two separate air defence and anti-submarine designs, and finally another international collaborative project. The United Kingdom had not backed out of the FAMS project, so the new ship would be armed with this missile system.[108] After another two years of feasibility studies and concepts work it was eventually decided to group together with the French and the Italians to develop a joint air defence ship named the Common New Generation Frigate or 'Horizon', which would be based around the PAAMS (Principal Anti-Air Missile System), the new development name for FAMS.[109] The Ministry of Defence would ultimately back out of Horizon, and a purely national air defence destroyer, the Type 45, was eventually ordered with the first of class, HMS *Daring*, commissioning in 2009, 11 years after the planned acceptance date of the first British NFR90.

Battle-Loss Replacement Frigates
It had been quickly agreed that the four destroyer and frigate losses in the Falklands conflict should be replaced by Type 22 frigates.[110] The Type 42 was a design whose flaws were clear and had contributed to the loss of two ships, the Type 21 was no longer in production and was anyway too small to fit the modern Sea Wolf point defence missile system, whilst the new Type 23 frigate was still under development and the design would not be ready for ordering for another year or more. By contrast the Type 22 was in production, had been proven to be capable in the conflict and was a ship optimised for the Royal Navy's core role of anti-submarine warfare in the Eastern Atlantic. In order to replace the medium gun capability lost with the four sunk ships, it was proposed that a new batch of the Type 22 be developed that included a medium gun armament and incorporating some of the lessons of the conflict. Politically, it was important to confirm the construction of these ships quickly, so major design changes would not be possible. The new batch, Batch 3, would not have the Outboard surveillance and information-gathering system, which would free up considerable space for additional weapon systems. With a 4.5in medium gun forward (with a magazine for 500 rounds below the waterline), the anti-ship missiles would have to be moved, ideally to amidships behind the bridge where the Outboard offices had previously been located. The fitting of close-in weapon systems such as Phalanx was also considered a possibility. The Batch 2's CACS command system would be given minor updates, whilst the propulsion chosen was two SM1A Spey and two Tyne gas turbines. Four SM1A had been preferred but this would have required a major redesign of the machinery spaces and this would not be possible in the timescales envisaged for ordering the new ships. The total crew would be 21 officers and 273 ratings, which could increase by another 12 if Phalanx or a similar system were fitted. The post-Falklands internal changes to the design included reductions in aluminium use, additional fire pumps, improved firefighting and smoke

screening, the removal of dangerous linings, the repositioning of fuel tanks, the installation of an emergency diesel generator forward, improved firefighting in machinery spaces and clipped watertight doors. It was estimated that a single ship of this type would cost £134 million at 1981–2 prices, with an additional £14.7 million for the first ship of this batch. Another £4.8 million would be needed if a close-in weapon system was fitted.[111]

In an indication of where power lay within John Nott's Ministry of Defence, Sir Ronald Mason, the Chief Scientific Adviser and General Johnston, the Deputy Chief of the Defence Staff, both demanded to have a meeting with the Naval Staff to discuss the proposed replacement ships and their weapon systems. Ostensibly about why both Sea Wolf and a close-in weapon system would be necessary, in reality it was expected that the Chief Scientific Adviser would ask why the ships needed to be ordered at all, and whether a new satellite or enhanced electronic systems ashore or on existing ships might be more useful instead. As the ships would be approved at great speed, the usual Ministry central approval processes would not be used, so *if* the informal approval of Johnston could be gained, who chaired the important Operational Requirements and Defence Equipment Committees, it would be beneficial to smoothing the way to the ordering of the ships. The final meeting with the Secretary of State to approve the ships would occur in December 1982.[112] The meeting with Mason and Johnston seems to have taken place without any major problems. The Naval Staff had prepared for Mason's expected questions by arguing that any other options proposed could not involve the direct spending of the new Treasury money to fund battle-loss replacements, some additional money would have to found from later years' programmes. In addition, the government had committed to a fifty escort navy and these ships were needed to help fulfil this commitment.[113]

At that point, the ninth and tenth Type 22 frigates had not yet been formally approved. The Secretary of State had stated before the Falklands that he was planning to approve the ninth ship, whilst the tenth was expected to have been ordered under the 1983 estimates. As a result, it was planned that Nott would announce four ships if he approved the order: one Batch 2 ship which was an ordinary order as planned, one Batch 2 ship which would be a battle-loss replacement, and two Batch 3 ships which would also be battle-loss replacements. This would leave the fourth battle-loss replacement to be ordered at another time, alongside the ship that had been planned for the 1983 estimates all along. If this last ship were ordered at all, it would now be a Batch 3 vessel.[114]

The meeting with Nott was also successful. The First Sea Lord was accompanied by both VCNS and the Controller. Nott questioned why the first battle-loss replacement could not be a ship from the new gun-armed batch. Fieldhouse answered that a total of six Outboard ships were needed to ensure that two would be available to support each of the two anti-submarine groups declared to NATO, and that six Outboard systems had been purchased already. Nott then asked why four Type 22s were to be ordered? Why could the order not include three Type 22s and, say, three or four 'Castle' class offshore patrol vessels instead? VCNS answered that the 'Castle' class did not have the capability, nor the space to fit the capability, to fulfil the anti-submarine mission in the Eastern Atlantic. Nott then asked why additional conventional submarines could not be built instead in order to improve the Navy's shallow-water capability, and VCNS answered that this area was being covered by improved hull-mounted sonar and the new EH101 helicopter. After this interrogation, Nott finally agreed to the four ships and asked for further discussions about the ordering of the last battle-loss replacement.[115] The Prime Minister was informed and agreed the orders in December 1982.[116] The last battle-loss replacement and the 1983 Estimates ship were both approved some months later and were ordered in January 1985.[117]

Swan Hunter had provided the lowest tender for the ninth and tenth ship and therefore secured those orders. Yarrow as the lead yard for the class, and therefore best placed to deal with new equipment fits in the Batch 3, gained the first Batch 3 order. It also obtained the second Batch 3 order by arguing that a double order would save £3 million from the total price. The last two Batch 3 ships were given to Swan Hunter again, and to Cammell Laird.[118] The weapon fit for the Batch 3 ships was only finalised in early 1984, well after construction was underway. It had been initially been assumed that the surface to surface missile system would probably be the latest MM40 version of Exocet, which allowed for eight cannisters and right-angle firing as envisaged for the ships. In the event, the US Harpoon missile system was chosen. The Operational Requirements Committee had preferred the Vulcan Phalanx as the close-in weapon system for the ships, but the Naval Staff favoured the Dutch Goalkeeper which had better performance, and also because a Dutch purchase might encourage them to purchase British Rolls-Royce gas turbines for their new 'M' class frigates, and possibly even Sea Wolf. Goalkeeper was chosen.[119] The first Batch 3 ship was named HMS *Cornwall*. Her keel was laid the day that she was ordered and she was completed in April 1988. Her three sisters were all completed within three years. The ships were successful in service and often used as task group command ships during the 1990s and 2000s. The Navy had been particularly lucky that the only available and appropriate escort design also happened to be the largest and most expensive frigate it had ever operated. As a result it gained four extremely capable ships replacing four battle-losses, two of which had been relatively low-capability stopgap frigates of the Type 21 class (*Antelope* and *Ardent*).

The Type 23 Frigate

Following the end of the Falklands conflict, the new Type 23 design had gradually increased in size, cost and capability. The addition of a second Sea Wolf tracker radar, a second SM1A gas turbine and an additional three metres to the flight deck, so that the Sea King helicopter could land on it, had added another £5.9 million to the cost (in 1981 prices). These had been approved by the Secretary of State as the design was going through the Ministry's internal committee process whilst the fighting in the South Atlantic was still occurring. The need to accommodate the Sea King was down to the delays in the replacement EH101 which meant that the first Type 23 might enter service and have to operate the older, but slightly larger, Sea King instead. After the Falklands another £5 million (in 1982 prices) was added to the cost, when various ship and weapon improvements reflecting fighting experience were added, in addition to another 5m length.[120] Further improvements in the first months of 1983 increased the costs again: the ship's sonar would now be in the bow rather than under its keel, the number of torpedo tubes would be increased from two to four in order to improve self-defence against submarines, and the ship's surveillance radar would have a height-finding capability added, which would improve the performance of the Sea Wolf missile system. Following Falklands experience it was decided to add a medium gun, but initially it was not thought that there was space for a 4.5in gun, so the smaller OTO Melara 76mm was chosen instead.[121] A few months later, it was confirmed that the 4.5in could be adapted and made both smaller and lighter, so it was added to the design.[122] The ship would now cost £98 million in 1982 prices. General Johnston, the DCDS, still supported the Type 23 despite these price rises, as it was only two-thirds the price of the Batch 3 Type 22 and would still have a crew of only 145 compared to 282.[123] The modified ship was now sufficiently developed for an order to be placed, and the first ship, HMS *Norfolk*, was ordered from Yarrow Shipbuilders in October 1984, and completed in June 1990.

Outside lobbying for an alternative design, dubbed the 'short, fat' frigate, by the entrepreneur and aircraft engineer David Giles, operating under the name of Thornycroft, Giles and Associates, gained much publicity and some high-profile supporters including Geoffrey Pattie, a junior minister, and John Moore, the editor of *Jane's Fighting Ships*.[124] Following the submission of his plans and a meeting with members of the Ship Department and the Naval Staff it became clear that their 'competing design' was undeveloped and little thought had been given to many key elements required for an anti-submarine frigate. There was little detail on weight, space, layout, machinery, power generation, stores and complement, and not much more information could be volunteered at the meeting.[125] Giles was able to continue pushing for his design for a number of years and it was not until Lloyd's Register completed an independent enquiry into the merits of different hull shapes for warships, that the issue was finally resolved in favour of the Ministry of Defence.[126]

The Navy, through the various adjustments set out above, had been able to obtain a ship that had an armament and sensor fit not too dissimilar to a Type 22 but for much less cost; an impressive achievement given that the ship concept had begun as a minimum vessel for towed-array operations. However, there was a significant catch: the Type 23 was designed only for maximum 30-day deployments and would be much more dependent on its attendant auxiliary, the new AOR, and shore support than its predecessors. This problem was only fully acknowledged by the Navy Board in 1987, as the construction of four ships of the class was already underway. Given the requirements of the Navy's operational programme, it was now expected that the new ships would have to undertake the same types of general purpose deployments as other frigates in the fleet for at least 60 per cent of the time. These deployments generally involved a standard six-month operational cycle, six times the length of time as that planned for the Type 23. The ship, which had a formal complement of 145 but had space for another 40 added during changes to the design in 1982, did have some space for augmentations. Another five crew members were added to the complement in July 1987 and by the time the ship was commissioned most of these empty berths had been filled. Additional crew meant that there would be extra personnel for basic ship husbandry, plus additional skilled or semi-skilled personnel to maintain equipment. The stowage arrangements for the ships were modified to enable more stores to be crammed in, but there were still doubts that the ships would be able to operate on a 90-day pattern. Major design changes would have to wait until a second batch was designed.[127]

The increase in both the cost of the Type 23 and its complement meant that the original plans for an ordering rate of three per year to enable the replacement of the ageing *Leander* class and Type 21 frigates, would be increasingly difficult to fulfil in the prevailing atmosphere of constrained budget in the mid and late 1980s. The Navy Department's most senior civil servant had warned of this problem as early as 1983, but there was little appetite across the Ministry to reduce or remove the newly gained capabilities of Type 23, nor was the Navy happy to relinquish the fifty figure voluntarily.[128] As a result, it should not have been too surprising that the order rate was almost half that originally envisaged by the Naval Staff's planners. A total of only ten ships had been ordered by the end of the Cold War. It was now almost inevitable that the destroyer and frigates levels would not be able to keep to fifty with an ordering rate at this level.

HMS *Norfolk* was accepted from her builders in November 1989, and her new commanding officer described her as the 'most radically different ship to pass through FOST [Flag Officer Sea Training] since the first of the Type 21 frigates almost twenty years earlier'. The greatest difference was the new, leaner, crewing philosophy. Not only had the size of the crew decreased, but a number of measures had been taken to create an 'all one company' mentality for the crew. Messdecks for ratings were mixed amongst the branches, meaning that no longer were operations ratings placed in one messdeck and marine engineers in another. The allocation of communal tasks for junior rates, which usually involved ship husbandry, was no longer on the basis of parties made up of the most junior personnel but spread across the ship and allocated daily.[129] However, there were other aspects of the ship's design that betrayed its origins as a utility vessel. The standards of paint and preservation on the exterior were not up to the levels expected on Royal Navy ships and would result in corrosion, as would the placing of dissimilar metals together on some of the external fittings. Too little space had been allocated to laundry spaces, whilst the allocation of ship's offices seemed to show a rushed design, with some departments having too much space and others, such as the Operations Department, not receiving any office space at all.[130] The greatest concerns came regarding maintenance and support. The additional staff allocated to the shore-based Fleet Maintenance Group supporting the ship were inadequate for the work required, whilst the support provided from the ship's squadron was also too little for the work required when *Norfolk* came alongside.[131] Many more personnel would be needed ashore in the future as more Type 23s entered service and eventually became the backbone of the escort fleet. In these circumstances, it would be difficult to continue with the ship-based squadron structures as the main way to support individual ships. The end of the squadrons and their replacement with a dedicated shore-based support structure, would eventually come to pass in a series of reforms during the late 1990s and early 2000s.[132] These reforms were made almost inevitable by the introduction of the Type 23s into the fleet and were the final step away from the 'self-supporting' concept for warships that had persisted into the late 1960s and early 1970s.

Norfolk's military capabilities were impressive, however. The reductions in her radar signature through the use of oblique angles on the ship's superstructure were considerable, whilst the new Sea Wolf vertical launch system had proved itself on trials although missile reliability needed improving. The ship's seakeeping and shiphandling was good, whilst in anti-submarine terms the ship was deemed 'very impressive', not only with her weapon systems and sensors but also with noise reduction across the ship.[133] The most pertinent operational issue was the lack of a functioning tactical command system. The Ferranti CACS 4, the system developed for the Type 23, had been cancelled in 1987 as it became clear that it was not technologically advanced enough to deal with the requirements imposed by the sensors and weapons feeding into it. In what turned out to be a major mistake, the contract for the manufacture of the CACS 4 hardware was awarded to Ferranti before the development contract was awarded in 1985, on the assumption that the hardware would only need a minor change from that used for CACS 1 on the Batch 2 Type 22 frigates. As the sensor and weapon fit of the Type 23 increased during 1981 and 1982, it became clear that the hardware capacity would not be sufficient. It was initially thought that adding some capacity to the existing system would resolve the problem but it eventually emerged that it would not. A major redesign was deemed to take too long, so the contract was cancelled in July 1987.[134] By the summer of 1988 it had been accepted that at least the first two Type 23s would be completed without their tactical command system, although due to delays with the CACS 4 successor, DNA 1, the first Type 23 to enter service fitted with a fully-functioning command system was HMS *Westminster*, the eighth ship of the class, in 1994.[135]

Offshore Patrol Vessels
In both the 1983 and 1984 estimates the Royal Navy had hoped to procure more 'Castle' class offshore patrol vessels to undertake the Falklands patrol task. These orders never materialised, and in the event the two existing ships of that class were taken off fishery protection duties from 1986 onwards and sent to the South Atlantic. In the meantime, plans had been developed for an 'enhanced' offshore patrol vessel, later known as 'OPV 3', in order to replace more capable and expensive frigates in routine patrol tasks worldwide, such as the West Indies Guardship commitment. Admiral Fieldhouse, the First Sea Lord, seems to have been the originator of the concept, as a way to circumvent the fifty-escort figure as the fleet gradually shrank over the 1980s. He took a clear-eyed view of the likelihood of sustaining a fleet of fifty destroyers and frigates, when unrealistically large numbers of Type 23s would need to be ordered over the next five to seven years.[136] By the summer of 1983, a basic concept had been developed. Described by VCNS as a 'huntin', shootin' and fishin' warship' designed to conduct low-level patrol duties worldwide, it would be a 'force multiplier' and fill a gap in the sea training pyramid by giving Lieutenant Commanders junior command opportunities. The ship would have a close-in weapon system for self-defence, a medium gun, anti-ship missiles, underwater and air defence countermeasures, a Lynx helicopter able to fly 25 hours a month for 45 days, a basic target indication radar, as much automation as possible, a speed of 21 knots, a range of 8,000 nautical miles, moderate shock and firefighting capabilities, but no radar signature reduction. Somewhat optimistically, it was hoped that these ships would have a unit cost of no more than £50 million in 1983 prices, less than half that of a Type 23 frigate.[137]

The concept gained early support from John Stanley, the Minister for the Armed Forces,[138] but it came up against the opposition of General Johnston, the DCDS. In the safe knowledge that he had the ear of the Secretary of State, he stated that even if OPV 3 gained ministerial approval from Stanley, 'I would oppose such [an] agreement [as] being taken to imply anything in the way of [a] commitment to what is currently only a speculative project.'[139] His main objection was that he did not see what role it could play in a general war, and taking a quintessentially Cold War British Army view of military capability, he therefore found it difficult to understand why it should be funded. He did raise the more pertinent question of what the Navy proposed to take out of its existing programme in order to fund the new class. Sure enough, the new Secretary of State, Michael Heseltine, backed up Johnston's line and ordered that no outside discussion of OPV 3 should take place until Johnston's concerns about the project had been answered.[140]

The retirement of General Johnston in late 1983 appears to have removed the main block to the further development of the OPV 3, and by May 1984 the shipbuilding industry was asked to register their interest in participating in the potential procurement. The next step was to write a competitive procurement document setting out the design brief for a conceptual study for OPV 3. This would include the Naval Staff's requirements and tasks for the proposed class. The answers from industry would then provide the basis from which a Naval Staff Target (the step before the issuance of a Naval Staff Requirement). The aim would then be to produce a concept paper to the Operational Requirements Committee at the centre for discussion.[141] The OPV 3 would therefore not be an in-house design but one developed from start to finish by the shipbuilding industry. Hall Russell, the builders of the previous OPV classes, submitted a design derived from the 'Castle' class, Yarrow submitted pared down versions of the Type 23, whilst Vosper Thornycroft submitted variants on their corvette classes developed for export.[142] At this point however, all forward momentum on the project stopped. The unexpected ending of the annual 3 per cent increases in defence spending meant that a series of other projects now had to be given priority over the OPV 3 if they were to get funding at all. The OPV 3 lingered on for a few years in the Navy Department's list of potential items for funding, but never got further than this. In retrospect, General Johnston's question about what would be removed from the programme if the OPV 3 were added, was crucial. In Fieldhouse's early conception of the project, he had implicitly assumed that the fifty-escort figure would be given up, and the reduction replaced by this enhanced OPV. DUS(N), the Navy Department's most senior civil servant, had pointed out this issue in 1983, optimistically hoping that a reduction of the destroyer and frigate force to forty might provide space for many more than ten OPVs in compensation.[143] However, the fifty number was never renounced, and the removal of the 3 per cent increase in 1985 is likely to have been instrumental in this. Even if OPV 3 had been placed at the top of the Navy's priority list, the environment was so difficult for securing additional funding, that if the fifty number had been given up and OPV 3s ordered instead, it would have been even more difficult to argue for additional Type 23s. The irony in this decision was that without OPV 3 orders, the Type 23s would have to be deployed outside the Eastern Atlantic on more general duties and for longer than the planned 30-day deployment cycle. This then resulted in the measures described above, which increased the complement and running costs of the ship to enable such operations.

Fort Victoria Class AORs

From the start of the development of the Type 23 design, the role of the 'AOR' (the NATO designation for a replenishment oiler, or 'one stop' auxiliary, that could provide fuel, stores and ammunition) had been central in ensuring that the costs of the new frigate remained controlled. It would be a 'mothership' for deployed helicopters, even when it was decided to provided hangars on the Type 23, be able to defend itself with its own Sea Wolf air defence system, and have the operations room facilities to command an ASW group of four Type 23 frigates. The operational concept of the Type 23 therefore depended in no small measure on the AOR; her nearly permanent presence near the frigate would therefore mean that stores on board could be reduced, as top-ups could always be transferred from the AOR.[144] In short, the Type 23 and the AOR were envisaged as having something close to a symbiotic relationship operationally.

The AOR, partly because of this, would be a large and sophisticated ship, much more so than earlier classes of Royal Fleet Auxiliaries. Swan Hunter had undertaken the feasibility study for the design, and the resultant ship was 33,000 tons, 200m long, armed with vertical-launch Sea Wolf and most of the radars, electronics and other surface and air sensors that would be fitted to a Type 23. Each vessel would cost £96 million in 1982 prices, a similar cost to a Type 23. The complement would be 178 Royal Fleet Auxiliary and 73 Royal Navy.[145] Given the unprecedented militarisation of the AOR, at an early stage the replacement of the RFA crew with further RN officers and ratings was considered. However, this resulted in a larger crew (even if there were fewer officers) that would cost 25 per cent more than an RFA equivalent, not including the expected costs of making a high proportion of RFA personnel redundant.[146]

This was an expensive and sophisticated vessel, and it was initially expected that the AOR design would eventually replace all other RFAs, up to a total of eleven. From the start it was known that the AOR would be vying for space in the Navy's programme with the Trident submarines, the Type 23 frigates and the new conventional submarines. The planned updates to the Sea Harrier would also be taking up space in the programme as well, so it was expected to be difficult to find space for the AOR.[147] This was a prescient assessment, as the class was indeed squeezed out of the programme until as late as April 1986, when the first of the class, *Fort Victoria*, was ordered. A second ship was ordered in December 1987 and after this no more vessels of the class were constructed.[148] After delays in completing the first of class, both ships were accepted for service in 1993. In a post-Cold War world, they appeared over-sophisticated and were extremely expensive. This therefore had a knock-on impact on the Type 23, which was seen above. No longer would the Type 23 only be operating with an AOR nearby, the symbiotic link was broken and the Type 23 would therefore need greater stores capacity than had originally been envisaged.

Mine Warfare Vessels
The 1980s were both frustrating for the mine-warfare specialism and also a period of great reinvestment and reinvigoration. The numerous and very aged 'Ton' class ships were replaced by three new classes of mine countermeasures vessels. The thirteen ships of the 'Hunt' class were completed between 1980 and 1989, bringing a range of new capabilities in much larger vessels that could be deployed overseas much more easily; their worth was demonstrated in the mine countermeasures force sent to the Gulf in 1988 and which has remained there ever since. If with the frigate force, the Type 23s were favoured before the OPV 3 and AOR, so with the mine warfare capability. The 'Hunts' were ordered on a regular basis through the 1980s, but both the new 'River' class minesweepers and the *Sandown* class single role minehunters were delayed repeatedly. With the 'River' class, the concept of trawlers in the sweeping role to deal with Soviet rising mines had been proven by the end of 1979, but the first orders of the class were not made until December 1982, with a total of twelve ships being completed between 1984 and 1986.[149] The operational concept behind the 'River' class had always been that they would be supplemented on a two-to-one or three-to-one basis by ocean-going stern trawlers taken up from trade in an emergency. Given the delays in ordering the 'Rivers', by the time they had begun to enter service, the British ocean-going trawler industry was in terminal decline, with only a very small number of ships remaining. This threatened to undermine the purpose of the 'River' class, and more importantly hugely complicate the Royal Navy's ability to deal with Soviet mines in times of high tension or war. The Navy Board considered the issue in 1986 just as the full class had entered service. The next best option, which was not considered the ideal, was to take up from trade British-registered oil rig support vessels. They had long, clear stern areas in which sweeping

rigs could be set up, but these would need to be used with 'bolt-on' winches provided by the Navy. Plenty of oil rig support vessels were currently available as a downturn in the oil industry had caused many to be laid up or left idle. Once the oil industry picked up again, the ability to charter such vessels would fall off significantly, so this was only a short to medium-term expedient.[150]

For the Single Role Minehunters, the problem was more fundamental: too few were being ordered. The first of class, HMS *Sandown*, was ordered in August 1985, but although the next four ships followed soon after, no further orders were placed until after the Cold War had ended.[151] Given that these vessels had been designed to be cheaper and more specialised versions of the 'Hunts', it was galling that the earlier class had been ordered in relatively good numbers but the *Sandown*s were not. The ultimate reason for this was that the *Sandown* class were not that much cheaper than the 'Hunts'. Although they lacked sweeping gear and were somewhat smaller, they had an improved (and more expensive) mine-hunting sonar and excellent manoeuvrability due to a combination of bow thrusters, computer-aided ship control and cycloidal propellors. The ships therefore ended up being better hunters than the 'Hunts'.[152] A further blow was the decommissioning, without replacement, of the exercise minelayer, HMS *Abdiel*. She was over 20 years old, so her disposal was not surprising, but the lack of a successor meant that the Royal Navy, for the first time since the First World War, lacked any defensive minelaying capability. Offensive minelaying could be undertaken by submarines, but the creation of minefields to protect port approaches against enemy submarines – the standard defensive minelaying task – was best undertaken by surface ships. This meant, that despite much attention theoretically being given to port defence in time of war, it would be difficult to undertake the most simple and effective ways to protect the country's maritime approaches. *Abdiel* had also acted as a support and command ship for mine warfare forces, so this dedicated capability was lost as well, although survey vessels could and now did undertake this role instead, not least in the 1990–1 Gulf War.[153]

Shipbuilders

The shipbuilders that were being entrusted to construct the new ships for the 1980s were undergoing as much wrenching change in this decade as they had done in the preceding one. The Conservative Party's 1979 general election manifesto had pledged to de-nationalise British Shipbuilders, but although this had not been achieved by the next general election in 1983, the government had managed to pass the British Shipbuilders Act which permitted the privatisation of the warship building yards within that nationalised corporation. However, once these yards had been privatised they would be ineligible for subsidies to build merchant ships, effectively forcing these companies down the route of building only warships.[154] Given the huge losses that the remaining merchant shipbuilding yards with British Shipbuilders were making, and their dependence on subsidies for any successful commercial contracts, this made it clear that the government saw no future in merchant shipbuilding. They saw the sole role of those yards fit to survive as supplying the Royal Navy and foreign navies with naval vessels. The three long-standing warship-only yards, Vickers at Barrow building submarines, Yarrow at Scotstoun building frigates and destroyers and Vosper Thornycroft in Southampton building mine warfare vessels, were joined by four other yards by being designated 'warship yards' fit for privatisation. These were Cammell Laird and Swan Hunter, which had been mixed yards building larger warships and merchant ships for many years, and the smaller Brooke Marine and Hall Russell Yards. The former built minor craft and small landing ships and the latter had built the 'Island' and 'Castle' class OPVs. By adding these four yards, the government was apparently signalling that it wished to instil a certain amount of competition into the warship bidding process, rather than handing construction monopolies to Vickers, Yarrow and Vospers.[155]

Unfortunately for these four yards, any sense of real competition was undermined by the government's continued willingness to award contracts on political rather than cost grounds, and the much lower than promised number of ships that were ordered. Brooke Marine was sold in May 1985 to its management team but gained few warship contracts and left the sector in 1987. Hall Russell, sold to the Aberdeen Shipbuilding Company in 1986, achieved no substantive orders either, largely due to the Navy's decision neither to build any more 'Castle' class OPVs nor to proceed with the OPV 3 project. Hall Russell went bankrupt in 1988.[156] With the departure of these two builders, Vosper Thornycroft now had a monopoly in the small ship side of warship building. Cammell Laird could theoretically have provided competition both in frigate building and submarine construction, but it was in fact bought by Vickers a few months after it had been awarded the contract to build one of the Batch 3 Type 22 frigates, a decision that the government admitted that it had undertaken in order to save the builder from bankruptcy. Cammell Laird was based near Liverpool, which was one of the government's test cases for redevelopment; its going under would not have helped the cause for this particular policy. The Prime Minister also wanted to reward those of its workers that had not gone on strike some months earlier.[157] The yard then gained the contracts for the three follow-on boats of the *Upholder* class but after the end of the Cold War, VSEL (the former Vickers) closed Cammell Laird after these vessels had been completed.

Swan Hunter should have been the obvious competitor with Yarrow for frigate construction and was also one of the few yards able to build surface ships of capital ship size, but the industrial policies of the government managed to undermine it following sale to its management team in January 1986. After building a number of Type 42 destroyers, and the second and third *Invincible* class carriers, all of which had been completed by 1985, Swan Hunter gained the contract to build two Batch 2 Type 22s, the new *Sir Galahad* and the replacement *Atlantic Conveyor* (enabled for future STUFT if necessary) for Cunard.[158] After this, things became increasingly difficult for the yard. It had been heavily involved in work to develop the new *Fort Victoria* class AORs but the contract for the first ship went to the Belfast yard, Harland and Wolff, instead. Harland and Wolff had remained outside British Shipbuilders and as a major employer of the Protestant working classes of Belfast, its survival was regarded as crucial support for that community in the province, despite its relatively poor record in delivering orders within budget and on time. In the event, Harland and Wolff proved a disastrous choice; the ship would eventually be completed by Cammell Laird.[159] Swan Hunter had hoped to secure two Batch 3 Type 22 orders following a successful competition, but the second of these two orders was awarded to Cammell Laird instead, as described above, based on a technicality relating to tender issuance.[160] Swan Hunter managed to gain one order for a Type 23 frigate out of a tranche of three placed in 1986, but failed to gain any two years' later when another tranche of three went out to tender.[161] It was successful in securing all three orders in a further group of three placed in December 1989, but it is telling that all were laid down within 13 months of each other: the shipyard clearly had sufficient empty slips and underemployed workers to build the ships almost simultaneously.[162] This 'feast and famine' approach to Type 23 orders at the end of the 1980s might have reduced contract costs for the Ministry of Defence in the short-term, but it resulted in stop-start work for Swan Hunter, a painful and potentially terminal situation for any shipyard which needed to plan for the long-term and retain skilled workers. No attempt appears to have been made to permit 'managed competition' where both Yarrow and Swan Hunter would be likely to gain one ship out of a tranche of three frigates, enabling competition between the two for the third ship, thus helping keep some form of limited competition alive and at least giving the Ministry some choices. Instead, Swan Hunter staggered into the 1990s but finally called in the receivers in 1993, having failed to gain the contract for the new helicopter carrier, HMS *Ocean*, which went to VSEL amid unproven accusations that the latter had deliberately underbid in order to force its competitor out of the market.[163]

As a result, through governmental policies that unevenly and unpredictably pursued a mixture of preferential contracts based on political factors combined with cut-throat competition and too few orders to sustain all seven yards, a series of de facto monopolies had been created. Vickers controlled all submarine and large ship production, Yarrows all frigate and destroyer construction and Vosper Thornycroft all mine warfare construction. Vickers had been privatised under an employee consortium and was later listed, Yarrow had been bought by British Aerospace in 1985, whilst Vospers had been sold to its management in the same year.[164] Their entrenched positions meant that Vickers would build all four *Vanguard* class and all seven *Trafalgar* class submarines during the 1980s and 1990s, Yarrow would build twelve of the sixteen Type 23s and then build all six Type 45 destroyers in the 2000s, whilst Vospers built all but one ship in the 'Hunt' class and every ship in the *Sandown* class. It is difficult to see how this could have benefitted the British taxpayer in the longer term even if government decisions over contracts had helped deal with short-term political difficulties in the mid-1980s and then hold down prices for a few years in the late 1980s.

* * *

The 1980s, as with the previous decade and many of the decades that have followed, demonstrated the difficulties keeping spending on naval, or for that matter defence, procurement within projected budgets. A just-about-adequate situation was maintained up to 1985, when the 3 per cent real terms growth commitment was ended. Although a shock at the time within Defence, in retrospect it is unsurprising that the government was uncomfortable with extending this forward indefinitely. The proportion of government spending devoted to defence would have increased well above 5 per cent of GNP if this had been sustained over the long-term, and although economic growth was strong in the mid- and late- 1980s, other parts of government spending were growing faster, not least supporting the unemployed, who were at historically high levels until 1988. Spending on care for the elderly, disabled and mentally ill was also rising significantly during this period; all areas where spending reductions were extremely difficult to achieve, both politically and practically.[165]

This occurred for many of the reasons seen in previous chapters: over-optimism with uncertain costings, the stretching out of procurements to save money in the short-term even if they increase much more in the long-term, or changes to designs at the later stages of development. Underlying all of this was a stubborn level of 'defence inflation' that was significantly above standard inflation. What was most significant in this case was that many of these procurements were interlinked in complex ways. The new diesel boats had been developed as more cost-effective alternatives to nuclear-powered attack submarines, whilst the attack submarines not only supported the SSBNs operationally and tracked enemy SSBNs, they also helped sustain the shipbuilding expertise in building nuclear submarines in the gaps between SSBN programmes. The Type 23, AOR and EH101 were designed symbiotically from the start, whilst the OPV 3 was an attempt to compensate for the Type 23's limited Eastern Atlantic zone of operations by providing a ship that could undertake worldwide patrol and presence work. Both the 'River' class minesweepers and the Single Role Minehunter were meant to be more cost-effective alternatives to the 'Hunt' class mine countermeasures vessel, to ensure that enough hulls were available for all the mine warfare tasks required by NATO.

The increase in costs and difficulties experienced in operating within existing budgets meant that not enough ships were ordered, and those that were, were primarily of the most capable and expensive types, resulting in unbalanced and sub-optimal capability mixes in the 1990s. The delays in the SSBN programme meant that although the number of SSNs would reach eighteen by 1991, after this point the five older *Valiant* class attack boats would have to be withdrawn from service whilst any replacements could not be built until after the last Trident SSBN had been completed. As a result, it was inevitable that the SSN fleet would have reduced to thirteen or fewer by the mid-1990s. The slow procurement of the *Upholder*s then meant that there would be fewer such SSKs to substitute for SSNs during the 1990s just when they would be most needed, which given the need to sustain numbers of trained and experienced submariners for the new generation of SSNs, was as good as confirming that the SSN fleet would have to reduce in size over the long-term and probably never reach eighteen boats again.

The Type 23 was heavily affected by the slow procurement of the AOR and the non-procurement of the OPV 3. It would now have to undertake general purpose presence deployments that would have been undertaken by the OPV 3, and do so without the support (or with limited support) from the small number of AORs that were ordered. As a result, the complement of the Type 23 had to be increased, more stores placed aboard, and deficiencies in self-repair and maintenance would become a significant feature of their service, forcing larger number of personnel to operate ashore in support roles, which in turn reduced the number of personnel at sea, undermining a major objective of the Secretary of State who had pushed the development of the Type 23 into the type of ship that it became.

The delayed procurement of the 'River' class minesweepers meant that their operational concept was partly undermined when the STUFT trawlers they were meant to operate alongside, had largely disappeared from the British registers of shipping when the ships finally entered service. The Single Role Minehunter was meant to be a cheaper alternative to the 'Hunt' class, and a key part of plans to ensure a fleet of forty to fifty mine warfare vessels that could protect routes for naval and merchant vessels entering bases and major ports during war, but this was undermined by their escalating capability (and cost). The issue was therefore not just the lack of orders, but the unbalanced nature of the orders that were made, creating additional problems and difficulties that had to be worked around or resolved as the new ships entered service. The alternative would have been balanced orders of every type, which itself would have created problems of supporting and maintaining small numbers of ships from multiple classes. This can therefore be seen as the final playing out of the original decisions many years before to create the multiple classes in an attempt to save money or in the case of the submarine programme, a lack of nuclear submarine-building capacity. They highlight the complexities of procurement decisions, their inter-linkages and cross-dependencies, and then the different ways in which unbalanced procurements have to be resolved once the vessels enter service.

20

To the End

The difficulties the Royal Navy faced in dealing with escalating equipment costs and insufficient ship orders in the mid- and late-1980s were paralleled by equally serious problems in retaining personnel. A range of remedies were considered and implemented, and the decision to integrate the Women's Royal Naval Service into the Navy and allow women to go to sea was heavily influenced by this overriding need to retain personnel. Issues of diversity began to be acknowledged, albeit reluctantly, and the sometimes-overlooked area of Fleet Support underwent its greatest changes since the 1960s: the dockyards were contracted out and digital storekeeping was introduced. This chapter will review these important areas, and then follow with another somewhat neglected area in the 1980s: 'out of area' operations in the Gulf, Mediterranean, Caribbean, West Africa and Hong Kong. In addition, the Navy was affected by the political and economic changes in the Soviet Union of the late 1980s: it became increasingly apparent that the Soviet military machine, including its navy, was suffering its own serious internal problems. The first tentative dialogues began behind closed doors between the Soviet Navy and the Royal Navy, just as the USSR began its final descent into collapse and dissolution. This chapter will therefore bring this study of the Royal Navy in the Cold War years to a close, with the next chapter finishing with some general conclusions.

Personnel

The Mounting Retention Crisis
In order to provide sufficient space in the Navy's budget to procure the vessels and weapon systems approved following the Falklands conflict, in 1983 the Admiralty Board had proposed an artificial limit on naval personnel

numbers which had then been agreed by the Secretary of State. Known as the Authorised Manpower Ceiling (or 'AMC') it would match the actual requirement for personnel until 1988, but from this point onwards the AMC would reduce to 66,400 by April 1988 and 64,500 a year later, reducing by 1 per cent a year until April 1993 when total personnel numbers would be 63,000. In addition, the ratio of personnel on shore postings in comparison to sea going posts would shift from 60:40 to 50:50, and then ideally to 40:60.[1] When these reductions had been agreed, it had been assumed that new classes of ship with smaller complements would be entering service by 1988 which would help reduce the total 'Naval Manpower Requirement' (or 'NMR') in line with the reductions in the AMC. Unfortunately, the Type 23 frigates, with their complements of 185 compared to around 250 for an old *Leander* class frigate, were not being ordered in sufficient numbers, whilst the OPV 3 which would have had an even smaller complement was not procured at all. As a result, ageing ships were remaining in service for many years longer than planned. Not only was this resulting in increased maintenance costs, as was discussed in the previous chapter, but these elderly ships required larger crews and the continuation of the training pipeline for operators and maintainers of the ageing and increasingly obsolescent systems, from steam turbines to Sea Cat missile systems. It became increasingly clear that there would be a large and growing mismatch between the Admiralty Board's self-imposed personnel ceiling, and the numbers of personnel required to keep fifty destroyers and frigates in commission, in addition to a growing submarine fleet and a Fleet Air Arm supplemented by additional aircraft purchases following the Falklands.[2]

Between 1983 and 1985 the situation had seemed bad enough when both the ongoing Falklands and Gulf commitments had resulted in long periods of sea time for personnel, which had in turn, caused retention problems, but by 1986 the impending mismatch between the ceiling and the required numbers was combined with a lopsided economic boom in the rest of the economy. This created a retention crisis of a type that had not been seen in recent decades. The mid-1980s economic boom provided many opportunities for skilled and educated workers, particularly in the prosperous south of England. When opportunities outside the Navy were combined with long periods of sea time in a stretched fleet, the result was large numbers of the Navy's best trained and most capable officers, artificers and ratings leaving the service, especially those with families who were irked by long periods of separation. However, the mid-1980s boom occurred in a period of unprecedently high unemployment, particularly in the old industrial areas of the Midlands and the North, hitting those with lower skills the greatest. As a result, the Navy had no problem recruiting large numbers of new personnel from the unemployed and from school leavers in depressed areas, but their educational levels were not as high as the cohort leaving, and in any case would take many years to train up to the level of skills required to act as replacements. The numbers of personnel leaving were so great that in 1986, the proportion under training was as high as 9.8 per cent of the Navy's total personnel numbers.[3] This was adding a particular strain on training staff and there were fears that numbers of trainers would leave and further slow the throughput of new joiners into the fleet.[4] The level of 'under-bearing' in some of the most demanding and skilled roles in the navy was at or near crisis levels. In 1986 there were 27 per cent too few command-qualified submariner officers, 28 per cent too few submarine watch leaders, 40 per cent too few Sea Harrier pilots and 14 per cent too few Principal Warfare Officers.[5] Two years later, the situation with Sea Harrier pilots was less severe, as the shortfall had reduced to a, still serious, 17 per cent, but the shortfalls in submariners and PWOs had persisted.[6] By 1989, the retention issue looked at risk of becoming a recruitment problem as well: the economic boom was now reaching the point where unemployment was falling and service in the Navy did not look attractive in comparison to the jobs becoming available in the civilian world.[7]

Other longer-term societal factors were also at work: the population cohort coming of age in the late 1980s and early 1990s would be smaller than those of previous generations, whilst social changes in the 1980s had accentuated the importance of individuality, job mobility and what was termed 'home-centredness'.[8] A career that involved long periods away from home and demanded up to 10 to 20 years' of a person's life working for a single employer, combined with the subordination of the self into a disciplined hierarchy, did not fit well with this new approach to working and family life. In this important respect the armed forces, and the Navy especially, were drifting further away from the rest of society.

There would also be very specific problems at certain points in the future: the shift from Polaris submarines to Trident submarines would create a 'bulge' in the requirement for submariners in the early 1990s, as two training pipelines and two groups of skill-sets would have to exist side by side during the transition period. Similar but less extreme problems would be experienced in the mid-1990s during the transition from the Sea King helicopter to the EH101 (the future Merlin) and for an 18-month period in the early 1990s when it was planned that all three aircraft carriers would be in service at the same time.[9] Given the fundamental importance of the Trident programme to defence, the Navy was able to negotiate an uplift in the ceiling for submariners during the early 1990s but could not do so to cover the helicopter transition or the three-carrier problem.[10] The Second Sea Lord recommended pushing for an increase in the AMC across the board, but the cost that this imposed made the Navy Board baulk at such a move in 1985. ACNS noted, when this was first proposed, that the cost of lifting the AMC to deal with the mismatch into the 1990s would be more than the price of building two Type 23 frigates.[11] This was one of the apparently insoluble dilemmas of the looming personnel crisis: without substantial additional funding, the only way to ostensibly solve the crisis would be to slow down even further the arrival into the fleet of new and less personnel-intensive warships, thus increasing the problem further.

Other ways of dealing with the issue included a series of remedies to mitigate the factors that pushed service personnel out of the Navy: ensuring a better balance between shore and sea postings, as well as reducing the number of times personnel would have to move across the country to new postings. These were important objectives, but some fundamental issues made resolving this difficult. Most of the shore postings were focussed in the Portsmouth area where there was a concentration of shore establishments, many of which were dedicated to training. However, the majority of sea postings involved being assigned to ships or submarines that were home ported at Devonport, Rosyth or Faslane. Therefore, for many sailors an increase in shore postings would in fact mean an oscillation between shore establishments in Hampshire followed by a return to sea postings in Devon or the central belt of Scotland. This 'turbulence' could do almost as much damage to retention as multiple sea postings.[12] Attempts to save money within the personnel budget, and increase the proportion of naval personnel at sea, also appeared to worsen the retention situation. The contracting out of over 300 catering/cook positions ashore towards the end of the decade only served to force naval cooks into an increasing cycle of one sea-posting after another, a sure way of pushing out those who could earn as much or more in commercial or hospitality catering roles outside the Navy, without any disruption to personal or family life.

Married quarters had been seen in the mid-1970s as a way of reconciling younger sailors to regular moves of house: the Ministry-wide Leitch Report of 1976 had aimed actively to discourage personnel from buying their own homes until they were in their mid-30s, by spending more money on the quarters and providing more flexibility in furnishings and decor. However, that same report had also proposed the sale of some married quarters to older service personnel as a way to reduce the stock of surplus Ministry-owned housing.[13] These proposals had not been implemented when the new Conservative government came to power, with its radical policy of selling council houses to tenants as a way of creating a 'property owning democracy'. As a result, most aspects of the Leitch Report were quietly shelved, but the married quarter sales proposal was enhanced and linked to the council house sales policy, with service personnel often receiving first refusal on the sale of surplus estates.[14] By 1990 over 7,000 quarters had been disposed of,[15] 2,600 of which had been sold to service personnel.[16] During the 1980s the strain on the defence budget had meant that less money was spent on the upkeep of accommodation and it was acknowledged that the relatively run-down appearance of some quarters had become an additional factor in personnel leaving the Navy.[17] However, it was only as late as 1990 that this was publicly acknowledged by the Ministry of Defence and the emphasis on sales was lessened and refurbishment increased.[18]

There were two obvious but painful solutions to the seemingly intractable problem of long-running retention issues. The first was to allocate more money to the personnel budget: either to increase pay, or to increase personnel numbers, or improve 'quality-of-life' provision such as accommodation and family facilities, or a mixture of all three. This was however, an extremely difficult case to argue: increased funding would do no more than keep existing naval capabilities fully crewed but more expensively than before, which would just suggest inefficiency in the minds of decision-makers, either on the Navy Board or at the Centre of the Ministry. The costs would not be trifling either. As seen above, the Second Sea Lord's request for additional funds to deal with the existing and expected personnel issues was the price of two state-of-the-art frigates, and all just to keep the existing 'show on the road' without any tangible enhancements. The problem of 'defence inflation' rising higher than ordinary inflation was not just caused by the spiralling cost of equipment procurement, but was also due to the rising costs of recruiting personnel and then discouraging them from leaving and joining the civilian workforce. Some improvements were agreed, including a 'Long Service at Sea' bonus and other benefits for long periods of separation from family, but these were relatively minor increments rather than fundamental changes that could resolve the underlying problems.[19]

The other solution was to shrink the requirement for personnel at sea by reducing the number of warships and submarines. In one of the many Navy Board discussions on personnel policy during the 1980s, this solution was raised by the Controller of the Navy (who as the Board member responsible for procurement, was grappling with a painfully slow production line of new warships and submarines). In the last years of the 1980s this seemed to be the only way to stave off a crippling retention crisis that delivered quick and tangible results without spending large additional sums of money. The commitment to fifty destroyers and frigates was watered down to 'around fifty' and this allowed the total to fall to forty-seven by April 1990.[20] The end of the Cold War, and the 'Options for Change' Defence Review – which falls outside the purview of this book – resolved many of the personnel problems faced by planners in the late 1980s (at least for a few years): the destroyer and frigate force was reduced by ten, the submarine fleet was reduced by more than a third, the three carriers were never all in service together, and the EH101 transition occurred many years later and with a shift to fewer helicopters.[21] With these changes the mismatch between the requirement and number of personnel rapidly fell away, so much so that tranches of redundancies were begun across Defence to resolve a new mismatch in the other direction. The beginnings of recession in 1991 also served to keep service personnel in the military as the private sector looked less alluring. Reducing the personnel requirement by shrinking the size of the fleet had been undertaken during the two previous periods of personnel strain in the mid-1960s and late-1970s, and would be resorted to again in the future.

Women at Sea
One underused segment of the Navy's workforce was the Women's Royal Naval Service ('WRNS'). They were better educated than the average sailor and were now staying in the service for longer than in the 1970s (now at an average of six years up from three) with many seeing it more as a long-term career. A proportion were continuing to serve after marriage, a significant change from the previous decade.[22] Although the number of WRNS who cited their inability to go to sea as a reason for leaving was not high at 24 per cent, it was increasing, and those who were leaving were giving reasons such their work being boring (77 per cent), their abilities and skills not being made best use of (77 per cent) and poor advancement (74 per cent).[23] A report into the possibility of WRNS going to sea was commissioned by the Navy Board in November 1987, just as the extent of the retention issue was becoming clear.[24] The report, which was completed in March 1989, argued that women in the naval service were a valuable but underused human resource that could be an important factor in ensuring that the personnel requirement matched the personnel available into the 1990s. The main area of concern was judged to be 'psycho-sociological' and it was seen as an 'emotive topic' for some male personnel. Despite this, it was recommended that the shift towards female sea-going should be undertaken, and undertaken rapidly, with the first women going to sea by April 1990 and the WRNS disbanded and women integrated fully into the Navy by April 1991. The number of WRNS personnel (at 3,000) was not too far in size from the expected shortfall in personnel numbers in the early 1990s, and it is clear from the report that the driving force behind its recommendation to send women to sea was the long-standing retention problem in the Navy.[25] The Report, after having been distributed to two-star commands for comment, was received by the Navy Board in January 1990 and approved by them 'out of committee' – in other words without meeting to discuss the matter, suggesting that its conclusions were not controversial amongst Board Members – and five ships, initially to have been non-combatant vessels, were to be chosen as the test vessels for implementation.[26] However, behind the scenes there seems to have been considerable pressure to shift from non-combatant ships such as survey vessels to a general integration across all sea-going roles. This would therefore see

the end of the policy that women should not be placed in posts where they could see combat, and it would also ensure that the decision would have the quickest and widest possible impact on the personnel crisis. With both the Armed Forces Minister, Sir Archie Hamilton, and the Director General of Naval Manpower and Training, Rear Admiral Neville Purvis, pushing for this change, the new policy was announced in Parliament in February.[27] As a result, amongst the first ships selected for integration were the carriers *Invincible* and *Ark Royal*, and a selection of destroyers and frigates, of which the frigate HMS *Brilliant* was the first.[28] HMS *Norfolk* would be the first ship with a female officer.[29] The formal integration of the WRNS into the Royal Navy took a little longer, being agreed by the Crown on 1 November 1993, and implemented on the 12th. By this time 25 warships had facilities for women and 760 women were serving at sea. However, three areas still remained closed to women: the submarine service, the Royal Marines and divers.[30]

Race and Ethnic Monitoring
From the Second World War the Royal Navy had operated a de facto 'colour bar' for potential non-white personnel,[31] and by the mid-1960s the situation was not too dissimilar, with non-white applicants having to demonstrate that they were *more* able than white entrants to have a chance at joining the Navy. In a report commissioned by the incoming Labour Government of 1964 it was stated that: 'In HM Ships communal life is intimate, constricted and confined to a far greater degree than the other two services, and for this reason coloured candidates are required to have outstanding personal qualities so as to overcome any prejudices they might meet. High standards are accordingly applied to coloured candidates for entry.'[32] In the same report it was argued that across all three services, issues of 'morale and man management' amongst white personnel would be affected if non-white personnel achieved positions of responsibility such as non-commissioned officers or warrant officers, implying a policy of not promoting non-white ratings and other ranks where possible.[33] In short, the senior personnel managers of the armed services, the Navy included, were unwilling to do anything to challenge the assumed racism of their soldiers, sailors and airmen, and then on top of this the progression of non-white personnel within the services would be held back despite the superior personal qualities they would have had to demonstrate in order to get in. This was a recipe for frustration and early release from the armed forces of talented personnel and a deliberate foregoing of any attempt to make the armed forces reflect the changes in civilian society in the post-war years.

During the 1970s and 1980s a small cohort of non-white personnel did join the Navy and a number were able to prosper, whilst the Race Relations Act of 1975 should have ensured that the discriminatory recruiting practices in place in the mid-1960s were removed, but attitudes amongst senior officers do not seem to have progressed significantly. In 1972, when the carrier HMS *Eagle* visited Durban in apartheid South Africa, the brave decision of the ship's padre to invite black priests to a formal reception on the carrier resulted in those invitations being rapidly rescinded for fear of offending the white South African officials invited to the same event. The Senior Naval Officer South Africa ('SNOSA') argued that a 'uni-racial' policy for such events was necessary, despite a recent Foreign Office decision that all formal diplomatic entertainments should be multi-racial, due to the difficulties this would cause with apartheid officials. SNOSA, who rather mystifyingly blamed the black priests for the incident, also argued that the Navy's 'run ashore' policy in South Africa should just accept that non-white sailors would have to stay aboard ship when the rest of the crew went ashore in racially-segregated areas.[34]

In the late 1980s an indication of the attitudes of senior personnel managers towards recruiting greater numbers of non-white personnel as a way of dealing with Navy's retention issues, was given in the report that had recommended integrating the WRNS into the Navy. It stated that 'previous experience of the Police and Army's efforts in this direction do not hold out hopes of a significant increase in recruiting from this group: its members' social patterns and perceptions of authority do not normally lead them into Service careers.'[35] External consultants were commissioned by the Ministry of Defence in 1989 to review why the recruitment of ethnic minorities across the three services remained low, and the results were not encouraging. Only the prison service or the police were less popular career options for ethnic minority young people interviewed by the consultants, whilst parents and careers officers tended to steer ethnic minority students away from a military career for fear of racial discrimination, the danger involved or the long periods away from family.[36] The consultants recommended a strategy of 'image building to address perceptions of racism in the Services, [and] increasing the frequency and quality of Service contact with ethnic minority young people'.[37] They also recommended that recruitment literature should emphasise equal opportunities and show ethnic minorities, neither of which was being done to any significant degree at the time; it was also important to demonstrate to recruits a real desire to tackle racial discrimination within the military.[38]

Throughout the 1980s, the Chiefs of Staff had opposed 'ethnic monitoring' in the armed forces, despite its introduction across the rest of the public sector.[39] Ethnic monitoring would at least have enabled the collation of firm statistics on non-white personnel and the progress of their careers through the services. It seemed that the Chiefs did not even want to know whether there might be a problem. It was only in 1992, after the 1991 census had included questions relating to ethnicity for the first time and had shown that 5.5 per cent of the population was non-white,[40] whilst non-white entrants into the armed forces stood at 1.1 per cent, that ethnic monitoring was finally conceded, but it would be another three years before the monitoring process was undertaken.[41] It was only in the late 1990s when targets for the recruitment and total numbers of non-white ethnicities were set for the armed forces.[42]

Homosexuality[43]

Whilst the position of women changed dramatically and rapidly during the 1980s, and that of ethnic minorities improved in a halting and relatively minor way, the Navy's attitude towards homosexuality seemed to go backwards. Since 1967 and the passing of the Sexual Offences Act which had decriminalised homosexual acts in private by those over the age of 21, there had been a significant difference between the norms regarding homosexuality in the civilian world and those in the military, where such acts were still an offence.[44] January 1987 saw a retrograde step in the Navy's formal position on homosexuality. For the first time, homosexuality was explicitly included in the Queen's Regulations for the Royal Navy, the volume that set out regulations and instructions for naval personnel. Prior to this, it had only been referred to indirectly in the Naval Discipline Act 1957, and had been directly referred to in the Manual of Naval Security (homosexuality was seen to make personnel vulnerable to blackmail and security compromise).[45] The language used in the update to the Queen's Regulations was blunt: homosexuality was described as 'the unnatural tendency of a man or a woman to have sexual inclinations towards a member of his or her own sex' and homosexual practices would normally result in discharge from the Service; 'other forms of sexual deviancy such as sadism and transvestism' were also bracketed into the same category.[46] It was accompanied by two new Defence Council Instructions (Royal Navy) which provided more detail.[47] Why this change was made is not clear, but it might have reflected the more conservative attitudes prevalent in the Conservative government and parts of the media at the time, which would also result in amendments to the Local Government Act which prevented local councils and schools from 'promoting' homosexuality in any way under the notorious Section 28.[48] It would take until the 1990s, when a combination of public campaigning, a more liberal attitude in government and a European Court of Human Rights judgement, would result in the ban on homosexuality being lifted. The Navy's approach to both homosexuality and race in the 1980s, aside from the moral and legal issues it raised, appears to have been both self-defeating and an unnecessary waste of talent which could have been put to good use across a fleet that was increasingly suffering from a personnel retention crisis as the decade wore on.

Support for the Fleet

The Dockyards and Contractorisation

The 1981 Defence Review had reduced the Royal Dockyards in number but had not changed their management structures or operating methods. Keith Speed's proposal to turn the dockyards into trading funds still stood as official policy and had the support of the Treasury, even if the Ministry's own finance officers were sceptical that this approach would make a significant difference to efficiency.[49] The Navy would, however, soon disavow the trading fund proposal. A report by the newly-created Royal Dockyard Policy Board, chaired by the Chief of Fleet Support, stated in September 1982 that a trading fund would not give the Navy the flexibility it needed in order to manage the dockyards effectively. Instead, an 'agency' would be created to establish 'customer requirements' for work by the dockyards and that the headquarters of the Chief Engineer's Department, which supervised the yards, would be slimmed down. A 'senior overseeing body' would be set up consisting of both 'customer' and 'supplier' representatives in order to manage work at a high level. This appears to have been an arrangement that would introduce many of the elements of a trading fund, but would also retain the ability of the Chief Engineer's Department to reach down into the dockyard organisations and direct work in detail when it was needed. The Defence Review's ending of mid-life refits and its reduction in the refit load generally had left the dockyards in flux, and the Navy Department did not want to lose its flexibility to influence how the dockyards operated before the new post-Review environment had bedded down.[50]

The Treasury did not approve of the proposals, which would have involved the abolition of the separate Dockyard Vote, only recently introduced, and this brought the issue to the attention of the Secretary of State who was keen to move entirely in the other direction and consider contracting out the two remaining dockyards at Rosyth and Devonport (Portsmouth no longer formally included a dockyard, although it retained considerable fleet maintenance facilities).[51] From late 1983 Peter Levene, the Secretary of State's personal adviser on efficiency matters, worked on the new proposals.[52] This would result in even less flexibility than the trading fund approach, but it was argued by Levene that contractorization would 'make the radical change in working habits which was needed to improve efficiency and effectiveness'.[53] Contracting out the dockyards, with a private company leasing buildings and equipment from the Ministry of Defence on a four-year contract, would give managers the flexibility to introduce the efficiency measures they needed to save money, speed up work and make the workforce more effective. The accounting system for the dockyards would be aligned with standard commercial practice, and the Navy's refitting needs would be confirmed through contract negotiations before each four-year renewal. In order to keep the contractors on their toes, 20 per cent of refits would also be tendered from commercial yards.[54]

The Admiralty Board appears to have been particularly nervous of the implications of contracting out. They were worried about disruption to Polaris submarine refits, the shift from one monopoly supplier to another, the impact on efficiency during the transition period, the speed at which Levene wanted to move (to have the new contracted yards in operation by 1 May 1987), and the extent of trades union disruption of activities in the two dockyards.[55] When the time came for a final decision, the Secretary of State decided to make a rare appearance at the Admiralty Board. He was accompanied by Levene and two junior ministers. In the interim a working party of senior civil servants had assessed Levene's plans and had ascertained that there were no legal or practical obstacles. However, both the Chief of Fleet Support, Vice Admiral Tippet, and the First Sea Lord, Admiral Fieldhouse, expressed their concerns and what they saw as the risks. The two junior ministers reassured the Board about potential disruption to Polaris refits, with John Stanley, the Minister for the Armed Forces, suggesting legislation to prevent the dockyard workers from striking. John Lee, the Under Secretary of State for Defence Procurement, took a more emollient line and suggested union consultations. Establishing a trading fund was seen as a halfway house that would be just as opposed by unions, require the same numbers of redundancies to make plausible, but result in fewer incentives for efficiency. Michael Heseltine was clear that there could be only one decision, stating that contractorization was the 'only approach to the problems of the dockyards which met the Board's objective' of a more efficient and cost-effective dockyard system.[56] The Controller argued that Devonport and Rosyth should have different contractors and that contracts should be renewed regularly – a comfortable commercial monopoly could not be allowed to develop. He also wanted a guarantee that the costs of redundancies would not have to be met by the Navy Department. The actual cost savings from contracting out were still ambiguous. Levene was certain that a 20 per cent increase in efficiency could be achieved, but the Chief of Fleet Support's Working Party on contractorization could not pin down the financial benefits even though they acknowledged that the transfer could work. Those dockyard employees transferred to the private sector would keep their existing conditions of service and therefore their working practices, unless they were changed with the agreement of the workforce. It was acknowledged that this would only be possible by offering significant pay rises with the new terms and conditions.[57]

Despite expressing his concerns at the uncertainties involved, Fieldhouse agreed to the proposals as did the Admiralty Board as whole.[58] They were then approved by Cabinet Committee and the Dockyard Services Act was passed on 25 July 1986, with the redundancies of dockyard personnel occurring before contracting out.[59] Legislation was not needed for the contracting out *per se*, but it was necessary in order to facilitate the transfer of the workforce to the contractor.[60] As predicted, the trades unions did strongly oppose contractorization, and they also attempted to undermine private refitting by refusing to work on ships that had been refitted this way. Demonstrations and attempts to obstruct tours by potential contractors and visits by ministers ended up undermining the unions' campaign. In one such situation the Minister for Defence Procurement, Norman Lamont, was trapped in an office building at Rosyth Dockyard for half an hour, whilst damage was caused to buildings and vehicles, and both police and demonstrators were injured.[61]

A joint venture between the engineering company Babcock and the electronics company Thorn EMI was awarded the contract in Rosyth, whilst Devonport Management Ltd, a joint venture between the US contractor Brown and Root and the shipbuilder Vickers, won the contract for Devonport.[62] The Rosyth contractor was appointed in January 1987 and the Devonport contractor one month later. Both had been given a seven-year contract to operate the dockyards under leases, and the formal transfer to commercial management occurred on 6 April 1987. Issues were complicated by changes to the Devonport consortium at the last minute as Vickers backed out and was replaced by three other companies, Balfour Beattie, Weir Group and Barclays Bank's investment banking arm.[63] The early months appear to have been chaotic: new processes and information systems were not yet in place, the commercial managers had only a short time to familiarise themselves with the dockyards, materials which would remain with the Ministry had not been properly accounted for, whilst records of loaned equipment were unsatisfactory. The quality of work by the disgruntled workforce in the build-up to vesting day had also suffered: a board of inquiry was necessary to investigate the poor standards of a submarine refit at Rosyth dockyard.[64] The Ministry also had to pay at least some of the redundancy costs prior to vesting, coming to a total of £30 million.[65] A new customer authority within the Ministry had to be set up, employing a total of 760 staff, about three times as many as the old Chief Engineer's Department headquarters.[66]

The new arrangements at least improved management-worker relationships. The new contractors gave significant pay increases to the remaining workers in return for new terms and conditions, new processes for industrial relations, and localised pay bargaining. The unions' local leadership either took voluntary redundancy or were promoted and integrated into the contractors' new industrial relations organisations. This canny approach managed to diffuse any remaining union militancy, although it was only possible by the generous use of money – up to £200 million – to oil the wheels of good industrial relations.[67] Improving dockyard efficiency appeared to be a longer-term task. In the first two years of contractor management of the dockyards thirty-nine out of fifty-five 'projects' undertaken for the Ministry of Defence were late. Many of the reasons were identical to those that had bedevilled the pre-contractorised yards: additional work needed on ships that was only spotted once the refit had started, late delivery of components and new equipment, and last-minute changes by the 'customer'. The late completion of refits in 1987 resulted in a total loss of two and a half 'hull years' of escort availability. Matters did appear to be improving by the end of the decade: refit specifications from the Ministry were improving as was cost control by the dockyard contractors. One major area where improvements were still 'in-progress' was the culture change required in a new commercial environment. For example, in 1990, 'slack timekeeping' by workers was still considered to be a problem by management in ensuring timely completion of work.[68]

Whether much money was being saved was another matter. The National Audit Office was pessimistic that forecast savings of £39 million at Rosyth and £123 million at Devonport would be achieved.[69] Even if these savings *were* achieved, they would not be that significant. For example, the Rosyth saving of £39 million would be from a total ten-year budget for that dockyard of £2.8 billion: less than 1.5 per cent.[70] This was a paltry sum that could easily be reached through a few years of efficiency 'wedges' that were the standard, and generally effective, tool of Ministry finance managers to achieve incremental savings over time. It is likely that the savings at Devonport would have been similarly minor. It was noted that in at least one area the new contractors were being charged less than their public sector predecessors: the contractors were charged £216 million over seven years as a license fee to use Ministry assets, whereas under the same terms and for the same period, the former public sector yards had been charged the equivalent of £312 million. As with the shift from four- to seven-year contracts and the allocation of redundancy costs back to the Ministry, the new contractors had clearly been able to negotiate important concessions from government. On the other side of the ledger, a complicating factor in assessing efficiencies and savings was a reduced refit load compared to that projected by the Ministry prior to the awarding of contracts.[71] Overall therefore, the jury was still out on the long-term value of the contracting-out of dockyards by 1990, suggesting that alternative approaches such as a trading fund or a government-owned company could have been more effective in saving money in the long run. It also raised the possibility of outright privatisation as a way to reduce costs, the option that would eventually be chosen in 1997. At least one tangible benefit had resulted from the upheaval of contracting out: there had been a significant reduction in the industrial tensions and disputes that had been a recurring factor within the dockyards since the end of the Second World War.

Fleet Maintenance Reform

Whilst the civilian side of shore maintenance was undergoing the most significant changes to its structure and management since the establishment of the dockyards many centuries ago, the naval side of shore maintenance was struggling to measure what it was doing and how efficiently it was doing it. In 1980 condition-based maintenance ('CBM') had been launched within the Navy, but trials only started on seven vessels including four submarines in 1985. The aim of CBM was to monitor equipment directly in order to identify and diagnose faults before they fully manifested themselves. Unfortunately, the record-keeping to manage this process efficiently was lacking: only when one knows when a piece of equipment was fitted, how often it has been used, its design life and the last time it was inspected, could condition-based maintenance work properly. As things stood in 1980s this was not yet possible, so maintenance remained a much more ad hoc, and therefore resource-intensive, process. Maintenance was still undertaken on input: budgeting focussed on the cost of inputs such as material, equipment and labour, not on tracking exactly that happened to individual pieces of equipment or components. As a result, it was not possible to calculate exactly what was spent on each individual ship during maintenance, nor was it possible to track what was spent at different levels of maintenance. The IT to support maintenance was rudimentary and had been developed piecemeal across the Navy.[72] In time, it was hoped that the computerisation of the logging of maintenance work would eventually enable real and effective condition-based maintenance but in 1990 the Navy was not yet at this stage ashore. Afloat, the situation was much more advanced.

Project Oasis

Whilst support functions ashore were still operating in the paper era, during the 1980s the Royal Navy spent considerable time and effort establishing a computer-based system for on-ship storekeeping. Tactical command systems and weapon systems had been computerised for many decades (although the shift from analogue to digital computing had only been recent), despite the rest of a warship's non-fighting systems remaining largely paper based. Ledgers, binders, forms and chits dominated the other aspects of ship management, from storekeeping through to weapon maintenance and marine engineering at sea. As ships and their supporting systems became more complex, so the old paper approaches began to come under strain. Effective information recording, filing and retrieval became increasingly slow and cumbersome, requiring more sailors working in administrative roles. The signs of administrative overload included rising instances of operational defects resulting from the lack of the right stores aboard ships when they were needed. By the early 1980s, each frigate-sized ship held over £2 million worth of stores, most of which were never used and was discarded after having expired. The Navy's answer was to start the development of a computerised storekeeping system. Named Oasis, development work was approved at the start of 1979, a contract having been awarded to the Digital Equipment Company Ltd. Trials of the Oasis system were conducted at the submarine base HMS *Dolphin*, on the old destroyer HMS *Kent* and at the Royal Navy Supply School. It was found that Oasis carried out basic stores transactions more accurately and quicker than the manual paper-based systems. It had been deliberately designed to be easy to use, so that specialist computer programming skills were not necessary and as many personnel as possible would be able to use it. This meant that inputs into the system would occur as and when a transaction occurred, rather than existing systems involving chits which were then sent to stores accountants for manual inputting into card indexes. With the successful trialling of Oasis, the project was expanded to include two more phases: Oasis II with cash management and catering and Oasis III for the management of engineering information.[73] This last development should have helped to resolve the dilemmas in implementing CBM.

By 1984 Oasis I had been fitted to seventeen warships, twelve shore establishments and three training installations, whilst Oasis II would start deploying in April 1985, with Oasis III arriving some time afterwards. Later work included more basic versions for minor war vessels, and the extension of the system to include armament stores.[74] Although at one level the computerisation of the Navy's support functions might appear to be a mundane change, it was also marked the beginning of an important shift towards a wholly 'digital navy'. How robust such systems would be in a conflict situation was not yet clear. When the new Type 23 frigate, HMS *Norfolk*, conducted first-of-class shock trials in 1993, her new Oasis system had to be landed prior to the trials as it was obvious that the equipment had not been designed to withstand the type of shock that could be induced by battle damage.[75] The digital navy was bringing many benefits, but it could also be adding vulnerabilities.

Out-of-Area Deployments

Group Deployments

By 1980 it had seemed that the annual group deployments that had taken place during much of the 1970s had run their course. As was seen in Chapter 11, the later deployments were often accompanied by indifference from the Foreign and Commonwealth Office and poor co-ordination with the defence industry to support arms sales. Despite this, the 1981 Defence Review had surprisingly given group deployments a new lease of life. They were mentioned in the 'Way Forward' command paper, and by the middle of 1981, planning was underway for a group deployment to the Indian Ocean and Australia led by *Invincible*, and another the following year to Latin America, including – ironically – planned ship visits to Argentina and the Falkland Islands.[76] It is not entirely clear why they were resuscitated by the Defence Secretary, but defence sales were clearly a driver in the planning. It is also possible that they were a response to United States' lobbying for a greater worldwide Royal Navy presence during the Defence Review.

The Falklands conflict put paid to the 1982 deployment, whilst it was clear that a Latin American group deployment in 1983 would be diplomatically out of the question. Instead, it was decided to capitalise on the positive outcome of the conflict and undertake a deployment in 1983 and early 1984 across the Indian Ocean and to Australia and East Asia. Named 'Orient Express 83/84', HMS *Invincible* would lead the group and be accompanied by four destroyers and frigates and a similar number of Royal Fleet Auxiliaries. The ships would transit through the Suez Canal, and make port visits in India, Malaysia, Singapore, Australia, New Zealand, The Philippines, South Korea, Japan, Hong Kong and a number of Pacific Island states. The Lebanon crisis (described below) came close to derailing the deployment entirely but the diversion of the force to stand off Lebanon did not in the event occur. Instead RAF Buccaneers and Phantoms were deployed to Cyprus, and Orient Express proceeded through the Canal and into the Indian Ocean. The visit to India was particularly successful: *Invincible* had just proved herself in the Falklands conflict, and this cachet gave the carrier and the group a certain celebrity status. Soon after a very positive visit to Bombay (now Mumbai), the Indian government placed orders for twelve Sea Harriers and in 1985 they would purchase HMS *Hermes* as a 'Harrier carrier' from which to fly these aircraft. After this point the fortunes of the group changed as *Invincible* developed serious problems with her port shaft which would require dry docking in Australia. This caused controversy given dockyard union resistance to the docking of a ship which was probably carrying nuclear weapons (*Invincible* had the capability to operate both WE177 freefall tactical nuclear weapons and anti-submarine nuclear depth bombs). The dry docking failed to resolve the problem and the crippled *Invincible* had to return home. Visits to Japan and South Korea by the carrier were cancelled, as were plans to fly out relatives of the crew to Singapore and Hong Kong which caused significant morale issues. The total time away from base port was nine months and Rear Admiral

Black, the Flag Officer leading the deployment, was certain that Orient Express, despite its diplomatic success in India and other countries, would have an impact on personnel retention as exhausted crew members decided to leave the sea-going life for good.[77]

Although the breakdown of HMS *Invincible* was an embarrassment, it did have the positive effect of shifting the policies of both Australia and Japan about docking ships that might have nuclear weapons on board. The United States was very keen to ensure that similar problems did not occur with any of its ships in the future, so an Australia/United Kingdom/United States agreement was signed that ensured that this would not happen again.[78] The embarrassment had been as much Australian as it was British, and in retrospect it had a role in helping to end a certain Australian ambiguity about nuclear issues since the early 1970s, and thus – in a small way – beginning to pave the way for the 2021 AUKUS nuclear submarine agreement many years later.[79]

The 1983 deployment had been sufficiently successful for another to be planned for 1986. This time the deployment would take a 'westabout' route, with a transit of the Panama Canal, involvement the US-led RIMPAC exercise, attendance at the Royal Australian Navy's 75th anniversary fleet review at Sydney, and then taking part in the first Saif Sareea exercise with Omani armed forces in December 1986. This last was a demonstration of the government's new commitment to 'out of area' operations and would have been almost unthinkable as a defence priority before the South Atlantic operation.[80] Named 'Global 86' the deployment was led by HMS *Illustrious*, accompanied by three destroyers and frigates and three RFAs, and a particular effort was made to visit states that had been left out of Orient Express, with Pakistan, Mauritius, Tanzania and even Jordan added to the planned itinerary. The deployment was shorter than its predecessor at seven and a half months. It managed to include 36 port visits in 25 countries, 100,000 members of the public visiting the ships involved, 110 TV slots and 250 newspaper articles. Even though *Illustrious* suffered a gearbox fire at the beginning of the deployment, she re-joined the rest of the group in the Indian Ocean four months later, missing the Pacific leg (including RIMPAC 86) but managing to attend the Australian fleet review and most of the other states on the Indian Ocean itinerary.[81]

The Global 86 deployment had been particularly successful in Australia, and as a result the Australian government had extended an invitation to the Royal Navy to attend Australia's bicentennial celebrations. The 1988 deployment would be led by HMS *Ark Royal*, and included within its escort would be HMS *Sirius*, the namesake of one of the ships in Australia's 'First Fleet' of ships that had arrived to settle the future country in 1788. This deployment would take a standard route through Suez, and include visits to China and Japan, as well as involvement in two major Five Power Defence Arrangements Exercises in July and September 1988.[82] The Australian focus of this deployment was made specific in its name: 'Outback 88' and it was much more focussed on South East Asian port visits, including Singapore, Australia, The Philippines, Brunei, Malaysia, Indonesia. Visits were also made to Hong Kong (but not Japan or South Korea) and to Sri Lanka, India and Pakistan. Although *Ark Royal* had an Olympus turbine changed during the group deployment, this had a little impact on her itinerary, although the escorting destroyer HMS *Edinburgh* had to have propeller repairs undertaken in dry dock in Sydney.[83]

The post-Falklands group deployments were much more successful and higher profile affairs than those of the 1970s. It helped that the United Kingdom, following the Falklands conflict, was no longer considered a country in decline, and that the deployments were led by aircraft carriers rather than aged cruisers or obsolescent 'County' class destroyers. By deploying every three years, they did not tax the resources of the Royal Navy beyond what it could bear, and had the advantage of being seen as major events by the port cities that received the ships, rather than an annual routine. Defence sales continued to be important to these deployments, with a more professional approach than in the 1970s, which now encompassed glossy brochures and a more engaged Foreign and Commonwealth Office.[84]

The Gulf: Operations 'Armilla', 'Cimnel' and 'Calendar'
Between 1980 and 1984, the Armilla Patrol had been a relatively low-key operational deployment. As was described in Chapter 11, it began as a two-ship deployment under extremely restrictive rules of engagement. The ships generally remained outside the Gulf but aimed to 'maintain a British presence and give ships, particularly British ships, confidence that assistance is available if required' but 'without giving credence to any rumours that military intervention was planned'.[85] The ships which were due protection from Royal Navy vessels – which took the form of 'accompaniment' rather than convoying – were British-registered ships, British dependent territory registered ships (which included Hong Kong and Bermuda-registered vessels), and ships which were wholly or predominantly British-owned. This last criterion was because of the complex and often changing nature of ownership and chartering in the shipping industry, which was extremely difficult to discern in practice.[86]

In order to ensure that two warships were available on patrol at any one time, four ships had to be deployed East of Suez. Whilst two were on patrol, the other two would be either at, or on passage to or from, a scheduled maintenance period at Mombasa in Kenya. After a 28-day patrol, the first two ships would be relieved by the two returning from Mombasa, and they would then in turn go to Mombasa for maintenance. Each pair of ships would spend a total of 84 days with Armilla (one 28-day patrol, one 28-day period for maintenance, and a second 28-day patrol) before returning to the United Kingdom via the Suez Canal.[87] From 1982 to early 1984 this patrol pattern was scaled back: at that time the Iran-Iraq War was not providing a major threat to merchant shipping. As a result, only two ships were East of Suez most of the time, spending 30 per cent of their time at two days' steaming from the patrol area. The rest of the time, the ships undertook port visits and exercised with friendly navies. The Omani armed forces proved particularly helpful in this regard: exercising with the vessels with their British-built Jaguar aircraft, and providing exchange officers for the two ships.[88] During and after the Falklands conflict, when most of the Navy's destroyers and frigates were either in the South Atlantic, in transit or under repair after the fighting, the Royal New Zealand Navy provided two of its frigates on rotation to the Armilla patrol in place of British ships; a gesture that was greatly appreciated by the British government.[89] Via the General Council of British Shipping, and their equivalents in Hong Kong and Bermuda, the Director of Naval Operations and Trade provided guidance notes for owners and masters of merchant ships, along with regular updates on the war, advice on how to respond when challenged by Iranian craft, and recommendations for defending their ships against attack.[90] The links with the shipping industry, which had been sustained in order to support Cold War exercises and transition to war planning, were now being used in very different circumstances to support merchant shipping in the Gulf.

At the start of 1984 the situation began to change, as what became known as the 'Tanker War' began. Iraq had been suffering in the land campaign, and in order to keep the pressure on the Iranians, it decided to step up its campaign to attack commercial shipping ferrying Iranian oil in the Gulf. Using French-built Mirage strike aircraft armed with Exocet anti-ship missiles and Soviet-built 'Badger' bombers armed with Silkworm missiles, the Iraqis attacked tankers within an exclusion zone near the Iranian coast, which included their main oil terminal on Kharg island. The Iranians lacked sufficient numbers of air defence aircraft to both support the land campaign and defend shipping, so they escalated the naval campaign by stating that any ships suspected of carrying Iraqi oil would be attacked by Iranian naval or Revolutionary Guard maritime forces, whether they were inside or outside the exclusion zone. As the Iraqis lacked a shipping industry, their oil was generally transported via Kuwaiti or other Gulf states' ships, which meant direct attacks on the shipping or wider interests of the other Gulf states. Before 1984 most Gulf shipping had not been affected by the conflict between Iran and Iraq, but now almost all of it could be at risk, especially as the Iranians often lacked the means to determine clearly whether ships were, or were not, carrying Iraqi oil. Through 1985 and 1986 this tanker war gradually escalated further as the Iraqis attempted to counter setbacks in the land war (including the loss of their only access to sea as a result of Iranian advances in the Al Faw Peninsula) by escalating their attacks on shipping further, and the Iranians responded in kind by ramping up their own attacks on shipping, in particular on Kuwaiti vessels. A second level of naval escalation employed by the Iranians was the use of mine warfare from January 1987 as Iranian fishing vessels were used to lay mines near off the coasts of Oman, the United Arab Emirates and Qatar.[91]

The first response of the British government to the Tanker War was to place the patrol back onto its original four ship (two on/two off) footing, increase the armament requirements for ships on the patrol, and – initially at least – only permit entry into the Gulf after ministerial approval. The enhanced armament requirements meant that only Sea Wolf or Sea Dart and Phalanx -armed ships, with increased electronic warfare capabilities, could be deployed on the patrol.[92] This excluded most *Leander* class and all Type 21 frigates, just as the patrol requirement was increasing. For the next four years, the demands of Operation 'Armilla' would primarily be borne by the more modern and capable ships in the fleet, reducing the time they had available to take part in NATO exercises and other Cold War, Eastern Atlantic, activities. The requirement for Ministerial approval before entering the Gulf also proved impracticable, not least because it could prevent or unnecessarily delay a naval response to a distress signal, thus potentially breaching the International Convention for the Safety of Life at Sea. It would also, more significantly, delay a response to a request for support from a merchant ship. As it became clear that the increase in attacks would be sustained, the Rules of Engagement were loosened somewhat, even if the approach was still cautious: 'Action is to be avoided whenever possible. Defensive fire in response to deliberate attack on HM Ships or ships entitled to RN protection is not to be opened unless it is immediately necessary in self-defence ... the force used should be that necessary to protect HM Ships and the lives of her men.'[93] Ships were however permitted to lock their fire-control radars onto aircraft or ships acting with hostile intent, something which had not been permitted under the previous Rules. A year later, the Rules of Engagement were tweaked again, this time to allow force to be used to protect not only HM Ships and their crews but also the ships and crews of protected vessels. It was now possible, five years into the patrol, for Armilla ships to engage in activities that could meaningfully protect shipping that came under Iranian attack.[94]

Fears that the Iranians were starting a mining campaign caused the activation in March 1984 of a contingency plan that had been in place since 1980 to send minehunters to the Gulf. Operation 'Armilla Accomplice' resulted in four 'Ton' class minehunters, *Brinton*, *Wilton*, *Kirkliston* and *Gavinton*, being sent into the Mediterranean, led by the MV *Oil Endeavour*, an oil rig support ship taken up from trade to act as command and support ship to the small force with Naval Party 1015 embarked. The lack of availability of HMS *Abdiel*, which would normally have undertaken this role, had meant that a STUFT option had been necessary.[95] In the event, the expected Iranian mining campaign did not occur so the small force reached the Mediterranean but was reassigned to support Egypt in continued clearance operations in the Gulf of Suez. Operation 'Harling', as it was called, therefore became in effect a successor to Operations 'Rheostat I' and 'II' of 1975–6 described in Chapter 9. A number of mines were detected and made safe by the minehunters over two months, and the operation ended in October 1985.[96]

Further intensifications of Iranian activity at the end of 1986 and the start of 1987 resulted in further changes in the role and posture of the 'Armilla' ships. In November 1986, British warships operating under Operation 'Armilla' entered the Gulf for the first time to accompany a British merchant ship. The patrol area was extended and now included a portion beyond the Straits of Hormuz and within the Gulf.[97] The nature of the threat meant that the two ships would patrol together when this was practicable, and the patrol was enhanced by the addition of a third 'back-up' ship in the Arabian Sea (which did not have to be Sea Wolf or Sea Dart armed). It could undertake the regional engagement activities that were now impossible for the two front-line ships, as well as providing additional support in the patrol area in the event of an emergency.[98] There would now be up to six destroyers or frigates East of Suez operating under Operation 'Armilla', the largest number of escorts permanently operating beyond the Suez Canal since the early 1970s. The Rules of Engagement were loosened again, by the addition of a new definition of self-defence as actions 'necessary to meet an attack or imminent threat which cannot be met in other ways and [which is] proportional to the attack or threat'.[99]

The Iranian use of mines to disable tankers and other ships from 1987, resulted in the decision to send a mine hunting force under Operation 'Cimnel', the successor to 'Armilla Accomplice'. The 'Hunt' class mine countermeasures vessels, *Brecon, Bicester, Brocklesby* and *Hurworth* sailed on 17 August and arrived in the Gulf on 21 September, this time with HMS *Abdiel* as support and command ship.[100] Almost as soon as they had arrived on station, the United States Navy requested their use to clear mines, after helicopters from the USS *Jarrett* had intercepted and damaged the Iranian minelayer *Iran Ajr* after it was found laying mines north-west of Bahrain. US Rules of Engagement were much less restrictive than those of the Royal Navy, and by this stage of the campaign the US Navy was undertaking offensive operations against Iranian naval vessels. US forces boarded the ship, gathered intelligence, detained the surviving crew members and scuttled the burnt-out vessel.[101] The mine warfare vessels arrived in the former location of the *Iran Ajr* on 29 September to undertake their first clearance operation, with 'Armilla' vessels in attendance for protection.[102]

This operation, combined with an earlier attack on the Hong Kong registered vessel, the MV *Gentle Breeze*, resulted in a full review of the Rules of Engagement for both the 'Armilla' and 'Cimnel' forces. Although the presence was still described as 'de-escalatory' and remained a purely 'national' task to avoid too close an association with the United States and its much more aggressive policy towards Iran, two changes to the Rules of Engagement were proposed. Up until this point, Royal Navy ships could only act against a vessel laying mines if it 'constituted an immediate threat' to HM ships or to a merchant ship entitled to RN accompaniment. However, the recent US actions – which had been heavily reported in the news – had created an expectation among the British public that British naval action might be similarly robust. As a result, it was recommended that the definition of 'imminent threat' be expanded to include the authority of a ship's commanding officer to use proportionate force against a minelaying vessel if it had not responded to clear warnings.[103] Other changes included a clearer emphasis on the importance of timely self-defence: aircraft approaching in an attack profile could be engaged within three nautical miles and Armilla ships could also attack aircraft that were providing targeting information for missile-launching aircraft.[104]

In the spring and summer of 1988, it did, for a time, appear that the Iran-Iraq war could escalate even further. The mining of a US frigate, the *Samuel B Roberts*, in April 1988 resulted in a large scale retaliatory attack by the US Navy, Operation 'Praying Mantis', which destroyed three Iranian Navy warships including the frigate *Sahand* and two oil rigs.[105] The 'Cimnel' force was tasked with clearing the minefields that had damaged the *Roberts*, and it included one minehunter each from the Netherlands and Belgian Navies, who were now working alongside the Royal Navy to clear mines under Operation Calendar.[106] The mistaken destruction of an Iranian airliner by the US cruiser *Vincennes*[107] in July could have marked a further stage in escalation, but the continued stalemate on the battlefield combined with the growing risk of full conflict with the United States pushed the Iranians into negotiating a ceasefire with the Iraqis in the following month.[108]

Only a few weeks after the ceasefire the destroyer HMS *Southampton* was involved in a collision with the MV *Tor Bay* whilst preparing to accompany the ship. The tanker's bow caused flooding and considerable damage to the ship's Sea Dart magazine, and after her ammunition was removed she was returned to the United Kingdom on the *Mighty Servant I* heavy lift vessel.[109] With the end of the war, the Armilla patrol remained in place but reduced to two vessels, which were now free to visit ports in the northern Gulf. The

Operation 'Cimnel' force was withdrawn, although with a commitment to return to region if necessary.[110] With the Iraqi invasion of Kuwait only 20 months later, the mine warfare force would soon return, with additional destroyers and frigates under Operation 'Granby', but that falls outside the remit of this book.

During the conflict only two British-registered, two Bermudan-registered and two Hong Kong-registered vessels were hit in attacks by either Iran or Iraq.[111] There were four other 'entitled ships' which were hit, overseas-registered but assessed to be British-owned. Those hit by Iraqi forces (two Bermudan-registered and two overseas-registered) had deliberately decided to sail outside the designated Armilla patrol areas. A total of 1,020 entitled ships were accompanied by British warships between January 1986 and November 1988 through some of the most dangerous waters near the Straits of Hormuz. None of these suffered any damage, and in no circumstances did British warships find it necessary fire their weapons.[112] Although deliberately low-key, the restrained approach, combined with a judicious and gradual adjustment of the Rules of Engagement as warfare escalated, served to protect British interests as a neutral in the conflict between Iran and Iraq whilst also upholding freedom of the seas and the passage of vital world trade.

Lebanon: Operation 'Offcut'
In the 1980s the Mediterranean regained an importance it had not had since the 1960s as a transit zone between East of Suez duties and home waters. Emergencies in the Mediterranean Sea could therefore be met either by ships in transit, or by ships at or near Gibraltar which might either be passing to or from the Falklands, or involved in NATO exercises in the Azores or the mouth of the Mediterranean. The deteriorating situation in Lebanon in 1983 resulted in the despatch of two ships from Gibraltar on 18 November 1983 under Operation 'Offcut'. The older HMS *Glamorgan* was able to arrive off Lebanon first on the 22nd as she had greater endurance at higher speed, whilst the new frigate, HMS *Brazen*, arrived a day later. Their role was to support the small British peacekeeping force ('BRITFORLEB') in Lebanon, and if necessary evacuate the force, as tensions reached boiling point following the assassination of the president-elect in September and the attack on the US and French peacekeeping headquarters which killed 241 US and 58 French personnel on 23 October.

BRITFORLEB had arrived in February that year to take part in a four-nation Multi-National Force ('MNF') which was meant to support the implementation of a US-negotiated peace plan. BRITFORLEB comprised just over 100 personnel based in Hadath in the outskirts of east Beirut. *Glamorgan* and *Brazen* were tasked with providing logistic support for the

British peacekeepers as normal port and road routes were no longer safe. Consideration was also given to providing 'recreational breaks' for groups of fifty peacekeepers on board the warships. RAF Wessexes based in Cyprus were able to ferry stores from that island to the British warships, but because these aircraft were only search and rescue helicopters, their aircrew were not trained in the tactical low-level flying necessary to minimise the risks of attack from militants on the ground in Lebanon. The logistical stores were therefore transferred to *Glamorgan* and *Brazen*, and then to their RN Lynx helicopters for flying to Hadath. Twenty-six such sorties were undertaken by the naval helicopters under 'extremely testing operational conditions'.[113] Luckily no Lynxes were attacked but one helicopter was damaged by a collision with a wire during low-flying manoeuvres on 24 November. Plans to ferry soldiers to the two ships for recreational breaks were 'put on ice' on 23 October as it was felt that the risks being run ferrying such large numbers of troops, combined with placing the ships only 20 miles off the coast so that they could receive them as quickly as possible, were too great.[114]

Glamorgan and *Brazen* only remained on station for five days until they were replaced by the assault ship *Fearless* escorted by the frigates *Andromeda* and *Achilles* and supported by RFA *Grey Rover* (in transit from Armilla duties). *Fearless* would be much better equipped to manage an evacuation, whilst the two frigates were deemed to be necessary as a Libyan 'Foxtrot' class submarine was known to be operating the area, and might be tempted to attack the naval forces from many countries now operating off the Lebanese coast. Soon, RAF Chinooks had been flown to Cyprus, and these were able to take over much of the logistics role from the naval helicopters: they had much greater capacity and would therefore need to undertake the journey less often, thus reducing the risks of attack from the ground. By the end of the first week of December, the Libyan 'Foxtrot' had left the area so the two frigates were returned to their previous duties. *Fearless* was now operating further away from Lebanon whilst her Commando Sea Kings were largely tasked with ferrying fuel for BRITFORLEB's Ferret patrol cars. The 'recreational breaks' which were now called 'dormitory options' (reflecting their main role was now to provide a good night's sleep for beleaguered peacekeepers) were undertaken for three nights. The extractions occurred at 1600 Beirut time and the returns from *Fearless* at 0800 the next morning. *Fearless* came closer to Lebanon in order to make the flights as rapid as possible. After this, the fighting near Hadath reduced somewhat, and considerable efforts were made to improve the safety and habitability of the facilities at the small peacekeeping base and at the British Embassy. On 11 January 1984 *Fearless* was relieved by RFA *Reliant*, the ARAPAHO helicopter carrier described in Chapter 17, which had been diverted from her first deployment to the Falklands.[115]

The situation had not improved in either December or January: the Lebanese government was less able to assert its authority, whilst US forces had bombed and shelled Syrian positions in Lebanon after the Syrian forces had fired at US reconnaissance aircraft, and any form of peace agreement seemed further away than ever. US and French public opinion was unlikely to support their troops remaining in Lebanon when the situation was at risk of becoming even more dangerous. As a result, it was decided to withdraw MNF to ships offshore and then once this was done, disband the force and leave residual monitoring and peacekeeping efforts to the small UN peacekeeping force which was already in place. Given the deteriorating security situation this evacuation did run the risk of, in the Foreign Secretary's words, 'precipitating a bloodbath' if it went wrong, so considerable time was spent planning how it would work.[116] A roll-on roll-off ship was chartered to load up the peacekeeping force's Ferret armoured cars from the port of Jounieh, whilst the remaining personnel would be air-lifted by Chinook from Hadath and onto RFA *Reliant*, and then from *Reliant* to Cyprus. British diplomatic personnel and other citizens would leave from west Beirut. RAF Phantoms and Buccaneers operating from Cyprus would be held at readiness in case the situation deteriorated.[117] In the event, the operation proceeded without difficulty: the militants were happy for the foreigners to leave and thought better of a confrontation. All the British peacekeepers had left by helicopter for RFA *Reliant* or by a chartered ship with their vehicles by the end of 8 February.[118] Although very much a tri-service operation that benefitted considerably from the relative closeness of British bases in Cyprus, naval forces had played a crucial role in the first days of the crisis by providing a first response capability until the right land-based air capabilities became available, and at the end by providing the reception platform for the evacuated forces.

South Yemen: Operation 'Balsac'
Two years later another evacuation operation was undertaken, but this time in the Arabian Sea, much further away from British bases: it gained much more publicity than Operation 'Offcut' and involved similar dangers and uncertainties. On 13 January 1986, a faction within the Soviet-backed government of South Yemen attempted a coup to overthrow the president, Abdul Fattah Ismail. Fighting within the capital, Aden City, and the approach of rebel tanks along the isthmus that separated the core of the capital from the mainland, meant that the route to the airport was cut off and the evacuation of foreign civilians became an urgent necessity.[119] The nearest Royal Navy vessel was HMY *Britannia*, on passage to support a Royal visit to Australia and New Zealand (with no members of the Royal Family on board at the time).[120] She arrived off Aden on 15 January, and was joined two days later

by the frigate *Jupiter*, which had been detached from Armilla patrol duties. Rear Admiral John Garnier, the Flag Officer Royal Yachts, led the British evacuation force, which was joined by the destroyer *Newcastle*, survey vessel *Hydra* and RFA *Brambleleaf*.[121]

The Soviets had the largest number of foreign nationals in the city; their embassy was in the greatest danger as it was positioned on the isthmus, and their ships were already conducting an evacuation of their own nationals when *Britannia* arrived. *Britannia* anchored off Khormaksar, the part of the city that covered the isthmus and its beaches. The ship's boats went ashore on the 18th and a total of 152 foreign civilians were evacuated this way from the beaches to the Royal Yacht until the fighting reached the embarkation points. The 160 remaining civilians awaiting the boats were guided into the Soviet embassy compound for their safety. From the 19th, negotiations were started with those authorities still operating ashore such as Aden's harbourmaster, discussions which were helped considerably by the arrival of the British Ambassador and Vice Consul in *Newcastle*. *Britannia* then started her second evacuation, this time from the city of Zinjibar to the east of Aden. The MV *Diamond Express* had been chartered by the British government and was also being used in the evacuations, supporting *Newcastle* off Al Mukalla much further up the coast. The evacuees were then ferried to Djibouti, allowing the ships to return to pick up more people. More were picked up from Aden City and from the oil refinery jetties at Little Aden to the west, whilst HMS *Hydra* evacuated foreign nationals at the city of Nishtun close to the Omani border. By the 22nd the fighting had eased sufficiently for the remaining foreign nationals stuck in Khormaksar to be convoyed by road to jetties at the Port of Aden to be picked up by ships' boats. With the attempted coup nearing defeat, the airport was then re-opened and the remaining foreign nationals still wishing to leave departed by air.[122]

A total of 1,379 foreign nationals had been evacuated by British ships during Operation 'Balsac' with 640 being evacuated by *Britannia* and *Jupiter* between the 17th and 19th, and the rest being evacuated by all the ships involved on the 22nd and 23rd.[123] A further 5,000 were evacuated by the Soviets and 300 by the French.[124] Initially, the Soviet naval forces were unwilling to co-operate with British and other Western ships but communications improved as the evacuations continued. The vast majority of those evacuated were neither British nor Western.[125] The largest number of foreign nationals taken aboard the British vessels were 211 Indians, 185 Pakistanis, 163 Filipinos and 109 Chinese. One hundred and three British were evacuated, alongside 58 French and 56 Danes, with the other significant nationalities represented being Sudanese, Bangladeshi, Egyptian and Brazilian.[126] From the perspective of Admiral Garnier, the most important lesson from the evacuation was that it was not possible to evacuate 'selectively' in such circumstances and that taking on board large numbers from many countries had to be expected and planned for from the start.[127] The success of the British evacuation had been partly down to the unusual nature of *Britannia*: the South Yemeni authorities only permitted her arrival at Aden because 'she was so obviously not a warship (and therefore [not] a threat to combatants ashore)'. Her large numbers of ships' boats, considerable space on board and wide range of 'sophisticated communications facilities' meant that she was ideally suited for the operation that then unfolded.[128]

The Caribbean and West Africa
The 1980s saw an important shift in the Royal Navy's operations in the Caribbean. Throughout the 1960s and 1970s the West Indies Squadron, and its successor, the Belize Guardship, had undertaken a variety of roles, many of which had supported Britain's many colonies in the region during the transition to independence. As was seen in Chapters 9 and 17 this might involve standing offshore over the horizon ready to provide support to local police if disturbances broke out, or to be a visible presence anchored within sight of major settlements or placed alongside. With only a handful of territories remaining, the West Indies Guardship (renamed after the independence of Belize in 1981) increasingly focussed on two quite separate tasks from the late 1980s: counter-narcotics patrols in partnership with the United States Coastguard and relief work during the annual hurricane season as these storms became more devastating and their impact on the islands of the region greater.[129]

In 1983 the largest British naval force to visit Belize since the 1960s took place, as *Invincible* and the large destroyer *Bristol* visited the newly-independent state and undertook a series of exercises alongside the British garrison. The port visit to Belize was the most southerly part of an itinerary that included port visits along the eastern seaboard of the United States and a series of trials at AUTEC in the Bahamas during February and March.[130] The successful Falklands campaign probably had a significant deterrent effect on any Guatemalan thoughts about a possible invasion of Belize, and during the 1980s tensions did ease somewhat, with the Guardship being used to host regular liaison discussions between Guatemalan military commanders and the Commander of British Forces Belize under Operation 'Nolan'.[131] However, tensions did not dissipate entirely: in November 1988 the survey ship *Fawn* was fired upon by a Guatemalan patrol craft as the former undertook surveys to confirm the borders of the territorial waters and Exclusive Economic Zone of the two states.[132] This incident appears to have been isolated, and as was noted in Chapter 17, five years later the British garrison was withdrawn, although

Belize has continued to host visits by British army contingents undertaking jungle training.

In the same year as the *Invincible* visit, Grenada, following a coup by Communist-backed forces in October 1983, was invaded by a United States amphibious force and the government removed. Even though Grenada was a member of the British Commonwealth, the US did not inform the British government in advance. The destroyer *Antrim*, which was acting as West Indies Guardship at the time and fortuitously had the Flag Officer Second Flotilla ('FOF2') flying his flag on board, had not been far away and had stood offshore ready to help evacuate British citizens if the coup descended into civil strife or the Communists sought to expel Western citizens. *Antrim* saw the arrival of the US force and observed the landings at a distance, and during these early days provided the British government with its only reliable information on the US invasion. As the military situation steadied – opposition by Cuban forces on the island had initially been stronger than expected by US military commanders – FOF2 visited the US flagship and liaised with US military commanders, relaying the information he could glean back to Whitehall.[133] In February 1986, HMS *Apollo* stood off Haiti ready to evacuate British nationals under Operation 'Cosmos' as protests mounted against Jean-Claude 'Baby Doc' Duvalier's regime, but these proved unnecessary after Duvalier fled the island and tensions decreased. The frigate was stood down on 21 February.[134]

1985 and 1986 marked the start of an important transition for the British naval presence in the Caribbean, as a major political crisis began to take shape on the British overseas territory of the Turks and Caicos islands to the east of the Bahamas. The Chief Minister of the Turks and Caicos, Norman Saunders, along with legislature members Stafford Misick and Aulden 'Smokey' Smith, were arrested in Miami and charged with facilitating drug smuggling on the islands on 5 March 1985.[135] As Saunders refused to resign, causing a constitutional crisis, and concerns grew about stability on the island, the West Indies Guardship, HMS *Arrow*, was placed over the horizon under Operation 'Eschew', ready to intervene should the Governor request.[136] On New Year's Eve that year, a government building was burnt down, which was linked to drugs trafficking and corruption by politicians and officials. A QC was sent from the United Kingdom to undertake an enquiry and his report stated that the Chief Minister and other ministers were unfit to hold public office. In June 1986, in anticipation of possible disturbances following the announcement of the findings, the new Guardship HMS *Apollo* was ordered proceed to the Turks and Caicos and remain there in support of the Governor until tensions lessened.[137] In the event it was found that the conspirators numbered less than fifty and after a few days *Apollo* was able to leave and was held within 72 hours steaming from the Turks and Caicos for another week.[138] These deployments were very similar to the numerous military aid to civil government operations undertaken in previous decades in the Caribbean, but the Turks and Caicos crises heralded the beginnings of a major shift. Since the 1970s, US Coastguard vessels had been attempting to intercept drug smugglers arriving in the USA by sea and by air.[139] Following such clear evidence of drug trafficking on a British overseas territory, it is unsurprising that during 1987 and 1988, the Foreign and Commonwealth Office worked with US government agencies to undertake a 'Drugs Survey' of the Caribbean. It covered both British overseas territories and former colonies, many of which still had legal and law enforcement links with the United Kingdom.[140] Recommendations that flowed from this survey included training programmes, improved forensics in the region and increased joint operations with US, British and local authorities.[141] It was also suggested that 'more use [should be made] of ... coastguard vessels (and US/UK ships)' in the region,[142] and it was not long before Royal Navy vessels were involved in such counter-narcotics work.

As a precursor to this new tasking, in January 1987, HMS *Cardiff* on Guardship duties was alerted by a yacht to the ditching of a light aircraft half a mile away from the Jamaican coast. When the destroyer arrived on the scene there was only aircraft debris floating on the surface accompanied by forty-six large bales of marijuana estimated to be worth up to £500,000.[143] Just over a year later, Royal Navy warships were operating alongside US Coastguard cutters as part of Operation 'Ocean Tracker'.[144] US Coastguard officers would be embarked on board the Guardship, and the British ship's radars and operations room would help direct US high speed cutters onto targets for interception and inspection. The first success in which a British warship was involved occurred in April 1988 when the Ice Patrol Ship, HMS *Endurance*, temporarily detached to the Caribbean, joined with USCGC *Escanaba* to locate smugglers' boats, the latter finding six tons of marijuana on the *Luz Maria* on 27 April.[145] In the autumn of 1989, HMS *Alacrity*, accompanied by RFA *Brambleleaf*, ran the *Miss Beverly Ann* to a stop, which was subsequently boarded by USCGC *Petrel*. 14,000lb of marijuana were found, and its crew of three was arrested.[146] Co-operation with the US Coastguard had clearly reached a marked closeness after only a short time working together under Operation 'Ocean Tracker'. Operation 'Seawolf', where foreign ships operated with Colombian naval headquarters ashore to track and locate helicopters, aircraft and boats was somewhat less successful, as a notable 'cooling-off' of co-operation with Colombian authorities had been evident during the late 1980s.[147]

In the closing years of the 1980s the annual Caribbean hurricanes became stronger and caused much more damage across the region. Hurricane Gilbert in 1989 was the first of these more devastating storms and HMS *Active* was able to provide help to the government of Jamaica after the hurricane. The ship's crew cleared debris, reroofed vital buildings, helped restore services including electricity and provided 1,750 meals a day to those whose houses had been damaged. The ship's Lynx helicopter also undertook medical evacuation duties to ferry injured people from around the island to hospital.[148] The next year, when Hurricane Hugo struck, HMS *Alacrity* provided help and support to the overseas territory of Montserrat which had been hit hard by the storm: the island's main jetty had been washed away, the only runway was blocked by debris, all telephone and radio communications had been lost, the power station had been flooded and disabled, the mains water was not working, the hospital badly damaged and 95 per cent of the island's buildings had suffered roof damage. On 18 September, *Alacrity* anchored off Montserrat and emergency relief supplies along with 100 of the ship's crew were transferred to the island by helicopter, the weather still being too rough to use the ship's boats. Work began to repair the power station's generator and re-roof its building, the hospital was re-roofed as well and an emergency generator started whilst six miles of roadway were cleared between the capital Plymouth and the airport. *Alacrity* was joined by the French patrol ship *Capricieuse* and the US Coastguard Cutter *Dauntless*, and by 20 September the runway had been cleared and a US Hercules was able to land more supplies on the island, followed by an RAF Hercules once the US aircraft had shown that such a landing was safe. By the 22nd the weather had improved sufficiently for personnel and supplies to be ferried by boat as personnel from all three ships continued to restore vital services. On the 24th a new temporary jetty was constructed to allow the landing of more supplies to support disaster relief. With both the runway and jetty repaired and basic service restored, *Alacrity* returned to normal duties.[149] The Royal Navy's response to Hurricanes Gilbert and Hugo were the first instances of what would be many such hurricane and disaster relief operations in the Caribbean up to the present day.

The West African coast, with its former British colonies long since independent, was generally seen as a transit zone for British warships steaming to or from their Falklands patrols during the 1980s. However, the beginning of the long-running civil war in Liberia put foreign nationals at risk of being caught up in the fighting as rebels began to besiege the capital Monrovia, the head of the Liberian Army fled and the military began to collapse.[150] US forces under Operation 'Sharp Edge' and two British frigates, HM Ships *Andromeda* and *Phoebe*, under Operation 'Eldorado', stood offshore for five weeks in anticipation of conducting evacuations, that might have mirrored Operations 'Offcut' and 'Balsac' in their complexity and danger. The US force was built around a significant amphibious capability, which would have provided the main means of removing civilians, but the two British frigates included small detachments of Royal Marines and would have been able to bring people from ashore with their helicopters or ships' boats. It soon became apparent that no more than 100 evacuees were expected (60 British subjects and 40 from countries for which the UK had consular responsibility).[151] In the event, the two frigates were stood down on 21 July 1990, after it became clear that the sixty British subjects would be 'staying put', that consular obligations had been discharged, and it had been agreed that US, if necessary, would evacuate British subjects if they so wished.[152] A month later an African-led peacekeeping force was landed in Monrovia and helped stabilise the situation, but not before US naval forces had evacuated their diplomats and citizens as fighting intensified in the weeks before the peacekeepers arrived.[153]

Hong Kong

The British naval presence in Hong Kong underwent significant changes during the 1980s: not only did the shape of the small naval force change considerably, but the attitude of the Hong Kong government underwent a dramatic change following the signing of the Sino-British Joint Declaration in December 1984. As was described in Chapter 9, five new Hong Kong patrol craft were built in Britain to replace the elderly 'Ton' class minesweepers. The five craft aimed not only to replace the 'Tons', but also to have some of the capabilities of the former guardship, HMS *Chichester*, which had departed in 1976. They had a medium gun and a speed close to that of a frigate. The construction and operation were 75 per cent funded by the Hong Kong government and their capabilities fitted those requested by the then governor, who wanted vessels which would able to warn off Chinese warships from Hong Kong waters. However, just as the new force of patrol vessels were entering service, the political environment changed radically.

The signing of the Sino-British Joint Declaration, which confirmed that the United Kingdom would hand back both Hong Kong and the New Territories in 1997, meant that Chinese naval vessels were no longer attempting incursions, removing one of the main roles for the craft. In addition, the Hong Kong Legislative Council was soon to be given more powers and as a result decisions made by the Hong Kong government were placed under much greater scrutiny and with much less deference to London's wishes.[154] The new governor questioned the need for these expensive vessels (despite the fact that they had been largely designed to meet criteria set by his predecessor), whilst the Hong Kong Police emphasised the extent to which their own small craft could undertake many of the roles for which the Royal Navy craft had been procured.[155] Pressure was placed on the other armed services on the island as well: the Hong Kong government was keen that British Army patrols on the border were replaced by police patrols as much as possible. With the handover only 13 years away, there was now much greater self-assertion by the local Hong Kong authorities, and a quiet awareness that any British military personnel in place in 1997 would be replaced by People's Liberation Army personnel. A smaller British military establishment would also mean, it was optimistically hoped, a smaller Chinese military presence after the handover.[156]

As a result, two of the five patrol craft were returned to the United Kingdom in 1988. It was hoped that the two craft might be used for Operation 'Grenada' patrols off Northern Ireland, but the Hong Kong government was keen for sales receipts for the two vessels (of which they would receive 75 per cent), so these almost new warships were eventually sold to the Irish Navy instead.[157] The three remaining vessels were fitted with facilities for fast launches as a partial compensation for the loss of their two sisters, and to make them more useful in support of the Hong Kong Police.[158] In a sign of the changing times, it was even queried whether the three remaining boats could be refitted by a Hong Kong shipyard owned by a Chinese state-owned company. The request was refused.[159] The Tiananmen Square uprising in 1989 increased Hong Kong concerns about the pending Chinese handover,[160] but the trajectory of the colony had been set and eight years later Hong Kong became a Special Administrative District of China, and the last three patrol craft were sold to the Philippines.

Leadership

After nearly four years as First Sea Lord, Admiral Staveley was replaced by Admiral Sir Julian Oswald. He in turn was replaced as Commander-in-Chief Fleet by Admiral Sir Benjamin Bathurst, a former helicopter pilot who had been naval assistant to the First Sea Lord in 1976, had been Director of Naval Air Warfare in the Naval Staff and then Flag Officer Second Flotilla. He would succeed Oswald as First Sea Lord in 1993. Bathurst had previously held the post of Chief of Fleet Support, and he was replaced by Vice Admiral Sir Jock Slater, a navigator by training and former commanding officer of HMS *Illustrious*, who would later follow in Bathurst's footsteps as Commander-in-Chief Fleet and then First Sea Lord. Admiral Sir Sandy Woodward, the commander of the Falklands task force, succeeded Admiral Stanford as Commander-in-Chief Naval Home Command in 1987, and he in turn would be succeeded by a fellow Falklands veteran, Admiral Sir Jeremy Black, former captain of *Invincible*, in 1989. The long-serving Controller, Admiral Sir Derek Reffell, retired in 1989 and he was replaced by Admiral Sir Kenneth Eaton, a weapons engineer who had spent considerable portions of his career at the Admiralty Surface Weapons Establishment before taking leading posts in underwater warfare, and then becoming Flag Officer Portsmouth in 1987. He would be only the second engineer to hold the post of Controller. Admiral Fitch was replaced by Admiral Sir Brian Brown as Second Sea Lord, a Fleet Air Arm pilot who had changed branches to become a supply officer half way through his career, rising to be the Secretary to the First Sea Lord between 1979 and 1982. Having held a number of senior personnel posts in the past, Brown therefore became the first personnel specialist to be Second Sea Lord.[161] These changes saw a welcome return of Fleet Air Arm, submariner, engineer and supply officers to the Navy Board, and it would be these senior officers who would lead the Navy as the Cold War ended.

The Soviet Navy under Glasnost[162]

Confidence-building
The arrival of Mikhail Gorbachev as General Secretary of the Communist Party of the USSR saw a rapid thawing in superpower relations at the diplomatic level. Gorbachev and President Reagan relaunched strategic arms limitation talks and signed the Intermediate-range Nuclear Forces Treaty in December 1987. Domestically, Gorbachev attempted to reform the Soviet economy, bring in elements of pluralism into government and reduce censorship.

Multiple links began to be made between East and West during 1987 and 1988, and one of these resulted in a consultation in Moscow in April 1988 that had been organised by two think tanks: one British, the Foundation for International Security, and one American, the American Committee for US-Soviet Relations. This then led to an agreement that confidence-building talks on naval issues could be productive. Stanley Windass, of the Foundation for International Security, offered his house in the village of Adderbury in Oxfordshire, and in July 1988 a delegation led by Admiral Nikolai Amel'ko, a retired former Deputy Chief of the General Staff, arrived at Windass's house to launch a secret dialogue with the aim of furthering understanding and diffusing tensions between the two sides.[163] These discussions were clearly only a first step, but what was also obvious was that the Soviets were rattled by the 'forward' aspects of the US Maritime Strategy: the recent Teamwork 88 Exercise had included significant elements within the north Norwegian Sea close to the Soviet Union. The Soviet Navy saw this as aggressive and provocative, and the delegation called for naval arms control as a way to constrain such exercises.[164] A few weeks earlier Marshal Sergei Akhromeyev, the Chief of the Soviet General Staff (the head of all Soviet armed forces, not just the Army), on a visit to the United States had made it clear to Admiral Trost, the US Chief of Naval Operations, that 'You, you the United States Navy, are the problem', pointing to the threat of US carriers and cruise missile submarines against the Soviet northern flanks in the east and west.[165] He also called for naval arms limitations talks. The Maritime Strategy had clearly achieved its intent in causing nervousness amongst the Soviet military leadership and not just within its Navy.

The second set of talks in the Adderbury series occurred in Sevastopol and Moscow later that year, with the Western delegation visiting the Soviet cruiser *Kerch*.[166] In May 1989, the Dartmouth Training Squadron, consisting of HMS *Bristol* and HMS *Achilles*, undertook a tour of the Baltic, with *Bristol* visiting Leningrad and Gdynia in Poland, and *Achilles* visiting Rostok in East Germany. Captain Franklyn of *Bristol* described the visits, the first by British warships to the Eastern Bloc since 1976, as an 'exploration into the unknown'.[167] The Soviets did not want any external publicity from these ship visits: foreign journalists were not permitted to visit Leningrad to report on the visits, whilst the only other route to sending photographs or material to the media – via the British naval attaché – had been cut off by the coincidental expulsion of the attaché from the USSR a few days before. Five thousand members of the public visited *Bristol* in Leningrad and 8,000 in Gdynia. A total of 2,000 visited *Achilles* when she was alongside at Rostok, where the East German press had been given much more freedom to report, resulting in coverage that was described by Franklyn as 'enormous'.[168] Captain Franklyn had been accompanied by Rear Admiral J F Coward during the trip to Leningrad, and Coward met, and presumably had talks with, Rear Admiral K A Tulin of the Soviet Navy although the nature and content of these talks is not known.[169]

In November 1989 the Adderbury talks returned to Windass' home. They now had a much more official flavour, with greater numbers of senior Soviet, US and UK naval officers attending and taking a much more prominent role. In addition to Admiral Amel'ko, Vice Admiral D P Komarov and Rear Admiral Markov attended from the Soviet Navy. The United States was represented by Admiral Wesley MacDonald and Vice Admiral James Lyons, recently retired former commanders of the US Atlantic and Pacific Fleets, whilst the Royal Navy attendees included the new First Sea Lord, Admiral Oswald, Admiral Eberle, the retired former Commander-in-Chief Fleet, Rear Admiral J R Hill, now an author and naval analyst, and Vice Admiral John Webster, the Flag Officer, Plymouth.[170] The meetings, which would be soon known as the 'RUKUS' talks, built up further momentum during 1990, with Admiral Chernavin, the Commander-in-Chief of the Soviet Navy, meeting Admiral Oswald in July of that year. At the same time the Soviet destroyer, the *Bezuprechny*, visited Portsmouth, with Rear Admiral V P Yeryomin on board. Four months later, Admiral Makarov, the Chief of the Soviet Naval Staff, visited Oswald and was given a tour of HMS *Trenchant*, one of the newest of the Royal Navy's nuclear submarines, and the Outboard frigate, HMS *London*.[171] These regular reciprocal visits, which continued the following year, did much to build confidence between the two sides just as the USSR was beginning to disintegrate. Despite the dissolution of the USSR they would endure, with the RUKUS talks continuing through the 1990s and into the early 2000s.

Collapse

Whilst the Adderbury process was beginning to build up momentum, the Soviet Union itself was undergoing a series of destabilising wrenches that would lead to its collapse. Gorbachev's economic reforms, some of which initially focussed on harnessing the supposed efficiency of military procurement to major civilian sectors such as food production, and then shifted in stages towards a more market-led approach, were beginning to result in inflation and economic dislocation.[172] As Gorbachev's faith in the defence industry began to falter towards the end of the decade, he then started shifting resources out of the sector entirely: the defence budget suffered a reduction of around 15 per cent between 1988 and 1991.[173]

Even before Gorbachev's reforms, there had some significant problems in the Soviet defence industry, notwithstanding the impressive-looking equipment they were producing. It was not accidental that almost all new major warships in the 1980s were handed over to the Navy in the last few weeks of December each year: targets for handover would be met for the production complexes to receive their bonuses, even if it meant that the ships were delivered with a significant portion of their main armament not fitted (which would then have to be added by the Navy at its dockyards rather than by the shipbuilder).[174] As was seen in Chapter 18, only relatively small numbers of some of the most important new classes of ship and submarine were completed. Production bottlenecks occurred within the Soviet 'shortage economy' even when the defence industry was given the highest prioritisation for supply. Targets focussed on quantitative rather than qualitative results with production managers being happier to produce large numbers of established types of equipment than push for innovation.[175] Technologically, the Soviet sector was some distance behind that of the West, especially in electronics.[176] The defence industry was also a major producer of consumer goods, which took up 40 per cent of the industry's productive capacity by 1985 and distracted it from its core role.[177]

Soviet military backwardness began to be appreciated fully as the Adderbury process started to involve reciprocal visits on Soviet and Royal Navy ships. The aforementioned visit of the modern destroyer *Bezuprechny* (commissioned 1985) to Portsmouth in July 1990 gave British naval officers a chance to see inside a modern Soviet warship for the first time. She appeared to be a paper tiger to the visitors:

Whilst outwardly impressive, she was characterised by the one RN PWO [Principal Warfare Officer] who got into her operations room as 'Batch 2 County class vintage technologically' (i.e. resembling RN designs of 20 years ago). The general RN evaluation was that this was a technologically dated and not particularly well-maintained warship.[178]

Comments were also made about how the crew was treated. In a scene that seemed more appropriate to navies of the eighteenth century, corporal punishment was 'roughly administered on the destroyer's upper deck' at one point, and it was later discovered that a sailor had died from a brain haemorrhage during the visit. It was not known why or how this had occurred, or whether it was linked to the physical punishment that had been meted out on the upper deck.[179] A British visit to *Gromky*, a Soviet 'Krivak II' class frigate (commissioned 1979), in 1991 resulted in an even less complementary report:

> From a distance the ship looked smart, well painted and tidy. Closer inspection reveals poor paintwork (no chipping takes place, many layers of grey paint over hinges, brasswork, pre-wetting system, door seals) ... Ship's boats looked unused and hoisting gear beneath the paint was rusty and poorly maintained.

In the ship's galley the situation was even worse:

> Hygiene is not a consideration. The deck was filthy with food remnants, tins and grease. Sailors in unwashed uniform peeled potatoes in stagnant water with unwashed hands. Utensils were caked in last year's leftovers. No fridges – meat, cheese, yoghurt left out all week ... cockroaches everywhere. Rats lived in the dry provision stores and bakery.[180]

Seen up close, the mighty Soviet Navy looked much less menacing, although there was the risk that by focussing on insanitary conditions and rudimentary-looking equipment, this could mask the fact that these ships were still armed with missile systems that were sufficiently effective to cause a serious military threat. Also, this was only a picture of the surface navy, which relied heavily on conscripts; the submarine arm, and the Soviet Navy's main offensive capability, was likely to have been much better looked after. Despite this, the state of these relatively new warships gave an indication of the problems faced by the Soviet Navy, the much lower standards that they accepted as a matter of course, and the implications for operational effectiveness.

* * *

In the summer of 1989 Gorbachev began the inadvertent unravelling of the Warsaw Pact: he ended Soviet backing for the Communist states of Eastern Europe, their regimes rapidly collapsed, and they began the democratic transition as the Red Army started to leave. Fighting between the Armenian and Azerbaijani Republics within the USSR broke out, whilst the three Baltic republics began their own independence movements.[181] The power of the Soviet Communist Party began to ebb away as a more pluralistic politics, just as much focussed on the constituent republics, began to develop. For the Soviet defence industry, whose relations with the Kremlin had been mediated through the Party, these changes were of considerable importance. It is therefore not surprising that party leaders of the Severnaya Verf shipyard in Leningrad were amongst those leading the attempt to create an autonomous Russian Communist Party in spring 1990.[182] A bungled coup attempt in August 1991 to stop the unravelling of Soviet power by deposing Gorbachev disintegrated when it became clear that the coup leaders could not control Moscow. After this, the power of the Soviet organs of state began to ebb away as the leaders of the major republics started planning for independence. By the end of December 1991, the USSR had ceased to exist; so too had the Soviet Navy. The expected foe of the Royal Navy for at least 45 years was no more, and the expectations and strategic assumptions of that era would have to change in a Western world that now seemed to lack any existential adversaries.

21

Conclusions

This book has aimed to produce a comprehensive history of the Royal Navy between the cancellation of the CVA01 aircraft carrier in 1966 and the end of the Cold War. It has therefore sought to provide not only a history of naval operations, strategy and high level policy, but also to cover other areas that have been much less prominent in the existing academic and general literature, such as personnel policy, procurement and fleet support. This chapter will draw together the main findings from this book: in some areas they modify or significantly change existing academic assessments, in a few others they confirm or augment them, and in a significant number of areas they cover new ground that it is hoped will be developed by scholars and researchers in future years.

Retreat
This book has shown that the failure to procure the CVA01 strike carrier during the 1965–6 Defence Review was in significant part due to poor decision-making within the Naval Staff. It was unwilling to compromise at the right time and contemplate fall-back positions, and it managed to alienate neutral and even supportive outsiders. When it did finally make concessions they were too late and too incoherent to make a difference, and it failed to exploit gaps in the arguments of those lobbying against the carrier. The planned 60,000-ton carrier was almost certainly never going to be built, but a smaller carrier – probably at 30,000–40,000 tons – was a distinct possibility, and for a time had the support of a number of senior officials and military officers close to the Secretary of State. But the Admiralty Board and Naval Staff refused to accept what turned out to be their only chance to procure a carrier. The result was an unnecessary catastrophe that not only resulted in the cancellation of CVA01 but a decision to withdraw all remaining carriers by 1975; it was

followed by the resignation of the First Sea Lord and Navy Minister. After the withdrawal of the carrier force, the fleet's air defence, long-range maritime strike and airborne early warning would all be dependent upon the Royal Air Force's land-based maritime air capabilities. The serious ramifications of this decision for much of the ocean-going surface fleet would be seen across the rest of the period covered by this book.

Picking up the pieces after this traumatic episode, the Royal Navy instituted a series of reforms in its organisation, its personnel and fleet support policies whilst pushing ahead with procuring a new fleet of cruisers, destroyers and frigates. Self-confidence gradually returned to the senior service as it adjusted to a world without strike carriers. The Navy's growing fleet of nuclear-powered submarines, including four ballistic missile boats which took over the role of carrying the country's strategic nuclear deterrent in 1969, epitomised this new navy and the formidable capabilities that it possessed. The procurement of three small aircraft carriers (initially described as cruisers) was achieved despite some scepticism within the Ministry, but these ships and the Sea Harrier aircraft that they carried, would ensure that an element of organic fixed wing air power remained, even if it was not until the early 1990s that the Sea Harriers were capable of effective air defence against the most modern Soviet long-range strike aircraft. The successful recapture of the Falkland Islands would have been impossible without them. The long-term outcomes of the various reforms were, however, mixed: the new organisational structure of a single fleet and a split between the 'user' and 'provider', was a logical approach but achieved strangely few economies in either spending or posts. The personnel reforms resulted in a welcome leap ahead in understanding what would recruit and keep sailors in the Navy as civilian society changed rapidly, but the after-effects of a promotion policy that had penalised officers interested in and well-suited to staff work, would be felt many years after that policy had been changed. The later creation of the Principal Warfare Officer and the sustaining of a comprehensive and effective system of tactical doctrine were other, much more positive, developments, as was the fostering of the science of oceanography. In retrospect, the decision to procure two new classes of escort (the Type 42 and Type 21) as quickly as possible, which was made for perfectly sensible policy reasons, resulted in the approval of under-developed designs which soon escalated in cost, and with capabilities designed for the lower threat world that seemed likely before the Soviet suppression of the Prague Spring. The ships proved unsuited to the high-threat maritime environment of the mid to late 1970s Eastern Atlantic when they finally entered service.

This book has shown that the final naval withdrawal from East of Suez was more complex than had previously been assumed. The new Conservative government elected in 1970 did wish to retain capabilities East of Suez after the planned withdrawal from Singapore and the Gulf in 1971, but this created substantial problems for the Navy. It had already reformed both its deployment and its 'harmony' rules on the expectation of a full withdrawal, so the government announcement of plans to keep five frigates at Singapore created substantial strains on a new system designed on the basis of home porting in the United Kingdom. Such a large portion of the frigate force was now tied up on roulement to and from East of Suez, that a new policy was instituted by the Navy in 1973 that replaced the five frigates with annual 'Group Deployments' complemented by two permanently-based lightly-armed frigates in Singapore and Hong Kong. Thus, the Navy itself partly reversed the limited return-to-East of Suez policies of the new government, but created a force posture of forward deployed presence vessels combined with regular group deployments to the region that was not too dissimilar to that developed nearly half a century later. That same government's 'dash for growth' policy also disrupted the Navy's procurement pipeline for frigates and destroyers and further increased the costs and delays to the Type 42 and 21 programmes.

A Defence Review in 1974–5 continued the shift in strategic focus of defence towards Europe and the Atlantic. This book has shown that the Navy did not suffer badly in the Review, but intimations of future vulnerability were increasingly apparent, albeit largely unrecognised by the service's leadership. The Royal Air Force clearly saw the maritime Eastern Atlantic theatre as secondary to that in Central Europe and wished to minimise its investment in capabilities for the former. Officials were openly asking rhetorical questions about whether a Navy was needed any longer. The effectiveness of the Chief of the Defence Staff's 'critical level' negotiating position and his stamping on inter-service rivalry, protected the Navy in the short-term, but these issues would return with a vengeance only half a decade later.

In an environment where NATO's Central Front dominated not only the thinking of the Army but also that of the Royal Air Force, and where the old worldwide role was associated with both the imperial past and the Navy, the strategic culture of the majority of the Ministry increasingly narrowed to one in which only a short-warning and short war scenario against the Warsaw Pact across the Central European Plain could be contemplated. This was despite the experience of the Cuban Missile Crisis of 1962 and US-Soviet Yom Kippur naval stand-off of 1973, both of which came as close as anything during the Cold War to provoking a conflict between the USA and USSR, and which were characterised by prolonged periods of high tension confrontation involving maritime forces manoeuvring, marking and counter-marking in support of allies well beyond the Central European Front. This 'strategic myopia' which involved only preparing for the expected where it was expected, resulted in an environment in which it was extremely difficult for the Navy's arguments to gain traction. There was no understanding in the Ministry of what would later be termed the 'Quinlan Paradox': that effective deterrence against a primary threat (such as that presented by the Soviets in Central Europe), therefore makes secondary, and therefore much less expected and predictable, threats *more* likely to occur.

Crisis

It has also been shown that during the late 1970s the Navy did not prepare itself well for a future reckoning within the Ministry over its role in a NATO-focussed environment. Its own initial concept of operations did not align with the realities of the defence budget. Later, a centrally developed strategic concept reflected the splits over the future role of the Navy within both the Ministry and the Navy itself, whilst the Naval Staff was unable to develop a new concept of operations that reflected the new centrally developed concept. As a result, the Navy would begin the 1981 Defence Review without any satisfactory concepts – strategic or operational – from which to base its arguments. These failures reflected increasingly serious splits within the Navy itself: some argued that the future Navy should focus on its underwater capabilities and retain only a fleet of light frigates for Eastern Atlantic duties, whilst others emphasised the continued significance of a balanced fleet, surface task forces and the importance of preparing for the unexpected. These splits not only prevented the completion of key concepts within the Navy Department, but leached out beyond the Ministry. They ultimately resulted in the creation of a 'negative briefing environment' around the Prime Minister due to effective direct lobbying by a former naval officer and prominent defence journalist, John Moore, against the Navy Department and its policies just prior to the 1981 Defence Review.

It is therefore unsurprising that such splits affected the procurement programme as new and more capable vessels were needed to counter the growing Soviet air threat and to deal with the dangerously inadequate submarine detection abilities of the surface fleet. Both the large Type 22 frigate and the unbuilt Type 43 destroyer gave the Navy a reputation for producing very expensive but not especially capable warships. At the same time, it failed to be sufficiently innovative in the development of warship types to reflect the new more threatening maritime environment: equipping ships with the US Aegis air defence system was rejected whilst attempts to get as many anti-submarine helicopters to sea as possible were half-hearted, subordinated to the frigate programme and ultimately failed. By contrast, the continued programme of nuclear submarine building produced increasingly impressive and capable boats (of the *Swiftsure* and *Trafalgar* classes), even if their Achilles heel remained the lack of an effective heavy torpedo until the introduction of Spearfish in the 1990s. There was one additional area of particular success:

the new British shipborne towed-array sonar proved to be a revolutionary step forward in the detection of nuclear submarines by surface ships, far in excess of previous capabilities and more effective than existing US towed-arrays. It was this innovation that ensured that surface ships now had a realistic chance of countering the underwater threat.

Pay freezes during a period of high inflation created a major personnel recruitment and retention crisis during the late 1970s, resulting in the early retirement of vessels and the placing of significant numbers of ships in reserve. This and a similar but more serious crisis in the mid to late 1980s, reflected the sometimes-pre-eminent role that personnel shortages can play in determining the effectiveness and, ultimately, the shape of the fleet. The importance of recruitment and retention difficulties in naval (and defence) policy has often been under-recognised and this book has attempted to place these more clearly in the foreground. The crucial influence of external factors largely outside the control of the Ministry of Defence – such as economic recessions and booms – has to be recognised to understand the pressures under which recruitment and retention policies worked (and still work today).

It has also been shown that between 1979 and 1980 the Navy's message did land well with a Conservative Defence Secretary, Francis Pym, but his attempts to reduce the British military burden on the continent in order to focus more on maritime and air capabilities were prevented by the diplomatic ramifications of such a change, and the protection afforded to British Forces Germany by the limits set by the Brussels Treaty. This failure emphasised the primary role of symbolism and performative assurance to allies of British forces in Central Europe, rather than their intrinsic capability (they were only 10 per cent of NATO forces in that theatre, compared to the 70 per cent of ready naval forces contributed by the Navy to the Eastern Atlantic). Pym's failure to reset the strategic focus of British defence was combined with another failure to control defence spending in the Department. The Prime Minister's loss of confidence in him also damaged the Navy as he had been so closely associated with the senior service, thus turning attention towards the viability of the eastern Atlantic role of the Navy when a new Secretary of State arrived at the Ministry.

It has been demonstrated that John Nott's Defence Review was undertaken at great speed and based on extremely shaky conceptual and technological foundations. His key decision to rapidly shrink the size of the surface fleet had been arrived at before any significant analyses had been completed. Much of his rationale was based on the misrepresented abilities of maritime patrol aircraft both to undertake barrier patrols in extremely challenging oceanographic conditions without cueing from long-range detection systems, and also to protect surface task groups. Nott forced through re-written estimates based on these conclusions, but the gradual unravelling of his assumptions and heavy lobbying from the United States resulted in two major changes. The first change was an increase in the planned numbers of destroyers and frigates from 'around 40' up to 'around 50', and the second was that US analysis helped to support the reinstatement of the medium anti-submarine helicopter in the programme and a more realistic understanding of the capabilities of the maritime patrol aircraft. Finally, it is almost certain that US lobbying also saved the two amphibious assault ships from early withdrawal from service. The overheated equipment programme and the need to procure Trident had meant that the Defence Review would always have been painful for the Royal Navy, but Nott's self-defeating, aggressive approach made the outcomes more painful – for both the Navy and ultimately for the Defence Secretary – than they needed to have been.

The direct and effective lobbying of the United States has been under-represented in the existing literature, and this book has made clear the significance of this whilst the British government was negotiating to procure the US Trident ballistic missile system and new submarines. The Navy's leadership and the Naval Staff were neither imaginative nor radical in the defence of their position, and they had difficulties articulating their arguments, but they were dogged and determined and benefitted significantly from US support at key moments. They were also extremely fortunate that the review occurred under a new pro-navy Republican administration. The previous Carter administration would not have pressured Nott to change the review outcomes significantly, as many of Nott's presumptions had been shared by that of the earlier US administration.

Revival
The Falklands conflict has been covered many times, not least in a two-volume official history, but the successful retaking of the islands following an Argentine invasion tested the Royal Navy in many ways. It demonstrated the crucial role of sea power in undertaking operations in unexpected places in unexpected circumstances, far from fixed bases. The campaign also demonstrated the singular abilities of the Navy's cadre of experienced operational commanders, especially at the level of ship and small-group command. In addition, it was a powerful demonstration of the ability of the nuclear-powered submarine to make a major tactical and strategic impact on the campaign, and justified the significant investment in technology, infrastructure, training and personnel in this formidable capability. It vindicated the Navy's concerted and successful push for an organic fixed-wing air capability in the 1970s in the shape of the Sea Harrier, which was a significant part of the successful mission to prevent Argentine air forces from jeopardising the amphibious landings and attacking British troops once ashore. It also showed the value of a large and capable

logistics chain, and of the importance of ships taken up from trade as force multipliers and adjuncts to warships. Less positively, it also showed the intense vulnerability of British warships to air attack, although the highest value units were all successfully protected, and (in a pre-towed-array surface force) the relative ineffectiveness of surface ship anti-submarine capabilities.

The Falklands had a longer-term impact on the Navy. It was no longer on the defensive within the Ministry, with the gains already achieved no longer at risk of being pushed back. It also helped to reverse some significant decisions that had still stood despite US lobbying: the sale of the carrier *Invincible* was cancelled, and much less well known, the guided missile destroyer was saved from its long-term demise by the decision to take part in the NFR90 NATO escort programme. The provision of battle-loss replacements in ships, aircraft and weapons worked to the benefit of the Navy, not least because the only practical replacement ships that could be built were modified, and more capable, versions of the very expensive Type 22 frigate. The post-conflict lessons-learnt process provided the Navy with a series of capability improvements derived directly from South Atlantic operations that were used successfully to lobby for capability enhancements through the mid-1980s.

The development of the United States' Maritime Strategy in the early 1980s was also beneficial to the Navy, by re-emphasising the importance of the Eastern Atlantic and High North in NATO, and providing it with a specific and crucial role as the providers of two NATO anti-submarine groups, one of which would protect the US carrier strike group. The Strategy was also successful in unnerving the Soviets and showed the flexibility of sea power to threaten the USSR's flanks in the north rather than merely focus on the theatre of its choice, the Central European Front. However, the escalatory nature of elements of the Strategy, not least those focussed on strategic anti-submarine warfare in the Soviet Navy's bastions, did add an additional element of risk if it had come to open conflict. Even here though, strategic anti-submarine operations in a period of tension might be just as likely to de-escalate if they were successful in reducing Soviet confidence that they could successfully launch a strategic nuclear strike.

The further centralisation of the organisational structure of the Ministry of Defence in the mid-1980s nominally reduced the influence of the single-services in defence policy-making, but in practice – at least during the rest of the decade – the single-services were still able to wield similar levels of influence through the system, albeit indirectly. In budgetary terms the mid and late 1980s were a frustrating time for the Navy, as increases in the budget did not feed through to significant capability enhancements and procurement programmes progressed slower than planned. Earlier attempts to produce cheaper variants of ship types to save money – such as the *Upholder* class conventional submarines, the OPV 3 light frigate and the Single Role Mine Hunter – often failed to fully achieve their aims, due to delays in orders, cancellation or cost escalations that meant that they did not produce significant savings.

This book has shown that the sending of women to sea alongside men was primarily driven by a mounting retention crisis within the Navy, but also that there was little interest in promoting racial or sexual diversity, despite the potential benefits to recruitment and retention, and that with respect to sexuality, policies became more regressive in the late 1980s. The 1980s also saw a transformation in many aspects of support to the fleet. The dockyards were contracted out, which did not save much money but improved industrial relations, whilst the computerisation of storekeeping was introduced in order to aid efficiency and relieve a paper system straining under the more complex requirements of a modern Navy. From the 1960s to the end of the 1980s, major changes in ship maintenance also occurred: at the start of the period covered by this book, ships were nominally self-sufficient outside of refits but in practice were partially reliant on a growing infrastructure of ad hoc maintenance services when alongside. In the late 1960s this was formalised and rationalised into the use of Fleet Maintenance Units, and by the end of the period covered here, the substantial shore-based support required by the new Type 23 frigates heralded a further and final shift away from self-maintenance towards even greater dependence on facilities ashore.

'Out of area' deployments in the 1980s underwent a fundamental shift from earlier post-colonial operations, such as the over-the-horizon or visible support to authorities in colonies as they made the sometimes bumpy transition to independence, to a new set of priorities in the Caribbean, where counter-narcotic operations and hurricane and disaster relief work gained prominence; priorities which remain to this day for the British naval presence in that region. The 'Armilla' deployment to the Gulf during the Iran-Iraq war also provided the foundations for today's deployment to the region: supporting the free passage of shipping by the presence of both frigates and mine countermeasures vessels. Group deployments were also transformed in the 1980s from annual into occasional deployments led by higher-profile aircraft carriers as flagships, with more committed involvement from the Foreign and Commonwealth Office, and a greater impact on the countries visited. They would continue into the 1990s and be revived with an almost identical approach in the early 2020s. Finally, this book has shown that the Navy, initially through indirect channels, played a notable part in the rapprochement between the naval leaderships of East and West in the last years of the Cold War.

* * *

The period from 1966 to 1990 was amongst the most politically testing that the Royal Navy had faced in the modern era. When dealing with a growing threat from a formidable enemy whilst also undertaking a range of peacetime roles, it also had to deal with the realisation that many within government, including the Ministry of Defence, did not see the utility of most of its capabilities, aside from those of its nuclear submarines. The Ministry therefore underappreciated the flexibility and significance of sea power in both deterring the Soviet Union and upholding British interests globally. The Falklands crisis re-awoke an understanding in some of the importance of globally deployable navies and provided political protection from further serious reductions through the rest of the 1980s, but the strategic myopia of a department focussing only on the expected never completely dissipated. The Navy dealt skilfully with elements of the challenges that it faced: the development of a high-quality nuclear submarine force – from the boats through to the personnel – was the most important example, closely followed by the production of a superlative surface towed-array capability, the re-acquisition of an organic fixed-wing aviation capability and the maintenance of a highly experienced and effective operational leadership cadre supported by effective training and doctrine. In other areas, the Navy had to cope with complex and interlinked problems in personnel, procurement and support that also plagued the other armed services but in somewhat different ways. Sometimes it dealt with these well, sometimes adequately, and on occasion poorly, but not necessarily dramatically worse than the other services, with the exception of the catastrophe of the carrier cancellation analysed at the start of this book. What also stands out was the role of chance and circumstance, particularly during the period of acutest crisis in 1981 and 1982: the Navy was lucky that the Trident negotiations gave the US administration unusual leverage over John Nott, and lucky that the review had occurred during a Republican administration and not a year earlier when the Carter administration would have taken a very different position. The victory in the Falklands also required its own element of luck, but it is an important skill for any sailor to make the most of the good fortune that comes their way, and this was clearly the case with the Navy during the quarter century covered by this book.

The Royal Navy survived these most difficult years with a balanced and flexible fleet that also proved to be well suited to the more unpredictable times of the post-Cold War era. It now faces a shift back towards more conventional threats from major military powers. In the move to reorientate towards countering a land-based threat from the East, it should not be forgotten that threats can emerge from unexpected directions where pre-positioned land and air forces are unavailable or not easily amassed quickly. And when the threat does emerge from the expected direction it can often be more productive, as was the case with the Maritime Strategy of the 1980s, to challenge those threats in the maritime flanks rather than just in the theatre and on the terms of your adversary's choosing.

Appendices

Appendix 1: Organisation

1.1: Navy Department Organisation 1971[1]

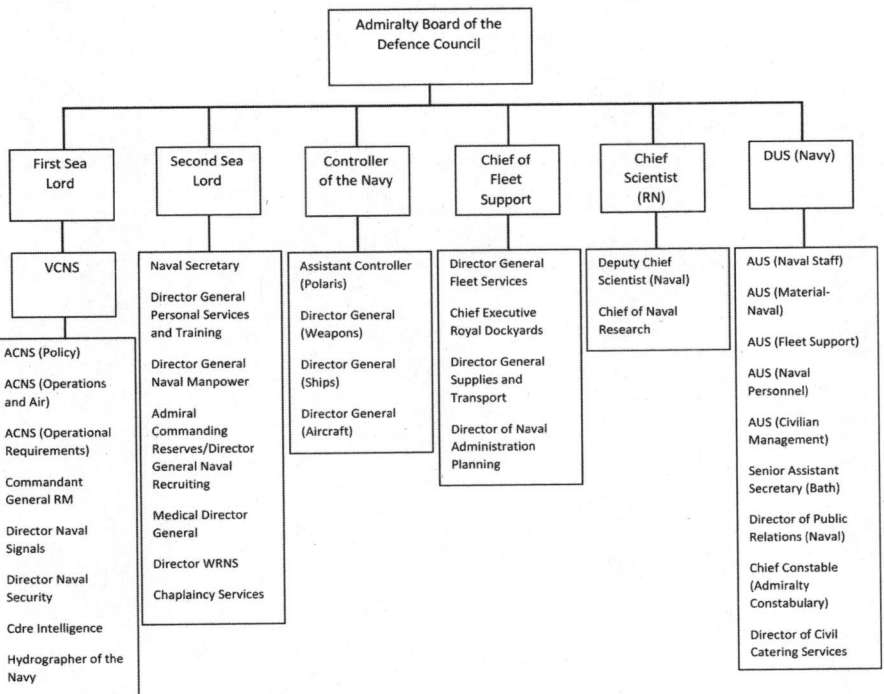

1.2: Navy Department Organisation 1989[2]

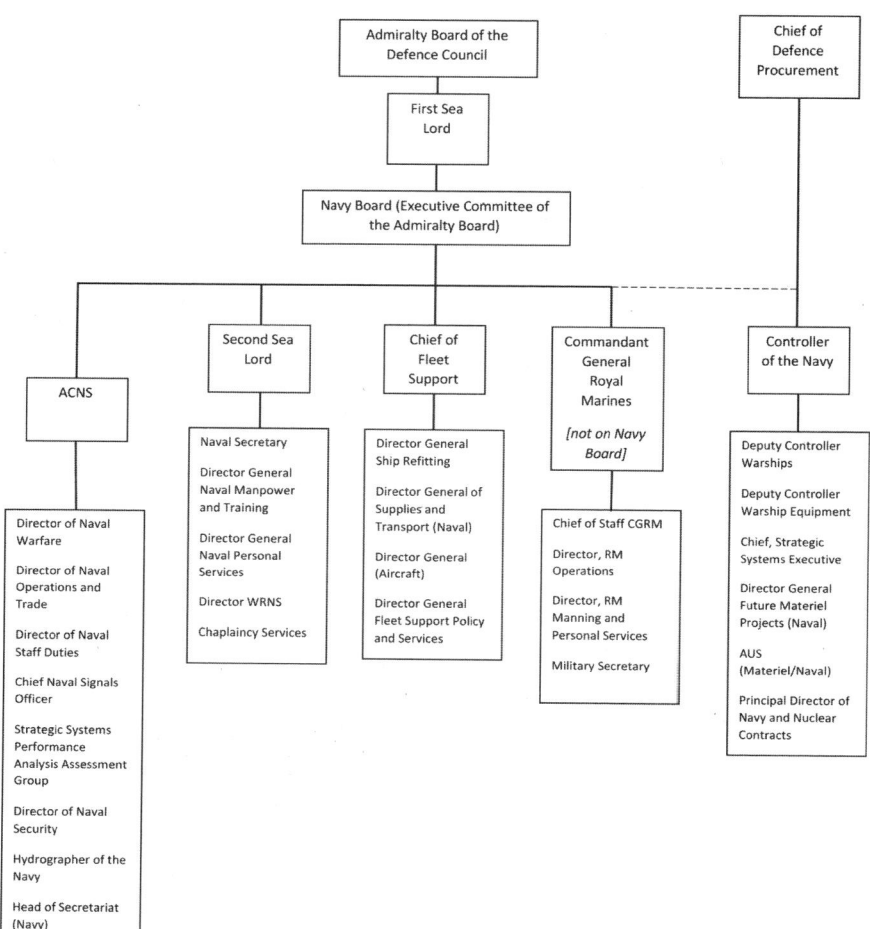

APPENDIX I: ORGANISATION

1.3: Fleet Organisation 1968[3]

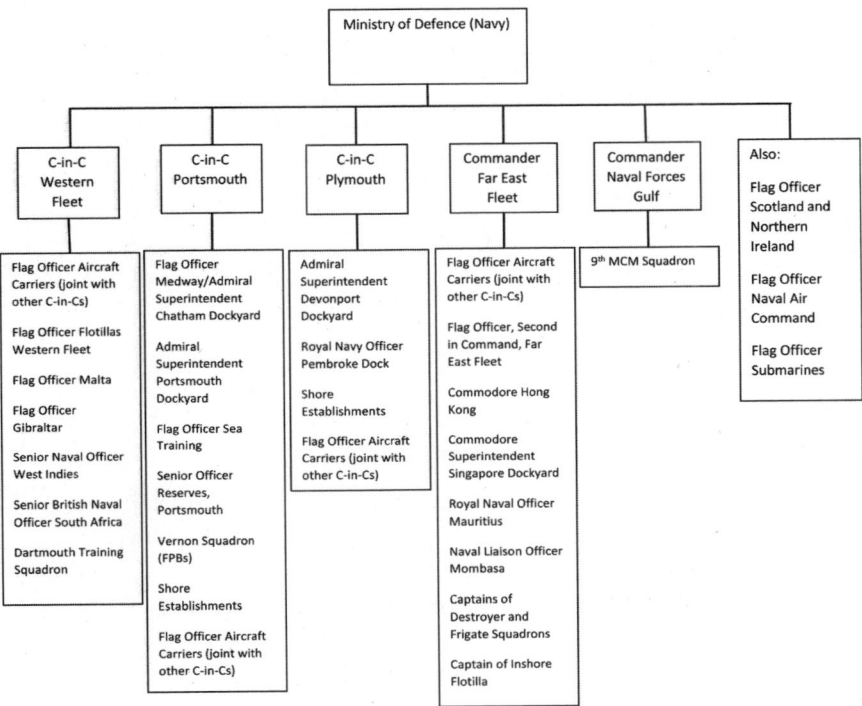

1.4: Fleet Organisation 1988[4]

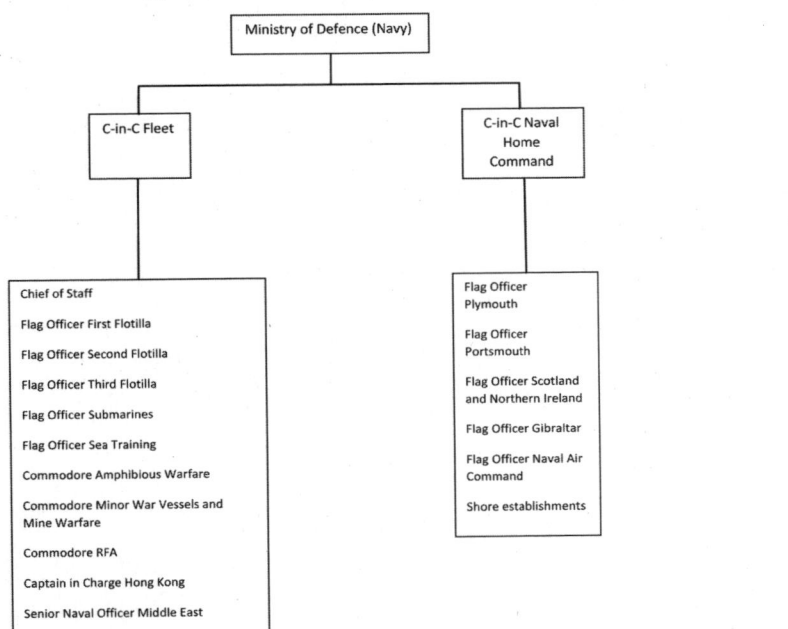

Appendix 2: Budget

2.1: Four ways of seeing defence expenditure[1]

	A	B	C	D
	Defence spending (current prices, £ billions)	*Defence spending (1990 prices, £ billions)*	*Defence as % of public spending*	*Defence as a % of GDP*
1964–5	1.9	13.6	14.5	5.5
1965–6	2.0	13.7	13.7	5.4
1966–7	2.2	14.5	13.6	5.4
1967–8	2.3	14.8	12.4	5.4
1968–9	2.3	14.2	11.8	4.9
1969–70	2.2	12.9	10.7	4.4
1970–1	2.4	13.3	10.5	4.2
1971–2	2.7	13.8	10.6	4.2
1972–3	3.0	14.4	10.5	4.1
1973–4	3.5	15.4	10.5	4.2
1974–5	4.2	16.1	9.6	4.2
1975–6	5.2	16.3	9.3	4.3
1976–7	6.1	16.6	9.5	4.3
1977–8	6.7	15.9	9.5	4.1
1978–9	7.7	17.0	9.7	4.0
1979–80	9.5	18.9	10.0	4.1
1980–81	11.6	20.1	10.1	4.3
1981–2	12.9	20.1	10.0	4.3
1982–3	14.8	21.3	10.4	4.5
1983–4	15.9	21.9	10.4	4.4
1985–6	18.4	23.0	10.7	4.3

	A	B	C	D
	Defence spending (current prices)	Defence spending (1990 prices)	Defence as % of public spending	Defence as a % of GDP
1989–90	21.0	22.4	9.6	3.3
1990–1	22.0	22.0	9.2	3.2

2.2: Defence Budget Split Amongst the Three Services (by Percentage)[2]

%	RN	Army	RAF	Other
1964	26	30	28	16
1965	27	30	29	13
1966	29	29	27	14
1967	30	30	27	13
1968	31	30	27	12
1969	30	30	28	12
1970	27	31	28	14
1971	27	33	29	11
1972	26	32	27	15
1973	26	32	32	10
1974	25	34	31	10
1975	25	35	29	11
1976	26	35	28	11
1977	27	34	28	11
1978	28	35	28	11
1979	28	33	29	10
1980	28	32	29	11
1981	29	32	30	9
1982	29	31	31	9
1983	29	31	31	9
1984	29	31	31	9
1985	29	31	31	9
1986	29	30	30	11

Commentary

Appendix 2.1 sets out four different ways of looking at defence spending. Column A shows spending at current prices and tells the reader little because it does not adjust for inflation. Column B is inflation adjusted (to 1990 prices) and shows defence spending broadly at a £13–14 billion plateau until the early 1970s, when it rises gradually until reaching a £21–23 billion plateau from 1982 onwards. This particular measure would understandably be the Treasury's favoured figure, as it would emphasise the real-terms increases Defence had secured through most of this period, although the fall at the end of the 1960s and drift downwards towards the end of the 1980s would have been painful. Columns C and D show different methods of looking at defence spending, emphasising defence spending as a percentage of either total public spending or GDP. At different times these measures would often be deployed by Defence in order to push for increased spending, to recognise the importance of defending the country when compared to the 'public purse' or its total wealth. Both figures have their problems: during an economic recession GDP would shrink thus *increasing* Defence as a percentage of GDP without any real increase in spending. Relying on pegging defence spending to a particular level of GDP can therefore result in calls for real *reductions* in defence spending during periods of economic stress. Defence as a percentage of public spending is even more problematic, as public spending is likely to increase during a recession (as benefits payments increase to those in economic difficulty), and different governments can take different perspectives on public spending – either aiming to reduce or increase such spending depending upon ideology or economic circumstances. What is most notable about Columns C and D is their general stability during much of this period. Defence as a percentage of public spending, after a period of reduction in the 1960s, stabilises at between 9.2 and 10.7 per cent, with dips within this band during the late 1970s and end of the 1980s. Defence as a percentage of GDP generally sits within 4 to 4.9 per cent during this period, except during the late 1960s and late 1980s, both being periods of strong economic growth. Overall, this author is struck by the relative stability of spending, however it is measured, across the period in question.

Appendix 2.2 then allows the Navy's position within Defence to be understood. Gaining information on spending by service is extremely difficult after 1968 as both the Estimates and the Appropriation Accounts no longer split out spending by service, whilst this author has not seen consistent figures across this period in archival sources (although it might be possible to collate figures from each department's budget bids during the annual Estimates round). The data here comes from a short book written by Ewen Broadbent, a recently retired Second Permanent Under-Secretary at MOD, so one presumes that he was able to source this information from his former department. It would have required a considerable amount of reallocation of spending, with procurement spending being allocated back to departments after 1971 following the creation of the Procurement Executive. The book does not provide any data after 1986. Above all, it shows a certain amount of budgetary stability amongst the three services but with the Navy being somewhat behind the Army and RAF in most years; this being most pronounced in the 1970s. The three services were in near equipoise between 1982 and 1986.

Appendix 3: Personnel

3.1: Regular Personnel[1]

000s	Male (RN and RM)		Female (WRNS and QARNNS)		Enlisted outside UK	Total
	Officers	*Ratings/Ranks*	*Officers*	*Ratings/Ranks*		
1965	11.2	83.8	0.4	3.2	2.0	100.6
1966	11.5	82.7	0.4	3.2	1.9	99.7
1967	11.5	81.7	0.4	3.4	1.9	98.9
1968	11.4	79.9	0.4	3.4	1.8	96.9
1969	11.2	75.5	0.5	3.0	1.6	91.8
1970	10.9	71.9	3.3		1.6	87.7
1971	10.6	68.6	3.3		1.5	84.0
1972	10.4	68.5	3.5		1.1	83.5
1973	10.2	67.4	3.6		0.8	82.0
1974	10.2	64.5	3.6		0.8	79.1
1975	10.0	62.5	0.5	3.2	0.8	77.0
1976	9.9	62.3	0.5	3.4	0.7	76.8
1977	9.8	62.4	0.5	3.5	0.5	76.7
1978	9.6	61.6	0.4	3.6	0.4	75.6
1979	9.6	59.1	0.4	3.4	0.3	72.8
1980	9.7	58.4	0.4	3.4	0.3	72.2
1981	10.1	60.2	0.5	3.6	0.3	74.7
1982	10.0	59.0	0.5	3.5	0.3	73.3
1983	9.7	58.1	0.4	3.5	0.4	72.1
1984	9.4	58.0	0.4	3.5	0.4	71.7
1985	9.5	57.1	0.4	3.3	0.4	70.7

000s	Male (RN and RM)		Female (WRNS and QARNNS)		Enlisted outside UK	Total
	Officers	Ratings/Ranks	Officers	Ratings/Ranks		
1987	9.9	53.4	0.4	3.0	0.4	67.1
1989	9.8	51.4	0.4	3.1	0.3	65.0
1990	9.8	49.9	0.4	3.2	0.3	63.6

3.2: Royal Marines[2]

From 1981 (backdated to 1977), the strength of the Royal Marines was set out separately in the Statements on Defence Estimates:

000s	Officers	Other Ranks	Total
1977	0.6	7.1	7.7
1978	0.6	6.8	7.4
1979	0.6	6.8	7.4
1980	0.6	6.9	7.5
1981	0.7	7.3	8.0
1982	0.7	7.2	7.9
1983	0.6	7.1	7.7
1984	0.6	7.0	7.6
1985	0.6	7.0	7.6
1986	0.6	7.0	7.6
1987	0.7	7.2	7.9
1988	0.7	7.1	7.8
1989	0.7	7.0	7.7
1990	0.7	6.9	7.6

3.3: Reserves[3]

000s	Regular reserves	Volunteer reserves	Total
1965		9.9	
1966		9.5	
1967		9.1	
1968	20.9	9.2	30.1
1969	22.0	8.9	30.9
1970	23.5	8.6	32.1
1971	25.1	8.4	33.5
1972	26.9	8.1	35.0
1973	27.8	7.1	34.9
1974	28.1	7.1	35.2

000s	Regular reserves	Volunteer reserves	Total
1975	30.1	7.0	37.1
1976	29.7	6.8	36.5
1977	30.3	6.3	36.6
1978	28.7	6.4	35.1
1979	30.8	6.3	37.1
1980	29.2	5.8	35.0
1981	28.7	6.3	35.0
1982	26.9	6.5	33.4
1983	26.1	6.5	32.6
1984	25.7	6.2	31.9
1985	25.6	6.3	31.9
1986	26.7	6.7	33.4
1987	26.8	6.9	33.7
1988	27.1	6.9	34.0
1989	27.7	6.9	34.6
1990	28.4	7.0	35.4

Commentary

In Appendix 3.1 the change in ratio between officers and ratings/other ranks during this period is significant: from approximately 1:8 to 1:5 in only 25 years. As ships' systems became more complex and greater automation was introduced, a higher proportion of more highly-trained personnel were required (including a higher proportion of senior rates within the total number of ratings) even if numbers were falling in total. These more highly-qualified personnel would need to be paid more, would require more money spent on their training and greater accommodation space and facilities both afloat and ashore. These factors should not be under-estimated when assessing the reasons for defence inflation rising higher than general inflation during this period (see Chapter 20). Automation does reduce the need for personnel, but those that remain are generally more highly trained and proportionately paid more, so the net budget savings might be less than initially assumed. Personnel enlisted outside the United Kingdom mostly included those enlisted in Singapore, Malta and Hong Kong. The last Maltese enlistees left the service by 1979 and those from Singapore probably by 1976.

In Appendix 3.2 the relatively static size of the Royal Marines during this period, in comparison to the shrinkage of the Royal Navy as a whole, should be noted. This appears to have been driven by the tasking of the Royal Marines (with the commitment to supply units for tours of Northern Ireland from the early 1970s onwards) and the personnel numbers required to sustain four (later three) Commandos. In Appendix 3.3 the total figures should be treated with care. The numbers in the regular reserve are more a function of those who had left the naval service in recent years rather than any success in reserve recruitment and retention. Numbers of regular reserves from 1965 to 1967 are not known.

Appendix 4: The Fleet

4.1: Composition of the Fleet (Major Fighting Vessels Only)[1]

Numbers = active/trials and training/refit and reserve Tonnage = standard tons, total of active vessels only		1 April 1970		1 April 1980		1 April 1990	
Type	Class	Numbers	Tonnage	Numbers	Tonnage	Numbers	Tonnage
SSBN	Resolution	3/0/1	22,500	3/0/1	22,500	3/0/1	22,500
SSN	Dreadnought/Valiant	2/0/1	7,625	5/0/1	20,825	3/0/2	13,200
	Swiftsure			4/0/1	16,800	5/0/1	21,000
	Trafalgar					5/0/1	23,500
SSK	'A' class	5/0/1	5,600				
	Porpoise	6/0/2	9,630	2/0/1	3,210		
	Oberon	10/0/3	16,100	9/0/4	14,490	8/0/2	12,880
	Upholder					0/1/0	
All submarines		*26/0/8*	*61,455*	*23/0/8*	*77,825*	*24/0/7*	*93,080*
CVA	Eagle/Hermes	2/0/1	86,060				
LPH	Bulwark	2/0/0	46,600				
CVS	Hermes/Bulwark/Invincible			2/0/1	39,300	2/0/1	32,000
LPD	Fearless	2/0/0	22,120	1/0/1	11,060	1/1/0	11,060
CL	Tiger	1/0/2	9,500	0/0/1			
All carriers/amphib/cruisers		*7/0/3*	*164,280*	*3/0/3*	*50,360*	*3/1/1*	*43,060*
DD	Daring/'Battle'/'Ca'	1/1/5	2,106				
DLG	'County'/Type 82	3/0/3	18,300	4/0/2	24,600	1/0/0	6,300
DDG	Type 42			6/0/0	21,000	10/1/1	35,000
FF	Type 15	1/4/0	2,240				
	Type 14	5/1/2	5,900				
	Type 12	7/3/4	16,660	3/1/4	7,140		
	Types 41/61	7/0/1	15,580	0/0/2			

Numbers = active/trials and training/refit and reserve Tonnage = standard tons, total of active vessels only		1 April 1970		1 April 1980		1 April 1990	
Type	Class	Numbers	Tonnage	Numbers	Tonnage	Numbers	Tonnage
FF	Type 81	6/0/1	13,800	2/0/5	4,600		
	Leander (unmodernised)	20/1/1	50,000	7/0/4	17,500	1/1/0	2,500
	Leander (Ikara)			8/0/0	19,600		
	Leander (Exocet)			6/0/1	14,700	3/0/0	7,350
	Leander (Sea Wolf)					4/0/1	9,800
	Leander (Towed Array)					3/0/1	7,350
	Type 21			8/0/0	19,250	6/0/0	16,500
	Type 22			2/0/0	7,000	11/2/1	35,400
	Type 23					0/1/0	
All destroyers and frigates		50/10/17	124,586	46/1/18	135,390	39/5/4	120,200
MCMV	'Ton'/ 'Ham'/ 'Ley'	26/18/10	9,360	28/5/2	10,080	11/0/3	3,960
	'Hunt'			1/0/0	625	11/2/0	6,875
	'River'					12/0/0	10,680
	Sandown					0/1/0	
All mine countermeasure vessels		26/18/10	9,360	29/5/2	10,705	34/3/3	21,515
Total tonnage			359,681		274,280		277,855

Commentary

This table sets out the size of the fleet in 1970, 1980 and 1990 in both numbers and tonnage. The reduction in tonnage from 1970 to 1980 is significant and reflects the withdrawal from service of the last fleet carriers and the reduction in active commando ships and assault ships. The shift from 1980 to 1990 is more nuanced. The total tonnage is similar, but there has been a reduction in the total tonnage of major surface ships, destroyers and frigates, and an increase in submarines and mine countermeasures vessels. Although the number of active submarines has only increased by one, their tonnage has increased by approximately 20 per cent as conventional boats have reduced in number and nuclear boats increased. In mine countermeasures, the small vessels of the 1950s have been replaced by more capable and larger vessels. This shift during the 1980s is a reflection of the significant sustained investment in nuclear submarine building and the re-equipping of the mine warfare fleet with larger and more capable vessels. This was achieved, to some extent, at the expense of the main surface fleet.

Appendix 5: Warship Procurement

5.1: Comparison of 1970 Long Term Costing Assumptions ('LTCA') with Reality[1]

Class	Number ordered 1970–1980			Number accepted into service 1970–1980		
	LTCA	*Actual*	*+/-*	*LTCA*	*Actual*	*+/-*
Cruiser (*Invincible*)	3	3	0	3	1	-2
Commando Ship	2	0	-1	1	0	-1
SSN	9	7	-2	11	8	-3
'County'				2	2	0
Type 82				1	1	0
Type 42	16	13	-3	13	7	-6
Leander				5	5	0
Type 21	5	7	+2	6	8	+2
Type 22	17	6	-11	10	2	-8
Mermaid		1	+1		1	+1
Wilton				1	1	0
'Hunt'	20	6	-14	18	1	-17
Ocean Patrol Vessel	6	0	-6	6	0	-6
'Bird'		4	+4		4	+4
Offshore Patrol Vessel ('Island')		7	+7		7	+7
Offshore Patrol Vessel ('Castle')		2	+2		2	+2
Hong Kong Patrol	5	0	-5	5	0	-5
Scimitar				3	3	0
Speedy		1	+1		1	+1
Tenacity		1	+1		1	+1

Class	Number ordered 1970–1980			Number accepted into service 1970–1980		
	LTCA	Actual	+/-	LTCA	Actual	+/-
MCM Forward Support Ship	1	0	-1	1	0	-1
Inshore Survey Craft	5	0	-5	5	0	-5
'Rover'	2	2	0	3	4	+1
Armament Support Ship	2	0	-2	2	0	-2
Stores Support Ship	1	0	-1	1	0	-1
Fleet Replenishment Ship ('Fort')		2	+2		2	+2

5.2: Comparison of 1980 Long Term Costing Assumptions ('LTCA') with Reality[2]

Class	Number ordered 1980–1990			Number accepted into service 1980–1990		
	LTCA	Actual	+/-	LTCA	Actual	+/-
Invincible				3	3	0
SSBN		3	+3			
SSN	11	4	-7	10	7	-3
SSK	9	4	-5	4	1	-3
Type 42				9	7	-2
Type 43	12	0	-12	3	0	-3
Type 22	16	8	-8	19	12	-7
Type 23 ('large' 6,000-ton)	6	0	-6			
Type 23 ('small' 3,500-ton)		10	+10		1	+1
'Hunt'	21	7	-14	20	12	-8
Sandown		5	+5		1	+1
EDATS trawlers ('River')		12	+12	12	12	0
MCM Hovercraft	4	0	-4	1	0	-1
'Castle'	6	0	-6	8	2	-6
Hong Kong Patrol	5	5	0	5	5	0
Challenger				1	1	0
'Bird'		3	+3		3	+3
Falklands Patrol		3	+3		3	+3
Inshore Survey Craft	3	1	-2	3	1	-2
AOR (*Fort Victoria*)	5	2	-3	5	0	-5
Small Fleet Tankers	3	0	-3	3	0	-3
Support Tankers ('Leaf')				2	2	0
Fleet Replenishment Ship	2	0	-2			

Class	Number ordered 1980–1990			Number accepted into service 1980–1990		
	LTCA	Actual	+/-	LTCA	Actual	+/-
Stores Support Ship	2	0	-2			
Reliant		1	+1		1	+1
Diligence		1	+1		1	+1

Note: LTCA 80 (which was drafted in March 1979) had assumed that the 15th and 16th Type 42 destroyers would be ordered in April 1979, as would all twelve EDATS trawlers (the future 'River' class). In the event, no further Type 42s were ordered and the EDATS trawlers were ordered in 1982.

Commentary

The Long Term Costing Assumptions were created in order to provide equipment and procurement data from which to build the annual Long Term Costings. They would attempt to look ahead up to ten years to predict the likely numbers and types of ships that would be needed, when they would be ordered and when they would enter service. Estimates of the costs of these procurements would be made and then fed into the planning process. These two tables compare the numbers of vessels estimated in two LTCA documents, those for 1970 and 1980, with the reality of what was ordered. It is unsurprising that plans changed and different classes were procured instead of those envisaged in 1969 and 1979, but the overriding impression given is the extreme over-optimism of the number of ships of different types that could be afforded. In 1969 it had been hoped that seventeen Type 22 frigates and twenty 'Hunt' class mine warfare vessels would be ordered, when instead only six and six were respectively. This was in no way compensated for by the order of two additional Type 21 frigates and HMS *Mermaid* instead. In 1979, the disparity was even greater as it had been envisaged that sixteen Type 22s would be ordered as well as twelve Type 43 destroyers and six 'large' Type 23 frigates. As was seen in Chapter 11 each Type 43 would have cost as much as a nuclear-powered attack submarine, whilst the original 'large' Type 23 would have shared a hull with the Type 43 and probably cost almost as much. The Type 22 was also an expensive ship, with the first of class costing almost three times as much as the last *Leander* class vessel.[3] The actual number of submarines ordered was also much less than envisaged during this decade.

It is not as if a much larger budget was envisaged either, in fact quite the reverse. The Navy's projected annual budget under the 1970 Long Term Costings was calculated to be £571 million in 1980–1 in 1970 prices.[4] When adjusted for inflation between 1970 and 1980, this would mean that it was expected to be £1.825 billion, when in reality the 1980–1 sketch estimates set out a planned budget of £2.277 billion (the finalised budget would not have been too different from this figure).[5] Similarly, in the 1980 Long Term Costings the 1989–90 budget was planned to be £2.679 billion (£4.985 billion in 1989 prices),[6] whilst the 1989–90 sketch estimates 'bid' was in fact £5.517 billion.[7] The last part of Chapter 7 discusses the reasons for such significant underestimates in the cost of procurements.

Notes

Introduction
1 British Newspaper Archive: *Daily Mirror* front pages, 16 and 17 March 1966. 2 Grove, *Vanguard to Trident*. 3 Roberts, *Safeguarding the Nation*. 4 Hennessy and Jinks, *The Silent Deep*; David Hobbs, *The British Carrier Strike Fleet after 1945*. See also Duncan Redford, *The Submarine, A Cultural History*. 5 Childs, *Age of Invincible*. 6 Dockrill, *Britain's Retreat from East of Suez*; Young, *The Labour Governments 1964–1970: International Policy*; Dorman, *Defence under Thatcher*; Peden, *Arms, Economics and British Strategy*; Stoddart, *Losing an Empire, Finding a Role*; Stoddart, *The Sword and the Shield*; Stoddart, *Facing Down the Soviet Union*; Jones, *The Official History of the British Nuclear Deterrent, Volume II*; Dyndal, *Land Based Air Power or Aircraft Carriers*; Hampshire, *From East of Suez to the Eastern Atlantic*; Boren, 'Britain's 1981 Defence Review' (PhD Dissertation), Dyson, 'The Limits of Influence' (MA Dissertation). See also Jackson and Bramall, *The Chiefs*, for an excellent institutional history of one part of the defence structures of the UK. 7 Brown, *The Royal Navy and the Falklands War*; Freedman, *The Official History of the Falklands Campaign*, 2 volumes. 8 Brown and Moore, *Rebuilding the Royal Navy*; Friedman, *British Carrier Aviation*; Friedman, *British Destroyers and Frigates Since 1939*; Friedman, *British Submarines in the Cold War Era*. 9 Healey, *The Time of My Life*; Mason, *Paying the Price*; Nott, *Here Today, Gone Tomorrow*; Ziegler, *Mountbatten*; Smith, *Mountbatten*; Baker, *Dry Ginger*; Ashmore and Grove, *The Battle and the Breeze*; Hill, *Lewin of Greenwich*; Leach, *Endure no Makeshifts*; Watson, *Commander-in-Chief*; Treacher, *Life at Full Throttle*; Lygo, *Collision Course*; Black, *There and Back*.

Chapter 1: February 1966
1 TNA: ADM 187/66-68, Pink Lists 1955. 2 Grove, *Vanguard to Trident*, pp. 245–50, 262–3, 265–7; TNA: ADM 234/1068, 'Naval Staff History: Middle East Operations, Jordan/Lebanon 1958, Kuwait 1961' (1968) BR 1736(55). 3 Names given for Commanders-in-Chief, Flag Officers and other senior naval officers in this chapter are from HMSO, *The Navy List, Spring 1966* (London, 1966), pp. 302–05 and 456–7. 4 TNA: ADM 187/101, Pink List 15 February 1966, pp. 1, 4 and 27. 5 Mobley, 'The Beira Patrol', pp. 5–8, 15–17. 6 TNA: ADM 187/101, Pink List 15 February 1966, pp, 27–27B. Table excludes ships under Flag Officer Middle East, as well as hydrographic vessels, RFAs and PAS craft. 7 Ibid., pp. 1, 27–29. 8 Ibid., pp. 7, 27–27B. 9 Ibid., pp. 27A, 27B, 28A, 33, 34–8. 10 Watson, *Red Navy at Sea*, p. 148. 11 TNA: ADM 223/724, Quarterly Intelligence Report March to June 1963, pp. 6–12; NHB: Naval Intelligence Report, January to March 1965, pp. 35–8. 12 Grey, *Up Top*, pp. 52–3. 13 French, 'Dire Straits', pp. 115–124; NHB: Naval Intelligence Report, January to March 1965, pp. 35–8. 14 TNA: ADM 187/101, Pink List 15 February 1966, pp. 25–6. 15 Ibid., p. 23. 16 The sensitivities of this issue are set out in Young, 'The Wilson Government and the Debate over Arms to South Africa', pp. 62–86. 17 TNA: ADM 187/101, Pink List 15 February 1966, p. 24. 18 Ibid., p. 24. 19 Johnson, 'The British Caribbean from Demobilisation to Constitutional Decolonisation', pp. 620–1. 20 NHB: Home Station narrative, Volume 4 (1965–67), pp. 403–09. 21 TNA: ADM 187/101, Pink List 15 February 1966, pp. 10–1.3. 22 TNA: Ibid.,

pp. 5–13. List excludes hydrographic vessels, RFAs and ships under local Commanders-in-Chief (which include most of the reserve fleet, PAS craft etc). **23** TNA: Ibid., pp. vi–xii, 10–13. **24** TNA: Ibid., p. 9. **25** TNA: Ibid., p. 28. **26** TNA: ADM 182/192, AFO 659/54, 'Reduction of Periods of Foreign Service', 12 March 1954. **27** Sayle, *Enduring Alliance*, pp. 147–60. **28** Polmar and Moore, *Cold War Submarines*, pp. 71–82, 96–9, 111–13. **29** Apal'kov, *Podvodniye Lodki*, pp. 87–92; Huan, *La Marine Sovietique*, pp. 38–9, 42. **30** Polmar and Moore, *Cold War Submarines*, pp. 75, 79. **31** Gardiner, *Conway's All the World's Fighting Ships 1947–1995*, pp. 416–17. **32** Gordon and Komissarov, *Soviet Naval Aviation 1946–1991*, pp. 301–04. **33** Baer, *One Hundred Years of Sea Power*, pp. 394–9; Herrick, 'The USSR's Blue Belt of Defence Concept', pp. 169–78. **34** In particular see Herrick, *Soviet Naval Strategy*. Note how his analysis jars heavily with the preface written by Admiral Arleigh Burke, pp. vii–ix. **35** NHB: Naval Intelligence Report, No. 8, April 1966, 'Review of the Soviet Navy 1965–70', pp. 3–4. **36** Ibid., pp. 25–6. Note that in 1964 Naval Intelligence did include 'attacks on allied shipping' as a third role after attacking NATO carriers and Polaris submarines, but again only *after* these vessels had been destroyed. ADM 223/727: Quarterly Intelligence Report for January to March 1964, pp. 3–4. **37** TNA: ADM 223/723: Quarterly Intelligence Report for January to March 1963, No. 35, 8 April 1963, 'Review of the Soviet Navy 1962', p. 3. **38** Sayle, *Enduring Alliance*, Chs 6 and 7. **39** TNA: ADM 187/101, Pink List 15 February 1966, pp. 1–3. **40** Air Historical Branch, SD161/1966(1) Location of Units of the RAF, 1 January 1966, pp. 36–7; Ashworth, *RAF Coastal Command 1936–1969*, pp. 212–22, 235–40; Gibson, *Nimrod's Genesis*, pp. 81–90. **41** TNA: ADM 187/101, Pink List 15 February 1966, pp. 5–6. **42** TNA: Ibid., p. 7. **43** NHB: 'The Organisation of the Naval Staff within the Admiralty and Ministry of Defence, 1927–2000', p. 136. **44** TNA: ADM 187/101, Pink List 15 February 1966, pp. 29–31. **45** Blackman, *Jane's Fighting Ships 1970–71*, p. 359. **46** ADM 182/210, AFO 2282/58, Flag Officer Sea Training, 19 September 1958; Hampshire, *The Royal Navy since 1945*, p. 176. **47** Until 21 January 1966 Admiral Begg had 'double-hatted' as NATO's Commander-in-Chief Channel, but this role had recently been transferred to the C-in-C Home Fleet, giving the latter Admiral two NATO roles in addition to his RN responsibilities. See HMSO: *The Navy List, Spring 1966* (London, 1966), p. 303. **48** TNA: ADM 187/101, Pink List 15 February 1966, pp. 14–20. **49** Evans, *Arming the Fleet*, pp. 9–11, 237–43. **50** NHB: BR 1868, 'Notes on the Royal Navy' (December 1964), p. 12–2. **51** HMSO, Defence Estimates 1965–1966, Vote 7, pp. 32–3 and Appendix IV, p. 58. Another 15,712 locally-engaged staff were employed at Singapore, Gibraltar, Malta and other overseas naval bases; the plurality of these probably worked in the dockyards. **52** HMSO, The Navy List, Spring 1966, pp. 604–07. **53** Ibid., pp. 596–7. **54** HMSO, The British Imperial Calendar and Civil Service List 1964, columns 53–57. The 1964 Calendar has been chosen as, from 1965 and the incorporation of the Admiralty into the Ministry of Defence, far less detail on naval establishments is given in later publications. See also Evans, *Arming the Fleet*, p. 9 and HMSO: The Navy List, Spring 1966, pp. 590–1. Note that Ditton Priors was in the process of being wound down in 1966; it shut in 1968. **55** NHB: BR 1868, 'Notes on the Royal Navy' (December 1964), p. 12–3; BR 1029(1) 'Regulations for the RNSTS' (1975), Annex 3.1; HMSO, The British Imperial Calendar and Civil Service List 1964, columns 84–85; Value of Stocks of Naval Stores ledger, Return D323, value on 31 March 1966. **56** Corsham Civic Society: 'Demise of the Copenacre Site', 25 July 2016: https://www.corshamcivicsociety.co.uk/demise-of-the-copenacre-site/ (accessed 15 February 2022). **57** HMSO: The Navy List, Spring 1966, pp. 587–8; NHB: BR 1029(1) 'Regulations for the RNSTS (1975), Annex 3.1. In addition, there were two further RNSTS-run oil depots for NATO use at Loch Striven and Campbeltown. **58** TNA: ADM 167/164, A/M(64)10, Item 2, 5 November 1964; NHB: Admiralty Board Memoranda, A/P(64)23, 27 October 1964, p. 4. **59** HMSO: Defence Estimates 1965–66, Vote 6, pp. 29–31 and Appendix IV, p. 58. **60** Sleat, 'The Royal Navy Contracts 1869–1969', p. 17. **61** NHB: Research Establishments Box/T27816, 'Admiralty Engineering Laboratory Golden Jubilee 1920–1970 Open Days' (1970). **62** NHB: Research Establishments Box/T11834, 'Admiralty Experiment Works' (1972). **63** NHB: Research Establishments Box/T11835, T27721, 'Admiralty Research Laboratory' (1967, 1976). **64** HMSO: The Navy List, Spring 1966 (London, 1966): pp. 592–3. **65** HMSO: Defence Estimates 1965–66, Appendix IV, p. 58. The number of scientists working with the Navy Department (many probably working at the Ship Department in Bath, the RN Scientific Service headquarters or in operational analysis) was 547 in 1965 but was expected to fall to 488 in 1966 (ibid., Vote 3, p. 24). **66** Johnman and Murphy, *British Shipbuilding and the State Since 1918*, pp. 149–50, 160. **67** Murphy, *Shipbuilding in the United Kingdom*, p. 38. **68** Ibid., pp. 8–12. **69** Johnman and Murphy, *British Shipbuilding and the State*, pp. 158–65. **70** Murphy, *Shipbuilding in the United Kingdom*, p. 119. **71** Johnman and Murphy, *British Shipbuilding and the State*, pp. 155 and 209. **72** Gorst and Johnman, 'British Naval Procurement and Shipbuilding 1945–64', pp. 139, 142. **73** TNA: DEFE 69/327, Shipbuilding Inquiry Committee, Paper (i), July 1965. **74** Gardner, *The British Aircraft Corporation*, p. 163. **75** NHB: Value of Stocks of Naval Stores ledger, Return D323, value on 31 March 1966. **76** Compare the 1947 and 1958 editions of the Naval War Manual: NHB: 'Naval War Manual 1947' (BR 1806), pp. 25–6 and TNA: ADM 234/590 (BR 1806), pp. 46–9. **77** Cooper, 'Sir Michael Cary', p. 448. **78** HMSO: *The British Imperial Calendar and Civil Service List 1966* (London, 1966), columns 166–189; NHB: 'The Organisation of the Naval Staff', p. 137. **79** Goldsmith, *A History of the Ministry of Defence Financial Organisation*, Ch 4; Sleat, *Royal Navy Contracts*, p. 5. **80** Davies, *Intelligence and Government in Britain and the United States, Volume 2*, pp. 181–6. **81** HMSO: The British Imperial Calendar and Civil Service List 1966, columns 166–167. **82** NHB: 'The Organisation of the Naval Staff', p. 140; Jackson and Bramall, *The Chiefs*, pp. 356–7. **83** HMSO: Defence Estimates 1965–66, Navy Section Appendix IV, pp. 53–4. **84** NHB: Manning Ratings, Box 6/T826, 'Naval Manpower Statistics Annual Abstract as at 30 September 1965' (17 January 1966). Officers column from Table 2, totals from Table 1 and ratings/other ranks column from subtracting Table 1 from Table 2 totals. This table includes recalled reservists and those compulsorily retained. **85** Ibid., Tables 1 and 2. **86** Ibid., Table 4. **87** Ibid., Tables 3 and 19. **88** Ibid., Tables 33 and 34. **89** Ibid., Table 19. **90** Ibid., Tables 13, 17, 18 and 20. **91** NHB: BR 1868, 'Notes on the Royal Navy' (December 1964), p. 13–9. **92** Ibid., pp. 13–10 to 13–12. **93** NHB: Manning Ratings, Box 6, 'Naval Manpower Statistics', Table 11. Similar changes were occurring in the Army but to a lesser degree: by the mid-1960s just over 50 per cent of other ranks were classed as 'tradesmen' (a wider categorisation than the RN's artificer), French, *Army, Empire and Cold War*, p. 178. **94** NHB: Manning Ratings, Box 6, 'Naval Manpower Statistics', Table 32. **95** Ibid., Tables 27 and 28. **96** Ibid., Table 30; NHB: BR 1868, 'Notes on the Royal Navy' (December 1964), pp. 13–5 and 13–6. **97** Ibid., Table 9. **98** Ibid., Table 23. **99** TNA: ADM 182/200, AFO 1/56, 'The New Officer Structure' (January 1956); NHB: BR 1868, 'Notes on the Royal Navy' (December 1964), pp. 13–1 to 13–6; see also Admiralty Library: Da 1101, 'Promotion of Seaman Officers to Commander and Captain on the General List' May 1959. **100** Fiennes, *Britannia's Voices*, pp. 23–6. **101** NHB: Manning Ratings, Box 6, 'Naval Manpower Statistics', Tables 23 and 24. **102** Ibid., Table 25. **103** Ibid., Table 20. **104** Ibid., Table 29. **105** Ibid., Tables 12, 26. **106** Stanley, *Women and the Royal Navy*, pp. 129–42, 205. **107** NHB: BR 1938, 'Naval Ratings Handbook 1965', pp. 19–20. **108** Adams and Smith, *The Royal Fleet Auxiliary*, p. 20. **109** HMSO, Defence Estimates 1965–1966 (London, 1965), p. 59. **110** NHB: Port Defence, Box 1/T71336, 'Port Auxiliary Service: Portland Establishment' 29 December 1970; T71337, Portsmouth 7 July 1970; T71338, Chatham 3 July 1969; T71339, Devonport/Pembroke Dock 14 May 1969; T71340, Rosyth 14 August 1969; T71341, Gibraltar 18 September 1968. **111** Murray, *The Royal Naval Auxiliary Service*, pp. 5–18. **112** Ibid., p. 37. **113** For the origins and wartime service of RNV(S)R officers see Lavery, *In Which They Served*, pp. 9–44; Jones, *Uncommon Courage*. **114** HMSO: *Defence Estimates 1965–66*, Navy Section Appendix III, pp. 48–52; for the dissolution of the RNV(S)R, see Howarth, *The Royal Navy's Reserves in War and Peace*, p. 130.

Chapter 2: The Battle for the Carrier
1 The author has written about this subject in greater detail in Hampshire, *From East of Suez to the Eastern Atlantic*, pp. 41–139. **2** NHB: Admiralty Press Notice 66/62; Luce had also known Lord Mountbatten, the Chief of the Defence Staff and former First Sea Lord, for many years. He, Mountbatten and Charles Lambe, who himself became First Sea Lord in 1959, had visited Vienna together, presumably on leave from the Mediterranean Fleet, when they were junior naval officers. This long-standing friendship could have been decisive in his promotion to First Sea Lord whilst Mountbatten was still Chief of the Defence Staff. University of Southampton Library ('USL') MS62/MB1/K176, Lord Mountbatten to Luce, 3 July 1968. **3** National Museum of the Royal Navy: NMRN 2004.48, 'My bit of Navy, a love story', unpublished memoirs of Admiral Sir William O'Brien, pp. 347–8; National Maritime Museum, Greenwich, London ('NMM'), Lewin Papers, LWN 6/5 Leach to Lewin, 3 January 1999. **4** Admiral Frank Hopkin, a former Swordfish observer was, in 1966, Vice Chief of the Naval Staff; during the 1970s a series of talented former FAA pilots would rise to the rank of Admiral such as Desmond Cassidi and John Treacher, both of whom held senior posts in the Naval Staff as Captains in 1966. **5** NMRN: 2004.48, Admiral O'Brien memoirs, p. 348. **6** King's College London: Liddell Hart Centre for Military Archives ('LHCMA'), Mayhew 8/2, Handwritten note, 24 February 1966, pp. 1–2. **7** LHCMA: Mayhew 8/2, Handwritten note, 24 February 1966, pp. 1–7. **8** Grove, *Vanguard to Trident*, pp. 93–4, 203. **9** Friedman,

The Postwar Naval Revolution, pp. 104–05; Friedman, *British Carrier Aviation*, pp. 305–11. **10** TNA: DEFE 13/477, Thatcher to Nairne, 30 November 1965. **11** Spey-engines for the Phantoms had been approved in 1965: TNA: DEFE 69/340, Harbord to MAT 3(N), 29 September 1965. **12** Grove, 'Partnership spurned', pp. 227–41. **13** TNA: CAB 148/25, OPD(66) 6th meeting, 21 January 1966. **14** Jackson and Bramall, *The Chiefs*, pp. 114, 117 and 119. **15** Dockrill, *Britain's Retreat from East of Suez*, p. 139. **16** Peden, *Arms, Economics and British Strategy*, pp. 304–10. **17** TNA: T225/2600, Clarke to Armstrong, 12 March 1965. **18** Dockrill, *Britain's Retreat from East of Suez*, pp. 50–1. **19** TNA: CAB 128/37, 50th meeting, 30 July 1963. **20** Trend had initially been sceptical of a hard £2,000 million limit, but changed his mind after discussions with the Chancellor of the Exchequer and the Secretary of State for Economic Affairs. TNA: PREM 13/18, Trend to Wilson, Chequers briefings, Section A and conclusions, 19 November 1964; Trend to Wilson, 31 December 1964. **21** Labour Party: General Election Manifesto, 'A New Britain' (September 1964), Section C, Defence. **22** Dockrill, *Britain's Retreat from East of Suez*, pp. 56–7, 63. **23** Healey, *The Time of My Life*, p. 270. **24** TNA: AIR 41/93 'Defence Policy and the Royal Air Force 1964–1970', pp. 2.1–2.4, 2.8–3.1; Dockrill, *Britain's Retreat from East of Suez*, pp. 80–104. **25** TNA: T 225/2600, Downey to Nicholls, 8 March 1965; Clarke to Armstrong, 12 March 1965. **26** Jackson and Bramall, *The Chiefs*, pp. 343–5; Healey, *The Time of My Life*, pp. 257–9; Ziegler, *Mountbatten*, pp. 528, 586. For an example of RN special treatment in the new structures, see the exemptions given to warship procurements: TNA: DEFE 10/484, OR/M(66)14, item 3, 8 November 1966. **27** TNA: AIR 8/2355, Quinlan to Elworthy, 6 January 1965. **28** Healey, *The Time of My Life*, pp. 258–9. **29** In one of the early studies into the role of the carrier in intervention operations, Mountbatten used his control of the Chiefs of Staff structures in an attempt to stifle RAF opposition and Army concerns: TNA: DEFE 4/180, CoS(65)7, 4 February 1965; DEFE 32/10, CoS 7th mtg/65, confidential annex, 4 February 1965. **30** Ziegler, *Mountbatten*, p. 637; TNA: CAB 130/213, MISC 17 2nd meeting, p. 7. **31** Ziegler, *Mountbatten*, pp. 633–5. **32** This was the view of Christopher Mayhew after the carrier had been cancelled, LHCMA: Mayhew 2/3, Mayhew to Mountbatten, 7 April 1966. **33** TNA: DEFE 69/481, Mayhew to Healey, 16 December 1965. **34** TNA: DEFE 5/123, CoS(62)1, 9 January 1962. **35** TNA: DEFE 13/114, handwritten note by Healey, June 1965. **36** TNA: AIR 20/11561, Brief for Elworthy at Chiefs of Staff meeting, 12 April 1965. **37** DEFE 25/173, VCDS to CDS, 28 October 1965; Draft note Hull to Chiefs of Staff, October 1965. Phantoms had been able to undertake 'touch and go' landings and take-offs from the 35,000-ton *Victorious* in January 1965, whilst similar landings would be shown to be possible from the 29,000-ton *Hermes* in May 1968, Hobbs, *British Aircraft Carriers*, pp. 280–3. **38** TNA: DEFE 69/481, Private Office notes 2 November and 16 December 1965; Healey to Mayhew, 13 December 1965. **39** For the development of the Buccaneer, see Hobbs, *The British Carrier Strike Fleet after 1945*, pp. 302–09. **40** TNA: CAB 148/45 OPD(O)(65)82, 20 December 1965, marks the first time that the Naval Staff conceded a noticeably smaller escort force. The proposed programme for future destroyers and frigates was also in a mess that would not bear close scrutiny. The planned Type 82 destroyer – originally conceived as a small air defence frigate derived from the *Leander* class – had grown into a heavily-crewed 6,000-ton behemoth during design development. Because of future personnel constraints, the planned small, fast Type 19 frigate, which would have to make up the large numbers required to keep the escort fleet at eighty ships, became smaller, cheaper and impossibly leanly manned as the Type 82 grew. It was therefore clear that if the Navy wanted sophisticated ships like the Type 82 it would be impossible to keep the number of escorts at eighty into the 1970s. The Naval Staff did not appear to be able to acknowledge this until the dying stages of the battle for the carrier. T 225/2667, Frazer to Mountfield, 30 January 1964, Gough to Lawrence-Wilson, 3 March 1964; DEFE 69/446, DNPlans to VCNS, 4 November 1965; NMM, LWN/6/5 'My impressions of DNTWP' Admiral Sir R Macdonald to Lewin, 20 October 1998. **41** TNA: CAB 148/42, OPD(O)(65)16, Annex, Appendix 4, Reserve Forces. **42** TNA: DEFE 69/481, Mayhew to Healey, 17 November 1965; Healey, *The Time of My Life*, p. 275. **43** TNA: DEFE 4/183, CoS (65) 19, item 2A, 13 April 1965; DEFE 69/481, Report by Joint Service Study Group covered by DCNS to CNS, 8 April 1965; AIR 20/11561, DCNS to VCAS, 9 March 1965; Quinlan to ACAS(Ops) 11 March 1965; AUS(P&B) to Hardman, 8 April 1965; Report by Joint Service Group (ACSG(P))8; AIR 8/2355, Quinlan to Cooper, 11 February 1965. **44** TNA: AIR 20/11561, AUS(P&B) to Hardman, 8 April 1965. **45** TNA: AIR 20/11561, Brief for Elworthy at Chiefs of Staff meeting, 12 April 1965. **46** TNA: AIR 8/2355, Quinlan to Elworthy, 10 December 1964. **47** Neubroch, 'The Great Carrier Controversy 1964–65', p. 65. **48** The main groups of studies included three intervention studies, a maritime airpower study, a threat to shipping study, various versions of a carrier plan, case for and case against the carrier papers, a navy without carrier study, and various scenario studies, all between March and October 1965. See Hampshire, *East of Suez to Eastern Atlantic*, pp. 51–89. **49** TNA: DEFE 13/114, Healey to Wilson, 2 July 1965. **50** TNA: DEFE 10/511, DC/P(65)20, 5 October 1965; DC/M(65)7, item 2, 7 October 1965. The possibility of using the old US carrier *Shangri-La* until 1980 was put forward by Zuckerman but rejected due to the personnel requirements for this ship. By 1980 it was assumed that the relevant technologies would be in place that would make carriers obsolete. **51** TNA: DEFE 69/481, Healey to Mayhew, 13 December 1965. **52** TNA: DEFE 69/481, Mayhew to Healey, 16 December 1965. **53** TNA: T 225/2711, Bell to Walker, 4 January 1966. **54** TNA: CAB 148/53, OPD(O)(66), 1st meeting, 6 January and 2nd meeting, 7 January 1966; T 225/2711, Daniel to Henley and Wiggins, 5 January 1966. **55** TNA: CAB 165/28, Trend to Wilson, 18 January 1966. **56** TNA: CAB 148/25, OPD(66) 4th to 13th meetings, 19 January to 13 February 1966; PREM 13/744, Mayhew to Wilson, 28 January 1966, WKR to Mitchell, 28 January 1966. **57** TNA: CAB 148/25, OPD(66) 12th meeting, 11 February 1966. **58** LHCMA: Mayhew 8/1, Mayhew to Wilson 7 December 1965; Wilson to Mayhew 28 December 1965; Mayhew to Wilson, 3 January 1966; Mayhew 8/2, typed note by Christopher Mayhew, 29 December 1965. **59** TNA: CAB 148/25 OPD(66) 9th meeting, 1 February 1966. **60** TNA: CAB 128/41, CM(66) 8, 14 February 1966. **61** LHCMA: Mayhew 2/3, Mayhew to Luce, 7 March 1966. **62** Dyndal, *Land based Air Power or Aircraft Carriers?*, pp. 177–9. **63** Grove: *Vanguard to Trident*, p. 280.

Chapter 3: Recovery and Rebuilding 1966–1968
1 Hobbs, *The British Carrier Strike Fleet after 1945*, p. 399. **2** TNA: DEFE 24/128, Head DS4, Note on CNS's No 213A of 22 July; Grove, *Vanguard to Trident*, pp. 280–2. **3** NHB: Royal Navy Press Release no 40/36, 24 March 1966. **4** TNA: DEFE 24/128, Head DS1 to DUS(P&B), 20 July 1966; Cass to DUS(P&B), 27 July 1966. **5** Ibid., Peck to P/S PUS, 21 July 1966. **6** TNA: DEFE 24/149, Begg to Healey, 2 May 1966. **7** TNA: DEFE 24/128, Healey to Hull, Begg to Dunnett, 8 August 1966. **8** Ibid., Jaffray to Dunnett, 26 July 1966. **9** TNA: ADM 167/166, A/M(66)10th meeting, 20 July 1966, item 1. **10** TNA: DEFE 24/149, Healey to PUS, 25 November 1966. **11** TNA: DEFE 13/591, 'Concept of Maritime Operations Until the Early 1980s', 21 July 1966. **12** TNA: DEFE 24/128, Head BS4, Note on CNS's No 213A of 22 July. **13** Ibid., Summary Conclusions and Recommendations, FFWP Report, 30 August 1966. **14** Ibid., Annex B, see handwritten note para. 12; Peck to Head DS1, 27 September 1966. **15** Ibid., brief for PUS, 14 March 1967, p. 3. **16** TNA: DEFE 24/149, Note of meeting with Secretary of State, 2 August 1966. **17** TNA: Ibid., Begg to various, 26 September 1966; DEFE 24/150, Jaffray to Committee Members, 27 September 1966; Grove, *Vanguard to Trident*, p. 282. **18** TNA: DEFE 24/149, 'Concept of Future Naval Operations', 18 October 1966, Annex 1, p. 2. **19** The Standard Frigate would later become the Type 22. Friedman (*British Destroyers and Frigates*, pp. 291–2), states that the Standard Frigate, which he correctly describes as a derivative of the Type 19, became the Type 21. However, what became the Type 21 was termed by Navy Department planners as 'the RN/RAN frigate' between 1966 and 1968, whilst the 'Standard Frigate' was described separately. By March 1969 the RN/RAN frigate had been renamed the Type 21 and the Standard Frigate the Type 22. For example, see NHB: Finance Box 5, '1968 Long Term Costing Assumptions', March 1968, Appendix A, pp. 1–2, T48738; '1969 Long Term Costing Assumptions', February 1969, Appendix A, pp. 2–3, T48739. **20** TNA: DEFE 24/150, Begg to Admiralty Board Sub-Committee, 11 October 1966; DEFE 24/149, enclosure 10, Annex 2, 'Shape of the Future Fleet'. **21** TNA: DEFE 24/149, The Future Fleet: Note on Minister (RN)'s submission of 28 October 1966, para. 13; Jaffray to Peck and Dunnett, 4 November 1966. **22** TNA: DEFE 24/149, Mallalieu to Healey, 28 October 1966 covering The Future Fleet, Note on Minister(RN)'s submission of 28 October 1966. **23** TNA: ADM 167/166, A/M(66)16th meeting, 9 November 1966; DEFE 24/149, note by Healey to Dunnett, 14 November 1966. **24** TNA: DEFE 4/207, 53rd meeting, item 6, 11 October 1966; DEFE 4/210, 68th meeting, 20 December 1966. **25** TNA: DEFE 25/111, Healey to Hull, 10 February 1967, and note of meeting 9 February 1967. **26** TNA: T 225/2963, White Paper draft December 1966, note of meeting 2 January 1967, Bancroft to Nicholls, 16 January 1967. **27** TNA: DEFE 13/585, Dunnett to Healey, 10 March 1967. **28** Ibid., Peck to Dunnett, 6 March 1967, forwarded to Healey with comments by Nairne, 14 March 1967. **29** Ibid., Note of Wilson-Healey meeting, 14 March 1967. **30** For the importance of the ending of the Confrontation to the eventual decision to withdraw, see Dockrill, *Britain's Retreat from East of Suez*, pp. 128–30, and James, 'Global Britain's strategic problem East of Suez', pp. 171–89; for the

actual discussions and decisions to withdraw, see Saki Dockrill, *Britain's Retreat from East of Suez*, Chs 8 and 9. **31** TNA: DEFE 4/214, CoS(66)24/1, 17 March 1967. **32** DEFE 24/149, Defence Council minutes extract, 20 March 1967. **33** TNA: DEFE 24/128, Brief for Dunnett, 14 March 1967. **34** TNA: CAB 148/31/22 OPD(67)46, 21 June 1967. **35** TNA: DEFE 4/222, CoS(67)81, 21 November 1967. **36** TNA: FCO 46/9 telegram Washington to FO, 13 September 1967; FCO 46/10 telegram Washington to FO, 11 October 1967; Wilford to Sykes, 12 October 1967; Sykes to PUS, 17 November 1967; PUS to Foreign Secretary, 17 November 1967; Healey, *The Time of My Life*, p. 292. **37** TNA: CAB 128/43, CC(68)7, 15 January 1968. **38** Ibid., CC(68)6, 12 January 1968; CC(68) 7, 15 January 1968. **39** In 1966 there were fourteen *Leander* class, seven Type 81 and one modernised Type 12 with hangars and flight decks for Wasp helicopters, five years earlier there had been no frigates in the fleet with such capabilities. **40** TNA: DEFE 45/27, DCI(RN)67/35, 'Officers – General List Seamen – Fixed Wing Aircrew – Future', 13 January 1967. **41** NHB: Manning Officers Box 2, 'Report of the Fleet Air Arm Working Party' April 1968, Annex N, T16775. **42** Sturtivant, Burrow and Howard, *Fleet Air Arm Fixed Wing Aircraft Since 1945*, pp. 44–75. **43** Ibid., pp. 470–9. **44** HMSO: Statement on the Defence Estimates 1967 (Cmnd 3203), February 1967, p. 34. **45** TNA: ADM 167/166, A/M(66)4, Item 2: Ark Royal: Three Year Special Refit, 3 March 1966; A/M(66)5, Item 1: Matters Arising, 17 March 1966; NHB: Admiralty Board Papers, A/P(66)7, 'HMS Ark Royal: Three Year Special Refit', 1 March 1966. **46** TNA: ADM 167/166, A/M(66)18, item 2: Special Refit of Ark Royal, 13 December 1966. **47** Hobbs, *British Aircraft Carriers*, p. 280. **48** TNA: ADM 167/167, A/M(67)8, Item 2, Sketch Estimates 1968–69, 22 November 1967; NHB: Admiralty Board Papers, A/P(67)2, 'Sketch Estimates 1968–69', 17 November 1967, Annex A. **49** NHB: Admiralty Board Papers, A/P(66)17, 'Implications of Increased Phantom Prices', Appendix B. **50** TNA: ADM 167/167, A/M(67)8, Item 3: HMS Victorious, 22 November 1967. **51** NHB: Victorious Box 1: 'Future of HMS Victorious', T2268: Wilde to Sargeant, 4 July 1968; Watt, 'Note on the Victorious sale', 18 December 1968; Pestell to DUS(E), 14 March 1969; Ashmore to DUS(N), 2 April 1969. *Victorious* was sold for scrap on 3 July 1969 (not 1968 as stated in some publications) and towed from Portsmouth eight days later for breaking up. *Marine News*, August 1969, p. 233, cited in NHB: *Victorious* Chron Card 13. **52** For the decision to purchase Polaris, see Matthew Jones, *The Official History of the UK Strategic Nuclear Deterrent, Volume 1* (Abingdon, 2017), Chs 9–11. **53** TNA: DEFE 24/238, Report of the Future Fleet Working Party, Volume 1, 12 September 1966. The author would like to thank Duncan Redford for pointing out the significance of this illustration. **54** TNA: ADM 167/166, A/M(66)16th meeting, 9 November 1966. **55** The incoming Labour government had discussed whether three, four or five boats should be constructed; the previous Conservative government had envisaged a force of five. Following discussions between October 1964 and January 1965, four was finally decided upon. See Jones, *The Official History of the UK Strategic Nuclear Deterrent, Volume 2*, pp. 28–31, 34–7, 44–5. **56** Hennessy and Jinks, *The Silent Deep*, pp. 248–50. **57** Ibid., pp. 254–8. **58** Jones and Young, 'Polaris East of Suez', pp. 847–70. **59** Henry, 'A CO's Story', p. 248. **60** Some in the Navy during the late 1950s and 1960s had been concerned about the impact that the costs of Polaris would have on the balance and shape of the fleet, not least its impact on the budget available for the surface fleet. Jackson and Bramall, *The Chiefs*, p. 343; Jones, *UK Strategic Nuclear Deterrent Volume 1*, p. 155. **61** Hennessy and Jinks, *The Silent Deep*, pp. 249–53. **62** TNA: ADM 167/166, A/M(66)1, Item 2, 'Nuclear submarine hull defects', 27 January 1966; A/M(66)10, item 3, 'Steel for nuclear submarines', 20 July 1966. **63** Hennessy and Jinks, *The Silent Deep*, pp. 302–03. **64** TNA: ADM 167/166, A/M(66)11, item 2, Improved Valiant Class Nuclear Submarine – Sketch Design, 4 August 1966; ADM/167/167, A/M(67)3, item 2, SSN-07 – Improved Valiant Class: Building Drawings, 16 March 1967; NHB: Admiralty Board Papers, A/P(66)24, 'Improved Valiant Class Nuclear Submarines – Sketch Design', 13 June 1966. See also Friedman, *British Submarines in the Cold War Era*, pp. 155–8; Friedman uses the same sources as the author but provides much more detail than space allows in this book. **65** HMSO, 'Statement on Defence Estimates 1968 (Cmnd 3540, February 1968), p. 29. **66** TNA: T 225/3324, Swain to Patterson, 24 February 1967. **67** NHB: *Swiftsure* Box, Ministry of Defence News Release 38/73, 10 April 1973. Unfortunately, most records relating to the naming history of the *Swiftsure* class have not survived. However, this class saw a shift from traditional capital ship names with the first three boats (*Swiftsure*, *Sovereign* and *Superb*) to names associated with submarines from the Second World War such as *Sceptre* and *Splendid* (the name of the fifth boat, *Spartan* had been used both for a cruiser and a submarine in the War). This shift marked an increased self-assertiveness amongst submariners in the 1970s, and the re-use of wartime submarine names continued with most of the succeeding *Trafalgar* class. See Redford, *The Submarine: A Cultural History*, pp. 190–9. **68** Friedman, *British Carrier Aviation*, pp. 349–50. **69** TNA: DEFE 24/149, enclosure 10, Annex 2: 'Shape of the Future Fleet'. **70** TNA: T 225/3200, Patterson to Nicholls et al, 29 June 1967. **71** As at March 1968 the tentative particulars of the cruiser were 12,500 tons, three Olympus gas turbines driving three shafts, Sea Dart, 4.5in Mk 8 gun, six Sea King, and a suite of radar and sonar similar to the Type 42. Finance Box 5/T48738, '1968 Long Term Costing Assumptions', March 1968, p. A1. **72** Friedman, *British Destroyers and Frigates*, pp. 181–92; Morton, *Fire Across the Desert*, pp. 342–4. **73** Friedman, *British Destroyers and Frigates*, p. 182. **74** Poole, *History of Acquisition in the Department of Defense, Volume II*, pp. 312–16. **75** NHB: Exercises Box 7, 'Analysis of Exercise Phoenix 1964', 30 April 1964, III-1, T47410. **76** Gjessing, *Anglo-Australian Naval Relations 1945–1975*, pp.178–82. **77** TNA: ADM 167/166, A/M(66)6, item 3, County Class modernisation, 20 April 1966; NHB: Admiralty Board papers, A/P(66)11, 'First Long Term Refits of County Class GMDs 01–04', 18 April 1966. **78** TNA: ADM 167/168, A/M(66)8, item 2, First Long Refits of County Class DLGs, 18 July 1968. **79** Morton, *Fire Across the Desert*, p. 345. **80** NHB: VCNS Papers Box 52, VCNS 40/1/7, VCNS to 1SL, 16 March 1973. **81** TNA: DEFE 24/128, enclosure 4B, Options for Concept of Operations, pp. 3–6, July 1966. **82** TNA: DEFE 24/149, enclosure 29, Healey to Begg, 10 February 1967. **83** TNA: DEFE 24/238, Report of the Future Fleet Working Party, Volume 3, August 1966, pp. 13, 15 and 17. **84** TNA: T 225/ 3323, Nicholls to Bancroft, 8 February 1968; DEFE 10/533, OR25/67 NSR 6528, 22 June 1967; OR55/67 NST 7096, 4 December 1967. **85** TNA: DEFE 13/584, Begg to Admiralty Board 28 December 1966; cover note by Hastie-Smith, 2 January 1967. **86** TNA: ADM 167/168, A/M(68)10, item 3, Type 42, 21 November 1968; NHB: Admiralty Board Papers, A/P(68)24, 'Type 42 Destroyer – Final Design, Building Drawings', 30 October 1968. **87** TNA: ADM 167/166, A/M(66)3, Item 3, 18 February 1966; A/M(66)4, Item 5, 3 March 1966. **88** HMSO, Statement on the Defence Estimates 1966–67 (Cmnd 2902), February 1966, p. 102. **89** Gjessing, *Anglo-Australian Naval Relations*, p. 160; Loxton, 'DDL – The Concept Develops', pp. 12–13. **90** The new version of the DDL was now developed in partnership with YARD (the Yarrow-Admiralty Research Department) as a 4,200-ton Tartar-armed destroyer with some family resemblance to the Type 42 and Type 22. Loxton, 'DDL – The Concept Develops', pp. 13–17. **91** TNA: ADM 167/169, A/M(69)3, item 2, Type 21, 24 March 1969; NHB: Admiralty Board Papers, A/P(69)4, Type 21, 3 March 1969. **92** Brown, *A Century of Naval Construction*, p. 258. **93** Friedman, *U.S. Amphibious Ships and Craft*, pp. 364–5; Speller, *The Role of Amphibious Warfare in British Defence Policy*, pp. 204–06. **94** TNA: DEFE 69/325, 'Naming Ship after Sir Winston Churchill' 1965–66. **95** Blackman, *Jane's Fighting Ships 1967–68*, p. 296. **96** Kuzin and Nikol'sky, *Voyenno-Morskoy Flot SSSR*, Ch 7.4. **97** TNA: DEFE 69/333, Bryars to FOSNI 2 February 1966 for approval of HMS *Exmouth* to be converted into the Olympus/Proteus trials ship. The first Type 19 frigate had also been considered but rejected as the trials vessel: Edge-Partington to DS4, 3 November 1965. **98** Preston, *Power for the Fleet*, pp. 5–22, 48–51, 64–6. **99** Ibid., pp. 70–6. **100** Admiralty Library, Pam. 2709: Central Office of Information, 'Notes on Science and Technology in Britain: Hovercraft' (December 1962); Russell, *The Interservice Hovercraft (Trials) Unit*, Foreword. **101** Preston, *Power for the Fleet*, pp. 37–9. **102** Russell, *Interservice Hovercraft (Trials) Unit*, p. 1. **103** Ibid., after foreword; HMSO, 'Statement on Defence Estimates 1968', (Cmnd 3540, February 1968), p. 24; 'Statement on Defence Estimates 1969', (Cmnd 3927, February 1969), p. 27. **104** Russell, *Interservice Hovercraft (Trials) Unit*, pp. 7–9; Preston, *Power for the Fleet*, p. 43; HMSO, 'Statement on Defence Estimates 1967' (Cmnd 3203, February 1967), p. 22; HMSO, 'Statement on Defence Estimates 1968', (Cmnd 3540, February 1968), p. 17. **105** Preston, *Power for the Fleet*, p. 46. **106** NHB: Equipment (General) Box 1: N/TW 911/40/64, 'Report on Instrumented Body Trials of Sonar Type 195 from Hovercraft SRN-3', September 1964; minute by DUSW(N), 6 July 1966. **107** Mobley, 'The Beira Patrol', pp. 63–7; Mlambo, 'Honoured more in the Breach than in the Observance', pp. 371–93. **108** Mobley, 'The Beira Patrol', pp. 67–73. **109** NHB: Beira Patrol Box, Volume 1, 'Revised Instructions to the Beira Patrol' DS5, 20 December 1967 and Annex pp. 26–7. **110** Mobley, 'The Beira Patrol', p. 76. **111** The political process of preparing for independence was complex and can only be touched here, not least the failed attempts to merge the colony and two protectorates into a single Federation before independence. Ducker, 'Historical and Constitutional Background', pp. 8–59. **112** Walker, *Aden Insurgency*, pp. 239–70. **113** NHB: FO2 FE Box, Report of Proceedings, Ashmore to CinC Far East Fleet, 22 December 1967, Annex A: Diary of Events. **114** Ibid., paras 5–20; for a history of the introduction of the teleprinter system ('RATT': Radio Teletype), see RN

Communications Branch Museum website, 'Introduction to RATT': https://www.commsmuseum.co.uk/ratt/pdfs/rattintro.pdf (accessed 24 August 2021). **115** NHB: FO2 FE Box, Report of Proceedings, Ashmore to CinC Far East Fleet, 22 December 1967, paras 16–18. **116** NHB: FO2 FE Box, Report of Proceedings, Ashmore to CinC Far East Fleet, 21 January 1968. **117** NHB: FO2 FE Box, Report of Proceedings, FOAC to CinC Far East Fleet, 29 January 1968. **118** Watson, *Red Navy at Sea*, pp. 149–50, 161. **119** NHB: Naval Intelligence Report for January to March 1966, No. 8, 12 April 1966, pp. 5–9. **120** The 'Z' class War Emergency Destroyers were identical to the 'Ca' class destroyers. Four 'Ca' class and one 'Z' class (converted to a frigate) were still active in the fleet in October 1967. TNA: ADM 187/107, Pink List 2 October 1967, pp. 11 and 26. **121** Polmar and Gresham, *Defcon 2*, pp. 60, 159–66. **122** Watson, *Red Navy at Sea*, pp. 148–60; NHB: Naval Intelligence Report, Winter 1968, No.19, p. 20. **123** Polmar and Moore, *Cold War Submarines*, pp. 168–71; Zaloga, *The Kremlin's Nuclear Sword*, pp. 117–18. **124** CIA Online Reading Room: 'Soviet Capabilities to Counter US Aircraft Carriers', May 1972, pp. 13–16, 35–8: SOVIET CAPABILITIES TO COUNTER US AIRCRAFT CARRIERS (cia.gov) (accessed 27 June 2023); Polmar and Moore, *Cold War Submarines*, p. 164. **125** NHB: Naval Intelligence Report, Spring 1967, No. 12, pp. 2–4. **126** Il'in and Kolesnikov, *Otyechyestvyennyye Atomnyye Podvodnyye Lodki*, p. 40. **127** Theberge, *Russia in the Caribbean*, Ch 12; Dismukes and McConnell, *Soviet Naval Diplomacy*, Ch 3; Hill, 'The Cold War Soviet Navy in Sub-Saharan Waters', pp. 109–30. **128** Watson, *Red Navy at Sea*, pp. 133–6. **129** NHB: Naval Intelligence Report for January to March 1966, No. 8, pp. 3–26 was the last annual review of the Soviet Navy in this publication. Up to 1970 the only substantive mention of Soviet intentions was given in an extract of a speech by SACLANT: 'The degree of emphasis placed in this evaluation [a paper on Soviet Seapower by SACLANT's staff] on the defensive maritime aims of the Soviets should not be interpreted as any justification for a diminished concern within NATO of the active maritime threat discussed in the paper … the ever growing maritime threat to NATO's flank, to the out-flanking of NATO, and to the free use of the world's oceans, is today and will increasingly be in the future, one of the most menacing with which NATO is faced, and we shall disregard it at our peril.' NHB: Naval Intelligence Report, October 1969, No. 22, pp. 14–16. **130** Herrick, *Soviet Naval Doctrine and Policy 1956–1986, Volume 1*, pp. 224–83.

Chapter 4: A New Navy
1 Baker, *Dry Ginger*, p. 217. **2** Le Bailly, *From Fisher to the Falklands*, pp. 172–3, Healey, *The Time of My Life*, p. 266. **3** Benjamin, *Five Lives in One*, p. 132. **4** For Twiss's perspective on his time as 2SL, see Twiss, *Social Change in the Royal Navy*, Ch 10. **5** TNA: DEFE 45/35, DCI(RN)543/68, 'Changes in Service Board Membership', 3 May 1968. **6** Twiss, *Social Change in the Royal Navy*, pp. 194–7. **7** TNA: ADM 167/167, A/M(67)5, item 3, 8 June 1967; NHB: Admiralty Board Papers, A/P(67)14, 'Rum', 1 June 1967; at an informal meeting of the Board in December 1967 it was provisionally agreed to abolish the tot afloat, but this plan was delayed by objections and concerns by the Treasury and Customs. These are set out in Moore, 'We are a Modern Navy', pp. 73–4. **8** NHB: Admiralty Board Papers, A/P(69)13, 31 October 1969; the money allocated is set out in Appendix D. **9** Twiss, *Social Change in the Royal Navy*, pp. 200–01; Moore, 'We are a Modern Navy', pp. 76–8. **10** TNA: ADM 167/168, A/M(68)1, item 2, 1 February 1968; NHB: Admiralty Board Papers, A/P(68)4, 'Full Bunk Sleeping in Existing Ships', 22 January 1968. **11** TNA: ADM 167/169, A/M(69)8, item 3, 13 November 1969; NHB: Admiralty Board Papers, A/P(69)11 Revise, 'HM Ships – Accommodation Standards for Ratings', 29 September 1969. **12** TNA: ADM 114/155, Holden to Morris, 30 October 1970; NHB: Admiralty Board Papers, A/P(71)12, 'Trials of New Uniform', 3 November 1971. **13** TNA: ADM 167/171, A/M(71)8, Item 3, 11 November 1971; NHB: Admiralty Board Papers, A/P(71)12, 'Trials of New Uniform', 3 November 1971; Admiralty Library: Folio Pamphlet A013, 'Review of Class II Uniform July 1971'; for detail of sailors' views on uniform see also NHB: Board Bulletin, January 1972, pp. 9–10. **14** TNA: ADM 167/174, A/M(74)7, Item 2, 12 December 1974. **15** Hobbs, 'The Hobbs Report', pp. 9–10; Lavery, *All Hands*, pp. 226–7. **16** NHB: Admiralty Board Papers, A/P(69)9 Paper I, 'Review of Engagement Structure', 8 July 1969. **17** TNA: ADM 167/169, A/M(69)6, Item 2, 17 July 1969. **18** NHB: Admiralty Board Papers, A/P(70)4, Sketch Estimates 1971–72, 4 November 1970, p. 2. **19** TNA: DEFE 24/422, 'Report of the Committee on boy entrants and young servicemen', August 1970, pp. 1–2. **20** TNA: ADM 167/170, A/M(70)7, item 3, 14 October 1970; NHB: Admiralty Board Papers, A/P(70)12, 'Report of the Donaldson Committee', 17 September 1970. **21** Other Donaldson recommendations included widening of the window in which an under-18-year-old undergoing training

could apply for discharge if it was clear that he would not 'settle down' into a career in Defence. TNA: DEFE 24/619, 'Measures needed to man the Fleet post-Donaldson', October 1971, p. 1. **22** TNA: ADM 167/172, A/M(72)2, Item 2, 1 March 1972. **23** The Armed Forces Pay Review Body remains in existence today. HMSO: Statement on Defence Estimates 1970 (Cmnd 4290, February 1970), pp. 1 and 13; Statement on Defence Estimates 1971 (Cmnd 4592, February 1971), p. 38; NHB: A/P(69)5, '1969 Pay Review', 6 May 1969. For the X Factor, see TNA: ADM 167/169, A/M(69)2, 27 February 1969, Item 2 and Hansard Parliamentary Debates, HC Deb, 13 November 1969 Vol. 791 c. 631, Mr Hattersley. **24** TNA: DEFE 45/35, DCI(RN)551/68, 'Ratings – Drafting – General Service Ratings – New Drafting Rules', 3 May 1968; NHB: Admiralty Board Papers, A/P (69) 14, 'Service Conditions and Ship's Programmes', 10 October 1969; A/P(70)6, 'Types of Commission', 4 March 1970; TNA 167/169, A/M(69)8, item 4, 13 November 1969. **25** TNA: ADM 182/192, AFO659/54, 'Reduction of Periods of Foreign Service', 12 March 1954. **26** TNA: DEFE 69/299, Director General of Naval Manpower to CinC Home Fleet et al, 10 September 1964. **27** NHB: Admiralty Board Papers, A/P(70)6 'Types of Commission', 4 March 1970. **28** TNA: DEFE 45/47, DCI(RN)534/70, 'Commissions – Introduction of Continuous Commissions', 1 May 1970. **29** NHB: Admiralty Board Papers, A/P(70)6 'Types of Commission', 4 March 1970. **30** TNA: DEFE 45/47, DCI(RN)534/70. **31** TNA: ADM 167/170, A/M(70)4, item 3, 12 March 1970; NHB: Admiralty Board Papers, A/P(70)7, 'Service Conditions and Ship's Programmes', 5 March 1970. **32** NHB: Admiralty Board Papers, A/P(70)6 'Types of Commission', 4 March 1970; TNA: TNA: DEFE 45/47, DCI(RN)534/70. **33** TNA: ADM 182/200, AFO1/56, 'The New Officer Structure', January 1956, paras 38–41; Admiralty Library: Da 1101, Promotion of Seaman Officers to Commander and Captain on the General List, May 1959. **34** TNA: DEFE 45/14 DCI(RN)1605/65. **35** TNA: ADM 167/168, A/M(68)4, item 3, 28 March 1968; NHB: Admiralty Board Papers, A/P(68)10, 'The Split List', 25 March 1968; TNA: DEFE45/35 DCI(RN)651/68. **36** Among his books were, *Maritime Strategy for Medium Powers* (London, 1986), *Arms Control at Sea* (London, 1989) and *Lewin of Greenwich: the authorised Biography of Admiral of the Fleet Lord Lewin* (London, 2000). **37** Hore, 'Rear Admiral Richard Hill 1929–2017'. **38** TNA: ADM 167/171, A/M(71)5, item 1, 5 August 1971; NHB: Admiralty Board Papers, A/P(71)5, 'Seaman Officers – Promotion to Commander and Captain and Sea Appointments', 22 July 1971. **39** TNA: DEFE 45/62 DCI(RN)955/71. For an overview of the Split List from 1956 to 71 see also NHB: Manning (Officers) Box 10/T777590, Claro to Sec (ACNS), D/NHB/9/8/11, 10 December 1998. **40** The leading defence scientist Ralph Benjamin, who worked alongside and for senior naval officers for nearly 30 years, noted that 'it obviously was a good thing for a naval officer to *be* clever, but he had to take care not to show it' [Benjamin's emphasis]. Although there is a note of flippancy in the statement, it does reveal much about the pervading culture amongst senior naval officers in 1960s and 1970s. Benjamin, *Five Lives in One*, p. 131. **41** Livsey, 'The Royal Navy's Principal Warfare Officer Course', pp. 300–03. **42** NHB: Admiralty Board Papers, A/P(71)4, 'Seaman Officer Training – The Principal Warfare Officer concept', 30 June 1971. **43** TNA: ADM 167/171, A/M(71)4, item 2, 8 July 1971; Livsey, 'Royal Navy's Principal Warfare Officer Course', pp. 304–05; TNA: ADM 167/174, A/M(74)1 Item 2, Seaman Officer Structure and Training, 11 February 1974. **44** Penn, *HMS Thunderer*, pp. 148–9; see also pp. 122–30 for the pre-1966 system linked to universities. **45** TNA: DEFE 69/391, 'Independent Enquiry into the Service Colleges', 29 July 1966, p. 38; HMSO: Supplementary Statement on Defence Policy 1968 (Cmnd 3701, July 1968), pp. 18–19. **46** NHB: Admiralty Board Papers, A/P(69)10, 'In-service Degree Training for Junior Seaman and Supply Officers', 11 July 1969; A/P(70)5, 13 February 1970. **47** NHB: Admiralty Board Papers, A/P(70)13, 'Future of In-service Degrees', 7 October 1970; Dickinson, *Wisdom and War*, pp. 234, 238. **48** Twiss, *Social Change in the Royal Navy*, pp. 192–3. **49** HMSO: Statement on The Defence Estimates 1969 (Cmnd 3927, February 1969), pp. 30–1; Holdsworth and Pugsley, *Sandhurst*; Haslam, *Royal Air Force Cranwell*, pp. 112–13 and 125 (fn 1). **50** TNA: ADM 167/174, A/M(74)2, Item 3, 26 February 1974. **51** Dickinson, *Wisdom and War*, pp. 222–34. **52** TNA: ADM 167/174, A/M(74)2, Item 3, 21 February 1974. **53** TNA: ADM 167/173, A/M(73)7, item 1, 3 October 1973; NHB: Admiralty Board Papers A/P(73)11, 'Formation of an Operations Branch', 23 August 1973. For implementation, see TNA: DEFE 45/85, DCI(RN)S1/74, 'Introduction-Operations Branch-Ratings', 4 January 1974; DCI(RN)S114/74, 'Ratings-Operations Branch-Implementation', 2 August 1974; NHB: Naval News Summary 8/74, pp. 1–2. **54** TNA: DEFE 69/306, NA to 2SL to DGNM, 16 May 1969; DGNM note 'Branch Structures' 29 August 1969; NHB: Admiralty Board Papers, A/P(69)19, 'Branch Structures', 12 December 1969. **55** TNA: DEFE 45/86, DCI(RN)S142, 'Extension of the user/

maintainer scheme in the under-water weapons field', 13 September 1974; NHB: Admiralty Board Papers, A/P(72)8, 'Introduction of a Limited User-Maintainer Scheme into the Royal Navy' 18 October 1972; TNA: ADM 167/172, A/M(72)7, item 2, 2 November 1972. **56** TNA: ADM 176/178, A/M(75)8, item 5, 10 July 1975. **57** NHB: Admiralty Board Papers, A/P(70)1, 'Introduction of Warrant Officers into the Rating Structure of the RN', 8 January 1970. **58** NHB: Admiralty Board Papers, A/P(70)4, 'The system of advancing ratings', 10 February 1970. **59** TNA: DEFE 45/86, DCI(RN) S114, 'Ratings-Operations Branch-Implementation', 2 August 1974. **60** The 1960–1 figures were £794,000 for the RN compared to £5.9 million for the Army and £5.4 million for the RAF. In 1968–9 the figures were: £3.9 million RN, £7.2 million Army and £6.2 million RAF. TNA: DEFE 13/363, Powell-Chandler to DUS(PL), 13 September 1969, Annexed table. Comparative personnel numbers in 1968–9 were 98,000 for the RN and 125,000 for the RAF. These were the strengths voted for by Parliament, actual levels would have been a little lower. HMSO: Defence Estimates 1968/69, 21 February 1968, pp. 21, 145. **61** NHB: Board Bulletin August 1971, 'Married Quarters', pp. 7–8. **62** TNA: DEFE 13/363, PS USofS(RN) to PS SofS, 5 March 1968. **63** House of Lord Debates, 'Social Services: The Seebohm Report' (HL Deb 29 January 1969, Vol. 298, cc. 1168–1175). **64** TNA: ADM 167/173, A/M(73)11, Item 1 Seebohm Report on Naval Welfare, 13 December 1973; NHB: Admiralty Board Papers A/P(73)17, 'Seebohm Report on Naval Welfare: Memorandum by the Second Sea Lord', 7 December 1973. The report was published by the Ministry of Defence the following year: HMSO, 'Report of the Naval Welfare Committee; Chairman: Lord Seebohm' (Ministry of Defence, 1974). **65** NHB: Admiralty Board Papers A/P(76)12, 'Naval Personal and Family Service' Second Sea Lord, 15 November 1976; Admiralty Board Minutes A/M(76)8, Item 3, 24 November 1976; Hill, *Lewin of Greenwich*, pp. 294–5. Hill suggests that Lewin was somewhat favourably inclined towards the reforms but only had differences with Admiral Williams, the Second Sea Lord, over control of the new service. Admiralty Board records show that in fact Lewin led the opposition to the Seebohm proposals and was instrumental in blocking their implementation. **66** Royal Navy website: Press Release 2 July 2020: 'Social Worker Trial on Carrier Proves A Success': https://www.royalnavy.mod.uk/news-and-latest-activity/news/2020/july/02/20200702-social-worker-trial-on-carrier-proves-a-success (accessed 17 May 2021). **67** Andrew Sackville, 'The British Association of Social Workers 1970–88', section 2.8. **68** HMSO: 'The Navy List: Spring 1970', p. 176. **69** TNA: DEFE 69/239, 'Economies in Shore Training: CONSTRAIN', March 1969. **70** TNA: DEFE 69/239, A/P(69)8, 16 May 1969, 'Economies in Shore Training: CONSTRAIN', Annex A; for concerns about shutting HMS *Caledonia*; Lummis to Edwards, 22 May 1969 and Healey to Ross, 30 January 1970. **71** NHB: DCI(RN)498/79, 'HMS *Vernon* – Weapons Section – Transfer of Responsibility', 3 August 1979; diving training and other functions would remain at *Vernon* (renamed HMS *Nelson* (Gunwharf) in 1986) until 1996. See also Poland, *Torpedomen*, pp. 339–40, 364–8. **72** TNA: ADM 167/173, A/M(73)2, Item 1, 22 February 1973; Harrold and Porter, *Britannia Royal Naval College*, p. 155. **73** TNA: ADM 167/172, A/M(72)1, Item 2, 13 January 1972; NHB: Admiralty Board Papers, A/P(72)1, 'Ship Fighting and Management Training Centre', 6 January 1972; Warlow, *Shore Establishments of the Royal Navy*, pp. 55, 107, 109. **74** TNA: DEFE 69/239, AUS(PS) to Head of Home (N), 27 June 1969; ADM 167/173, A/M(73)10, item 3, 22 November 1973.

Chapter 5: Structures, Doctrine and Deployments

1 TNA: ADM 167/167, A/M(67)1, Item 3, 19 January 1967; NHB: Admiralty Board Papers, A/P(66)35, 'Naval Home Command Structure', 28 December 1966. **2** TNA: ibid. **3** TNA: ADM 167/167, A/M(67)4, Item 2, 31 March 1967. **4** NHB: Admiralty Board Papers, A/P(66)35, 28 December 1966; A/P(67)23, 'Home Command Re-Organisation: Report of the Way Ahead Committee', 1 December 1967; TNA: DEFE 45/30, DCI(RN)1255/67, 'Flag Officers – FO Second in Command Western Fleet – Change of Title', 27 October 1967. The new Flag Officer Flotillas, Western Fleet, would become Flag Officer First Flotilla when the Far East Fleet was abolished in late 1971. **5** TNA: DEFE 45/27, DCI(RN)334/67, 24 March 1967 and DEFE 45/28 DCI(RN)613/67, 2 June 1967. **6** TNA: ADM 167/167, A/M(67)9, item 1, 15 December 1967; NHB: Admiralty Board Papers, A/P(67)23, 'Home Command Re-Organisation: Report of the Way Ahead Committee', 1 December 1967; A/P(67)24, 'Reorganisation of Western Fleet Command', 1 December 1967; TNA: DEFE 45/34, DCI(RN)204/68; DEFE 45/35, DCI(RN)407/68; DEFE 45/40, DCI(RN)380/69. **7** TNA: ADM 167/167, A/M(67)9, Item 2, 15 December 1967; NHB: Admiralty

Board Papers, A/P(67)24, Reorganisation of Western Fleet Command, 1 December 1967. **8** Hill, *Lewin of Greenwich*, p. 278; Treacher, *Life at Full Throttle*, p. 164; Watson, *Commander-in-Chief*, pp. 134–5. It is however worth noting that between 1967 and 1989 only one former Fleet Air Arm officer, Admiral Treacher, was appointed Commander-in-Chief Western Fleet or Commander-in-Chief Fleet (the successor post to CinC WF). It was within the Fleet Air Arm that the wounds of 1966 were the rawest, and for whom, clearly with some exceptions, the relationship with the RAF could be at its most difficult. **9** TNA: ADM 167/173, Admiralty Board Minutes, A/M(73)10, item 2, 22 November 1973; ADM 167/178, Admiralty Board Minutes, A/M(75)8, item 4, 10 July 1975; ADM 167/176, Admiralty Board Papers, A/P(75)14; T 225/4386, Cassell, note on OpCon presentation 19 July 1974; T 225/4387 Lambert to Hansford 15 August 1974; Thomas to Hansford 4 September 1974. The delay in shifting Flag Officer Submarine's HQ from Gosport to Northwood in the mid-1970s was perhaps as much due to the expectation that CINCFLEET would come south rather as any nostalgic or conservative desire to stay at the submarine service's old HQ at HMS *Dolphin* as stated in Hennessy and Jinks, *The Silent Deep*, pp. 345, 365. **10** TNA: T 225/4386, 'A Command Control and Information System for the HQ of CINCFLEET, CINCCHAN (NASR 7954)', 4 January 1973. **11** TNA: DEFE 45/28, DCI(RN)487/67, 'Commands – Naval Command Structure – New Titles and Station Limits', 28 April 1967. **12** TNA: DEFE 45/28, DCI(RN)613/67, 'Commands – Naval Command Structure – Closure of Mediterranean Command', 2 June 1967. **13** TNA: DEFE 45/34, DCI(RN)204/68, 'Commands – Naval Home Shore Command Structure – Reorganisation', 23 February 1968; DEFE 45/36, DCI(RN)928/68, 'Commands – Western Fleet – Operational Command and Control', 2 August 1968. **14** TNA: ADM 167/167, A/M(67)2, item 1, 2 March 1967; A/M(67)9, Item 2, 15 December 1967; NHB: Admiralty Board Papers, A/P(67)23, 'Home Command Re-organisation: Report of the Way Ahead Committee', 1 December 1967, Attachment: WAC/P(67)6; A/P(67)9, 'Naval Home Command Structure', 23 March 1967. **15** NHB: Admiralty Board Papers, A/P(67)9, 'Naval Home Command Structure', 23 March 1967. **16** HMSO, Statement on the Defence Estimates 1968 (Cmnd 3540), February 1968, p. 22. **17** Between 1966–7 and 1969–70 the total number of civil servants under the Navy Department shrank from 120,523 to 111,020, but half of this reduction can be accounted for by a one-third reduction in locally employed staff, with more attributed to staff reassigned from the Navy Department to the Centre. From 1970–1 the Defence votes were combined, so tracking personnel sizes becomes more difficult, but between 1969–70 and 1970–1 the numbers of staff at 'Naval Establishments' (not the same as Navy Department staff) reduced from 105,899 to 103,088. HMSO: Defence Estimates 1967–8, 10 February 1967, pp. 60–1; Defence Estimates 1969–70, 19 February 1969, pp. 60–1; Defence Estimates 1970–1, 18 February 1970, pp. 74–5. **18** TNA: DEFE 45/28, DCI(RN)487/67, 'Commands – Naval Command Structure – New Titles and Station Limits', 28 April 1967; DCI(RN)568/67, 'Commands – Future of Middle East Station and Gulf Naval Command', 19 May 1967. **19** TNA: DEFE 45/61, DCI (RN)439/71, 23 April 1971. On 1 May 1971 control of the Far East Fleet actually passed to CinC Western Fleet, who then immediately delegated that control to the Commander Far East Fleet. This would allow for a smoother assumption of direct command by CinC Western Fleet (who was renamed CinC Fleet) later that year. The downgrading to a 2* (rear admiral) post allowed for a smoother transfer to the new Five Power Defence Arrangements command, which was held by an Australian 2* who stepped into position following the hauling down of Commander FEF's flag. **20** TNA: ADM 187/157, Pink List, 10 March 1970, pp. 24–6. **21** HMSO: Supplementary Statement on Defence Policy 1970 (Cmnd 4521) October 1970, pp. 4–5. **22** NHB: Naval News Summary, November 1971, pp. 13–14. **23** NHB: Pink Lists, 4 November to 16 December 1971; see also TNA: ADM 187/168–170, Pink Lists, 26 October 1971, 29 December 1971 and 22 January 1972. **24** NHB: Eagle Box 1, Reports of Proceedings 1968–78 volume, p. 285A. **25** TNA: ADM 187/123–131, Pink List volumes 1971 to 1973. **26** TNA: ADM 167/173, A/M(73)4, item 1, 16 May 1973; NHB: Admiralty Board Papers, A/P(73)5, 'Operation and Deployment of the Fleet', 9 May 1973. **27** Ibid. and Hill, *Lewin of Greenwich*, pp. 248–51. **28** TNA: DEFE 11/839, 'Force levels in Hong Kong' Commander British Forces, 3 July 1974, p. 11. **29** NHB: Hong Kong RoP, registered file 'HK Guardship, policy and replacement', Pritchard to CinC Western Fleet, 20/9/71. **30** NHB: Chichester Box/T74150, RoP *Chichester*, 25 April to 17 September 1973. **31** NHB: Chichester Box/T74147, RoP *Chichester*, 8 June to 4 September 1974. **32** Borthwick, *Yarrow and Company Limited*, p. 118; Marriott, *Royal Navy Frigates Since 1945*, pp. 102–04. **33** NHB: Mermaid Box/T112943, Mermaid RoP, 25 August to 7 December 1974. **34** TNA: ADM 167/173, A/M(73)4,

Item 1, 15 May 1973; NHB: Admiralty Board Memoranda, A/P(73)5, 'Operation and Deployment of the Fleet', 9 May 1973; Group Deployments Box 2, Fleet Deployments 1969–78 volume, pp. 32–5. **35** NHB: Group Deployments Box 2, Fleet Deployments 1969–78 volume, pp. 32–62; Roberts, *Safeguarding the Nation*, pp. 100–01. Roberts erroneously gives the TG number as 317.1. **36** Mobley, 'Beira Patrol', p. 17. **37** NHB: Group Deployments Box 2, Fleet Deployments 1969–78 volume, pp. 64–115; Roberts, *Safeguarding the Nation*, pp. 101–02. **38** Ibid., pp. 103–04. **39** NATO Archives: MC03/IMSWM-181-69 'Exercise Peace Keeper', Military Committee Memorandum, 25 July 1969: https://archives.nato.int/uploads/r/nato-archives-online/0/e/6/0e645fd8ae290cf77b693760695e38387dd787ff050079a4ae2fd43b7933a616/IMSWM-181-69_ENG_PDP.pdf (accessed 23/3/22). **40** NHB: Exercises Box 11/T83812, ACNS(O&A) to VCNS, 30 September 1969. **41** Zumwalt, *On Watch*, p. 467. **42** NHB: Exercises Box 5/T56527, Naval Control of Shipping Underway Indoctrination, 1 September 1970. **43** Ibid., Exercise Northern Wedding, NCS Helicopter Trial, Report, 22 October 1970. **44** NHB: Exercises Box 11/T47311, 1SL brief 'Exercise Peace Keeper', 3 September 1969. **45** TNA: ADM 187/60, Pink List July 1970. **46** NHB: Exercises Box 10/T24701, Strong Express 72 Press Pack. **47** NHB: Exercises Box 10/T47289, Exercise Swift Move, Fieldhouse to Sec 1SL, 25 September 1973. **48** NHB: Exercises Box 10/T47286, Exercise Northern Merger, Skinner to Sec 1SL, 6 September 1974. **49** TNA: DEFE 67/66, Lime Jug 70 Exercise Report Vol 1, pp. 1–3 to 1–5. **50** NHB: Exercises Box 9/T83241, Lime Jug 70, DNW to Sec VCNS and Sec 1SL, 16 November 1971. **51** TNA: DEFE 67/66, Lime Jug 70 Exercise Report Vol 1, pp. 1–7 to 1–12. **52** TNA: DEFE 67/67, Lime Jug 70 Exercise Report Vol 2, pp. 1–5 to 1–7, 5–1 to 5–5. **53** NHB: Exercises Box 9/T83219, Exercise High Wood 71, DNW to Sec 1SL, 24 November 1971. **54** TNA: DEFE 67/69, Window Delta in Exercise High Wood 71, 1 April 1972. **55** TNA: DEFE 67/71, Exercise High Wood 71: Command and Control Evaluation, April 1972, pp. v–x. **56** TNA: DEFE 58/113, Joint Report: Exercise High Wood 71, September 1972, p. H-2. **57** TNA: DEFE 58/54, Operational Evaluation of Exercise High Wood 71 (RAF Strike Command), May 1972, p. 2. **58** Ibid., p. 4. **59** TNA: DEFE 67/72, Exercise High Wood 71: ASW, August 1972, p. 54. **60** Ibid., p. 5. **61** TNA: DEFE 58/113, Joint Report: Exercise High Wood 71, September 1972, p. J-1. **62** One ship, HMS *Hermione*, was credited as a 'paper Ikara' firing ship – Ikara had not yet entered service – and she undertook seven simulated attacks but all of these simulations were misses as well. TNA: DEFE 67/72, Exercise High Wood 71: ASW, August 1972, pp. 19–29. **63** NHB: Diary of Principal Naval Exercises 1973, 30 April 1973, p. 22 (November). **64** TNA: DEFE 67/102, Exercise High Wood 75, November 1975, pp. 11–20; NHB: Exercises Box 8/T83162, Exercise High Wood 75, DNW to Sec 1SL, 16 September 1975. **65** NHB: Exercises Box 8/T83164, Exercise High Wood 77, DNW to Sec 1SL, 30 June 1977. **66** NHB: Exercises Box 8/T83166, Exercise High Wood 79, DDNW to Sec 1SL, 11 June 1979. **67** TNA: DEFE 67/108, Exercise High Wood 1977, December 1977, pp. 11–26. **68** Watson, *Commander-in-Chief*, pp. 78–9. **69** Hattendorf, 'NATO's Policeman on the Beat', pp. 187–95. **70** HMSO: Statement on the Defence Estimates 1973, February 1973 (Cmnd 5231), p. 17; NHB: Submarine Warfare Box 5, Signal FOSM to CO HMNLS *Tonijn*, 27 October 1972, T4774. **71** Karreman, *In Deepest Secrecy*, p. 83; 'Dutch Submarines Base in Britain' *Daily Telegraph*, 18 August 1972. **72** Compare Blackman, *Jane's Fighting Ships 1968–69*, p. 200, with *Jane's Fighting Ships 1971–72*, p. 238. **73** Ministry of Defence website: 'Press release: UK and Netherlands confirm future relationship', 30 June 2023: UK and Netherlands confirm future amphibious relationship – GOV.UK (www.gov.uk) (accessed 25/7/23). **74** Ministry of Defence, 'Joint Doctrine Publication 0–01: UK Defence Doctrine' 6th edition, November 2022, p. 55: JDP 0–01, UK Defence Doctrine, 6th Edition (publishing.service.gov.uk) (accessed 7 December 2022). **75** For a comprehensive, and definitive, discussion of RN tactical doctrine in this period, see Livsey, 'Thought Leadership', draft article 2022. The author thanks Cdr Livsey for allowing him to read and cite this article before submission and publication. **76** NHB: BR 1806, 'The Naval War Manual', January 1969; for the earlier 1958 version, see TNA: ADM 234/590, 'The Naval War Manual', 1958 (1961 Reprint). **77** Livsey, 'The Royal Navy and Julian Corbett, 1990–2020', p. 2. **78** Churchill College, Cambridge, Witness seminar: 'Overstretched? The making and impact of the UK's defence reviews since 1957', transcript, p. 29 (ACM Sir John Willis). **79** TNA: ADM 239/785, CB 04487(1), 'The Fighting Instructions Volume I', June 1969. **80** TNA: ADM 239/786, CB 04487(2), 'The Fighting Instructions Volume 2: Tactical Problems', June 1970. **81** Livsey, 'Thought Leadership', pp. 14–15. **82** FOTIs are not publicly-available, although some titles have been declassified, such as the examples given here. Titles taken from TNA: ADM 239/786, 'Fighting Instructions Volume 2', pp. 34, 82. **83** Livsey, 'Thought Leadership', p. 11. **84** TNA: DEFE 69/197 1SL to Sec St, 2 November 1971; see also Hampshire, 'Naval Intelligence', pp. 161–4. **85** Books of Reference can be found in TNA: ADM 234, and Confidential Books in TNA: ADM 239. **86** Williamson, *The US Navy and its Cold War Allies*, pp. 148–62; Livsey, 'Thought Leadership', pp. 5–10, 12–14. **87** TNA: DEFE 45/62, DCI(RN)1022/71, 17 September 1971. **88** NHB: Admiralty Board Papers, A/P(68)23, 'Review of Home Dockyards', 11 October 1968. **89** Coats, *20th Century Naval Dockyards*, pp. 153–75, 189–91. **90** Boarer, 'The Devonport Frigate Complex', pp. 505–21. **91** NHB: Admiralty Board Papers, A/P(69)18, 'Fleet Maintenance Bases', 12 December 1969. **92** NHB: Admiralty Board Papers, A/P(69)17, 'New Construction in Dockyards', 9 December 1969. **93** HMSO: Defence Appropriation Accounts 1975–76 (Volume 1: Classes I-III). Prior to 1964 there had been a separate dockyard vote within the Navy Estimates. **94** Goldsmith, 'History of Ministry of Defence Finance', pp. 10–1 to 10–10, 23–1 to 23–4.

Chapter 6: Sea Control
1 Obituary, *The Guardian*, 2 October 2006. **2** Richard Hill, 'Sir Michael Pollock', *Dictionary of National Biography*, 7 March 2013; see also HMSO: Navy List, various years 1955–1971. **3** Jones, *UK Strategic Nuclear Deterrent, Volume II*, pp. 399–400. **4** Stoddart, *Losing an Empire and Finding a Role*, pp. 128–36; Jones, *Strategic Nuclear Deterrent Volume II*, Chs 10 and 11. **5** As a NATO capability, the targeting of the UK's strategic nuclear deterrent was co-ordinated with the US's Single Integrated Operations Plan which provided combined targeting for the US deterrent across land, air and sea-launched capabilities. Kristin Stoddart, 'Maintaining the Moscow Criterion', pp. 898–9. **6** Jones, *UK Strategic Nuclear Deterrent, Volume I*, pp. 283–97; *Volume II*, pp. 368–71; Stoddart, 'Maintaining the Moscow Criterion', pp. 898–9. **7** Spinardi, *From Polaris to Trident*, pp. 66–72. **8** Ibid., pp. 86–112; Stoddart, *Sword and the Shield*, p. 54; Polmar and Moore, *Cold War Submarines*, pp. 123–4. **9** Healey, *The Time of My Life*, p. 313. **10** Robb, 'Antelope, Poseidon or a Hybrid', pp. 806–09. **11** Jones, *Strategic Nuclear Deterrent Volume II*, pp. 210–17, 316, 353; Hennessy and Jinks, *The Silent Deep*, p. 463–4; Stoddart, *Sword and the Shield*, pp. 47–8; Baylis and Stoddart, 'Britain and the Chevaline Project', pp. 128–9. **12** Baylis and Stoddart, 'Britain and the Chevaline Project', pp. 129–30; Stoddart, *Sword and the Shield*, p. 48. **13** Robb, 'Antelope, Poseidon or a Hybrid', pp. 803–05; Parr, 'The British Decision to Upgrade Polaris', pp. 263–7. **14** Stoddart, *Sword and the Shield*, p. 63; for earlier (1969) discussions of a fifth boat, see Jones, *Strategic Nuclear Deterrent Volume II*, p. 503. **15** Parr, 'The British Decision to Upgrade Polaris', pp. 256–7. **16** Stoddart, *Sword and the Shield*, pp. 21–5. **17** Ibid., pp. 49–51, 66–9. **18** Robb, 'Antelope, Poseidon or a Hybrid', pp. 802–03. **19** Ibid., pp. 806–08. **20** Jones, *Strategic Nuclear Deterrent Volume II*, pp. 507–09; Baylis and Stoddart, 'Britain and the Chevaline Project'; Daniel, *The End of an Era*, p. 199. **21** Robb, 'Antelope, Poseidon or a Hybrid', pp. 809–13. **22** Parr, 'The British Decision to Upgrade Polaris', p. 269. **23** Baylis and Stoddart, 'Britain and the Chevaline Project', pp. 135–6. **24** In 1975 the Royal Navy and RAF in the maritime role operated tactical nuclear bombs and air-launched nuclear depth bombs. The US navy operated a much wider range of nuclear-tipped weaponry including anti-submarine missiles and air defence missiles. The Dutch also used nuclear depth bombs. TNA: DEFE 69/468, DN Plans, The Use of Tactical Nuclear Weapons at Sea, Appendix 1 to Annex A, 11 November 1975. **25** Sayle, *Enduring Alliance*, pp. 82–4; Westad, *The Cold War: A World History*, pp. 303–04; Friedman, *The Fifty Year War*, pp. 285–7. **26** NATO: 'NATO Strategy Documents 1949–1969', MC14/3 (Final), 16 January 1968, pp. 345–70. **27** Stoddart, *Losing an Empire and Finding a Role*, pp. 223–4. **28** Hennessy and Jinks, *The Silent Deep*, p. 307. **29** Polmar and Moore, *Cold War Submarines*, pp. 297–300; Gordon and Kommissarov, *Soviet Naval Aviation 1946–1991*, p. 153. **30** TNA: DEFE 11/471, ACDS(Pol) to CDS, 23 May 1972. **31** TNA: ADM 239/785, Fighting Instructions 1970, Chapter 10, Annex 10B. **32** Ibid. **33** Ibid. **34** Quoted in TNA: ADM 239/785, Fighting Instructions 1970, Chapter 10, Annex 10B. **35** TNA: DEFE 68/468, Use of Tactical Nuclear Weapons at Sea, Annex B, 11 November 1975. **36** TNA: DEFE 11/471, Nuclear Planning Group minutes of 10th, 11th, 12th and 13th meetings, held 26–27 October 1971, 18–19 May 1972, 26–27 October 1972 and 15–16 May 1973 respectively. **37** Freedman and Michaels, *The Evolution of Nuclear Strategy*, pp. 332, 403–16, 528–30. **38** Gordon and Kommissarov, *Soviet Naval Aviation 1946–1991*, pp. 153–4. **39** Friedman, 'Elmo Russell Zumwalt Jr', pp. 367–8. **40** Watson, *Red Navy at Sea*, pp. 73–130, 147–67. **41** Friedman, 'Elmo Russell Zumwalt Jr', pp. 366–7, 375–7. **42** The term 'sea control' was

derived from the more traditional term 'control of the sea' but emphasised the difficulties in asserting such control in the contemporary environment. 'Missions of the US Navy', in Hattendorf, *US Naval Strategy in the 1970s*, pp. 38–42. **43** Zumwalt, *On Watch*, p. 363. **44** 'Project Sixty' in Hattendorf, *US Naval Strategy in the 1970s*, pp. 3–17. **45** Nott, *Here Today, Gone Tomorrow*, p. 231. **46** 'Project Sixty' in Hattendorf, *US Naval Strategy in the 1970s*, p. 13. **47** TNA: DEFE 13/880, Carrington to Hill-Norton, 16 August 1971; Hill-Norton to Carrington, 3 December 1971. **48** Friedman, 'Elmo Russell Zumwalt Jr', pp. 371–5; 'Project Sixty' in Hattendorf, *US Naval Strategy in the 1970s*, pp. 18–21; Zumwalt, *On Watch*, pp. 74–7. **49** TNA: DEFE 24/160, Le Bailly to DUS(RN), 9 July 1968. **50** Gardner, *Anti-Submarine Warfare*, pp. 39–45; Garrison, *Oceanography*, pp. 154–6; Laite, *Maritime Air Operations*, pp. 36–42; TNA: ADM 239/785, Fighting Instructions Volume 1 (CB08847(1)), pp. 10–7 to 10–11. **51** Garrison, *Oceanography*, p. 155. **52** TNA: ADM 239/785, Fighting Instructions Volume 1 (CB08847(1)), p. 10–8; Gardner, *Anti-Submarine Warfare*, pp. 43–4. **53** Gardner, *Anti-Submarine Warfare*, pp. 46–8. **54** TNA: ADM 239/785, Fighting Instructions Volume 1 (CB08847(1)), p. 10–7. **55** Ibid., p. 10–8; Gardner, *Anti-Submarine Warfare*, pp. 51–2. **56** Gardner, *Anti-Submarine Warfare*, pp. 48–9; NHB: Board Bulletin (August 1971), 'ASW in the 1980s', pp. 21–2. **57** Laite, *Maritime Air Operations*, pp. 41–2. **58** Ibid., pp. 40–41; TNA: ADM 239/785, Fighting Instructions Volume 1 (CB 08847(1)), pp. 10–7 to 10–8; NHB: Board Bulletin (August 1971), 'ASW in the 1980s', p. 21. **59** Garrison, *Oceanography*, pp. 161–2. **60** TNA: DEFE 67/67, Lime Jug 70 Exercise Report, August 1971, pp. 3–10 and 3–11. **61** Ibid., p. 3–2. **62** The 'Charlie II' class submarine (Soviet designation: Project 670M), the first of which entered service in 1973, could fire the SS-N-9 'Siren' (P-120 Malakhit) anti-ship cruise missile with a maximum range of 65 nautical miles; Kuzin and Nikol'sky, *Voyenno-Morskoy Flot SSSR*, section 6.3 and table 6.2. **63** TNA: DEFE 67/67, Lime Jug 70 Exercise Report, August 1971, p. 2–4. **64** NHB: CB04826, Particulars of War Vessels 1973, pp. 14, 69–79, 89–90. The Type 199 differed from the Canadian SQS-504 primarily by its British-designed handling equipment. The ships were *Leander, Ajax, Aurora, Euryalus, Galatea, Naiad, Arethusa, Bacchante, Charybdis, Hermione, Jupiter, Ashanti* and *Gurkha*. **65** NHB: KSM Anti-Submarine Warfare Box 1, FO Flotillas, Home Fleet to Commander-in-Chief, Home Fleet, 6 December 1957. T2356. **66** The Royal Navy's disillusionment with VDS had become clear by 1971, when Canadian and US research into the next generation of VDSs was not producing encouraging results. NHB: Board Bulletin August 1971, 'ASW in the 1980s', p. 21. See also Osborne and Sowden, *Leander Class Frigates*, p. 65. It is notable that the Type 199 only had a maximum depth of around 100m, meaning that in the Eastern Atlantic it might not reach the thermocline. Conditions were apparently more favourable in the western Atlantic. TNA: ADM 239/785, Fighting Instructions 1970, p. 10–5, fig. 10.1. **67** TNA: ADM 239/785, Fighting Instructions, Volume I, June 1969, p. 10–40; see also Jeram-Croft, *The Royal Navy Lynx*, p. 3. **68** TNA: ADM 239/786, Fighting Instructions Volume II, 1970, p. 31. It was assessed that an 'Attack carrier squadron' could keep a screen of two ASW helicopters on task continuously for three days, whilst a '*Tiger* class squadron' would find it 'difficult' to do the same. Making use of Wessexes from two or three 'County' class would presumably help fill the gap between carrier and *Tiger* class helicopter numbers, although the Wessex had a much shorter endurance than the Sea King. **69** NHB: Home Commands Box/T71792: Fell to O'Brien, 14 July 1970. **70** TNA: ADM 239/785, Fighting Instructions, Volume 1, June 1969, p. 10–40; ADM 239/786, Fighting Instructions Volume II, 1970, p. 30. **71** Allen, *Sea King*, pp. 7, 28; Friedman, *Naval Institute Guide to Naval Weapons 1989*, p. 364. **72** NHB: DOR(RN) Note 6/66: 'some detection equivalence values of different ASW vehicles' July 1966. **73** TNA: DEFE 67/67, Lime Jug 70 Exercise Report, August 1971, pp. 1–5. **74** Grove, 'The Royal Navy and the Guided Missile', p. 203; NHB: Boscombe Box 40/T151036, RNIK 60 – Issue 6: RN Ikara Anti-Submarine Weapon System: Agreed Characteristics, March 1973. **75** The 'Ikara destroyer' was removed from the Long Term Costing Assumptions in 1968 and replaced by Ikara *Leander* conversions. NHB: Finance Box 5, '1968 Long Term Costing Assumptions', March 1968, para. 15, appendix C, Frigates-*Leander* pages. See also Friedman, *British Destroyers and Frigates*, pp. 271–4, 285. **76** TNA: ADM 1/28254, SASS Working Party remarks on Staff Requirement USW 158/62, Stage 1, Section 5, p. 25, 16 January 1963. **77** The cost of converting an older *Leander* was put at £1.5 million in January 1968 and cost of a converting a *Leander* whilst building was £0.7 million. By May 1968 the cost of the older *Leander* conversion had risen to nearly £3 million. TNA: DEFE 10/484 OR43/67 Ikara, 16 August 1967; DEFE 10/533 OR meeting 13, item 6, Ikara, 31 August 1967; DEFE 10/941 OR2/68 Ikara in *Leander*s, 8 January 1968; T 225/3323, Adams to Paterson, 30 May 1968. **78** Another unexpected advantage of the Nimrod was that it sounded like an airliner to a surfaced submarine, which would be much less likely to dive quickly, rather than propeller aircraft, which by the 1960s were rare to hear at sea and would be a tell-tale sign of a nearby Shackleton (or US P3 Orion MPA). The author would like to thank Andrew Livsey for this information. **79** Air Historical Branch: ASR 381 file, Air Staff Requirement for interim Shackleton replacement, 4 June 1964; Gibson, *Nimrod's Genesis*, pp. 156–77. **80** TNA: DEFE 67/72, 'Exercise High Wood 71: ASW', August 1972, p. 51. **81** Air Historical Branch: ASR 875 file, Air Staff Requirement: acoustic processor for Nimrod MR2, 20 March 1973. **82** TNA: ADM 239/785, Chapter 10, para. 18; Air Historical Branch: ASR 782 file, Air Staff Requirement: Nimrod upgrade, 19 January 1972. **83** TNA: DEFE 67/67, Lime Jug 70 Exercise Report, August 1971, p. 5–7; ADM 239/785, Chapter 10, para. 18. **84** Air Historical Branch: ASR 875 file, Air Staff Requirement: acoustic processor for Nimrod MR2, 20 March 1973. **85** TNA: ADM 239/785, Chapter 10, para. 18; Gibson, *Nimrod's Genesis*, pp. 28–31. **86** The new R29 missile had a range of 4,300 nautical miles, whilst its predecessor, the R27, had a range of only 1,350 nautical miles. By way of comparison, the distance between Murmansk and New York City is just under 3,500 nautical miles as the crow flies. Regular Soviet deterrent patrols, which began in 1969, usually consisted of two boats in the Atlantic and one in the Pacific. Polmar and Moore, *Cold War Submarines*, pp. 171, 175–6; Zaloga, *The Kremlin's Nuclear Sword*, pp. 116–18, 155–6; Shirokorad, *Oruzhiye Otyechyestvyennogo Flota 1945–2000*, p. 422. **87** Hennessy and Jinks, *The Silent Deep*, pp. 346–7. **88** Ford and Rosenberg, *The Admirals' Advantage*, p. 62. **89** Hennessy and Jinks, *The Silent Deep*, pp. 327–8. **90** TNA: DEFE 69/529, 'Visit … to the USA to discuss SOSUS and possible UK participation', pp. 1–2 and Annex 1, pp. 1–2, 6. **91** Ibid., p. 2. **92** Ibid., p. 3. **93** Ibid., p. 4. **94** Hennessy and Jinks, *The Silent Deep*, pp. 326–7. **95** TNA: DEFE 24/160, Le Bailly to DUS(RN), 9 July 1968; Le Bailly to Lewin, 30 August 1968; Signal CBNSW to MOD(N), 1945Z 4 October 1968. **96** Ford and Rosenberg, *The Admirals' Advantage*, pp. 56–61. **97** Ibid., p. 61. **98** Hennessy and Jinks, *The Silent Deep*, pp. 345–6. **99** NHB: 'Board Bulletin', 1972, p. 14. **100** TNA: DEFE 69/484, Head CE2(N) to Head RDF(N), 31 August 1965. **101** TNA: DEFE 69/484, 'Report of the Navy Department Panel on Oceanography', 5 August 1965; DEFE 69/485, 'Review of PASWEPS in the Eastlant Area', 9 March 1967; 'Board Committee for Oceanography: Note for meeting 25 July 1966'; Morris, *Charts and Surveys in Peace and War*, p. 209. **102** TNA: ADM 167/164, A/M(64)7, Item 2, 16 July 1964; A/M(64)9, Item 1, 8 October 1964. **103** TNA: DEFE 69/485, 'Board Committee on Oceanography – Progress Report', May 1967; for a detailed analysis of oceanographers' interactions with NERC and Defence in the late 1960s, see Robinson, 'Between the Devil and Deep Blue Sea' (PhD Dissertation), pp. 237–58, 265–6. **104** Hamblin, *Oceanographers and the Cold War*, pp. 144–53. **105** TNA: DEFE 69/485, 'Board Committee on Oceanography – Progress Report', May 1967; 'Board Committee on Oceanography: Note by RDF(N) for Second meeting, 5 January 1966'.

Chapter 7: Cost Control

1 Jackson and Bramall, *The Chiefs*, p. 377; Grove, *Vanguard to Trident*, p. 310. **2** For the Royal Navy's Long Term Costing Assumptions see NHB: Finance Boxes 3 to 5, LTCAs 1968–1984. **3** HMSO, 'Statement on the Defence Estimates 1970' (Cmnd 4290, February 1970), p. 32. **4** HMSO, 'Statement on the Defence Estimates 1972' (Cmnd 4891, February 1972), pp. 5–7; HMSO: Supply Estimates 1972–73, Class XII Ministry of Defence, 15 February 1972, Vote 9: Sea Systems, pp. 26–7; for the internal version of Rayner's Report, see TNA: DEFE 13/767, First Interim Report, 12 March 1971. **5** NHB: Admiralty Board Papers, A/P(69)6 Long Term Costings 1969, 9 May 1969. **6** NHB: Admiralty Board Papers, A/P(69)16 Sketch Estimates 1970/71, 5 November 1969. **7** NHB: Admiralty Board Papers, A/P(70)9 Long Term Costings 1970, 23 April 1970, p. 4. **8** Carrington: *Reflect on Things Past*, p. 228. **9** HMSO: Supplementary Statement on Defence Policy 1970, October 1970 (Cmnd 4521), pp. 5–6. **10** NHB: Finance Box 5/T48736, 1971 Long Term Costing Assumptions, January 1971, p. 1. **11** HMSO: Supplementary Statement on Defence Policy 1970, pp. 6–10. **12** TNA: PREM 15/844, Macmillan to Heath, 1 October 1971; Trend to Heath, 11 October 1971. **13** NHB: Admiralty Board Papers, A/P(70)14 Sketch Estimates 1971/72, 4 November 1970. **14** NHB: Board Bulletin, August 1971, p. 23. **15** Polmar and Moore, *Cold War Submarines*, p. 144. **16** NHB: Admiralty Board Papers, A/P(71)2 Long Term Costings 1971, 22 April 1971, p. 8. **17** Ibid., pp. 6–7. **18** Ibid., p. 3. **19** TNA: ADM 167/171, A/M(71)2, item 2, 29 April 1971. **20** NHB: Admiralty Board Papers, A/P(71)11 Sketch Estimates 1972/73, 2 November 1971, p. 1. **21** TNA: ADM 167/171, A/M(71)8, item 2, 11 November 1971. **22** NHB: Admiralty Board Papers, A/P(72)4, Long Term Costings 1972, 12 April 1972; TNA: ADM 167/172, A/M(72)4, item 1, 20 April 1972. **23** NHB: Admiralty Board Papers, A/P(72)9, Sketch Estimates 1973/74, 9 November 1972. **24** TNA: ADM 167/172, A/M(72)8 Item 2, 16 November 1972. **25** See TNA: DEFE 13/971, Hill-Norton to Carrington, 17 May 1973 for similar reductions of excesses by the other services; the Navy and Army departments were in similar positions but the RAF was somewhat better off. For Admiralty Board concerns about its portion of spending, see ADM 167/172, A/M(72)8 Item 2, 16 November 1972. **26** TNA: DEFE 13/971, Mumford to Carrington, 11 May 1973; DP16/73 (Final) 'LTC 1973: The Savings Study', 16 May 1973. For the wider background of the expenditure cuts, see Dell, *The Chancellors*, p. 396. **27** TNA: DEFE 13/971, Hill-Norton to Carrington, 4 June 1973; Mumford to Carrington, 21 September 1973. **28** TNA: DEFE 69/348, Implications of the Geddes Report (draft), 21 March 1966; Chapman, 'Geddes Report: Naval Orders', 7 April 1966; Note of meeting, AUS/MAT(N), 25 August 1967. **29** Johnman and Murphy, *British Shipbuilding and the State*, pp. 195–6, 201–02. **30** Ibid., p. 200. **31** Ibid., pp. 197–8, 203–04. **32** HMSO: Supply Estimates 1972–73, Class XII MoD, 15 February 1972, Vote 9: Sea Systems, p. 26. **33** Johnman and Murphy, *British Shipbuilding and the State*, pp. 202–03. **34** T 225/3324, Patterson to Swain, 2 March 1967; HMSO, Supplementary Statement on Defence Policy 1968 (Cmnd 3701, July 1968), p.10; T 225/3324, Note for Record, 6 August 1970. **35** Hennessy and Jinks, *The Silent Deep*, pp. 290–1. **36** TNA: T 225/3324, Patterson to Bancroft, 30 November 1966; Patterson to MoD, 5 December 1966. **37** Hennessy and Jinks, *The Silent Deep*, pp. 365–7; Brown and Moore, *Rebuilding the Royal Navy*, pp. 127–8. **38** Brown and Moore, *Rebuilding the Royal Navy*, p. 188. **39** NHB: Finance Box 5/T48739, 1969 Long Term Costing Assumptions, February 1969, p. 2; Finance Box 4/T48734, 1973 Long Term Costing Assumptions, November 1972, p. A5. **40** NHB: Finance Box 5/T48736, 1971 Long Term Costing Assumptions, January 1971, p. 4. **41** The earliest sketch design studies envisaged a 1,000-tonne boat, 60m in length with a complement of 29–30. By late 1972 the design had enlarged to 1,500 tonnes and was potentially more than just a training boat having 'possibly limited inshore capability in war'. NHB: Finance Box 5/T48736, 1971 Long Term Costing Assumptions, January 1971, p. A5; Finance Box 4/T48734, 1973 Long Term Costing Assumptions, November 1972, p. A5. **42** TNA: T 225/3200, Nicholls to Barratt, 21 October 1969; T 225/3471, Draft DOPC paper, January 1970. **43** TNA: T 225/3200, Hall to Barratt, 16 October 1969; T 225/3471, Barratt to Pyrie, 19 January 1970. **44** TNA: T 225/3471, Healey to Jenkins, 8 January 1970. **45** Compare NHB: Finance Box 5/T48735, 1972 Long Term Costing Assumptions, January 1972, p. A2, with Finance Box 4/T48734, 1973 Long Term Costing Assumptions, November 1972, p. A3. **46** NHB: Finance Box 5/T48738, '1968 Long Term Costing Assumptions', March 1968, p. A1; T48739, '1969 Long Term Costing Assumptions', February 1969, p. A1. **47** NHB: Finance Box 4/T48734, '1973 Long Term Costing Assumptions', November 1972, p. A3. **48** Brown and Moore, *Rebuilding the Royal Navy*, p. 89. **49** Ibid., p. 90. **50** NHB: Bristol Box/T73097, Macdonald to CinCFleet, 29 November 1973. **51** NHB: 'Board Bulletin', January 1971, p. 16. **52** NHB: Bristol Box/T73093, Squires to CinCFleet, 14 June 1976, Annex B. **53** TNA: DEFE 69/782, O'Hara to ACNS(P), 4 November 1982. **54** NHB: Bristol Box/T73091, Casdagli to CinCFleet, 6 November 1980. **55** NHB: CNGF Box 46/T125239, History of Type 21 and 42 – Draft Summary, 28 May 1976, Annex A. **56** NHB: Finance Box 5/T48738, 1968 Long Term Costing Assumptions, March 1968, para. 12. **57** NHB: Finance Box 5/T48739, 1969 Long Term Costing Assumptions, February 1969, p. 2 and p. B4. **58** NHB: Finance Box 5/T48737, 1970 Long Term Costing Assumptions, January 1970, p. 2. **59** NHB: CNGF Box 46/T125239, History of Type 21 and 42 – Draft Summary, 28 May 1976, Annex A. **60** Ibid., p. 1. **61** Ibid., Annex B(2). **62** Ibid., Annex A. **63** Ibid., p. 7. **64** Ibid., p. 6. **65** NHB: CNGF Box 47/T125260, History of the Type 21 and Type 42 frigates: Volume 1, 1975, p. 5. **66** NHB: CNGF Box 46/T125239, History of Type 21 and 42 – Draft Summary, 28 May 1976, p. 13. **67** For the Vospers perspective see, Barry Stobart-Hook, *Warships for the World* (Newport, 1994), pp. 39–41; for the Ship Department perspective see NHB: CNGF Box 46/T125239, History of Type 21 and 42 – Draft Summary, 28 May 1976, p. 8. **68** NHB: CNGF Box 46/T125239, History of Type 21 and 42 – Draft Summary, 28 May 1976, p. 11. **69** Ibid., pp. 7–8. **70** NHB: CNGF Box 46, History of the Type 21 and Type 42 frigates: Volume 2, 1975, Ch II, p. 2. **71** NHB: CNGF Box 47/T125260, History of the Type 21 and Type 42 frigates: Volume 1, 1975, p. 5. **72** Ibid., p. 7; Daniel, *The End of an Era*, pp. 216–17. **73** NHB: CNGF Box 46/T125239, History of Type 21 and 42 – Draft Summary, 28 May 1976, p. 10. **74** Ibid., p. 9. **75** NHB: CNGF Box 47/T125260, History of the Type 21 and

Type 42 frigates: Volume 1, 1975, p. 15. **76** NHB: CNGF Box 46, History of the Type 21 and Type 42 frigates: Volume 2, 1975, Ch II, pp. 34–5; Ch III, pp. 11–12. **77** For example, the building of the National Theatre on the South Bank in London at almost exactly the same time was hit by similar shortages in electricians and problems with strikes, Calder, *Raw Concrete*, p. 311. **78** NHB: CNGF Box 46/T125239, History of Type 21 and 42 – Draft Summary, 28 May 1976, p. 7. **79** Ibid., p. 6. **80** For the Type 21's popularity, see Lippiett, *Modern Combat Ships 5: Type 21*, pp. 76–9. **81** TNA: DEFE 67/107, Type 21 Frigate Operational Evaluation, December 1977, pp. 15–18. **82** Gordon and Komissarov, *Soviet Naval Aviation 1946–1991*, p. 329. **83** TNA: DEFE 48/974, DOAE M77122: An Assessment of Type 42 variants in Ship Group Defence, September 1977, pp. 5–11. The Report assumed that the Type 42s would have been fully modernised with radar replacements for the ageing Type 965 radar and an updated version of Sea Dart. The Report also assessed air defence by other air defence ship variants: ships with two Sea Dart launchers had a better success rate, as did those air defence ships also equipped with Sea Wolf point defence missile launchers to defend themselves. Despite this poor performance, a somewhat earlier analysis still concluded that Type 42s would be more effective in defending unarmed units than Type 22s, although a mix of both types was optimum when defending against the Soviet AS-6 (KSR-5) missile. TNA: DEFE 48/693, DOAE WP 154/112: Comparison of the Type 42 and Type 22 in the air defence role, July 1974, p. 5. **84** NHB: Finance Box 5, '1968 Long Term Costing Assumptions' March 1968, para. 42, and Appendix C, Frigates-*Leander* page, T48738. **85** NHB: 'Particulars of War Vessels 1973', p. 77. The Ikara *Leander*'s variant of ADAWS was ADAWS 5, with the associated DAE data handling and weapon control outfit and the JZR display system (see p. 20). **86** NHB: Group Deployments Box 2, Vol. 145A, Fieldhouse to CinCFleet, 18 December 1975, para. 23. **87** NHB: *Leander* Box/T113992, Shattock to CinC Fleet, AUTEC Trials, 3 May 1974. **88** TNA: ADM 239/785, Fighting Instructions Volume 1, 1970, p. 10–37. **89** Kuzin and Nikol'skiy, *Voyenno-Morskoy Flot SSSR*, pp. 548–55. **90** TNA: ADM 239/786, Fighting Instructions Volume 2, 1970, p. 40. **91** NHB: Tactical Doctrine Box 2: 'Fighting Instructions Volume 2', 1975, p. 26. **92** TNA: ADM 239/786, Fighting Instructions Volume 2, 1970, pp. 33–4; ADM 239/785, Fighting Instructions Volume 1, 1969, p. 10–14. **93** Polmar and Moore, *Cold War Submarines*, p. 144. **94** NHB: Tactical Doctrine Box 2: 'Fighting Instructions Volume 2', 1975, p. 20. **95** NHB: Finance Box 5/T48739, 1969 Long Term Costing Assumptions, February 1969, p. 5. **96** TNA: DEFE 13/819, Cook to Min Def, 17 July 1970; Cook to Min Def 29 July 1970; Balniel to Carrington, 7 August 1970; Macmillan to Balniel, 8 March 1971. The comparison between Exocet and Ship Martel was undertaken again in 1971, with the time benefits of Exocet being more marked and the cost differences between the two missiles probably being minimal but difficult to predict, DEFE 13/820, Controller to Min Def, 1 April 1971. **97** NHB: VCNS Box 53, VCNS 40/1/4, FRC/P(73)1 DNOR: revised Exocet fitting policy, 4 July 1973. In the event a total of thirty-three ships were fitted with quadruple Exocet between 1973 and 1988. **98** The range of the 'Styx' (P15/P15U) was 40km with the later improved version having a range of 80km (P15M), Kuzin and Nikol'skiy, *Voyenno-Morskoy Flot SSSR*, Ch 6.3 and Table 6.2. **99** NHB: Finance Box 5/T49873, 1970 Long Term Costing Assumptions, January 1970, p. 2; the addition of Exocet to the Type 42s was dropped in 1973 as it was considered that the existing Batch 1 ships could not accommodate the system given their extremely tight margins for additional equipment, NHB: VCNS Box 53, VCNS 40/1/4, FRC/P(73)1 DNOR: revised Exocet fitting policy, 4 July 1973; Exocet had been considered for the *Tiger* class, in place of their remaining 6in mounting, but were removed from the programme due to CINCFLEET's belief that the problem-prone 6in was improving in reliability and was becoming a more viable anti-ship weapon, NHB: VCNS Box 53, VCNS 40/1/4, Head of DS4 to VCNS, 28 January 1975. **100** NHB: VCNS Box 53, VCNS 40/1/4, FRC/Misc (71)9, Secretary FRC to committee, 20 May 1971. **101** The last planned Exocet refit, of HMS *Juno*, was cancelled just as the ship was entering dockyard hands. She was partly disarmed and became a navigation training ship, emerging from her refit in 1985. Marriott, *Royal Navy Frigates since 1945*, p. 90. **102** NHB: Norfolk Box 1, Wemyss to CinCFleet, 22 July 1974. **103** NHB: VCNS Box 53, VCNS 40/1/4, VCNS to Controller 29 August 1975. **104** NHB: Fleet Requirements Committee Box 1, 'Destroyer and frigate programme in the short-term', 6 December 1974, pp. 7–8. **105** TNA: DEFE 69/1409, DG Ships to DSDE et al, 1 March 1979. **106** NHB: Finance Box 5/T48738, '1968 Long Term Costing Assumptions', March 1968, p. A2. **107** TNA: DEFE 10/483, OR/P(66) 31, NST 6522 Sea Wolf, 8 November 1966. **108** TNA: DEFE 24/457, Anglo-Dutch Frigate: Costs of Sea Wolf, 1969. A Type 22 would have deep magazine space for thirty missiles, twelve already loaded into both launchers and a further twelve in ready-use magazines near the launchers. **109** TNA: DEFE 24/457, E6, Sea Wolf and Sea Sparrow: ORC and WDC endorsement, 1969. **110** TNA: DEFE 10/483, OR/P(66)31 NST 6522, 8 July 1966; DEFE 10/942, OR 61/68 NSR 6522, 8 November 1968. **111** TNA: DEFE 24/457, Bryars to PS/USofS, 2 June 1969, Annex A. **112** TNA: DEFE 24/457, Penney to PS/USofS, 30 June 1969; Alvey to Owen, 17 September 1969; DNOR to VCNS, 5 November 1969, Brief for Controller. **113** NHB: Finance Box 5/T48736, '1971 Long Term Costing Assumptions', January 1971, p. A3. **114** NHB: Finance Box 4/T48733, '1974 Long Term Costing Assumptions', June 1973, p. A7. **115** NHB: Finance Box 5/T48731, '1976 Long Term Costing Assumptions', May 1975, p. A7. **116** NHB: Finance Box 5/T48735, Long Term Costing Assumptions 1972, pp. 7–8. **117** The large ASW ship, when it first appeared in the Long Term Costing Assumptions in 1971 was armed with Sea Dart, Sea Wolf and only two Lynx helicopters at 9,000–10,000 tonnes. In 1973 the ship had jumped to 12,000 tons after the Lynxes were replaced by six Sea Kings or successors – a clear indication of what was now considered the most effective means of detecting and attacking submarines. NHB: Finance Box 5, 1971 Long Term Costing Assumptions, January 1971, p. A9, T48736; NHB: Finance Box 4/T48734, 1973 Long Term Costing Assumptions, November 1972, p. A3. **118** Friedman, *The World's Naval Weapon Systems 1997–98*, pp. 611–12. **119** A cheaper version of the SSGW frigate was also mooted at the same time, costing £13 million and with no medium gun and 3 knots slower. NHB: Finance Box 5/T48735, 1972 Long Term Costing Assumptions, January 1972, p. 8, p. A10, pp. B11-B11B. **120** In 1968 the Long Term Costing Assumptions set out ten fast patrol boats (for acceptance early 1971 to early 1974) plus three training craft (acceptance 1970). FPBs costing no more than £0.8 million. An alternative plan was set for nine patrol boats (costing £0.9 million each), three FPBs and three training craft (involving a reduction in the planned MCMV programme by two ships). The fast patrol boat's tentative particulars were: 100–120ft long, gas turbine propulsion, 50 knots deep and dirty, 400 miles range at 45 knots, radar Type 978, crew of 23. The Patrol Craft's particulars were: 150–200 ft long, endurance of 1,000–2,000nm at 15 knots, one gun, crew of 34–55. NHB: Finance Box 5/T48738, 1968 Long Term Costing Assumptions, March 1968, paras 20–22, appendix A p. 6. **121** TNA: ADM 239/785, Fighting Instructions Volume I, pp. 9–1 and 9–2. **122** NHB: Coastal Forces Pictorial History Volume 1, 1949–52 sections. **123** The six oceangoing vessels (to be ordered 1972–3 and delivered 1973–5) were very tentatively to have been 45 to 60m long, with either gas-turbine or diesel propulsion, a gun and perhaps even anti-ship missiles. The four inshore patrol craft would be ordered in 1972 and delivered 1973–4. Also, five replacements for the HK patrol craft were placed in the programme for the first time (to be in service from 1975). NHB: Finance Box 5/T48739, 1969 Long Term Costing Assumptions, February 1969, p. 2; T48737, 1970 Long Term Costing Assumptions, January 1970, p. A5. **124** Initially there were to be up to nineteen *Seal* class, to be ordered 1972–5 and entering service 197–79. There were two hydrofoil options: ten US-built vessels to a NATO design armed with four Exocet and one 76mm gun (and a tentative ASW version with a variable-depth sonar), with the first in service in 1976, or a total of nine craft – two US *Tucumcari* class purchased in 1973, plus seven built in the UK (ordered between 1978–81). NHB: Finance Box 5/T48735, 1971 Long Term Costing Assumptions, January 1971, p. 5, p. A8, p. B11. **125** NHB: Finance Box 5/T48735, 1972 Long Term Costing Assumptions, January 1972, p. 9. **126** At sea state five 'movement within the ship is excessive and crew fatigue becomes a major consideration'. NHB: Kingfisher Box, Forbes to CFP, 5 January 1976. **127** The author has not been able to ascertain whether *Tenacity* had been built with a Royal Navy order in mind, but that might explain the Navy's eventual purchase, although attempts to support Vospers whilst it dealt with the Type 21 and Brazilian frigate orders during Barber's 'dash for growth' is just as likely. Dawson, *A Quest for Speed at Sea*, pp. 68–70; NHB: Ship Boxes 'T' Box 1/T21925, Tenacity data; DS5 notification 3/80, dated 20 June 1980 (cited in NHB Chron Cards). **128** NHB: 'Board Bulletin', August 1971, p. 15. **129** Harris, 'The Hunt Class Mine Countermeasures Vessels', pp. 486, 491–2. **130** Brown and Moore, *Rebuilding the Royal Navy*, pp. 137–9. The name *Wilton* was selected as a 'bridge' name between the older 'Ton' class vessels whose name ended in -ton, and the theme for the new class, hunts. NHB: RW310/56/1/6, DG Ships to DNE et al, 14 August 1970. **131** TNA: DEFE 69/447, PS/Chief Scientific Adviser to APS/Minister of State, 22 April 1975. **132** NHB: 'Board Bulletin', August 1971, pp. 16 and 18. **133** Harris, 'The Hunt Class Mine Countermeasures Vessels', pp. 485–92. **134** Brown and Moore, *Rebuilding the Royal Navy*, p. 139. **135** NHB: 'Board Bulletin', August 1971, p. 16. **136** NHB: Finance Box 5, 1968 Long Term Costing Assumptions, March 1968, paras 19–22, T48738. **137** Harris, 'The Hunt Class Mine Countermeasures Vessels', pp. 494–6. **138** NHB: Finance Box 5/T48738, 1968 Long Term Costing

Assumptions, March 1968, appendix A, p. 5; T48734 '1973 Long Term Costing Assumptions', November 1972, p. A8; T48731, '1976 Long Term Costing Assumptions', 1975, p. A8. **139** The sketch design in 1970 consisted of a 18,290-tonne, 195.07m long ship with a speed limited to 20 knots, flying eighteen Wessex helicopters or their replacements, accommodation for 1,500 crew and marines, a Type 965P search radar and the CAAIS tactical command system with six display screens. Two ships would have been ordered to replace *Albion* and *Bulwark*. NHB: Finance Box 5/T48737, '1970 Long Term Costing Assumptions', January 1970, pp. 1–2, p. A7. **140** NHB: Finance Box 5/T48736, 1971 Long Term Costing Assumptions, January 1971, p. 3. **141** NHB: Finance Box 5/T48735, 1972 Long Term Costing Assumptions, January 1972, p. 3, p. B4. **142** NHB: Finance Box 4/T48734, 1973 Long Term Costing Assumptions, November 1972, p. A3. **143** NHB: Finance Box 5/T48732, 1975 Long Term Costing Assumptions, May 1974, p. A3. **144** Basic particulars were: 22,000 tons deep, 16 knots (diesel-electric), 640ft long, crew of 1,018, no armament but a helicopter, hangar and 30-ton crane NHB: Finance Box 5/T48738, 1968 Long Term Costing Assumptions, March 1968, para. 16 and appendix A3. **145** TNA: DEFE 69/348, Whittuck to Leckie, 9 August 1967; Baylis to Whittuck, 14 August 1967. **146** NHB: Finance Box 5/T48739, 1969 Long Term Costing Assumptions, February 1969, p. 2. Proposals to retain the capability to deploy Polaris boats East of Suez were considered in an internal review of the nuclear deterrent in 1967, and can be seen as a hangover from British attempts to retain influence with the US in East Asia by permanently basing V Bombers at Singapore. The proposals were finally rejected in June 1968. Jones, *UK Strategic Nuclear Deterrent, Volume II*, pp. 270–1, 283, 387; see also Jones, 'Up the Garden Path? Britain's Nuclear History in the Far East', for British nuclear policy East of Suez pre-Polaris. **147** Tentative particulars in 1968 were 10,000 tons, 18 knots, 202 crew plus accommodations for two Fleet Maintenance Units each; in 1970 this had changed to 13,310 tonnes, 19 knots, 466 crew including 1 Fleet Maintenance Unit, plus 149 berths for SSK crews. NHB: Finance Box 5/T48738, 1968 Long Term Costing Assumptions, March 1968, appendix A, p. 4; T48737, 1970 Long Term Costing Assumptions, January 1970, p. A6. **148** NHB: Finance Box 5/T48735, 1972 Long Term Costing Assumptions, January 1972, p. B15, T48735; Finance Box 4, 1974 Long Term Costing Assumptions, June 1973, p. B15. **149** Tentative particulars in 1968 were: 6,000 tons, 16 knots, 350ft long, crew of 377, providing forward support for ten MCMVs. NHB: Finance Box 5/T48737, 1968 Long Term Costing Assumptions, March 1968, para. 18 and appendix A, p. 4; T48738, 1970 Long Term Costing Assumptions', January 1970, p. A7; T48735, 1972 Long Term Costing Assumptions, January 1972, p. B15. **150** NHB: Finance Box 4/T48734, 1973 Long Term Costing Assumptions, November 1972, p. A11. **151** For an admittedly anecdotal assessment from a naval officer, see Thompson, *On Her Majesty's Nuclear Service*, p. 223. **152** NHB: Naval News Summary, April 1972, p. 3. **153** Burgess, 'HMS *Defiance* 400 years on', pp. 194–200. **154** MoD, *Joint Services Recognition Journal*, March 1980, p. 64, cited in NHB Ships Card Index. **155** Grove, *Vanguard to Trident*, pp. 378–9. **156** Adams and Smith, *The Royal Fleet Auxiliary*, pp. 105, 112–13 and 117. **157** Ibid., pp. 122, 131; NHB: Finance Box 5/T48738, 1968 Long Term Costing Assumptions, March 1968, paras 28–32. **158** The 'Leaf' and 'Dale' classes often looped round to Singapore in the early 1970s as well. See Pink Lists 1972–75, TNA: ADM 187/124–136. **159** NHB: Finance Box 4/T48734, 1973 Long Term Costing Assumptions, November 1972, p. B20; T48743, 1978 Long Term Costing Assumptions, April 1977, p. B20. **160** This was broken down into orders for two *Leander* class, three RAN/RN frigates (future Type 21), thirteen Standard Frigates (future Type 22), and fifteen Sea Dart destroyers (future Type 42); and acceptances into service of two 'County' class, one Type 82 destroyer, ten *Leander* class, three RAN/RN frigates, eight Standard Frigates and eleven Sea Dart destroyers. NHB: Finance Box 5/T48738, 1968 Long Term Costing Assumptions, March 1968, Appendix B, pp. 1–4. **161** Broken down into orders for two *Leander*s, eight Type 21s, four Type 22s and eleven Type 42s; and commissioning of two 'County' class, one Type 82, ten *Leander*s, eight Type 21s and four Type 42s, Moore, *Jane's Fighting Ships 1979–1980*, pp. 589–615. **162** Broken down into orders for twenty Type 42s and its successor class and seventeen Type 22s; and acceptances into service of seventeen Type 42s, eight Type 21s and nine Type 22s. NHB: Finance Box 4/T48733, 1974 Long Term Costing Assumptions, June 1973, pp. B7–B9. **163** Broken down into orders for eight Type 42s and twelve Type 22s; and commissioning of one Type 82, eleven Type 42s, eight Type 21s and four Type 22s. Moore, *Jane's Fighting Ships 1984–1985*, pp. 594–618. **164** Between 1968 and 1978: the LTCAs assumed three cruisers to be ordered and three accepted into service (compared to three ordered and none in service in reality), and nine SSNs ordered and six accepted into service (seven and four in reality). Between 1973 and 1983 the LTCAs assumed three cruisers ordered and three in accepted into service (three and two in reality), and ten SSNs ordered and nine in accepted into service (seven and seven in reality). NHB: Finance Box 5/T48738, 1968 Long Term Costing Assumptions, March 1968, Appendix B, pp. 1 and 5; Finance Box 4/T48733, 1974 Long Term Costing Assumptions, June 1973, pp. B2, B5; John Moore, ed. *Jane's Fighting Ships 1979–1980*, pp. 589–615; *Jane's Fighting Ships 1984–1985*, pp. 594–618. **165** Between 1968 and 1978: the LTCAs assumed five depot/maintenance/support ships ordered and five accepted into service (reality: none); nineteen MCMV ordered and thirteen entered into service (reality: three ordered and one commissioned); and thirteen FPBs ordered and thirteen in service (reality: three FPBs and four *Seal* class patrol vessels ordered, and three FPBs and four Seals commissioned). Between 1973 and 1983 the LTCAs assumed three maintenance/support ordered and three accepted into service (reality: none); twenty-five MCMV ordered and thirteen entered into service (reality: fifteen and seven); and twenty-two patrol vessels ordered and twenty-six accepted into service (reality: eighteen and thirteen). NHB: Finance Box 5/T48738, 1968 Long Term Costing Assumptions, March 1968, Appendix B, pp. 8–9; Finance Box 4/T48733, 1974 Long Term Costing Assumptions, June 1973, pp. B10–B15; Moore, *Jane's Fighting Ships 1979–1980*, pp. 589–615; *Jane's Fighting Ships 1984–1985*, pp. 594–618. **166** For optimism bias, see Gray, 'Review of Acquisition for the Secretary of State for Defence', p. 19; for defence inflation, which was more usually called 'the relative price effect' in the 1970s and 1980s, see MOD: 'Evidence Summary: The Drivers of Defence Cost Inflation' (February 2022). **167** The tonnage differences were 2,500 tons and 3,500 tons standard. The differences in cost were '£8–9m' for the last *Leander* class (1973), compared to '£68.9m' for *Broadsword* (1979), the first Type 22 (£9 million adjusted for inflation to 1979 figures would be £19.87 million). These can only be very rough comparisons as costs might not be internally adjusted for inflation (i.e. tranche payments to builders over 3–4 years might not be inflation adjusted) and this is a comparison between last of class and first of class costs (the latter always being much higher). However, the cost difference is nonetheless significant despite these uncertainties. Blackman, *Jane's Fighting Ships 1973–74*, p. 323; Moore, *Jane's Fighting Ships 1980–81*, p. 558.

Chapter 8: The Critical Level
1 Ashmore, *The Battle and the Breeze*, pp. 104–85. **2** TNA: DEFE 13/971, Hill-Norton to Carrington, 17 May 1973. **3** Timmins, *The Five Giants*, pp. 285, 291–3, 299–300 and 305. **4** TNA: T 225/4376, Hall to Pliatzky 12 March 1973, see also Philip Dyson's master's dissertation on the Defence Review. It is particularly valuable for its setting out of the Treasury's position, especially in 1973 and the early stages of the Review: Dyson, 'The Limits of Influence' (Master's dissertation). **5** Dyson, 'The Limits of Influence', p. 11. **6** TNA: DEFE 11/805, Mumford to PUS, 25 January 1974. **7** TNA: T 225/3903, Dunnett to Allen, 8 January 1973. **8** TNA: T 225/3903, Allen to Dunnett, 22 December 1972. **9** TNA: DEFE 68/116, Report of LTSG, 3 January 1973. **10** TNA: T 225/4376, Economic Growth and Defence Spending to 1985 of Certain European Allies, 9 April 1973. **11** TNA: T 225/4377, Hall to Pliatzky 23 May 1973. **12** TNA: DEFE 11/805, Carver to COSC, 19 November 1973. **13** TNA: DEFE 11/805, Hockaday to Carrington, 28 November 1973. **14** TNA: DEFE 11/805, Taylor to SECCOS, 23 November 1973. **15** TNA: DEFE 11/805, Asst Sec 1 to SECCOS, 30 November 1973. **16** TNA: DEFE 4/280, CoSC minutes, item 4, 5 February 1974; Labour Party website, 'February 1974 Labour Party Manifesto': http://www.labour-party.org.uk/manifestos/1974/feb/1974-feb-labour-manifesto.shtml (accessed 23 December 2022). **17** TNA: T 225/4161, Hunt to Dunnett, 25 February 1974; Hunt to Wilson, 5 March 1974. **18** TNA: T 225/4161, Hansford to Pliatzky, 27 March 1974. **19** NHB: Defence Review 1974, Volume 1B: OPD(74)7, Defence Review: Note by the Steering Committee, 1 April 1974. **20** TNA: T 225/4161, Pliatzky to Allen, 3 April 1974; NHB: Defence Review 1974, Volume 1B: MISC 16(74), Defence Review Steering Group, 1st meeting, 25 March 1974. **21** NHB: Defence Review 1974, Volume 1B: OPD(74)7, Defence Review: Note by the Steering Committee, 1 April 1974. **22** The term 'shopping list' was used by Carver in his autobiography; Carver, *Out of Step*, p. 448. **23** NHB: Defence Review 1974, Volume 1B: Mayne to ACDS(Pol) et al, 15 March 1974. **24** Carver, *Out of Step*, pp. 448–9. **25** TNA: DEFE 25/221, Carver to Mason, 13 May 1974; DEFE 25/223, Carver to Mason, 13 June 1974. **26** Mason, *Paying the Price*, pp. 123–4. **27** NHB: Defence Review 1974, Volume 1B: PS/SofS to PS/CDS, 11 March 1974. **28** NHB: Defence Review 1974, Volume 7, Note of Defence Review Presentation at SHAPE, 4 December 1974. **29** TNA: T 225/4165, Hall to Henley, 17 July 1974. **30** Dyson, 'The Limits of Influence', September 2012, p. 25. **31** NHB: Defence Review 1974, Vol. 1D: DNP to ACNS(P), 26 April 1974, Annex A,

pp. 2–3. **32** Ibid., pp. 3–4. **33** Ibid., p. 4. **34** NHB: Defence Review 1974, Vol. 4A: DSWP(P)51(Final Revise), 'The 1974 Defence Review', July 1974, pp. 3–4. **35** NHB: Defence Review 1974, Vol. 1C: DNP to ACNS(OR) et al., 26 March 1974. **36** Ibid. **37** NHB: Defence Review 1974, Vol. 1C: DNP to Head of Mat. Co-Ord(N), 16 April 1974. **38** NHB: Defence Review 1974, Vol. 4A: DSWP(P)51(Final Revise), '1974 Defence Review', July 1974, pp. 14–16. **39** Ibid., p. 14. **40** NHB: Campaign: Armilla Box 1: Draft Staff Naval History, Volume 1, p. 13. **41** NHB: Defence Review 1974, Vol. 4A: DSWP(P)51 (Final Revise), '1974 Defence Review', July 1974, pp. 21–2. **42** Gov.uk website: 'Allied Joint Publication-5: Allied Joint Doctrine for the Planning of Operations' AJP-5, May 2019, p. 4–2: Allied Joint Publication-5, Allied Joint Doctrine for the Planning of Defence, Edition A Version 2, UK Change 1 (publishing.service.gov.uk) (accessed 23 December 2022). **43** NHB: Defence Review 1974, Vol. 4A: DSWP(P)51(Final Revise), '1974 Defence Review', July 1974, p. 23. **44** Ibid. **45** NHB: Defence Review 1974, Vol. 4A: DSWP(P)52(Revise), '1974 Defence Review: Annexes', July 1974, Annex L1. **46** NHB: Defence Review 1974, Vol. 4A: DSWP(P)51(Final Revise), '1974 Defence Review', July 1974, pp. 24–6. **47** NHB: Defence Review 1974, Vol. 4A: DSWP(P)52(Revise), '1974 Defence Review: Annexes', July 1974, Annex L1. **48** NHB: Defence Review 1974, Vol. 4A: DSWP(P)51(Final Revise), '1974 Defence Review', July 1974, p. 28. **49** Ibid., pp. 29–34. **50** Ibid., pp. 35–7. **51** NHB: Defence Review 1974, Vol. 4A: DSWP(P) 52 (Revise), '1974 Defence Review: Annexes', July 1974, Annexes P, Q and R. **52** NHB: Defence Review 1974, Vol. 4A: DSWP(P) 51 (Final Revise), '1974 Defence Review', July 1974, p. 37. **53** Ibid., pp. 38–9. **54** HMSO, Statement on Defence Estimates 1975 (Cmnd 5976), March 1975, pp. 9–10. **55** TNA: T 225/4161, Howard note for record, 3 May 1974. **56** TNA: T 225/4165, Henley to PPS, 17 July 1974. **57** Howard, *The Continental Commitment*. Although concerning the period 1914 to 1945, this book, based on Howard's 1971 Ford lectures, helped create the conception of a longstanding 'continental commitment' for Britain just as this commitment was becoming pre-eminent in contemporary defence policy. **58** NHB: Defence Review 1974, Vol. 4D: OPD(74)23, 'Defence Review', 15 July 1974. **59** NHB: Defence Review 1974, Vol. 5A: MISC 16(74) 9th meeting, 11 September 1974. **60** NHB: Defence Review 1974, Vol. 5A: 'Presentation to the DOPC by CDS', attachment to COS(MISC) 582/130I/2, 13 September 1974, paras 12–16. **61** Ibid., para. 15. **62** Ibid., paras 16–17. **63** NHB: Defence Review 1974, Vol. 5A: MISC 16(74) 9th meeting, 11 September 1974. **64** TNA: CAB 148/145, OPD(74) 15th meeting, 18 September 1974. **65** Donoughue, *Downing Street Diary*, pp. 188–90. **66** TNA: CAB 148/145, OPD(74) 16th meeting, 23 October 1974. **67** Donoughue, *Downing Street Diary*, pp. 230–41. **68** Hansard: 'Defence Review', HC Deb 3 December 1974, Vol. 882, cc. 1351–69; HMSO: Statement on Defence Estimates 1975 (Cmnd. 5976), March 1975. **69** HMSO: Statement on Defence Estimates 1975 (Cmnd. 5976), March 1975, pp. 1–2. **70** Ibid., pp. 4, 23–4. **71** Ibid., p. 24. **72** TNA: DEFE 13/974, Mayne to PS/SofS, 2 December 1974; NHB: Finance Box 4, 1974 Long Term Costing Assumptions, 15 June 1973, p. 3, T48733. **73** HMSO: Statement on Defence Estimates 1975 (Cmnd. 5976), March 1975, pp. 20–1. **74** Ibid., pp. 10–12. **75** TNA: DEFE 13/1084, Judd to Mason, 14 April 1975. **76** HMSO: Statement on Defence Estimates 1975 (Cmnd. 5976), March 1975, pp. 15–16. **77** NHB: Finance Box 5/T48732, Long Term Costing Assumptions 1975, pp. A-2 to A-3; compare with T48731, Long Term Costing Assumptions 1976. **78** TNA: DEFE 13/973, Mason to Wilson, 19 November 1974; DEFE 13/974, Cary to Carver, 6 January 1975. **79** TNA: DEFE 13/973, Carver to Ashmore, 23 December 1974; Mason, *Paying the Price*, pp. 133–4. **80** There had nominally been a flight of four Nimrods based in Singapore, but in practice only two had been present. This two-aircraft force had cost £300,000 per annum. TNA: DEFE 13/974, Hudson to PS/SofS, 28 January 1975. **81** TNA: DEFE 13/1005, COS 22/74, 'Accommodation of non-NATO and Mediterranean commitments within the critical level', 15 October 1974, p. A-2. **82** HMSO: Statement on Defence Estimates 1975 (Cmnd. 5976), March 1975, pp. 14–15. **83** Mallinson, 'Cyprus, Britain, the USA, Turkey and Greece in 1977', pp. 742–4. **84** TNA: DEFE 13/1005, COS 22/74, 'Accommodation of non-NATO and Mediterranean commitments within the critical level', 15 October 1974, p. A-3. **85** TNA: DEFE 13/974, Carver to Mason, 12 February 1975. **86** TNA: PREM 16/733, Mason to Wilson, 19 June 1975. The author would like to thank Andrew Harris for bringing this document to his attention. **87** TNA: DEFE 13/1005, Mason to USofS(N), 18 October 1974. **88** TNA: DEFE 5/201, COS 19/76, Appendix 1 to Annex A, 4 May 1976. RAF service personnel, dependents and locally employed were expected to be 1,145, 2,890 and 1,123 respectively on 1 April 1977. RN numbers were 959, 1,710 and 1,316 respectively. **89** NHB: Singapore Naval General Orders, March 1975, Chapter 1. **90** TNA: DEFE

13/1121, CA to Rodgers, 4 April 1974. **91** TNA: DEFE 13/1121, APS to Rodgers, 4 April 1974; PS to Rodgers, 12 February 1975. **92** TNA: DEFE 13/973, Ashmore to Cary, 12 November 1974. **93** TNA: DEFE 13/973, Cary to Mason, 18 November 1974; CA to CSA, 12 November 1974. Cary's support for the maritime Harrier is interesting, and might well have been decisive, as only Ashmore had been pushing strongly for the aircraft before his intervention. Cary had been the Deputy Under-Secretary of State for the Navy during the battle over the CVA01 carrier in 1966 and in its aftermath as the new cruiser design was developed and Admiral Begg pushed for its approval. **94** TNA: DEFE 13/973, Mumford to Mason, 21 November 1974. **95** Ibid. **96** TNA: DEFE 13/973, Mason to Rodgers, 22 November 1974; DEFE 13/974, Mason to Rodgers 27 January 1975. **97** TNA: DEFE 13/1121, Bondi and Carver to Rodgers, 23 January 1975, Annex A. **98** The first-generation cruise missile submarines of the 'Juliett' and 'Echo II' classes as well as missiles fired from Tu-16 'Badger' bombers depended on mid-course correction of this type. The Tu-22 'Blinder' also relied on reconnaissance aircraft, but in the 'pathfinder' role and not mid-course correction. Friedman, *Seapower and Space*, pp. 141–55. **99** TNA: DEFE 13/1121, Bondi and Carver to Rodgers, 23 January 1975, Annex A. **100** Ibid., Annexes B and C. **101** TNA: DEFE 13/1121, PS to Rodgers, 24 January 1975; for the operational availability of the Sea Harrier, see DEFE 13/1121, Bondi and Carver to Rodgers, 23 January 1975, Annex A. **102** Compare HMSO, Statement on Defence Estimates 1975 (Cmnd. 5976), March 1975, p. 101, with Statement on Defence Estimates 1976 (Cmnd. 6432), March 1976, pp. 27, 96. **103** TNA: PREM 16/1974, Hunt to Wilson, 12 May 1975. **104** Donoughue, *Downing Street Diary*, pp. 379–80. **105** TNA: DEFE 24/1551, DP 21/76 (Revised Final), 22 September 1976. **106** TNA: DEFE 24/1551, DDNOR to DDAP et al, 22 October 1976. **107** TNA: DEFE 48/243, DOAE Report 7624, June 1976, pp. 2–5, 20. **108** Ibid., p. i–ii. **109** Ibid., pp. ii, 15. **110** Ibid., pp. iii, 17. **111** Ibid., p. 36. **112** Ibid., pp. ii, 10, 32–3. **113** Ibid., pp. 38, 43. **114** Ibid., p. 37. **115** Ibid., p. 32. **116** Ibid., p. ii. **117** Gordon and Komissarov, *Soviet Naval Aviation 1946–1991*, pp. 360–3; Kuzin and Nikol'skiy, *Voyenno-Morskoy Flot SSSR 1945–1991*, Ch 9.2, table 9.2. **118** TNA: DEFE 48/243, DOAE Report 7624, pp. ii, 66. ECM was considered to be more effective against the AS-5 anti-ship missile than with the AS-6. **119** Thompson, *The Royal Marines*, pp. 532–3. **120** Thompson mentions the southern flank role in passing but focusses much more on the development of the Marines' Arctic warfare capabilities, Thompson, *The Royal Marines*, pp. 529–3. Ladd briefly mentions 41 Cdo's base in Malta and the deployment to Cyprus, but not the wider southern flank commitment. Ladd: *By Sea, By Land*, pp. 332–45. Carter, in his history written for the Royal Marines Historical Society, *does* mention the pre-eminence of the southern flank in the early 1970s, but – perhaps understandably for a short overview history – does not provide any detail. Carter, *Short History of the Royal Marines*, p. 79. **121** For example, see NHB: Exercises Box 10/T47310, Deep Furrow 71 Exercise Brief, Hepworth to Sec 1SL, 4 October 1971; Exercises Box 11/T83801, Deep Furrow 73 Exercise Brief, Fieldhouse to Sec 1SL, 7 September 1973; Exercises Box 11/T83803, Deep Express 75 Exercise Brief, Skinner to Sec 1SL, 2 September 1975. **122** NHB: Home Commands Box/T71792: Fell to O'Brien, 14 July 1970. **123** Carter, *A Short History*, pp. 76–8. **124** HMSO: Statement on Defence Estimates 1975 (Cmnd 5976), March 1975, p. 11. **125** Ladd, *By Sea, By Land*, p. 332; HMSO: Statement on Defence Estimates 1975 (Cmnd 5976), March 1975, p. 11. **126** TNA: DEFE 13/1392, Mulley to Callaghan, 17 June 1977; Owen to Callaghan, 20 June 1977. **127** TNA: DEFE 49/95, 'Report of the RNR and RNXS Review Committee', December 1974. **128** TNA: ADM 167/178, A/M (75) 7, item 3, 26 June 1976; Howarth, *The Royal Navy's Reserves*, pp. 136–43. **129** Howarth, *The Royal Navy's Reserves*, p. 144. The Reserve QARNNS had already been integrated into the RNR in 1971, p. 133. **130** HMSO: Statement on Defence Estimates 1976 (Cmnd. 6432), March 1976, pp. 60–1. **131** HMSO: Statement on Defence Estimates 1979 (Cmnd. 7474), February 1979 Annex H, p. 83. **132** For example, see the promotion of Capt B K Perrin of the Sussex Division to Commodore, NHB: Press Releases Box 13, MOD(RN)18/77, 'New Commodore for Royal Naval Reserve', 8 February 1977. **133** Howarth, *The Royal Navy's Reserves*, p. 144; for an example of NCS involvement in major NATO exercises, including NCS work in Australia and Norfolk, Virginia, see NHB: Reserves Box 1/T9829, 'London Log: The Journal of HMS *President*' June 1977, pp. 7–8; TNA: DEFE 45/93, DCI(RN)S170/75, 'Future of RNR and WRNR', 24 October 1975. **134** ADM 167/176, A/P(75)4, WRNS Study Group Report; see also Stanley, *Women and the Royal Navy*, pp. 142–4. **135** In discussion with the Second Sea Lord, Talbot specifically stated that she was not asking for WRNS to go to sea. TNA: DEFE 69/1366, Talbot to 2SL, 12 September 1973; Secretary to 2SL to PS DUS(N), 21 November 1973. **136** TNA: ADM 167/178, A/M(75)3, item 2, 17 February 1975. **137** TNA: DEFE 69/1366, Head of Naval Manpower Future

Policy Division to Director of WRNS, 23 June 1970. The tenor of these initial investigations can be gauged from the note sent out by HNMFPD asking for contributions to his memo to DWRNS which began with 'This is not a joke!', HNMFPD to various, 1 June 1970. **138** TNA: DEFE 69/1366, Scott to Lewin, 18 August 1972. **139** Taaffe, 'We suffered in silence' (PhD Dissertation), pp. 42–3. The author would like to thank Ann Coats for making me aware of this dissertation. **140** TNA: DEFE 69/1366, Sherriff to DNMP, 15 June 1973; Sherriff to FP1, 18 July 1973; Sherriff draft brief for DGNMT, 19 July 1973; DGNMT to 2nd Sea Lord, 7 August 1973. **141** TNA: DEFE 69/1366, unknown to DGNMT, undated, covering Sherriff draft brief for DGNMT, 19 July 1973. **142** TNA: DEFE 69/1366, minutes of meeting held 7 July 1975. **143** TNA: DEFE 69/1366, Robinson to DNMR, 12 September 1975. **144** TNA: DEFE 69/1366, Hydrographer of the Navy to AUS(NP), 3 February 1976; Hydrographer to NP1a, 29 April 1976; Reynolds to DWRNS, 13 October 1977. **145** TNA: DEFE 69/1366, Sherriff to Hydrographer et al, 28 September 1977; note of meeting of 4 November 1977. **146** TNA: DEFE 69/1366, minute by Ames, FP3, 2 February 1978. **147** TNA: DEFE 69/1366, note by DNMP, 3 February 1978. **148** TNA: DEFE 13/1068, draft note for OPDO(S) covered by Judd to MinState, 17 April 1975. **149** TNA: ADM 167/174, A/M(74)6, Item 2, 14 November 1974. **150** TNA: CAB 148/156 OPDO(S) (75) 11, Report of Hydrographic Study Group, 1 May 1975. **151** Increasing the costs of charts was strongly opposed, as 'the whole system of free exchange of surveying information among nations, on which the Hydrographer depends for 80 per cent of his charts, would be jeopardised', TNA: DEFE 13/1068, draft note for OPDO(S) covered by Judd to MinState, 17 April 1975. **152** TNA: CAB 148/149, OPDO(S) 4th Meeting, 21 May 1975. **153** TNA: DEFE 13/1068, draft note for OPDO(S) covered by Judd to MinState, 17 April 1975. **154** TNA: DEFE 13/1068, Jaffray to VCNS, 9 April 1975; Balogh to Barnett, 29 April 1975. **155** HMSO: Statement on Defence Estimates 1977 (Cmnd 6735), February 1977, p. 22. **156** TNA: DEFE 23/190, Humphreys to PS/Min St, 21 March 1978, Annex. **157** Thompson, *The Royal Marines*, pp. 534–7; Ladd, *By Sea, by Land*, pp. 336–7. **158** Ibid., pp. 537–46; Ibid., pp. 338–41. **159** NHB: *Fearless* Box 1/T50963, Cassels to FOCAS, 2 August 1972. **160** Ladd, *By Sea, by Land*, p. 339. **161** TNA: DEFE 24/945, Ingham to MO4, 9 July 1976. **162** TNA: DEFE 24/945, Bryant to various, 20 November 1973, pp. 2–5 and Annex C. **163** TNA: DEFE 24/945, Holder to DNE, 16 December 1974; DS5 to CINCFLEET, 7 March 1975. **164** TNA: DEFE 24/945, Bryant to various, 20 November 1973, p. 5. **165** MOD: BR 1736(57) 'Naval Staff History: The Cod War, Naval Operations off Iceland in Support of the British Fishing Industry (1958–1976)', 1990, pp. 1–35. See also Welch, *The Royal Navy in the Cod Wars*, pp. 93–156. **166** 'Naval Staff History, The Cod War', pp. 35–42. **167** Ibid., pp. 42–54; for the trawler fishing crews' ultimatum and the RN ships entrance into the 50-mile limit, see NHB: Fisheries Box 2, RoP 88B, Iceland, HMS *Plymouth*, Rawlinson to FOSNI, 15 June 1973. **168** 'Naval Staff History, The Cod War', pp. 55–62. **169** Ibid., pp. 62–77. **170** Ibid., pp. 77–96.

Chapter 9: Retreat to the Four Pillars

1 Polmar and Moore, *Cold War Submarines*, p. 164; Il'in and Kolyesnikov, *Otyechyestvennyye Atomnyye Podvodnyye Lodki*, p. 40. **2** Watson, *Red Navy at Sea*, pp. 89–90, 124–6. The Syrian ports of Latakia and Tartus were also used regularly used for port visits, more so after 1973 when Soviet forces were expelled from Egypt. **3** Watson, *Red Navy at Sea*, p. 183. 'Warship days' include transits as well as ships stationed in the sea, although it should be noted that the Suez Canal was impassable for all shipping between 1967 and late 1974. **4** TNA: DEFE 13/635, DS12 to APS SofS, 3 July 1968; DEFE 25/253, Burrows to Brosio, 12 July 1968. **5** For the relatively muted impact of the deployment, see Hampshire, *From East of Suez to Eastern Atlantic*, pp. 177–9. **6** NHB: Exercises Box 11/T47327, DN Plans to NA 1SL, 6 October 1971. **7** For example, see Deep Furrow 71, Deep Furrow 73 and Deep Express 75. NHB: Exercises Box 10/T4731, Hepworth to Sec 1SL, 4 October 1971; Exercises Box 11/T83801, Fieldhouse to Sec 1SL, 7 September 1973; T83803, Skinner to Sec 1SL, 2 September 1975. **8** For example, see Dawn Patrol 70 and Dawn Patrol 75. NHB: Exercises Box 10/T47302 and T47303, short memoranda; Exercises Box 11/T83804, Skinner to 1SL, 16 June 1975. **9** NHB: Exercises Box 10/T83800, Skinner to Sec 1SL, 16 April 1974. **10** NHB: Exercises Box 11/T47327, DN Plans to NA 1SL, 6 October 1971. **11** Goldstein and Zhukov, 'A Tale of Two Fleets', pp. 27–9. **12** Zumwalt, *On Watch*, pp. 446–7. **13** Goldstein and Zhukov, 'A Tale of Two Fleets', pp. 44–6. **14** Ibid., pp. 46–53. **15** Quoted in Goldstein and Zhukov, 'A Tale of Two Fleets', p. 54. **16** Goldstein and Zhukov, 'A Tale of Two Fleets', pp. 53–5. **17** O'Flaherty, *Naval Mine Warfare*, pp. 105–09. **18** Mallinson, *Cyprus: A Modern History*, pp. 31–74. **19** *The Times*, '35,000 fled to British bases during fighting', 25 July 1974. **20** NHB: Hermes Box 1/T83347, Branson to FOCAS, Report of Proceedings, 2 April to 6 August 1974. **21** NHB: Naval News Summary, July 1974, p. 1. **22** Pedaliu, 'A Sea of Confusion', pp. 747–9. **23** Harris, *Lebanon*, pp. 224–35. **24** NHB: Bulwark Box 2/T73475, Extract from 40 Cdo Newsletter, 1975, p. 20. **25** Harris, *Lebanon*, pp. 237–8. **26** NHB: Mermaid Box/T112909, Stephens to CinC Fleet, 23 July 1976. **27** HMSO: Treaty Series No. 44 (1972), 'Agreement ... with respect to the Use of Military Facilities in Malta', 26 March 1972 (Cmnd 4943). **28** NHB: Exercises Box 6: Withdrawal of British Forces from Malta, DP 21/75 (Final), 24 March 1975. **29** NHB: London Box/T92377: Report of Proceedings, Ram to CinCFleet, 11 July 1979. **30** NHB: Defence Review 1974, Volume 4D: OPD(74)23, 'Defence Review', 15 July 1974, p. 11. **31** Gibraltar mainly undertook routine short refits of *Leander* class frigates and MCM vessels. NHB: Admiralty Board Papers, A/P(76)9, Long Term Review of Dockyard Load and Capacity, 18 October 1976, p. 18. **32** HMSO: Supplementary Statement on Defence Policy 1970, Cmnd 4521; Statement on Defence Estimates 1971, Cmnd 4592, p. 5. **33** Borthwick, *Yarrow and Company Limited*, pp. 118, 155. **34** NHB: Singapore Naval General Orders, March 1975, 1–4; Mermaid Box/T112936, Reports of Proceedings 3 to 26 April 1975; and T112929, 14 July to 24 September 1975. **35** NHB: Singapore Naval General Orders, March 1975, 21–2 and 21–5. **36** TNA: DEFE 13/1084, CPL to CDS, 28 January 1976. **37** Huxley, *Defending the Lion City*, p. 207. **38** TNA: DEFE 11/839, 'Force levels in Hong Kong' Commander British Forces, 3 July 1974, p. 11. **39** NHB: Hong Kong RoP, registered file 'HK Guardship, policy and replacement', Cdre Hong Kong to MoD, 23 November 1971, annex B. **40** TNA: DEFE 11/839, 'Force levels in Hong Kong' Commander British Forces, 3 July 1974, p. 11. **41** TNA: DEFE 11/840, cypher telegram, Foreign Secretary to Governor Hong Kong, 15:40, 1 August 1975; DEFE 11/842, minutes of first plenary meeting on defence costs, 28 October 1975. **42** Moore, *Jane's Fighting Ships 1986–1987*, p. 665. **43** NHB: Hong Kong RoP, registered file 'Contingency Study of the Reintroduction of the Hong Kong Guardship', DNPlans to VCNS, 18 June 1976. **44** Harland, *The Royal Navy in Hong Kong*, p. 70. **45** TNA: DEFE 11/840, Parrish to Dinwhiddie, 24 July 1975. **46** The communications hub at Mauritius, which was at the core of British defence communications East of Suez until the advent of the Skynet satellite system, had been established in 1962 following the closure of a similar station in Ceylon. NHB: Press Release Box/T127144, 16 February 1962. For a general history, see: Royal Navy Communications Branch Museum website: 'HMS Mauritius: Now a Memory' HMS Mauritius (commsmuseum.co.uk) (accessed 22/11/22). **47** Legislation.gov.uk: British Indian Ocean Territory Order 1976, SI 1976/893. The islands separated from the Seychelles were returned in 1976 on that colony's independence. **48** NHB: Hydra Box 1: RoP Volume 15A, Morris to CinCFleet, 27 February 1972, ff. 134–140; Falmouth Box, Giles to CinCFleet, 19 March 1975. In the latter instance the Royal Navy had stiff competition from other navies when offering disaster-relief help: the USS *Enterprise* and the French carrier *Clemenceau* had just left the islands when *Falmouth* arrived, whilst the Soviet cruiser *Dmitri Pozhorski* had arrived and her crew were busily helping with repairs across the islands. Many major powers were fighting for influence over the small but strategically placed islands that made up Mauritius. **49** NHB: Devonshire Box/T74741, Sandford to CinCFleet, 22 January 1973; Group Deployments Box 2, Volume 145A, Clayton to CinCFleet, 18 October 1974. **50** NHB: Euryalus Box/ T92172, Roome to CinCFE, 2 February 1968. **51** NHB: Arethusa Box 1/T29621, Skinner to CinCFleet, 29 June 1972; Leopard Box, Whyte-Melville Jackson to CinCFleet, 12 June 1974. **52** NHB; Hydra Box 2, Volume 15A, see RoPs 1972–76. **53** TNA: DEFE 69/2051, signals COMFEF to various 1 June 1970 1715Z, 2 June 1970 0522Z; 73A1 Sitrep 7 June 1970. **54** NHB: Eagle Box 1, Reports of Proceedings 1968–78 Volume, Cecil to CinCFleet, 21 January 1972, plus attachments and following papers, pp. 286–300. **55** Rehman, 'Indian Aspirational Naval Doctrine', pp. 73–4; Hiranandani, *Transition to Eminence*, pp. 17–18; Dockrill, *Britain's Retreat from East of Suez*, pp. 111–12. **56** Dockrill, *Britain's Retreat from East of Suez*, p. 112. **57** Young, *The Labour Governments 1964–70*, pp. 64–6. **58** Hiranandani, *Transition to Eminence*, pp. 71–3, 114–20. **59** NHB: Group Deployments Box 2: Group Deployments Volume, Fieldhouse to CinCFleet, 1 September 1975. **60** NHB: Group Deployments Box 2: Group Deployments Volume, Morton to CinCFleet, 6 December 1976. **61** Mobley, 'The Beira Patrol', *Naval War College Review*, p. 17. **62** In 1972, HMS *Mauritius* is reported as having employed 750 local personnel: Mauritius News website, 'Farewell heritage: HMS Mauritius, the last vestiges swept away by the SMF gymnasium' *Mauritius News* (mauritiushindinews.com) (accessed 22/11/22). **63** TNA: DEFE 13/1084, CPL to CDS, 28 January 1976; DEFE 13/973, Dales to Bridges,

27 November 1974; DEFE 13/974, Bridges to Brown, 16 December 1974. **64** Dockrill, *Britain's Retreat from East of Suez*, pp. 128–9, 150. **65** Cooper, '1955–1972: The Era of Forward Defence', pp. 190–2. **66** Gjessing, *Anglo-Australian Naval Relations*, pp. 182–3. **67** 'New Equipment Preview' edition, *Navy Quarterly*, October 1972, pp. 1–19; Gjessing, *Anglo-Australian Naval Relations*, pp. 160–1. **68** Berlyn and Foster, 'New destroyer for the RAN', pp. 4–6. **69** NHB: Group Deployments Box 2, Fieldhouse to CinCFleet, 18 December 1975. **70** Howard, *The Navy in New Zealand*, pp. 91–2, 161. **71** Ibid., pp. 132–6. **72** Morey, *Service from the Sea*, p. 217. **73** McIntyre, *Winding up the British Empire in the Pacific Islands*, pp. 9–15. **74** NHB: Hydra Box 2, Volume 15A, Read to Hydrographer, 1 March 1975. **75** NHB: Hydra Box 2, Volume 15A, RoPs 1972–74. **76** NHB: Military Task Events, 2015 edition, 1970, pp. 17–18; 1971, p. 18; 1974, pp. 29–30; 1976, pp. 3–10. **77** Poland, *Torpedomen*, p. 360; NHB: Military Task Events, 1977, pp. 2 and 18. **78** McIntyre, *Winding up the British Empire in the Pacific Islands*, pp. 253–5. **79** NHB: Hermione Box, Brown to COMANZUKNAV, 30 November 1973. **80** NHB: West Indies RoP Box, Volume 55A, extract from Director of Naval Plans 'Major Matters', May 1975, folio 7. **81** Johnson, 'The British Caribbean from Demobilisation to Constitutional Decolonisation', pp. 618–20. **82** Ashton, BDEEP, 'Introduction', pp. lxxx–lxxxi. **83** NHB: West Indies RoPs Box, Volume 55A, Pritchard to SNOWI, 16 January 1972. **84** NHB: Intrepid Box 1/T114870, Kidd to FOCAS, 27 March 1973. **85** NHB: Fearless Box 1/T50954, Rumble to FOCAS 23 May 1975. **86** Hansard, Parliamentary Debates: HC Deb 10 April 1963, Vol. 675, cc. 1261–2, Bahamas Cays (Patrols). **87** NHB: Sirius Box/T109838, Penny to SNOWI, 25 May 1971; Fox Box, Volume 11A, Hope to Hydrographer of the Navy, 31 July 1970. **88** Theberge, *Russia in the Caribbean*, pp. 99–108; Watson, *Red Navy at Sea*, pp. 43–9. **89** NHB: Admiralty Board Memoranda, A/P(73)13, Sketch Estimates, 8 November 1973, p. 2. **90** NHB: Plymouth Box 1/T111042, Livesay to SNOWI, 31 October 1972. **91** NHB: West Indies RoPs Box, Volume 55A, Garnier to SNOWI, 12 September 1973, folio 16. **92** NHB: Rhyl Box/T92047, Duffay to SNOWI, 16 December 1968. **93** NHB: Bacchante Box/T33839, Oswald to SNOWI, 20 April 1971. **94** NHB: West Indies RoPs Box, Volume 55A, McKeown to SNOWI, 7 December 1972. **95** NHB: Scylla Box/T91928, Bacchante to CinC Fleet, 14 March 1979. **96** *Minerva* first landed British officials in an attempt to negotiate with the leaders of the rebellion, then covered the arrival of another by private plane. After the 'ignominious retreat' of this second party, Marines from HMS *Minerva*, HMS *Rhyl* and HMS *Rothesay*, supplemented by additional forces, landed at Road Bay on 19 March 1969. NHB: Minerva Box/T92287, Armytage to SNOWI, 20 May 1969. The author would like to thank his father, who was aboard *Rothesay* at the time, for additional information on this operation. **97** NHB: West Indies RoPs Box, Volume 55A, Cole to SNOWI, 10 July 1975, folio 333. **98** Ashton, BDEEP. 'Introduction', p. lxxx. **99** NHB: West Indies RoP Box, Volume 55A, extract from Director of Naval Plans 'Major Matters', May 1975, folio 7. **100** TNA: DEFE 13/1084, CPL to CDS, 28 January 1976. **101** NHB: Dockyards and Establishments (Overseas) Box 3/T27790, 'HMS Malabar; a Brief History…'. **102** Schirmer, *The Guatemalan Military Project*, pp. 9–17. **103** TNA: DEFE 11/889, Hawley to Director of Plans, November 1973; Mellersh to Director of Plans, 28 August 1973; DEFE 11/822, Green to CoS Secretariat, 17 July 1975; DOPS paper 'Increased Threat to Belize', 18 August 1975; telegram Commander BF Belize to MoD, 19 May 1975. **104** White, *Phoenix Squadron*, pp. 199–200, 205. **105** TNA: PREM 15/1625, Consul General Guatemala City to Douglas-Home, 26 January 1972. **106** TNA: PREM 15/1625, Douglas-Home to Governor British Honduras, 26 January 1972. **107** White, *Phoenix Squadron*, p. 209; TNA: PREM 15/1625, Douglas-Home to Consul General Guatemala City, 26 January 1972. **108** TNA: PREM 15/1625, Note for record, 28 January 1972. **109** TNA: FCO 7/3108, Guatemala Annual Report 1975, pp. 7–9. **110** TNA: DEFE 11/822, Posnett to Lamour, 12 September 1975. **111** Foreign Relations of the United States 1969–76, Volume E-11, Part 1, document 195, pp. 553–4; TNA: DEFE 11/822 'The Guatemalan Threat' CBF Belize, 15 September 1975. **112** TNA: DEFE 11/824, Posnett to FCO, 2 November 1975. **113** TNA: DEFE 11/822, telegram, CBF Belize to SNOWI, 9 September 1975; telegram, SNOWI to CBF Belize, 9 September 1975. **114** TNA: DEFE 11/822 'The Guatemalan Threat' CBF Belize, 15 September 1975. **115** TNA: FCO 7/3108, Guatemala Annual Report 1975, pp. 9–11, annex A, p. 5. **116** Hore, *Royal Navy and Royal Marines Operations 1964 to 1996*, p. 40. **117** TNA: DEFE 13/1131, Owen to Mulley, 1 July 1977; Whitmore to PS, Secretary of State, 4 July 1977; Wall to Cartledge, 21 July 1977. **118** TNA: DEFE 13/1131, 'The military risks in Belize' attachment to 1018/1, 4 July 1977. **119** Cable, *Gunboat Diplomacy 1919–1991*, p. 204; TNA: DEFE 13/1131,

Owen to Mulley, 1 July 1977. **120** TNA: DEFE 11/890, telegram MOD to BDS Washington, 2 December 1977, 1420Z. **121** TNA: DEFE 13/1131, Defence Situation Centre, Belize sitrep, 0830Z 8 July 1977; Owen to Mulley 8 July 1977.

Chapter 10: The Eastlant Navy

1 NHB: Fleet Requirements Committee Box 2/T63576: 'A Concept of Operations for UK Maritime Forces 1985–99', FRC(75)(P)1(Final). **2** Watson, *Red Navy at Sea*, see especially Chs 4, 6, 7 and 10. **3** NHB: FRC Box 2: 'Concept of Operations', paras 7–9, 12–13. **4** Ibid., para. 10. **5** Ibid.. para. 16. **6** Ibid., para. 18. **7** Ibid., paras 22–23. **8** Ibid., paras 30–109. **9** Ibid., paras 110–114. **10** Poole, *Joint Chiefs of Staff 1973–1976*, pp. 57, 74–9, 80–3. **11** Zaloga, *The Kremlin's Nuclear Shield*, p. 175; Gordon and Komissarov, *Soviet Naval Aviation 1946–1991*, p 283. **12** Although able to carry three missiles, they increased drag and reduced speed significantly: 'seasoned crews always insisted on one missile per plane'. It is not clear the extent to which this was known by NATO at the time. Tokarev, 'Kamikazes: The Soviet Legacy', p. 72. **13** NHB: FRC Box 2/T56373, FRC(75)(P)4, 'Size and Shape of the fleet', pp. 24–5, 29–31. **14** Ibid., pp. 16–24. **15** Ibid. **16** Ibid., pp. 26–9. **17** Ibid., p. 37. **18** Ibid., pp. 36–7. **19** Ibid., annex C. **20** Ibid., pp. 43–8. **21** Ibid., Annexes A and B. **22** NHB: Admiralty Board Memoranda 1972: A/P(72)4, 'Long Term Costings 1972', 12 April 1972, p. 3. Given in 1971 prices (£629 million), transferred to 1973 prices using Bank of England inflation calculator and rounded upwards. **23** French, *Army, Empire and Cold War*, Ch 10 and conclusion. **24** TNA: FCO 46/2170, 'Defence Priorities', 21 January 1980. **25** TNA: DEFE 69/637, DP18/77 (Final), cover note, 3 March 1978. **26** Ibid., pp. A-21 to A-25. **27** Ibid., pp. A-30 to A-31. **28** Ibid., p. A-27. **29** Ibid., p. A-29. **30** Ibid., p. A-27. **31** Ibid., p. A-2. **32** TNA: DEFE 69/1387, Fitch to DN Plans, 30 May 1979; ADNFPS to various, 28 April 1980. **33** TNA: DEFE 69/1387, Newman to AD NFPS, 8 May 1980. **34** TNA: DEFE 69/1387, White to DN Plans, 15 May 1980. **35** TNA: DEFE 69/1387, DN Plans to various, 22 August 1980, attached paper. **36** TNA: DEFE 69/637, FRC80(P)5, 'The roles of UK Maritime Forces', October 1980. **37** TNA: DEFE 69/643, DN Plans to Sec VCNS, 23 September 1977; see comments by DNOR about the concept's inadequacy if used to help justify operational requirements: DEFE 69/644, DNOR to DN Plans, 15 August 1978. **38** TNA: DEFE 69/644, ACNS(Pol) to Burgoyne, 6 July 1978. **39** TNA: DEFE 69/643, Livesay to DN Plans, 12 December 1977, Annex, Threat section; DEFE 69/644, DN Plans to DNW et al., 25 April 1978, Chapter 3. **40** TNA: DEFE 69/643, Gunning to Cdre(Int), 21 December 1977, Annex A. **41** TNA: DEFE 69/643, Livesay to DN Plans, 12 December 1977, Annex, Threat section. **42** TNA: DEFE 69/644, DN Plans to DNW et al., 25 April 1978, Chapter 2. **43** TNA: DEFE 69/643, Straker to Crowe, 24 October 1977, Annex A. **44** TNA: DEFE 69/644, DN Plans to DNW et al., 25 April 1978, Chapter 4. **45** There was a valid criticism of the paper on the basis that the distinction between the short and long-warning scenarios would be difficult to make in practice: when a crisis began it would not be clear how long it would last before escalating into conflict and also how long that conflict would last. Therefore, in practice, operational commanders would have to attempt to prepare to both long and short scenarios simultaneously, at least initially until the character of the crisis became more evident. TNA: DEFE 69/644, NFPS to DN Plans, 12 May 1978. **46** For example, see Nott, *Here Today, Gone Tomorrow*, p. 231; Baer, *One Hundred Years of Sea Power*, p. 412. **47** TNA: DEFE 69/644, DN Plans to DNW et al., 25 April 1978, pp. 25–6. **48** Rearden, *Joint Chiefs of Staff 1977–80*, pp. 172–5; Keefer, *Harold Brown*, pp. 378–89, 411–16. **49** Even the conception of what a 'long war' might look like was contested between the two most senior US commanders in NATO: SACEUR and SACLANT. The former argued for a 30-day long war and the latter a 40–70-day long war (presumably including a period of confrontation or increased tension). TNA: DEFE 69/137, Fisher to DN Plans, 15 May 1980. **50** Keefer, *Harold Brown 1977–81*, pp. 231–8. **51** TNA: AIR 6/194, AFBSC(76)8, 19 October 1976, Annex F. The author would like to thank Alastair Noble for bringing this document, and other AIR 6 papers from the late 1970s, to his attention. **52** CIA, 'The role of interdiction at sea in Soviet naval strategy and operations' (February 1978), https://www.cia.gov/library/readingroom/docs/DOC_0005390331.pdf (accessed 24 September 2019); note that Soviet open-source literature written by Admiral Gorshkov and others in professional journals such as *Morskoy Sbornik* had been indicating that anti-SLOC operations were a secondary priority as far back as the mid-1960s. See Herrick, *Soviet Naval Doctrine and Policy Volume 2*, pp. 278–83. **53** HMSO: 'Statement on Defence Estimates 1976' (Cmnd 6432), March 1976, p. 18. **54** NHB: Admiralty Board Sub-Committee Memoranda 1976, ABSC/P(76)1, 12 January 1976. **55** HMSO, 'Statement on Defence Estimates 1976', p. 27. **56** Ibid., p. 29. **57** HMSO, 'Statement on the Defence Estimates 1977' (Cmnd 6735), February

NOTES TO PAGES 269–282 671

1977, p. 1. **58** TNA: DEFE 13/1026, Whitmore to PS/SofS, 7 December 1976; Hudson to Mulley, 6 December 1976. **59** TNA: DEFE 13/1026, Chiefs of Staff to Callaghan, 10 December 1976. The previous direct meeting with the Prime Minister had been in 1968 in protest against the speed of defence reductions following the completion of the Defence Expenditure Studies: Facer to Mulley, 9 November 1976. **60** HMSO, 'Statement on Defence Estimates 1977', p. 60. **61** HMSO, 'Statement on Defence Estimates 1978' (Cmnd 7099), February 1978, p. 32; 'Statement on Defence Estimates 1979 (Cmnd 7474), February 1979, p. 31. **62** In 1976 service personnel gained a net pay rise of between £3.27 and £4.39 a week. This would be a 10 per cent pay rise for the very lowest ranks (whose pay had been set at £32.76 per week in 1975), but much less than that for leading seamen and those more senior. In 1977 the pay rise was 5 per cent across the board. Inflation in 1976 was 16.5 per cent and in 1977, 15.8 per cent. *The Times*, 4 May 1976, p. 3; 21 June 1977, p. 2. **63** HMSO, 'Statement on Defence Estimates 1978', p. 16; 'Statement on Defence Estimates 1979', p. 15. **64** Apal'kov, *Podvodniye Lodki*, pp. 21–39. **65** Polmar and Moore, *Cold War Submarines*, pp. 159, 179. **66** TNA: DEFE 13/1357, Operational Concept for ASW, 1978. **67** The Commanding Officer of *Matapan* neatly summarised what his ship's experimental sonar could and could not do: it 'has the capability only of denying the surface duct [i.e. the isotherm] to the submarine and a CZ [convergence zone: usually 30nm in the Eastern Atlantic] capability over a narrow annulus [bottom bounce detection zone].'NHB: Matapan Box: Cdr Hoskin to Capt 2nd Frigate Squadron, 'Bottom Bounce Sonar Project – Summary of Trials', 23 July 1976, T113065. **68** Friedman, *Naval Weapon Systems 1997–98*, pp. 611–12. **69** TNA: DEFE 13/1026, Hudson to PS/SofS, 28 January 1977, Annex A. **70** Hennessy and Jinks, *The Silent Deep*, pp. 375–7; Hervey, *Submarines*, pp. 99–100. **71** Friedman, *Naval Weapon Systems 1997–98*, p. 612. **72** NHB: Lowestoft Box/T113358-T113362, reports of proceedings 29 July 1977, 22 March 1978, 2 August 1978 and 13 August 1979. **73** NHB: Boscombe Box 57/T151727, 'Sonar Type 2031 Optrial' OEG Report 8/78. **74** NHB: Fleet Requirements Committee/ T56345, 'Sonar 2031 Shipfitting Policy', 15 March 1978. **75** Osborne and Sowdon, *Leander Class*, pp. 74–8. **76** NHB: VCNS Papers, VCNS 40/11/4, AP/S Minister (DP) to Sec/CofN, 16 March 1982. **77** Gibson, *Nimrod's Genesis*, pp. 175–9. **78** Allen, *Sea King*, pp. 30–1. **79** Ibid., p. 40; Lambert, ed., *Jane's All the World's Aircraft 1991–92*, p. 328. **80** TNA: DEFE 24/605, Campbell to Commanders in Chief, 12 June 1968; DEFE 13/985, Piper to Secretary of State, 4 December 1973. **81** Hampshire, 'From Malin Head to "Okean 75"', pp. 659–74. **82** Watson, *Red Navy at Sea*, pp. 30–2. **83** NHB: Danae Box, Operation Algy RoP, 27 April 1975, T74609. **84** Ford and Rosenberg, *Admiral's Advantage*, p. 61. **85** Potter, *Electronic Greyhounds*, pp. 137–8; Friedman, *Naval Weapon Systems* (1991), p. 5; Ford and Rosenberg, *Admirals' Advantage*, pp. 61, 114 and plate 10. The radio frequency sensors were designated SLR-16 and the direction finders SRD-19 by the United States Navy. **86** Ashmore and Grove, *The Battle and the Breeze*, p. 223. **87** NHB: Fleet Requirements Committee Box 2, FRC79(P)1, Batch 2 Type 22, 15 February 1979. **88** Hennessy and Jinks, *The Silent Deep*, pp. 353, 377–83, 520–7. **89** TNA: PREM 16/1181, Mason to Wilson, 18 September 1975; for sustaining the Moscow criterion see: Hunt to Wilson, 28 February 1974. **90** Stoddart, *Facing Down the Soviet Union*, pp. 18–21. **91** TNA: PREM 16/1181, Cartledge to Vile, 20 July 1977; Mulley to Callaghan, 21 July 1977. **92** TNA: PREM 16/1181, Owen to Callaghan, 26 July 1977. **93** Stoddart, *Facing Down the Soviet Union*, pp. 26–30; Hennessy and Jinks, *The Silent Deep*, pp. 464–8. **94** Stoddart, *Facing Down the Soviet Union*, pp. 21–6. **95** TNA: PREM 16/1181, meeting of ministers, 29 September 1976. **96** Calculations for cost increases: £337 million at 1975 prices (Stoddart, *Facing Down the Soviet Union*, p. 15) and £1,000 million at 1981 prices (Stoddart, *Facing Down the Soviet Union*, p. 102). The 1975 figure was then re-based to 1981 prices using the Bank of England Inflation Calculator. **97** NHB: Exercises Box 11/T47290, 'Ocean Safari 75'. **98** NHB: Exercises Box 11/ T47291, 'Teamwork 76'. **99** NHB: Exercises Box 11/T83805, 'Ocean Safari 77'. **100** NHB: Exercises Box 11/T47293, 'Northern Wedding 78'. **101** NHB: Exercises Box 10/T83792, 'Ocean Safari 79'. **102** NHB: Exercises Box 10/T47295, 'Teamwork 80'. **103** NHB: Exercises Box 8/T83162, 'High Wood 75'; T83164, 'High Wood 77'; T83166, 'High Wood 79'. **104** NHB: Ministry of Defence: 'The Cod War: Naval Operations off Iceland in Support of the British Fishing Industry (1958–76)', BR 1736(57), pp. 95–9. **105** Ibid., pp. 102–04, 107. **106** Ibid., Appendices J and K, pp. 206–11. **107** Ibid., pp. 128, 135, 148–50, 161 Appendix K, pp. 210–11. **108** Ibid., pp. 159–64, 177–8. **109** NHB: Offshore Tapestry Box/T47959, D/DNPlans 22/2/5B, 'The Protection of Offshore Interests' covered by Lang to Defence Sales 2, 31 January 1979. **110** Ibid., paras 5–6. **111** TNA: T 225/4212, 'Background brief: Protection of North Sea Oil and Gas Installations', 7 May 1975. **112** TNA: DEFE 13/1068, Judd to Erickson, 17 February 1975. **113** The highest profile loss to the Navy was the early retirement of Lieutenant

Commander Peter Cobby, amongst the Navy's most experienced diving instructors, so that he could lead the new cross-industry Underwater Training Centre at Fort William which had been set up by the Department of Energy and the Offshore Supplies Office. The losses were so serious that measures such as delaying premature voluntary release for recently trained divers were considered. TNA: DEFE 13/1068, Bailey to DUS(N), 11 February 1975; Head of Naval Personnel Dvn 2 to AUS(NP) et al, 17 March 1975, plus appended note; Mason to Varley, 26 March 1975; Poland, *Torpedomen*, pp. 361–2. **114** NHB: Offshore Tapestry Box/T47958, Resources for Offshore Tasks – Brief for ACNS(P), DNPlans to VCNS, 'Offshore Tapestry, the Next Steps', 22 January 1976, Tab A. **115** TNA: DEFE 13/1068. Yeeles to APS/MinSt, 18 June 1975, appended background note. **116** Moore, *Jane's Fighting Ships 1978–79*, p. 588. **117** TNA: DEFE 23/190, PS/USofS(N) to PS/Min St, 17 August 1977; Jackling to PS/MinState, 16 September 1977; NHB: 'Protection of Offshore Interests', paras 7–8, T47959. **118** TNA: T 225/4212, Ross to Anson, 24 June 1975, covering 'Resources for Offshore Tasks'. **119** NHB: Offshore Tapestry Box/T47958, Resources for Offshore Tasks – Brief for ACNS(P), DNPlans to VCNS, 'HMS *Kingfisher* Report – Future of the Bird Class', 17 June 1976, Tab H. **120** NHB: Fleet Requirements Committee Box 2, 'Offshore Patrol Vessel NST 7040' FRC 77(P)6(Revised), 15 September 1977. **121** Brown and Moore, *Rebuilding the Royal Navy*, pp. 135–7. **122** HMSO, 'Statement on Defence Estimates 1979', Cmnd. 7474, February 1979, p. 33; John Moore, ed. *Jane's Fighting Ships 1981–82*, p. 577; The first two *Jersey* class cost £3.3 million together at 1976 prices, with inflation added this translates to £5.5 million at 1980 prices, therefore giving the price of four *Jersey* class at c. £11 million. **123** Gibson, *Nimrod's Genesis*, p. 217. **124** Ibid., pp. 211–17; NHB, T47959: 'Protection of Offshore Interests', paras 9–10, 13–16. **125** NHB: Offshore Tapestry Box, D/DNPlans 22/2/5B, Hamil to DN Plans, 'Brief for VCNS Designate' 1 May 1980. **126** A hoax bomb was blown up by a RN bomb disposal team on the Claymore Alpha rig, *The Times*, 5 July 1978; the Sullom Voe oil terminal in Shetland was attacked by the Provisional IRA, *Guardian* 12 May 1981; and a bomb threat, allegedly by the Palestinian Liberation Organisation, against British and Norwegian oil rigs was made in the same year; it was later deemed to be a hoax, *Daily Telegraph*, 7 December 1981. **127** TNA: DEFE 13/1068, Judd to Mason, 6 June 1975 and Annex. **128** NHB: Offshore Tapestry Box/T47959, D/DNPlans 22/2/5B, Hamil to DN Plans, 'Brief for VCNS Designate' 1 May 1980; 'Protection of Offshore Interests', paras 28–29. **129** Gibson, *Nimrod's Genesis*, p. 210. **130** That the Ship Department were trying to use the OPV2 to show the Naval Staff how a smaller hull could be 'up-gunned' into a light frigate or corvette is shown in Daniel, *The End of an Era*, pp. 247–8. The shift to other Government Department funding was agreed with the Treasury in 1975 when it became clear that the 200-mile EEZ limit would be agreed at the UN Conference on the Law of the Sea. NHB: Fleet Requirements Committee Box 2, 'Offshore Patrol Vessel NST 7040' FRC77(P)6(Revised), 15 September 1977, T56358; Offshore Tapestry Box/T47959, D/DNPlans 22/2/5B, Cann to Moss, 30 January 1979; TNA: DEFE 13/1068, Barnett to Shepherd, and appended report, 30 July 1975; Bishop to Barnett, 6 August 1975. **131** Ashmore and Grove, *Battle and the Breeze*, p. 225. **132** Ibid., p. 219. **133** Ibid., pp. 257–9; Hill, *Lewin of Greenwich*, pp. 301–02.

Chapter 11: After *Ark Royal*
1 NHB: Ark Royal Box 1: Report of Proceedings for 5/4 to 15/12/78, 9 January 1979, T29899. **2** BBC Website: 'History of the BBC: Sailor 5 August 1976': https://www.bbc.com/historyofthebbc/anniversaries/august/sailor (accessed 20/11/2020). **3** For the Silver Jubilee review, see Dunn, *The Power and the Glory*, pp. 247–52. **4** NHB: Admiralty Board Minutes, A/M(77)2, item 2, 17 February 1977, Leppard to DUS(RN). **5** NHB: Admiralty Board Minutes, A/M(79)3, item 3, 26 April 1979. **6** TNA: DEFE 13/1134, Pritchard to Antrim, 15 December 1978. **7** NHB: Naval sales for scrap: Davey to Kitson Vickers Ltd, 23 July 1980. **8** NHB: Ark Royal Box 1/T29899, Anson to FOF3, 9 January 1979. **9** Ibid. **10** Sturtivant, Burrow and Howard, *Fleet Air Arm Fixed Wing Aircraft since 1946*, pp. 44–75, 470–9. **11** Ballance, Howard and Sturtivant, *Squadrons and Units of the Fleet Air Arm*, pp. 128–31, 263–5. **12** Wilson, *Blackburn/BAE Buccaneer*, p. 86. **13** Sturtivant, Burrow and Howard, *Fleet Air Arm Fixed Wing Aircraft*, pp. 324–37; Ballance, Howard and Sturtivant, *Squadrons and Units of the Fleet Air Arm* pp. 228–34. **14** Ashmore and Grove, *The Battle and the Breeze*, pp. 261–2; HMSO, Statement on Defence Estimates 1977, Cmnd 7099, February 1978, p. 13. **15** Hansard HC Deb 18 December 1986, Vol. 107, cc. 1351–1359, 'Airborne Early Warning Aircraft'. **16** NHB: VCNS Papers Box 73, VCNS 40/7/1, 'Westland Helicopters: Study in AEW Developments' November 1972. **17** TNA: DEFE 10/484, ORC meetings 6/66, 21 April 1966; 4/67,

6 April 1967; 9/67, 11 July 1967. **18** Ashmore and Grove, *The Battle and the Breeze*, pp. 222–3. **19** Ibid.; NHB: VCNS Papers Box 73, VCNS 40/7/1, Jungius to VCNS 1974; Capt L E Middleton to VCNS 20 March 1978. **20** TNA: DEFE 13/1134, Duffy to Mulley, 10 August 1977; Duffy to Mulley, 12 December 1977; DEFE 23/190, Mulley to Callaghan, 22 December 1977; NHB: Admiralty Board Sub Committee Memoranda 'HMS *Bulwark*', ABSC/P(77)5, 21 April 1977; 'HMS *Bulwark*', ABSC/P(77)12, 19 October 1977; Admiralty Board Sub Committee Minutes, meeting 9, item 1, 7 November 1977. **21** Watson, *Commander-in-Chief*, pp. 102–15; NHB: Group Deployments Box 2, Rear Admiral J D E Fieldhouse to CinCFleet, 1 September 1975, 18 December 1975, 9 March 1976, 5 April 1976; Captain R D de Leathes to CinCFleet, 22 October 1975. **22** NHB: Group Deployments Box 2, Group Deployments volume, Vice Admiral A Morton to CinCFleet, 6 December 1976; Royal Navy Press Release 75/76, 24 September 1976. **23** Livingstone, *Britain and the Dictatorships*, pp. 150–2. **24** NHB: Group Deployments Box 2, Rear Admiral M Wemyss to CinCFleet, 17 June 1977. **25** NHB: Group Deployments Box 2, Rear Admiral M Wemyss to CinCFleet, 30 December 1977 and 16 May 1978; Captain S Cassels, 23 January 1978. **26** Roberts, *Safeguarding the Nation*, pp. 127–8. **27** NHB: Group Deployments Box 1/T83472: Rear Admiral D C Jenkin to CinCFleet, 12 December 1980. **28** Ibid. **29** Ibid. **30** Ibid. **31** RN involvement in the 1981 Midlink Indian Ocean/Persian Gulf exercise – which previous Group Deployments had often been involved – had been indicated in early 1979, but had been removed by the following year. The Iranian revolution would also have had an impact. NHB: Diary of Principal Exercises 1979–81, 20 April 1979. **32** NHB: Hong Kong Reports of Proceedings, *Scimitar*, 19 April 1980 and 14 January 1981, also FOST 2 June 1980, Capt Moland 2 June 1980. **33** NHB: Hong Kong Reports of Proceedings, Naval Party 1009, 24 September 1982, DS5 notification 4/82 26 March 1982, closure notice 19 July 1982; *Daily Telegraph* cutting, May 1980, folio 293. **34** Tripp, *History of Iraq*, pp. 230–5; El-Shazly, *Gulf Tanker War*, Ch 2. **35** NHB: Operation Armilla 1980–1990 Draft Staff History, pp. 11–12. **36** Ibid., p. 13. **37** TNA: PREM 19/813, Gillmore to Graham, 9 October 1980. **38** NHB: Operation Armilla 1980–1990 Draft Staff History, pp. 12–15. **39** NHB: Coventry Box, Report of Proceedings, Operation Armilla, 3 November 1980. **40** NHB: Fleet Operations Programme 11/80 to 3/81. **41** NHB: DCI(RN)3/79, 5 January 1979. **42** NHB: Fleet Requirements Committee Box 2, FRC 79(M)3, item 1 'Future VSTOL', Annex B 17 May 1979. **43** TNA: AIR 6/196, AFBSC(76)9th conclusions, 7 October 1976, item 2; Air Historical Branch: AFBSC(77)12, RAF Maritime Programmes, 28 October 1977. **44** Sturtivant, Burrow and Howard, *Fleet Air Arm Fixed Wing Aircraft since 1946*, p. 84. **45** NHB: VCNS Papers Box 73, VCNS 40/6 Annex, APS/MinState to PS/CA 5 October 1979; AUS(NS) to Head DS1 9 April 1980. **46** The author would like to thank Andrew Livsey for this analogy to help describe the difference between radar and passive intercept. **47** TNA: T 225/4056, Operational Requirements Committee, OR30/67, 'NSR7151: Passive Search Receiver (Abbeyhill)', 21 June 1967. **48** Keily, *Naval Electronic Warfare*, pp. 17–18. **49** Peter West, '50 Years of Instantaneous Frequency Measurement', Y1PWE website: http://www.y1pwe.co.uk/IFM per cent20RECEIVERS50G.pdf (accessed 14 June 2021). **50** Friedman, *Naval Weapon Systems 1991*, pp. 514–17; and NHB: VCNS Papers, Box 51, VCNS 40/14 Part IV; Slater to Sec VCNS, 4 May 1979. **51** NHB: VCNS Papers Box 52, VCNS 40/1/7, Sea Slug, VCNS to 1SL 16 March 1973. **52** NHB: Defence Policy Box 2/T47393: Fleet Requirements Committee Minutes, 3rd meeting 1977, item 4: 'Type 42 – redesign and successor', 17 October 1977, 2nd meeting 1978, item 3: 'Type 42 – major refits', 24 February 1978, 2nd meeting 1979, items 2–4: 'Type 42 refit', 11 May 1979; Fleet Requirements Committee Box 1/T56347, 'Type 42 refit options' FRC 78(P)1, 2 February 1978. **53** TNA: DEFE 24/3200, ACSA(S) to DCDS(OR), 5 August 1980. **54** TNA: DEFE 69/1231, Controller to VCNS, 5 June 1974; AD Ships to DGWP et al, 6 March 1975. **55** TNA: DEFE 69/1231, DG Ships to Controller, 23 June 1976; DEFE 23/3200, Controller to MinState, 13 December 1977. **56** NHB: NHB: Defence Policy Box 2: Fleet Requirements Committee Minutes, 3rd meeting 1977, item 4: 'Type 42 – redesign and successor', 17 October 1977, T47393. **57** TNA: DEFE 69/1231, Rydill to DG Ships and DGW(N), 12 September 1977. **58** NHB: Defence Policy Box 2: Fleet Requirements Committee Minutes/T47393, 3rd meeting 1977, item 4: 'Type 42 – redesign and successor', 17 October 1977; Fleet Requirements Committee Box 1/T56350, Type 42/43 programme', FRC(P)3, 4 and 5, 24 April 1979; T56346, 'Type 42 Successor, Timing' FRC(78)2, 2 February 1978, T56346. **59** NHB: Fleet Requirements Committee Box 1/T56326, FRC 79(P)16, 7 May 1980, 'Maritime Anti-Air Warfare Policy Paper'. **60** TNA: DEFE 69/1580/1, DUWP(N) to

various, 28 February 1979. **61** Brown and Moore, *Rebuilding the Royal Navy*, p. 100. **62** NHB: Fleet Requirements Committee Box 1/T56325, FRC 79(P)17, 1 November 1979, 'Type 43 Destroyer'. **63** NHB: Tactical Doctrine Box 2, Fighting Instructions Volume 2 1975, p. 20. **64** TNA: DEFE 69/1577, Power to DUS(N), 6 September 1979. **65** TNA: DEFE 69/1577, DUS(N) to Head DS4, 2 August 1979. **66** TNA: DEFE 24/2840, OR-/80, NST 7007: Type 43 Destroyer (draft), 19 November 1979. **67** TNA: DEFE 24/2840, Poole to Harvey-Samuel, 22 August 1980. **68** TNA: DEFE 69/772, Newman to Black, 13 June 1980. **69** TNA: DEFE 69/772, ACSA(P) to ACNS(Pol), 25 June 1980. **70** The preceding holders of the post had been Admirals Lygo and Treacher. **71** Jerram-Croft, *The Royal Navy Lynx*, pp. 1–34. **72** Friedman, *British Destroyers and Frigates*, p. 339. **73** NHB: Finance Box 4/T48743, 1979 Long Term Costing Assumptions, April 1978. **74** NHB: Finance Box 4/T48740, 1980 Long Term Costing Assumptions, May 1979. **75** NHB: Finance Box 4/T48740, 1981 Long Term Costing Assumptions, May 1980. **76** Fleet Requirements Committee Box 2, 'Garage Ship', FRC 79(P)5, 10 May 1979, Defence Policy Box 2/T47393: Fleet Requirements Committee Minutes, 3rd meeting 1979, item 2, 17 May 1979, T47393. **77** NHB: Fleet Requirements Committee Box 2, 'Garage Ship', FRC 79(P)5, 10 May 1979, Defence Policy Box 2: Fleet Requirements Committee Minutes, 3rd meeting 1979, item 2, 17 May 1979; 4th meeting 1979, item 3, 5 July 1979. **78** NHB: Defence Policy Box 2/T47393, Fleet Requirements Committee Minutes, 3rd meeting 1980, item 2, 12 May 1980. **79** Johnman and Murphy, *British Shipbuilding and the State*, Ch 7; Murphy, *Shipbuilding in the United Kingdom*, pp. 85–7, 93–4. **80** TNA: PREM 16/1769, Varley to Barnett, 29 June 1978. **81** TNA: CAB 130/1067, GEN 156(78) 1st meeting, item 1, 12 December 1978; GEN 156(79)28, 2 March 1979. **82** TNA: PREM 16/2185, Hunt to Callaghan, 27 November 1978. **83** TNA: CAB 130/1067, GEN 156(78), 1st meeting, item 1, 12 December 1978; PREM 16/2185, Downey to Berrill, 29 November 1978. The Polish order, which was twenty-four ships, is described in Murphy, *Shipbuilding in the United Kingdom*, pp. 87–8. **84** TNA: CAB 130/1067, GEN 156(79)28, 2 March 1979. **85** TNA: DEFE 69/1409, Oughton to AUS(MatN), 14 February 1979. **86** TNA: DEFE 69/1409, Admiralty Board Sub-Committee 22 January 1979. **87** TNA: CAB 130/1067, GEN 156(79), 4th meeting, item 1, 15 February 1979. **88** For example, see TNA: DEFE 69/1409, Coates: Ship Department Instruction, 9 April 1979. **89** The Department of Industry wanted the long leads to be absorbed back into MoD stock if the ships were not ordered, the MoD made positive noises, but did not commit to this unequivocally. Given the extent to which MoD was going slow on the Type 24, and that the Department of Industry would have required MoD expertise to place the long lead orders, it is possible that the orders were never placed. TNA: DEFE 69/1409, Brief for Minister of State, 15 February 1979, Annex A. **90** TNA: DEFE 24/1379, Controller to Griffin, 6 June 1979; NHB: Admiralty Board Sub Committee Papers, 'The Type 24 and the Naval Programme', ABSC/P(79)6, 15 May 1979; NHB: VCNS papers, Box 123, 'The Light Frigate/Type 24' VCNS 40/72, Pt III, 'Type 24 Customer Panel Report' November 1979, VCNS to 2SL et al. (draft), February 1980, 'Brief for VCNS, Defence Policy Priorities' White to DNPlans, 13/3/80. **91** Corlett, 'Can British Torpedoes stay the course?', pp. 84–92. **92** NHB: VCNS Papers Box 48: VCNS 40/12 Annex: Mk 24 Torpedo – Kiely Report 2/82, Executive Summary and Annex B. **93** For a personal, and more positive, view of Tigerfish from an officer involved in its trials, see Thompson, *On Her Majesty's Nuclear Service*, pp. 93–108. **94** NHB: VCNS Papers, Box 48, VCNS 40/12 Part II, Nott to Thatcher, 15 December 81; VCNS 40/12/4 Part VI, Pringle to 1SL, 4 September 81. **95** For the reliability problems of the 'Forger', see Gordon and Kommissarov, *Soviet Naval Aviation 1946–1991*, pp. 272, 338–9. **96** Hennessy and Jinks, *The Silent Deep*, pp. 373–4; Polmar and O'Connell, *Strike from the Sea*, p. 139. See also, TNA: T 225/4030, Defence Equipment Policy Committee, NSR 6533, 4 February 1975; Cassell to Hansford, 10 February 1975; Cassell to Kellett, 29 September 1975. **97** Hobbs, *The British Carrier Strike Fleet after 1945*, pp. 485–7. **98** NHB: VCNS Papers Box 52, VCNS 40/1/6, NPB(P) 1/76, Naval Projects Board Minutes, Item 2; CSA to MinState 13 January 1977; APS/MoS to PS/CSA, 19 January 1977. **99** NHB: VCNS Papers, VCNS Box 53, VCNS 40/1/4, Cassels to Controller, 12 January 1979. **100** NHB: VCNS Papers, VCNS Box 53, VCNS 40/1/12/1, Sec/VCNS to Sec/COS 9 October 1979; Sec/COS to Chiefs, 11 January 1982. **101** TNA: CAB 130/1105, MISC 2(79)1, 17 May 1979; CAB 148/183, OD(79) 7th meeting, 19 September 1979; Friedman, *Naval Institute Guide to Naval Weapon Systems 1997–98*, p. 687. **102** NHB: Press Releases Box 2/T119306, 102/79, 'Two Eras Collide', 3 December 1979. **103** NHB: Brecon Box 1, Report of Proceedings, Capt Fox to CinCFleet, 27 May 1980. *Brecon* also had trouble meeting her design speed of 15 knots and remained a slow vessel compared to her sisters. The former Deputy Director of Naval Construction, D K Brown, has stated that the crew's seasickness was due to a propensity for the crewmembers themselves to have seasickness, not any design fault. Brown and Moore, *Rebuilding the Royal Navy*, p. 140. **104** TNA: DEFE 69/447, 'Mine Countermeasures: A Concept of Operations for the Future', October 1975. **105** NHB: Fleet Requirements Committee Box 1/T56321, FRC80(P)4, MCM Concepts and Numbers, 1 September 1980. **106** Spassky, *Russia's Arms Catalog, Volume III*, pp. 445–6, 449; Kuzin and Nikol'skiy, *Voyenno-Morskoy Flot SSSR*, section 6.10; TNA: DEFE 69/447, Mine Countermeasures: a Concept of Operations for the Future, October 1975. **107** NHB: Fleet Requirements Committee Box 1, 'NSR 7008 – EDATS Trawlers' FRC 78 (P) 14, 20 October 1978, pp. 3–4. **108** NHB: Exercises Box 11/T47293, Armytage to Sec/1SL, 22 August 1978. **109** NHB: 'NSR 7008-EDATS Trawlers', pp. 5–11; by 1983 the estimated cost per ship was £4.25 million: HMSO, 'Statement on Defence Estimates 1983' (Cmnd 8951-I), p. 10. **110** NHB: DCI(RN)773/78 and 774/78, 8 December 1978. **111** NHB: Boscombe Box 59/T151732, OEG 7/79, Exercise Centex 79, 12 October 1979. **112** Moore, *Jane's Fighting Ships 1983–84*, p. 600; HMSO, 'Statement on Defence Estimates 1983' (Cmnd 8951-I), p. 12. **113** NHB: DCI(RN)63/85, 15 February 1985. **114** TNA: DEFE 23/190, DCA(PN) to PS/Min St, 15 February 1978; Groom, *Diver*, pp. 274–82. **115** Fleet Requirements Committee Box 2/T56374, FRC(75)(P)3, Saturation Diving Vessel, 15 July 1975. **116** NHB: Admiralty Board Paper, A/P(79)3, 'Seabed Operations Vessel' 10 April 1979. **117** Murphy, *Shipbuilding in the United Kingdom*, pp. 107–108. **118** NHB: Admiralty Board Minutes, A/M(79)4, item 4, 14 June 1979. **119** Murphy, *Shipbuilding in the United Kingdom*, pp. 115–18; for Scott's relationship with the Ministry of Defence in the 1960s and 1970s, see Murphy, 'Scott's of Greenock', pp. 196–211. **120** NHB: Challenger Box, Buchanan to Controller, 30 July 1984; T73974, signal CO Challenger to FOF3, 1958Z 6 October 1984; T73973, Captain Submarine Acceptance to DOR(Sea), 5 July 1985; T1637, Operation Perintis, 14 May 1989, annexes C and E. **121** NHB: DCI(RN)291, 2 November 1990. **122** NHB: Equipment/Hovercraft Box 1/T57110, VCNS 40/95, Advanced Naval Vehicles, 'ANV: RN/USN Working Level Discussions 9-13/6/80', pp. 7–11. **123** NHB: Fleet Requirements Committee Box 2, 'Hovercraft in the Royal Navy' FRC77(P)4, 1 June 1977. The role of hovercraft in mine countermeasures had first been considered seriously in 1974 under Naval Staff Target 7002. At this early stage the need for precursor MCMVs was raised, as were the additional costs of 'open beach advance bases' needed to support the hovercraft. Fleet Requirements Committee Box 1, 'Hovercraft in the Royal Navy' FRC/P(74) 2 July 1974, see also Hunsley to Sec/FRC, 17 July 1974, attached to the above. **124** Moore, *Janes Fighting Ships 1979–80*, pp. 612–13; *Flight Deck*, March 1979, p. 36; NHB: DCI(RN)192/81 27 March 1981; *Navy News*, August 1981, p. 4; DS5 Notification 4/82, dated 26 March 1982 (cited in Chron Cards). **125** NHB: Ships Boxes, 'S' Box 1, Cox to DPR(N), 20 November 1979; Brown, 'Hydrofoils', 12 February 1980, pp. 49–56. **126** NHB: Ships Boxes, 'S' Box 1/T110392, 'Ship's Captain's Record: HMS Speedy', Cavanagh to NHB, 28 February 1980; Nicholls to PS/USofS(AF), 30 March 1982. **127** NHB: Ships Boxes, 'S' Box 1/T110386, Roach, Operation Foilbait, 15 December 1981; Extract from *Orkney* RoP, 3 April 1981; T110393, briefing note to Villar, 26 January 1982; Equipment/Hovercraft Box 1, VCNS 40/33 Part III, AUS(NS) to PS/US of S(AF), 19 May 1982, Coward to Head DS5, 3 May 1984. **128** TNA: DEFE 13/1346, DUS(Navy) to USofS(RN), 26 May 1976; Head DS5 to AUS(NS), 29 July 1976. **129** NHB: Admiralty Board Sub Committee, 'HM Dockyards: Long Term Load / Capacity Review 1978', under cover of ABSC/P(77)11, 6 October 1977, diagrams, sheet 11. **130** NHB: Admiralty Board, Item 2, A/M(77)7, 16 November 1977. **131** TNA: ADM 167/177, 'Long-term review of dockyard load and capacity 1977/78 to 1988/89' A/P(76)9, 18 October 1976; NHB: Admiralty Board Sub Committee, 'The Dockyard Programme over the Next Decade', ABSC/P(77)4, 14 April 1977, paras 26–28; Admiralty Board, 'Long Term Review of dockyard Load and Capacity 1979/80 to 1990/91', A/P(78) 6, 26 October 1978; TNA: DEFE 13/1346, A/P(75)20 'Long Term Review of Dockyard Load and Capacity', 14 October 1975; A/P(75)21, 'Warship construction in Royal Dockyards', 14 October 1975. Also, if the then boom in export building continued, then RN capacity could have been squeezed out. In the event, the boom ended after Vosper's delivered their Brazilian order and Vickers their various submarine orders. **132** NHB: Admiralty Board Sub Committee, Item 1, ABSC/M(78)5, 31 July 1978; Admiralty Board, item 3, A/M(79)4, 20 June 1979. **133** TNA: ADM 167/177, 'The Future of Chatham Naval Base' A/P(76)10, 27 September 1976. **134** NHB: Admiralty Board Sub Committee, Item 2, ABSC/M(77)8, 19 October 1977, para. 15. **135** TNA: DEFE 13/1346, Evans to PS/USofS, 7 April

1976. **136** NHB: Admiralty Board Sub Committee, 'Consequences of Industrial Disruption', ABSC/P(78)11, 19 October 1978. **137** NHB: Admiralty Board, Item 2, A/M(78)4, 28 June 1978; 'The Royal Dockyards: Proposed White Paper', A/P(78)5, 8 June 1978. **138** NHB: Admiralty Board, 'Long Term Review of Dockyard Load and Capacity 1979/80 to 1990/91', A/P(78)6, 26 October 1978. **139** NHB: Admiralty Board, 'Interim Review of Dockyard Load and Capacity', A/P(79)4, 29 March 1979; 'HM Dockyards: Long Term Load and Capacity Review 1980', A/P(79)9, 24 October 1979, diagrams, sheet 16.

Chapter 12: False Hope
1 Jackson and Bramall, *The Chiefs*, p. 389; Dorman, Kandiah and Staerk, 'The Nott Review', pp. 36–7, comments by Frank Cooper; 'Conservative General Election Manifesto 1979' (Conservative Party, April 1979), section 6: https://www.margaretthatcher.org/document/110858 (accessed 9/9/19); for comments by Conservative spokesmen in opposition concerning defence, see CCAC: THCR 2/1/3/15, speech of 8 March 1979 by Francis Pym; THCR 2/6/1/80, 'Towards a new Defence Policy' Geoffrey Pattie. **2** TNA: PREM 19/15, Larking to Lever, 13 June 1979. **3** Hampshire, 'Margaret Thatcher's First U-Turn', pp. 359–79. **4** NHB: Admiralty Board Sub Committee, ABSC/M(76)10 'Middle Management Working Party', 27 October 1976. **5** NHB: Admiralty Board Sub Committee, ABSC/M(76)6, Item 1, 'Officers Study Group', 19 September 1976. **6** NHB: Admiralty Board Sub Committee, ABSC/M(76)5, 22 July 1976; ABSC/M(76)6, 10 September 1976; ABSC/M(77)2, 20 January 1977; ABSC/M(77)3, 27 January 1977; ABSC/M(77)10, 1 December 1977, all 'Officers Study Group'. **7** HMSO, *The Navy List 1975 Appendix*, p. 13; *The Navy List 1977 Appendix*, p. 13. For an ordinary rating on pay band B, pay stayed static at £4.98 per day between 1975 and 1977. During this period inflation averaged 16.2 per cent over this period. If pay had risen to match inflation an ordinary rating on pay band B should have been on £6.72 per day. However, a rate of £4.98 placed him at only 74 per cent of this amount. **8** HMSO, *The Navy List 1978 Appendix*, p. 13: 6.92/7.28=0.95. **9** Ibid., p. 13: 8.98/6.92 = 1.2977. **10** Bank of England Inflation Calculator: https://www.bankofengland.co.uk/monetary-policy/inflation/inflation-calculator (accessed 9/9/19). **11** NHB: Admiralty Board Sub Committee Minutes, ABSC/M(79)5 item 2, 7 June 1979. **12** NHB: Admiralty Board Minutes, A/M(79)4, item 2, 20 June 1979. **13** CCAC: THCR 2/6/46, part 1, Clemens to Britto, 9 November 1979. **14** NHB: DCI (RN)118/80, Introduction of 3 ½ Year Short Career Commission, 15 February 1980; Admiralty Board Minutes, A/M(79)7, item 3, 13 November 1979. **15** NHB: Admiralty Board Minutes, A/M(79)6, item 3, 15 October 1979. **16** Oxford, Bodleian Libraries: MS Howe dep. 140, PG/11/76/40, 'First Draft Report: Public Sector Policy Group', undated, probably 1977. **17** Grove, *Vanguard to Trident*, p. 306; 'Conservative Party General Election Manifesto: A Better Tomorrow' (Conservative Party, 1970), http://www.conservativemanifesto.com/1970/1970-conservative-manifesto.shtml (accessed 11 September 2019). **18** TNA: FCO 36/2170, Franklin to Braithwaite, 11 February 1980; Acland note for record, 3 March 1980. **19** TNA: FCO 46/2170, Acland to Gillmore, 25 January 1980. **20** TNA: DEFE 69/637, VCNS note on Maritime Strategy, 23 April 1980. **21** Jackson and Bramall, *The Chiefs*, p. 396. **22** Hill, *Lewin of Greenwich*, pp. 342–9. **23** Ibid., pp. 270–1, 319–20. **24** Leach had been singled out by Air Chief Marshal Beetham as the person most likely to break Carver's tri-service consensus and begin 'feuding in front of ministers', Boren, 'Establishing Civilian Supremacy', p. 253. **25** Hill, *Lewin of Greenwich*, p. 320; HMSO, *The Navy List 1978*, pp. 5 and 300; *The Navy List 1979*, p. 303. **26** See Hampshire, 'Margaret Thatcher's First U-Turn' pp. 359–79 for coverage of these disputes, and those of 1980, in more detail. **27** TNA: CAB 130/1113, MISC 11(79) 2nd meeting, item 2, 13 July 1979; PREM 19/161, Pym to Thatcher, 2 July 1979; Lankester to Thatcher, 6 July 1979. **28** TNA: PREM 19/161, Biffen to Pym, 11 September 1979; Howe to Thatcher, 16 October 1979; Hunt to Thatcher, 19 October 1979; Whitmore to Thatcher, 22 October 1979; Hunt to Armstrong, 24 October 1979; Howe to Thatcher, 24 October 1979; Howe to Thatcher, 30 October 1979; Whitmore to Battishill, 9 November 1979. **29** TNA: CAB 148/183, OD (79) 13th meeting, item 3, 3 December 1979. **30** TNA: FCO 48/2170, Goulden to Moberly and Acland, 4 January 1980. **31** TNA: FCO 48/2170, Palliser to PS/Foreign Secretary, 22 February 1980. **32** TNA: FCO 48/2403, Synnott to Richards, 31 October 1980; see also FCO 48/2171, Moberly to Gillmore, 27 March 1980. **33** TNA: PREM 19/335, Rayner to Thatcher, 21 December 1979. **34** TNA: PREM 19/335, Laughlin to

Pattison, 21 December 1979. **35** TNA: PREM 19/161, Moore to Gow, covered by Lankester to Wiggins, 17 January 1980. **36** TNA: PREM 19/161, Lankester to Wiggins, 17 January 1980. **37** CCAC: THCR 2/6/2/46 pt 3, Moore: 'Aspects of the British Defence Problem', 16 June 1981. **38** TNA: PREM 10/335, Whitmore to Thatcher, 2 January 1980. **39** TNA: FCO 48/2170, Goulden to PS/PUS, 29 February 1980. **40** Hansard volume 977, column 681, 24 January 1980. **41** Stoddart, *Facing Down the Soviet Union*, pp. 95 and 102. **42** Salisbury, 'From Silence to Showmanship' (PhD dissertation), pp. 221–4. Salisbury does however suggest that the announcement was co-timed with a discussion on the cutting of child benefits, which would have been a different political driver. He also notes that disclosing the cost of Chevaline, alongside projected costs for Trident, was a way to open up debate on Chevaline's ultimate successor. **43** Stoddart, *Facing Down the Soviet Union*, pp. 95–9, 105. **44** Hennessy and Jinks, *The Silent Deep*, pp. 469–89. **45** Stoddart, *Facing Down the Soviet Union*, pp. 116–17. **46** Ibid., pp. 118, 120–2, 131. **47** Ibid., pp. 122–4. **48** Ibid., pp. 134–5. **49** Ibid., pp. 122–4, 134–6. **50** Ibid., pp. 136–43. **51** TNA: PREM 19/161, Howe to Thatcher, 11 December 1979. **52** TNA: PREM 19/162, Whitmore to Hall, 21 January 1980. **53** TNA: PREM 19/163, Lankester to Thatcher, 27 June 1980, marginal note by Thatcher. **54** TNA: PREM 19/161, Armstrong to Lankester, 11 December 1979. **55** TNA: CAB 164/1506, Hastie-Smith to Wade-Gery, 28 February 1980. **56** TNA: CAB 148/183, OD(79)29, 'Future United Kingdom Defence Policy: the Background', 5 October 1979. **57** For the concept of the 'warfare state', see Edgerton, *Warfare State*, pp. 1–14. **58** NHB: Finance Box 4: 1980 Long Term Costing Assumptions, May 1979, pp. B2-B16, T48740. **59** TNA: PREM 19/162, Armstrong to Thatcher, 18 January 1980. **60** TNA: FCO 46/2403, telegram Wright to FCO 1110Z, 6 October 1980; Synott to Richards, 31 October 1980. **61** TNA: PREM 19/163, Hall to Lankester (draft), 28 January 1980; Whitmore to Hall, 30 January 1980. **62** NHB: Admiralty Board minutes, A/M(80)1, item 3, 30 January 1980. **63** NHB: Admiralty Board minutes, A/M(80)1, item 3, 30 January 1980; Admiralty Board papers, 1980 Long Term Costing, A/P(80)2, 11 January 1980, annex D; the Admiralty Board had foreseen likely problems in the new year, and some of these items had been provisionally taken out of the programme in the preceding November: NHB: Admiralty Board minutes, A/M(79)8, item 2, 15 November 1979; the nature of *Tarbatness*' conversion is set out in NHB: Royal Navy Press Release/T119462, 'New Role for *Tarbatness*' 26 February 1979. It would have enabled her to transport 1,300 Royal Marines plus supporting arms and vehicles and six landing craft (presumably LCVPs on davits). Other deferred orders included two support tankers (later cancelled), the first AOR and RMAS tugs, whilst mooring vessels were cancelled as was early development for a cruise missile programme. The UK also dropped out of the NATO anti-ship missile programme. **64** TNA: CAB 164/1506, Draft OD paper 27/6/80, annex B 'measures already taken'. **65** NHB: Admiralty Board papers, 1980 Long Term Costing, A/P(80)2, 11 January 1980, paras 21–2. **66** The actual wording of the 1954 revision of the 1948 Brussels Treaty referred to four divisions and the RAF's Second Tactical Air Force, but this had been interpreted since 1957 as 54,000 military personnel across British Forces Germany, when the British Army of the Rhine shifted to a Brigade Group structure with only two divisions. In 1961 BAOR was reorganised again into a three divisional structure; this remained in place until the end of the Cold War. Western European Union: Brussels Treaty, Protocol II, Article 1(b), p. 18, 23 October 1954: Modified Brussels Treaty (Paris, 23 October 1954) – CVCE Website (accessed 30/3/23); French, *Army, Empire and Cold War*, pp. 203–05. **67** TNA: CAB 148/189, OD(80) 9th meeting, item 1, limited circulation annex, 20 March 1980. **68** NHB: Finance Box 4/T48740, Long Term Costing Assumptions 1981, pp. B4–B5. **69** NHB: Finance Box 4/T48740, Long Term Costing Assumptions 1980, pp. A1-10-13 and B8-9, 23 May 1979; Long Term Costing Assumptions 1981, pp. A1-9-10 and B8-9. **70** NHB: Finance Box 4/T48740: Long Term Costing Assumptions 1981, pp. B10–B11. **71** TNA: CAB 164/1506, Draft OD paper, 27 June 1980, annex B 'further measures'. **72** TNA: PREM 19/162, Armstrong to Thatcher, 18 January 1980. **73** Ministry of Defence, Statement on Defence Estimates 1980, volumes I and II (Cmnd 7826 I and II), London HMSO, pp. 27–37. **74** TNA: CAB 148/189, OD(80) 9th meeting, item 1, limited circulation annex, 20 March 1980. **75** TNA: PREM 19/163, Conservative Research Department paper, 24 April 1980. **76** TNA: PREM 19/163, Pym to Thatcher, 9 July 1980. **77** TNA: DEFE 13/1418, Cooper to Pym, 28 August 1980; Mottram to PS/USofS(Army), 9 October 1980; Omand to various, 29 October 1980.

Chapter 13: The 'Bermudagram'

1 Hampshire, 'Margaret Thatcher's First U-Turn', pp. 373–4. **2** Thatcher, *Downing Street Years*, pp. 26–7, 131; Young, *One of Us*, p. 144; Nott, *Here Today, Gone Tomorrow*, pp. 168–73, 185–201. **3** Noble, *British Defence Policy and the RAF*, pp. 103–04; TNA: PREM 19/415, Nott to Thatcher, 11 March 1981 **4** TNA: DEFE 13/2020, Lewin to Nott, 9 Jan 1981. **5** Ibid., Cooper to Nott, 15 Jan 1981. **6** Young's method of note taking immediately after a discussion with a politician or official is set out in Trewin, *Hugo Young Papers*, pp. xxi–xxii. **7** Trewin, *Hugo Young Papers*, p. 280. **8** Boren, 'Britain's 1981 Defence Review', p. 257. **9** Healey, *The Time of My Life*, pp. 268, 299. **10** Quinlan, a former civilian assistant to CAS during the 1964–6 Defence Review, was DUS(Policy) during the 1981 Defence Review and PUS between 1988 and 1992, whilst Michael Mottram was Cooper's private secretary until 1982 when he became private secretary to John Nott and then to the next two succeeding Secretaries of State. He was PUS between 1995 and 1998. Omand was Nott's private secretary in 1981–2, and rose to become DUS(Policy) by 1994 before transferring to GCHQ to head up that agency in 1996. **11** The Army suffered the most from the 1990–1 Options for Change review, which was led on the civil service side by Quinlan and Mottram: the Army lost a quarter of its personnel: BAOR was halved in size. The RAF was hit hard, losing eleven squadrons. In comparison the Navy's escort force was reduced from forty-six to forty, but it did suffer a significant reduction in its submarine force. HMSO: Statement on the Defence Estimates 1991: Britain's Defence for the 1990s, Cm 1559-I, July 1991. **12** NHB: VCNS Box 61, ACNS(P) 10/1/14i, DP1/81, CDS to CoS, 13 February 1981, p. 16. **13** Hill, *Lewin of Greenwich*, pp. 322–4. The cost of Polaris and the *Resolution* class were not split out from the rest of the Navy's accounts during their procurement (at least not publicly). For example, see HMSO, 'Defence Accounts 1967–68' (21 January 1969), pp. 13–60. Given the extreme secrecy surrounding Chevaline procurement in the 1970s, these would not have been split out either (definitely not publicly; internally only a very small number of MoD accountants would have even been aware). **14** CCAC: NOTT 4/8/1, p. 6. **15** Dorman, *Defence Under Thatcher*, p. 69. **16** TNA: DEFE 13/2020, Norbury to PSO/CDS et al, 13 Jan 81. **17** Boren, 'Defence Review', p. 250. **18** Ibid., pp. 252–3; Dorman, *Defence Under Thatcher*, p. 67. **19** Dorman, *Defence Under Thatcher*, pp. 66–7. **20** NHB: VCNS Box 61, ACNS(P) 10/1/14i, DP1/81, CDS to CoS, 13 February 1981, pp. 1–2. **21** Ibid., pp. 4–9. **22** Ibid., pp. 18–20. **23** Ibid., pp. 24–7. **24** Ibid., pp. 30–1. **25** White, *Never Ready*, pp. 79–82; French, *Army, Empire and Cold War*, p. 241. **26** Dorman, *Defence Under Thatcher*, p. 68. **27** NHB: VCNS Papers Box 61, ACNS(P), 10/1/13/4, Woodward, 'Maritime or Land?' 23 January 1981, pp. 12, 21. **28** Ibid., p. 30. **29** Ibid., p. 2. **30** NHB: VCNS Papers Box 61, ACNS(P), 10/1/13/7, 'Size and Shape Review 1981–2000', 23 February 1981, p. 2. **31** Ibid., pp. 3–10. **32** NHB: VCNS Papers Box 61, ACNS(P), 10/1/13/7, DN Plans to DNW et al, 3 March 1981. **33** HMSO: *London Gazette*, supplement 44851, p. 1561, 3 February 1981. **34** TNA: DEFE 13/2020, 'Force Mix Study – A Paper by DCDS (OR)' 23 Feb 81, p. 1. **35** Ibid., p. 4. **36** Ibid., pp. 8–11. **37** Ibid., p. 5. **38** Ibid., p. 6. **39** Ibid., pp. 6–7. **40** Boren, 'Britain's 1981 Defence Review', p. 275, quoting from an interview with Nott 13 Nov 1991. **41** For example, see NHB: Cleopatra Box/T74280, Liardet to CINCFLEET, 26 July 1984, for DOAE's pre-existing attitude towards the irrelevance of military judgement. **42** TNA: DEFE 13/2020, 'Force Mix Study', p. 1. **43** Boren, Britain's 1981 Defence Review', pp. 253–4. **44** TNA: DEFE 12/2021/2, Omand to Nott, 4 March 1981. **45** Ibid., AUS(NS) to AUS(OR), 5 March 1981. **46** Ibid., AUS(GS) to AUS(OR), 5 March 1981. **47** Boren, 'Britain's 1981 Defence Review', pp. 274–8; Nott, *Here Today, Gone Tomorrow*, p. 228. **48** TNA: PREM 19/414, Note for Record, 10 February 1981. **49** Ibid. **50** TNA: DEFE 13/2021/2, Omand to Nott, 4 March 1981. **51** TNA: DEFE 13/2020, APS SoS to PSO/CDS, 3 March 1981. **52** Ibid., Reffell to PS/Secretary of State 'Maritime Operations Presentation' 6 March 1981, pp. 1–4. **53** Ibid., 'Maritime Operations Presentation', pp. 4–6. **54** Ibid., 'Maritime Operations Presentation', pp. 6–8. **55** Friedman, *Seapower and Space*, pp. 169–71. **56** TNA: DEFE 13/2020, 'Presentation to Secretary of State on Maritime Operations' Deputy Director of Air Plans, 5 March 1981. **57** Hine's point might carry some weight with air defence aircraft, but much less so with the strike aircraft: aircrews would need training and experience in land strike operations – usually with different weaponry – before they could be effective in this domain, Laite, *Maritime Air Operations*, pp. 5–6; Lake and Crutch, *Tornado*, pp. 106–07. **58** Without SOSUS to provide initial detection and to limit search areas, Nimrod MR2s would have had considerable problems locating Soviet submarines. The Nimrod's strengths lay in localisation and attack, not in broad-ranging surveillance of large sea areas. NHB: Lowestoft Box/T113354, Buckle to CINCFLEET, 8 February 1982. **59** TNA: DEFE 13/2020, 'Presentation to Secretary of State' and 'Nimrod ASW Operations' map. **60** Ibid., Beetham to Nott, 20 February 1981. **61** CCAC: NOTT 4/8 file 1, 'Start of the defence review' and 'Defence policy and programmes'; see also TNA: PREM 19/415 Nott to Thatcher 16 March 1981. **62** TNA: DEFE 13/2021/2, Cooper to Nott, 13 March 1981; 'First weeks'; CCAC: NOTT 4/8 file 1, 12–14; Boren, 'Defence Review' p. 267. Both Boren, and Nott commenting three years later, stated that Michael Quinlan, as the DUS(P), who would normally be responsible for drafting high-level policy documents including White Papers, was involved. The TNA documents show that he was not (or at least Cooper did not tell Nott that he was). Despite the authorship of the 'Bermudagram' by his officials, many did believe that it had been written by Nott directly or at least under his active direction. For example, see Hill, *Lewin*, p. 333. **63** TNA: DEFE 13/2021/2, 'Facing up to the Future: Supplementary Statement on Defence Policy 1981', 13 March 1981. **64** TNA: DEFE 13/2021/2, Nott to CDS, PUS, 16 March 1981, pp. 1–2. **65** Ibid., pp. 2–3. **66** Ibid., p. 4. **67** Ibid., p. 4. **68** Ibid., p. 5. **69** Ibid., p. 5. **70** Ibid., pp. 5–6. **71** Ibid., pp. 6–10. **72** Ibid., Annex. **73** TNA: DEFE 13/2021/2, Cooper to DUS(N) et al, 19 March 1981. **74** Boren, 'Britain's 1981 Defence Review', pp. 310, 312. **75** This flaw in Nott's reasoning is picked up in Dorman, *Defence Under Thatcher*, pp. 70–1. **76** Baer, *One Hundred Years of Sea Power*, pp. 406–07, 424–6. **77** NHB: 'Home Station, Volume 1', p. 62. **78** TNA: PREM 19/415: Nott to Thatcher, 14 May 1981. **79** TNA: PREM 19/415, Norbury to Whitmore, 17 March 1981.

Chapter 14: The Way Forward
1 TNA: DEFE 13/2021/2, Speed to Nott, 1 April 1981. **2** Boren, 'Defence Review', pp. 299–300. **3** TNA: DEFE 13/2021/1, Cooper to Nott, 10 April 1981. **4** Ibid., DUS(RN) to DUS(FB), 3 April 1981. **5** Ibid., AUS(P&B) to DUS(FB), 10 April 1981. **6** Ibid., Omand to Nott, 10 April 1981. **7** Ibid., Cooper to Nott, 13 April 1981. **8** Ibid., DUS(N) to APS/SecSt, 15 April 1981; Cooper to Nott, 13 April 1981. **9** Ibid., Cooper to Nott, 13 April 1981. **10** Ibid., three draft notes from Nott to PUS and CDS, undated but surrounding documents suggest c. 10–15 April 1981. Nott investigated abolishing specialist reinforcement forces across all three services completely (the Royal Marines, ACE mobile force, the UK mobile force, RAF enablers and GR1 Harriers etc). The savings would have been considerable but the political costs with NATO allies were considered too great. DEFE 13/2304/2, Cooper to Nott, 12 May 1981. **11** NHB: VCNS Papers Box 123, ACNS(P) 40/17 Fid II, Hallifax to Reffell, 10 September 1981. **12** TNA: DEFE 13/2021/1, Mason to Nott, 14 April 1981. **13** Ibid. **14** NHB: Boscombe Box 10/T150197, DOAE Note 279/200, 'Present ASW systems comparison', 23 October 1980, pp. 44–5. **15** Ibid., p. 21. **16** Admiralty Library: UKHO: NP 526, Underwater Handbook: Western Approaches to British Isles (April 1970), plate 2. **17** Ibid., plate 3. In the summer the surface layer would become even shallower before falling to around 400ft. **18** TNA: DEFE 13/2021/1, Mason to Nott, 14 April 1981, hand annotations by Nott. **19** Ibid., DP 8/81 (Revise) 10 April 1981. **20** TNA: DEFE 13/2304/2, DUS(N) to DUS(FB), 1 May 1981, Annex B. **21** Ibid., Annex A. **22** The Frigate Support Ship appears to have been a version of the 'garage ship' concept considered in the late 1970s, although like the 15th and 16th Type 42s, it seems to have been an optimistic inclusion in earlier costings. **23** TNA: DEFE 13/2304/2, DUS(N) to DUS(FB), 1 May 1981, Annex B. **24** Ibid., Annex D. **25** Ibid., Annex D. **26** TNA: DEFE 13/2304/2, DUS(N) to Nott, 11 May 1981. **27** The attendees were the Admiralty Board members, Nott, DUS(N), Head of DS4 (the Central Secretariat's branch leading on Naval matters and co-located with the Naval Staff) and the 2nd PUS; TNA: DEFE 13/2304/2, Record of meeting in Nott's room, 6 May 1981. **28** TNA: DEFE 13/2304/2, Record of meeting in Nott's room, 6 May 1981. **29** Ibid. **30** TNA: DEFE 13/2304/2, DUS(N) to Nott, 8 May 1981. **31** TNA: DEFE 13/2304/1, undated note, 'Views of the Chief of Defence Staff', surrounding documents indicate 8 May 1981. **32** TNA: PREM 19/415, Leach to Nott, 11 May 1981. **33** TNA: DEFE 13/2022, Whitmore to Norbury, 15 May 1981; PREM 19/415, Nott to Thatcher, 13 May 1981, annotations by Whitmore. **34** TNA: DEFE 13/2022, Leach to Thatcher, 18 May 1981; Leach, *Endure No Makeshifts*, p. 210. **35** TNA: PREM 19/416, Whitmore to Norbury, 8 June 1981; Leach, *Endure No Makeshifts*, p. 211. **36** Speed, *Sea Change*, pp. 106–07. **37** TNA: DEFE 13/2022, Speed to Nott, speech transcript, 15 May 1918. **38** Speed, *Sea Change*, p. 108. **39** Thatcher, *Downing Street Years*, p. 250; Nott, *Here Today, Gone Tomorrow*, p. 233; Speed, *Sea Change*, pp. 108–09; TNA: PREM 19/415, TPL to Whitmore, 17 May 1981. **40** TNA: PREM 19/415, Nott to Thatcher, [cover note] 14 May 1981, p. 1. **41** Ibid., p. 5. **42** Ibid., pp. 4–5. **43** TNA:

PREM 19/415, Nott to Thatcher, [main note] 14 May 1981, Annex A. The reductions in destroyers and frigates would actually be more brutal than Nott's paper set out. By April 1985 four 'County' class destroyers and sixteen *Leander* class frigates (those neither equipped with towed-array nor Sea Wolf) would be withdrawn from service and by April 1991 the last 'County' class, HMS *Bristol* and the five Sea Wolf *Leander*s would also be withdrawn. DEFE 13/2022, Sec/CNS to APS/SofS, 19 May 1981. **44** TNA: PREM 19/415, Nott to Thatcher, [main note] 14 May 1981, Annex C. **45** Ibid., pp. 5, 7, Annex A. **46** TNA: PREM 19/415, Nott to Thatcher, [cover note] 14 May 1981, p. 5. **47** Ibid. **48** TNA: PREM 19/415, Armstrong to Thatcher, 15 May 1981. **49** TNA: DEFE 13/2022, Whitmore to Norbury, 19 May 1981. **50** TNA: PREM 19/415, Armstrong to Thatcher, 15 May 1981. **51** TNA: DEFE 13/2022, Whitmore to Norbury, 19 May 1981. **52** TNA: FCO 46/2571, Brief for Carrington, 28 April 1981. **53** Carrington, *Reflect on Things Past*, p. 228. **54** TNA: DEFE 13/2022, Whitmore to Norbury, 19 May 1981. **55** Ibid., Omand to DUS(FB), 21 May 1981. **56** Ibid., DUS(FB) to APS/SofS, 27 May 1981, Table 3. **57** TNA: DEFE 13/2023/2, Omand to PS/PUS, 15 June 1981. **58** Ibid., Nott to Cabinet, 15 June 1981, Appendices A, D and G. **59** TNA: PREM 19/416, OD(81)29 'The Defence Programme' Draft, from surrounding documents probably early June 1981. **60** Ibid., Appendices G and I. **61** TNA: CAB 129/213, C(81)31 'The Defence Programme', Appendix J. **62** TNA: PREM 19/416, Wade-Gery to Thatcher, 5 June 1981. **63** Ibid. **64** TNA: PREM 19/416, Trefgarne to Nott, 11 June 1981. **65** Ibid., Nott to Joseph, 17 June 1981, plus annotations by Whitmore. **66** Ibid., Nott to Thatcher and Howe, 17 June 1981. **67** TNA: CAB 129/213, C(81)31, 'The Defence Programme', 15 June 1981. For a more detailed explanation of the Cash Limits system and its application in a high-inflation economy, see Hampshire, 'Margaret Thatcher's First U Turn', pp. 362–3. **68** TNA: CAB 128/71, CC(81) 24th Conclusions, 18 June 1981, item 4. **69** Boren, 'Britain's 1981 Defence Review', p. 328 citing the *Financial Times* and *Guardian*, 19 June 1981. **70** TNA: PREM 19/416, Nott to Thatcher 18 June 1981, covering Draft White Paper, 18 June 1981, para. 27. **71** TNA: DEFE 13/2023/2, Cooper to Nott, 17 June 1981. **72** TNA: PREM 19/416, telegram Henderson to FCO, 19 May 1981, 1610Z. **73** TNA: DEFE 13/2023/2, Cooper to Nott, 17 June 1981. **74** Ibid., Nott to Thatcher, 17 June 1981. **75** Hattendorf, *Evolution of the US Navy's Maritime Strategy*, pp. 50–1. **76** TNA: DEFE 13/2023/2, Leach to Nott, 12 June 1981, plus annotations by Omand; Sec/1SL to PS/SofS, 16 June 1981. **77** TNA: DEFE 13/2023/1, Cragg to Omand, 12 June 1981 and 16 June 1981. **78** Ibid., Omand to Nott, 17 June 1981. **79** This core fleet would mean: cancelling the seventh *Trafalgar* class; running on the first two *Invincible* class with only normal refits; cancelling *Ark Royal*; disposing of *Hermes*, *Fearless* and *Intrepid* between April 1982 and April 1984; disposing of the five 'County' class and HMS *Bristol* between December 1981 and December 1986, although *Antrim* would be run on as a minelayer; undertaking normal refits only for the fourteen Type 42s; cancelling the Type 44; building only eight Type 22s but they would have just normal refits over their service lives; withdrawing all eight Ikara *Leander*s between December 1981 and July 1985; three of four non-towed-array Batch 2 *Leander*s would go into deep reserve with the fourth (*Juno*) becoming a training ship as originally planned; disposing of unmodernised Batch 3 *Leander*s between December 1981 and April 1984 and the modernised ships between April 1988 and April 1991; disposing of all *Rothesay*s between December 1981 and August 1984; disposing of *Britannia* in October 1983 and *Endurance* in May 1982. The four towed-array *Leander*s would continue in service into the 1990s. This would mean a frigate force of eight Type 21s and seven Type 22s with four towed-array *Leander*s and five Sea Wolf *Leander*s in 1985–6, which by 1990–1 would include the first four Type 23s, the last Type 22 but no Sea Wolf *Leander*s. The first Type 23 would be accepted into service in January 1989 and the first new SSK in August 1987; all three *Echo* class and all four *Fox* class survey ships would be withdrawn by April 1985. It is not clear in the table why the destroyer numbers tick up to 16 in 1990/91, nor why the 1985/86 figure for frigates and destroyers had increased from 38 to 39. TNA: DEFE 13/2032/1, Cragg to Omand, 12 June 1981, Annex A. **80** Ibid., Omand to Nott, 17 June 1981. **81** Ibid., Cragg to Omand, 12 June 1981, Annex A, handwritten annotations citing DUS(N) note dated 19 June 1981. **82** TNA: DEFE 13/2023/1, Programme for visit to Washington, 20–21 June 1981. **83** TNA: FCO 46/2574, Record of conversation over dinner on 20 June 1981. **84** Ibid. **85** Ibid. **86** Ibid. **87** TNA: FCO 46/2574, Record of discussions on 21 June 1981. **88** Ibid., Quinlan to AUS(D Staff) et al, 25 June 1981. **89** Ibid., Record of discussions on 21 June 1981. **90** Ibid., Quinlan to AUS(NS), 2 July 1981. **91** Ibid., Note of meeting between Nott and Luns, 23 June 1981. **92** Boren, 'Defence Review', abstract and p. 437. For an overview of the post-Falklands newspaper backlash against Nott, particularly in the *Times*, see Noble, *Defence Policy and the RAF*, pp. 192–6. **93** Another, even earlier, analysis of the Review was undertaken by Grove in *Vanguard to Trident* (pp. 345–56), based on contemporary accounts. Much of Grove's analysis is astute: he correctly emphasises the difficult financial situation in 1980 and 1981 and the importance of the Chief Scientific Adviser, but perhaps inevitably, much of the detail of the review process does not fully accord with the documentary record. **94** Boren, 'Defence Review', pp. 426–31, 436–7. **95** Dorman, 'The Nott Review: Dispelling the Myths?', pp. 103–04. **96** Boren, 'Defence Review', p. 433. **97** Ibid., pp. 431–2. **98** Churchill College, Cambridge and Centre for Contemporary British History: 'Overstretched? The making and impact of the UK's defence reviews since 1957', 2008, transcript, p. 22. **99** Dorman, 'The Nott Review: Dispelling the Myths?', pp. 103–09, 117–18. **100** Ibid., pp. 116–17. **101** Boren, 'Defence Review', abstract. **102** Ibid. **103** Ibid. **104** Nott, *Here Today, Gone Tomorrow*, p. 212. **105** Scholars have argued that the Reagan administration's approach to Trident negotiations was transactional, but have not provided much detail on what concessions the US was able to gain from the UK, beyond some minor support to Belize post-independence. This chapter has shown that the concessions were indeed relatively substantial: a 25 per cent larger destroyer and frigate force than Nott had originally planned. Stoddart, *Facing Down the Soviet Union*, pp. 200, 232; Doyle, 'United States sale of Trident to Britain'; Doyle, 'A Foregone Conclusion? The United States, Britain and the Trident D5 Agreement'. **106** TNA: PREM 19/414, Note for Record, 10 February 1981.

Chapter 15: Pushing Back
1 NHB: VCNS Papers Box 57, ACSN(P) 40/102, 'The Way Ahead for the AOR', September 1981, p. 9. **2** TNA: DEFE 13/2025, Cragg to PS/Min(AF), 30 June 1981. **3** Ibid., Young to PS/PUS, 29 June 1981, Annex B, Appendix 1. **4** TNA: DEFE 69/1478, DN Plans, A Policy for the Standby Squadron, 21 January 1981. **5** NHB: Fleet Operations Programme, June 1981. **6** The Standby Squadron was temporarily reactivated during the Falklands conflict, as a place for ships in the process of being reactivated to backfill those ships sent to the South Atlantic. This was a temporary and short-term measure driven by circumstances and had not been planned. NHB: Fleet Operations Programme, July 1981-June 1982. **7** NHB: Naiad Box, DS5 Notification 4/81, 17 September 1981. **8** TNA: DEFE 13/2025, AUS(NS) to DUS(P), 28 August 1981. **9** Ibid., Norbury to AUS(NS), 24 August 1981. **10** TNA: DEFE 13/2025, AUS(NS) to DUS(P), 28 August 1981. **11** Ibid. **12** Ibid., hand annotation by Nott. **13** Ibid., note of meeting, item 3. **14** TNA: DEFE 13/2025, Omand to Nott, 4 September 1981. **15** TNA: DEFE 13/1950, Norbury to PS/PUS, 24 August 1981, annotations by Nott. **16** Ibid., Cooper to Nott, 12 October 1981. **17** Ibid. **18** TNA: DEFE 13/1950, CS(RN) to VCNS, CSA, CER, 29 September 1981. **19** Ibid., Blaker to Nott, 13 October 1981. Lehman and Train's thinking is emblematic of the early stages of the Maritime Strategy which emphasised forward *surface* operations into the Norwegian Sea. **20** TNA: DEFE 13/1950, Power to DUS(P), 7 October 1981. The dollar/sterling exchange rate on 12 October 1981 was $1 to £0.5312, with $600 million therefore meaning £319 million. **21** Ibid. **22** NHB: VCNS Papers, VCNS 63/3 Pt III, Hastie-Smith to Perle, 4 December 1981; VCNS 63/3 Pt IV, Cragg to Sec/VCNS, 18 August 1982, UK/US discussion of DD/FF numbers since Cmnd 8288. **23** NHB: Fleet Operations Programme, January 1982. **24** NHB: VCNS Papers Box 37, VCNS 10/26/18(F), Wrigley to CFS et al, 19 October 1981, Annex A. These eight ships would be the five unmodernised Batch 3 *Leanders* and the three Batch 2 *Leanders* without towed-array. They would stay in the Standby Squadron for four to five years before being replaced by the five Sea Wolf-armed Batch 3 *Leanders*. **25** NHB: VCNS Papers, Box 110, VCNS 63/3 Pt III, Beaumont to Pakenham, 4 February, covering UK position paper No.4/82. **26** TNA: DEFE 13/3169, Sec/1SL to PS/SecSt, 12 March 1982, covering draft signal. **27** NHB: VCNS Papers, Box 110, VCNS 63/3 Pt IV, Cragg to Sec/VCNS, 18 August 1982, UK/US discussion of DD/FF numbers since Cmnd 8288, Annex C, The Future, DPQ 82. **28** Stoddart, *Facing Down the Soviet Union*, p. 175. **29** Hennessy and Jinks, *Silent Deep*, p. 511; Brown and Moore, *Rebuilding the Royal Navy*, p. 129. **30** Stoddart, *Facing Down the Soviet Union*, pp. 179–85, Doyle, 'A Foregone Conclusion?', pp. 874–8. **31** Stoddart, *Facing Down the Soviet Union*, pp. 187–91, Doyle, 'A Foregone Conclusion?', pp. 880–1. **32** Doyle, 'A Foregone Conclusion?', pp. 881–90. **33** NHB: VCNS Papers Box 112, 63/2 Part VII, Brief for Nott, 1 April 1982. **34** Thatcher, *The Downing Street Years*, p. 248. **35** Hill, *Lewin*, p. 341; Dorman, *Defence Under Thatcher*, p. 85. **36** TNA: DEFE 13/1950,

Leach to Nott, 18 December 1981, annotations by Nott and Omand. **37** CCAC: NOTT 4/8ii, transcript of discussion with Nott, 'Nuclear-Trident', p. 24. **38** Boren, 'Britain's 1981 Defence Review', p. 337. **39** Hill, *Lewin*, p. 341; Leach, *Endure No Makeshifts*, p. 203. **40** Stoddart, *Facing Down the Soviet Union*, p. 193. **41** TNA: DEFE 13/1950, Leach to Nott, 18 December 1981. The price was later negotiated down to £70 million, but the important point here is that Nott was minded to keep the two ships when the price was still estimated to be £120 million. In addition, to retain the two ships even at a cost of £120/£70 million would mean the withdrawal from service of two destroyers, which then had a cost impact on the commitment to retain fifty destroyers and frigates. TNA: DEFE 13/3169, VCNS to Nott, 4 February 1982; Cragg to PS/SecSt, 18 February 1982. **42** CACC: NOTT 4/8ii, transcript of discussion with Nott, 'Nuclear-Trident', p. 24. **43** TNA: DEFE 13/3169, Hastie-Smith to PS/SecSt, 4 March 1982; Nott to Weinberger, 5 March 1982; Hastie-Smith to PS/SecSt, 9 March 1982. **44** NHB: Exercises Box 10/T83786, Webster to Sec/1SL, 28 July 1981. **45** Ibid. **46** Lehman, *Oceans Ventured*, pp. 6–74. **47** Ibid., pp. 78–9; see Friedman, *Seapower and Space*, pp. 193–4, for how deception worked in practice. **48** Lehman, *Oceans Ventured*, p. 76. **49** NHB: Exercises Box 10/T83786, Webster to Sec/1SL, 28 July 1981; T47296, Briggs to Sec/1SL, 17 August 1981. **50** NHB: Bristol Box/T73086, Grose to CINCFLEET, 14 October 1981. It is possible that Admiral Fox had his flag in *Bristol* rather than *Invincible* because her internal communication system (ICS 3) was almost certainly non-operational, making her unsuitable for a flag staff. ICS 3, as will be seen, was still inoperable during Operation 'Corporate' eight months later. **51** Patrick Allen, *Sea King*, p. 40. **52** NHB: Fleet Operations Programme, August 1981. **53** Polmar and Moore, *Cold War Submarines*, pp. 205, 214–16. **54** NHB: *Invincible* Box 1/T51267, Livesay to CINCFLEET, 4 January 1982. **55** Polmar and Moore, *Cold War Submarines*, pp. 136–40. **56** NHB: Arethusa Box/T59047, Jameson to CINCFLEET, 10 November 1981. **57** NHB: London Box/T59105, Garnier to CINCFLEET, 18 December 1981. **58** Lehman, *Oceans Ventured*, pp. xv–xvii. **59** A similar intelligence gathering operation had been undertaken by the US landing ship *Fairfax County* in March. Lehman, *Oceans Ventured*, p. 100. **60** Hampshire, 'From Malin Head to Okean 75', p. 66; Hampshire, *Soviet Cold War Guided Missile Cruisers*, p. 40. **61** NHB: Exercises Box 10/T47296, Briggs to Sec/1SL, 17 August 1981. **62** TNA: DEFE 13/1950, Power to DUS(P), 7 October 1981. **63** TNA: DEFE 13/1950, Blaker to Nott, 13 October 1981. **64** NHB: *Invincible* Box 1/T51267, Livesay to CINCFLEET, 4 January 1982. **65** NHB: Illustrious Box 1/T51438, Kerr to CINCFLEET, 20 April 1984. **66** NHB: VCNS Papers Box 75, Norman to Sec/1SL et al, 16 July 1980; Reffell to VCNS, 21 October 1980. **67** NHB: Fleet Requirements Committee Box 1/T56312, 'Type 23 Light Frigate: March 81 Report', 4 March 1981. **68** The first modern AORs had been the US *Wichita* class replenishment oilers which entered service in the late 1960s and 1970s. **69** NHB: VCNS Papers Box 57, ACNS(P) 18/11/3 Part 3, 'Review of Future Afloat Support Requirements' 8 October 1982, p. 4. **70** NHB: VCNS Papers Box 57, ACNS(P) 40/102, 'The Way Ahead for the AOR' September 1981, pp. 13–15. **71** NHB: Fleet Requirements Committee Box 1/T56311, 'Type 23 frigate: Concept of Operations', 13 March 1981. **72** NHB: VCNS Papers Box 75, Rowe to DNOR et al, 11 June 1981, 'The Way Ahead for the Type 23', p. 6; HMSO, 'The United Kingdom Defence Programme: The Way Forward' (Cmnd 8288), June 1981, p. 10. **73** NHB: VCNS Papers Box 75, Mumford to PS/CDP, 18 June 1981; VCNS Papers Box 89, DG Ships to Controller, 1 July 1981. **74** NHB: VCNS Papers Box 89, ACNS(P) 40/17 Fid I, Record of meeting between Sir John Rix and Nott, 14 July 1981. **75** NHB: VCNS Papers Box 123, ACNS(P) 40/17 Fid II, Hallifax to Reffell, 10 September 1981. **76** Ibid., Reffell to Hallifax, 26 November 1981. There is a good chance that this was a joke at the expense of the un-named minister, probably either Peter Blaker or Lord Trenchard. **77** NHB: VCNS Papers Box 123, ACNS(P) 40/17 Fid II, Controller to DG Ships, 25 September 1981; VCNS to ACNS(OR), 9 October 1981. **78** Ibid., Hogg to DDSD et al, 20 November 1981. **79** NHB: VCNS Papers Box 124, VCNS 40/72/1 Pt V, DEPC/ORC 'NSR 7069 – Type 23 Frigate', p. 18. **80** Ibid., DG Ships to Controller, 23 June 1982; Brief for ACNS(OR), 14 July 1982. **81** The author would like to thank Andrew Livesy for this information. **82** NHB: VCNS Papers Box 123, ACNS(P) 40/17 Fid II, DCDS(OR) to CDS et al, 6 November 1981. **83** NHB: Boscombe Box 248/T154028, SCICON Consultancy International, 'Type 23 Frigate Operational Studies', 16 March 1981, Section 3. **84** NHB: VCNS Papers Box 123, ACNS(P) 40/17 Fid II, Stanford to VCNS, 7 January 1982. **85** NHB: VCNS Papers, Box 39, VCNS 10/57 Pt II, CSA to Nott, draft, 30 June 1981; Reffell to VCNS, 14 August

1981. **86** Ibid., DN Plans to VCNS, 19 June 1981. **87** NHB: VCNS Papers, Box 123, ACNS(P) 40/17 Fid II, Fuller, Briefing on Type 23 Frigate, 28 September 1981. **88** Ibid., USofS(DP) to Nott, 15 October 1981. **89** NHB: VCNS Papers, Box 39, VCNS 10/57 Pt II, Spellar to ACNS(P), Annex A, pp. A5, A15. **90** SeaMix I was a 1973 study, so would probably have carried less weight than SeaWar 85, but its conclusions were nonetheless useful as the study was based on a postulated 1981 conflict. NHB: VCNS Papers, Box 39, VCNS 10/57 Pt II, Spellar to ACNS(P), Annex B. **91** NHB: VCNS Papers Box 124, VCNS 40/72/1 Pt V, ORC 4th Meeting/82, 6 May 1982, pp. 6–8. **92** NHB: Fleet Requirements Committee Box 1/T81546, 'Naval Staff Requirement 7069', 15 September 1983. **93** NHB: VCNS Papers Box 123, ACNS(P) 40/17 Fid II, Osborne to Sec/VCNS 6 November 1981, covering brief by McKnight. **94** Brown and Moore, *Rebuilding the Royal Navy*, p. 111. **95** NHB: Finance Box 4/T48745, 1982 Long Term Costing Assumptions, compare pre- and post-Defence Review versions, pp. B3–B4. **96** TNA: DEFE 13/1950, Blaker to Nott, 7 December 1981. **97** Ibid. **98** TNA: DEFE 13/1950, Evans to PS/Min(AF), 14 December 1981. **99** TNA: DEFE 13/3169, Signal Lewin to Train, 5 February 1982 0830Z. **100** Ibid., Pattie to Nott, 3 February 1982; Hennessy to Macdonald, 7 December 1981. **101** Ibid., Pattie to Nott, 10 February 1982. **102** Ibid., New Patrol Class Submarine, NSR 7029. **103** Ibid., Type 2400 presentation, 15 March 1982. **104** Brown and Moore, *Rebuilding the Royal Navy*, pp. 118–19. **105** Brown, *Century of Naval Construction*, p. 267. **106** Polmar and Moore, *Cold War Submarines*, pp. 293–4. **107** TNA: CAB 148/198, OD(81)41, The Heavyweight Torpedo, 4 September 1981. **108** TNA: CAB 148/197, OD(81) 14th meeting, 8 September 1981. **109** TNA: DEFE 13/2025, Young to PS/PUS, 29 June 1981. **110** Ibid. **111** TNA: DEFE 13/2024, AUS(GS) to APS/Sec St, 23 June 1981. **112** TNA: DEFE 13/1950, Omand to Nott, 9 September 1981. **113** Ibid., annotations by Nott; Evans to Head DS 1, 14 September 1981. **114** NHB: Admiralty Board Sub Committee Memoranda, ABSC/P(82)1, Future Policy for the Royal Marines, VCNS cover note, 19 February 1982. **115** NHB: Admiralty Board Sub Committee Memoranda, ABSC/P(82)1, Future Policy for the Royal Marines, 16 February 1982, pp. 2–21. **116** Ibid., pp. 22–9. **117** George Gelder, 'The Royal Marines and Sea Service since 1900', *Globe and Laurel* (the author would like to thank George Gelder for making the author aware of this article). **118** NHB: Admiralty Board Minutes, A/P(80)5, The Dockyard Study, 2 May 1980, pp. 57–9. **119** For Chatham, see Chapter 5, for Gibraltar, see TNA: CAB 148/167/2, DOP(77)24, Future of Gibraltar Dockyard, 18 October 1977. **120** NHB: Admiralty Board Memoranda, Annex to A/P(81)4, HM Dockyards Long Term Load/Capacity Review 1981, August 1980, pp. 21–2, sheets 11–18. **121** TNA: DEFE 13/2022, Nott to Thatcher, 14 May 1981, Annex I. **122** NHB: T204489, HM Naval Base Chatham Development Plan, Volume 2, September 1975, pp. 17–19. **123** Ibid., pp. 5–7. **124** TNA: CAB 148/197, OD(81) 17th meeting, 12 November 1981, item 3; CAB 148/198, OD(81)50, Future of Gibraltar Dockyard, 4 November 1981; DEFE 24/2867, White to Head DS12, 6 January 1982. **125** NHB: VCNS Papers, Box 41, VCNS 10/15/34/1 Part 1, DGW(N) to Controller, 28 September 1981. **126** Ibid., Controller to CFS, 25 March 1982; CFS to Controller, 5 April 1982. **127** Ibid., Nott to Thatcher, 19 April 1982. **128** Ibid., Rowe to Sec/VCNS, 20 April 1982. **129** Ibid., VCNS to Controller and CFS, 23 June 1982; Controller to VCNS, 8 July 1982. **130** Ibid., VCNS to CFS, 16 July 1982. **131** NHB: Admiralty Board Memoranda, A/P(82)10, Dockyard Overload, 18 November 1982; Admiralty Board Minutes, A/M(82)3, 27 January 1983, Item 1. **132** NHB: Admiralty Board Memoranda, Annex to A/P(83)11, HM Dockyards Long Term Load Capacity Review 1984, September 1983, sheets 12–16. **133** TNA: DEFE 13/3169, Sec/1SL to PS/SecSt, 12 March 1982, Draft Message to Fleet. **134** NHB: Admiralty Board memorandum, 'Restructuring the Navy' A/P(82)2, 26 February 1982. **135** TNA: DEFE 13/1950, Leach to Nott, 16 December 1981; NHB: Admiralty Board memorandum, 'Restructuring the Navy' A/P(82)2, 26/2/82; VCNS/ACNS papers, 'Way Ahead Executive Sub-Committee' ACNS(P) 10/26/18 Pt II, Rr Adm Dalton to Sec WAC, 6 September 1982; NHB: VCNS/ACNS papers, 'Way Ahead Executive Sub-Committee' ACNS(P) 10/26/18 Pt II, Way Head presentation script, Cdr Lees, para. 32, 2 June 1982. **136** HMSO: 'The United Kingdom Defence Programme: The Way Forward' (Cmnd 8288), p. 11. **137** NHB: Admiralty Board memorandum, 'Restructuring the Navy' A/P(82)2, 26 February 1982. **138** NHB: VCNS/ACNS papers, 'Way Ahead Executive Sub-Committee' ACNS(P) 10/26/18 Pt II, Automation and Manning in the Future Fleet, Dalton to VCNS 20 May 1982; NHB: Admiralty Board minute, A/M(82)1, item 2, 23 March 1982. **139** The MoD's adjustment of cash prices into 'volume' numbers was more complex that just using a price increase based on inflation. They took each type of item and compared the previous and current year's prices, and where this was not possible, they took 'indices appropriate to the industrial sector concerned' as an inflator. These were then fed into to an extrapolated assumption of future costs. Apart from being hugely resource intensive, this approach was also more of an art than a science and provided many opportunities for small errors to compound themselves, or for optimistic assumptions to be made. It is not surprising that Nott referred to volume figures as 'funny money' and that the Treasury was keen to stamp out the practice in the Ministry of Defence. TNA: PREM 19/687, Defence Prices: Note by Officials, 20 November 1981; Nott, *Here Today, Gone Tomorrow*, p. 207. **140** TNA: PREM 19/687, Nott to Thatcher, 16 October 1981. **141** Ibid., Matthews to Thatcher, 19 October 1981. **142** TNA: DEFE 13/1950, Hastie-Smith to PUS and CDS, 27 November 1981, Scrutiny of Sketch Estimates, see also Annex A. **143** TNA: PREM 19/687, Kerr to Scholar, 2 November 1981. **144** Ibid., Gregson to Thatcher, 19 November 1981. **145** Ibid., Defence Prices: Note by Officials, 20 November 1981. **146** TNA: CAB 128/71, CC(81) 38th meeting, 26 November 1981, item 5, Confidential Annex. **147** TNA: CAB 148/205, OD(82) 1st meeting, 27 January 1982. **148** TNA: CAB 148/205, OD(82)2, The Defence Estimates, 21 January 1982, see also Annexes A and B; see also Noble, *British Defence Policy and the RAF*, pp. 185–8, for the detail of the RAF's reductions. **149** Noble, *British Defence Policy and the RAF*, pp. 188–9. **150** Nott, *Here Today, Gone Tomorrow*, pp. 238–41.

Chapter 16: Operation 'Corporate'

1 Brown, *Royal Navy and the Falklands War*, pp. 55–64; Freedman, *Official History Vol. 2*, pp. 3–14; Middlebrook, *Fight for the Malvinas*, pp. 13–39. **2** The official history of the campaign is a comprehensive two-volume account of the conflict and its background. Freedman, *Official History Vols 1 and 2*. The most detailed published account of the Royal Navy's war is still David Brown's *The Royal Navy and the Falklands War*, published in 1987. Hugh Bicheno, *Razor's Edge*; John Shields, *Air Power in the Falklands Conflict*; Santiago Rivas, *Wings of the Malvinas*; Paul Brown, *Abandon Ship*; and Kenneth Privratsky, *Logistics in the Falklands War* are all important accounts and analyses of different aspects of the war and are strongly recommended. **3** Fursdon, *Falklands Aftermath* and Dutford, ed. *Falklands Aftermath: Forces '85* touch on these issues but do not systematically discuss the Navy's force levels, structure and deployment patterns. **4** For the background to the claims on the Falklands and the diplomacy preceding the conflict, see Freedman, *Official History Vol 1*; Burns, *Land that Lost its Heroes*, Chs 1–4; Beck, *Falklands as an International Problem*, Chs 1–5. **5** Freedman, *Official History Vol. 1*, Chs 16–17; Middlebrook, *Battle for the Malvinas*, Chs 2–3; Perkins, *Operation Paraquat*, Ch. 3. **6** Nott, *Here Today Gone Tomorrow*, pp. 257–8; Leach, *Endure No Makeshifts* pp. 218–21; Thatcher, *Downing Street Years*, p. 179; Moore, *Margaret Thatcher*, p. 667; for Leach's apparent motivation to 'demonstrate the Royal Navy's continued worth', see Freedman, *Official History Vol 2*, p. 24. **7** NHB: 'The Falklands War: Operation Corporate', Ch. 1, pp. 11–15, Ch. 3, p. 1; Nott, *Here Today Gone Tomorrow*, p. 256; Woodward and Robinson, *One Hundred Days*, pp. 70–1; Watson, *Commander in Chief*, pp. 144–6. **8** NHB: Fleet Operations Programme, March 1982. **9** NHB: Battleaxe Box, Nolan to CINCFLEET, 26 November 1982. **10** NHB: 'Falklands War', Ch. 1, pp. 12–13; Brown, *Royal Navy and the Falklands War*, pp. 67–8. **11** Ibid., p. 65. **12** Ibid., pp. 65, 68. **13** NHB: 'Falklands War', Ch. 3, p. 1. **14** Hennessy and Jinks, *Silent Deep*, pp. 394–9. **15** TNA: DEFE 69/846, FOSM to CINCFLEET, 5 October 1982. **16** Hennessy and Jinks, *Silent Deep*, pp. 442–4. **17** TNA: DEFE 69/981, Cox to DRP(S), 16 April 1982. **18** Brown, *Royal Navy and the Falklands War*, pp. 361–2, 365–70. **19** Ibid., pp. 350–6. **20** Privratsky, *Logistics*, pp. 60–4, 68–9. **21** Ibid., p. 84; Brown, *Royal Navy and the Falklands War*, pp. 216, 236. **22** Privratsky, *Logistics*, pp. 71–2. **23** TNA: DEFE 69/885, White to Mackay, 11 June 1982; McLoughlin to DS11, 9 April 1982. **24** Ibid., Stevens to Head CFS Coord(N), 9 July 1982. **25** Brown, *Royal Navy and the Falklands War*, p. 354. **26** Freedman, *Official History Vol. 2*, pp. 771–2. **27** TNA: DEFE 69/981, Garnier to ACNS(O), 13 May 1982. **28** Ibid., CFS to VCNS, 29 April 1982. **29** Freedman, *Official History Vol. 2*, pp. 29–33; Stephen Prince, 'Command and Control in the Falklands Campaign', *Defence Analysis*, Vol. 18, No. 2, 2002. **30** TNA: DEFE 69/785, Livesay to various, 20 April 1982. **31** TNA: DEFE 69/789, Kendall to DNW et al, 27 April 1982. **32** The operation was formally known as Operation 'Paraquet', after a type of small parrot, although it became more generally known by those involved as Operation 'Paraquat', presumably assuming that it had been named after the effective but highly toxic herbicide. **33** Freedman, *Official History Vol. 2*, p. 226. **34** Brown, *Royal Navy and the Falklands War*, pp. 98–9; Perkins,

Operation Paraquat, pp. 131–53. **35** Perkins, *Operation Paraquat*, pp. 154–68. **36** Ibid., pp. 168–80. **37** Freedman, *Official History Vol. 2*, pp. 87–8; Brown, *Royal Navy and the Falklands War*, p. 84. **38** Freedman, *Official History Vol. 2*, pp. 261–3. **39** Hennessy and Jinks, *Silent Deep*, pp. 415–17. **40** Freedman, *Official History Vol 2*, p. 286; Brown, *Royal Navy and the Falklands War*, pp. 130–3; Rivas, *Wings of the Malvinas*, pp. 242–3, 250–1, 268–71. **41** Freedman, *Official History Vol 2*, p. 285. **42** Freedman, *Official History Vol 2*, pp. 279–86; Brown, *Royal Navy and the Falklands War*, pp. 118–19; Rivas, *Wings of the Malvinas*, p. 206; Middlebrook, *Battle for the Malvinas*, pp. 76–8; Craig, *Call for Fire*, pp. 58–60. **43** Brown, *Royal Navy and the Falklands War*, pp. 123–6; Middlebrook, *Battle for the Malvinas*, pp. 81–2; Rivas, *Wings of the Malvinas*, pp. 166–74, 184–5. **44** Sciaroni and Smith, *Go Find Him*, pp. 51–5; Middlebrook, *Battle for the Malvinas*, pp. 80–1. **45** Brown, *Royal Navy and the Falklands War*, p. 126; Rivas, *Wings of the Malvinas*, pp. 88–92. **46** Hennessy and Jinks, *Silent Deep*, p. 419; Woodward and Robinson, *One Hundred Days*, pp. 154–6. **47** Freedman, *Official History Volume 2*, pp. 296–8; Brown, *Royal Navy and the Falklands War*, pp. 134–7; Boveda, *All for One*, pp. 52–3; Robert Sheina, 'The Malvinas Campaign' *USNI Proceedings*, May 1983, pp. 106–07. Freedman and Sheina give the total dead as 321, Boveda gives 323. **48** Brown, *Royal Navy and the Falklands War*, pp. 140–1; Freedman, *Official History Vol 2*, pp. 302–04. **49** Freedman, *Official History Vol. 2*, pp. 304–05. Sounding the general alarm might not have made much difference and could have made the situation worse: personnel would have been going through watertight doors just as the missile hit. The author would like to thank Andrew Livsey for this insight. **50** Paul Brown, *Abandon Ship*, pp. 62–72; Brown, *Royal Navy and the Falklands War*, pp. 141–4, 154–5. **51** Brown, *Royal Navy and the Falklands War*, pp. 144, 148. **52** Rivas, *Wings of the Malvinas*, pp. 62–3. **53** Freedman, *Official History Vol 2*, p. 426; Middlebrook, *Fight for the Malvinas*, pp. 219–23. **54** Brown, *Royal Navy and the Falklands War*, p. 154; Rivas, *Wings of the Malvinas*, p. 120. **55** Brown, *Royal Navy and the Falklands War*, pp. 158–61; Rivas, *Wings of the Malvinas*, pp. 134–5. **56** NHB: Glasgow Box 1/T91597, Hoddinott to ComTF317, 19 June 1982. **57** Brown, *Royal Navy and the Falklands War*, pp. 151–3. **58** Craig, *Call for Fire*, pp. 76–84; Brown, *Royal Navy and the Falklands War*, p. 156. **59** Brown, *Royal Navy and the Falklands War*, p. 166. **60** Ibid., pp. 163–4; Freedman, *Official History Vol 2*, p. 435; Rivas, *Wings of the Malvinas*, p. 106. **61** Craig, *Call for Fire*, p. 82; Brown, *Royal Navy and the Falklands War*, pp. 156–7. **62** Brown, *Royal Navy and the Falklands War*, pp. 171–2. **63** Ibid., p. 171. **64** Freedman, *Official History Vol. 2*, pp. 445–51, Southby-Tailyour, *Reasons in Writing*, pp. 173–5. **65** Freedman, *Official History Vol. 2*, pp. 467–8; Brown, *Royal Navy and the Falklands War*, p. 174. **66** Freedman, *Official History Vol. 2*, pp. 468–9; Brown, *Royal Navy and the Falklands War*, p. 178. **67** Freedman, *Official History Vol. 2*, p. 469; Brown, *Royal Navy and the Falklands War*, p. 184; Southby-Tailyour, *Reasons in Writing*, pp. 206–08. **68** Clapp and Southby-Tailyour, *Amphibious Assault Falklands*, p. 136. **69** Brown, *Royal Navy and the Falklands War*, pp. 178–83; Freedman, *Official History Vol. 2*, pp. 469–470; Southby-Tailyour, *Reasons in Writing*, pp. 188–209; Clapp and Southby-Tailyour, *Amphibious Assault Falklands*, pp. 138–40; Julian Thompson, *No Picnic*, pp. 52–5. **70** Brown, *Royal Navy and the Falklands War*, pp. 184–7; Rivas, *Wings of the Malvinas*, pp. 108–10, 237–9. **71** Rivas, *Wings of the Malvinas*, pp. 175–6, 186–7; Brown, *Royal Navy and the Falklands War*, pp. 186–8; Rivas states that *Brilliant* was attacked, but the target was more likely to have been *Broadsword*. **72** Brown, *Royal Navy and the Falklands War*, pp. 190–1; Rivas, *Wings of the Malvinas*, pp. 136–7. **73** Brown, *Royal Navy and the Falklands War*, p. 191; Rivas, *Wings of the Malvinas*, pp. 120–1. **74** Brown, *Royal Navy and the Falklands War*, p. 193; Rivas, *Wings of the Malvinas*, p. 176. **75** Brown, *Royal Navy and the Falklands War*, p. 192; Rivas, *Wings of the Malvinas*, pp. 137–8. **76** Rivas, *Wings of the Malvinas*, pp. 176–8. **77** Paul Brown, *Abandon Ship*, pp. 91–106; Martin Higgitt, *Through Fire and Water*, pp. 186–246; Brown, *Royal Navy and the Falklands War*, pp. 194–6; Boveda, *All for One*, pp. 55–8; Rivas, *Wings of the Malvinas*, pp. 252–9. **78** Rivas, *Wings of the Malvinas*, pp. 83–5; Brown, *Royal Navy and the Falklands War*, pp. 201–02. **79** Brown, *Royal Navy and the Falklands War*, pp. 202–04. **80** Paul Brown, *Abandon Ship*, pp. 126–9; Rivas, *Wings of the Malvinas*, pp. 139–41; Brown, *Royal Navy and the Falklands War*, pp. 205–09. **81** Rivas, *Wings of the Malvinas*, pp. 260–1. Rivas argues that the second bomb in *Antelope* had come from the A4Qs, on the basis that the two bombs must have been different as the bomb disposal team failed to disarm the second bomb effectively. Paul Brown, on the other hand, states that the Argentine Air Force had been supplied with four different types of triggers when the bombs had been transferred many years earlier, thus explaining the different bomb types. This author inclines to the latter explanation, although proving either is probably close to impossible.

Paul Brown, *Abandon Ship*, p. 133. **82** Rivas, *Wings of the Malvinas*, p. 189. **83** Paul Brown, *Abandon Ship*, pp. 130–8; Underwood, *Our Falklands War*, pp. 63–6; Brown, *Royal Navy and the Falklands War*, pp. 209–10. **84** Brown, *Royal Navy and the Falklands War*, pp. 211–14; Rivas, *Wings of the Malvinas*, pp. 141–4. **85** Brown, *Royal Navy and the Falklands War*, p. 214; Rivas, *Wings of the Malvinas*, pp. 189–90. **86** Brown, *Royal Navy and the Falklands War*, p. 214; Rivas, *Wings of the Malvinas*, pp. 179–80. **87** Brown, *Royal Navy and the Falklands War*, pp. 214–15; Rivas, *Wings of the Malvinas*, p. 123. **88** Rivas, *Wings of the Malvinas*, p. 144. **89** Brown, *Royal Navy and the Falklands War*, pp. 218–20; Rivas, *Wings of the Malvinas*, pp. 123–4. **90** Paul Brown, *Abandon Ship*, pp. 164–77; Hart-Dyke, *Four Weeks in May*, pp. 1–4, 145–69; Rivas, *Wings of the Malvinas*, pp. 144–9; Brown, *Royal Navy and the Falklands War*, pp. 221–3. **91** Paul Brown, *Abandon Ship*, pp. 192–201; Brown, *Royal Navy and the Falklands War*, pp. 227–31. **92** Brown, *Royal Navy and the Falklands War*, p. 238; Rivas, *Wings of the Malvinas*, pp. 150–3. **93** Brown, *Royal Navy and the Falklands War*, pp. 248–50, 259–60; Rivas, *Wings of the Malvinas*, pp. 73–7. **94** Brown, *Royal Navy and the Falklands War*, p. 251. **95** Wrecksite.eu website: 'Amerada Hess Shipping Corporation v. Argentine Republic' (US Court of Appeals for the Second Circuit, Case No. 334, decided 11 September 1987), pp. 2-3: PlainSite :: Flashlight.... v. Argentine Republic (wrecksite.eu); *New York Times*: 'Tanker Attacked in South Atlantic', 9 June 1982: TANKER ATTACKED IN SOUTH ATLANTIC - The New York Times (nytimes.com) (accessed 4 October 2023); Rivas, *Wings of the Malvinas*, pp. 77, 80. Rivas, *Wings of the Malvinas*, 80. **96** Rivas, *Wings of the Malvinas*, pp. 126–30; Brown, *Royal Navy and the Falklands War*, pp. 254–7; Freedman, *Official History Vol 2*, pp. 545–6. Argentina also attempted to procure further air-launched Exocet during the conflict but was unsuccessful. See West, *The Secret War*, pp. 99–100, 114–15; Freedman, *Official History Vol 2*, pp. 390-391. **97** Freedman, *Official History Vol. 2*, p. 586. **98** Ibid., pp. 468, 552–82. **99** Brown, *Royal Navy and the Falklands War*, p. 249. **100** Brown, *Royal Navy and the Falklands War*, pp. 247, 251, 253–4, 259; Pook, *RAF Harrier Ground Attack Falklands*, Chs 14–16. **101** Freedman, *Official History Vol. 2*, pp. 548–9, 621, 638. **102** Brown, *Royal Navy and the Falklands War*, pp. 242–3, 245, 252–3, 258, 262, 270, 272, 276–7, 279, 285–6, 289. **103** Rivas, *Wings of the Malvinas*, pp. 70–1; Brown, *Royal Navy and the Falklands War*, pp. 272–4. **104** Brown, *Royal Navy and the Falklands War*, pp. 283–4, 286. **105** Freedman, *Official History Vol. 2*, p. 601. **106** Southby-Tailyour, *Reasons in Writing*, pp. 257–300; Paul Brown, *Abandon Ship*, pp. 214–23. **107** Brown, *Royal Navy and the Falklands War*, pp. 297–301; Rivas, *Wings of the Malvinas*, p. 192. **108** Rivas, *Wings of the Malvinas*, pp. 153–5. **109** Brown, *Royal Navy and the Falklands War*, pp. 302–04; Rivas, *Wings of the Malvinas*, pp. 154–60; Southby-Tailyour, *Reasons in Writing*, pp. 300–07. **110** Freedman, *Official History Vol. 2*, pp. 596, 601. According to Nott it was Bramall's decision to send the Welsh and Scots Guards, Nott, *Here Today, Gone Tomorrow*, p. 306. **111** Rivas, *Wings of the Malvinas*, pp. 95–7; Brown, pp. 327–8. **112** Brown, *Royal Navy and the Falklands War*, p. 323. **113** Freedman, *Official History Vol. 12*, p. 623. **114** Inskip, *Ordeal by Exocet*, pp. 150–85; Brown, pp. 318–19. **115** Brown, *Royal Navy and the Falklands War*, pp. 329–30. **116** NHB: 'Falklands War', Ch. 17, pp. 1–9. **117** Ibid., Ch. 17, pp. 9-11; Brown, pp. 339-340. **118** HMSO: 'The Future Defence of the Falkland Islands'. House of Commons Defence Committee, 1982-83, HC-154, 12 May 1983, p. xv. **119** TNA: DEFE 69/764, Hogg to CED Ships, Draft Loose Minute, December 1982. **120** TNA: DEFE 69/969, Nott to Thatcher, 2 September 1982. **121** TNA: DEFE 69/764, Nott to CDS, 29 October 1982. **122** HMSO: 'The Future Defence of the Falkland Islands', House of Commons Defence Committee, 1982-83, HC-154, 12 May 1983, p. xiv. **123** NHB: VCNS/ACNS Box 54, ACNS(P) 40/55, Morgan to DN Plans, 31 March 1982. **124** Ibid., Smith to DNOR, 23 April 1982. **125** Ibid., Jago to ACNS(OR), 2 December 1982. **126** Ibid., Report of Project ARAPAHO sea trials, September 1982. **127** Ibid., Bathurst to ACNS(OR), 16 December 1982; VCNS 40/55 Pt 3, 'Lease of One (1) Arapaho Unit', 7 April 1983. **128** NHB: Fleet Operations Programme, September 1983 to February 1984. **129** Brown, *Royal Navy in the Falklands War*, p. 345. **130** TNA: DEFE 69/764, ACNS(P) to DG Ships, 30 November 1982; Mottram to AUS(NS), 16 December 1982; Dalton to Sec/1SL et al, 26 January 1983; Dalton to ACNS(OR) et al, 27 January 1983. **131** NHB: Fleet Operations Programme, various months 1984-87. **132** HMS *Dumbarton Castle* was in the South Atlantic for just over two years before being relieved by her sister. NHB: Fleet Operations Programme, October 1986 to December 1988. **133** NHB: Fleet Operations Programme, various months 1984-87.

Chapter 17: Lessons Learnt

1 NHB: 'The Falklands War: Operation Corporate', Chapter 18, pp. 1–2. **2** NHB: Falklands Box 3/T48293, Nott to Lewin, 14 June 1982. **3** Ibid., CSA to ACDS (Ops), 15 June 1982, TORs Annex A. **4** Ibid., Scientific Analysis of Corporate, Central Staff Co-ordination Group, meeting notes, 1 July 1982. **5** NHB: 'The Falklands War: Operation Corporate', Chapter 18, p. 2. **6** NHB: Falklands Box 6, Operation Corporate, FOF1 Formex 100, 30 June 1982. **7** The first draft of the CTF317 report was produced two weeks after Woodward's. TNA: DEFE 69/777, Anson to DCDS, 15 July 1982. **8** TNA: DEFE 69/792, PUS and CDS to VCDS(P&L) et al, 24 June 1982. **9** Ibid., ACNS(P) to VCNS, 30 June 1982. **10** NHB: Falklands Box 3/T48293, Scientific Analysis of Corporate, Central Staff Co-ordination Group, meeting notes, 3 August 1982. **11** Ibid., Bawtree loose minute, 29 June 1983. **12** TNA: DEFE 69/695, NATO Naval Armaments Group: The Falklands Campaign – Material Lessons Learnt, 18 October 1983. **13** TNA: DEFE 69/899, 'Lessons of the Falklands, Summary Report', Department of the Navy, February 1983. This report is also available online: https://apps.dtic.mil/sti/pdfs/ADA133333.pdf (accessed 3 May 2023); DEFE 69/907, Mottram to AUS (D Staff), 29 June 1983. **14** TNA: DEFE 69/899, Middleton to D of DPS(OR), 20 April 1983. **15** TNA: DEFE 69/907, Aldred to FLS(Air), 16 September 1983. **16** TNA: DEFE 69/779, DCDS to VCNS, VCGS, VCAS, 28 July 1982. **17** TNA: DEFE 69/795, CINCFLEET to various, 8 March 1983, Annex A. **18** Ibid. FOTI 2024 was the relevant RN ROE document. **19** NHB: Boscombe Box 60, UAA1 Opeval Interim Report, OEG 1/80, 7 January 1980, p. 5 and Annex D, T151733. This report noted that SCOT interference of the UAA1 passive intercept was not well known within the fleet, and it recommended promulgating this issue in the relevant FOTI. It is not known whether this was done. For the inability of MOD to procure a solution to this problem before the Falklands, see Andy Beckett, *Promised You a Miracle* (London, 2015), pp. 277–9. **20** TNA: DEFE 69/781, Knight to D/Mat Co-Ord(N), 18 October 1982; DEFE 69/795, CINCFLEET to various, 8 March 1983, Annex C. **21** NHB: VCNS Box 46, VCNS 40/13 Pt V, NSR 7113 Supporting Paper, January 1984; Sec/VCNS to PS/Min(AF), 14 October 1983; TNA: DEFE 69/764, Hogg to CED Ships, Draft Loose Minute, December 1982. **22** TNA: DEFE 69/908, ACNS to AUS (Systems), 9 October 1985; Aldred to APS/Min(AF), 2 January 1987. **23** TNA: DEFE 69/908, ACNS to AUS (Systems), 9 October 1985. **24** Hansard, 'Falkland Islands (Gazelle Helicopter)', statement by Mr Stanley, Vol. 100, Col. 62, 25 June 1986. **25** NHB: Falklands Box 4/T49422, ASWE Analysis of Operation Corporate: Command, Control and Communication, 15 September 1982, section 1. **26** TNA: DEFE 69/778, Falklands Interim Report, 2 August 1982, p. B-20-9. For the history of the HP 9845, see: https://www.hp9845.net/9845/history/story (accessed 3 May 2023). **27** TNA: DEFE 69/780, Whetstone to VCNS, 23 September 1982. **28** Moore, *Margaret Thatcher*, pp. 697–8; Thatcher, *Downing Street Years*, p. 226; Hill, *Lewin*, pp. 371, 375. **29** Clapp and Thompson, *Amphibious Assault Falklands*, p. 44; Thompson, *No Picnic*, p. 25. **30** HMSO, *The Navy List 1982* (Corrected to 31st October 1981), p. 148. **31** Finlan, *Falklands Conflict and Gulf War*, pp. 75–9. **32** Ibid., pp. 74–5. **33** Woodward and Robinson, *One Hundred Days*, pp. 58–9. **34** Prince, 'British Command and Control', p. 241; Watson, *Commander in Chief*, p. 157. Commodore Clapp had served at sea during the Korean War as a midshipman. To this author's knowledge he was the only senior naval officer at sea in the campaign with either Second World War or Korean War experience. Clapp and Southby-Tailyour, *Amphibious Assault Falklands*, p. 129. **35** Freedman, *Official History, Vol 2*, pp. 586, 730–1. **36** Hastings and Jenkins, *Battle for the Falklands*, pp. 348–51. **37** Those captains who had commanded two major ships (submarines, frigates or larger) before their current command in the Falklands were: Captains J J Black, M G T Harris, H M Balfour, A P Hoddinott, S Salt, J F Coward, W R Canning, H M White, J L Weatherall and P G V Dingemanns. Captains A Grose, B G Young, D Hart-Dyke, C H Layman, D Pentreath and N J Barker had commanded one major vessel before their current command. Sources: *Who's Who* (London), various editions; HMSO, *The Navy List*, various editions. **38** NHB: Falklands Box 17/T48483, Staveley to 2SL and VCNS, 'Preparation for the Stress of Battle', 6 February 1984. **39** Shields, *Airpower*, pp. 186–7. **40** For example, see Inskip, *Ordeal by Exocet*, p. 194. **41** TNA: DEFE 69/908, 'Operation Corporate – The Intelligence Lessons Learnt', 10 July 1985. **42** NHB: 'The Falklands War: Operation Corporate', Chapter 18, pp. 15–16. **43** NHB: Falklands Box 4/T49422, ASWE Analysis of Operation Corporate: Command, Control and Communication, 15 September 1982, section 1. **44** TNA: DEFE 69/795, CINCFLEET to various, 8 March 1983, Annex A. **45** Shields, *Airpower*, pp. 129–31. **46** NHB: Falklands Box 4/T49447, ASWE Analysis of Operation Corporate: Ship Weapon Systems Aspects, 15

September 1982. **47** HMSO, Statement on the Defence Estimates (Cmnd 9227-I, 1984), p. 28. **48** NHB: Falklands Box 4/T49447, ASWE Analysis of Operation Corporate: Ship Weapon Systems Aspects, 15 September 1982; TNA: DEFE 69/777, Anson to DCDS, 15 July 1982, Annex C. **49** TNA: DEFE 69/780, Equipment Performance Report draft, Appendix 3, 28 September 1982. **50** NHB: Falklands Box 4/T49447, ASWE Analysis of Operation Corporate: Ship Weapon Systems Aspects, 15 September 1982. **51** Ibid. **52** TNA: DEFE 69/795, CINCFLEET to various, 8 March 1983, Annex B. **53** TNA: DEFE 69/756, Stanford to CofN, 28 April 1982. **54** HMSO, Statement on the Defence Estimates 1983 (Cmnd 8951-I, 1983), p. 11; Statement on the Defence Estimates 1984 (Cmnd 9227, 1984) p. 28. **55** Johnston-Bryden, *Illustrious*, p. 25. **56** TNA: DEFE 69/760, Sec/1SL to APS/SofS, 4 June 1982. **57** Friedman, *World Naval Weapon Systems 1997-98*, pp. 523–5; NHB: VCNS Box 65, ACNS(P) 40/18, Ad Hoc Group on Type 42 Destroyer: Paper by DSWP(N), 31 August 1982. **58** TNA: DEFE 69/777, Anson to DCDS, 15 July 1982, Annex J; DEFE 67/778, Falklands Interim Report, 2 August 1982, pp. B-16-1 to 2. **59** TNA: DEFE 69/795, CINCFLEET to various, 8 March 1983, Annex A; DEFE 69/777, Anson to DCDS, 15 July 1982, Annex J. The rushed fitting of AAR would, two decades later, result in a tragic accident over Afghanistan when fuel leaked after AAR refuelling, causing the aircraft to crash and kill its crew. TSO: 'The Nimrod Review' (HC 1025, October 2009). **60** TNA: DEFE 69/907, Whetstone to various, 17 January 1983, Annex B. **61** HMSO, Statement on the Defence Estimates 1984 (Cmnd 9227-I, 1984), p. 33. **62** TNA: DEFE 69/777, Anson to DCDS, 15 July 1982, Annexes D and I. **63** Ibid., Annex I. **64** Shields, *Airpower*, pp. 173–6, 198–9; Pook, *RAF Harrier*, pp. 96, 147–8, 164. The holding back of GR3s from further ground-attack missions could have been related to concerns that they might have to fulfil their original role as air defence back-ups to the Sea Harriers if the latter had suffered greater attrition. **65** Freedman, p. 297; Hennessy and Jinks, *Silent Deep*, pp. 421–2. **66** TNA: DEFE 69/777, Anson to DCDS, 15 July 1982, Annex A; DEFE 69/778, Falklands Interim Report, 2 August 1982, pp. B-1-1 To 8. **67** TNA: DEFE 69/846, FOSM to CINCFLEET, 5 October 1982, Annex B. **68** TNA: DEFE 69/777, Anson to DCDS, 15 July 1982, Annex A. **69** TNA: DEFE 69/778/T48185, Falklands Interim Report, 2 August 1982, pp. B-1-1 to 8; NHB: Falklands Box 4, Herbert to CINCFLEET, 5 October 1982. **70** TNA: DEFE 69/780, Equipment Performance Report draft, Appendix 1, 28 September 1982. **71** NHB: Falklands Box 3/T48294, Bartlett to CinCFleet, 2 August 1983; 'Draft Working Paper 3 August 83', Annex B, 8 September 1983. **72** TNA: DEFE 69/777, Anson to DCDS, 15 July 1982, Annex A. **73** Ibid. **74** Friedman, *World Naval Weapon Systems 1997-98*, pp. 609–10. **75** Ibid., p. 610. **76** TNA: DEFE 69/777, Anson to DCDS, 15 July 1982, Annex A. **77** Ibid. MAD for naval helicopters had been successfully trialled just before the Falklands conflict in the Atlantic west of Ireland. NHB: Boscombe Box 60, Opeval helicopter towed MAD, OEG 1/82, January 1982. **78** TNA: DEFE 69/778, Falklands Interim Report, 2 August 1982, pp. B-1-1 to 8. **79** Brown, *Royal Navy and the Falklands War*, pp. 151–3, 166. **80** TNA: DEFE 69/778, Falklands Interim Report, 2 August 1982, p. B-2-1; Brown, *Royal Navy and the Falklands War*, pp. 138, 205. **81** TNA: DEFE 69/780, Equipment Performance Report draft, Appendix 2, 28 September 1982; Elliott, *A Gulf Record*, pp. 19–20, 28; Pokrant, *Desert Storm at Sea*, pp. 87–9. **82** TNA: DEFE 69/795, CINCFLEET to various, 8 March 1983, Annexes A and B. **83** TNA: DEFE 69/777, Anson to DCDS, 15 July 1982, Annex B. **84** NHB: 'The Falklands War: Operation Corporate', Chapter 18, p. 17. **85** TNA: DEFE 69/795, CINCFLEET to various, 8 March 1983, Annex B; NHB: Falklands Box 4, Chair AWESC to various, 16 December 1982, Annex A. **86** TNA: DEFE 69/782, O'Hara to ACNS(P), 4 November 1982. **87** TNA: DEFE 69/791, Scientific Evaluation Serial 2, September 1982, section C2. **88** TNA: DEFE 69/780, Equipment Performance Report draft, Appendix 2, 28 September 1982. **89** TNA: DEFE 69/795, CINCFLEET to various, 8 March 1983, Annex. **90** TNA: DEFE 69/898, Grey to ACNS(P), 15 September 1982, Annex A. **91** TNA: DEFE 69/781, VCNS to DCDS, 8 October 1982. **92** TNA: DEFE 69/777, Anson to DCDS, 15 July 1982, Annex G. **93** TNA: DEFE 69/898, Hogg to ACNS(P), 20 September 1982, covering 'Draft: Operation Corporate – Reports'. **94** Ibid., Grey to ACNS(P), 15 September 1982, Annex A. **95** Clapp and Southby-Tailyour: *Amphibious Assault Falklands*, pp. 33, 47, 77, 81. **96** Johnstone-Bryden, *Ocean*, pp. 19–48. **97** TNA: DEFE 69/781, Jago to AUS (RP), 6 October 1982, attached draft chapter, para. 19. **98** TNA: DEFE 69/759, DCDS(OR) to CDS, 27 May 1982. **99** TNA: DEFE 69/777, Anson to DCDS, 15 July 1982, Annex H. **100** TNA: DEFE 69/907, Whetstone to various, 17 January 1983, Annex B. **101** Ibid. **102** TNA: DEFE 69/780, VCNS to DCDS, 29 September 1982. **103** Privratsky, *Logistics*, pp. 76–9. **104** TNA: DEFE 69/777,

Anson to DCDS, 15 July 1982, Annex H. **105** Hennessy and Jinks, *The Silent Deep*, pp. 436–7; TNA: DEFE 69/777, Anson to DCDS, 15 July 1982, Annex H. **106** TNA: DEFE 69/779, Cardy to ADC Pol, 5 August 1982. **107** Ibid. **108** TNA: DEFE 69/779, McMaster to Sec/C of N, 30 July 1982, covering D/S DDNSP/3/20. **109** TNA: DEFE 69/795, CINCFLEET to various, 8 March 1983, Annex A. **110** TNA: DEFE 69/898, Hogg to ACNS(P), 20 September 1982, covering 'Draft: Operation Corporate – Reports'. **111** TNA: DEFE 69/777, Anson to DCDS, 15 July 1982, Annex G. **112** TNA: DEFE 69/795, CINCFLEET to various, 8 March 1983, Annex D. **113** Ibid. **114** Ibid. **115** HMSO, Statement on the Defence Estimates 1982 Volume 2 (Cmnd 8529-II, June 1982), p. 25; NHB: Intrepid Box 1/T49005, Dingemans to CINCFLEET, 30 July 1982. **116** TNA: DEFE 69/795, CINCFLEET to various, 8 March 1983, Annex D. **117** Ibid. **118** Ibid. **119** TNA: DEFE 69/795, CINCFLEET to various, 8 March 1983, Annex F. **120** TNA: DEFE 69/795, CINCFLEET to various, 8 March 1983, Annex D. **121** TNA: DEFE 69/907, DGST(N) to CINCFLEET, 17 June 1983. **122** NHB: T175822, 'Operation Corporate: Recollections from SNO Atlantic Conveyor'. **123** TNA: DEFE 69/795, CINCFLEET to various, 8 March 1983, Annex D. **124** NHB: Falklands Box 4, 900/210/1/38/7, Chair AWESC to various, 16 December 1982, Annex A. **125** Ibid. **126** NHB: Falklands Box 17/T4848, Staveley to 2SL and VCNS, 'Preparation for the Stress of Battle', 6 February 1984. **127** Ibid. **128** Ibid. **129** Ibid. **130** Ibid. **131** TNA: DEFE 69/777, Anson to DCDS, 15 July 1982, Annex M-2. **132** Ibid. **133** TNA: DEFE 69/778, Falklands Interim Report, 2 August 1982, p. B-6-1 to 5. **134** For an example of reportage on this subject just after the conflict, see Robert Fox, 'Welcome Home and After', *The Listener*, 22 July 1982 in Hanrahan and Fox, *I counted them all out*, p. 130. **135** TNA: DEFE 69/795, CINCFLEET to various, Annex E, 8 March 1983; 'Material Lessons Learnt', 31 May 1983; DEFE 69/777, Anson to DCDS, 15 July 1982, Annex M-2. **136** TNA: DEFE 69/782, Trenchard to DUS(N), 28 October 1982. **137** TNA: DEFE 69/782, Trenchard to DUS(N), 20 October and 28 October 1982. **138** TNA: DEFE 69/795, 'Material Lessons Learnt', 31 May 1983. **139** TNA: DEFE 69/764, Griffiths to NA/CFS, 24 January 1983. **140** TNA: DEFE 69/777, Anson to DCDS, 15 July 1982, Annex M-3. **141** TNA: DEFE 69/795, 'Material Lessons Learnt', 31 May 1983; for steel in place of wood and new accommodation standards, see TNA: DEFE 69/764, DG Ships to Controller, 24 January 1983; for light armour, see Rawson to NA/Controller, 6 January 1983. **142** TNA: DEFE 69/777, Anson to DCDS, 15 July 1982, Annex M-3. **143** TNA: DEFE 69/695, DG Ships to Controller, 18 October 1982. **144** Brown and Moore, *Rebuilding the Royal Navy*, p. 111. **145** TNA: DEFE 69/777, Anson to DCDS, 15 July 1982, Annex L. **146** TNA: DEFE 69/795, CINCFLEET to various, 8 March 1983, Annex B. **147** NHB: Falklands Box 5/T48221, British Aerospace: 'Operational analysis of mine hunting activities in the South Atlantic', February 1983. **148** TNA: DEFE 69/777, Anson to DCDS, 15 July 1982, Annex M-1. **149** TNA: DEFE 69/795, 'Material Lessons Learnt', 31 May 1983. **150** TNA: DEFE 69/777, Anson to DCDS, 15 July 1982, Annex M-1. **151** TNA: DEFE 69/795, CINCFLEET to various, 8 March 1983, Annex F. **152** TNA: DEFE 69/764, Hammersley to the Editor, *Journal of Naval Engineering*, 12 August 1982. **153** NHB: Fleet Operational Programme, December 1986 and January 1987. **154** TNA: DEFE 69/779, McMaster to Sec/C of N, 30 July 1982, covering D/S DDNSP/3/20. **155** TNA: DEFE 69/780, Baird-Murray to Sec C of N, 31 August 1982. **156** TNA: DEFE 69/780, DG Defence Contracts to DUS (Pol) PE, 6 September 1982; DEFE 69/782, DGW(N) to SO/WAESC, 25 October 1982. **157** TNA: DEFE 69/779, Flowers to Sec/C of N, 29 July 1982, Annex A. **158** Hastings and Jenkins, *Battle for the Falklands*, pp. 331–3; Badsey, 'The Falklands War as a Media War'. **159** Badsey, 'The Falklands War as a Media War', p. 45, citing Harris, *Gotcha!*, pp. 94, 110–14. **160** TNA: DEFE 69/795, CINCFLEET to various, 8 March 1983, Annex A. **161** Badsey, 'The Falklands War as a Media War', p. 50. **162** In 1977 and 1978 there were a number of warhead failures during Exocet missile firings by HM Ships *Phoebe*, *Alacrity* and *Sirius*. NHB: VCNS Box 53, VCNS 40/1/4, Reffell to NA/1SL, 11 October 1977; Gerard-Pease to VCNS, 15 March 1978; DNW to ACNS(O), 10 May 1978. Manley, 'The Loss of HMS Sheffield'. **163** NHB: VCNS Papers, Box 61, VCNS 10/1/20, VCNS to 1SL, May 1982; VCNS to DN Plans, 10 May 1982. **164** Ibid., Wood to DWRP(N), 11 May 1982; Dalton to VCNS, 18 May 1982. **165** HMSO, The Falklands Campaign: The Lessons, Cmnd 8758 (December 1982). **166** Sturtivant, Burrow, Howard, *Fleet Air Arm Fixed Wing Aircraft*, pp. 88–9. **167** HMSO, The Falklands Campaign: The Lessons, pp. 32–5. **168** HMSO, Statement on the Defence Estimates 1983 (Cmnd 8951-I), p. 14; Statement on the Defence Estimates 1984 (Cmnd

9227-I), p. 28. **169** HMSO, Statement on the Defence Estimates 1985, Volume 1 (Cmnd 9430-I), p. 10. **170** HMSO, Statement on the Defence Estimates 1983, Volume 1 (Cmnd 8951-I), pp. 11, 14; Statement on the Defence Estimates 1984, Volume 1 (Cmnd 9227-I), p. 28. **171** NHB: VCNS Papers, Box 41, VCNS 10/15/34 Part 1, VCNS to CFS, 16 July 1982. **172** TNA: DEFE 69/783, CDS 7/82 (Revised), Principal Military Lessons of the Falkland Islands Campaign, 3 December 1982. **173** Ibid. **174** Ibid. **175** TNA: DEFE 13/1785, Cooper to Nott, 18 June 1982. **176** CCAC: NOTT 4/8/iv, 'Discussion US Strategy', p. 24. **177** Hennessy, *Cabinet*, pp. 166–7; Hennessy, *Whitehall*, p. 609. **178** TNA: PREM 19/4012, Major to Price, 30 April 1993. **179** TNA: DEFE 69/783, CSA to DCDS, 27 August 1982. **180** TNA: DEFE 69/939, various reports by Breeze, April-July 1982. **181** TNA: DEFE 69/783, CSA to DCDS, 27 August 1982. **182** NHB: Falklands Box 17, DNW to DN Plans, 6 December 1982. **183** For government statements on 'Out of Area' operations, see HMSO, Statement on the Defence Estimates 1983 (Cmnd 8951-I), p. 15; Statement on the Defence Estimates 1984 (Cmnd 9227-I), pp. 7, 29–33.

Chapter 18: Maritime Strategy
1 NHB: MoD (Royal Navy) Press Release, 37/78, 12 May 1978. **2** *The Times*, 30 May 1991, Obituary. **3** *The Daily Telegraph*, 20 October 2019, Obituary. **4** NHB: MoD (Royal Navy) Press Release, 28D/80, 30 July 1980. **5** Ibid., 41B/80, 16 October 1980. **6** Ibid., 7A/81, 19 March 1981. **7** This assessment was most pronounced amongst external analysts in the 1970s: see Eller, *The Soviet Sea Challenge*; Wegener, *The Soviet Naval Offensive*; Villar, 'Future Trends in Maritime Warfare', pp. 199–200. For US official publications, see Department of Defense, *Soviet Military Power* (Washington, 1981), p. 51 and Department of the Navy, *Understanding Soviet Naval Developments* (4th edition, Washington, 1981), p. 13. See also Ranft and Till, *The Sea in Soviet Strategy* pp. 12, 146–52, 205–13; although they caveat their more nuanced analysis with a warning that 'it is difficult to produce simple conclusions about the rise of the modern Soviet Navy' (p. 205). **8** Polmar and Moore, *Cold War Submarines*, pp. 194–8; Zaloga, *Kremlin's Nuclear Sword*, p. 186; Kuzin and Nikol'sky, *Voyenno-Morskoy Flot*, section 3.1. **9** Zaloga, *Kremlin's Nuclear Sword*, pp. 183–6, 188–90. **10** Cote, *The Third Battle*, pp. 60–2. **11** Polmar and Moore, *Cold War Submarines*, pp. 278–81. **12** Ibid., pp. 286–8. **13** Central Intelligence Agency, 'The Komsomelets Disaster' (CIA, 2007). **14** Polmar and Moore, *Cold War Submarines*, pp. 281–4. **15** Il'in and Kolesnikov, *Otechestvennye Atomnye Podvodnye Lodki*, p. 22. **16** Polmar and Moore, *Cold War Submarines*, p. 137. **17** Ibid., p. 284. **18** Apal'kov, *Podvodnye Lodki VMF SSSR*, p. 514. **19** The term 'saved by the bell' is used in Cote, *Third Battle*, p. 78. **20** Wells, *Tale of Two Navies*, pp. 116–18. **21** Polmar and Moore, *Cold War Submarines*, pp. 284–6. **22** Wells, *Tale of Two Navies*, pp. 121–8, 131–2; Polmar and Whitman, 'Russia poses a non-acoustic threat to US subs'. **23** Polmar and Moore, *Cold War Submarines*, pp. 214–18. **24** Kuzin and Nikol'skiy, *Voyenno-Morskoy Flot*, section 4.1; Apal'kov, *Udarnye Korabli*, pp. 27–36. **25** Apal'kov, *Udarnyye Korabli*, pp. 36–40; The US Government in 1983 was publicly predicting the completion of a large nuclear-powered carrier much earlier, in the late 1980s. US Department of Defense, *Soviet Military Power 1983*, p. 62. **26** For example: Villar, 'Weapon Development in the 1980s: Sea', p. 200; Moore, ed., *Jane's Fighting Ships 1982-1983*, p. 477. **27** Pavlov, *Warships of the USSR and Russia*, p. 96. **28** Kuzin and Nikolskiy, *Voyenno-Morskoy Flot*, section 4.2; Apal'kov, *Udarnye Korabli*, pp. 74–87. **29** Apal'kov, *Udarnye Korabli*, pp. 62–73. **30** Kuzin and Nikolskiy, *Voyenno-Morskoy Flot*, section 4.3. **31** Apal'kov, *Udarnye Korabli*, pp. 93–110. **32** Kuzin and Nikolskiy, *Voyenno-Morskoy Flot*, section 4.3; Apal'kov, *Protivolodochnye Korabli*, pp. 119–32. **33** Apal'kov, *Udarnye Korabli*, pp. 88–93. **34** Sharpe, ed., *Jane's Fighting Ships 1989-1990*, pp. 591–3. **35** Apal'kov, *Udarnye Korabli*, pp. 162–83. **36** Gordon and Kommissarov, *Soviet Naval Aviation*, pp. 327–30. **37** Kuzin and Nikol'skiy, *Voyenno-Morskoy Flot*, section 9.2; Gordon and Kommissarov, *Tupelov Tu-22M*, Appendix 2. **38** Gordon and Kommissarov, *Soviet Naval Aviation*, pp. 132–4. **39** On a standard high-low-high mission profile (gradually descending to, and gradually ascending from, the middle leg). Gordon and Kommissarov, *Tupelov Tu-22M*, p. 213. **40** Tokarev, 'Kamikazes: The Soviet Legacy', p. 15; Gordon and Kommissarov, *Tupelov Tu-22M*, p. 226. **41** Hattendorf, *Maritime Strategy*, pp. 12–13. **42** Ibid., pp. 4–7. **43** Ibid., pp. 17–20. **44** Hattendorf, *US Naval Strategy in the 1970s*, pp. 103–24; Hattendorf, *Maritime Strategy*, pp. 13–17. **45** Hattendorf, *Maritime Strategy*, pp. 36–44. **46** The production of PD 59, a new Presidential Directive on nuclear targeting policy also marked a change in the Carter administration's approach to the Soviet threat. Keefer, *Harold Brown*, pp. 142–5, 351–75. **47** Hattendorf, *Maritime Strategy*, p. 9. **48** Lehman, *Oceans Ventured*, pp. 20–4; Inboden, *The Peacemaker*, pp. 21–49. **49** Polmar, 'Working

for John Lehman, Part 1'; NHB: Invincible box 1/T91264, Gerken to CINCFLEET, 28 April 1983. **50** Hattendorf, *Maritime Strategy*, pp. 38–9, 48–57. **51** Friedman, *US Destroyers*, pp. 391–4. **52** Ford and Rosenberg, 'The Naval Intelligence Underpinnings of Reagan's Maritime Strategy', pp. 381–7; Hattendorf, *Maritime Strategy*, pp. 23–32. **53** Hattendorf, *Maritime Strategy*, pp. 33–6. **54** Following the end of the Cold War, the picture of a strategically-defensive Soviet Navy fighting to protect its bastions has not been contradicted, although the picture was clearly more nuanced. In the late 1950s Marshal Zhukov had pushed for the Soviet Navy to create capabilities to interdict transatlantic shipping, but the number of submarines and torpedoes required were beyond the capabilities of the Soviet economy. The interdiction of shipping remained a secondary role for the Soviet Navy through the Cold War. Kuzin and Nikol'skiy, *Soviet Navy 1945-91*, sections 1.2 and 1.3 (cited by Friedman in *Seapower and Strategy*, pp. 207, 331 (fn. 18)). For Soviet public pronouncements on the anti-SLOC mission from the 1960s onwards, see Herrick, *Soviet Naval Doctrine and Policy*, Volume 1, pp. 278–83; Volume 2, pp. 668–82; Volume 3, pp. 1149–71. From Herrick's compilation and analysis of open-source documents, it seems that by the 1980s the role of anti-SLOC operations had increased in prominence somewhat, although there were splits between the Navy and the General Staff over how this would be undertaken (Volume 3, pp. 1165–71). **55** For example, during USN war games undertaken in 1983, Hattendorf, *Maritime Strategy*, p. 35. **56** Hattendorf, *Maritime Strategy*, p. 84. Hattendorf states that 'the attack, which was envisaged against Soviet SSBNs, failed in the [war] games to have the hoped-for result, leading some of the [war gamers playing] Soviets to terminate a war'. This author has interpreted 'to terminate a war' to mean resort to nuclear weapons, but the meaning here is somewhat opaque. **57** Hattendorf, *US Naval Strategy in the 1980s*, pp. 203–06; citing United States Naval Institute *Proceedings*, The Maritime Strategy (Annapolis, January 1986). **58** Hennessy and Jinks, *Silent Deep*, pp. 546–7, 562–71. **59** NHB: VCNS Papers Box 110, VCNS 62/3 Pt III, Whetstone to VCNS, 22 October 1981. **60** Ibid., Dalton to VCNS, 3 March 1982. **61** NHB: VCNS Papers Box 110, VCNS 62/3 Pt IV, Dalton to VCNS, 25 May 1983. **62** NHB: VCNS Papers Box 110, VCNS 62/3 Pt III, Whetstone to VCNS, 22 October 1981. **63** TNA: DEFE 69/1116, Draft Operational Concept for Maritime Anti-Air Warfare, November 1982, pp. 5–6. **64** Grove and Thompson, *Battle for the Fjords*, p. 24. **65** TNA: DEFE 69/1116, Operational Concept, pp. 6–7. **66** Ibid., pp. 7–8. **67** Ibid., p. 18. **68** Ibid., p. 36. **69** TNA: DEFE 69/1116, ROW5 to AD(ME), 15 November 1982. **70** This particular concept document does not seem to have been fully endorsed by the Chiefs of Staff, as it was overtaken by an entirely different document on the same subject by the newly raised Concepts group within the Central Staffs. Written by an Army 1*, the document was not the carefully crafted compromise between the RN and RAF that previous such iterations had been, so both services felt free to criticise it heavily and pick up on its poor understanding of elements of both the naval and air aspects. It does not seem to have proceeded any further either. The Sharpe document does nonetheless provide an important statement of the Navy's thinking in the early 1980s. TNA: DEFE 69/1116, Beckett to Various, 31 May 1983, covering 'An Operational Concept for Maritime Anti-Air Warfare 1990-2005' (annotations by DN Plans); Walker to Beckett, 17 June 1983. **71** NHB: Admiralty Board Papers, A/P(84)16, 'The Naval Programme', 29 November 1984. **72** Ibid. **73** Ibid., Annex A. **74** Hennessy and Jinks, *Silent Deep*, pp. 375–7; Friedman, *Naval Weapon Systems 1997-98*, p. 612. **75** TNA: DEFE 13/1357, Controller to Minister of State, 20 October 1977, Hennessy and Jinks, *Silent Deep*, p. 375; Friedman, *Naval Weapon Systems 1997-98*, pp. 612–13. **76** Hennessy and Jinks, *Silent Deep*, pp. 376–7. **77** The Naval Staff permitted the public dissemination of the 100km figure in April 1984: NHB: VCNS Papers Box 49: VCNS 40/11/1 Part 6, VCNS to Gueritz, 9 April 1984; Friedman, *Naval Weapon Systems 1989*, p. 366, mentions 100 nautical miles. Both should be caveated with the fact that a number of factors effect detection range, although bearing accuracy generally decreases as the range increases. **78** NHB: Boscombe Box 59/T151727, Sonar Type 2031 Optrial, OEG Report 8/78. **79** NHB: Lowestoft Box/T113360, Smy to CINCFLEET, 2 August 1978; T113359, Smy to CINCFLEET, 13 August 1979; T113358, Chestnutt to CINCFLEET, 22 September 1980. See also TNA: DEFE 13/1357, Controller to Minister of State, 26 October 1978. **80** NHB: Cleopatra Box/T74280, Liardet to CINCFLEET, 26 July 1984. **81** NHB: Lowestoft Box/T113352, Howat to CINCFLEET, 30 January 1984. **82** NHB: Lowestoft Box/T113350, Howat to CINCFLEET, 17 October 1984. **83** NHB: Fleet Requirements Committee/T56345, 'Sonar 2031 Shipfitting Policy', 15 March 1978; VCNS Papers Box 49: VCNS 40/11/4, Controller to Minister (DP) 11 February 1982; also see Osborne and Sowdon, *Leander Class Frigates*, pp. 74–8. **84** NHB: VCNS Papers Box 49: VCNS 40/11/1 Part 6, ACNS(OR) to Controller, 26 March 1982. **85** NHB: VCNS Papers Box 49: VCNS 40/11/1 Part 6, DNOT to DNOR,

19 December 1983; Fleet Operations Programmes, 1985-86. **86** NHB: VCNS Papers Box 49: VCNS 40/11/4, APS/Minister (DP) to Sec/CofN, 16 March 1982. **87** *HMS Illustrious: the first two years*, pp. 21–2; NHB: Illustrious Box 1/T51438, Kerr to CINCFLEET, 20 April 1984. **88** NHB: Illustrious Box 1/T51438, Kerr to CINCFLEET, 20 April 1984. **89** Ibid. **90** NHB: Cleopatra Box/T74280, Liardet to CINCFLEET, 26 July 1984. **91** Ibid. **92** NHB: Sirius Box/T190805, Melson to CINCFLEET, 12 June 1984. **93** NHB: Cleopatra Box/T74280, Liardet to CINCFLEET, 26 July 1984. **94** Ibid. **95** NHB: Lowestoft Box/T113354, Buckle to CINCFLEET, 8 February 1982. **96** The author would like to thank his father, who served aboard a towed-array *Leander*, for this information. **97** *HMS Illustrious: the first two years*, pp. 20–1. **98** NHB: Illustrious RoP 20 April 1984, T51438. **99** NHB: Boscombe Box 57/T151704, FOAS: Trial Gypsum report, 1984. **100** NHB: Sirius Box/T109805, Melson to CINCFLEET, 12 June 1984. **101** Friedman, *World Naval Weapon Systems* (1989), p. 366. **102** NHB: Cleopatra Box/T143280, Newman to CINCFLEET, 13 June 1985. **103** NHB: Cleopatra Box/T74278, Dalrymple-Smith to CINCFLEET, 17 June 1986. **104** NHB: Argonaut Box/T29690, de Halpert to CINCFLEET, 4 November 1987. **105** NHB: Argonaut Box/T29691, Barton to CINCFLEET, 9 October 1987. **106** NHB: Fleet Operations Programmes, 1987-89. **107** TNA: DEFE 13/1357, VCNS to MinState, 24 August 1978. **108** Although the North Atlantic remained the core area for RN involvement in NATO exercises, it did still contribute to NATO Mediterranean exercises, although generally at a much lower level than in the early 1970s. One exception to this was the RN involvement in Exercise Display Determination in September 1983, which involved *Illustrious, Hermes* in the commando carrier role (40 Cdo embarked) and the frigates *Leander, Ariadne* and *Arethusa*. NHB Exercises Box 10/T47298, Rogers to Sec/1SL, 15 September 1983. **109** NHB: Fleet Operations Programme, September 1982. **110** NHB: Fleet Operations Programmes, March 1985 and March 1987. **111** NHB: Fleet Operations Programmes, March 1989, September 1989, March 1990, September 1990; See also Grove and Thompson, *Battle for the Fjords*, p. 34. This account was written as this transition was taking place and as a result did not anticipate the ending of Ocean Safari and its replacement by North Star. **112** NHB: Exercises Box 10/T83797, O'Riordon to Sec/VCNS, 29 March 1984, section d. **113** Ocean Safari 83, Northern Wedding 86 and Teamwork 90 all saw two mine countermeasures squadrons involved; more normally there would be one; in the early 1980s they were sometimes supplemented by STUFT stern trawlers operating as deep ocean sweepers. NHB: Fleet Operations Programmes, 1983-90. **114** NHB: Fleet Operations Programme, September 1990. **115** Grove and Thompson, *Battle for the Fjords*, p. 34. **116** Johnstone-Bryden, *HMS Illustrious*, p. 35. **117** For example, Teamwork 86 included *Intrepid*, three LSLs and nine ships taken up from trade for the amphibious role. NHB: Liverpool Box/T51034, Bracelin to CINCFLEET, 13 October 1986. **118** The only major exception seems to have been in 1989 when SNFL was not involved in North Star 89, although it was present at Sharp Spear 89. NHB: Fleet Operations Programme, March and September 1989. **119** NHB: Invincible Box 1/T51260, Layman to CINCFLEET, 26 July 1985. **120** Grove and Thompson, *Battle for the Fjords*, pp. 24–6. **121** Ibid., p. 26. **122** Ibid., pp. 34–6. **123** NHB: Ark Royal Box 3/T29910, Weatherall to CINCFLEET, 20 November 1986. **124** Ibid., Annex D. **125** Freedman and Michaels, *Evolution of Nuclear Strategy*, pp. 532–3. **126** The 1963 MoD War Book was declassified in 2000 and is referred to in Hennessy, *Secret State*, pp. 193–8. **127** TNA: DEFE 24/1418, Gerard-Pearse to various, 2 June 1978; for the Hilex Exercise series, see NATO website, Antoine Gott, 'NATO crisis management exercises: preparing for the unknown', 7 February 2020: NATO Review (accessed 2 November 2023). **128** TNA: DEFE 24/1418, Brinn to Various, 4 October 1978, Annexes B, C1 and C5. **129** Ibid., Annex C2. **130** Ibid., Annexes C3, C6, C7, C8 and C11. **131** Ibid., Annexes C15, C16 and C17. **132** Ibid., Annex C18. **133** NHB: Logistics Box 2/T47977, 'The Logistic Support of Naval War Operations', 26 March 1976, p. 2. **134** Ibid., pp. 2–3. **135** Ibid., pp. 3–8. **136** Murray, *Royal Naval Auxiliary Service*, p. 17. **137** TNA: DEFE 69/643, Turner to ACNS(O), 15 February 1978.

Chapter 19: Reform and Overstretch
1 NHB: MoD Navy News Release, 17A/81, 1 June 1981. **2** NHB: Naval biographies boxes, Anthony Tippet. **3** NHB: MoD Navy News Release, 31B/80, 7 August 1980; *The Independent*, obituary, 22 February 1994. **4** Johnston, 'More Power to the Centre'. The author would like to thank Stephen Prince for drawing his attention to this article. See also Hill, *Lewin of Greenwich*, pp. 342–4. **5** Hill, *Lewin of Greenwich*, pp. 344–5. **6** Johnston, 'More Power to the Centre', p. 9. **7** Boren, 'Britain's 1981 Defence Review', pp. 431–2. **8** HMSO, Statement on the Defence Estimates 1984, Volume 1 (Cmnd

9227-I, 1984), p. 12. **9** Broadbent, *The Military and Government*, pp. 67–9. **10** Heseltine had first introduced MINIS at the Department of the Environment, where he had been Secretary of State until moving to the Ministry. Heseltine, *Life in the Jungle*, pp. 190–4. **11** Thatcher, *Downing Street Years*, p. 424. **12** Broadbent, *Military and Government*, pp. 69–70; NHB: 'The Organisation of the Naval Staff 1927-2000', p. 151. **13** NHB: VCNS Papers, Box 44, ACNS(P) 13/21 Fid III, Farnfield to MINIS Unit, 12 June 1984. **14** Ibid., Heseltine to PUS, CDS et al, 8 September 1983. **15** Broadbent, *Military and Government*, pp. 70–1. **16** HMSO, Statement on the Defence Estimates 1984, Volume 1, (Cmnd 9227-I, 1984), pp. 12–14. **17** NHB: 'Evolution of the Naval Staff', pp. 153–5. In later reforms during the 1990s DNOT would be transferred out of the Naval Staff and into the new Permanent Joint Headquarters. **18** HMSO, Statement on the Defence Estimates 1984, Volume 1, (Cmnd 9227-I, 1984), p. 14. **19** NHB: 'Evolution of the Naval Staff', pp. 152–3. **20** *Flight Deck*, Issue 1, 1988, pp. 2–5; NHB: 'Evolution of the Naval Staff', p. 155. **21** NHB: Navy Board Minutes and Papers, 1985-90. **22** Compare the 1984 and 1985 Board discussions and decisions on the Sketch Estimates and Long Term Costings. NHB: Admiralty Board Minutes, A/M(84)1, item 2, 1 February 1984; A/M(84)4, item 2, 13 November 1984; Navy Board Minutes, NAVB/M(85)1, item 1, 14 February 1985; NAVB/M(85)8, item 3, 31 October 1985. **23** Having nominal control over the operational requirements and planning side of the old single-service Staffs was not the panacea to the Ministry's problems that some at the Centre might have thought. Following further reforms in the 2010s, operational requirements for equipment were devolved back down to the single-services. **24** NHB: VCNS Papers Box 45, VCNS 13/21/7 Pt II, 'Overall Star Count', Appendix 2 to DGMA 322/84, 12 June 1984; Broadbent, *Military and Government*, pp. 218–19. **25** Broadbent, *Military and Government*, pp. 73–4. **26** NHB: 'Evolution of the Naval Staff', p. 156. **27** Ibid., pp. 157–8. **28** HMSO: Statement on the Defence Estimates 1989, Volume 1 (Cm 675-I, May 1989), pp. 43–4. **29** D K Brown, *A Century of Naval Construction*, pp. 328–9, 366–7. **30** NHB: Admiralty Board Sub-Committee Minutes: ABSC/M(82)4, item 2, 7 October 1982; Admiralty Board Minutes: A/M(84)5, item 5, 5 December 1984. The nine sites were: Portsdown, Portland, Teddington, Gosport, Poole, Portsmouth (laboratory in the Dockyard, diving at HMS *Vernon*), Devonport and Rosyth. HMSO: *Civil Service Yearbook 1986* (London, 1986), columns 177-181. **31** The RAF's first post-reform Chief of the Air Staff, Sir David Craig, found that the new structures did not significantly diminish the RAF's power and influence within the system, the situation was very likely the same for the Navy. See Noble, *British Defence Policy and the RAF*, p. 216, fn. 74. **32** NHB: Admiralty Board Minutes: A/M(82)1, 4 March 1982, item 3; Admiralty Board Papers: A/P(82)1, 26 February 1982, '1982 Long Term Costing'. **33** NHB: Admiralty Board Minutes: A/M(82)3, 25 November 1982, item 2; A/M(83)1, 3 February 1983, item 2; Admiralty Board Papers: A/P(82)9, 19 November 1982, 'Sketch Estimates 1983/84'; A/P(83)1, 27 January 1983, '1983 Long Term Costings'. **34** TNA: DEFE 24/2729, A/P(83)1, 27 January 1983, '1983 Long Term Costings', and Annex A. **35** Ibid. **36** TNA: DEFE 24/2702, A/M(83)1, 3 February 1983, item 2. **37** TNA: PREM 19/1187, Policy Unit note of 20 October 1983, covered by Turnbull to Galloway, same date. **38** Ibid. **39** TNA: PREM 19/977, Gieve to Scholar, 14 October 1982. **40** TNA: DEFE 24/2702, A/M(83)3, 24 November 1983, item 4; Admiralty Board Papers: A/P(83)3, 14 November 1983, 'Sketch Estimates 1984/85 and LTC 84'. **41** For the decision to end the 3 per cent rises, see Noble, *British Defence Policy and the RAF*, pp. 205–06, 209–11, 213. **42** For example see, Noble, *British Defence Policy and the RAF*, pp. 217–26. **43** NHB: Navy Board Papers, NAVB/P(85)1, 11 February 1985, '1985 Long Term Costing'; DPSG(85)1 (Revised), 5 February 1985, Annex C. **44** NHB: Navy Board Papers, NAVB/P(85)7, 25 June 1985, 'Audit of the Royal Navy'. **45** These procurements were all listed as unfunded, and aside from the amphibious capability, were classed as category II priorities. NHB: Navy Board Papers, NAVB/P(85)7, 25 June 1985, 'Audit of the Royal Navy', Annex G. **46** TNA: DEFE 69/908, Abbott to Sec/1SL, 21 March 1986, Annex A. **47** TNA: DEFE 69/908, Abbott to ACNS, 4 March 1987, enclosure 1, Annex A. **48** NHB: Bristol Box/T73075, West to CINCFLEET, 12 November 1987. **49** Friedman, *British Destroyers and Frigates*, p. 339. **50** Sharpe, ed., *Jane's Fighting Ships 1993-1994*, p. 723. **51** NHB: Navy Board Minutes, NAVB/M(88)1, 7 January 1988, item 2. **52** NHB: Navy Board Minutes, NAVB/M(89)1, 5 January 1989, item 2. **53** HMSO: 'Statement on the Defence Estimates 1990, Volume 1' (Cm 1022-I, 1990), p. 53. **54** NHB: Navy Board Minutes, NAVB/M(90)1, 4 January 1990, item 2. **55** In the late 1980s, the Defence Secretary, George Younger, was seen by the Prime Minister's Office as insufficiently hard-nosed and willing to countenance effective cost controls and if necessary project cancellations. TNA:

PREM 19/2073, Robson to Butler, 24 March 1987; Norgrove to Thatcher, 1 May 1987. Even Charles Powell, who was sympathetic to the Ministry, had some doubts about Younger's ability to push the Chiefs of Staff into economies: PREM 19/3252, Powell to Thatcher, 28 June 1988. **56** Stoddart, *Facing Down the Soviet Union*, p. 198. **57** Pound Sterling Live Website: British Pound / US Dollar Historical Reference Rates from Bank of England for 2000 (poundsterlinglive.com) (accessed 24 November 2023). **58** HMSO: 'Statement on the Defence Estimates 1991', Volume 1 (Cm 1599-I, July 1991) p. 65. **59** Saunders, ed., *Jane's Fighting Ships 2001-2002*, p. 754. **60** Hennessy and Jinks, *Silent Deep*, pp. 540–1. **61** Wells, *Tale of Two Navies*, pp. 165–7. **62** HMSO: 'Torpedo Programme and Design and Procurement of Ships', Committee of Public Accounts, 1985-86 session, 40th report, p. vi. **63** NHB: Finance Box 3: 'Long Term Costing Assumptions 1984', Appendix B4. **64** HMSO: 'Statement on the Defence Estimates 1992' (Cm 1981, July 1992) p. 33. **65** Moore, ed. *Jane's Fighting Ships 1987-1988*, p. 660. **66** Hobbs, *British Aircraft Carriers*, pp. 321, 326. **67** The test aircraft had been XZ450. It was lost in the Falklands campaign. Sturtivant, Burrow and Howard, *Fleet Air Arm Fixed Wing Aircraft*, p. 80. **68** HMSO: 'Statement on the Defence Estimates 1985, Volume 1' (Cmnd 9430-I, 1985) p. 26. **69** Sturtivant, Burrow and Howard, *Fleet Air Arm Fixed Wing Aircraft*, pp. 86–90. **70** Hobbs, *British Carrier Strike Fleet*, pp. 483–9. **71** Friedman, *Seapower and Space*, pp. 166–72. **72** HMSO: 'Ministry of Defence: The Annual Statement on Major Defence Projects', Committee of Public Accounts, Session 1989-1990, 9th Report, 14 March 1990, p. 19. **73** Lake and Crutch, *Tornado*, pp. 40–4. **74** Morris, 'UK Control and Reporting System', pp. 99–101. **75** RAF Historical Society, *Defending Northern Skies 1915-1995* (Newcastle, 1996), Figure VI, p. 107. **76** Noble, *British Defence Policy and the RAF*, pp. 241-250; HMSO: Statement on the Defence Estimates 1985, Volume 1 (Cmnd 9430-I, 1985), p. 21; Statement on the Defence Estimates 1986, Volume 1 (Cmnd 9763-I, 1986), p. 31; Statement on the Defence Estimates 1987, Volume 1 (Cm 101-I, 1987), p. 45. **77** Franks, *Shackleton*, p. 59. **78** Lake and Crutch, *Tornado*, pp. 107–09. **79** HMSO: 'Minutes of Evidence: Air to Air Refuelling', Committee of Public Accounts, Session 1988-89, 14 December 1988. **80** Balance, Howard and Sturtivant, *Squadrons and Units of the Fleet Air Arm*, p. 150. **81** Jerram-Croft, *The Royal Navy Lynx*, pp. 148–56. **82** Allen, *Sea King*, p. 50. **83** HMSO: 'EH101 Anglo-Italian Helicopter Project', Committee of Public Accounts, Session 1987-88, 29th Report, 15 June 1988. **84** Sharpe, ed., *Jane's Fighting Ships 1989-90*, p. 679. **85** Johnston-Bryden, *HMS Ocean*, pp. 18–19; HMSO: Statement on the Defence Estimates 1987, Volume 1, (Cm 101-I, 1987), p. 25. **86** Adams and Smith, *Royal Fleet Auxiliary*, pp. 142–3, 146. **87** NHB: VCNS Papers, Box 36, ACNS(P) 10/13 Fid IV, Oswald to ACNS(P) et al, 3 April 1984. **88** NHB: VCNS Papers, Box 36, VCNS 10/13/pt III, Larken to ACNS(P), 25 November 1983. **89** Ibid., DCFMP(N) to ACNS(P) et al, 10 February 1984. **90** NHB: VCNS Papers, Box 36, ACNS(P) 13/1/3/2, Wilson to Sec/VCNS, 20 June 1984, Annex A. **91** TNA: DEFE 69/1321/1, Cobbold to various, 25 April 1983; Oswald to ACDS(C) et al, 15 November 1984. **92** TNA: DEFE 69/908, Ross to DN Plans, 13 February 1986. **93** Hansard: HC Deb 9 December 1986, vol. 107, cc. 178-179; HMSO: Statement on the Defence Estimates 1989, Volume 1 (Cm 675-I, 1989), p. 24. **94** Johnston-Bryden, *Ocean*, pp. 20–1. **95** TNA: DEFE 69/1916, DCDS(S) and Controller to CSA, 2 August 1991. **96** HMSO: Statement on the Defence Estimates 1988, Volume 1 (Cm 334-I, 1988), p. 26; Johnston-Bryden, *HMS Bulwark*, pp. 9–10. **97** NHB: Navy Board Minutes, NAVB/M(90)1, 4 January 1990, item 2. **98** Johnston-Bryden, *Bulwark*, pp. 10–11. **99** Adams and Smith, *Royal Fleet Auxiliary*, p. 145. **100** TSO: National Audit Office, The Landing Ship Dock (Auxiliary) Project, 30 November 2007, HC 98-III, session 2007-08, p. 6. **101** Johnston-Bryden, *Ocean*, pp. 21–44; Johnston-Bryden, *Bulwark*, pp. 12–14, 20–33. **102** Improvements during the 1990s included the updating of the command system from ADAWS to ADIMP, and improved radar systems. Sharpe, ed., *Jane's Fighting Ships 1995-1996*, p. 765. **103** HMSO: Statement on the Defence Estimates 1985, Volume 1 (Cmnd 9430-I, 1985), p. 18; NHB: CNGF Box 106/T145831, Lessons Learnt from the Premature Termination of the Programme NATO Frigate for the 1990s, 8 February 1990, pp. 2–5. **104** NHB: CNGF Box 106/T145831, Lessons Learnt from the Premature Termination of the Programme NATO Frigate for the 1990s, 8 February 1990, pp. 5–7. **105** NHB: Navy Board Minutes, NAVB/M(88)1, 7 January 1988, item 2. **106** NHB: CNGF Box 106/T145831, Lessons Learnt from the Premature Termination of the Programme NATO Frigate for the 1990s, 8 February 1990, pp. 8–10. **107** NHB: CNGF Box 96/T145525, Marsh to Oswald, June 1990; Box 72/T144908, Future Frigate First Progress Report, Draft, September 1990, pp. 2–3. **108** TNA: DEFE 69/1803, Cox to Sec/Controller, 26 June 1990; Burleigh to PS/USofS(DP), 25 January 1991; Future Frigate

Procurement Strategy (5th draft), July 1990. **109** HMSO: Defending our Future: Statement on the Defence Estimates 1993 (Cm 2270, July 1993), p. 63. **110** Hansard: HC Deb, 14 December 1982, Vol. 34, cc. 129-130. **111** NHB: VCNS Papers, Box 123, ACNS(P) 40/17 Fid III, Hogg to Sec VCNS et al, 22 October 1982, covering draft ORC submission. **112** Ibid., Mason to Controller, 28 October 1982; Hogg to VCNS, 5 November 1982. **113** Ibid., Hogg to ACNS(OR), 4 November 1982. **114** TNA: PREM 19/977 Mottram to Coles, 10 December 1982; NHB: VCNS Papers, Box 123, ACNS(P) 40/17 Fid III, Cragg to Head DS11, 6 December 1982. **115** NHB: VCNS Papers, Box 123, ACNS(P) 40/17 Fid III, Record of Meeting to discuss Battle Loss Replacements, 2 December 1982. **116** TNA: PREM 19/977, Nott to Thatcher, 6 December 1982. **117** Friedman, *British Destroyers and Frigates*, p. 309. **118** NHB: VCNS Papers, Box 123, ACNS(P) 40/17 Fid III, Nott to Thatcher, 6 December 1982; Hughes loose minute, 16 December 1982; DG Ships to Controller, 18 February 1983. **119** Ibid., Controller and VCNS to Min(DP), 1 December 1983; DCDS to CoS, 12 January 1984. **120** NHB: VCNS Papers, Box 123, ACNS(P) 40/17 Fid III, DUS(N) to 1SL et al, 17 January 1983. **121** NHB: VCNS Papers, Box 123, ACNS(P) 40/17/2 Fid I, Controller to Min(DP), 10 February 1983. **122** Ibid., Morgan to Controller and VCNS, 27 June 1983. **123** Ibid., DCDS to SecSt, 31 March 1983. **124** TNA: PREM 19/977, Moore to Thatcher, 1 October 1982; Nott to Thatcher, 12 November 1982. **125** NHB: VCNS Papers, Box 123, ACNS(P) 40/17/2 Fid I, Morgan to ACNS(OR), 15 June 1983. **126** Brown and Moore, *Rebuilding the Royal Navy*, p. 111. **127** NHB: Navy Board Papers, NAVB/P(87)14, Increased autonomy for the Type 23, 6 July 1987. In the event, further improving stowage on the same hull enabled the Type 23 to have deployability patterns not too dissimilar to previous classes. **128** DUS(N) warned that the Navy was at risk of reinforcing its reputation for 'extravagance in our surface ships' which had been gained with the Type 22 procurement. NHB: VCNS Papers, Box 123, ACNS(P) 40/17 Fid III, DUS(N) to 1SL et al, 17 January 1983. **129** NHB: Norfolk Box 1/T81544, Band to FOF1, 5 July 1991; T81538, First of Class Report, 1 March 1991, section 1, paras. 40–57. The author understands that both the mixed messdecks and the communal tasks soon reverted to earlier practices (the author would like to thank Andrew Livsey for pointing this out). **130** NHB: Norfolk Box 1/T81538, First of Class Report, 1 March 1991, section 1, paras. 40–57. **131** Ibid., paras. 103–112. **132** NHB: *Broadsheet 2000/2001* (London, 2000), pp. 16-18, 107; *Broadsheet 2001/2002* (London, 2001), pp. 30–3, 107. **133** NHB: Norfolk Box 1/T81538, First of Class Report, 1 March 1991, section 1, paras. 1-13; T81544, Band to FOF1, 5 July 1991. **134** HMSO: 'The Procurement of Major Defence Equipment', Defence Committee, 5th Report, Session 1987-88, pp. xi–xiii. **135** Friedman, *British Destroyers and Frigates*, p. 309; Friedman, *Naval Weapon Systems 1997-98*, pp. 113–14. **136** NHB: VCNS Papers, Box 61, VCNS 10/1/13/7, '1SL Notes on Size and Shape', 7 April 1983. **137** NHB: VCNS Papers, Box 83, ACNS(P) 40/26, Fid II, Hogg to VCNS, 26 May 1983. **138** Ibid., Stanley to USofS(DP). **139** Ibid., DCDS to VCNS, 4 October 1983. **140** Ibid., Mottram to PS/USofS(DP), 10 October 1983. **141** Ibid., Controller to DCDS, 11 June 1984. **142** Newcastle University Marine Technology Special Collection: OPV 3 submissions, Hall Russell, Yarrow and Vosper Thornycroft, 1984. **143** NHB: VCNS Papers, Box 83, ACNS(P) 40/26, Fid II, DUS(N) to VCNS, 10 November 1983. **144** NHB: VCNS Papers, Box 57, VCNS 40/102 Pt II, Fleet Requirements Committee, Minutes 11 April 1983. **145** Ibid., Marsh to VCNS, 28 February 1983, enclosure, 'The AOR'. **146** Ibid., Dalton to Secretary, Way Ahead Committee, 7 December 1982. **147** NHB: VCNS Papers, Box 57, VCNS 40/102 Pt II, Marsh to VCNS, 28 February 1983, enclosure, 'The AOR'. **148** Sharpe, ed. *Jane's Fighting Ships 1989-90*, p. 678. **149** Ibid., p. 669. **150** NHB: Navy Board Papers, NAVB/P(86)7, 'Alternative Vessels for Auxiliary Minesweepers', 13 June 1986. **151** Sharpe, ed. *Jane's Fighting Ships 1989-90*, p. 670. **152** Brown and Moore, *Rebuilding the Royal Navy*, pp. 142–3. **153** Elliott, *Royal Navy Task Force 321.1*, pp. 8–9, 24–5, 36–7. **154** Murphy, *Shipbuilding in the United Kingdom*, pp. 118–19. **155** Johnman and Murphy, *British Shipbuilding and the State*, pp. 217–19. **156** Murphy, *Shipbuilding in the United Kingdom*, pp. 127–8. **157** Ibid., p. 126. **158** Tyne built ships website, Swan Hunter page: Swan Hunter Group Tyne (tynebuiltships.co.uk) (accessed 19/11/23). **159** Johnman and Murphy, *British Shipbuilding and the State*, p. 239. **160** NHB: VCNS Papers, Box 123, VCNS 40/17 Pt IV, Tebbit to Heseltine, 9 April 1984; Heseltine to Tebbit, 10 April 1984; Evans to AUS(MAT N),13 April 1984; Tebbit to Heseltine, 13 April 1984. See also Heseltine, *Life in the Jungle*, pp. 277–9, for his perspective on the Cammell Laird Contract. **161** Johnman and Murphy, *British Shipbuilding and the State*, pp. 221, 223. **162** Friedman, *British Destroyer and Frigates*, p. 339. **163** Johnman and Murphy,

British Shipbuilding and the State, pp. 224-225. **164** Murphy, *Shipbuilding in the United Kingdom*, p. 127. **165** ONS website: An overview of the UK Labour Market, 27 February 2015: An overview of the UK labour market - Office for National Statistics (ons.gov.uk) (accessed 3/12/23); Timmins, *Five Giants*, pp. 414–15.

Chapter 20: To The End
1 NHB: Navy Board Papers, NAVB/P(85)3, Naval Manpower Strategy, 1 May 1985. **2** Ibid., NAVB/P(87)4, Audit of the Royal Navy: Manpower, 5 June 1987. **3** NHB: Navy Board Minutes, NAVB/M(86)6, item 2, 18 September 1985. **4** NHB: Navy Board Papers, NAVB/P(88)5, Audit of the Royal Navy: Manpower, 25 May 1988. **5** Ibid., NAVB/P(86)13, Audit of the Royal Navy: Manpower, 30 June 1986. **6** Ibid., NAVB/P(88)5, Audit of the Royal Navy: Manpower, 25 May 1988. **7** Ibid., NAVB/P(89)5, Naval Manpower, An Approach for LTC 90, June 1989. **8** Ibid., NAVB/P(88)5, Audit of the Royal Navy: Manpower, 25 May 1988. **9** Ibid., NAVB/P(86)16, Meeting the Naval Manpower Requirement, 18 September 1986. **10** Ibid., NAVB/P(87)4, Audit of the Royal Navy: Manpower, 5 June 1987. **11** NHB: Navy Board Minutes, NAVB/M(85)2, item 3, 9 May 1985. **12** NHB: Navy Board Papers, NAVB/P(87)4, Audit of the Royal Navy: Manpower, 5 June 1987. **13** TNA: DEFE 24/1003, 'Housing the Married Serviceman' (Leitch Report), November 1976, pp. 101–03; Draft PPO committee minutes, May 1977. **14** TNA: DEFE 25/392, Draft PPO committee minutes, October 1979. **15** HMSO: Statement on the Defence Estimates 1989, Volume 1 (Cm 675-I, May 1989), p. 43. **16** NHB: Principal Personnel Officers Committee, PPO 25/90, 'Sale of Surplus Married Quarters', 2 July 1990. **17** NHB: Navy Board Papers, NAVB/P(88)10, Retention of RN Personnel, 27 May 1988. **18** HMSO: Statement on the Defence Estimates 1990, Volume 1 (Cm 1022-I, April 1990), p. 26. **19** NHB: Navy Board Papers, NAVB/P(88)5, Audit of the Royal Navy: Manpower, 25 May 1988. **20** HMSO: Statement on the Defence Estimates 1990, Volume 1 (Cm 1022-I, April 1990), p. 53. **21** HMSO: Statement on the Defence Estimates 1991, Volume 1 (Cm 1559-I, July 1991), p. 47. **22** TNA: DEFE 69/1616, 'Report of Study into employment of WRNS Personnel in the Royal Navy', March 1989, pp. 10–13. **23** Ibid., p. 11. **24** NHB: Navy Board Papers, NAVB/P(90)1, 'Employment of WRNS Personnel in the RN', January 1990. **25** TNA: DEFE 69/1616, 'Report of Study into employment of WRNS Personnel in the Royal Navy', March 1989, pp. i–iii, 8–10. **26** NHB: Navy Board Papers, Oughton to Sec/CNS et al, 22 February 1990, covering NAVB/P(90)1, 'Employment of WRNS Personnel in the RN', January 1990. **27** Stanley, *Women and the Royal Navy*, pp. 156–8. **28** Ibid., pp. 179–82. **29** NHB: Norfolk Box/T81544, Band to FOF1, 5 July 1991. **30** In addition, women would not be able to go to sea in minehunters, at least initially, as some had not yet been converted to mixed crewing. NHB: DCI RN 259/93, 12 November 1993. **31** Houghton, '"Alien Seamen" or "Imperial Family"?', pp. 1429–61. **32** TNA: DEFE 13/782, PPO Committee: PPO 83/65, 28 May 1965. **33** Ibid. **34** NHB: Eagle Box 1, Reports of Proceedings 1968-78 Volume, Cecil to CinCFleet, 21 January 1972, plus attachments and following papers, pp. 286–300. **35** TNA: DEFE 69/1616, 'Report of Study into employment of WRNS Personnel in the Royal Navy', March 1989, p. 9. **36** NHB: Manning (Ratings) Box 8/T8265, Peat Marwick McLintock, Ethnic Minority Recruitment to the Armed Services, Volume 1 (July 1989), pp. 18, 21, 23. **37** Ibid., p. 2. **38** Ibid., pp. 27, 31–2. **39** Hansard: Armed Forces (Discipline), 17 June 1991, Volume 193, Column 91, John Reid. **40** Gov.uk website: Richard Laux, '50 years of collecting ethnicity data', 7 March 2019: 50 years of collecting ethnicity data - History of government (blog.gov.uk) (accessed 7 January 2024); Local Government Chronicle, 'Ethnicity in the 1991 Census, Volume 2', 11 June 1996: ETHNICITY IN THE 1991 CENSUS: VOLUME 2 | Local Government Chronicle (LGC) (lgcplus.com) (accessed 7 January 2024); Hansard: Armed Forces (Discipline), 17 June 1991, Volume 193, Column 114, Archie Hamilton. **41** HMSO: 'Statement on the Defence Estimates 1992' (Cm 1981), July 1992, p. 52; 'Statement on the Defence Estimates 1995: Stable Forces in a Strong Britain' (Cm 2800), May 1995, p. 86. **42** TSO: 'Ministry of Defence: Performance Report 1999/2000' (Cm 5000), December 2000, p. 26. **43** This section is heavily indebted to the author's colleague, Kate Brett, whom he thanks for letting him make use of her research in this area. **44** Sexual Offences Act 1967, the exemption for the three services was set out in subsection five. **45** NHB: CB 4005, The Manual of Navy Security (1970, with changes up to 1987). **46** NHB: BR 31, The Queen's Regulations for the Royal Navy (first issued January 1967), Change 72, January 1987. **47** NHB: DCI(RN) 75/87 and DCI(RN) (In Confidence) 2/87. It is probably the latter that is referred to in anonymous testimony to the Etherton Review: Terence

Etherton, 'LGBT Veterans Review: Final Report' (May 2023) p. 64: 6.8313_CO_LGBT Veterans Review (publishing.service.gov.uk) (accessed 1/11/23). **48** Buckle, *The Way Out*, pp. 27–9. Testimony to the Etherton Review suggests that homophobic attitudes were widespread in the Navy at this time, so the new promulgation of policy could well have gone 'along the grain' of service opinion. Terence Etherton, 'LGBT Veterans Review: Final Report' (May 2023) pp. 58–70: 6.8313_CO_LGBT Veterans Review (publishing.service.gov.uk) (accessed 1/11/23). **49** Goldsmith, 'History of the Ministry of Defence Financial Organisation', p. 23-4. **50** NHB: Admiralty Board Sub-Committee Papers, ABSC/P(82)7, 'Management of Ship Maintenance and Repair', 1 October 1982. **51** Goldsmith, 'History of the Ministry of Defence Financial Organisation', pp. 23-3 to 23-4. **52** TNA: DEFE 13/2028, CFS to PS/SofS, 29 December 1983. **53** NHB: Admiralty Board Minutes, A/M(84)2, 7 March 1984, item 2. **54** TNA: DEFE 13/2028, Levene to Heseltine, 9 February 1984, covering 'Future of the Royal Dockyards'; NHB: Admiralty Board Papers, A/P(84)2, 'Future of the Royal Dockyards', 27 February 1984. **55** NHB: Admiralty Board Minutes, A/M(84)2, 7 March 1984, item 2. **56** Ibid., A/M(84)3, 25 June 1984, item 2. **57** NHB: Admiralty Board Papers, A/P(84)9, 'Future of the Royal Dockyards', 18 June 1984. **58** NHB: Admiralty Board Minutes, A/M(84)3, 25 June 1984, item 2. **59** Legislation.gov.uk website: Dockyard Services Act 1986, Chapter 52, 25 July 1986. **60** TNA: DEFE 69/1268, Haworth to Ellis, 4 January 1985. **61** Law, 'Neither Colonial, Nor Historic', pp.169–71. **62** At Portsmouth, in parallel to the contracting-out of the dockyards, a civilian Fleet Maintenance and Repair Organisation was set up in October 1984 alongside the service Fleet Maintenance Base to undertake '3rd and 4th level repair work' and 'residual' refit work. It had a workforce of 2,600, and by the 1990s it was very close to being a refit organisation (i.e. a dockyard) in all but name. When the remaining dockyards were fully privatised in the late 1990s, the FMRO was privatised alongside Devonport. TNA: DEFE 13/2029, Lee to Viggers, 14 March 1984; HMSO: 'Ministry of Defence: Fleet Maintenance', Committee of Public Accounts Session 1989-90, 42nd Report, 24 October 1990, p. xiii. **63** HMSO: 'Ministry of Defence: Transfer of Royal Dockyards to Commercial Management', Committee of Public Accounts, Session 1988-89, 2nd Report, 30 November 1988, pp. v–vii. **64** Ibid., pp. vii–viii. **65** Ibid., p. 3. **66** Ibid., p. viii. **67** TNA: DEFE 13/2029, PUS to Heseltine, 16 April 1984; Law, 'Neither Colonial, Nor Historic', pp. 171–3. **68** HMSO: 'Ministry of Defence: Fleet Maintenance', Committee of Public Accounts Session 1989-90, 42nd Report, 24 October 1990, pp. xii–xiii. **69** HMSO: 'Ministry of Defence: Transfer of Royal Dockyards to Commercial Management', National Audit Office, 3 March 1988, pp. 4–5, 20–3. **70** J Burgess, 'The Dockyard Will Provide the Pipes', p. 252. **71** HMSO: 'Ministry of Defence: Transfer of Royal Dockyards to Commercial Management', Committee of Public Accounts, Session 1988-89, 2nd Report, 30 November 1988, pp. x–xi; HMSO: 'Ministry of Defence: Transfer of Royal Dockyards to Commercial Management', National Audit Office, 3 March 1988, pp. 4–5, 20–3. **72** HMSO: 'Ministry of Defence: Fleet Maintenance', Committee of Public Accounts Session 1989-90, 42nd Report, 24 October 1990, pp. viii–xii. **73** NHB: Admiralty Board Sub Committee Papers, ABSC/P(82)2, 'The Oasis Project', 18 June 1982; Admiralty Board Sub Committee Minutes, ABSC/M(82)2, 1 July 1982, item 1; Royal Navy: *Broadsheet 82*, pp. 36–7. **74** NHB: Admiralty Board Sub Committee Papers, ABSC/P(84)1, 'The Oasis Project', 1 August 1984. **75** NHB: Norfolk Box/T81541, Perowne to FOSF, 26 November 1993. **76** NHB: VCNS Papers Box 100, ACNS(P) 30/13, Nichols to PS/Min(AF), 31 July 1981; AUS(NS) to APS/SofS, 6 April 1982. **77** NHB: Group Deployments Box 1: Black to CINCFLEET: Orient Express 83/84 Deployment Report, 30 April 1984. **78** TNA: PREM 19/2072, Heseltine to Thatcher, 15 October 1985. **79** For Australia's nuclear 'renunciation' in 1973, see Walsh, 'Surprise Down Under', pp. 12–13. **80** TNA: PREM 19/2072, Heseltine to Thatcher, 15 October 1985. **81** NHB: Group Deployments Box 1/T83476: Kerr to CINCFLEET: Global 86 Deployment Report, 11 February 1987. **82** TNA: PREM 19/7072, Younger to Thatcher, 15 October 1987. **83** NHB: Group Deployments Box 1: Woodhead to CINCFLEET: Outback 88 Deployment Report, 15 December 1988. **84** For an example of these brochures, see NHB: Group Deployments Box 2: Global 86 defence sales catalogue. **85** NHB: Operation Armilla Draft Staff History, p. 14. **86** Ibid., p. 14. **87** Ibid., p. 19. **88** Ibid., pp. 25–7. **89** Ibid., pp. 30, 33–6. **90** Ibid., p. 43. **91** Chin, 'Operations in a War Zone', pp. 184–6. **92** NHB: Operation Armilla Draft Staff History, pp. 44–6. **93** Ibid., p. 47. **94** Ibid., p. 72. **95** NHB: Brinton Box/T72996, White to Capt MCM, 1 October 1984. **96** NHB: Gavinton Box/T116379, Bruen to SO 3rd MCM Sq, 20 February 1985; Brinton Box/T72994, Wall to SO 3rd MCM Sq, 16 July 1985. **97** NHB: Operation Armilla Draft Staff History, pp. 90–2. **98** Ibid., pp. 101, 106–07. **99** Ibid., p. 112. **100** The aged *Abdiel* soon developed problems with her generators and was replaced by oceanic survey vessels of the *Hecla* class. TNA: DEFE 69/1554, Taylor to PS/Min(AF), 3 December 1987. **101** TNA: DEFE 69/1554, Crowe to Fieldhouse, 23 September 1987. **102** Ibid., Howe to Powell, 28 September 1987. **103** Ibid., Davies to PS/SofS, 30 September 1987. **104** NHB: Operation Armilla Draft Staff History, p. 129. **105** Ibid., pp. 154–5. **106** TNA: DEFE 24/3271, Wray to Slade, 16 May 1988, Background note; NHB: Operation Armilla Draft Staff History, pp. 161–2. **107** TNA: DEFE 24/3271, Reagan to Thatcher, 11 July 1988. **108** El-Shazly, *The Gulf Tanker War*, pp. 255–9. **109** NHB: Operation Armilla Draft Staff History, pp. 167–70. **110** TNA: DEFE 24/3271, Howe to Thatcher, 15 December 1988; Younger to Thatcher, 20 December 1988. **111** El-Shazly, *The Gulf Tanker, War*, p. 40. **112** NHB: Operation Armilla Draft Staff History, p. 184. **113** NHB: Glamorgan Box/T91511, Burns to CINCFLEET, 16 December 1983, Annex B. **114** Ibid. **115** NHB: Fearless Box/T50930, Trussell to CINCFLEET, 20 January 1984. **116** NHB: VCNS Papers Box 119, VCNS 65/11/Pt III, Howe to Thatcher, 2 February 1984. **117** Ibid., MODUK to CBF Cyprus and Com BFL, 1515Z, 7 February 1984. **118** Ibid., CTG 321.2 to MODUK, 1648Z, 8 February 1984. **119** NHB: Britannia Box 9, Garnier to CINCFLEET, 6 February 1986, see also maps in Annexes B1 and B. **120** TNA: FCO 46/4954, Howe to Athens, 29 January 1986 1030Z. **121** Hansard: HC Deb, Vol. 91, cc. 472-743, 6 February 1986, John Stanley. **122** TNA: FCO 46/4954, Howe to Athens, 29 January 1986 1030Z; NHB: Britannia Box 9, Garnier to CINCFLEET, 6 February 1986. **123** NHB: Britannia Box 9, Garnier to CINCFLEET, 6 February 1986, Annex E. **124** TNA: FCO 46/4954, Howe to Athens, 29 January 1986 1030Z. **125** NHB: Britannia Box 9, Garnier to CINCFLEET, 6 February 1986. **126** Ibid., Annex E. **127** NHB: Britannia Box 9, Garnier to CINCFLEET, 6 February 1986. **128** TNA: FCO 46/4954, Howe to Athens, 29 January 1986 1030Z. **129** NASA website: 'A Force of Nature: Hurricanes in a Changing Climate', 1 June 2022: A Force of Nature: Hurricanes in a Changing Climate – Climate Change: Vital Signs of the Planet (nasa.gov) (accessed 6 January 2024). **130** NHB: Invincible Box 1/T91264, Gerken to CINCFLEET, 28 April 1983. **131** NHB: Active Box/T238812, Canter to FOF1, 19 December 1988. **132** Ibid. **133** NHB: Antrim Box/T29474, Bathurst to CINCFLEET, 5 December 1983. **134** NHB: Apollo Box/T28521, de Halpert to CINCFLEET, 21 March 1986. **135** TNA: PREM 19/5104, Appleyard to Powell, 6 March 1985. **136** Ibid. **137** TNA: PREM 19/5104, Cradock to Powell, 20 June 1986. **138** NHB: Apollo Box/T28521, de Halpert to CINCFLEET, 21 March 1986. **139** See Fuss, *Sea of Grass* for US counter-narcotics operations since 1970. **140** TNA: FCO 183/125, Smith to Edmonds-Brown, 15 April 1987. **141** Ibid., Eggar to Mellor, 15 May 1987. **142** Ibid., 'UK/US Drugs Survey', undated, probably May 1987. **143** NHB: Cardiff Box/T50890, Burns to CINCFLEET, 9 March 1987. **144** NHB: Newcastle Box/T51125, Davies to FOF1, 30 March 1988. **145** NHB: Endurance Box 1/T117314, Sunter to FOF3, 27 May 1988. **146** Fuss, *Sea of Grass*, p. 263; NHB: Alacrity Box/T29011, Ferbrache to FOF2, 14 December 1989. **147** NHB: Alacrity Box/T29011, Ferbrache to FOF2, 14 December 1989. **148** NHB: Active Box/T28812, Canter to FOF1, 19 December 1988. **149** TNA: DEFE 69/1853, Ferbrache to FOF2, 27 September 1989. **150** TNA: DEFE 24/3283, Monrovia to MODUK, 1930Z 1 July 1990. **151** Ibid., Mason to DMO, 4 July 1990; Hatfield to MA/Min(AF), 18 July 1990. **152** NHB: Andromeda Box 2/T57289 et seq.; Phoebe Box/T1728, Smith to FOF1, 15 February 1991; TNA: DEFE 24/3283, Hatfield to MA/Min(AF), 18 July 1990. **153** National Museum of the US Navy webpages: 'August 5, 1990: Liberia (Operation Sharp Edge)': August 5, 1990 – Liberia (Operation Sharp Edge) (navy.mil) (accessed 1 December 2023). **154** TNA: DEFE 69/1364, Boam to Fieldhouse, 28 May 1986. **155** Ibid., Hum to Sills, 3 October 1986; Hong Kong Phase 3 Steering Committee minutes, 4 September 1986, item 4. **156** Ibid., Scicluna to ACDS(O), 3 March 1986. **157** TNA: DEFE 69/1476, Essenhigh to DNSD et al, 6 March 1987; Watkins to ACNS et al, 23 December 1987; Invitation to Tender for Surplus Vessels: HMS *Swallow* and HMS *Swift*, 31 March 1988; Walmsley to Hd RP(N), 21 April 1988. **158** NHB: Hong Kong Box 1/T71705, Dalrymple-Smith to CINCFLEET, 23 January 1990; Plover Box/T111086, Whinney to CAPIC HK, 10 October 1988. **159** TNA: DEFE 69/1476, Glennie to DOR(Sea), 5 February 1988. **160** NHB: Hong Kong Box 1/T71705, Dalrymple-Smith to CINCFLEET, 23 January 1990. **161** *Who's Who*, various editions. **162** The author would like to thank both Robert Avery and David Fields for allowing me to make use of their papers relating to UK-Soviet naval liaison visits to write this section. **163** Email to the author from David Fields, 14 November 2023. The Western delegation included British defence academics Geoffrey Till and Eric Grove. **164** Lehman, *Oceans Ventured*, p. 239. **165** Ibid., p. 236. **166** Robert Avery, 'RN-RFN Flag/Delegation Visits 1988-2014', email to author from Robert Avery, 16 September 2022. **167** NHB: Bristol Box/T73090, Franklyn to FOF1, 5 July 1989. **168** Ibid. **169** Robert Avery, 'RN-RFN Flag/Delegation Visits 1988-2014', email to author from Robert Avery, 16 September 2022. **170** Ibid. **171** Ibid. **172** Cooper, *Soviet Defence Industry*, pp. 30–4, 51–9; Gaddy, *The Price of the Past*, pp. 55–61. **173** Davis, 'Defence Sector in the Economy of a Declining Superpower', p. 18; Gaddy, *Price of the Past*, pp. 61–5. **174** The most obvious example of the handover of ships without all their equipment was the completion of the destroyer *Sovremenny*, without her air defence or anti-ship missile systems in place. Moore, ed., *Jane's Fighting Ships 1981-82*, p. 497. **175** Davis, 'Defence Sector', pp. 8–9. **176** Ibid., p. 16; Kuzin and Nikol'skiy, *Voyenno-Morskoy Flot*, Ch. 8.4. **177** Gaddy, *Price of the Past*, p. 134; Davis, 'Defence Sector', pp. 15–16. **178** Robert Avery papers: 'Soviet Destroyer "Bezuprechny" pays an official visit to Portsmouth', RPA, August 1990. **179** Ibid. **180** NHB: Soviet Navy Box 2/T83485: Naval Attaché Moscow to Eberle, 'Operation Dervish 91', 24 October 1991. **181** Odom, *Collapse of the Soviet Military*, pp. 260–71. **182** Cooper, *Soviet Defence Industry*, pp. 71–4.

Appendix 1: Organisation

1 NHB: Ministry of Defence Staff Directory Volume 2: Navy Department (1964, updated to 1971). **2** NHB: Ministry of Defence Directory (February 1989) pp. 7-2 and 12-2. **3** NHB: T70529, Organisation of the Navy Department 1960, 1964 and 1968. **4** NHB: T29240, Bridge card, June/July 1988.

Appendix 2: Budget

1 Sources for columns A and D: Office for Budget Responsibility, '300 years of UK public finance data' (spreadsheet download), 20 July 2023: 300 years of UK public finance data (obr.uk) (accessed 21/2/24). Column C is derived from column A and 'Total Public Sector Spending' figures given in '300 years of UK public finance data' spreadsheet (through the formula = 100(A/Total Public Sector Spending)). Column B is created by using the Bank of England inflation calculator to adjust Column A to 1990 prices. **2** Broadbent, *Military and Government*, p. 225. Broadbent states that 'Other' is made up of 'R&D and other services not readily attributable'.

Appendix 3: Personnel

1 Statements on the Defence Estimates 1965–1979, Statements on the Defence Estimates Volume 2, 1980–1991. Numbers given are total strength of personnel, not trained strength (which is also given in SDE from 1980) on 1 April of the relevant year. Note that between 1970 and 1974 SDE did not separate out female officers and ratings, so these are given together for those years. **2** Statement on the Defence Estimates 1981–1991. **3** Statements on the Defence Estimates 1966 to 1991. As per 1 April of relevant year, except for 1965-7, which are as per 1 January. Figures for the regular reserves were only given in the SDE from 1971 onwards (backdated to 1968). Regular reserves consist of those ex-service personnel on the Retired and Emergency Lists of officers, the Royal Fleet Reserve (ex-RN ratings) and equivalents. Volunteer reserves consist of the volunteer reserve forces for the Royal Navy, Royal Marines and Women's Royal Naval Service.

Appendix 4: The Fleet

1 Sources: Statements on the Defence Estimates 1970, 1980 (Part I) and 1990 (Part I). *Jane's Fighting Ships*, various editions, for tonnage. Standard tonnage has been used. Where not known for submarines, surfaced tonnage has been used instead.

Appendix 5: Warship Procurement

1 NHB: Finance Box 5/T48737, *Jane's Fighting Ships 1981/82*. **2** NHB: Finance Box 4/T48740, Long Term Costing Assumptions 1980; *Jane's Fighting Ships 1991/92*. **3** See Chapter 7, endnote 167. **4** NHB: Admiralty Board Papers, A/P(70)9, Long Term Costings 1970, 23 April 1970. **5** NHB: Admiralty Board Papers, A/P(79)11, Sketch Estimates 1980/81, 5 November 1979. **6** NHB: Admiralty Board Papers, A/P(80)2, Long Term Costings 1980, 11 January 1980. **7** NHB: Navy Board Papers, NAVB/P(88)19, Sketch Estimates 1989/90 and LTC 89, 20 December 1988.

Bibliography

Archival Sources

Admiralty Library, Portsmouth
Central Office of Information, 'Notes on Science and Technology in Britain: Hovercraft' (December 1962), Pam. 2709.
Goldsmith. John, 'A History of the Ministry of Defence Financial Organisation 1964–1985' (Ministry of Defence, 1988).
Hobbs. David, 'The Hobbs Report, Part 1: An Historical Analysis of RN Clothing' (Ministry of Defence, February 1995).
'Review of Class II Uniform, July 1971', Folio Pamphlet A013.
Sleat. A J, ed, 'The Royal Navy Contracts 1869–1969' (Ministry of Defence, 1969).
United Kingdom Hydrographic Office ('UKHO'): NP 526, Underwater Handbook: Western Approaches to British Isles (April 1970).

Air Historical Branch, Northolt
SD161: Location of Units of the Royal Air Force.
Air Staff Requirement Files.

Bodleian Library, Oxford
Archive of (Richard Edward) Geoffrey Howe, Baron Howe of Aberavon: MS Howe Dep. 140, PG/11/76/40.

Churchill College, Cambridge, Churchill Archives Centre
Nott Papers: NOTT 4/8/files 1, 2, 4.
Thatcher Papers: THCR 2/1/3/15, 2/6/1/80, 2/6/2/46 pt. 3, 2/6/46, pt. 2.

Liddell Hart Centre for Military Archives, King's College, London
Mayhew Papers: Mayhew 2/3, 8/1, 8/2.

National Archives, Kew ('TNA')
ADM 1: Admiralty, Correspondence and Papers.
ADM 114: Admiralty/MOD Navy Department, Victualling Department.
ADM 167: MOD Navy Department, Admiralty Board, Minutes and Papers.
ADM 182: Admiralty Fleet Orders.
ADM 187: Admiralty/MOD Navy Department, Stations and Movements of Royal Navy Ships (Pink Lists).
ADM 223: Admiralty, Naval Intelligence Division, Intelligence Reports and Papers.
ADM 234: Admiralty/MOD Navy Department, Books of Reference.
ADM 239: Admiralty/MOD Navy Department, Confidential Books.

AIR 6: MOD Air Force Department, Air Force Board, Minutes and Papers.
AIR 8: MOD Air Force Department, Chief of Air Staff Department Registered Files.
AIR 20: MOD Air Force Department, Air Historical Branch Papers.
AIR 41: MOD Air Force Department, Air Historical Branch, Narratives and Monographs.
CAB 128: Cabinet Conclusions.
CAB 129: Cabinet Papers.
CAB 130: Cabinet Miscellaneous Committees, Minutes and Papers.
CAB 148: Cabinet Oversea Policy and Defence Committee.
CAB 164: Cabinet Office, Subject Files.
CAB 165: Cabinet Office, Committee Files.
DEFE 4: Chiefs of Staff Committee Minutes.
DEFE 5: Chiefs of Staff Committee Memoranda.
DEFE 10: MOD Major Committees, Minutes and Papers.
DEFE 11: Chiefs of Staff Committee Registered Files.
DEFE 13: MOD Ministerial Private Offices, Registered Files.
DEFE 23: MOD Permanent Under Secretary's Private Office, Registered Files.
DEFE 24: MOD Defence Secretariat Branches and Successors, Registered Files.
DEFE 25: MOD Chief of Defence Staff's Private Office, Registered Files.
DEFE 32: Chiefs of Staff Committee, Secretary's Standard Files.
DEFE 45: MOD Defence Council Instructions (Navy).
DEFE 48: MOD Defence Operational Analysis Establishment, Reports and Files.
DEFE 49: MOD Navy Department Personnel Division, Registered Files.
DEFE 58: MOD Royal Air Force Strike Command, Reports and Papers.
DEFE 67: MOD Navy Department, Operational Evaluation Group/Joint Anti-Submarine School.
DEFE 68: MOD Central Staffs, Registered Files.
DEFE 69: MOD Navy Department, Registered Files.
DEFE 70: MOD Army Department, Registered Files.
DEFE 71: MOD Air Force Department, Registered Files.
DEFE 72: MOD Procurement Executive, Registered Files.
FCO 7: FCO American and Latin American Department, Registered Files.
FCO 46: FCO Defence Department, Registered Files.
FCO 183: FCO Narcotics Control and AIDS Department, Registered Files.
T 225: Treasury Defence Policy and Materiel Division, Registered Files.

National Maritime Museum, Greenwich, London
Lewin Papers: LWN 6/5.

National Museum of the Royal Navy, Portsmouth
O'Brien Papers: Admiral O'Brien Memoirs, NMM 2004.48.

Naval Historical Branch, Portsmouth ('NHB')
Admiralty Board/Admiral Board Sub-Committee/Navy Board minutes and papers (duplicate sets).
Admiralty Fleet Orders ('AFOs')./Defence Council Instructions ('DCIs') (duplicate sets).
Admiralty Pink List (duplicate set).
Admiralty Press Releases/Ministry of Defence (Navy). Press Releases.
Board Bulletin/Board Report, 1971–79.
Books of Reference ('BR'), various.
Boscombe Boxes (mostly Defence Operational Analysis Establishment ['DOAE'] material).
Common New Generation Frigate ('CNGF') Boxes.
Confidential Books ('CB'), various.
Defence Review 1974 Binders (mostly collated duplicates).
Exercises Boxes.
Fleet Operations Programme, 1971–90.
Fleet Requirements Committee ('FRC'). Papers, 1974–85.
General Orders and Standing Orders, various commands.
Key Subject Matter ('KSM'). Boxes, various series by subject.
Naval Intelligence Reports, 1962–74.

Naval Internal Newsletters/Magazines, various branches.
Naval News Summary, 1963–76.
Ship Boxes (by name of ship, mostly Reports of Proceedings).
Staff Histories: Home Station Narrative (Volume 4), The Cod War, Falklands War, Operation Armilla, History of the Development of the Naval Staff.
Vice Chief of the Naval Staff ('VCNS'). Papers, 1974–84.

University of Southampton Library
Mountbatten Papers: MS62/MB1/K176.

Official Publications

United Kingdom Government
Legislation.gov.uk website.
Hansard: House of Commons Debates, House of Lords Debates.
House of Commons Defence Committee.
House of Commons Public Accounts Committee.
House of Commons Library Research Papers.
Defence: Supply Estimates 1966–1992.
Statement on the Defence Estimates 1965–1992.
Defence Accounts/Defence Appropriation Accounts 1965–1991.
Armed Forces Pay Review Body Reports 1971–1991.
Imperial Calendar/Civil Service List/Civil Service Yearbook 1945–1994.
Navy List 1945–1991.
National Audit Office: Major Projects Reports 1983–1992
TSO: 'The Nimrod Review' (HC 1025, October 2009).
Grey, Bernard, 'Review of Acquisition for the Secretary of State for Defence' (October 2009).
MOD, 'Defence Reform: an Independent Report into the Structure and Management of the Ministry of Defence' [Levene Report] (June 2011).
MOD: 'Evidence Summary: The Drivers of Defence Cost Inflation' (February 2022): Evidence Summary: The Drivers of Defence Cost Inflation - GOV.UK (www.gov.uk). (accessed 4/7/23).

United States Government
Central Intelligence Agency, 'The Komsomelets Disaster' (CIA, 2007).
Central Intelligence Agency, CIA Electronic Reading Room: 'CIA Analysis of the Soviet Navy' (CIA, 2017): CIA Analysis of the Soviet Navy | CIA FOIA (foia.cia.gov). Research guide for collection: Soviet Navy - Intelligence and Analysis During the Cold War (cia.gov).
Department of Defense, *Soviet Military Power* (Washington, 1981–1990).
Department of the Navy, *Understanding Soviet Naval Developments* (3rd-6th editions, Washington, 1975, 1978, 1981, 1991).

Dissertations

Dyson, Philip, 'The Limits of Influence: The Treasury, the Ministry of Defence and the 1975 Defence Review', King's College London, MA Dissertation, 2012.
Boren, David, 'Britain's 1981 Defence Review', Doctoral Thesis, King's College London, 1992.
Robinson, Samuel, 'Between the Devil and Deep Blue Sea: Ocean Science and the British Cold War State' Doctoral thesis, University of Manchester 2015.
Salisbury, D B, 'From Silence to Showmanship: The British Government's presentation of nuclear policy, 1974–83' Doctoral Thesis, King's College London, 2016.
Taaffe, Emma, 'We suffered in silence: Health and Safety in Chatham Dockyard 1945–1984', Doctoral Thesis, University of Hull, 2013.

Published Secondary Sources

Adams, Thomas, and James Smith, *The Royal Fleet Auxiliary: A Century of Service* (London, 2005).
Allen, Patrick, *Sea King* (1993).
Apal'kov, Yu V, *Podvodniye Lodki VMF SSSR* (Moscow, 2006).

Apal'kov, Yu V, *Protivolodochnye Korabli* (St Petersburg, 2010).
Apal'kov, Yu V, *Udarnyye Korabli* (St Petersburg, 2010).
Ashmore, Edward, and Eric Grove, *The Battle and the Breeze* (Stroud, 1997).
Ashton, S R, 'Introduction' in Ashton and David Killingray, eds. *British Documents on the End of Empire: The West Indies* (London, 1999).
Ashworth, Chris, *RAF Coastal Command 1936–1969* (Yeovil, 1992).
Badsey, Stephen, 'The Falklands War as a Media War' in Stephen Badsey, Rob Havers and Mark Grove, *The Falklands Conflict Twenty Years On* (Abingdon, 2005).
Baer, George, *One Hundred Years of Seapower* (Stanford, 1993).
Baker, Richard, *Dry Ginger* (London, 1977).
Ballance, Theo, Lee Howard and Ray Sturtivant, *The Squadrons and Units of the Fleet Air Arm* (Air-Britain, 2016).
Baylis, John, and Kristan Stoddart, 'Britain and the Chevaline Project: The hidden nuclear programme, 1967–1982', *Journal of Strategic Studies*, Vol. 26, No. 4 (2003).
Beck, Peter, *The Falklands as an International Problem* (London, 1988).
Benbow, Tim, ed, *British Naval Aviation: The First 100 Years* (Aldershot, 2011).
Benbow, Tim, 'Royal Navy defence engagement during the Cold War', *Naval Review*, Vol. 108, No. 1, February 2020.
Benjamin, Ralph, *Five Lives in One: An Insider's View of the Defence and Intelligence World* (Speldhurst, 1996).
Berlyn, N, and J Foster, 'New destroyer for the RAN', *Navy Quarterly*, Summer 1974.
Bicheno, Hugh, *The Razor's Edge: The Unofficial History of the Falklands War* (London, 2007).
Black, Jeremy, *There and Back: the Memoirs of Admiral Sir Jeremy Black* (London, 2005).
Boarer, A C, et al, 'The Devonport Frigate Complex', *Transactions of the Royal Institution of Naval Architects*, 1980.
Boren, David, 'Establishing Civilian Supremacy: Influence within Britain's Ministry of Defence 1972–1982', in Paul Smith, ed, *Government and the Armed Forces in Britain 1856–1990* (London, 1996).
Borthwick, Alastair, *Yarrow and Company Limited 1865–1977, Yarrow Shipbuilders Limited 1977–1990* (Glasgow, 1990).
Boveda, Jorge, *All for one, one for all* (Warwick, 2021).
Boyd, Andrew, *British Naval Intelligence Through the Twentieth Century* (Barnsley, 2020).
Broadbent, Ewen, *The Military and Government* (London, 1988).
Brown, David, *The Royal Navy and the Falklands War* (London, 1987).
Brown, David K, 'Hydrofoils, a review of their history, capability and potential', *Transactions of the Royal Institution of Naval Architects*, Paper No 1427, 12 February 1980.
Brown, David K, and George Moore, *Rebuilding the Royal Navy: British Warship Design since 1945* (Barnsley, 2004).
Brown, Paul, *Abandon Ship: The Real Story of the Sinkings in the Falklands War* (Oxford, 2021).
Buckle, Sebastian, *The Way Out: A History of Homosexuality in Modern Britain* (London, 2015).
Burgess, J, 'HMS *Defiance* 400 years on', *Journal of Naval Engineering*, Vol. 27, No. 2, June 1982.
Burgess, J, '"The Dockyard will Provide the Pipes": a Review of the Dockyard Scene', *Journal of Naval Engineering*, Vol. 30, No. 2, June 1987.
Burns, Jimmy, *The Land that Lost its Heroes* (London, 2002).
Cable, James, *Gunboat Diplomacy 1919–1991* (Macmillan, London 1994).
Calder, Barnabas, *Raw Concrete: the Beauty of Brutalism* (London, 2016).
Carrington, Peter, *Reflect on Things Past: The Memoirs of Lord Carrington* (London, 1988).
Carter, B L, *A Short History of the Royal Marines 1664–2012* (4th edition, 2013).
Carver, Michael, *Out of Step, The Memoirs of Field Marshal Lord Carver* (London, 1989).
Childs, Nick, *The Age of Invincible* (Barnsley, 2009).
Chin, Warren, 'Operations in a War Zone: The Royal Navy in the Persian Gulf in the 1990s', in Ian Speller, ed, *The Royal Navy and Maritime Power in the Twentieth Century* (Abingdon, 2005).
Christenson, Joel C, Anthony R Crain and Richard A Hunt, *The Decline of Détente: Elliott Richardson, James Schlesinger and Donald Rumsfeld 1973–1977* (Secretaries of Defense Historical Series, 1973–1977).
Clapp, Michael, and Ewen Southby-Tailyour, *Amphibious Assault Falklands* (London, 1996).
Churchill College, Cambridge and Centre for Contemporary British History: 'Overstretched? The

making and impact of the UK's defence reviews since 1957', 2008, transcript of witness seminar.
Coats, Ann, *20th Century Naval Dockyards: Devonport and Portsmouth Characterisation Report* (Naval Dockyards Society, 2015).
Cooper, Alastair, '1955–1972: The Era of Forward Defence', in David Stevens, ed, *The Royal Australian Navy* (Melbourne, 2001).
Cooper, Frank, 'Sir Michael Cary', in *The Oxford Dictionary of National Biography*, Volume 10 (Oxford, 2004).
Cooper, Julian, *The Soviet Defence Industry: Conversion and Reform* (RIIA, London 1991).
Corlett, Roy, 'Can British Torpedoes stay the course?' in ed. John Moore, *Jane's Naval Review 1983–84* (London, 1983).
Cote, Owen, *The Third Battle: Innovation in the US Navy's silent Cold War struggle with Soviet submarines* (Newport, 2002, Naval War College Newport Papers, 16).
Craig, Chris, *Call for Fire* (London, 1995).
Daniel, R J, *The End of an Era* (Penzance, 2003).
Davies, Philip H J, *Intelligence and Government in Britain and the United States, Volume 2: The Evolution of the U.K. Intelligence Community* (Santa Barbara, 2012).
Davis, Christopher, 'The Defence Sector in the Economy of a Declining Superpower: The Soviet Union and Russia, 1965–2000' (Oxford, Department of Economics Discussion Paper No. 8, April 2000).
Dawson, Christopher, *A Quest for Speed at Sea* (Hutchinson, 1972).
Dell, Edmund, *The Chancellors* (London, 1997).
Dickinson, Harry, *Wisdom and War, The Royal Naval College Greenwich 1873–1998* (Farnham, 2012).
Dismukes, Bradford, and James McConnell, eds. *Soviet Naval Diplomacy* (New York, 1979).
Dockrill, Saki, *Britain's Retreat from East of Suez: The Choice between Europe and the World?* (Basingstoke, 2002).
Donoughue, Bernard, *Downing Street Diary: With Harold Wilson in No. 10* (London, 2005).
Dorman, Andrew, ed, *The Changing Face of Maritime Power* (London, 1999).
Dorman, Andrew. 'The Nott Review: Dispelling the Myths?' *Defence Studies*, Vol 1, No 3, autumn 2001, pp. 103–04.
Dorman, Andrew. Michael Kandiah and Gillian Staerk, eds, 'The Nott Review' (ICBH Witness Seminar Programme, 2002).
Dorman, Andrew. *Defence under Thatcher* (Basingstoke, 2002).
Doyle, Suzanne, 'A Foregone Conclusion? The United States, Britain and the Trident D5 Agreement', *Journal of Strategic Studies*, Vol. 40, No. 6 (2016), pp. 867–94.
Doyle, Suzanne, 'The United States sale of Trident to Britain 1977–1982: Deal making in the Anglo-American Nuclear Relationship', *Diplomacy and Statecraft*, Vol. 28, No. 3 (2017), pp. 477–93.
Doyle, Suzanne, "Preserving the Global Nuclear Order: The Trident Agreements and the Arms Control Debate, 1977–1982', *The International History Review*, Vol. 40, No. 5 (2018), pp. 1174–90.
Ducker, John, 'Historical and Constitutional Background' in Peter Hinchcliffe, John Ducker and Maria Holt, *Without Glory in Arabia: the British Retreat from Aden* (London, 2006).
Dunn, Steve, *The Power and the Glory: Royal Navy Fleet Reviews from earliest times to 2005* (Barnsley, 2021).
Dutford, Mark, ed. *Falklands Aftermath: Forces '85* (London, 1984).
Dyndal, Gert Lage, *Land Based Air Power or Aircraft Carriers? A Case Study of the British Debate about Maritime Air Power in the 1960s* (Farnham, 2012).
Edgerton, David, *The Warfare State: Britain 1920–1970* (Cambridge, 2006).
Edmonds, Martin, ed, *100 Years of the Trade: Royal Navy Submarines Past, Present and Future* (Lancaster, 2001).
Eller, Ernest, *The Soviet Sea Challenge* (New York, 1971).
Elliott, T D, *Royal Navy Task Force 321.1: A Gulf Record* (Dubai, 1991).
El-Shazly, Nadia El-Sayed, *The Gulf Tanker War* (Basingstoke, 1998).
Evans, David, *Arming the Fleet: The Development of the Royal Ordnance Yards 1770–1945* (Gosport, 2006).
Fiennes, Joseph, *Britannia's Voices: Sixty Years of Training at Dartmouth* (Dartmouth, 2017).
Finlan, Alastair, *The Royal Navy in the Falklands Conflict and Gulf War* (London, 2004).
Ford, Christopher, and David Rosenberg, 'The Naval Intelligence Underpinnings of Reagan's Maritime

Strategy', *Journal of Strategic Studies*, Vol. 28, No. 2.
Ford, Christopher, and David Rosenberg, *The Admirals' Advantage* (Annapolis, 2005).
Franks, Richard, *Shackleton: Guardian of the Sea Lanes* (Stamford, 2005).
Freedman, Lawrence, *The Official History of the Falklands Campaign: Revised and Updated Edition*, 2 Volumes (Abingdon, 2007).
Freedman, Lawrence, and Jeffrey Michaels, *The Evolution of Nuclear Strategy* (4th edition, London, 2019).
French, David, *Army, Empire and Cold War: The British Army 1945–71* (Oxford 2012).
French, Paul, 'Dire Straits: The Transit of the Lombok Strait, September 1964', in Antony Preston, ed. *Warship 1999–2000* (London, 1999).
Friedman, Norman, 'Elmo Russell Zumwalt Jr' in Robert William Love, ed. *The Chiefs of Naval Operations* (Annapolis, 1980).
Friedman, Norman, *The Postwar Naval Revolution* (London, 1986).
Friedman, Norman, *British Carrier Aviation* (Annapolis, 1989).
Friedman, Norman, *The Naval Institute Guide to Naval Weapons* (Annapolis, 1989).
Friedman, Norman, *The Naval Institute Guide to Naval Weapon Systems* (Annapolis, 1991).
Friedman, Norman, *The Naval Institute Guide to Naval Weapon Systems 1997–98* (Annapolis, 1997).
Friedman, Norman, *The Fifty Year War: Conflict and Strategy in the Cold War* (London, 2000).
Friedman, Norman, *Seapower and Space* (London, 2000).
Friedman, Norman, *Seapower and Strategy: Navies and National Interests* (Annapolis, 2001).
Friedman, Norman, *U.S. Amphibious Ships and Craft* (Annapolis, 2002).
Friedman, Norman, *US Destroyers, Revised Edition* (Annapolis, 2004).
Friedman, Norman, *British Destroyers and Frigates Since 1939* (Barnsley, 2012).
Friedman, Norman, *British Submarines in the Cold War Era* (Barnsley, 2021).
Fursdon, Edward, *Falklands Aftermath* (London, 1988).
Fuss, Charles, *Sea of Grass: The Maritime Drug War 1970–1990* (Annapolis, 1996).
Gaddy, Clifford G, *The Price of the Past: Russia's Struggle with the Legacy of a Militarized Economy* (Washington, 1996).
Gardiner, Robert, ed, *Conway's All the World's Fighting Ships 1947–1995* (London, 1995).
Gardner, Charles, *The British Aircraft Corporation* (London, 1981).
Gardner, W J R, *Anti-Submarine Warfare* (London, 1996).
Garrison, Tom, *Oceanography: An Invitation to Marine Science* (Pacific Grove, 2002).
Gibson, Chris, *Nimrod's Genesis: RAF Maritime Patrol Projects and Weapons since 1945* (Manchester, 2015).
Gjessing, Mark, *Anglo-Australian Naval Relations 1945–1975: A More Independent Service* (Cham, 2018).
Goldrick, James, and Steven Haines, ed. *Maritime Strategy for Medium Powers in the 21st Century* (forthcoming, 2024).
Goldstein, Lyle, and Yuri Zhukov, 'A Tale of Two Fleets: A Russian Perspective on the 1973 Naval Standoff in the Mediterranean' *US Naval War College Review*, Spring 2004, vol. 57, No. 2.
Gordon, Yefim, and Dmitriy Komissarov, *Soviet Naval Aviation 1946–1991* (Manchester, 2013).
Gordon, Yefim, and Dmitry Komissarov, *Tupelov Tu-22M* (Atglen, PA, 2022).
Gorst, Anthony, and Lewis Johnman, 'British Naval Procurement and Shipbuilding 1945–64', in David Starkey and Alan Jamieson, eds. *Exploiting the Sea: Aspects of Britain's Maritime Economy since 1870* (Exeter, 1998).
Gorst, Anthony, 'CVA-01: a case study in innovation in Royal Navy aircraft carriers, 1959–1966' in Richard Harding, ed, *The Royal Navy 1930–2000: Innovation and Defence* (London, 2004).
Grey, Jeffrey, *Up Top: The Royal Australian Navy and South East Asian Conflicts 1955–1972* (St Leonards, 1998).
Groom, Tony, *Diver* (Rendlesham, 2007).
Grove, Eric, *Vanguard to Trident: British Naval Policy Since World War Two* (Annapolis, 1987).
Grove, Eric, *The Future of Sea Power* (Annapolis, 1990).
Grove, Eric, *Maritime Strategy and European Security* (London, 1990).
Grove, Eric, and Graham Thompson, *The Battle for the Fjords: NATO's Forward Maritime Strategy in Action* (Annapolis, 1991).
Grove, Eric, 'Partnership spurned: the Royal Navy's search for a Joint Maritime Air Strategy East of Suez

1961–63', in N A M Rodger, ed, *Naval Power in the Twentieth Century* (Basingstoke, 1996).
Grove, Eric, 'The Royal Navy and the Guided Missile' in Richard Harding, ed. *The Royal Navy 1930–2000: Innovation and Defence* (Abingdon, 2005).
Hamblin, Jacob Darwin, *Oceanographers and the Cold War: Disciples of Marine Science* (Seattle, 2005).
Hampshire, Cecil, *The Royal Navy since 1945* (London, 1975).
Hampshire, Edward, 'Naval Intelligence', in *British Intelligence: Secrets, Spies and Sources* (Kew, 2009).
Hampshire, Edward, 'Air Intelligence', in *British Intelligence: Secrets, Spies and Sources* (Kew, 2009).
Hampshire, Edward, 'The Battle for CVA01' in Benbow, Tim, ed, *British Naval Aviation: The First 100 Years* (Aldershot, 2011).
Hampshire, Edward, *From East of Suez to the Eastern Atlantic: British Naval Policy 1964–70* (Farnham, 2013).
Hampshire, Edward, 'Margaret Thatcher's First U-Turn: Francis Pym and the Control of Defence Spending 1979–81', *Contemporary British History*, Volume 29, No. 3 (2015).
Hampshire, Edward, *British Guided Missile Destroyers* (Oxford, 2016).
Hampshire, Edward, 'Strategic and Budgetary Necessity, or Decision-making "Along the Grain"? The Royal Navy and the 1981 Defence Review', *Journal of Strategic Studies*, Vol. 39, No. 7, 2016.
Hampshire, Edward, 'Missing the Klondike Rush: Defence Sales and British Foreign Policy towards China 1971–79' in *The Foreign Office, Commerce and British Foreign Policy in the Twentieth Century*, ed. John Fisher, Effie Pedaliu and Richard Smith (London, 2016).
Hampshire, Edward, *Soviet Cold War Guided Missile Cruisers* (Oxford, 2017).
Hampshire, Edward, *Soviet Cruise Missile Submarines of the Cold War* (Oxford, 2018).
Hampshire, Edward, 'From Malin Head to "Okean 75": shadowing and intelligence collection operations by Royal Navy surface ships 1975–85' *Intelligence and National Security*, Vol. 33, No. 5, 2018.
Hampshire, Edward, *British Amphibious Assault Ships* (Oxford, 2019).
Hampshire, Edward, *Soviet Cold War Attack Submarines* (Oxford, 2020).
Hampshire, Edward, 'The Rise of the Chinese Navy: Past, Present and Future', *The Naval Review*, Vol. 108, No. 3 (2020).
Hampshire, Edward, *The Falklands Naval Campaign 1982* (Oxford, 2021).
Hampshire, Edward, 'Is Russia a Medium Maritime Power?' in James Goldrick and Steven Haines, ed. *Maritime Strategy for Medium Powers in the 21st Century* (forthcoming, 2024).
Hanrahan, Brian, and Robert Fox, *I counted them all out and I counted them all back* (London, 1982).
Harding, Richard, ed. *The Royal Navy 1930–2000: Innovation and Defence* (Abingdon, 2005).
Harland, Kathleen, *The Royal Navy in Hong Kong since 1841* (Liskeard, 1985).
Harris, John, 'The Hunt Class Mine Countermeasures Vessels', *Transactions of the Royal Institution of Naval Architects* (1980).
Harris, Robert, *Gotcha! The Media, the Government and the Falklands Crisis* (London, 1983).
Harris, William, *Lebanon: A History 600–2011* (Oxford, 2012).
Harrold, Jane, and Richard Porter, *Britannia Royal Naval College 1905–2005: A Century of Officer Training at Dartmouth* (Dartmouth, 2005).
Hart-Dyke, David, *Four Weeks in May* (London, 2007).
Haslam, E B, *The History of Royal Air Force Cranwell* (HMSO, 1982).
Hastings, Max, and Simon Jenkins, *The Battle for the Falklands* (London, 1983).
Hattendorf, John, 'NATO's Policeman on the Beat: The First Twenty Years of the Standing Naval Force Atlantic 1968–88', in Hatterndorf, ed, *Naval History and Maritime Strategy* (Malabar, 2000).
Hattendorf, John, *The Evolution of the US Navy's Maritime Strategy* (Rhode Island, 2004).
Hattendorf, John, *US Naval Strategy in the 1970s: Selected Documents* (Rhode Island, 2007).
Hattendorf, John, *US Naval Strategy in the 1980s*, Naval War College Newport Papers, No. 33 (Newport, 2008).
Healey, Denis, *The Time of My Life* (London, 1989).
Hennessy, Peter, *Cabinet* (London, 1986).
Hennessy, Peter, *Whitehall* (London, 2001).
Hennessy, Peter, *The Secret State: Preparing for the Worst 1945–2010* (London, 2010).
Hennessy, Peter, *Cabinets and the Bomb* (Oxford, 2007).
Hennessy, Peter, and James Jinks, *The Silent Deep, The Royal Navy Submarine Service since 1945* (London, 2015).
Henry, Michael, 'A CO's Story' in John Moore, ed. *The Impact of Polaris* (Huddersfield, 1999).

Herrick, Robert, *Soviet Naval Strategy: Fifty Years in War and Peace* (Annapolis, 1968).
Herrick, Robert, 'The USSR's Blue Belt of Defence Concept' in Paul Murphy, ed, *Naval Power in Soviet Policy* (Washington, 1978).
Herrick, Robert, *Soviet Naval Doctrine and Policy 1956–1986*, 3 volumes (Lampeter 2003).
Hervey, John, *Submarines* (London, 1994).
Heseltine, Michael, *Life in the Jungle: My Autobiography* (London, 2000).
Higgitt, Martin, *Through Fire and Water* (London, 2000).
Hill, Alexander, 'The Cold War Soviet Navy in Sub-Saharan Waters', in Timothy Stapleton, ed, *African Navies: Historical and Contemporary Perspectives* (Abingdon, 2022).
Hill, Richard, *Anti-Submarine Warfare* (London, 1984).
Hill, Richard, *Maritime Strategy for Medium Powers* (London, 1986).
Hill, Richard, *Air Defence at Sea* (London, 1988).
Hill, Richard, *Arms Control at Sea* (London, 1989).
Hill, Richard, *Lewin of Greenwich: the authorised Biography of Admiral of the Fleet Lord Lewin* (London, 2000).
Hinchcliffe, Peter, John Ducker and Maria Holt, *Without Glory in Arabia: the British Retreat from Aden* (London, 2006).
Hiranandani, G M, *Transition to Eminence: The Indian Navy 1976–1990* (New Delhi, 2005).
HMS Illustrious: the first two years: 20th June 1982 to 20th June 1984 (Grosvenor Press, Portsmouth, 1984).
Hobbs, David, *British Aircraft Carriers* (Barnsley, 2013).
Hobbs, David, *The British Carrier Strike Fleet after 1945* (Barnsley, 2015).
Holdsworth, Angela, and Chris Pugsley, *Sandhurst: A Tradition of Leadership* (London, 2005).
Hore, Peter, ed, *Royal Navy and Royal Marines Operations 1964 to 1996* (Naval Historical Branch, 1999).
Hore, Peter, ed, Seapower Ashore: 200 Years of the Royal Navy and Operations on Land (London, 2001).
Hore, Peter, 'Rear Admiral Richard Hill 1929–2017', in James Goldrick and Steven Haines, ed. *Maritime Strategy for Medium Powers in the 21st Century* (forthcoming, 2024).
Houghton, Frances, '"Alien Seamen" or "Imperial Family"? Race, belonging and British sailors of colour in the Royal Navy 1939–47', *English Historical Review*, Vol. 137, No. 588, 3 January 2023.
Howard, Grant, *The Navy in New Zealand: An Illustrated History* (London, 1981).
Howard, Michael, *The continental commitment: the dilemma of British defence policy in the era of the two world wars* (London, 1972).
Howarth, Stephen, *The Royal Navy's Reserves in War and Peace* (Barnsley, 2003).
Huan, Claude, *La Marine Sovietique* (Nantes, 2002).
Hunt, Richard A, *Melvin Laird and the Foundations of the Post-Vietnam Military 1969–1973* (Secretaries of Defense Historical Series, 2015).
Huxley, Tim, *Defending the Lion City: The Armed Forces of Singapore* (London, 2000).
Il'in, V, and A Kolesnikov, *Otyechyestvyennyye Atomnyye Podvodnyye Lodki* (Moscow, 2000).
Inboden, William, *The Peacemaker: Ronald Reagan, The Cold War, and the World on the Brink* (New York, 2022).
Inskip, Ian, *Ordeal by Exocet* (London, 2002).
Jackson, William, and Dwin Bramall, *The Chiefs: The Story of the United Kingdom Chiefs of Staff* (London, 1992).
James, Williams, 'Global Britain's strategic problem East of Suez', *European Journal of International Security*, Vol. 6 (2021).
Jeram-Croft, Larry, *The Royal Navy Lynx: An Operational History* (Barnsley 2017).
Johnman, Lewis, and Hugh Murphy, *British Shipbuilding and the State Since 1918: A Political Economy of Decline* (Exeter, 2002).
Johnson, Howard, 'The British Caribbean from Demobilisation to Constitutional Decolonisation', in Judith Brown and Wm Roger Louis, eds, *The Oxford History of the British Empire, Volume 4: The Twentieth Century* (Oxford, 1999).
Johnston, Maurice, 'More Power to the Centre: MOD Reorganisation', *RUSI Journal*, October 1982
Johnstone-Bryden, Richard, *HMS Illustrious (V)* (2015).
Johnstone-Bryden, Richard, *HMS Ocean (VI)* (2018).
Johnstone-Bryden, Richard, *HMS Bulwark (VII)* (2018).

Jones, Julia, *Uncommon Courage: The Yachtsmen Volunteers of World War II* (London, 2022).
Jones, Matthew, 'Up the Garden Path? Britain's Nuclear History in the Far East', *International History Review*, Vol. 25, No. 2 (2003).
Jones, Matthew, and John Young, Polaris East of Suez: British Plans for a Nuclear Force in the Indo-Pacific, 1964–68, *Journal of Strategic Studies*, Vol. 33, No. 6, 2010.
Jones, Matthew, *The Official History of the UK Strategic Nuclear Deterrent, Volume 1* (Abingdon, 2017).
Jones, Matthew, *The Official History of the British Nuclear Deterrent, Volume II: The Labour Government and the Polaris Programme, 1964–1970* (London, 2017).
Karreman, Jaime, *In Deepest Secrecy: Dutch Submarine Espionage Operations from 1968 to 1991* (Amsterdam, 2018).
Keefer, Edward C, *Harold Brown, Offsetting the Soviet Military Challenge 1977–1981* (Secretaries of Defense Historical Series, 2017).
Keefer, Edward C, *Caspar Weinberger and the US Military Buildup 1981–1985* (Secretaries of Defense Historical Series, 2023).
Keily, D G, *Naval Electronic Warfare* (London, 1988).
Kuzin, V P, and V I Nikol'sky, *Voyenno-Morskoy Flot SSSR 1945–1991* (St Petersburg 1996).
Ladd, James, *By Sea, By Land: The Royal Marines 1919–1997* (London 1998).
Laite, B C, *Maritime Air Operations* (London, 1991).
Lake, Jon, and Mike Crutch, *Tornado: The Multi-Role Combat Aircraft* (Leicester, 2000).
Lambert, Andrew, *Seapower States: Maritime Culture, continental empires and the conflict that made the modern world* (New Haven, 2018).
Lambert, Mark, ed, *Jane's All the World's Aircraft 1991–92* (Coulsdon, 1991).
Lavery, Brian, *In Which They Served* (London, 2008).
Lavery, Brian, *All Hands: The Lower Deck and the Royal Navy since 1939* (London 2012).
Law, Alex, 'Neither Colonial, Nor Historic: Workers' Organisation at Rosyth Dockyard 1945–95', in Kenneth Lunn and Ann Day, eds, *History of Work and Labour Relations in the Royal Dockyards* (London, 1999), pp. 169–71.
Le Bailly, Louis, *From Fisher to the Falklands* (London, 1991).
Leach, Henry, *Endure no Makeshifts: Some Naval Recollections* (London, 1993).
Lehman, John, *Oceans Ventured* (New York, 2018).
Lippiett, John, *Modern Combat Ships 5: Type 21* (Shepperton, 1990).
Livingstone, Grace, *Britain and the Dictatorships of Argentina and Chile, 1973–1982* (Cham, 2018).
Livsey, Andrew, 'The Royal Navy's Principal Warfare Officer Course 1972–2015', *Mariner's Mirror*, Vol. 103, No. 3 (August 2017).
Livsey, Andrew, 'The Royal Navy and Julian Corbett, 1990–2020', *The RUSI Journal* (October 2022).
Livsey, Andrew, 'Thought Leadership: the development of Royal Navy doctrine in the Cold War', draft article 2022.
Loxton, B H, 'DDL – The Concept Develops', *Navy Quarterly*, Vol. 1, No. 4, October 1972.
Lygo, Raymond, *Collision Course* (London, 2002).
McIntyre, W David, *Winding up the British Empire in the Pacific Islands* (Oxford, 2014).
Mallinson, William, *Cyprus: A Modern History* (London, 2005).
Mallinson, William, 'Cyprus, Britain, the USA, Turkey and Greece in 1977: Critical Submission or Submissive Criticism', *Journal of Contemporary History*, Vol. 44, No. 4 (October 2009).
Manley, David, 'The Loss of HMS Sheffield – A Technical Reassessment', RINA Warship Conference, Bath, June 2015.
Mason, Roy, *Paying the Price* (London, 1999).
Marriott, Leo, *Royal Navy Frigates Since 1945* (2nd edn. Shepperton, 1990).
Middlebrook, Martin, *The Fight for the Malvinas* (London, 1990).
Mlambo, Alois S, 'Honoured more in the Breach than in the Observance': Economic Sanctions on Rhodesia and International Response, 1965 to 1979', *South African Historical Journal*, Vol. 71, No. 3 (2019).
Mobley, Richard, 'The Beira Patrol', *Naval War College Review*, Vol. 55, No. 1, Article 5 (2002), pp. 5–8, 15–17.
Moore, Charles, *Margaret Thatcher: the Authorised Biography, Volume 1* (London, 2013).
Moore, John, ed. *Jane's Fighting Ships*, 1979–1980 to 1987–1988 editions (London, 1979–1987).

Moore, Patrick A, *The Greenie: The History of Warfare Technology in the Royal Navy* (Staplehurst, 2011).
Moore, Richard, '"We are a modern Navy": Abolishing the Royal Navy's rum ration', *Mariners Mirror*, Vol. 103, No. 1, February 2017.
Morey Kelly Ana, *Service from the Sea/Nga Mahi No Te Moana* (North Shore, 2008).
Morton, Peter, *Fire Across the Desert* (Canberra, 1989).
Morris, Alec, 'UK Control and Reporting System from the End of WWII to ROTOR and beyond', in RAF Historical Society, *Defending Northern Skies 1915–1995* (Newcastle, 1996).
Morris, R O, *Charts and Surveys in Peace and War: The History of the RN Hydrographic Service 1919–1970* (London, 1995).
Murphy, Hugh, 'Scott's of Greenock and Naval Procurement 1960-77', *Mariner's Mirror*, Vol. 87, No. 2 (Mary 2001).
Murphy, Hugh, *Shipbuilding in the United Kingdom: A History of British Shipbuilders Corporation* (Abingdon, 2021).
Murray, John, *The Royal Naval Auxiliary Service: The First Twenty Five Years* (Liskeard, 1988).
Neubroch, H, 'The Great Carrier controversy 1964–65, a Defence Planner's recollections' in *Royal Air Force Historical Society Journal, No. 27* (2002).
Noble, Alastair, *British Defence Policy and the Royal Air Force, May 1979-April 1988* (Northolt, 2022).
Nott, John, *Here Today, Gone Tomorrow* (London, 2002).
Odom, William, *The Collapse of the Soviet Military* (New Haven, 1998).
O'Flaherty, Chris, *Naval Mine Warfare: Politics to Practicalities* (2019).
Osborne, Richard, and David Sowdon, *Leander Class Frigates* (World Ship Society, Kendal, 1990).
Parr, Helen, 'The British Decision to Upgrade Polaris, 1970–74', *Contemporary European History*, Vol. 22, No. 2, (2013).
Pavlov, A S, *Warships of the USSR and Russia 1945–1995* (Annapolis, 1997).
Pedaliu, Effie, '"A Sea of Confusion": The Mediterranean and Détente, 1969–1974', *Diplomatic History*, Vol. 33, No. 4 (September 2009).
Peden, Geoffrey, *Arms, Economics and British Strategy: from Dreadnoughts to Hydrogen Bombs* (Cambridge, 2007).
Penn, Geoffrey, *HMS Thunderer: The Story of the Royal Naval Engineering College Keyham and Manadon* (Emsworth, 1984).
Perkins, Roger, *Operation Paraquat: The Battle for South Georgia* (London, 1986).
Pokrant, Marvin, *Desert Storm at Sea* (Connecticut, 1999).
Poland, Nicho, *The Torpedomen* (Emsworth, 1993).
Polmar, Norman, and K J Moore, *Cold War Submarines* (Dulles, 2004).
Polmar, Norman, and John Gresham, *Defcon 2: Standing on the Brink of Nuclear War during the Cuban Missile Crisis* (Hoboken, 2006).
Polmar, Norman, 'Working for John Lehman, Part 1' NavyHistory.org website, 14 August 2013: Norman Polmar's Corner: Working for John Lehman, Part 1 | Naval Historical Foundation (navyhistory.org). (accessed 12/11/23).
Polmar, Norman, and Edward Whitman, 'Russia poses a non-acoustic threat to US subs', *USNI Proceedings*, No. 143/10, October 2017.
Polmar, Norman, and John O'Connell, *Strike from the Sea* (Annapolis, 2020).
Pook, Jerry, *RAF Harrier Ground Attack Falklands* (Barnsley, 2007).
Poole, Walter S, *History of Acquisition in the Department of Defense, Volume II: Adapting to Flexible Response 1960–1968* (Historical Office of Department of Defense, Washington, 2013).
Poole, Walter S, *The Joint Chiefs of Staff and National Policy 1973–1976* (Washington, 2015).
Potter, Michael, *Electronic Greyhounds: The Spruance Class Destroyers*, (Annapolis, 1995).
Preston, C E, *Power for the Fleet* (Eton, 1982).
Prince, Stephen, 'Command and Control in the Falklands Campaign', *Defence Analysis*, Vol. 18, No. 2 (2002).
Privratsky, Kenneth, *Logistics in the Falklands War: A Case Study in Expeditionary Warfare* (Barnsley, 2016).
RAF Historical Society, *Defending Northern Skies 1915–1995* (Newcastle, 1996).
Ranft, Brian, and Geoffrey Till, *The Sea in Soviet Strategy* (London, 1983).
Rearden, Steven L, *The Joint Chiefs of Staff and National Policy 1977–80* (History of the Joint Chiefs of Staff, Office of the Chairman of the Joint Chiefs of Staff, 2015).

Redford, Duncan, *The Submarine, a Cultural History from the Great War to Nuclear Combat* (London, 2010).
Redford, Duncan, and Philip Grove, *The Royal Navy: A History since 1900* (London, 2014).
Rehman, Iskander, 'Indian Aspirational Naval Doctrine', in Harsh Pant, ed, *The Rise of the Indian Navy: Internal Vulnerabilities and External Challenges* (Farnham, 2012).
Rivas, Santiago, *Wings of the Malvinas* (Manchester, 2012).
Robb, Thomas, 'Antelope, Poseidon or a Hybrid: The Upgrading of the British Strategic Nuclear Deterrent', 1970–1974, *Journal of Strategic Studies*, Vol. 33, No. 6 (2010).
Roberts, John, *Safeguarding the Nation: The Story of the Modern Royal Navy* (Barnsley, 2009).
Rowlands, Kevin, *21st Century Gorshkov: The Challenge of Sea Power in the Modern Era* (Annapolis, 2017).
Russell, Brian, *The Interservice Hovercraft (Trials). Unit* (Gosport, 1979).
Sackville, Andrew, 'Professional Associations and Social Work: Working Paper 15 – The British Association of Social Workers 1970–88', section 2.8 (1988): https://www.kcl.ac.uk/scwru/swhn/2013/sackville-wp15-british-association-of-social-workers-1970-1988.pdf (accessed 17 May 2021).
Saunders, Stephen, ed, *Jane's Fighting Ships 2001–2002* (Coulsdon, 2001).
Sayle, Timothy Andrews, *Enduring Alliance: A History of NATO and the Postwar Global Order* (Ithaca, 2019).
Sciaroni, Mariano, *Carrier at Risk* (Warwick, 2019).
Sciaroni, Mariano, and Andy Smith, *Go Find Him and Bring Me Back His Hat* (Warwick, 2020).
Schirmer, Jennifer, *The Guatemalan Military Project: a Violence called Democracy* (Philadelphia, 1998).
Sharpe, Richard, ed, *Jane's Fighting Ships,* 1989–1990 to 1995–1996 editions (London, 1989 to 1992, Coulsdon, 1993 to 1995).
Shields, John, *Air Power in the Falklands Conflict* (Barnsley, 2021).
Shirokorad, A B, *Oruzhiye Otyechyestvyennogo Flota 1945–2000* (Moscow, 2001).
Smith, Adrian, *Mountbatten, Cold War and Empire 1945–79* (London, 2023).
Smith, Paul, ed, *Government and the Armed Forces in Britain 1856–1990* (London, 1996).
Southby-Tailyour, Ewen, *Reasons in Writing* (London, 1993).
Spassky, Nikolai, ed, *Russia's Arms Catalog, Volume III, Navy* (Moscow, 1996).
Speed, Keith, *Sea Change* (Bath, 1982).
Speller, Ian, *The Role of Amphibious Warfare in British Defence Policy 1945–1956* (Basingstoke, 2001).
Speller, Ian, ed, *The Royal Navy and Maritime Power in the Twentieth Century* (Abingdon, 2005).
Spence, Daniel Owen, *Colonial Naval Culture and British Imperialism, 1922–1967* (Manchester, 2015).
Spence, Daniel Owen, *A History of the Royal Navy: Empire and Imperialism* (London, 2020).
Spinardi, Graham, *From Polaris to Trident: The Development of US Fleet Ballistic Missile Technology* (Cambridge, 1994).
Stanley, Jo, *Women and the Royal Navy* (London, 2018).
Stevens, David, ed, *The Royal Australian Navy* (Melbourne, 2001).
Stobart-Hook, Barry, *Warships for the World* (Newport, 1994).
Stoddart, Kristin, 'Maintaining the Moscow Criterion': British Strategic Nuclear Targeting 1974–1979', *Journal of Strategic Studies*, Vol 31, No. 6, 2008
Stoddart, Kristin, *Losing an Empire, Finding a Role: Britain, the USA, NATO and Nuclear Weapons 1964–1970* (Basingstoke, 2012).
Stoddart, Kristin, *The Sword and the Shield: Britain, America, NATO and the Nuclear Weapons 1970–1976* (Basingstoke, 2014).
Stoddart, Kristin, *Facing Down the Soviet Union: Britain, the USA, NATO and Nuclear Weapons 1976–1983* (Basingstoke, 2014).
Sturtivant, Ray, Mick Burrow and Lee Howard, *Fleet Air Arm Fixed Wing Aircraft Since 1945* (Air-Britain 2004).
Thatcher, Margaret, *The Downing Street Years* (London, 1993).
Theberge, James, *Russia in the Caribbean* (Georgetown, 1973).
Thompson, Eric, *On Her Majesty's Nuclear Service* (Oxford, 2018).
Thompson, Julian, *3 Commando Brigade in the Falklands: No Picnic* (London, 2008).
Thompson, Julian, *The Royal Marines: from Sea Soldiers to a Special Force* (London, 2000).
Till, Geoffrey, *Maritime Strategy and the Nuclear Age* (London, 1982).

Till, Geoffrey, *The Future of British Seapower* (London, 1984).
Till, Geoffrey, ed, *Britain and NATO's Northern Flank* (London, 1988).
Timmins, Nicholas, *The Five Giants: A Biography of the Welfare State*, Revised Edition (London, 2001).
Tokarev, Maksim Y, 'Kamikazes: The Soviet Legacy', *Naval War College Review*, Vol. 67, No. 1, 2014
Treacher, John, *Life at Full Throttle: from Wardroom to Boardroom* (Barnsley, 2004).
Trewin, Ion, ed, *The Hugo Young Papers* (London, 2008).
Tripp, Charles, *A History of Iraq* (2nd ed. Cambridge University Press, 2002).
Twiss, Frank, *Social Change in the Royal Navy 1924–1970* (Stroud, 1996).
Villar, Roger, 'Future Trends in Maritime Warfare – NATO and the Warsaw Pact', in Edward Gueritz and Jennifer Shaw, *Brassey's Defence Yearbook 1982* (London, 1982).
Underwood, Geoffrey, *Our Falklands War* (Callington, 1983).
Villar, Roger, 'Weapon Development in the 1980s: Sea' in Edward Gueritz and Jennifer Shaw, *Brassey's Defence Yearbook 1982* (London, 1982).
Walker, Jonathan, *Aden Insurgency: The Savage War in South Arabia 1962–1967* (Staplehurst, 2005).
Walsh, Jim, 'Surprise Down Under: The Secret History of Australia's Nuclear Ambitions', *The Nonproliferation Review* (Vol. 5, No. 1, Fall 1997).
Ward, [Nigel] 'Sharkey', *Sea Harrier over the Falklands* (London, 1993).
Warlow, Ben, *Shore Establishments of the Royal Navy* (Liskeard, 2000).
Watson, Basil, *Commander in Chief: A Celebration of the Life of Admiral of the Fleet The Lord Fieldhouse of Gosport* (Gosport, 2005).
Watson, Bruce, *Red Navy at Sea: Soviet Naval Operations on the High Seas, 1956–1980* (Boulder, 1982).
Wegener, Edward, *The Soviet Naval Offensive* (Annapolis, 1975).
Welch, Andrew, *The Royal Navy in the Cod Wars* (Liskeard, 2006).
Wells, Anthony, *A Tale of Two Navies* (Annapolis, 2017).
Westad, Odd Arne, *The Cold War: A World History* (London, 2017).
White, Kenton, *Never Ready: Britain's Armed Forces and NATO's Flexible Response Strategy, 1967–1989* (Warwick, 2021).
White, Rowland, *Phoenix Squadron* (London, 2009).
Williamson, Corbin, *The US Navy and its Cold War Allies 1945–53* (Kansas, 2020).
Wilson, Keith, *Blackburn/BAE Buccaneer All Marks 1958–1994* (Yeovil, 2018).
Woodward, Sandy, and Patrick Robinson, *One Hundred Days* (London, 1992).
Young, Hugo, *One of Us: Final Edition* (London, 1993).
Young, John, *The Labour Governments 1964–1970: International Policy* (Manchester, 2003).
Young, John, 'The Wilson Government and the Debate over Arms to South Africa in 1964', *Contemporary British History*, Vol. 12, No. 3, 1998, pp. 62–86.
Zaloga, Steven, *The Kremlin's Nuclear Sword* (Washington, 2002).
Zeigler, Philip, *Mountbatten, the Official Biography* (London, 1985).
Zumwalt, Elmo, *On Watch* (New York, 1976).

Index

3 Commando Brigade, Royal
  Marines, 15, 442, 461–2
18 Group, RAF, *see also* Coastal
  Command, 109–10
148 Commando Forward Observation
  Battery, 484

Aberdeen Shipbuilding Company,
  578
Abidjan, Ivory Coast, 441
Adams, Rear Admiral John, 51–3,
  55, 71
ADAWS tactical command system,
  69, 148, 171–3, 300, 302, 478
Adderbury process, 615–7
Aden, *see also* Yemen, 5, 15, 58, 76,
  79–81, 83, 85
Aden City, Aden, 79–81, 607–9
Admiral Commanding Reserves, 629
Admiral Superintendent Chatham
  Dockyard, 16, 107
Admiral Superintendent Devonport
  Dockyard, 16, 108
Admiral Superintendent Portsmouth
  Dockyard, 16
Admiral Superintendent Rosyth
  Dockyard, 16
Admiral Superintendents of
  Dockyards, 16
Admiralty, 21–3, 38, 42, 68, 158,
  347–8,
Admiralty Board, *see also* Navy Board,
  21–2, 24, 36, 43, 45–6, 53, 55–6,
  67, 70–1, 74, 87–9, 91, 94, 96,
  98, 100, 102–3, 107, 111, 115,
  129–30, 132, 157–8, 162, 188,
  218, 220–2, 288, 297, 301, 309,
  318, 323–4, 327–9, 378–80,
  382–3, 420, 426, 429, 431, 470,
  506, 541, 545, 548–50, 583–4,
  593, 620, 629–30
Admiralty Board Sub-Committee,
  545
Admiralty Board Sub-Committee on
  Oceanography, 154
Admiralty Board Sub-Committee on
  the future of the Royal Marines,
  424–5
Admiralty Cable Layers, 155
Admiralty Compass Laboratory,
  Slough, 19
Admiralty Engineering Laboratory,
  West Drayton, 18
Admiralty Experimental Diving Unit,
  Portsmouth, 19
Admiralty Experimental Works,
  Haslar, Gosport, 18, 548
Admiralty Fuel Establishment Station,
  Haslar, Gosport, 19
Admiralty Hydro-Ballistic Research
  Establishment, Helensburgh, 19
Admiralty Interview Board, 95
Admiralty Marine Engineering
  Establishment, 548
Admiralty Marine Technology
  Establishment, 548
Admiralty Materials Laboratory,
  Holton Heath, Dorset, 19, 548
Admiralty Oil Laboratory, Brentford,
  19
Admiralty Reactor Test Establishment,
  Dounreay, 19
Admiralty research establishments,
  268, 333, 548
Admiralty Research Establishment,
  548
Admiralty Research Laboratory,
  Teddington, 18–9, 154, 548
Admiralty Surface Weapons
  Establishment, Portsdown, 18, 443,
  548, 614
Admiralty Underwater Weapons
  Establishment, Portland, 18, 147,
  311–2, 524, 548
Advanced Warfare Officer, 96
Aegean Islands, 216
Aegean Sea, 217
Aegis air defence system, 301, 358,
  384, 392–3, 397, 517, 623
Aero engines, *see* Gas Turbines
AFNORTH, NATO command, 189,
  217, 278, 410–1, 525
Africa, 62, 255, 353
  East, 3, 10, 13, 110; Horn of, 5;
  Southern, 76–8; West, 6, 276,
  292, 583, 612–3
AFSOUTH, NATO command, 193
Afghanistan, 292, 337, 410
Age of Invincible, The (book), xiii
Agriculture, Fisheries and Food,
  Ministry of ('MAFF'), 226, 282,
  284, 467
Agusta helicopters, 561
Air Defence, *see also* Ballistic Missile
  Defence and Electronic Warfare,

INDEX

125, 259–61, 296–304, 357–8, 362–4, 406, 501, 503, 519, 558, 559
By shipborne aircraft, 41–2, 63, 67–8, 77, 80, 210–3, 257–8, 266, 297–8, 307, 324, 341, 357, 362, 383, 511, 531–2, 558, 621; by land-based aircraft, 49, 52, 55, 59, 119–20, 122, 192, 200–1, 208, 211–6, 266, 289, 296–7, 347, 352, 357, 363–4, 521, 558, 560, 601, 621; by shipborne weapon systems, 52, 55, 68–71, 84, 142, 168, 171–2, 175, 177, 213–6, 257, 260–1, 299–304, 324, 341, 344, 357–8, 362, 368, 383–4, 392–3, 397, 443, 500, 503, 512–3, 517, 550, 553, 565–7, 623; in Falklands Campaign, 448, 450, 452, 460, 461–2, 467, 471–2, 477–80; of Belize, 251–2; ships, impact of missile systems on, 33; training and exercises, 8
Air Defence Area, United Kingdom, 559
Air Force Board, 297, 373
Air Force Department, Ministry of Defence, 44, 162, 212, 262, 290, 361, 371, 432–3
Air Ministry, 22, 38, 347–8
Air Staff, 38, 40, 42, 44–5, 49, 109, 150, 192, 211, 213, 264, 272, 313, 362, 418, 544
Air Staff Target, 313
Air to air refuelling, 215, 364, 366, 383–4, 413, 450, 459–60, 480–1, 560
Airborne Warning and Control System (AWACS), 259, 289, 559
Aircraft, fixed wing (British operated, unless otherwise stated)
  Aermacchi MB339 (Argentine), 454
  Anglo-French Variable Geometry Aircraft, 47
  Britannia, 228
  Boeing 707 (Argentine), 456
  Buccaneer, 13, 21, 37–8, 42–3, 47, 49, 60–2, 119–21, 138, 208, 212, 251, 289, 291, 312–3, 357, 383, 559–60, 598, 607
  Canberra (British and Argentine), 70, 119–20, 238, 447, 460, 462–3

Dagger (Argentine), 447, 454–7, 461–2
Eurofighter Typhoon, 565
F-14 (US), 558
F-15 (US), 558
F-111 (US), 38, 40–2, 47, 49, 59, 299
F/A-18 (US), 558
Gannet, 2, 13, 47, 289–90, 559
Harrier/P1127, *see also* Sea Harrier, 40, 52, 54, 165–6, 178
Harrier GR1/GR3, 198, 251–2, 365, 452, 454, 458, 460–1, 464, 476, 481
Hastings, 280
Hercules (British, Argentine and US), 40, 450, 459–60, 612
HS681, 40
Jaguar, 47, 159, 601
Lancaster, 14
Lightning, 119–120, 296–7, 558
Maritime patrol aircraft, *see also* Nimrod, Shackleton and Orion, 2, 13–4, 77, 83, 119–20, 122, 139–40, 149–53, 200, 206, 231, 238, 258–61, 263, 271–5, 282, 284, 295, 305, 355–6, 358, 362, 367–8, 374–5, 382–4, 412, 415, 418, 434, 448–9, 479, 483, 511, 524, 526, 529, 559, 624–5
MiG-15 'Fagot' (Soviet), 11
MiG-17 'Fresco' (Soviet), 11
MiG-23 'Fitter' (Soviet), 514
Mirage (Argentine), 447, 470, 601
Nimrod, 14, 119–22, 138, 149–50, 152, 206, 208, 211, 228, 231, 238, 259, 272–3, 280, 282, 284, 289–90, 363–4, 366–7, 383–4, 404, 415, 417–8, 479–80, 521, 559–60
Orion (US), 366
P1127, *see* Harrier
P1154, 40
Phantom F4K, 42, 46–7, 60–1, 63, 119–21, 214–5, 289, 291, 296–7, 363, 465, 558, 598, 607
Pucara (Argentine), 451, 454
Scimitar, 2, 13
Sea Harrier, 201, 208–15, 257–60, 262, 266, 290–1, 297–300, 306–7, 325, 341, 348, 357–8, 362, 366, 368, 373, 383, 446–7, 450–2, 454–6, 458, 460, 464, 470, 476, 477, 481, 484, 500,

526, 531–3, 550, 557–8, 560, 576, 585, 598, 621, 625
Sea Vixen, 2, 13, 21, 47, 61–3
Shackleton, 14, 77, 119–20, 149–50, 231, 272, 289–90, 363, 479–80, 559
Skyhawk (Argentine), 442, 446, 450–1, 454–7, 459, 461–2
Skyvan (Argentine), 451
Su-15 'Flagon' (Soviet), 514
Su-33 'Flanker' (Soviet), 511
Super Etendard (Argentine), 449, 458–9, 470, 477, 479
Tankers, 200, 208, 210–5, 259, 262, 364, 481, 521, 560
Tornado, 159, 214–5, 259, 297, 303, 357, 364, 366, 383, 396, 433, 558–60
Tristar, 481, 560
TSR2, 38, 40
Tu-16 'Badger' (Soviet), 119, 172, 215, 272, 601
Tu-22M 'Backfire' (Soviet), 172, 214–5, 257, 259, 270, 301–2, 344, 514, 521, 532, 558
Tu-95 'Bear' (Soviet), 201, 210–1, 413
Turbo Mentor (Argentine), 451
VC10, 246, 481, 560
Victor, 481, 560
VSTOL aircraft, 38, 142, 159, 209, 257–8, 357
Vulcan, 119–20, 446, 460, 481
Yak-38 'Forger' (Soviet), 313, 511
Ajax Bay, Falkland Islands, 453, 458
Akhromeyev, Marshal Sergei, Soviet Army, 615
Al Faw, Iraq, 602
Al Mukalla, Yemen, 608
Aldabra, Indian Ocean, 59
Alexandria, Egypt, 83, 231, 233
Alexandria Torpedo Factory, Dunbartonshire, 18
Allied Tactical Publications, 126
Amel'ko, Admiral Nikolai, Soviet Navy, 615
America, 232, 255
  Central, 247, 250, 407, 502; Latin, 6, 251, 502, 598; North, 117, 142, 257, 379, 404, 507, 521; South, 7, 247, 292
American Committee for US-Soviet Relations, 615

Amphibious operations, 12, 15, 42, 45, 262, 279, 357, 424, 453–7, 460–2, 466, 474, 513, 522
Andropov, Yuri, 534
Andros Island, Bahamas, 7
Andros Trench, Bahamas, 248
Angola, 84
Anguilla, 247, 249
Anguilla Cays, Bahamas, 248
Annual Management Plan, Navy Department, 545
Antigua and Barbuda, 247
Anti-air warfare, *see* Air Defence, Maritime
Anti-ballistic missile systems, 134, 136, 277, 336
Anti-Ballistic Missile Treaty, 136, 140
Anti-ship warfare, 4, 11, 42, 46–7, 67, 70–1, 84, 121, 138, 140, 145, 159, 166, 173–6, 179, 211, 213, 215–6, 231–2, 234, 258–9, 278, 301, 311–4, 316, 342, 357, 362–4, 374, 412, 415, 420–2, 442–4, 446, 449, 451, 478–80, 484–5, 508, 511–4, 519, 532, 557, 559–60, 567
Anti-Submarine Group Two, NATO, 412, 520, 525
Anti-submarine warfare (ASW), *see also* Mortars, Anti-Submarine; Sonar; Torpedoes; 8, 14, 17, 26, 72, 99, 104, 121–2, 125, 143–55, 178, 192, 200–1, 213, 215–6, 221, 229, 232, 248, 256–8, 263, 269–74, 278, 286, 292, 334, 361–4, 369, 372, 375, 403, 414, 443, 505, 510–1, 518–9, 522, 525, 538, 567, 569

By hovercraft, 76; by ship-borne aircraft, 2, 13, 68, 119–22, 138, 146–7, 165, 178, 186, 201, 258, 260, 262, 270–1, 273, 291, 301, 304–7, 325, 355–8, 362, 367–8, 383–4, 397, 412, 416, 418, 434, 465–6, 483, 486, 526–7, 532, 560–1, 598, 623, 625; by shore-based aircraft, 13–14, 121–2, 138–9, 149–50, 192, 263, 270, 272–3, 282, 356, 358, 362–4, 366, 375, 383, 418, 434; by submarines, 122, 151, 262–3, 482, 520;by surface ships, 3, 8–10, 60, 71–2, 145–9, 172–4, 178–80, 186, 198, 201,

212, 217, 258–60, 263, 270, 279, 301–2, 304–5, 307–10, 333, 342, 349, 355–6, 358, 362, 367–8, 382–3, 395, 397, 403, 412, 414–6, 419, 482–3, 512–3, 519, 522–9, 566, 570, 572, 598, 626; strategic ASW, 151, 517, 520, 626
Antrim armament depot, 17, 268
ANZUK command, Singapore, 113
Apartheid, 6, 77, 242, 441, 590
Apprentices, *see also* Artificers, 17, 26, 91, 103, 128, 219, 427
ARAPAHO system, 466, 606
Arbroath, Scotland, 216
Arctic region, 216, 267, 517, 531
Argentina, 169, 292, 411, 598
Air Force, 454, 459, 625; Army, 484; 'Dirty War', 437; Falklands dispute and conflict, 199, 436–502, 557, 625–6; Marines, 436; Military Junta, 437, 442, 445–8, 451, 481–4; Naval Air Arm, 459: Navy, 437
'Argus', Project, Soviet Navy, 509
Argyll and Sutherland Highlanders, 79
Armagh, Northern Ireland, 224
Armed Forces Minister, *see* Minister of State for the Armed Forces
Armed Forces Pay Review Body, 338
Armilla Patrol, *see* Operations, codenames; Armilla
Armstrong, Sir Robert, 340, 384
Army, British, *see also* British Army of the Rhine, 5, 15, 24, 30, 38–40, 43, 52–3, 57–8, 68, 74, 76, 80, 88, 90–1, 97, 100–1, 103, 159, 187, 197–8, 200, 205–6, 217, 223–4, 247–8, 261, 334, 341–2, 349, 351, 352, 358, 365–6, 369, 372–3, 379, 382, 385–6, 395, 423–5, 434, 461, 462, 472, 513, 535, 563, 574, 590, 610, 613, 622, 633–4
Army Air Corps, 38, 460
Army Department, Ministry of Defence, 162, 371, 433
Artificers, *see also* Apprentices, 17, 25–8, 62, 91, 99–100, 327, 489, 584
Ascension Island, South Atlantic, 440–1, 444, 449, 460, 480, 487, 489
Ashmore, Admiral Sir Edward, *see also* First Sea Lord, 79–81, 87, 96,

133, 189, 209–10, 285–6, 290, 505, 541
Asia, South East, 39, 53, 59, 116, 207, 239–40, 244, 255, 600
Assistant Chief of the Defence Staff (Commitments), 544
Assistant Chief of the Defence Staff (Operations), 473
Assistant Chief of the Defence Staff (Policy), 261
Assistant Chief of the Defence Staff (Signals), 189
Assistant Chief of the Naval Staff, 133, 544, 630
Assistant Chief of the Naval Staff (Operational Requirements), 629
Assistant Chief of the Naval Staff (Operations and Air), 629
Assistant Chief of the Naval Staff (Policy), 51, 361, 540, 629
Assistant Chief Scientific Adviser (Projects), 303
Assistant Chief Scientific Adviser (Studies), 300
Assistant Controller, Polaris, 629
Assistant Under Secretary (Civilian Management), 629
Assistant Under Secretary (Fleet Support), 629
Assistant Under Secretary (Material-Navy/Materiel-Naval), 629–30
Assistant Under Secretary (Naval Personnel), 629
Assistant Under Secretary (Naval Staff), 359, 629
Assisted Maintenance Periods, 92–3, 240, 439, 528
Associated States, Caribbean, 247
ASW Striking Force, NATO, 520
Athens, Greece, 8
Atlantic Council, NATO, 256
Atlantic Ocean, 4, 14, 64, 117, 122, 143, 149, 151–3, 203, 215, 221, 225, 232, 250–1, 255, 266–8, 278, 288, 291–2, 319, 321, 330, 335, 340, 342, 344, 364–5, 368, 380, 382, 384, 390, 392, 398, 403, 409–10, 412, 418, 424, 439, 505, 517–9, 521–2, 533, 560, 622
Eastern Atlantic (i.e. NE Atlantic), xii, 8, 52, 82, 85, 106, 113, 116–9, 123, 141, 146–7, 152–3, 178, 189, 195–6, 200–4, 207–8, 211–7, 220, 229, 230, 252,

INDEX

254–7, 261, 266, 268–70, 278, 291, 293, 297, 332, 339–42, 347, 349, 351–3, 356, 359, 361, 363–5, 373, 375, 379, 383, 393–5, 398, 410–1, 415–6, 467, 472, 476, 480, 488–9, 505, 510, 520–1, 523–4, 528–30, 533, 560, 567, 569, 575, 581, 602, 621–4, 626; North Atlantic, 12, 59, 144, 148, 151, 255, 276, 286, 310, 361–2, 384, 448, 516, 519, 524; South Atlantic, xii, 6–8, 116, 193, 253, 255, 386, 409–12, 436–42, 444, 448, 460, 462, 464–7, 469, 472, 475, 479, 489, 491, 495, 529, 549, 561, 570, 573, 599, 601, 626; Western Atlantic (i.e. NW Atlantic), 152, 247, 255, 413
Atlantic Undersea Test and Evaluation Centre ('AUTEC'), Bahamas, 7, 248–9, 533, 609
Atomic Weapons Research Establishment, 277
AUKUS nuclear submarine agreement, 599
Australia, *see also* Royal Australian Navy, 5, 14, 58, 69, 73, 113, 148, 168, 208, 239–40, 244–6, 278, 292, 310, 407, 598–600, 607
Automated Flight Control System (helicopter), 147
Azores, The, 10, 117, 214–5, 279, 365, 404, 410, 412, 424, 441, 525, 605

Bab al-Mandab straits, 80
Bahamas, 7, 247–51, 609–10
Bahamas Patrol, 248–50
Balfour Beattie, contractors, 594
Bally-Kelly RAF air station, 14
Baltic Sea, 180, 230, 255, 321, 351, 410–2, 414, 509, 513–4, 616, 619
Bandeath Armament Depot, 268
Bangkok, Thailand, 3
Bangladesh, 608
Barbados, 247
Barber, Anthony, MP, 162
Barclays Bank plc, 594
Barents Sea, 10, 230, 274, 282, 362, 413, 514, 516, 518
Barrow, Captain Michael, 475
Basic Operational Sea Training, 538

'Bastion Strategy', Soviet naval, 267–8, 317, 507, 517, 519, 626
Bath, Somerset, 18, 22, 24, 333, 536
Bathurst, Admiral Sir Benjamin, 541, 614
Bathurst, Gambia, 6
Batista regime, Cuba, 248
Battle of the Atlantic, 12, 267, 491, 517
Bedenham Armament Depot, Gosport, 16
Begg, Admiral Sir Varyl, *see also* First Sea Lord, 15, 51–3, 55–9, 64, 68, 71, 85–6, 168–9, 178
Beira Patrol, 2–3, 13, 76–9, 85, 112, 116, 185, 243–4, 488
Beirut, Lebanon, 237–8, 605–7
Beith Armament Depot, Ayrshire, 17
Belfast, 17, 19, 21, 223–4, 579
Belfast Aircraft Repair Yard, 17
Belgium, 191
Belize, *see also* British Honduras, 198, 207, 248, 250–3, 369, 388, 394, 407, 411, 423, 439, 476, 502–3, 609–10
Belize City, 251
Berlin Crisis (1958–61), 82
Berlin Wall, fall of, 566
Bermuda, 7, 152, 236, 247, 249–50, 252, 537, 600, 601, 605
'Bermudagram' document, *see also* Defence Reviews, 1981, 347, 360–1, 364–73, 375, 394, 398, 407–8, 504
Best, Rear Admiral Thomas, 6
Bickleigh, Devon, 15
Bingham, Sub Lieutenant David, 125–6
Biscay, Bay of, 411
Black Sea, 230–3, 513–4
Blackham, Rear Admiral J L, 16
Blaker, Peter, MP, 414, 421
'Blue Belt of Defence' concept (Soviet Navy), 12, 85
Bluff Cove, Falkland Islands, 461–2
Board of Admiralty, 21
Boeing Marine Services, 320
Bombay, *see* Mumbai
Bombs, aerial free fall, *see* Nuclear Weapons for nuclear armed bombs, 14, 37, 40, 446–7, 451, 454–60, 462–3, 477–8, 481, 492–3, 495–6, 532, 557.
Bonn, West Germany, 62

Books of Reference, 126
Booz, Allen and Hamilton, 163
Boren, David, 394–7, 408
Borneo, Malaysia, 1, 3, 5, 15, 246
Bosphorus Straits, 216
Brawdy Naval Air Station/RAF air station, 13, 153, 418
Brazil, 170, 411, 608
Brezhnev, Leonid, 10
BRITFORLEB, peacekeeping force, 605–6
British Aerospace, 302, 313, 339, 580
British Aircraft Corporation, 21
British Army of the Rhine, *see also* British Forces Germany, 197, 200, 329, 349, 352, 361, 365, 381, 534
British Broadcasting Corporation (BBC), 287, 292, 440
British Carrier Strike Fleet after 1945, The (book), xiii
British Empire Medal, 32
British Forces Germany, *see also* British Army of the Rhine; Royal Air Force, RAF Germany, 329, 351–3, 385, 624
British Honduras, *see also* Belize, 7, 247, 250–1
British Indian Ocean Territory, *see also* Diego Garcia, 241
British Petroleum, 163, 284
British Shipbuilders Corporation Ltd, 285, 308–10, 322, 329, 416, 577–9
British Shipbuilders Act 1977, 577
British Virgin Islands, 247
British-India Steam Navigation Company, 241
Broadbent, Sir Ewen, 634
'Broadsheet' magazine, 288
Brooke Marine, shipbuilders, 578
Broughton Moor Armament Depot, Cumberland, 17
Brown, Admiral Sir Brian, 615
Brown, David K, 301, 320
Brown, Harold, 266, 516
Brown and Root, contractors, 594
Brunei, 246–7, 423, 600
Brussels, 326, 470
Brussels Treaty, 187, 261, 329, 342, 361, 365, 376, 380, 392, 395, 398, 624
Bryson, Admiral Sir Lyndsey, 506, 540

Bubiyan, Battle of, 1990–91 Gulf War, 484
Bulgaria, 216
Bunk sleeping (aboard ship), 88–9
Burdwood Bank, South Atlantic, 447
Bush, Vice Admiral Sir John, 23, 65

CAAIS tactical command system, 172, 175, 181, 478
Cabinet, xi, 39–40, 48, 59, 385, 387–91, 401, 406, 408–9, 422–3, 433
Cabinet Committees, 309, 343, 594
  MISC 2 (shipbuilding policy), 315;
  MISC 7 (deterrent renewal), 336, 406; Oversea Policy and Defence Committee (OPD, OD), 46–7, 49, 58, 193, 203–4, 379, 381, 385, 387, 389, 391, 401, 408, 422
Cabinet Office, 49, 190, 332, 498
Cabinet Secretary, 39, 46–7, 49, 136, 192, 309, 340, 384
Cable and Wireless Ltd., 440
CACS tactical command system, 300, 302, 567, 572–3
Caerwent Propellant Factory, Monmouthshire, 18
Callaghan, James, MP, *see also* Prime Minister, 278, 323, 336
Cambridge, University of, 97, 516
Cameron, Air Chief Marshal Sir Neil, 285
Cammell Laird, shipbuilders, 19, 65–6, 163–4, 309, 342, 344, 466, 556, 569, 578–9
Canada, *see also* Royal Canadian Navy, 126, 146, 153, 236, 251, 292, 310, 369, 411, 423
Cape Canaveral, United States, 278, 335
Cape Kennedy, United States, *see* Cape Canaveral, 11
Cape Province, South Africa, 6
Cape Town, South Africa, 6, 242
Cape Verde Islands, 276, 441
Captain in Charge, Hong Kong, 631
Captain, Mine Counter Measure Vessels, 108
Captain of Inshore Flotilla, Far East Fleet, 631
Captain of the Dockyard, Portsmouth, 16
Cairn Ryan, Scotland, 288

Caribbean, 7, 153, 193, 207, 221, 230, 242, 246, 247–53, 292, 320, 380, 409–12, 519, 583, 609–12, 627
Carlingford Lough, Northern Ireland, 224
Carrington, Lord Peter, *see also* Secretary of State for Defence, 136, 142, 158, 190, 329, 361, 385, 389, 406
Carter, Jimmy, 266, 295, 337, 365, 390, 397, 403–4, 434, 515–6, 625, 628
Carver, General Sir Michael, 191–2, 194–5, 197, 202, 205–9, 394
Cary, Sir Michael, 22, 210, 347–8
Cassels, Admiral Sir Simon, 506, 541
Cassidi, Admiral Sir Desmond, 506, 541
Cassidy, Rear Admiral T J, USN, 519
Castro, Fidel, 248
Cayman Islands, 247
Cecil, Rear Admiral O, 239
Center for Naval Analyses (US), 418, 515
Central Dockyard Laboratory, Portsmouth, 548
Central European Front (NATO), *see* North Atlantic Treaty Organisation
Central Front (NATO), *see* North Atlantic Treaty Organisation
Central Policy Review Staff, 190
Central Staffs, *see also* Defence Operations Staff; Defence Planning Staff; Defence Policy and Operational Staff; Defence Staff; 211, 262–3, 303, 348, 351, 358, 376, 396, 468–70, 473, 541–2, 546
Chancellor of the Exchequer, 192, 204, 212, 277, 315, 332, 334, 338, 344, 346, 385, 386, 388, 399
Charles, Prince of Wales, 249
Chatham Dockyard/Naval Base, 16, 20, 31, 107–8, 127–8, 322–4, 372, 378, 386–7, 401, 420–1, 426–8, 537
Chernavin, Admiral Vladimir, Soviet Navy, 616
Chief Constable, Admiralty Constabulary, 629
Chief Engineer's Department, Navy Department, 487, 592, 594

Chief Executive, Royal Dockyards, 629
Chief Naval Signals Officer, 630
Chief of Defence Procurement, 350, 542, 546, 630
Chief of Fleet Support, *see also* Vice Controller of the Navy, 87, 129, 133, 322–4, 329–30, 428–9, 506, 540, 592–3, 614
Chief of Naval Operations (United States Navy), 141–3, 233, 515, 518, 615
Chief of Naval Research, 629
Chief of the Air Staff, 40, 42, 44–5, 192
Chief of the Defence Staff, 23, 41, 49, 131–2, 189, 191, 285–6, 329–30, 346, 350, 355, 366, 394, 437, 452, 469, 473, 501, 506, 540–4, 546–7, 622
Chief of the Naval Staff, *see* First Sea Lord
Chief Scientific Adviser, Ministry of Defence, 45, 49, 350, 359, 367, 374, 376, 418, 422, 503–4, 521, 542, 546, 568
Chief Scientist (Royal Navy), 21–2, 629
Chief, Strategic Systems Executive, 630
Chief Technician, Artificer, 100
Chiefs of Staff Committee, 42, 57, 127, 191, 541–2
Chiefs of Staff Secretariat, 192
Childs, Nick, xiii
China, Peoples' Republic of, 4, 64, 84, 114, 240, 243, 292–3, 476, 511, 599, 614
Choiseul Sound, Falkland Islands, 453–4, 457
Churchill, Winston, 74
City University, London, 97
Civil Service Department, 332
Clapp, Commodore Michael, 442, 474, 486,
Clarke, Sir Richard 'Otto', 39
Clayton, Admiral Sir Richard, 115–6, 285, 309–10, 330
Clyde, River, 19, 20, 163, 318, 537
Coastal Command, Royal Air Force, *see also* 18 Group, 8, 13–14, 107, 109–10
Cockerell, Sir Christopher, 75
'Cod Wars', 189, 225–9, 279–82, 322

INDEX

Colombia, 611
Comacchio Company, Royal Marines, 284
Commandant General, Royal Marines, 15, 424, 630
Commander Amphibious Forces, 108
Commander Far East Fleet, 112, 631
Commander Maritime Air Eastern Atlantic (NATO), 109
Commander Naval Command South (NATO), 110
Commander Naval Forces, Gulf, 631
Commander South East Mediterranean (NATO), 110
Commander Strike Fleet Atlantic (NATO), 117
Commander Submarines Eastern Atlantic (NATO), 123
Commander-in-Chief
  Allied Forces Mediterranean (NATO), 110; Channel (NATO), 107, 141, 256; Eastern Atlantic (NATO), 8, 109, 138, 141, 274, 297, 324, 531; Far East (tri-service), 112, 132; Far East Fleet, 87, 110, 112; Fleet (CINCFLEET), 109–10, 113, 139, 141, 189, 256, 285, 323–4, 410, 429, 431, 438, 442, 470, 473–5, 477, 489, 498, 505–6, 531, 533, 535–6, 540, 544, 614, 616; Home Fleet, 8, 14, 107, 110; Mediterranean Fleet, 6, 110; Middle East (tri-service), 5, 79, 112; Naval Home Command (CINCNAVHOME), 102, 108–9, 111, 218–9, 285, 330, 506, 536, 541, 545, 614; North (NATO), 118; Pacific Fleet (US), 515; Plymouth, 108; Portsmouth, 15, 51, 104, 107–8; Western Fleet, 64–5, 110, 133, 139, 189
Commanders-in-Chief Committee (West), 107
Commando Logistics Regiment, 217
Commissions (Officers), *see also* Officers, Naval
  General List, 27–9, 33, 94–5, 98; Post List, 29, 94–5; Special Duties Officers, 17, 27–30, 104, 126; Split List, 94–6, 98; Supplementary List Officers, 27–8, 33, 104

Commissions (Ships)
  Foreign Service Commissions, 10, 93–4, 113; General Service Commissions, 10, 93; Home Sea Service Commissions, 10
Commodore, Amphibious Warfare, 631
Commodore, Hong Kong, 241, 631
Commodore, Minor War Vessels and Mine Warfare, 631
Commodore, Royal Fleet Auxiliary, 631
Commodore Superintendent, Singapore Dockyard, 631
Commonwealth, 3, 6, 41, 202, 247, 610
Communications Branch, Royal Navy, 26, 99
Communism, 4, 84, 114, 226, 228, 255, 360, 516, 534, 610, 619
Concept of Maritime Operations, NATO, *see* North Atlantic Treaty Organisation
Concept of Maritime Operations, US-UK, 264–8
Concepts of Operations, Royal Navy/ Ministry of Defence, 51–7, 250, 254–9, 261–6, 286, 305, 348, 356, 396, 398, 520, 563, 623
Condition-Based Maintenance, 596
Confidential Books, 126
Congress, United States, 59, 136–7, 392, 402, 409, 518
Conservative Party and governments, 36, 39, 79, 112, 135, 158, 165, 168, 190, 205, 209, 216, 229, 231, 239, 310, 314, 326–9, 336, 361, 379, 434, 501, 542, 577, 586, 591, 621, 624
CONSTRAIN report and process, 103–4
Continental Shelf Act 1964, 284
Contracts Department, Navy, *see* Navy Department
Controller of the Navy, 21–2, 72, 87, 132–3, 157, 161, 285, 309, 330, 428–9, 506, 540, 548, 568, 587, 593, 614
Convergence zone, 144–5, 523
Convoys, *see also* Naval Control of Shipping, 32, 42, 72, 117–9, 122, 137, 147, 151, 214–15, 219, 232, 238, 257–8, 262–3, 265–8, 279, 306–7, 317, 344, 354–5, 365–8,

375–6, 403–4, 414, 418–19, 466, 488, 522, 537, 600
Cook, Joy, 32
Cooper, Sir Frank, 347–8, 364, 367–8, 371–2, 376–9, 390, 394, 397, 403–4, 406, 408, 424, 469, 498, 502–3, 541
Copenacre Stores Depot, Wiltshire, 18
Coral Sea, Battle of, 37
Corfu, Greece, 8
Costa Rica, 250
Coward, Rear Admiral John, 616
Coward, Captain, Peter, 295
Cox, Vice Admiral John, 410
Crater City, Aden, 79
Crete, Battle of, 111
Crossmaglen, Northern Ireland, 224
CTF 311, *see* Task Forces, TF 311
CTF 317, *see* Task Forces, TF 317
Cuba, 84, 247–8, 407, 610
Cuban Missile Crisis, 11, 12, 82–3, 142, 230, 233, 235, 266, 268, 379, 395, 622
Culdrose Naval Air Station, 13
Cunard, shipping line, 579
Curtis, Dr T E, 524–5, 527
Cyprus, 119–20, 138, 198, 207, 232, 236–8, 388, 423, 476, 598, 606–7
Czechoslovakia, 84, 231

Dakar, Senegal, 441
Dalatangi, Iceland, 227
Damascus, Syria, 238
Dannreuther, Commodore H, 7
Dartmouth, Britannia Royal Naval College, 17, 97, 103–4, 283
Dartmouth Training Squadron, *see* Squadrons, Naval
Darwin, Falkland Islands, 452
DATUM 'data highway' project, 434
Dean Hill Armament Depot, Hampshire, 17
Decca Radar, 21, 273
Declaration of Independence (US), 287
Decoys, torpedo: Type 182 'Foxer', 452, 483
Deep layer, sea, 143–5
Deep sound channel, ocean, 145
Defence budget, 39, 43, 49, 53–4, 58, 156–62, 186–7, 192, 204, 209, 259, 261, 268–9, 307, 331–4, 338, 340, 345, 351, 353, 355, 367, 383,

385, 387, 389, 396, 404, 423, 432–4, 465, 549–55, 563, 586, 617, 623, 632–4
Defence Council, 21, 45, 58, 168
Defence Council Instructions (RN), 591
Defence Equipment Committee (MOD), 568
Defence Estimates, Annual, 16, 157–8
'Sketch' estimates, annual, 157–8, 161, 545, 643–4
Defence Expenditure Studies, *see* Defence Reviews
Defence Industry, *see also* Shipbuilding Industry
British, 19–21, 34, 191, 311–2, 333, 470, 565–6, 598; Soviet, 617, 619
'Defence Inflation', 187, 387, 551–2, 580, 587, 637
Defence Intelligence Staff (MOD), *see also* Intelligence, 23, 265, 361, 476
Defence, Ministry of, *see also* Defence Budget, Defence Council, Secretary of State for Defence, Chiefs of Staff Committee, Army Department, Air Force Department, Navy Department, Procurement Executive
As a civilian employer, 16, 31, 58, 112, 183–4, 329, 592–6; Finance Department of, 62, 130; Organisation and structure, 21–4, 38, 41, 55, 87, 105, 112, 158, 394, 539, 541–8, 592–6, 626
Defence Operational Analysis Establishment, West Byfleet, 356, 358, 375, 469
Defence Operations Staff (MOD), 473
Defence Planning Committee (NATO), 207
Defence Planning Staff (MOD), 232, 336, 376
Defence Policy and Operational Staff (MOD), 544
Defence Reviews
1957 ('Sandys Review'), 1; 1965–66 ('Healey Review'), 22, 39–50, 54, 67, 71, 74, 111, 133, 176, 190, 201, 205, 216, 231, 363, 620–1; 1966–67 ('Defence Expenditure Studies'), 57–9, 86, 111, 190, 205, 216, 231; 1974–75 ('Mason Review'), xii, 179, 182–3, 189, 191–210, 212–3, 216–9, 221–222, 229–30, 232, 237–41, 244, 249, 252, 254, 260–261, 267, 269, 319, 323, 340, 348, 353, 357, 367, 369, 375, 427, 622; 1980 ('Pym Mini-Review'), 338–43; 1981 ('Nott Review'), xii, xiv, 195, 201, 207, 229, 264, 288, 346–99, 402, 404, 409, 414–6, 419–20, 424–6, 430, 434, 443, 446, 485–6, 489, 499–502, 506, 521, 541–2, 549, 556–7, 592, 598, 623–5; 1990–91 ('Options for Change'), 555, 565, 587
Defence Sales Organisation (MOD), 62, 293
Defence Secretariat (MOD), 23, 193
DS1 (Defence Secretariat, Branch 1), 52; DS4 (Defence Secretariat, Branch 4), 23; DS5 (Defence Secretariat, Branch 5), 23
Defence Secretary, *see* Secretary of State for Defence
Defence Staff, *see also* Central Staffs, 23, 545–7
Defence Studies Working Party, *see also* Defence Reviews, 1974–75 Review, 162, 190–2
Defence White Paper, *see also* Statement on the Defence Estimates, 55, 137
'The Way Forward' (June 1981), 393
Defense, Department of, US, 390, 397–8, 402, 404, 409, 466, 470, 504, 518
Deltic diesel engine, 181
Denmark, 119, 279, 351, 411, 424, 535
Denmark Strait, 149
Depth Charges, *see also* Nuclear Weapons, Nuclear Depth Bombs, 149–50, 444, 462, 483
Deputy Chief of the Defence Staff, 132, 213, 355, 542, 545, 568
Deputy Chief of the General Staff (Soviet Union), 615
Deputy Chief of the Naval Staff, 87
Deputy Chief Scientist (Naval), 629
Deputy Controller, Warship Equipment, 630
Deputy Controller, Warships, 630
Deputy Director of Naval Construction, 301, 320
Deputy Under Secretaries, 546
Deputy Under Secretary (Budgets and Plans), 58
Deputy Under Secretary (Navy), 380
Détente, *see* Soviet Union
Devonport Dockyard/Naval Base, 16, 20, 31, 127–8, 184, 287–8, 292, 322–3, 420, 426–9, 439, 537, 586, 592–5
Devonport Management Ltd, 594
Diego Garcia, *see also* British Indian Ocean Territory, 241, 244, 476
Diesel generators on board ships, 496, 568
Diesel surface ship propulsion, 75, 114, 181, 239, 306–7, 321, 415
Digital Equipment Company Ltd, 597
Director General, Aircraft (Naval), 629–30
Director General, Fleet Services, 629
Director General, Fleet Support Policy and Services, 630
Director General, Future Materiel Projects (Naval), 630
Director General, Naval Manpower, 101, 629
Director General, Naval Manpower and Training, 589, 630
Director General, Naval Personal Services, 630
Director General, Naval Personal Services and Training, 629
Director General, Naval Recruiting, 629
Director General, Ship Refitting, 630
Director General, Ships, 176, 487, 629
Director General, Supplies and Transport, 18, 629–30
Director General, Weapons (Naval), 506, 629
Director of Civil Catering Services, 629
Director of Naval Administration Planning, 629
Director of Naval Air Warfare, Naval Staff, 290, 545, 614

INDEX

Director of Naval Manpower Planning, 221
Director of Naval Operational Requirements, Naval Staff, 544
Director of Naval Operations and Trade, Naval Staff, 544, 601, 630
Director of Naval Plans, Naval Staff, 189, 353, 474, 540, 544
Director of Naval Security, 630
Director of Naval Signals, 629
Director of Naval Staff Duties, Naval Staff, 630
Director of Naval Warfare, Naval Staff, 541, 545, 630
Director of Public Relations (Naval), 629
Director of Undersea Warfare, Naval Staff, 66
Director, Operational Requirements (Sea), 544
Director, Plans and Programmes (Sea), 544
Director, Royal Marine Manning and Personal Services, 630
Director, Royal Marine Operations, 630
Director, Women's Royal Naval Service, 219, 629
Directorate of Naval Operations and Trade, Naval Staff, 487
Distinguished Service Cross, 86, 132
Distinguished Service Order, 35
District Transport Movement Operation Centres, 534
Ditton Priors Armament Depot, Shropshire, 17
Djibouti, 80
DNA 1 tactical command system, 573
Docking and Essential Defects periods, 240, 391, 428, 430, 438, 489, 528, 537
Dockyard Services Act 1986, 594
Dockyard Vote, 16, 130, 592
Dockyards, Royal *see also* Naval Bases, Chatham Dockyard/Naval Base, Devonport Dockyard/Naval Base, Gibraltar Dockyard/Naval Base, Portsmouth Dockyard/Naval Base, Singapore Dockyard/Naval Base, 15–7, 20, 22, 106, 127–30, 176, 207, 219, 229, 239, 321–5, 327, 338, 372, 383, 425–30, 487, 583, 592–6, 617, 627

Contractorisation, 592–6; Royal Dockyard Policy Board, 592; White Paper, proposed, 324
Doctrine, 81, 106, 120, 123, 124–6, 139–40, 174, 178, 213, 217, 234, 266, 302, 520–1, 621, 628
Dominica, 247
Donaldson, Lord, 91
Donoughue, Bernard, 212
Dorman, Andrew, 396
Douglas Home, Sir Alec, MP, *see also* Prime Minister, 39
Down, County, Northern Ireland, 224
Dreyer, Admiral Sir Desmond, 22
Druze Muslims, Lebanon, 237–8
Duff-Mason Report (nuclear deterrent), 336–7
Dundee, Scotland, 122
Dunlop Tyres Ltd., 20
Duvalier, Jean-Claude 'Baby Doc', 610
Dyndal, Gert Lage, 49

Eaglescliffe Stores Depot, County Durham, 18
East of Suez, *see* Suez, Royal Navy East of
Eaton, Admiral Sir Kenneth, 614
Eberle, Admiral Sir James, 330, 616
Education and Science, Department of, 91
Egypt, 79–80, 82–4, 141, 231, 233–6, 603, 608
Electrical Branch, Royal Navy, 26
Electronic Warfare, 26, 33, 61, 96, 99, 114, 119, 125, 167, 298–300, 362, 368, 415, 433, 449, 468, 480, 503, 558, 602
'Abbeyhill', *see* UAA-1; Corvus 'Chaff', 120, 293, 442, 449, 458–9, 480; 'Orange Crop', 560; Super RBOC chaff launchers, 498; Type 670 jammer, 480; Type 675 jammer, 480; UA8/9 'Porker' passive intercept, 298; UAA-1 passive intercept, 167, 298–9, 413, 449, 465, 480
Elizabeth II, Queen, 41, 170–1
Elizabeth, Queen Mother, 378, 382, 386
Elworthy, Sir Charles, Air Chief Marshal, 42, 46, 132
Empress State Building, London, 22

Empson, Admiral Sir Derek, 112, 133, 285
Energy, Department of, 222–3, 284
Engineering Mechanic Branch, Royal Navy, 26
English Channel, 75, 117–8, 204, 255, 265, 274, 284, 298–9, 343, 351–2, 365, 520, 534
Esbjerg, Norway, 279
Ethnic minorities, in the armed forces, 589–91
European Court of Human Rights, 591
Exclusive Economic Zones
 Belize, 60; British, 256, 282, 284; Icelandic, 280
Exercises
 Alloy Express 82, 439
 Avalanche Express 84, 525
 Busy Eagle 84, 525
 Cadnam (British Honduras 1972), 251
 Centex (Deep sweep 1979)
 Cold Winter 79, 323
 Cold Winter 85, 530, 532
 Cold Winter 87, 530
 Cold Winter 89, 530
 Cold Winter 90, 530
 Cold Winter series, 530
 Compass 77, 292
 Dawn Patrol 74, 232
 Dawn Patrol 78, 323
 Dawn Patrol series, 217, 232
 Deep Express 75, 237
 Deep Express series, 216, 232
 Deep Furrow series, 216, 232
 Display Determination 79, 323
 Fettle (Bahamas 1971), 248
 High Wood 71, 120–2
 High Wood 75, 121, 279
 High Wood 77, 121–2, 279
 High Wood 79, 121–2, 279
 High Wood series, 120–3
 Hilex 8 (NATO HQ), 534
 Lime Jug 70, 119–20, 123, 145, 147
 Magic Sword North 81, 410–11
 Magic Sword South 81, 411
 Midlink 74, 116
 Midlink 76, 292
 Midlink 77, 292
 Mill Stream (1966), 3, 10
 North Star 89, 530
 Northern Merger 74, 119, 217

Northern Wedding 70, 117–18
Northern Wedding 78, 279, 288, 317, 323,
Northern Wedding 82, 529
Northern Wedding 86, 532–3
Northern Wedding series, 529–30
Ocean Safari 75, 279
Ocean Safari 77, 279
Ocean Safari 79, 279
Ocean Safari 81, 410–4, 529
Ocean Safari 83, 523, 530–1
Ocean Safari 87, 532
Ocean Safari series, 529–31
Ocean Span 73, 121
Ocean Venture (1981), 409–14, 511, 516, 519, 529
Open Gate 78, 323
Peacekeeper (1969), 117–8
Purple Oyster 75, 284
RIMPAC 86, 599
Rip Tide series, 117, 119
Roast Beef 82, 320
Sailor's Pride (1966), 8–10, 14
Sharp Spear 89, 530
Sindex 77, 292
Snow Scene (Belize 1975), 251
Springtrain 82, 438–9, 474, 490
Strong Express 72, 119, 127, 410
Swift Move 73, 119, 121, 217
Teamwork 76, 279
Teamwork 80, 279
Teamwork 84, 524–6, 530–1
Teamwork 88, 532, 615
Teamwork 90, 530–1
Teamwork series, 529–30
United Effort 83, 523
United Effort 84, 524–5
Whiskey Venture 79, 279

Faeroe Islands, 121–2, 363, 424, 559
Fairfield's, shipbuilders, 19–20
Falkland Islands, *see also* Falklands Campaign, 6–7, 76, 198, 253, 386, 388, 394, 425, 437, 465–7, 496, 501, 550, 573, 584, 598, 605–6, 612
  East Falkland, 436, 451–2, 456, 458, 460–1, 463, 472, 475
  West Falkland, 451–2, 456–7, 461
Falkland Sound, Falkland Islands, 451, 454–5, 460
Falklands, Battle of (1914), 506
Falklands Campaign (1982), *see also* Atlantic Ocean, South Atlantic; Task Forces; Task Groups; Task Units; xii–xiv, 81, 116, 167, 184, 199, 288, 299, 305, 369, 393–4, 419, 428–9, 434, 436–505, 519, 524, 526, 529, 531–2, 537–8, 540, 544, 549, 557, 561, 562, 567–8, 570, 583–4, 598, 600–1, 609, 614, 621, 625, 628
  Exclusion Zones, Maritime and Total, 445, 452, 471; Rules of Engagement, 471
Falklands Campaign, Lessons Learnt; 468–504, 553, 625–6, 628
  Air defence, 477–80, 557, 565; Air operations, other, 480–1, 560; Amphibious warfare, 485–6, 562; Anti-ship operations, 484; Anti-submarine warfare, 482–4; Battle stress, 491–2; Command and control, 471–6; Communications, 471–2; Damage control, 492–5; Electronic warfare, 480; Engineering, 495–6; FORMEX 100, Admiral Woodward's, 469; Intelligence, 476–7; Logistics, 486–9; Media Relations, 498–9; Mine warfare, 495; Naval gunfire support, 484–5, 567, 570; Personnel and training, 489–91; Procurement processes, 497–8; Ship survivability, 492–5, 499, 567–8, 570; Submarine operations, 481–2; White Paper, 500
Falmouth, Cornwall, 537
Fanning Head, Falkland Islands, 453
Far East Fleet, *see also* Commander-in-Chief Far East Fleet, Commander Far East Fleet, Flag Officer Second in Command Far East Fleet, 1–5, 7, 10, 35, 51, 79, 87, 92–3, 96, 110, 112–3, 189, 216, 239, 244
Farnfield, Commander Richard, 276
Faslane Naval Base, 14, 123, 439, 586
Federation of the West Indies, 247
Felixstowe, Essex, 537
Fell, Vice Admiral Sir Michael, 147, 217
Ferranti Defence Systems, 21, 302, 572–3
Fieldhouse, Admiral Sir John, *see also* First Sea Lord, 110, 245, 291–2, 330, 410, 438, 442, 448, 469, 471, 473–5, 505–6, 540, 544, 569, 573–4, 593
Fighting Instructions, *see also* Doctrine, 125–6, 180
Fiji, 246
Finance Department (MOD), *see* Defence, Ministry of
Finance Department (Navy), *see* Navy Department
First Lord of the Admiralty, 158
First Sea Lord, *see also*, Luce, Admiral Sir David; Begg, Admiral Sir Varyl; Le Fanu, Admiral Sir Michael, Hill-Norton, Admiral Sir Peter, Pollock, Admiral Sir Michael; Ashmore, Admiral Sir Edward; Lewin, Admiral Sir Terrence; Leach, Admiral Sir Henry; Fieldhouse, Admiral Sir John; Staveley, Admiral Sir William; Oswald, Admiral Sir Julian; xi, 1, 21–3, 35–6, 41, 45, 47, 49–50, 53, 55, 56, 60, 64, 68, 71, 75, 86, 94, 106, 126, 130, 132, 156, 165, 189, 192, 206, 210, 285, 290, 329–30, 333, 350, 369–70, 381, 391, 397, 405, 407, 422, 438, 446, 505–6, 540–1, 544, 546, 554, 568, 573, 593, 614–6, 621
Fisher, Admiral of the Fleet Sir John 'Jackie', 114
Fishery Protection Squadron, *see* Squadrons, Naval
Fitch, Admiral Sir Richard, 525, 541, 614–5
Fitzroy, Falkland Islands, 460
Five Power Defence Arrangements, 112, 239–40, 600
Flag Officer
  Aircraft Carriers, 13, 108, 631; Carriers and Amphibious Ships, 108, 147, 217, 296, 506; First Flotilla, 108, 116, 353, 438, 631; Flotillas Western Fleet, 108, 631; Gibraltar, 6, 108, 631; Malta, 110, 239, 631; Medway, 107–9, 631; Middle East, 5, 112; Naval Air Command, 13, 36, 108, 506, 545, 631; Plymouth, 108–9, 506, 631; Portland, 108–9; Portsmouth, 614, 616, 631; Rosyth, 109; Royal Yachts, 608; Scotland and Northern Ireland, 15–16, 109,

INDEX

227, 281, 631; Sea Training, 15, 108, 111, 572, 631; Second Flotilla, 113, 115, 291, 610, 614, 631; Second in Command Far East Fleet, 2, 79, 96, 113, 189, 631; Second in Command Home Fleet, 108; Spithead, 108; Submarines, 14, 66, 107, 123, 133, 139, 330, 442, 469, 631; Third Flotilla, 296, 410, 474, 525, 533, 540–1, 631
Flag Officers, in general, 21, 95, 100, 102–3, 106–7, 125, 130, 473–4, 476, 535–7
Fleetlands Aircraft Repair Yard, Gosport, 17
Fleet Air Arm, xiii, 2, 13, 35–6, 38, 51, 59–60, 63, 87, 111, 165, 214, 217, 288, 304, 506, 545, 584, 615
Fleet Contingency Ships, 323, 528
Fleet Maintenance Units, 129, 183–4, 240, 242, 627
Fleet Operational Analysis Staff, 470
Fleet Operational and Tactical Instructions, *see also* Doctrine,
Fleet Requirements Committee, 254, 260, 264, 300–2, 306, 310, 357, 416
Flexible Response, NATO strategy, 138–40, 196
Florida, United States, 247
Foley, Vice Admiral Bob, USN, 519
Ford, Gerald, 516
Foreign and Commonwealth Office, *see* Foreign Office
Foreign Office, 22, 39, 56, 191, 197, 206, 241, 249, 293, 330, 385, 590, 598, 600, 611, 62
Foreign Secretary, *see* Secretary of State for Foreign and Commonwealth Affairs
Fort Lauderdale, United States, 287, 533
Forth, Firth of, 9
Fortuna Glacier, South Georgia, 444
Foundation for International Security, 615
'Four Pillars', of British Defence, 202–3, 229, 330–2, 339, 342, 347, 359, 395
Fox Bay, Falkland Islands, 451, 460, 464
'Foxer', *see* Decoys, torpedo

France, 7, 47, 77–8, 135, 159, 174, 176–7, 181, 191, 205, 235, 245–6, 281, 295, 304, 313–4, 337, 352, 368, 411, 414, 447, 449, 470, 531, 566–7, 601, 605, 607–8, 612
Franco, General Francisco, 323
Franklyn, Captain P M, 616
Frater Armament Depot, Gosport, 16
Freetown, Sierra Leone, 441
Frewen, Vice Admiral Sir John, 8
Front for the Liberation of South Yemen, Aden/Yemen, 81
Frost, Rear Admiral Philip, 15
Future Fleet Working Party, 51–8, 63, 68, 70, 179

Gallipoli, Turkey, 216
Gambia, 6
Gan, Maldives, 207, 241
Garnier, Rear Admiral John, 608–9
Gas turbines, naval/aero propulsion, 11, 74–5, 129, 167, 169, 179, 307, 321, 415, 451, 495–6, 513, 554, 569
Gnome, 75, 147, 273; Olympus, 75, 451, 496, 600; Proteus, 74; Spey/SM1A, 37, 567, 570; Tyne, 75, 163, 567
Gdynia, Poland, 616
Geddes, Lord Raey, 20, 162–3
Gemini 8 space craft, xi
General Council of British Shipping, 601
General Electric Company plc (GEC), 273, 312, 559
General Staff, British, 352, 360
General Staff, Soviet, 140, 508
Geneva, Switzerland, 280
George VI, King, 133
Germany, Democratic Republic of (East Germany), 117, 616
Germany, Federal Republic of (West Germany), 58, 62, 74, 117, 159, 187, 191, 202, 205, 212, 231, 254, 261, 268, 289, 314, 330–1, 340, 342–4, 351–2, 361, 370, 376, 382, 392, 395, 398, 411, 421, 424, 443, 535, 566,
West German Navy, 320–1, 361, 531; Inner German Border (with East Germany), 142, 234, 267, 351, 501, 504
Germany (pre-1945), 12, 62, 114, 133, 175

Ghana, 115, 239
Gibraltar 8, 16, 17, 232, 238, 254, 323, 330, 338, 427, 439, 464, 476, 529, 605
Gibraltar Dockyard/Naval Base, 6, 9, 16, 32, 239, 323–4, 372, 378, 386–7, 426–8, 537
Gibson, Rear Admiral Donald, 13
Gilbert, John, MP, 324
Gilbert and Ellice Islands, 246
Giles, David, 570–1
Graseby Instruments, 21
Glasgow, 20, 506
Glass Reinforced Plastic (GRP), 181–2, 197, 315–7, 325
Good Hope, Cape of, 115, 241–2
Goodpaster, General Andrew, US Army
Goose Green, Falkland Islands, 452–4, 456
Goose Green, Battle of, 460
Gorbachev, Mikhail, 615, 617, 619
Gork'iy, Soviet Union, 509
Gorshkov, Admiral Sergey, Soviet Navy, 274, 379
Gosport, Hampshire, 14, 16–8, 102–3, 107
Government Communications Headquarters (GCHQ), 348
Gow, Sir Ian, MP, 333
Grantham Sound, Falkland Islands, 455
Gray, Vice Admiral John, 6
Grechko, General Andrei, Soviet Army, 274
Greece, 78, 232, 236–7
Greenland, 363
Greenland-Iceland-United Kingdom Gap, 117–9, 149, 208, 228, 255–8, 263, 278–9, 297, 356, 363–5, 375, 379, 383–4, 411–3, 427, 517, 520–1, 524–5, 529, 533
Greenwich, Royal Naval College, 17, 98, 350, 352, 431
Gregory, Vice Admiral Sir George, 15
Grenada, 247, 610
Griffin, Admiral Sir Anthony, 133, 285
Grimsby, Yorkshire, 538
Grog money, 87
Group Deployments, 114–6, 229, 239, 291–3, 296, 431, 488, 597–600, 622, 627

1973–74 Group Deployment (Task Group 321.1), 115–6; 1974 Group Deployment (Task Group 317.1), 116; 1975 Group Deployment (Task Group 317.2), 116, 245, 291–2; 1976 Group Deployment, 243, 292; 1977 Group Deployment, 292; 1978 Group Deployment, 292; 1979 Group Deployment, 292; 1980 Group Deployment, 292–3, 295; 1982 Group Deployment (cancelled), 598; Orient Express 83/84, 598–9; Global 86, 599–600; Outback 88, 600

Grove, Eric, xii, 50
Grytviken, South Georgia, 444–5
Guardships, 187, 254
   Belize, 207, 252, 411, 609; Gibraltar; Hong Kong. 112, 116, 240–1, 613; Singapore, 116, 239; South Georgia, 459; West Indies, 249–50, 407, 573, 609–11
Guatemala, 7, 247, 250–3, 476, 502–3, 609–10
Guided Missiles, for nuclear missiles, see Nuclear weapons
   AMRAAM, 477, 557
   Anti-Ship Euro-Missile (NATO), 314; AS12, 444
   AS-4 'Kitchen'/Kh-22 (Soviet), 215, 514
   AS-5 'Kelt'/KSR-2 (Soviet), 215
   AS-6 'Kingfish'/Kh-26 (Soviet), 215
   AS-7 'Kerry'/Kh-23 (Soviet), 313
   Blowpipe (British and Argentine), 342, 434, 454, 457
   Confessor, see Sea Wolf
   Exocet, 159, 161, 166, 171, 174–6, 178, 272, 276, 301, 305, 313–4, 357, 372, 417, 442–3, 449–50, 458–60, 463, 468, 470, 472, 477, 479, 494, 499, 569, 601, 640
   Future Air Defence Missile System, 566; Harpoon, 314, 480, 569
   Ikara, 54, 56, 72, 99, 148–9, 166–7, 172–5, 178, 270, 301–4, 401, 412, 438, 524, 529, 640
   Martel, 47, 174, 313, 363
   Phoenix (US), 214

   Principal Anti-Air Missile System, 567
   PX-430, see Sea Wolf
   Rapier, 341, 406, 453, 456, 457, 472; Sea Cat, 3, 21, 33, 61, 71–2, 148, 158, 175–6, 305, 443, 455, 457, 463, 478, 487, 498, 584
   Sea Dart, 21, 54–7, 68, 70–2, 148, 160, 166–8, 171–2, 176, 257, 259–60, 299–303, 307, 341, 357–8, 362, 366, 383, 393, 442–3, 446, 450–2, 456–2, 465, 472, 477–8, 498, 500, 565, 602–4
   Sea Eagle, 313, 342, 357, 366, 383, 386, 446, 557, 560
   Sea Skua, 305, 342, 456, 484, 560
   Sea Slug, 21, 68–70, 160–1, 206, 299, 454, 463
   Sea Sparrow (US), 176–7
   Sea Wolf, 21, 72, 158, 171, 175–7, 300–2, 305, 307–8, 362, 368, 372, 415, 417, 419, 442–3, 450–1, 454–5, 457, 458, 478, 484, 496, 552–3, 565, 567–70, 572, 575, 602–3, 640
   Sidewinder, 454–6, 477, 480, 487, 557
   Silkworm (China, Iran), 601
   Skyflash, 214
   Stinger, 454
   Sub-Harpoon, 313, 372
   Sub-Martel, 313
   SA-N-1 'Goa' (Soviet), 11
   SA-N-6 'Grumble'/S-300 (Soviet), 512
   SS-N-2 'Styx' (Soviet), 11
   SS-N-3 'Shaddock'/P-6, P-35 (Soviet), 11
   SS-N-7 'Amethyst' (Soviet), 231
   SS-N-12 'Sandbox'/P-500 (Soviet), 313, 512
   SS-N-19 'Shipwreck'/P-700 (Soviet), 313, 508
   SS-N-22 'Sunburn' (Soviet), 313
   Standard (US), 301–2, 393
   Tartar (US), 176, 245
   Tigercat, 251
   Tomahawk (US), 278, 314
Guided Missile Systems
   GWS 1 (Sea Slug), 68–9; GWS 2 (Sea Slug Mark II), 69–70; GWS 25 (Sea Wolf), 177; GWS 30 (Sea Dart), 166–7, 171–2, 301, 477–8; GWS 31 (Sea Dart Mark II), 300, 302–3; GWS 41 (Ikara), 166, 173

Gulf, The, see Persian Gulf
Gulf War (1990–91), 484, 577
Guns, Army: SP70 self-propelled, 356
Guns, Naval
   4.5in, Mk 6, 485; 4.5in, Mk 8, 68, 166–7, 172, 174–5, 300, 460, 567, 570; BMARC light guns, 498; Goalkeeper close-in weapon system, 479, 569; OTO Melara 76mm, 415, 570; Vulcan Phalanx close-in weapon system, 479, 498, 553, 565, 569
Gurkhas, Brigade of, British Army, 247, 460

Hadath, Lebanon, 605
Haiti, 247, 610
Hall Russell, shipbuilders, 283, 574, 578
Hamburg, West Germany, 566
Hamilton, Archie, MP, 589
Hamilton, Admiral Sir John, 6
Hammocks, 88–9, 316
Harland and Wolff, shipbuilders, 19, 561, 579
'Harmony' rules, 93–4, 113, 622
Haslar, Royal Naval Hospital, Gosport, 17, 537
Hastie-Smith, Richard, 404–5
Hawker Siddeley Group, aircraft manufacturers, 21, 37, 209, 313
Hawthorn Leslie, shipbuilders, 19
Hawkins, Vice Admiral Sir Raymond, 22
Hayward, Admiral Thomas, USN, 515–8
Head of Secretariat (Navy), 630
Healey, Denis, MP, see also Secretary of State for Defence, 21, 36, 40–9, 52–3, 55–9, 64, 70, 164–6, 190, 204, 212, 231, 277, 361
Heath, Edward, MP, see also Prime Minister, 135–7, 158, 228, 231, 329
Helicopters
   Airborne early warning, 289–91, 325, 479–80, 500; Anti-submarine, 13, 68, 76, 120, 146–7, 149, 186, 201, 258, 260–2, 271, 273, 291, 301, 304,

INDEX

306–7, 325, 355–8, 367–8, 383–4, 416, 418, 434, 465, 623, 625; Commando, 13, 30, 206, 343, 486, 550, 552, 563, 606; EH101/Merlin (Sea King Replacement), 366–8, 371–2, 378, 380, 395, 397, 418, 560–1, 569–70, 581, 585, 587; Gazelle, 434, 453, 461, 472; Lynx, 174–8, 259, 304–6, 356, 415, 444–5, 456, 483–4, 490, 526, 550, 560, 573, 606, 612; Sea King, 54, 61, 68, 119, 121–2, 147, 161, 165–6, 178, 259, 273, 283, 289–91, 304–7, 318, 367–8, 412, 415, 452, 465–6, 479, 483, 486, 500, 526–7, 550, 552, 560, 570, 585, 606; Wasp, 13, 72, 121, 146–8, 162, 173–4, 178, 249, 304, 444–5; Wessex, 2–3, 13, 30, 61, 76, 147, 206, 237, 343, 444–5, 458, 486, 550, 606; Whirlwind, 13
Hennessy, Peter, xiii, 199, 421
Herbert, Vice Admiral Peter, 442
Heseltine, Michael, MP, *see also* Secretary of State for Defence, 542–3, 546–7, 574, 593
Hewlett Packard, 473
High North region, 16, 180, 189, 279, 357, 407, 410, 413–4, 421, 475, 489, 505, 507, 513, 517–20, 530–2, 556, 626
High Wycombe, Buckinghamshire, 109
Hill, Rear Admiral J R, 95, 616
Hill-Norton, Admiral Sir Peter, *see also* First Sea Lord, 2, 131–2, 142, 191
Himalayan mountains, 243
Hine, Air Vice Marshal P B, 362–4
HMS Ark Royal Preservation Society, 288
Hobbs, David, xiii
Holts, shipowners, 163
Home, Sir Alec Douglas, MP, 39
Homosexuality, 591
Hong Kong, *see also* Commodore, Hong Kong; Captain in Charge, Hong Kong; Guardships, Hong Kong, 4, 112, 114–6, 179–80, 197–8, 221, 230, 239–41, 252, 261, 268, 292–4, 319, 424–5, 466, 476, 490, 583, 598, 600–1, 604–5, 613–4, 622, 637, 641–2

Hopkins, Vice Admiral Sir Frank, 23, 43–5, 49
Hormuz, Straits of, 294–5, 603, 605
House of Commons, *see* Parliament
Hovercraft Trials Unit, 75, 319–21, 434
Howe, Sir Geoffrey, MP, 334, 338
Howes, Rear Admiral Peter, 5
HP 9845 desktop computer, 473
Hull, General Sir Richard, later Field Marshal, 42, 49
Humphrey, Marshal of the Air Force Sir Andrew, 285
Hunt, Admiral Sir Nicholas, 540
Hurricane Gilbert, 611
Hurricane Hugo, 612
Hydrographer of the Navy, 220
Hydrographic Branch and Service, *see also* Warships, Hydrographic vessels, 189, 220, 221–3
Hydrographic Department, MOD, 22, 154
Hydrographic Office, 536
Hydrography, *see also* Oceanography, 153–5, 242, 246, 253, 388–9

Ibbs, Sir Robin, 547
IBM corporation, 473
Iceland, 113, 152, 204, 214, 225–9, 279–82, 363, 559
ICS3 internal ship communications system, 472
Improvised Explosive Devices, 224
Independent Study of Defence Organisation, 106
India, 84, 211, 241–4, 598–600, 608
Indian Ocean, *see also* Indo-Pacific, 2–5, 39, 53, 59, 62, 81, 83–4, 116, 141, 153, 185, 198, 206–7, 230, 241–4, 246, 255, 292–3, 295, 390, 402–3, 519, 598–9
Indonesia, 3, 4–5, 11, 600
Indonesian Confrontation, 1, 3, 5, 52, 58
Indo-Pacific region, 39, 56, 115, 293
Industry, Department of, 309–10
Intelligence, *see also* Defence Intelligence Staff; Falklands Campaign, Lessons Learnt, Intelligence; Naval Intelligence Division; Ocean Surveillance Information System (OSIS), 4, 82, 84–5, 153, 207, 233–4, 251, 256, 265, 267, 269–70, 274–7, 301,

308, 359, 361, 379–80, 446, 448, 469, 484, 509–10, 515, 517–9, 531, 540, 556, 603
Intelligence Branch (RN), 476–7
Interagency Committee on Oceanography, US, 154
Intermediate-range Nuclear Forces Treaty, 615
International Convention for the Safety of Life at Sea, 602
International Law of the Sea Conferences, 225–6, 228
International Monetary Fund, 268
Interrogator Friend of Foe transmitters, 472
Invergordon Oil Depot, Ross and Cromarty, 18
Iran, 6, 198, 210–12, 292
Iran-Iraq War (1980–88), 198, 294–5, 600–5, 627
Iraq, 2, 80, 484, 531, 605
Ireland, Republic of, 121, 224
Irish Sea, 16, 117, 121, 225, 279, 284
Island Strategy, Indian Ocean, 59
Isle of Wight, 19
Ismail, Abdul Fattah, 607
Isotherm layer, sea, 143, 151, 270–1, 483
Israel, 82, 136, 191, 196, 231, 233–4, 237, 242, 421, 447
Italy, 154, 159, 191, 232, 270, 368, 418, 459, 561, 566
Ivory Coast, 441
Izmir, Turkey, 8

Jakarta, Indonesia, 4–5
Jamaica, 7, 247, 611–2
Jane's Fighting Ships (publication), 74, 333, 570
Janvrin, Rear Admiral Hugh, 13
Japan, 19, 37, 84, 116, 239, 308, 330, 598–600
Java, Indonesia, 4
Jenkin, Rear Admiral D C, 292–3
Jinks, James, xiii
John Brown, shipbuilders, 19
John, Admiral Sir Caspar, 35, 60, 138
Johnson, Lyndon, 138
Johnston, General Sir Maurice, 347, 355–60, 367, 397, 418, 422, 568, 570, 574
Joint Maritime Operational Procedures, 119

Joint National Operations Planning Centre, 109
Joint Service Publication 4 (JSP 4), 81
Joint Tactical Information Distribution System (JTIDS), 558
Jordan, 82, 231, 237, 599
Joseph, Sir Keith, MP, 190
Jutland, Denmark, 279
Jutland, Battle of, 175, 417

Kamaran Island, Aden, 80
Kamchatka, Soviet Union, 516
Kaufmann, Gerald, MP, 309
Kelley, General Paul USMC, 518
Kennedy, John F, 138
Kennon, Vice Admiral Sir James, 506, 540
Kent, 323
Kenya, 2, 18, 241, 422, 600
Kevlar armour, 494
Khor Al Quawi, Oman, 81
Khormaksar, RAF Air Station, 79–80
Khormaksar, Aden/Yemen, 79–80, 608
Khrushchev, Nikita, 10, 56, 59
Kiel, Germany, 320
Kiely Report (into Tigerfish torpedo), 311–2
King George VI Dock, Singapore, 2
Kinloss, RAF Air Station, 14, 121, 272
Kiribati, 246
Kola Peninsula, Soviet Union, 507
Komarov, Vice Admiral D P, Soviet Navy, 616
Komsomol'sk-na-Amure, Soviet Union, 510
Kosygin, Andrei, 10
Kuwait, *see also* Gulf War (1990–1), 1, 80, 531, 601–2, 605
Kynaston, David, 407
Kyparissia, Greece, 232
Kyrenia, Cyprus, 236

Labour Party and governments, xi, 20, 36, 39–41, 48, 77, 79, 137, 157–8, 162, 192–4, 204–5, 211, 231, 277, 308, 310, 323, 327, 335–6, 343, 379, 589
Labuan, Malaysia, 3
Lafonia, Falkland Islands, 452
Lagos, Nigeria, 44
Lake Point, Falkland Islands, 436

Lamberton secure speech communications system, 465, 471, 560
Lamont, Norman, MP, 594
LAPADS sonar processor, 273
Larken, Captain E S J, 475
Latakia, Syria, 233
Law, Admiral Sir Horace, 22, 87, 133
Lawrence Livermore National Laboratory, United States, 278
Le Bailly, Admiral Sir Louis, 86
Le Fanu, Admiral Sir Michael, *see also* First Sea Lord, 68, 79, 81, 86–7, 106, 130–2, 165, 178
Leach, Admiral Sir Henry, *see also* First Sea Lord, 116, 330, 350, 369, 381–2, 397, 403, 407–8, 438, 505–6
Leader of the House of Commons, 344, 406
Lebanon, 237–8, 526, 598, 605–7
Lee, John MP, 593
Lee-on-Solent, Hampshire, 17, 75
Leeward Islands, Caribbean, 247
Lehman, John, 404, 410, 414, 515–8, 533
Leitch Report on married quarters, 586
Leith, South Georgia, 445
Leith Cardle ship compartment doors, 494
Leningrad, Soviet Union, 513, 616, 619
Leppard, Captain Keith, 288
Leuchars, RAF Air Station, 121
Levene, Peter, 592–3
Lewin, Admiral Sir Terence, *see also* First Sea Lord, 102–3, 110, 113, 115–6, 133, 161, 285–6, 329–30, 346, 350–2, 360, 369, 376, 380, 385, 408, 410, 421, 437, 469, 473, 498, 501, 505, 541–2, 544
Lewis, Admiral Sir Andrew, 91, 97, 133
Liberia, 6, 459, 612–3
Libya, 76, 533, 606
Link 10 tactical communication system, 172, 471
Link 11 tactical communication system, 167, 173, 558
Link 14 tactical communication system, 473
Link 16 tactical communication system, 305, 558

Little Aden, Yemen, 608
Liverpool, 20, 537, 578
Lloyd's Register, 571
Local Government Act 1988, 591
Lofoten, Norway, 118
Logistics, *see* Assisted Maintenance Periods; Condition Based Maintenance; Docking and Essential Defects Periods; Dockyards; Falklands, Lessons Learnt, Logistics; Fleet Maintenance Units; Replenishment at sea; Royal Fleet Auxiliary
Logistics and Loitering Area, South Atlantic, 441
Lombok, Straits of, 5
Londonderry, Northern Ireland, 8, 14, 145, 224
Londonderry Squadron, *see* Squadrons, Naval
Long Term Costing Assumptions, 156–7, 165, 178, 186–7, 305–6, 353, 641–3
Long Term Costings, 156–8, 161–2, 186, 190, 348–9, 365, 368–76, 387, 429, 521, 545, 549–50, 552–5, 564, 643–4
Long Term Studies Group, 191
Long War/Long Warning scenarios for war, 264–8, 353, 360, 370, 397, 403, 522, 536, 538
Lossiemouth Naval Air Station/RAF Air Station, 13, 214
Luce, Admiral Sir David, *see also* First Sea Lord, xi–xii, 1, 35–6, 41, 44–9, 51, 60, 397, 506
Luns, Josephy, 228
Luqa, RAF air station, Malta, 238
Lygo, Vice Admiral Sir Raymond, 290, 306
Lympstone Commando Training Centre, Devon, 425
Lyness Oil Depot, Orkneys, 18, 268
Lyngenfjord, Norway, 532
Lyons, Vice Admiral James, US Navy, 616

McDonnell Douglas, aircraft manufacturer, 37
McGeoch, Rear Admiral Ian, 14
McIntyre, W David, 246
MacDonald, Admiral Wesley, US Navy, 616
Macao, 115

INDEX

Madagascar, 77
Madeira, 424
Magnetic Anomaly Detector, 149–50, 302, 305, 418, 483, 526
Majunga, Madagascar, 77
Makarios, Archbishop, 236
Makarov, Admiral Konstantin, Soviet Navy, 616
Malacca, Straits of, 4
Malakhit, submarine design bureau, Soviet Union, 509
Malayan Insurgency, 1
Malaysia, 3, 5, 76, 159, 239, 246, 598, 600
Malaysian Navy, 239–40
Maldives, 207, 241
Malta, 6, 8, 14, 17, 32, 110, 119, 198, 206–8, 216–8, 223, 231, 236, 238–9, 284, 637
Malta Convoys, Second World War, 111, 189
Manadon, Royal Naval Engineering College, 17, 97–8
Manila, Philippines, 239
Manning Directorate, Navy Department, 220
Manpower Planning Directorate, Navy Department, 220–1
Manual of Naval Security, 591
Marchwood Military Port, Hampshire, 439
Marconi, electronics company, 21, 177, 273, 290, 302, 312, 315, 422–3, 524
Maritime Contingency Force, NATO, *see* North Atlantic Treaty Organisation
Maritime Strategy, US, 264, 403, 505, 514–22, 532–3, 538, 615, 626, 628
Maritime Tactical School, RN, 306
Markov, Rear Admiral, Soviet Navy, 616
Marks and Spencer Ltd, 332
Maronite Christians, Lebanon, 237–8
Married quarters policy, 101–2, 110, 115, 240, 586–7
Martin, Captain T L, 16
Mason, Sir Ronald, *see also* Chief Scientific Adviser, 355, 367, 374–6, 379, 394, 502–4, 542, 568
Mason, Roy, MP, *see also* Secretary of State for Defence, 194, 205, 210, 211–2

Matapan, Battle of Cape, 111
Mauritius, 17, 198, 207, 241–2, 244, 476, 599
Mayhew, Christopher, MP, xi, 21, 36, 45, 47–9
MBT 80 tank, 341
Medical Branch, Royal Navy (officers and ratings), 29, 352, 366, 492
Medical Director General, Royal Navy, 629
Mediterranean Fleet/Station (Royal Navy), 1, 6–7, 10, 83, 107–8, 110
Mediterranean Sea, xiii, 6–9, 33, 52, 83–4, 106, 111, 113–4, 116, 119, 130, 140–3, 145, 151, 159, 175, 181, 193, 199, 203–4, 207, 216–7, 221, 229–39, 252–3, 255, 268, 278, 284, 288, 291–2, 380, 410–2, 427, 438, 474, 516, 519, 526, 583, 602–3, 605
Mention in Despatches, 86
Merchant Marine, 31, 124, 487
Merchant Navy Training Board, 31
Merchant vessels
  Astronomer, 466
  Atlantic Conveyor, 458, 491, 579
  British Wye, 459
  Canberra, 440, 447, 453, 460, 464
  Container ships, 440, 458, 466
  Contender Bezant, 561
  Diamond Express, 608
  Europic Ferry, 453
  Everton, 227
  Gentle Breeze, 604
  Hercules, 459
  Lloydsman, 227
  Lord St Vincent, 228
  Luz Maria, 611
  Lycaon, 441
  Mighty Servant I, 604
  Miss Beverly Ann, 611
  Narwhal, 451
  Norland, 453, 456, 460, 464
  Oil Endeavour, 602
  Oil tankers, 6, 77–8, 232, 423, 440–1, 459, 601, 603–4
  Queen Elizabeth II, 440
  Roll-on roll-off ships, 440, 561–2, 607
  Salvageman, 464
  Seaforth Clansman, 318–19
  Stena Inspector, 184, 466, 496
  Stena Seaspread, 184, 451, 466–7, 487, 489, 496

Suffolk class stern trawlers, 317
Tor Bay, 604
Trawlers, 225–9, 279–81, 283–4, 317–8, 440, 451, 464, 484, 488, 495, 576, 581
Tugs, 226–8, 280, 440, 464
Messina, Straits of, 232
Metcalf, Admiral Joseph, US Navy, 525
Mexico, 247, 250
Mexico, Gulf of, 365
Miami, United States, 610
Michael Heseltine, MP, 542–3, 546–7, 574, 593
Middle East Station (RN), 6, 9, 112
Middleton, Captain Linley, 290–1, 475–6
Midway, Battle of, 37
Milford Haven, Pembrokeshire, 17, 537
Military Aid to the Civil Authorities, 284
Military Aid to the Civil Power, 247–8
Military Branch, Admiralty, 23
Military Sealift Command, United States, 403
Military Secretary, Commandant General Royal Marines, 630
Mine warfare, 76, 118, 180–2, 184, 186, 218–9, 235–6, 259–60, 315–20, 325, 371–2, 380, 464, 488, 495, 522, 530, 576–7, 581–2, 602–5, 640
Mines, naval
  PMR-2 rising mine (Soviet Navy), 316; Rising mines, 316–7, 320, 530, 576; RM-2 rising mine (Soviet Navy), 316
MINIS, 542–4
Minister of State for Defence, 209, 324, 529
Minister of State for the Armed Forces, 589, 593
Minister of State for the Navy, xi, 21, 36, 45, 47–8, 50, 56, 621
Minister of State for Defence Procurement, 297, 493
Ministry of Defence, *see* Defence, Ministry of
Misick, Stafford, 610
Mitchell, Rear Admiral Geoffrey, 123, 218
Mombasa, Kenya, 2, 241, 600

Mombasa Armaments Depot, Kenya, 18
Monrovia, Liberia, 6, 612–3
Montserrat, 247, 612
Moody Brook, Falkland Islands, 436
Moore, Major General Jeremy, 442, 460
Moore, Captain John, 333–4, 570, 623
Mortar, anti-submarine, 71–2, 121, 145, 147–8, 462, 483
Morton, Vice Admiral A S, 243, 292, 304
Moscow, Soviet Union, 134, 233, 277–8, 336, 406, 615–6, 619
'Moscow Criterion', 134–6, 277, 336, 406
Mottram, Sir Richard, 348, 364
Mount Batten, RAF air station, 14
Mount Harriet, Falkland Islands, 460
Mount Kent, Falkland Islands, 460
Mount Rosalie, Falkland Islands, 461
Mount Soufriere, St Vincent, 248
Mountbatten, Admiral of the Fleet, Lord Louis, 1, 41–2, 73, 75–6, 94, 285, 506
Mozambique, 2, 77–8, 84, 243–4
Mullard Research Laboratories, 299
Mulley, Fred, MP, *see also* Secretary of State for Defence, 285
Multi-National Force, Lebanon, 605–7
Mumbai, India, 241, 293, 598
Murray, Bob, 390
Mururoa Atoll, French Polynesia, 245
Mutual Defence Agreement (US-UK), *see also* Nuclear Weapons, 337

Nab Tower, Solent, 76
Nairne, Sir Patrick, 23, 42, 47, 49, 192, 348
National Aeronautical and Space Agency (NASA, United States), 440
National Audit Office, 595
National Health Service, 190
National Liberation Front, Aden, 80
National Research Development Corporation, 75
National Security Council (US), 136
National Service, 33
National Union of Seamen, 424
Naval Administrative Planning Division, Naval Staff, 23
Naval Air Mechanic Branch (RN), 26

Naval Air Squadrons (RN)
  800 NAS, 13; 801 NAS, 13; 803 NAS, 2, 13; 809 NAS, 2, 13, 289; 814 NAS, 13, 526; 815 NAS, 2, 13; 819 NAS, 13; 820 NAS, 13; 829 NAS, 13; 845 NAS, 13; 848 NAS, 3, 13; 849 NAS, 13; 890 NAS, 13; 892 NAS, 13, 289; 893 NAS, 13; 899 NAS, 13
Naval Air Stations, *see* Brawdy, Culdrose, Lossiemouth, Portland, Yeovilton
Naval Air Warfare Division, Naval Staff, 23, 290, 545, 614
Naval Aircraft Materials Laboratory, Fareham, 19
Naval Airman Branch, Royal Navy, 26
Naval Armaments Group, NATO, *see* North Atlantic Treaty Organisation
Naval Bases, *see* Bermuda, Chatham, CONSTRAIN, Devonport, Faslane, Gibraltar, Malta, Portland, Portsmouth, Rosyth, Shore Establishments
Naval Construction Research Establishment, Dunfermline, 19, 548
Naval Control of Shipping, *see also* Convoys, 32, 219, 535, 537
Naval Discipline Act 1957, 30, 219, 591
Naval gunfire support, *see also* Falklands, Lessons learnt, Naval gunfire support, 73, 445, 463–4, 470
Naval Intelligence Division, Admiralty, 23
'Naval News Bulletin' magazine, 288
Naval Operational Research Department, MOD, 22
Naval Operations and Trade Division, Naval Staff, 23, 487, 544, 601, 630
Naval Operations Staff, 473
Naval Ordnance Inspection Laboratory, Caerwent, 19
Naval Party 1015, *see also* Mine Warfare, 603
Naval Plans Division, Naval Staff, 23
Naval Secretary, 36, 629–30
Naval Staff (RN), *see also* Fleet Requirements Committee, 15, 22–4, 36, 51, 53, 55, 57, 61, 65–6,

86, 140, 176, 178–80, 185–6, 259, 261, 263–4, 290, 297–8, 301, 304–6, 308, 321, 404–5, 416, 418–9, 423, 428, 443, 468, 470, 486–7, 503–4, 541, 550, 553, 568–71, 574, 614
  And the battle for CVA01, 38, 41–5, 47, 49, 620; and the 1974–75 Defence Review, 197, 202, 208; and the 1981 Defence Review, 347–50, 353–5, 357–9, 370, 373, 380, 391, 396–7, 625; and defence reform (1984–85), 544–8
Naval Staff Requirements, 209, 315, 574
Naval Staff Targets, 300, 307, 574
Naval Tactical and Weapons Policy Division, Naval Staff, 23
Naval War Manual, *see also* Doctrine, 124
Naval Weather Service, 23, 154
Navigation and Tactical Control Division, Naval Staff, 23
Navy Board, Ministry of Defence, 545, 548, 571, 576, 585, 587–8, 615
Navy Department, MOD, 19, 52–3, 62, 68, 76, 89, 157, 161–2, 200, 209, 211–2, 290, 297, 303, 305, 309–11, 329, 333, 356–8, 361, 370, 378, 380, 396–7, 400, 402–3, 430, 432, 468–70, 483, 491, 493, 498–9, 544–6, 548, 552, 571, 574, 592–3, 623, 629–30
  Contracts Department, 22, 157; creation of, 1964, 21–3; budget of, 62, 70, 156–8, 161–2, 261, 341–2, 367, 371–2, 376, 404, 423, 433; Finance Department, 22; Ship Department, 22, 52, 56, 72–3, 75, 130, 148, 158, 169–70, 176, 180, 285, 303, 309, 320, 333, 417, 419, 422, 487, 493, 499, 570; Trident, bearing the costs of, 349, 355, 366
Navy Department, US Department of Defense, 514–5, 517
Navy Minister, *see* Minister of State for the Navy
'Navy News' newspaper, 288
Netherlands, The, *see also* Royal Netherlands Navy, 70, 123–4, 166,

INDEX

176–7, 191, 411, 417, 479, 520, 523, 535, 569, 604
Nevada, US, 136
New Hebrides, 246
New Management Strategy, Ministry of Defence, 547
New Zealand, *see also* Royal New Zealand Navy, 113, 208, 239–40, 245, 246, 292, 310, 437, 598, 607
Newcastle, 20
Newman, Captain R T, 263–4
Nicaragua, 250
Nigeria, 441
Nixon, Richard, 136
Nkrumah, President Kwame, 115
Norfolk, United States, 152, 366
Normandy Landings (1944), 35
North Atlantic Treaty Organisation (NATO), 11–3, 52–3, 57, 84, 109–10, 113–4, 117–8, 122–3, 136, 141–2, 180, 189–91, 193–5, 198–200, 203, 205, 207, 215, 225, 228–9, 231, 237, 239, 249, 252, 255, 257, 263–70, 275, 282, 298, 314, 316, 326, 331, 340, 344, 347, 351–3, 356, 359–61, 363, 379–80, 383, 390, 394, 396, 399, 403, 410–2, 414, 420–1, 427, 470, 472–3, 507–8, 510–1, 513–5, 517, 520–1, 529, 532, 534–7, 623
Air Mobile Force, 198; Article 5 commitment, 118; and British nuclear deterrent, 64, 134, 136–7, 139; Central European Front/Central Front, xii, 117, 119, 138, 195, 204, 207, 213, 215, 229, 232, 234, 253–4, 261, 267–8, 297, 329–31, 342, 347, 349, 351–3, 358, 360–1, 373, 379–80, 385, 395, 504, 515–6, 622, 626; carrier strike fleet/groups, 12, 255–6, 262–3, 265, 278–9, 291, 296, 306, 312, 362, 410, 508, 522, 531, 538; commands held by RN officers, 6, 8, 14, 107, 109–11, 123–4, 141, 256, 324, 412, 531; commands, other, 110, 118, 124, 141–2; Concept of Maritime Operations, 520, 522; doctrine, 123, 126, 139–40, 521; maritime Contingency Force, 522; Military Committee, 410; NATO exercises, *see also* Exercises, 7, 33, 106, 114, 117, 121, 131, 217, 219, 229, 232, 278–9, 368, 410, 413, 489, 505, 511, 524, 527, 528, 529–33, 602, 605; Naval Armaments Group, 314; naval forces, 63, 82–5, 118–9, 140–1, 151, 180, 210, 256, 265–6, 269, 272, 301, 314, 317, 340, 413, 508, 514, 517, 518, 520, 530, 539; Northern Flank, 196, 198–200, 216–7, 256, 354, 439, 485, 489, 501; Nuclear Planning Group, 140; Secretary General, 228, 389, 393; Royal Marine commitments to, 424–5; Royal Navy commitments to, 10, 57, 161, 178–9, 193–5, 197, 200, 203–4, 222, 255, 284, 296, 342–3, 351, 353, 373, 377, 390–3, 404, 540, 563, 569, 581, 626; Southern Flank, 196, 198, 207, 216, 229, 232, 237; standardisation and joint procurement, 177, 500, 565–7, 626; Standing Naval Force Atlantic, 122–3, 131, 411, 413, 531; strategy, 114, 116–7, 119, 124, 137–8, 140, 142–3, 155, 194–6, 199, 201, 213, 261–2, 265, 343, 520, 532
North Cape, 413
North Cape, Battle of the, 133, 330
North, Ian, 491
North Sea, 35, 121, 148, 151, 180, 221, 255, 274, 282–4, 321, 323, 388, 411, 520
North-Western Approaches, 317
Northern Ireland, 15, 17, 189, 218, 223–5, 229, 423, 425, 614, 637
Northwood, United Kingdom, 8, 14, 64, 107, 109–10, 153, 161–2, 274, 297, 442, 448, 452, 471, 473, 475, 489, 531
Norway, 19, 49, 113, 117–9, 123, 216–8, 256, 278–9, 282, 306, 357, 407, 411, 424, 485, 513, 525, 530–2
Norwegian Sea, 10, 120, 122, 151, 180, 225, 256, 274, 279, 357, 362, 404, 410–1, 413, 505, 509–10, 514, 516, 518, 520–3, 529–30, 533, 615

Nott, Sir John, *see also* Secretary of State for Defence, xiv, 142, 344, 346–7, 349–50, 352–3, 355, 358–61, 364–76, 378–400, 402–4, 406–10, 416, 420–4, 426, 428, 430–5, 465, 500, 502–4, 541–2, 549–50, 568–9, 624–5, 628
Nuclear propulsion, 14, 65, 158, 164–5, 406, 511, 555
Nuclear weapons, *see also* Duff-Mason Report, Mutual Defence Agreement, Polaris Sales Agreement
Antelope, 135; Chevaline, 137, 277–8, 330, 335–7, 341; Multiple Independently targetable Re-entry Vehicle, 134–7, 337, 405; Multiple Re-entry Vehicle, 134–5; nuclear bombs, freefall, 137–8, 598; nuclear depth bombs, 125, 137, 139–40, 149–50, 598; penetration aids, 135, 277, 335; Pershing (US), 140; Polaris, 12, 22, 62–5, 83, 107, 125, 131–5, 137, 154, 158, 183, 201, 277–8, 330–1, 335–7, 340, 378, 405, 585, 593; Poseidon (US), 134–7, 335, 337, 405; R-27 (Soviet), 151; R-29 (Soviet), 151, 517; R-29RM (Soviet), 507; R-39 (Soviet), 507; Red Beard, 138; Skybolt, 63; Stag, 135; Super-Antelope, 135–7; tactical nuclear weapons, 137–9, 201, 357, 417, 598; Trident, 336–8, 349, 355, 365–7, 371, 379, 381, 390, 392, 394, 402–9, 420, 434, 549–50, 552–6, 575, 581, 585, 625, 628; WE177, 138, 598

O'Brien, Rear Admiral Sir William, 36
Oasis, computerised stores management system, 596–7
Ocean Surveillance Information Centre, US Embassy, London, 153
Ocean Surveillance Information System (OSIS), 153, 269, 275
Oceanography, *see also* Convergence zone, Deep layer, Deep sound channel, Isotherm, Thermocline, 18, 146, 153–5, 221, 223, 270, 374–5, 448, 534–5, 621, 624

Office of Management and Budget, MOD, 546
Officers, Naval, *see also* Commissions (Officers), 24, 27–30, 87, 94–8, 101–2, 104, 124, 126, 228, 327–9, 371, 378, 387, 401, 475–6, 489, 492, 567, 575, 584–5, 621, 635–7
  Branches, 29; Retired List, 32; Emergency List, 32, 219
'Offshore Tapestry', 282–5
Oil and gas, industry and supply of, *see also* Iran-Iraq War
  Gulf, 6, 142, 185, 198, 232, 236, 294–5, 351, 601, 604; North Sea, 180, 203, 221–3, 282–4, 321, 323, 362, 425, 577; Rhodesia, supply of oil to, 77–8, 243; warship fuel, oil as, 18, 185, 240, 268, 306, 378, 440–1, 459, 493, 499
Oil Crisis, 1973, 156, 171, 190–1, 232, 255, 279, 308
Old Admiralty Building, Whitehall London, 22, 547
Old Kilpatrick Oil Depot, Dumbartonshire, 18
Oman, 81, 295, 599, 601–2, 608
Oman, Gulf of, 295
Omand, Sir David, 348, 359, 364, 372–3, 378, 391–2, 403, 408–9, 424
Operational Analysis, *see also* Defence Operational Analysis Establishment, Fleet Operational Analysis Staff, 44, 45, 52, 57, 172, 174, 213–6, 257, 259, 356, 358, 367–8, 375, 395, 398, 542
Operational Concept, *see* Concept of Operations
Operational Defects (OPDEFs), 484, 537, 597
Operational Evaluation Group, Royal Navy, 272, 470, 523
Operational Requirements Committee, MOD, 209, 312, 418, 561, 569, 574
Operations, codenames (British or NATO unless otherwise stated)
  Activate (Barents Sea 1981), 413
  Algy (Okean 75 shadowing), 274–5
  Armilla (Persian Gulf 1980 onwards), 293–6, 359, 488, 528, 600–6, 608, 627

Armilla Accomplice (Gulf 1984), 602–3
Balsac (Yemen 1986), 607–9, 612
Cimnel (Gulf 1987–88), 603–5
Corporate (Falklands 1982), *see also* Falklands campaign, 436–67
Cosmos (Haiti 1986), 610
Dewey (Cod Wars), 227–9, 280–2
Eldorado (Liberia 1990), 612–3
Eschew (Turks and Caicos 1985), 610–1
Glasscutter (Northern Ireland 1972), 224
Granby (Kuwait liberation 1990–91), *see* Gulf War (1990–91)
Grenada (Northern Ireland), 225, 614
Harling (Gulf of Suez 1984–85), 603
Heliotrope (Cod Wars), 280
Hemicarp (Gilbert and Ellice Islands 1977), 246
Hemicarp II (Gilbert and Ellice Islands 1977), 246
Impresario (towed-array patrol 1987), 528
Interknit (Northern Ireland 1972 onwards), 225
Keyhole (Southern Thule 1982), 464–5
Larder (shadowing), 274
Magister (Aden 1967), 79–81
Mimulus (towed-array patrol 1987), 528
Monitor (Aden 1967–68), 81
Motorman (Northern Ireland 1972), 224
Nolan (Belize 1980s), 609
Ocean Tracker (Caribbean 1988 onwards), 611
Offcut (Lebanon 1983–84), 605–7, 612
Okean 70 (Soviet Navy), 412
Okean 75 (Soviet Navy), 274–5, 475
Optic (Belize 1970s), 250
Praying Mantis (US, Gulf 1988), 604
Rheostat (Suez Canal 1974), 235–6, 603
Rheostat II (Suez Canal 1975), 235–6, 603
Seawolf (Colombia 1980s), 611

Sharp Edge (US, Liberia 1990), 612
Sheepskin (Anguilla 1969), 249
Titan (New Hebrides 1980), 246
Tornado (Falklands 1982), 453
Operations, Royal Navy, *see also* Aden, Armilla Patrol, Beira Patrol, Cod Wars, Falklands Conflict; 1–5, 7, 76–81, 223–9, 235–8, 246, 248–52, 274–7, 279–82, 294–5, 413, 436–67, 600–13
Operations Branch, 101, 126, 430
Operations Room Working Party, 96
Order in Council, secondary legislation, 487
Order of the British Empire, 35
Orkney Islands, *see also* Scapa Flow, 18
Orthodox Christians, Lebanon, 237
Osorio, Colonel Carlos Arana, 250
Oswald, Admiral Sir Julian, *see also* First Sea Lord, 533, 614, 616
'Out of Area' operations, 116, 189, 252, 261, 263, 351, 357, 359, 361, 373, 384, 394–5, 425, 434, 502, 504, 583, 599, 627
'Outboard' surveillance system, 272, 275–6, 305–6, 308, 380, 383, 413, 415, 528, 567, 569, 616
Outer Hebrides, 559
Overseas Development, Department of, 222
Owen, Dr David, MP, 130, 277, 292
Oxford, University of, 97

Pacific Ocean, *see also* Indo-Pacific, 6–7, 12, 141, 153, 230, 242, 244–6, 266–7, 292, 365, 368, 390, 516, 598, 599
Packer, Rear Admiral S H, US Navy, 519
Pakistan, 116, 243, 292, 391, 599–600, 608
Palestinian Liberation Organisation (PLO), 237
PanAm Airways, 440
Panama Canal, 7, 292, 365, 439, 599
P&O, 163
'Panorama' television documentary, 292
Papua New Guinea, 246
Parachute Regiment, 373, 424
  2 Para (2nd Battalion), 453, 461; 3 Para (3rd Battalion), 453, 460

Parkhill secure speech communication system, 471
Parliament, British, 24, 88, 157, 204–5, 222, 322, 333, 393, 408–9, 423, 472, 543, 564, 589
Pattie, Geoffrey, MP, 421–2, 570
Pearl Harbor, Japanese attack on, 37
Pebble Island, Falkland Islands, 451, 457, 460
Peck, A D, 58
Peloponnese, Greece, 232
Pembroke Dock Oil Depot, Pembrokeshire, 18, 268
Penang, Malaysia, 3
Pentagon, Washington, *see* Defense, Dept. of, US
Perim Islands, Aden, 80
Perle, Richard, 408
Permanent Joint Headquarters (MOD), 473
Permanent Under-Secretary (MOD), 23, 44, 53, 55–6, 190, 206, 328, 347, 350, 373, 469, 502, 542–3
Persian Gulf, 1–2, 5–7, 81, 84, 111, 116, 142, 185, 198, 232, 242, 292–5, 351, 359, 390, 438–9, 488, 519, 576, 583–4, 600–5, 622, 627
Personnel policy, Naval, *see also* Training, 24–33, 43, 86–105, 112–3, 218–21, 269, 326–9, 432, 489–92, 583–91, 624, 627–8, 635–8
  Authorised Manpower Ceiling, 584–5; Naval Manpower Requirement, 584–5; pay, 25–7, 30, 32–3, 90–2, 99–100, 105, 153, 157, 269, 283, 326–9, 338, 340, 587, 624; promotion, 27, 90, 94–6, 100–1, 327, 621; recruitment, 25–6, 34, 43, 89, 90–1, 98, 102, 105, 112, 167, 219, 221, 322, 326, 338, 340, 342, 585, 590–1, 624, 627; retention, 27, 34, 43, 88–92, 98, 105, 112–3, 130, 167, 219–21, 229, 326–9, 338, 340, 583–8, 590–1, 599, 624, 627, 638
Perth Stores Depot, Scotland, 18
Philippines, 608, 614
Phoenix air surveillance drone, 356
Pillar, Vice Admiral William, 330
Piper Alpha oil rig, 284
Pitcairn Islands, 246
'Plan Loft', 534–5

Plessey Electronics, 21
Plymouth, Devon, 15–7, 97, 111, 216, 537
Plymouth, Montserrat, 612
Plymouth Sound, 287
Poland, 309, 616
Polaris Executive, Ministry of Defence, *see also* Nuclear Weapons, 22
Polaris Sales Agreement, US-UK, *see also* Nuclear Weapons, 337, 406
Pollock, Admiral Sir Michael, *see also* First Sea Lord, 132–3, 156, 189
Poole Royal Marine training base, Dorset, 425
Port Auxiliary Service, 4, 16, 31, 268
Port Fitzroy, Falkland Islands, 460
Port Howard, Falkland Islands, 460
Port King, Falkland Islands, 451
Port Said, Egypt, 234–5
Port San Carlos, Falkland Islands, 453
Port Stores and Transport Officer, 127
Portland, 8, 15–6, 18, 31, 102, 111, 117, 121, 439, 495, 537, 548
Portland Naval Air Station, 13
Porton Down chemical defence establishment, Wiltshire, 493
Portugal, 77, 243, 411
Portsmouth, 14, 16–7, 19, 103–4, 110, 127, 133, 333, 548, 586, 616
Portsmouth Dockyard/Naval Base, 8, 14, 16, 20, 31, 127–8, 292, 323, 333, 372, 378, 387, 407, 426–9, 439, 499, 501, 537, 592, 616–7
Power, M G, 359
Prague Spring, 621
Priddy's Hard Armament Depot, Gosport, 16
Prime Minister, Belize, 250
Prime Minister, British, *see also* Douglas Home, Alec; Wilson, Harold; Heath, Edward; Callaghan, James; Thatcher, Margaret; 39, 45–8, 58, 64, 74, 136–7, 158, 191–2, 204, 206, 212, 228, 244, 269, 277–8, 309, 315, 326, 331–4, 336, 340, 341, 343–6, 360–1, 368, 381–5, 388–90, 398–9, 408–9, 423, 428, 434, 436, 438, 473, 503, 542, 569, 578, 623–4
Principal Director of Navy and Nuclear Contracts, 630
Principal Warfare Officer, 96–7, 490, 585, 618, 621

Prior, Jim, MP, 389
Pritchard Report on WRNS, 219
'Proceedings' US Naval Institute magazine, 518
Procurement, Royal Navy, *see also* Shipbuilders, Warships, 19–20, 37–57, 63–76, 158, 160–2, 166–88, 200–1, 206, 297–321, 342–3, 349, 353–5, 371–2, 382–4, 386, 497–8, 500–1, 555–82
  Aircraft, *see* Aircraft, fixed wing, and Helicopters; aircraft carriers, xi, 37–9, 41–50, 557, 620–1; amphibious vessels, 54, 73–4, 182–3, 206, 333, 486, 552, 554–5, 562–5; auxiliaries and other support ships, 183–5, 206, 318–9, 415–6, 418, 554, 562–3, 575–6; cruisers, Large ASW ships, 'Garage Ships', 52, 54–6, 67–8, 158, 165–6, 178–9, 196, 200–1, 206, 306–8, 353–5, 361, 371, 377–8, 380, 383, 386; destroyers and frigates, 20, 43, 52, 54–7, 68–73, 148, 158, 160–3, 166–72, 176–9, 196, 206, 269, 300–11, 333, 342–3, 349, 353–5, 358, 366, 368, 371–4, 377, 380, 383–4, 386, 415–9, 433–4, 493–5, 500–1, 550, 552–4, 565–73, 621–3, 626; mine warfare vessels, 158, 180–3, 197, 315–8, 333, 343, 353–5, 372, 549, 576–7; minor vessels, 75–6, 179–80, 197, 319–21, 380, 434, 550, 553, 573–5, 626; propulsion, *see* Diesel surface ship propulsion, Gas Turbines, Nuclear propulsion; sensors, *see* Electronic Warfare, Radar, Sonar; submarines, 20, 54, 56, 63–7, 163–5, 197, 200–1, 206, 336–8, 342, 349, 353–5, 373, 380, 386, 405, 419–22, 552–7, 621, 623, 626; weapons, *see* Guided Missiles; Guns; Nuclear weapons; Torpedoes; Mortars, anti-submarine
Procurement Executive, 157, 181, 303, 332, 366, 367, 543, 546, 548, 634
Provisional Irish Republican Army (IRA), 284

Public Expenditure Survey, 339, 389, 554
Puerto Rico, 247
Pump Jet propulsor, 66, 556
Purvis, Rear Admiral Neville, 589
PWR 2 Pressurised Water Reactor, 406
Pym, Sir Francis, MP, *see also* Secretary of State for Defence, 326, 329, 331–2, 334–5, 338–44, 346–8, 353, 355, 370, 385, 388–9, 395–6, 406, 425, 439, 550, 624

Queen Alexandra's Royal Naval Nursing Service, 24, 31, 635–6
Queen's Regulations for the Royal Navy, 591
Quinlan, Sir Michael, 348, 392, 394
'Quinlan Paradox', 199, 623

Racal Electronics, 21
Radar
  Blue Fox, 477, 557; Blue Vixen, 557; 'Broomstick' *see* Type 988; Ecko, 147; Sea Searcher, 273, 412; Searchwater, 479–80, 500; Type 909, 167, 443, 478; Type 965, 61, 166, 299; Type 984, 69; Type 988, 70, 166; Type 992, 496; Type 1022, 166, 300; Type 1030, 300; VM40, 417
Ras al Ara, Aden, 80
Ratings, Naval, *see also,* Personnel, 17, 24–32, 62, 87–94, 98–104, 115, 126, 220, 316, 328, 372, 378, 430–1, 473, 489–90, 568, 572, 575, 583–91, 635–8
  Able Seamen, 27; Leading Seamen, 26–7, 101, 327, 492; Petty Officers, 17, 26–7, 31, 89, 101, 103–4, 430; Chief Petty Officers, 26–7, 31, 89, 100–1, 432; Warrant Officers, 90, 99–101, 432, 589
Rayner, Sir Derek, 332, 334
Reagan, Ronald, 390, 404–6, 434, 505, 515–6, 533, 615
Red Sea, 80
Reffell, Admiral Sir Derek, 361–4, 474, 540, 614
Regional Military Commanders, United Kingdom, 537
Registrar General of Shipping and Seamen, 31

Regulating Branch, Royal Navy, 26
Reinforcement Port Naval Parties, 534
Replenishment at sea, 31, 497, 561
Replenishment, Vertical, 31, 184
Republican Party (US), 136, 390, 409–10, 515, 625, 628
Research and Development, 18–9, 33, 68, 157–8, 161, 352, 406, 469–70, 548
Reykjavik, Iceland, 227
Rhodesia, 2, 76–8, 243
Ridley, Nicholas, MP, 437
Rio de Janeiro, Brazil, 441, 459
Roberts, John, xii
Rodgers, Bill, MP, 209–11
Rolls-Royce, engine manufacturer, 37, 75, 147, 273, 569
Rostok, East Germany, 616
Rosyth Dockyard/Naval Base, 16–7, 31, 104, 127–8, 280, 322–3, 420, 426, 428–9, 537, 586, 592–5
Rowlands, Ted, MP, 249
Rowner Estate, Gosport, 102
Royal Air Force, 24, 76, 79, 100, 159, 165–6, 180, 208, 212, 236, 248, 282–3, 285, 290, 298, 313, 334, 342, 433, 520, 535, 558–9, 561, 612, 633–4
  And battle for CVA01, 38–44, 46–7, 49, 110; and Beira Patrol, 76–8; and Belize, 251–2; and Brussels Treaty, *see also* British Forces Germany, 342; and Cod Wars, 228, 280, 282; and co-operation with RN, 109–10, 119–23, 212–3, 279, 284; and Falklands conflict, 440, 446, 452, 460, 465, 469, 479–81, 487; and Indo-Pacific region commitments, 5, 207, 241, 244; and 'Island Strategy', 58–9; and Lebanon crisis (1983–4), 598, 605–7; and long war/short war arguments, 267; maritime air capabilities and role, *see also* 18 Group and Coastal Command, 8, 13–4, 52–3, 55, 106, 149–52, 159, 165, 192, 208, 210–5, 258, 261–2, 266, 272–4, 289, 296–7, 303, 312, 324, 413, 417–9, 521, 558–60, 621; and Mason defence review, 198, 200, 205–8; and Mediterranean commitments,

207–8, 231, 238, 284; and Nott defence review, 352, 356–8, 360–4, 372–5, 382–3, 386, 396, 398; and nuclear weapons, 63, 65, 133, 137–8; personnel issues, 88, 90–1, 98, 101, 103; and prioritisation of Central European Front, 208, 215, 349, 395, 622; RAF Germany, *see also* British Forces Germany, 215, 329, 342, 352; and transfer of aircraft and personnel from Fleet Air Arm, 51, 60, 63, 288–9
Royal Air Force Squadrons, 14
Royal Aircraft Establishment, Farnborough, 289, 481
Royal Artillery, 15
Royal Australian Navy, 14, 69, 73, 113, 168, 244, 292, 393, 486, 599
Royal Canadian Navy, 14, 117–8, 292
Royal Clarence Victualling Yard, Gosport, 16
Royal Defence College, 97
Royal Fleet Auxiliary, 4, 6, 9, 31, 74, 78, 162, 184–5, 200, 203, 206, 259–60, 306–7, 354, 377–8, 403, 411, 413, 423, 438–9, 441, 444, 459, 462, 465–6, 486–7, 496, 503, 526, 575, 599
Royal Fleet Auxiliary, Ships
  AOR, *see Fort Victoria* class
  Appleleaf, 439
  Argus, 561–2
  Blue Rover, 280, 438
  Brambleleaf, 439, 608, 611
  'Dale' class, 185
  Diligence, 184, 466–7, 496, 463
  Engadine, 561
  Ennerdale, 242
  Fort Austin, 438
  Fort Austin class, 185, 642
  Fort Grange, 459
  Fort Victoria, 576
  Fort Victoria class, 185, 307, 354, 400, 416, 554, 571, 575–6, 579, 581, 642
  Gold Rover, 274
  Grey Rover, 238, 438, 606
  'Improved Tide' class, 184, 403
  'Leaf' class, 185, 642
  LSLs, *see Sir Lancelot* class
  Lyness, 184
  'Ness' class, 403
  Oilers, *see* Tankers

INDEX

Olmeda, 464
Olwen, 121, 280, 295, 413
Olynthus class, 184
Replenishment/stores ships, 9, 54, 78, 184–5, 197, 252, 341, 400, 403, 416, 439–40, 467, 496, 642–3
Regent, 252
Reliant, 466–7, 561, 606–7, 643
Resource, 439
Resource class, 184
'Rover' class, 184, 439, 465, 467, 642
Sir Bedivere, 80, 439, 457, 564
Sir Caradoc, 562
Sir Galahad (1970–82), 80, 457, 461–2, 482, 500, 562
Sir Galahad (1987–2006), 500, 562, 579
Sir Geraint, 80
Sir Lamarock, 562
Sir Lancelot, 457, 459, 563–4
Sir Lancelot class, 15, 74, 183, 197–8, 354, 366, 369, 371, 377, 423–4, 428, 439, 485–6, 490, 562–4
Sir Tristram, 439, 461–2, 500, 562
Stromness, 238, 439, 441, 453, 456
Tankers, 4, 9, 54, 68, 78, 161–2, 184–5, 197, 206, 242, 280, 343, 403, 415–6, 440, 444, 465, 467, 642
Tarbatness, 341
Tidepool, 280
Tidereach, 280
Tidespring, 438–9, 44
Royal Fleet Reserve, 32
Royal Flight, 206
Royal Marine Commandos
40 Commando, 3, 15, 224, 453, 464; 41 Commando, 15, 206, 216–8, 223, 238, 248, 425; 42 Commando, 3, 15, 224, 453, 464; 43 Commando, 15; 45 Commando, 15, 216, 223–4, 453
Royal Marines, 3, 7, 13–5, 24–5, 30, 33, 37, 58, 103, 118, 123, 183, 189, 198, 200, 206, 216–8, 223–4, 246–8, 279, 284, 351, 357, 366, 372–3, 402, 408, 424–5, 431, 436, 444, 452, 464, 469, 474, 486, 525, 545, 562–3, 589, 613, 635–7

Royal Marines Band Service, 352, 372, 425
Royal Marines Reserve, 200
Royal Maritime Auxiliary Service, 268, 280, 283, 466
Royal Naval Auxiliary Service, 32, 537, 117
Royal Naval Officer, Mauritius, 631
Royal Naval Physiological Laboratory, Alverstoke, 19
Royal Naval Reserve, 9, 32–3, 43, 117, 189, 200, 218–9, 283, 317–8, 490, 636–8
Royal Naval Special Reserve, 33
Royal Naval Supply and Transport Service, 18, 22, 486
Royal Naval Volunteer (Supplementary) Reserve, 33
Royal Navy Officer, Pembroke Dock, 631
Royal Netherlands Navy, 73, 118, 123, 176, 531
Royal New Zealand Navy, 4, 112, 122, 245, 292, 601
Royal Ordnance Factories, 338
Royal Technical College, Glasgow, 506
RUKUS talks, see also Adderbury process, 616
Rules of Engagement, 78, 125, 139, 227–8, 295, 471, 600, 602–3, 604–5
Rum tot, 87–9
Rumsfeld, Donald, 516

Sabah, Malaysia, 3
SACLANT ASW Research Centre (SACLANTCEN), La Spezia, Italy, 154, 270
Safeguarding the Nation (book), xii
'Sailor' television documentary, 227–8
Sailors' Fund, The, 88
St Athan, RAF air station, 289
St Johns, Antigua, 249
St Kitts and Nevis, 247, 249
St Lucia, 247
St Mawgan, RAF air station, 272
St Vincent, Cape Verde Islands, 441
St Vincent, Caribbean, 247–9
Salalah, RAF air station, Oman, 81
Sampson, Nicos, 236
San Carlos, Falkland Islands, 451–4, 460–2, 478, 484

San Carlos Bay, Falkland Islands, 452, 532
San Carlos, Battle of, 453–8, 476, 498
San Carlos Water, Falkland Islands, 453–7, 459, 462, 489, 486
Sandhurst, Royal Military Academy, 97
Sarawak, Malaysia, 246
Saros Bay, Turkey, 216
Saunders, Norman, 610
Saunders Roe, hovercraft builders, 75
Scilly Islands, 284
Schlesinger, James, 134, 207
Schleswig-Holstein, West Germany, 351, 424
Scapa Flow, Orkneys, 323
SCOT satellite communications system, 449, 471, 480
Scotland, 13–4, 18, 121, 163, 214, 216, 272, 274, 279, 284, 288, 316, 322, 586
Scots Guards, British Army, 460–1
Scottish Department of Agriculture and Fisheries, 283–4
Scotts Shipbuilding, 19, 318–9
Sea Appointments Board, 95
Sea Control, 12, 72, 119, 141–3, 153, 155, 255, 262, 265, 367, 470, 488, 507, 511
Sea Denial, 12, 201, 265, 521
Sea Lines of Communication, 12, 85, 117, 265, 507, 515–7
Sea Strike plan, US Navy, 515–16
Sea Systems Controllerate, MOD, 303, 548
Sea-Air Warfare Committee, MOD, 213–6, 257, 375
Seaforth, shipping operator, 467
Seaman Branch, Royal Navy, 26, 94, 99, 101
SeaPlan 2000, US Navy, 515–6
Second Permanent Under Secretary for Defence, 545–7, 634
Second Permanent Under Secretary for the Royal Navy, 22
Second Sea Lord, 21–2, 63, 86–7, 90–1, 94–5, 97–8, 101–2, 132–3, 218–9, 327, 506, 541, 585, 587, 615
Second World War, 3, 6, 8, 12, 15, 17, 21–2, 33, 35, 37, 52, 62, 68, 73–4, 83, 105, 111, 126, 128, 150, 189, 321, 323, 330, 389, 422, 436,

446, 448, 474, 482, 485, 488, 492, 494–5, 589, 596
Secret Intelligence Service, 476
Secretary of State for Defence; see also Denis Healey, Lord Carrington, Roy Mason, Fred Mulley, Francis Pym, John Nott, Michael Heseltine, George Younger, 21, 24, 36, 40–1, 45, 48, 51–3, 55–7, 61–3, 68, 70–2, 82, 86, 91, 106–7, 160, 164, 190, 212, 285, 312, 326, 329, 340, 342, 347–8, 350, 356, 359, 361–4, 370, 373, 382, 385, 388, 392–4, 396, 398, 402, 404, 408–9, 420, 422, 424, 433–4, 469, 541–4, 546, 559, 568, 570, 574, 581, 584, 592–3, 620, 624
Secretary of State for Foreign and Commonwealth Affairs, 204, 227, 292, 329, 331, 359–1, 385, 398, 406, 607
Secretary of State for Industry, 309–10, 385
Seebohm, Frederic, Baron, 102–3
Seebohm Report, 102
Senegal, 441
Senior Assistant Secretary, Bath, 629
Senior Naval Officer Middle East, 631
Senior Naval Officer South Africa, 590, 631
Senior Naval Officer West Indies, 7, 108, 207, 247, 249–50, 252, 631
Senior Officer Reserves, Portsmouth, 631
Services Electronics Research Laboratory, Baldock, 19
Services Valve Test Laboratory, Haslemere, 19
Sevastopol, Soviet Union, 616
Severnaya Verf shipyard, Soviet Union, 619
Severodvinsk, Soviet Union, 509
Seychelles, 241–2, 292
Sexual Offences Act 1967, 591
Shanghai, China, 292–3
Sharpe, Captain Richard, 276, 520
Shatt Al 'Arab, Iraq, 294
Shattock, Commander B K, 173
Sheerness, Kent, 537
Shetland Islands, 122, 279, 284, 559
Shia Muslims, Lebanon, 237
Ship Department, see Navy Department

Ships Taken up from Trade (for individual ships, see Merchant Vessels), 384, 429, 440, 466, 487, 495, 497, 503, 531, 563, 626
Shipbuilding Industry, see also Defence Industry, 19–21, 65, 73, 158, 160, 162–4, 169–70, 183, 185–6, 303, 308–11, 322, 324, 336, 339–40, 342–3, 371, 373–4, 383, 416, 497, 566, 574, 577–81
Shipbuilding Industry Board, 163
Shipping Federation, 31
Shore Establishments, see also CONSTRAIN, 17–9, 26, 31, 103–4, 323, 489, 535, 586, 597
Caledonia (Rosyth), 17, 104, 431
Collingwood (Fareham), 17, 103
Daedalus (Lee-on-Solent), 17
Dauntless (Reading), 17
Dolphin (Gosport), 14, 17, 597
Dryad (Southwick), 17, 103–4
Excellent (Portsmouth), 17, 103–4, 431
Fisgard (Torpoint), 17, 103, 431
Ganges (Ipswich), 17, 26
Jufair (Bahrain), 5
Lochinvar (Firth of Forth), 9
Malabar (Bermuda), 247
Mercury (East Meon), 17, 103
Nelson (Portsmouth), 16
Pembroke (Chatham), 104, 431
Phoenix (Portsmouth), 104, 431
Raleigh (Torpoint), 17, 103–4
Royal Arthur (Corsham), 17, 104
St George (Eastney), 104
St Vincent (Gosport), 17, 26
Sheba (Aden), 5, 80
Sultan (Gosport), 17, 103–4
Terror (Singapore), 2
Vernon (Portsmouth), 17, 104, 108, 110, 431
Victory (Portsmouth), 17
Short War/Short Warning scenarios, see also Long War/Long Warning scenarios, 263–8, 349, 360, 398, 515–6, 522, 536, 538, 622
Shorts, missile manufacturer, Belfast, 21
Sick Berth Branch, RN, 26
Sierra Leone, 441
Silent Deep, The (book), xiii
Silver Jubilee Fleet Review, 287
Simbang, Malaysia, 3
Simonstown, South Africa, 6, 441

Sinai, Egypt, 233
Singapore, 2–5, 9, 13–6, 76, 112–6, 138, 159, 184, 206, 208, 229–30, 232, 239–41, 244, 246, 292, 598, 600, 622, 637
Singapore Dockyard/Naval Base, 1–4, 6, 16, 32, 112, 240
Singapore Maritime Command, 239
Sino-British Joint Declaration 1984, 613
Sirte Gulf, Battle of, 111
Six Day War, Arab-Israeli, 82, 231, 242
Skagerrak, 255
Skynet communications satellite system, 372, 471
Slater, Admiral Sir John 'Jock', 541, 614
Smeeton, Vice Admiral Sir Richard, 36
Smith, Aulden 'Smokey', 610
Social Services, Head of Naval, 102–3
Social workers, 102–3
Socotra, Aden/Yemen, 5
SOKS, non-acoustic underwater detection system, Soviet, 510
Solomon Islands, 246
Somalia, 141
Sonar, see also Oceanography, 8, 19, 21, 33, 76, 83, 96, 99, 122, 143–5, 153–5, 174, 248, 300, 314, 363, 383, 447, 483, 510, 529, 577
  Active, 143, 151, 260, 271, 415, 419, 526, 532; 'Barra', 273, 418; 'Bottom bounce', 149, 178, 270; CAMBS, 273; dipping, 13, 76, 147, 149–50, 178, 273, 302, 356, 358, 415, 418–9, 483, 526, 560; hydrophone, see Passive; 'Jezebel', 150, 273, 526; Mk 1C sonobuoy, 150; passive, see also SOSUS and Towed arrays, 143, 149, 152–3, 164, 258, 260, 415, 532; shipborne hull sonars, 121, 145–7, 149–50, 172–3, 178, 186, 213, 258, 260, 269, 305, 356, 419, 483, 526, 569–70; sonobuoys, 14, 121, 150, 358, 415, 526, 560; Sound Surveillance System (SOSUS), 151–3, 258, 260–1, 270–1, 318, 362–4, 367, 374–5, 384, 395, 418, 448; SQR-15 (US), 525; SQR-18a (US), 525; SQS-

504, 146; submarine sonars, 151, 414, 482, 555; towed arrays, 213, 223, 258, 260–1, 263, 270–2, 302, 304–5, 310, 356, 364, 368–9, 375, 415, 417, 505, 522–9, 624; Type 184/184M/184P, 172–3, 178, 483; Type 193M/193T, 181, 320; Type 195, 76, 147, 273, 483; Type 199, 146; Type 2001, 482, 555; Type 2016, 178, 270, 483–4; Type 2020, 555; Type 2024, 271, 482, 522–3, 555; Type 2026, 271, 523, 555; Type 2031I/2031Z, 272, 305, 415, 523–5; Type 2038, 415; Type 2046, 523; Type 2050, 305; Type 2069, 483, 560; variable depth, 146, 412
Sorreisa, Norway, 118
South Africa, 6–7, 77–8, 242–3, 441, 590
South Atlantic and South America Station, 6, 108, 110
South China Sea, 4, 37
South Georgia, 436–7, 440–5, 459–60, 464, 484
South Korea, 308, 598
South Yemen, *see also* Aden, 607–9
Southampton, 18, 20, 439, 578
Southby-Tailyour, Major Ewen, 64
Southern Rhodesia, *see* Rhodesia
Southern Thule, South Atlantic, 464
Sovereign Base Areas, Cyprus, 236–7, 476
Soviet Army, 619
Soviet Navy, 10–12, 59, 70, 74, 82–4, 118, 125, 131, 137, 140–2, 153, 180–1, 195–6, 202–3, 216, 230–1, 233–5, 254–5, 258, 262, 265, 270, 274, 279, 293, 316–7, 343, 353, 361–3, 365, 367, 373, 410, 412–3, 505–5, 520, 533, 576, 583, 608, 615–6, 619, 622, 626
Air threat, 119–20, 140, 151, 172, 201, 210–1, 214, 233, 290, 297, 299, 303, 307, 341, 344, 356–7, 362, 375, 383, 393, 413, 479, 514, 521, 524, 531–2, 557–8, 560, 601, 621, 623; Black Sea Fleet, 233; Northern Fleet, 10–1, 84–5, 254, 260, 269, 274, 410, 414; Pacific Fleet, 4, 84, 515; strategy, 12, 85, 264–5, 267–8,

360, 507, 517; submarines, 10–12, 65, 82–4, 117, 118, 121, 131, 137, 139–41, 145–6, 149, 151–2, 160, 173–4, 195–6, 202, 230–1, 233, 255, 257–8, 262, 267, 269–70, 272–4, 276, 301, 311–2, 314–5, 343, 356, 362–3, 365, 373, 375–6, 379–80, 395, 412, 418–20, 422, 439, 474, 507–11, 518–9, 523, 525, 539, 560; warships, 4, 10–11, 74, 81–4, 118, 137, 141, 174–5, 179–181, 231, 233–4, 235, 244, 248, 256, 258, 274–5, 295, 312–13, 357, 375, 413, 475, 511–13, 528
Soviet Union, 1, 4, 10, 12, 18, 82–4, 119, 125, 134–5, 140, 142, 195, 203–4, 219, 229, 231–3, 255, 258–9, 261, 266–7, 269, 277, 279, 326, 330, 336–7, 343, 346, 351–2, 356, 358–60, 380, 403, 405, 410, 425, 468, 476, 501–4, 516, 520–2, 530, 534, 536, 538, 583, 608–9, 615–17, 622–3, 626, 628
Collapse, xiii, 617–9; détente, 53, 82, 84, 279, 292, 343, 410, 529; espionage, 125–6, 510; Glasnost, 615–7; invasion of Afghanistan, 292–3, 337, 410; invasion of Czechoslovakia, 84–5, 231, 629; support for developing states, 4–5, 13, 233, 235–6, 242–3, 353, 607; support for insurgencies, 1, 78–9, 81
Spain, 288, 323, 411, 427, 476
Special Air Service (SAS), 373, 444–5, 451–2, 460, 476
Special Boat Service (SBS), 439, 476
Speed, Keith, MP, 370, 382, 390, 397, 425, 592
Squadrons, Naval (Royal Navy unless otherwise stated), 295–6, 475, 572
1st Frigate Squadron
1st Mine Countermeasures Squadron
1st Submarine Squadron, 14
2nd Frigate Squadron, 8, 184
3rd Frigate Squadron, 113, 116
3rd Mine Countermeasures Squadron
3rd Submarine Squadron, 14, 123
4th Frigate Squadron, 296
5th Frigate Squadron, 115

6th Frigate Squadron, 115
6th Squadron/Eskadra (Soviet Navy), 83, 231
6th Submarine Division
7th Frigate Squadron, 8, 113, 116
7th Submarine Squadron, 3
8th Frigate Squadron, 113
9th Frigate Squadron, 5, 9
10th Mine Counter Measures Squadron, 318
17th Escort Squadron, 8
20th Frigate Squadron, 8
21st Escort Squadron, 3, 9
23rd Escort Squadron, 2
24th Escort Squadron, 3
26th Escort Squadron, 3, 10
27th Escort Squadron, 9
29th Escort Squadron, 3, 9
Dartmouth Training Squadron, 8, 616
Fishery Protection Squadron, 9–10, 16, 145, 225, 282, 321
Hong Kong Squadron, 241
Londonderry Anti-Submarine Training Squadron, 8–10, 145
Standby Squadron, 328, 391–3, 401–5, 409, 428, 500, 538, 549–50
West Indies Squadron, 248, 609
Sri Lanka, 600
Staff Course, Naval, *see* Greenwich Royal Naval College
Stalin, Josef, 243
Standing Naval Force Atlantic, *see* North Atlantic Treaty Organisation
Stanford, Admiral Sir Peter, 506, 541, 614
Stanley, Falkland Islands, 7, 436, 441, 450, 452–4, 458, 460–1, 463–4
Stanley, John, MP, 574, 593
Stanley Airfield, Falkland Islands, 445–6, 450, 454, 460, 464–5
Statement on the Defence Estimates, 137, 205, 209, 218, 343
Stationery Office, Her Majesty's
Statue of Liberty, New York, 533
Staveley, Admiral Sir William, *see also* First Sea Lord, 330, 476, 488, 506, 540, 614
Steel Production Hall, Portsmouth Naval Base, 128
Stephens, shipbuilders, 19
Stoddart, Kristan, 408
Stonehouse barracks, Plymouth, 216

Stonehouse, Royal Naval Hospital, Plymouth, 17
Strategic Arms Limitations Talks I/II, 135–6, 140, 257, 337, 615
Strategic Concept, British Maritime, *see also* Maritime Strategy, 196, 261–4, 286, 623
Strategic Systems Performance Analysis Assessment Group, 630
Strategy, British Maritime, *see also* Concept of Operations; Strategic Concept, British Maritime, 521–2
Strike Command, RAF, 109
Sturdee, Admiral Sir Doveton, 506
Subic Bay, Philippines, 239
Submarines (Royal Navy unless otherwise stated)
  'A' class, 3, 14, 369
  'Akula' class (Soviet Navy), 301, 509
  'Alfa' class (Soviet Navy), 160, 174, 269, 276, 315, 509
  Ambush, 3
  Amphion, 3
  Anchorite, 3
  Andrew, 3
  Auriga, 3
  Billfish (US Navy), 122
  'Charlie'/'Charlie II' class (Soviet Navy), 83–4, 121–2, 145, 173, 230–1, 269, 508, 523
  Churchill, 66, 74, 121
  Conqueror, 118, 164, 439–40, 447–8, 487, 518
  Courageous, 66, 276, 440
  'Delta'/'Delta II'/'Delta III'/'Delta IV' class (Soviet Navy), 151, 227, 269, 276, 507
  Diesel-electric powered, 2–3, 9, 144, 165, 183, 239, 272, 348, 415, 428, 483, 523, 555, 580
  Dreadnought, 14, 63, 66, 115, 118, 122, 420–1, 434, 523, 639
  'Echo'/'Echo II' class (Soviet Navy), 11, 82–3, 276, 508
  'Foxtrot' class (Soviet, Libyan Navies), 11, 606
  'Hotel' class (Soviet Navy), 11, 82–3
  K-162 (Soviet Navy), 412
  K-278 (Soviet Navy), 509
  K-284 (Soviet Navy), 509
  K-313 (Soviet Navy), 231
  'Kilo' class (Soviet Navy), 412, 511
  Komsomolets (Soviet Navy), *see K-278*
  'Mike' class (Soviet Navy), 301, 509
  'November' class (Soviet Navy), 11, 82–3
  Nuclear powered, attack (SSN), 11, 54, 56–7, 83, 118, 158, 164–5, 197, 200–1, 259, 311–2, 339, 342, 354–5, 362, 366–7, 372–3, 377, 380, 386, 403–4, 411, 415, 426, 429, 448, 509, 517–9, 523, 525, 530, 540, 553, 555–6, 580–1, 639, 641–3
  Nuclear powered, ballistic missile firing (SSBN), 11, 14, 38, 64–5, 83, 85, 124, 141, 151, 197, 199, 255, 262, 265, 267, 269, 274, 276, 322–3, 337, 353–5, 377, 406, 426, 429, 507–8, 517–8, 554–5, 580–1, 621, 625, 639, 642
  Nuclear powered, cruise missile firing (SSGN), 11, 83, 121, 145, 151, 174, 255, 269–70, 274, 276, 356, 412, 508–9, 523, 615
  Oberon, 3
  Oberon class, 422, 639
  Ohio class (US Navy), 406
  Onyx, 440, 482
  Oracle, 324
  'Oscar' class (Soviet Navy), 269–70, 276, 508
  'Papa' class (Soviet Navy), 160, 174, 412
  Porpoise class, 14, 197, 639
  Renown, 65–6, 335–6
  Repulse, 65, 336
  Resolution, 64–5, 133, 336
  Resolution class, 64–5, 128, 133–4, 137, 164, 227, 335–6, 406, 420, 507, 556, 639
  Revenge, 65–6, 336
  'Romeo' class (Soviet Navy), 11
  San Luis (Argentine Navy), 447
  Santa Fe (Argentine Navy), 444
  Sceptre, 276
  Seawolf (US Navy), 556
  'Sierra' class (Soviet Navy), 301, 509–10
  Sovereign, 276, 523
  Spartan, 276, 439–40, 482
  Splendid, 67, 439–40, 446–7, 518
  SSN0X, *see Swiftsure* class
  SSN0Y, *see Trafalgar* class
  SSN0Z design, 165, 339, 342
  Superb, 276, 439, 518
  Swiftsure, 66–7, 164, 523
  Swiftsure class, 66–7, 85, 156, 164–5, 306, 555–6, 623, 639
  'T' class, 14
  'Tango' class (Soviet Navy), 412
  TK-208 (Soviet Navy), 507
  Torbay, 518
  Trafalgar, 518, 555
  Trafalgar class, 164–5, 306, 339, 342, 372, 377, 380, 386, 420, 554–6, 580, 623, 639
  Trenchant, 616
  Type 209 class (Argentine Navy), 443
  'Typhoon' class (Soviet Navy), 507–8, 518, 565
  Upholder, 556–7
  Upholder class, 165, 554, 556–7, 578, 581, 626, 639
  Valiant, 66, 439
  Valiant class, 64, 66–7, 164, 555–6, 581, 639
  Vanguard class, 555–6, 580
  Vengeance, 555
  'Victor'/'Victor II'/'Victor III' class (Soviet Navy), 83, 230, 269, 509–10, 518
  Warspite, 66, 116
  'Whiskey' class (Soviet, Indonesian Navies), 4–5, 11
  'Yankee' class (Soviet Navy), 83, 85, 151
  'Zulu' class (Soviet Navy), 11
Submersibles, 181, 318
Sudan, 608
Suez, Gulf of, 603
Suez, Royal Navy East of, xii–xiii, 1, 5–6, 39, 42, 45, 52–3, 55–9, 62, 64, 73, 76, 82, 86, 106, 112–6, 129–30, 138, 153, 182, 221, 230, 232, 242, 292, 348, 488, 600–1, 603, 605, 621–2
Suez, Royal Navy West of, 53, 55–7, 82, 87, 106–12
Suez Canal, 181, 235–6, 242, 292, 598–9, 601, 603
Sunda Strait, 5
Sunni Muslims, Lebanon, 237
Supply and Secretariat Branch, Royal Navy, 26, 29, 31, 97, 104, 506, 540–1, 615

INDEX   735

Supreme Allied Commander Atlantic (SACLANT), 139–40, 142, 212, 215, 232, 268, 289, 297, 363–4, 383, 404, 410, 421
Supreme Allied Commander Europe (SACEUR), 64, 117, 142, 212, 297, 363
Surabaya, Indonesia, 4
Surface layer, sea, *see* Isotherm
Surface Action Group, 122, 125, 137, 140–1, 413, 475, 512
Surface and Amphibious Warfare Division, Naval Staff, 23
Sussex Mountains, Falkland Islands, 453
Swan Hunter shipbuilders, 19, 163, 170, 309, 569, 575, 578–9
'Swing Strategy', US Navy, 266
Syria, 82, 141, 231, 233, 237–8, 607

Tactical Data Handling System, submarine, 66
Tailyour, Lieutenant General Norman, 15
Talbot, Vice Admiral Sir Arthur, 15
Talbot, Commandant Mary, WRNS, 219
Tanganyika, 2
Tanzania, 599
Taranto, Battle of, 111
Task Forces
  TF 311 (Submarine C2), 153; TF 317 (Falklands), 442, 469; TF 318 (Aden), 79
Task Groups
  TG 321.1 (1973 Group Deployment), 116; TG 317.0 (Falklands Campaign: Amphibious Group), 442; TG 317.1 (1974 Group Deployment), 116; TG 317.1 (Falklands Campaign: Carrier Battle Group), 442; TG 317.1 (Falklands Campaign: Land Forces Theatre Commander), 442; TG 317.2 (1974–75 Group Deployment), 116; TG 317.9 (Falklands Campaign: South Georgia Group), 442; TG 324.3 (Falklands Campaign: Submarines), 442
Task Units
  TU 317.1.1 (Falklands Campaign: 3 Commando Brigade), 442; TU

317.1.2 (Falklands Campaign: 5 Infantry Brigade), 442
Tawau, Malaysia, 3
Teal Inlet, Falkland Islands, 458
Territorial Army, 159
Territorial Waters
  Argentina, 481; Belize, 609; Hong Kong, 114, 240–1; Iceland, 225; Soviet Union, 413; United Kingdom, 16, 179, 282, 347
Thailand, 76
Thatcher, Margaret, MP, *see also* Prime Minister, 112, 295, 315, 326, 332–4, 336, 338, 340, 346, 361, 382, 404, 407–8, 436, 438
Thermocline layer, sea, 143–4, 146, 152, 178, 412
Thompson, Brigadier Julian, 442, 474–5, 486
Thorn EMI, contractors, 594
Thornycroft, Files and Associates, 570
Tiananmen Square uprising, China, 614
Tippet, Vice Admiral Anthony, 540–1, 593
Tokyo, Japan, 293
Toledo province, British Honduras/Belize, 251
Tonga, 246
Top Level Budgets, Ministry of Defence, 547
Torpedoes (in British service unless otherwise stated)
  53-65M (Soviet), 173; Mark 8, 139, 422, 448, 482; Mark 23, 312; Mark 24, *see* Tigerfish; Mark 31, 158, 160; Mark 44, 160, 173, 314–5; Mark 46, 160, 173–4, 314–5; Mark 48 (US), 422; Ondine, *see* Tigerfish; Spearfish, 312, 552–3, 623; Stingray, 160, 302, 314–5, 366, 372, 423, 480; Tigerfish, 139, 158, 311–2, 448, 482
Trade, Department of, 206, 346, 423, 440
Train, Admiral Harry, US Navy, 404, 421
Training, *see also* Dartmouth Training Squadron and Londonderry Squadron
  Belize Armed Forces, 407; British Army, 369, 423, 462, 610; Caribbean law enforcement,

611; NATO, *see also* Exercises, 534; Dockyard workforce, 323, 427; Royal Air Force, 282, 363; Royal Australian Navy, 244; Royal Canadian Navy, 14; Royal Fleet Auxiliary, 31, 503; Royal Marines, 425, 486; Royal Navy, 8, 10, 13, 15, 17, 22, 26, 91, 93, 96–9, 103–5, 106–8, 111, 124–6, 145, 161, 165, 198, 218–9, 238, 248, 289, 293, 329, 358, 375, 387, 401, 410, 417, 421, 430–2, 439, 467–9, 486, 489–92, 503–4, 538, 553, 561, 573, 584–6, 597, 625, 628, 637; United States Navy, 319
Transition to War, MOD, 349, 357, 425, 487–8, 490, 505, 533–8, 601
Transport, Ministry of, 15
Treacher, Admiral Sir John, 110, 285
Treasury, *see also* Defence Budget, Public Expenditure Survey, 39–40, 45–6, 53, 57–9, 61, 68, 71, 87, 130, 157, 162, 164–6, 187, 190–1, 193–5, 199, 202, 204–5, 208, 222, 269, 312, 315, 326, 331–2, 339–40, 345–6, 349, 387–8, 401, 408, 432–4, 465, 550–2, 566, 568, 592, 633
Trecwn Armament Depot, Milford Haven, 17
Trenchard, Lord Thomas, 297
Trend, Sir Burke, 39, 47, 136
Trewby, Vice Admiral G F A, 134
Trieste, Italy, 8
Trinidad and Tobago, 7, 247
Tromso, Norway, 16, 525
Trondelag, Norway, 279
Trost, Admiral Carlisle, USN, 615
Troup, Rear Admiral John, 112–3
Tugs, Repair and Logistics Area, South Atlantic, 441
Tulin, Rear Admiral K A, Soviet Navy, 616
Tunisia, 309
Turks and Caicos Islands, 247, 610–1
Turner, Admiral Sir Francis, 8
Tuvalu, 246
Twiss, Admiral Sir Frank, 2, 86–7, 90, 97, 99–100
Tyne, River, 19, 163

Undersurface Warfare Division, Naval Staff, 23

Uniform policy, 89–90
Unilateral Declaration of Independence, Rhodesian, 76
Union of Soviet Socialist Republics (USSR), *see* Soviet Union
United Nations, 250–1
  Convention on the Law of the Sea, 95; General Assembly Resolution, 251; Security Council Resolution, 77
United States of America, *see also* America, North; Kennedy, John F; Johnson, Lyndon; Nixon, Richard; Ford, Gerald; Carter, Jimmy; Reagan, Ronald, xi–xii, 19, 38, 40, 45, 64, 69, 141, 151–2, 154, 198, 241, 245, 247, 250, 255, 267, 269, 278, 287, 335, 353, 379, 412, 510, 518, 525, 531, 555, 562, 609, 616
  Johnson administration, 59, 135, 152–3; Nixon administration, 133–7, 152–3, 233–5, 255; Ford administration, 207, 236, 257, 275; Carter administration, 257, 295, 308, 331, 337; Reagan administration, 367, 380–1, 389–93, 400, 402–4, 406–7, 409, 414, 420–1, 434, 438, 441, 470, 487, 505, 516–7, 519–20, 549, 598–9, 604, 610, 615, 625–6
United States Air Force, 440
United States Coastguard, 609–11
United States Embassy, Grosvenor Square, London, 153, 275
United States Marines, 319, 390, 518, 562
United States Military Sealift Command, 403
United States Navy, 12, 64, 66, 69, 73, 83, 94, 141–3, 152, 203, 219, 233–4, 240, 244, 245, 248, 257, 264–7, 275, 292, 313, 319–20, 365, 366–8, 390, 392–3, 397, 402, 404–5, 407, 410, 414, 514, 417, 465, 511, 514–20, 525, 529, 531, 556, 558, 562, 603–4
  Atlantic (2nd) Fleet, 117, 203, 410, 531, 616; Mediterranean (6th) Fleet, 84, 231–3, 410; Pacific Fleet, 515–6
Upper Yardmen, 27
Urgent Operational Requirements, 479, 497
User-maintainer, 99

'V Force' bombers, RAF, 133
Vancouver, Canada, 439
Vanguard to Trident (book), xii
Vanuatu, *see also* New Hebrides, 246
Varley, Eric, MP, 309
Venezuela, 247, 292
Vertical envelopment (amphibious helicopter assault), 37, 486, 562
Vestfjord, Norway, 531–3
Vice Chief of the Defence Staff, 546–7
Vice Chief of the Naval Staff, 21–3, 63, 87, 94, 96, 98, 113, 132–3, 161, 189, 221, 290, 303–4, 306, 328, 330, 429, 468, 476, 488, 506, 521, 529, 541, 544–5, 568–9, 573
Vice Controller of the Navy, *see also* Chief of Fleet Support, 21, 22, 129
Vickers, shipbuilders, 20, 65, 163–4, 166, 169–71, 421–2, 556, 578–80, 594
Vietnam, South, 240
Vietnam War, 84, 141, 244, 255, 266, 279, 294, 368, 515
Vladivostok, Soviet Union, 292–3
Volga, River, Soviet Union, 509
Vosper Thornycroft, shipbuilders, 20, 73, 163–4, 166, 169–70, 180–1, 245, 309, 315–6, 320–1, 416, 574, 578, 580
VSEL shipbuilders, *see* Vickers

Wade-Gery, Sir Robert, 388
War Book, British Government, 534, 536–8
War Office, 38
Warsaw Pact, 10, 56, 84, 124, 141–3, 180, 191, 195, 216, 231, 234, 265–6, 279, 331, 349, 351, 356, 359, 476, 488, 501, 515, 534–5, 619
Warship classes and designs, *see also* Submarines
  Aviation Support Ship design, 562–4
  'Battle' class destroyers, 72, 639
  'Brave' class fast training craft, 179
  Bulldog class hydrographic vessels, 154
  'Ca' class destroyers, 72, 639
  'Castle' class (OPV 2) patrol vessels, 283, 285, 341, 434, 466–7, 550, 569, 573–4, 578, 641–2

Charles F Adams class destroyers (US and Australian Navies), 244
Command cruiser designs, *see also Invincible* class, 54–8, 68, 75, 85, 178, 260
Commando carrier (new design 1969–74), 159, 182–3, 206, 216–7
Common New Generation Frigate designs, 567
'County' class destroyers, 20, 52, 68–9, 74, 114, 116, 146, 156, 159, 167, 173, 175, 196, 244, 291, 296, 341, 354, 377, 401, 412, 430, 438, 463, 475, 600, 618, 639–40
Cruiser-carrier, 54, 67
CVA01 aircraft carrier, see *Queen Elizabeth* class
Daring class destroyers (1952–70), 72, 639
DDL (Australian Navy), 73, 244–5
Dock Landing Ships, *see Fearless* class
EDATS trawlers, see 'River' class
Enhanced Offshore Patrol Vessel, *see* OPV 3
Essex class aircraft carriers (US Navy), 414
Fearless class assault ships, 366, 485, 639
Fleet depot ship design, 183
Fleet maintenance ship design, 183
Future Frigate design (1990–3), 566–7
'Garage Ship' design, 306–8, 325, 358, 384, 397, 416
'Ham' class minesweeper, 640
Hecla class hydrographic vessels, 154–5, 220
Helicopter Support Ship design, 354–5
'Horizon' design, *see* Common New Generation Frigate
'Hunt' class mine countermeasure vessels, 182, 315–7, 333, 339, 342, 354, 495, 549, 576–7, 580–1, 603, 640–3
Invincible class cruisers/aircraft carriers, 212, 258–9, 288, 296–8, 306–7, 353, 357, 361, 368, 372, 378, 383, 393–4, 402, 404, 414, 428, 479, 511, 557, 579, 639, 641–2

INDEX

'Island' class (OPV 1) patrol vessels, 283, 285, 574, 578
Jura class patrol vessels (SDAF), 283
'Kanin' class destroyers (Soviet Navy), 11, 274
'*Kara*' class cruisers (Soviet Navy), 313
'Kashin' class destroyers (Soviet Navy)
Kiev class aircraft carriers (Soviet Navy), 313
'Kildin' class destroyers (Soviet Navy), 11
Kingfisher class patrol vessels, *see Seal* class
Kirov class cruisers (Soviet Navy), 313, 512–3
'Komar' class fast attack craft (Soviet Navy, Indonesian Navy), 4, 11
Kortenaer class frigates (Netherlands Navy), 177
'Kotlin' class destroyers (Soviet Navy), 11, 84
'Kresta'/'Kresta II' class cruisers (Soviet Navy), 84, 274, 313
'Krivak' class frigates (Soviet Navy), 274, 295, 313, 413, 513, 618
Landing Ships, Logistic, *see* Royal Fleet Auxiliaries, *Sir Lancelot* class
Large ASW Ship design, 178–9, 182, 197, 206
LCT, *see* Tank Landing Craft
Leander class frigates, 3, 8, 13, 20, 51, 56–7, 72–3, 146, 148, 156, 168, 172, 176, 184, 187, 243, 259, 305, 322, 391, 401, 405, 438, 452–3, 478, 554, 571, 584, 602, 640–1, 643
Leander class 'Exocet' (Batch 2) modernisations, 174–6, 197, 377, 391, 640
Leander class 'Ikara' (Batch 1) conversions, 99, 148–9, 167, 172–4, 377, 401, 412, 438, 524, 529, 640
Leander class 'Sea Wolf' (Batch 3) modernisations, 175–6, 197, 270, 341, 377, 391, 640
Leander class 'Towed array' (Batch 2A) modernisations, 272, 305, 377, 415, 524–9, 640

'Ley' class minehunters, 640
Light Destroyer design (Australian Navy), *see* DDL
Lion class cruisers, 67
LPDs, *see Fearless* class
LST, *see* Tanking Landing Ships
'M' class frigates (Netherlands), 417, 569
Mark 18 frigate design (Vosper Thornycroft), 73
Mine Countermeasures Forward Support Ship design, 183
'Nanuchka' class fast attack craft (Soviet Navy), 513
NATO Frigate Replacement design (NFR 90), 500, 565–7, 626
Oliver Hazard Perry/FFG-7 class frigates (US Navy), 142
OPV 1 patrol vessels, see 'Island' class
OPV 2 patrol vessels, see 'Castle' class
OPV 3 patrol vessels/light frigates, 553, 573–6, 578, 581, 584, 626
'Osa' class fast attack craft (Soviet Navy), 11
Pegasus class hydrofoils (US Navy), 320–1
Queen Elizabeth class aircraft carriers (1964–6), xiii, 39–50, 63, 85, 166–7, 348, 620
'Riga' class frigates (Soviet Union, Indonesia), 4
'River' class (EDATS trawlers) minesweepers, 316–8, 339, 343, 372, 380, 576, 581, 640, 642–3
Sandown class minehunters, 182, 316, 342, 380, 549, 552, 576–7, 580–1, 626, 640, 642
Scimitar class fast training craft, 179, 321, 641
Sea Dart Frigate design, *see* Type 42
Seal class patrol vessels, 180, 225, 283
Single Role Minehunters, *see* Sandown class
Skory class destroyers (Soviet Navy, Indonesian Navy), 4
Slava class cruisers (Soviet Navy), 512
Sovremennyy class destroyers (Soviet Navy), 313, 513
SR.N1 hovercraft, 75
SR.N3 hovercraft, 76

SR.N5 hovercraft, 75
SR.N6 hovercraft, 75
SSGW frigate design, 176, 178–9
Standard Frigate, *see* Type 22
Support helicopter carrier design (1973–4), 182–3, 197, 199, 206
Sverdlov class cruisers (Soviet Navy, Indonesian Navy), 4, 11
Tank Landing Craft (LCT), 5, 73
Tank Landing Ships (LST), 5, 15, 73–4
Ticonderoga class cruisers (US Navy), 517
Tiger class helicopter cruisers, 54, 114–15, 146, 159, 175, 273, 296
'Ton' class mine countermeasure vessels, 3, 5–6, 9, 16, 179–81, 282–3, 294, 315, 317, 495, 576, 602, 613, 640
Towed-Array Corvette design, 366, 368, 371, 374
'Tribal' class frigates, *see* Type 81
Type 12 (*Whitby/Rothesay*) class frigates, 3, 8, 206, 438–9, 453, 524, 550, 639
Type 14 (*Blackwood*) class frigates, 16, 74, 173, 282–3, 639
Type 15 class frigates, 72, 639
Type 17 destroyer design, 148
Type 19 frigate design, 52, 54, 56, 70, 176, 275
Type 21 (*Amazon*) class frigates, 73, 75, 85, 99, 133, 148, 156, 160–3, 167–71, 174–6, 179, 185, 245, 259, 272, 275, 280, 292, 296, 305, 371, 377–8, 401, 438–9, 452–3, 456, 463, 478, 493, 500, 553, 567, 569, 571–2, 602, 621, 640–1, 643
Type 22 (*Broadsword*) class frigates, 73, 75, 85, 89, 130, 156, 158, 160–1, 168, 171, 175–9, 185–7, 196–7, 206, 245, 259–60, 269–70, 272, 275–6, 303–8, 310, 333, 339, 341–2, 356, 366, 371–2, 374, 377, 380, 383, 400–1, 413, 415, 419, 426, 433, 438, 453, 475, 479, 484, 494, 500, 524, 527–8, 566–71, 573, 578–9, 623, 626, 640–3
Type 23 (large) frigate design, 305–6

Type 23 (*Norfolk*) class frigates, 306, 310, 339, 342, 357–8, 366, 368, 371–4, 377, 380, 384, 386, 391–2, 395, 397, 400, 415–9, 432–3, 435, 494–5, 524, 528, 550, 552–4, 561, 566–7, 570–6, 579–81, 584, 586, 597, 627, 640, 642–3
Type 24 frigate design, 308–1, 330, 333, 416
Type 25 frigate design, 310, 354
Type 41 (*Leopard*) class frigates, 6, 8, 115, 206, 401
Type 42 (*Sheffield*) class destroyers, 56, 58, 68, 71–2, 75, 85, 99, 133, 148, 156, 160–3, 166–76, 185, 196, 206, 214–5, 245, 259–60, 270, 275, 299–304, 307, 310, 322, 324, 339, 341–3, 358, 366, 371–2, 377–8, 383–4, 393, 400–1, 412, 428, 432, 438–9, 441, 446, 449–50, 458, 475, 477–9, 483–5, 493, 494, 499, 500, 503, 552–3, 565–7, 579, 621–2, 639, 641–3
Type 43 destroyer design, 300–3, 305–7, 339, 341–3, 419, 623, 642–3
Type 44 destroyer design, 303–4, 342–3, 349, 358, 366, 368, 377, 380, 415, 419
Type 45 (*Daring*) class destroyers, 567, 580
Type 61 (*Salisbury*) class frigates, 3, 8, 114–5, 401
Type 81 (*Ashanti*) class frigates, 5, 8, 13, 72, 74, 146, 175, 640
Type 82 (*Bristol*) class destroyers, 52, 54–6, 67, 70–1, 133, 148, 156, 166–8, 172, 259, 441, 639, 641
Udaloy class destroyers (Soviet Navy), 513
VT2 hovercraft, 320
'Weapon' class destroyers, 72
Warships (all RN unless otherwise stated, *see also* Submarines)
25 de Mayo (Argentine Navy), 446–7
Abdiel, 183, 235, 552, 577, 603
Achilles, 240, 252, 606, 616
Active, 438, 442, 463, 611
Admiral Isakov (Soviet Navy), 413

Admiral Kuznetsov (Russian Navy), see *Riga*
Aegir (Iceland), 227
Agincourt, 9
Aisne, 8
Ajax, 3
Alacrity, 295, 439, 446, 451–2, 611–2
Albion (1954–73), 3, 13, 37, 52, 61, 73, 79, 113, 118, 159, 161
Albion (2003–), 565
Amazon, 73, 168–9, 171
Ambuscade, 441, 452, 458, 463
Andromeda, 227–8, 236, 442, 606, 612
Antelope, 439, 441, 452, 456, 569
Antrim, 292, 341, 438, 444–5, 453–4, 459, 475, 610
Apollo, 228, 412, 610
Arethusa, 8, 227, 242, 412, 524, 527–9
Argonaut, 272, 441, 453–6, 459, 495, 524, 528
Ariadne, 438
Ark Royal (1955–78), 2–3, 37–8, 60–3, 118–9, 133, 159, 182–3, 197, 206, 216, 251, 278, 287–9, 291, 296, 315, 323, 430, 479, 506
Ark Royal (1985–2011), 288, 298, 371, 373, 377–8, 380, 382, 386, 530, 532, 533, 557, 589, 599–600
Arrow, 412–3, 438–9, 446, 449, 452, 463–4, 610
Ashanti, 8
Aurora, 8, 438
Avenger, 442, 459–60, 463–4, 496, 501
Bacchante, 249
Bahia Buen Suceso (Argentine Navy), 451, 484
Baku (Soviet Navy), 511
Baldur (Iceland), 281
Barrosa, 3
Bastion, 5
Battleaxe, 179, 438
Beaver, 528
Berwick, 3, 248
Bezuprechny (Soviet Navy), 616–17
Bicester, 603
Birmingham, 171, 496
Bismarck (German Navy), 62, 175
Blackpool, 9

Blackwood, 16
Blake, 8, 116, 118, 146, 159, 197, 291, 315, 328, 430
Bossington, 235
Brazen, 497, 605–6
Brecon, 181, 315–6, 603
Brighton, 8, 123
Brilliant, 438–9, 444–5, 447, 451, 453–6, 484, 589
Brinton, 602
Bristol, 166–7, 173, 299, 377, 411–3, 441, 452, 485, 519, 553, 609, 616
Britannia, 7, 118, 371–2, 377, 392, 426, 428, 607–9
Broadsword, 179, 304, 305, 412–3, 438–9, 450, 453–5, 457–8, 484
Brocklesby, 603
Bullfinch, 155
Bulwark (1955–81), 13, 37, 61, 73, 112, 119, 159, 197, 206, 217, 237, 291, 323, 341, 442, 639
Bulwark (2004–), 565
Cambrian, 3
Capricieuse (France), 612
Cardiff, 170, 441, 456, 461–2, 464, 472, 611
Carysfort, 8
Centaur, 8, 37, 61–2
Challenger, 318–9, 426, 429, 642
Chichester, 3, 114–6, 240–1, 613
Cleopatra, 174–6, 227, 272, 524–8
Cornwall, 569
Coventry, 295, 412, 436, 450, 456–8, 478
Dainty, 7
Danae, 274
Daring (2009–), 567
Dauntless (US Coastguard), 612
Decoy, 8
Defender, 6
Defiance, 184
Delight, 9
Derriton, 181
Devonshire, 3, 113, 236
Diana, 118
Dido, 3, 172, 401, 438, 529
Dumbarton Castle, 283
Dundas, 8
Dwight D Eisenhower (US Navy), 411, 413
Eagle, 2–3, 37–8, 46, 60, 63, 69, 77, 79–81, 113, 118, 146, 590
Eastbourne, 8

INDEX

Edinburgh, 565, 600
Eilat (Israeli Navy), 82
Empire Fulmar, 80
Empire Grebe, 80
Empire Guillemot, 80
Empire Petrel, 80
Endurance, 197, 220, 377, 386, 392, 437–8, 444–5, 464–5, 553, 611
Escanaba (US Coastguard), 611
Eskimo, 5
Euryalus, 242, 438, 529
Exeter, 441, 452, 458–9
Exmouth, 16, 74–5, 238
F4 (LCU), 462
Falmouth, 8, 281
Fawn, 609
Fearless, 15, 74, 79–80, 112, 118, 159, 175, 182, 217, 224, 248, 407–8, 425, 439, 452–3, 457, 460–1, 472, 475, 529, 606
Foch (French Navy), 531
Forrestal (US Navy), 411, 413
Forth, 183–4
Fox, 248
Galatea, 9
Gavinton, 602
General Belgrano (Argentine Navy), 447–8, 481–2, 484
Glamorgan, 291–2, 401, 438, 446, 453, 463–4, 475, 605–6
Glasgow, 413, 438, 449, 451, 495–6, 519
Grafton, 8
Gurkha, 5, 249, 281
Gromky (Soviet Navy), 618
Guardian, 467
Hampshire, 8, 93, 159, 196, 206, 323, 328
Hardy, 8
Hecate, 13
Hecla, 13, 222
Herald, 155
Hermes, 8, 37–8, 46, 62, 69, 81, 119, 121–2, 146, 159, 182, 197–8, 206, 216–7, 236–7, 252, 278, 291, 377, 424, 439, 449, 452, 461, 464, 472, 475, 481, 486, 541, 564, 598, 639
Hermione, 247
Hood, 417
Hubberston, 235
Hurworth, 603
Hydra, 242, 246, 608

Illustrious, 291, 414, 464, 472, 479, 497, 525–6, 557, 599, 614
Independence (US Navy), 526
Intrepid, 15, 74, 80, 159, 182, 197, 224, 248, 407, 425, 439, 452–3, 464, 489, 530
Invincible, 166, 291, 361, 403, 407, 409, 411–4, 439, 449, 460–1, 464, 472, 496, 499–501, 519, 526, 530, 532, 557, 589, 598–9, 609–0, 614, 626
Iran Ajr (Iranian Navy), 603
Irian (Indonesian Navy), 4
Isla de los Estados (Argentine Navy), 451, 484
Jaguar, 6–7, 227–8, 246
Jarrett (US Navy), 603
Jersey, 283
John F Kennedy (US Navy), 118
Juno, 401
Jupiter, 227, 608
Jura (SDAF), 283
Kent, 8, 341, 597
Keppel, 16
Kerch (Soviet Navy), 616
Kirkliston, 602
Kirov, 512
Laioning (Chinese Navy), 511
Leander, 9, 529
Leeds Castle, 283
Leopard, 8, 242
Lincoln, 3, 227
Lion, 8, 159
Llandaff, 8
Loch Fada, 3
London (1963–81), 8, 239, 401, 412
London (1987–99), 616
Londonderry, 9, 434
Lowestoft, 3, 263, 272, 305, 415, 438, 523–4, 526, 529
Lynx, 8
Maidstone, 17
Manxman, 4, 183
Matapan, 220, 270
Maxton, 235
Medway, 4
Melbourne (Australian Navy), 378
Meon, 73
Mermaid, 115–6, 206, 238–40, 281, 641, 643
Minerva, 78, 249, 251, 442, 524
Mohawk, 8
Monsunnen (Argentine Navy), 456

Mount Whitney (US Navy), 531
Murray, 8
Naiad, 8, 401
Newcastle, 608
Nimitz (US Navy), 352
Norfolk (1930–50), 133
Norfolk (1970–82), 175, 341, 401
Norfolk (1989–2004), 570–2, 589, 597
Nubian, 5, 251, 274
Ocean, 565
Odinn (Iceland), 227
P234, 320
P236, 294
P237, 294
Palliser, 16
Pellew, 8
Penelope, 8, 442, 463
Petrel (US Coastgard), 611
Phoebe, 248, 251, 272, 524, 528, 612
Plover, 9
Plymouth, 3, 227, 412, 438–9, 444–5, 453, 456, 461–2, 464
Prince of Wales, 37, 330
Protector (1936–68), 6, 13
Protector (1983–86), 467
Puma, 6
Pyetr Vyelikiy (Russian Navy), 512
Reclaim, 9, 318
Relentless, 8
Repulse, 37
Reward, 283
Rhyl, 3, 236, 249, 438
Riga (Soviet Navy), 511
Rio Carcarana (Argentine Navy), 451, 454, 456, 484
Rio Iguazu (Argentine Navy), 456
Rothesay, 7, 249, 272, 377, 391, 401
Russell, 8
Sahand (Iran), 604
St Davids, 318
St Margarets, 155
Salisbury, 3, 244
Samuel B Roberts (US Navy), 604
Sandown, 577
Scarborough, 8
Scharnhorst (German Navy), 133
Scimitar, 294
Scylla, 129
Sentinel, 467
Sheffield, 71, 168–71, 300, 438, 449–50, 468, 471, 478–9, 493–4, 499

Sheraton, 235
Sirius, 228, 248, 272, 524–5, 527–8, 599
Southampton, 604
Speedy, 321, 434, 641
Striker, 5
Tartar, 9
Tenacity, 180
Tenby, 8
Thor (Iceland), 228
Tiger, 8, 159, 197, 291, 430
Tobruk (Australian Navy), 486
Torquay, 8
Triumph, 3–4, 113, 129, 159, 183–4
Troubridge, 9
Tucumcari (US Navy), 180
Tyr (Iceland), 281
Ulster, 8
Ul'yanovsk (Soviet Navy), 511
Undaunted, 8
Ursa, 7
Varyag (Soviet Navy), 511
Venturer, 318
Verulam, 8
Victorious, 8, 37–8, 62, 69
Vigo, 133
Vincennes (US Navy), 604
Wakeful, 8
Waveney, 318
Westminster, 573
Whirlwind, 8
Whitby, 8
Wilton, 181, 235, 602, 641
Yarmouth, 8, 281, 438–9, 447, 449, 453, 456–7, 463–4
Zealous, 82
Zest, 8
Zulu, 9
Watkins, Admiral James (US Navy), 518

Wavell communications system (British Army), 386
Weapons Department (Navy), Ministry of Defence, 157, 285
Webster, Vice Admiral John, 616
Weinberger, Caspar, 389–3, 398, 402–3, 409, 516, 533
Weir Group, contractors, 594
Wells, Anthony, 556
Wells, Rear Admiral D C, RAN, 113
Welsh Guards, British Army, 460–2
Welsh Office, 284
West Indies, *see* Caribbean
West Indies Station (RN), 6–7, 9, 242, 247
Western Approaches, 8, 117, 121, 215, 279, 317, 404, 410–2, 427, 520, 529
Westland Helicopters, 147, 273, 289–90, 561
White, Captain Hugo, 263–4, 501
White Sea, 10, 509
White's, shipbuilders, 20
Whitmore, Sir Clive, 334
Wigg, George, MP, 48
Williams Island, Bahamas, 248
Williams, Admiral Sir David, 113, 330
Wilson, Harold, MP, *see also* Prime Minister, 39, 41, 48, 77, 137, 157, 189, 192, 204, 212, 231, 243
Wilson, Brigadier Tony, 442
Windass, Stanley, 615
Windward Islands, Caribbean, 247
Women's Royal Naval Reserve (WRNR), 33, 218
Women's Royal Naval Service (WRNS), 17, 24–5, 30–1, 33, 103, 105, 189, 219–21, 583, 588–90, 635–6

Wood's Hole, Oceanographic Institution (US), 154
Woodward, Admiral Sir John 'Sandy', 353, 355, 438–9, 442, 447–8, 464, 469, 473–5, 614
Woolston Stores Depot, Southampton, 18
Woomera, Australia, 69, 278
Wrabness Armaments Depot, Essex, 17
Wreford-Brown, Commander Christopher, 448, 482
Wroughton Royal Naval Aircraft Yard, 268

Yarrow Shipbuilders, 20, 73, 115, 163, 166, 171, 309, 316, 569–70, 574, 578–80
Yarrow-Admiralty Research Department, 245
Yeovilton Naval Air Station, 13
Yeryomin, Rear Admiral V P (Soviet Navy), 616
Yom Kippur, War of (and US-Soviet naval stand-off), 136, 191, 196, 233–5
Young, Captain Brian, 274, 442, 444, 475
Younger, George, MP, *see also* Secretary of State for Defence, 559
Youngsfield, Cape Town, South Africa, 6

Zakheim, Dov, 402, 404–5, 518
Zambia, 77
Zuckerman, Sir Solly, 45, 49
Zumwalt, Admiral Elmo, US Navy, 141–3, 233, 267, 367, 514